ORGANIZED CRIME

ORGANIZED CRIME

Mitchel P. Roth

Sam Houston State University

Prentice Hall

Upper Saddle River, New Jersey
Columbus, Ohio

Library of Congress Cataloging-in-Publication Data
Roth, Mitchel P.
  Organized crime / Mitchel P. Roth.
    p. cm.
  ISBN-13: 978-0-20-550827-3
  ISBN-10: 0-20-550827-8
  1. Organized crime—History.   2. Organized crime—United States—History.   I. Title.
  HV6441.R68 2010
  364.106—dc22

                                                                    2008051990

Editor in Chief: Vernon R. Anthony
Acquisition Editor: Tim Peyton
Assistant Editor: Dan Trudden
Editorial Assistant: Alicia Kelly
Marketing Manager: Adam Kloza
Senior Marketing Coordinator: Alicia Wozniak
Production Manager: Wanda Rockwell
Full Service Project Coordination/Composition: Ravi Bhatt / Aptara®, Inc.
Manager, Visual Research: Beth Brenzel
Image Permission Coordinator: Ang'John Ferreri
Cover Design: Margaret Kenselaar
Printer/Binder: Hamilton Printing Co.
Cover Printer: Demand Production Center

Pearson Education Ltd., London   Pearson Education Australia Pty, Limited
Pearson Education Singapore, Pte. Ltd.   Pearson Education North Asia Ltd., Hong Kong
Pearson Education Canada, Inc.   Pearson Educación de Mexico, S.A. de C.V.
Pearson Education—Japan   Pearson Education Malaysia, Pte. Ltd.

Prentice Hall
is an imprint of

www.pearsonhighered.com

10 9 8 7 6 5 4 3 2 1
ISBN-13: 978-0-20-550827-3
ISBN-10:   0-20-550827-8

*This book is dedicated to Earl Dachslager (1934–2007)
and Bernie Stableford (1951–2007)*

PREFACE

Almost 25 years ago, I was introduced to the topic of organized crime by Professor Alexander Callow at the University of California, Santa Barbara. The author of what for many years was the standard biography of William "Boss" Tweed, Alex held the rapt attention of the always-filled auditorium as he regaled students with lectures about the Sicilian Mafia and its impact on organized crime in America. Virtually every textbook from the 1970s and well into the 1990s focused on Italian-American organized crime over all others; however, a new generation of historians revealed the emergence of other examples of organized crime well before the Italian version. Chinese, Irish, Protestant, and Jewish mobsters were on the scene well before their better-known Italian counterparts. However, these groups never received their due in earlier eras. None of these other groups were memorialized in popular culture the way the Italian permutation was through popular culture and films from 1930's *Little Caesar* to 1970's *The Godfather.*

The landscape of organized crime continues to shift. Forces such as globalization, the World Wide Web, the fall of the Soviet Union and South African apartheid, and the explosion of Yugoslavia, unimaginable in the not-too-distant past continue to shape the changing nature of worldwide organized crime and crime in general. It is the intention of this textbook to look beyond many of the outdated interpretations of organized crime; it is also the hope of the author that it contributes to a better understanding of the multitude of forces shaping organized crime in the 21st century.

After transferring most of its sources to the "War on Terror" after September 11, 2001, American law enforcement is finally marshalling its sources once more to confront organized crime, which has slipped under the radar in recent years. The number of terrorist groups has multiplied since the beginning of the new millennium, as has their lethality. With few state sponsors willing to foot the bill, the overwhelming majority of terrorist organizations have borrowed pages from the organized crime playbook to fund their operations, further demonstrating the complicated nature of organized crime in the 21st century. It was formerly *de rigueur* to study terrorism, white-collar crime, and organized crime as distinct forms of criminality. These distinctions have become increasingly blurred in recent years, and it is only through acknowledging the overlapping nature of much of this criminality that one can truly understand the complicated nature of organized crime today.

No one writes a book alone. From its inception to conclusion, writing a textbook is a prodigious undertaking that cannot be accomplished without the help and input of a number of individuals. First, I thank my original editor, Dave Repetto, who shepherded the project through its earliest stages. Dan Trudden and Tim Peyton stepped in and have seamlessly directed the project to conclusion, and I cannot thank them enough. Dan has been my lifeline to Pearson over the past year, and his prompt communications and feedback have made this project an enjoyable effort for this author. Having written books for a number of other presses, this experience has been the best by far. Furthermore, copy editor Mercedes Heston made sure that any gaffes on my part were corrected before publication. Finally, I want to thank project manager Ravi Bhatt for his assistance in creating the final product.

I have had the good fortune to use several pioneers in organized crime research as sounding boards. Conversations with Joseph Albini at the 2007 annual meeting of the American Society of Criminology as well as with guest lecturer William Chambliss at Sam Houston State University convinced me that I took the proper tact in using an interdisciplinary approach to writing this book. As a trained historian and professor of criminal justice, I was influenced tremendously by the research methodologies and skill sets of both disciplines. No one contributed more to my increasing academic interest in organized crime than my former professor, Alex Callow, at the University of

California, Santa Barbara. Thanks are surely due five anonymous reviewers who made valuable suggestions and saved me from several embarrassing and erroneous statements.

Two of my doctoral students, now PhDs themselves, played important roles in my education in organized crime. Murat Sever, who is returning to the Turkish National Police this summer as Dr. Sever, helped me in my research on the PKK and Turkish organized crime in Europe, and Minwoo Yun, formerly with the South Korean National Police, shared his expertise on human smuggling and trafficking in the former Soviet Union. Russian organized crime scholar Joe Serio kept me updated on the changing nature and rampant mythology surrounding Russian organized crime, and I owe him a debt of gratitude for his ever-present willingness to keep me posted on the latest information on organized crime in the states of the former Soviet Union. My graduate assistants, James Phelps and Brett Finn, played important roles cadging articles and sources that I might otherwise never have found.

Longtime organized crime expert introduced me to a number of the leading international figures in the study of organized crime and was truly influential in my progress as a scholar of organized crime. He played an important role in spreading the gospel of international organized crime scholarship and the study of comparative criminal justice systems with study-abroad programs and his involvement in the Organization of International Criminal Justice and the International Association for the Study of Organized Crime. I also thank him for suggesting me as a source for the *Lords of the Mafia* series. His direct and indirect efforts have also allowed me to study criminology in Cuba, Israel, Italy, and England.

Finally, since the early part of 2000 I spent a significant amount of time in Sicily, where my wife's family treated me like a son, uncle, and brother. I learned so much about civility and the best of human nature from Maria, Daniela, Pietro, Luigi, Paola, and Pongo. Together with literally dozens of extended family members, they have proved an imposing counterweight to the stereotypical image of the Sicilian Mafia that sadly is still so prevalent around the world. My experiences in Sicily allowed me to observe the detrimental nature of organized crime to southern Italy, and to understand its truly anomalous nature (not to be construed as synonymous with Italian and Sicilian society).

In the end, none of this would have been possible without the love and support of my wife and life-partner, Ines, and the joy and affection provided by my Sicilian-born daughter Erica. Writing books is a wonderful endeavor, but its rewards pale in comparison to the joys of family and friends.

CONTENTS

CONTENTS

CHAPTER 1

Defining and Recognizing Organized Crime

Academics, public and government officials, and journalists have been among those attempting to define organized crime and its various manifestations for more than a century. As early as 1898, the Illinois State Supreme Court had ruled that racketeering activity was illegal. In 1915, several years before Prohibition began, a Chicago crime commission was investigating local racketeering activities and found that a number of "well-organized criminal gangs, often in conjunction with legitimate business, were operating not only in Chicago but also in numerous other cities throughout the country" (Bequai 1979,1). However, there were few references to *organized crime* prior to the 1930s. During the 1920s the term *organized crime* was mentioned briefly in the pioneering works of Frederic Thrasher and John Landesco, albeit without any definitional attribution.

In the tumult of globalization, cyberspace, and the information superhighway, organized crime continues to defy definition. Organized crime groups, according to various theories and definitions, come in all shapes and sizes. It is clear that one shape or structure does not fit all. This chapter demonstrates that today's groups, particularly nontraditional groups that do not conform to the Italian Mafia paradigm (discussed in Chapters 3 and 4), are much more fluid, flexible, and pragmatic than past exemplars, with few regards to restricting membership by ethnicity and other related criteria.

The first major effort to forge an official definition was by the National Commission on Law Observance and Enforcement, more commonly known as the Wickersham Commission (1929–1931). At the highest level of government, President Herbert Hoover was the first president to use the term *organized crime* when he spoke to the commission prior to its research. In the course of contributing to the Wickersham Reports, Goldthwaite Dorr and Sidney Simpson made major strides toward developing a definition of *organized crime* by elaborating on four specific categories of losses caused by criminal activity, including "losses due to other crimes affecting wealth" (Standing 2003), such as commercial fraud and extortion, basically placing criminal businessmen in the same category as the era's gangsters.

RACKETEERING AS ORGANIZED CRIME

The 1920s and 1930s found a number of authorities alluding to *rackets* rather than *organized crime,* and there was just as much badinage as to its meaning then as today. In his 1931 follow-up to the first biography of Al Capone, Fred D. Pasley confronted the distinctions between traditional crimes and organized crime, or in the parlance of the day, what was referred to as *the rackets.* The term was applied by the Employers' Association of Chicago to two distinct types of crime against business. The first was called the *collusive type of racket,* which featured "an unscrupulous businessman," a "crooked leader of organized labor," a "crooked politician," and members of the underworld employed by the first three individuals to ensure that "racket price schedules or methods of competition"

Rackets and Racketeering

There are a host of explanations for the provenance of the word *racket*. According to one recent authority, *racket* in reference to underworld activities can be traced back to eighteenth-century England (Raab 2005, 37). The more scrupulous etymologist Eric Partridge traced the term to 1811, when it was used to refer to "an underworld trick or means of livelihood" (Partridge 1950, 551). Between the 1860s and 1905, any individual who was regarded *in the racket* was engaged in a criminal enterprise. By the 1920s, it referred to professional criminals and criminal big shots, as in *racket guy* or *racket-man*. Contemporary researchers have suggested that *racket* refers to the new cornucopia of crimes that syndicates turned to after Prohibition, including bookmaking, loansharking, narcotics dealing, cargo hijackings, and the numbers game. Still others associate it with the noise or "racket" produced by Irish-American gangs during wild parties. What seems clear is that the derivative *racketeer* is "a totally American invention, probably coined by a newspaper reporter" during the 1930s. T. J. English, a chronicler of the Irish American gangster, noted the irony that New York police and firemen "still refer to retirement parties and in-house fundraisers as rackets" (2005, 34).

are under control. The second type of racket was "The Simon Pure Type of Racket [that] is headed by professional criminals . . . whose sole purpose is to exploit business or employees by driving them, by force, into trade associations, so-called, or 'Unions'" (Pasley 1931, 234–235). Of these two, the collusive type was most difficult to destroy, because its links to legitimate political and business leaders lends its subterfuge a mask of respectability.

Nonetheless, despite attempts by law enforcement officials and academics to define organized crime in Chicago in the 1930s, the mission went unfulfilled. One noted academic of the era lamented in 1930 that "today many law enforcement officers have no clear picture of the racket, nor do they find in the law any exact definition of the activities that constitute the racket" (Pasley 1931, 236).

Former New York Governor Alfred E. Smith perhaps made one of the biggest strides toward understanding the complexity of racketeering and its distinction from former types of criminal activity when he traced its origins to 1920s Prohibition. Reminiscing about a simpler time, Smith recounted the various gangs of his youth in the late nineteenth century, noting, "Whatever form of organization they maintained was more for their own protection. . . . Their line of business was not any racket as we understand it today [1930]." As Smith remembered it, these gangs "were not commercially organized for personal profit," and it was not until Prohibition "that so-called gangs became menacing by perfection of organization" (Pasley 1931, 250–251).

Racketeering: Organized Crime Control Act of 1970

The landmark legislation of the Organized Crime Control Act of 1970 includes a detailed definition of what *racketeering activity* means (Section 901 (A) Chapter 96, Title 18, United States Code, 1961. Definitions). *Racketeering* includes the following activities:

- Any act or threat involving murder, kidnapping, gambling, arson, robbery, bribery, extortion, or dealing in narcotic or dangerous drugs, which is chargeable under State law and punishable by imprisonment for more than one year.
- Any act which is indictable under any of the provisions of title 18, United States Code and Relating to:
  - bribery, sports bribery
  - counterfeiting
  - theft from interstate shipment
  - embezzlement from pension and welfare funds
  - extortionate credit transactions

The Debate: Is Organized Crime Non-ideological or Politically Motivated?

Howard Abadinsky, a leading authority on organized crime, created perhaps the most influential definition of organized crime. A linchpin of his definition has been the notion that because organized crime groups are profit-driven, they are not ideologically motivated, and if this is so, it removes them from the equation. In the early 1990s, Abadinsky opined that organized crime is non-ideological, disregarding the possibility that although the profit motive is most evident, criminal syndicates often "align themselves with political power structures that reinforce their value system" (Clark 2004, 104).

- transmission of gambling information
- mail or wire fraud
- obstruction of justice or criminal investigations
- transportation of wagering paraphernalia
- illegal gambling businesses
- interstate transportation of stolen property
- white slave traffic

WHAT IS ORGANIZED CRIME? THE ACADEMIC DEBATE

In 1984, Thomas Schelling posited that organized crime does not simply mean "crime that is organized" (1984, 180). If this was so, an argument could be made then that any gang of thieves could be regarded as such. However, academics including criminologists would probably deride this notion. As Alan Wright noted, "Unfortunately, the official documentation and the critical literature set out almost as many definitions as there are people with an interest in the subject" (Wright 2006, 2–3).

One of the most important epiphanies made by organized crime researchers is the fact that these groups are like chameleons, shifting from one activity to another, depending on geopolitics and changing markets, both legitimate and underground in nature. Attempts at arriving at a legal definition can become counterproductive, because no definition can simultaneously address present and future forms of criminality.

Beginning in the early 1950s (with the Kefauver Hearings) and continuing well into the next decade, criminal justice officials and academics labored to come up with a convincing organizational structure with which to gauge the activities of organized crime groups, focusing almost exclusively on criminals of Italian descent. A number of observers found inspiration in governmental and business structures that favored a bureaucratic model. The 1960s was a boon decade for the study of organized crime, as academics and policymakers searched for ways to explain and contain the complex criminal enterprises revealed by the McClellan Commission and the Oyster Bay Conference.

The academic debate over the structure of organized crime in the 1960s revolved around a handful of conceptual models that were either influenced by or a reaction to the findings of the Kefauver and McClellan Hearings. The following three models are usually at the center of any discussion of the issue in the late 1960s. Because of the academic component offered by each, this carried a continuing resonance into the following decades. For a number of contemporary observers, this academic debate has done much to impede the discussion, or, as one authority noted, "had the unfortunate consequence of stopping the process of model building in its tracks" (Smith, Jr. 1994, 126).

Donald Cressey and the Bureaucratic/Corporate Model

Like the large legitimate corporations which it resembles, Cosa Nostra has both kinds of positions, making it both a business organization and a government . . .

—DONALD CRESSEY, Theft of a Nation: The Structure and Operations of Organized Crime in America, *1969, p. 110*

Cressey on Organized Crime in America (1967)

- There is a nationwide alliance of at least 24 tightly knit Mafia "families" that control organized crime in the United States.
- All of the members of these families are Italians and Sicilians or of Italian or Sicilian descent.
- Each family has a hierarchical structure of positions that regulates power in that family.
- These families are linked together by "understandings, agreements, and obedience to a nine-member commission."
- The names of at least 2,000 members of these 24 families are known to law enforcement officials.
- Members of these families control most of the nation's illegal gambling and loan-shark operations and are heavily involved in drug trafficking.
- These families either own or are "behind-the-scenes owners" of most Las Vegas casinos.
- They have infiltrated labor unions and made liaisons that give them power over state and federal legislators and other officials at every branch of government.[1]

As advisor to the U.S. President's Commission on Law Enforcement and the Administration of Justice, criminologist Donald Cressey became one of the first academics "to set out a formal structure for organized crime" (Wright 2006, 4). Central to Cressey's thesis was that because of its bureaucratic nature, organized crime (La Cosa Nostra) is efficient and represents the most advanced form of criminal organization. For Cressey, the term *organized crime* became synonymous with syndicated crime—the Mafia and La Cosa Nostra—traditional Italian American organizations that were characterized by a well-defined hierarchy of roles for members and leaders, with specific goals and unwritten laws that determined one's behavior. His findings were adopted by the Commission, which buttressed the claims that organized crime was "a society that seeks to operate outside the control of the American people and their governments."

In Cressey's view, organized crime was closest to a hierarchical bureaucracy. The new interpretations central to Cressey's thesis gave a patina of "academic legitimacy" to the study of organized crime (Standing 2003). His report to the 1967 President's Commission offered new definitions of organized crime based on what has become popularized as the so-called La Cosa Nostra model, a social system-cum-structure designed with an eye for maximum profits and the provision of illicit goods and services. Further characterizing this bureaucratic model was an accompanying code of behavior, with rules and procedures carried out by individuals filling various occupational roles based on expertise, a division of labor that mimicked corporate bureaucracies. The bureaucratic structure gave this model its self-perpetuating character, giving the organization a permanence that lasted beyond the tenure of any one leader or officer. Cressey borrowed this structure to explain the organizational chart of Italian-American organized crime "families" in the United States. According to one of Cressey's critics, "From a theoretical standpoint, the structural model was thus based on classical concepts concerning the division of labor, scientific management and bureaucratic attributes of precedence, rules, procedures and functional role" (Smith, Jr. 1994, 127).

In 1969 (the same year of publication as Mario Puzo's *The Godfather*), Cressey used the Task Force Report for the Commission as the foundation for his widely read *Theft of the Nation*. One observer has commented that the representation of organized crime in each book was "highly consistent"—a case of art imitating reality or reality imitating art. During the 1970s, Cressey continued to expand on this topic and became an important influence on U.S. government policies against organized crime for the next 30 years. Nonetheless, a number of "skeptics" recognized that by involving a scholar of Cressey's stature, it was a gesture, "one merely designed to boost the credibility of a model that was previously constructed by a group of law enforcement officials" (Standing 2003, 5).

Joseph Albini and the Patron-Client Relationship (1971)

"Mafia then is not an organization. It is a system of patron-client relationships that interweaves legitimate and illegitimate segments of Sicilian society."

—JOSEPH ALBINI, The American Mafia: Genesis of a Legend, *1971, p. 135*

Several critics of the bureaucratic interpretation offered alternatives that focused more "on behavioral dynamics rather than organizational structure." In his pioneering work on organized crime, Joseph Albini asserted that the key ingredient to this phenomenon is "organized," calling it the "basic distinguishing element between organized crime and other types of crime" (Albini 1971, 35). Albini's examination of organized crime in Detroit contrasts sharply with Cressey's model. Albini suggests that organized crime is made up of a "network of patrons and clients," rather than "rational hierarchies or secret societies." These networks are characterized by a loose system of power relationships; "rather than being a criminal secret society, a criminal syndicate consists of a system of loosely structured relationships functioning primarily because each participant is interested in furthering his own welfare" (Albini 1971, 288).

According to Albini, organized crime was "an indigenous phenomenon," one that developed out of "patron-client" relationships central to Sicily's stratified culture (see Chapter 3) and brought to the United States by Italian immigrants (Smith 1994, 128). So on one hand, Albini concurred with Cressey when it came to identifying their family-like structures; however, Albini diverged from Cressey's findings by arguing that syndicates are not bureaucratic in structure, and if they were, this would be a major weakness. As one leading expert rightly points out, because an organization based on the bureaucratic/corporate model requires "extensive written rules and regulations" and "communication from the top of the hierarchy to the persons on the bottom, usually in written form," this structure would leave too much of a paper trail and be impractical for organized crime groups trying to avoid scrutiny from investigators (Abadinsky 2007, 6).

Francis A. J. Ianni and Elizabeth Reuss-Ianni and Mafia as Social System

"Secret criminal organizations like the Italian-American or Sicilian Mafia families are not formal organizations like governments or business corporations. . . . Rather, they are traditional social systems organized by action and cultural values which have nothing to do with modern bureaucratic virtues."

—FRANCIS A. J. IANNI, A Family Business: Kinship and Social Control in Organized Crime, *1973, p. 120*

Francis Ianni researched organized crime in the United States in the late 1960s and into the 1970s and was among the critics questioning the validity of Cressey's corporate/bureaucratic model for organized crime. Like Albini, Ianni agreed that the southern Italian immigrants brought their

---

What is a **patron?**   Any person who is in a position of power and influence and thereby can help or protect others who are not in this position.

What is a **client?**   The person who seeks and receives assistance or protection for which he in return offers services to the patron.

What is **patronage?**   Refers to the system of intricate relationships that develop between those who provide the services inherent in their position and power and those who receive and in turn reciprocate whatever services they are capable of providing.

(Adapted from Albini 1971, 110)

Organized Crime Definitions on American Borders

Mexico: According to its 1996 Federal Law against Organized Crime, when three or more persons agree to organize themselves or to be organized to carry out, in an ongoing or repeated way, actions that they or others to them have as a goal or result to commit one or more of a variety of crimes, they will be prosecuted for that fact, as members of organized crime.

Canada: *Organized crime* is "economically motivated illicit activity undertaken by any group, association or other body consisting of two or more individuals, whether formally or informally organized, where the negative impact of said activity could be considered significant from an economic, social, violence generation, health and safety and/or environmental perspective" (Porteous 1998, 1–2). Porteous goes on to assert that organized crime groups "tend not to have centralized controlled rigid organizational structures," but "can be highly organized despite the fact that those engaged in the activity are acting in fluid groups and alliances" (Porteous 1998, 10).

cultural values and social system with them to the United States. However, according to Ianni, this social system had no specific structure outside of providing a "mediation structure" for the patron-client milieu (Smith Jr., 1994, 128). In his analysis of the definitional debate, Dwight Smith Jr. acknowledged that the southern Italian tradition of dealing with individuals in "personal terms" reinforced a patron-client relationship in which the patron was viewed more as a "benefactor" rather than a representative of an "impersonal organization" (Smith, Jr., 1994, 128).

After a detailed "participant-observation" field study of the pseudonymous "Lupollo family," Ianni came to the conclusion that such organized crime syndicates were not tightly structured organizations but adhered more closely to traditional social networks or kinship ties that were common and traditional in southern Italy, referring to Italian Mafia families as "traditional social systems, organized by action and by cultural values which have nothing to do with bureaucratic virtues" (Ianni 1972, 108).

According to Ianni, the family operated as a social unit merging both social organization and business functions. In the Lupollo family, positions of leadership were based on kinship from the top to the "middle-management" level of the hierarchy. It was in this way that that the higher one was in the organization, the closer the kinship ties (Ianni 1972, 118).

Later, Francis A. J. Ianni built on his original work exploring organized crime activities among African-American and Hispanic-American groups (Ianni 1972). There are some who would argue that Ianni is merely updating the "alien conspiracy thesis" to reflect changes in the modern urban environment (Wright 2006, 131). Nonetheless, Ianni recognized, when few others did, that organized criminal activities were among the few alternative routes allowing African-American and Hispanic-American inner-city dwellers to move above their status at the bottom rung of the ladder of economic opportunity.

Why Is Important to Arrive at a Consensus on a Definition?

In order to create laws to effectively combat organized crime on national and international levels, it is important to have an agreed-on definition that distinguishes it from other criminal activities. The lack of consensus on a definition has hindered international law enforcement. However, this should not be unexpected, because there are such national differences between judicial systems and police strategies, as well as a lack of information sharing. By operating in a number of countries simultaneously, international criminal organizations exploit these variations to their own advantage.

DEFINING INTERNATIONAL/TRANSNATIONAL ORGANIZED CRIME

The United Nations Convention against Transnational Organized Crime (2003)

In September 2003, the UN Convention against Transnational Organized Crime (TOC) became law after being introduced some three years earlier. It is too early to make any substantive conclusions about its effectiveness; however, what has done has been to come up with a legal definition of organized crime acceptable to most countries and offering only "'a minimum common denominator definition' with no strict criteria in terms of number of members and group structure" (Finjaut and Paoli 2004, 40).

Prior to the 1990s, organized crime definitions revolved around central characteristics such as the nature and severity of offenses committed, the numbers of individuals involved, and the enduring nature of the enterprise. In the 1990s, the concept of transnational organized crime emerged as one of the most challenging issues confronting law enforcement. Beginning in this period the "transnational dimension of organized crime [became more] strongly emphasized" (Fijnaut and Paoli 2004, 23). In 2000, the United Nations defined *organized crime* broadly "as a structured group of three or more persons existing for a period of time and acting in concert with the aim of committing one or more serious crimes or offenses in accordance with this Convention in order to obtain, directly or indirectly, a financial or material benefit" (United Nations [UN] 2000, Article 2). A *serious crime* refers to "conduct constituting a criminal offense punishable by a maximum deprivation of liberty of at least four years or a more serious penalty" (TOC Convention, Article 2 (b)).

At the 2000 Convention against Transnational Organized Crime (TOC), international representatives did not arrive at a consensus on a definition or a list of criminal acts, but decided to adopt a broad definition of *organized criminal groups,* and "not limit the scope of application to hierarchically structured or mafia type organizations but also to cover more loosely organized criminal groups, committing serious crimes which are transnational in nature" (United Nations Office on Crime and Drugs, September 2002, 4–5).

An offense that would be considered transnational is one that

> (a) is committed in more than one state; (b) is committed in one state but a substantial part of its preparation, planning, direction or control takes place in another state; (c) is committed in one state but involves and organized criminal group that engages in criminal activities in more than one state; or (d) is committed in one state but has substantial effects in another state. (TOC Convention, Article 3 (2))

The United Nations has identified 18 categories of transnational offenses whose inception, perpetration, and direct or indirect efforts involve more than one country. These categories include the following:

Money laundering	Computer crime
Terrorist activities	Environmental crime
Theft of art and cultural objects	Trafficking in persons
Theft of intellectual property	Trade in human body parts
Illicit arms trafficking	Illegal drug trafficking
Aircraft hijacking	Fraudulent bankruptcy
Sea piracy	Infiltration of legal business
Insurance fraud	Corruption and bribery of public or party officials

GLOBALIZATION AND THE NEW WORLD OF ORGANIZED CRIME

A number of accepted notions about organized crime have fallen by the wayside in recent years in response to globalization and the tremendous changes wrought by post-industrial economies. These new economies have emerged in a number of incarnations, including failed states, underground economies and black markets, shell states, and others discussed in later chapters on Africa, Latin America, and Asia. Prior to the 1970s, most organized crime groups operated within the boundaries of their countries of origin. The globalization of the world economy has occurred coincident with the globalization of organized crime. In the 1980s, a number of traditional culture–bound syndicates such as the Japanese Yakuza, the Chinese Triads, and the Sicilian Mafia diversified into new markets. In the 1990s, the fall of the Soviet Union opened up the doors to a cornucopia of ethnic gangs with deep roots and traditions, many of which emerged on the scene later as prominent smugglers.

By most accounts, the emergence of new technologies and other factors related to globalization "have lowered the barriers to entry in respect to some criminal activities, and have as a result diversified the nature and types of activities that criminal groups are involved in" (UN Office on Drugs and Crime, September 2002, 6). Further complicating this issue is the fact that most of the data collected by law enforcement "is biased towards more visible and prominent groups as opposed to less visible, unconventional and smaller groups (which often resemble more complex and fluid networks)" (UN Office on Drugs and Crime, September 2002, 6; Williams 2001).

A 2002 United Nations pilot survey of 40 selected organized criminal groups in 16 countries has contributed to a better understanding of the changing nature and structure of twenty-first century organized crime. An interesting new typology emerged from this research: According to the study conducted by Mark Shaw (2002), future analysis of trends in transnational organized crime could benefit by investigating the following three components:

- *Groups:* At the lowest level, the collection of data on individual criminal organizations.
- *Clusters:* The collection of information around the various clusters of criminal groups, often originating from specific geographic localities.
- *Markets:* Information on regional criminal markets (Shaw 2002).

Russian Mafiya or Criminal Clusters?

Distinguishing clusters from more monolithic structures of organized crime is an important component for the study of organized crime. Some criminologists posited that it would be more useful to examine Russian and West African crime groups as clusters rather than labeling them as "less-definable" groups (Finckenauer and Waring 1998; Shaw 2002). One explanation is that it is easier for the media to label them as such "for ease of reference." Clusters can often be viewed as "interconnected criminal groups" with the same regional background. In the United States, where it has been fashionable for years to identify all Russian organized crime as the Russian Mafiya and all West African crime as Nigerian, it is clear this is counterproductive in any attempt at arriving at a meaningful understanding of what constitutes organized crime groups (Shaw 2002).

The media, law enforcement, and academics began referring to a number of different loosely structured crime syndicates as the Russian Mafiya in the 1980s. These gangs or clusters featured representatives from a number of Eurasian countries including Russia, Armenia, Ukraine, Lithuania, Chechnya, Dagestan, and Georgia. Hundreds of gangsters were affiliated with more than a dozen of these groups in the United States. As criminologists demonstrated in recent years, these groups were not part of a monolithic organized crime group with clear leadership and structure, but were closer to a hodgepodge of networks that were flexible and "opportunity-driven" in nature. The fluid structure explains "why Russian organized crime groups are quick at adapting to, and diversifying into, new criminal markets" (Shaw 2002, 8).

Profile of Forty Selected Organized Crime Groups in Sixteen Countries

- Most had some form of hierarchy in their structure.
- Groups tended to have between 20 and 50 members (just fewer than half had more than 50).
- Most viewed violence as essential to group's activities.
- Less than half of the groups had no strong social or ethnic identity (23 cases from same social background or ethnic group).
- Majority engaged in only one primary criminal activity.
- Most groups spread activities across five or more states.
- Corruption was essential to the primary activity of group in just less than half the cases.
- In just under half the cases, there was no evidence of political influence.
- In the largest number of cases (18), it was recorded that there was extensive cross-over between legitimate and illegitimate activities (Shaw 2002).

The Structure of Organized Crime Groups (UNDOC September 2002)

In a study of 40 organized crime groups in 16 countries, a survey revealed five types of structures exhibited by prominent groups:

1. *Rigid hierarchy:* Typically headed by a "single boss," this type of organization is divided into "several cells reporting to the centre" and adhering to "strong internal systems of discipline."
2. *Devolved hierarchy:* Has a hierarchical structure and chain of command. "However, regional structures, with their own leadership hierarchy, have a degree of autonomy over day to day functioning."
3. *Hierarchical conglomerate:* Is an "association of organized crime groups with a single governing body," which can range from "an organized umbrella type body to more flexible and loose oversight arrangements."
4. *Core criminal group:* "Range from relatively loose to cohesive group of core individuals who generally regard themselves as working for the same organization." In addition, it is typically horizontal rather than vertical in structure.
5. *Organized criminal network:* "Defined by the activities of key individuals who engage in illicit activity together in often shifting alliances. They do not necessarily regard themselves as an organized criminal entity. Individuals are active in the network through the skills and capital that they may bring" (adapted from UNDOC September 2002, 19).

In many societies, organized crime can exist without identifiable or traditional structured hierarchies, adhering to more modern tendencies to be "dynamic and often relatively loose structures," which presents a nearly impossible challenge to law enforcement entities trying to keep tabs on these forms of criminality (UN 2002, 6).

DEFINING ORGANIZED CRIME: AN INTERNATIONAL PERSPECTIVE

Since the mid-1980s, a number of international experts have contributed to the challenging task of defining organized crime. Not surprisingly, there are a number of parallels with the previously mentioned interpretations.

A Survey of Selected International Definitions

Interpol: "Any group having a corporate structure whose primary objective is to obtain money through illegal activities, often surviving on fear and corruption" (Bresler 1993, 319).

Egypt: Organized crime is

> crime practiced by an institutional body that comprises a large number of professional individuals who work within it in accordance with a work system that divides the work in very precise, complex, and secret ways, and which is governed by an extremely severe law, whose sanctions go up to and include murder or the perpetration of bodily harm on those who disobey it. (El-Aboudy 2002).

By definition, the organized crime group plans activities with "great precision," and is usually "characterized by violence, depend on the corruption of certain officials and leading statesmen, and aim to make huge profits." Unlike American organized crime, the definition suggests that the organized crime group "often exists for many centuries, society co-existing with it and seeking its protection out of fear of its brutality" (El-Aboudy 2002).

India: Organized crime means

> any continuing unlawful activity by an individual, singly or jointly, either as a member of an organized crime syndicate or on behalf of such syndicate, by the use of violence or threat of violence or intimidation or coercion, or other unlawful means, with the objective of gaining pecuniary benefits, or gaining undue economic or other advantage for himself. (Maharashta Control of Organized Crime Act, 1999).

Russia: "Organized crime is defined as the functioning of stable, hierarchical associations, engaged in crime as a form of business, and setting up a system of protection against public control by means of corruption" (Gilinskiy 2006, 278).

Germany: Organized crime

> is the planned commission of criminal offences determined by the pursuit of profit and power which, individually or as a whole, are of considerable importance and involve more than two persons, each with his/her own assigned tasks, who collaborate for a prolonged or indefinite period of time a) by using commercial or business-like structures; b) by using force or other means of intimidation or c) by exerting influence on politics, the media, public administration, judicial authorities or the business sector. (quoted in von Lampe, 2006, p. 16)

Italy: Despite repeated calls for inquiry into the Italian Mafia phenomenon in the late 1940s and throughout the 1950s, the general consensus in Rome was that, "it was an unimportant phenomenon peculiar to Sicily" (Servadio 1976, 197). In reality, most politicians were too wary of losing Sicilian votes to investigate such matters. In 1962, the Italian Parliament approved the creation of the Anti-Mafia Commission in the aftermath of a series of high-profile murders—50 murders in 50 days. The Commission is considered the first in Italy "to include the word Mafia in its title" (Servadio 1976, 198). Also noteworthy were the implications that this criminal activity was no longer a regional problem, but had ramifications for the rest of the country. The Anti-Mafia Commission was composed of 31 Parliament members representing all political factions. Although it began its investigations in 1963, it took almost a decade for their findings to be published. Its findings included the conclusion that the traditional Sicilian Mafia had evolved into a "national, sophisticated crime cartel with international contacts and heavy involvement in the narcotics trade." Among its most troubling findings was the fact that at least three members of Parliament, including a former cabinet minister, had consorted with the criminal cartel. (Adapted from von Lampe, 2006)

Historical Roots of Organized Crime: An International Perspective

Organized crime has existed in one form or another throughout much of recorded history. It flourished in a number of preindustrial societies, drawing support from the hinterlands rather than the cities and urban centers that would become strongholds much later. Agricultural societies, among them Italy and China, gave impetus to the rise of groups such as the Mafia, the Camorra, the

Characteristics of the Mafia (Anti-Mafia Commission, 1971)

1. Ruthless elimination of "awkward" rivals through commissioned murders.
2. Use of threats and intimidation in order to obtain what was wanted.
3. Formal and false respect for authority.
4. Ability to obtain favors and illegal measures whenever they are useful.
5. Continuous and compromising help to the political authorities.
6. Non-proved verdicts.
7. Relationships with people who are able to provide information and collusive administrative concessions.
8. Enrichment achieved by any means.

'Ndrangheta, and Triads. Most early accounts of their origins are shrouded in myths and half-truths, as are the origins and development of newer groups such as the La Cosa Nostra, America's version of the Sicilian Mafia.

Piracy, highway robbery, and banditry were precursors to modern organized crime, all products of rapidly changing conditions in earlier historical eras. As far back as 1931 and in the concluding years of the Prohibition era, *The Saturday Evening Post* opined,

> There is really nothing new about it. Organized robber bands preyed on merchants in the past and exacted tribute from them. Pirates took their toll from commerce on the high seas. It is almost beyond belief, however, that in this present day [1931] the methods of the robber gangs can still be applied so successfully. (Quoted in Pasley 1931, 258)

Although some of the characteristics of modern organized crime may seem familiar to these earlier groups—violence, hierarchy, strict rules and regulations, entrepreneurial activities, corruption of officials, and profit motivation—others, such as monopolization, longevity, racketeering and infiltration of legitimate business, restricted membership, and self-perpetuating leadership, reflect more complex and urbanized societies.

As early as 1304, England created trailbaston commissions to deal with an escalating organized crime problem in rural localities. The trailbaston commission was a special judicial commission of judges empowered to visit crime-plagued villages and set up grand juries that would help stem local gang activity tied to a combination of factors, including rural unemployment, demobilized soldiers, and social unrest. Historians have compared the work of the trailbaston to the crime commissions led by 1930s New York racket-buster Thomas E. Dewey and later Rudolph Giuliani, who successfully targeted organized crime in New York City in the 1980s (Roth 2005).

Medieval justices of the peace, similar to their modern-day counterparts, made headway through the use of informants who were convinced to turn state's evidence and testify against former colleagues in return for lighter sentences, much like twentieth-century mob informers broke organized crime's reputed oath of silence in order to make deals with the authorities.

Eighteenth-century gangster Jonathan Wild rose to crime-boss prominence in London's underworld, dominating the understrata for a brief decade from 1715 until his death in 1725. Novelist and police reformer Henry Fielding once said of Wild, "Nature intended Jonathan Wild for a sleuth, and had he been born two centuries later it is probable that he would have won a responsible position at Scotland Yard" (Bleackley 1929, 47).

With the onset of the Industrial Revolution, first in England toward the beginning of the nineteenth century and then in other parts of the Western world, rural peasants flocked to newly urbanized settings in search of better jobs and sustenance. This, together with developments in faster forms of transportation, hastened the evolution of longer-lasting and more efficient crime syndicates that allowed them "to adapt to rapidly changing markets, consolidate their power, accumulate capital, expand from their original bases, and continue to operate in the modern world" (Lunde 2005, 17).

JONATHAN WILD: THIEF TAKER AND HIGHWAYMAN   Toward the end of the seventeenth century, the profession of *thief taking*, or bounty hunting, was created by the Act for the Encouraging the Apprehending of Highwaymen. English highwaymen operated on horseback and usually wore masks as they robbed seemingly at will along the roads leading into London. By most accounts, equestrian bandits killed less victims than their bipedal counterparts due to their ability to escape quickly. Although they occasionally engaged in gun battles with their victims or soldiers, treacherous accomplices and informers represented a much greater danger, as the chronicle of Jonathan Wild demonstrates.

Without a regular police presence and suffering a recurring outlaw problem, the English government began offering a £40 reward for the arrest and successful prosecution of any highwayman. On top of this, thief takers were permitted to claim the highwayman's horse, weapons, and other possessions (unless they were proved to be stolen). Initially, thief takers were bandits who informed on their accomplices for the promised reward. Despite the best intentions of the new legislation, highway robbery continued undiminished.

During the 1720s, London experienced one of its sporadic crime waves. Prior to the inauguration of public policing and because most major criminals were protected from prosecution thanks to the corruption of various officials, the only response the government could muster was to begin offering rewards for the capture of robbers and the threat of the death penalty for most offenses. After Wild served a criminal apprenticeship with the London city marshal, he was well versed in the trade of receiving stolen goods. Subsequently, he set up an office near the Old Bailey, where he acted as agent between thief and victim. Wild had learned a very important lesson in the vagaries of crime—that the original owners of stolen goods were willing to pay the highest prices to retrieve their possessions. Wild improvised an ingenious system for receiving stolen goods based on one developed by the notorious "Moll Cutpurse" in the previous century. He improved the system by posing first as a private thief taker who went after offenders to subsequently collect a reward once the objects were returned. He then organized bands of thieves whom he directed in his various schemes.

A master of self-promotion, Wild would have engendered a certain amount of respect from modern hoods such as Chicago's Al Capone and New York Gambino crime family boss, flashy John Gotti, to be sure. By 1718, Wild regarded himself that era's "boss of bosses" or *capo di tuti,* taking the sobriquet *Thief Taker General* as he exploited the limits of the law to the fullest. Some police historians consider his posse of thief catchers to be a precursor to early police departments, but Wild is better known for having elevated thief taking to a science, and over his ten years he was credited with sending more than 100 criminals to the gallows. His success was ensured by his ability to set up for arrest and execution any thief who tried to compete in like fashion. Therefore, by aiding the law in his capacity as thief taker, he sued the law to fatten his own coffers. Testament to his success was the fact that London highwaymen gave London a wide berth between 1723 and 1725, evidenced by the fact that none were hanged during this period. Wild enjoyed the protection of influential patrons, survived attempts on his life, and acquired massive real estate holdings. However, despite supporters who argued he helped control the crime problem, Wild was sent to the gallows in 1725 following the implementation of more punitive anti-thief legislation (Roth 2005).

QUESTION: WAS JONATHAN WILD INVOLVED IN ORGANIZED CRIME?   Since the early 1980s, most definitions of *organized crime* have included common characteristics, including

- Structure
- Continuity
- Violence
- Discipline

- Involvement in legitimate enterprises
- Multiple enterprises
- Corruption
- Monopolization
- Sophistication[2]

Of course, organized crime groups might share all or some of these features as well as others, but the consensus is that if a criminal group displays a number of these features it can be considered an organized crime group. In the chronicle of Jonathan Wild, we can discern a number of these characteristics, especially structure, violence, discipline, involvement in legitimate enterprises, monopolization, and sophistication. However, does this equate thief taking in the eighteenth century with organized crime? What is clearly missing here is the continuity aspect that accompanies the better-known exemplars of this activity. As Thief-Taker General, Wild dominated the London underworld for almost a decade, but, when he was gone from the scene, so was his organization, although other individuals would fill the void. Herein lies the dilemma for criminologists, journalists, policymakers, and police authorities—it is virtually impossible to come up with a definition that stands the test of time. Organized crime groups are flexible enterprises that can change shape and structure to take advantage of opportunities. However, these opportunities are always changing, paralleling the development of new markets, consumer demands, and the changing legal climate.

PIRATES: THE ORIGINAL GANGSTERS?

Organized crime expert Donald Lunde recently suggested that "Reading 17th century Spanish complaints about English and Dutch pirates is curiously like reading accounts of modern reports on organized crime" (2005, 17). Indeed, piracy and other crimes of the preindustrial era plagued an earlier world much as organized crime does the modern one. Although most pirate organizations lasted about as long as their captains, with few having any type of continuity in leadership, while they did exist they shared a number of attributes with modern syndicates—bribing officials, operating sometimes with state support, and selling stolen booty to legitimate businessmen in a type of pre-modern money laundering system.

Colonial Piracy As Organized Crime

Like organized crime, an exact definition of piracy universally acceptable over time and between places has eluded criminologists. Over the past several decades a broad definition has emerged from historical research that suggests piracy "is essentially indiscriminate taking of property with violence, on or by descent from the sea" (Rediker 2004, 83). Others refer to piracy as a form of "maritime macro-parasitism" (Anderson 2001, 82; McNeil 1980). For students of organized crime, parallels to the modern era can be discerned during the so-called Golden Age of Piracy in the seventeenth and eighteenth centuries, a time which has been referred to as "a period of unrestrained murder, robbery and kidnapping on the high seas" (Millard 2007, 28).

Beginning in the 1950s, at the height of the first federal investigations into American organized crime (the Kefauver Hearings), writers began acknowledging piracy as a progenitor to modern racketeering (Karraker 1953). As long as ships bearing cargoes have plied the high seas, there have been those who would like to have said ships and all they carried. Phoenicians and Vikings engaged in piracy, and pirates have ranged the oceans from the Roman era well into the modern one. In the enormous archives of such lore, these men were referred to as *pirates, privateers, corsairs,* and *freebooters,* to name just a few.[3] This quantity of names is not unlike the modern attempts to affix a proper name to organized crime through monikers such as *mafia, syndicate, cartel, mob, rackets, gang,* and so forth. In any case, an examination of the persistence of *piracy* into the American colonial era offers a number of parallels to organized crime acts and activities of a more modern era.

What Constitutes Piracy Today?

According to the International Maritime Bureau that serves as an international clearinghouse for piracy data, in 2005, *piracy* was defined as "Any act of boarding or attempting to board any ship with the apparent intent to commit theft or any other crime and with the apparent intent or capability to use force in the furtherance of that act" (Walters 2007, 10).

Chroniclers of piracy have tended to stereotype pirates and their activities in the pre-modern era. Because pirates rarely left records or diaries, the tendency has been to view all pirates through the prism of the best-known accounts dating back to the eighteenth century.[4] According to one account, by basing the stereotypical pirate on a handful of well-known pirates, "this approach backfires" (Turley 199, 93).

THE GOLDEN AGE OF PIRACY (1650–1730)   Recent scholarship suggests that there were three distinct generations of pirates between 1650 and 1730, the so-called Golden Age of Piracy. Between 1650 and the 1680s, most pirates, or buccaneers, were Protestant "sea dogs" from England, Northern France, and the Netherlands, who typically targeted ships from Catholic Spain. Then, beginning in the 1690s, Captain William Kidd and others moved their operations into the Indian Ocean and built a pirate base on the island of Madagascar (Rediker, 2004).

The third and most successful era of piracy was between 1716 and 1726, an age dominated by larger-than-life figures like Bartholomew Roberts and Edward Teach. It was this era that generated most of the familiar images in popular culture, including Long John Silver of *Treasure Island* fame, the black flag of the *Jolly Roger,* and the sinister Blackbeard (Rediker 2004, 9). This era is the most heavily documented of the pirate periods, rife with accounts produced by newspapers, diaries, court records, pirate interviews, and colonial and naval correspondence. During this decade there were an estimated 2,000 to 4,000 pirates representing a potpourri of ethnicities. Together and apart, they disrupted trade in what was then considered a "strategic zone of capital accumulation," namely the West Indies, North America, and West Africa (Rediker 2004; Earle 2003).

Rules and Regulations

Most historians of piracy have explained the process by which pirate organizations wrote up articles of rules for behavior and the distribution of ill-gained profits. By agreeing to such oaths of honor, new members joined the subculture of the pirate crew, thereby cementing their loyalty to the group. Going one step further, Hans Turley suggested that the pirate oaths and articles expressed "the terms of camaraderie in their own transgressive world" while demonstrating that ocean-going outlaws had "their own cultural and legal system" (Turley 1999, 94–95). Rediker called these articles "one of the most egalitarian plans for the disposition of resources to be found anywhere in the eighteenth century" (1987, 264). He describes a criminal hierarchy and organization in which the spoils were typically shared according to position. In the pirate hierarchy, there was apparently less disparity between the top and bottom ranks (Rediker 1987). By most accounts, the reason given for pirate articles was that the pirates were outside "the laws of God and Man," and were only attempting to inject some order as they created their own society or subculture.

An examination of pirate "articles," or rules and regulations, reveals a number of parallels with their modern gangland counterparts. Pirate articles "allocated authority, distributed plunder, and enforced discipline" (Rediker 1987, 142). As Turley notes, "The pirates' articles demonstrate the extent to which the pirate milieu opposed the political structures of conventional society" (1999, 93).

Few original *Articles of Regulation* have survived, but most are similar in content. Those that more closely parallel the rules of modern gangland are intended to ensure harmony in the pirate crews and confederations. Items include how to resolve quarrels; theft of booty; and the banning of gambling, cowardice, desertion, drunkenness, and certain disrespect to women captives. Similarly, a

FIGURE 1.1 Captain Kidd hanging in a gibbet after death on gallows as a warning to all potential pirates
Source: Dorling Kindersley Media Library/Tina Chambers

number of modern criminal syndicates have written or well-understood prohibitions against drug use and addiction as well as against disrespecting women. In the milieu of some modern crack houses, rules and potential punishments are even posted on the walls inside. In other organizations there are often unwritten prohibitions that members don't steal or fight among themselves. Like the pirate bureaucracy, these rules were meant to maintain discipline (Rediker 1987; Turley 1999).

Many potential buccaneers were lured by the "organization" of most pirate ships, which contrasted favorably to life in the British navy. Over time, pirate crews developed certain codes that formed the nucleus of later pirate articles. By most accounts there was a striking similarity between the rules and customs of different pirate ships. Pirate compacts were usually drawn up either at the beginning of the voyage or the election of a new captain and then were voted on by the crew. According to these written agreements, crews allocated authority; decided how plunder, food, and other resources would be divided; and enforced discipline (Rediker 2004, 65). Historians suggest that the best-known pirate articles, written by Bartholomew Roberts, became a model for other pirates. Virtually every book on piracy mentions these early eighteenth-century rules. One of the popular conceptions about modern organized crime is that members must swear to a code of behavior as well as participate in a variety of rituals (see Chapter 3 for Mafia, 'Ndrangheta, and Camorra). By most accounts, Bartholomew Roberts' crew was required to swear over a Bible to obey his rules.

Summary of Bartholomew Robert's Ship Articles (1720s)

  I. Every man shall have an equal vote in affairs of moment. He shall have an equal title to the fresh provisions or strong liquors at any time seized, and shall use them at pleasure . . .
 II. . . . But, if they defraud the company to the value of even one dollar in plate, jewels or money, they shall be marooned. If any man rob another he shall have his nose and ears slit, and be put ashore where he shall be sure to encounter hardships.
 III. None shall game for money either with dice or cards.
 IV. The lights and candles should be put out at eight at night, and if any of the crew desire to drink after that hour they shall sit upon the open deck without lights.
  V. Each man shall keep his piece, cutlass and pistols at all times clean and ready for action.
 VI. No boy or woman to be allowed amongst them. If any man shall be found seducing any of the latter sex and carrying her to sea in disguise he shall suffer death.
VII. He that shall desert the ship or his quarters in time of battle shall be punished by death or marooning.
VIII. None shall strike another on board the ship, but every man's quarrel shall bended on shore by sword of pistol in this manner.
 IX. No man shall talk of breaking up their way of living till each has a share of 1000 pounds. Every man who shall become a cripple or lose a limb in the service shall have 800 pieces of eight from the common stock and for lesser hurts proportionately.
  X. The captain and the quartermaster shall each receive two shares of a prize, the master gunner and boatswain, one and one half shares, all other officers one and one quarter. . . .

PIRATE CAPTAIN AS CAPO: CONTINUITY IN LEADERSHIP   Pirate captains enjoyed their position only with the full support of their crews. Although there was continuity in leadership, captains would do well to remember that they served at the discretion of their crews and were eminently replaceable. A successful captain was typically a formidable presence who held his position through sheer force of personality. There are a number of examples of captains being "snatched from their positions" for cowardly or cruel behavior, and many ships experienced frequent changes of command. In at least one case, a captain was overthrown by the "class conscious wrath of his crew for being too 'Gentleman-like'" (Rediker 2004, 65). In other cases, some crews executed captains considered too "despotic." Pirates were just as willing to replace their leaders with more visionary leaders as their modern day organized crime counterparts. Daniel Defoe chronicled the lives of many of these men. In the first decades of the eighteenth century, Edward England had been the scourge first of the Caribbean and then the African coast. However, when he began to exercise leniency toward prisoners, his crew saw this as a sign of weakness, and they decided to get rid of him.

PIRATES AS GOODFELLAS   Many a child has been brought up on the romanticized exploits of pirates. More than 130 films have been made heralding this antisocial lifestyle, a faraway second to the movies that have chronicled the lives of traditional gangsters. Most of these pirate films were little more than flights of fancy, with little regard for accuracy. The same can probably be said about most films based on organized crime. Nevertheless, at one time or another both genres of films have proved to be good box office.

Ask almost anyone about organized crime and they will respond with "Mafia," codes of honor, and the usual accounts made popular by the alien-conspiracy theories—and they will typically be wrong. Ask the same question about the pirates and you will probably hear something about walking the plank and buried treasure—also dubious history.

Organized piracy has thrived throughout history. By the Middle Ages, piracy was already an ancient occupation for certain men (and a few women). As trade increased over the centuries, so did the volume of piracy. Why? That was where the money was! With the expansion of oceanic trade routes during the commercial expansion of the sixteenth and seventeenth centuries, pirates too ex-

Gangster Violence, Eighteenth-Century Style

There is a notorious scene in Nicholas Pileggi's *Casino* in which gangster Anthony Spilotro places his victim's head in a vise and presses it until his eyeballs pop out. The pirates of the Golden Age were no pikers either when it came to brutality, as witnessed by the various methods that were used to convince victims to hand over their valuables. In one particularly resonant act called *woolding*, a pirate wrapped a knotted cord around a man's head until his eyes popped out. Other cases have chronicled pirates placing burning matches inside a victim's eyelids and even slicing off a prisoner's lips and making him watch as they were cooked over hot coals (Woodard 2007).

panded their trade routes, following the money trail from the Old World to the New. Quite often, the European competition for trade monopolies led to war between nations on the high seas as the British, French, and Spanish attempted to expand their empires into the Americas. These wars often deteriorated into unconventional warfare and piracy (Karraker 1953).

Best known as the author of *Robinson Crusoe,* author Daniel Defoe also penned one of the best early accounts of English piracy. His critique of the phenomena has an eerie resonance if one considers various modern reactions to the growing problem of transnational crime. Defoe warned his readers in the early eighteenth century that "The pirate destroys all government and all order, by breaking all those ties and bonds that unite people in a civil society under any government" (Perotin-Dumon 2001, 40). By most accounts, pirates were indeed violent and antisocial. Both writers and popular culture have unduly romanticized pirates, ensuring that like modern gangland's so-called men of respect, both have enjoyed a kind of Jeckyl-and-Hyde immortality. In popular culture, the gangsters of the Godfather seem rather benign, as do the pirates of *Treasure Island;* however, the reality was far more grotesque. Both archetypes had blood on their hands. Violence, corruption, robbery, and torture were never far from their underworld purview.

CREATING A PIRATE PROFILE   Due to the economic conditions of the seventeenth and eighteenth centuries, there was always a large population of mostly unemployed young men who probably felt exploited and provided a group of willing recruits. Marcus Rediker convincingly demonstrates that piracy "was a way of life voluntarily chosen, for the most part, by large numbers of men who directly challenged the ways of the society from which they excepted themselves" (2004, 139–140). For ordinary sailors, piracy offered a better but probably shorter life that promised respite from poor quarters and food, brutal discipline and the low wages that characterized conditions in legitimate ocean-going occupations. "Life for these men" according to historian Peter Earle, "may have been dangerous, harsh, and usually short, but it had its compensations" (2003, 180). Remuneration came in the form of decent food and ale, sailing in good weather, and better pay than could be expected in "honest service," where food and wages were marginal and labor demanding (Earle 2003, 169). Much like their modern-day counterparts, most accounts indicate that as soon as they captured a ship they insisted on dividing up the plunder. Similarly, most of the profits were probably quickly gambled away or spent, because it was "doubtful that any invested much for the future due to the short-lived careers that were the norm" (Ritchie 1986, 229).

One recent scholar discovered that the typical pirate served only from one to two years under the skull and crossbones, and "almost without exception came from the lowest social classes" (Rediker 2004, 50). However, a pirate ship could not succeed without a coterie of skilled seamen and artisans such as carpenters, surgeons, and sailmakers.

Although some similarities can be discerned between pirates and gangsters, these comparisons fade when placed in their contemporary worlds. Although it is true that pirates were indeed uneducated and had little opportunity for employment, "modern gangsters have had public money spent on their education and never live within a few days of possible starvation" (Thrower 1980, 89).

WHY PIRACY? ENGLAND'S NAVIGATION ACTS: PROHIBITION, SEVENTEENTH-CENTURY STYLE   The Navigation Acts were to seventeenth-century organized piracy and smuggling what Prohibition and the Harrison Act were to narcotics and alcohol prohibition in twentieth-century America. England's Navigation Acts were much like American Prohibition and the modern "war on drugs," which in most cases only stimulated the law-breaking behavior of the American people. The first Navigation Acts were a series of acts enacted by Parliament between 1651 and 1696 that made it virtually impossible to bring into the colonies certain luxury items legitimately. Smugglers, pirates, and black marketers were only too happy to challenge these barriers for a reasonable price.

The Navigation Acts sought to control colonial trade to England's benefit by stipulating that no goods could be imported into England or her colonies unless on British ships manned by British subjects. Other onerous features of the legislation included stipulations that certain colonial products could only be shipped to the English market; almost all goods bound to or from the colonies had to unload in England, in the process paying customs duties that pushed up prices on the major staple crops of the American colonies, such as tobacco, sugar, and dyestuffs. The Acts in effect created a near English monopoly on both shipping and trade. The people in the colonies resented this and had no problem trading with oceanic outlaws, establishing in effect an unrestricted market for cheaper goods, undercutting legitimate markets in the process. New Navigation Acts served only to inflame colonial tensions—particularly in 1663, when it was mandated that virtually all European products destined to the colonies must be landed in England first and then reloaded on English ships for the conclusion of the voyage—items that included Portuguese salt, Irish and Scottish horses and linens, and wines from Madeira and the Azores. Luxury goods were marked up in the process, creating a healthy smuggling economy (Hoffer 2000).

As a result of this system, colonial officials and entrepreneurs in the New World were drawn into the smuggling system. So, although colonial governors were expected to enforce the law, more often than not they participated in the smuggling and corruption behaviors that exemplified early organized crime 200 years later. The unwillingness of American colonists and officials to obey the Navigation Acts, not unlike the enforcement of Prohibition laws in the 1920s, created parallel systems of justice. Colonists were willing to follow the letter of the law for traditional crimes such as treason, murder, and robbery. However, when it came to traditions of free trade, they essentially nullified the law by creating organized smuggling ventures. New England merchants, in particular, routinely participated in trade with non-English ports. Others adopted brilliant scams—ships would arrive in their first port of call, then secretly unload and load at neighboring steams and inlets. Here, small boats would ferry goods illegally to and from shore. Ship captains contributed to the subterfuge by carrying false sets of papers to get by the customs officials.

By the Revolutionary era of the mid-1700s, the American colonies were home to a number of clandestine economies, thanks to organized smuggling rings and black markets. By the early 1700s, smuggling and black-markets "had become a way of life" in America (Hoffer 2000, 412). By most accounts, merchants in New England became most prosperous in this manner, some making considerable fortunes smuggling in Dutch linens and French brandies. According to one estimate, in order to avoid import taxes, British colonial businessmen probably smuggled two million gallons of illegal molasses into port cities between 1738 and 1750. Other sources indicate that "Five-sixths of the tea consumed in most colonies had been smuggled" (Williams 1961, 145). Another interesting parallel with Prohibition is the fact that there were always too few agents to enforce the law. Similarly, despite pleas for additional customs inspectors, Parliament made no effort in that direction. Yet even if they had increased the manpower, most sources indicate that like their Prohibition era counterparts in the twentieth century, eighteenth-century customs officials were easily bribed.

PIRACY AND THE LEGITIMATE BUSINESS COMMUNITY   At various stages in their development, English, French, and Spanish colonies in the New World teetered on the brink of extinction. In order to make up for the unstable resupply of provisions, some colonies purchased contraband from pirates. In other cases, pirate crews were not tied to the various commercial treaties imposed by foreign nations, and could therefore sell their illicit goods below the usurious prices imposed by charter companies.

This relationship was particularly fruitful at the local level—at ports and docks along the colonial trade routes. New England's famous shipyards flourished by building and outfitting pirate ships, whereas local merchants did a thriving business selling exotic pirate plunder to eager colonists.

North America proved to be the greatest markets for pirate plunder in the seventeenth century. In the early colonial years that spanned the late seventeenth and early eighteenth centuries, pirates engaged in lucrative commerce with New York City and other colonial ports. Organized piracy flourished due to the exigencies of international geopolitics and trade patterns. By the mid-1680s, pirates were familiar visitors to North Atlantic ports. In fact, their visits were looked forward to by a number of merchants. According to Mueller and Adler, there was an incredible amount of greed and corruption in North America that "Facilitated this unholy and bloody trade" between the pirates and the merchants (1985, 297). In one account, a pirate ship stocked with treasure worth 700 pounds per pirate docked in Boston. Local merchants sent out a pilot to help navigate it into the harbor. During the ensuing transactions, the pirates purchased "most of the choice goods in Boston" (Karraker 1953, 66). Apparently, the Boston businessmen were more than happy to relieve the outlaws of their bounty, which they could then resell for a huge profit.

New England merchants rightfully felt exploited by English trade rules. Forced trade with the English at exorbitant fixed rates set by English merchants gave merchants little opportunity for what traditionally had been high profits. Some of colonial America's leading families consorted with pirates as fences of pirate plunder. Merchants often maintained legitimate businesses while engaged in the illegitimate brokering of stolen property (Gottschalk and Flanagan 2000, 11).

In 1699, a New York courtroom sat in rapt attention as the pirate-cum-merchant Adam Baldridge described his illegitimate business arrangements on the island of Madagascar. Testifying before the Court of Vice Admiralty, he explained how he left the British colony of Jamaica in 1685 one step ahead of murder charges and decided that the pirate life offered him the best opportunities for economic advancement. When he first arrived on the Madagascar coastal enclave of St. Mary's (off the coast of southeastern Africa), he had planned to stay only temporarily. One thing led to another, and he made the transition from high-seas piracy to island merchant. He found his new status as island mogul and patriarch more profitable than chasing down ships at sea.

Between 1691 and 1697, Madagascar became an important destination for pirate and merchant ships alike. Pirate ships such as the *Bachelor's Delight* would dock here to sell cargoes plundered in the Red Sea. Here, Baldridge sold cattle and provisions to pirate crews for beads, cannons, barrels of flour, and iron bars. One merchant ship unloaded a cargo from a New York businessman named Frederick Philipse, regarded by some as "Probably the greatest" of New York's profiteers (Botting 1978, 74). In court, Baldridge regaled his listeners with how illicit pirate lucre was traded and sold to the New York merchant in return. Philipse shipped seeds, wine, and clothing intended for the pirate customers. Baldridge served as a willing and ready middleman to the pirates, happy to mark up the price of such goods in the bargain. Baldridge supplied the resident pirates with rum, tobacco, and weapons while purchasing pirate plunder at bargain rates, which he then conveyed to Philipse in New York to be marketed there at much higher prices.

Frederick Philipse: Patron to the Red Sea Pirates

Frederick Philipse was a respected church member, landholder, and a respected councilor to New York's governor. He also happened to be the main middleman and broker for the Madagascar pirates in the 1690s. By the time he enlisted in this enterprise, he already owned a huge estate along the Hudson River, thanks in part to marrying well. For well over a decade, he supplied the pirates with all types of essentials in return for slaves and stolen treasures. However, he could not have survived without the collusion of colonial authorities, who reportedly arranged for customs inspectors "not to be strict with what goods" came to Philipse (Botting 1978, 74). All the while, Philipse ran legitimate businesses as a front. Although he was eventually tied to the pirate trade, he was never prosecuted and died a wealthy man in 1702, thanks in no small part to his piracy activities.

Piracy and Modern Organized Crime: Some Shared Characteristics

Modern Criminal Organizations	Colonial	Piracy
Corruption	✗	✗
Violence	✗	✗
Continuity	✗	
Structure	✗	✗
Discipline	✗	✗
Lack of ideology	✗	✗
Multiple enterprises	✗	✗
Rules and regulations	✗	✗
Codes of conduct	✗	✗
Sophistication	✗	✗

CHARACTERISTICS

Geographically, piracy occurred on a global scale. Illegal pirates and state-sponsored privateers had vast economic incentives to participate in the looting of cargoes of gold and jewels, grain, and even wine and drugs. The import and export market of these goods was often heavily restricted, thus in order for the system of piracy to succeed, it needed the willing participation of corrupt officials and greedy merchants, especially when it came for pirates to launder their ill-gotten profits. Law enforcement was almost nonexistent outside the various naval vessels and the handful of customs officials, and with little in the way of international agreements or jurisdictional demarcation, the seas were a vast frontier for freebooters. The very regulations and organization of a pirate ship and the ways in which a ship selected a new crew in the eighteenth century guaranteed continuity and ensured a certain social uniformity that one pirate historian referred to as an "elaborate social code" or "consciousness of kind" that in effect perpetuated "the social world that pirates had creatively built for themselves" (Rediker 2004, 152).

CORRUPTION   Piracy flourished for quite some time in the New World because of the active participation of colonial politicians, business merchants, and the colonists themselves. According to several criminologists, "for piracy truly to flourish, a corrupt officialdom and/or merchant class is needed, especially to 'launder' ill-gotten gains" (Mueller and Adler 1985, 300). Corruption existed at every level of the fledgling colonial economies. Merchants dined with pirate chieftains; governors sold special government commissions to pirates that allowed them to attack and loot enemy ships; customs officers were bribed; and leading citizens sold them rum, weapons, and provisions. Reports also indicated that farmers as well as local merchants supplied pirate crews with provisions, arranged local transportation for them, warned them of patrolling constables, hid them in safehouses, and even helped pirates escape from wooden jailhouses (Karraker 1953, 85). Collusion was so pervasive that honest citizens felt powerless to enforce the law in the face of official obstruction. Pirate trials held in Philadelphia in 1699 revealed the influence of pirate groups over government and business interests. Bostonian participation extended to setting up a mint just to stamp plundered metals into coins. New York was considered even worse. Among the many accounts of collusion with the pirates from the period was one reporting the existence of a syndicate of respected businessmen who employed a resident agent on Madagascar who supplied goods to the ocean outlaws for high profits while shipping plundered goods back to New York (Winston 1969, 35).

As the leading representatives of the crown in America, colonial governors in some cases lamented their limited abilities to suppress piracy due to the complicity between the business

The Killigrew Family

In the Elizabethan era of the late 1500s, the English crown led a campaign against piracy at home that was largely ineffective. Piracy flourished in England and other European cities often due to collusion between the pirates and constables, sheriffs, and justices of the peace—the law enforcement apparatus of the day. Farther inland rural gentry became involved in the pirate machinery as well. In the sixteenth century, the Killigrew family pirate organization of Cornwall, England, was perhaps the largest operation of its kind in the British Isles. As the "President of the Commissioners for Piracy," the Killigrew Family, a wealthy landowning clan with influential friends in government, controlled pirate syndicates along the southwestern British coast. The Killigrew enterprise flourished due to the insulation of the family from outsiders. By most accounts it was a "closely knit organization of relatives, retainers, and agents" (Williams 1961, 55). However, the major source of the family lucre was its support of pirate ships and crews that plied the seas off the British Isles.[5]

community and local merchants with pirate crews. What made matters worse was the fact that some governors actively participated in the underground economy. New York Governor Benjamin Fletcher was removed from office for such corruption in the 1690s. One expert has even pondered that in 1699, "It is conceivable that not the lieutenant governor and his council but pirate racketeers were the real rulers of New York" (Karraker 1953, 104).

Pirates were able to flourish up and down the Eastern coast of the American colonies in part because piracy was so well organized. One observer remarked, "Almost everywhere one looks along the Atlantic seaboard in 1699 politicians and merchants are obstructing efforts of honest officials" (Ritchie 1986). By some accounts, the "pirate industry" was the foundation for economic prosperity in some colonies. Despite accounts of Massachusetts' Puritans, Philadelphia's Quakers, and New York's Anglicans, who "loudly condemned piracy as a social evil and cancer on the body politic," evidence suggests that these very same individuals secretly profited from trading with pirates, eager to smuggle goods restricted under English trade laws (Ritchie 1986, 66). Americans were only too happy to partake in the two-way exchange as colonial entrepreneurs lined their pockets with pirate gold. Pirate trials in Philadelphia in 1699 revealed the influence of pirate groups over government and business (Karraker 1953). Some accounts revealed that American merchants loaded ships with rum, beer, European apparel, guns, and other goods and trade them for slaves with pirates in the Red Sea region often the coast of Africa (Earle 2003).

THREAT OF OR USE OF FORCE   By most accounts pirates depended on the use of force or the threat of force in the pursuance of their operations. Today it is popular to ascribe terrorist tendencies to pirates and other freebooters, with authors citing the frequent use of brutality and images of the Skull and Crossbones, not unlike "Black Hand" extortionists of the late nineteenth century who furthered their extortion operations with the use of sinister Black Hand notes. Rediker makes the case that, "Pirates consciously used terror to accomplish their aims—to obtain money, to punish those who resisted them, to take vengeance against those they considered their enemies, and to instill fear in sailors, captains, merchants, and officials who might wish to attack or resist pirates" (2004, 5). There is also indeed the possibility that pirates fostered this perception in order to avoid fighting; using their reputation to win early capitulation.

ORGANIZED HIERARCHY   The quartermaster, who was elected by the crew to protect its interests, balanced the power of the ship's captain. He was responsible for discipline, supervised distribution of food and loot, called meetings to discuss future policy, and acted as judge in trials of with jury of 12 men, half chosen by the accused (Earle 2003, 173). Loot was allocated according to each member's skills and standing. The largest shares went to the Captain and Quartermaster and then in descending order to the gunners, boatswains, mates, carpenters, doctors, and finally the others.

COLORS AND EMBLEMS   One of the more accepted customs in organized crime is the maintenance of secrecy. However, certain forms of organized crime follow other practices. Among African-American street gangs such as the Bloods and Crips, the wearing of blue or red items is a clear message of their identity. Hispanic street gangs use hand signals and tattoos, whereas in Japan a Yakuza member stands out with a missing finger digit or elaborate tattoos. In outlaw motorcycle gangs the group's colors instantly identify their association. Similarly, pirate organizations used colorful flags on the high seas to announce their intentions and affiliations. However, they rarely sailed under the black flag and crossbones in the seventeenth century. They were likely to use a *ruse de guerre* in which a flag representing another country was presented to convince potential victims to close with the ship. The "Bloodie Red Flag," or *Jolie Rouge,* was hoisted to let a fleeing ship know that if they fled, no quarter would be shown to its passengers and the ship best sidle close (Zacks 2002, 43). Designs varied from ship to ship. Most incorporated symbols related to death such as skulls, crossbones, bleeding hearts, and skeletons. Explorer and sea captain William Dampier recorded the colors of a number of pirate flags. Bartholomew Sharp announced his presence with a red and green one, whereas John Coxon's was plain red, and John Hawkins was readily identifiable by his red striped with yellow (Thrower 1980).

One pirate expert describes the pirate flag as a "triad of interlocking symbols—death, violence, limited time," all representing the meaningful parts of seaman's life. Although the flag varied from ship to ship, almost all were black, adorned with "white representational figures, sometimes an isolated human skull, or 'death's head' but more commonly an entire skeleton" (Rediker 2004, 98). In any case the persistence of such a symbol should be considered "an advanced state of group identification."

MONOPOLIZATION   English pirate captain John Hawkins acquired a rather cumbersome cargo on one occasion in the 1590s. Intent on selling it to merchants in Spanish America's Hispaniola, he used a strategy of forcing the colonists to do business by preventing other cargo from reaching the colony from other sources (Andrews 1979).

FIGURE 1.2   Pirate flag or "Jolly Roger" skull and crossbones
Source: Dorling Kindersley Media Library/Tina Chambers

PIRATE DISCIPLINE   Most accounts suggest that in "organized piracy," everything that was captured was to be pooled. This was followed by what was called a *shareout* (Thrower 1980). Similar to modern syndicate members who fail to pay a percentage to the higher powers, if any of the crew held out or failed to contribute in any way, the consequences were deadly. Some pirates were marooned on uninhabited islands; others were executed on board ship.

Modern Piracy

Maritime piracy has come a long way since the halcyon Golden Age some 300 years ago. Today's pirates are likely to possess a combination of ancient sailing skills along with the latest in high-tech equipment, including high-performance speedboats, modern weapons, and radio intercept technology capable of identifying and locating the position of large valuable vessels chock-full with modern booty. However, most evidence suggests that the majority of pirates are rather low tech, more likely to favor a gun or knife than other weapons. These types of crimes are increasing at an alarming rate. According to the International Maritime Bureau (IMB),[6] more than 3,300 cases of piracy were reported between 1993 and 2004. In these instances, 334 people were killed, 152 reported missing, and 2,791 taken hostage or held for ransom (Walters 2007). In the first nine months of 2005 alone, more than 200 acts of piracy were reported around the world, triple the number of incidents from a decade previously, resulting in the killing, kidnapping, and disappearance of more than 280 crew members (Knight and Crystall 2005). During the first nine months of 2007, pirate activity rose 14 percent from Africa to Southeast Asia, with the largest increases in Somalia and Nigeria (Harris 2007, A21).

A variety of groups and individuals commit acts of piracy at a number of levels. For example, one criminologist suggests that low-level piracy is committed by "coastal-dwelling, sea-knowledgeable, poverty-stricken individuals who find piracy a viable career option" (Walters 2007, 11). Such miscreants steal virtually anything of value on a ship. From an organized crime perspective, a number of crime syndicates have been identified as pirates, especially off the coasts of South America, Africa, and Southeast Asia. One of the more interesting aspects of modern piracy is that the majority of pirate attacks (50.2 percent) take place while the ship is anchored, with ships steaming at sea accounting for only 26.1 percent of these attacks (Walters 2007, 12). Criminologist Stephen Walters explains that most cases occur at anchor because this is when the ship is most vulnerable; ships that are berthed at a dock are usually protected by lighting and security patrols. Ships steaming on the high seas are typically moving at speeds that are difficult to match. Ships at anchor are connected by one anchor line running from the water to the deck, offering an inviting method for getting on board. While anchored, the ship has no ability to maneuver and is often too far away from other ships for security (Walters 2007, 11).

Modern piracy tends to occur in regions with weak and impoverished governments, such as in Africa, where there are few land-based police resources, let alone sufficient police to patrol territorial waters. As one recent investigation makes clear, "the lack of security near major shipping lanes has created fertile ground for hijackers" (Harris 2007, A21). In a number of cases, the U.S. Navy has been called in to aid hijacked ships from North Korea and Japan.

Modern shipowners have begun to respond in kind to the new wave of high-tech pirates. Where once ships responded to these threats with cannons and muskets, some modern vessels are just as likely to be armed with a host of new security devices, including antitheft intruder alarms and thermal cameras, and deterrents such as high-powered water cannon, electrified fences, and in the case of the *Seabourn Spirit*, attacked off the coast of Somalia in November 2005, an acoustic weapon that emits eardrum-shattering blasts of noise that often leaves the attackers too stunned to complete the mission. In the late 1990s one research group even experimented with infrasound—low-frequency noises that were intended to induce involuntary bowel movements. However, ships with such weapons are far from the norm due to the high cost of such systems (Knight and Crystall 2005).

Today, the 900-kilometer long Strait of Malacca between Indonesia and Malaysia is considered one of the more treacherous regions. With more than 50,000 ships passing through each year bearing half of the world's oil supply, the possibilities for plunder are limitless. The pirates have taken advantage of the proximity to a coastline with hundreds of inaccessible islands and isolated harbors. The Horn of Africa,

(continued)

traditionally a target for maritime criminals, continues in that role today with more than 25 attacks off the coast of Somalia during a seven-month period in 2005.

In the past, pirates often relied on luck, weather, and ancient shipping routes to find their plunder. Today, they are more likely to bribe shipping agents for information on cargo and routes or to use VHF radios to intercept messages. Although many ships use radar, it is often useless against the wooden vessels and wetsuits often worn by criminals to protect themselves from infrared security cameras. Sometimes they resort to the old standby of masquerading as a ship in distress to draw a target ship into range and then go aboard and destroy communications equipment. Once the treasure is in hand, it is often off-loaded to waiting merchants eager to act as middlemen and take advantage of porous security and lack of taxes.

However, once intruders manage to storm a vessel, it is likely that "most captains and crew do what victims of piracy have done for centuries—simply comply with their captors' demands" (Knight and Crystall 2005). According to the best estimates, there are more than 200 "phantom vessels" navigating the world's oceans, many of which are vessels that have been hijacked and are enjoying a second life with a new name, new paint, and false documents. Shipping firms have responded to this worst-case scenario by developing a tagging technology such as ShipLoc, owned by a French satellite company, which uses a satellite transmitter hidden on board ship and regularly sends off information on its position to a central control office.

LEGISLATING ORGANIZED CRIME IN AMERICA: INFLUENTIAL ORGANIZED CRIME COMMISSIONS, COMMITTEES, AND INVESTIGATIVE BODIES

Since the late nineteenth century, a number of crime commissions, committees, and investigative bodies at all levels of government—state and federal especially—have attempted to contribute to the body of knowledge concerning organized crime. As can be seen by the following descriptions of organized criminal activities, a number of characteristics have remained unchanged over time.

LEXOW COMMITTEE AND THE TESTIMONY OF GEORGE APPO (1894) Due to pressure from reformer Reverend Charles Parkhurst and others, in January 1893, New York City's Chamber of Commerce adopted a resolution calling for an investigation of the city police department and municipal mismanagement. Subsequently, the Lexow Committee was created, a special senate committee consisting of five Republicans and two Democrats, including one who was considered independent from the Tammany machine. Under the leadership of Judge Clarence Lexow, the hearings began on March 9, 1894, and established the existence of organized crime and vice rackets under the sanction and protection of the police and the city's powerful Democratic political machine operating out of Tammany Hall between 1855 and the 1930s. According to one historian, the investigations revealed the existence of widespread political and police malfeasance that "extended beyond simple toleration of saloons, brothels, and gambling dens" (Gilfoyle 2006, 244), citing examples of a veritable police extortion racket in which police officials extorted kickbacks and other payments from a litany of steamboat operators, produce merchants, sailmakers, bootblacks, pushcart peddlers, and other small-scale merchants.

The subsequent investigation revealed the existence of a menu of bribes for promotion through the ranks of the New York Police Department as well as an established system for shaking down illegitimate businesses. Under the ongoing system, prostitutes and brothel madams paid fees to policemen to solicit and operate. Gambling establishments were expected to pay for protection, and pool halls could operate for $300 per month. Saloon owners paid $20 per month, an "established custom," according to Parkhurst (1895, 96–97).[7]

The Lexow Committee lasted through 74 sessions and produced 10,576 pages of testimony, which one historian called "a mosaic of personal and institutional corruption" (Jeffers 1994, 54). Although numerous officers were dismissed and the Tammany machine was replaced by reform-minded politicians, there were no enduring achievements; just four years later, Tammany was back in the hands of the bosses, and the police force had reverted back to its former corrupt excesses. Lest there be uncertainty as to the impact of the hearings, one only need observe Tammany's slogan during the city's first

The New York Police Department–Tammany Hall Promotion Racket (1890s)

To join NYPD	$300
Promotion to Roundsman	$300
Promotion to Sergeant	$1,600
Promotion to Captain	$14,000

mayoral election in 1898, which read, "To Hell with Reform." It easily vanquished the reform ticket in this pivotal election for mayor of the city's five boroughs under the new consolidation plan.

One of the most revealing witnesses to testify before the Lexow Committee was George Washington Appo, the son of Chinese and Irish immigrants. Before he was out of childhood, his father was in Sing Sing Prison for murder and his mother dead and barely a memory. A lifetime criminal, a guest at numerous prisons beginning at the age of 14, a denizen of the notorious crime-plagued Five Points neighborhood, Appo never spent a day in school. A well-known pickpocket, now almost 40 years old, his testimony before the Committee on June 14, 1894, offered revelations about a New York City demimonde that only supported what many had long assumed. During his three hours on the witness stand, Appo offered what historian Timothy J. Gilfoyle called "a virtual lecture on the argot and behavior of the confidence man, describing the purposes of circulars, backers, steerers, writers, ringers, turners, tailers, turning joints, and guys" (2006, 244), as well as the role played by cooperative police officials and telegraph operators.

Appo's testimony enumerated a street organization of con artists that had been in existence since shortly after the Civil War. By most accounts, what made bunco rings such as the Green-Goods Scam so successful was the participation of legitimate telegraph operators, postal employees, and policemen. The Green-Goods Swindle, or the Sawdust Game, hit town in the late 1860s. The Green-Goods Man first had to obtain the names of individuals who regularly subscribed to lotteries and similar activities. Other potential victims were retrieved from the *Bradstreet's* or *Dunn's* mercantile agencies and other city directories. A "writer" selects the names and mails them circulars describing the Green Goods (see the following example of a Green-Goods Letter). Letters were then sent "claiming that they possessed stolen or discarded currency engraving plates from the U.S. Treasury. The circular offered genuine-looking counterfeit money or 'green goods' to prospective buyers at cut-rate prices" (Guilfoyle 1927, 196). An agent was then sent out to scout for the most promising marks, and as Herbert Asbury succinctly put it some 80 years ago, "In due time those chosen for sacrifice received one of several circular letters" (1927:196).

There were a number of permutations of the Green-Goods Scam. The trial of George Appo revealed one of the more popular ones, which involved a type of bait-and-switch in which the victims would be shown a bag of money in which they were told were counterfeit bills. The victim then

Typical Green-Goods Letter

Dear Sir: I will confide to you through the circular a secret by which you can make a speedy fortune. I have on hand a large amount of counterfeit notes of the following denominations: $1, $2, $10 and $20. I guarantee each note to be perfect . . . I furnish you with my goods at the following low price . . .

For $1,200 in my goods (assorted) I charge . . . $100

For $2,500 in my goods (assorted) I charge . . . $200

For $5,000 in my goods (assorted) I charge . . . $350

For $10,000 in my goods (assorted) I charge . . . $600

bought the counterfeit bills with real ones for pennies on the dollar, only to find out once the scammers left the scene that they were holding a bag of worthless paper clippings or sawdust. One of the brilliant conceits of this con was that there were few chances that the victim would report the ruse to law enforcement, because the swindle would implicate both parties in the exchange of counterfeit bills. In the event that a victim decides to return to the scene of the crime to confront the conmen, the team employs a "lookout" who is expected to scare him into believing he is a policeman and to scold the victim by telling him "that he is just as bad as they are, and puts himself more liable to the law" than other members of the fraud ring (Lexow Committee, Vol. II, 1895, 1632).[8]

Selections from the Testimony of George Appo (June 14, 1894)

Q. Let us see; in the green goods business there are quite a number of men engaged, are there not?
A. Yes, sir.

Q. Now, we will say, first, there is the backer, is there not?
A. Yes, sir.

Q. Or the bank-roll man as he is called?
A. Yes, sir.

Q. He is the man that supplies the capital?
A. Yes, sir.

Q. He is the man with the money?
A. Yes, sir.

Q. Then there is the writer?
A. Yes, sir.

Q. Now, what does the writer do?
A. Well, he sends out his mail; send out these circulars.

Q. Then there is the steerer?[9]
A. Yes, sir.

Q. What does the steerer do?
A. He goes after the victim.

Q. And the victim is the man that comes way from the backwoods here to New York to buy the green goods; that is what he is called?
A. Yes, sir; and from towns, too, and cities all over the United States.

Q. There is a man called the ringer, is he not?
A. Yes, sir.

Q. What does the ringer do?
A. He is behind the partition; he takes the good money away and puts the green goods back.

Q. He takes the good money from the victim?
A. Yes, sir.

Q. And puts the bad money?
A. Yes, sir.

Q. Or the counterfeit money—?
A. Yes, sir.

Q. Or the bricks?
A. Yes, sir.

Q. In its stead?
A. Yes, sir.

Q. Is there any other man that has to do this thing; isn't there a turner?
A. A turner.

Q. What does the turner do?

A. Well, he is supposed to be the son of the old man; and he sells the goods.

Q. He does the selling of the green goods?

A. Like a salesman over the counter.

Q. He handles the green goods over the counter and sells them to the victim.

Q. Now, we will see; what is the man that takes charge of the victim after he finds out that he has been fleeced, has been robbed?

A. Well, a steerer takes him away, and then there is the tailer that tails him up in case he should open up.

Q. Now, is there not a place called the "turning joint"?

A. It is a store, just an empty store with a desk in it, like an office.

Q. That is the place where the job is done?

A. Yes, sir.

Q. But there are more places than the turning joint that the victim is brought to, are there not?

A. He is instructed to come to a hotel 50 or 100 miles from New York, say Elizabeth, N.J., Poughkeepsie, Fishkill, or any of those towns out of New York City; they send a steerer after him; he is supposed to be a messenger.

Q. Can you tell us how these various persons divide up the proceeds of the money that is taken from the victims?

A. Well, the writer gets 50 per cent; and the backer gets 50 per cent; and the steerer gets 5 per cent, but he is supposed to get 10 per cent.

Q. Out of which 50 per cent does the steerer get his percentage?

A. Both of them; each gives $2\frac{1}{2}$ per cent.

Q. How do the other men get paid?

A. They get $5 for each man; the turner gets $10, and the ringer gets $5, and the tailer gets $5.

(Appo's testimony from pp. 1622–1664, Vol. II, of Lexow Hearings).

CHICAGO CRIME COMMISSION   In 1919, the Chicago Crime Commission (CCC) was formed by a consortium of Chicago businessmen anxious to rid Chicago of its gangland reputation. It was credited as being the oldest and longest lasting of the country's 16 citizens' crime commissions (Lindberg 1999, 38). Although Chicago mob historian Gus Russo most recently referred to it as "a self-serving exercise in hypocrisy" (2001, 45), it successfully heralded the city's crime problems through a public relations campaign that produced the "Public Enemy" list, well in advance of J. Edgar Hoover's rendition of it. Al Capone would become the first organized crime figure to reach number one on the list.

Nine Recognizable Signs that Organized Crime Is Moving into a Community:

- Social acceptance of hoodlums in decent society.
- Your community's indifference to ineffective local government.
- Notorious mobster personalities in open control of business.
- Deceptive handling of public funds.
- Interest at very high rates to poor risk borrowers (the juice loan).
- Close association of mobsters and local authorities.
- Arson and bombings.
- Terrorized legitimate businesses.
- Easily found gambling, narcotics, and prostitution.

Adapted from Pace and Styles (1975).

ILLINOIS CRIME SURVEY (1929) In 1929, following three years of investigation, the 1,100-page Illinois Crime Survey was published. Sponsored by the Illinois Association for Criminal Justice, it was a statistical and historical examination of the Chicago and Illinois criminal justice systems. Published as *Organized Crime in Chicago,* it is most remembered for Part Three of the survey, written by John Landesco, a research director of the American Institute of Criminal Law and Criminology. One of the most important aspects of Landesco's work was his recognition that organized crime did not originate with Prohibition, but had existed for decades, noting that between 1905 and 1928 there had been both continuity and change within the organized crime milieu. Landesco cited the changing rackets—from gambling and vice to bootlegging and labor union racketeering. He also recognized the all-powerful financial motivations that led gangsters into closer contacts with police and politicians while moving away from the traditional values that governed neighborhood relationships.

SEABURY INQUIRY (1930) The Seabury Investigation began as a probe of the New York Magistrate's Court after several judges were linked to underworld figure Arnold Rothstein and other reputed organized crime stalwarts. It turned into a series of three probes that lasted into 1932. Judge Samuel Seabury[10] concluded that not much had changed since the Lexow Committee investigation 36 years earlier. A law school graduate at the age of 20, Seabury had started his career as a champion of the poor and the labor unions before serving terms on the New York State Supreme Court and the court of pleas. The Seabury hearings proved that a number of judges were involved in illicit enterprises and consorted with gamblers and other underworld characters. During the first hearings in 1930, "solid evidence emerged of the presence in the women's court of an infamous ring of policemen, bondsmen, lawyers, and an assistant district attorney engaged in wholesale extortion from women" (Peterson 1983, 171), most of whom were prostitutes. Forty members of the New York City vice squad were implicated, as were 23 lawyers and 48 bondsmen.[11] Ultimately, the Seabury Commission's findings led to the dismissal of 20 members of the vice squad and the exposure of rampant political bribery and corruption among city leaders, including police commissioners and Tammany Mayor Jimmy Walker, who was forced to resign in 1932.[12]

AMEN REPORT (1939) In 1938, Judge John Harlan Amen was selected to conduct hearings into suspicions that members of the New York City's District Attorney Geoghan's staff were rigging cases. According to the Citizen's Committee on the Control of Crime in New York, of the close to 14,000 cases handled by the court since 1937, a startling number of them were marked by what was termed *irregularities.* Subsequently, more than half of these records disappeared from the 78th police precinct office. Over the next four years Amen's staff found evidence of widespread corruption in the DA's office. The Amen inquiry revealed corruption in the bail bond system, an abortion ring, and gambling rackets operating with police protection (Peterson 1983, 224).

ORGANIZED CRIME HEARINGS: THE 1950s AND 1960s

The FBI, the FBN, and the Kefauver Commission

During the 1940s the Federal Bureau of Narcotics (FBN) took the lead in attacking organized crime, but by doing so linked the underworld to Italians, an unfortunate conclusion that would resonate in the findings of the 1950–1951 Kefauver Hearings. Under the direction of Harry Anslinger, a campaign was conceived (and believed) after the war to link Lucky Luciano and the Mafia to a mythical communist drug-smuggling conspiracy (Valentine 2004, 80).

Shortly after it was announced that Senator Estes Kefauver would be chairing a Special Committee to Investigate Organized Crime in Interstate Commerce, he ran into opposition from J. Edgar Hoover, who feared that such an investigation might sidetrack or perhaps detract from his campaign against communism. The avid racetrack devotee prohibited FBI agents from serving as investigators for the Committee, claiming that his organization's resources were stretched too thin to investigate "what he deemed to be consensual crimes" (Valentine 2004, 85).

Kefauver knew that without the assistance of federal agents there was little chance that his investigation would uncover interstate criminal networks. In his recent history of the FBN, Douglas Valentine suggests that just when it seemed that Kefauver "had committed political suicide," Anslinger "stepped out of the shadows with a solution that saved the day" (2004, 85). At that time, the FBN had the most extensive files on interstate crime networks that were kept in what was described as the "Mafia Book," full of suspected Italian gangsters as well as members of other marginalized minorities. Anslinger saved the day when he gave each member of the committee a copy of it, thereby making it "possible for them to agree to try to sell Anslinger's proposition that the Mafia controlled crime in America" (2004, 85)

Senate Crime Investigation (Kefauver Hearings), 1950–1951

At the start of these hearings few Americans outside of his home state of Tennessee had heard of Senator Estes Kefauver, the soft-spoken bespectacled senator from the state's hill country. Most political observers could little have imagined the subsequent repercussions of the hearings. Kefauver had introduced a bill to investigate organized crime in the United States in early 1950. According to his earliest biographer, Kefauver did not pull this crusade out of a hat, but had a simmering interest in organized crime and judicial corruption since 1945, when as a Congressman he chaired a committee investigating a corruption case involving a Pennsylvania judge (Anderson and Blumenthal, 1956, 140). It was during this period that Kefauver had conversations with various mayors who thought racketeering had become extremely well organized and was even operating on a national basis. Mayors confided in the senator that the local syndicates had become too powerful to be handled by local law enforcement. So, five years before making his own headlines, Kefauver had uncovered "links between the underworld and the judiciary" (Ibid. 140).

Kefauver and several investigators then began a study of crime commission reports from California, Illinois, and elsewhere looking for evidence of trans-state criminal operations. He took particular aim at gambling, and in 1949, he championed several bills directed at organized crime. According to his biographers, his efforts went unrewarded because prior to the 1950s "nobody knew how the gangs operated nationally" and "the public was not interested enough" (Ibid. 141).

The freshman senator was unwavering on this issue, and in January 1950 proposed a Senate Resolution to investigate organized crime at the national level.[13]

U.S. Senate Committee (McClellan Committee), 1963–1964—La Cosa Nostra

The 1963 organized crime hearings helmed by Senator John McClellan were notable for the testimony of mobster Joseph Valachi, the first "made member" of a New York City crime family to testify about Italian-American organized crime in detail. Although his testimony has been hammered for its inconsistencies for years, its conclusion that organized crime operated as a hierarchical structure created the stereotypical view of the modern Mafia. According to Attorney General Robert Kennedy, the results of these hearings were "the biggest intelligence breakthrough yet in combating organized crime and racketeering in the U.S." (Goldfarb 1995, 149). He might have celebrated too quickly, because Valachi's testimony failed to result in a single conviction.

The McClellan Committee famously resolved

> there exists . . . today a criminal organization that is directly descended from and is patterned upon the centuries-old Sicilian terrorist society, the Mafia. This organization, also known as La Cosa Nostra, operates vast illegal enterprises that produce an annual income of many billions of dollars. This combine has so much power and influence that it may be described as a private government of organized crime. (U.S. Senate Report on Organized Crime, p. 117)

The Kefauver Hearings: A Landmark Television Event (1951)

When the Kefauver Committee arrived in New York City on March 12, 1951, not many Americans had paid attention to the commission and few expected anything of importance to come out of it. However, much to the surprise of an entire nation, it became a landmark, "not so much in the history of crime or crime fighting as in the history of television and the coming of a national political theater" (Halberstam 1993, 190). These were the first Congressional Hearings to be broadcast to a national audience. As serendipity would have it, the hearings were not even going to be televised until the last minute. It must be remembered that as a new medium, there were few choices on television, but the hearings coincided with the meteoric rise of television ownership. Over the previous year, in New York City alone the number of homes with televisions had risen from 29 percent to 51 percent. David Halberstam, who chronicled the 1950s, recently pointed out that these figures "meant that for the first time in any metropolitan area in any city of the world there were more homes with televisions than without" (Halberstam, 1993, 190). Filmed live and in black and white, a cast of unforgettable characters paraded before the cameras and left an indelible impression on the American public. On March 13, Frank Costello, "The Prime Minister" of organized crime, objected to having his face appear on camera. After consultation the committee agreed not to show his face. One enterprising television technician suggested that they should televise his hands. Viewers were captivated by his hands, which some thought "relentlessly reflected his tension and guilt—drumming the table, gripping a water glass, tearing paper to bits, hands sweating"—a performance that failed to convince anyone that he was only a law-abiding businessman. *Life* magazine probably said it best when it suggested that, "Never before had the attention of the nation been so completely riveted on a single matter. The Senate investigation into interstate crime was almost the sole subject of national attention" (quoted in Halberstam 1993, 192). It should not be so surprising then that the findings of this committee received so much attention and were so readily accepted by Americans. For his endeavors, Kefauver won an Emmy Award from the Academy of Television Arts and Sciences for special achievement in "bringing the workings of our government into the homes of the American people" (Halberstam 1993, 193–194).

Oyster Bay Conference on Combating Organized Crime (1965)—The Confederation

In 1965, a series of confidential meetings were held by the country's leading organized crime experts in Oyster Bay, New York. This seldom-mentioned conference produced a number of consultants and revealing information that would appear in the organized crime report in 1967 heralding the accomplishments of the President's Commission on Law Enforcement and Administration of Justice (Salerno and Tompkins 1969). According to attendee Donald Cressey, the conference members sought to "find a name for the organization which operates organized crime in America" (1969, 17). One of the most important conclusions drawn at this meeting was that the American syndicates "should not be confused with the Sicilian Mafia" (Ibid.). It was during these meetings that various names were bandied about, including *Mafia*. The consensus was that because many organized crime actors are not Sicilian and that the Sicilian Mafia does not have an American "branch office," the term should be rejected as a term for American organized crime. The term *Cosa Nostra* was likewise rejected. In the end, the conference attendees agreed that *confederation* was the most applicable term to the American incarnation of organized crime, and defined *organized crime* as

> The product of a self-perpetuating criminal conspiracy to wring exorbitant profits from our society by any means—fair or foul, legal and illegal. Despite personnel changes the conspiratorial entity continues. It is a malignant parasite, which fattens on human weakness. It survives on fear and corruption. By one or other means it obtains a high degree of immunity from law. It is totalitarian in its organization. A way of life, it imposes rigid discipline on underlings who do the dirty work while the top men of organized crime are generally insulated from the criminal act and the consequent danger of prosecution. (*Combatting Organized Crime,* 1966, 19)

Characteristics of Organized Crime, According to Oyster Bay Conference (1965)

1. Organized crime is a *business* venture.
2. The principal tool of organized crime is *muscle*.
3. Organized crime seeks out every opportunity to *corrupt* or *have influence* on anyone in government who may do favors for organized crime.
4. *Insulation* serves to separate the leaders of organized crime from illegal activities which they direct.
5. *Discipline* of a quasi-military character.
6. An interest in *public relations*.
7. A *way of life* in which members receive services which outsiders either do not receive or receive from legitimate resources. (Cressey 1969, 315)

By adopting the term *confederation* to refer to what the attendees (mostly law enforcement) thought was a "national criminal cartel" (Salerno and Tompkins 1969, 90–91), they sought to adopt a word that implied "a voluntary arrangement or alliance in which the leaders of various groups meet together for consultation, but without any boss of bosses at the top" (Ibid.).

President's Commission on Law Enforcement and Administration of Justice (Task Force), 1967—Gambling Is the Greatest Source of Revenue

In 1967, criminologist/sociologist Donald Cressey advised the U.S. President's Commission on Law Enforcement and rose to prominence as one of the first academics to delineate the formal structure of organized crime. Cressey later posited in his 1969 book *Theft of the Nation* that "the organized criminal, by definition, occupies a position in a social system, an 'organization' which has been rationally designed to maximize profits by performing illegal services and providing legally forbidden products demanded by the broader society within which he lives" (1969, 72).

In an introduction to its report published in 1968, the Commission stated, "The extraordinary thing about organized crime is that America has tolerated it for so long" (quoted in Cressey 1969, 8). At the same time, it admitted that although law enforcement "deplores the Mafia" and society tolerates its activities, "we can't quite define it." The report goes on to describe organized crime is a "rather loose confederation of highly organized 'families,' governed by a commission of from 9 to 12 men. It controls such activities as gambling, loan-sharking and wholesale importation of narcotics" (President's Commission on Law Enforcement and the Administration of Justice 1972, 29). The Commission asserted that gambling was organized crime's greatest source of revenue (Ibid. 440). Second largest source was loan sharking (Ibid. 441), followed by narcotics trafficking (Ibid. 442).

President's Commission on Organized Crime (1986)—Expanding the Definition

Over the course of more than two years, President Ronald Reagan's Commission on Organized Crime published seven volumes of hearings and reports. To facilitate the investigation, the committee held hearings in several large cities where local law enforcement weighed forth on the prevalence of organized crime in their cities. The Commission's final four reports focused separately on money

Organized crime is a society that seeks to operate outside the control of the American people and their governments. It involves thousands of criminals, working within structures as complex as those of any large corporation, subject to laws more rigidly enforced than those of legitimate governments. Its actions are not impulsive but rather the result of intricate conspiracies carried on over many years and aimed at gaining control over whole fields of activity in order to amass huge profits. (Ibid.1972, 437)

Executive Order 12435: Establishing the President's Commission on Organized Crime (July 28, 1983)

The commission was established to

> make a full and complete national and region-by-region analysis of organized crime; define the nature of traditional organized crime as well as emerging organized crime groups, the sources and amounts of organized crime's income, and the uses to which organized crime puts its income; develop in-depth information on the participants in organized crime networks; . . . evaluate Federal laws pertinent to the effort to combat organized crime[;] . . . advise the President and the Attorney general with respect to its findings and actions which can be undertaken to improve law enforcement efforts directed against organized crime[;] . . .

laundering, labor racketeering, drug use, and drug trafficking. However, for the purpose of defining *organized crime,* the Commission broadened the government's interpretation of the organized crime problem by moving beyond the parameters set by the earlier Kefauver and McClellan investigations.

Moving beyond the parochial view of the Italian Mafia as synonymous with organized crime, the Reagan Commission, in marked contrast to other investigations over the previous 20 years, expanded its emphasis to include outlaw motorcycle gangs; prison gangs; and Chinese, Vietnamese, Japanese, Cuban, Columbian, Irish, Russian, and Canadian criminal organizations.

Overview

The findings of the President's Commission on Organized Crime (PCOC) in 1986 marked a major step toward moving away from the traditional Italian model of organized crime. A number of scholars were forced to reevaluate their opinions about the nature of organized crime in the United States as a host of emerging crime groups rose to prominence, including Jamaican Posses, Outlaw Motorcycle Gangs, Prison Gangs, Russian *Mafiya,* and various Asian groups. However, a number of authorities continued to try and define groups according to ethnic, racial, and cultural characteristics. For some observers this was simply a repeat of earlier attempts to paint organized crime as some type of alien conspiracy. Others were more critical, including Michael Woodiwiss, who made a cogent argument that the period from the 1950s to the mid-1980s saw the "dumbing down of discourse" on the topic (2001, 227–311).

Scholars, journalists, commissions, and law enforcement agencies have offered and debated explanations and definitions of organized crime since the early twentieth century. Most attempts to define organized crime come from criminologists, law enforcement agencies, former syndicate members, and economists. Although this chapter details a number of common factors in the definitions of organized crime, there is actually only limited concurrence

between law enforcement, policymakers, and scholars concerning the real nature of organized crime. Yet for many years, law enforcement had a monopoly on the data, which gave them and their related commissions a prominent position in the development of strategies regarding organized crime. What hamstrung those attempting to identify organized crime have been the enduring myths that have characterized and held back the debate over what is and is not organized crime. More recently, the discussion of organized crime has centered on transnational syndicates, failed states, regional wars, and global insecurity. The success of stateless and decentralized terrorist and crime networks underscores not only the difficulty in identifying modern organized crime groups, but even identifying strategies to inhibit their operations as well. Today's organized crime almost makes one nostalgic for the simpler definitions of the mid- to late twentieth century.

The fact remains that there is not one list of criteria that meets with universal approval. From an international perspective, represented by the United Nations definition, most of the earlier Americanized versions have been ousted. Even the most venerable definitional requirements have met resistance and skepticism from international scholars and policymakers. For many years, one of the most sanctified and accepted characteristics of organized crime was the lack or absence of political or ideological motivation; another has been the notion of limited or exclusive membership. Any close inspection of modern organized crime groups demonstrates that these are, for the most part, quaint reminders of a less-complicated world of crime. As one academic notes, the misunderstandings often begin with the acceptance of the term *organized crime* as a "well-defined phenomenon" (Van Duyne 1996, 53; Wright 2006, 13). If there is any international consensus in the twenty-first century, it is a general agreement that organized crime groups are chameleon like—ever-changing and flexible structures and alliances that take advantage of whatever opportunities exist to make money and avoid the scrutiny of an often myopic law enforcement apparatus.

Key Terms

Racketeering	Devolved hierarchy	*La Cosa Nostra*
Wickersham Commission	Hierarchical conglomerate	Oyster Bay Conference
Organized Crime Control Act	Core criminal group	The Confederation
Donald Cressey	Organized criminal network	President's Commission on
Bureaucratic/Corporate Model	Howard Abadinsky	Organized Crime (1986)
Theft of a Nation	Lexow Committee	President's Commission on Law
Joseph Albini	Tammany Hall	Enforcement and Administration
Patron–client relationship	Chicago Crime Commission	of Justice (1967)
Francis and Elizabeth Ianni	Illinois Crime Survey	Jonathan Wild
Lupollo Family	Seabury Inquiry	Thief taking
Transnational organized crime	Amen Report	Golden Age of Piracy
Globalization	Kefauver Commission	Pirate Articles and Rules
Criminal clusters	McClellan Committee	Bartholomew Roberts
Rigid hierarchy	Joseph Valachi	English Navigation Acts

Critical Thinking Questions

1. Compare and contrast racketeering and organized crime?
2. When did the academic debate on defining organized crime begin?
3. What are the characteristics of Donald Cressey's model, and what most influenced his ideas?
4. What were the main structural criticisms of Cressey's model?
5. Which structural model best explains modern organized crime groups?
6. Why is it important to arrive at an international consensus on a definition?
7. Compare and contrast international perspectives on organized crime. Do they conform to the modern United Nations' definition?
8. What examples demonstrate the persistence and growth of organized crime through history?
9. Was Jonathan Wild truly an organized crime figure?
10. Were pirates the original gangsters? Discuss their structure and activities in terms of organized crime characteristics.

Endnotes

1. Adapted from Donald R. Cressey, "The Structure and Functioning of Criminal Syndicates," in *Task Force Report: Organized Crime, 1969,* Appendix A, pp. 25–60.
2. See, for example, Pennsylvania Crime Commission (1980). *A Decade of Organized Crime: 1980 Report,* St. Davids: Pennsylvania.
3. Pirates based in the Mediterranean were usually called *corsairs,* most famously along North Africa's Barbary Coast, whereas *buccaneer* refers to pirates based in the Caribbean.
4. Of these accounts, Daniel Defoe (1720; 1725) and Charles Johnson (1724; 1734) stand out.

5. The Killigrew pirate syndicate is well chronicled in David Mathew, "Cornish and Welsh Pirates in the Reign of Elizabeth," *English Historical Review,* July, 1924.

6. The IMB is part of the International Chamber of Commerce and operates the Piracy Reporting Center in Kuala Lumpur, Malaysia.

7. Charles Parkhurst, (1895), *Our Fight with Tammany,* New York: Charles Scribner's Sons, pp. 96, 97.

8. These reports are known formally as the Report and Proceedings of the Investigation of the Senate Committee Appointed to Investigate the Police Department of the City of New York, hereafter cited as Lexow Committee Hearings. The report contains the most detailed description of the green-goods operation.

9. The steerer meets the victim and gives him the "pointers," the password with which to contact the next link in the nefarious chain.

10. Judge Samuel Seabury initially came to prominence when he presided over the second trial of mobbed-up police lieutenant Charles Becker in May 1914. Becker's conviction was upheld and he was executed that same July at Sing Sing Prison.

11. See Virgil W. Peterson (1983), *The Mob: 200 Years of Organized Crime in New York,* Ottawa: Green Hill, pp. 161–197.

12. For a detailed account of Seabury and his crusade against corruption, see Herbert Mitgang (2000), *Once Upon a Time in New York: Jimmy Walker, Franklin Roosevelt, and the Last Great Battle of the Jazz Age,* New York: Free Press.

13. Investigative journalist Jack Anderson and co-author Fred Blumenthal summarize the complex negotiations navigated by Kefauver before getting acceptance, pp. 138–144.

CHAPTER 2

Explaining Criminal Subcultures and Actors

Chapter 1 examines the ongoing definitional debate over what is and what is not organized crime activity. There is an even more contentious debate over why individuals turn to criminal careers. Sociologists, psychologists, criminologists, and economists have ranged forth with various theories on why individuals join organized gangs and crime groups. This chapter examines, gives perspective, and attempts to reconcile the often conflicting explanations that have been part of a debate that began in earnest in the eighteenth-century Enlightenment and continues today.

At the height of the Cold War, 1950s scholars from a variety of disciplines applied a cornucopia of methods to studying various types of crime, particularly organized crime. Building on earlier studies and assumptions, criminologists, sociologists, and ethnographers cited explanations such as biological and hereditary dispositions, poverty and the environment, greed, and even the fears of an omnipresent nuclear war that threw certain people out of their more rational temperaments. Regardless of the explanations, urban Americans had become more fearful of crime, although the fear of rising crime rates was more perception than reality.

Some of the greatest minds of the classical world jousted over why certain individuals turned to criminal behavior. One Greek aristocrat blamed the common people for most crimes, noting, "Within the ranks of the people will be found the greatest amount of ignorance, disorderliness, rascality—poverty acting as a strong incentive to base conduct, not to speak of lack of education and ignorance." The esteemed philosopher Plato pondered the cause of crime, suggesting, "tendencies to violence and crime were found in communities where the juxtaposition of wealth and poverty produced feelings of envy and jealousy" (Robinson, Jr. and Robinson 1980, 21–22).

So, of course the question is often raised as to, "If wealth was distributed equally, would there be crime?" Aristotle opined, "But want is not the only cause of crimes, men also commit them simply for the pleasure it gives them, and just to get rid of an unsatisfied desire." Foreshadowing the biological theories of the nineteenth century, the poet Theognis of Megara noted, "No man has ever devised a method to make a fool wise or a bad man good."

CLASSICAL AND NEO-CLASSICAL THEORY

Free Will and Rational Choice

Until the eighteenth century and the so-called Enlightenment, most interpretations or explanations of human behavior and actions were couched in a theologically based worldview provided by the power of the Church and its clergy. However, during the Enlightenment, there was a groundswell of challenges to these predominant notions. A mélange of European philosophers promoted new and more scientific theories, including Italian Cesare Beccaria, Englishmen

---
Rational Choice Theory[2]

Rational Choice Theory, rooted in the eighteenth-century ideas of Beccaria and Bentham, assumes that before many people commit crimes, they consider the risks and rewards. During the late twentieth century, a number of psychologists, economists, and sociologists adopted the rational choice perspective on crime, and postulated that criminal offenders make decisions and choices to benefit themselves through criminal activity. Decision-making ability is sometimes limited by the offender's cognitive abilities that limit the ability to make a rational decision.

Jeremy Bentham and Samuel Romilly, and German Johann Anselm von Feurbach, laid the intellectual foundations for what would become known as the Classical School of Criminology. Chief among the ideas was the notion that humans had the capacity to make appropriate decisions based on observation and reason.

According to the rational philosophy and economic presumptions of such eighteenth-century philosophers as Cesare Beccaria (1735–1795) and Jeremy Bentham (1748–1832),[1] one decided to commit a crime after measuring the possibilities and ramifications of being caught versus the pleasure and financial gains of getting away with the crime. The Enlightenment focus on the power of free will was accompanied by the tenet that individuals should be responsible for their own actions; that one's behavior was motivated by a "hedonistic rationality," in which individuals weighed the potential pleasure and financial gains of getting away with a crime against the unpleasant ramifications of being caught and punished.

BIOLOGICAL THEORIES AND CRIMINAL ANTHROPOLOGY

Although long since discredited, for many years biological theories were used as a theoretical foundation by social scientists attempting to explain why some individuals are drawn to criminality whereas others are not. In earlier years, physical appearance and low intelligence were two of the more popular explanations for criminal behavior. In the nineteenth century, several Italian criminologists[3] challenged this earlier-held belief that an individual made a rational choice as to whether to commit a crime. However, for the new generation of Italian criminologists, their investigations into anthropological and biological explanations seemed to them to demonstrate that crime was caused and not chosen. After examining both convicted criminals and cadavers, these "pioneers" claimed to have discovered that crime was caused by biological defects in inferior atavistic individuals who were throwbacks to an earlier evolutionary stage of human development. Others theorized that criminals were physically different from the more law-abiding members of the population hundreds of years before Lombroso. As early as the sixteenth century, J. Baptiste della Porte was investigating the criminal physiognomy, and by the early nineteenth century, Gall and Spurzheim were pursuing the "science" of phrenology, in which personality traits of an individual were revealed by interpreting the bumps and fissures of the skull. Building on the foundations of these and others, Lombroso built on the advances in science during his era.

Observers as far back as antiquity have commented on the notion that children tend to resemble their parents in numerous ways. Several early biological theories on crime explained that some individuals act a certain way because they were structurally different from others. Of these investigations, the "rural studies" of the purported Juke (1877) and Kallikak (1912) families were among the most prominent.[4] In recent decades, popular science writer Stephen Jay Gould discovered that the photos in the Kallikak study had been doctored, and most of the research has been discounted (Gould 1981, 171; Rafter 1988). Despite the questionable value of studies like these, in their day they were used to support the development of a *defective delinquency* theory, thus offering an equation that connected high-grade mental defects with criminality. Although these studies have been dismissed as a pseudo-scientific fad, they were "much too complex and significant to allow [such] simplistic historical judgments to go unchallenged" (quoted in Rafter 1988, 30). As noted criminologist Nicole Rafter makes clear,

> Instead of dismissing the family studies as the fantasies of a handful of crackpots, we should recognize that they explored issues of fundamental and enduring concern: the relationship between humans and nature, biology and society, heredity and environment, and the meaning of evolution. (1988, 30–31)

Scientific studies beginning in the 1850s introduced a number of theories concerning the development of criminal tendencies. Among the more prominent pioneers in this arena was Charles Goring, who concluded that criminal traits are inherited in much the same way, as are ordinary physical traits and features. Goring noticed a high correlation between height and criminality as predisposing factors. He also surmised that the length of imprisonment and number of sentences served by parents and children indicated a propensity for inherited criminality. By associating criminality with inherited factors, environmental factors were effectively ruled out. Like Sir Francis Galton before him, Goring supported prevention of reproduction as the best way to prevent crime (Driver 1972, 439–440). Over time, Goring became one of the first theorists to postulate that crime might be the result of an interaction between heredity and environment, rather than one or the other.

Although the theories of Lombroso, Sheldon, and others linking body characteristics to delinquency have been for the most part been discounted modern biological theories have evolved that consider the entire spectrum of biological characteristics, including genetic defects that are noninherited, and those environmentally produced. For the most part, modern biological theories do not suggest that biological characteristics cause crime directly, but argue that certain biological factors simply increase the likelihood that an individual will engage in antisocial behavior, including criminal behavior. Some recent biological explanations have gained currency as ways in which to describe an individual's predisposition to criminal behavior.

Cesare Lombroso (1835–1909)

SOME INDIVIDUALS ARE BORN CRIMINALS   Italian physician Cesare Lombroso is considered the founder of the Positivist school of criminology and is often mentioned as the father of modern criminology. Lombroso believed that criminals had a criminal personality and were different from normal civilized people. Later in life he acknowledged social and psychological factors, but always held that these were less important than biological factors in respect to criminality.

Lombroso was consumed with resolving the "problem of the nature of the criminal" (quoted in Wolfgang 1960, 184). His theories, although widely dismissed today, owe much to Charles Darwin's *The Origin of Species* (1859) and *The Descent of Man* (1871), which suggested that some

---

Modern Biological Explanations for Criminal Behavior

- Chromosomal abnormalities
- Glandular dysfunction
- Chemical imbalances
- Nutritional deficiencies

Lombroso "Discovers" the Criminal Type (1876)

At the sight of that skull, I seemed to see all of a sudden, lighted up as a vast plain under a flaming sky, the problem of the nature of the criminal—an atavistic being who reproduces in his person the ferocious instincts of primitive humanity and the inferior animal. Thus were explained anatomically the enormous jaws, high cheekbones, prominent superciliary arches, solitary lines in the palms, extreme size of the orbits, handle-shaped or sessile ears found in criminals, savages, and apes, insensitivity to pain, extremely acute sight, tattooing, excessive idleness, love of orgies, and the irresistible craving for evil for its own sake.

men are closer to their primitive ancestors than others. Earlier speculations on degeneracy can be traced back to research conducted in France as early as the 1820s.

During the last decades of the nineteenth century, Europe's so-called first scientific criminologists applied social Darwinist theory to Italy and its regions, which many impugned as backward, attributing the gap between Italy and Anglo-Saxon Europe to a "compromised biology" that made southern Italians and Sicilians a threat to the more progressive and superior northern Italians. Lombroso experienced an epiphany while performing a post-mortem on a prominent Italian bandit, when he recognized there was a relationship between the physical characteristics of a criminal and his behavior. He went on to collect a mass of evidence based on the close examination of a number of criminals to support his theory that the criminal can be distinguished from the non-criminal by a variety of physical anomalies that were of an atavistic or degenerative origin. Arguing that some individuals were born criminals, his conclusions flew in the face of penal reformers who argued that criminals could be reformed in the proper environment.

There is a great deal of debate regarding exactly what Lombroso contributed to the field of criminology. No less an authority than Edwin Sutherland suggested in 1947 that "by shifting attention from crime as a social phenomenon to crime as an individual phenomenon, it delayed for forty years the work which was in progress at the time and made no lasting contribution of its own" (Sutherland 1947, 57). Others were kinder, crediting Lombroso, who promoted the post-mortem examination of criminal brains, with providing the impetus for the study of clinical criminology and the basis for the methodology of cadaver identification later employed in the field of legal medicine (Rafter 1997).

Lombroso's contention that there is a criminal type, demonstrable by certain physical anomalies—that the criminal was identifiable on the basis of certain cranial, facial, and body measurements—may have seemed like a great advance in the late nineteenth century. However, a growing number of challengers to his ideas began to view crime as the product of certain social factors. Lombroso's legacy was the shifting of the focus of criminology toward the scientific study of the criminal and the conditions under which a crime is committed. No less an authority than Marvin Wolfgang suggests that Lombroso's greatest contribution to the emerging criminology discipline was his recognition "that it is the criminal and not the crime we should study and consider; that it is the criminal and not the crime we ought to penalize" (Wolfgang 1961, 287).

Gabriel Tarde (1843–1904)

CRIME AS A NORMAL LEARNED BEHAVIOR The French-born Gabriel Tarde showed an early affinity for mathematics but gravitated toward the legal profession after contracting a serious eye disease. Mathematics' loss proved a gain for the developing criminology and sociology disciplines, where he would come to prominence for his theories attempting to explain the criminal mind. Tarde's theory was couched in terms of *laws of imitation,* a learning process by which individuals imitate the behavior of those they closely interact with. Tarde rejected Lombroso's biological determinism, which suggested that an individual's behavior was determined by laws of nature and

Charles B. Goring (1870–1919)

Goring began his career as a medical officer in the English correctional system. Over more than a decade, he studied some 3,000 convicts and in his subsequent book, *The English Convict*, repudiated much of Lombroso's positivist theories regarding the notion of the hereditary criminal. His detailed examination concluded that there was no such animal as the born criminal, placing the onus for criminal behavior on adverse environmental factors instead. Goring employed a laborious methodology that utilized the most sophisticated statistical and physical measurements of the era to compare prison inmates to soldiers, college students, hospital patients, and other non-prisoners and found that except for differences in height and weight, there were no significant statistical differences between behavior and 37 different physical characteristics.

inevitable social influences rather than any sort of free will. Tarde's major contribution was asserting that an individual's predisposition to criminal behavior reflected the physical environment that he grew up in rather than a biological predisposition to it as Lombroso suggested. Tarde suggested through a sort of contagion process potential criminals gravitated toward the criminal milieu where, through a process of informal training, a criminal apprenticeship of sorts, individuals would be drawn to a life of crime unless society intervened. Tarde's theory was important at its time for challenging Lombroso's theories and as a pioneering work in the association of criminal behavior with the normal learning process (Vine 1972; Curtis 1953).

ANTHROPOLOGISTS: BODY-TYPE THEORIES

A number of researchers attempt to demonstrate that an individual's mental capacity and behavior can be explained by physical characteristics. Lombroso was the best known of these. Body-type's theorists argued that there is an empirically proved correspondence between an individual's body type or physical appearance and the person's temperament, often expressed as criminal behavior or delinquency. In the late nineteenth and early twentieth centuries, several American criminal anthropologists, Arthur McDonald, Henry Boies, and Charles Henderson among them, were influenced by Lombroso, who believed individual body differences determined one's criminal bent. Following in their footsteps, others such as Earnest Hooten and William Sheldon, called *constitutional theorists,* explained crime was the result of decisions made by feeble minds with inferior physical constitutions.

Earnest Albert Hooten (1887–1954)

AN INDIVIDUAL'S PHYSICAL CHARACTERISTICS DETERMINED THE TYPES OF CRIMES HE WAS LIKELY TO COMMIT   Earnest Hooten was a controversial—and, to some, infamous—Harvard anthropologist who spent twelve years studying criminals and published his findings in *The American Criminal* (1939). The genesis of his anthropological research began in 1926 as an examination of county jail prisoners in Massachusetts. He went on to expand his study to include prison and reformatory inmates from ten states selected to represent a cross-section of racial and ethnic groups mirroring the rest of the country (Hooten 1939), He ended up studying the anthropometric records of more than 17,000 individuals. Harking back to Lombroso and his ilk, Hooten, a confirmed positivist, claimed that an individual's physical characteristics determined the type of crimes he was likely to commit. Sounding straight out of Lombroso, Hooten claimed, "Low and sloping foreheads are excessively present among criminals" (Hooten 1939).

Hooten's first book only focused on "native white criminals of native parentage" and "civilian check samples of similar origin." One of his research questions asked, "Are criminals physically different from law-abiding citizens of the same ethnic origins?" (Hooten 1939). Ultimately,

The Gluecks

In the 1950s, Harvard-affiliated criminologists Eleanor and Sheldon Glueck reached similar conclusions to Sheldon, and as late as the 1970s others also found an association between mesomorphy and delinquency.[5] The Gluecks partnered in research for more than three decades. In 1959, they published their most controversial work, *Predicting Delinquency and Crime,* which introduced the Social Prediction Table, a measuring tool intended to help determine signs of incipient delinquency in children as young as two. Despite its provocative reputation, in its time it was regarded as an advance in the detection of early delinquency.

he discovered that criminals were inferior to civilians when it came to bodily measurements, no matter the crime (Hooten 1939).

In his later research, Hooten examined "native whites of foreign parentage" and whites from foreign countries. Among his later claims were that tall, thin men tended toward murder and robbery; tall and heavy men preferred killing, forgery, and fraud; and undersized, thin men were drawn to stealing and burglary. However, short, heavy men tended toward assault, rape, and other sex crimes, "whereas men of mediocre body build tend to break the law without obvious discrimination or preference" (Hooten 1939, 84–104).

Hooten's greatest academic lapse was a rejection of social and economic factors over biological explanations. His assumptions incorporating hereditary criminality and the use of sterilization and biological control turned him into a pariah in part of the scientific community, although he continued to publish until his death.

William H. Sheldon (1898–1977)

HUMANS CAN BE DIVIDED INTO THREE BASIC BODY TYPES   William Sheldon was also influenced by the body-type theories advanced by Lombroso. Writing in the 1940s, Sheldon is considered one of the foremost proponents of this theory. Sheldon insisted that humans could be divided into three basic body types, which he called *somatypes.* These included the *endomorphic,* or soft and fat; the *mesomorphic,* or athletically built and muscular; and the *ectomorphic,* described as thin and delicate. Sheldon noted that most people have parts of all three types, but usually one of these predominates. Between 1939 and 1949, Sheldon studied 200 Boston delinquents and reported that they were typically more mesomorphic than non-delinquents, and that serious delinquents were more mesomorphic than less-serious offenders.

A widely held critique of the body-type theories is that "biological differences between human beings reflect hereditary factors and the influence of natural and social environments" (AAPA Statement 1996, 569–570) Simply stated, the reason mesomorphs might be regarded as more likely to be delinquent than non-delinquents is just because their body type would be more attractive for gang selection due to its physical superiority. In addition, the notion that delinquents are more likely to be mesomorphs flies in the face of the generally held belief that criminals are biologically inferior in terms of physique.

PSYCHOLOGICAL THEORIES

It became a popular and academic notion during the first decades of the twentieth century that crime was typically committed by individuals with low intelligence. (This idea made a comeback of sorts in the 1990s with the publication of Herrnstein and Murray's *The Bell Curve.*) Among the early proponents of this idea was H. H. Goddard (1866–1957), who in 1914 published *Feeblemindedness:*

Its Causes and Consequences, in which he argued that criminals in the parlance of the day were *feebleminded,* or had below-average intelligence. Goddard and others tested this theory in a variety of populations, especially in prisons and jails (where there was a captive audience). Although IQs varied considerably, Goddard found that 70 percent had substandard IQs.[6]

In 1931, Edwin Sutherland perused hundreds of investigations into the link between intelligence and criminality/delinquency (totaling 175,000 criminals). His findings rebuked Goddard and his constituents by arguing that although intelligence indeed played a part in some cases, ultimately the distribution of the intelligence scores of criminals and delinquents is not much different from the general population. Sutherland's findings seemed to have ended the debate until the 1970s, when new studies suggested that IQ *was* an important predictor of delinquency, and should be included with race and social class in any discussion of the issue. Sociologists supported such findings by examining the impact of low IQ in school performance and the subsequent cycle of anger at school followed by truancy and concomitant delinquency (Hirschi and Hindelang 1977; Gordon 1976).

The debate over intelligence and its relation to criminal behavior continues to fester. However, if one were to accept this notion, it follows then that whenever there is a spike in crime rates, there should also be a corresponding spike in the decline of intelligence of the offenders. Clearly, some of America's most intelligent people have transgressed into criminal behavior—witness the increase in white collar prosecutions since the mid-1990s.

The Antisocial Personality

A number of theorists suggest that criminal behavior originates in the personality of the offender rather than in an individual's biology or environment. The term *antisocial personality* is often used interchangeably with *sociopath* and *psychopath,* two expressions that are often too broadly used. According to the 1994 *Diagnostic and Statistical Manual–IV* (*DSM-IV*) of the American Psychiatric Association, "the essential feature of the Antisocial Personality Disorder is a pervasive disregard for, and violation of, the rights of others that begins in childhood or early adolescence and comes into adulthood" (*DSM-IV* 1994, 645–650). According to this definition, a diagnosis can be made for this "disorder" when at least three of the following six characteristics are present:

- Repeated violations of the law that are grounds for arrest
- Repeated lying, use of aliases, or conning others for personal profit or pleasure
- Impulsivity or failure to plan ahead
- Repeated physical fights or assaults
- Repeated failure to sustain consistent work behavior or honor financial obligations
- Lack of remorse (*DSM-IV* 1994, 645–650)

These characteristics become less evident as one grows older, and is particularly true in gangs where individuals typically "age-out" of the activities.

There is still a lack of consensus over predicting an individual's future criminality. Some recent studies indicate one of the strongest predictors for later delinquency can be found in the classroom demeanor of children, particularly those who demonstrate early childhood behavior problems such as disruptive classroom conduct, aggressiveness, lying, and dishonesty. Later in this chapter we examine gangs and gang behavior, and the reader can well understand why, as some gang researchers suggest, these previously mentioned personality characteristics may not be personality characteristics at all; rather, they may be viewed as behavioral mechanisms that a gang leader needs "to create and maintain leadership over a gang" (Short and Stodtbeck 1974, 248–264).

Cleckley's Characteristics (1964)

- Superficial charm and good intelligence
- Absence of delusions and other signs of irrational thinking
- Absence of nervousness or psychoneurotic thinking
- Unreliability
- Untruthfulness and insincerity
- Lack of remorse and shame
- Inadequately motivated antisocial behavior
- Poor judgment and failure to learn by experience
- Pathologic egocentricity and incapacity for love
- General poverty in major affective reactions
- Specific loss of insight
- Unresponsiveness in general interpersonal relations
- Fantastic and uninviting behavior with drink and sometimes without
- Suicide rarely carried out
- Sex life impersonal, trivial, and poorly integrated
- Failure to follow any life plan

(Adapted from Schmalleger 1996, 202)

Hervey Cleckley

In his 1964 book *Mask of Sanity,* Hervey Cleckley introduced sixteen behavioral characteristics of a *psychopath* that he adapted from clinical interviews and other corroborating sources (see the box above). In Cleckley's view, the *psychopath* was "a moral idiot," who featured immature, unemotional, and thrill-seeking behavior. Just four years later, the *DSM* discontinued the use of the term *psychopath* in favor of *antisocial* and *asocial personality*. Although most psychologists more or less agree on the nature of psychopathic traits, not all agree that it fits the description of the antisocial personality or whether personality disorders indicate a criminal mind.

Anthony Spilotro: Case Study of an Antisocial Personality

One of six sons, Anthony "Tony" Spilotro was born to hard-working Italian immigrants in Chicago in 1938. According to his biographer, Tony, the fourth born, "was the worst of the litter" (Roemer 1994, 9). Early on, Spilotro chose older boys who always seemed to have lots of ready cash as role models. Once in high school, Tony went about making a name for himself as a tough guy. What he lacked in size he made up for in confident aggressiveness. He was smart enough not to try to intimidate athletes, preferring to pick on the weak and timid. When Tony's father died in 1954 at the age of 55, the younger Spilotro was free from familial constraints that had kept him in line.

In high school, Tony rarely cracked a book and did not participate in extracurricular activities. He dropped out of school in his sophomore year, after which he met a gang of like-minded kids and got involved in petty crimes such as shoplifting and purse snatching. In 1955, at the age of sixteen, he was arrested for the first time. Before the decade was out, he was arrested more than a dozen times. As veteran FBI investigator William F. Roemer put it, "These were the formative years for young Tony Spilotro. This was his education—from a grade and high school bully to a common petty thief" (1994, 12). Spilotro grew up to become one of the Chicago Outfit's most prominent button men. He came to national prominence during his ill-fated turn in Las Vegas, chronicled in Nicholas Pileggi's book *Casino*. On June 14, 1986, Tony and his brother Michael failed to come home on time. Their bodies were discovered a week later in a shallow grave in a cornfield in northwest Indiana. By most accounts, few missed him.

- Crime is a normal aspect of society.
- Crime is functional for society.
- Crime promotes social solidarity by uniting people against crime.
- Under certain circumstances, crime provides a means of achieving necessary social change.

SOCIOLOGICAL THEORIES

Emile Durkheim (1858–1917): Anomie

IS A SOCIETY WITHOUT CRIME POSSIBLE?   Emile Durkheim has been credited with introducing a number of sociological theories of delinquency, including, but not limited to, anomie/strain theory, differential opportunity, theories of culture conflict, cultural transmission, and social disorganization. Writing some twenty years after Cesare Lombroso, Durkheim took exception to the classical notion that humans were free and rational in a contract society and rejected the notion that the world is simply the result of individual human actions. Unlike Lombroso, Durkheim focused on the organization and development of society rather than the determinants of human behavior. Durkheim insisted that inequality as well as crime was a natural part of the human condition.

One of the most influential classical European theorists, French sociologist Emile Durkheim argues that crime rates and related behavior cannot be adequately explained without examining the breakdown in the norms that operate throughout society. In his classic study *The Rules of Sociological Method* (1895), Durkheim ascribes a certain functionalism to the ubiquity of crime and criminals in societies. He suggests that crime must serve some social function if it exists in all societies, because if it did not serve such a function, then it would not exist. According to Durkheim, "Crime is present not only in the majority of societies of one particular species but in all societies of all types" (1938, 65). Durkheim was more interested in explaining that crime is inherent in society rather than examining why crime occurred. He explains that society produces individuals who resort to crime; therefore, these individuals represent certain characteristics of society, and crime, like death and taxes, is a normal condition. At the same time, Durkheim suggests that crime is beneficial to society because it allows society to evolve its legal system continually; without crime, the law would not evolve at all (Lunden 1958). A number of the major sociological theories of delinquency are rooted in Durkheim's ideas, including anomie/strain theory, differential opportunity, cultural transmission, culture conflict, and control theories.

What Is the Chicago School?

Between the 1920s and 1940s, American sociology and criminology was overwhelmingly dominated by the contributions and methods of the members of the University of Chicago's Department of Sociology.[7] The faculty reads like a *Who's Who* of sociology. The influence of such theorists as Robert E. Park, Ernest Burgess, Clifford R. Shaw, Henry D. McKay, and others was so pervasive that they were collectively referred to as the "Chicago School." It was no fluke that the 1920s and 1930s produced so many studies focused on deviance and social problems. During these co-called Crisis Decades, crime emerged as one of the nation's greatest political and social issues. Compared to previous eras, in the 1920s and 1930s, Americans were much more concerned with crime, thanks in part to an omnipresent news media and the impact of Prohibition.

During the first decades of the twentieth century, America's rapidly changing demographics led academics and social commentators to lament the new social ills such as juvenile delinquency and other urban problems that were seen by many as the by-product of new waves of immigrants from Southern and Eastern Europe. A number of sociologists were inclined to believe that the best way to study these problems was through the laboratory of an urban setting. As a center for most of these issues, Chicago proved an excellent place to start their ecological studies. Using this ecological

Social Disorganization Theory

According to Clifford Shaw and other theorists, the areas of highest delinquency were *socially disorganized*. It was here that the usual controls over delinquent behavior were largely absent. Social disorganization theorists suggested an ongoing relationship between America's increasing urban complexity and higher rates of deviance, especially in large urban communities. Social scientists recorded the predominance of deviance in certain urban environments, typically those featuring large immigrant communities, poor housing, poverty, transient residents, and a lack of reliable community institutions. Such settings often featured the breakdown in effective social control of behavior and a dearth in close personal relationships. A number of social disorganization theorists concentrated on the political, economic, and social changes sweeping the country affecting almost every aspect of life. Most noticeable for some of these observers was the weakening in the fabric of social life in the face of rapid industrialization, urbanization, immigration, and internal migration.

perspective, sociologists studied the social order of the city—examining in terms of competition, change, cooperation, and symbiosis. Instead of focusing on rapid change in society, investigators focused their research on rapid change in neighborhoods, particularly in Chicago.

Robert E. Park spent a quarter of a century as a newspaper reporter investigating local social conditions. He joined the University of Chicago Sociology Department in 1914, where he developed the concept of *human ecology,* viewing the city as a super organism that had many natural areas where different types of people lived. Together, this area had an organic unity of its own, not unlike an ecosystem in the natural world. In nature, ecologists investigate jungles, swamps, and grasslands, whereas those studying the ecology of crime explore racial and ethnic communities ranging from Little Italy and Chinatown to the Barrio and Skid Row. Park, together with Burgess, later explored the ecology of cities in more detail, finding that cities tended to expand radially from center in patterns of concentric circles or zones. As pioneers in the ecological approach, Park and Burgess (1925) saw society as an organism, and expanded the concept of the environment to include social as well as physical environments.

In the late 1980s, Sampson and Groves tested Shaw and McKay's social disorganization theory. They found five indicators of social disorganization:

- Residents were of low economic status
- There were many different ethnic groups
- High frequency of residency turnover
- Dysfunctional families
- Urbanization[8]

As early as 1915, Dr. William Healey, in *The Individual Delinquent,* found after examining the case histories of 1,000 juvenile repeat offenders that poverty was rarely a factor. Ten years later, a follow-up investigation found that 73 percent of the juveniles actually came from families with average or above-average incomes (Healy and Bonner 1926). However, by the 1930s McKay and Shaw (1931, 111) observed a different trend, at least in Chicago:

> Children who grow up in these deteriorated and disorganized neighborhoods of the city are not subject to the same constructive and restraining influences that surround those in the more homogeneous residential communities farther removed from the industrial and commercial centers. These disorganized neighborhoods fail to provide a consistent set of cultural standards and a wholesome social life for the development of a stable and socially acceptable form of behavior in the child.

During the 1920s, despite the prominence of bootlegging gangs and syndicates, there was a sense that juveniles committed most crimes. Others believed that delinquency was rooted in

Cultural Transmission Theory

Cultural Transmission Theory argues that delinquency is culturally transmitted. It has been heavily criticized over the years for its bias and overprediction. One of the problems with Shaw and McKay's research strategies was neglecting to personally inspect the neighborhoods that they theorized about, and in the process they failed to acknowledge that a neighborhood might possibly be organized according to a different set of values than those followed by the dominant culture. Suggesting that certain neighborhoods were susceptible to the transmission of delinquent values no matter who lived there failed to explain, for instance, why Jewish and Chinese children in these areas did not have high rates of delinquency; nor did it explain why only a small number of youths were delinquent in these zones of social disorganization.

psychological explanations. Social scientists and criminologists pointed out the shortcomings of biological explanations for deviance. Much of their criticism focused on the inability of biological explanations to account for variables such as geography, age, sex, ethnicity, race, and social class. Much of the criticism of the biologically based theory came from the ecologically influenced sociological approach, which saw crimes as being caused more by place than by person.

Clifford R. Shaw (1896–1957) and Henry D. McKay (1899–1980)

SOME NEIGHBORHOODS ARE CHARACTERIZED BY THE SAME CRIMES OVER A LONG PERIOD OF TIME   Both sociologists were familiar with the theories of Chicago sociologists Robert E. Park and Ernest W. Burgess, who concluded that social problems were due to environmental factors. Similar to Lombroso, Shaw, and McKay believed that to understand crime and deviance, one must focus on the individual more than the crime. Their focus was on juveniles and groups rather than adults and individuals, for by the time one was late into the delinquent years, he began "to identify himself with the criminal world, and to embody in his own philosophy of life the moral values which prevailed in the criminal groups with which he had contact" (Shaw 1931, 228).

McKay and Shaw met in 1926 when both were working at the recently created Chicago Institute for Juvenile Research. They went on to collaborate on a number of projects in the 1930s and 1940s, including the compiling of autobiographical narratives from delinquents and a geographic study of the distribution patterns of delinquency (Shaw and McKay 1942). Together, Shaw and McKay concluded that the highest rates of delinquency were found in areas of the lowest economic status (Shaw and McKay 1931; 1942). Their findings indicated that delinquents were not much different from most of their counterparts in society when evaluating such factors as intelligence, physical condition, and personality traits (Shaw, 1938:350). What was most intriguing was their conclusion that there was continuity in certain neighborhood traditions that included the transmission of different criminal techniques, including car theft, shoplifting, and muggings (Shaw and McKay 1969). This epiphany was the result of noticing that despite a changing population, Chicago's highest delinquency rates between 1900 and 1906 were the same areas with the highest rates between 1917 and 1923.

Wickersham Report, Chicago: 1929

"The influx of great numbers of people of such widely different social and cultural backgrounds implies not only lack of homogeneity but also disorganization and reorganization affecting a large proportion of the population. Chicago is, in brief, a new and rapidly changing commercial and industrial city, whose population is a most varied assortment of racial and national groups in various stages of assimilation and adjustment."[9]

Robert K. Merton (1910–2003): Strain Theory

WHERE THE DISCREPANCY BETWEEN GOALS AND MEANS IS GREATEST, A CONDITION OF ANOMIE PREVAILS, AND INDIVIDUALS RESORT TO ILLEGITIMATE MEANS TO ACHIEVE GOALS   Merton's theory of anomie was first proposed by the previously Emile Durkheim, who conceptualized it as a condition of *normlessness* in society. Not unlike the Chicago theorists, Durkheim argued that as social rules become less binding due to decreasing consensus in a complex society, individuals feel less bound by social norms. Subsequently, evidence of deviance such as crime and delinquency is bound to increase. This social condition was termed *anomie* or *normlessness* by Durkheim (although Chicagoans called it *social disorganization*). Both the Chicagoans and Durkheim theorized that increasing rates of deviance are the result of structural conditions in society. However, Durkheim diverged to the extent that he believed that crime was both necessary and normal in a society, for without it, law would not evolve in response to it.

Building on Durkheim, Merton argued, in a journal article that has been called "the most frequently quoted single paper in modern sociology" (Clinard 1964, 10), that crime and deviancy occur when individuals feel blocked from achieving success and happiness in society. Following up on this research, Merton concluded that when most people in society are taught to seek culturally prescribed goals such as occupational and financial success, higher rates of crime and deviancy result when some individuals lack access to legitimate means of securing such goals. It is in these areas with such a juxtaposition of wealth and poverty where the discrepancy between goals and means is greatest and a condition of anomie prevails. It is here that individuals are most likely to resort to illegitimate means to achieve these goals when legitimate opportunities are blocked (hence *blocked opportunities*). Merton thus concluded that deviance is more common among the lower socioeconomic classes because they are less likely to have access to legitimate paths to success. Therefore, these individuals would be under strain to use legitimate means to reach culturally prescribed goals, and would feel forced to engage in nonconformist rather than conformist conduct such as gang delinquency to reach these goals.

Marvin E. Wolfgang (1924–1998) and Franco Ferracuti

In 1981, Marvin E. Wolfgang and Franco Ferracuti completed their general theory of criminal violence. Published in 1982 as *The Subculture of Violence*, the book has been influential in a number of disciplines. The theory was in part based on Wolfgang's 1958 study of homicide in Philadelphia that revealed that a significant number of homicides are the result of rather trivial incidents that took on "great importance because of mutually held expectations how people would behave" (Wolfgang 1958). Wolfgang referred to these types of killings as *victim precipitated*. More important, he discovered that in many of these killings the victim had the same characteristics as the offender, noting that it is often by chance that one becomes the victim and the other the offender.

Building on this previous research, Wolfgang and Ferracuti proposed that there are subcultures (such as the gang subculture) in which a different value system exists aside from the traditional and more civil value system. Individuals are expected to respond with violence to seemingly petty provocations such as staring someone down or bumping into someone. These take on added significance when committed within the confines of a particular subculture or neighborhood. These homicides, which account for a substantial portion of annual killings, are neither planned nor the result of some major mental disorder. Some observers suggest that there are certain neighborhoods where life is valued less highly and where those who follow these norms are respected and those who do not are reviled. The authors of the subculture of violence theory posit that these types of homicide are the result of a peculiar set of values, norms, and expectations of behavior that are transmitted from generation to generation.

> ## Learning Criminal Behavior: The Nine Propositions of Differential Association
>
> 1. Criminal behavior is learned.
> 2. Criminal behavior is learned in interaction with other persons in a process of communication.
> 3. The principal part of the learning of criminal behavior occurs within intimate personal groups.
> 4. When criminal behavior is learned, the learning includes
>   a. techniques of committing the crime.
>   b. the specific direction of motives, drives, rationalizations, and attitudes.
> 5. The specific direction of motives and drives is learned from definitions of legal codes as favorable and unfavorable.
> 6. A person becomes delinquent because of an excess of definitions favorable to violation of law over definitions unfavorable to violation of law.
> 7. Differential associations may vary in frequency, duration, priority, and intensity.
> 8. The process of learning criminal behavior by association with criminal and anti-criminal patterns involves all of the mechanisms that are involved in any other learning.
> 9. Although criminal behavior is an expression of general needs and values, it is not explained by those general needs and values because non-criminal behavior is an expression of the same needs and values.

SOCIAL PROCESS THEORIES: LEARNING THEORY

Differential Association: Edwin Sutherland (1883–1950)

CRIMINAL BEHAVIOR IS A LEARNED BEHAVIOR; THE PRINCIPAL PART OF THE LEARNING OCCURS WITHIN INTIMATE PERSONAL GROUPS   Edwin Sutherland is considered one of the first twentieth-century criminologists to argue forcefully that criminal behavior was learned. A critic of positivist criminology, Sutherland was also among the sociologists who differed with Merton's anomie theory.[10] He contended that criminal behavior was a result of an individual identifying more closely with a criminal group than with a non-criminal group. According to his cultural transmission theory of differential association, criminal behavior is learned in a pattern of communication, in which individuals acquire patterns of criminal behavior through the same learning process by which they acquire patterns of lawful behavior (see box above).

Between 1934 and 1947, Sutherland developed his theory of differential association. He listed the nine basic propositions of his theory in his textbook, *Principles of Criminology* (1947, 6–8).

CRIMINOLOGISTS WEIGH IN

Criminologists gravitated to sociostructural explanations to explain crime patterns by seeking complex explanations for the social, political, and economic inequalities that shaped both criminal behavior and the perspectives of society at large.

In the process they took major steps toward deconstructing older biological, or positivist explanations, that viewed crime through the prism of the human anatomy. One scholar refers to this as "the rejection of positivist distinctions by criminologists" (Bernstein 2002, 41).

Delinquency Subculture: Albert K. Cohen

BLOCKED FROM STATUS WITHIN THE LARGER SOCIETY LOWER CLASS YOUTHS BECOME INVOLVED WITH GANGS TO CREATE THEIR OWN, MOSTLY DELINQUENT SUBCULTURE   Albert Cohen rose to prominence with the 1955 publication of *Delinquent Boys: The Culture of the Gang*, in which he attempts to modify Merton's theory with his own theory of delinquent subcultures. Although he accepts the notion that delinquency occurs because of the discrepancy between culture goals and institutional means, Cohen suggests that the "delinquent subculture is a reaction forma-tion to socially induced stresses that our social class system inflicts on working class boys" (Cohen 1955). Cohen suggested that youths from a lower socioeconomic class are blocked from status within the larger society and become involved with gangs to create their own, mostly delinquent subculture, in which they can achieve a measure of status. Although making it clear that not all delinquents were gang members, Cohen viewed gangs as a subculture with a value system different from the dominant ones found in inclusive American culture.

Differential Opportunity: Richard Cloward and Lloyd Ohlin

IF ILLEGITIMATE OPPORTUNITY IS AVAILABLE TO THEM, MOST WILL FORM CRIMINAL GANGS TO MAKE MONEY   One of the more widely held theories explaining gang delinquency and forma-tion has been Cloward and Ohlin's Opportunity Theory, their subculture theory published in 1960. Among its more important claims was that limited opportunity structures influenced gang involve-ment and delinquency. Cloward and Ohlin embroidered Merton's and Cohen's theories on anomie, suggesting that not all gang delinquents adapt to anomie in the same fashion. He asserted that prospective gang members have differential opportunities, either legitimate or illegitimate. Their adaptation often depends on the illegitimate opportunity structure available to them. According to one recent study, Cloward and Ohlin's new model was a "theoretical advance over the classical social disorganization explanations, not least because it brought back the race/class dialectic left untheorized by both Thrasher and the subculturists" (Brotherton and Barrios 2004, 33).

The researchers made distinctions between the various *delinquent subcultures,* explaining that variations exist because "socially structured anomie based on interclass conflict and the availability of legit and illegitimate opportunity structures differentially organized on an ethnic and neighborhood basis" (Cloward and Ohlin 1960). According to Cloward and Ohlin, the type of subculture that emerges in a neighborhood depends on the level of criminal and non-criminal opportunity structures that exist in the community at the time. The theorists identified three delinquent subcultures (see box below). In essence, if illegitimate opportunity is available to delinquent youths, most form criminal gangs to make money. However, if neither illegitimate nor legitimate opportunities are available, this often leads to frustration and dissatisfaction that finds expression in the organization of violent gangs to vent their anger.

Howard Becker: Labeling Theory and Outsiders

THOSE WHO ARE LABELED AS DEVIANT ARE MORE LIKELY TO TAKE ON THAT IDENTITY THAN IF NOT LABELED   During the 1950s, America experienced one of its periodic crime hysterias, this time focusing on increasing juvenile delinquency. Howard Becker was one of the earlier proponents of what became known as *labeling theory.* In his 1963 book, *Outsiders: Studies in the Sociology of Deviance,*[11] Becker suggested that deviance should not be considered a quality of an individual, but is actually dependent on the reaction of others. Edwin Lemert originally introduced this theory in 1951. Its essence is that "when society acts negatively to a particular individual [such as adjudication], by

---

Cloward and Ohlin: Three Dominant Types of Delinquent Gangs (1960)

The *criminal gang:* devoted to theft, extortion, and other illegal means of securing income; some of whose gang members may graduate into the ranks of *organized crime* or professional crime.

The *conflict gang:* where the participation in acts of violence becomes an important means of securing status.

The *retreatist gang:* the most enigmatic group, where the consumption of drugs is stressed and addiction is prevalent.

means of the label [delinquent], we actually encourage future delinquency" (Lemert 1951, 75–78). Therefore, for Lemert and Becker, the labeling process depended less on the behavior of the delinquent and more on the way others respond to their actions—or, as sociologist George Herbert Mead (1934) suggested, an individual's self-worth is derived from how others define him. One might commit a criminal/deviant act, but unless the act is noticed and responded to by others, the individual is not considered deviant. However, once an individual is stigmatized in association with a negative label, there is a strong possibility that the youth will take on a deviant identity and engage in deviant behavior. So, basically an individual might not necessarily be guilty of a criminal act, but if others think that person is indeed guilty, he or she is labeled deviant. Deviance then is a quality attached by an outside reaction. This means that deviance is a caused by the reaction to it.

Becker was also concerned with the perception of status on a relationship. Just as the labels *doctor* or *lawyer* affords an individual a certain cachet in society, so too do such negative status indicators as *criminal, delinquent,* and *ex-con.* It is the latter negative status that labeling theorists argue often restricts life opportunities available to these individuals. Such individuals might find their only alternative careers lie in criminal activity. Becker recognized, as did others, that certain adolescents were predestined for delinquent status—especially those who frequently appeared before the courts and were told that they were indeed delinquent for engaging in minor vandalism and petty shoplifting. Ultimately, the delinquent label was likely a ticket to the next level of criminality because the label restricted their opportunities to mature out of the associated delinquent behaviors. However, statistics indicate otherwise—that most juveniles do commit crimes, but generally do not become adult criminals.

Labeling theorists have suggested that lower-class individuals were more likely than individuals from the middle and upper classes to be officially labeled delinquent. The process by which individuals react to various labels and the effect it has on the person being labeled was referred to as *criminogenesis,* or the later creation of crime from the initial labeling of a person as a criminal. In addition, once a person is labeled a criminal, the criminal justice system pays more attention to them, increasing the potential of recidivistic arrest.

Social Control: Travis Hirschi

PEOPLE WILL COMMIT CRIME UNLESS THEY ARE PROPERLY SOCIALIZED   Among the more enduring questions posed by social control theorists is, "Why do people commit crime?" and "Why don't people commit crime?" Studies demonstrate that individuals commit crimes and acts of delinquency unless they are prevented from doing so or they are properly socialized. Travis Hirschi (1969) enumerated several criteria for measuring the socialization process and posited that without these, delinquency was likely to occur:

- Attachment (parents and school)
- Commitment (educational and occupational success)
- Involvement in such conventional activities as scouting and sports leagues
- Belief in legitimacy and morality of law

More than twenty years later, Hirschi and Gottfredson (1990) argued that the primary cause of deviant behavior, including crime, was ineffective childrearing, which can produce low self-control in such children. Low self-control is characterized in a number of ways, including

- Impulsivity
- Insensitivity
- Physical risk-taking
- Short-sightedness
- Lack of verbal skills

With low self-control, an individual is less able to calculate the consequences of his actions. Furthermore, if everyone has a predisposition toward criminality, as a number of scholars have insisted over the centuries, those with low self-control will have the hardest time resisting their criminal urges.

Labeling: Charles Wellford

SOCIAL CONTROL AGENTS RATHER THAN CORRECTING DEVIANT BEHAVIOR MAY INSTEAD BE PERPETUATING IT BY SOLIDIFYING AN INDIVIDUAL'S SELF-IMAGE AS DEVIANT According to the perspective of Charles Wellford, society seeks out its deviants and stigmatizes them before assigning them delinquent status. Similar to Becker, he suggested that those labeled are more inclined to see themselves as outcasts, or *outsiders,* and behave accordingly. Once tagged as deviant due to an unsavory reputation, it should not be unexpected the individual would find numerous barriers to seeking a non-deviant role. Once someone is placed in this position, evidence suggests that the delinquent tends to seek moral and physical support from others similarly stigmatized.

According to Wellford, there are groups in society who are responsible for sanctioning an individual's conduct. When these groups find it necessary to label someone *deviant,* the conditions are created to enable deviant subcultures to flourish at the group level by establishing the need of those labeled deviant to find physical and moral support from others.

Social Bonding: Gresham Sykes and David Matza

In 1957, Sykes and Matza extended Sutherland's learning theory in their article "Techniques of Neutralization: A Theory of Delinquency." They offered a thesis that the deviant rationalizes his behavior so that he can simultaneously violate a rule or law while maintaining his belief that what he did was not wrong through a process of *neutralization.* Once the individual's impulses are neutralized, he or she becomes free to commit the act in question. Sykes and Matza classified their excuses and justifications (the neutralization) into five types:

- Denial of responsibility (*It was not my fault because I was drunk*).
- Denial of injury (*No one was injured*).
- Denial of victim (*They deserved it*).
- Condemnation of the condemned (*Everybody does it*).
- Appeal to higher loyalties (*I didn't do it just for myself*)[12].

Sykes and Matza's *subculture of delinquency* is distinct from the traditional and oppositional notion of a *delinquent subculture.* In later research, they applied these findings to the world of youth gangs and concluded that most delinquents are not full gang members, but are *mundane delinquents* who afterward express remorse for their actions and in many cases admire those who obey the law. For Sykes and Matza, delinquency and mainstream subcultures, rather than inhabiting two different worlds, exist side by side. Delinquents, who are aware of the difference between right and wrong are influenced by both sets of values and make a choice whether to victimize and who the target will be (Matza and Sykes 1961; Lanier and Henry 1998).

THE GANG: A HISTORICAL PERSPECTIVE

A recent study of the Almighty Latin Kings, which the authors describe as the "archeology of gang theory," traces the term *gang* back to Scottish agricultural society, when it meant "a walk for cattle (Brotherton and Barrios, 2004)." In Old English *gang* took on more of an association with group formation, as in "a gang of sailors," reflecting the mercantile society of the British Isles. By the early 1800s when someone proffered *gangs,* it usually referred to individuals socially displaced by the industrial revolution, as in "a company of persons acting together for some purpose, usually criminal, as in 'gang of thieves'" (Brotherton and Barrios 2004, 26). In any case, by the nineteenth century, *gang* "had a well-established connotation in Europe" (Brotherton and Barrios 2004).

According to gang scholar Lewis Yablonsky, "One of the earliest applications of the term 'gang' to youth groups in America was made by Henry D. Sheldon in 1898" (1962, 73; 1997). However, the term *gang,* when applied to crews or groups of persons with associated ideas, can be traced back as far as the seventeenth century (Partridge 1950, 279). Citing the London gangs of pre-Dickensian London, one scholar noted, "Gangs did not originate in the United States" (Hagedorn 2006, 183). Sheldon, however, deserves credit for classifying American gangs according to their activities, characterizing most as social and athletic clubs, industrial associations, philanthropic associations, and literary and musical organizations. Sheldon asserted "predatory organizations [were] a poor second" (Sheldon 1898, 425–428).

Some of the earliest allusions to youth gang activity in America come to us from the post-Revolutionary 1790s. One Philadelphia editor lamented the hordes of adolescents parading through the nighttime streets, complaining,

> The custom of permitting boys to ramble about the streets by night is productive of the most serious and alarming consequences to their morals. Assembled in corners, and concealed from every eye, they can securely indulge themselves in mischief of every kind. The older ones train the up the younger, in the same path, which they themselves pursue. (quoted in Sanders 1970, 325)

In the 1790s, according to one explanation for the proliferation of homeless juveniles on the streets, there were so many slaves and wage laborers that the customary path of apprenticeship was no longer open for the growing population, and children found themselves on the streets among the unwanted. In a time before modern police forces, young boys could escape to areas of the city without fear of apprehension. Despite the apparently large numbers of homeless juveniles, America would not have a gang problem until the years of the Industrial Revolution and urbanization in the 1840s.

It is impossible to separate several themes from the development of gangs in America. Urbanization, immigration, ethnicity, and poverty are the most frequently cited for the development of myriad gangs in the late nineteenth and early twentieth centuries. Rising tides of Irish, Italian, Polish, and Russian immigrants faced almost insurmountable challenges in their attempts to join the American economy. With few social and economic outlets, social commentators and reformers such as Jacob Riis turned their attention to social conditions faced by the children of immigrants—poverty, disease, poor housing, and even poorer educational opportunities. As a result, "'Gang life was a natural outcome for such youth" (Decker and Van Winkle 1996, 4). Jewish mob historian Jenna Weisman Joselit quoted one early twentieth-century gang member who explained why one would join a gang, "It was the exceptional, almost abnormal boy who did not join the gang. The gang was romance, adventure, had the zest of banditry, the thrill of camp life, and the lure of hero-worship" (1983, 26).

Alien Conspiracy Theory

The *alien conspiracy theory* has been adopted by commentators sporadically throughout American history to explain why certain ethnic groups predominated in urban organized crime. However, critics have blasted this ethnocentric theory, referring to it as "a smokescreen for a product that was homegrown" (Woodiwiss 2001, 104). In the late nineteenth century and at different times in the twentieth century, new immigrant groups have been targeted by officialdom for threatening the sanctity of American institutions. However, more recent research reveals that as early as the mid-1920s few observers emphasized ethnicity and alien conspiracy theories as a key to understanding the evolution of organized crime. In fact, says Woodiwiss, there were few if any responsible observers prior to the 1940s who believed that the Italians, Jews, or any other group that conspired to control urban organized crime. A new generation of historians now argues that certain conditions in American society exemplified by business competition and notions of the self-made man popularized in the accounts of the "Robber Barons" such as Andrew Carnegie and John Rockefeller functioned as models for criminal entrepreneurs of the era. Contributors to the 1930s Wickersham Report even postulated that rather than the result of immigration and alien conspiracies, *gangsterism* should be understood as more of a homegrown product, an unfortunate result of America's "political, economic, sociological and legal structures" (quoted in Woodiwiss 2002, 235). As early as 1930, Fred Pasley subtitled his biography of Al Capone, *The Biography of a Self-Made Man.* He describes Capone not in terms of his Italian-American roots, but as "the John Rockefeller of some twenty-thousand anti-Volstead filling stations" (quoted in Woodiwiss 2001, 229), referring to the Volstead Act that ushered in the age of Prohibition.

DANIEL BELL AND THE "QUEER LADDER OF SOCIAL MOBILITY"   In 1953, two years after the inauguration of the Kefauver Committee Hearings, Columbia University sociologist Daniel Bell first described urban organized crime as "one of the queer ladders of social mobility in American life" (1961, 129).[13] Bell's thesis was built on previous notions that immigrants moved up the social ladder to better, working-class jobs and were often able to move out of the worst communities, only to be replaced by the newest incarnations of the poor, who would spawn new ethnic gangs. Bell argued that early twentieth-century Italian immigrants often found their legitimate paths to success blocked by other ethnic groups that wanted to keep the new group out. Like previous newcomers, gangs provided access to individual wealth and opened doors to economic and political power in cities such as Chicago and New York City. Therefore, in Bell's eyes, it was only natural that like the Irish and Jews before them, Italians would eventually take their turn in the ethnic succession.

Bell, a critic of Kefauver's findings about a national crime syndicate known as the Mafia, and other conspiracy theories observed, "Unfortunately for a good story—and the existence of the Mafia would be a whale of a story—neither the Senate Crime Committee in its testimony, nor Kefauver in his [subsequent] book, presented any real evidence that the Mafia exists as a functioning organization" (quoted in Anderson 1979, 9). Bell posited that eventually, Italian organized crime activity would fade from the scene, only to be replaced by other groups. However, Bell was never able to explain why Italians remained prominent in urban organized crime circles for the next half century, even though the vast majority of Italians found legitimate social status and advancement attainable. Critics of Bell's thesis, such as Michael Woodiwiss, argue that the queer ladder theory lacks empirical support, noting that many choose lives of crime because it offers exciting paths to wealth and represents a personal decision more than a reaction to blocked opportunities (2001).

Too often, Bell's thesis has not been thoroughly understood. Most prominent supporters of his thesis focus on the often-chronicled succession of Irish gangsters, succeeded by Jewish criminals, and then Italians. One glaring misread of Bell's work is that this ethnic succession is applicable to all regions of the United States. In fact, he notes that immigration in the South and on the West Coast was an altogether different story and that most accounts of the process of ethnic succession focus on the Northern states, which offered a "distinct ethnic sequence in the modes of obtaining illicit wealth" (Bernstein 2002, 22).

Although widespread skepticism persists as to the viability of the ethnic succession thesis, "with the possible exception of Italian-Americans the broad process of one ethnic group's supplanting and succeeding another in certain types of criminal activity appears discernible and seems generally plausible" (Kelly et al. 1994, 2). However, extending this thesis to the dynamics of organized crime groups remains questionable, in part because immigration demographics are much more complex than earlier waves of specific ethnic and racial groups. The important lesson presented by Bell's "queer ladder of social mobility" thesis is the "reminder that organized crime was a multiethnic phenomenon at a time when professional and media opinion was moving towards a perception that significant organized crime was ethnically exclusive to Italian Americans" (Woodiwiss 2001, 256).

THE GANG, THE NEIGHBORHOOD, AND ETHNIC SUCCESSION   The very word *gang* summons up mostly pejorative connotations. For some, it means a bunch of juveniles hanging outside a local store; to others, the benign youths of *West Side Story;* for still others, it depicts highly organized crime families. By the 1920s, pioneering investigators such as Frederic Thrasher were focusing on immigration as a source for early youth gangs. The notion that the ethnicity of gangs might change but their location did not has become an accepted tenet in the field of research. Still, in 1955, Cohen focused on gangs generically without reference to ethnicity or specific communities. However, since the late 1960s, class, race, ethnicity, and particular communities have been regarded as key variables for studying gangs (Moore 1988).

Most discussions of the theory of ethnic succession revolve around the immigration of roughly thirty million immigrants from Ireland and Eastern and Southern Europe in the nineteenth and early twentieth centuries.[14] According to the traditional interpretation, members of each immigrant group acquired money and social standing from the illegal marketplace, and then used their newfound wealth to move into more legitimate society. Once this occurs, a vacuum is left in the illegal market sector that is filled by another marginalized group.

By the 1960s, the ethnic changes became less European and more African American and Hispanic. However, also during that time, America's changing economic order meant there were less opportunities for newcomers—whether European, Hispanic, or Black. Observers noticed that minority youths were less able to move up the industrial ladder and mature out of the gang. Therefore, in effect, the deindustrialization of urban America led to a narrowing of opportunities for those who in earlier years would have matured "out of delinquent and deviant ways" (Hagedorn 1988, 44).

In the late 1920s, Frederic Thrasher described the ethnic succession of one Chicago neighborhood known as the *Old Nineteenth Ward, Moonshine Valley,* or the *Bloody Nineteenth.* Here he describes a neighborhood that in 1889 was largely German and Irish. These nationalities gradually moved out giving way to an influx of Italians, Russians, Jews, and Greeks and more recently (in the 1920s), "gypsies, negroes, and Mexicans" (Thrasher 1927, 11). Obviously, this is just one of hundreds of examples that can be brandished to demonstrate the ethnic succession of a cornucopia of racial and ethnic groups in poor neighborhoods throughout the United States since the late 1850s.

Subsequent findings by the National Commission on Law Observance and Enforcement (NCLOE) in 1931 acknowledged "the succession of cultural groups in delinquency areas" (NCLOE, 1931) in Chicago during the first decades of the twentieth century. Among its most lasting findings was the observation that "the composition of the [delinquent] population was paralleled by a corresponding change in the racial and nationality groupings among children brought before the juvenile court of Cook County" (NCLOE, 1931) during this era. This demonstrated to the researchers of the so-called Wickersham Report that the "relative magnitude of the rates of delinquents in the areas having the greatest concentration of delinquent boys" (No. 13, 1931, 82–83) changed hardly at all between 1900 and 1920.

Succession of Cultural Groups in Delinquency Groups (1930)

On first arriving in the city, an immigrant group tends to settle in a very compact community near the industrial areas adjacent to the center of the city. These regions are known as areas of first settlement and are characterized culturally by the perpetuation of many European traditions and habits of life. After some years of residence in such an area of initial settlement, the group tends to move outward to some new district, establishing an area of second settlement. In such a district, the group is characterized by less concentration and by a closer approximation of urban-American living standards. As individual members of these immigrant communities become more fully assimilated, they tend to move away from their particular communities into cosmopolitan American residential areas. Thus the length of time an immigrant group has been in the city is reflected by the pattern of distribution. The oldest immigrant groups in the city are the least highly concentrated and are found farthest removed from the center of the city.[15]

Jewish Immigrants and Ethnic Succession in Organized Crime

According to one leading organized crime observer, major Jewish involvement in organized crime was, for the most part, "a one-generation phenomenon" (Volkman 1998, 48). The Jewish immigrant community never considered criminal syndicates to be a by-product of their folkways or cultural experience (baggage), and had vocally expressed its disapproval over the years, making it even more intent on sacrificing for the benefit of a future generation that would go to college and bring pride to the small community. Meyer Lansky's wife reportedly told him after their son was born with cerebral palsy, "God is punishing you for all the rotten things you're doing" (Volkman 1998, 48). Another factor playing a role in the diminished presence of Jewish organized crime was the federal government's 1924 Reed-Johnson Act, which stemmed the flood of Jewish immigration from Eastern Europe, and "drying up the pool from which the Jewish gangs drew young recruits." Conditions became so bad, one gangster reportedly lamented, "We lost our farm system" (Volkman 1998, 48).

By the beginning of the 1970s, many observers still cited the ethnic succession continuum as part of the explanation for the persistence of organized crime in America. In 1972, Ramsey Clark (p. 59) posited,

> The earlier markets for criminal operations of the Mafia, the ethnic ghettos of recent immigrants have disappeared. The new market, Negro, Puerto Rican, Mexican-American, have proven more difficult. As the Jewish merchant in the black ghetto yields to small businesses owned by blacks, the monopoly of the Mafia in organized crime gives way to the black or Spanish-speaking entrepreneur.

Pointing to the large numbers of Italian, Irish, and Jewish immigrants who have prospered through legitimate channels, since the mid-1980s several prominent scholars have argued that the trail of upward mobility was not as narrow as previously thought. According to Lupsha and others (1981, 3–4), organized criminal behavior was not based on either "a narrow or limited status or mobility ladder for early twentieth century immigrants, or frustration or anger at the thwarting of mobility desires of immigrants by the dominant culture."

By the approach of the post-industrial 1980s, gangs had become an enduring attribute of a burgeoning minority underclass. Jobs that had formerly offered lifetime careers to those with minimal education and skills were by the 1980s more likely to be part time, temporary, low paying, and with little opportunity for advancement. The decline of full-time labor union jobs meant a tectonic shift in the urban economic landscape.

What Is a Gang?

Several criminal entities have been saddled with the nom de guerre of *gang*—ranging from the more traditional Italian exemplars of La Cosa Nostra and the Mafia, to newer gangs representing any number of racial or ethnic groups—African American, Hispanic, Asian, Jamaican, and so forth. Other cliques include white skinheads, outlaw motorcycle gangs, and prison gangs. In any case, all seem rather removed from what *gang* conjured up in earlier eras. Sanchez-Jankowski suggested that each historical era defines its contemporary gangs through the prism of the times (1991). When one mentions gangs in the 1920s and 1930s, what comes to mind are the bootleggers and machine-gun killers of the Capone era. Herbert Asbury used *gangs* and *gangsters* to describe the syndicates of the previous century, whereas Frederic Thrasher used *gang* and *mob* interchangeably. Later writers adopted the term *syndicate* to distance the definition from the more amateur world of youth street gangs. Therefore, over time terms such as *mob, syndicate,* and other catchwords were used to distinguish genuine formal criminal groups from the generic *youth gang.* However, no matter which era one evaluates in American history, the term *gang* has had mostly negative connotations.

If there was ever such thing as an original gangster, it is the western outlaws of the nineteenth century, many of whom entered the pantheon of criminal mythology—the James-Younger Gang, the Dalton Gang, and the Reno Gang just for starters. The social, economic, and moral problems that gave rise to the criminal landscape of the nineteenth century were replicated in succeeding generations as the term *gang* was transferred from the western desperadoes to the urban gangs of the twentieth century (Thrasher 1927; Yablonsky 1997).

Trying to define a gang runs into the same definitional problems faced by those defining organized crime. The very nature of the term is so imprecise that it can refer to any group of individuals, regardless of numbers, interests, goals and motivations, race and ethnicity, class and occupation. The fact remains that there is no consensus of definition or even the most important elements of the definition. Authorities cite the presence of illegal activity (Ball and Curry 1995), solidarity and territoriality (Thrasher 1927), and territoriality and self-identification (Klein 1971) among the attributes of prototypical gangs.

Throughout most of recorded history, the word *gang* has not implied criminal activity, but simply referred to a group of individuals working together. Some definitions emphasize the importance of territoriality (Decker and Van Winkle 1996), but where does this place Asian gangs that are highly mobile and do not claim turf for the most part, but meet other criteria? By most accounts, modern gangs are not shy about projecting visible symbols of gang association, whether it is tattoos, hand signals, jargon, or colors. Even law enforcement has failed to come up with a widely accepted definition. The following are some of the more widely accepted official and law enforcement definitions of modern street or youth gangs (Delaney 2006).

OFFICE OF JUVENILE JUSTICE AND DELINQUENCY PREVENTION   In 2000, the Office of Juvenile Justice and Delinquency Prevention (OJJDP) identified a number of criteria used to identify a group as a gang. These characteristics have been widely cited and at least offers a starting point. Among its most important criteria are the following:

- The group must have more than two members (gangs always have more than two members).
- Group members must fall within a limited age range, generally acknowledged as ages twelve to twenty-four.
- Members must share some sense of identity, which can be accomplished by naming the gang after a local geographic feature, or through the adoption of specific colors and symbols.
- Youth gangs require some permanence.
- Involvement in criminal activity is a central element of the youth gangs.

CALIFORNIA PENAL CODE   According to the California Penal Code, Section 186.22 (1987, 3–4), a *gang* is

> a group of associating individuals which (a) has an identifiable leadership and organizational structure; (b) either claims control over particular territory in a community, or exercises control over an illegal enterprise; and (c) engages collectively or as individuals in acts of violence or serious criminal behavior.

NEW MEXICO STATE PENAL CODE   New Mexico's State Penal Code, Section 11-9-4, defines *street gangs* as

> any ongoing organization, association in fact, or group of three or more persons, whether formally or informally organized, or any sub-group thereof, having as one of its primary activities the commission of one or more criminal acts or illegal acts, which has an identifiable name or symbol, and whose members individually or collectively engage in or have engaged in a pattern of criminal gang activity for a one year period.

Academics and the Gang

Between the 1920s and the present, various criteria have been accepted or discarded by a wide range of scholars. Miller (1975), for example, suggests that youth gangs are distinct from simple groups when it comes to organization, identifiable leadership and identification with a territory, and had a continuous association and a specific purpose. Almost a half century earlier, Thrasher found most gangs had between six and twenty members and formed spontaneously in poor and socially disorganized neighborhoods. However, unlike their modern counterparts, he found those of the 1920s were formed to fulfill a youthful need for fun and adventure, rather than for purely criminal reasons, and that this playacting often resulted in acts of delinquency (Thrasher 1927). Others such as Cloward and Ohlin posited that gangs emerged as the result of blocked opportunities.

Of those who assert that street gangs are not actually organizations, Lewis Yablonsky is most prominent in defining most youth gangs as "near groups," in which they are not groups in a strictly social sense, but fit somewhere between a group and a mob, or "spontaneous short-lived crowd with no roles or membership status" (Yablonsky 1962, 1997). Revisiting his groundbreaking earlier work from 1997, Yablonsky went as far as to define a *group* as "an identifiable, coherent, and finite entity made up of people who relate to each other on the basis of defined norms and rules for interaction—the role of each member is clearly defined and entails certain rights, duties, and obligations" (1997, 191).

A number of gang scholars agree with Yablonsky to the extent that street gangs are indeed not well organized. Martin Klein (1995, 61), for example, found Los Angeles street gangs to be a loosely organized and "rather amorphous collection of subgroups, cliques, pairs and loners." In their ethnographic studies of St. Louis gangs, Decker and Van Winkle found gangs to be "a loosely organized confederation of individuals bound together through common action, experiences, symbols, and allegiances" (1996, 271–72).

Others have jettisoned the notion of organized street gangs all together, arguing that "the idea of sophisticated gang organizations is still largely a product of the self- or organizational-interested musings of gang leaders, certain police officials, academic researchers, and media reporters" (Spergel 1995, 79–80).

Frederic Thrasher

JUVENILE GANGS ARE TRAINING GROUNDS FOR PROSPECTIVE ORGANIZED CRIME MEMBERS
Most studies of the gang begin with the pioneering work of Frederic Thrasher (1892–1962). His groundbreaking book was an extensive examination of Chicago's myriad (1,313) gangs, including their social structure, and even examined the social gap that gangs fill. Subsequent studies built on the foundation built by Thrasher, and indeed accepted a number of his conclusions. In his pioneering work, *The Gang* (1927), Thrasher extensively chronicled the gangs of Chicago, finding that gang activity accounted for about 95 percent of all juvenile delinquency in Chicago during the period of his investigation. Unlike the prototypical gangs of the 1950s, he found gangs to be much smaller, with ages averaging between 10 and 17 years old. More than 80 percent of juveniles committed delinquent actions in collaboration with other gang members. Compared to later years their activities were rather benign, consisting of common offenses such as truancy and begging. He also found a continuum in which older boys taught younger boys techniques for more serious crimes.

Since the halcyon days of film land's *Our Gang* and *Bowery Boys*, the term *gang* has garnered an increasingly pejorative connotation. There are no universal definitions for *gang*. Pioneering gang researcher Frederic Thrasher made one of the earliest attempts in 1927, writing, "A gang is an interstitial[16] group, originally formed spontaneously, and then integrated through conflict" (1927, 57). The following types of behavior characterize a *gang*:

- Meeting face to face
- Milling
- Moving through space as a unit

- Conflict
- Planning

The result of this collective behavior is the development of tradition, "an unreflective internal structure, esprit de corps, solidarity, morale, group awareness, and attachment to a local territory" (Thrasher 1927, 57).

Selected Academic Definitions of the Gang (1971–1996)

MALCOLM KLEIN (1971)   Building on the research of Thrasher and others, Klein (1971, 13) added the dimension of *delinquency* to his definition, describing a *gang* as

> any denotable adolescent group of youngsters who (a) are generally perceived as a distant aggregation by others in the neighborhood; (b) recognize themselves as a denotable group (almost invariably with a group name); and (c) have been involved in a sufficient number of delinquent incidents to call forth a consistent negative response from neighborhood residents and/or enforcement agencies.

CARTWRIGHT, THOMSON, AND SCHWARTZ (1975)   Building on Thrasher's foundation, Cartwright, Thompson, and Schwartz argue that the gang was indeed "an interstitial and integrated group of persons who meet face to face more or less regularly and whose existence and activities as a group are considered an actual or potential threat to the prevailing social order" (1975, 4).

WALTER B. MILLER (1980)   Cultural anthropologist Walter B. Miller (1958) suggests that lower-class boys are virtually unaffected by middle-class traditions, and that much of lower-class delinquency is simply a reflection of certain "focal concerns" that are characteristics of the urban lower-class way of life. Miller posits that gang involvement and delinquency are simply an extension of lower-class culture, asserting that the lower class has a separate identifiable culture distinct from the culture of the middle class, and that this culture is at least as old as that of the middle class.

Because not all children who live in criminogenic environments turn to deviant behavior, there must be other explanations. In the mid-1970s, Miller surveyed a number of police departments and youth service workers in six large urban areas with acknowledged gang problems. The following list contains the five most common responses to the question, "How would you define a gang?" He later added a sixth response after another survey (see box below).

Miller combined the aforementioned criteria in what he referred to as the *consensus-based* definition of gangs. More influenced by criminal justice system professionals than the others, he defines a *gang* as

> a self-formed association of peers, bound together by mutual interests, with identifiable leadership, well defined lines of authority, and other organizational features, who act in concert to achieve a specific purpose or purposes which generally include conduct of illegal activity and control over a particular territory, facility, or type of enterprise. (1980, 121)

1. Violent or criminal behavior as a major activity of group members.
2. Group organization, with functional role division and chain of command.
3. Identifiable leadership.
4. Continuing and recurring interaction among group members.
5. Claims of control over specific territory.
6. Specific purpose.

GEORGE KNOX (1993)   According to George Knox, a group can be considered a gang if

> it exists for or benefits substantially from the continuing criminal activity of its members. Some element of crime must exist as a definitive feature of the organization for it to be classified as a gang. That need not be income-producing crime, because it could also be crimes of violence (1993, 5).

SCOTT DECKER AND VAN WINKLE (1996)   Decker and Van Winkle describe a *gang* as "an age graded peer group that exhibits some permanence, engages in criminal activity, and has some symbolic representation of membership" (1996, 31).

KINNEAR (1996)   Kinnear explains that creating a definition "is often a highly political issue that reflects the interests and agendas of the various individuals and agencies involved with gangs, including law-enforcement personnel, politicians, advocates, social workers, the media, and researchers" (1996, 1–2).

Gang Characteristics

An evaluation of most definitions of contemporary street gangs reveals a number of elements that are usually verifiable and include the following:

- Some type of organization
- Identifiable leadership
- Identifiable territory
- A specific purpose
- Continual association
- Participation in some type of illegal activity

Today, most gangs share similar behaviors, including

- Use of graffiti to mark territory and communicate with other gangs
- Dress alike, often adopting gang color (Crips/blue; Bloods/red)
- Often tattoo selves with gang names or symbols
- Abide by a specific code of conduct
- Have own specific argot
- Own set of hand signs that help recognize other members

Are Today's Gangs as Territorial as Gangs in the Past?

The shifting demographics of immigration and the rapidly changing nature of urban America represents a sea change in the definitional criteria once accepted as part and parcel of the gang experience. Perhaps none has changed more than the notion of territoriality as a mainstay of the definition. A number of scholars point to modern transportation, urban renewal, and other factors that have gone a long way to weakening the relationship between gangs and their neighborhoods. Ko-Lin Chin was among the first to recognize that Asian gangs that proliferated in the 1980s were no longer confined to singular neighborhoods, but were more likely to cruise other communities and were considered extremely mobile (1990). Others posit that the precipitous decline of some Black neighborhoods has diminished the value of turf, making some neighborhoods no longer deemed worthy of defending (Hagedorn 1988).

Impact of Gangs on Popular Culture

Urban street life has gone mainstream in recent years, giving rise to stores such as Urban Outfitters and styles reflecting gang culture as viewed through the prism of pop culture. Gang identifiers from a decade ago are no longer dependable measures of gang membership with its sartorial eccentricities and graffiti subsumed by the money machine known as popular culture. Using symbols, dress, and mannerisms as criteria for gang membership is considered outdated due to the diffusion of gang culture. Some have even gone as far as to suggest that most gangs today are poorly organized, purposeless, and without clear hierarchical leadership (McCorkle and Miethe 2001, 207).

Are Most Urban Street Gangs Highly Structured Organizations?

One of the more controversial examinations of gangs came out of the barrios of Los Angeles, where one gang scholar found highly structured gangs that served both individual and collective interests through a variety of illegal activities (Sanchez-Jankowski 1991). Over the course of nearly ten years, Sanchez-Jankowski studied thirty-seven gangs in three cities and discovered that most youths joined gangs there to take part in the drug trade, where they found employment conditions that surpassed the legitimate market when it came to earning potential, working conditions, and financial security.

Others would disagree, suggesting that claims of organized drug trafficking by street gangs are "weak and anecdotal" (McCorkle and Miethe 2001, 216). During the 1960s and 1970s, most studies suggested that few gangs had organizational qualities, but were marked by loose cohesion and changing leadership, held together by what Thrasher referred to as *esprit de corps* (Yablonsky 1962; Klein 1971). One study by the Los Angeles District Attorney's Office described street gang involvement in drug activity to be "minimal, episodic, and completely disorganized," whereas academics such as Martin Klein found "the world of crack in Los Angeles belonged principally to the regular drug dealers, not to street gangs" (Klein, Maxson and Cunningham. 1991, 647). St. Louis gang experts found that few members joined gangs to sell drugs or to use drug money for gang objectives. Furthermore, they found little evidence that gangs ran most drug houses or that most dealers were gang members. Counter to the claims who view street gang members as organized drug traffickers, the St. Louis research indicated that these members could not control the illegal drug market in St. Louis because "they lacked the skills or commitment to organize for a long range profit making venture" (Decker and Van Winkle 1996, 159).

Gangs and Organized Crime

In his 1927 book *The Gang,* Thrasher found it useful to use the terms *gang* and *mob* interchangeably because according to Yablonsky, he was "dealing with formal youth groups and their relationship to formal crime organizations and found it useful to use both terms" (Sanchez-Jankowski 1991, 3). Thrasher is considered among the first to treat gangs as an organizational phenomenon and process by which certain individuals are socialized into organized adult gangs: "Both Herbert Asbury and Thrasher identified youth gangs as the socialization agents for the graduation of young delinquents to organized crime" (Sanchez-Jankowski 1991, 3).

Thrasher tried to explain why adolescents become delinquent and break the law. For the student of organized crime, one of the most important notions was that juvenile gangs were simply

---

Some Differences between Street Gangs and Organized Crime

- Street gangs have younger members.
- Street gangs are social most of the time.
- Organized crime groups operate differently, in that they are created for economic gain through illegal acts (Shelden, Tracy, Brown, 1997).

training grounds for future organized crime career. Thrasher compared it to an apprenticeship of sorts, where some gang members found social mobility through criminal activities and utilized youth gangs "as feeder groups for the Mafia" (Thrasher 1927, 281–312). The next step was for organized syndicates to recruit from these for the gangster major leagues. However, there is little evidence beyond the anecdotal that this continuum has actually existed. More likely gang membership was just one of many responses of immigrant youths to a disorganized community.

It is often difficult to distinguish between youth crime and organized crime from the outside looking in (Howell and Decker 1999). What has become clear is that the more formally structured and organized a youth gang becomes, the more likely it will eventually become embroiled in organized crime enterprises such as drug dealing and trafficking. Experts have observed that if a youth gang has a formal organization with clear leadership and rules and operates within a framework of expectations and sanctions for non-compliance it is more likely to embrace and succeed at a more advanced level of organized criminality (Duffy 2004, 4).

Once gangs began working for the urban political machines in the nineteenth century, they became part of the organized crime continuum (see Chapter 5). In cities such as Boston and New York City, a system emerged that was exemplified by consistent and direct contact between gang representatives and city politicians. However, studies of cities such as Los Angeles, which has no political machine tradition, were marked by inconsistent or intermittent contact between the two organizations. According to Jankowski-Sanchez's ten-year study of the relationship between modern politicians and gangs, a pattern of symbiosis emerged that allowed gangs and politicians to flourish. Among the most often cited services provided by the gangs were

- Dissemination of literature for candidates
- Place signs at public places and carry signs at polling booths
- Active in getting out the vote on election day—either physically or by reminding
- Pressure to vote through intimidation
- Make donations (very rare)
- Undertake crude fundraising by coercing local merchants to donate to campaign

In return, members received patronage jobs; this was particularly true with Irish gangs who had grown up in this tradition. Other groups received money or perhaps protection for various illegal activities or even free rental spaces in small buildings (Sanchez-Jankowski, 1991).

Juvenile versus Adult Gangs

In terms of studying organized crime, it is essential to distinguish between the activities of groups of juveniles who engage in street crimes from their more organized adult counterparts. Herbert Asbury ([1927], 1970) and Frederic Thrasher (1927) were among the first to make a distinction between those who grow up in a gang and criminals who organize to perform illegal acts more effectively. Frederic Thrasher asserted that "a striking fact which bears directly upon the relation of juvenile delinquency to mercenary crime is the early age at which professional criminals, gangsters, gunmen, and racketeers begin their criminal careers" (1927). Thrasher and others purported to show that that there was an inexhaustible supply of young street criminals hoping to join gangs at the next level. Over the years, organized crime groups were distinguished from adolescent gangs by the use of the term *mob*. One pioneer in the field posited that it was necessary to make this distinction to separate analytically two related but distinct social problems—organized crime and delinquency (Sanchez-Jankowski 1991, 3–4).

Following on the heels of Thrasher, Frank Tannenbaum examined the evolution of Chicago youth gangs, concentrating on the metamorphosis of some young gang members into gangsters. Tannenbaum suggested that boys made the transition to gangster as they aged, turning from simple crimes such as shoplifting to more lucrative ventures such as stealing cars and robberies (Tannenbaum 1938; Yablonsky 1997). Like other so-called representatives of the Chicago School, Tannenbaum

How Modern Gang Activity Diverges from Past Gang Activity

Modern Gang Activity	Example
Lethality of weapons	Uzis instead of knives and zip guns[17]
Intraracial violence instead of interracial	Black-on-Black or Hispanic-on-Hispanic violence
Participation in the drug business	Drug trafficking and addiction
Variability of activities	Organized crime activities

Adapted from Yablonsky 1997, pp. 2–3.

placed heavy weight on theories of family disorganization, explaining that in poor neighborhoods, gang activity became a normal activity; that most crimes were committed by gang members; and that gangs emerged when communities failed to integrate youths into law respecting society.

Overview

The Gang in the Twenty-First Century: An International Perspective

Some early studies note that urbanization was a prime ingredient for the growth of gangs (Park 1924; Thrasher 1927). However, as the world becomes increasingly urbanized, the gulf separating the poor from the middle and upper classes continues to expand. From an academic perspective, what was once mostly a Western phenomenon has become a worldwide concern, particularly in countries with a growing underclass of young men who operate "outside the control of formal state authority" (Hagedorn 2006). Most recently, Hagedorn (2006) noted that in most cities of the developing world, unsupervised groups of teenagers come under the influence of a variety of criminal groups and are often recruited by nationalist and religious militias. Also contributing to the dilemma are the links between prison gangs and street gangs. For example, the United States, South Africa, and South America have huge prison populations. Many new prisoners enter gang life for the first time in prison. Once free, they use their prison credibility and connections to recruit back on the streets.

The tumult from urbanization and immigration has reached virtually every urban corner of the globe. In 2003, one United Nations report (Short and Hughes 2006) found almost one billion people living in urban slums. Slum dwellers make up 43 percent of the total population in developing nations, compared to only 6 percent in their developed counterparts. In Latin America, 80 percent of the population lives in cities; sub-Saharan African cities slums house more than three quarters of the city dwellers.

If one were to go back to the early work of the Chicago School theorists, one would not be surprised to find that urbanization accelerated the growth of gangs throughout the world, particularly in Latin America, Africa, and Asia. As previously noted, gangs are not a new phenomenon, but "have formed all over the world whenever and wherever industrialization and related processes drive people into cities" (Short and Hughes 2006, 183).

Almost a century has passed since Thrasher, Park, and the Chicago School chronicled the impact of unprecedented urbanization on the development of gangs—a process now being replicated throughout the developing world. The process of industrialization and its concomitant developments pushed and pulled individuals from the countryside to the city. It should not be surprising that the majority of today's gang members are located in Africa, Asia, and Latin America. There is an incredible diversity of gangs worldwide; so many that it is beyond the scope of any book chapter to cover in detail. Recent studies examined South Africa's 100-year history of gangs, including more recently the *skollies* (Pinnock 1984; Shurink 1986). New Zealand has its Maori gangs, and Sierra Leone is plagued by *rarry boys* (Hazlehurst 2002; Abdullah 2002).

International gang expert Hagedorn sees gangs as a universal phenomenon with millions of members. He suggests that the sequence of steps leading to gang membership is akin to the "voice of those marginalized by processes of globalization" (Hagedorn 2006, 181). Indeed, one cannot examine most street gangs today without viewing them in a global context. Similar to the vacuum left in crime-prone neighborhoods as one group replaces another, in many parts of the world, "the state has retreated, leaving a vacuum to be filled by gangs and groups of individuals who fill the void left by the retreat of the social policies of the state" (Hagedorn 2006, 181).

Key Terms

Cesare Beccaria
Rational choice theory
Biological/anthropological
  theories
Cesare Lombroso
Criminal types
Gabriel Tarde
Ernest A. Hooten
Body-type theories
William H. Sheldon
Antisocial personality
Emile Durkheim
Psychological theories
Sociological theories

The Chicago School
Robert E. Park
Ernest Burgess
Clifford Shaw
Henry McKay
Social disorganization theory
Cultural transmission theory
Robert Merton
Edwin Sutherland
Learning theories
Albert Cohen
Delinquent subcultures
Richard Cloward
Lloyd Ohlin

Anomie
Differential association
Differential opportunity
Labeling theory
Howard Becker
Travis Hirschi
The gang
Ethnic succession
Daniel Bell
Queer ladder thesis
Frederic Thrasher
Turf and territoriality

Critical Thinking Questions

1. How did philosophers in the eighteenth-century Age of Enlightenment explain crime and criminality?
2. How were biological and anthropological theories used to explain criminality?
3. What did Lombroso contribute to the study of criminality?
4. Can an individual's body type determine whether one turns to crime?
5. How are these aforementioned theories viewed today?
6. What is an *antisocial personality,* and what does this have to do with crime and criminality?
7. Is a society without crime possible? Discuss Durkheim and his impact on the study of this problem.
8. What is the Chicago School and who were its leading contributors? Discuss the various sociological theories and theorists.
9. What did the Chicago School have to do with the notion of *ethnic succession?* Is the ethnic succession a viable theory?
10. Is crime a learned behavior?
11. Can being stigmatized as a criminal lead one to become a criminal?
12. When did gangs first appear in America? What conditions led to their development, and have they been repeated in other countries?
13. What is a *gang*? Are gangs the same as *organized crime groups?* Are gangs highly structured?
14. Are gangs the products of certain neigh-borhoods or specific behavior types?

Endnotes

1. See Cesare Beccaria, *An Essay on Crime and Punishments,* translated with an introduction by Henry Paolucci, New York: Macmillan Publishing, 1963; Jeremy Bentham, *An Introduction to the Principles of Morals and Legislation,* edited with an introduction by Laurence J. Lafleur, New York: Hafner Publishing, 1948.

2. See, for example, Derek B. Cornish and Ronald V. Clarke (1987), "Understanding Criminal Displacement: An Application of Rational Choice Theory," *Criminology,* 25(4): 933–947.

3. These included Cesare Lombroso, Raffaele Garofalo (1852–1934), and Enrico Ferri (1856–1928). Together, the three were sometimes referred to as the *Italian Triumvirate.*

4. Nicole Hahn Rafter brings together in one volume the most important eugenic family studies in her 1988 book, *White Trash: The Eugenic Family Studies, 1877–1919,* Boston: Northeastern University Press.

5. Juan B. Cortes, *Delinquency and Crime: A Biopsychological Approach*, New York: Seminar, 1972.

6. His testing methods ran into trouble after the U.S. Army adopted them for determining the fitness of draftees during World War I. According to the Goddard test, one third of the draftees would not have made the cut. The Army could not afford to lose these men, and a decade later Goddard revised his conclusions.

7. The University of Chicago inaugurated the nation's first college-level sociology department in 1892.

8. Sampson and Groves, 1989.

9. According to the census of 1920, the population of Chicago was 95.8 percent White, with 29.98 percent of the total population foreign-born and 42.2 percent "native white of either foreign or mixed parentage." The city's "native white of native parentage" was less than 24 percent of the total population. See Shaw and McKay, *National Commission on Law Observance and Enforcement, Report on Causes of Crime,* Vol. II, No. 13, June 26, 1931, pp. 24–25.

10. The originator of the term *white-collar crime,* Sutherland's earlier theory raised several important questions, not the least was how it explained crime outside the lower class, such as white-collar crime. How does one, for instance, explain crime among those who do have access to legitimate means of success?

11. As late as 1997, this book was the best-selling book on crime and delinquency authored by a sociologist (Gans 1997).

12. Adapted from Lanier and Henry 1998, 149.

13. It originally appeared in a 1953 article, "Crime as an American Way of Life," in *Antioch Review,* using the Italian experience as an example.

14. Although this might be true for these groups, most historical studies argue this is not applicable to the early Chinese experience and other groups not accounted for in the traditional understanding of ethnic succession.

15. In 1930, the oldest immigrant groups were German, Irish, and Swedish. Closest to the center were Italians, African Americans, Russian Jews, Poles, and Czechs. For similar comparisons of other American cities at this time, see *Report on the Causes of Crime*, Vol. II, No. 13, June 26, 1931, pp. 140–188.

16. This means that the gangs are formed on the periphery of society. As members of the lower economic orders, members do not have the advantages others have, and often feel ignored by mainstream society.

17. A *zip gun* was a primitive facsimile of a handgun. According to Yablonsky (pp. 4–5), because handguns were hard to come by before the 1950s, early gang members might make these in a school shop class. The weapon consisted of a metal pipe as barrel, a wooden handle, and a clump of heavy elastic bands providing the firepower to launch a bullet.

CHAPTER 3

Italian Organized Crime

WHAT IS THE MAFIA? OLD WORLD AND NEW WORLD INCARNATIONS

It should be clear to everyone that the Mafia is an exquisitely criminal organization.

(JUDGE GIOVANNI FALCONE, 1986)

Journalist George De Stefano begins his recent book, *An Offer We Can't Refuse: The Mafia in the Mind of America*, with the proclamation, "The Mafia Is Dead" (2006, 3). Perhaps no other five-letter word conjures up more images, misconceptions, and misguided ethnic stereotypes than the Italian term *mafia*. Indeed, although there is no agreed-on or simple definition for the word, or a consensus as to its murky origins—it is a word that is routinely applied to a wide range of criminal enterprises and behaviors. *Mafia* has been applied to groups and individuals so widely that its origins and historical roots have lost their importance. More recently, historian Denis Mack Smith suggested, "Mafia is the only word from the Sicilian dialect to be incorporated into all the main world languages" (Smith, Nov. 30, 1995, 7). However, although both the Sicilian and American permutations of this criminal enterprise share some tendencies and occasionally cooperate in the drug trade, they operate in different dimensions—the American version has always stood at the periphery of society, whereas the Sicilian version has long been a dominant presence in the region's politics and economic life.

Definitions and explanations for the persistence of the Sicilian mafia vary widely among anthropologists, sociologists, historians, and policymakers. For a number of years it was convenient for Italian magistrates to view the Sicilian mafia as a single, monolithic, hierarchical organization directed by a commission of top bosses. The members of such an organization expressed their solidarity by accepting unwritten rules that included strict internal discipline, job specialization, and a strong sense of duty. When it became a criminal offense to belong to a mafia organization in 1982, it was made much easier for the criminal justice establishment to use this convenient gauge for measuring who is and who is not a member of the vaunted Cosa Nostra.

During the 1970s and 1980s, other academics applied a different set of standards; rather than viewing the mafia as a monolithic organization, sociologists and anthropologists and others described

> a fluid network of competing "families," each loosely organized and subject to constant conflicts and reversals of fortune and alliance. Moreover, their activities are very closely linked to varying local economies, values, administrations and public security traditions.

A number of authorities were swayed by a more minimalist interpretation of the Mafia popular before the mid-1980s. For them, *mafia* meant a set of common values and attitudes that made it convenient for Sicilian criminals to communicate and cooperate with each other. The Mafiosi,

There Is No Secret Society Called *Mafia*

Many authors have tried to write the "history of the mafia." But once the term "mafia" has been properly understood the problem of a history appears in a new light. Since there is no organization, no secret society called mafia, one cannot write the history of such an institution. All that can be traced is the behavior pattern of Mafiosi in various historical situations, the role they played in the history of Sicily. Thus, the so-called 'histories of the mafia' are for the most part histories of Sicily, of the peasant movement, of the successes and failures of the various political parties, etc., combined with reports of a few sensational trials. (Hess 1971, 155)

according to this then-popular view, worked through informal relationships of kinship, friendship, and clientage (Hess 1971). When contrasted to the notion that the Mafia was this vast, centralized conspiracy as outlined by Joseph Valachi in his 1963 testimony before the McClellan Commission, it seemed a plausible response.

Interpretations changed drastically in the wake of testimony by Sicilian kingpin and informer Tommaso Buscetta in 1984, when he violated the oath of *omerta* by divulging the secrets of the Mafia in America and Sicily. The first testimony by a major figure in the Sicilian Mafia was considered the biggest challenge to the Mafia since Mussolini cracked down on the organization in the 1920s. However, although a number of authorities believed Buscetta's testimony implicitly, there were those such as leading Italian mafia researcher Pino Arlacchi, who insisted that the Sicilian syndicates were not as centrally organized as portrayed and that "There is a danger that we will make the same mistake the United States made 20 years ago when Joe Valachi made the whole of organized crime look like a tightly organized syndicate of five Cosa Nostra families."

Since the mid-1980s, most authorities have become less reluctant to use the term *Mafia* or *Cosa Nostra* to describe a highly structured organization with specific rules, procedures of admission, and a hierarchy of leadership. Perhaps organized crime authority Letizia Paoli explained it best when she noted:

Up until the early 1980s a major branch of the scientific and popular discourse understood the term mafia as an attitude and behavior typical of Sicilians, denying a corporate dimension. Since then however, thanks to judicial investigations, it has become clear that organized crime groups lie at the core of the mafia phenomenon. (1998, 186).

What Is a Mafia Family?

Some anthropologists and sociologists compare the Sicilian Mafia family metaphorically to a *cosca* (*cosche,* plural), the tightly bunched leaves of an artichoke (Ianni and Ianni 1972).[1] This organizational model reflects the *kinship model* of organization, where membership can be passed from father to son and uncle to nephew. However, there is always certain pragmatism at work, with family members carefully weeding out inappropriate kin who may lack criminal reliability. In such cases, they are urged to find another calling. Some *cosche* even have rules that prohibit admitting too many relatives at one time for fear they are planning to usurp the power within the *cosca*. These

Mafia or Cosa Nostra?

In his 1984 testimony, Buscetta claimed that the word *Mafia* was a "literary creation," and that it was called *Cosa Nostra* ("Our Thing") in Sicily, just like in America (Stille 1995).

> **The FBI Discovers the Mafia**
>
> America's leading law enforcement organization had denied the existence the Mafia for more than 50 years, but following the revelations of the 1957 Apalachin Conference in upstate New York and the sensational testimony of Genovese Family hitman Joe Valachi at the 1963 McClellan Hearings, the FBI was forced to acknowledge the existence of Italian-American organized crime.

cosche are territorial and are identified by either the names of their towns or urban locales. Two of the leading authorities on the subject assert that

> Each commonly extorts tribute (a *pizzo*) from businesses in its territory and demands that the territory's employers hire mafia dependents. At the same time, through entrepreneurial coalitions that cut across the *cosche* and include many strategic outsiders, Mafiosi pursue more far-flung activities from animal rustling to the commerce of contraband tobacco, arms, and drugs. Meanwhile, their carefully cultivated political connections and capacity for violence give them considerable leverage in competing for access to and control over public goods. (Schneider and Schneider 2005, 502)

Legendary Origins

Any discussion of the etymology of the word *mafia* begins on the island of Sicily. A strategic island at the crossroads of Mediterranean civilization, Sicily has been home to Arab, Roman, Byzantine, Norman, Catalan, French, Greek, Austrian, and Spanish invaders over the past millennia. For almost 3,000 years the island's location has been a potent lure due to its commercial and military opportunities. Foreigners came and went; some were more imperious, whereas others were more permissive.

The word *mafia* has not been found in an Italian dictionary prior to the 1860s. Nonetheless, the concept has long resonated among Sicilians. By some accounts it is a Sicilian dialect term that was born out of the poor streets of Palermo in western Sicily. The use of the words *mafioso* and *mafiosa* were often used to express respect for excellence, grace, or beauty. According to Fentress, it was first used as slang to refer to something that was "flashy" or "eye-catching" (2000, 152). When applied to men, the term *mafiusu* went further, connoting an individual's strength, honor, self-reliance, and manliness as well as his predilection to use physical force to stand up for himself.

The most frequently cited myth in relation to Mafia beginnings in Sicily, and the most frequently discounted, has been the more than 700-year-old tale of the Sicilian Vespers. The Angevin French ruled Sicily until 1282, when a Palermo bride was reportedly raped and killed by a French soldier. In the aftermath of this act, the Sicilians rose up and killed thousands of Frenchmen. One source suggests that the nationalist uprising was led by the chant "*Morte alla Francia, Italia anela*" ("Death to France, Italy groans")—creating the acronym MAFIA.[2] Others suggest the word was tribute to the laments of the bride's mother, who repeated over and over, "*Ma fia, ma fia*," or "My daughter, my daughter."

Words derived from *mafia* entered the Italian dictionary after an 1863 play entitled *I Mafiusi della Vicaria* appeared in Sicily. The play glorified the daring of certain prisoners in Palermo's Vicaria penitentiary. In the 19th-century English translation of the play, *mafiusi* meant "heroes." The play's popularity, according to some sources, led to the adoption of this word in the common patois of Sicily and mainland Italy as the word *mafiusi* morphed into *Mafiosi*.

Despite a plethora of possible origins, modern scholars opine that it probably had Arabic origins, most likely either the term *mahias*, or bold man, or *Ma afir*, referring to an Arabic tribe that ruled Palermo in the period between the 9th and 11th centuries. No matter its origins, the word *mafia* entered the American lexicon with the arrival of Italian immigrants in the 19th century. By the late 19th century, the word *mafia* summoned up man's more sinister behaviors, including gambling, racketeering, extortion, prostitution, and murder.

Etymologies of Mafioso and Mafia

Arabic:

maha: quarry or cave (In Trapani and Marsala they are referred to as *mafie* in the Sicilian dialect.)

mahyas: bold man, braggart, arrogant

mahfil: meeting or meeting place

mu'afa: safety of protection

Ma'afir: name of a Saracen tribe that once ruled Palermo

Sicilian Dialect:

mafuisu, marfusu: arrogant, bully; also could be bold, brave, courageous, handsome

Florentine Dialect:

mafia, mafia: poverty, deprivation

Piedmontese:

mafi, mafio, mafiun: little, badly shaped, rude, rough, stubbornly silent, careless (Gambetta 1998, 259–261)

By most accounts and despite its modern connotation, *mafiusu* was not initially synonymous with criminal or gangster nor did it refer to a criminal conspiracy. Etymologists and criminologists seem to concur that the prototype of the early *mafiusu* was a young man who demanded respect from everyone he came in contact with and expected the appropriate respect for himself and his associates. Moreover, his lifestyle was such that it often involved physical confrontations that would often result in a prison sentence. This next stage of the journey allowed the young man to come into contact with the criminal population in prison who would indoctrinate his entry into the criminal underworld (Fentress 2000).

SICILY

The man to be respected and admired was the man who resisted.

(ITALIAN ADAGE)

For three millennia, Sicily proved an attractive lure to a succession of conquerors. Phoenicians, Greeks, Carthaginians, Romans, Byzantines, Arabs, Normans, Catalans, Spaniards, Austrians, and French all laid claim at various times to this island strategically located at the crossroads of the Mediterranean trade routes. In order to understand Sicily, one must be cognizant that central to its history is its legacy of foreign occupation. However, each time the island was conquered, it was usually ruled from a great distance—Athens, Rome, Constantinople, Vienna, and so forth.

Sicily Enters the 19th Century

Recently, one journalist proclaimed: "The story of rebels and mafiosi is also the story of the people of Sicily" (Fentress 2000, 8). Most recent scholarship suggests that the mafia as understood today is not an ancient set of customs but rather the product of 19th-century Sicily, a time of failed social rebellions and reform efforts. By the turn of the 19th century, the ancient feudal system of rural Sicily was beginning to crumble. Since the Romans introduced the feudal system sometime in the third and second centuries BC, the island's most arable lands were divided into large estates, each owned by powerful nobles. However, their relationship with the native Sicilians could only be described as parasitical, as the rich reaped the bounty while giving little in return—there would be no Hadrian's Wall or Appian Way left as a reminder of their time on the island.

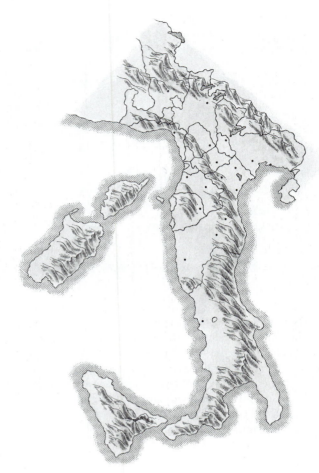

FIGURE 3.1 Map of Italy and Sicily
Source: Dorling Kindersley Media Library

Feudalism was ended in Sicily in 1812 by order of King Ferdinand, whose lands included the Kingdom of the Two Sicilies (Naples and Sicily). He was chased out of Naples one step ahead of Napoleon's troops and was given shelter in Sicily, which he repaid by consenting to allow reforms and the abolition of feudalism. The abolition of the vast feudal state transformed much of the island into a welter of large private estates owned by the island's aristocracy—the barons. Over time, the landed gentry moved to the more alluring cities, leaving in their wake absentee landlords who would play an important role in the development of the traditional Sicilian Mafia. These middlemen were respected and feared, as they protected the interests of the absentee landlords. The so-called *gabelloti* (from *gabella,* for "tax") were hired by the nobles to run their estates in their absence and they soon became the de facto power in the hinterland.

Gabelloti rented lands from the absent barons for a percentage of the harvest. In return, they rented out small pieces of property to tenant farmers who paid with part of the harvest. This kept the peasantry fully in line, for whoever controlled the lands controlled the people. It was not long before these "men of respect" adapted their power to exploiting those positioned both above and below them. There were many instances where they fenced off common grazing lands, usurped water rights, and organized gangs of cattle rustlers. The *gabelloti* figured out that by controlling the food supply in the agricultural regions they controlled the urban food supply as well. It was a short leap to extorting residents of the Sicilian cities and gaining a foothold in urban centers as well. Like the

FIGURE 3.2   Sicilian agricultural landscape today
Source: Dorling Kindersley Media Library/Demetrio Carrasco

various incarnations of the mafia that would develop in the United States and elsewhere, the *gabelloti* were able to master the boundary between capital and labor and independently exploit both.

Italy's unifier, Giuseppe Garibaldi, led his 1,000 Redshirts onto the island in 1860, where he received rousing support from the historically disenfranchised residents and the following year Sicilians voted in favor of union with Italy. However, with the new government situated in northern Italy in Turin, the new administrators seemed to be almost as alien as preceding outsiders.

When it came time to fulfill military service many young men disappeared into the rugged terrain and joined bandit gangs. Along with these changes came the familiar discontent, and soon poverty levels had risen as well. As the government responded with punitive measures, it served only to intensify Sicilian identification with its own provincial world and the traditions of *omerta* and the *mafia*—which many regarded as their only protection from the national government.

Sicilians of all walks of life united against efforts by the central government to modernize their island. Paralleling this was the growth of Mafia membership, which by the last decades of the 19th century now included mountain brigands and urban aristocrats. Soon the Mafia had achieved

The *Gabelloto* and Men of Respect

The *gabelloti* became power brokers and patrons to the rural peasantry. In some cases a more benevolent *gabelloto* might provide protection, food, or other necessities for subsistence, whereas in other cases he might settle disputes between landowners and tenants like a mediator. However, he was just as likely to use his position to extort protection money from landlords and peasants alike. In order to impose his power, it was necessary to assemble a coterie of henchmen, or *campieri*, who supervised day-to-day activities, collected taxes, and enforced brutal discipline. These overseers soon became better known as "men of respect."

Omerta

Omerta, the code of silence, evolved naturally as a firm social contract between Sicilian citizens and criminals, born in no small part from their fear of the power of the Mafiosi, only heightened by their distrust of the belligerent absentee landowners. This subculture was governed by a conventional system of norms; the private use of violence, respect, refusal to cooperate with the state in any way—the rule of silence.

Sicilian proverbs are rich in extolling the importance of silence and contempt for the loquacious. For example, *Bell'arti parrari picca* translates to, "To speak little is a beautiful art." Another way of putting this would be, *L'omu chi parra assai nun dici nienti; l'omu chi parra picca e' sapienti*, or, "The man who speaks much says nothing; the man who speaks little is wise."

> The word *omerta* comes from the Sicilian omu, meaning "man." Its main connotation is the idea of the true man: in the Sicilian view a real man knows how to make himself respected through his own efforts, defend his property through his own efforts, if necessary restore his honour and that of his family through his own efforts, and solve problems and controversies through his own efforts without having to seek the help of others or have recourse to any kind of State organ. (Hess 1971, 99–100).

such power that it had almost become a state within a state, or what one observer described as an "antistate, with its own rules, laws, and economy" (Lunde 2005, 57).

A riotous uprising in Palermo in 1866 led "witness after witness, northerners and Sicilians alike" to surmise that it was a "mafia uprising" (Fentress 2000, 148). Testifying just a year after the first official reference to the "so-called Maffia," a witness at the subsequent trials, former Palermo mayor and prefect Marquis di Rudini remarked that "crime in the region was stronger than the law and stronger than the government" (Fentress 2000, 147). This he explained was the main reason that the mafia existed. If citizens expected to work safely, they needed some type of protection, and for

FIGURE 3.3 Palermo (2008)
Source: Dorling Kindersley Media Library/Nigel Hicks

this they turned to the "Men of Honor." However, the marquis recognized that the mafia was basically selling Sicilians protection from itself, and that as a matter of Old World respect, alluded to it in a more judicious manner as protection instead of extortion. Rudini acknowledged that, "In order to defend one's life and property in the countryside it is necessary to seek out the patronage of criminals," an unholy alliance of sorts (Fentress 2000, 148).

Palermo was not the only 19th-century city with a criminal underworld. Palermo's Mafia would be hard pressed to match the machinations of the Camorra in Naples and New York City's Tweed Ring. Internationally, the transformation of urban locales into more capacious cities insured that criminal underworlds would be more common than in times past.

During the Italian reunification years between 1863 and 1870, Italian crime rates soared, but no region could match the levels of violence and murder in Sicily.[3] The contrast was stark as witnessed by Lombardy's ratio of 1 murder for every 44,673 inhabitants, compared to the Sicilian rate of 1 per 3,194. Matters became so dire than in 1874, the Italian government called a state of emergency and sent in a military detachment to police the region. Subsequently the country's first left-wing government came to power in the next elections, including Sicily's 48 deputies (representatives), most of who were Mafiosi. In the wake of these changes, the Sicilian faction in government offered to use their own to police the island, and the government was more than willing to cut costs by pulling out the army. Here again, the island's mafia played the middle, profiting in its relationship with the central government and their own constituents, and in the process clamped down on non-Mafia-affiliated criminal gangs.

In the last decades of the 19th century, the barons and the Mafia brutally suppressed a growing worker's movement and the reforms that it engendered. This only added to the harsh conditions that launched massive Sicilian immigration to America in the first decades of the 20th century. Of the more than 1 million immigrants (not including illegal immigrants) that left Sicily between 1900 and 1913—roughly one quarter of the island's population—more than three-quarters ended up in America.

Contrary to popular lore, during the first decades of the 20th-century mafiosi were just as likely to extort money from local peasants as they were the large landowners. They were also just as likely to cooperate with the state when it suited their purposes, such as when they helped authorities brutally suppress nascent socialist reform movements.

Why Is Mafia Activity Less Common in Eastern Sicily?

Over the years there has been a vigorous debate as to whether the Mafia reaches into Eastern Sicily. Throughout most of the 19th and 20th centuries, Mafia activities were centered more often than not in western Sicily, in the provinces of Palermo, Agrigento (formerly Girgenti), Trapani, and Caltanisseta. Although he compared Sicilian peasants in the interior to the "savages" of North America, and suggested they were incapable of civilization unless guided by outsiders, in a groundbreaking report in 1876, Tuscan parliamentarian Leopoldo Franchetti referred to the eastern region of Catania, Messina, and Syracuse as "the tranquil provinces," where one could travel "without fear of being killed or blackmailed" (Schneider and Schneider 2005; Nelli 1976). At least one historian has suggested that a number of factors were at work here that went a long way toward delineating these differences, including the fact that eastern Sicily experienced "the factory age earlier, because of the decline of local handicrafts and increasing competition from northern industry" (Nelli 1976, 9). This in turn offered the inhabitants "greater recourse to group action as a means of self-protection" (Nelli 1976, 9). Geography also played an important role in that the eastern half of the island was blessed with richer soil that allowed for diversified agriculture, and helped perpetuate conditions that caused the estate owners "to live on their land and take a personal interest in their tenants and farms" (Nelli 1976, 9). More recently, a leading scholar noted that there were 15 anti-racket associations in eastern Sicily and only 1 in the western side of the island. Some observers have taken this as a sign that it was weaker in the east where many groups vie with each other for control and none had been able to take control over the entire territory.

Mafia Nemesis: Cesare Mori (1880–1942)

Cesare Mori received much of the credit for chasing Mafiosi from Sicily to the United States during the reign of Benito Mussolini. His war against the Mafia, which he chronicled in his book *The Last Struggle with the Mafia*, demonstrated a prescience of the Mafia phenomena unmatched to that time. Among his observations was that the syndicates were not an "association in the sense of being a vast aggregate organized and incorporated on regular principles" (quoted in Sifakis 1987, 228). Rather, he noted, the Mafia could best be understood as a "potential state which normally takes concrete form in a system of local oligarchies, closely interwoven, but each autonomous in its own district" (quoted in Sifakis 1987, 228). He had already made his name for suppressing socialist unrest in Bologna and had been with the future dictator since his rise to power in the early 1920s. Once securely in power, Mussolini rewarded his protégé by selecting him as prefect of Palermo, where he was given the task of replacing the city's administrators with more zealous Fascists, and in so doing earned the sobriquet "Prefect of Iron." However, it turned out that many of them were in fact affiliated with the Mafia, and soon the "men of honor" went to war with the fascists using the same strategy of terror used against previous enemies. Many of Mori's appointments were assassinated; others were killed in broad daylight on the streets of Palermo. In 1924, Mussolini ordered Mori to make quick work of the Mafia and imbued him with the powers and forces to do it. During a 4-year campaign of torture and other extra-legal methods, he obtained hundreds of confessions and elicited false testimony from residents. Hundreds were jailed and just as many probably fled to the United States, where many of them hooked up with Italian-American syndicates. Mori's campaign wound up in 1929 with the arrest and conviction of the most prominent Mafia leader, Don Vito Cascio Ferro.[4] Those Mafiosi who had not been arrested or had fled pledged their support to the new regime, and the Mafia was, for the most part, a thing of the past until the Allied invasion of the island in 1943.

The Mafia during Mussolini's Fascist Dictatorship (1921–1943)

Written in 1969, the authors of *The Crime Confederation* remarked that any list of Italian-American organized crime's heroes would have to rank "Benito Mussolini at the top" (Salerno and Tompkins 1969, 270). The ascendance of Mussolini to the leadership of Italy in 1922 would shake the Sicilian Mafia for the first time in its modern history. In 1924, the dictator was humiliated by the Mafia establishment on a visit to the island and recognized there was room in Italy for only one absolute power. Like most dictators, Benito Mussolini would not allow any autonomy in his empire, and this included the traditional Sicilian Mafia. During the 1920s and 1930s, he ruthlessly suppressed its members, chasing many of them overseas.

Post-War Sicily and the Mafia

Recent scholarship argues that Mussolini's anti-Mafia program might have worked out if the U.S. Army intelligence and military government did not intercede. However, they were evidently taken in by local and U.S.-based Sicilian mobsters such as Lucky Luciano, who they found to be ideal advisors, interpreters, and administrators. There are a number of indications that the Mafia was indeed resurrected in the aftermath of the Allied invasion in 1943, with the U.S. rewarding them for their services, allowing various families to penetrate cities, where they gained control over public contacts and expanded into other criminal activities, including prostitution, extortion, and smuggling.

However, writing in 1997, one Sicilian historian labeled this a myth, adding that "the available sources do not confirm this view" (Lupo 1997, 21). Lupo explains, "such an explanation caters to a taste for conspiracies" and "nicely removes the responsibility [of the Italians] for what occurred in Sicily as a consequence of voting for fifty years for a party like the Christian Democrats" (Lupo 1997, 21).

In any case, the only incontrovertible fact is that in July 1943, American tanks and infantry rumbled into central Sicily. However, most recent scholarship argues that there was no American plot to enlist the Mafia as an ally in the invasion. As one source recently put it, "It is hardly likely that the Allies would entrust the secret of Operation Husky [the invasion], then the largest amphibious assault in history, to hoodlums" (Dickie 2004, 239). Others have suggested that if the liberal Italian state had been motivated to generate order and stability, the Mafiosi who reemerged after the war would have been redundant (Schneider and Schneider 2005).

Relations between the mafia and the Allies during the war paved the way for the next 50 years of Sicilian politics, one in which the Mafia made sure that the island's residents voted for the Christian Democratic Party and keeping socialists and communists at bay. In return, the Mafia was given freedom to pillage Sicily for the next half century. Dozens of left-wing leaders were murdered in the decade following the war. Once the Christian Democrats came to power, they were able to prevent the Communist Party from holding office. The Mafia in turn became a more powerful player in both Sicily and mainland Italy as it moved away from its rural roots and took over much of the lucrative urban underground economy.

Toward the end of the war it was fashionable for former fascist supporters to vocally denounce their former fascist patrons. By doing so, they were able to ingratiate themselves with the island's invaders. Although it is still hotly debated as to whether the Mafia deserved kudos for their efforts, the Allies took over Sicily with great speed. The end of the war signaled a new era in organized crime as Mafiosi moved their operations from inland pastures to the streets of Palermo—from cattle rustling and extortion to the international drug market.

The Mafia and the Christian Democrats: Getting Out the Vote

At the end of World War II, the emergent Christian Democratic Party (CDP) was well aware that American aid for rebuilding post-war Italy depended on preventing communists from participating in national politics. By turning to the island's Mafia leaders for votes, the CDP was able to keep the communists out of power and at the same time reinforced its omnipresence in rural and urban communities (Arlacchi 1993).

Once the Mafia was restored to its former power and prestige in Sicily, any hopes of land reform for the island's peasants were dashed. An unwritten agreement existed by which the Mafiosi protected the landed estates from bandits and peasant protests; in return, they killed any

---

"Don Vito" Cascio Ferro (1862–1943) to Calogero "Don Calo" Vizzini (1877–1954)

Born in Palermo, Don Vito Cascio Ferro first became accustomed to power as *gabelloto* collecting revenue on the feudal estate where he was born. He became an international figure in 1901 when he visited New York City and advised Black Hand extortionists on various rackets. He was arrested by the Italian-American policeman Joseph Petrosino in 1903, but returned to Sicily. Nine years later, Petrosino began investigating links to the Black Handers in Palermo, but was almost immediately assassinated. Ferro took credit for the murder, further cementing his status in the eyes of the local mafia. Despite almost 70 arrests, Ferro stayed out of jail and even became a regular on the Palermo society circuit. His career ended during the Mafia purges in the late 1920s, and he died in prison during an Allied bombing raid in 1943.

The scion of peasants, Don Calo Vizzini rose above his provincial roots to become a respected Mafia boss following the death of Don Vito Cascio Ferro in 1943. At the time of the Allied invasion of Sicily, he was probably the most respected Mafioso in Sicily and one of the few anti-fascists to have weathered the Mori purges of the 1920s. The year following the invasion, Vizzini supporters seriously wounded a communist leader as he addressed a crowd. During the next decade more than 40 communists and left-wing leaders were systematically eliminated as the Mafia fulfilled their part of the "wicked deal" to keep the Christian Democrats in power. During the war, he won accolades for assisting the Allies and was even made an honorary colonel by the U.S. Army. However, his one goal went unfulfilled—making Sicily an American state. His subsequent funeral was one of the largest ever recorded on the island.

FIGURE 3.4 Corleone Today
Source: Dorling Kindersley Media Library/Nigel Hicks

leftist leaders. More than 50 peasant and union leaders were killed in 1950 when land reforms seemed on the horizon.

In what has been referred to as "that wicked deal," the Mafia offered electoral support to the CDP. By insuring that islanders voted for the CDP, it effectively excluded the Communist Party, which had supported the peasants from cementing any governmental alliances (Schneider and Schneider 2005). Recent research suggests that each Mafiosi was able to collect 40 to 50 supporters from their friends, kin, and clients, which added up to close to 100,000 "friendly votes" in the province of Palermo alone (Arlacchi 1993, 182–83). As a result, the Mafia gained de facto immunity from prosecution and long jail terms and were given the green light to enter new rackets revolving around the administration of land reform, urban produce markets, new house construction, and public works projects. However, what was probably the least anticipated and most consequential outcome of the "wicked deal" was the failure of the government to prevent the Mafia from organizing global heroin trafficking networks in the 1970s (Arlacchi, 1993).

The Corleone Mafia: The Rise of Luciano Leggio

Allied occupiers made one of their biggest mistakes in 1943 when they granted Michele Navarra a trucking concession in Palermo that would help Sicily's Corleone family control much of the city's black market. Navarra, despite his criminal connections, was a man of some achievement. His resume showed he was a physician and hospital director, and leader of the local landowners' association. However, an important position had been purposely left off his impressive vita—leader of the Corleone family. Under Navarra's leadership, more than 150 men were killed by his acolytes between 1944 and 1948, many committed by the up and coming Luciano Leggio.[5] Born in rural poverty in 1925, Leggio had a well-earned reputation as a stone-cold killer and even kept a ravine on his property to get rid of his victims. By 1958, Navarra had his fill of the brutal subordinate and dispatched more than a dozen men to kill Leggio at his country home. Leggio escaped and went into hiding. It was not long before two of Leggio's most loyal killers—Salvatore Riina and Bernardo Provenzano—murdered Navarra near his estate. Leggio subsequently had Navarra's supporters hunted down. In the ensuing war between the two factions, Navarra's was clearly the loser, losing its leader and 28 men, whereas the Leggio group lost only 12. This war signaled a new chapter in the history of the Sicilian Mafia as it moved away from many of the traditions that evolved in an agrarian society and made the jump to a post-war era in which all that mattered was profit, and Luciano Leggio would be the man to see in this new era. Few dared cross Leggio during his heyday. One *pentiti* suggested that he "had a look that struck fear even in us mafiosi" (Dickie 2004, 332). Stories of his malevolence were widely circulated, including an incident when he killed a mafioso and his lover, and then raped and killed her teenage daughter.

One need only drive across Sicily in the 21st century and observe abandoned homesteads on virtually every rural road and highway to understand the titanic shift of the 1940s, after the large estates were broken up and peasants exercised their independence by often moving to the cities or overseas.[6] In their wake, they left a generation of former *gabelloti*, protectors, and exploiters who needed to seek new opportunities in the burgeoning urban chaos of Palermo and elsewhere. By the 1950s, Palermo was a city of 1 million, divided up among 39 Mafia families, all contesting for control of various food markets and a booming construction industry and collecting protection money from every business in their territory.

Leggio moved into this complex scene with unrestrained violence in 1955. His ability to avoid arrest over the years won him the nickname of the "Scarlet Pimpernel" of Corleone, until he was arrested in 1974 for the final time, where he remains today. Leggio is considered a transitional figure in the story of the Sicilian Mafia, having straddled two different eras. He came up as a cattle rustler in the feudal countryside and participated in the transformation of the Mafia into an international player in the emerging world drug trade.

The Sicilian Commission: The Cupola

At its inception in 1957, the Sicilian Commission, or *Cupola* (meaning "dome" or "big heads"), was helmed by Salvatore "Little Bird" Greco, who, along with 12 members representing the three Palermo families, headed Sicilian Mafia matters. Under Palermo's direction, it was a horizontal

The Grand Hotel des Palmes Meeting (October 12, 1957)

By some accounts it was deported mob luminary Lucky Luciano who suggested this historic meeting between American and Sicilian mob bosses in Palermo (Stille 1995, 102). It has also been assumed that it was at this meeting that Luciano suggested that the Sicilians should form their own governing commission to regulate the affairs of the more than 150 Sicilian families. Back in Italy since 1946, Luciano attended the meeting with American representatives Joe Bonanno and others as they met with the stalwarts of Sicilian organized crime. More recently, however, Sicilian insider Tommaso Buscetta recalled that it was Bonanno who actually suggested that they adopt the commission structure, telling Buscetta, "You should set up a commission like we have," adding, "in the United States no man of honor can be killed without the approval of the commission. This system works very well" (Blumenthal 1989, 65). In any case, within a year a commission had been set up in the main cities of Palermo, Agrigento, and Trapani—an arrangement that would run smoothly until 1962. The meeting retains a prominent place in the history of the modern drug trade, because it was here that the international heroin trade was organized and it was here that it was recognized that America was the largest consumer of heroin. Luciano, an old hand at the heroin trade having had a hand in its organization in Cuba since the 1940s, predicted that this important transit point would probably have to be replaced as the Cuban Revolution loomed on the horizon. Ironically, during this period the American version of the Commission still formally opposed narcotics trafficking, but informally accepted the huge profits from the trade. It was hoped both commissions could collaborate in controlling the import of heroin into the United States.

The Ciaculli Massacre

Due to the quite public displays of violence, a massive police presence was brought into the region. However, after a car bomb meant for a rival family accidentally killed seven policemen[7] and three citizens in Ciaculli on June 30, 1963, an onslaught by the government not seen since the days of Cesare Mori led to the arrests of almost 2,000 men and the confiscation of hundreds of weapons, and like the previous era, launched a wave of Mafia emigration to other countries where they only broadened the global reach of the Mafia. In the wake of the bombing, the government passed new anti-Mafia laws and established what was hoped would be a more effective Anti-Mafia Commission. As was usually the case, the trials were anti-climactic, with many defendants receiving amnesty and acquittals.

federation: each family kept its own structure and territory and the bosses remained more or less equal. All were supposed to follow the Cupola's rulings.

When war broke out between Palermo's syndicates in 1962, the Cupola's grip on the families was shattered. A number of theories have risen to explain the conflict, but most probably it was either over drugs or rivalries between the established Palermo families and the newcomers from the farmlands—Luciano Leggio and the Greco family. Despite its creation to prevent these conflicts, the *Cupola* proved powerless, and the streets of Palermo were littered with victims of the internecine feuding. It would be more than a decade before the *Cupola* was revived in 1975.

The new *Cupola* oversaw important changes in the structure of the Mafia, as it became more hierarchical and centrally organized, in no small part due to the necessity required by its involvement in increasingly complex activities in weapons and drug smuggling as well as its myriad construction rackets. To ensure control of what had become a complex multinational organization, murder became the solution for every problem, as Sicilian Mafia leaders moved more and more toward transforming itself into a virtual dictatorship called *La Cosa Nostra*.

The Fall of the French Connection

The combined French-American assault on the French heroin trade in the early 1970s transformed the Sicilian Mafia. (For more on the heroin trade and the French Connection, see Chapter 6.) With the end of the "French Connection" run by Corsican mobsters out of Marseilles, the Sicilians took over and opened their own laboratories in Palermo and other cities. Corsicans were the main narcotics suppliers in the 1950s. Having established their base of operations in southern France, they opened factories to refine morphine base. With their U.S. connection, the Sicilian Mafia became the Corsicans' best customers. Heroin was transhipped through Sicily to the United States, usually hidden in shipments of Italian specialty items such as oranges, olives, and olive oil.

At first, Sicilians tolerated the presence of the drug trade under an unwritten social contract in which the mobsters promised to keep heroin off the island's streets in return for a vow of silence. However, like all other drug networks that made similar promises, it reneged on the deal when they realized how much lucre could be made by selling some of the heroin at retail prices at home instead of sending all of it to markets abroad. As a result of this betrayal, Palermo's population of addicts climbed from 100 in 1976 to more than 8,000 in 1984. However, the exponential growth of the heroin trade contained the seeds for the demise of the heroin consortium as the mob families came into bloody internecine conflict with one another. It was not long before Sicilian labs were turning out as much as 40 kilos a week. These new market forces required organization that surpassed what the traditional families could offer. As a result, new syndicates were created and old unwritten rules were forgotten. By the 1980s, wives and children were being murdered along with Mafia husbands and fathers; troublesome officials were similarly dispatched. However, this would not prevent the Sicilians centered in Palermo from bringing in close to $9 billion a year in profit.

The Corleonese

In the 1980s, the western town of Corleone became synonymous with the Sicilian Mafia. Long a stronghold for traditional organized criminal gangs, author Mario Puzo was inspired by its rich history to name the leading figure of his novel *The Godfather* (1969), Don Corleone, played by Marlon Brando in the film version, after this town. One of the more unique characteristics of the Corleonese was that few actually knew the identities of its members. It was not uncommon to hear bosses of other Mafia groups complain that this family did not reveal the names of its members (Stille 1995, 106). Many of America's leading mobsters of the 20th century had roots either here or in the nearby bucolic seaside town of Castellemmare del Golfo. Corleone once boasted a population approaching 20,000, but has lost much of its luster over the decades due to the Corleone family's propensity for going to war with other families. Among its more prominent contributions to mob lore are Ignazio "Lupo the Wolf" Saietta, Ciro Terranova, and the Morello clan featuring Joe Morello, who for a short time was considered one of New York City's crime bosses. However, all of these examples combined could not compare to the body count and power wielded by its most recent exemplars such as Leggio, Riina, and Provenzano, fortunately now all behind bars.

With the Mafia's growing participation in the international heroin trade in the 1970s and 1980s, its traditional role in Sicilian society was jeopardized. Until the mid-1970s there were about 100 top Mafia families, often interrelated by marriage. Most of their traditional criminal activities revolved around areas such as construction, agriculture, extortion, prostitution, and some drug trafficking.

History demonstrates that although the Mafia has often been overly romanticized, they did abide by a set of principles that included cultivating relationships with politicians and police instead of killing them; likewise, until the 1980s women and children were considered off limits as targets, and heroin was delivered only to the American market. However, these scruples were challenged on every level after the French Connection was busted in the mid-1970s and Sicily succeeded Marseilles as the world heroin capital.

Sicilian War of the Godfathers

Between 1971 and 1978, Gaetano Badalamenti was considered the chief of the Sicilian Cupola. The heroin business had become such a cash cow by the 1980s that the Cupola was powerless to prevent a war between the Mafia families from 1980 to 1983. The Commission hierarchy began crumbling during this period when the three leading Corleone families who had moved their operations to Palermo allied themselves with a second group of Palermo and Catania families to seize control of the commission. Led by Luciano Leggio, Salvatore "Toto" Riina, and Michele "The Pope" Greco, the Corleonese challengers were formidable.

By most accounts, Salvatore "Toto" Riina was regarded as the new "boss of bosses." However, his unremitting use of violence led some family members to break the code of *omerta*. No murder upset the status quo more than the killing of Palermo's new prefect General Carlo Alberto Dalla Chiesa and his wife in 1982. He was a widely respected Italian hero, having won recent success and fame stamping out left-wing terrorists known as the Red Brigades in northern Italy. However, just months after his arrival in Palermo, his car was ambushed by machine gunners, leaving him, his wife, and their escort dead in the streets of Palermo. Emboldened by their newfound heroin wealth and confident that the central government was not willing to crack down on the syndicates, the Corleonese soon added more "eminent corpses" to the carnage.

Much of what is known about the so-called "War of the Godfathers" comes from the testimony of Mafia turncoat, or *pentiti* Buscetta, who blamed the conflict on the emergence of the over-ambitious Michele Greco, whose family undertook a number of counterproductive political killings without the permission of the Cupola. Buscetta and Badalamenti considered themselves moderates who opposed these assassinations as unnecessarily provocative. The war between the two factions

Bernardo "The Tractor" Provenzano (born 1933)

With only a second-grade education Provenzano ascended from hitman to shadowy crime boss of the Corleone Family during a half-century career. He joined the Corleone Family after World War II and while still in his teens became a trusted enforcer. Known more for is brawn than his brains, one mobster described him as having "the brains of a chicken but shoots like an angel." He earned his nickname "Tractor" reportedly for his inclination for mowing down people, or as one well-known Sicilian writer suggested, "like a tractor, wherever he passed he never so much as left a blade of grass in his wake" (Camilleri 2006, A 23). Provenzano later became a hitman for boss Luciano Leggio and was in on the assassination of the former mob boss Navarra that paved the way for Leggio's ascendance. Many mafiosi felt this unsanctioned killing violated the so-called Mafia code, and they went gunning for Leggio and his accomplices. By the 1960s, Provenzano had gone underground but still remained active, both socially by fathering two sons, and professionally by collecting mob money. By the outbreak of the early 1990s and the murders of judges Falcone and Borsellino, most authorities thought he was dead. With the arrest of his childhood pal and fellow Corleonese Toto Riina in 1993, Provenzano was elevated to its top spot and ruled the syndicate with an iron hand, albeit while in hiding. Italian police suggested that he attempted to move the family away from violent activities to focus on the traditional mainstays of extortion and muscling in on public works projects (Emsden, 2001). In 2001, police intercepted some cryptic letters indicating he was still alive. However, each time the police moved in, he managed to escape—until April, 11, 2006, when he was finally apprehended on the outskirts of his hometown after 40 years in hiding. Police explained he was able to run the syndicate while in hiding for 43 years by transmitting orders on little scraps of paper, or *pizzini*, folded over several times. Trusted couriers with no tangible links to the mafia were entrusted with passing them on hand to hand along meandering, lengthy, and random routes. These messages informed members who would be rewarded with government contracts, who one should vote for in elections, and other matters (Camilleri 2006).

resulted in the deaths of at least 500 mobsters, wives, and children, as well as a number of public figures. Some experts have compared the bloodletting to a scorched earth policy in which the Corleonese went on the warpath to eliminate entire Mafia families. In the end, only the Corleonese faction was standing—but not for long.

Perhaps no family suffered more than that of Tommaso Buscetta, who had cast his lot against the winning faction. Beginning in 1981, the gang boss lost 14 family members, including his two sons, a brother, a brother-in-law, a son-in-law, and a nephew. Disillusioned by his personal losses and attempting to save his own skin, Buscetta would later testify against the Mafia, leading to the arrest of 360 suspected mafiosi—at that time the largest mob crackdown in modern Italian history. His damaging revelations would challenge the existence of the Mafia in a series of trials in the 1980s.

Tommaso Buscetta: *Pentito*

Born in 1928, the youngest of 17 children born to a middle-class Palermo family, Tommaso found his calling in the post-war Mafia. He was first arrested in 1959 for bootlegging cigarettes. Later he began traveling to Brazil and United States. At one point he opened a chain of pizza parlors in New York's Little Italy, using them as cover for drug trafficking. In 1970, he was arrested as an illegal alien, but escaped to Brazil after jumping $750,000 bail. As the 1970s came to an end he was arrested and extradited to Italy to serve a sentence for conspiracy and kidnapping. Buscetta returned to Brazil in 1980 under the alias of Jose Roberto Escobar, and once more became involved in the heroin and cocaine trafficking with the Sicilian and American Mafias.

Buscetta would not be the first informant, or *pentito*, in mafia history, but he was the first executive-level one. His revelations, according to Alexander Stille, "revolutionized mafia prosecutions on both sides of the Atlantic" (1995, 121). Until the 1980s it was considered downright suicidal to denounce the Mafia in Sicily. This became patently clear in March 1973, when Leonardo Vitale walked into Palermo's police headquarters and volunteered to chronicle a tale of murder and extortion and reveal Mafia secrets. The police listened but took no action, and Vitale was declared insane and the accusations dismissed. In return for his information, Vitale was given a prison sentence (Suro 1986). Shortly after his release in 1984, he was shot dead on his way home from church. However, the 1980s signaled a new era of Mafia informers, revealing both its power and the increasing chinks in its armor.

During Buscetta's 1984 interrogation and subsequent trial testimony, he described in detail the workings and machinations of Sicilian Mafia families. In his words, the traditional family was led by the boss or *capofamiglia*, who was elected by the members. The boss than appoints an underboss or *sotto capo* and one or two *consiglieri*, or counselors. Under them are group leaders or *capodecima*, each in charge of a crew or number of "men of honor" or *uomini d'onore*. Under these are a number of associates who are entrusted with minor tasks and who hope to one day be elevated to official family status.

For some observers, the results of Buscetta's testimony were mixed. However, investigators such as magistrate Giovanni Falcone reported that before Buscetta's testimony that he had "only a superficial understanding of the mafia phenomenon," but in time allowed law enforcement for the first time "see inside" the Mafia, confirming various notions about its recruitment techniques, structure, and function (Stille 1995, 121). Some authorities asserted that Buscetta's revelations indicated that the balance of power of the traditional Mafia had been broken down. Conversely, this has also led to a dispersion of power that is harder to trace. Critics of his testimony have suggested that Buscetta testimony might have been influenced by the Valachi revelations in the 1960s, citing the liberal use of terms such as *soldiers, a commission of bosses*, even *cosa nostra*, but not once did he mention the term *Mafia*. Among the foremost critics is the scholar and former official Pino Arlacchi who utilized thousands of documents and telephone transcripts and had interviewed legions of informers, leading him to discount Buscetta, reportedly commenting, "The simple fact is, they don't talk like that. They don't say *cosa nostra* or call themselves soldiers." Furthermore, he opined that he believed "Buscetta's terminology springs from the fascination of many Mafiosi with the image of themselves that has been created by the press."

The Palermo Maxi-Trials (1986–1987)

Magistrate and future Mafia victim Giuseppe Falcone helped extradite Tomasso Buscetta from Brazil to Italy in June 1986. Following the confessions of Mafia boss Tommaso Buscetta (and Salvatore Contorno), preparation for the Palermo Maxi-trials became a national priority. Buscetta testified in two prominent trials, including the Maxi-trial and (later) the Pizza Connection Trial. As a result of Buscetta's testimony, arrest warrants were issued on 366 mafiosi. A special police squad was formed to hunt down the suspects. Eight suspects were captured in short order, but not before several high-ranking investigators were murdered. Both Falcone and his fellow prosecutor Paolo Borsellino were on the Mafia hit list and they were transported to a safe location while they prepared the indictments for what would become the largest Mafia trial in history. More than 340 mafiosi and their associates were eventually convicted, including the head of the Cupola, Michele "The Poet" Greco.

The Maxi-trials were held in a specially constructed courtroom in Palermo's Ucciardone Prison. The maximum-security courtroom included 30 steel cages fronted by partitions of bulletproof glass to hold the hundreds of defendants. Defendants jeered and spat at journalists and other observers while threatening those who testified. Some went as far as stapling their lips closed to demonstrate they would not break the code of silence. More than 2,000 police were stationed around the fortified and supposedly bomb-proof courtroom.

More than 1,000 witnesses testified revealing an international network of drugs and weapons trafficking. Of the hundreds of convictions carrying sentences totaling more than 1,500 years, the most important were the 12 life sentences handed down to the members of the Cupola. Following the trial, a prescient Falcone hardly rejoiced, commenting, "I have opened an account with the Mafia which can only be closed with my death—natural or otherwise" (Stille 1995). Less than 6 years later,

Inside the Sicilian Mafia: The Revelations of Don Antonino Calderone

Born in 1935, Antonino and his brother Pippo ran the Catania "family" from the 1960s into the 1980s. After the murder of his brother, Antonino fled to France, where he was arrested and jailed, then decided to cooperate with the Italian justice department. His revelations led to the arrest of more than 200 individuals and today he lives under an assumed identity outside Italy.

In his autobiography written with the assistance of Mafia expert Pino Arlacchi, we get a rare first-hand glimpse into the hierarchy of a Sicilian crime family. According to Calderone, "a family's hierarchy begins with the men of honor," the so-called soldiers. In Palermo they are referred to as *picciotti*, which translates to "boys" in Sicilian dialect. Above the soldiers are the *decina* bosses, referring to the heads of anywhere from 5 to 30 soldiers (although there are no limits in numbers). Next in ascending order are the vice-representative and the representative. Describing these positions in his own family, Calderone noted that "the vice-representative has no right to vote at all" (Arlacchi 1993, 33–35). He has such little standing that he is not even called to attend council meetings. However, if the representative is unavailable, he is the one who decides in his place.

The Council and the Consigliere

The Council is composed of representatives and *consigliere*.

> The consigliere is always elected by the family's men of honor, and his duty is to stand beside and even to control the representative. If the representative's head swells and he becomes a despot and starts to give absurd orders, making mistakes that affect the whole family, it's the duty of the consigliere to slow him down, to make him see reason. (Arlacchi 1993, 33–41)

The consiglieri are entities to themselves and have nothing to do with the decina bosses. Consigliere is an important position, and "in some cases he is as important as his representative, since he is very close to him, influences him, informs him, and presents things to him in a certain light" (Arlacchi 1993, 33–35). Calderone was familiar with Mario Puzo's *The Godfather* and admitted that he and the rest of the family members had seen the film. He suggested that the character of consigliere Tom Hagen, as played by Robert Duvall in the movie, was "in certain respects accurate" (Arlacchi 1993, 35).

The Decina Boss

> He has specific duties: he commands men and follows orders; he has to "take care" of his *decina;* he's the channel between the representative and the men of honor. The representative can say to a *decina* boss: Pass on to your *decina*, to someone in your *decina* that this specific operation needs to be carried out [murder, extortion, blackmail, etc.]. Pick one of your men and let him do it. (Arlacchi 1993, 33–35)

Likewise if a man of honor wanted authorization from the head of the family he was expected to go through the channels—first through his *decina* boss, who forwards the request to the representative, who either approves it or turns it down. Calderone explained that the main difference between the modern era and the past is that "No one went over his superiors' heads" (Arlacchi 1993, 33–35). Calderone explained: "If there's only one *decina* boss, or two at the maximum, they are also called in to council meetings. When there are many *decina* bosses—four, five, or even up to ten—they are not called in" (Arlacchi 1993, 33).

"If a problem concerning a decina has to be discussed, the boss of that group is often called in" and questioned on the matter. "Otherwise, it's the council that decides" (Arlacchi 1993, 35).

in 1992, his prediction came true. Just 2 months after Falcone's murder, Prosecutor Borsellino was assassinated as well.

In the aftermath of the trials, the Italian Supreme Court, headed by Judge Corrado Carnevale, nicknamed "The Sentence Killer," began to overturn the hard-won convictions. When he had finished unraveling the work of the prosecutors, only 60 of the original 344 convictions were still in force. It did not take a sleuth to figure out that official support was being withdrawn from the investigations. One plausible explanation for the about face was that feeling betrayed by the

Christian Democratic government's prosecution, fugitive boss Toto Riina ordered Sicilians to switch their votes from the traditional Christian Democratic Party to Mafia-supported candidates in the next election. With new elections on the horizon, the government seemed less willing to pursue the revelations of the Maxi-trials. This was especially true for politicians who counted on the western Sicilian electorate. Nonetheless, by 1989, few of the Maxi-trial defendants were still behind bars (Stille 1995).

The Murders of Giovanni Falcone and Paolo Borsellino (1992)

The murders of Giovanni Falcone and Borsellino in 1992 galvanized the Italian government into action by mounting a sustained and coordinated attack on the island's Mafia. The Palermo-born anti-Mafia judge rose from urban poverty to heroic status during a career that ended on May 23, 1992, when he along with his wife and three bodyguards were virtually vaporized when their cars were blown up on the highway between Palermo and the city airport. Most evidence suggests the hit was ordered by Corleone boss Toto Riina. Not long afterward, Borsellino and five bodyguards were killed by a car bomb in front of his mother's apartment building. The murders ignited a tinderbox of long-simmering rage among the Sicilians. Mass demonstrations spontaneously erupted on the streets of Palermo and throughout Sicily, demanding justice. The state responded by sending several thousand troops to Sicily to protect members of the judiciary and suppress the out-of-control violence. The murders of both men led to the creation of the *Direzione Investigativa Anti-Mafia* (DIA) and the passage of a witness protection law. The subsequent investigation identified 18 "men of honor" in the slayings and led to the arrest of Riina in January 1993, ending his more than 20 years on the run. The most unexpected result of the witness protection program was the wave of more than 600 informers who came forth to testify against the Mafia families.

FIGURE 3.5 Headquarters of *Direzione Investigativa Anti-Mafia* in Corleone
Source: U.S. Department of the Treasury

Michele Sindona (1920–1986): The Bank of Italy Scandal

In the 1970s Michele Sindona, financial advisor to the Vatican, was picked by Sicilian crime bosses to put his creative and criminal imagination to work, taking care of the huge drug profits coming in from the then emerging international drug trade. To his credit or discredit, Sindona became the most prominent international banking criminal of the modern era, in the process ruining the financial lives of thousands of investors. In 1974, he engineered the crash of the prominent Franklin National Bank in New York, which at that time was the biggest fraud in American history, totaling a loss of $1.7 billion. This was soon followed by the failure of *Banca Privata Italiana*, in which the bank losses almost bankrupted the Italian state. Responsible for laundering and investing more than $1 billion a year, he went bankrupt on his way to prison in 1979, the same year that an investigator following his financial affairs was murdered in Milan. Staring at 99 counts of fraud, perjury, and misappropriation funds, and probably at least a 25-year prison stint, he went on the lam while out awaiting trial. Gambino crime family members reportedly helped by faking his kidnapping and getting him out of the country to Palermo, where unhappy Mafia representatives awaited him. According to Lunde, in Palermo, Sindona consulted with bosses Stefano Bontate and Salvatore Inzerillo, who wanted their money back. In an attempt to pay them back, Sindona concocted a blackmail scheme targeting his former associates by threatening to reveal their financial misdeeds. However, this strategy went disastrously wrong (2004). Held under virtual house arrest, Sindona spilled the goods on compromising misdeeds by the Vatican Bank as well as gave his captors incriminating information on 500 prominent Italian businessmen and politicians—all information that could be used for blackmail purposes for years to come. They released him after a month, and he was sent back to New York to stand trial and was hit with a 25-year sentence. Sent back to Italy, he was given a life sentence. However, like the future Ken Lay of 21st-century Enron fame, he cheated the criminal justice system by dying in his cell the day after his trial, the victim of strychnine poisoning.

The Pizza Connection Trial

No case illustrates the contacts between Old World and New World Italian organized crime better than the notorious "Pizza Connection" case of the 1980s,[8] when the Mafia used pizzerias to distribute some $1.6 billion in proceeds from heroin sales. The operation was later tied to New York's Bonanno family (see Chapter 4), but the actual operation was largely run by Sicilian emigrants, mostly in the American Midwest, who distributed drugs manufactured in Sicily.

Investigators, policymakers, journalists, and the academic community were rewarded with major insights into the workings of the Italian and Sicilian Mafias during the Pizza Connection Trial. This case also catapulted the future FBI chief Louis J. Freeh and future mayor of New York City Rudolph Giuliani to national prominence.

Both are distinct groups; they were not subservient to one another—but separate—parallel during the 1970s a number of poor Sicilian criminals made their way to the States. Other mobsters referred to them as *zips*.

The Zips

During his infiltration of the Bonanno Family, FBI agent Joseph Pistone, AKA Donny Brasco, uncovered a new dimension to Italian-American organized crime—the arrival of the heroin-dealing Sicilian newcomers, referred to in pejorative fashion as *zips*. Coined by their American counterparts, the term's origin remains obscure. One study of the phenomena claims it is in reference to a favorite Sicilian pasta dish called *ziti*; others suggest it was derived from the silent, homemade zip gun. What is far more likely is that it referred to their rapid way of speaking Sicilian dialect (Blumenthal 1988).

Sicilians began coming to the United States in 1970s, and instead of joining the domestic Mafia, most reported to Sicilian boss Gaetano Badalamenti. Badalamenti used pizza parlors as fronts for heroin trafficking, establishing a multimillion-dollar undercover operation. Speaking in code and placing their orders in quantities of cheese, tomato paste, and pizza dough, they distributed heroin with the help of the Bonanno family, which had the strongest ties to Sicily.

The Sicilian Mafia Redux

Despite the setbacks handed the Mafia prosecutors in the late 1980s and early 1990s, this period was followed by an almost decade of stringent law enforcement leading to a number of victories for prosecutors and investigators. The emergence of Prime Minister Silvio Berlusconi in 2002 short-circuited the war on the Mafia after his party spearheaded new legislation that made it more difficult to convict mafiosi. Among the new laws were limits on the use of *pentiti* testimony and restrictions on using bookkeeping evidence to prove frauds and extortion schemes. To capitalize on the new climate, Sicily's bosses adopted a new low-profile stance referred to as *Pax Mafiosi*, or Mafia Peace. This essentially rested on avoiding bloody confrontations with non-Mafia personnel and prohibitions against the murders of prosecutors, judges, police, and politicians—a cast formerly referred to as "excellent cadavers." However, it is too early to write the obituary of the traditional Mafia, for as one Italian prosecutor put it, "The silence of the Mafia is a strategy, not an absence" (quoted in Raab 2005, 703).

SOUTHERN ITALY

The Camorra

"The camorra is cynically and opportunistically present whenever there is something useful to obtain, a service to ensure, or a profitable business to do."[9]

During the 19th century, Italian officials tended to use the terms *Mafiosi* and *Camorristi* interchangeably. One explanation for this is that in the 19th century, officials and others "were unable to interpret many [criminal] phenomena other than in terms of the work of a secret society" (Hess 1973), and over time both terms became synonymous with organizations that were little known. In time, the Neapolitan Camorra model and other "extra-Sicilian models were transferred to Sicily" (Hess 1973, 94). Like the word *Mafia,* the etymology of the term *Camorra* is imprecise, with some individuals tracing its origins back to the 14th-century Arabic game of dice called *Kumar*, outlawed in the Koran. Others suggest that it is derived from *ca(po)* and *morra*, a gambling game. In any case, it first appeared in Italian dictionaries in a 1735 document chronicling gambling halls in Naples (Lunde 2005, 74).

Although most explanations for the origin of the term are simply speculation, there is little argument among experts that the Camorra was the product of urban delinquency and gangsters involved in gambling and extortion schemes. The most probable setting for its creation was the jails of Naples, an apt setting for the fraternization of the burgeoning delinquent population and professional criminals. By most accounts then, the Camorra originated in the prisons of Naples sometime during the 19th century. Here, like the Sicilian Mafia, they played both sides, keeping order in the jails for the administration for a fee while collecting taxes from prisoners as well. As members were released back into society the gangsters were able to extend their reach beyond prison walls into Naples.

Around 1820, police found papers documenting the organization's policies and rituals. Other evidence indicated that the Camorra took a 10% cut of all cargo unloaded at the docks of Naples and a percentage of the city's gambling and theft rackets. During the reunification efforts of the 1860s, one member was rewarded with the position of police chief for keeping the city under control. However, it was not long before the government realized what they had here, and a large number of *camorristi* were arrested, whereas others left for America, opening a branch of the Camorra in New York City sometime toward the end of the 19th century.

Recent estimates place the number of Camorra gangs at around 100. Each has a hierarchical structure, with a boss at the top and in descending order capos in charge of crews of members and associates. Until the 1970s, these gangs preferred to engage in gambling, loan sharking, extortion, tobacco smuggling, and political corruption. Since the later 1970s, they have become more involved in international crimes such as drug trafficking and money laundering. Along with its newfound wealth has come a rise in violence between the various Camorra groups, making Naples one of the bloodiest cities in the country. According to some authorities, "it is the least active of all Italian organized crime groups in the United States" (Capeci 2002, 5).

Like other exemplars of Italian organized crime the Camorra enjoyed a recrudescence after the fall of the fascists and the end of the Second World War. Deported to Naples previously, Italian-American mobsters Vito Genovese and Lucky Luciano "made Naples a magnet for Sicilian criminals" (Lunde 2005, 75) as it became the center of Italian smuggling operations thanks to the leadership of the Sicilians. However, the tough work on the streets remained in the hands of the indigenous Neapolitans who would fill the ranks of the post-war Camorra.

The Camorra eventually took over the movement of the food supply from the farms to the city through a strategy of extortion and intimidation. It was not until the gangs latched onto tobacco smuggling that they could claim to have achieved status as a major player in urban organized crime. In order to comprehend the profits that could be made in this line of work, consider that in 1959, a case of cigarettes could be purchased in Morocco for only $23 and sold in Europe for $170. By taking over this trade from the Corsicans in the 1960s, the Camorra vaulted to the top ranks of Europe's organized crime groups.

Today, Naples is perhaps the most violent city in Italy, as a network of Camorra gangs each made up of 30–40 members battle for control of various rackets. One expert has gone as far as to suggest that the Camorra gangs "form a kind of parallel government intricately interwoven with regional politics and business" (Lunde 2005, 75–76).

'Ndrangheta

The' Ndrangheta is even more powerful and well established internationally than previously thought.[10]

Based in the Calabrian province located in Italy's southern boot, the 'Ndrangheta, (also referred to as the Honored Society or brotherhood) has been compared to the Sicilian Mafia. However, both have unique structures. In Sicily, the groups are typically hierarchical, whereas the 'Ndrangheta has no single leader or *capo* and operates through a variety of cooperative strategies. Despite the fact that "loose mechanisms of communication, coordination, and dispute settlement have existed" for more than a century, attempts at duplicating "a Sicilian Mafia–style regional commission" have met with varying degrees of success (Varese 2006, 423).

Both regions have featured a legacy of resistance to government repression. Encumbered with a backward economy and forgotten by the central government, Calabria remains the poorest and most crime-plagued region of Italy. The name for the group is of Greek origin, from '*ndrina*, or "a man who does not bend" (Varese 2006, 422). The 'ndrina, then, "is the basic organizational unit and is the equivalent of the Sicilian Mafia's family, or cosca. The 'ndrina typically controls a small town or community and if more than one 'ndrina is operating on the same territory, they form a *locale* (Paoli 2003, 29). Each 'ndrina is autonomous on its territory; no formal authority stands above the 'ndrina boss, and each 'ndrina unit is composed of men belonging to the same family unit (Varese 2006, 422–423).

Members have merged into families with a hierarchical structure, strict rules of behavior, and a vow of secrecy. Law-enforcement sources suggest that the organization's structure is both its weakness and its strength. On one hand, the group is very difficult to infiltrate due to its family-based structure; however, to its detriment, when feuds between rival families do break out, they "are difficult to distinguish" (Holmes 2007).

One leading authority asserted that, "The 'Ndrangheta is a specific confederation of 'mafia' families that is located in southern Calabria and has been documented since the late nineteenth century" (Varese 2006, 422; see also Paoli 2003, 37). Over time, the 'Ndrangheta adopted some of the earlier traditions of Calabrian bandit gangs. Following a government crackdown on the bandits in the 1880s, those who survived sought sanctuary in the region's small towns and cities; by the next century, they had formed organized gangs in a number of these communities. By the 21st century, these precursors to the modern 'Ndrangheta formed the early nucleus with what would become, according to organized crime expert Donald Lunde (2005), one of the largest and most violent Italian criminal associations.

Historically, it has remained more rural than its counterparts in Naples and in the Apulian region, home to the Sacra Corona Unita. Due to its geographic proximity to Sicily, there are sporadic contacts with the Sicilian Mafia, but both are clearly distinct organizations in their own right.

Dating back at least a half century, it has been a tradition for 'Ndrangheta leaders to hold annual summits called *crimini*. One former member described these annual meetings as a chance for the bosses to recount that year's activities in his territory, including kidnappings, murders, and other major crimes (Paoli 2003, 59). Bosses have attended these gatherings from as far as Canada and Australia (Varese 2006). Every year, a director for the summit, or *capo crimine*, is selected to put the meeting together. However, other than this task, the individual has little authority beyond his own group. Despite these yearly meetings, as separate gangs they have often been at war with each other, as witnessed by the bloody events in Germany in 2007. Although most of the 'Ndrangheta's operations have been conducted in southern Italy, in 2007 an outbreak of violence between groups members in Germany left close to 20 dead, including 6 in one murder alone.

'NDRANGHETA GANG WAR (2007)   The 'Ndrangheta was thrust into the international spotlight in August 2007 after six men, including one only 16 years old, were killed in a machine gun drive-by as they left a pizzeria in the German city of Duisburg.[11] Although Italian law enforcement had been aware of the organization's migration to Germany and elsewhere, it was less known to other law enforcement agencies. However, what was clear was that members had started business ventures in Germany in order to launder illicit profits far from Italian investigators. By most accounts there has been a strong Italian presence here for at least a half century, with many migrating to work in Germany's factories and steel mills during the war. Germany is now home to more than 500,000 Italian immigrants, second only to Turkey. Although most Italians are considered well integrated into German society, their numbers indicate a strong recruitment pool for organized crime groups.

In the subsequent investigation it was revealed that most of the cocaine that enters Europe comes through the Calabrian port of Gioia Tauro, which is controlled by the 'Ndrangheta. The bloody feud that erupted in Germany was traced back to its origins in the Calabrian town of San Luca. Investigators have traced the roots to a 1991 celebration in which gang members hurled eggs and insults at each other, leading to a fight that left two dead and two wounded. The feud that transpired was between the Pelle-Romeo and Nirta-Stangio families. Other observers suggest that something more was at stake here—hegemony over all of the 'Ndrangheta criminal operations (Holmes 2007). What has become clear is that Italian criminal organizations have taken advantage of the Sicilian Mafia crackdowns since the 1990s and have flourished thanks to the drug trade and

The Getty Kidnapping (1973)

The Calabrian gangs achieved international prominence in 1973 when they kidnapped the heir to the Getty fortune. Members kidnapped J. Paul Getty III, who lived in Italy. However, the oil billionaire refused to pay up, and as a result he was sent one of his grandson's ears, convincing him to meet the ransom request. The $2 million ransom was paid, and no one was ever called to account for the crime.

How Do the 'Ndrangheta Differ from Other Mafia-Style Groups?

According to one Italian investigatory commission, "Marriages help cement relations within each 'ndrina and to expand membership. As a result, a few blood families constitute each group, hence 'a high number of people with the same last name often end up being prosecuted for membership of a given 'ndrina'" (Varese 2006, 423). The heavy influence of kinship ties in the 'Ndrangheta distinguishes this form of organized crime from the mafias of Sicily, America, Russia, and Hong Kong. One of the distinctions of the 'Ndrangheta is the fact that unlike other groups, it does not try to limit the amount of blood members in a group. Other groups view this as a weakness due to the fact that too many blood relatives can create cabals within a group or lead to dissension between members due to favoritism and the like. However, as Federico Varese recently noted, "each family, blood family and membership of the crime family overlap"; furthermore, he suggests that this arrangement stimulates solidarity and closer allegiances between members, resulting in less informers than other groups. Varese points to several studies in the mid-1990s that assert that the 'Ndrangheta has indeed produced less *pentiti* than the Sicilian Mafia (2.6% vs. 6.9% of membership) (Varese 2006, 423–424).

direct connections with the Colombian cocaine trade. The vice chairman of the Italian parliament's anti-Mafia commission recently summed it up by saying, "Its looks like we underestimated them" (Aloisi 2007, 2).

'Ndrangheta members have been active in tobacco smuggling, gambling, kidnapping, and extortion. More recently, they have entered legitimate business related to construction, restaurants, and supermarkets. By the 1970s they had become active in the international heroin and cocaine trade. They are well respected for their money-laundering acumen. Members have been identified in a number of countries, including the United States and Canada. Today, there are an estimated 100 'Ndrangheta families with more than 5,000 members in Italy, with at least another 10,000 in branches outside Italy. These have been established primarily through migration. 'Ndrines have been identified in Germany, Belgium, Holland, France, eastern Europe, the United States, Canada, and Australia. Most of the groups in Italy (70 of 86) operate in the province of Reggio Calabria, with most families centered in poor villages, and San Luca is considered the stronghold (Varese 2006). One former member admitted that "almost all the male inhabitants belong to the 'Ndrangheta" (Paoli 2003, 29), noting that Sanctuary of Polis has long been the meeting place of affiliates who attend meetings here from as far as Canada and Australia.

The 'Ndrangheta have staved off prosecution in recent years by systematically threatening politicians, some of who have been wounded or killed; Mafia bosses successfully run for office, corrupt politicians, and systematically run protection rackets (Varese 2006). Italian judges and prosecutors avoid service in this region whenever possible. Generally, those who score highest on exams can choose their postings, and if any are assigned to Calabria they immediately request a transfer.

SACRA CORONA UNITA Little mentioned outside of Italy, this recent crime group is based in the heel of the southern Italian boot in the region of Puglia (Pulia). The Sacra Corona Unita (SCU) achieved national notoriety in 1990 when it bombed the law courts in Lecce, placing it on the government's radar as a major organized crime group. It was established in Bari Prison in 1983 in response to the encroachment of another gang, the New Organized Camorra (NCO), that was moving in on Puglia's smuggling rackets. During the late 1970s, other Italian organizations had begun making overtures to Puglia as well, especially the 'Ndrangheta and the Sicilians.

The structure of the SCU combines the features of both the previously mentioned 'Ndrangheta and Camorra. Leading the organization is the boss or *crimine* and at the bottom are the soldiers or *camorristi*. In between in ascending order are the enforcers, or *sgarristi*; then saints, or *santisti*; the *evangelisti*, or evangelists; and below the boss what are called the *trequartini*, the three-quarters.

The New Organized Camorra (NCO)

In response to Sicilian encroachments on Naples and Campania in the 1970s, gangster Raffaele Cutolo created the New Organized Camorra (NCO). In part, it was also an attempt to revive the faltering power of the Camorra, which had seen better days. Observers suggest it was a combination of regional pride and profit that led to its formation. Cutolo adopted a number of features from the 19th-century Camorra, including its structure and violence. Its favored rackets were extortion and cocaine trafficking, in contrast to the Naples Camorra, which preferred tobacco and heroin smuggling and was then moving into more sophisticated enterprises, including real estate and construction. However, the NCO would prove rather transitory, as Camorra groups united against it, resulting in a war that left some 500 dead. A subsequent police campaign in 1983 led to almost 1,000 arrests and put the finishing touches on the short-lived NCO. With the fledgling group out of the way, the Neapolitan Camorra continued to flourish.

The SCU divided Puglia into territories, each corresponding to its three major regions of Lecce, Brindisi, and Taranto. During the 1980s each region developed into an autonomous organization that was often at war with one another. However, when it came to interlopers, they were usually inclined to unite to keep out competition. Recent estimates place SCU membership at close to 1,000. Its main sources of income come from drug and tobacco smuggling, human trafficking, extortion, weapons dealing, and gambling. This organization took advantage of its strategic location on the Salento Peninsula during the Yugoslavian conflict in the 1990s when the Balkan heroin smuggling routes to Europe were no longer tenable and traffickers used the ports on the peninsula as a major transit point for smuggling contraband into Europe.

The Sicilian Stidda

Some authorities consider this Sicilian group as the "fastest growing organized crime group in Italy" (Lunde 2005, 77). Others disagree, suggesting that the *Stidda*, meaning "star,"[12] is used by Sicilian Mafia members to refer to criminal syndicates that challenge them. In any case, there are a number of authorities who allude to the nascent Sicilian *Stidda*. Established in Sicily in the 1980s, the Stidde has spread to a number of Sicilian cities and even to northern Italy. Its creation can be traced to Toto Riina's internecine war with the other Mafia families. In its aftermath, a number of soldiers from the losing families, as well as "disaffected" men of honor from Riina's own family, fled to southern Sicily, especially the towns of Caltanisseta, Agrigento, and Gela, where they created their own gangs under the guidance of Giuseppe Croce Benventuto and Salvatore Calafato. Unlike other organizations, the Stidda eschewed "charismatic leaders and a hierarchical structure" (Lunde 2005, 79) and by offering quicker membership, promotion, and flexibility, its democratic façade led to its meteoric growth leading into the new century.

Women and the Mafia

Traditionally, women have been excluded from most Mafia activities—"not only meetings but events such as banquets and hunting parties in which masculine identity is asserted through men's affectionate, even homoerotic, horsing around" (Schneider and Schneider 2005, 503). According to *pentiti* Antonino Calderone, the women of mafiosi are often themselves from Mafia families, so they are well-versed in what is and what is not expected of them, because "they have breathed [that] air since they were born" (quoted in Schneider and Schneider 2005, 503; Arlacchi 1993, 147).

Unwritten rules expected a mafioso's wife to play host to her husband's friends while allowing her to enjoy "the refinements that his money and status can provide and knowingly shelters his assets from the confiscatory power of the state" (Schneider and Schneider 2005). In return, she is expected to shelter fugitives at her husband's discretion or courier messages from prison. The

Italian Organized Crime in the 21st Century

In 2006, Robert Saviano rocked the Mafia underworld with his best-selling book *Gomorra*,[14] which sold more than 100,000 copies in Italy during its first 6 months in bookstores. In it, he convincingly reveals the scope of Italy's biggest enterprise, made up of the Camorra, the 'Ndrangheta, the Sicilian Mafia, and the Sacra Corona Unita. Furthermore, he argues that today's sprawling Camorra gang network is now the most formidable in terms of both violence and power. Not surprisingly, Saviano has received a number of death threats since the publication of his book, and has been assigned a brace of bodyguards by Naples police.

Mafia has had a reciprocal agreement that has included punishing those who cheat on wives and caring for the "widows and orphans" of imprisoned members (Schneider and Schneider 2005; Arlacchi 1993).

Until the late 1990s or so, traditional rules prohibited the killing of women and the participation of women in internal Mafia affairs. Reflecting a changing world in which informants, or *pentiti* as they are known in Italy, have upset the old order of things, a number of cases in the 1990s chronicle the killing of women. Most observers chalk up the new conditions to the appearance of the first informants in the 1980s, leading to the dropping of the old taboo against harming women. According to journalist Alessandra Stanley, "The stereotype of the mob wife—loyal, deferential and tight-lipped—began changing when the role of women organized crime became more prominent, most noticeably as targets of mob-style hits as old honor codes protecting women broke down" (Stanley, Jan. 11, 2001).

More tantalizing are recent cases of women entering the organized crime business in Naples, Italy. In one noteworthy 2001 case, Naples police arrested Carmela Marzano, wife of jailed crime boss Luigi Giuliani, formerly a top leader inside the Camorra crime network. Marzano was charged with taking over some of her husband's duties and with threatening to kill the widow of a rival mob boss who wanted to testify against some of her family members, whom she accused of killing her husband in 1999. This arrest came only weeks after the arrest of Erminia Giuliano, the mob boss's sister. She was considered even more powerful, and investigators asserted that she had taken over the family business after the arrest of her five brothers. Others have emerged as well, including Maria Licciardi, known as the *Camorra Princess*, the sister and heir-apparent of a dead Camorra crime boss, who police charged with heading one of the most violent Camorra factions (Stanley 2001). As to why this has been more noticeable in Naples than Sicily, a Naples police spokesman explained, "Family ties are very tight here, and women have always had a far more dominant role in the family here than in Sicily" (Stanley, Jan. 11, 2001).[13]

Overview

Organized crime, in all of its permutations has been devastating for parts of Italy. In his book *Excellent Cadavers,* journalist Alexander Stille chronicled the impact of the modern Mafia on Sicily since the late 1970s. Most damning is evidence that of the enormous grants given by the European Union to subsidize southern Italy's decaying infrastructure, millions are unaccounted for. By most accounts, organized crime groups have established a virtual monopoly over the island's public works projects, raising costs to astronomical levels. One estimate suggests that Mafia involvement raises the costs of constructing roads, hospitals, and office buildings four to five times the free market price. On top of this, almost every business is expected to pay protection, a regular extralegal tax to local "men of honor." Few are surprised then that outside investment in Sicily remains minimal as a chorus of northern Italians lobbies for severing the island from the rest of the country (Stille 1995).

The term *Mafia* has been used to describe a number of different forms of international organized crime, such as in the case of the so-called Russian, Sicilian, Asian, and Albanian mafias (Gambetta 1993; Varese 2006; Hill 2003). In most cases, there has been a tendency to view these groups as the products of undeveloped and disordered social systems. Most academic investigations into the Mafia phenomenon suggest that these types of groups emerge in societies on the brink of modernization and embroiled in economic transformation. However, at the same time these developing societies have not quite arrived at the point where they have created a legal apparatus capable of protecting individual property rights and settling business disputes between its citizens. The perception that Mafias materialize "in times of rapid but flawed transitions to [a] market economy" has been bolstered by recent studies of Japanese and post-Soviet organized crime groups (Varese 2006, 411–412; Gambetta 1993).

Anthropologists, sociologist, criminologists, journalists, and historians have long grappled with trying to explain the public's identification of the Italian people with the mafia and organized crime. The more perceptive observers recognize that Sicily is culturally plural, and viewing it as synonymous with organized crime was to criminalize its entire culture (Schneider and Schneider 2005). More recently, a number of authorities have demonstrated that the notion of the Italian-American Mafia was in great part a product of the now discredited alien conspiracy theory of organized crime advanced by the Kefauver Commission and the early work of Donald Cressey. As Federico Varese notes, if only the mere presence of immigrants from Mafia enclaves such as southern Italy was a prerequisite for establishing new Mafias, then "we would find mafias in every country to which southern Italians have migrated in the past" (Varese 2006). In his groundbreaking research on Mafia migration, Varese explored how the Italian government punished mafiosi by forcing them to relocate to areas outside their purview. Italy established this policy in 1956 with the hopes that by transporting southern Italian criminals to northern Italy, they would abandon their traditional ways and adopt the more law-abiding culture of the north. However, contrary to the government's goals, according to one Mafiosi informant, this resettlement policy turned out to be "a good thing, since it allowed us to contact other people, to discover new places, new cities" (Varese 2006, 417).

The American and Sicilian versions of the mafia remain distinct, with members linked on occasion by personal contacts and associations (Stille 1995). For example, a Sicilian Mafioso could not expect to come to the United States and become a made member without the traditional long waiting period that used to be the rule. Conversely, when Lucky Luciano was deported to Naples, he had no formal status in Mafia matters in his native country. According to journalist Alexander Stille (1995), Luciano chose to remain in Naples rather than relocate to Sicily, where he might be suspected of becoming involved in Mafia business.

This chapter demonstrates that Italy is home to a variety of organized crime groups. The 'Ndrangheta, the Sicilian Mafia, and the Camorra are all rooted in the world of the 19th century, whereas the Sacra Corona Unita is a more recent incarnation. Family and kinship ties play an important role in some of these societies, mirroring the strength of such ties in the legitimate world. Like other cultures featured in this text, waves of Italian immigrants have relocated throughout the world in the 19th and 20th centuries, sometimes accompanied by small numbers of criminals. Western Europe, the United States, Canada, and Australia have been especially popular destinations.

Informer Tommaso Buscetta described a once well-ordered and rule-bound criminal hierarchy gone haywire from rapid over-expansion and the greed of many of its new, drug-enriched bosses, a process in which they "traded honor" for the "more trivial pursuit of wealth" (Paoli 1998, 171; Arlacchi 1988). However, in 1971 one pioneering researcher described the emergence of a new type of Mafia, the product of the emigration of millions of southern Italians to the United States. According to Hess, this movement of people, which he called "a process of extensive cultural exchange" (1971, 155), led to the evolution of a new subculture within American society as immigrants assimilated to the social and economic conditions of the American system. The Italians might have introduced a new subculture, but it was only one of many new subcultures that made the jump from foreign shores to the United States.

The late Italian prosecutor Giuseppe Falcone debunked the myth of the "new Mafia" in his book *Cose di Cosa Nostra,* writing, "We must learn that there is always a new Mafia ready to replace the old" (quoted in Varese, 2001, 248, fn. 12). Falcone added that as late as the 1950s it was common for people to speak of a Mafia without principles that had transformed the old respectable rural Mafia into a criminal organization more interested in urban rackets such as public works construction projects than in the old standbys of extortion and cattle rustling. Later in this book, we demonstrate the Italians were just one of a host of immigrant groups—Russian, Irish, Chinese, Jamaican, West African, and countless others that came to America since the late 18th century. The overwhelming majority took the legitimate route toward assimilating into American society, while a micro-percentage found it easier to take the low road through organized criminal activities. However, most of these groups would each adopt a patina reflecting the opportunities incumbent in American culture.

Key Terms

Mafia	Don Carlo Vizzini	Michele Greco
Tommaso Buscetta	Christian Democrats	Pizza Connection
Omerta	Corleone	Zips
Cosche	Luciano Leggio	Giovanni Falcone
Cosca	Salvatore Riina	Paolo Borsellino
Pizzo	Bernardo Provenzano	Camorra
Gabelloti	Grand Hotel del Palmes	'Ndrangheta
Men of respect	Meeting	Getty kidnapping
Giuseppe Garibaldi	The Cupola	Naples
Benito Mussolini	Ciaculli Massacre	Palermo
Cesare Mori	*Pentiti*	Calabria
Fascism	*Pentito*	Sacra Corona Unita
Don Vito Ferro	Palermo Maxi-Trials	*Stidda*

Critical Thinking Questions

1. What is a *Mafia family*? Do they really exist in Italy?
2. When and where did the term *Mafia* originate? Discuss its possible origins and meanings.
3. What makes Sicily such a distinct culture? Discuss its strategic location.
4. How did the *gabelloti* originate, and what was their position in agricultural Sicilian society?
5. Who were the "Men of Respect"?
6. How did the code of *omerta* evolve? What is its significance to understanding the Sicilian Mafia?
7. What has been the historical relationship between the central government in Rome and the island of Sicily?
8. Why is Mafia activity less common in East Sicily?
9. What was the impact of Mussolini's regime on the Sicilian Mafia?
10. What was the impact of the American invasion of Sicily in World War II on the local Mafia families?

11. Describe the political relationships after World War II that hastened the resurgence of the Mafia.
12. What was the significance of the Grand Hotel del Palmes Meeting in 1957? Who attended?
13. Describe the impact of heroin on Sicilian organized crime after World War II.
14. Who were the Corleonese, and what was the "Sicilian War of the Godfathers"?
15. Regarding question 14, who were the losers and winners? What role did the war have on the *pentiti* phenomenon?
16. Compare and contrast the structural differences among the Sicilian Mafia and the Camorra, the 'Ndrangheta, and Sacra Corona Unita.
17. How has the Italian government responded to organized crime since the early 1980s?

Endnotes

1. According to Schneider and Schneider (2005), the term *family* should be understood metaphorically rather than literally.
2. This explanation is highly unlikely, because it would be almost another 500 years before the Sicilians would consider themselves Italian after unification in the 1860s; nor would this phrase have been appropriate for the dialect of the era. In addition, those residing in what are now southern Italy and Sicily would have known that their occupier was from Anjou, and not "France." The Second House of Anjou was given the kingdoms of Naples and Sicily in 1266 by the Pope. Most historians assert that Anjou did not consider itself French, nor was it regarded as such by others.
3. The first official reference to the "so-called Maffia or delinquent association" appeared in a report in April 1865 (Fentress 2000, 146).

4. Some sources suggest he was recalled in 1929 when he turned his attention to investigating links between the Mafia and the Minister of War.
5. His name is also often spelled *Liggio,* which was the original spelling of the name.
6. The author has traveled widely over the island during the past 7 years.
7. The bomb was so powerful that the only remains recovered from the policemen were one pistol, one beret, and a finger wearing a wedding ring.
8. For more on this trial, see Chapter 5 for the heroin trade and Chapter 12 for the investigative strategies and players.
9. Italian *carbinieri* Brigadier General Carlo Alfiero, quoted in Lunde 2005, 75.
10. According to the Italian Antimafia police and the Guardia di Finanza.
11. All six either worked in the pizzeria or had an ownership interest.
12. According to Lunde (2005, 74), the symbol of a star is tattooed on the right hand of members for instant recognition of their association with the group.
13. In her 1997 book *Mafia Women,* author Clare Longrigg describes the testimonies of more than 1,200 women over a 5-year period. She interviewed women representing the Sicilian Cosa Nostra, the Neapolitan Camorra, the Calabrian 'Ndrangheta, and American crime families.
14. This title is used to connote the similarity of the Camorra and the lawless situation in Naples with the biblical Gomorrah.

CHAPTER 4

The Mafia in America: Origins of an Alien Conspiracy

The first inklings of a Mafia presence in America did not come out of New York City, Chicago, or Miami, but from the historic streets and docks of the Mississippi River port of New Orleans. Although there is still debate concerning the first appearance of the Mafia in America, most accounts lean toward New Orleans sometime in the 1880s.

New Orleans is seldom mentioned in the same breath as New York when it comes to talking about early Italian-American organized crime. However, both were the most popular ports of entry for Italian immigrants. Most discussion of immigration in the late 19th century accepts the probability that along with the tens of thousands of new immigrants were some Italian criminals with associations with the Mafia in Sicily or the Camorra in Naples. The problem is that so much of the public record is enveloped in anti-Italian bias.

In his popular history of the New Orleans underworld, Herbert Asbury described a city that by the late 19th century was "afflicted with [the] hoodlums" and gangs of thieves (Asbury 1938, 403). Among the more notorious gangs were the Yellow Henry and Spider gangs. However, criminals had been attracted to the Crescent City decades earlier. In 1860, New Orleans had the sixth highest percentage of foreign-born residents (Jackson 1969, 11). As the decade wore on, local newspapers warned of the growing presence of "an organized gang of Spanish and Sicilian thieves and burglars" (Asbury 1938, 406). More recently, however, one gang chronicler asserted that the earliest gang activity in New Orleans dated back to 1834, when an Irish gang named the Corkonians "waged a war with another Hibernian gang known as the United Irishmen" (English 2005, 50). Journalist T. J. English compares the early warring Irish gangs of New Orleans to the New York's Five Points Gangs. Conflict between the groups was often over economic issues entailing undercutting each other to win bids on labor contracts (English 2006).

The heyday of New Orleans' Irish gangs gave way to new immigrant gangs, as the former Irish laborers became contractors and entrepreneurs, moving up the ladder of respectability. Irish gangs continued to persevere into the 1870s, but by the 1880s waves of new immigrants from Italy and Sicily changed the demographics of the Crescent City. Newspapers and city rumor mills worked overtime conjuring sensational accounts of sinister Mafia and Camorra groups. Until recently, most chroniclers of American organized crime have somehow overlooked the importance of New Orleans as a center of immigration and organized crime activities prior to the 20th century.[1] In fact, some of the earliest journalistic coverage of Sicilian organized crime and Mafia activities took place here. Herbert Asbury plumbed every corner in extrapolating stories of vice and crime in old New Orleans. His research suggests that what were regarded as Mafia activities surfaced in 1861. Asbury claims that by 1885, the Mafia had an inner membership of at least 300 (Asbury 1935; Sondern 1959). In 1939, historian John S. Kendall dated the first Mafia-related crime in New Orleans to 1878 (1939, 504). One Italian journalist noted, "The first time that the word 'Mafia'

Giuseppe Esposito in New Orleans (1881)

In his homeland of Sicily, Giuseppe Esposito achieved a formidable reputation for his brutality and cunning as a bandit chieftain. In 1881, word was received by the New Orleans police that he was in the vicinity and had been wanted by Italian authorities for 5 years, following the kidnapping of a British clergyman traveling in Sicily. The Englishman was forced to write a ransom letter to his wife in England. To make sure that his family was attuned to the seriousness of the situation, the kidnappers cut off the clergyman's ears and mailed them home with the letter. Esposito was captured but escaped to New Orleans before he could face trial. The case was placed in the hands of detective and future police Chief David Hennessey. Hennessey was considered a veteran sleuth at the age of 24, and lived up to his reputation by capturing Esposito and sending him back to New York City to await extradition to Italy. He would eventually be returned and sentenced to life in prison (Smith 2007).

appeared abroad was in *The Times* of London in October 1890 (Servadio 1976, 55), in connection with the murder of New Orleans Police Chief David Hennessey. Although the subsequent trial failed to reveal any conspiracy by Sicilian criminals, the term *Mafia* was increasingly cited whenever a crime involving anyone of Italian decent occurred, and added *Mafia* to the American lexicon less than thirty years after it appeared in Italy (Smith 2007).

Sicilian and other Old World immigrants had been debarking at New Orleans docks since before the Civil War. In the aftermath of the war, immigration quickened. Although some newcomers prospered and rose to political prominence, high homicide rates accompanied the Italian immigrant experience. New Orleans was the largest city in the post–Civil War South, and was a natural destination for Italians due to its warmer climate and a tradition of Latin-Catholic culture, a legacy of earlier French and Spanish rule (Reppetto 2004, 7).

According to the census of 1890, Italians made up more than a tenth of the population of New Orleans. Census reports indicate that years later, the city's Italian population, including foreign-born residents and their children, was "the largest of sixteen white ethnic groups in the city" (Gambino 1977, 49). The vast majority had come from Sicily and southern Italy. Beginning in the 1880s, the Italians established a formidable presence in the Crescent City as they intermingled and settled among earlier immigrants from Ireland and Germany, as well as the Black communities.

THE HENNESSEY AFFAIR

The events behind the murder of New Orleans police chief David G. Hennessey (1857–1890), allegedly by Mafia assassins, remains rather obscure—clouded in ethnic stereotyping, bigotry, and allegations of police corruption. Hennessy's father and namesake had been a policeman, and like his son, had been murdered in the line of duty in 1866. The younger son had large boots to fill, and in 1881 he achieved local prominence for his role in the apprehension of Sicilian fugitive Giuseppe Esposito, wanted in Italy for murder and kidnapping (see box above). However, Hennessey derailed his career by becoming embroiled in police politics. After a shoot-out that left his competitor for chief of detectives dead, Hennessy (with his brother) was placed on trial for murder, leading to his resignation from the force in 1882.

Following the mayoral election of Joseph Shakspeare[2] in 1888, Hennessy was appointed chief of the newly reorganized police department, making him one of the nation's youngest police chiefs (Pitkin 1977; Gambino 1977). However, his term was ill fated. By the late 1880s the city was teeming with Italian immigrants. Nativist local newspapers ran headlines claiming the presence of "1,100 Dago Criminals," fomenting tensions and contributing to the image of Sicilian criminality (English 2005, 64). At the time of his appointment, two Italian gangs were in an intense competition to control the docks. Most accounts suggest that the roots of the murder germinated in events that occurred 5 months earlier, when two gangs of Italian dockworkers, the Provenzanos and the Matrangas (named after their stevedore bosses) clashed over the control of the loading and unloading of ships.[3] The faction led by the Provenzano brothers had controlled the operations for a decade. However, the Charles Matranga[4] led gang, which ran a local gambling parlor/dance hall, began to show interest after police pressure on his gaming business forced him to look for new opportunities. Conflict between the two groups resulted in the Matrangas taking over the docks by the time Hennessey took office.

In May 1890, several members of the Matrangas were ambushed with shotguns after unloading a cargo at the Levee. Tony Matranga lost a leg and several others were seriously wounded. Initially, the victims adhered to old-country *omerta* and refused to identify the assailants. Presaging the future epidemic of mob informants, they broke down and identified their attackers, and six members of the Provenzanos were arrested and convicted that June.

Hennessey had a long relationship with the Provenzanos and was soon able to have the investigation reopened. The year following his death, all of convictions of the Provenzanos were overturned. Popular accounts suggest that Hennessey contacted Italian police officials and was told the Matranga gang was actually a branch of the Mafia. Rumors were rampant at this time, and word leaked out that the police chief was to present evidence supporting the Provenzanos. It has been a widely accepted theory that the Matranga faction had him murdered 1 week before the date of the new trial to keep him from appearing.

Pioneering Mafia historian Humbert S. Nelli suggests that the two immigrant factions indeed "shared some of the characteristics of the Sicilian organization, like involvement in politics and desire to control activities in a particular line of work." However, he noted their divergence from the Sicilian ethos—violation of the code of silence and lack of support from the Italian community (Nelli 1976, 37).

Hennessey was returning home late on the night of October 15, 1890, when he was ambushed and mortally wounded. Before dying the following day, he reportedly said, "The dagos shot me," although the only person to report this was Detective William O'Connor. Investigators jumped to the conclusion that the attackers had to be affiliated with the Matrangas. The police rounded up family leader Charles Matranga and 18 associates and family members. After a jury failed to convict any of them on March 13, 1891, rumors led city leaders to suspect that the fix was in and that the jurors were bribed. The next day, not willing to let the "truth" get in the way of the facts, a mob estimated at between 5,000 and 20,000 people gathered to protest the verdicts and stormed the jail, where they unceremoniously killed 11 Italian prisoners. These included three who had been acquitted, three who had received a mistrial, and five awaiting trial.

Despite the brutality of the vigilante attack, there was a lack of opprobrium in the nation's newspapers.[5] Some papers editorialized that these deaths made "life and property safer," whereas New Orleans Mayor Shakspeare saw it as "a necessity and justifiable" (English 2005, 68). The strongest condemnation by far came from the international press and almost resulted in hostilities between Italy and the United States in 1891. However, quick actions by President Benjamin Harrison, which included a public declaration deploring the incident and an offer of indemnity payments, ended the affair. As for Charles Matranga (1857–1943), he survived the bloodbath and is believed by some observers to have taken over the New Orleans family from 1891 until stepping down in 1922.[6]

Charles Matranga mentored Sylvestro "Sam" Carolla (1896–1972), who would succeed him in 1922 during the early years of Prohibition. The era of Carolla and then Marcello established several organized crime anomalies in New Orleans. On one hand, the city has probably the oldest Italian-American syndicate, but it has experienced less government heat than other municipalities. In addition, New Orleans has a long tradition of barring outside incursion by other Mafia families. Since the introduction of legal gambling in the 1990s, New Orleans has continued its love affair with corruption and organized crime.

Carlos Marcello (1910–1993)

The son of Sicilian parents, born in Tunisia, Carlos Marcello was baptized Calorso or Calogero Minicari in 1910. His parents immigrated to America before he was a year old, and by the time he was 20 had come to the attention of the authorities after an arrest (along with his father and a brother) for bank robbery. Marcello entered the world of organized crime in New Orleans, and by the 1930s was considered a comer by boss Sam Carolla. Marcello would fill in for him when he served a stint in prison. Following Carolla's deportation to Italy in 1947, Marcello took over the myriad New Orleans rackets.

Despite arrests for narcotics trafficking, gambling, income tax evasion, robbery, and assault, Marcello maintained good relations with local and state politicians throughout his long criminal career, even earning a full pardon from the Louisiana governor for an assault rap. Marcello fended off a number of deportation attempts over the years until Attorney General Robert Kennedy forcibly removed him to Guatemala in 1961.[7] Following a labyrinthine course of events, Marcello stepped on a plane and returned to America for good despite promises by Attorney General Robert Kennedy to send him back. The feud between the two has led conspiracy buffs to claim that Marcello had a role in the assassination of John F. Kennedy. For after all, the death of the president nipped the attorney general's attempts to deport him in the bud when Lyndon Johnson took over the White House in 1963, leading to a new Attorney General.

Over a-year period, Marcello extended his criminal reach from the Mississippi Delta up to Dallas, taking in the Ozark foothills and the Florida Panhandle as well. It was here that he gave up some of his power in deference to the formidable Santo Trafficante, with whom he maintained cordial relations over the years. In the 1970s, Marcello found himself once more under federal scrutiny when Congressional hearings into the assassinations of President Kennedy and Martin Luther King, Jr., linked Marcello and the Mafia to the killings. Marcello was also overheard on tape discussing a bribery operation and was indicted for attempting to bribe a judge, leading to a 17-year prison sentence in 1982. He was released early due to deteriorating health, and died in 1993. Since his death, no prominent Italian-American organized crime figure has emerged in New Orleans. Ironically, in 1991, Louisiana legalized a state lottery and video poker in saloons. Riverboat gambling and casinos soon followed.

BLACK HAND GANGS/LA MANO NERA

Before Italian-American organized crime became synonymous with *Mafia,* it was known by a handful of other identifiers. Perhaps, best known was the *Black Hand* extortion gangs. However, other terms were common as well, including *Mala Vita, Unione Siciliana,* and ultimately *La Cosa Nostra.* More like small gangs or cells than organized crime syndicates, the late 19th and early 20th centuries witnessed a phenomenon known as the *Black Hand.* Although these gangs have been confused with the Mafia or viewed as precursors to modern organized crime, there was nothing monolithic about it. Composed of Italian and Sicilian immigrants, their major activity revolved around extorting money from fellow immigrants. Gangs were estimated to range in size from 6 to 10 members under one leader. The gangs typically extorted money by sending sinister letters threatening injury or death if the victim did not comply with demands. Letters often featured crude drawings of daggers, skulls, coffins, and black hands in the margins. Originally Black Hand letters were simply signed with the imprint of a hand in black ink. With the advent of fingerprinting, this signature was discontinued. By Prohibition, most of these operations had fallen out of favor as gangsters were drawn into more lucrative rackets (Roth 2005).

Crime news has always been a staple of the printed media—"If it bleeds, it leads," goes the popular adage. Newspapers were complicit in creating the "Black Hand Society" in late 19th-century America. An important cog in the alien conspiracy theory that blamed recent immigrants such as the Italians for the rise in crime of the 1880s and 1890s, the Black Hand phenomenon was willingly accepted by most native-born Americans looking for an explanation for the country's rapidly changing demographics.

Ignazio Saietta, AKA "Lupo the Wolf" (1877–1914)

Ignazio Saietta, or "Lupo the Wolf," was the best-known Black Hander of the early 20th century. A leader in New York's Morello gang, Saietta arrived in the Big Apple from Sicily shortly before the turn of the 20th century. His reputation was such that Italians were known to cross themselves at the bare mention of his name. He was credited with at least 60 victims, many of whom were extortion victims who refused to pay up, whereas others were members of competing gangs. By most accounts, his victims were forcibly taken to the "Murder Stable" at 323 East 107th Street. Despite nightly screams from the location, the police rarely responded. Like Al Capone, who got away with dozens if not hundreds of murders only to be put behind bars by the Internal Revenue Service, it took the federal government's Secret Service to arrest Lupo on charges of counterfeiting, leading to a 10-year stint in prison. Lupo went back to Sicily but returned to New York's Little Italy with a vengeance in 1922, where he opened a bakery as a front for criminal activities. However, with the reorganization and emergence of the Americanized Mafia in the early 1930s, Lupo's methods were considered outdated and crude, and he was consigned to the sidelines as organized crime blossomed. Except for a protection racket he set up in the bakery trade, Lupo's last crime-prone years, except for a stint in the federal pen in Atlanta, were rather uneventful.

Although the Black Hand is identified with Italian extortionists in the turn of 20th-century urban America, the name actually originated with a Spanish anarchist secret society that spread into a number of countries with the intention of assassinating heads of state and members of the monarchies. According to Italian journalist Arrigo Petracco, "the symbol of the Black Hand was introduced into America by European anarchists" (Petracco 1974, 27). By the late 19th century, small gangs of Italian criminals had adopted the Black Hand symbol, particularly in the use of extortion letters adorned with the print of "a hand and bordered with designs of skulls and crossed daggers" (Petracco 1974, 27). Anyone in the local Italian community who made strides toward prosperity was sure to receive one of these letters. The Italian communities were tight-knit parochial worlds, where it became common knowledge (especially among Black Handers) when someone inherited money back home in Italy or was awarded a cash insurance settlement. If one was brave enough to face down the extortionists, he risked being bombed out of his home or business and worse. No less a celebrity than opera star Enrico Caruso paid a $2,000 extortion payment in the 1910s.

Contrary to most accounts of early Italian-American organized crime there was never a Black Hand Society on American shores. This is not to say there was no Black Hand. These small extortion gangs operated with relative impunity in Italian neighborhoods in urban America during the late 19th and early 20th centuries. The Italian immigrants that arrived in cities such as New Orleans, New York, Boston, and Philadelphia quickly gravitated to "Little Italy" enclaves that emerged in the late 1870s and 1880s. Here they congregated with their compatriots in a zone that seemed safe and familiar, where Italian was the first language and where Old World culture predominated.

In 1912, the New York City Assistant District Attorney wrote, "We have the 'Black Hand' gangs among the Italian population of our largest cities" (Train 1912, 231), and describes what he calls "men of honor" as "native Italians" (Ibid.).

According to the biographer of Black Hand nemesis, New York Police Department detective Joseph Petrosino, in the early 20th century a New York City reporter queried Petrosino about the existence of the Black Hand criminal organization. He responded:

> I've told you many times before that the Black Hand doesn't exist as a functioning organization.
> It's the newspapers that have built up the myth of an octopus that's supposed to have the whole
> city of New York in its tentacles. What does exist is gangs, mostly very small, and not connected
> with one another. (Petracco 1974, 5)

By the second decade of the 20th century, virtually any crime committed by an Italian was viewed as a Black Hand crime. Former Italian squad member Mike Fiaschetti, writing about the

Black Hand Nemesis: Giuseppe "Joe" Petrosino (1860–1909)

Born in Padua, Italy, Giuseppe "Joe" Petrosino immigrated with his family to New York at the age of 13. Ten years later he joined the New York Police Department. In 1905, he was placed in charge of the newly created Italian Squad, which was tasked with suppressing rising crime in the Italian community. His native background and familiarity with Italian language and customs made Petrosino the ideal choice to lead the squad. Petrosino earned a reputation for his investigative skills, often donning disguises such as a blind beggar, a day laborer, and even as a gangster. During its first 5 years the new squad was credited with thousands of arrests and hundreds of convictions, with a number resulting in deportations. Under Petrosino, the Italian Squad targeted much of its efforts at cracking the Black Hand extortion gangs that preyed on the Italian-American community in New York. By 1896, he was commanding 50 men. In 1909, he sought permission to gather information on Sicilian organized crime groups and went to Palermo. Although no one was ever charged in his death, he was shot down on March 12, 1909, soon after landing on the island. He was the first NYPD member to be killed outside the United States. More than 200,000 mourners paid their respects on the funeral route that winded through the streets of Manhattan to his funeral (Petacco 1974).

Black Hand toward the end of the 1920s, suggested that Prohibition helped get rid of the Black Handers, by taking a bad thing and turning it into something much worse. According to Fiaschetti,

> The Black Handers operated in obscurity and for comparatively little money among the Italians. . . . The Eighteenth Amendment endowed the Black Hand with fabulous funds and took it from the isolated Italian quarters and bestowed it on the cities at large—hence the splendors and crimes of the racket. (Fiaschetti 1930, 14–15)

Mob and Myth: The Castellammarese War and the Purge of the Mustache Petes

The deaths of New York's Sicilian bosses Salvatore Maranzano and Joe Masseria in 1931 were to be sure pivotal moments in American mob lore. Beginning in the early 1940s, the so-called Americanization of the New World mob on the night of September 10, 1931, was an accepted foundation in the saga of organization crime. Perpetuated by the likes of Mafia informer Joseph Valachi; Murder, Inc., prosecutor Burton Turkus; sociologist Donald Cressey; and numerous others, the so-called Castellammarese War[8] was accepted as the catalyst for the birth of New York's Five Mafia Families and the ascendance of Lucky Luciano for more than a quarter century.

In his 1951 bestseller *Murder Inc.: The Story of the Syndicate,* Turkus and co-author Sid Feder gave new life to the legend that Lucky Luciano engineered the murders of leaders of the Mafia's older group over a 3-day period in 1931. In his bestseller *The Valachi Papers,* author Peter Maas relates Valachi's 1963 testimony in front of the McClellan Committee:

> The murder of Maranzano was part of an intricate, painstakingly executed mass extermination engineered by the dapper, soft-spoken, cold-eyed Charlie "Lucky" Luciano. On the day Maranzano died, some forty Cosa Nostra leaders allied with him were slain across the country, practically all of them were slain across the country, practically all of them were Italian born old-timers eliminated by a younger generation making its bid for power. (Maas 1968; McClellan 1962)

No less an expert and academician than Donald Cressey bought into this tale, noting in *Theft of the Nation,* on September 11, 1931, and over the next several days "some forty Italian-Sicilian gang leaders across the country lost their lives in battle," including boss Salvatore Maranzano (Cressey 1969, 44). A great story, but is there anything to it? For almost 25 years virtually every chronicler of the organized crime saga regurgitated the same story with little modification or

Salvatore Maranzano: He Had a "Caesar Complex"

Compared to the almost illiterate "Joe the Boss" Masseria, Salvatore Maranzano was a veritable Renaissance man. The university-educated Maranzano was fluent in several languages and boasted of a fine library at home. Much of his collection was devoted to his idol and role model, Julius Caesar. Crime bosses were never without a fawning audience when they wanted one and Salvatore was no different. One of the early tribulations faced by his gangsters was sitting through a dinner with the boss and listening to seemingly endless soliloquies on the Roman leader. However, the worst was yet to come. Ever ready to demonstrate his classical education, Maranzano followed up his interminable lectures on Caesar with long passages in Latin from various ancient classics.

After the death of Masseria, Maranzano decided to replace the old interethnic cooperative structure of organized crime with the modern "Five Families" approach Maranzano once more went to his Julius Caesar playbook. He decided that the reorganization should be based on the Roman legion model, which featured a boss and an underboss; a *capodecine* (ranks of 10), or a street crew; a *caporegime,* on par with the captain in a legion, with each in charge of a *capodecine.*

inquiry. Even the 1962 Pulitzer-Prize winning investigative journalist David Chandler repeated this tale in his 1975 book *Brothers in Blood: The Rise of the Criminal Brotherhoods*, embellishing the body count closer to 60, including a cast of conspirators numbering in the hundreds (1975, 160).

In the 1970s historian Humbert S. Nelli attempted to unravel the full story of the purge through intensive research into Italian organized crime activity in 14 different cities. His subsequent book, *The Business of Crime: Italians and Syndicate Crime in the United States,* was the first major attack on the long accepted theory. He was able to trace the origins of the story to a 1939 *Collier's Magazine* story (Davis 1939, 44). The article was based on an interview with Dutch Schultz killer Abe "Bo" Weinberg, who recounts his participation in the Maranzano murder that was followed by the murders of 90 old-timers. The next step for Nelli was to identify the 90 casualties for those several days in September. His extensive examination of newspapers in Baltimore, Boston, Chicago, Cleveland, Denver, Detroit, Kansas City, Los Angeles, New Orleans, Philadelphia, Pittsburgh, and San Francisco for the months of September–November 1931 found only one killing that could be tied in to the "bloodletting"—a murder in Denver (Nelli 1976, 181–183).

ORIGINS AND GENEOLOGY OF THE FIVE FAMILIES/AMERICAN MAFIA

Prior to the shake-up after the deaths of Masseria and Maranzano in 1931 most references to Italian organized crime syndicates in New York City were prefaced with the name of the region in Italy where members emigrated from—in this case the Castellamare and Villabate families (Capeci 2002). As immigration increased new gang members were drawn from immigrants arriving from various other areas of southern Italy and Sicily. Gangs were soon identified by the name of the boss. However, most experts cite the testimony of Joseph Valachi in 1963 as providing the public and the criminal justice community with the names of the five reigning families of New York City: the Bonanno, Genovese, Gambino, Luchese, and Profaci (Colombo) families.[9]

Prior his death in 1931, Giuseppe "Joe the Boss" Masseria was considered New York City's leading Mafia boss. Born in Palermo, Sicily, in 1880, he made a fortune in the Prohibition liquor trade by the time of his killing at the hands of his rival and syndicate upstart Salvatore Maranzano (1868–1931). Maranzano came from Castellammarese del Golfo, Sicily, a cradle for other mob luminaries including Joe Bonanno and future Apalachin meeting host Joseph Barbara. By most accounts, he was sent to the United States by the Sicilian Mafia with the intention of organizing all of the American groups (of all ethnicities) under the aegis of Old World Don Vito Cascio Ferro.

CASTELLAMMARESE DEL GOLFO: HOME TO MOB LUMINARIES

Masseria, who had arrived in the United States one step ahead of a murder charge in Sicily in 1903, eventually took over the Morello crime organization by 1920. He earned a reputation for invincibility after several close escapes, and was awarded the sobriquet as "the man who could dodge bullets." However, like a cat, his lives were numbered with the outbreak of war between the two factions. Maranzano rallied other Mafiosi from his home region, including future mob stalwarts Joe Profaci, Joe Bonanno, Stefano Maggadino, and Joe Aiello, against the Masseria contingent that was brutally attempting to impose tribute on the Castellammarese group. Masseria's stable of gunmen was impressive at this time, counting Charles "Lucky" Luciano, Meyer Lansky, Benjamin "Bugsy" Siegel, Frank Costello, and Vito Genovese—a virtual *Murderer's Row.*

The conflict between the two factions seemed counterproductive to earning profits, and young hoodlums from both factions began to meet secretly to remedy the situation. It was left to Luciano to betray his boss by setting up a dinner at a fancy Coney Island restaurant on April 15, 1931. Luciano apparently left the table to use the men's room when four gunmen pounced on "Joe the Boss" and shot him dead. The four killers would enter mob lore—Bugsy Siegel, Joe Adonis, Albert Anastasia, and Vito Genovese. By the time Luciano left the john, his boss was dead. Like the waitresses and customers who were in the restaurant that day, Luciano told police he saw nothing.

Luciano continued the charade by joining with Maranzano and as second-in-command assured the new boss of his fealty. It was at this point that Maranzano made his mark in a meeting with hundreds of mobsters where he shared his vision for the American Cosa Nostra. Influenced by the lives of the Roman emperors, the well-read Mafioso announced that from here on he would be "the boss of bosses," or *capo di tuti capi,* and the nascent organization would be *La Cosa Nostra,* or "Our Thing." Under the boss, gangsters, or "men of honor," would be arranged in five "families" led by their own captains or *capos,* who in turn were answerable to the boss. Prospective members of *La Cosa Nostra* were expected to undergo an initiation ritual and promise to follow the code of *omerta.*

FIGURE 4.1   Charles "Lucky" Luciano
Source: U.S. Department of the Treasury

Maranzano was murdered just months after Masseria when four Jewish gunmen disguised as federal tax inspectors killed him in his midtown Manhattan office after Luciano discovered that he was on a list of prominent gangsters targeted by his boss for assassination. The death of Masseria and Maranzano signaled the end of Old World dons, the "Mustache Petes," and proved a watershed for the development of modern organized crime in America. The added dimension that Luciano contributed with the likes of his childhood cohorts Meyer Lansky and Bugsy Siegel was a "rainbow coalition" of sorts that would include all ethnicities.

La Cosa Nostra: The American Mafia

Sometime around the late 1950s and early 1960s, federal wiretap surveillance picked up the term *Cosa Nostra*. The FBI apparently took the next step in coining the phrase *La Cosa Nostra* to distinguish Italian-American organized crime from its variations in Italy. The term *La Cosa Nostra*, which translates as "the our thing," has been used incorrectly for almost a half century but remains firmly lodged in the language of popular culture. Therefore this text uses *La Cosa Nostra* (LCN) when referring to the American Mafia.[10] The organizational structure of LCN is well-chronicled. Virtually every account lists 24 separate gangs or "families." Membership is restricted to men of Italian-American descent. At one time, both parents had to be Italian, but apparently one Italian-American parent is sufficient in the modern era. During Genovese Family member Joseph Valachi's testimony before the McClellan Commission in 1963, he revealed the initiation rituals and customs and identified LCN and the national commission.

America's version of the Sicilian Mafia has no "Boss of Bosses," although some ambitious mob bosses have unsuccessfully attempted to claim this honor. It was during Prohibition and the accompanying "Americanization" of Italian-American organized crime that a number of gangs in major American cities emerged and eventually cooperated through a national commission. In times past, the commission held things in check by mediating interfamily disputes and setting general policies. In its heyday, perhaps two-thirds of the country's Mafia members were affiliated with the New York crime families.

MEMBERSHIP   In order to become a member of LCN, one must have an Italian-American or Italian father. In times past, both parents had to be Italian. One stands a much better chance of being inducted if a parent or close relative is already a made member. John Gotti, Joseph Bonanno, Carlo Gambino, Santos Trafficante, and Joseph Profaci were among the leading members who watched their sons become parts of their crime families. For those without the lineage, Mafia families are always looking for prospects who have reputations as earners and have no compunction with committing violence. In one of the best-known cases, Joseph "Donnie Brasco" Pistone ingratiated himself with the higher-ups with his skills as a jewel thief. Of course, it did not hurt his cause that he was always ready with wads of cash for his sponsors. It has been a tradition that to become a member, one must either commit a murder or participate in one—a security precaution for keeping out law enforcement infiltration, because they could not obviously let the murder happen. During U.S. Senate hearings in 1988, a leading Cleveland underboss admitted that the murder rule was not really sacrosanct—that there were occasions when members have been admitted without involvement in a murder. By most accounts, when a member is ready for induction, he is told by his *capo* and prepared for the ceremony for the following day.

Before the 1980s, when the recruit pool was much deeper, Mafia families could be more selective in who was proposed for leadership. Since the late 1990s, the pool has become so diminished that those who would have been rejected in times past are now eagerly recruited. Most recruits begin their ascent to membership performing criminal tasks such as collecting debts, running gambling and other vice rackets, and strong-arming competitors. No matter where one starts in the criminal rackets, the ultimate achievement is to become an official member, or "being made."

LCN STRUCTURE   During the first century of LCN, most of the families adhered to a similar hierarchy. Each family was led by a boss, who earned his position in several ways. Often when a boss died from natural causes, his second-in-command or underboss succeeded him. In other cases, after a crime boss was sent to prison, he might appoint someone to run the family in his absence or even vacate the position altogether, which was most preferable. However, Carlo Gambino gained the top spot by entering into alliances with other family leaders to guarantee his appointment as boss following the murder of Albert Anastasia.

The boss typically appoints his underboss, a selection that suggests that he has the potential to be the family boss. However, it is much more tenuous position than that of boss. Although the boss insulates himself from family internal business, the underboss is expected to arbitrate family grievances on his own. However, no matter the situation or decision, the boss is the final arbiter.

The position of *consigliere* has often been nebulous to outsiders. Some suggest he is elected by the membership to protect the interests of the rank and file, rather than by the boss. According to one gang authority, intelligence on this position was spotty before 1960 (Capeci 2002). Wiretap surveillance has revealed that it is doubtful that the *consigliere* is elected by the members. In 1979, a wiretap on New England boss Ray Patriarca, Jr., revealed him explaining his selection of his new *consigliere*.

Family bosses appoint their *capos* or captains. The larger the membership, the more *capos* a family has. The *capo* runs his gang or crew of soldiers and associates. Not all *capos* are considered equals. The more productive the *capo* and his crew, the more clout he has within the organization. A percentage of the family rackets is dispersed hierarchically. For example, the underboss takes a percentage of the profits handed him by his *capos* before passing on the remainder upstairs. Conversely, the boss may decide to cut his underboss on profits from activities outside the family purview.

Under the *capos* are the soldiers, the lowest level of family membership, but still a position envied by those in the criminal milieu. To be a soldier, one must demonstrate some capacity for bringing in money. However, most of it flows upward to the *capo,* the underboss, and the boss. Similar to other family positions, not all soldiers are considered equals. For example, a mob boss might have his son inducted as soldier. However, most in the know can easily understand that he is being groomed for a higher position. There is a tremendous difference between being a soldier or a crew associate, who is not officially connected to the family. Associates, for example, are not protected by family protocol. Every mob family has a large number of associates, what one source has compared to an army of worker ants (Capeci 2002, 11). Most are affiliated with a soldier for various ventures before moving on to other opportunities. There is no single associate prototype. Some just hang around doing odd jobs such as physical labor, unloading hijacked trucks or getting rid of stolen cars. History has shown that an associate was always more likely to be killed than a bona fide member, simply because their loyalty was always in question.

THE UNWRITTEN RULES OF THE AMERICAN MAFIA: "WE ONLY KILL EACH OTHER"   Members were expected to adhere to the vaunted code of silence, or *omerta,* as well as to stay away from members' wives under the threat of death. Conspicuous consumption should be avoided at all costs, and members were only to kill each other—in other words, cops, journalists, and politicians were off limits. Any violation of these tenets was a capital offense in the Americanized Mafia world view. The death of mobster Arthur "Dutch Schultz" Flegenheimer was probably the best example of this understanding. Schultz controlled a bootlegging empire and formed his own numbers racket in Harlem. Never a team player, Schultz was a general thorn in the side of his more organized and orderly counterparts. However, in 1935, Schultz went too far when he threatened to kill Special Prosecutor Thomas E. Dewey, who was on a virtual one-man crusade against New York City's syndicates. After Dewey confiscated thousands of his slot machines and had them publicly smashed apart, Schultz went to the newly created Commission and asked for permission to kill the young lawyer. Luciano knew that such a killing would draw so much heat that it could permanently affect syndicate operations throughout the city. Not content with the answer, Schultz left promising to kill him anyway. In turn, Luciano received permission from the Commission to have Schultz killed, and on October 23, 1935, two hitmen mortally wounded him at Newark's Palace Chop House. Schultz lingered for several days, but held to at least one part of the gangster code by not identifying the shooters.

La Cosa Nostra Commandments

LCN comes before God, country, and family; do not disobey an order.

Keep silent about LCN around outsiders.

Show respect toward wives and daughters of LCN members.

No fighting between members.

Get permission from the *capo* before taking a vacation or entering new businesses.

Don't get caught dealing drugs.

Make money and share it with your bosses.

The National Crime Commission

In 1928, a national crime syndicate was inaugurated at a meeting held at Cleveland's Statler Hilton Hotel. Here at least 23 prominent mobsters from New York, Chicago, St. Louis, Tampa, Philadelphia, and elsewhere met to discuss how future problems would be mediated. Of those who attended, a handful would go on to command crime families, including Joseph Profaci, "Lucky" Luciano, Vincent Mangano, and Joseph Magliocco. However, it was not until 1931 and the end of the so-called Castellammarese conflict that the Commission was brought back to life. Just five days after the demise of the Mustache Petes on September 15, 1931, the new Mafia godfathers agreed there would be no "boss of bosses," that New York would be divided up into 5 crime families, with 24 others scattered around the country, and nine members would sit on the Commission to settle disputes in the Americanized Mafia. In the beginning, there was no restriction in membership in most of the families, with members of various faiths—including Jews and Protestants—playing prominent roles in their operations. In fact, the original 1931 Commission had three Jewish and Italian delegates.

Although opinions vary as to whom exactly should be credited with the idea of an organized crime "commission," as the most respected mob boss in New York City after the "purge," most credit is given to Luciano. Al Capone hosted the 1931 Commission meeting at the ornate Congress Hotel. Here, Luciano unveiled his plan to organize and Americanize organized crime by establishing a seven-member commission composed of the five New York City bosses at the time—Joe Bonanno, Gaetano "Tommy" Gagliano, "Lucky" Luciano, Vincent Mangano, and Joe Profaci—as well as Chicago's Al Capone and Buffalo boss Stefano Maggadino. Shortly after the conference, Frank Nitti replaced Capone after he was convicted of tax evasion and sentenced to more than a decade in prison. With only seven seats, this left most of the nation's crime bosses out of the picture, so a protocol was established by which these bosses could have their voices heard through specific Commission members. Chicago, for example, represented Los Angeles, San Francisco, San Jose, Milwaukee, and other families, whereas the Genovese Family spoke for Philadelphia, Pittsburgh, and Cleveland. Due to rumblings that the Commission was like a private club, beginning in 1956, the Commission was increased to nine members, adding Philadelphia's Joseph Bruno and Joseph Zerilli of Detroit.

If one is to accept the testimony of Valachi before the 1957 McClellan Committee, the Commission is sometimes referred to as the "High Commission, "the Grand Council, the "Administration," the "Round Table," and the "Inner Circle." Attorney General Robert F. Kennedy, criminologist Donald Cressey, and many others bought into the notion that "This body serves as a combination board of business directors, legislature, supreme court, and arbitration board [made up of the] rulers of the most powerful families which are located in large cities" (Cressey 1969, 111). The release of more than 2,000 pages of wiretap transcripts from the electronic surveillance of Sam "The Plumber" De Cavalcante in 1969, including various references to "the Commission" and "Cosa Nostra," suggested that not all of Valachi's testimony could be discounted. However, as more than one authority has pointed out, the recordings focus mostly on the New York–New Jersey corridor, and "does not establish the existence of a tightly knit national organization" (Moore 1974, 253).

The Rise and Fall of Murder, Inc.

The elite hit squad known as Murder, Incorporated was awarded its sinister moniker by New York journalist Harry Feeney.[11] Prior to this, it had no name, just a purpose—providing contract killers for gangland murders in the 1930s. Murder, Inc., familiarized generations of Americans with the terms *contracts* and *hits*. Jewish gangster Louis "Lepke" Buchalter is usually credited as the originator of this concept (Raab 2005). Lepke,[12] a reprobate during his teenage years, served stints in reform school for minor crimes before graduating to Prohibition racketeering in the 1920s. He initially found employment with Arnold Rothstein as an enforcer, and became involved in strikebreaking activities in the garment district with other Jewish hoodlums. Toward the end of the 1920s, Lepke was in command of a gang of mostly Jewish gangsters called the Gorilla Boys. One of the gang's greatest achievements was being selected by boss Albert Anastasia to kill Arthur "Dutch Schultz" Flegenheimer. In the 1930s, Lepke held sway over the Brownsville section of Brooklyn, a predominately Jewish neighborhood. His crew performed contract killings under various mob bosses, and together with Albert Anastasia, they came up with the blueprint for Murder, Inc. They came up with a scheme where Anastasia would contact Lepke's "Boys from Brooklyn" whenever a Mafia associate or member needed killing. By using mostly Jewish killers, law enforcement had a hard time connecting the dots between the Italian gangsters and the killers (Raab 2005).

By most accounts, the killer had a contact first point out the intended victim, who was killed at the appropriate moment. The system worked like clockwork for almost 5 years, and as the 1930s moved toward closure, Lepke could count more than 200 men under his control, involved in everything from labor racketeering and loan sharking to dealing drugs. Mob expert Selwyn Raab estimated that of these, 12 were considered the nucleus of the killing machine. Several of them were little known outside organized crime circles, such as Philip "Farvel" Cohen, Abe "Pretty" Amberg, Samuel "Tootsie" Feinstein, and Seymour "Red" Levine, who refused to take assignments on Jewish holidays. Better known were such killing machines as Harry "Pittsburgh" Strauss and Charles "the Bug" Workman,[13] one of the participants in the Schultz hit. Like much of organized crime in that era, Italian-Americans and Jews cooperated frequently— that is, when they weren't killing each other. Italian killers of Murder, Inc., included Harry "Happy" Maione, Frank "Dasher" Abbandando, and Vito "Chicken Head" Gurino, who used live chickens for target practice.

Authorities have never been able to come up with the total number of slayings attributed to Murder, Inc., but estimates range from 60 into the hundreds. Of all the killers, the most famous was Abe "Kid Twist" Reles, who earned his moniker with his dexterity at slipping a rope around a victim's neck and strangling him with one twist (Volkmann 1998). When not killing, the contract killers hung out at Midnight Rose's Candy Shop in Brooklyn, comparing notes on ways to kill. Techniques varied, often depending on the reason for the killing. Sexual predators would be killed and castrated (maybe not in that order), or informants usually were found with a canary or rat stuffed in their mouths. A number favored the ice-pick through the ear, causing massive brain damage that often spoke of a cerebral hemorrhage to the medical examiner.

Lepke was in great part responsible for the demise of Murder, Inc. In 1938, he had seven potential witnesses against him murdered. However, in this situation, he was only protecting his own assets. This violated the rules of the Murder, Inc., canon, which prohibited killing for personal business reasons. Not only was Lepke being hounded by a Thomas Dewey–led investigation, but also there was a separate manhunt going after him for drug dealing. He had become a major distraction and liability for New York City's gang bosses. Rather than kill him, they went through legitimate channels. A plan was hatched in which Lepke would surrender to newspaper columnist Walter Winchell (and J. Edgar Hoover). Beforehand, Anastasia had told Lepke a plan had been approved for him to be charged only on federal drug trafficking. He indeed was charged and convicted of this offense and sentenced to 13 years, plus, much to the chagrin of Lepke, an additional 30 years for other crimes. There had been no deal!

During the course of the legal proceedings, Lepke's participation in the murder of a trucker was revealed. The linchpin to the government's case was Murder, Inc., killer Abe Reles. In order to save his own life, Reles agreed to testify against Lepke. In 1941, Lepke was convicted of murder and sentenced to the electric chair. Despite several years trying to make a deal for his life, his time ran out, and he was executed in 1944. To this day, Lepke is considered the only major American organized crime figure to be executed.

Reles' testimony also led to the executions of six other colleagues[14] in the killing club. However, shortly before he was to appear at Lepke's murder trial, Reles went head first out of a sixth-story window of the Half Moon Hotel in Coney Island. A number of explanations for his death have been offered over the years. However, perhaps the press had the last word, when one journalist described the incident as, "The canary who could not fly." What was most perplexing was that Reles and three other witnesses were under 24-hour police protection. Only Reles had a room to himself. The five police guards all claimed to be in various stages of sleep, and not one person heard a thing. Police officials claimed Reles was either trying to escape or was playing around, trying to lower himself to the floor below and then coming back upstairs to surprise his guards. In any event, his death ended further investigation into Murder, Inc., and prevented Reles from testifying against Anastasia. For several years, rumors abounded that a $100,000 contract had been placed on Reles before he could testify.

The Apalachin Conference (1957)

Joseph Barbara had come to America from Sicily in 1921. Except for several arrests on suspicion of murder in the 1930s, his record had been clean prior to 1957, although state law enforcement in upstate New York suspected the owner of the local Canada Dry Bottling Company of involvement in illicit bootlegging using his business as a front. His 18-room home was considered one of the more lavish ones on the outskirts of the hamlet of Apalachin, New York. However, his local reputation seemed solid—so solid that the Endicott police chief had recommended him for a gun permit.

On November 14, 1957, New York State Police Sergeant Edgar D. Croswell, acting on a lead he had developed on the previous day, along with another state trooper and two men from the Alcohol Tax Bureau decided to pay Barbara a visit. When they pulled up to the house, they observed a number of cars with out-of-state plates next to the house and perhaps two dozen cars parked in a field behind Barbara's horse barn and began writing down license numbers. Suddenly, several of the visitors saw them while others began to jog from a backyard barbecue into the house. Croswell and his team set up a roadblock on the only passable road to check out the attendees on their way out while sending for a back-up. After the element of surprise was gone, many of the attendees began running for the woods while others piled into cars and were stopped at the roadblock. Croswell's plan netted luminaries such as Vito Genovese, Joe Profaci, and Carlo Gambino, while Joe Bonanno and Santo Trafficante were collared scampering for the woods. Once the dragnet concluded, the 65 suspects were brought to a police substation, where they were searched and questioned (there could have been dozens more, but Barbara's house was never searched). Although they carried plenty of greenbacks, they were free of contraband—not even a gun. Questioned as to his occupation after uncovering a roll of almost $10,000 in his pocket, one suspect replied "Unemployed."

The big question has always been "Why they were they all there?" By most accounts, the meeting had been convened to discuss the Vito Genovese–ordered murder of Albert Anastasia (just 3 weeks earlier) as well as the attempted killing of Frank Costello earlier that same year. Others have suggested that it was set up to mediate a long-simmering dispute over the drug trade. In later years, "Lucky" Luciano claimed that the police had been tipped off to the meeting as part of a plan to discredit Genovese. When it came to explaining their meeting to local law enforcement, they most politely explained that they were there to pay respects to their sick friend Barbara, and that it was a coincidence they all arrived at the same time. Ironically, if this is true, only four of them showed up to his funeral two years later (Kelly 2000). The police were forced to release them—none were fugitives and they had not violated any laws. Although no crime had been committed, it finally gave tangible proof to most Americans that the unsubstantiated revelations of the 1951 Kefauver Hearings were, in fact, true.

WHAT REALLY HAPPENED AT THE APALACHIN MEETING?   The press had a field day with the Apalachin meeting. Contemporary accounts claimed that "national and international racketeers [from] as far away as California, Florida, Texas, Cuba, and Italy [were having] one of their periodic meetings" (Sondern 1959, 3) at the home of local businessman Joseph Barbara, Jr. Such a conference undermined J. Edgar Hoover's contention that organized crime was merely a local problem to be handled by local police. Apalachin called out the dogs, and the FBI entered the fray with such strategies as the Top Hoodlum program that helped shape the public's perception of organized crime.

So much emphasis is placed on the Apalachin Conference in upstate New York that it obscures previous meetings that were probably more influential in the creation of modern organized crime in America. By most accounts, since 1931 and the "purge of the Mustache Petes," national organized crime figures had been holding mostly clandestine meetings every 5 years. One post-Apalachin wiretap revealed Chicago's Sam Giancana telling Buffalo boss Sam Maggadino, "Well, I hope you're satisfied, sixty-three of our top guys made by the cops." Maggadino replied, "I gotta admit, you're right, Sam. It never would have happened in your place" (quoted in Fox 1989, 326).

Rather than a meeting of representatives from every corner of the country, the overwhelming majority of attendees came from east of the Mississippi River—from Detroit, Cleveland, New Jersey, Pennsylvania, and New York (Moore 1974). Although most of the attendees were indeed from the east, who authorities referred to as "the hierarchy of the Eastern Seaboard criminal world," several had, in fact, traveled from California, Colorado, Illinois, Missouri, and even Havana (Bernstein 2002).

Recent scholarship has uncovered much about the attendees in the last half of the 20th century. We now know that there were "sixty-five Italian-Americans (only 58 arrested) with a combined total of 153 arrests and 74 convictions for homicide, narcotics, gambling, alcohol, and other violations" (Bernstein 2002, 3).[15] We know that half were born in Italy, mostly in Sicily. We know that only nine were without criminal records and several had testified before the Kefauver Committee earlier in the decade. However, what was perhaps most disturbing about the subsequent round-up by the police was that none of the "suspects" were wanted men.

Although there were a number of nationally known organized crime figures, many of the attendees were legitimate businessmen and pillars of their communities. Of the trades listed for each attendee, the garment trade was the most common. Others listed their occupations as owning bars or restaurants, cheese and olive oil importation, beer distributorships, and even funeral homes (Kelly 2000). Among them was a cheese company executive from Colorado, a well-known labor official, and the owner of one of western New York's biggest taxi companies, who in 1956 had been selected as Man of the Year by the Erie Club, the social organization of the Buffalo Police Department (Fox 1989, 328; Bernstein 2002, 6).

J. Edgar Hoover and the Aftermath of Apalachin

During a crime-fighting career that lasted almost half a century, John Edgar Hoover made his name in the 1920s and 1930s chasing hoodlums with monikers such as "Pretty Boy" Floyd, "Machine Gun" Kelly, "Baby Face" Nelson, and John Dillinger, many of whom he glamorized and elevated in status to Public Enemies. Hoover's enemies, who were legion, suggested that the chief wanted quick and easy-to-solve crimes that would improve the Bureau's arrest-and-conviction record (Cook 1964; Turner 1970). While FBI resources were lavished on chasing these one-man crime waves, urban gangland was feasting on the American public's insatiable thirst for bootleg booze, prostitution, and gambling. It was not until the 1957 Apalachin Conference that Hoover, with his back against the wall, was forced to admit there was such a thing as organized crime in the United States. What made the Apalachin revelations so damaging to Hoover was the fact that he had denied the existence of organized crime for some years, even calling it "baloney" in the 1950s. Critics of the FBI chief had a field day following the event, and quickly distributed statements made by him over the years denying the existence of national crime syndicates.

Explanations for Hoover's recalcitrance on the subject have run the gamut from rumors of mob blackmail over his rumored homosexuality to his fondness for horse racing and an unwritten agreement that he did not have to pay off his losses (Summers 1993). However, all of this is shrouded in conjecture. Despite a number of recent biographies, Hoover's indiscretions have never been substantiated and are highly unlikely (Messick 1972; Cook 1964). A more convincing explanation for the lapse was proposed by Hoover biographer Richard Gid Powers, who asserted that the FBI chief was worried that if he admitted that organized crime was a national problem, he might have to concede power to others, because "it would require a task force strategy using personnel drawn from all available branches of government" (1987, 333). Hoover had learned over the years that for him to survive in his role as the nation's "top cop," he had to have complete control over the operations of his agents and all of the Bureau's operations.

According to at least one authority, Hoover's judgment was rooted in the disastrous Red Scare of 1919 and 1920, when American civil rights were violated and he came under the harshest criticism of his young career. He was intent on not repeating his mistakes. However, with Apalachin and the McClellan Senate Rackets Committee hearings, both in 1957, Hoover's main response was to set up the FBI "Top Hoodlum Program," which required every field office to draw up a list of the 10 most important underworld figures to target for intensive investigation. Throughout the 1950s, he opposed such ideas as the Justice Department's Special Group on Organized Crime. Testament to his obstinacy, in 1959 the FBI's New York office had 400 agents specifically chasing Communists and only four relegated to organized crime detail (Cook 1964).

Hoover finally relented in 1960 and began to pay more than lip service to the evidence given him by his aides. In late 1959, Hoover even gave permission to the Chicago office to begin microphone surveillance in order "to make up for lost time in expanding his knowledge of organized crime" (Powers 1987, 335). He had better luck this time than in the hunt for radicals in the 1920s. The biggest dividend was developing "a complete list of the names of members of the Mafia's 'national commission'" (Powers 1987, 335). The battle had finally been joined.

NEW YORK CITY'S FIVE FAMILIES

Luciano/Genovese Family

Charles ("Charley Lucky," "Charley Ross") Luciano (1897–1962) took over Joe Masseria's domain and inaugurated a number of innovations that Americanized and brought organized crime into the modern era, including the creation of the Commission. Born Salvatore Lucania in Naples, Italy, Luciano is easily one of the most significant mobsters of the 20th century, eclipsing the more public and ostentatious Al Capone and John Gotti. In 1906, he moved with his family to the United States, where he fell in with the wrong crowd in his teens, earning his first arrest before the age of 18 for heroin possession. After serving a 6-month sentence, he was released and became one of the leaders of the Five Points Gang. With the onset of Prohibition, he became, with friends Meyer Lansky and Bugsy Siegel, a formidable presence in New York's bootlegging trade. It was during this era that he created friendships with a variety of ethnic hoodlums as well as the old-time tradition-bound Sicilian gangsters. Despite warnings to cut his ties with non-Italian criminals, he continued to develop them instead. During the 1931 "Castellammarese War," he led a revolt against the Old World "Mustache Petes" and is generally credited with leading the wave of Americanization in New York City that saw increased cooperation between Italian and non-Italian mobsters.

With the demise of Maranzano and Masseria in 1931, the Old World mobsters lost their foothold in America, and Luciano and a new generation of hoodlums took organized crime to unimagined levels of power and fratricide. Luciano's Commission concept made the transition from theory to practice in the 1930s and helped guide a new type of organized crime—more businesslike—into developing lucrative rackets such as construction and narcotics trafficking. The alliances Luciano forged with Jews, Irish, African Americans, and other groups facilitated his short-lived rise to the pinnacle of American organized crime.

Luciano was not shy about spending his illicit income, living in unimagined luxury for a poor Sicilian immigrant in the New York's Waldorf Astoria Hotel, where he probably at one time or another shared an elevator ride with such neighbors as General Douglas MacArthur and former President Herbert Hoover. However, when the young racket-buster Thomas Dewey set his sights on the city's most eminent crime bosses, Luciano's days were numbered. In 1935, Luciano was convicted of organized prostitution and sentenced to 50 years in prison. Little did Dewey know that he owed his life to Luciano, who short-circuited a plot to kill the prosecutor by ordering the murder of Dutch Schultz before he could fulfill a promise to kill Dewey. After Luciano went to prison, his partners Siegel and Lansky headed to milder climes in California and Florida. However, despite his confinement, Luciano still called the shots through Frank Costello.

By overlooking Genovese and placing Costello in charge in 1936, Luciano had set into motion a series of events that would culminate in the busy year of 1957—one that proved a hectic one for newspaper scribes who chronicled the crime beat: in short order, Albert Anastasia was shot dead in a barbershop, Frank Costello barely survived an attempted hit by future "oddfather" Vincent Gigante, and the Apalachin Conference all signaled trouble in the New York City underworld. Indeed, the reins of mob leadership were at stake as Luciano's clout diminished and less-adept pretenders to mob royalty fought over control over New York City's rackets.

By most accounts, Vito Genovese (1897–1969) engineered the shooting of Costello in order to take over the family, which he did just two years later. The Genovese crime family emerged as a major player in American and international organized crime under the leadership of its namesake and his successors.

Vito Genovese was born in Naples toward the end of the 19th century and arrived on New York's lower East Side sometime in his mid-teens. Here he made the acquaintance with other future gangsters and became affiliated with Luciano. Although he participated in bootlegging and other rackets, his soft spot was always narcotics smuggling. Genovese was forced to flee back to fascist Italy in 1937, one step ahead of an unsuccessful murder, where he ingratiated himself with Mussolini. Most sources agree that *Il Duce* convinced Genovese to arrange the murder of anti-Fascist journalist Carlo Tresca in New York in 1943. Genovese also convinced the American military authorities that he could help them in Sicily as an interpreter, which allowed him to increase his familiarity with drug-trafficking networks and other black market operations in the Mediterranean region.

With the end of the war and his documented service in support of the Allies in Sicily, Genovese was returned to America to face his 1937 charges. However, with all potential witnesses to his earlier crime silenced, attempted murder charges were dropped, paving the way for Genovese to take over the family from Costello, who was running the family with Luciano out of the picture. Costello's star was on the wane with the murder of Anastasia and the public carnival in Apalachin.

With Luciano now deported to Italy, only Frank Costello and Luciano partner Meyer Lansky stood in the way of Genovese, who aspired to take over the Luciano crime family. As the highest ranking member of the family, Costello, who virtually ran the organization since Luciano had been arrested 20 years earlier, was first targeted. Genovese hired future Genovese crime boss Vincent

La Cosa Nostra or La Causa Nostra?

During the interrogation of Valachi in 1962, the FBI were slowly able to muscle in on the case, basically pulling the rug right from under the Federal Bureau of Narcotics (FBN), who had made the original inroads in the case. By early 1963, FBN agents were not even allowed to talk to Valachi. It must be understood here that the FBN employed a number of Italian-speaking agents and knew the various dialects, whereas the FBI agents had little knowledge of the language. One of the FBN agents later suggested that it was the FBI agents that came up with the term *La Causa Nostra,* which translated to "The Our Cause." Later, according to the agents, they changed it to the more palatable *La Cosa Nostra,* or "The Our Thing." FBN agents claimed that this term was merely used by Valachi in regard to the drug dealing activities of his faction within the crime family, as "drug dealing was 'our thing' at the time." FBN agent George Gaffney later explained, "The FBI felt they needed a different name, because we'd been calling it the Mafia for years, and they didn't want to appear to be stealing our [the FBN's] thunder" (Valentine 2004, 285).

"Chin" Gigante, a failed boxer and an even worse killer. As Costello was entering his New York City apartment, he heard a voice warning him, "This one's for you, Frank," giving his target enough warning to move sideways and escaping with only a minor bullet crease on his scalp. Although he lived, Costello realized it would be good time to step away from the family. Most mob experts posit that the main reason for the 1957 Apalachin summit just months later was the brainchild of Genovese, who was looking to gain the support of other bosses for his ascendance to the leadership of the family. Apalachin was a well-documented debacle, and Genovese received much of the blame for it.

Only two years into his reign as boss of the newly named Genovese crime family, in 1959, Vito was arrested for drug trafficking. Police and mob experts have been long convinced that he was framed by Luciano and Costello (and probably Lansky as well). He was sentenced along with more than a dozen others to 15 years in prison, where he continued to direct family affairs until his death in 1969. During his prison years, Genovese had become increasingly paranoid and had ordered the murder of several associates. Among those he suspected of being an informer was low-ranking family member Joseph Valachi (see box).

During the 1970s and 1980s, a number of lesser-known figures ran the Genovese Family as it competed with the Gambino Family for the New York underworld top spot. Vincent Gigante led the crime family from the 1980s until sentenced to prison in 2003. When Gambino boss John Gotti was

Vincent "Chin" Gigante: Genovese Family "Oddfather" (1928–2005)

Born in the Bronx, one of five sons of Italian immigrant parents, Vincent "Chin" Gigante entered mob lore as a hitman for the Genovese crime family after he botched an assassination attempt on then-boss Frank Costello in 1957. Costello refused to identify his assailant and stepped down, leaving the family in the hands of Vito Genovese. Gigante proved more resilient than "Teflon Don" John Gotti, who despite winning two acquittals was sent to prison after informants and surveillance tapes led to his demise. Gigante, however, had only served 5 years for heroin trafficking during a half-century stint in organized crime prior to his 2003 sentencing. The passing of the shuffling, pajama-clad, and supposedly mentally ill Genovese crime boss known as the "Oddfather" in 2005 signaled an end of an era. *The New York Times Magazine* accorded him the accolade of "the last great Mafioso of the century" (quoted in the *New York Times,* Dec. 20, 2005, B6). He had avoided imprisonment for decades through a carefully crafted charade of insanity, but after almost a 25-year performance, he admitted his insanity ruse and pled guilty at a federal hearing in 2003 to obstructing of justice. His plea led to his imprisonment for a 1997 racketeering conviction as well as an added 3 years for his 2003 plea. Mob experts noted that at the height of his power, his empire reached from New York City's Little Italy to the ports of Miami.

sentenced to life in prison, the Genovese Family seemed to have become the most powerful LCN Family. Although the Gambino Family saw its fortunes waning by the mid-1990s, the Genovese Family had maintained its hierarchy and membership numbers. With its increasing prominence came increasing power on the Commission, which allowed the family to earn the largest share of the profits when cooperating in activities with other families. Nowhere was this truer than in the construction and gambling rackets previously dominated by the Gambinos (Raab 1995). On top of this, the Genovese Family created the largest bookmaking and loan-sharking rings in the region.

According to the FBI, Genovese associates stayed active in drug trafficking, murder, gambling, extortion, loan sharking, labor racketeering, money laundering, gasoline bootlegging, and infiltrating legitimate businesses into the 21st century. During a 2002 FBI investigation named "Mobstocks," members were found to be active in stock market manipulation and other illegal frauds. Membership continues stabile at between 225 and 400 members (Capeci 2002, 56).

Genovese Family Informer: Joseph Valachi (1903–1971)

Joe Valachi became an instant celebrity and an embarrassment to the FBI and the Mafia when he testified before the 1963 McClellan Commission. Although his testimony never directly sent anyone to prison, he was the first official member of the Mafia to describe in chilling detail the most secret machinations of Italian-American organized crime. Valachi got his start associated with the Maranzano organization in the late 1920s and was officially inducted into La Cosa Nostra in 1930. He was the first American Mafia member to describe a number of rituals that became popular culture mainstays such as the "kiss of death" and the initiation ceremonies, as well as the term for the Italian-American mob—*La Cosa Nostra*. Although his position at the lowest ranks of the crime family led a number of academics to discount a number of his revelations, this began to change in the 1980s with the testimony of important Sicilian turncoats Tommaso Buscetta and Antonino Calderone, both high-level bosses who buttressed Valachi's testimony with similar revelations while on trial in Italy and America. Valachi had functioned as a hitman, enforcer, numbers operator, and drug dealer for the Luciano–Genovese crime family before being sentenced to 15 to 20 years in federal prison on drug-trafficking charges in 1959. While ensconced in the Atlanta Federal Penitentiary, he shared a cell for a time with his boss, Vito Genovese. Although he was probably privy to many of the secrets of the national crime syndicates from an Italian point of view, the main questions about Valachi's testimony have been the degree to which he understood the roles played by non-Italian criminals such as Meyer Lansky, Longy Zwillman, and Moe Dalitz. As one source noted, "The lower one goes in the Mafia structure, the more one finds the will to believe in the all-powerfulness of the Italian society" (Sikafis 1999, 370).

Valachi agreed to testify against his family and organized crime soon after he assumed that Genovese suspected him of becoming an informer and giving him the kiss of death. Terrified within the tight paranoia-inducing structure of prison confinement, Valachi even went as far as beating to death an individual he incorrectly suspected of plotting his death. For this, his sentence was increased to life, and he decided to testify before the McClellan Committee. Recent scholarship asserts there were reasons for both Genovese and Valachi to be wary of the other, rather than just a case of two paranoid mob sociopaths in a cell together. Valachi had indeed been convicted in a major narcotics case (the Rinaldo-Palmieri case) and was continually hounded by agents from the Federal Bureau of Narcotics (see Chapter 14 for more on the FBN and the FBI). They thought they could "soften him up" by putting him a cell with Genovese, who they knew already suspected him of informing (because other inmates had reported through the prison grapevine that he was meeting with FBN agents). It was then that he was given the kiss of death in front of everyone (Valentine 2004, 281–286). The rest is history.[16]

In his recent history of the Lucchese Family, investigative journalist Ernest Volkman claims that Valachi had sought help in his predicament from boss Gaetano Lucchese. He apparently wanted nothing to do with Genovese and never replied to his childhood friend. It was after this that Valachi killed the prisoner, forcing him to become an informer to escape a lifetime prison sentence (Volkman 1998, 91).

For the rest of his life and before the inception of the modern witness protection program, Valachi would be guarded by U.S. marshals to protect him against anyone wanting to claim a $100,000 bounty for

(continued)

his killing. When he was finished singing, he had identified more than 300 Mafia members and was credited by Attorney General Robert F. Kennedy with giving "a significant addition to the broad picture" (Bernstein 2002). Valachi collaborated with Peter Maas on the bestselling book *The Valachi Papers*. According to one FBN agent, the Peter Maas book was based on his reports that were used to write "the FBI-approved biography of Joe Valachi" (Valentine 2004, 285).

As a postscript: Most contemporary accounts noted Valachi's nickname "Joe Cargo" was the result of his youthful preoccupation with building scooters out of wood crates. Cargo was then modified to the more Sicilian sounding *Cago*. In later years mobsters loved explaining that his moniker *Cago* was actually dialect for "excrement," as a way of sullying his reputation. Nonetheless, a 1966 New York City Police Department report revealed that in the 3 years following Valachi's testimony, more syndicate-affiliated criminals were jailed than in the previous 30 years (Sifakis 1999). As Valachi's star faded, so did his boss Vito Genovese, who would soon lose control of his family from behind bars and see the power of the competing Gambino Family overtake its position at the pinnacle of the New York City underworld.

Mangano/Anastasia/Gambino Family

The Mangano family was the precursor to the modern-day Gambino Family. It emerged out of the Castellammarese under the leadership of the Sicilian-born brothers Vincent and Philip Mangano, who were heavily embroiled in the Brooklyn waterfront rackets. However, ambitious underboss Albert Anastasia usurped leadership in 1951 following the disappearance and presumed death of Vincent Mangano and the murder of his brother (whose body was found).

Known as the "Lord High Executioner" and the "Mad Hatter," Albert Anastasia was born Alberto Anastasio in Tropea, Italy, in 1902. He arrived in the United States illegally sometime in his early teens and soon after was arrested for murder. Some sources indicate he changed the spelling of his last name to save his family the embarrassment. His brother Anthony "Tough Tony" Anastasio would keep the original spelling as he made a similar reputation as head of the Brooklyn waterfront. Albert was never one to shy away from violence and played an inextricable role with Lepke Buchalter in the running of Murder, Inc.

Anastasia's relationship with Luciano, Costello, and other mob stalwarts held him in good stead with the Commission for a number of years. However, he crossed the line in 1952, when he ordered the murder of Arnold Schuster, a young unaffiliated salesman who had turned in wanted bank-robber Willie Sutton and seemed to bask too much in his newfound celebrity. Like Dutch Schultz and others who either killed or threatened to kill outside the boundaries of the underworld, this killing brought unwanted heat on the organization. On top of this, the "Mad Hatter" had upset the traditionalists by selling mob memberships in a separate scheme.

However, the reasons for Anastasia's murder were predicated on a more Byzantine level. Frank Costello had been running the Genovese crime family with Luciano deported to Italy. Anastasia had a good working relationship with Costello, helping to keep his ambitious underboss Vito Genovese in check. With Anastasia out of the picture, Genovese had fewer obstacles to gaining the top spot in Costello's organization (the future Genovese crime family). Anastasia's murder on October 25, 1957, in midtown Manhattan's Park Sheraton Hotel barbershop is one of the most memorable hits in mob lore (committed in same hotel that Arnold Rothstein had been killed in).

With the death of Albert Anastasia in 1957, the reins of the family were passed to Carlo Gambino (1900 or 1902–1976), and during the next two decades he led it to underworld pre-eminence. After Frank Costello was forced into retirement by the rival Genovese Family (thanks to the Anastasia hit and the failed murder of Costello), Luciano partner Meyer Lansky transferred his backing to Gambino, and in the process gave him access to the nationwide network of the National Syndicate.[17]

Gambino entered the underworld during the Prohibition era, when he familiarized himself with the bootlegging and gambling rackets. During World War II, he amassed a fortune trading black market food ration stamps and gasoline, and by the end of the war he had been elevated to

Anastasia underboss. At the 1957 Apalachin Conference held soon after the murder of Anastasia, he was confirmed as Anastasia's replacement.

As boss, most sources indicate that Gambino attempted to change the image of organized crime to one closer in spirit to the legitimate business world, stepping once and for all out of the shadows of nefarious street killings and gang violence. Among his most personal edicts was the rule against narcotics trafficking, afraid it would only further stigmatize the image of Italian-American organized crime. As a result, death was mandated for any family member involved in the drug trade. Gambino trod a path to the future with such old pursuits as loan sharking, gambling, racketeering, and fencing stolen goods while becoming increasingly immersed in the more modern crimes related to the construction industry, garbage disposal, and the garment and seafood industries.

As the family prospered, he continued to ensure the security of the family by relying on personal relationships achieved through marriage and long friendships. However, when his health deteriorated in the 1970s, he hoped to ensure the continued power of his immediate family by appointing his brother-in-law, Paul Castellano, as his successor. Recognizing that this might be an unpopular move among the younger members, he made a countermove by getting all sides to agree on appointing the more popular Aniello Dellacroce as underboss. To solidify the agreement, he also gave Dellacroce the organization's most profitable turf in Manhattan. Gambino died of natural causes in 1976, but his death ushered in an era of decline not just in the Gambino Family fortunes, but the entire world of Italian-American organized crime as well.

Over the next decade the Castellano and Dellacroce factions managed an uneasy truce. However, Castellano's position in his own family and among other crime bosses had begun to crumble, especially when he went on trial and tapes were played of him openly insulting the other crime bosses. After Dellacroce died of cancer in 1985, Castellano lost his protection.

Born in the South Bronx in 1940, John Gotti quit school at 16 and fell in with a gang of car thieves before gaining induction into the Gambino crime family. He achieved a measure of underworld notoriety in 1972 when he took part in the murder of Jimmy McBratney, who had killed Carlo Gambino's nephew. Arrested in 1974, he was out of prison two years later and stepped into the role of lieutenant in the family the same year its namesake died and leadership was placed in the hands of Paul Castellano. Gotti was of the mind that Dellacroce should have been elevated, having made his reputation on the streets, unlike the more businesslike Castellano, who conducted himself like a CEO. However, when Gotti found out that Thomas Bilotti was next in line for the family leadership, he orchestrated an almost Shakespearean plot to take over the family. In 1985, two weeks following the death of Dellacroce (the last person capable of keeping the Gotti faction in check), Gotti engineered the assassinations of Castellano and Bilotti in front of Sparks Steak House.

Gotti was never far from the limelight during his short career as Gambino crime boss—typically either in court or under indictment. The Gambino Family saw its fortunes decline in the 1990s after boss John Gotti was sentenced to life in prison in 1993 on federal charges of murder and racketeering. In prison, his hold on the family diminished, and with poor leadership the organization was virtually rudderless. At the same time membership plummeted from 400 to 200 between 1990 and 1995, and its number of active crews dropped from 22 to 10 (Raab 1995). When Gotti selected his son John Jr. as acting boss, he made one of his biggest errors. Lacking any respect or claim to authority, most of the Gambino captains reportedly acted on their own authority. Although the family still brought in income from gambling, loan sharking, and drug trafficking, recent prosecutions and investigations weakened their hold on various labor rackets, including private garbage hauling, trucking, and garment businesses.

Demonstrating the change in Gambino fortunes and the waning attraction of street life, in 2004, John Gotti, Jr., declared he was done with the mob. It was no wonder to most mob observers who commented regularly on the intellectually vacant and charisma-challenged son of the "Teflon Don" as he faced one charge after another while his "deepest" thoughts were captured by police surveillance, his observations becoming daily fodder for New York City tabloids. As far back as the late 1990s he was captured on tape, admitting, "I'm a two-bit leg breaker for a loan shark"

Gambino Family Informer: Sammy "The Bull" Gravano

When Gambino Underboss Sammy "The Bull" Gravano agreed to testify against his own crime family in 1992, he became the highest ranking Mafiosi informer in the United States (up to that time). Prior to the conspiracy to murder boss Paul Castellano, John Gotti and Sammy Gravano knew each other but had not yet participated in any joint criminal activities. The only son of Sicilian immigrants, Gravano, born in 1945, was 5 years younger than Gotti. Growing up in Bensonhurst in the late 1950s, the 5'5" Gravano dropped out of school and took up boxing, where he earned the nickname of "The Bull" for his fighting style and compact muscular physique. Gravano committed petty crimes and served a stint in the Army before entering the ranks of organized crime. He originally was an associate with the Colombo crime family before receiving permission to switch to the Gambino Family, a rare move. Gravano earned a reputation as an "earner" for extorting construction companies, loan sharking, and a host of other rackets. During the 1980s he was living the high life with profits from illicit activities and legitimate businesses that allowed him to launder mob money. He rapidly rose through the ranks of the Gambino Family to captain of his own crew. His loan-sharking operation alone was bringing in $200,000 to $300,000 a year in profits. By 1986, a series of RICO convictions depleted much of the hierarchy of the Gambino Family, and as a result, Gravano was promoted from soldier to one of the family's three acting street bosses. Once Castellano was out of the picture and Gotti was boss, the family came under pressure from a well-orchestrated assault by the FBI. Gotti won several highly publicized court cases (by bribing jurors) in the 1980s, winning the moniker "The Teflon Don," because the charges never stuck. Before the Gotti era, Gravano had already killed 8 people during a 14-year period. Under Gotti, he killed 11 in almost half that time. In 1990, Gotti went on trial for the last time. It so happens the Feds had bugged Gotti's headquarters and had Gotti on tape bad-mouthing Gravano and was thinking of setting Sammy up to take the fall for several murders. Once Gravano heard the tapes, he made a deal with the FBI to testify against Gotti. His testimony ensured Gotti would never walk the streets again (he died of cancer in prison in 2002) and sent scores of other mobsters to prison. Gravano spent a short time in jail for his 19 murders and went into the federal Witness Protection Program. Not content to have escaped with his life and little prison time for 19 murders, Gravano threw away his second chance at life by getting arrested for trafficking in the drug ecstasy in 2000 and is currently serving 12 years in prison (Raab 2005; Maas 1997).

(Glaberson 1998). Some of his more trenchant observations on contemporary issues included in reference to Dr. Kevorkian and euthanasia: "I believe Dr. Kevorkian. I agree with that." On growing older, he managed this gem: "Every decade after you turn 30 years old your testosterone falls 10 percent." In 2004, at the age of 40, Gotti, Jr., was responsible for five children and declared that he would have walked away from the life years earlier if not for his father; this as he was waiting to get out of jail after serving 5 years for a 1999 racketeering conviction (McShane 2004).

The Gambino Family had not yet fully recovered from the debacle that was the John Gotti era when it was hit with a federal indictment in February 2008. Among the more than 60 members and associates indicted were three of its highest-ranking members as well as the brother and nephew of the late John Gotti. These devastating raids were the biggest setback for New York's Five Families since the mid-1980s Commission Trial. However, some observers cite the fact that after the 1985–1986 trial, a vacuum in leadership made room for a new generation of hoods like John Gotti. It is yet to be seen who will step up to the fill the void in the Gambino Family (Feuer 2008; Hays 2008).

Maranzano/Bonanno Family

Namesake Joseph Bonanno (1905–2002) attended the Salvatore Maranzano–led meeting in 1931 in the small Hudson Valley hamlet of Wappingers Falls, where the doomed "boss of bosses" offered his vision of the future Mafia. Like Maranzano, Bonanno was born in Castellemmare del Golfo, Sicily. Bonanno was only 26 in 1931, when Maranzano was murdered and the Five Families emerged. He had arrived in America in 1924 and drifted into extortion and bootlegging activities in Brooklyn. Bonanno was already a proven commodity when Luciano tabbed him to lead one of the

Five Families (composed of the nucleus of the former Maranzano faction). As of 2007, the Bonanno Family is the only one of the original Five Families to still identify with its founder.

Known to the public as "Joe Bananas," a moniker he detested, he fell from grace during the 1960s for what most experts believed was his attempt to become "boss of bosses" through the so-called "Banana War." He was ultimately exiled to Tucson, Arizona, by the other families. Bonanno lived a miraculously long life for someone who violated so many tenets of *omerta*. Besides trying to become a modern-day Maranzano (whose goal of becoming boss of bosses was also cut short), Bonanno went on to collaborate on his autobiography, *A Man of Honor: The Autobiography of Joseph Bonanno*, which became a huge bestseller in 1983. To sell the book, he even appeared for an interview on CBS's *60 Minutes*. The well-publicized appearance might have boosted his ego and bank account, but also drew increasing attention from law enforcement. In the book, he admitted, "I am not a Father anymore and there is no Bonanno Family anymore." Although he admitted having sat on "the Commission," he denied engaging in such "unmanly" activities as narcotics trafficking or prostitution (law enforcement vehemently disagreed). Fellow syndicate members were apoplectic at his revelations, and peace officers were left scratching their heads why someone who has avoided jail for so long would leave himself open for prosecution. U.S. attorney in New York City Rudolph Giuliani used the autobiography as an outline for his 1986 "Commission Case" against organized crime (see Chapter 14). As Giuliani put it, "If Bonanno can write about the Commission, I can indict it" (quoted in Jacobs 1994, 80).

Bonanno was forced into retirement in 1968 due to medical problems and the events related to his kidnapping by a cousin, Buffalo Mafia boss Stephano Magaddino, as well as the "Banana War" within his own family. Bonanno was followed by a succession of bosses before Carmine Galante tried to take over in the late 1970s. Known as "the Cigar" for his omnipresent stogie, the brutal Galante had spent many years in prison for drug trafficking, and when he was released wanted to become head of the Bonanno Family if not "boss of bosses." In 1979, his ambitions were cut short when he was killed execution style on orders from the other bosses.

Today, the Bonanno Family continues to keep its hand in a variety of enterprises both illicit and legitimate. In his lifetime, Bonanno made millions from dairy and cheese processing plants, the garment industry, a funeral parlor, a laundry service, and a soft drink company. At present, they are just as likely to be running chains of pizzerias, as witnessed by the infamous "Pizza Connection" case. During the 1990s, information provided by the infiltration of Joe Pistone (AKA "Donnie Brasco") revealed the family had about 125 members and more than twice that number in associates (Pistone 1987).

The Bonanno Family saw its fortunes rise in the mid-1990s after John Gotti was imprisoned and the Gambino Family fell into deep disarray. When Joseph Charles Massino left prison in 1992, he reenergized the family by putting together 12 active crews. Leading New York mob expert Selwyn Raab suggested that by 1995, the Bonanno and Genovese families were "the only New York families operating with a full hierarchy of boss, underboss and *consigliere* who are not behind bars" (1995, 12).[18]

In 2003, the family's fortunes were in the hands of Joseph C. Massino, although he was back in federal custody (after 11 years) on charges of racketeering and murder. Massino deserves mention because he was the only New York Mafia boss to evade prosecution during the previous decade. One of the more secretive bosses, unlike his more public counterparts such as John Gotti, Massino discouraged his members from bringing cell phones into meetings and instituted other stringent rules for family members to avoid government detection. According to one reporter, the Bonanno Family had become so insular by 2003 that its leaders held meetings in other countries to avoid American law enforcement. In addition, they began recruiting new members from Sicily who more carefully clung to old world traditions. After the Donnie Brasco fiasco, the family became harder to infiltrate because so many more of its members were related by blood and marriage (Rashbaum 2003). Today, the Bonanno Family has somewhere between 130 and 300 members (Capeci 2002, 53).

Bonanno Family Informant: Joe "Donnie Brasco" Pistone

Joseph Pistone worked as a civilian special agent for the Office of Naval Intelligence prior to joining the FBI in 1969. He spent his first 7 years investigating gambling, bank robberies, truck hijackings, and prostitution. In 1976, he was selected to go undercover as thief "Donnie Brasco" and try to penetrate organized crime fencing operations in New York City. Few could have imagined that for more than 6 years he became an important associate with the Bonanno Family, the deepest penetration of law enforcement into a New York crime family in history. He had gained the trust of top capos to the extent that he was promised that as soon as the membership books were opened again he would be proposed for induction into La Cosa Nostra.

Gagliano/Lucchese Family

According to one leading authority, the Lucchese Family "proved to be the most stable and least divisive of the New York Families" since its inception in the 1930s. It also remains the only one of the Five Families to have never had an assassination attempt on its boss (Raab 2005, 476). Variously known as "Three-Finger Brown,"[19] "Thomas," and "Tommy Brown," Gaetano Lucchese (1900–1967) became one of the most successful New York City crime bosses. Born in Palermo, Sicily, at the turn of the 20th century, Lucchese ended up in America shortly before his teens, but managed to earn a rap sheet more than 20 years before getting his citizenship. He served a short prison stint in 1921 for car theft before moving into the garment industry rackets later in the decade. All the while, he was diversifying into legitimate businesses such as fruit importation—a façade for his bootlegging schemes.

Lucchese got his start with the Masseria syndicate and became an associate of "Lucky" Luciano, and reportedly was in on the murder of Salvatore Maranzano in 1931. Luciano paid him back by appointing him the number two man under Boss Gaetano "Tommy" Gagliano's new family. By the end of Prohibition, he was considered to be one of the prominent movers in the garment industry. During World War II, he continued to serve as underboss to Gagliano as he ascended the criminal ladder into the more respectable construction and garment industries. With the death of Gagliano in 1953, Lucchese became boss.

Lucchese's dexterity at courting the legitimate world allowed him to move away from his mob roots when it suited him—such as when he was able to gain his son an appointment to West Point. Intermarriage between the Lucchese- and Carlo Gambino–led families strengthened the bonds between the two. By most accounts, Lucchese was one of the more popular family bosses of the 20th century, while keeping his hand in gambling, loan-sharking, narcotics, and construction rackets.

Lucchese succumbed to brain cancer and heart disease in 1967. The more than 1,000 people who attended included individuals from all walks of life—dope dealers, judges, politicians—testimony to the high regard in which he was held. Lucchese was succeeded by Carmine Trumanti, before stepping aside for Anthony "Tony Ducks" Corrallo when he left prison in 1970. According to journalist Selwyn Raab, Corrallo was a "dedicated Lucchese student" who matriculated through the basic Mafia curriculum, gaining expertise in loan sharking, hijackings, and union corruption along the way (2005, 237). Between 1941 and 1960, Corrallo was arrested numerous times but was acquitted each time, leading Lucchese to comment each time "Tony ducks again," hence his nickname, "Tony Ducks." Corrallo would be undone by a federal wiretap and subsequent conviction during the 1986 Commission case (see Chapter 14). The following regimes degenerated into a modern version of Murder, Inc. Under the administration of Vittorio "Vic" Amuso and his underboss Anthony "Gaspipe" Casso, the family strategy was simply to kill anyone that got in the way. Numerous family members ended up doing deals with the government to save their skins from the homicidal bosses. Both ended up being sentenced to life in prison. In the late 1980s, family membership was at nearly 120 made men, with a supporting

Lucchese Family Informer: Henry Hill

Henry Hill was involved with the Lucchese Family as an associate for a number of years. He participated in several major crimes, including the 1978 Lufthansa Heist that netted almost $6 million. The following years he was involved in the Boston College point shaving scandal. During his long career, he had his hand in rackets ranging from drug trafficking to extortion and hijacking. Hill eventually turned informer, and his testimony led to the conviction of mobster Jimmy Burke for murder. The saga of Henry Hill provided the linchpin for Nicolas Pileggi's bestselling *Wiseguy*. Hill joined the Witness Protection Program in 1980, but was kicked out of it 7 years later for cocaine use and dealing. Today, he enjoys the limelight as an author and avid self-promoter, even to the extent of running an Internet site devoted to his life and mobster memorabilia.

cast of perhaps 1,000 associates. What was once the smallest of the Five Families emerged shortly before 1990 as "the third largest Mafia dominion in New York" (Capeci 2002; Raab 2005, 478). However, the self-destruction of the Amuso and Casso regime by the end of the 1990s had left the family in tatters, with perhaps half of its membership dead, in prison, or helping the government (Raab 2005, 528).

The Lucchese Family received unwanted prominence when members were linked to the 1978 Lufthansa Heist, depicted in the book *Wiseguy* by Nicholas Pileggi and the subsequent movie version *Goodfellas* by Martin Scorsese.

Profaci/Colombo/Persico Family

The Sicilian native Joseph Profaci (1897–1962) headed up one of the original Five Families (at the behest of Salvatore Maranzano) for more than three decades. He arrived in America at the age of 25 and had the rare fortune of never serving a day in prison for a felony conviction. His daughter married Joseph Bonanno's oldest son, further cementing a friendship between the two bosses that had begun during the 1931 Castellammarese War. Profaci was typically referred to as the "Old Man," and was regarded as a relic of the old Mustache Petes. Despite a zeal for church and family, he could be brutal when required, as in a case when some expensive jewels were stolen from a Bensonhurst church religious statue. The jewels were quickly recovered and the perpetrator was found murdered, with rosary beads draped around his neck. With few hobbies and interests outside his two families, he devoted much of his time to his olive oil importation business, becoming the largest one in the country. However, his Old World ways did not go over well with his plainly New World constituents, many of whom had grown tired of his inclination to favor relatives and friends over his soldiers. He also did not ingratiate himself as the only boss to demand a $25 monthly tax from each member (which he supposedly pledged to a legal defense fund for his members). In the end, it became an open secret that he pocketed the tax.

Profaci's imperious ways soon alienated a faction of the family led by the hot-headed Joseph Gallo, and in 1961 the animosity led to war within the crime family between the two elements. Furthermore, the Gallo brothers—Joey, Larry, and Albert—had also participated in the killing of Albert Anastasia, and felt they had not been properly rewarded for the act. The conflict began when the Gallos kidnapped Profaci's brother and several others. After securing their release through intermediaries, Profaci's killers began gunning down anyone affiliated with the Gallos. The Profaci-Gallo war between 1961 and 1963 left scores of gangsters (and, on occasion, innocent onlookers) wounded or killed. Profaci who died in 1962, and Joey Gallo, who was imprisoned for extortion in 1961, was on the sidelines when the war ended in 1963.

Profaci was succeeded by his brother-in-law (married to his sister) Joseph Magliocco, who is barely remembered as a footnote in mob lore after succumbing to a heart attack just a year later. Joseph Bonanno made overtures to his former friend's (Profaci) family, hoping to consolidate some type of understanding between the two, worried about inroads being made by the Lucchese and Gambino families. By most accounts, a plan was concocted by Bonanno and Magliocco to kill the chiefs of the Lucchese and Gambino families, but it was exposed beforehand by Joseph Colombo, one of the planned killers (1914–1978). Magliocco was called before the Commission shortly before his death, and was fined $50,000 and forced to retire (Lunde 2003). To return their gratitude, they supported Colombo's selection as the next boss of the Profaci Family. This not only stifled the conflict between the Gallo and Profaci cliques for the time being, but also bestowed the Colombo title on the crime family, which it holds to this day.

Joe Colombo was considered many things in life—killer for the Profacis, youngest Mafia boss, first of the modern bosses, and youngest to be killed by the mob. He became a member of the Profaci Family, like his father before him who was murdered in 1938, sometime in the late 1930s. He introduced several of new strategies to lend the impression of respectability to his organization, including making sure all members had legitimate paying jobs. Although he reported his own occupation as a real estate salesman, his soldiers claimed employment as butchers, bakers, bar owners, and truck drivers. Of all of his decisions, the one that would cost him most dearly was his active participation in creating the Italian-American Civil Rights League (IACRL) in 1970 to deal with negative stereotyping of Italian Americans. However, it was little more than a thinly veiled attempt to harass the FBI, whose surveillance led to the arrest and prosecution of his son (Kelly 2000).

Colombo's public crusade embarrassed the more tradition-bound bosses who preferred to handle grudges of all persuasions privately. When he organized a rally that attracted 50,000 people in New York, he crossed the line of propriety. After he announced similar plans the following year, Carlo Gambino warned him to cancel it, which he refused. On June 28, 1971, Colombo was enjoying the huge turnout (and the attention) when an African-American gunsel named Jerome Johnson shot him three times in the head. Johnson was gunned down by Columbo's bodyguards, but not before Colombo was put into a coma that he would die from 7 years later.

Most mob experts concede that the mob hit on Colombo was ordered by the venerable Carlo Gambino. Joey Gallo, who had been released from prison the previous year, is thought to have arranged the hit. However, following the errant shooting, Gallo went into hiding. On April 7, 1972, Gallo was shot down at Umberto's Clam House in New York's Little Italy. Subsequently, close to a dozen men would be killed. However, the war took a brutal turn when members of the Bonanno and Lucchese families became targets. This bloodshed was never good for business, and it did not stop until Carlo Gambino stepped in. As a result, he was recognized as the "boss of bosses," a title that had eluded all others since the 1930s.

Among the Five Families none has seen as much turmoil since the early 1960s as the Colombo Family. The most important faction to rise to the top slots has been Carmine Persico and his college-educated son Alphonse. However, they have spent more time in prison than outside the walls.

Recent Mafia Convictions

Family	Boss	Conviction Date	Sentence
Genovese	Vincent Gigante	1997	12 years (died in prison 2005)
Gambino	Peter Gotti	2003	9½ years
Colombo	Alphonse Persico	2003	13 years
Lucchese	Steven Crea	2004	3–6 years
Bonanno	Joseph Massino	2005	Life

(Adapted from Willing 2006.)

The Five Families in the 1990s

With prosecutions and informers taking a toll on membership rosters, all the families opened the books just 5 years after closing them in 1990 in an attempt to stave off mob informers. Law enforcement estimated that by 1995, the number of made members had shriveled from 1,000 in the late 1980s to just 700. No family was hit harder than the formerly preeminent Gambinos. By the mid-1990s, the Genovese and Bonanno families were flourishing in comparison.

Mafia Initiation Ceremonies: Fact or Fiction?

Early accounts of "Mafia-like" initiation rituals can be traced to an 1877 description of a fraternal organization referred to as the *Stuppagghiari,* located in Palermo. It bears a remarkable similarity to the various other examples that have been recorded in Italy and the United States between 1877 and 1990. The most common traits include the pricking of a finger to draw blood, taking an oath, and burning the image of a sacred saint. Variations are recorded among the Fratellanza near Agrigento (1884), the Fratuzzi of Bagheria (1889; 1918), and others. Well into 1970s, scholars remained skeptical of these accounts, regarding them as products of the prosecutorial imagination. However, the depositions of *pentiti* in the 1980s and later prompted a reassessment. One feature has constantly been featured in every description—a ritual in which an initiate holds the burning paper image of a saint while his sponsor pricks his finger. The sponsor then mixes the "symbolically laden blood and ashes" and has the novice swear an oath of lifelong loyalty to solidarity and silence in front of outsiders (Schneider and Schneider 2005).

Joseph Valachi (1930)

The landmark description was made public during Joe Valachi's testimony before the 1963 McClellan Committee when he revealed the first account of the ritual in the United States. Describing his 1930 initiation, he recounted what was about a 10-minute ceremony:

> The table was about five feet wide and maybe thirty feet long. . . . It was set up for dinner with plates and glasses and everything. I'd say about forty guys were sitting at the table, and everybody gets up when I come in. . . . Now Mr. Maranzano said to everybody around the table, "This is Joe Cago."[20] Then he tells me to sit down in an empty chair on his right. When I sit down, so does the whole table. Someone put a gun and a knife on the table in front of me. . . . After that, Maranzano motions us up again, and we all hold hands and he says some words in Italian. Then we sit down, and he turns to me, still in Italian, and talks about the gun and the knife. "This represents that you live by the gun and the knife and you die by the gun and the knife." Next he asked me, "Which finger do you shoot with?" I said, "This one," and I hold my right forefinger. I was still wondering what he meant by this when he told me to make a cup of my hands. Then he put a piece of paper in them and lit it with a match and told me to say after him, as I was moving this paper back and forth, "This is the way I will burn if I betray the secret of this Cosa Nostra." All of this was in Italian. . . . [The Cosa Nostra] comes before anything—our blood family, our religion, our country. (Quoted in Gambetta, 1993, 264–265).

Then, a member is selected to serve as a mentor to the new recruit and in this case it was future boss Joe Bonanno, who orders Valachi to "Give me the finger you shoot with." He hands him the finger, and he pricks the end of it with a pin and squeezes it until blood seeps out. After this happens, Maranzano says, "This blood means we are now one Family." Maranzano then explains how to determine whether another person is a member, telling him that if he is with a member and he meets another member, but the two members do not know each other, he should say, "He is a friend of ours." However, if he is just a friend and not an actual member he should say, "He is a friend of mine" (adapted from Gambetta 1993, 265–266; Maas 1970, 86–89).

Over the next 20 years, Valachi's testimony was mostly discredited due to a lack of substantiation and other reasons. However, when high-ranking Sicilian informers such as Tommaso Buscetta and Antonino Calderone gave testimony in the 1980s, a number of academics gave Valachi a second look after discovering some remarkable substantiation in their initiation stories.

(continued)

Tommaso Buscetta (1948)

Prominent Sicilian *pentiti* Tomasso was inducted in 1948. Recounting the ceremony in 1984, he remembered:

> The recruit is taken to a secluded location, in the presence of three or more men of honor of the family, and then the oldest informs him that the goal of "this Thing" is to protect the weak and eradicate abuses. Afterward one of the candidate's fingers is pricked and the blood is spilled onto a sacred image. Then the image is placed in the hand of the novice and set on fire. At this point, the novice, who must endure the burning by passing the sacred image from one hand to the other until it is completely extinguished, swears to be loyal to the principles of "Cosa Nostra," solemnly stating, "May my flesh be burned like this sacred image if I do not keep faith with my oath." (Quoted in Gambetta 1993, 266)

Antonino Calderone (1962)

Antonino Calderone, the Catania, Sicily, Mafia boss and *pentiti,* provided one of the most detailed descriptions of the ritual ceremony in 1987:

> When the appropriate moment comes, the candidate or candidates are led to a room, in a secluded location, in the presence of the *rappresentante* and those who hold certain positions within the family, and also the ordinary men of honor of the family. . . . At this point the *rappresentante* of the family tells the novice the rules which discipline the Cosa Nostra, beginning by saying that what is known as "Mafia" is, in reality, called "Cosa Nostra." After being told the rules and prohibitions of Mafia protocol and giving the initiate the possibility of withdrawing, the candidate takes part in an oath ceremony. First, the candidate is asked which hand he shoots with and the index finger of that hand is pricked to release a small trickle of blood. The candidate is told never to betray the family, because "in the Cosa Nostra one enters with blood and leaves only with blood." The blood from the index finger is then used to mark a holy card.[21] The card is the set on fire, "and the novice, preventing the fire from going out and holding the card in his cupped hands, solemnly vows never to betray the 'commandments' of the Cosa Nostra, or else he will burn like the *santina.*" (Adapted from Gambetta 1993, 268–269)

Overview

The traditional Italian-American Mafia continues to flourish into the 21st century. Despite continued efforts by law enforcement, according to one FBI source, it is "wrong to suggest that La Cosa Nostra or LCN is no longer a threat to public safety or the economic vitality of New York City" (Rashbaum 2008, A1). By most accounts, recent setbacks such as the massive attack on the Gambinos in February 2008 by the federal government, organized crime remains a fact of life in much of the region's construction business. In addition, these venerable crime organizations continue to rake in millions of dollars from old standbys such as loan sharking, labor racketeering, gambling, drugs, and securities fraud (see Chapter 7).

The recent rash of indictments against the Gambinos and other families reflected in part the cooperation between Italian and American police agencies. Sicily has been a traditional recruiting ground for organized crime. In the operation dubbed "Old Bridge," police forces on both sides of the Atlantic found a rare opportunity to break the ties between the two. This demonstrates that despite almost a century, ties are still strong between the Old World and New World versions of the Mafia. Although authorities claimed the two investigations were "technically unconnected," it was still considered "an international attempt to disrupt Sicilian ties to the Gambino Family" (Hays 2008, A3).

Key Terms

David Hennessey
The Matrangas
Carlos Marcello
Black Hand gangs

Ignazio Saietta
Joe Petrosino
Castellammarese War
Mustache Petes

Salvatore Maranzano
Joe Masseria
Joseph Valachi
Meyer Lansky

Bugsy Siegel
La Cosa Nostra
Dutch Schultz
Thomas Dewey
The Commission
Lucky Luciano
Murder, Inc.
Lepke Buchalter
Albert Anastasia

Boys from Brooklyn
Apalachin Conference
Vito Genovese
Vincent Gigante
Carlo Gambino
Frank Costello
John Gotti
Paul Castellano
Sammy Gravano

Joseph Bonanno
Donnie Brasco
Thomas Lucchese
Henry Hill
Joseph Profaci
Gallo Brother
Joe Colombo
Five Families

Critical Thinking Questions

1. Which U.S. city reported the first significant Mafia activity? What were its activities, and what was the Mafia's success in that city?
2. Were Black Hand gangs the beginning of the Mafia in America? What was the structure of Black Hand gangs? How were they similar or different from Mafia families?
3. What did the New York Police Department do in response to the Black Hand?
4. What was the Castellammarese War, and why is it central to the "mythic" evolution of the Mafia in America? What actually happened to the Mustache Petes on September 11, 1931?
5. Discuss the formation of the Five Families. What role did "Lucky" Luciano play?
6. What were the ethnic restrictions of early organized crime groups, and how did this change over time?
7. What is the origin of the term *La Cosa Nostra*?
8. What are the unwritten rules of the American Mafia?
9. What kind of structure do the New York crime families have? Is it similar to the Chicago Outfit?
10. What was the "Commission"? How was it formed, and who belonged to it?
11. Discuss the rise and fall of Murder, Inc.
12. What was the impact of the 1957 Apalachin Conference on the war against organized crime? Who attended the meeting, and why was it held?
13. Compare the evolution of the Gambino and Genovese crime families. Discuss important leaders and events.
14. Discuss the controversy over Joe Valachi's testimony before the McClellan Commission. Has academic and official opinion changed regarding the veracity of his testimony? What impact has recent testimony by Sicilian crime bosses had on the discussion concerning Valachi's testimony?
15. How did John Gotti rise to the top of the Gambino Family? Was he successful as crime boss? Explain.
16. What were the results of "Donnie Brasco's" infiltration of the Bonanno Family?
17. Discuss the state of the Five Families since the 1990s.

Endnotes

1. For example, any mention of New Orleans prior to 1890 is all but absent in Howard Abadinsky's, *Organized Crime,* 2003, 7th ed.; Kenney and Finckenauer, 1995, *Organized Crime in America*; and Jay S. Albanese, *Organized Crime in America*, 1996.
2. His name is also spelled "Shakespeare" by some sources.
3. Because neither group was from Naples, they would not be considered Camorra. Incidentally, both clans knew each other from their hometown in Sicily.
4. According to Jerry Capeci, the Matrangas were "the forerunners of the Mafia family that Carlos Marcello" led in the 1960s (2002, 104).
5. One examination of 105 the nation's newspapers found the opinion divided. Of these, 58 opposed it and 42 approved it, with the rest expressing no opinion. The mob action found its greatest support in the West and South (Nelli 1976; Karlin 1941).
6. Humbert Nelli is among those that disputes this, noting that "If indeed he had ever headed a *mafia* group, he lost this prominent position" after the mass killing. There was, according to Nelli, "nothing occurring in the remaining fifty-two years of his life [that] connected him with criminal activities" and "he led a quiet life as a stevedore" until his retirement in 1918 (1976, 64).

7. Marcello traveled on what was probably a false Guatemalan passport contrived from an equally forged birth certificate, but as a resident alien, the federal government knew this was his Achilles' heel.

8. A number of early Sicilian mobsters emigrated from the Sicilian town of Castellemmare del Golfo to America, as did future stalwarts such as Joe Bonanno.

9. Joseph Profaci ran the family for years and was replaced by Joseph Magliocco in 1963, so the Senate Hearings used Valachi's testimony relegating the former boss Profaci to mob boss. In reality, Joseph Colombo replaced Magliocco after he died in December 1963. According to gangland expert Jerry Capeci, Joe Colombo "remains the only Mafia boss whose name has replaced that of the one that came into common usage in 1963" (Capeci 2002).

10. *La Cosa Nostra* translates to "This thing of ours."

11. Although some sources credit Burton Turkus and Sid Feder, the authors of the 1951 bestseller *Murder, Inc.: The Story of the Syndicate* as the originators of the expression, it is in this book that the association with Feeney is expounded on.

12. Buchalter's better-known moniker *Lepke* is derived from the Yiddish word *Lepkele,* or "Little Louis."

13. Strauss, who would later be executed, was a mean actor. In one oft-repeated incident, Strauss was so unhappy with dinner service one night, he poked a waiter in the eye with a fork.

14. These included Phil Strauss, Louis Capone, Mendy Weiss, Bugsy Goldstein, Happy Maione, and Dasher Abbandando.

15. It has been suggested that as many as 50 might have escaped, including Sam Giancana from Chicago, Joe Zerilli of Detroit, San Francisco's James Lanza, and Stefano Maggadino of Buffalo.

16. It was standard FBN procedure at this time to call convicted drug traffickers to prison meetings that were usually unproductive, but would give the appearance to other inmates that they were cooperating with the authorities.

17. It is widely believed that it was Gambino, along with Lansky, Luciano, and Costello, who framed Genovese on the drug charge that sent him to prison.

18. At that time, Bonanno's boss was Massino, underboss Salvatore A. Vitale, and *consigliere* James Tartaglione.

19. During a stint working at a machine shop, the only legitimate job he would ever hold, Lucchese managed to crush his right index finger. The injury convinced him that crime was safer than legitimate employment. While being fingerprinted for car theft, a police officer jested that that he should be called "Three-Finger Brown," in deference to the Chicago Cubs star pitcher "Three Finger" Brown.

20. Valachi's childhood nickname was "Cargo"; Cago was probably a corruption of the word.

21. According to Gambetta, the holy card typically features Annunziata, the patron saint of the Cosa Nostra.

CHAPTER 5

Historical Roots of Organized Crime in America

CREATING A CLIMATE FOR ORGANIZED CRIME

Following the first wave of Irish immigration to America in the early 1800s, alliances between politicians, gamblers, and gangsters in urban settings began laying the foundations for the evolution of complicated criminal syndicates. Waves of Irish immigrants entered America beginning in the 1820s and 1830s. It was during the so-called Jacksonian era that property barriers to voting (white men) had become diminished enough to allow the Irish to become a powerful voting bloc. The Irish immigrants came from a cultural tradition that had pitted them against the English for centuries. Their experience with mass action and direct action politics came into play between the 1820s and 1880s as they created perhaps America's most famous political machines. The strength of the Irish community was multiplied by ethnic and religious unity. Irish politicians learned that the road to power could be attained through the requisite career paths of street captain, district and precinct leadership, aldermen, and then higher office beyond the municipal confines.

Because most Irish immigrants lacked industrial skills, patronage jobs such as policeman, fireman, and public works were attractive to a constituency that became economically dependent on big city political machines. Irish Catholic politicians ascended the social ladder to lead political machines in cities as diverse as New York City, Boston, Cleveland, Chicago, Baltimore, St. Louis, and New Orleans.

Between 1880 and 1920, the ethnic composition of urban America shifted from Irish and German immigrants to newcomers from southern and eastern Europe, a mélange of Russians, Jews, Poles, Italians, Greeks, and others. Compared to earlier immigrants, these new ones were more inclined to remain in the cities. If one was to create a profile, the typical post-1880 immigrant was from rural peasantry, poor, often illiterate, and unfamiliar with American political and social institutions. The relationship between the immigrant and the political boss was an urban symbiotic relationship that blossomed because each needed the other. Until the advances of the Progressive era (1900–1920), America's urban immigrants were vulnerable to the opportunities offered by the political boss.

SALOON CULTURE

In the late-18th century there were few American communities without a church and a local tavern. With social and political activities of small communities scattered over often vast territories, American communities became much more centered on the twin meeting places of the church and the tavern than its European counterparts. Diametrically opposed to one another in spirit, the tavern became the most accessible local institution for the male world of the early 19th century.

In order to understand the American permutation of social interchange, one must put American drinking habits into the context of the 18th and early-19th centuries. Unlike Europe in this era, America (until the sectional debate before the Civil War) was not permanently plagued by bitter ideological conflicts. In stark contrast, European cities offered, unlike an overwhelmingly rural and sparsely populated America, countless examples of social, literary, and political groups who met in drinking establishments, but there are "few references to the political clout" of these European café or pub owners (Behr 1996, 11). However, not all Americans were well-disposed to this evolving institution. In the late-18th century, John Adams and other idealists openly expressed their disdain for the early political power of the tavern owner.

In the first half of the 19th century and beyond, no community attained the prominence of New York City's Five Points for crime and criminality. More than a century ago, one observer noted that he had traveled through every large city in America, but had "no hesitancy in pronouncing" the Five Points neighborhood the worst in terms of "abject poverty and vice" (Buell 1883, 107–108). It would be in such neighborhoods as Five Points that early connections were forged "between politics and liquor," predating Prohibition by more than a century. As early as the 1820s and 1830s, saloon-keepers in New York City were considered among the ranks of the political elite, and in Five Points and other poor neighborhoods, they were the most esteemed men in the area.

Saloonkeepers built their reputations by stepping in for local residents when they most needed it—feeding the hungry, offering clean toilets, and giving first aid to victims of accidents or fights. Besides their benevolence, they offered a place of recreation during an era with few urban amusements. Saloons became virtual neighborhood social clubs. Many taverns featured billiard tables and bowling alleys, and were more than willing to make their backrooms available for union meetings, Saturday night dances, and family celebrations (Cashman 1981; Kobler 1974).

One historian compares saloonkeepers to a combination of "guide, philosopher, and creditor" (Anbinder 2001, 145). Because the tavern owner saw his customers regularly and was probably on a first-name basis with them, it was more than likely that his customers trusted him more than any other member of the merchant class, and often relied on him for news concerning city politics and events. In an era without mass media, tavern keepers and ministers were considered the consensus builders of the community—influential personas whose opinions were not to be lightly digested. The saloonkeeper, often regarded as the most informed member of the community, was often responsible for convincing these very same people to vote for the "right" candidate on Election Day. There was also a darker side to this power. As saloon owners attained more power, there was a tendency for them to create working relationships with members of various gangs. Any recalcitrant voters on Election Day could be easily persuaded by these "shoulder hitters" to vote for the favorite candidate. Some saloonkeepers rode their popularity to public office themselves.

In the late 1800s, urban reformer Jacob Riis asserted, "The rumshop turns the political crank in New York" (1957, 159). Perhaps the earliest exemplar of the saloonkeeper–politician was Captain Isaiah Rynders, a former gambler and knife fighter who carved a reputation along the Mississippi River before arriving in New York City in the 1830s. In quick succession, he purchased six grocery stores, which sold little more than alcohol and offered a similar route to power as the saloon (Cashman 1981, 43). He rose to Tammany (democratic political) leader of the Sixth Ward. It became one of the city's worst-kept secrets that he also coordinated most gang activities that had to do with politics from his saloon. He was one of the first saloon owners to organize the surrounding slums into anything resembling a voting bloc. Rynders' winning strategy was to meet immigrants as they got off the boat, give them a place to stay, find them a job, and pledging them to vote for Tammany candidates.

Neighborhood taverns became increasingly identified as centers of political activity and a key to Tammany power in the post–Civil War era. During the late 19th century, many New Yorkers would have agreed with John Adams' lamentations in the previous century as they observed powerlessly the corrupting influence of the saloons. Periodic attempts were made to close them or even limit their hours, but these were in vain and hard to enforce in a city whose police force had become increasingly Irish and whose officers probably received their jobs as favors from the saloon owners in the first place (Allen 1993).

The Godmother: Fredericka "Marm" Mandelbaum (1818–1894)

A number of authorities have described Fredericka, better known as "Marm," Mandelbaum as the leading criminal in America during the second half of the 19th century. One historian of Jewish crime described her as one of New York City's "leading fences" (Joselit 1983, 35), while another writer described her as "the most influential American criminal after the Civil War" (MacIntyre 1997, 31). However, popular crime historian Carl Sifakis was probably carried away when he suggested that it was Mandelbaum, "rather than Lucky Luciano and Meyer Lansky, who first put crime in America on a syndicated basis" (Sifakis 1992, 470). In any case, there is little doubt that she actively financed and plotted many of the era's capers. The more successful she became, the more her reputation grew, albeit often being accorded unsubstantiated credit for directing the operations of gangs of bank robbers, blackmailers, confidence men, as well as offering advanced courses in burglary and safe blowing and teaching kids the ins and outs of street crime in a sort of Fagin-school for delinquents (Macintyre 1997; Sifakis 1982, 470; Fried 1980, 26).

What is most remarkable was that an immigrant Jewish woman from Prussia was able to earn a place in the century's criminal pantheon. Arriving in New York with her husband Wolfe in tow, she bought a dry goods store and home on the Lower East Side. Within 5 years, her legitimate business had become only a façade for her criminal operations that ranged throughout the United States. Like other Jewish criminals of the era, Mandelbaum was drawn to the garment industry. Jewish crime historian Albert Fried posited that, "Dealing in stolen goods or fencing was an integral part of the criminal activities of New York Jews in the nineteenth century" (1980, 35).

Mandelbaum's name first appeared on New York City's ledger books in 1862. Following the 1863 Draft Riots, she was suspected of being "the biggest receiver of stolen goods looted, much of which she disposed of as far as Chicago; fittingly enough a good portion of loot taken during the subsequent Chicago fire (1871) ended up in her warehouses in New York" (Sante 1992, 210–211). Over the next two decades, estimates placed the amount of goods going through her three-story building on the corner of Clinton and Rivington streets at between $5 million and $10 million.

She was handling so much merchandise by the late 1860s that she had to purchase several other warehouses in Manhattan and Brooklyn to store the goods. By most accounts it was here that confederates removed labels, trademarks, and other identifiers from the stolen lucre. After removing any trademarks that might identify its origins, a buyer was found and the deal completed. Furthering her success were her close relationships with major underworld figures as well as upstanding members of the legitimate business community. What helped maintain these links was Marm's business acumen—businessmen at every level of society knew they could count on her for the cheapest wholesale prices for goods she typically purchased at from one-fifth to one-tenth the wholesale price. She was so tuned into the criminal demimonde that she was almost immediately notified of a robbery. She or one of her agents would then examine the goods and, if approving, always paid in cash. There were few commodities she would not handle, including selling stolen horses transferred from upstate New York by the region's Loomis Gang. The venerable Pinkerton Detective Agency had reports of her activities from the East Coast to Cincinnati.

Her dry-goods (or haberdashery) shop was regarded as an out-and-out market for crimes of larceny. Others have described it as "a gigantic operation, citywide, indeed nationwide" (Fried 1980, 26). Historian Timothy Gilfoyle went as far as to depict it as "an underworld haven attracting the nation's most famous criminals" (2006). Even New York City Police Superintendent George Walling sarcastically referred to Mandelbaum's business "as the 'Bureau for the Prevention of Conviction'" (2006, 151).

Marm Mandelbaum was unique in a city of probably of hundreds of fences. Her organized operation allowed her to amass a small fortune that gave her a leg up on her less-prosperous counterparts. Compared to other fences who rarely could afford to fight prosecution, Mandelbaum's wealth gave her access to lawyers, police, and even prosecutors. Few were above accepting what was called *fall money* in the parlance of times. Among her more prominent lawyers were two of the era's best—Howe and Hummel, whom she kept available with a $5,000 retainer each year (Asbury 1928). The more successful she became, the better able she was able to insulate herself from the crimes she supported by conducting her business affairs through messengers and other intermediaries.

(continued)

New York City's police had come to some type of arrangement with Mandelbaum during her 20-year career. They pretty much ignored her as long as she continued to set up small-time operations and other underworld competitors (see Jonathan Wild and thief taking in Chapter 1). However, it would be the nation's premier police organization that ended her American criminal career after the Pinkertons infiltrated her criminal network in 1884. She fled to Canada soon after jumping bail on a grand larceny indictment. Because existing extradition laws could not force her return to the United States, she was able to live out the remainder of her life north of the border. After she died in 1894, her body was returned to New York for burial.

URBAN YOUTH GANGS

Arriving in the United States shortly after the Civil War, Danish immigrant Jacob Riis wandered New York City's streets in semi-poverty before settling in as a police reporter in 1877 for the *New York Tribune* and then the *Evening Sun*. Over the next 22 years he chronicled the city's teeming immigrant East Side slums. Riis, who would go on to write 10 books, reported from the city's most dangerous streets—places such as Bandit's Roost, Bottle Alley, Thieves Alley, and Kerosene Bend. Fellow reformer Lincoln Steffens famously reported, "Riis was interested not at all in crime and vice, [but] only in the stories of people in the conditions in which they lived" (Steffens 1931, 223).

Riis' most prominent work was *How the Other Half Lives*, published in 1890. In it, he lamented, "The one thing you shall vainly ask for in the chief city of America is a distinctively American community" (1900, 21). An amateur sociologist and without academic training, Riis was influenced by the prejudices of the day, insisting that immigrants assimilate or "Americanize" as soon as possible.

Of all New York City's neighborhoods, none summons up images of early gangs more than the Five Points section. More than 50 years after it achieved a sort of nefarious prominence, the Irish had all but moved out, replaced by Italians, Poles, Greeks, Russians—a cornucopia of cultures that made Riis ponder how a "queer conglomerate mass of heterogeneous elements" had taken the place of the "earlier Americans" (Riis 1900).

Riis reserved his greatest scorn for the gangs of Hell's Kitchen. Riis plums fertile ground here, making the connections between poverty and gang culture, one of the earliest observers to do so. He describes the lack of opportunities and adult supervision, noting, "With no steady hand to guide him, the boy takes naturally to idle ways" (Riis 1900, 181). In a later book, Riis made it clear that over the previous decade conditions were still rife for the creation of gangs. He describes the genesis of one gang member named Jacob Beresheim in particular, reporting, "As a kid he hunted with the pack in the street. As a young man he trains with the gang" (Riis 1899, 305).

The Gangs of New York

It did not take long for local politicians to recognize the criminal talents of New York City's myriad gangs. As many of the ward and district leaders acquired grocery stores, saloons, and dance halls in the Bowery and Five Points neighborhoods, they found a waiting supply of young gangsters ready

The Gang Is an Institution in New York (1900)

Along the water-fronts, in the holes of the dock-rats, and on the avenues, the young tough finds plenty of kindred spirits. Every corner has its gang, not always on the best of terms with the rivals on the next block, but all with a common programme: defiance of law and order, and with a common ambition: to get "pinched," i.e. arrested, so as to pose as heroes before their fellows. A successful raid on the grocer's till is a good mark, "doing up" a policeman cause for promotion. The gang is an institution in New York. . . . The gang is the ripe fruit of tenement-housegrowth. (Riis 1900, 217–218) to use violence to bring out the vote and harass competitors for financial compensation. It was in this way that some gangsters were able to neutralize their vicious reputations and become part of the establishment. For politicians it was also a way to control the teeming number of gang members, estimated at 35,000 by 1855 (Haskins 1974).

New York City had been a breeding spot for gangs since the era of the American Revolution. As New York City grew more urban in the 19th century, a new class of servants, orphans, and indigents for whom no one felt responsibility began to clamor across the municipal landscape. As early as 1766, one city resident lamented the "children nightly trampouze the streets with lanthorns upon poles and halloing . . . the magistry either approve of it, or do not dare suppress it" (quoted in Stokes 1915, 760). Initially more a nuisance than a public hazard, youth gangs would gradually evolve into an urban menace by the early 19th century.

Although dates of origin are speculative, a handful of White and Black gangs existed by the late 18th century, including the Smith's Vly gang, the Bowery Boys, and the Broadway Boys, and such Black gangs as the Fly Boys and the Long Bridge Boys (Sante 1992). However, these early gangs were more social organization than crime syndicate. Most members had regular jobs, typically as butchers, carpenters, mechanics, and dockworkers. It is probable that there was always a scant minority drawn to illicit activities, such as gambling, or toward the tavern trade.

To trace back the origins of New York City's numerous syndicates is to travel back to the early decades of the 19th century to a fetid neighborhood known as Five Points. It was home to a number of gangs, including what many consider the city's first organized gang—Edward Coleman's Forty Thieves, which can be traced back to at least 1826 (Ellis 1966; 1997, 231; Sante 1992, 105).[1] By the early 1820s, the Five Points district (so-named for the intersection of five streets) was a breeding ground for every type of criminal element. It is generally accepted that some of America's earliest organized crime groups were born out of this locale, where thieves, cutthroats, and pickpockets found refuge from a society intent on bringing order to the chaos that was urban America (Gilfoyle 2006).

By the 1820s, overcrowding and rising immigration in the Five Points district created new opportunities for the developing gangs. Besides the Forty Thieves there were the Kerryonians from County Kerry, Ireland, and reputedly the city's second organized gang; the Chichesters; the Roach Guards, who supposedly formed in a liquor store owned by a man named Roach; the Plug Uglies, beefy men who wore plug hats that they filled with batting and wool like a leather helmet used in battle; and the Shirt Tails, to name but a few. Their benign names belied their predilection for brutal fighting and bellicosity. By the 1830s, a number of gangs had developed that "varied greatly in strength, importance and raison d'être" (Sante 1992, 200).

The New York gangs presaged some of today's gangs that wear a particular color or distinctive clothing. For example, the Roach Guards wore a blue stripe on their pants, and the Dead Rabbits a red stripe. The anti-Catholic nativist gangs, such as the True Blue Americans, were easily recognizable with their preference for stovepipe hats and ankle-length frock coats (Haskins 1974). Weapons were deadly but inventive—most anything at hand could be converted into a bludgeon or stabbing instrument—ice picks, knives, brickbats, brass knuckles, and worse contributed to the violence of the bloody gang wars of the era.

The developing slums of American cities paralleled the growing disparity between the living conditions of the native born and the more marginalized mostly Irish immigrants. Although the Five Points district tended to foster the development of Irish Catholic gangs, the Bowery produced a welter of gangs that shared a violent antipathy for the Five Points realm—gangs that included the Bowery Boys, the O'Connell Guards, the Atlantic Guards, the American Guards, and the True Blue Americans (Sante 1992). For a while, the Bowery gangs found common ground against the Five Pointers. However, ethnic tension was on the horizon as the groups diverged according to whether their allegiances were to the Irish-bound Tammany Hall or the nativist Know Nothing Party. Most of the Five Points gangs reached their apogee in the aftermath of the 1863 Civil War Draft Riots.

During its first century, "no Five Points immigrants had ever assimilated to an extent that would have satisfied native-born Americans" (Anbinder 2001). The succession of ethnic groups—from the Irish, Germans, and Italians to the Jews and Chinese—"all tended to recreate their Old World culture in New York rather than adopt American habits and values" (Anbinder 2001, 422). Historians of immigration have long noted how immigrants tended to join their compatriots in the slums of urban America, where they felt more secure. However, what has been less reported was the fact that that of these entire immigrant groups, "Only the neighborhood's Jews gave little thought to returning" to the pogroms and anti-Semitism of the old country (Anbinder 2001, 423). By the turn of the 20th century, the Chinese were the only one of these groups to call the neighborhood home. Since then, Chinatown has occupied the former Five Points netherworld.

In the years leading up to the Civil War, the only significant gang presence could be found along the waterfront "where gangs were much more single mindedly criminal" (Sante 1992, 204). By one 1850 estimate, there were between 400 and 500 "river pirates" and close to 50 gangs in the Fourth Ward alone. Most of New York City's early gangs were unsophisticated compared with what was to come. Most crimes were accomplished with at least a modicum of violence, preferring such activities as mugging and robbery when they weren't fighting with each other.

Following the Civil War, several German gangs emerged in the Hell's Kitchen neighborhood, robbing residents, extorting protection payments, and burglarizing businesses. Within a half century, the first Italian gangs were operating on Mulberry Street in what was to become known as "Little Italy." The Chinese population grew from 700 in 1880 to more than 10,000 in 1910. The burgeoning Chinatown gave birth to tongs, combination community leaders–benevolent society–criminal entrepreneurs (see Chapter 9). Tong leaders used grocery stores and other legitimate businesses to mask gambling and opium smoking dens. Jacob Riis estimated there were 200 gambling houses in New York's Chinatown in the 1890s.

By the 1890s, the Whyos[2] were considered the city's most powerful gang (Asbury 1928). It is somewhat hard to believe that Herbert Asbury, writing in the heyday of the Chicago mobs, wrote that the Whyos were "the most ferocious criminals who ever walked the streets in an American city" (Gilfoyle 2006, 185; Asbury 1928, 225). Although the gang's origins are obscure, it was a force from at least the early 1880s. The Whyos demonstrated a criminal acumen that presaged the growth of the Prohibition-era mobs. They were part of a complex system in which they kept their "power by intimidation, terror, and political favoritism" and in effect "were early racketeers" (Gilfoyle 2006, 191). One of its members was arrested while in the possession of a list of prices for services provided by the gang (see box next page). However, the gang's ascendance went into a tailspin throughout the 1890s as law enforcement cracked down on the Whyos.

Moving toward the turn of the century four large gangs emerged with an estimated membership of more than 1,200. The gangs included the Eastmans, the Five Pointers, the Gophers (pronounced Goofers), and the Hudson Dusters.[3] These gangs differed from the earlier incarnations in respect to their increasing sophistication (Asbury 1928; Sante 1992). For example, the Eastmans were required to turn in written summaries of their activities and contract jobs. According to gang historian Luc Sante, they copied the "Tammany practice of operating locally through the fronts provided by neighborhood chowder clubs and baseball teams" (1992, 220).

The emergence of the mega-gangs in the 1890s also marked the appearance of several major Jewish- and Italian-led gangs, which were in the process of supplanting the Irish gangs such as the Whyos. Monk Eastman was one of New York City's first prominent Jewish gangsters. Born Edward Osterman in Brooklyn in 1873, his Eastman gang furnished voters for local politicians in return for police protection, and was one of the first underworld gangs to provide strikebreakers to unions and employers undergoing labor conflict (Joselit, 1983). Released after a stint in jail in 1909, Eastman never again reached the prominence that he once enjoyed. He served time in jail next for an opium rap, but got out in time to distinguish himself in the French theater of World War I.

Paolo Vaccarelli, who went by his better-known moniker, Paul Kelly, led the Five Pointers, the avowed rivals of the Eastmans. Despite the fact that both had business accommodations with

Whyo Take-Out Menu[4]

Punching	$2
Both eyes blacked	$4
Nose and jaw broke	$10
Jacked out	$15
Ear chawed off	$15
Leg or arm broke	$19
Shot in leg	$25
Stab	$25
Doing the big job	$100 and up

Tammany Hall, both gangs were bent on killing each other. In his recent history of Irish American organized crime, T. J. English noted that it was common for Italian criminals to adopt Irish surnames in the early 20th century, citing the examples of New York City mob boss Frank Costello (Francesco Castiglia); Chicago hitman Machine Gun Jack McGurn (Vincenzo DeMora); and Sam Giancana's assistant, Charles "Chuckie" English, born Salvatore Inglese (English 2005, 107). In Kelly's case, the adopted name was an attempt to improve his image during a mediocre boxing career (Reppetto 2004, 26). Some of the best-known Italian organized crime figures of the Prohibition years graduated from Kelly's Five Points gang.

Beginning a tradition that J. Edgar Hoover's FBI would continue up until the late 1950s, the federal Secret Service was more focused on small bands of Black Handers (due to their participation in counterfeiting), whereas Vaccarelli and the nascent organized criminal gangs such as the Five Pointers and the Eastmans slipped under the national radar.[5] The first to recognize their growing threat was New York City finest.

Jewish/Eastern European Organized Crime

An ethnic shift in gang activity took place in the first decades of the 20th century as Jewish and Italian gangsters came to prominence, first with Irish monikers like Eastman and Kelly, and later under their real names. At the turn of the 20th century, Jewish crime was dominated by Russian and Eastern European immigrants on New York's Lower East Side. According to the crime patterns of the era, Jewish criminals favored property crimes such as burglary, pick-pocketing, fencing, arson, and horse poisoning (an extortion racket). New York City crime figures demonstrated that New York Jews committed 15.9% of all felonies in 1900; by 1905, it rose to 25.4%. In other words, they committed 80% of the city's reported property crimes.

The advent of Prohibition offered Jewish gangsters an astonishingly rewarding form of property crime. During the first decades of the 20th century, a flourishing Jewish underworld existed in New York City, Boston, Cleveland, Detroit, and Philadelphia (Fried 1980). Throughout Prohibition, much of the nation's bootlegging was centered in New York City, home to 1.6 million American Jews—46% of the nation's Jewish population (Fox 1989).

Arnold Rothstein (1882–1928)

Arnold Rothstein was regarded as the most prominent gangster in New York during the 1910s and 1920s and served as mentor to a generation of Jewish (and Italian) gangsters, including Benjamin "Bugsy" Siegel, Meyer Lansky, Arthur "Dutch Schultz" Flegenheimer, and Waxey Gordon.

Arnold Rothstein gets lost in a cacophony of names like Al Capone, John Gotti, and Joe Bonanno that seem to dominate any account of the development of modern American organized crime. However, he should be remembered as a pioneering presence as both a gambling and narcotics kingpin in the years leading up to Prohibition. Several recent biographies testify to the growing appreciation he is finally receiving from crime historians (Tosches 2005; Pietrusza 2003). The recent groundbreaking history of the Federal Narcotics Bureau described Rothstein as "America's premier labor racketeer, bookmaker, bootlegger, and drug trafficker" during the 1920s (Valentine 2004, 6). An opium smoker as a teenager, he knew people would buy drugs on the black market following the passage of the Harrison Narcotics Act in 1914, just as he knew people would hire prostitutes although "happily" married and drink alcohol during Prohibition.

Throughout his run during the 1920s, Rothstein bought police and political protection while developing new strategies to reorganize the corrupting of the upper-world with payoffs, bribery, and graft. He also pioneered the indiscriminate pairing of various ethnic groups without restrictions of nationality, ethnicity, race, or religion. He proved a willing mentor to the best minds of the underworld including "Lucky" Luciano, Meyer Lansky, and Frank Costello. By some accounts his presence was so strong at city hall that more than 6,000 bootlegging cases were dropped, and it was believed that he could fix any court case through his political connections.

However, Rothstein's vision for the future of American syndicates contrasted sharply with the Italian-dominated one that predominated beginning in the 1930s. Rothstein had envisioned a loose confederation of gangs with their own territories supervised by a board of directors and little hierarchy, rather than a heavily hierarchical model featuring bosses, underbosses, counselors, and soldiers that became fashionable for some after his death. In the end, Rothstein was murdered in 1928, perhaps because of unpaid gambling debts, but Luciano and Lansky put many of his strategies into practice, including the notion of a national Commission made up of powerful bosses who would mediate disputes and function as an advisory board.

Did Arnold Rothstein Fix the 1919 World Series?

The Black Sox Scandal of 1919 is considered America's greatest sports betting scandal. What lent it its lasting resonance was what one authority has called "the ultimate corruption of our sports heroes, the ultimate corruption of American heroism" (Pietrusza 2003, 147). It has been a long-accepted fact among popular histories of organized crime that Arnold Rothstein bribed baseball players to fix the 1919 World Series in the so-called Black Sox Scandal (Asinof 1963). Typical allegations assert without much substantiation that it was "almost certainly Rothstein who persuaded eight players of the Chicago White Sox to lose the World Series against the infinitely inferior [Cincinnati] side" (Morton 1998, 29). Even a well-researched 2003 biography is entitled *Rothstein: The Life, Times, and Murder of the Criminal Genius Who Fixed the 1919 World Series* (Pietrusza 2003). The scandal turns up in F. Scott Fitzgerald's *Great Gatsby* (1925),[6] and is immortalized in the expression, "Say it ain't so, Joe!" referring to fallen idol "Shoeless" Joe Jackson.

What most authorities agree on is that a coterie of Chicago White Sox players felt underpaid and conspired to throw the World Series in which they were heavily favored. By most accounts, including Rothstein's, two sets of gamblers put their financial backing behind the fix. Players apparently took money from both. However, when both gambling groups didn't follow through with the agreed-on money, the Reds retaliated by winning the third game and in the process bankrupted one of the cabals. However, gangland messengers threatened them with violence if they didn't follow through with the fix—which they did. Although suspicions were raised almost immediately, it took a year before the plot was exposed publicly. Eight of the Reds and a number of gamblers went on trial in Chicago, but to the chagrin of the baseball hierarchy, all won acquittal. Nevertheless, none of the players would play professional baseball again (Tosches 2005; Pietrusza 2003).

Rothstein's presence looms large over the scandal, although his participation has always been questionable. Several gamblers did approach him about backing the fix, but he turned them down flat. Despite his demurral, the fix went on without him. In the most recent biography of Rothstein, Nick Tosches proclaims, "Of all the transgressions of which he has been accused, this, the most celebrated of them, was perhaps the only one of which he was innocent" (2005, 266). This is a far cry from suggesting that he couldn't have done it if he wanted to. On October 26, 1920, Rothstein appeared voluntarily before a Cook County grand jury and was "officially exonerated of any blame" (Tosches 2005).

Rothstein's wife Carolyn would later give her impressions of the scandal in her 1934 book, *Now I'll Tell*. In it, she paints a portrait of her late husband as a cautious man who, if "sounded out on the subject of bribing baseball players," would probably have been inclined to use "inside knowledge that they were going to be bribed to make winning bets" (Rothstein 1934, 170).

In 1923, just four years after the disputed World Series, Rothstein was called to testify as a hostile witness in an unrelated "bucket shop"[7] case. Attorney William M. Chadbourne, representing the bankrupt bucket shop owners, in which Rothstein owned a large share, went on the attack, as Rothstein, acting as his own attorney, brilliantly parried the questions.

Chadbourne (WC): Did you wager on the 1919 World Series?

Rothstein (AR): I object on the ground that the question is irrelevant and immaterial. . . .

WC: I am seeking to prove that the witness had full knowledge that the series was fixed and that, with the knowledge, he won various wagers including some from [my client]

AR: This baseball thing has been the sore spot of my career. I faced a Grand Jury and was vindicated.

WC: Didn't you hire counsel to appear in your behalf in the investigation?

AR: You ought to be ashamed to ask me that. This is no place to ask me that kind of question. You ought to be ashamed. Before I'd be a tool like you, I'd jump in the Hudson River. . . .

WC: Did you bet [with my client] on the 1919 Series?

AR: I made a lot of bets. It's a long time. I'm not sure I remember.

WC: Check your records.

AR: [checks records] Yes.

WC: How much did you bet?

AR: The bet was $25,000.

WC: Then you won $25,000 from [my client] on a Series that was fixed?

AR: I didn't win. I lost.

(Katcher 1959, 199ff.; Alexander 2001, 194).

RISE OF URBAN AMERICA: CITY BOSSES AND URBAN REFORMERS

An American Original: The City Boss

Citing the impact of city bosses on the growth of the American city in the 19th century, urban historian Alexander B. Callow noted in 1976, "The city boss is an American original" (1976, 3). Prominent examples included men like William Magear Tweed and Richard Croker in New York City, George Cox in Cincinnati, Tom Pendergast in Kansas City, "Bathhouse" John Coughlin and "Hinky Dink" Mike Kenna in Chicago, and the list goes on. However, none exemplified the Big City Crime Boss like the New York City bosses.

Prior to the ascendance of the City Boss, urban concerns were the purview of the respectable gentry, or "aristocracy, . . . whose political credentials [were established by] family fame, grandeur of fortune, or eminence as professional, merchant, or businessmen" (Callow 1976, 4). However, they viewed public office a duty rather than a calling, in a time when city services were not a given, but were solely the province of voluntary organizations, policemen, and firemen.

Until the mid-19th century, cities were much smaller and less diverse, both ethnically and racially. However, a curious transformation took hold in the 1850s as the country became more urbanized, and the new urban and industrial society that required new types of city leaders and municipal services. Between 1860 and 1900, urban residents increased from roughly 6 million to more than 30 million. Cities such as Chicago, New York, Philadelphia, and Cleveland saw populations increase exponentially in the 1880s. Chicago doubled in size, whereas New York City increased twice that.

The political system helmed by the City Boss could only have flourished in an era with few civil service rules or social services for the downtrodden. During the 19th century, waves of immigrants flocked to whichever political banners offered jobs and solutions to their social miseries.

In the 1880s, the Democratic ward boss on Manhattan's Lower East Side, George Washington Plunkitt, conducted his business from a bootblack stand outside the New York County Courthouse. Plunkitt is best remembered for coining the term *honest graft*. Testament to his skill in this direction was the receiving of four salaries simultaneously for serving as a magistrate, alderman, county supervisor, and state senator (Mitgang 2000). Writing in 1905, Plunkitt explained,

> It makes me tired to hear of old codgers back in the thirties [1830s] and forties [1840s] boastin' that they retired from politics without a dollar except what they earned in their profession or private business. If they lived today, with all the existen' opportunities, they would be just the same as twentieth century politicians. There ain't any more honest people in the world just now than the convicts in Sing Sing. Not one of them steals anything. Why? Because they can't. . . . The politician who steals is worse than a thief. He is a fool. With the grand opportunities all around for the man with a political pull there's no excuse for stealing a cent. (Riordan 1905, 32)

Plunkitt famously remarked several times, "As for me, I see opportunities and I take them. Honest graft" (Riordan 1905, 32).

Although the Democrats seemed at times to dominate urban corruption in this era, in his 1931 autobiography, Lincoln Steffens (1931) suggested that neither party at the turn of the 20th century had a monopoly on corruption, finding as many corrupt Democrats as Republicans in his peregrinations. As the following examples suggest, urban America at the turn of the 19th century was rife with opportunities for honest graft. In fact, after the jailing of Boss Tweed in the 1870s, a new generation of city bosses sometimes adopted the title *Honest* instead of *Boss*, including "Honest John" O'Neill and "Honest John" Kelly (Mitgang 2000). However, this did not protect them from Tweed's fate in the end.

In 1904, *McClure's Magazine* reporter Lincoln Steffens traveled into the darkest corners of urban America. He emerged with six pieces of reportage that would make up *The Shame of the Cities*, revealing corruption in St. Louis, Minneapolis, Pittsburgh, and Philadelphia, as well as some of the steps taken toward urban reform in New York City and Chicago. He detailed who gave and received bribes, the "managers and protectors of condoned criminality" (Steffens 1968), and revealed the various payment schemes that specific city officials received for favors. In terms of journalism, it was a monumental achievement. However, the articles offered more questions than solutions to these problems.

By the 1920s and 1930s, America's city bosses had changed little. Frank Hague in Jersey City told anyone that would listen, "I am the law," whereas Ed Crump ran Memphis and much of Tennessee from the safe confines of a real estate office. James Michael Curley was even re-elected while ensconced in a Boston jail cell. Huey Long, according to at least one historian, ran Louisiana "like a banana republic," while Tom Pendergast of Kansas City lived to see one of his own men, Harry S. Truman, elected President.

By mid-century, there was little that the remaining city bosses could offer America's immigrants and impoverished that was not available through mammoth social services at most levels of government, courtesy of four decades of social reform. A number of factors contributed to the decline of the "American original," most significant has been the creation of social security and welfare legislation that offers protection against many of the risks posed by the industrial era—protection against work-related accidents, unemployment, old age, and other types of poverty. In times past, the ward boss or other city representatives doled out gratuities while increasing the dependence of these potential voters on the political system. Other observers point to changing immigration patterns and a reduction in urban poverty. Still others invoked the strength of the unions at mid-century, which gave members protection from poor working conditions, low wages, and long hours, improving the lives of workers in ways the city boss could not.

A ROGUES' GALLERY OF BOSSES

New York City: Richard Magear "Boss" Tweed[8]

Richard Magear (not Marcy) Tweed and his association with Tammany Hall have become synonymous with corruption and urban graft, "a metaphor summing up the symbiosis of politics and crime" (Block 1980, 19). Several authorities suggest that he "was the first city politician in the United States to be called Boss" (Ellis 1997, 328; Mitgang 2000, 42). By the age of 50, and only 5 years before his death, Tweed was New York City's third largest landowner; director of the Erie Railway, the Tenth National Bank, and the New York Printing Company; proprietor of the Metropolitan Hotel; and President of the Americus Club. His wealth was estimated in the millions of dollars, including two fancy steam-powered yachts, a mansion, a Greenwich estate, as well as a stickpin valued at $300,000 in 21st-century cash (Ackerman 2005). City officials eventually estimated that during the 3-year apogee of the Tweed "ring," he took $45 million from the city treasury. A recent biographer compared this to "an amount larger than the entire annual U.S. federal budget before the Civil War" (Ackerman 2005, 2).

Similar to the campaigns against other 19th-century city bosses, it was the power of the press that eventually brought down Tweed, as it did most corrupt political machines. Conversely, like many of his counterparts, "he had built as grandly as he'd stolen" (Ackerman 2005, 7). One only need visit the construction of the new Brooklyn Bridge or enjoy the wide paved streets on Broadway and circling Central Park to get a glimpse of this side of the Tweed enigma. Pioneering Tweed historian Alexander Callow noted that the state legislature appropriated more than $2 million for private charities between 1852 and 1869. However, over the next 2 years Tweed surpassed this, wrangling more than $2,225,000 from the state for the same purposes (Callow 1966; Sante 1991).

FIGURE 5.1 Thomas Nast Cartoon Satirizing Boss Tweed
Source: Prentice Hall School Division

FIGURE 5.2   Boss Tweed Coin Bank
Source: Dorling Kindersley Media Library/Chas Howson

Tweed entered New York City's political maelstrom in 1851, losing an election for alderman. The following year he came out on top, and in 1853 he was elected to Congress. When Tweed was elected alderman in 1852, the city council was composed of 20 aldermen and 20 assistant aldermen. Their corruption was so well known they were referred to as the "Forty Thieves." Although aldermen were not paid salaries, they more than made up for it by appointing police officers, awarding saloon licenses, and doling out franchises—all for the right price. Tweed rapidly became bored in the nation's capital and returned to New York. After he declined a nomination for office by the anti-immigrant Know Nothing Party in 1854, he won a following in the growing Irish and German immigrant communities. Between 1856 and 1861, he served on the school commission, as county supervisor, and deputy street commissioner. He left electioneering after losing a sheriff's race and turned to law. He opened an office and began his career using contacts at city hall to "fix problems" for businessmen and others for kickbacks and other forms of reimbursement. By the 1860s, virtually every contractor and merchant who wanted city business had to kick back to Tweed and his compatriots 15% of the total bill, even before the contract was granted (Ackerman 2005).

Tweed was not the first to turn foreigners into citizens so they could vote for the city machine. Fernando Wood had accomplished this years earlier, and as one historian noted, "Plunder of the city treasury, especially in the form of jobbing contracts, was no new thing in New York" (Bryce 1908, 387). The difference with Tweed was that he took the corruption to unimaginable levels.

Come Election Day, Tweed's ward leaders were expected to hire enforcers and arm-breakers to intimidate the city's Republican voters. This, combined with making sure transients and drifters

What Is Tammany Hall?

Founded by William Mooney, a veteran of the American Revolution, Tammany Hall, New York City's headquarters for the Democratic machine, was named after a legendary Delaware Indian Chief Tamenend.[9] According to the popular legend, the Indian chief signed a treaty with William Penn that gave Pennsylvania to the Quakers. The original Tammany Society started as a patriotic club or fraternal organization during the Revolutionary era. Tammany leaders created 13 *tribes*, one in each of the 13 states, and designated their leaders by Indian titles such as *Sachem*, and they referred to their meeting places as *wigwams*. Tammany moved beyond its revolutionary roots and threw its considerable influence into political campaigns during the early 19th century. In its heyday, *Tammany Hall* actually referred to two separate entities that combined ran the city's Democratic Party. One was a social organization made up of clubs dispersed throughout New York City. This arm was responsible for filling the needs of citizens at the community level. The other was a political organization, or the New York County Democratic committee. In all practicality, the second organization was the seat of power. Tweed managed to control both, allowing him to control both party patronage and elections. Following Tweed's death, Tammany managed to regain its position in the New York City power structure and remained a force into the 1960s.

voted several times each, usually insured a Tammany victory. In the process, these voters became known as *Tweed repeaters* (Ackerman 2005). Judges appointed by Tweed assisted by naturalizing thousands of new immigrant voters if they promised to vote Democratic.

Tweed indulged in a variety of rackets. During the Civil War, if one story is to be believed, he purchased 300 benches at $5 each, and then turned around and authorized the city to buy them back from him at $600 each (Ackerman 2005, 29). Another report indicated that the Tweed administration paid $10,000 for $75 worth of pencils. Luc Sante, in his magisterial history of New York City's "low life," reported that members of the "Tweed Ring" supported a Zachariah Simmons, who "ran about three-quarters of the six hundred or seven hundred [policy] operations in the city at that time and opened franchises as far west as Milwaukee" in the aftermath of the Civil War (Sante 1991, 155). Tweed's most egregious spending was lavished on a new courthouse behind City Hall, which still stands today—testament to his avarice. Tweed wasted more than $12 million on it, including almost $2 million on a $50,000 plastering job and close to $7 million on furniture and decorations (Sante 1991, 264).

During Tweed's 1873 trial, he admitted in detail how he bribed state political figures, rigged elections, skimmed money from municipal contractors, and methodically diverted funds from the city treasury into his own pockets. However, his contributions to the city poor in the form of new hospitals, orphanages, schools, churches, and public works projects did not go unforgotten. He has been even credited with devising an extralegal "social security program" in which he doled out $1,000 to each alderman, who in turn was expected to deliver it to indigent constituents (Sante 1991). It should be no less surprising then, that after Tweed's ignominious demise that representatives of the dispossessed responded to the effect, "Well, if Tweed stole, he was at least good to the poor" (Sante 1991, 265).

Recent scholarship has attempted to separate Tweed from the other members of the so-called Tweed Ring, instead arguing that the Boss never controlled this group, who were simply political hucksters and racketeers in their own right (Hershkowitz 1977; Ackerman 2005). Tweed's reign also coincided with the "Gilded Age," a corrupt era that produced "Robber Barons" and built also on the patterns of corruption that already existed in New York City for generations (Ackerman 2005, 357). Much of the blame for creating this shadow over Tweed was his omnipresence over Tammany and the power of newspapers to manipulate public perceptions. Political cartoonist Thomas Nast's crusade against city racketeering was an almost unrelenting chronicle of New York City graft, personified by hundreds of caricatures of Boss Tweed. In an interview from his jail cell,

Tweed told one reporter, "If I could have bought newspapermen as easily as I did members of the Legislature, I wouldn't be in the fix I am now" (Ackerman 2005, 359).

Boss Tweed surely was corrupt—he bribed state legislators, fixed elections, skimmed money from city contractors, and diverted public funds on an unprecedented scale. He controlled the police, judges, mayors, and governors. Tweed was the last of the Protestant Tammany leaders. He was followed by a succession of Irish-American Catholic politicians (Raab 2005). As his most recent biographer has concluded, "Tweed didn't invent civic corruption or ballot-box stuffing, but he and the Tammany crowd elevated the techniques to stunning proportions" (Ackerman 2005, 356).

A Day in the Life of a Tammany Boss

2 A.M.: Aroused from sleep by the ringing of his doorbell; went to the door and found a bartender, who asked him to go to the police station and bail out a saloonkeeper who had been arrested for violating the excise law. Furnished bail and returned to bed at three o'clock.

6 A.M.: Awakened by fire engines passing his house. Hastened to the scene of the fire, according to the custom of the Tammany district leaders, to give assistance to the fire sufferers, if needed. Met several of his election district captains who are always under orders to look out for fires, which are considered great vote-getters. Found several tenants who had been burned out, took them to a hotel, supplied them with clothes, fed them, and arranged temporary quarters for them until they could rent and furnish new apartments.

8:30 A.M.: Went to the police court to look after his constituents. Found six "drunks." Secured the discharge of four by a timely word with the judge, and paid the fines of two.

9 A.M.: Appeared in the Municipal District Court. Directed one of his district captains to act as counsel for a widow against whom dispossess proceedings had been instituted and obtained an extension of time. Paid the rent of a poor family about to be dispossessed and gave them a dollar for food.

11 A.M.: At home again. Found four men waiting for him. One had been discharged by the Metropolitan Railway Company for neglect of duty, and wanted the district leader [boss] to fix things. Another wanted a job on the road. The third sought a place on the Subway and the fourth, a plumber, was looking for work with the Consolidated Gas Company. The district leader spent nearly three hours fixing things for the four men, and succeeded in each case.

3 P.M.: Attended the funeral of an Italian as far as the ferry. Hurried back to make his appearance at the funeral of a Hebrew constituent. Went conspicuously to the front both in the Catholic Church and the synagogue, and later attended the Hebrew confirmation ceremonies in the synagogue.

7 P.M.: Went to district headquarters and presided over a meeting of election district captains. Each captain submitted a list of all voters in his district, reported on their attitude toward Tammany, suggested who might be won over and how they could be won, told who were in need, and who were in trouble of any kind and the best way to reach them. District leader took notes and gave orders.

8 P.M.: Went to a church fair. Took chances on everything, bought ice cream for the young girls and the children. Kissed the little ones, flattered their mothers and took their fathers out for something down at the corner.

9 P.M.: At the clubhouse again. Spent $10 on tickets for a church excursion and promised a subscription for a new church bell. Bought tickets for a baseball game to be played by two nines from his district. Listened to the complaints of a dozen pushcart peddlers who said they were prosecuted by the police and assured them he would go to Police Headquarters in the morning and see about it.

10:30 P.M.: Attended a Hebrew wedding reception and dance. Had previously sent a handsome wedding present to the bride.

12 A.M.: In bed.

Record of an actual day in the life of ex-Senator and Tammany leader of the Fifteenth district, George Washington Plunkitt, at the turn of the 20th century. Passage from *Plunkitt of Tammany Hall*, pp. 91–93, 1963 edition.

Cincinnati: George B. Cox

George B. Cox (1853–1916) was the political boss of Cincinnati between 1904 and 1912, presiding over what muckraking journalist Lincoln Steffens called "one great graft" and "the most perfect thing of the kind in this country" (Miller 1968, 823). Another critic called Cox "The Biggest Boss of Them All," describing the Cox machine as "more compact and closely knit than any of the political; machines which have dominated New York, Philadelphia, Chicago, St. Louis or San Francisco" (Miller 1968, 823). Hyperbole or not, Cox was surely one of the late 19th and early 20th centuries' most powerful city bosses.

Born in 1853, Cox matriculated through a variety of urban occupations, rising from bootblack and newsboy to lookout at a gambling joint, bartender, and tobacco salesman. By the early 1870s, Cox had saved enough money to purchase a Cincinnati saloon in the "Dead Man's Corner" neighborhood, so-named for its numerous unsolved murders. As a saloon owner, traditional mainstay of the 19th-century political landscape, Cox rode his prominence into politics, serving two stints on the Cincinnati city council, beginning in 1879. By most accounts Cox explained that he sought city office so he could suppress police raids on his bar. Coincidentally or not, police raids on his establishment ended with his election to city office (Miller 1968). However, after several failed campaigns for higher office, Cox decided his future lay in working on the periphery of politics as a power broker.

Cox was a stalwart Republican in an age of Democratic bosses. By the turn of the 20th century, Cox had been able to get a number of his "clients" elected to higher city offices, including the police judge. Although Cox ended his political aspirations as far as holding office, he remained chair of the county Republican Committee, which allowed him to preside as "City Boss." Anyone seeking political office in Cincinnati needed Cox's endorsement. Of course, this could be purchased for cash and gifts. Once in office, these candidates were then expected to appoint Cox supporters to fill other city positions, including policemen, firemen, street cleaners, secretaries, and other positions.

Cox reached outside his party in 1905 by appointing Democrats to almost 40% of the municipal offices; in return, these appointees were expected to kickback 2.5% of their salaries to the Republican Committee. Cox used this money to buy votes on Election Day. When the vote was too close to call, the ever-prescient Cox paid residents from other states to come to Cincinnati to vote illegally (Miller 1968). Voters were encouraged to cast their votes more than once for his candidate using false names as well. Cox also allowed prostitution and gambling establishments to operate openly, as long as their owners supported his machine. However, he allowed only a limited number of individuals to control these operations. Not unlike his counterparts in other cities, Cox could point to improvements in his city funded by his political machine, offering some improved city services such as street cleaning.

Cox's power eroded as the city annexed surrounding communities. Many of the new constituents were middle class and opposed to machine politics. The ascendance of Progressive reformers also turned the tide away from vice districts and toward more traditional and moral values. In the end, the avalanche of new voters, uncontrolled by Boss Cox, led to his candidate for mayor being rejected, and by 1911, Cox had lost his power base and he retired from the political arena.

Chicago: Michael "Hinky Dink" Kenna and John "Bathhouse" Coughlin

In the words of one perceptive urban historian, "Crime and politics were wedded in unholy matrimony on the spit of land" (Smith 1954, 20) that would eventually be home to Chicago, one of the nation's most storied cities. For much of the 19th century, Chicago's "underworld, its police, and its politicians were dominated by one man" (Smith 1954, 20)—the city boss. Two of its earliest exemplars were First Ward committeeman Michael "Hinky Dink" Kenna (1869–1938) and Alderman John "Bathhouse" Coughlin (1857–1946).[10] To understand the Chicago system of politics, one must acknowledge its peculiar ward system. The city is carved up into 50 wards and 3,000 voting precincts (Russo 2001). The main players of the ward are the aldermen, who are elected, and the committeemen, who are appointed. Although the alderman performs a multiplicity of traditional duties—voting on ordinances and budgets, acting as legislator—it is the committeeman who offers "a powerfully seductive invitation to corruption" (Russo 2001, 14).

Like most metropolitan cities of the post–Civil War era, Chicago offered a segregated vice district. The "Levee," on the city's South Side, had been expanded and redistricted over time, eventually becoming the nation's largest *tenderloin district*, so named because the choicest cuts of graft were available here. One authority suggested that the Levee and the prostitution trade grew due to the presence of six railroad depots in the area, which in fact insured a steady stream of potential clients (Pacyga 1986). The denizens of the Levee included gamblers, prostitutes, thugs, pickpockets, pimps (known as *cadets*), and customers looking for excitement. According to one crime commission estimate, in 1910, prostitution grossed $30 million annually, with half going into the pockets of politicians and police (Johnson and Sautter 1998, 8).

Kenna and Coughlin earned the sobriquet "Lords of the Levee." Chicago crime historian Gus Russo asserts that they were "among the earliest architects of political corruption [in Chicago and] set the standard and constructed the template for all the official chicanery that would follow" (Russo 2001, 15). Through their control of the First Ward vote, they were able to offer protection to all comers. With their almost total control over city jobs and the police force, no one would challenge the bosses. They acted as patrons to clients in almost every city, county, and state office, and controlled the dispensing of jobs to city workers, including the postmaster and the police. By paying the duo thousands of dollars, any financier or politician could be assured that for the right price, the aldermen would get the vote out for their clients on election day. Whether a businessman needed a permit, a zoning variance, a tax reduction, or city services, he knew he could purchase it from the bosses of the Levee. By most accounts, Kenna and Coughlin never lost an election in 40 years. Kenna served as First Ward Committeeman for 49 years, and reportedly "spent his last days guarded by police and the mob both, compulsively counting and hiding coins in his hotel room lest they be stolen" (Merriner 2004, 69).

The bosses worked a variety of voting scams that ensured the votes for their candidates and proposals. For $0.50 a vote and several days of room and board, on election day, Democratic Party workers marched the flotsam and jetsam of the First Ward and its Levee district to the polls, including "railroad hands, stevedores, tramps, thugs, thieves, cadets, rounders, and other warm bodies that might be available" (Merriner 2004; Johnson and Sautter 1998, 10). All of the voters had already been provided with stolen ballots marked for their candidates. After this army of "floaters" turned in their ballots, they left the polling places with the new empty ballots that were given them to vote on entering. They then took the second ballot to another polling place and repeated the procedure.

Two of the Levee bosses' "collectors," Mont Tennes and Jim Colosimo, would build on the foundations of organized crime set by Kenna and Coughlin. In the 1920s, they extended organized crime's "tentacles beyond anything as parochial as the vision of Bathhouse and the Little Fellow" (Russo 2001, 16). It was Colosimo that the two turned to when they decided to look outside the Irish neighborhoods for votes, and thus paved the way for bringing Italian-Americans into Chicago's next chapter of corruption and graft.

New Orleans: Martin Behrman

Until the ascendance of Huey Long, no one dominated New Orleans politics like Martin Behrman did between 1900 and the 1920s. Behrman's biographer asserted that as New Orleans mayor, Behrman "controlled almost every aspect" of its political life (Kemp 1981, 170). During this period he was elected mayor five times, dying in office in 1926. According to one historian, Behrman's first election in 1904 "was the beginning of 16 years of uninterrupted Tammany Hall–styled machine politics in New Orleans" (Kemp 1981, 158). The New Orleans *Times-Democrat* (later *Picayune*) became one of his most prominent critics. That same year, one editorial strongly opposed

Times-Picayune editorial, January 15, 1920

Under TWENTY YEARS OF RING RULE, this crawling, fetid, contaminating monster of the UNDER-WORLD, has grown and grown, poisoning and corrupting all it touches. It has spread beyond the city. It has planted its cancerous colonies of lechery and vice across the city lines—reached out to spew its venom in the faces of Jefferson and St. Bernard! "The UNDERWORLD" of Orleans, Jefferson, and St. Bernard ARE ONE! And the "underworld" LIVES AND THRIVES under RING RULE.

his bid for mayor, stating that Behrman "represents the very elements that would assure misgovernment of the city and seriously hinder and check its prosperity," adding,

> When New Orleans falls into the hands of the ring, when the arch masters of the politicians, the bosses, get possession of its government and administer it in the interest of ward workers, hangers on and all of the others of the great army of janissaries who make up the machine, it suffers in every department, in every branch of government and in its business as well. (Quoted in Kemp 1981, 158)

Behrman represented the Regular Democratic Organization (RDO), which was also known in New Orleans as the *Choctaw Club, the Ring, machine*, and *Regulars*. After 1922, it became known as the Old Regulars, representing members from the entire spectrum of the working populace—from laborers and salesmen to lawyers and bankers—all of whom had a stake in the success of the Democratic machine.

During the 1930s, a Columbia University graduate student noted that the machine's secret of success was the "simplicity of its structure" and the political patronage system of that era (quoted in Kemp 1981, 158–159). According to George M. Reynolds, the RDO was composed of a caucus and a club. The *caucus*, or "ruling body of the machine" (quoted in Kemp 1981, 159), was made up of the city's 17 ward leaders. They made up the "Council of Seventeen" that made all of the decisions regarding who ran for office with RDO support (Kemp 1981). It was in this manner that each Ward boss selected his precinct captains and doled out his considerable political patronage.

The RDO machine became little more than a cooperative of ward bosses who selected precinct captains and distributed political favors. The precinct clubs made up the foundation of the political machine. Precinct leaders were expected to turn out the vote on election days. Thanks to their local knowledge, these leaders were able to inform the RDO on local problems and issues, and who needed a job or a loan. In this way, precinct leaders knew what script had to be written to win the votes.

The RDO was an expensive organization. Members of the organization were expected to pay dues of $1 per month. All city employees had to belong. If anyone developed the urge to seek elected office with the support of the RDO, they were expected to kickback 10% of their salary once they won office. Major contributors to the RDO treasury included gambling proprietors and brothel madams (Kemp 1981). By most accounts, most of the city's liquor, gambling, and prostitution racketeers made payments to the RDO political machine (Vyhnanek 1998).

As mayor and city boss, Martin Behrman made sure the RDO enjoyed support of both the under and upper worlds. This was not uncommon. Historians chronicled how city bosses in San Francisco (Boss Abraham Ruef), Cincinnati (Cox), and St. Louis ("Colonel" Ed Butler), for example, maintained professional lives aside from political office—often as corporate presidents or directors (Kemp 1981; Zink 1930).

By the onset of Prohibition, New Orleans' newspapers and reformers were well into a campaign to diminish the power of the RDO Behrman machine. One opponent campaigned on a platform that promised public decency and free progress, while charging the Mayor with supporting "public vice, political bossdom and social and civil stagnation" (Kemp 1981, 162). Supporters of the opponent referred to Behrman as the "King of the Tenderloin" (referring to Storyville and the French Quarter). Leading papers carried front-page attacks based on Behrman's sordid record and affinity for protecting vice rackets. One newspaper even accused police officers of being staked out in vice establishments with the understanding they would protect gamblers and other members of the city's criminal milieu. Behrman would later write in his autobiography that he "didn't have enough time to go around investigating such foolishness" (quoted in Kemp 1981, 163).

Kansas City: Jim (1856–1911) and Tom Pendergast (1872–1945)

Except for New York City's Tammany Hall, no American political machine exceeded the continuity and unabashed power of Kansas City's Pendergast machine. In its heyday, the Pendergast syndicate controlled virtually every element of Kansas City organized crime. Born in Gallipolis, Ohio, in 1856, Jim Pendergast, the son of Irish immigrants, found himself penniless in Kansas City by the late 1870s. His fortunes changed when he won large on a long shot at the racetrack in 1881 and invested in a *barrelhouse*, a combination hotel–saloon business in the West Bottoms vicinity, not far from the Missouri River. Not surprisingly he named it after the winning horse—Climax.

Jim Pendergast entered the saloon business at a propitious time, when the growing city of 57,000 easily supported close to 200 drinking establishments (Steinberg 1972). It wasn't long before Jim branched out from the traditional hospitality business and began finding jobs for the unemployed, supplying food and clothing to the local indigent, and cashing checks without charge. According to one biographer, "there never was a winter in the last 20 years that he did not circulate among the poor of the West Bottoms, ascertaining their needs, and after his visit there were no empty larders" (quoted in Dorsett 1968, 21; quoted in May 2006, 25). In 1884, Jim gravitated to politics, successfully supporting a local mayoral candidate by getting out the vote. He branched out into party politics in county elections, and in 1892 was elected as alderman, besting his Republican opponent 5–1 in votes. He continually won re-election for the next 18 years. The local *Kansas City Star* awarded him the sobriquet "King of the First [Ward]" that would identify him until his death. It wasn't long until he expanded his power into the Second Ward as well.

Pendergast never forgot where he came from or where he was going. His popularity with the average workingman stemmed from his crusade to lower telephone rates, opposition to wage cuts for firemen, and the construction of a new city park. Like most drawn to political power, he also threw his lot in with local gamblers and was known to put up bond when bunco artists were jailed. Gambling was popular among his West Bottoms constituents, and his saloon could be counted on to act as a bank on payday for the hundreds of railroad and packinghouse workers, especially if they spent it in his gambling rooms upstairs (May 2006).

In 1892, the King of the First Ward closed his saloon, preferring to maintain his hotel separately. However, he wasn't done with the saloon business, subsequently opening two more, replete with upstairs gambling dens. Pendergast's power was such that when one of his gambling parlors was raided, he was able to go to the Missouri governor and have the Kansas City Police Chief replaced with a friendlier face. Despite a crusade by the local press and reform organizations to suppress gambling, Pendergast's clout ensured that only token cursory raids took place.

Pendergast's growing power coincided with the newspapers referring to him as "Boss Pendergast." Pendergast reportedly responded to the accusations with a succinct definition of political patronage, asserting, "I've been called a boss. All there is to it is having friends, doing things for people, and then later on they'll do things for you" (Dorsett 1968, 25; quoted in May 2006, 25). In the shifting tides of the late 1890s, Jim built a power base in the rapidly expanding North End, home to Little Italy and a new power elite that controlled gambling and liquor activities in that area. In 1898, he attempted to organize the Italian vote for the first time. He then targeted the Black vote by insinuating a vote for his candidate would lift police pressures in the community. Jim continued to solidify his power, and with it dispensing patronage jobs. No city position exemplified this practice more than the police force, where between 1900 and 1902 he appointed all but 50 of the 173 police officers.

Forced into a power-sharing arrangement in 1904 and with his health and power in decline, Jim increasingly relied on his younger brother and First Ward heir Thomas. Fortunately, he had brought his younger brothers Tom, Mike, and John into the fold in the 1890s. Tom worked as a cashier and bookkeeper in Jim's first saloon. Although all of the brothers played important roles in the machine, Jim would pass the reins to Tom, who "would make the machine the stuff of legend," and under whose direction would make "the Pendergast name synonymous with political corruption" (May 2006, 3). Posing as a successful businessman, Tom ran Kansas City and the political machine like a large corporation. Tom came to prominence in 1900, after he was selected as the Superintendent of Streets, a position that controlled 200 workers and the finances to supply materials for street paving, a lucrative patronage post indeed.

Sixteen years younger than his older brother, Thomas Joseph, or T. J., eschewed political office, preferring to run things from the safety of his position as head of the Democratic Party. Tom proved more than adept at using subterfuge and illegal voting strategies to put his men in office. Tom and Jim were a contrast in styles—Jim preferring persuasion to Tom's use of physical force. Jim once told his younger brother, "a saw was needed to shape wood, not a hammer" (quoted in Dorsett 1968; quoted in May 2006).

Jim left public office in 1910 due to ill health and died the following year. Tom won his seat as alderman. By 1910, Boss Tom was in control of the Jackson County Democratic Club and combined with the financial support of the local crime syndicate Pendergast was free to dispense protection to mobsters in the form of handpicking prosecutors and local judges. By most accounts, Tom controlled a number of illegal gambling parlors, the Riverside Race Track, and other properties.

During Prohibition, gambling and speakeasies flourished. By getting out the vote, often at close to 100%, and keeping his friends in office, Pendergast-controlled companies won sweetheart building contracts without bidding competition. Like his counterparts in other cities, T. J. could boast about his civic accomplishments, particularly in the dark days of the 1930s, when his support for the passage of a $40 million bond program led to a construction binge employing hundreds during the Depression. Pendergast is often credited with presiding over an era of unparalleled building construction in Kansas City.

For more than 30 years, T. J. ruled his machine from a simple, two-story yellow brick building at 1908 Main Street (Fox, 1989). Pendergast is probably most widely known for his early support of Harry S. Truman, who was derisively referred to as "the Senator from Pendergast" (Ferrell 1996, 124). Yet he must have been a shrewd judge of talent, as the unsuccessful haberdasher's son won a Senate seat in 1934 leading to the vice presidency under Franklin D. Roosevelt, and ultimately to almost two terms as president.[11]

During the 1920s, the ethnic composition of the city's north side made the transition from Irish to mostly Italian. Although the Italians had no problem prospering with the Pendergast machine, they insisted on their own ward leaders. It was at this point that Johnny Lazia rose to prominence. Born in the Little Italy neighborhood in 1897, by the late 1920s he was ready to challenge Pendergast protégé Mike Ross for the North End rackets. Pendergast had no choice but to provide him police protection in return for some of Lazia's bootlegging and gambling rackets. However, Lazia's greatest asset was getting out the Italian vote for the Pendergast candidates on election day. Although there had been an Italian organized crime presence in Kansas City since the onset of Prohibition, Lazia is credited with organizing the local rackets. According to mob historian Stephen Fox, "Under Pendergast by way of Lazia, Kansas City became an open town, a bigger, brassier

Backgrounds of Noted City Bosses

Boss	City	Nationality/Ancestry	Party
Abe Ruef	San Francisco	French-Jewish	Republican
Martin Behrman	New Orleans	German-Jewish	Democrat
George Cox	Cincinnati	English	Republican
William Tweed	New York City	Scots	Democrat
Michael Kenna	Chicago	Irish-Catholic	Democrat
John Coughlin	Chicago	Irish-Catholic	Democrat
Ed Vare	Philadelphia		Republican
Tom Pendergast	Kansas City	Irish-Catholic	Democrat

version of Hot Springs" (Fox 1989, 250). In 1934, while waiting for sentencing for a tax evasion case, Lazia was murdered.

Tom Pendergast reigned supreme until 1939, when he was convicted of tax evasion and sentenced to a year in prison, signaling the end of the family political machine. By the time he was released on probation in 1940, he had less than 5 years to live. It's doubtful that without his traditional power base that he would have wanted to live any longer in any case. Tom Pendergast left a mixed legacy as Kansas City political boss. Under his watch, the city became home to a growing legion of gangsters. At the same time, his influence and patronage helped the city survive the Great Depression and Prohibition eras. Harry S. Truman was among the mourners at the boss's funeral, despite warnings and pleadings from his aides to stay away.

GOVERNMENT CORRUPTION AT THE HIGHEST LEVEL

It would be disingenuous to suggest that corruption and criminal behavior has been solely the province of the city bosses. There is more than enough documentation to demonstrate these pursuits at every level of the government. More than a quarter century ago, William Chambliss wrote, "presidents, vice presidents, congressmen, senators, governors, and racketeers are implicated in a ubiquitous system of payoffs and favors, back-scratching, stealing, illegal campaign contributions, and personal aggrandizements" (Chambliss 1982, x). However, seldom has the highest office been targeted by law enforcement agencies. Since the administration of George Washington, presidents have used their offices to line their coffers and personal fortune (Chambliss 1982, 177). A number of scholars examined politicians "on the take," chronicling corruption schemes in various presidencies, including those of Martin Van Buren and Warren Harding (Chambliss 1982). However, none has been vilified as much as the Grant Presidency of 1868–1876. In his first term, his vice president was charged with collaborating with Union Pacific Railway officials in a plan to inveigle government bonds in what became memorialized as the Credit Mobilier scandal. However, it would be Grant's second term that would set the bar for corruption and fraud in the corridors of the nation's highest office, leading to the resignation of Grant's secretary of war and the indictment of Grant's personal secretary (Chambliss 1978; McFeely 1981; Miller 1998).

The Whiskey Ring (1875)

General John McDonald was convicted in 1875 for his role in the Whiskey Ring tax evasion conspiracy. McDonald would pen his account of the scandal after spending 18 months in the state penitentiary in Jefferson City, Missouri.[12] McDonald never wavered from his impression that the president was involved, writing, "I have briefly sketched in a hurried manner, the principal facts

> No ring was ever before formed embracing such a gigantic scope and membership, such distinguished Government officials. The original intention of the organizers, adopting from the highest authority in the land, was to make the ring co-extensive with the nation, with headquarters in all the large cities, for the purpose of raising a campaign fund with which to advance the interests of President Grant in his aspirations for a second term. (McDonald 1880, 17)

proving the connection of President U.S. Grant [and others] with the conspiracy organized in 1870 to defraud the Government out of the revenue on distilled spirits" (McDonald 1880, 337). Between 1870 and 1872, the tax would have been $0.50 per gallon on proof spirits, and would increase to $0.70 per gallon the following year. McDonald's district was in Missouri, where eight of the distilleries produced 9,600 proof gallons per day. McDonald calculated that the government was defrauded out of $2,786,000 in his district alone over a 6-year period (McDonald 1880, 338).

This scandal during the administration of President U.S. Grant was considered one the century's greatest political scandals. It further demonstrated that political corruption, which had been formerly considered a municipal phenomenon, could take place even in the highest levels of government. The plot revolved around the re-election of Grant. The conspirators included corrupt members of the Internal Revenue Service and a consortium of western whiskey distillers. The participants of the "Whiskey Ring" were charged with trying to evade the whisky tax. When these revelations were made public, more than 200 individuals were indicted—almost half would be convicted. During the trial, it was revealed how these unpaid taxes were used to help re-elect Grant to a second term in 1872. More money was being put aside for a third run in 1876. By most accounts, the president was not involved. In any case, as historian Nathan Miller noted, "The exposure of the 'Whiskey Ring' finally brought the dirty linen into the White House" (Miller 1998, 125), tarnishing the office and its occupants with the same dirty brush. Miller reported an anecdote by Bill Moyers, who commenting on the glum-looking photographic legacy of Grant, famously responded, "If you had his friends, you'd look glum too" (Miller 1998, 107).

URBAN ORGANIZED CRIME ORIGINS

Chicago

Local Indians referred to what would become America's "Second City"[13] as *Chicagou*, meaning "bad smell" or "stinking place" (Lewis and Smith 1929, 4).[14] In any case, the Indian term is loaded with sagacity, considering the city's reputation for corruption and criminality. Historian Perry R. Duis suggested, "Probably no other city in America has labored more than Chicago under a worldwide impression that it was filled with violence and crime" (Asbury 1986, xiii). Beginning as a frontier town in the 1830s and 1840s, by the end of the 1850s, visitors were well warned to be vigilant or avoid the city. Books such as *Tricks and Traps of Chicago* (1859), *Chicago after Dark* (1868), and later, *If Christ Came to Chicago* (1894) contributed to the growing apprehension with which travelers approached Chicago.

In the 1860s, Chicago was accorded the distinction of "the wickedest city in the United States" (Asbury 1986, 61). This was in no small part due to the almost utter lack of law enforcement. Due to the exigencies of the Civil War, the city was an easy lure for thousands of soldiers. By most accounts, English immigrant Roger Plant was the first prominent Chicago gang boss. A destination point for 10 railroads, by the mid-1850s the city had established itself as an important commercial depot (Russo 2005). Plant took advantage of the opportunities afforded by a growing city crowded with mostly young male adventure seekers. The foundation of his criminal empire was a two-story combination saloon, and living quarters that was known as "Under the Willow." Together with his wife, the Plants operated a 24-hour brothel containing 200 prostitutes. According to popular true crime writer Jay Robert

Nash, a blue curtain fronted each of the building's windows with the phrase "Why not?" painted on it. He suggested that, "this later became a catch phrase in U.S. bordellos" (Nash 1992, 323).

Roger Plant also established another Chicago custom by keeping the police on the *pad*, or his payroll, for 20 years. Despite pressure from civic groups to close down his establishment over the years, Plant's operations flourished in a labyrinth of underground tunnels. As legend has it, the growing criminal classes were skilled here in the criminal arts—picking pockets and fighting. Due to its location beneath the streets of Chicago, some began to refer to it as the *underworld*, an appellation that became synonymous for criminal gangs and organized crime over the ensuing decades (Nash 1992). By the late 1860s, Plant had socked away enough lucre to retire and make the transition from crime boss to country squire. His son and daughters carried the father's business into the 1890s.

"BIG MIKE" MCDONALD AND IRISH PRIMACY   Born in New York in 1839, "Big Mike" McDonald left home in his teens, for what today we would call to "find himself." He found himself working on the railroad in New Orleans. A den of gamblers and iniquity, McDonald was soon in their thrall. Having passed through Chicago several years earlier, he quickly understood "that the New Orleans model could be adapted" (English 2005, 73) to such a rapidly growing town. A prime example of "Big Mike's" business acumen was his creation of a bounty jumping racket in Chicago in the 1860s. During the Civil War, those who could afford it paid hundreds of dollars to usually poor Irish immigrants willing to accept the risks of the trade-off. McDonald organized a scam in which army deserters reenlisted and deserted over and over again, accepting a bounty each time. The bounty jumpers then split the commission with McDonald each time he assisted them in the process. During the 1860s, the city was awash in vice, including an estimated 2,000 street walkers in the downtown area alone (Smith 1954).

McDonald, according to one mob historian, "was the first true crime lord" (Russo 2001, 10), and by supporting winning candidates for mayor and other offices in the 1870s he became the first underworld figure "to recognize the importance of the political fix" (Russo 2001, 10).[15] By getting the vote out for his candidates for mayor and other offices on election day, he was rewarded with exclusive rights for certain gambling activities. Although he never held political office, Gus Russo noted that his gambling headquarters, The Store, was regarded as the city's unofficial City Hall. Known for his rabid dislike of policemen, legend has it that when he was asked by two policemen to make a $2 donation to bury a cop, McDonald replied, "Here's ten dollars. Bury five of them" (Russo 2001, 10–11).

By most accounts, McDonald was the first underworld boss to use the term *syndicate* when referring to a criminal organization (Russo 2001, 11). After several reversals, McDonald, flush with millions of dollars, retired from the scene in the early 1890s. In the last decades of the 19th century, Chicago underwent a metamorphosis from swampy frontier town to burgeoning "Second City." By 1900, the city boasted a population of more than 2 million, including numerous immigrants—Germans, Swedes, Jews, and Italians—each gravitating to their own communities. With close to 1,100 police officers for 2 million citizens and literally dozens of polyglot neighborhoods, the city became home to numerous vice districts.

BIRTH OF THE CHICAGO OUTFIT   In the 1930s, Chicago's Outfit had already become quite distinct from its New York City counterpart. One authority suggested that the Chicago syndicate eschewed the "elaborate ritual and internecine rivalry" (Russo 2001, 2) in order to avoid the spotlight that prevailed during the days of Al Capone. By most accounts, there is no consensus as to the origins of the moniker *The Outfit*. One Chicago gang expert has most recently argued that this expression for the Chicago Mob originated in the 1950s and "became popular some time later" (Binder 2003, 7).

When McDonald left the scene, gambler extraordinaire Jacob "Mont" Tennes inherited most of his operations. Tennes was already well known in the North Side milieu, but it was not until the early 1900s that he achieved citywide prominence. Throughout parts of the next two decades, Tennes had a virtual lock on the city's gambling rackets. The 1929, the *Illinois Crime Survey* asserted that he "maintained his position of dominance in the gambling fraternity by his control of the direct news from the tracks" (1929, 278).

Tennes, who is a forgotten figure in Chicago criminal annals compared to the more colorful Al Capone, Johnny Torrio, and Jim Colosimo, was every bit as influential in his heyday. No less an arbiter of 1920s crime than the 1929 *Illinois Crime Survey* suggested that "the complete life history of one man, were it known in every detail, would disclose practically all there is to know about syndicated gambling as a phase of organized crime in Chicago in the last quarter century. That man is Mont Tennes" (1929, 45).[16] By 1911, Tennes had risen from Chicago gambling king to "czar of all the race track gambling in the United States and Canada" (*Illinois Crime Survey* 1929, 59). Tennes retired from the rackets in the mid-1920s, only a step or two ahead of assassins and the judicial system.

The roots of modern organized crime in Chicago can be traced back to Tennes and the emergence of James "Big Jim" Colosimo in the 1890s, when he forged a gangster syndicate that became the most powerful prior to Prohibition. A native of southern Italy, Colosimo arrived in Chicago in 1894, where he found work digging ditches before gravitating to minor criminal activity. One Outfit historian explained the trajectory of his career as "graduating to Black Handing, moving quickly up the crime evolutionary ladder to the far more lucrative position of *ruffiano:* a pimp" (Russo 2001, 16). Colosimo had other flings with respectability—shoveling manure behind horse-drawn wagons, labor foreman, and union leader—none of which presaged his rise to gangland czar.

"Big Jim's" road to notoriety began when he came to the attention of Chicago's Irish political bosses—Michael "Hinky Dink" Kenna and John "Bathhouse" Coughlin. Anyone who could get the vote out on Election Day was a precious commodity, no matter his ethnicity. His work for the bosses became a steppingstone to becoming the city's vice lord. More important, according to Outfit historian Gus Russo, his ascendance was the first time an Italian American was brought into the game of political patronage in Chicago. Another Chicago mob authority insists that Colosimo's "multi-ethnic organized crime conglomerate served as the blueprint for the Torrio–Capone mob and the Outfit" (Binder 2003, 11). Colosimo carved his way into the top echelons of Chicago crime in a succession of positions for his Irish benefactors—running a saloon, collecting payoffs, and operating a gambling parlor.

In the course of his career, "Big Jim" cultivated an identity and style that would live on in the popular imagination as a sort of "mobster chic," which consisted of elaborate diamond ensembles, white linen suits, and a wide-brimmed hat. He came under the scrutiny of various Black Hand extortion rings and needed protection not from the law, but from his fellow thugs. In 1909, he imported his wife's nephew, Johnny Torrio, from Brooklyn to help protect his interests. By bringing in Torrio, he unknowingly had sown the seeds for his own demise.

In appreciation for fending off the extortionists, Torrio was placed in charge of a brothel and other operations. Torrio proved to be one of the most adept crime bosses in American history, and is sometimes credited as one of the fathers of modern organized crime. With the onset of Prohibition, Torrio grasped the new opportunities, but had one barrier to surmount before turning to bootlegging—"Big Jim." Like his cousin before him, Torrio looked to New York for help, and in 1919 summoned his pal Alphonse "Al Brown" Capone. Capone's life is perhaps the most documented of any gangster's, but at this point, he was only a hired gun and chauffeur to Torrio. Despite entreaties by Torrio to get on the Prohibition bandwagon, Colosimo desisted and forbade Torrio from becoming involved.

On May 11, 1920, just 3 days after marrying his teenage sweetheart, Colosimo was ambushed and killed in the lobby of his restaurant. Despite the interrogation of more than 30 suspects, the crime was never solved. Among mob historians and police officials, however, the consensus was that Torrio brought in an outside killer from New York—probably Frankie Yale, although others suggest that it was Capone (Russo 2001).

Torrio set out to create a bootlegging empire on the foundations laid by Colosimo, and immediately set on forging a bootlegging syndicate with other like-minded gangs. However, his attempts became bogged down in inter-gang bloodshed, especially with the Irish gang run by Dean O'Banion, who was famously killed in his flower shop on November 10, 1924.[17] Within 2 months, Torrio barely survived an ambush in retaliation. Lucky to be alive, he left town and turned the organization over to Al Capone. The gang war that followed the death of O'Banion and the attempted killing of Torrio took dozens of lives.

FIGURE 5.3   Rare View of Al Capone's Left Cheek with Scar
Source: Dorling Kimbersley Media Library

A Capone Chronology[18]

1899—January 18: Born in New York
1913—Leaves school to work for John Torrio
1915—Begins working for Frankie Yale at Harvard Inn
1918—Marries Mary "Mae" Coughlin; son Albert Francis born
1919—Murders for the first time, while collecting debts for Yale
1920—Prohibition officially begins
1920—Begins working for Torrio
1921—Moves to Chicago
1923—Torrio relocates headquarters to Cicero
1924—Capone brother Frank shot dead by police
1924—Torrio picks Capone to run organization
1925—Torrio retires after barely survives shooting
1926—Attempt on Capone's life at the Hawthorn Inn
1928—Purchases Miami home
1928—Orders assassination of Frankie Yale
1929—St. Valentine's Day Massacre
1929—March 12: Subpoenaed about financial transactions by grand jury
1929—May 13–16: Attends Atlantic City meeting with other crime bosses trying to create national commission
1929—May 17: To avoid possible attempts on his life, has himself jailed
1930—March 17: Released from jail
1931—Sentenced to 11 years in jail for tax evasion and failing to file income taxes
1933—Transferred to Alcatraz
1936—Stabbed by another inmate
1939—Transferred out of Alcatraz on medical orders
1939—Released from prison
1947—January 25: Dies at home from syphilis

Al Capone "was the last link in the evolutionary chain that gave rise to the Outfit" (Russo 2001, 24). According to a recent book by mob historians William J. Helmer and Arthur J. Bilek, "Capone seems to have been the first to refer to his criminal organization as an 'Outfit'" (2004, 281). In perhaps the earliest biography of Capone, journalist Fred D. Pasley described Capone in 1920 as "loud of dress, free of profanity; no paunch then; stout-muscled, hard knuckled; a vulgar person; a tough baby from Five Points, New York City; bouncer and boss of the Four Deuces; Torrio's all-around handy man" (1930, 10–11). This biography also established some of the myths of the Capone legend—that he was "Neapolitan by birth, [and] had served with the A.E.F. overseas in the World War" (Pasley 1930, 11). Born in New York City, Capone would tell anyone who asked about the scar on his face that he was wounded in World War I—he was never in the armed forces, or France (Pasley 1930, 11).

Capone, like those before him, took advantage of the cozy relationship among the vice world, the politicians, and the police, a consortium that was only sporadically threatened by a reform mayor; 1923 was just one of those rare years. William Dever was elected to mayor on the promise to rid the streets of bootleggers. At his side was a police chief who for once could not be bought off as well. Unable to pull the strings at Chicago's City Hall, the syndicate moved its headquarters to Cicero, on the western periphery of the city. There, the Capone mob set up its headquarters at the Hawthorne Inn and the gang proceeded to take over the town. It wasn't long before the suburbs, home to some 50,000 Bohemian immigrants, boasted of 100 saloons and 150 casinos (Russo 1992). The Capone syndicate was reaping a rapacious profit of more than $100 million some years.

In 1927, Bugs Moran took over the North Side Irish gang once led by Dean O'Banion.[19] Following the St. Valentine's Day Massacre in 1929, which saw the murders of several of his gang members, Moran's power declined and he left Chicago for good.[20] With the murder of Joe Aiello the following year, Capone got rid of the last Sicilian resistance to his organization as well (Capeci 2002).

After Capone was sent away for tax evasion in 1931, Frank "The Enforcer" Nitti succeeded him. Nitti led the Outfit into the post-Prohibition era, making the transition from bootlegging to gambling and labor racketeering. Although Nitti appeared to the public as the face of the Outfit into the 1940s, the real power was Paul "the Waiter" Ricca. In any case Nitti committed suicide in 1943,

Al Capone: Most Overrated Crime Boss?

No gangland figure in American history is more prominent than Al Capone. However, the reality is that he led Chicago's most powerful gang for only 3 years, during which tenure he was embroiled in gang wars, dodging hit men, or fighting with the law. His crowning misjudgment was the St. Valentine's Day Massacre, which led to a crackdown on organized crime and his eventual demise. Much of Capone's continued fame after his death in 1947 was his association with Eliot Ness. Interestingly enough, neither met each other in life. During Capone's lifetime, Ness was himself a rather innocuous presence. Both men were virtually resurrected when the hit television show *The Untouchables* in the 1950s made both men household names after they were both dead.

The real mastermind who gets lost in any discussion of Chicago's great mob bosses is Johnny Torrio, Capone's mentor. It was Torrio who saw the opportunities of Prohibition; it was Torrio who had "Big Jim" Colosimo eliminated, the first assassination of a major Italian crime boss; and it was Torrio who brought Capone to Chicago. So when Torrio retired, he handed over the operations to Capone, Al did little to improve the operation and was innocent of the art of cooperation and negotiation, and as historian-sports writer Allen Barra noted, Capone "never understood the idea of a syndicate" (Barra 1999).

At the relatively young age of 31, the IRS gave Capone a one-way ride to federal prison and his days as the nation's leading mob figure ended. In the words of one critic, "The TV series about him, *The Untouchables*, was at the top almost as long as he was" (Barra 1999).

FIGURE 5.4   Treasury Department Photos: St. Valentine's Day Massacre
Source: U.S. Department of the Treasury

a rare case in gang lore of a boss dying by his own hand.[22] Ricca was well regarded in mob circles. Al Capone served as his best man at Nitti's wedding, and during the 1950s the Kefauver Committee referred to him as "the national head of the Crime Syndicate" (Sifakis 1987, 281). Little had changed at the end of the decade when the McClellan Committee called him "the most important" criminal in America.[23]

The St. Valentine's Day Massacre (1929)

The meaning of St. Valentine's Day in Chicago changed forever on February 14, 1929, when the bodies of seven gunshot victims were found in the Chicago SMC Cartage Company Garage on 2122 North Clark Street. To the seven men in the garage, it seemed like a typical roust when the four men, two dressed like Chicago policemen, entered and ordered them stand facing the wall.[21] Two of the victims had nothing to do with crime—one was the garage mechanic and the other an optometrist who liked the company of mobsters. Considered the biggest gangland killing in Chicago history, the massacre was more significant for making Al Capone into a household name, marking the beginning of the end for "Scarface." The massacre had widespread impact. It helped revive the Chicago Crime Commission, whose members personally financed the country's first crime lab and also advanced the movement for the repeal of Prohibition. It also pointed to what everyone knew—law enforcement was unprofessional, corrupt, and out-of-date.

Eliot Ness and the Untouchables

Eliot Ness (1902–1957) came to the public's attention as head of the storied Untouchables unit in Chicago. He attended the University of Chicago prior to being selected to lead a special Prohibition unit in September 1929. Authorized to stamp out mob-controlled breweries and distilleries, Ness personally selected the nine members of his new unit, almost half of whom came from outside the city to guarantee a modicum of integrity. The Untouchables busted almost 20 distilleries and six breweries worth close to $1 million during their first year in operation. Despite the credit given the Ness legend, the Untouchables, like most Prohibition-oriented law enforcement units, were not entirely effective in bringing down Capone's bootlegging empire. Nonetheless, Ness's crew did achieve some victories, such as causing Capone's alcohol production to drop by 80%, forcing him to buy overpriced liquor elsewhere.

Source: U.S. Department of the Treasury

(continued)

The Untouchables received their moniker in 1930 following an incident when mobsters tossed a bomb into a vehicle bearing two members of the team. Tossing the bundle back into the gangster's car, the Prohibition agents rushed back and reported the incident to Ness. He wasted no time in relating the story to local newspapers that tabbed the crime-fighting unit with its famous name. With the crime lord out of the way thanks to the IRS in 1931, Ness focused on Capone associates such as Frank Nitti and later moonshine operations in the hills of Ohio, Kentucky, and Tennessee. Ness survived three assassination attempts, including a drive-by, a car bomb, and a runover.

Ness was more successful in his next position as public safety director for Cleveland. Following the repeal of Prohibition, he moved to Cleveland and in 1935 made short work of a police department riddled with corruption. Under his aegis, Moe Dalitz was forced to move his syndicate operations out of the city. By the 1940s his squeaky clean reputation was marred by divorce and a drunk-driving charge, leading him to leave law enforcement in 1942. Falling on hard times and living in obscurity as a salesman in Pennsylvania, he was visited by an old friend, journalist Oscar Fraley. They collaborated on the book *The Untouchables*, based on his Prohibition exploits. Ness, unfortunately, did not live to see the book published, dying of a heart attack shortly before it came out.

THE MODERN OUTFIT   Paul Ricca ended up spending several years in jail for a motion picture extortion scheme that went awry. While he was away, the Outfit was in the hands of perhaps its greatest boss, Anthony "Big Tuna" Accardo. A longtime member of the Outfit, Accardo would give the impression that both he and his good friend Ricca were in control until "The Waiter" died in 1972. Soon after Ricca got out of prison, he added his friend Sam "Mooney" Giancana to the Outfit hierarchy. In 1957, Accardo handed the reins of the Outfit to Giancana. It was great timing, because Giancana got pinched at the Apalachin meeting later that year, launching an all-out war on organized crime. Giancana found himself under constant FBI surveillance, and according to mob journalist Jerry Capeci, "The FBI often learned of Giancana's moves even before his men did" (2002, 83).

In the 1960s, Mooney came under increased FBI scrutiny and Accardo stepped in and told him to retire. He lived in Mexico until the government kicked him out in 1974. With mounting health problems and becoming increasingly frail, he returned to Chicago. Accardo probably thought Giancana might be a security risk at this point. On June 18, 1975, he was in his basement cooking sausages when a trusted friend murdered him. Accardo most probably approved Giancana's assassination in 1975, although fellow gangsters led the press to believe it was a CIA operation to quiet one of the insiders in the Castro assassination plots.

Under the Accardo regime, the Outfit increased its prominence in the labor rackets, gambling, and loan sharking. Although most bosses just paid lip service to various prohibitions against dealing drugs, Accardo backed up his words with violence. Despite a career that lasted seven decades, when he died in 1992. Accardo was probably most proud of having never served a night in jail.

Except for Joe "Doves" Auippa, a series of forgettable bosses led the Outfit from the 1970s into the 1990s. By most accounts, the organization is a mere shell of its earlier self, its power having been seriously eroded by a series of FBI investigations. Nonetheless, despite a reorganization of seven crews into only three or four, it is still a player on the organized crime scene. The diminished size of the Outfit "was not necessarily a bad thing" (Binder 2003, 102), because with less made members and more associates, there would be less potential informants to cause further damage. Unlike the New York Families, which were decimated by the Feds in the 1980s and 1990s, only two Chicago mobsters of any significance have been identified as informants (Binder 2003).

In 2005, 14 members of the Chicago Outfit, including several top level leaders, were indicted on a 9-count, 41-page racketeering conspiracy. Prosecutors reported that this was the first time that "the entire 'Chicago Outfit' [was] deemed a criminal enterprise under federal racketeering laws" (Davey 2005, A1). Outfit members were charged in 18 murders dating back almost 40 years. The best-known of these murders was the 1986 killings of enforcer Tony Spilotro and his brother, who were beaten and buried alive in a Midwestern cornfield. Spilotro played an important part in the bestselling book and 1986 movie of the same name, *Casino*. In September 2007, the final verdicts in the trial came in, ending one of Chicago's biggest mob trials in decades. Jurors found three of the men guilty of murder, including defendant Frank Calabrese, Sr., who was found guilty in seven of the murders.

Philadelphia

By the mid-19th century, the hometown and scene of the Declaration of Independence less than 75 years earlier was demonstrating all the characteristics of urban organized crime. By the 1850s, the "City of Brotherly Love" was home to criminal gangs such as the Buffaloes, Blood Tubs, Rugs, and Copper Heads. By this time, even the police were on the "pad." According to historian David Johnson, a Philadelphia grand jury offered evidence showing police officers bailing out felons "arrested by themselves [and] in some cases compounding felonies with thieves, and dividing the stolen property between themselves, thieves and the plundered" (Johnson 1979, 23–24). During Prohibition, according to one popular historian, a number of Philadelphia policemen making less than $4,000 per year had bank accounts with between $40,412 and $193,553 (Asbury 1950, 185).

Jewish gangsters dominated early 20th-century organized crime in Philadelphia. Of these the most notable was Max "Boo Boo" Hoff, who would commit suicide at the age of 48, was considered the city's premier bootlegger throughout much of the 1920s. After a bloody war with another gang of bootleggers, Irving Wexler, better known as "Waxey Gordon," and Harry Stromberg, AKA "Nig Rosen," emerged as the local crime bosses. With support from national syndicate boss Meyer Lansky, Rosen and Hoff rose to power when Waxey Gordon was sent to prison in 1933 (Eisenberg, Uri, and Landau 1979, 89). Rosen, who was originally from New York, had been "transferred to Philadelphia [in 1931], just as a corporation would move a key employee" (Fox 1991, 72). His friendship with Meyer Lansky and Bugsy Siegel implied that he had the backing of the New York syndicates. Rosen's clout went as far as Baltimore, Wilmington, and Atlantic City.

By the late 1920s, Philadelphia's gangland contained several prominent Italian and Jewish gangs, all vying to control operations in the city as well as in neighboring South Jersey and Delaware, as well as other parts of Pennsylvania. Both groups sporadically liaised with New York City gangs. In 1929, a major underworld conference was held in Atlantic City; however, only the Jewish racketeers Rosen and Gordon were invited to represent Philadelphia at this conclave (Salerno 1990; Eisenberg et al. 1979). Other notables in attendance included Al Capone, Frank Costello, Albert Anastasia, and Dutch Schultz.

Philadelphia's first prominent Italian organized crime boss was Salvatore Sabella, who came to power around 1920 and is credited with shaping the Philadelphia mob structure and introducing its ethnic rules. Sabella arrived on the scene in 1911—an immigrant looking for prosperity on the mean streets of Philadelphia. He was also on the run from a murder charge in Sicily (Salerno 1990). By most accounts, he created the city's first La Cosa Nostra (LCN) family, leading established gangsters who had been active in South Jersey and the city by the early 1900s. According to mob turncoat Joseph Salerno, the family was initially referred to as the Black Hand (1990, 13). Sabella was particularly miffed in 1929 when the Jewish members were selected over the Italians to attend the syndicate conference, suggesting that by the end of the 1920s, "Philadelphia was still controlled by the Jewish mob" (Salerno 1990, 15). In any case, Sabella presided over a number of criminal operations, including the usual suspects—protection and bootlegging,—but also branching out into the olive oil and cheese businesses. In the early 1930s, Sabella relocated to New York City and became embroiled in the Maranzano-Masseria conflict.

Sabella was replaced by his underboss, John Avena, who previously had been affiliated with local Jewish mobsters. Until his murder by rivals in 1936, he ran the family for five uneventful years. By most accounts, following the murder of Avena, Brooklyn-born Joseph Bruno (born Joseph LoCascio) was appointed by the New York commission to replace him. Bruno built up the family's gambling rackets and persevered with national syndicate backing until his death from heart disease in 1946. Nevertheless, Bruno left an important legacy for his successors by expanding Philadelphia control into Atlantic City and South Jersey. Next in succession was Joseph Ida, who was considered, at least by insiders, a "reluctant boss" (Capeci 2002, 72). Alarmed by all of the heat stoked by the Apalachin Conference, which he attended in 1957, Ida retired and returned to Italy.

By the time Angelo Bruno came to power in 1959, the Philadelphia LCN family had been one of the more respected American LCN families for more than 40 years (Machi 2006). Angelo was not related to Joseph Bruno, contrary to a number of sources that list him as his son. Bruno earned the nicknames the "Docile Don" and the "Gentle Don" during his more than two-decade reign. Compared to the succeeding regimes, the Bruno family kept violence to a minimum, preferring activities such as loan sharking, extortion, protection rackets, and labor racketeering. Philadelphia was one of the cities focused on by the Kefauver Committee in the 1950s.[24] The committee reported that the "Philadelphia story differs only slightly from the pattern of organized crime that the committee" had found in other cities. At this time, the numbers racket was preeminent, with little evidence of big gambling houses.

According to Mark Haller, who served as a consultant to the Pennsylvania Crime Commission, the Bruno Family was distinct from most other LCN families because they were involved in so much legitimate business and used less violence. Bruno's organization offered a governmental structure for settling disputes. He also refused to allow members to control prostitution—a dishonorable activity—and attempted to stay clear of drug dealing in order to escape and avoid federal heat (Haller 1991).

Despite Bruno's repugnance for violence, he was not above sanctioning murders if someone showed a lack of respect. Bruno was able to keep his power for so long in part due to his friendship with New York's most powerful boss, Carlo Gambino. When Gambino died in 1976, Bruno lost his "insurance" and was viewed as fair game by up-and-coming mobsters anxious to move the family into new territories. In 1980, Bruno was blasted into eternity while sitting in his car outside his home.

Since the late 1980s, the Philadelphia family has self-destructed under a sequence of ruthless bosses. In 1981, Philip "Chicken Man" Testa was killed with a bomb, leaving the mob in the hands of Nicodemo "Nicky" Scarfo, who one authority has suggested was "Philadelphia's answer to Crazy Joey Gallo" (Sifakis 1987, 294). Standing less than five-and-a-half feet tall, Scarfo made up for his lack in size with a hair-trigger temper and a violent temperament. By the mid-1980s, after a considerable amount of bloodletting, including dozens of murders, Scarfo emerged as the preeminent Philadelphia syndicate boss. Between 1987 and 1989, a handful of informants turned the tables on Scarfo and his upper echelon. Scarfo was sentenced to life in prison for murder in 1989. Since the 1990s, the leadership has been in a state of flux and has given up much of its Atlantic City rackets to the New York families.

Black Mafia

The term *Mafia* is bandied about so frequently it has led journalists, academics, and the public to conclude that whatever groups are referred to as *Mafias* conform to the traditional Italian characteristics discussed in Chapter 3. Since the late 1970s, several books have been written about the "Black Mafia." In most cases the authors have made a case for some monolithic organization that has had continuity over time. However, support for such an organization has been purely speculative.[25] Although there have been a host of syndicates run and often catering to African Americans, these organizations have always been "finite" in terms of lifespan.

One pioneer in the study of Black organized crime identified Harlem drug kingpin Leon Aiken as making "the first tentative steps toward forming a 'Black Mafia'" (Schatzberg and Kelly 1997). Not only did he traffic in drugs alongside the local Italian syndicates, but he also later diversified into legitimate business including real estate, restaurants, and dry cleaners. According to Schatzberg and Kelly, he used these businesses for money laundering and as "a springboard into New York's social and political life" (1996, 126). However, Aiken's ascendance was cut short when he was sentenced to a long stretch in prison in 1966. Other figures such as the legendary Nicky Barnes had delusions of creating "African-American gangs into a national syndicate along mafia lines" (Schatzberg and Kelly 1997, 98). However, these were pipedreams that never came to fruition. What would prove much more powerful in the evolution of Black organized crime was a "common sense of racial victimization [that was able] to generate and sustain an enduring criminal enterprise among African-American criminals" (Schatzberg and Kelly 1996, 98) during the racial and cultural upheaval of the late 1960s.

Of all of the groups identified as being a Black Mafia, the one that stands out in most recent studies has been an identifiable Black Mafia located in Philadelphia. That city's Black Mafia, or PBM, ran a number of illegal rackets in Philadelphia's Black communities from the late 1960s through the mid-1980s. According to the acknowledged expert on the subject, the group was founded in 1968 by a former Black Panther named Samuel "Sam" Christian (Griffin 2003). In 1990, the Pennsylvania Crime Commission identified the self-named group as "an outgrowth of 1960s street gangs in Philadelphia's impoverished African-American neighborhoods" (Griffin 2003). The original 14 members ranged in age from 28 to 34 and already had extensive rap sheets. Despite their backgrounds, their well-known use of violence usually kept any witnesses from testifying against them. It was in this way that they were able to control drug sales and distribution while engaged in widespread extortion rackets. By taking the name *Black Mafia*, there was obviously some deep wish fulfillment at work here. However, what distinguished this group from others was its flexibility and adaptability. During its less than 20-year run, it remained unique for branching out beyond narcotics trafficking to include organized auto theft, loan sharking, illegal lotteries, credit card fraud, and extortion.

During the 1970s, the PBM was deeply involved in the heroin and cocaine trade, branching out beyond its roots in South Philadelphia, expanding into the rest of the city. One authority asserted that it eventually controlled 80% of the city's heroin traffic at one time. Testament to its organizational structure the Black Mafia turf was divided into four territories, each directed by a Black Mafia lieutenant who had control of the territory but was expected to kick a percentage upstairs to the group's treasury (Kleinknecht 1996, 72).

What increased the visibility and reach of the Black Mafia was its decision in 1971 to become affiliated with Philadelphia's Black Muslim Mosque. According to Griffin, the Black Mafia became "the extortion arm of the Black Muslims" (2003, 20).[26] Similar to Chicago's El Rukns (see Chapter 10), the Black Mafia used its religious connection as a cover for its more sinister activities. This relationship not only increased the profile and prestige of the Black Mafia, but also caused problems for police authorities, because any attack on the group could now be considered not just "simply about race but religion as well that could be exploited as needed" (Griffin 2003, 24).

Throughout its halcyon days between 1968 and 1974, membership (peaked including associates) at 96, although a federal strike force identified 346 members and associates in 1976. In any case, the organization's structure remained rather nebulous because there was no way to distinguish members from associates, and no reference to identify who was an enforcer, a treasurer, and so forth. According to Griffin, the organization was better understood as being "operationally defined" rather than defined by specific positions (2003, 63). However, information gleaned from informants and others refer to a two-part structure, Part I and Part II. Part I is composed of members and associates; gang members and drug runners are considered Part II. Like everything else about the Black Mafia, there are conflicting depictions of its structure. Some sources refer to the low-ranking affiliates and drug runners as *Little Brothers* and mid-level members as *The Brothers*. The leaders, according to this source, are referred to as *The Big Brothers*. There is also an apparent policy for moving up in the ranks, with all who expected to become higher members having to convert to Islam. Griffin asserts that prisons, heavily influenced by Muslim prisoners, played an important cog in the recruitment and training process (Griffin 2003).

Although by the mid-1970s a federal crackdown led to the imprisonment of most of the Philadelphia Black Mafia leaders, it continued to operate various criminal enterprises, "a durability rare among black crime groups" (Griffin 2003). Around 1975, new national Muslim leadership led the Mosque to distance itself from criminal actors. A persistent effort by federal agencies finally put the Black Mafia out of business as "a functioning organization" by 1984 (Griffin 2003, 123).

Boston/Providence

The first organized crime families in New England emerged in the early 20th century in Providence, Rhode Island, and Boston. One of the more interesting characteristics of the organized crime groups of this region is the "decentralized nature of the Boston underworld," which mob chronicler T. J. English suggested "made for some strange bedfellows" (2005, 293). Beginning in the early 20th century, Jewish, Irish, and Italian mobsters collaborated but more often killed each other in the pursuit of illicit lucre. In the 1920s bootlegging and related rackets were a mainstay for the so-called New England Family.

According to mob historian Allan May, "Boston's Italian underworld has never approached the organizational level of its counterparts in other cities in the United States" (May 2006, 1). There is some debate as to the first Italian syndicate. One authority suggests that the first boss of the "Boston family" was Gaspare Messina, beginning in 1916. In 1924, Phil Buccola succeeded him. Buccola, whose gang thrived on the timeworn loan sharking, numbers, and bootlegging rackets, retired in 1954 (Machi 2006). However, the majority of experts assert that the earliest exemplars of the Italian-American mob tradition in New England were the five Morelli Brothers from New York who organized a syndicate in Providence, Rhode Island. The Morellis originally got their start in New York City before being drawn to the opportunities posed by the growing Italian community in Providence. By some accounts, the Morelli Brothers, who were active in southeastern Massachusetts, may have been responsible for the 1920 murders that sent Sacco and Vanzetti to the electric chair in 1927.[27] One of the brothers reportedly confided to New England boss Vincent Teresa, "These two suckers took it on the chin for us" (Teresa 1973, 57).

Other criminal syndicates emerged out of Boston in the Prohibition era. Among the earliest New England bosses was Charles "King" Solomon. According to one historian, Solomon, along with Joseph Linsey, Hyman Abrams, and Louis Fox, formed "the wealthiest liquor syndicate ever built up in New England" (Fried 1980, 104; Nelli 1976, 169). Solomon was among the mob luminaries who sat in on the first major meeting of mob chieftains held in Atlantic City in 1929, and ran gambling and prohibition rackets in the region until he was ambushed and killed in south Boston's Cotton Club in 1933.

Raymond Patriarca (1908–1984) took over the New England family in 1954 and is considered the most prominent mob boss to come out of this region. After taking control of what is often referred to as *The Office*, Patriarca moved the family headquarters to Providence, Rhode Island, selecting underboss Jerry Angiulo to oversee the Boston rackets (Machi 2006). However, his reign was plagued by illegal FBI wiretaps between 1962 and 1965, and in 1963, he was outed as the boss by Joseph Valachi. Patriarca was profiled in a *Life Magazine* article in the late 1960s that also included transcripts from the FBI surveillance. Between 1968 and 1974, Patriarca served stints in prison for gambling and murder conspiracy, but managed to run the family from behind bars. More charges followed in the 1980s, and in failing health, he turned control over to his son, Raymond, Jr., (Capeci 2002).[28] Since the death of Raymond, Sr., the New England family has been in turmoil and internecine conflict.

JAMES "WHITEY" BULGER AND THE WINTER HILL GANG   In his magisterial history of the Irish-American gangster, T. J. English declared Whitey Bulger holds "a special place in the U.S. gangland saga as the most revered and most vilified Irish American mobster of all time" (2005, 319). Born in 1929, his family moved to the Boston neighborhood of Southie in 1938. In the 1940s, Bulger ran with a local gang known as the Shamrocks. In the 1950s, he graduated to holding up banks and hijacking trucks. Considering his family background, the criminal trajectory of his career was unexpected. His parents were hard workers and his five siblings became solid middle-class citizens—brother William "Billy" even going on to a distinguished career in Boston politics.[29] Whitey, however, never graduated high school, deserted from the Air Force, and was jailed for a sexual assault in Montana. Returning to Boston, he joined a gang of bank robbers and got involved in other serious robbery sprees. He was finally arrested and sentenced to 20 years in a federal pen. In 1959, he was transferred from Atlanta to Alcatraz, where he developed a fondness for military history and became a fitness devotee. Alcatraz was closed in 1962, and after serving only 9 years he was released from federal custody in 1965 and returned to Southie; however, it was not the same Whitey that returned to the neighborhood—this one was mature, disciplined, and even more refined. By the early 1970s, he was most prominent Irish mobster in South Boston. By then, Boston was one of the few American cities with a major Irish-American crime presence.

Bulger's career took another unexpected turn when he became an FBI informant in the mid-1970s. This connection was born out of several underworld traditions. On one hand, "it was a relationship rooted in history, linked to an era when Irish American gangsters and Irish American cops were not infrequently cut from the same cloth" (English 2005, 378; Lehr and O'Neill 2000). However, more important, it occurred at a time when the New England Mafia was making serious inroads into the traditionally Irish-American communities of Boston. In what turned out to be a deal with the devil, the FBI agreed to protect Bulger from this threat if he agreed to relay information on Italian syndicates (English 2005; Lehr and O'Neill 2000).

Despite his deal with law enforcement, Whitey continued his killing ways unimpeded. The ink was barely dry on the agreement with the Feds when Bulger eliminated one of his gang rivals for the offense of having beaten Bulger up in a barroom fight in the past. The killing of the former Winter Hill gang member was accomplished with the help of the Italian-American gangster Steve "the Rifleman" Flemmi, formerly an expert sniper in the Korean War. What was most remarkable about this twosome is that neither one knew the other was an FBI informer. Flemmi had been turned 10 years earlier. Over the next 20 years, the relationship between the two would become the stuff of gangland legend, and "would become known as one of the most homicidal gangster partnerships in the history of the American underworld" (English 2005, 383). By one estimate, the twosome had perpetrated almost 20 murders, including two young women who had ended up on the wrong side of relationships with Flemmi.

Both Flemmi and Bulger had become major components of the Winter Hill gang, led by boss Howie Winter. In 1977, Bulger's handler in the FBI was informed that Flemmi and Bulger were about to be indicted in a major race-fixing operation engineered by the Winter Hill gang. Agent John Connolly managed to convince his bosses that this would endanger his investigation into Boston organized crime and the indictments were handed down without the names of Flemmi and Bulger.[30] In the end, virtually the entire hierarchy of the Winter Hill gang was convicted, leaving a leadership void that would be filled by Bulger. Bulger moved the headquarters of the Winter Hill gang and was kept up-to-date on government investigations into the activities of the gang by his FBI contact, a relationship that had clearly crossed the line. On one occasion, Agent Connolly[31] informed Bulger that the Massachusetts State Police had a bug inside his headquarters, ending the investigation before it had barely begun. In the 1980s the FBI had hidden a bug in the headquarters of Gennaro "Jerry" Angiulo, Boston's leading Mafia boss and Patriarca underboss. Revelations from this device led to the dismantlement of the Boston Cosa Nostra, leaving "Cadillac Frank" Salemme in charge in Boston. Much of the credit for the successful prosecution has been attributed to information provided by Bulger to the authorities (although this continues to be debated). The elimination of most of his Italian-American rivals and those within his own gang made Bulger the leading Boston mobster.

By the 1990s, Bulger's fabled luck was beginning to run out. In 1993, Bulger and Salemme were facing racketeering indictments. In 2000, New England boss Frank Salemme plea bargained, receiving 11 years. However, much to his chagrin, he found out that his two co-defendants, Steve Flemmi and James "Whitey" Bulger, were longtime FBI informants. Bulger is currently on the FBI's Most Wanted List and is regularly profiled on the television show *America's Most Wanted*. He was most recently spotted in the summer of 2007 strolling through the Sicilian seaside resort town of Taormina.

Street Corner Society, William H. Whyte

During the late 1930s, Harvard graduate student William H. Whyte began his sociological exploration of Boston's North End slums, which he called *Cornerville*. Despite a relative lack of knowledge about criminal justice matters and Boston's Italian syndicates, he was able to gain the trust of the tight-knit community, contributing to what would become a landmark study of a criminogenic neighborhood. In his book, Whyte detailed how the "Office" or the "Company" dominated local rackets with a combination of violence and business acumen. Particularly useful was his examination of the symbiotic relationship between cops and criminals in which mob informants tipped off police in order to shut down rivals and competitors, and in the process curtail violence.

Los Angeles

According to the special agent in charge of the Los Angeles FBI office in the 1980s, traditional Italian, Jewish, and Irish organized crime families never "had the kind of controlling influence over some elements of crime in Los Angeles, like the other Eastern [Mafia] families have had because of the absence of the type of political structures that you find back East" (Murphy 1987, 18). This has not prevented various federal investigators from labeling the Los Angeles Mafia family as one of the nation's 24 recognized families since the late 1960s.

By the beginning of the 20th century, Los Angeles was experiencing a series of Black Hand extortion cases (Reid 1969). However, it was again the enactment of national Prohibition in 1920 that stimulated the rise of organized crime activity in Southern California. To some observers, Jack Dragna (1891–1957), born Anthony Rizzoti, was considered the "Al Capone of the West," whereas his mob counterparts in New York City and Chicago were more inclined to refer to his syndicate as the "Mickey Mouse Mafia" for its failure to consolidate its power and to eliminate rival mobsters infringing on his turf. Dragna was born in Sicily and came to the United States with his brother around 1908, settling in California. Dragna rose to prominence following the disappearance of his boss Joe "Iron Man" Ardizonne in 1931. Although his disappearance is still unresolved, suspicion focused on Dragna, who had the most to gain. In any case, most mob experts assumed it was a sanctioned killing, because the Commission immediately recognized Dragna's ascendance (Capeci 2002).

Things got interesting in 1937, when Benjamin "Bugsy" Siegel was apparently sent west to look after Eastern syndicate interests, particularly its race wire business. There is no real consensus as to why he made the move, but most accounts suggest he was supported by the mob hierarchy. Siegel was no stranger to Los Angeles. He had made several trips there earlier in the decade to visit his brother and sister, who moved there in 1933. By 1934, Siegel was renting an apartment on the Sunset Strip and began casting about for opportunities in the post-Prohibition era. Following his 1937 move, Siegel began moving into other rackets in Southern California, muscling in on illegal gambling operations, as well as the legitimate California dog track and Tijuana's Agua Caliente racetrack. Siegel also branched out into narcotics trafficking opening up a network between Mexico and the United States.

With his good looks and dangerous allure, Siegel seemed a natural for the Hollywood scene. With the help of actor and childhood friend George Raft, Siegel ingratiated himself with the glitterati and even set his sights on a possible acting career. His circle of friends expanded outside gangland to include such luminaries as Gary Cooper, Jean Harlow, Cary Grant, and Clark Gable. His new Hollywood connections helped him establish a network of syndicate bookie joints, brothels, and illegal casinos.

When Siegel came to Los Angeles he had to contend with Dragna and his soldiers. Unlike the diversity of the New York City mob in the 1930s when Bugsy, Meyer Lansky, and Lucky Luciano cooperated for their mutual prosperity, the Sicilian gangsters in Los Angeles had an aversion to

FIGURE 5.5 Bugsy Siegel Sign Used by Bagel Shop in Las Vegas Flamingo Hotel
Source: Dorling Kindersley Media Library/Alan Keohane

interethnic cooperation—that is, until Luciano passed down the word that they should coexist. According to instructions by Lansky and Luciano, the city was to be divided up between them, with Siegel running the western side, which included the tony enclaves of Beverly Hills and Hollywood, while Dragna controlled the central city, the valley suburbs, and the Port of Long Beach.

While Dragna had Johnny Roselli at his side, Siegel hired former boxer Meyer "Mickey" Cohen as his enforcer. Conflict between the two factions was never far away. By the mid-1940s, Siegel had relocated to Las Vegas to oversee the Flamingo Hotel project that would ultimately lead to his murder in 1947. He left the Los Angeles operation in the hands of Mickey Cohen.[32] However, the mercurial Cohen was no Siegel, and was almost immediately at war with Dragna over local bookmaking operations. The real heyday of organized crime activity in Los Angeles was the 1940s, when Jack Dragna and Mickey Cohen battled over the town's bookmaking rackets and organized crime began extending its reach into Las Vegas. However, in the words of former L.A. mobster Jimmy "The Weasel" Frattiano, the Los Angeles family was probably the only major mob family that failed to gain a profitable interest in one of the city's new casinos. According to Frattiano, "Vegas was our town, we just could never get lucky up there" (Coll 1987, 4). Although Dragna flourished in the gambling and loan shark rackets, he still had his eyes on independent Jewish gangster Mickey Cohen's bookmaking network by the 1940s.

On several occasions Dragna's crew tried to kill Cohen, using both bullets and bombs. Dragna's death in 1956 saw his operation taken over by mob lawyer Frank DeSimone. However, DeSimone's private life was exposed following his arrest (along with his underboss) at the Apalachin debacle in November 1957. To make matters worse, in 1958, one of DeSimone's soldiers made national headlines after he was killed by movie actress Lana Turner's daughter. Johnny Stompanato was a well-known player on the L.A. bar scene, as well as a friend of Mickey Cohen's. Stompanato and Turner became lovers in early 1958, but the relationship quickly soured as Turner drank and Johnny replied with physical abuse. In any case, Turner's 14-year-old daughter claimed to have been defending Lana from her boyfriend when she plunged a kitchen knife into Stompanato's stomach, mortally wounding him. Following her trial, a jury came back with a verdict of justifiable homicide.

The IRS was able to accomplish what the Dragna family never could—put Mickey Cohen away. Cohen served 4 years beginning in 1952, and then began a 10-year stint in 1962. When he was released in 1972, he was a shell of a man, having been partially paralyzed after a convict beat him over the head with a lead pipe. His once lavish lifestyle hit the skids, and he was reduced to renting a downscale apartment. He died 4 years later (Rockaway 1993).

Detroit

Between the 1880s and Prohibition, thousands of eastern and southern Europeans entered the United States, drawn by the country's seemingly inexhaustible opportunities. Many ended up in Detroit, site of the then booming automobile industry. By 1927, Detroit was the nation's fourth largest city, with almost 2 million people.

First signs of immigrant criminal activity came in the person of small gangs of Black Hand extortionists, who preyed on their own communities. By the beginning of the 20th century, Detroit was home to its first Italian syndicates. These included the Gianolla and Adamo gangs that waged a bloody war over control of the city's lottery and extortion rackets (Burnstein 2006). Gang wars between Italian factions persisted into the 1920s, when the more diplomatic Salvatore "Singing Sam" Catalanotte rose to prominence, ensuring a relative peace for the rest of the decade (Kavieff 2000).

At the turn of the 20th century, Detroit had a thriving Jewish community located on the city's Lower East Side in the Hastings Street quarter, stretching from Jefferson Avenue to East Grand Boulevard. This "New Jerusalem" (Fried 1980, 103), became home to a number of Jewish gangs in the years before Prohibition. Of these, none rose higher in gangland prominence than the Purples (Nelli 1976, 170).[33] The predominantly Jewish Purples had a head start preparing for the Prohibition rackets because Michigan introduced Prohibition in 1918, two years before the rest of the country. At the start of Prohibition, the Detroit Purples already had created the semblance of an organization, and were in better position to take advantage of the new opportunities presented by the 18th Amendment. As the Purples prospered in bootlegging, they branched out into other mainstays of organized crime, including loan sharking, extortion, prostitution, and gambling (Driscoll 1933; Messick 1967, Nelli 1976).

The Purple Gang flourished in the early 1920s by shipping Canadian whiskey to Chicago's Capone syndicate. By the end of the decade, the Purple Gang had moved away from its provincial Jewish roots and now included Italian members as well, including Peter and James Licavoli and Joseph Zerilli. All would move on to mobland distinction in future decades. What had become clear is that the Italian faction soon superseded the Jews in Detroit's bootlegging rackets. According to the Kefauver Report, Zerilli's faction would become Detroit's dominant gangland faction (Nelli 1976). Moe Dalitz was one of the gang's most successful graduates, going onto gangland stardom in Cleveland and later Las Vegas.

The Purple Gang earned notoriety in a series of brutal killings in the late 1920s and 1930s. In 1926, the gang was linked to the machine-gun killings of three "St. Louis imports" (Messick 1967, 49). In 1929, Al Capone recruited several Purples as triggermen for what would become known as the St. Valentine's Day Massacre.[34] In 1931, their bootlegging partners of the "Little Jewish Navy" were targeted at the Collingwood Manor Apartments. The ensuing murders of three of them there entered mob lore as the "Collingwood Massacre." Three Purples were later convicted and sentenced to life imprisonment (Fox 1989). The Purple Gang was also involved in the shooting of crusading Detroit radio reporter Gerald Buckley in 1930 as well (Messick 1967). The Jewish-controlled Purple Gang era lasted from 1925 to 1933. During this period, the gang, under the direction of the four Bernstein Brothers, was responsible for an estimated 500 murders (Burnstein 2006, 23). Following the convictions for the Collingwood murders, most of the original Purples disbanded or went legit.

Jimmy Hoffa (1913–1975?): Detroit Made

Former Teamsters boss James R. "Jimmy" Hoffa disappeared on July 30, 1975, after leaving his house to meet three men at a suburban Detroit restaurant. His mob-connected life had seemed to come full circle. Hoffa was a product of Detroit (but born in Indiana). By most accounts, his ascendance to the head of the nation's largest union in the 1950s, the Teamsters Union, was assured with the backing of the Chicago and Detroit mob families. In prison for jury tampering, President Richard Nixon commuted Hoffa's sentence in 1971, with the tacit understanding that he would stay out of union politics for 10 years. Meanwhile, Frank Fitzsimmons had replaced Hoffa when he went to prison, and the syndicates had developed a cozy relationship with him due in no small part because he was easier to manipulate than the petulant Hoffa. No sooner did Hoffa get out of prison than he began making noise about getting his old job back, despite warnings by Mafia kingpins to leave it alone. Hoffa's wife was the last person to speak to him, when he called home wondering where his contact, Tony Provenzano, was. Soon after, Hoffa was last seen getting into a car. Suspicion immediately focused on the Detroit mob and boss Joe Zerilli. Despite a preponderance of theories and an exhaustive investigation, no one has ever been charged with Hoffa's disappearance. Hoffa was declared legally dead in 1983. In the 2004 book *I Heard You Paint Houses*,[35] an Irish-American gangster named Francis "The Irishman" Sheeran claimed on his deathbed to have participated in the killing of his "close friend." By most accounts, the FBI had always suspected him as being one of the last men to see Hoffa alive.

By the end of World War II, Italian-Americans not only dominated the once Jewish run rackets but also adopted the Purple Gang name. Joseph Zerilli supervised the Detroit mob for 40 years beginning in 1936. His longevity made the family "a model of underworld stability and efficiency" (Burnstein 2006, 43). Out of respect, Zerilli was made one of the only two non–New York members of the national commission (Angelo Bruno of Philadelphia was the other) (Fox 1989). Under his watch, the Detroit syndicate created lucrative ties with local labor unions and took over African-American rackets, and made inroads on Las Vegas casinos. Zerilli died in 1977.

Detroit's major organized crime syndicate declined in influence as so many others did in the 1980s and 1990s. In the 1980s, the Detroit mob relinquished its control of the inner-city drug trade that has been taken over by local Black cartels. Although still involved in loan sharking and bookmaking activities, the Detroit family has little at stake in the modern unions. In 1996, the family was decimated by an extensive RICO case that saw the boss and underboss jailed on federal charges (Burnstein 2006).

Cleveland

Cleveland became the terminus for waves of immigrants during the late 19th century—Irish, Italians, and Jews made communities there, and some drifted into the criminal milieu. Historian Stephen Fox suggests that at the onset of Prohibition, Irish gangsters were the first to recognize the opportunities it portended for organized crime (1989, 15). If this is true, then Thomas Jefferson McGinty should be considered its best exemplar (Messick 1967, 31). McGinty rose to prominence as a slugger in the newspaper rackets. In an era before television and radio, a number of newspapers battled to control the lucrative news industry. By using gangs of toughs and street fighters, the major newspaper dealers could intimidate competing newspapers and ensure their lucrative dominance over circulation. McGinty made the transition to bootlegging in the 1920s as the circulation wars cooled down and joined several family members in opening a saloon. In 1924, the McGintys were convicted of violating federal Prohibition statutes by conducting "a gigantic wholesale and retail conspiracy" (Fox 1989, 15). Thomas, who one U.S. Attorney referred to as "King of Ohio bootleggers" (Messick 1967, 31), ended up serving 18 months in the federal lockup in Atlanta, and when he got out returned to bootlegging.[36] However, this time he would take action to avert interference from Cleveland officials.

The Commission House District

During the 1920s, the Lonardo clan paid neighbors to operate stills to produce corn liquor. Cleveland crime bosses controlled the all-important corn sugar ingredient "essential to the distilling of whiskey" (Messick 1967). Typically, the Lonardos supplied local immigrants with the necessary raw materials and homemade stills to produce corn liquor. Each family that participated in this network was paid a commission for their products, leading the neighborhood to be referred to as the *commission house district* and each house a *commission house*. On one hand, decentralizing the production of illegal liquor through the use of thousands of small stills protected the overall business, but with poor quality control, the more successful bootleggers began to smuggle the good stuff from abroad. In any case, outright warfare over the control of corn sugar resulted in the bloody "Sugar War" in the late 1920s. When the commission system was implemented in 1925, Cleveland had the nation's ninth highest homicide rate. By the end of this era, the city was tied for third (Messick 1967; Porrello 1998).

Italian and Jewish gangsters eventually dominated Cleveland organized crime and the bootlegging rackets. A large Italian community evolved along Mayfield Road (Fox 1989). Among the early arrivals was the Lonardo family from Sicily in 1900. Joseph Lonardo became the city's "first known Mafia boss" (Capeci 2002, 96). He, along with his brothers, made the transition from a legitimate business selling ingredients for home-brewed liquor to bootlegging once Prohibition began. In 1927, Joseph and his brother were murdered in a barbershop owned by the next leader of the crime family. This initiated a series of revenge killings from both sides that ended with the ascendance of the Mayfield mob under Al Polizzi.

"Few racket groups in America have had a greater permanency of form or achieved a stronger organization than the one known as the Cleveland syndicate" (Peterson 1983, 422). The foundations for organized crime in Cleveland were set in the 1920s during the rum-running days of Prohibition. By 1950, the syndicate was operating the Desert Inn in Las Vegas, and subsequently for a number of years was a force in the Las Vegas gaming industry.

The Cleveland syndicate flourished in part because of its willingness to negotiate and work with various ethnicities. However, despite its predilection for working with others, it maintained a core leadership that was Jewish, including the so-called Cleveland Four—Moe Dalitz, Louis Rothkopf, Morris Kleinman, and Samuel A. Tucker. The alliance of the Cleveland Four with the Italian-American Mayfield Road Mob, led by Alfred "Big Al" Polizzi, was the linchpin for both its longevity and early successes. Beginning during Prohibition and lasting well into the 20th century, the organizations found solid ground in bootlegging activities in the Lake Erie region between Toledo and Buffalo. One historian suggested that the Four shipped so much illegal booze across the lake that it was referred to as "the Jewish Lake" (Fox 1989, 33). By most accounts, the partners were able to corrupt virtually every locality while enhancing their affiliation with other criminal gangs (Fried 1980).

According to the FBI, "the first known instance of a large meeting of Mafiosi" took place on December 5, 1928, when 23 important Sicilian-Italian hoodlums met at Cleveland's Statler Hilton Hotel (Reppetto 2004, 86). Considered the progenitor for future mob enclaves, Cleveland police got wind of the meeting and summarily arrested the group. Although 13 guns were found, most of those present were fined $50 and given 30-day suspended sentences. By most accounts the Cleveland

One interesting explanation for the affinity between the Mayfield Roaders and the Cleveland Four was that according to investigative writer Hank Messick, there were rumors that Polizzi's oldest brother Charles had been born to Jewish parents by the name of Berkowitz and after being orphaned was adopted by Polizzi's parents (Messick 1967).

Morris Barney "Moe" Dalitz (1899–1989): Godfather of Las Vegas

Next to Meyer Lansky and Arnold Rothstein, Moe Dalitz was probably one of America's most prominent Jewish organized crime figures. One Las Vegas journalist suggested that although he "never achieved Lansky's moniker of 'financial genius of organized crime,' it was not because he was less successful" (Smith 2006). Dalitz has been the subject of a number of enquiries and journalistic exposes over the years, but during his life was inclined toward reticence. Born in Boston, he moved with his family to Ann Arbor, Michigan, at age 4. A disinterested student, Moe left his Detroit high school before graduation, preferring the opportunities offered by the Purple Gang. All the while Moe ran a successful laundry business through which he met Jimmy Hoffa, whose Teamsters Pension Fund years later lent money to open many of Las Vegas' first casino resorts. Dalitz left Detroit for Cleveland in the 1930s, where he increased his national prominence through his activities with the Cleveland Four and the Mayfield Road mobs. Dalitz, Morris Kleinman, Sam Tucker, and Louis Rothkopf maintained a "friendly" partnership with Cleveland's Italian mobsters for decades. During Prohibition, Dalitz's syndicate operated gambling clubs in Cleveland and in the neighboring states of West Virginia, Kentucky, and Indiana. During the 1940s, he served in the Army, attaining the rank of lieutenant. After the war, Dalitz targeted Las Vegas, investing in the construction of the Desert Inn, which opened in 1950. During the 1950 Kefauver Hearings, Senator Kefauver asked Dalitz: "Now, to get your investments started, you did get yourself a pretty good little nest egg out of rum running didn't you?" Dalitz responded: "Well, I didn't inherit any money Senator. . . . If you people wouldn't have drunk it, I wouldn't have bootlegged it." Dalitz would become known as the "Godfather of Las Vegas" (Roemer 1994, 208). According to a number of sources, including the FBI, Dalitz served as a front for the Chicago Outfit and helped it run the Stardust Casino Hotel. Along with his three seemingly inseparable partners, the syndicate invested in other casinos and dominated the Vegas gambling world for a number of years. In order to stop other Mafia families from muscling in, he reportedly gave a piece of the action to the Cleveland syndicate. Payments were made by skimming cash from casino profits in order to avoid tax problems. Much of Dalitz's funding for his casinos came from the Teamsters Pension Fund. In the early 1960s, he refinanced the Stardust, the Desert Inn, and the Fremont Casinos. For his philanthropic activities and his support in the building of the Guardian Angel Catholic Cathedral, he was named "Humanitarian of the Year" in 1976. This partnership lasted into the 1980s. With the IRS at his door, he sold the Desert Inn to Howard Hughes in the 1960s. He eventually divested himself from all of his Vegas casino properties. Thus began the second incarnation of Dalitz—as "Mr. Las Vegas," philanthropist, and a political force in "Sin City." In 1982, *Forbes Magazine* listed him as one of America's richest men, with an estimated worth of $110 million.

meeting, which the Cleveland Police labeled the "Grand Council of the Mafia" (Reppetto 2004, 148), was called to discuss either the recent murders of Unione Siciliana presidents in Chicago and New York City that same year, or the control of corn sugar used in the distillation of whiskey. In any case, its intention was to stem the bloody rivalry over the Eastern and Midwestern bootlegging rackets. Two of the attendees, Joseph Profaci and Joseph Magliocco, later attended the 1957 Apalachin meeting.

In 1938, James T. "Blackie" Licavoli (1904–1985) arrived in Cleveland and entered the competitive world of organized crime, moving into the vending and gambling rackets (Nash 1992). Following the death of Cleveland boss John Scalish in 1976, Licavoli took charge of the organization. Except for an unsuccessful challenge from the "ambitious" John Nardi, Licavoli outlasted the competition, only to be brought down by the government in 1982. Licavoli's family members seemed to have a predilection for crime, because a number of them played prominent roles as gangsters in St. Louis and Detroit as well. Licavoli was well regarded among his peers and was respected for having been able to place an informant, a female clerk, inside the Cleveland FBI office—giving him a pipeline into the justice system. Among the most important tips were the names of several informers (Demaris 1981). In 1951, Licavoli, AKA "Jack White" (for his dark complexion), refused to answer questions at the Kefauver Hearings, and in 1982, he became one of the first major organized crime figures to be convicted under the RICO statutes. By most accounts, the Cleveland mob was diminished by RICO convictions, deaths, informants, and its loss of control of the lucrative Central States Pension fund (Capeci 2002).

Hot Springs, Arkansas

Located in the Ouachita Mountains, by the 1920s Hot Springs, Arkansas, earned a reputation as the "Baden Baden of America" due to its popularity among the rich as a vacation spa, offering mineral springs and gambling. Well-heeled tourists cavorted in clubs such as the Southern Club and the Belvedere. Underworld characters referred to it as "Bubbles" due to its sparkling hot springs. When the railroad reached town in 1874, its prominence as a national health and recreational center was all but assured. Over the next few decades, Hot Springs became "the wickedest city in the United States," due in no small part to the existence of a "tightly corrupt political machine" (Fox 1989, 222). Gambling proved a mainstay well into the 20th century.

Hot Springs also had a long reputation as a place for gangsters on the lam to hide out. Mayor Leo McLaughlin, who presided over the corrupt administration, was known to drive a buggy towed by horses "Scotch" and "Soda" through the center of town (Nown 1987). During his 20 years as mayor, he kept the peace by allowing mobsters and anyone willing to contribute to the local economy to take in the sights without molestation from local police. He also probably elicited a promise that gangsters would not try to take over the town or compete with the mayor and his coterie of rich racketeers known as the "Little Combination" for the lucrative criminal enterprises (Nown 1987).

Hot Springs became a popular vacation spot for Al Capone, who had discovered its charm reportedly while purchasing liquor from local stills for his Chicago speakeasies. In 1927, Capone narrowly escaped with his life when one of his competitors followed him from Chicago and just missed him with a blast from a shotgun (Hornung 1998). Once in town with his entourage, Capone typically reserved room 442, facing the Southern Club directly across the street.

When out-of-town criminals arrived in Hot Springs in the 1920s and 1930s, they typically asked waiting cab drivers to whisk them to "The Cigar Store," a reference to an establishment called the White Front Cigar Store owned by expatriate mobster Dick Galatas. Here, hoods could enjoy a combination casino–pool hall–bookie shop and "underworld clearinghouse rolled into one" (Fox 1989, 225–226), where gangsters could find out who was in town, and then arrange to buy a gun from an ever-reliable chief of detectives named Dutch Akers (Fox 1989). However, Akers warned that they could enjoy the town unimpeded as long as they did not interfere in the local rackets. Akers performed the dual role as peacekeeper and racketeer, responsible for collecting payoffs from local prostitutes and selling guns to criminals with the understanding that they would only be used outside of Hot Springs. Underworld visitors to the resort included Lucky Luciano, members of the Barker and Purple gangs, and Alvin "Creepy" Karpis. After the "Kansas City Massacre" in 1933, federal law enforcement closed down the White Front Cigar Store (Nash 1992).

Following the repeal of Prohibition and while other mobsters were on the hunt for greener pastures, the notorious Owney Madden (1891–1965) had saved millions of dollars, and by different accounts decided to relocate or retire or was banished to Hot Springs, lured by its openness and reputation for corruption (Reppetto 2004; Fox 1989; Nown 1987). In reality, according to Madden's wife, Owney had made a deal with New York authorities to be paroled to Hot Springs rather than New York in 1933, where he stayed in self-proclaimed exile for the remainder of his days. Although it is unsubstantiated, Madden reportedly left his rackets in New York in the hands of Frank Costello, who promised to look after his interests in return for a cut of Madden's operations in Hot Springs (Nown 1987).

Madden entered an arrangement with Meyer Lansky to open several casinos there. Close to the lair of Carlos Marcello in New Orleans, the two engaged in business as well. In 1943, Madden married a postmaster general, and over the last two decades of his life became an American citizen and made the transition, by some accounts, from urban gangster to southern gentleman.

The end of World War II also signaled the end of the corrupt McLaughlin administration, as soldiers returned home unwilling to bend to the power structure that seemed so much like the one they fought against in the war. Some referred to McLaughlin as "Der Fuehrer of Hot Springs" (Nown 1987, 174). On election day, several trains brought thousands of poor Whites and Black workers from outlying districts at Hot Springs. As late as 1946, Arkansas law allowed representatives of the mayor to buy blocks of poll tax receipts by proxy for voters who otherwise could not afford to vote. These shipped-in voters typically turned elections into a rout and allowed him to stay in power for so long. However, in 1946, war veterans instigated a government investigation that led to the dismissal of forged proxy votes and to the demise of the McLaughlin machine.

In the wake of the election, in 1947, the new city administration closed down most of the gambling joints, but not all. Most of the gambling joints that dotted the vicinity had been little more than shelters with roofs or roadhouses, but the more exclusive clubs were allowed to continue to operate to a more discrete clientele. However, national crime syndicates targeted Las Vegas, which in the 1920s was little more than a dusty weigh station in the Nevada desert, as the next "Hot Springs" in the 1940s. Although the Hot Springs casinos operated sporadically in the 1940s and 1950s, mob influence and interest shifted to Florida. In the 1950s and 1960s, members of both the Kefauver Committee and later the McClellan Committee met in Hot Springs to investigate the continuing presence of organized crime activity.

St. Louis

Black Hand extortionists were threatening fellow Italians in St. Louis by the late 1870s (Nash 1992, 321; May 2005). In the years leading up to the 20th century, a number of Italian mobsters gravitated from New Orleans, hoping to avoid the same outcome as the 11 Italians lynched in New Orleans after the murder of the city police chief in 1890. In the years leading up to Prohibition, the "Pillow Gang," under Carmelo Fresina, was the most formidable Italian gang. Egan's Rats had banded together as early as 1907, when criminal supporters of St. Louis Fifth Ward Democratic Committeeman Thomas Egan engaged in such "political activities" as burglary and theft from train boxcars (May 2005).

It was not until the 1920s that the Italians dominated organized crime in St. Louis. The "first known St. Louis family La Cosa Nostra boss" was Vito Giannola (Capeci 2002, 90). Giannola made his presence known in St. Louis in the 1920s, after fleeing to the United States several steps ahead of a murder charge in Sicily. Giannola's crew was imposing a tax on all goods sold in the Italian neighborhoods in the early 1920s before moving to monopolize wholesale meat industry. However, bootlegging presented too many opportunities. During Prohibition, his gang, the "Green Ones,"[37] was embroiled in a bloody bootlegging war with the Cuckoos Gang, reportedly costing dozens of lives over a 5-year period (Nash 1992). According to mob expert Jerry Capeci, St. Louis was one of only "three Mafia families" without a representative at the 1957 Apalachin Meeting (Capeci, 2002, 91). The others included Chicago and Detroit.

Predominately Irish in its early years, during Prohibition, Egan's Rats adopted a stance that many successful operations did in the era, by cooperating with other ethnicities, eschewing the traditional restrictions in gang membership. Jewish mob historian Alfred Fried suggested that the gang "adapted to the changing times and admitted to its ranks young Eastern European Jews and Southern Italians" (Fried 1980, 95). Among the best-known graduates of the Rats were safecracker Morris "Red" Rudensky (1908–1986) and killer Leo Brothers (1899–1951).

Organized crime became a more powerful presence in St. Louis during the 1940s, especially after Anthony Giordano (1914–1980) came to power in 1946. Giordano himself compiled a rap sheet with more than 50 convictions between 1938 and his death. (May 1999). Giordano's organization engaged in the usual litany of mob rackets—loan sharking, narcotics dealing, and extortion. However, it was his control over several local labor unions that gave him a legitimate front for money laundering and other perks. In 1967, Giordano and others were featured in a two-part expose in *Life Magazine*. This unwanted attention led to his conviction in 1975 for illegal behind-the-scenes machinations in the Las Vegas casino world.

During the 1950s, St. Louis was one of 14 cities where Kefauver held hearings, this time focusing on the gambling rackets. The hearings revealed that organized gambling thanks to the race wire service was the biggest law enforcement problem. Efforts to cut off the wire service had been in the works since 1938. Nonetheless bookmaking activities were estimated to bring in $20 million per year on one operation alone.

Following Giordano's death in 1980, he was replaced by his nephew Matthew "Mike" Trupiano (1938–1997), who just so happened to be president and international representative of Laborers Local 110 of the Laborers International Union (Nash 1992). The St. Louis mob had been on the decline since the 1970s as it became increasingly influenced by the Chicago Outfit. Just two years after taking over, Trupiano and four mob associates were indicted on racketeering charges, and in 1986 he was sentenced to 4 years in federal prison. Trupiano's health broke during another prison stint in the early 1990s. By then, "the St. Louis Mafia had been on life support for more than a decade," and with his death, "the switch was finally turned off" (Capeci 2002, 91).

URBAN SOUTH

Dallas

Carlo Piranio was the first prominent Dallas crime boss. He made the typical transition from bookmaking and gambling to bootlegging in the 1920s. Piranio had initially settled in New Orleans before relocating to Dallas. The Dallas family is sometimes regarded as "a satellite of the New Orleans mob" (Sleeper 2006, 87). Over time, Dallas became an important weigh station in smuggling operations between New Orleans and Chicago. Carlo Piranio was succeeded by his brother Joseph in 1930, and he ran the Dallas rackets for more than a quarter of a century before committing suicide in 1956.[38] Following Joseph's death, Joseph Frances Civello (1902–1970) took over the reins and went on to earn a reputation as the city's greatest crime boss (Gatewood 2004; Capeci 2002).[39]

Born in Louisiana, Civello earned his first federal narcotics conviction in 1928. He then moved to Dallas and went into legitimate business under Civello's Fine Foods and Liquor. The year after he was made boss Civello was caught up in the Apalachin fiasco in upstate, New York. The local *Dallas Morning News*, reported the story, noting that Civello was "a well-groomed man who is a partner in an Oak Lawn importing shop in Dallas specializing in liquors and foods, . . . was caught up in the New York State Police net" (January 21, 1958).

By most accounts, due to its lack of shipping, dockworkers, and the presence of strong labor unions, Dallas has never been considered "a traditional focal point for organized crime" (Sleeper 2006, 87); however, this did not preclude mob activity there. In the 1930s and 1940s, it was regarded as an important transit point for narcotics smuggled into the United States from Mexico, often through Galveston. Between the 1930s and 1950s, Lester Ben "Benny" Binion (1904–1989) was an important player in the world of Dallas organized crime. According to his biographer, Binion arrived in Dallas in 1923 and was hired by Civello to work in his bootlegging and protection businesses. Binion left Dallas for Las Vegas, but continued to oversee his numbers and bookie rackets as well as his hotels and gambling joints from the safe confines of Las Vegas, where he would achieve his greatest successes as a gambling entrepreneur. More recent scholarship suggests that Binion left due to a pending investigation of his gambling activities in Dallas by the Kefauver committee (Gatewood 2002).

In the years following the Kefauver proceedings and the concomitant embellishment of American organized crime by journalists, Civello was a frequent guest on the pages of Dallas newspapers. Some mob historians suggest that he was Carlos Marcello's underboss. Marcello and Civello were linked together by a record of toll phone charges (Scheim 1988). Similar to accounts of other mob bosses his influence was never near what was reported. Civello's name achieved a sort of immortality among Kennedy assassination buffs because of his testimony that he knew Jack Ruby, an important cog in the assassination continuum.[40]

Galveston's Maceo Family

Gamblers flocked to Galveston from New Orleans as early as the late 1830s, leading the City Council to introduce an ordinance to prohibit gambling by the end of the decade (Chalfant 1997). A tight rein was kept on gambling here until the turn of the century. By 1901, several gambling houses flourished. More than 50 establishments offered slot machines, or in contemporary parlance, "nickel-in-the-slot-machines." As a major southern port city prior to the Galveston Hurricane of 1900, Galveston had an established reputation for most types of vice, but little in the way of an organized crime presence until the ascent of the Maceo Family in the early 20th century. By the 1920s and 1930s, Galveston had earned such a reputation for criminal activity that the policing establishment referred to it as "the Free State of Galveston" (Sleeper 2006, 88).

Sicilian-born brothers Salvatore (Sam) and Rosario (Rose) Maceo moved to Galveston from New Orleans in 1910. They initially held legitimate jobs as barbers. At the onset of Prohibition, bootlegging, rum running, smuggling, gambling, and prostitution flourished in Galveston. Two prominent gangs had emerged before the 1920s—the Beach Gang, operating on the southern part of the island, and the Downtown Gang, which controlled operations on the north side. The Maceos became involved running rum for the Beach Gang, but soon branched out on their own. By the early 1920s, the Maceos were prosperous bootleggers and gamblers with their barbershop serving as a front. In 1926, the Maceos and partners opened the Hollywood Dinner Club on the outskirts of town. Some of showbusiness' leading stars performed there, and by the end of the decade, it was regarded as one of the nation's leading nightclubs (Chalfant 1997, 28).

The Maceos tried to play it safe by staying out of the prostitution rackets that they believed carried too much social stigma. By the early 1950s, most of the organized rackets were on the decline due in part to the enforcement of gambling laws and the increasing popularity of Las Vegas.

Tampa

In 1873, 52 years after becoming part of the United States in a treaty with Spain, Tampa officially was organized as a town. The introduction of a railroad line in the 1880s stimulated the town's ascendance to city-hood by the end of the century. During the Spanish-American War, the city became the main debarkation port for soldiers going to Cuba. During the early 20th century, immigrants from Cuba, Spain, and Italy settled down here where there were plenty of unskilled jobs in local cigar factories (Mormino and Pozetta 1987). Soon Tampa was the hub of the American cigar manufacturing business, leading to its moniker *Cigar City* (Deitche 2004). The center of syndicate activity was an area called Ybor City, which in the early 1900s was home to a growing number of Cuban, Spanish, and Italian immigrants.

According to Tampa mob expert Scott Deitche, "Unlike northern cities, Tampa had no established Jewish or Irish Gangs" (2006, 1). Much of the city's early mob activity revolved around gambling—particularly the bolita racket.[41] Deitche asserts that bolita was "the mob's predominant moneymaker until the 1960s" (Deitche 2004), when the narcotic trade supplanted it.

In the early 20th century, Tampa was experiencing a narcotics problem due to opium dens operating in a nearby vice area known as Fort Brooke, a wide open district replete with brothels and gambling houses. Contemporary police records estimated that problems associated with morphine and opium addiction cost the city more than $2 million per year (Deitche 2004). Among the early drug kingpins was Joseph M. "Jo-Jo" Cacciatore, who presided over an operation that "reached from Alabama through the Carolinas" (Deitche 2004). Besides running a number of legitimate businesses he used children to deliver drugs. Throughout the 1920s, Tampa harbor played an important role as a terminal for both narcotics and alcohol smuggling. One source suggests that it was second only to the port of New York as an entry point for illegal drugs (Deitche 2004, 12).

Similar to most other American cities, in 1920, the inauguration of Prohibition created bootlegging opportunities in Tampa. Although it rarely comes to mind in any discussion of this era, Tampa became an important destination and transit point for syndicates plying their trade between

Cuba and other Caribbean nations and the United States. Compared to New York City and other ports, Tampa's proximity to both Cuba and the Bahamas made it an easier destination for smugglers. According to Tampa mob historian Scott Deitche, "The Tampa Mafia remains one of the most enigmatic, least known and most influential Mafia organizations in this country" (2004, 267).

Tampa's involvement in organized crime activity was first revealed to law enforcement in 1928, after two Tampa gang leaders were among the arrested gangsters at the 1928 Cleveland meeting at the Statler Hilton. When a Cleveland police officer stumbled on a suspicious meeting of out-of-towners at the Hotel Statler on December 5, 1928, few could appreciate the significance of this occasion. By some accounts, this was the first national meeting of American syndicate bosses. When the authorities queried the visitors as to their *raison d'être* they gave widely divergent responses. The first inkling of Tampa organized crime beyond Florida was the identification of two well-known Italian-American businessmen from Tampa in attendance. More significantly other attendees included future New York bosses Joseph Profaci and Vincent Mangano. According to Tampa underworld authority Scott Deitche, there were several explanations for the meeting. One account suggests that it was a meeting to decide how to avenge the murder of Frankie Yale. Another explains that the meeting was held to organize the monopolization of corn sugar business, a vital ingredient for alcohol production during Prohibition (Dietche 2004, 4).

For a number of years, various syndicates fought each other over control of local rackets with no one boss emerging until the 1950s. Between 1930 and 1959, dozens of mob connected killings took place in Tampa, earning the era the sobriquet the "Era of Blood" (Dietche 2004).

Santo Trafficante, Sr. (1886–1954), a native of Sicily, arrived in Tampa in 1904 at the age of 22, and in 1925 became a naturalized citizen. Over the next three decades he became the most important boss in Tampa and central Florida (*US Senate, OC and Narcotics Hearings*, pp. 531–553). During the 1920s, he established himself as a prominent underworld figure in Tampa and central Florida. Subsequently, he affiliated himself with New York's crime families and syndicates in Kansas City, St. Louis, and New Orleans. With the violent death of his mentor Ignacio Antinori in 1940, Trafficante took over the heroin operations and extended his control over gambling operations. However, Trafficante had to draw a line on his expansion from the Gulf region into east-coast Florida when he ran into organized crime stalwart Meyer Lansky's domain. Following his death, the leadership of the Tampa syndicate was passed on to his son, Santo Trafficante, Jr. (1914–1987), who led the organization for another 30 years. Such a succession is indeed rare in mob history. Although the Tampa Bay mob never rose to prominence in the manner of Chicago and New York City, Santo Trafficante, Jr., succeeded his father and entered the pantheon of the country's most powerful crime bosses. Among the nation's major crime families, the Tampa syndicate remained one of the most difficult to penetrate. One leading authority chalked this up to the fact that a number of its members had grown up together, and that there was "a high rate of intermarriage among the different crime figures" (Deitche 2007, 128).

Santo Trafficante, Jr., played a crucial role in the operation of gambling casinos in Havana, and in 1954 relocated to Cuba. Recent scholarship asserts that at the same time, Trafficante was placed in charge of the training of clandestine operatives inside various Cuban political groups "in order to administer Mafia affairs in Havana" (Cirules 2004, 17). This had the twofold purpose of controlling organized crime interests as well as creating relationships with the leadership of various opposition parties that might have had future influence.

During his legendary career in organized crime, Santo Trafficante, Jr., was regarded as one of the country's most powerful bosses. Together with his father, the Trafficantes initiated early efforts to move into the Cuban casino business prior to the Cuban Revolution in 1959. The son moved to Cuba in 1946, and regarded it as his home until Castro came to power and closed down the casinos. He returned to Florida soon after and established ties in transnational crime activities, especially in the heroin trade.

Trafficante entered the public consciousness in a big way in 1975, when he testified that he had been deeply involved in CIA-brokered deals with the underworld to kill Castro. He admitted to a congressional committee that his coterie of conspirators tried "poison, planes, and tanks," but that each plot failed. The underworld–CIA connection is well chronicled, but fraught with inconsistencies.

By most accounts, it seemed Trafficante never seriously planned to kill the dictator, but was simply using the CIA. Since testifying 3 years later in front of the House Kennedy assassination committee in 1978, Trafficante has become a central figure in various assassination conspiracy theories due to his shadowy exploits in Cuba and with the CIA.

Organized Crime and the Assassination of JFK

In the late dinner hours of November 22, 1963, Tampa, Florida, boss Santo Trafficante shared several toasts with his longtime lawyer Frank Ragano in an upscale Tampa restaurant. It had been barely a month since Joseph Valachi had testified in front of a Senate Committee investigating organized crime. The room was rather subdued, for after all, the nation's youngest president had just been murdered earlier in the day in Dallas. Little concerned by the somber crowd, Trafficante repeated over and over again as he knocked glasses with his lawyer, "Isn't that something? They killed the son-of-a-bitch!" (Raab 2005, 126). They were not alone in the gangster community, because many were hoping this would end the unparalleled crackdown on organized crime that had been engineered by the attorney general, the president's brother Robert Kennedy.

There is a virtual cottage industry of books on the various conspiracy theories surrounding the assassination of President John F. Kennedy in 1963.[42] Prior to the late 1970s, most attention was focused on the backlash by the Cubans to attempts by the CIA to kill Fidel Castro using Mafia operatives in the former gaming capital of Havana. Of all the conspiracy theories, the notion that organized crime was involved in the Kennedy assassination has attained a prominent place among possible scenarios. More credence has been given to this conspiracy due to the eminent profiles of several of its proponents. Of these, G. Robert Blakey stands out (see Chapter 14 on RICO),[43] whose credentials include Chief Counsel of the 1979 House Select Committee on Assassinations (HSCA) and authorship of the RICO statute. The mob thesis continues to loom large as the most popular theory, in no small part due to the findings of the HSCA. The 2-year, $5 million investigation by the HSCA concluded that the murder of JFK was probably a conspiracy and the Mafia had the "motive, means, and opportunity" to kill him. The committee identified three prominent Mob figures (Marcello, Trafficante, and Hoffa) who, according to government informants, had each plotted or predicted the assassination, leading Blakey to write, "We concluded from our investigation that organized crime had a hand in the assassination of President Kennedy" (Blakey and Billings 1992, 205). Some of his evidence was based on a January 14, 1992, interview with Trafficante lawyer Frank Ragano by the *New York Post*. According to the interview, Ragano revealed knowledge of a plot involving Hoffa, Trafficante, and Marcello to assassinate the president (Benson 2003, 278).

Blakey's 1981 book and subsequent second edition, published in 1992 as *Fatal Hour: The Assassination of President Kennedy by Organized Crime*, presents a number of possible but unproved scenarios that have been accepted hook, line, and sinker by conspiracy buffs. These included Jimmy Hoffa possessing the motive and means to kill the president; an alleged deathbed confession by Santo Trafficante, Jr.; Sam Giancana's connection with JFK through the sharing of mistress Judith Campbell; Jack Ruby's and Lee Harvey Oswald's connections to Cuba and organized crime; and Carlos Marcello's almost pathological hatred for the Kennedy family after he was exiled to Guatemala in 1961 by Attorney General Robert Kennedy.

The "Organized Crime Did It" Lobby

Bill Bonanno, son of legendary mob boss Joe Bonanno, claimed in *Bound by Honor* that mob families outside of the Marcello–Trafficante–Giancana factions knew immediately the assassination was a mob hit and claimed that Jack Ruby "belonged to Sam Giancana like a pinkie ring" (Bonanno 1999, 110–111). He also claimed that certain members of the Dallas Police Department were on the payroll of Carlos Marcello, including J. D. Tippett, who was killed by Oswald. Tippett was supposedly charged with killing Oswald, but was beaten to the draw. The way Bonanno tells it, the task to kill Oswald was then given to Ruby (Bonanno 1999, 110–111).

Chicago Boss Sam Giancana's contacts with the CIA in an attempt to assassinate Fidel Castro have been well chronicled. Other motives for his involvement include the long-held contention that the Chicago syndicate was instrumental in providing the margin (118,000 votes) for victory in JFK presidential election in 1960. Giancana and others felt betrayed when Kennedy appointed his brother Robert attorney general. Bobby went on to become a major thorn in the side of organized crime throughout the country.

(continued)

Accordingly, Giancana and his ilk were of the mind that to get rid of RFK, they should hit the president. What makes the Giancana connection so perplexing was the fact that he was murdered while under police protection shortly before he was scheduled to testify to a Senate Intelligence Committee in 1975.

Santo Trafficante, Jr., was likewise linked to various CIA schemes to kill Castro, and reportedly made a number of references to his involvement in the murder. In 1959, while imprisoned in Cuba by Castro, a CIA memorandum to national security aide McGeorge Bundy reported that Jack Ruby visited Trafficante in jail. Much of the "evidence" for the mob connection has been based on a so-called deathbed confession that Trafficante made to his lawyer of 27 years, Frank Ragano, in which he admitted that he and Carlos Marcello were two of the architects of the assassination, reportedly telling Ragano, "Carlos [Marcello] fucked up. We should not have killed Giovanni [JFK]. We should have killed Bobby."

Carlos Marcello has frequently been tied to the murder of JFK. Five different individuals reported they overheard Marcello admit to his involvement; of these, at least two had mob connections. According to John H. Davis's *Mafia Kingfish*, Marcello told several associates that Attorney General Robert Kennedy had to be eliminated. However, he reasoned that if Robert Kennedy was killed, it would only make the president come down harder on organized crime. However, if JFK was eliminated, there was little doubt that Vice President Johnson, who "despised" the attorney general, would surely replace him. Marcello supposedly told his guests that the killing had to be accomplished with "fall guys" not associated directly with organized crime.

Naysayers

Despite the innuendoes and unsubstantiated claims of a parade of witnesses linking organized figures to the killing of JFK, the HSCA admitted at the conclusion of its investigation that it "had failed to turn up sufficient evidence to implicate anyone except Oswald" (Raab 2005, 146). The most influential and convincing debunker of organized crime involvement in the Kennedy assassination has been the respected lawyer-turned-investigative journalist Gerald Posner. In his best-selling 1993 book, *Case Closed: Lee Harvey Oswald and the Assassination of JFK*, Posner single-handedly attempted to demolish the leading conspiracy scenarios, including the notion of an organized crime angle.

Posner asserted that Trafficante's lawyer was lying, and that his story was merely his attempt to get back at his long-time client for his mistreatment at the hand of Florida boss after Ragano was disbarred and short on funds. Another suggestion was that Ragano had been close-mouthed about the case for 25 years. However, just 3 weeks before Ragano went public with his claims, the controversial film *JFK* opened up, initiating a national debate on the conspiracy theories regarding the assassination. It was probably no coincidence that Ragano was also attempting to sell his autobiography at this time. Posner has concluded that, "Those who have investigated and studied the mafia do not believe there is any credible evidence that the mob was involved in the JFK assassination" (1993, 463).

Perhaps the greatest argument against organized crime involvement in the murder of the president is the old adage attributed to Bugsy Siegel, "We only kill each other." Since before the time of Dutch Schultz, who was reportedly murdered after threatening to kill District Attorney Thomas Dewey, there has been an unwritten rule in mob circles that those outside of gangland circles were off limits. FBI agent Bill Roemer kept tabs on the mob for 30 years, and is considered an authority on gangster culture. According to Roemer, "The mob would never go after someone as high-ranking as RFK and JFK," in fact, he said, "They don't go after reporters, they don't go after judges, they don't go after FBI agents or cops—they will only go after these people when they have stolen money from them and double-crossed them." Roemer concluded that it would be "counterproductive" and would lead to the "end of the mafia if they went after the attorney general or the president and anything went wrong" (quoted in Posner 1993, 464).

Overview

No less than gangland specialist Jerry Capeci has asserted that a "unique American version of the Sicilian Mafia" emerged in the 20th century. Compared to its Sicilian counterpart, which is restricted to Sicilian males, the American La Cosa Nostra was open to men "whose roots went back to all parts of Italy" (Capeci 2002, iii). What makes the examination of the American permutation more complicated is the existence of thousands of multi-ethnic associates who provide the wheels that allow the rackets exist. This chapter examines a number of ethnic and racial organized crime groups that preceded and evolved alongside the modern Italian-American syndicates.

The passage of the 18th Amendment and the onset of Prohibition marked a turning point in the history of organized crime. Congress might have passed the Volstead Act, but it lacked the resolve to enforce it, allowing the underworld to control an entire American industry (see Chapter 6 for more on Prohibition). Prohibition, observed one writer,

> served as the gangsters' higher education, demanding as it did management skills, cooperation, planning, and high levels political contacts. It moved the gangs far beyond their neighborhood haunts. It eroded public respect for the law and turned street thugs into millionaires. By the mid-1920s the gangs, rather than serve the politicians as minions, were giving orders to mayors and congressmen. (Kelly 2000, 78)

When Prohibition ended in 1933, "A blood thread of ethnicity ran through every underworld empire" (Fox 1989, 75).

American organized crime groups can be traced back more than a century. Italian-American syndicates at their apogee influenced many sectors of the American system, from labor unions to presidential elections, and long-held interests in longshoring, trucking, gambling, construction, waste disposal, and garment manufacturing. Successful prosecutions under the RICO statutes during the 1980s decimated the country's leading Mafia families. By the end of the decade, less than half of the original 24 families still existed, with half of them still operating in New York. Virtually every boss of the fabled New York crime families had been indicted, imprisoned, or died, leaving the syndicates in the hands of individuals who would probably been passed over for membership just 20 years earlier. By most accounts, membership of the five major New York Families declined from 3,000 in the 1970s to 1,200 in the late 1990s. As of 2006, the decimated Commission had not even met in a decade (Kaplan 2006).

The age of terrorism has shifted law enforcement away from organized crime investigations in the 21st century and is in many cases allowing the regeneration of old crime families and the formation of new syndicates. The chief of the FBI's Organized Crime Section in New York recently noted that unlike their "fathers and grandfathers and uncles," this new generation is "smarter and better educated mobsters" (Kaplan 2006, 1). The most active families are still in New York, Chicago, Detroit, New England, New Jersey, Philadelphia, and Miami. Eschewing the brutal methods of their forbears, the new breed of mobsters prefers white-collar crimes using the Internet and stock market frauds. Perhaps the biggest change in American organized crime since the early 1990s has been the emergence of new ethnic gangs from Asia, Central America, Western Africa, and Eastern Europe, as well as the evolution of some urban street gangs such as the Gangster Disciples and Almighty Latin Kings into organized syndicates.

Key Terms

Saloon culture	Political patronage	Whitey Bulger and the
Urban youth gangs	The Whiskey Ring	Winter Hill Gang
Jacob Riis	Mike McDonald	Jack Dragna
Five Points	Chicago Outfit	Mickey Cohen
Gangs of New York	Mont Tennes	Bugsy Siegel
Whyos	Jim Colosimo	Mickey Mouse Mafia
Monk Eastman	John Torrio	Purple Gang
Arnold Rothstein	Al Capone	Mayfield Road Mob
1919 World Series	Bugs Moran	Moe Dalitz
City boss	Eliot Ness	Cleveland Statler Hilton Hotel
Boss Tweed	The Untouchables	Meeting
Tammany Hall	St. Valentine's Day	Hot Springs, Arkansas
George Cox	Massacre	Owney Madden
Hinky Dink Kenna	Sam Giancana	Egan's Rats
The Pendergasts	Salvatore Sabella	Benny Binion
Bathhouse John Coughlin	Angelo Bruno	Cigar City
Lords of the Levee	Black Mafia	Santo Trafficante, Sr.
Martin Behrman	Raymond Patriarca	Santo Trafficante, Jr.

Critical Thinking Questions

1. What was the importance of saloon culture in the development of American organized crime?
2. How can the gangs of New York be considered a progenitor to modern organized crime?
3. What conditions in the Five Points gave rise to organized crime activity?
4. How did Jews become involved in organized crime in the early 20th century, and what was their impact?
5. Why was Arnold Rothstein considered such an important crime figure? What were his contributions to the story of organized crime?
6. What role did the city boss play in urban America? What was his role in the evolution of modern organized crime?
7. Was Boss Tweed any different from other well-known city bosses? What distinguished him from the others?
8. Contrast the city bosses of at least three cities.
9. Who deserves the distinction the "Father of the Chicago Outfit"?
10. Why did Chicago become such a center of organized activity? What conditions contributed to its well-earned reputation as "the wickedest city in the United States"?
11. Who were the leading figures in Chicago organized crime between 1890 and 1970? Describe the evolution of the Outfit from the days of Mike McDonald.
12. Was Al Capone overrated? What was his role in the St. Valentine's Day Massacre?
13. How successful were Eliot Ness and the Untouchables?
14. What distinguished organized crime factions in Philadelphia, Cleveland, Detroit, St. Louis, and New England from each other?
15. Why was the L.A. mob described as the "Mickey Mouse Mafia," and who were its most prominent members?
16. Discuss the development of organized crime in the urban South, particularly the roles of Trafficante and Marcello.
17. Was the "mob" involved in the assassination of President John F. Kennedy? Discuss the various theories.

Endnotes

1. Coleman has the distinction of being the first criminal to be hanged at New York's Tombs Prison (1839).
2. The gang's name was reportedly attributed to the expression "Oh! Why! Oh! Why! Oh!" which gang members yelled to each other at the sign of approaching danger and policemen.
3. According to Luc Sante and others, the Dusters had a major cocaine problem, and this might explain the origin of their name.
4. This menu of services has been widely reported, including by Sante (1992, 215) and Asbury (1928).
5. Organized crime historian Thomas Reppetto (2004, 28) noted that Asbury's 1928 *Gangs of New York* concentrated on the Kelly gang, giving it 25 pages, compared to only 2 pages for the Black Handers.
6. Fitzgerald had met Rothstein once, but it made enough of an impression for him to inspire the creation of the character Meyer Wolfsheim for his greatest book.
7. A *bucket-shop* was a brokerage house geared toward investors of modest means. They typically handled small stock transactions and charged a slight premium over and above the listed stock prices. In many cases, bucket shops prospered by taking the money but not placing the stock orders.
8. According to Kenneth D. Ackerman, Tweed's most recent biographer, there are no primary documents with Tweed's middle name, only the initial *M.* Ackerman asserts that the initial "is doubtless for Magear, his mother's maiden name" (2005, 372). Both his son and grandson were baptized William Magear. Ackerman explained that the use of Marcy simply reflected the "then-common custom in the press of assigning political celebrities with middle names of famous people," as in the former New York State governor William L. Marcy. (See Ackerman, *Boss Tweed*, 2005, p. 371, n. 1.)
9. In the 20th century, Tammany Hall's official title became The Executive Committee of the New York County Democratic Committee.
10. Coughlin's moniker referred to his ownership of several bathhouses, which, like the saloons of the period, were places where political conversations were often conducted. Likewise, at 5'1", "Hinky Dink," in contemporary parlance, meant "a little fellow, well met."

11. Despite the taint from his affiliation with the Pendergast machine, Senator and later Vice President Harry S. Truman had a scrupulous reputation for honesty in Kansas City politics. Perhaps Truman put it best when he maintained, "Three things ruin a man: power, money, and women," quipping, "I never wanted power, I never had any money, and the only woman in my life is up at the house right now" (McCullough 1992, 181).

12. At this time, there was no federal prison system, so federal prisoners were housed in various state prisons.

13. Chicago's identification as "the Second City" came from A. J. Liebling's subtitle of his book, *Chicago: The Second City*, published in 1952.

14. There is some debate as to the origins of the word *Chicago.* Some accounts suggest the word came from a native wild onion or garlic called *chickagou;* others say it was from *chocago,* or destitute; or *shegahg,* for skunk.

15. By some accounts, McDonald was also the originator of the expression, "There's a sucker born every minute," traditionally attributed to the impresario P. T. Barnum. (See Smith 1954.)

16. In order to fill out the story of the birth of the Chicago Outfit, a well-researched biography of Tennes is overdue.

17. According to O'Banion biographer Rose Keefe, his killers included John Scalise, Albert Anselmi, and Frankie Yale. Capone later murdered Scalise and Anselmi at the infamous baseball bat–birthday party.

18. Compiled from Hornung, *Al Capone,* 1998; Kobler, *Capone,* 1971; Schoenberg, *Mr. Capone,* 1992; and Bergreen, *Capone: The Man and the Era,* 1994.

19. Virtually every textbook refers to O'Banion by the first name *Dion.* Where this comes from is anybody's guess, but according to his biographer Rose Keefe, he was born Dean Charles O'Banion in 1892, and was never called Dion during his career. One explanation is that newspapers sometimes referred to him as Dion during the Prohibition years (English 2005).

20. Arrested by the FBI in 1946, Moran died in prison from lung cancer in 1957.

21. According to ballistics evidence and insider information, the four gunmen were Fred "Killer" Burke, Gus Winkler, Ray "Crane Neck" Nugent, Bob Carey, and Fred Goetz.

22. Nitti was apparently depressed about a potential jail sentence. More probable was his embarrassment after a Hollywood motion picture studio extortion plot went awry.

23. The U.S. government tried to deport Ricca for years for using a false name when applying for citizenship.

By late 1963, 52 countries refused him entry. Ricca was cagey enough to send each Minister of the Interior his complete unabridged resume.

24. See, for example, Kefauver Report No. 3, May 1, 1951—Part I.

25. See, for example, Francis A. J. Ianni's *Black Mafia* (1974). Critics of his portrayal, such as Gus Tyler, have taken Ianni to task for concluding that Black organized crime fits neatly into the ethnic succession theory. According to Tyler, activities such as pimping, selling drugs, loan sharking, and gambling might be organized in African-American neighborhoods, but are not in the same class with the majority of accepted forms of organized crime "either qualitatively or quantitatively" (quoted in Sifakis 1987, 39).

26. For a detailed account of Philadelphia's Black Muslims, see Griffin (2003, 20–30).

27. For a remarkable early examination of the Morelli connection to the Sacco and Vanzetti case, see Herbert B. Ehrmann, *The Untried Case: The Sacco–Vanzetti Case and the Morelli Gang,* New York: Vanguard Press, 1933.

28. In 1989, virtually the entire Patriarca family leadership was caught on tape, allowing the FBI to record for the first time a mob induction ceremony in which four new members were made. The power of these tapes sent the leaders to jail, and a new boss, Francis "Cadillac Frank" Salemme, was appointed.

29. Having retired from the Senate in 1996, he was hired as president of the University of Massachusetts. However, after the 2003 hearings before a House Committee on Government Reform in Washington revealed a shadowy relationship with his brother Whitey as well as his FBI handlers, he was forced to resign and basically leave public life.

30. The relationship between FBI agent Connolly and Bulger is covered in fascinating detail in Dick Lehr and Gerald O'Neill's book, *Black Mass,* New York: Public Affairs, 2000.

31. In 2002, John Connolly was convicted of racketeering and obstruction of justice and sentenced to 10 years in a federal prison.

32. The best sources on Mickey Cohen include his book *In My Own Words*, as told to John Peer Nugent, Prentice-Hall, 1975, based on his own tape-recorded reminiscences and Steve Stevens and Craig Lockwood, *King of the Sunset Strip: Hangin' with Mickey Cohen and the Hollywood Mob,* Nashville: Cumberland House, 2006.

33. The term *Purples* was given to the gangsters when, after a series of drugstore thefts, an employee told a

newspaper reporter they were, in parlance of the era, "purple," meaning off-white or tainted.

34. Among the Detroit mobsters linked to the massacre was infamous hitman Fred "Trigger" Burke.

35. According to the gangland parlance of the 1950s, "to paint a house" meant to kill someone. Sheeran also claimed to have "painted" Joseph "Crazy Joey" Gallo at Umberto's Clam House in 1972.

36. One of the undercover agents in the McGinty Family case was Fred Rickey, whose brother Branch Rickey managed the St. Louis Cardinals.

37. Giannola's gang adopted this moniker because it reflected the agricultural roots of many of the gang members.

38. Besides the suicides of Chicago's Frank Nitti and Longy Zwillman, this was one of the few examples of this phenomenon in mob annals.

39. Kennedy assassination conspiracy buffs have claimed that Civello was the intermediary between Jack Ruby and New Orleans boss Carlos Marcello. Investigative journalist Anthony Summers claimed that Civello was "widely acknowledged to have been Texas representative" for Marcello (1981, 452).

40. For the best account of the Civello–Ruby relationship, see Scheim (1988, 98–99).

41. *Bolita* is a lottery-type game that, according to Dietche, was first brought to Ybor in the 1880s by Manuel Suarez.

42. See, for example, David E. Scheim, *Contract on America: The Mafia Murder of President John F. Kennedy,* New York: Shapolsky Publishers, 1988; G. Robert Blakey, *The Plot to Kill the President,* New York: Times Book, 1981; Brad O'Leary and L. E. Seymour, *Triangle of Death,* Nashville: WND Books, 2003; John H. Davis, *Mafia Kingfish: Carlos Marcello and the Assassination of John F. Kennedy,* New York: McGraw Hill, 1988; Seth Kantor, *Who Was Jack Ruby?,* New York: Everest House, 1978.

43. See G. Robert Blakey, *The Plot to Kill the President,* New York: Times Book, 1981.

CHAPTER 6

Vice Prohibition in America: Alcohol, Narcotics, Gambling, and Prostitution

The 1963 McClellan Hearings on Organized Crime and the Illicit Traffic of Narcotics are best remembered for the revelations of mafia hoodlum Joseph Valachi; however, the hearings also characterized a *crime syndicate* "as the combination of a number of persons who resort to criminal means in order to establish a monopoly in a financially profitable activity" (Committee on Government Operations 1963, 486), no matter if it was legal or illegal. The committee admitted that, "Organized crime stems from the various forms of vice operations, gambling, prostitution, and the illegal sale of narcotics and liquor. . . . Vice activities are now and always have been the seedbed of organized crime."[1]

American history is rife with well-intentioned, mostly Anglo-Saxon Protestant reformers who deemed themselves imbued with the moral imperative to determine what types of behavior should be recognized legally. At various points in time, they have targeted activities considered immoral and a threat to the sanctity of the American system. Moral reform movements began in America's earliest history, with clergymen speaking out against the vices of gambling, drinking, prostitution, and breaking the Sabbath. They believed that if they controlled these behaviors, "they would address the sources of poverty, crime, and other social evils" (Woodiwiss 2001, 171). It is doubtful that these moral crusaders could have predicted that organized crime would use the prohibitions of various vices to create unimagined criminal empires.

According to criminal justice historian Alan Block, "The networks within which vice entrepreneurs labored are but part of the history of the emergence of modern criminal syndicates" (1994, 62). Others have posited, "Yesterday's vice is frequently today's entertainment" (Zabilka 1995, 30). Any meaningful attempt to define what constitutes *vice* must contend with the changes of culture throughout American history. For example, at one time, a woman smoking a cigarette in public was considered morally repugnant. As America urbanized in the 19th century, few cities were without districts devoted to vice—typically involving sex, drugs, drinking, prostitution, and gambling. Some were formally or informally protected by public policy that was intended to isolate or at least contain illicit activities in segregated vice zones (Spillane 1998, 28).

Among the classes of people that profited most from America's urban growth were its professional thieves and vice entrepreneurs (Johnson 1979, 6). It wasn't long before vice entrepreneurs found common cause with urban politicians. New York City's John Morrissey typified the professional criminals of the mid-19th century, when "professional gamblers, gangs, and politicians of this era shared a growing affinity that ultimately led to the creation of gambling syndicates" (Schwartz 2006, 276).

Chicago: The Levee District

Chicago boasted a red-light district since the mid-19th century. It shifted from place to place over the years as residents wearied of the vice district and sporadically burned it down. It moved from the Sands to Little Cheyenne, then to Hell's Half Acre, and the Hair Trigger Block; however, the Levee lasted longer than any of them. The first levee in the early 1890s was home to more than 35 houses of prostitution, 46 saloons, 11 pawnbrokers, an obscene book store, and a shooting gallery. One modern observer remarked, "I think Rome at its worst had nothing on Chicago during those lurid days" (Lindberg 1985, 120). In the wake of a reform campaign in 1905, the vice resorts of the Levee were relocated farther south.

By the middle of the 19th century, many state legislatures had responded to pressure by reform leaders by passing anti-gambling, anti-prostitution, and other anti-racketeering laws. As a result of the reform movements, most forms of illegal vice were forced underground, laying the foundations for new criminal syndicates. Once forced underground, these pursuits became more expensive, but customers were willing to pay "a kind of value added tax based on risk." However, the success of developing organized crime syndicates was later based on their abilities to transcend local crime markets to forge national, regional, and international alliances that would expand the illegal markets as well as the sources of supply (Block 1994, 64).

At the turn of the 20th century, urban reformers could see that despite their victories in state legislatures, their efforts had clearly failed. What had not been forecast was that few city governments encouraged the police to enforce the laws (unless someone failed to pay protection money); more important, it soon became apparent that many politicians were in league with the vice entrepreneurs. Urban reformers and their allies saw signs everywhere that America was in need of a moral facelift, citing the popularity of alcohol, gambling, drugs, dances, new clothing styles, and the contaminating effects of the new motion picture industry.

By the 1920s and the end of the so-called Progressive era, a number of laws had been passed directed at eradicating the "vices" of millions of Americans. What happened instead was the reverse. The unforeseen consequences resulted in laws that fostered, facilitated, and sustained an illegal economy that was far more destructive and corrupting than any that existed in more tolerant societies. Although city governments charged local police forces with stamping out these vices, politicians often failed to support their efforts, and in effect, "licensed vice, enabling entrepreneurs to build up bookmaking, lottery, and policy syndicates, operate strings of gambling houses, or run houses of prostitution" (Woodiwiss 2001, 170–171).

ALCOHOL PROHIBITION IN AMERICA

The term *prohibition* is synonymous, at least in America, with the advent of the 18th Amendment and the subsequent Volstead Act, which paved the way for 13 years of alcohol prohibition. On January 16, 1919, the 18th Amendment to the Constitution was ratified, prohibiting the manufacture, sale, import, or export of intoxicating beverages. Ten months later, on October 27, Congress followed up with the Volstead Act, to enforce the amendment. It defined an *intoxicant* as "any beverage containing more than one-half of one percent alcohol by volume" (National Prohibition Act, 1920). It also authorized federal agents to prosecute all violations and mandated stiff penalties for those convicting in alcohol trafficking. January 1, 1920, was the last night to celebrate the New Year in bacchanalian tradition before the Volstead Act went into effect on January 16, beginning more than 13 years of prohibition.

Prohibition signaled a key triumph for the Women's Christian Temperance Union and gave voice to a decidedly rural constituency that looked at the cities of the era as a source of everything that was bad about America—factories polluting the air, immigrant hordes filling the tenements, and where organized crime reigned supreme. The urban centers produced their own supporters—

reformers, journalists, sociologists, and others who saw the need for a sober workforce in an era of saloons and rampant poverty.

In America, there is a rich tradition of making alcoholic beverages at home. From the first English colonies in the 17th and 18th centuries, colonists drank mostly beer and wine—probably from recipes brought with them from the Old World. By 1650, cider presses churned out gallons of hard cider—the better to help celebrate civic and social occasions. Soon the popularity of hard cider was surpassed by a new drink called *rum,* first distilled in America from pure cane sugar, or fermented molasses. By 1750, Massachusetts boasted more than 60 rum distilleries and an associated workforce of more than 1,000. The rum trade was international in scope; colonists preferred British sources of molasses to the cheaper versions available from French, Dutch, and Spanish traders in the Caribbean. Unwilling to compromise or lose the colonial trade, the English responded with the Molasses Act, which imposed high taxes on molasses purchased from foreign sources. This essentially stimulated the illegal smuggling of molasses. However, rum traders were willing to risk stern punishments and continued the underground trade. In 1763 alone, of the 150,000 hogsheads of molasses imported, duties were paid on only 1,000.

The Roots of Alcohol Prohibition

American temperance advocates had been crusading for anti-alcohol reform since the 1820s. However, unknown to its vociferous supporters, was the impetus it would provide for the creation of modern organized crime syndicates just 100 years later. Despite claims that alcohol prohibition was a response to the drinking cultures that immigrated to America beginning with the Irish in the 1820s and 1830s, and then the Italians, Jews, and other Eastern and South Europeans later in the century, America had a love affair with alcohol dating back to pre-immigration times. Following the American Revolution, it was common for almost every American community to have a village church and local tavern. Diametrically opposed to one another in spirit, the tavern was the most accessible local institution for the male world of the late 18th and early 19th centuries. Even the former Puritan communities of New England boasted more licensed taverns than meetinghouses. However, the problem was not necessarily the act of drinking, but the prodigious amount of libations consumed. According to one estimate, during the late 1700s each person consumed the equivalent of 3.5 gallons of pure, 200-proof alcohol. By the end of the 1790s, perhaps because of the anxieties generated by rapid social change, men were drinking even more heavily, with consumption increasing to an all-time high of 4 gallons per capita by the late 1820s (Rorabaugh 1979).

During the following two decades, liquor consumption declined in some regions of the country, in no small part due the temperance crusade led by New England clergymen. The campaign against drinking found a public voice in 1826, with the inauguration of the American Temperance Society. A highly charged crusade against "demon rum" and its resultant social disorder was supplemented by pamphlets written by the nation's leading doctors warning of the poisonous effects of alcohol, much in the vein of the materials used to propagandize "deadly marijuana" a century later. In 1838, temperance advocates won their first major victory when Massachusetts banned the sale of liquor in amounts under 15 gallons. This attempt to keep distilled liquor from taverns and the poor was repealed 2 years later. In any case, the crusade seemed to be working because by 1840, alcohol consumption had plummeted from 4 gallons per person per year to less than 1.5 gallons per person per year (Rorabaugh 1979; Walters 1978).

The transformation of American society in the first half of the 19th century was accompanied by growing clamor for a temperance movement (along with the growth of anti-immigrant hostility). During the 1840s and 1850s, nativist political parties, such as the short-lived American Republic Party and the Know-Nothing Party, founded on anti-Catholicism and anti-slavery, found common cause in the temperance movements of the era. By 1850, the Sons of Temperance claimed 250,000 dues-paying members. Whether religious or secular in nature, reform groups resorted to political action to accomplish their objective of taming demon rum.

Blue Laws

One consequence of the Prohibition era was a patchwork of laws, or *blue laws,* that exist today related to what people and businesses can do on Sundays, including the sale of alcohol that sometimes varies by county in certain states. Blue laws were introduced in Connecticut in the 17th century, so-named for the blue paper on which the laws were printed. Laws typically targeted drunkenness and excesses in dress. Today they are just as likely to restrict auto sales, hunting, or other activities (but you can still rent pornographic videos on Sundays). During the 19th and 20th centuries, a prohibition movement introduced more restrictive laws including bans on cigarette sales and entertainment, including books, movies, and plays. In 1961, the Supreme Court upheld the right of states to enact blue laws so long as their purpose was not religious (DeCuir 2007).

As of 2007, you still couldn't purchase beer or wine before noon in Texas, a holdover from the 1920s mindset. The legal sale of alcoholic beverages begins generally at noon, while the rest of the week its starts at 7 A.M. Texas' beverage code was drafted in the 1930s after Prohibition was repealed. Texas joined most other states in repealing Prohibition in 1933, and 2 years later voters ratified a repeal of the state dry law, leaving the issue to local communities. There are several counties that continue to remain dry by choice. Colorado has outlawed store sales of alcohol on Sunday since the repeal of Prohibition in 1933.

Proponents of repealing blue laws in Texas, Colorado, and elsewhere cite the desire to boost revenues and increase consumer convenience, whereas opponents typically refer to religious and family concerns and believe 6 days is plenty of time to buy booze. The move to change blue laws pertaining to alcohol picked up steam in 2006, when New Year's Eve and Christmas both fell on Sundays. Although 34 states permit Sunday alcohol sales, in 2007, proposals to lift it were defeated in Georgia, Missouri, Tennessee, and Minnesota.

After opponents of slavery joined the temperance crusade in the mid-1840s, Maine passed a law in 1846 that prohibited the sale of intoxicating beverages in less than 28-gallon increments. Enforcement of the law was added to the duties of each town's selectmen, although they were prone to look the other way when these infractions took place. Prohibitionists won their greatest victory up to that time when the Maine Law of 1851 was passed, prohibiting the sale and manufacture of all intoxicating beverages in the state. Over the next 5 years, 13 states passed similar laws, and New England, New York, and parts of the Midwest were considered *dry.* Although most prohibition laws were repealed by 1860, from this era on, the temperance crusade played an instrumental role in American politics and continued to challenge law enforcement on both the local and state levels.

Bootlegging

By most accounts, the term *bootlegging* came from the practice in various southern states in which *moonshiners* attempted to evade paying federal taxes on manufactured distilled spirits by delivering a pint or half-pint in the leg of his boot (Willing 1926, 40). Prohibition created the multimillion-dollar enterprise known as bootlegging. Like the current virtually unenforceable "war on drugs," attempts by the federal government (tasked) to patrol 18,000 miles of coastline; guard against the diversion of some 57 million gallons of industrial alcohol; oversee hundreds of millions of medical prescriptions; or monitor 20 million homes to prevent the manufacturing of home brew, wine, or bathtub gin were for naught. Chicago's Capone syndicate was among the many similar organizations bringing in tens of millions of dollars a year. It was in the country's largest cities where burgeoning ethnic enclaves sought "to keep their traditional drinking patterns alive" (Lender and Martin 1987, 141). The city offered all of the requirements necessary for a prospective bootlegging syndicate—lots of customers, transportation and storage facilities, distribution networks, and retail sales outlets (Lender and Martin 1987, 141).

One contemporary broke down the illegal alcohol trade into five specialties that included smuggling and transportation; redistillation or recooking; doctor and druggist complex; brewing of high-power beer; home brew and accessory stores; and homemade wine, ciders, and cordials (Willing 1926, 41).

Home Brew, Moonshine, and Bathtub Gin

In 1968, some 35 years after the end of Prohibition, the director of the ATF Division declared, "Moonshining is now an organized crime activity. It has specialists in production, transportation and in matters of finance" (quoted in Kellner 1971, 224). That same year, law enforcement seized and destroyed more than 13,000 moonshine stills—operations that produced more than 6 million gallons and accounted for more than $7 million in lost taxes (Kellner 1971, 224). According to Davis and Potter (1991), "there may be no purer form of organized crime enterprise than the rural bootlegging operations" they studied in rural Kentucky. Like other prohibitions in this chapter and other forms of criminal "entrepreneurship," moonshining developed out of the demand "for goods and services proscribed by law but in heavy demand in the community" (1991, 157). There was already a rich history of homemade alcohol in the United States prior to the advent of the 18th Amendment. As early as 1900, local and county prohibition laws started the process that would make several states dry by 1916, including Alabama, Arkansas, Georgia, North and South Carolina, Tennessee, Virginia, and West Virginia—southern states where moonshining morphed from "a little business into a big business" (Miller 1991, 187). Prices rose with Prohibition as moonshine stills sprung up in areas that were the driest. It was impossible to shut them all down; almost a half decade before national Prohibition, experiments in a handful of states "foreshadowed the difficulties of enforcing national prohibition in the twenties" (Miller 1991, 188).

Unlike the legitimate industry, moonshiners, bootleggers, and their ilk are rarely concerned with quality control, let alone paying social security taxes. In addition, few dollars went toward sanitation, advertising costs, or maintaining well-lighted retail establishments. The same factors that guarantee big profits for the manufacturers also create a product that is, on occasion, hazardous for human consumption. One of the biggest challenges facing both consumers and manufacturers of illegal alcohol was producing a beverage that would not kill the consumer—even today there are major dangers of lead poisoning in bootleg brew. There are a variety of sources for the lead; it is common for moonshiners to condense alcohol in the radiators (often containing a large amount of lead solder) of junked cars. Because the lead salts are undetectable through taste or sight, the imbiber of such brew has no protection. Unfortunately, only a small amount is enough to blind, paralyze, or kill the drinker. Revenue agents have even uncovered stashes of alcohol made with embalming fluid and grain alcohol.

In the 1920s, most upper-middle class drinkers were unwilling to risk their lives with home-made brew, preferring to pay a little more for liquors properly distilled and blended. This demand led to an international trade that although bringing in higher profits, was also more logistically complex and expensive. In order to make a profit, bootleggers often had to cut corners, even with the best booze, and it was not uncommon to cut liquor much like the drug dealer cuts dope. One ruse required identical labels and bottles and, to complete the façade, a little caramel coloring was added and combined with some pure alcohol. One formula used a bottle of top-shelf Scotch and a bottle of Canadian whiskey to make three bottles for the retail market. Canadian whiskey became so popular that at one time, almost 80% of all whiskey produced in Canada ended up south of the border.

Illegal beverages reached the market in a variety of ways. There is still some debate over this topic, with several studies suggesting that home distilling "was more prevalent on a small-scale, family basis than at any other time since the frontier days of the late 18th and early 19th centuries" (Lender and Martin 1987, 142). In large urban centers throughout the country, families purchased supplies for their $10 "alchy cookers" by which they produced several gallons of neutral spirits each day. This practice was so epidemic in some cities that Detroit was described by one historian as a "city upon a still" (Lender and Martin 1987, 142).

In many an Italian neighborhood it was estimated that hundreds of thousands of residents were involved in the production of bootleg wine—much of it purchased by organized crime groups. In some communities, local gangsters sold $2 cookers to prospective home producers; they later stopped back and bought homemade beverages for an average of $2 per gallon.

Deadly Brew in India (2008)

In May 2008, Indian media reported that more than 70 people in southern India died from alcohol tainted with lethal chemicals, and authorities arrest 8 people for selling illegal homebrewed alcohol. By most accounts, deaths from cheap alcohol are common here, with poor workers the typical victims.

Bootlegging Costs and the High Price of Illegal Booze

At the onset of Prohibition, the majority of smugglers were freelancers, often stealing each other's illegal booze shipments. However, then they began to get organized. More important, Irish, Jewish, and Italian gangsters found common ground in a trade that returned great profits if bloodshed was minimized. Chicago's John Torrio was among the more astute mobsters who grasped the opportunities presented by Prohibition. Torrio built his bootlegging empire on the foundations of the former Colosimo organization, and was credited with bringing stability and maximizing profits in the Windy City by bringing together most of Chicago's major gangs at the onset of Prohibition, forging them into a cartel that divided up the liquor business. In the heyday of the Torrio era, Chicago was divided up among the Northsiders, east of the north branch of the Chicago River, under Deanie O'Banion; the Genna brothers had the Near West Side, around Taylor Street; the West Side O'Donnells controlled the mostly Irish West Side; whereas the Druggan-Lake gang controlled the Near Southwest Side and west of there; and the Saltis-McErland gang ran the stockyards. Torrio controled the largest operation on the South Side areas to the south and west of the city. Theoretically, this arrangement was solid, but almost from the beginning, it was challenged by forces from within and without by those not accorded territories in this plan who sought more than their fair share. So, although the profits were highest as long as this arrangement was followed, it became clear that the promise of easy money was too strong to be resisted, and gangs began cheating on turf arrangements—most notably the "beer wars" between the non-Italian Northsiders and the Italians in 1924 (Binder 2003).

Meyer Lansky suggested that anyone could produce illegal liquor, but only good enough to sell to Skid Row alcoholics and low-grade speakeasies—few customers that could be counted on for repeat business. However, what was more important was to be able to provide an illicit alcohol that appealed to high rollers and socialites, those who could pay for the best. In what became known as *Lansky's Law,* the idea that "If you have a lot of what people want and can't get, then you can supply the demand and shovel in the dough." This mantra, according to one expert, became the centerpiece and "economic foundation of all modern organized crime" (Volkman 1998, 21).

Organized-crime groups faced enormous expenses and numerous risks getting their product to market. Costs came from a number of factors. Like the modern-day drug business, bootleggers had to hire strong-arm enforcers and security, chemists, workers for the distilleries, production equipment, shipping and trucks, and pay the ever-increasing payoffs to police and city officials. In order to make a profit, the price of drinking became substantially higher between the late 1910s and 1930s. Astute

Bathtub Gin

Most family operations used a recipe that mixed alcohol with 30%–40% water, adding several drops of glycerin and juniper juice to replicate the taste of gin. The mixture was then poured into bottles or jugs that were typically too tall to fill with water from the average water tap; so as an alternative they were filled from the bathtub tap—hence the term *bathtub gin* (Lender and Martin 1987).

observers suggested that "bootlegging activity was less a sign that drinking was rife than an explanation of why it was hard to drink cheaply" (Lender and Martin 1987, 145). Testament to this phenomenon was the fact that cocktails that cost a quarter in 1918 had tripled in price by the 1920s; as domestic lager beer rose from $10.40 to $160 per barrel, and domestic spirits surged from $1.39 to $4.01 per bottle by 1930.

If one fancied imported liquor, the prices were even higher. Scots distillers, for example, charged $17 for a 12-bottle case of Scotch before 1920, but raised it to $26 a case to American customers in what one pundit described as "revenge for Yorktown." Syndicates sold it for $30 a bottle; with the highest quality going for up to $175 a bottle. Meyer Lansky reported that each shipment of 3,000 cases returned a $1 million net profit. Regardless of the quality, by the mid-1920s, organized crime groups were raking in millions each month from overseas shipments alone.

Testimony to the expensive nature of the bootleg trade was Luciano's record of expenses for 1925, when he made $12 million. Costs included a payroll of about $1 million per year. Of the remaining $11 million, $5 million went to bribes and $2 million to liquor and operational expenses. Luciano and his partners still managed to pocket almost $4 million after expenses.

Luciano and his compatriots discovered early that to obtain the best liquor, they needed to set up huge smuggling operations that required purchasing the genuine article in Great Britain and Canada. They had to buy large ships to transport the goods to the 3-mile limit[2]; from there an armada of speed boats would be used to offload the booze to shore, where they would be met by an army of trucks responsible for moving it to the warehouses of wholesale bootleggers; security was needed to protect the stock; a distribution network was needed to move the liquor to retailers and thence to consumers; and finally a financial organization to keep track of it all and collect the profits.

Smugglers depended on a "Rum Row" that was active off the coasts of many large cities. Here ships lined up beyond the 3-mile territorial limit as they waited for fast boats to pick up the cargoes coming from Great Britain and the Caribbean. A number of American bootleggers established bases outside the country in such far-flung locales as the island of St. Pierre and Miquelon (south of Newfoundland), the Bahamas, British Honduras, Mexico, and even Papeete, Tahiti. Of these rum runners, none was immortalized more than Bill McCoy. He was renowned for his rum-running skills and the quality of his merchandise, earning the sobriquet of "the original Real McCoy." Between 1921 and 1925 he was credited with moving more than 175,000 cases of illegal liquor before being arrested (Woodiwiss 2001, 187).

Most of the liquor that was legally imported into the United States, whether from Italy, Spain, or France, had been "dealcoholized" by law to 0.1% by volume of ethyl alcohol. Complementing the flow of this product was a parallel import market that brought "essence" products to grocery stores—flavors that mimicked the tastes of crème de menthe, Benedictine, vermouth, scotch mash, sloe gin, and others, if one had the requisite imagination. All that was needed to complete the concoction was a little grain of sugar and a dash of pure ethyl alcohol.

Industrial alcohol was legally available throughout the Prohibition years. However, there was a catch: although it had to be *denatured*—in other words, *poisoned*—there was a relatively easy process that could be utilized to remove the poison. According to one recipe, a gallon of denatured alcohol could be treated to produce 3 gallons of counterfeit Scotch or gin. By law, denatured alcohol was still allowed for medicinal purposes, preparing photographic film, making smokeless gunpowder, and other products. Between 1920 and 1933, the production of denatured alcohol increased from 28 million to 180 million gallons, with an estimate that perhaps a third of it found its way into the illicit liquor business (Lender and Martin 1987). According to one account, this poisoned version was so profuse in the state of Pennsylvania that its governor complained that 150 firms in that state had been authorized to purchase it purportedly "to manufacture perfumes and hair tonic, [enough to] fill the needs of the entire world" (Woodiwiss 2001, 186).

A new type of organization was necessary to meet the needs required by this new approach to the distribution and sale of an illegal substance—one in which Lansky organized the financial network, Lucchese organized the transportation system, and Costello paid off police officers and other officials. One of the greatest reversals of Prohibition was the fact that the politicians who had originally controlled much of the criminal landscape and expected a share of organized crime activities were now the pawns of the gangsters who bought and controlled them. A main ingredient of a successful organization was the use of corruption, an essential mob tool. In its first year, the bribing of Prohibition agents and police officers was widespread. The agents were especially vulnerable; they were not law-enforcement professionals but served because of their proper dry credentials—selected because they had the requisite political and theological views. In any case, the bribing of Prohibition agents and cops became epidemic in urban America.

In May 1929, "Lucky" Luciano convinced approximately 30 fellow gangland kingpins to meet in Atlantic City to discuss a better game plan for the expansion of Prohibition operations, an early overture toward the creation of some type of national crime syndicate. Delegates to the meeting included some of the nation's most respected and feared crime lords. The largest contingent came from New York City, including Luciano, Lansky, Frank Costello, Joe Adonis, Dutch Schultz, Louis Lepke, and many others. Longy Zwillman traveled from New Jersey, Al Capone and Jake Guzik from Chicago, John Lazia from Kansas City, Moe Dalitz from Cleveland, and members of the Purple Gang came from Detroit. Besides establishing a syndicate of cooperation, discussion included the liquor business following the end of Prohibition. Most concurred that it would be reasonable to get into the legitimate end of the liquor business by purchasing breweries, distilleries, and import operations. However, most saw a future in gambling.

FIGURE 6.1 Prohibition-era corkscrew disguised as inside waiter trinket. Head lifts off and acts as handle
Source: Dorling Kindersley Media Library

FIGURE 6.2   Protesting against Prohibition
Source: U.S. Department of the Treasury

Impact of Alcohol Prohibition

The impact of alcohol prohibition on America is still a subject of intense debate among scholars. By most accounts, deaths from alcoholism increased in this era from 1 per 100,000 between 1914 and 1920 to 3.9 per 100,000 in 1926. In 1920, deaths from cirrhosis of the liver were about 6.2 per 100,000; 6 years later, they had risen to 7.3 per 100,000. A number of these deaths were no doubt the result of toxic ingredients (Cashman 1981). Bootleg alcohol was not restricted by the terms of the 1906 Pure Food and Drug Act.

In 1933, after the repeal of Prohibition, a news publication claimed that the final cost of Prohibition was more than one-third greater than the national debt of $22 billion, and $10 billion more than the cost of America's participation in World War I, which was $26.361 trillion. A tabulation of Prohibition killings surpassed 1,100 civilians and 512 Prohibition agents between 1920 and 1932 (quoted in Helmer and Mattix 1998, 65).

With criminal syndicates now deeply embedded in American society by the end of Prohibition, they were organized well enough to turn their talents to traditional vices such as gambling, drugs, and prostitution.

Not all bootleggers faded into obscurity or the shadows of the underworld following the repeal of the 18th Amendment, many reconverted their illegitimate operations into legitimacy. Joe Kennedy, for example, became the official distributor for Haig & Haig and Pinchbottle Whiskey and Gordon's Gin (even before repeal); however, Sam Bronfman, once Canada's largest bootlegger and Luciano's biggest supplier, went on to found Seagram's. Mobster Frank Costello and his associates set up Alliance Distributors, selling the same brands of Scotch that they smuggled during the 1920s and later acquired a controlling interest in the Scotch distributor J. Turnley and Sons (Behr 1996, 240).

FIGURE 6.3 Car with sign "Happy Days are BEER again"
Source: U.S. Department of the Treasury

Joseph Kennedy and Prohibition

Having grown up in a family that relied on the profits of liquor—his father owned a saloon—it should not be surprising that Joseph Kennedy, father of future President John F. Kennedy, quickly grasped the opportunities provided by the 18th Amendment. At the end of prohibition in 1933, Kennedy was regarded as the largest distributor of Scotch in the United States (Kessler 1996, 36). During the 1920s, Kennedy purchased liquor from international distillers and furnished it to organized crime syndicates that unloaded it from boats offshore. Frank Costello recalled that Joe approached him to help smuggle illegal alcohol and made an arrangement in which Kennedy dropped the liquor at a transhipment point known as "Rum Row," where police were paid to look the other way, and Costello took over. Other luminaries such as Meyer Lansky, "Lucky" Luciano, Dutch Schultz, and Longy Zwillman participated as well. Together, they fixed prices, distributed the booze, established quotas, and paid off corrupt police and politicians. Although Kennedy surrogates have always denied this relationship, it has been well-chronicled by a number of writers and mob bosses. For example, in 1983, Joe Bonanno told Mike Wallace on the CBS show *60 Minutes* that his employees unloaded whiskey for Kennedy at Sag Harbor in Long Island, New York. During Prohibition, Kennedy stockpiled liquor after receiving permission through Washington, D.C., contacts to import large quantities of Haig & Haig and Dewar's as medicine (Kessler 1996, 104). As a result, when the 18th Amendment was lifted in 1933, he possessed one of the largest inventories of premium liquor in the country.

A case of Scotch cost roughly $65, which included shipping, bribes, purchase, and delivery. It was estimated that one could earn $325,000 for a 5,000 case shipment. Typically, each bottle was diluted by half using other liquid ingredients. Once this was done, it was repackaged and sold to a wholesaler for

$85 a case. Once this process was completed, $525,000 could be earned on an investment of $325,000—a markup of almost two thirds. It should not be surprising the ease with which Kennedy was able to supply liquor to his 10th Harvard class reunion in 1922, according to former classmates. *Fortune Magazine* estimated in the mid-1920s that Kennedy was worth $2 million—or $15 million in 2008 dollars, a significant fortune. So although the legends suggested that Joe got rich playing the stock market in the years leading up to the Stock Crash of 1929, most sources agree that he could have only made his early fortune through organized bootlegging.

PROSTITUTION

Prostitution served as a lucrative source of income for organized crime syndicates in the United States for more than 150 years. By the middle of the 19th century, urban America offered "a wide variety of commercial sexual activity" (Gilfoyle 1992, 18). Houses of prostitution were available in most cities, visible to customers and non-customers alike. According to one leading historian, it had become so commercially viable by the mid-1850s that for the first time in American history, "with the opportunity to resort to prostitutes on a massive scale, sex became an objective consumer commodity" as an underground economy soon flourished (Gilfoyle 1992, 18).

Although some states lacked laws that explicitly criminalized prostitution in the 19th century, prostitution was nonetheless never accepted as a respectable profession. By the 1860s and 1870s, many Americans were beginning to view it as less a crime and more a public health problem, as reflected by St. Louis' experimentation with legalization between 1870 and 1874, when local health and police boards persuaded the state to give the city new powers, including the power to regulate or suppress "bawdy or disorderly houses, houses of ill-fame, or assignation" (Friedman, 1993, 225).

The passage of this ordinance gave police licensing authority over brothels. The public at first expressed approval as 1,284 prostitutes were legally registered to work in 136 licensed brothels, 9 houses of assignation, and 243 single rooms. In the end, regulation failed—it "looked too much like a bargain with the devil" (Friedman 1993, 225). According to one historian,

> The dirty little secret of the century was not prostitution itself, but the business of prostitution. Men (and women) ran houses as a business; policemen, from patrolmen to captains, were on the take. Most shocking of all (to some) was that many of the women looked on prostitution as simply a job, a way to keep from starving in an era with few opportunities for women. (Friedman 1993, 225)

Soon police and public officials in other cities talked about medical exams for prostitutes as bills for prostitution licenses were introduced in New York City between 1867 and 1871. However, these were all shot down by the state government in Albany. Despite sporadic outbursts of moral reform, law enforcement favored a policy of containment or "maintenance" rather than prohibition, in hopes it could control it by either "driving it underground, confining it to specific areas, or prosecuting only its most disorderly or lowly haunts" (Friedman 1993, 226).

America's urban areas have never lacked for places to sin, with a number hosting notable red light districts in the years leading up to the 20th century (Keire 2001). By the last quarter of the 19th

What Is Prostitution?

Prostitution can be generally defined as the granting of non-marital sexual access, established by mutual agreement of the woman/man, a client, and/or employer, for remuneration that provides part or all of his/her livelihood. In a number of states, a *prostitute* is defined as any person who participates in "indiscriminate sexual intercourse" for a fee or anything else of value" (Winick and Kinsie 1971, 3).

FIGURE 6.4 Prostitutes leaning out tenement windows in New York City
Source: Pearson Education/PH College/Laimute Druskis

century, a peaceful coexistence had been established by which prostitution was confined with other vices to specific vice districts, where it would not offend the sensibilities of the respectable classes. These red light zones remained "strongholds of organized vice" (Keire 2001, 12), but were mostly immune to police crackdowns thanks to a shadowy network of police corruption, shakedowns, and payoff schemes. Perhaps one authority put it best when he noted, "Organized crime has had a range of relationships to prostitution in the United States, reflecting the circumstances, formats, and degree of acceptance and law enforcement" of it in different periods of American history (Winick 1994, 289).

Organized Prostitution in the 20th Century

Prostitution served as an important source of income for organized crime groups during the early decades of the 20th century when America was one of the few countries in the world where it was illegal, and perhaps the only country where a customer could be tried for the criminal offense of seeing a prostitute. The "world's oldest profession" was a major business in most U.S. cities between 1900

The Tenderloin

The famously corrupt New York City policeman Alexander "Clubber" Williams has been credited with popularizing the term *tenderloin*. In 1871, promoted to captain, Williams famously exclaimed, "I've had nothing but chuck steak for a long time, and now I'm going to get a little tenderloin," referring to opportunities for corruption in the vice-zoned district (quoted in Roth, 2005, 173). Another source observed, "Borrowing from big city tabloids," Lexington, Kentucky, newspapers used *tenderloin* to refer to the local red light district, where handouts and bribes to policemen on this beat indicated they "were the only ones who could afford the better cuts of meat" (Thompson 1983, 87).

and 1920. Its organization varied from place to place, depending on official and unofficial polices of local law enforcement. Although some organized crime syndicates ran various sex-related operations, they never monopolized this business. In Chicago, prostitution was a mainstay of the Colosimo, Torrio, and Capone era, but once their time had passed, future leaders such as Frank Nitti and Paul Ricca were well aware of the criticism directed at the former mob bosses and "disengaged the mob from direct control of the sex business" in the 1930s (Reppetto 2004, 152). Most "made" members of Italian American organized crime were not directly involved with the business because they viewed it as low class and not a respectable business for a mobster. Instead, money was made by taking a weekly cut from brothels through protection rackets and bribery. According to some madams, "Gangster involvement tended to be more as extortionists than as organizers" (Woodiwiss 2001, 204).

At the turn of the 20th century, "an organized network of syndicates" (Gilfoyle 1992, 261) controlled and coordinated much of the prostitution trade. In the words of one authority, "the rise, after 1890, of large scale leisure institutions with commercial sex and the toleration of prostitution by police, politicians, and real estate interests facilitated the formation of organized networks of proprietors called syndicates" (Gilfoyle 1992, 261). Of these, the most prominent in New York City was the Independent Benevolent Association (IBA) on the city's Lower East Side. It was originally a conglomerate of local politicians, real estate agents, and saloon and brothel owners. The IBA eventually so dominated prostitution on the Lower East Side that one source described it as "a kind of enterprise syndicate that was structured around an illegal activity" (Gilfoyle 1992, 261). It prospered "by adopting an entrepreneurial approach to commercial sex," eschewing violence in favor of paying the protection fees, bonds, and legal costs of its more than 250 members and functioning as "an arbitration board settling disputes and conflicts over business" (Gilfoyle 1992, 261). According to the testimony of one pimp, members of the IBA were expected to turn over a percentage of their profits to the association.

Recent research indicates that the immigrant backgrounds of many of the IBA members facilitated its connection with affiliates in Europe, South America, and even South Africa. By 1906, the IBA had extended its reach from the Lower East Side of New York to Newark, Philadelphia, Chicago, Los Angeles, and San Francisco. Home to the country's largest Jewish community, a number of observers suggested that the Lower East Side Jews controlled a substantial proportion of the city's prostitution business (Gilfoyle 1992, 263–264).

As the demographics of American cities changed in the early 1900s after waves of Eastern European and Italian immigrants, it was popular to blame organized vice on "foreign" entrepreneurs. One 1912 investigation profiled a typical vice resort owner, revealing

> a large, well-fed man about forty years of age and five feet, eight inches in height. His clothes are the latest cut, loud in design, and carefully pressed. A heavy watch chain adorns his waistcoat, a large diamond sparkles in a flashy necktie, and his fat, chubby fingers are encircled with gold and diamond rings. (Kneeland 1913, 80)

However, there was no typical prostitution racket during this era. Sometimes it was a family affair, including brothers, uncles, brothers-in-law, and cousins, or in some cases, a "combine" of between 10 and 20 men might operate 30 houses of prostitution (Kneeland 1913, 80).

Jim Colosimo and Syndicate Prostitution in Chicago

The Chicago crime syndicate was "the most visible link between crime and prostitution" during the 1920s and 1930s (Winick 1971, 232). Under the direction of Colosimo, Torrio, and then Capone, Chicago mobsters operated a chain of brothels masked as hotels in cities from Chicago, Minneapolis, Fargo, and Bismarck, to Butte, Spokane, and Seattle. Jim Colosimo's ability to bring out the vote on election day for the Kenna-Coughlin machine, which became known as *The Trust,* protected him from police harassment. By 1912, he and his wife, the city's premier madam, Victoria Moresco, owned 200 brothels, making an estimated $600,000 in undeclared income per year. By most accounts, prostitutes accompanied by their pimps made the circuit starting in Chicago and

Commercialized Prostitution in New York City (1912)

During the first 11 months of 1912, New York City's Bureau of Social Hygiene conducted a survey of houses of prostitution in New York City. What they found were 142 parlor houses in Manhattan. Of these, 20 were known as $0.50 houses, 80 as $1 houses, 6 as $2 houses, and 34 as $5 and $10 houses.

However, the survey found that the actual business of prostitution in the city was conducted in buildings that were designated as *vice resorts*. The most prominent operations were conducted in the so-called parlor house or brothel, so-named for the practice in which the "inmates gather in the parlor to receive guests" (Kneeland 1913, 80). From there, every step in the process of arranging for and conducting an establishment of this character is taken in most businesslike fashion. In most cases, regular leases were drawn up between "usually two or more individuals [who] enter into a regular partnership agreement" to run the brothel (Kneeland 1913, 80).

> Their employees embrace a number of skills unrelated to the sex act, including servants, cooks, maids, porters, and bouncers. The partners hire a madame or housekeeper by the month or on a percentage basis to take charge (usually former prostitute) and keep daily profit reports (in early morning usually). The porter cares for the house, runs errands, and maintains a "lighthouse" to stand on the street for the purpose of procuring trade and to give warning of approaching law enforcement. (Kneeland 1913, 5–6)

"working" their way west, spending several weeks at each stop. One source suggests that the average brothel in the chain had no more than six prostitutes at any one time, insuring a ready supply of new faces. One investigation by local and federal law enforcement revealed a system for procuring and exchanging prostitutes between Chicago and other gangs in New York City, Milwaukee, and St. Louis as early as 1909.

When Torrio left the Outfit in the hands of Capone, he gave him the control of most prostitution in Chicago. Among his most lucrative properties was the suburban Speedway Inn, whose business was so brisk that turnstiles were required to regulate the foot traffic (Winick 1971, 233). Like other businesses, employees were periodically evaluated. Each prostitute's efficiency was regularly evaluated, and the less productive ones were fired. Customers were handed soap and towels as they passed went through the turnstile and proceeded up one side of a staircase—assigned a prostitute—and left premises by going down another flight of stars. At one time, the Speedway Inn was considered the largest brothel in the United States, employing 50 women whose prices ranged from $2 to $5, depending on services. One observer described the brothel as "a large pavilion-like building with a bar and cigar store on the ground floor" (Winick 1971). Prostitutes conducted business in small rooms on the upper floors. It was closed after Prohibition in 1934 (Winick 1971).

White Slavery

Although *white slavery*[3] was often equated with "compulsory prostitution" beginning in the late 19th century, the origins of the phrase have been traced to labor movements in the 1830s, when English and American laborers adopted the term as "a way to describe their low wages and intolerable conditions" in an era when criticism of the capitalist system was not uncommon (Keire 2001, 7). In her autobiography, former San Francisco madame Sally Stanford famously posited,

> Personally, I never met a white slave in my life—not a female one, that is. If captives were sold, drugged, or slugged into prostitution, I never knew a case. A far more common thing (and a continual nuisance) was the arrival at my various doors of numberless who wanted work. . . . The greatest number of candidates were women who just wanted to be prostitutes. (Stanford 1966, 95–96)

The Raines Law

The Raines Law was passed in an attempt to "minimize the evils connected with saloons." In terms of organized prostitution, its passage led to "the immediate growth [of this] social evil." The law raised the established saloon license tax from $200 to $800 and was designed to mobilize increased law enforcement, because as a state law it would be "beyond the reach of local influences" in an effort to enforce Sunday blue laws (quoted in Kneeland, 1913, 34). Saloon keepers got around this by adding hotels to their establishment with the requisite 10 bedrooms, kitchen, and dining room. They were called *Raines Law hotels* after an 1896 New York State ordinance that forbade the sale of alcohol on Sunday except in hotels, a *hotel* being defined as anything with at least 10 bedrooms, a dining room, and a kitchen. By 1905, there were 1,000 such places in Manhattan and the Bronx alone, adding 10,000 new bedrooms to the city total (Fried 1980, 13). However, there was no actual demand for the increase in hotel accommodations and owners were able to make ends meet by renting them out for prostitution. If investigators discovered that hotels were being used in such a way, it was labeled a *disorderly hotel*. During the early 20th century, the disorderly hotels became the scene of a number of crimes, from murder to theft (Kneeland 1913, 34–35). More recent research describes Raines Law hotels as "threadbare establishments consisting of several rooms and a saloon, a favorite place for a relaxed evening" (Fried 1980, 13).

White slavery conjures a number of images of women being held behind locked doors and barred windows. The reality was something different, although the term was so loaded with evil it energized the red light abatement movement and led to the passage of the Mann Act in 1910. Surely, there were women who wanted to leave the trade who were not barred physically from walking away, but as one investigator explained it, "Uneducated, with little or no comprehension of her legal rights or the powers which could be invoked to aid her, often an immigrant or at least a stranger, she is soon cowed by the brute to whom she has mistakenly attached herself" (Kneeland 1913). According to Kneeland, those who were responsible for finding women for the vice resorts were called *procurers,* or *white slavers.* They often prowled entrances to factories and department stores, or walked the streets at night looking for lonely girls "looking for adventure." Procurers also were known to proposition girls waiting tables at a restaurant, or working a cashier's desk; in other cases they haunted amusement parks and public dance halls, basically anywhere "girls congregate for business or for pleasure" (Kneeland 1913, 85–89).

The Mann Act, Progressive Era Reform Efforts, and Prostitution

There was a marked decline in public prostitution in the years following World War I, a reflection of the changing nature of American urban life, as new industries and construction projects pushed prostitution from mid-town tenderloin districts as real estate entrepreneurs found profit in other real-estate arrangements. The federal government played a crucial role in the decline of public prostitution when Congress passed the Mann Act in 1910, which prohibited the transportation of women across state lines for immoral purposes. This law signaled a turning point in the history of prostitution in America, suggesting that public opinion found its voice in federal legislation toward a vice that had formerly been partially zoned and confined to certain enclaves in towns. During the next decade, law enforcement closed down most vice areas in big cities in the red-light abatement crusade.

Historian Timothy Gilfoyle claims that the significance of the Mann Act was "more symbolic than real" in diminishing prostitution, but in any case did "hurt organized syndicates" most (1992, 308–309). Supporters of the Mann Act realized that the law would not cripple commercialized prostitution, because the only people being prosecuted were low-level pimps and madams; they then shifted their efforts from policing people to policing places. The best way to accomplish this was by closing down the red-light districts, the most visible reminders of the sex trade (Keire 2001).

FIGURE 6.5 Jazz Festival Program (1949) and 1905 Blue Book containing detailed directory of New Orleans brothels
Source: Dorling Kindersley Media Library/Dorling Kindersley

By mid-decade, New York had outlawed all forms of prostitution. As America prepared to enter World War I in 1916, one national commission saw prostitution and sex-related diseases as a threat to national security. In order to protect soldiers from its ravages, the Commission on Training Camp Activities launched "the most aggressive attack on prostitution in the nation's history" (Gilfoyle 1992, 309).

A number of other factors contributed to the decline of organized prostitution in New York City the 1920s. Among them were federal immigration acts that made a significant dent in the number of transients coming through the city (the terminus for most immigrants entering the country). The number of foreigners coming through the port of New York was cut in half between the first and

Storyville

Prostitutes first appeared in New Orleans during the 1700s, and several red light districts were established in the following century. However, none was more famous than Storyville, created by the New Orleans City Council in 1897 in an attempt to contain prostitution in a specific area of town. The district was named for Alderman Sidney Story, who introduced the ordinance, and was a respected businessman who was apparently mortified that his name became associated with the red light district. It operated from 1898 until it was closed by the Navy Department in 1917. According to one of its chroniclers, "It was unique in being the only legally established restricted district in the United States" (Rose 1974). Prostitution was illegal outside this 38-block district. In its heyday, the district was home to 2,000 prostitutes.

Satan's Circus

During the second half of the 19th century, so many sex-related establishments lined the blocks between Twenty-Fourth and Fortieth Streets, and between Fifth and Seventh Avenues in New York City's tenderloin, that this netherworld was referred to as *Satan's Circus* by local clergymen; however, most others referred to it simply as the *Tenderloin,* offering a "greater concentration of prostitutes than any equivalent are in the country" (Dash 2007). By one 1885 estimate, half of the buildings in this vicinity were used for some type of vice activity. Perhaps 5,000 prostitutes worked this area, with specific streets catering to different sexual entertainments. Sixth Street establishments allowed one to take in can-can shows from private booths, whereas West Fortieth Street was known for specializing in oral sex (Sante 1998; Dash 2007, 5). It was an open secret that most of the brothel owners paid police protection in an era when shakedowns and raids were regular and a part of the fabric of big-city vice districts. Recent research suggests that the average house of prostitution was lucky to keep more than 15% of its profits once payoffs were paid each week (Dash 2007, 383–384).

second decades of the 20th century, reaching a low of 23,068 in 1933 (after a zenith of 1.2 million in 1907). The demand for prostitutes plummeted with fewer transient males available. Also, the passage of the Volstead Act in 1919, according to one historian, played an important role in transforming the structure of prostitution by eliminating most of the saloons, concert halls, and cabarets where prostitutes formerly plied their trade. As a result, prostitutes increasingly sought less public venues such as speakeasies. Therefore, Prohibition led prostitution to join alcohol as an underground activity (Gilfoyle 1992).

The Prostitution Trial of the Century: Thomas Dewey v. "Lucky" Luciano

Thomas Dewey's prosecution of mob kingpin "Lucky" Luciano for prostitution in the 1930s was one of the most prominent organized crime court cases of the era. After declaring war on organized crime, Dewey targeted Luciano, who was familiar to the police but not yet a household name. Luciano proved elusive from the very beginning, eschewing recordkeeping and careful on the telephone, always circumspect about potential wiretaps.

Dewey's first lead came from an unexpected source—his only female staff member—Eunice Carter, who convinced him to examine the rampant corruption inside New York City's Women's Court. She correctly surmised that payoffs to judges, lawyers, and bondsmen meant few prostitutes were convicted. As a result of her urgings, Dewey grudgingly began a limited investigation. In reality, Dewey wished to convey a racket-busting image rather than "a puritanical prosecutor [chasing] fallen women and madams" (Raab 2005, 52).

Dewey soon discovered that the corruption of court personnel extended far up into the organized crime hierarchy. Wiretaps on city brothels revealed a number of references to something called the *Combine* and the *Combination,* which controlled hundreds of whorehouses and thousands of working girls in Manhattan and Brooklyn. Further investigation led to the discovery that a top Luciano associate was supervising much of the operation while collecting more than $10 million a year from organized prostitution.

By the 1930s, the Italians had replaced Jewish gangsters as the dominant force in the brothel business, "a pattern similar to the Mafia's takeover of other rackets in the city from Jewish and Irish hoodlums" (Raab 2005, 52). In 1936, Dewey's officers simultaneously raided 80 brothels and arrested hundreds of employees, ranging from hookers and madams to the "bookers," who helped manage the houses, recruit women, and assign them to different locations.

Under the threat of stiff sentences, many suspects cooperated, and during the ensuing trial and follow-up investigation dramatized the magnitude of the enterprise. Some witnesses fingered Luciano and several associates. Luciano fled to Hot Springs, Arkansas, when he found out. However, three prostitutes claimed to have firsthand knowledge of the involvement of Luciano in the enterprise. Dewey responded by obtaining an extradition order and bringing him back to face 90 counts of "aiding and abetting compulsory prostitution," code for white slavery. Luciano was charged with placing women in brothels and collecting money for it. Referring to prostitution as an "age-old institution," Dewey insisted the case "was not about prostitution but about its syndication" (Stolberg 1995, 134). He suggested that before mobsters organized it in New York, the activity was highly individualistic, describing how some women worked alone, whereas madames ran houses with one to four girls, noting, "They were separate, isolated, they kept the money they earned; they were not blackjacked, nor was the money stolen from them by anybody else" (quoted in Stolberg 1995, 134). He asserted that all of this changed in 1933, when several men took over houses by gunpoint with the aim of large-scale monopoly.

The subsequent trial revealed that the prostitution business was rather simple. Prostitutes lived in hotels with their pimps, who then booked them into whorehouses for about a week at a time, where they were expected to work 10 to 14 hours a day for less than 40% of earnings, out of which they paid board and other expenses. Meanwhile, mobsters taught them the fine art of lying to magistrates and set up a finely honed system where bail bondsmen got to court before the women. If the case could not be fixed, the girls were sent away until things cooled off. These methods seemed to work well, if 1935 was any indicator, when none went to jail after 170 arrests.

Dewey told the jury,

> All we can give you is a fragmentary picture of any great criminal enterprise. We can give you a fairly full picture of what happens at the bottom, a smaller picture of what happens at the next stratum. . . . and very little up at the top. (Quoted in Stolberg 1995, 135)

In the course of Luciano's 1936 trial for promoting compulsory prostitution, Dewey lined up 68 witnesses, promising them lenient sentences, immunity, or probation if they linked Luciano to the charges. His main strategy was to paint the prostitutes "as victims of the Depression, exploited and terrorized by the Combine's ruthless sentries" (Raab 2005, 53).

Luciano testified in his own defense, denying all charges, but was found guilty and sentenced to from 30 to 50 years. Despite the recantation of several witnesses, a new trial was denied, and Luciano became the "first major organized crime figure to serve a prison sentence for promoting prostitution" (Raab 2005, 55). Luciano always insisted he was framed, and 9 years later Dewey commuted his sentence.

Prostitution in the 21st Century

A number of authorities have suggested that the sexual revolution of the 1960s put the final nail in this once-profitable business. Others have pinned its decline on other social trends, including the decreased segregation of sexes, the equalization of the sex ratio, the women's movement, more effective contraception, the concept of crimes without victims, and the changing priorities of law

Is Prostitution Still Prohibited in the United States?

Today, Nevada is the only state where prostitution is legal, but even there, it is only in certain counties. It has the most unusual legal arrangements for prostitution in United States. Houses of prostitution may be established or maintained so long as they are not on principal business streets or within 400 yards of a schoolhouse or church, or do not disturb the peace of a neighborhood. Power is also given to incorporated cities and unincorporated towns and cities to regulate, prohibit, license, tax, and suppress them. Only 2 of Nevada's 17 counties prohibit houses of prostitution (Clark County, including Las Vegas, and Washoe, which is home to Reno).

enforcement (Winick 1994). As far back as 1967, *The President's Commission on Organized Crime* concluded that "prostitution played a small and declining role in organized crime operations" (1967, 189). In the 1970s and 1980s, prostitution ranked low as a revenue producer compared to other rackets such as loan sharking, drugs, and other activities. Today's domestic sex trade is segmented among disparate settings such as streets, bars, call houses, strip clubs, massage parlors—a range of locations not easily monitored by prospective criminal entrepreneurs.

Governments and private groups have been cooperating against prostitution as far back as the 1899 International Conference for the Suppression of Traffic in Women, which convened in England. In 1904, authorities from 13 countries agreed to coordinate their activities when they signed the International Agreement for the Suppression of the White Slave Traffic Act. In the Second International Convention for the Suppression of the White Slave Traffic, signatories in 1910 agreed to punish any person who helped a girl under the age of 20 enter a career as a prostitute, or who procured an adult by force or fraud (Winick and Kinsie 1971, 269). Between 1930 and 1933, the League of Nations ran a Commission of Enquiry into the trafficking of women and children in Far Eastern countries. Several resolutions were considered further regulating this trade before interruption of World War II (Winick and Kinsie 1971).

In every era (but increasingly so in modern times), organized prostitution and sex trafficking have "required a complex level of organization, arrangements, financing, and marketing" (Winick 1994). In 1999, the U.S. government estimated that 50,000 women were being trafficked into the country for sexual purposes. Five years later, in 2004, these numbers were reported to have declined to no more than 17,500 per year. However, despite the decline since 2000, 42 Justice Department task forces and $150 million in federal dollars, these efforts have resulted in the finding of only 1,400 individuals "certified as human trafficking victims" in the United States, a small portion of the estimated figures (Markon 2007, A25).

GAMBLING

Gambling is older than recorded history. Anthropologists and archeologists have discovered gambling artifacts in prehistoric Mesopotamia as well as among the native populations of Europe, Asia, Africa, and the Americas. Most early games were apparently precursors to modern dice games (Schwartz 2006). Although gambling has long flourished in the United States, "it took the nineteenth century to make it into a real business" (Sante 1991, 153). Prior to this period, gambling was typically a local racket where individuals bet on card games or wagered on races and dogfights. However, no game was as popular and widespread from the colonial period into the 1820s than lotteries.

From the time of the colonial era, the federal government supported various lotteries as a device for generating revenue. The First Continental Congress helped finance the American Revolution with lotteries, and Benjamin Franklin, George Washington, and Thomas Jefferson each sponsored private lotteries themselves. However, frequent charges of fraud drew the castigation of the "vice" by Protestant clergymen who were at the forefront of opposition to the lotteries. Nevertheless, the influence of the clergy could not stop the growth of lotteries, and by 1832, eight eastern states were spending more than $55 million on lotteries, more than four times the national budget. During the 1830s and 1840s, the lottery was increasingly regarded as a moral blight on society, and in 1833, New York outlawed lotteries and other states followed suit. Although early lotteries successfully brought in money to a cash-starved treasury, scandals energized anti-gambling forces, leading to its prohibition from 1894 to 1964, when New Hampshire introduced the first legal lottery of the 20th century, leading to an undiminished growth in gambling. By the end of the 1970s, 14 states were operating lotteries.

The campaign against the lottery was one of the early victories for reformers who became Progressives in 20th-century America. Except for legal lotteries, most gambling in the 18th and early 19th centuries was decentralized, with few resembling large-scale gambling syndicates.

FIGURE 6.6 Ancient Roman dice made from bone
Source: Dorling Kindersley Media Library/Dorling Kindersley

FIGURE 6.7 Chinese dice
Source: Dorling Kindersley Media Library/Geoff Brightling

Following the end of Prohibition in 1933, criminal syndicates were looking for the next big racket. Crime syndicates took little time in adapting to the new rackets, operating any type of game from penny-policy to slots, high stakes poker, horse and dog tracks, bookie parlors, and casinos. One observer even conceded, "excepting only unpopulated Western ranges, some kind of gambling institution, casino, horse parlor or numbers bank, was established within thirty miles of every home in America" (King 1969, 25).

The America of the 1930s was a far cry from the present day—especially when it game to gambling, better-known as *gaming* in upper-class parlance. The 21st century abounds with gambling venues—from Internet poker to legal lotteries in almost every state, and casinos from Las Vegas and Atlantic City to Indian reservations and Bible Belt riverboats, leading one observer to comment, "the Bible belt might as well be renamed the Blackjack Belt" (Popkin and Hetter 1994), as floating and land-based casinos dot the landscape from Florida to Texas. Sports gambling is probably the most widespread and popular form of betting, with newspapers publishing betting point spreads for a variety of professional and collegiate sporting events.

American acceptance of gambling varied from era to era. It was widely accepted during the colonial period and through much of the 19th century, but has been widely rebuked as immoral and deviant behavior throughout the early 20th century. During the first half of the 20th century, gambling was deemed an immoral activity that led one to associate with bad characters and possibly led to dissolution. However, since the late 1960s, attitudes have become more favorably disposed toward gambling, as evidenced by the number of states that have legalized lotteries, horse and dog racing, and casino gambling as sources of income. This major attitudinal change was first noted during 1940s war years, as more and more servicemen found relaxation and recreation playing various games of chance for money. Some found it an ideal way to control stress through the artificial world of cards and dice. Paralleling this was an increasingly ambivalent attitude among the public. Efforts were made by various lobbyists to remove the stigma from gambling after the war, as illegal gambling reached a larger population. Yet before it could be widely accepted, its association with crime and organized crime had to be laid to rest. If gambling could be separated from its association with mobsters, it could be sanitized as a form of recreation, and in the process diminish its attraction to organized crime groups. The drive to expand legal gambling was continuous since the post–World War II era, as seen by the expansion of race track betting in the 1950s, followed by the legalization of off-track gambling and the proliferation of legal casino gambling as it spread from Las Vegas to Atlantic City, the Indian reservations, and even the southern Bible Belt, where fixed "riverboats" became fixtures in a number of communities.

The Kefauver Hearings and Gambling

The mid-20th-century Kefauver Hearings arrived at several conclusions in which illegal gambling figured prominently. The Committee concurred that following Prohibition, organized crime groups paid more attention to bookmaking, policy (numbers), slot machines, as well as the usual standbys of trafficking in narcotics and prostitution, labor and union racketeering, and other black market activities. However, among the committee's most important revelations was the fact that most criminal syndicates "shifted their major criminal activities to gambling" (Senate Report 307, 1951, 1).

Little had changed by the time the President's Commission on Law Enforcement and Administration of Justice released its report in 1967, noting, "Law enforcement officials agree almost unanimously that gambling is the greatest source of revenue for organized crime" (President's Commission on Organized Crime 1972), estimating its yearly gross revenue at from $7 billion to $50 billion, in 1960s dollars.

Legal Gambling

Today, there are four main forms of legal gambling—charitable gaming, pari-mutuel betting, casino gaming, and lotteries. *Charitable gaming* is typically run for the benefit of various non-profit

---

Kefauver Committee on Gambling (1951)

- Gambling profits are the principal support of big-time racketeering and gangsterism.
- The legalization of gambling would not terminate the widespread activities of criminal syndicates.
- Gambling has historically been associated with cheating and corruption.
- Rapid transmission of racing information and gambling information about other sporting events is indispensable to big-time bookmaking operations.
- At the time of the hearings, this information was controlled by a monopoly operated by the Continental Press Service, which was controlled by the Chicago Outfit.
- This wire service is so crucial to bookmaking operations throughout the country that they are all forced to subscribe to the service at whatever price the market will bear.

---

groups, such as when the PTA has a Monte Carlo night or a church has a raffle, all to raise money for the institution. By most accounts, Bingo remains the most popular form of charitable gambling and is legal in 45 states. However, because this form of gambling is the least regulated, there has been criticism directed at it due to the numerous opportunities for fraud, theft, and cheating.

Over recent decades legal gambling has grown to include state lotteries, pari-mutuel betting on horses, greyhounds, and jai-alai; sports bookmaking, card games, keno, bingo, slot machines, video poker and blackjack machines, and a number of other games. However, there is little continuity in gaming in America, with each state allowing the type of gambling that it supports or least condones—some states have lotteries but no casinos, whereas other states allow casinos but no lotteries; some states even have both.

Pari-mutuel wagering involves betting on horse and dog races as well as the game of jai-alai. In these games, bettors bet against each other instead of against the "house," which is typified by casino gambling.

Casino betting is the mainstay of Las Vegas and Atlantic City. Newer land-based casinos have been established in Deadwood, South Dakota, some Colorado mining towns, and a number of Indian reservations. Riverboats have also entered the fray in Iowa, Illinois, Indiana, Missouri, Louisiana, and Mississippi.

The Gambling Revolution: The Telegraph, the Pari-Mutuel Machine, and the Slot Machine

One chronicler of America's love–hate affair with gambling suggested that three inventions in the late 19th century allowed gambling to grow from only a diversion and past-time to a full-fledged industry—citing the telegraph, the pari-mutuel system, and the slot machine. The telegraph was first developed in the 1830s, but further improvements by Samuel Morse and Thomas Edison broadened its capacity for relaying and obtaining racing results. This represented a great stride, as bookmakers found they could obtain racing results almost immediately, as well as link up with bookies in other cities. Many began forming their own powerful gambling syndicates that would allow them to move

---

Vicksburg, Mississippi: City of Chance?

By the mid-1990s, Vicksburg, Mississippi, supported at least four riverboat casinos, with more to come. Contrast this with 1835, when gambling equipment was smashed and five professional cheats were hanged, as citizens enraged by the proliferation of riverboat gamblers and gambling parlors took law into their own hands.

Gaming and Gambling

The origin of the word *gaming* can be traced back to the Saxon word *gamen,* which refers to "joy, pleasure, sports, or gaming." In Samuel Johnson's early dictionary, he defines the term *gambling* as playing "extravagantly for money." One 19th-century historian distinguishes *gambling* from *gaming* or *playing,* arguing that in gambling, chance assumes a more important role, and "the money motive increases, as chance predominates over skill" and is seen as a "quicker road to wealth than by honest industry" (Ashton 1969, 2).

money and bets. However, the upheaval in the horse racing industry from 1890 to 1910 brought these to a crashing halt. All those involved knew that if horse-race betting was not available, the industry was doomed.

In 1913, New York reenergized the business by adopting pari-mutuel machines. *Pari-mutuel betting,* French for "mutual betting" or "betting between ourselves," was the brainchild of the French perfume shopkeeper Pierre Oller, who in 1865 came on the idea of selling horse-race tickets so that all of the proceeds in the common prize pool could be split between the winners. Using this system, Oller took 5% of the bets as a handling fee and then distributed the rest to the bettors according to the established odds on each horse. By 1887, pari-mutuel wagering was the legalized method of betting at French race tracks. Forty years later, the system was adopted in Great Britain and the United States. Today, it is the accepted betting procedure at major horse-racing tracks throughout the world. Its success has led jai-alai games and greyhound tracks to adopt it as well. Experts suggest that the decline in its popularity is the result of the more complicated nature of modern sports, leading some race tracks to add casino games, hoping to attract non-track gamblers to pari-mutuel betting.

SLOT MACHINES   Invented in the late 19th century, the slot machine quickly established a presence in retail outlets and country clubs throughout the country. In private settings, they usually paid off in cash; in public, you won cigarettes or chewing gum. Toward the end of the 19th century, a forerunner to the slot machine was created and in the process went a long way toward reviving a sluggish gambling industry. The "Little Gem" was invented to produce poker hands on spinning reels. For as little as a nickel, gamblers could try their luck at pulling a lever with the hopes of lining up a royal flush and winning $5. Over time, fruit figures and other icons were added, giving the mind-numbing game an artistic flourish.

It was not uncommon to see signs posted near the machines declaring, "This is not a gaming device." However, it often "kept the authorities from enforcing anti-gambling laws" (Schwartz 2006, 330). Among the biggest challenges faced by operators was the ever-present threat of cheating, theft, and hijacking by criminal groups. Although the first two problems were fixed with mechanical solutions, it was found that one way to placate criminal gangs was to cut them in on the profits; besides, in the event they faced strong competition they could always rely on the strong arm of the mobsters (Schwartz 2006, 330).

One of the most indelible images of the 1930s is the photo of New York City Mayor Fiorello LaGuardia busting up slot machines with a sledgehammer and then having them dumped into East River/Long Island Sound. During the 1930s, the illegal but widespread slot machines were a major earner for the Frank Costello syndicate. Even before the end of Prohibition, Costello teamed up with Phil Kastel to acquire the New York territory from the Mills Novelty Company of Chicago—the largest producer of the machines in the country. The two hoods inaugurated their business under the aegis of the Tru-Mint Company, and within a short time had more than 5,000 slot machines in high-traffic spots throughout the city. By 1931, Costello controlled more than 25,000 New York slot machines (Schwartz 2006). Soon, slot machines took their place in candy shops, cigar stores, speakeasies, and grocery stores and were bringing in somewhere between $20 million and $40 million a year. However, not all of this was profit; as one observer noted, "There were

FIGURE 6.8 Slot Machines
Source: Rough Guides Dorling Kindersley/Greg Ward

very, very heavy expenses. Half the police department and all of Tammany Hall were on the pay-roll" (quoted in Nelli 1976, 223).

Once LaGuardia was elected mayor in 1933, he took on the slot machine rackets and its accompanying corruption. Costello attempted to stave off a total loss by removing the slot machines to the more-welcoming confines of New Orleans at the behest of then Senator Huey P. Long. Following Long's assassination in 1935, Costello won favor with the new mayor and had more than 8,000 machines in almost every business establishment in the city, bringing in more than $32 million over the next decade (Nelli 1976).

Low-skill games such as lotteries and slot machines proved to be the major revenue producers. With the saturation of new casinos throughout the country, the popularity of slot machines proved irresistible as a major revenue producer. From Las Vegas to the Indian Reservation casinos, a trend evolved in which these "one-armed bandits" have taken up more space from the lower revenue–producing table games such as poker. This transition actually began in the 1980s, when slot machine profits (versus table game profits) rose in Las Vegas casinos from 31.4% of profits in 1971 to 51.8% in 1984 (Rosecrance 1988).

VIDEO POKER   Video poker is one of the fastest growing illegal gambling games. Although there are a number of options, most are similar to the modern banking machine in that they have a video screen with buttons to control what is on the screen. They are often hidden in out-of-the-way locations inside restaurants and bars, or other locales where there is little foot traffic. Most operate as follows: A customer gives the bartender $20 to begin playing, and he is registered with 20 points on his screen. The player then attempts to beat the hand shown by the machine using the "draw poker" method, where he can pick between one and four cards by pushing a button. Although customers

Pari-Mutuel Betting

This system of cooperative wagering was invented in France around 1870, and refers to a type of gambling in which the total prize pool is based on the amount of money wagered—the more money wagered, the bigger the payoff. What distinguishes this type of betting is the idea that gaming public itself determines the payoff odds. Horse racing is the most prominent pari-mutuel event, although it is also used in less-popular dog racing and jai-alai. It still survives, in no small part because it is considered a major deterrent to illegal bookmaking.

typically lose and must buy more points, they can cash out whenever they want for whatever is on the screen. Organized crime makes its money by renting the machines to businesses for a percentage of the profits.

Horse Racing

Horse racing, the "sport of kings," can be traced back at least 6,000 years into antiquity. Early Assyrian tablet inscriptions suggest that chariot racing was already an established sport by 1500 B.C. Athenian texts indicate that the selective breeding of racing stock was taking place by 1000 B.C., and that the first mounted races were recorded during the 33rd Olympiad in 324 B.C. Organized racing closer to the modern prototypes was popular in 12th-century Norman England. Subsequent monarchs owned "running horses" in royal stables. However, King Charles II is generally credited with promoting the sport, earning the sobriquet "the father of the British turf." Following in the footsteps of the Puritan rule, Charles II catered to an English public eager for public festivities including the racing of horses (Rosecrance 1988; Schwartz 2006).

Horse-race betting became especially popular in Europe during the 19th century, leading to a rivalry between off-track bet-takers, or *bookies,* and the legitimate racing establishment. In America, horse racing was a popular form of gambling during the colonial era and into the first half of the 19th century. However, the anti-gambling crusade of the late 19th century adversely affected its availability. By the late 19th century, it had become increasingly controlled by professional gamblers. As a result, state after state prohibited horse racing completely. By 1906, it was legal only in Maryland, Kentucky, and New York; by 1911, only 6 states allowed betting at racetracks, although this number increased to 21 tracks in 1930. During the 1930s, states saw racing as a source of raising state revenues, and before the end of the decade, another 11 states had legalized pari-mutuel on-track betting. As the trend against horse racing reversed course, Las Vegas embraced the change by becoming the first state to legalize most forms of licensed gambling, including off-track betting in 1931 (Rosecrance 1988).

BOOKMAKING   *Bookmaking* originally referred to the process by which someone could place a bet on a horserace without being present at the event (this was illegal in every state except Nevada). Later, when state-run off-track betting was legalized, bookmakers extended their reach to other forms of sports betting, including baseball, football, basketball, and boxing. According to one Internal Revenue Service estimate, by 1940, there were at least 15,000 individual bookies across the nation (Russo 2001, 115).

Originally, bookmakers set up shop on and at race tracks, posting odds on chalkboards, but in the 1880s a number states responded to complaints of rigged races by banning bookmaking. Without on-track betting, attendance plummeted, so that by the 1890s, many tracks closed their gates. However, despite the track ban on betting, anyone who wanted to could place a wager away from the track using *handbooks,* basically bookmakers who operated from particular fixed locations—sometimes a business, a saloon, or a street corner. Others sought the company of other bettors in the friendly confines of what was then called a *poolroom* or *horseroom.* There were no pool tables here—just betting pools. Poolrooms were connected to a nationwide information network known as the *race wire.* The wire reached from the racetracks, where runners collected information, including updates on the status of horses, jockeys, and track conditions, which was in turn transmitted

FIGURE 6.9 Gamblers at betting windows at racetrack
Source: Pearson Education/PH College/Irene Springer

FIGURE 6.10 Gamblers leaving offtrack betting office in Chinatown
Source: Pearson Education/PH College/Stephen Capra

by telegraph to a central headquarters and then to poolrooms. The poolrooms allowed race devotees to be part of the action while living (in some cases) hundreds of miles away. When Western Union pulled out of the gambling business in 1904, racing opponents were thrilled; however, so were certain crime syndicates that saw a great opportunity (Schwartz 2006).

Chicago, Horse Racing, and the Wire Services: A Case Study

With the ascendance of Carter Harrison II to Chicago mayor in 1904, horse-race betting was virtually eliminated at local racetracks in an attempt at ending handbook activities. For the next 18 years, horse-race betting was a dead issue in Illinois—that is, until the creation of the race wire. The idea of a race wire service was the brainchild of a former telegraph operator from Cincinnati in the early 1900s. While working for the Western Union Telegraph, John Payne reacted to the company's decision to eliminate reporting racing results at the behest of major stockholders by striking out on his own and devising a simple relay procedure for processing horse-race results. Payne's procedure required a spotter at the racetrack who would use a mirror to flash back a coded race result to a telegrapher in a nearby building, who would instantly relay the results to handbooks, or *bookies,* throughout Cincinnati, thus establishing the Payne Telegraph Service of Cincinnati. Among the benefits of the Payne system was the fact that bookies could take bets on races in which they already knew the results. This way, if they knew the horse being bet on had lost, they would gladly accept the wager; conversely, if it was on a winner, the bookie could tell the prospective bettor they were too late.

In 1907, Chicago gangster Mont Tennes became one of the first to recognize the potential impact of long-distance communications on illegal horse racing when he tried to parlay, albeit unsuccessfully, an exclusive telegraph racing-news contract out of Cincinnati into a local monopoly of bookmakers (Moore 1974, 18). That same year, Tennes purchased the Payne System exclusively for Illinois for $300 per day. Initially, Tennes received racing results at the Forest Park train station using a switchboard made up of a trunk-line with 45 wires (May 2006). Coded results were then doled out to hundreds of poolrooms[4] and handbooks. Results from tracks around the country were then relayed to bookie joints, and in Chicago, no gambling joint could receive racing results by telephone or telegraph without paying half its daily net receipts to the Tennes syndicate.

According to the February 9, 1910, edition of the *Chicago Herald and Examiner,* Tennes' intention was to monopolize control of the country's racing news service. In doing so, he would supply this information to "handbooks and poolrooms throughout the country with racing information, such as entries, odds, jockeys, scratches and results" (Landesco 1978, 57). The Illinois Crime Survey Commission seemed to confirm his success when it offered, "If the complete life history of Mont Tennes were known in every detail, it would disclose practically all there is to know about syndicated gambling as a phase of organized crime in Chicago in the last quarter century" (Landesco 1978, 57). Once Tennes took control of the wire services, he entered into an unwritten agreement with the police that they would not interfere, and soon gamblers descended on Chicago from all over the country. Any gambling racket that expected to flourish under Tennes was expected to adhere to a protection rate that ranged from 40% to 60% of the winnings, depending on whether it was a pool-room,[5] roulette, faro, or craps game.

Making the transition from "king of the Chicago Gamblers to czar of all the race-track gambling in the United States and Canada" (Landesco 1978), by 1911, Tennes was making $3,600 weekly from 90 Chicago poolrooms and $4,000 a week from 70 New York poolrooms. More than 20 other cities across the country paid for the service as well. That same year, the Interstate Commerce Commission (ICC) began investigating the Payne and Tennes wire services, but determined they were not violating any laws by providing racing results. Despite bombings by rivals and police harassment, Tennes' syndicate continued to flourish. As America became embroiled in World War I, less attention was directed toward the country's gambling rackets.

In the spring of 1920, a Senate judiciary hearing on interstate race betting information revealed "that Chicago was the center of race track gambling in the United States," explaining

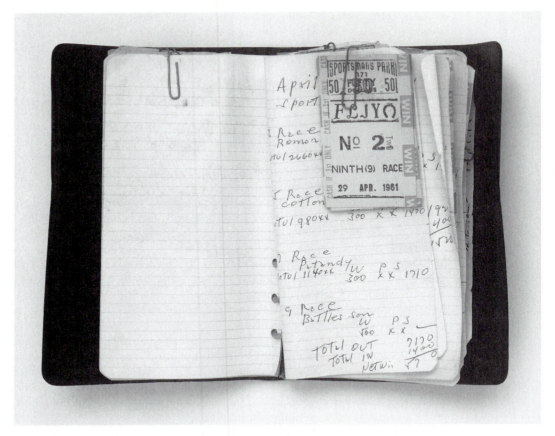

FIGURE 6.11   Chicago Outfit boss Sam Giancana's notebook detailing his bets with clipped-on horse racing ticket
Source: Dorling Kindersley Media Library/Andy Crawford

that this was made possible by "a system of trunk lines running all over the country: from a location on the top of one of Chicago's skyscrapers" (Landesco 1929, 77). It took the reform administration of Chicago Mayor William E. Dever in the early 1920s to finally clamp down on the city's gambling rackets, and in the first year of his term he closed more than 200 handbook parlors. During the last years, Tennes was faced with mounting competition from the Capone and Bugs Moran organizations as well as the appearance of a new race wire service, and in 1927, he decided to retire and sold his ownership of the General News Bureau. Its new major stockholder was newspaper tycoon Moses Annenberg, a veteran of the recent Hearst circulation wars. By the time he bought the wire service in 1927, nearly 20 other racing-wire services were in operation, leading to an intense competition and diminished profits. According to Kefauver historian William Howard Moore, by the end of the 1930s, Annenberg "had a powerful hold on a national gambling empire that included bookmaking, racing publications, and various 'scratch' sheets" (1974, 19). On trial for tax evasion in 1940, the prosecution was able to demonstrate that he "was American Telephone and Telegraph Company's fifth largest customer" (Moore 1974, 19).

Sports Betting

Sports betting is the most popular form of illegal wagering today. More money is bet on football than any other sport, and in Las Vegas the biggest gambling day is Super Bowl Sunday.

Moses Annenberg (1878–1942)

According to one crime historian, "Probably no fortune in America was built on a sturdier foundation of cooperation with organized crime and the Mafia than that of Moses Annenberg" (Sifakis 1999, 15). Born in Prussia in 1878, Annenberg immigrated to Chicago with his family in 1885, where he found early experience as a messenger for Western Union. He was then hired by William Randolph Hearst to lead his forces in the "newspaper circulation wars" before World War I, as eight newspapers vied for the city's circulation. In the course of the conflict, violence was used to prevent papers from being delivered, newsstands were destroyed, delivery trucks bombed, papers stolen, and carriers throttled. By most accounts, Annenberg was often at the center of the brawls. It was here that Annenberg (and his rival and brother, Max) turned to mobsters from the Torrio-Capone syndicate and the North Siders under Bugs Moran and Deanie O'Banion. More recently, one Chicago Outfit historian noted that during the circulation wars, the city was first divided up "along the geographical battle lines that would soon prevail in the beer wars of 1925" (Russo 2001, 198).

While still under the aegis of Hearst, Annenberg recognized the potential of providing racing information from both a legal and an illegal perspective. He bought the *Daily Racing Form* in 1922, and within 5 years had accrued enough income and businesses that he could leave Hearst. Over the years, Annenberg gained control of various newspapers, as well as *Radio Guide* and *Screen Guide;* however, none surpassed his profits from the Nation-Wide News Service, which he ran in collusion with various East Coast mobsters. His stock had risen so high in the underworld that some mob authorities claimed that Al Capone brought him to the famous 1929 Atlantic City Conference (although others dispute this), which set some of the guidelines for the structure of the modern underworld.

Most estimates place total wagers each year in the billions of dollars. Similar to the numbers business, organized crime syndicates make a profit by owning a sports betting operation and partnering with other bookies; and like numbers, they often layoff bets to other bookies if too much money is wagered on one team. Other gangsters let independent operators run the business while they take a percentage of the action, or what's called a *street tax,* by protecting them from other mobsters.

During the 1870s, baseball betting was regarded as the favorite of sports bettors. Of course, it also contributed to the game's reputation for corruption. In an era when ballplayers were hardly paid at all, it was not uncommon for them to accept bribes, following in the footsteps of mayors, policemen, and judges in most urban locales. No gambler was more prominent in this era of sports betting than Arnold Rothstein, the "Big Bankroll." Although his participation in the 1919 Black Sox Scandal is still debated, this case sullied further a sport falling into low repute among the betting public. Football and boxing soon took its place.

THE POINT SPREAD   The practice of point-spread betting "revolutionized sports betting," especially the sports of football and basketball, by allowing bookmakers to handicap teams. Its actual origins are still unclear, but according to the most recent history of gambling, the concept dates back to the early 19th century before conforming to its more modern incarnation in the 1940s. The *point spread* is a betting line set by odds makers (experts) who spend their entire careers gauging the differences among various teams and distill this information into a point rating. This figure is a balance between the differences of the teams and an estimate of how the public will bet. If a bookie believes that a team is likely to win, it must to win by a particular number of points. Conversely, if the bookie believes that a team is likely to lose, a bettor could pick a loser and if that team lost by less than the point spread, it would pay off. In this way, bookmakers could adjust the *line,* or point handicap, as bets came in.

Let's say that a looming game between Detroit and Boston is bringing in bets on mostly one team. Then the bookie adjusts the line by increasing it from a 6-point favorite to a 7-point favorite, hoping to attract more bets for the other team to offset the differential. If he is able to do so, the bookie will have *balanced his book* (equal bets on both teams). Although the bookie makes a profit, it nonetheless pales in comparison to the numbers racket.

From Policy to Numbers

Policy[6] *gambling* probably developed in London and the American colonies as an illegal alternative to the legal lotteries. Policy syndicates emerged as major gambling organizations from the mid-19th century at a time when state after state outlawed legal lotteries, and by the Civil War was a major component of illegal gambling in cities like New York (Haller 1991).

From the late 19th century until about 1940, policy wheels were the predominant lottery among urban Blacks and lower-class Whites (Light 1977). By the 1890s, New York was home to a well-organized policy racket. Financiers. or *policy kings,* divided the city into districts. They funded the operations, employed the runners, bribed precinct captains and police, provided protection, and supplied the winning numbers. Individual writers earned a 25% profit after rent and protection money was paid to the top backers (Fabian 1990).

In his examination of policy gambling in Chicago, historian Mark Haller found Black syndicates dominated it by the 1920s. Typically, a bettor placed money on one or more numbers that they hoped would be among the 12 numbers drawn between 1 and 78. A number of different bets paid off, including combinations of 2 and 4 numbers, and the *gig,* which was a bet on three numbers. If these 3 were among the 12 selected, the winner collected at odds of 100:1 or higher. Bets could be placed as low as a penny, and the game was regarded as the province of the poor.

Policy was directed by a syndicate, or a *policy wheel.* Although the odds favored the policy seller, there was always the chance that several individuals might pick the same winning numbers and bankrupt the game. To meet this challenge, policy *banks* or *backers* were developed to assume financial risks. It worked as follows: Every banker was responsible for perhaps 100 policy sellers conducting business at policy stations located in local saloons, barber shops, newspaper stands, and other places that received much foot traffic. Policy sellers kept a fixed percentage of each bet, approximately 20%, and delivered the remainder to the banker. Larger syndicates employed *runners,* who collected from the sellers and carried the betting slips and cash to the banker. Policy drawings were open to the public, and were often accomplished using a blindfolded boy who was tasked with picking 12 numbers from a wheel. Once the numbers were picked, the banker gathered the winning slips and returned it to sellers to pay the winners. It was in this way that sellers earned a regular income and operated without the risks associated with working outside a syndicate. On the other end, the bankers accepted the risks as well as the profits from thousands of small bets placed through sellers (Haller 1991).

NUMBERS   During the 1920s, recent West Indian immigrants introduced a new game called *numbers* to Harlem. Numbers was simpler than policy, because it involved only a single bet on one 3-digit number from 000 to 999. Eventually, policy was supplanted by the numbers business in cities such as New York, Boston, and Philadelphia, whereas in other cities such as Detroit, the two games existed simultaneously, with some syndicates even backing both. Still others like Chicago and St. Louis preferred the traditional policy game.

Instead of a wheel or a drum, the numbers were drawn from published numbers such as bank-clearing totals, volume on Wall Street, or pari-mutuel totals. By using a published figure, it eliminated a rigged outcome—a technical advantage over policy. Since this racket began in the 1920s operators have always tried to ensure that the winning numbers could not be fixed by players. The winning number was often decided by using the last three digits of the total mutual handle at a racetrack. What made this convenient was that the results were printed in the newspaper, so the players could easily find out if they won and at the same time gave the racket a patina of legitimacy due to its association with the press.

At its roots, numbers is a simple game, not much more than an illegal lottery. Bettors can place bets for relatively small amounts of money, under $1, and bet on a 3-digit number between 000 and 999. Payout rates are typically from 500:1 to 600:1, meaning that on a $1 bet, the bettor can earn from $500 to $600. When it was first introduced in the 1920s, bettors wagered pocket change as little as a nickel; today, the typical bet is $5 or $10. It differs from the legal state lotteries in that money generated from the game is not used to support retirees or pay for public works projects. It has been estimated that the "mob's daily number" has earned billions of dollars for corrupt politicians and criminals since its inception (Liddick 1999).

Criminal syndicates make money from the numbers racket in several ways, including either owning a percentage or all of a numbers operation or demanding a percentage from the profits made by unaffiliated numbers businesses. During a typical day, employees of the numbers bank keep track of the numbers being bet; occasionally, they might notice heavy action on a particular number. Perhaps 20 or 30 individuals are all placing bets on the number 234. The banker then makes a similar bet on the same number with another banker. This is called making a *layoff* bet, a type of insurance. Tracking the daily numbers bets and using an appropriate layoff in response to such a situation ensures against heavy losses. More recently, banks have begun to lower their odds from 100:1 to 500:1.

The numbers game remains a popular pursuit due mostly to its better payoff odds and the fact that winnings do not have to be reported as taxable income. Others have suggested that the game is culturally embedded in some communities, with some residents claiming to have played over many decades so that it has become an integral part of inner-urban life. In addition, residents usually know the local operators who are part of the community and have in the past maybe contributed to local charities. This seemed more important than funding state lotteries, in which little trickled down to the poorer inner cities.

Until the introduction of the legal state lotteries in 1964, the numbers game was one of the few outlets for poor bettors. In the early years, those less privileged often wagered on a single-digit number, bets that were available for less money and less of a payoff. With the rising popularity of legal state lotteries in the 1970s, most observers predicted the demise of numbers gambling, but all reports indicate that by the end of the 1990s the racket was still doing well. Often-cited explanations for its persistence include the ability for one to bet on credit and the very ease of phoning in a bet. Better yet, the odds are better than the legal lottery, and if you win, no tax money is withheld. For the operator, the odds are always in his favor; on occasion, when action is heavier on one number than others, he has the alternative of laying-off action on another bookie. So, by staying on top of all incoming bets and using the proper layoff strategy, the numbers business remains a moneymaker.

DUTCH SCHULTZ, STEPHANIE ST. CLAIR, AND THE BATTLE OVER THE HARLEM NUMBERS RACKETS   By most accounts, the numbers game was introduced in New York City in the 1920s by a coterie of enterprising immigrants—Caribbean Blacks from Cuba, Puerto Rico, the West Indies, and even France (Schwartz 2006). None was better known than Stephanie St. Clair, the "Madam Queen of Policy." One pioneering study of numbers argues that numbers began as an exclusive Black lottery and was eventually adopted by others (Light 1977, 894).

During the 1920s, several large Black organized gambling syndicates implemented a new method to determine winning numbers, and thus began the policy numbers racket. According to one expert, "This was the first time in American history that blacks were in a leadership role in an organized gambling activity" (Schatzberg 1993, xv). Most accounts indicate that Black numbers operators began as business entrepreneurs in a system with few economic opportunities for African Americans. However, what was most crucial were links to the corrupt political machines dominated by White politicians who catered to White syndicates; without their support, Black criminals were stymied from further organization. Eventually, White gangsters moved in on the racket and took over policy numbers.

Ellsworth "Bumpy" Johnson (1906–1968)

For nearly 40 years, Harlem's millionaire racketeer "Bumpy" Johnson flourished by working with instead of against La Cosa Nostra, but not without serving several prison stints for drug trafficking. Between the 1930s and 1960s, Johnson played it safe by serving as a middleman between various organized crime groups in New York. In the end, he died of natural causes, a rare occurrence for someone of his stature in the underworld. "Bumpy" supposedly inspired the portrait of the drug kingpin in the *Shaft* novels and films of the 1970s. Flashy as a Neapolitan don, Johnson loved to flaunt a large wad of cash, courtesy of his various criminal enterprises, which ran the gamut from prostitution and heroin to running numbers and extortion. Recent accounts paint a portrait of a charismatic gangster eager to improve himself by reading 4 hours every day (Chepesiuk 2007). Fellow inmates at New York's Dannemara prison were so impressed by his knowledge that they referred to him as the *Professor.*

In the 1930s, Dutch Schultz took over much of Harlem's numbers rackets through both violence and guile. One of his most successful strategies was offering large independent contractors police protection if they joined his organization. The takeover was then made possible by money his syndicate had in reserve from the bootlegging business. Further greasing his ascendance in Harlem was the timely conviction of several West Indian Harlem numbers entrepreneurs that allowed Schultz's syndicate to take control by Winter 1932 (Liddick 1999). Under Schultz, Harlem's numbers rackets grossed $20 million a year at its peak of centralization, but financial problems intervened when the end of Prohibition reduced his bootlegging empire. Compounding his problems was the fact that his expenses increased along with his legal problems. After Schultz was killed in 1935, the numbers business reverted to its pre-Schulz structure.

THE MODERN NUMBERS BUSINESS: THE LEADHOUSE   By the 1980s, the numbers business was going through a makeover with the rise of the leadhouse. In times past, a bettor typically placed a bet through a *numbers writer;* today, this would most likely occur at a *leadhouse,* which combines the features of betting by telephone and betting through a writer—and is now the dominant mode of numbers gambling. A bettor goes into a leadhouse, also called a *store place,* and places a bet with the cashier or window clerk who works there (usually middle-age woman) and is given back a receipt. She then telephones/faxes the information to a *phone lady,* who relays the information to headquarters. Observers have compared the environment of a Leadhouse to an old-age home, with "a living room with couches and a TV" (Steffensmeier and Ulmer 2006), coffee brewing, and lemonade and orange juice on hand; people can come in and visit, even sit and read the papers. Most of its denizens are older, from 45 to 60, even into their 70s—but few under 30. Playing the numbers in this setting is something to look forward to after getting a pension or Social Security check every 2 weeks (Steffensmeier and Ulmer 2006, 132).

One recent investigation of the changing numbers business suggests that the transition from writers and runners to the store or leadhouse has led to a major reduction in the workforce and makes retailing more efficient. However, by lowering expenses, leadhouses can afford to offer higher betting odds and greater potential winnings. For example, compared to the state lotteries, where bets are paid off 500:1 on a straight bet, illegal operators have been known to offer odds as high as 800:1 (Steffensmeier and Ulmer 2006). There is still considerable debate as to the state of the numbers business in the 21st century. Although some argue that it continues to flourish in the era of the leadhouse, others contend that it has lost considerable allure in the face of stiff competition from legal and illegal slot machines, video poker, and the expansion of the casino business and state-sponsored lotteries.

Bolita

The game of *bolita,* which is Spanish for "little ball," is another permutation of the lottery that was popular in the late 19th and early 20th centuries in Cuba and Florida. Some accounts suggest the game was brought to the Tampa area by Cuban immigrants in the 1880s. Over the years, several variations developed. At about the same time numbers was being introduced in New York City, Cuban immigrants were doing likewise with a similar game in the American South. Unlike its counterpart though, *bolita* required a sack filled with 100 numbered balls that was tossed back and forth between the players until a signal was given to retrieve a ball that was declared the winner. During the 1930s the game proved especially popular in the Cuban community of Ybor City near Tampa, Florida. It soon spread throughout Florida and became a popular gambling game among all races and ethnic groups. According to one recent history of gambling, by 1938, Tampa boasted 125 *bolita* operations, bringing in an estimated $20,000 per day (Schwartz 2006, 381). Over the years it spread north to other cities and further west. A number of ways for cheating at the game have been uncovered. Because bets were often taken well in advance, the game always had the potential for being rigged. For example, extra balls of a particular number could be included, or some numbers not at all. Others have filled balls with lead so they would sink to the bottom of the bag, whereas others have frozen balls beforehand so that they could be retrieved by touch by whoever was pulling the numbers from the bag.

CASINOS

Prior to the rise of legal gambling in Las Vegas, most casino betting was illegal. However, this didn't stop the construction and operation of grand casinos in various parts of the United States. Most of these catered to a high-end crowd, with elegant dining and top entertainers. Some of these clubs were run by Jewish gangsters in league with Mafia affiliates. However, the success of these operations always depended on corruption and political influence that was periodically erased during various reform efforts. This led in part to a movement into Cuba by a number of leading mobsters, including Meyer Lansky in the 1930s and 1940s. Santo Trafficante, Jr., opened a casino there in 1946. Once Fulgencio Batista came to power in a coup in 1952, more casino–hotels followed, with American mobsters as investors. However, in 1959, the Cuban Revolution sounded the death knell for both Batista and the gambling industry.

Various organized crime syndicates dominated the gambling profession since the era of the riverboat gamblers. Prohibition schooled gangsters in the finer points in promoting gambling concerns, mass merchandizing, and finance—skills that were put to use as the gangs gravitated toward gambling following Prohibition. By running large—but illegal—gambling halls, gangsters developed the skills and resources required for big-time betting operations that would be put to use once Las Vegas became a gambling mecca. The growth of gambling in Las Vegas lured illegal casino operators from Southern California, especially following the municipal reform efforts of the late 1930s. A number of floating casinos had once operated offshore from Los Angeles. However a concerted effort by law enforcement closed them down between 1939 and 1942, and professional gamblers swarmed toward Las Vegas, among them Benjamin "Bugsy" Siegel and Tony Cornero. They brought with them experience in large-scale gaming operations as well as the general business of vice, skills that would serve them well as they transformed gambling into a sophisticated and more successful form of entertainment.

One historian asserted that the migration of Los Angeles casino operators to Las Vegas was significant for bringing an "infusion of experience and skills to make gambling into a big business" (Findlay 1986, 122–123). Not only did they represent "the first clearly defined group of emigrants from the world of organized crime to set up legitimate businesses in Nevada," but they also "foreshadowed the arrival of seasoned personnel and tainted funds from underworld actors"; figures who "ranged from petty shills and dealers to full-fledges gangsters" (Findlay 1986, 122–123). Although these gambling emissaries came with the intention of reaping a fortune, their contributions were also formidable, for they provided financing at a time when few investors were willing to finance casinos in southern Nevada.

FIGURE 6.12 Downtown Las Vegas: Fremont Street, yesterday and today. Fremont Street Experience and relic from past
Source: Dorling Kindersley Media Library/Demetrio Carrasco/Rough Guides Dorling Kindersley/Greg Ward

Casino gambling, except for between 1910 and 1930, has been legal in Nevada since 1869. Between 1931 and 1945, licensing and regulation was the responsibility of local and county authorities. By most accounts, this was an era when a large amount of organized crime money was used to fund the early modern casinos. In 1945, the state took over licensing and tax collection, but it was not until after 1955 that the state established a separate gaming control agency.

In 1976, New Jersey legalized gambling, leading to the opening of Atlantic City's first casino 2 years later, and in 1992, Louisiana became the third state to legalize land-based casino gambling. A number of other states have followed suit, beginning with South Dakota in 1989, which legalized limited-stakes games ($5 maximum bet) in the historic town of Deadwood. In 1990, Colorado also legalized limited-stakes games in three historic mining towns of Cripple Creek, Black Hawk, and Central City. Iowa and Illinois became the first states to legalize riverboat casino gambling in 1989. Today, more than 60 boats offer legal gambling in at least 6 states. Like other forms of gambling, each jurisdiction varies, with most states permitting traditional games such as blackjack, roulette, and slots.

Las Vegas

While searching for a new route between Santa Fe, New Mexico, and Los Angeles in 1829, a young Mexican scout came across an oasis in the desert, which he named Las Vegas, Spanish for "The Meadows." However, it took another 15 years before it appeared on a map following the peregrinations of the explorer John C. Fremont in 1844. Except for a Mormon missionary group that was sent there to build a fort and teach agricultural techniques to the local Paiutes, the area remained isolated with few settlers until the coming of the railroad in 1905. Taking advantage of the local water supply, a town took shape here and soon saloons, stores, and boarding houses began popping up. By 1909, it was the new county seat for the recently created Clark County. Despite local prohibitions against gambling, underground gambling joints flourished over the next 20 years. On March 19, 1931, gambling was legalized in Nevada. Six gaming licenses were issued the next month. Over the next decade, the state's divorce laws were liberalized, allowing couples to get "quickie" divorces in only 6 weeks, thanks to shorter residency requirements. Early tourists flocked to the Las Vegas area to enjoy the dude ranches that were considered the precursors to the modern Strip (Griffin 2006). The construction of the Hoover Dam in the 1930s further added to a growing population, as it added jobs to one of the country's few regions boasting a booming economy during the Great Depression.

In April 1941, city's first casino, El Rancho Vegas, opened up on the Strip. It was followed by the Last Frontier the following year. However, it was the opening of Benjamin "Bugsy" Siegel's Flamingo in 1946 that organized crime first became intimately involved in Las Vegas gambling rackets. Although Siegel is often accorded the distinction of being the pioneer of the Las Vegas hotel–casino business, others had built similar business years earlier. Even Siegel's involvement in the Flamingo came only after another entrepreneur named Bill Wilkerson ran out of funding. Siegel first surfaced in Las Vegas in 1942 while attempting to sign bookmakers to subscriber contracts with the Trans-America wire service. He did not appear for any length of time until he moved to Vegas and took over the Flamingo project from Wilkerson in 1946. Partially completed, Siegel figured he would have no problem finding the financial backing to finish the project. However, when his $1.6 million luxury project escalated to $6 million, his project came under deeper scrutiny by his mob financiers (Reid and Demaris 1974; Griffin 2006).

Siegel had some understandable explanations for the cost overrun. Not willing to spare any expense in completing his luxurious hotel–casino, he insisted that only the best wood and marble would be used. However, he soon found out that not all of the products he wanted were available so soon after World War II; nonetheless, he paid black marketeers their ridiculous prices, which in some cases they stole back at night and sold it back to him again. Siegel soon exhausted his options and flew back to New York, where he gave the "Combination" an ultimatum

Either loan him $2 million (which he owed the construction company), or he would put their Trans-America wire service out of business. On top of the cost overruns, poor money management, and the larcenous black marketeers, Siegel was beleaguered by poor workmanship and design mistakes (Griffin, 2006).

On the night of December 26, 1946, the Flamingo had its grand opening. Although unfinished, customers could still choose from a casino, lounge, theater, and restaurant. What was supposed to be his salvation turned into his demise. Due to poor weather conditions, a lot of the high rollers and celebrities he expected from Los Angeles were grounded, and the night was a resounding debacle. Even worse, the casino hemorrhaged money during its first 2 weeks. Siegel ended up begging his cohorts for more time, and indeed, by May 1947, it was $300,000 in the black. Figuring that his vision had been realized and that Lansky, Luciano, and the others were satisfied with the conclusion of this scenario, on the night of June 20, 1947, as Siegel relaxed with the newspaper in the living room of his girlfriend Virginia Hill's mansion while she vacationed in Paris, two rifle slugs struck him in the face from a still unknown assailant. Siegel was dead at the age of 41, but Las Vegas was just getting started. Over the next decade, seven more casinos were constructed on the developing Strip, all reportedly backed by organized crime financing from Chicago and the East Coast.

From the end of World War II to 1960, several Cosa Nostra Families acted as silent partners in casinos started by others. For example, Frank Costello received part of the skim because he, like others, had invested money in the enterprise. So, it was more of a personal decision as to whether each mob boss decided to participate. However, this all changed in 1959, when Jimmy Hoffa began lending money to the bosses from the Central States Pension Fund. Using this as their bank, they no longer had to put up their own cash (Capeci 2002).

During the era of organized crime involvement in the Las Vegas casino business that lasted into the 1970s there was no better way to make money than the *skim*. Skimming could not have been accomplished without the connivance of the casino operators. In this way, they repaid silent partners and other gangsters and paid off corrupt officials and police. During the 1960s and 1970s, mobsters had their own people placed in charge of casinos in which they had an interest. This ensured that cash would be skimmed off the top without interference from the IRS, the FBI, and the Nevada Gaming Commission.

Frank Rosenthal, who was immortalized in Nicholas Pileggi's *Casino* and in the subsequent eponymous movie, knew the casino business perhaps better than anyone. In his estimation,

> There is no casino, in this country at least, that is capable of defending itself against a skim. There are no safeties. You can't prevent a skim if a guy knows what he's doing. On the other hand, there are two kinds of skims. One is what we call *bleeding*. And that's horseshit. You've got a guy who's a twenty-one manager. He's going to knock out his three hundred dollars, four hundred dollars a night. That's bleeding a casino. That takes only two people—the manager and the runner, the guy who runs the chips back and forth from the cage to the games. Now when you get into the organized skim, you're talking about something very, very sophisticated. You couldn't do it in my day unless the whole casino was corrupted. . . . An organized skim calls for at least no less than three people. At a high level. You cannot do it without. (Pileggi 1995, 212–213)

In late 2006, investigators broke up what one New York attorney described as "the largest illegal gambling operation we have ever encountered, [rivalling] casinos for the amount of betting" (Hays 2006). More than two dozen individuals, including a professional baseball scout, were charged with $1 billion-a-year gambling ring that relied on an Internet Web site called Playwithal.com. One of those arrested was considered a top earner in a network of 2,000 bookies that took in more than $3 billion in cash bets since 2004 from tens of thousands of customers. Much of the money taken in by the ring was laundered and banked using *shell corporations* throughout the world.

The Stardust Skim: A Case Study

Between 1970 and 1980, the Las Vegas casino industry experienced unimagined growth, doubling the number of visitors who left behind $4.7 billion, an increase of 273.6% over the previous decade (Pileggi 1996). More cash is handled in a casino than in any other business on a daily basis. Most major casino cash thefts have taken place behind the closed doors of the count rooms. So much cash is collected here on a daily basis that it is often weighed rather than counted in various denominations. For example, $1 million in $100 bills weighs 20.5 pounds, whereas $1 million in $20 bills weighs 102 pounds (Pileggi 1996, 16). Beginning in the 1960s, a number of casinos were victimized by the "illegal siphoning off of casino cash" (Pileggi 1996, 16), better known as *skimming*. In this era, a number of organized crime groups were intimately involved in the daily machinations of casino count rooms, but none more than the Stardust Casino and Hotel, built in 1959, and the first high-rise casino on the strip. According to federal investigators "It passed through several owners connected to the Chicago mob" (Pileggi 1996, 16).

Skimming has probably occurred throughout the history of casinos, but the taking of cash prior to declaring it for taxes or as corporate income has generated tens of millions of profits for organized crime groups. In his book *Casino,* Nicholas Pileggi chronicles the Stardust skim and the dozens of ways skimming can be accomplished. These include ticket skims, food and beverage kickbacks, and theft from the count room.

One new clique of casino executives had adopted such clever methods of skimming millions of dollars out of casinos that no one knew the money was missing. As Pileggi put it, they sometimes "skimmed for the owners; sometimes they skimmed from the secret owners; and sometimes they skimmed the money for themselves" (1996, 211).

In the early 1970s, new management for Argent Corporation, which owned the Stardust, the Fremont, and the Hacienda, removed the controls that protected the proper reporting of all cash coming into the casino count room and rigged slot machine meters to record one-third more wins than were actually paid out (Pileggi 1996, 178). After the slots were emptied, the coins were taken to the count room, where an electronic scale was used to weigh the coins; it had also been rewired to underweigh the coins by one third. The next step was finding a way to remove tons of coins out of the tightly controlled environment. His solution was to create secondary banks on the casino floor, where the skimmed coins were traded for paper money by slot machine change clerks. In this way, these auxiliary banks circumvented the accepted procedures, where the paper bills were taken to the cashier's cage to be counted with the rest of the casino's paper money. Small metal doors were built into the side of the auxiliary banks so that once the clerk slid the cash into a locked compartment, the door could then be opened from the outside and the bills taken away in manila envelopes. This money from the auxiliary banks in each of the Argent casinos was taken to Argent management office and handed to special couriers, who regularly transported the skimmed cash to mob families in Milwaukee, Cleveland, Kansas City, and Chicago (Pileggi 1996, 178–179). By most accounts, casino executives were aware of the skim, but were too cowed by organized syndicates to interfere. It was estimated that from 1974 to 1976, $7 million to $15 million was skimmed out of the Argent Corporation.

Las Vegas Gangster Museum

In December 2007, Las Vegas announced that it was building a museum that would acknowledge the role played by organized crime in developing the city into America's first gambling capital. Mayor and former mob-defense attorney Oscar Goodman acknowledged the city's somewhat schizophrenic relationship with its criminal past, admitting, "This is more than legend. It's fact." More surprising is the fact that the project has the support of the FBI and is even being guided by a retired agent. It is expected to open in 2010.

Macau: World's Number One Gambling Mecca (2007)

Playing on a recent Las Vegas promotional line, one journalist recently noted, "What happens in Vegas now happens in Macau" (Wiseman 2007, A1). Once a sordid alternative to close-by Hong Kong, in 2006, Macau surpassed Las Vegas as the world's number one gambling market. Taking advantage of the booming economy of China's more than 1 billion people who are prohibited from gambling legally, Macau reportedly took in more than $500 million more than Las Vegas between January and November 2006. Prior to 2002, Macau's gambling operations were a monopoly directed at high-rolling Chinese gamblers who played blackjack and baccarat for huge sums of money. A city of nearly 500,000 people, before the former Portuguese colony was turned over to China in 1999, it had a reputation for prostitution and gang wars. With the turnover, crime has been curtailed and American casino operations have begun targeting the new gambling mecca. According to one recent press release, the Sands opened up a complex in 2004, and earned back its $260 million investment in less than a year (Wiseman, 2007).

Nevada's Black Book and Organized Crime

Officially referred to as the "List of Excluded Persons," the Black Book was inaugurated in 1960 (but did not begin to list nominees until 1978). After an individual is consigned to the book, he or she is barred from entering licensed gambling sites in Nevada for life. Those selected to be excluded are selected by the state's gaming regulators. They are gubernatorial appointees and serve full-time on the Gaming Control Board and part-time on the Nevada Gaming Commission. The following is a list of the alleged criminal associations of nominees prior to 1995:

Associations	Number	Percentage
Associate of Black Book Member	20	44.4
Associate of organized crime	8	17.8
Organized Crime figure	24	53.3
Not mentioned	5	11.1
Syndicate affiliation		
Chicago	10	41.7
Kansas City	5	20.8
Los Angeles	4	16.7
New England	1	4.2
New York	4	4.2
Hawaii	2	8.3
Unknown	1	4.2
Syndicate position		
Boss	7	29.2
Lieutenant	4	16.7
Enforcer	3	12.5
Henchman	1	4.2
Loan Shark	4	16.7
Collector	1	4.2
Soldier	1	4.2
Unknown	3	12.5

(Adapted from Farrell and Case 1995, 248)

Indian Reservation Gambling

Having had a long and conflicted relationship with its Indian nations, in a measure of recompense, Congress passed the Indian Gaming Regulatory Act (IGRA) in October 1988, which gave the country's sovereign Indian tribes a rare opportunity toward attaining "tribal economic development, self sufficiency, and strong tribal governments" (Popkin 1993). By law, activities that are illegal in a state cannot be legal on any of its reservations; at the same time, tribes cannot be prohibited from engaging in activities that are legal in the state they are located in due to their sovereignty. Since the late 1970s, as the majority of states have legalized gambling options such as lotteries, bingo, and charity games, some Indian tribes have responded by building gambling casinos on their reservations. Utah, which bans all gambling, is one of the few states where Native Americans are prevented from opening gaming establishments.

The inauguration of legal gambling on Indian reservations did not escape the predatory eyes of organized crime groups. In the late 1980s, Chicago mobsters moved toward infiltrating and taking over San Diego's Rincon Reservation gambling business, located in a remote part of Northern San Diego County. Over a period of months, FBI wiretaps followed the machinations of the Chicago mobsters as they attempted to move into this new realm of operations. Eventually, the government compiled thousands of wiretap reports collected on 27 pay phones in and around San Diego. The mobsters had not counted evidently on the new federal roving wiretap law that allowed agents to monitor a series of phones used by gangland suspects.

In 1986, Stewart Siegel, long affiliated with casinos from Las Vegas to the Caribbean, was selected to run the Barona reservation's bingo hall in San Diego. Capitalizing on his record as a high-rolling casino manager, among his first actions was to set up some grand prizes, including tens of thousands of dollars in cash and luxury automobiles. However, it was later revealed the prizes were usually owned by associates (shills) who then returned the winnings to Siegel himself. In 1986, he pled guilty to four counts of grand theft. He turned state's evidence, and entered the witness protection program soon afterward. His identity obscured by a hood, "Marty" told a Senate Select Committee on Indian Affairs that he was aware of more than a dozen gambling halls controlled by organized crime groups, but "guessed that nearly half of all Indian casinos were tainted by it, either directly through management and investors or indirectly through suppliers" (Segal 1992, 26–30; Popkin 1993).

Due to the finances of opening a gaming establishment, Indians are at a disadvantage when it comes to dealing with organized crime groups. Because few financial institutions are willing to make loans to tribes (due to the fact that their lands are sovereign, they cannot be foreclosed), tribes are forced to look elsewhere for start-up funds—and with few alternatives, fall prey to the money lenders of organized syndicates (Segal 1992).

Urban mobsters had never faced the challenges of infiltrating Native America's inner sanctums where, by their own accounts, they endured the frustrations of dealing with the residents, their changing demands, longstanding family disputes, and suspicions of outsiders (Sound like the Mafia?).

At the time of this case in 1987, gambling was bringing in $1 billion a year to tribal economies on reservations that were considered the poorest places in America. Although the Chicago mob lost interest in this proposition, during a 2-year investigation, the FBI was treated to a tutorial on how the mob can infiltrate reservation gambling halls and "how it counts on skimming and lax oversight to cheat tribes out of the revenue" that should have gone toward bettering the lives of the country's poorest citizens (Lieberman 1991, A22). Today, between 150 and 200 Indian casinos operate in at least 22 states.

DRUGS AND NARCOTICS PROHIBITION

People have used narcotics for medicinal, recreational, and religious purposes for millennia. Although *narcotics* specifically refers to opium and its derivatives (including laudanum, morphine, and heroin), the term has been used broadly by some to encompass other restricted drugs, including cocaine, marijuana, ecstasy, and even LSD. It has become especially popular to categorize opium and coca-based drugs as narcotics, although they are medicinally distinct, one being a central nervous system depressant, and the other a stimulant. According to a leading historian of drug addiction, both were combined in early legislation against them "because of an assumption that both were potentially habit-forming and associated with crime" (Courtwright 1989, 8).[7]

As early as the 18th century, Spanish officials were taxing and selling the coca leaf to pay for New World expansion (Karch 1998, 1). America's first law directed at marijuana was passed by the Virginia Assembly in 1619, which required every family to grow it. Hemp was considered not just a valuable commodity, but also an important necessity because the plant itself can used to make sails, rigging, and material for caulking wooden ships. Other colonies used hemp as legal tender in times of currency shortages and to increase its production—but there is little if any evidence that the early colonists were aware of its psychoactive properties at the time (Schlosser 2003, 19).

During the 19th century, a number of new drugs were heralded as "miracle cures" and used to treat all kinds of ailments. It was not until the late 1800s that the public recognized that opiate-laden miracle drugs could be addictive. Unfortunately, without regulations in place, patent medicines often contained up to 50% morphine, and were estimated to have created 2 million drug addicts in the United States at the beginning of the 19th century.

During the Victorian era that coincided with the last half of the 19th century, Americans were more worried about excessive drinking, linking it to many of the leading social problems, including public drunkenness, domestic abuse, child abandonment, insanity, pauperism, early death, and certain damnation. The question comes up as to why alcohol prohibition was targeted over drugs. Most explanations suggest that it was easier for a tranquil opiate addict to remain inconspicuous in public and private than the inebriated drunk (Courtwright 1998).

Earlier studies have indicated that at the turn of the 20th century, American officials estimated that there were between 250,000[8] and 1 million addicts of opium and its derivatives in the country, leading one observer to describe the United States as "a nation of drug takers" (Morgan 1974, 8). With a population of 76 million in 1900, this would be the equivalent of 1 person out of 400. By contrast to today's illegal narcotics, drugs in the pre-Prohibition era were unadulterated and would probably kill the average heroin addict today. Taken together with the fact that doctors often overprescribed and patients self-medicated, it's little wonder that so many fell under the influence of drug addiction. More recently, studies have begun to suggest that the number of America's "dope fiends" was exaggerated at the turn of the 20th century, with the typical American addict represented by "a middle-aged southern white woman strung out on laudanum," a potion of opium and alcohol (Courtwright 1982, 1; Gray 1998, 43). In any case, by most accounts, addiction peaked in America around 1900. Explanations for this varied, but leaned heavily toward a growing awareness of the hidden potency of medical remedies combined with the adoption of the Pure Food and Drug Act in 1906, which forced manufacturers to list the ingredients of drugs on their labels. One expert surmised, "When people began to realize their favorite nostrums were laced with addictive drugs, they stopped using them" (Gray 1998, 43–44).

Although public concern about drug addiction peaked in the in the years from 1900 to 1920, this was a crucial period for shaping America's future drug policies. The passage of the Pure Food and Drug Act in 1906 heralded an important victory for those seeking federal standards for the manufacture of patent medicines. In 1909, Congress restricted the importation of opium except for certified medical purposes, but, reformers still remained unsatisfied, demanding a codified, nationally applied anti-drug law. Reformers of the so-called Progressive Era (1890–1920) idealized a society that did not tolerate drug addiction, just as it would not tolerate alcohol abuse and political patronage. Reflecting these concerns, on December 17, 1914, President Woodrow Wilson signed into law the Harrison Narcotic Act, which criminalized the non-medical use of opium, morphine, and coca-leaf derivatives. In contrast to alcohol prohibition, there was little political debate over its intentions. Written primarily as a tax law, the act made it illegal for any "non-registered" person to possess heroin, cocaine, opium, morphine, or any of their products. The following year, more than 100 individuals were arrested as drug enforcement went into practice. Although many indicators suggest that White women were the predominant users, during World War I, the Army rejected 1 man out of every 1,100 due to addiction (compared to 1 in 10,000 during World War II).

In response to the new legislation, physicians and pharmacists became more conservative in dispensing opiates as the public became more wary of their effects. In addition, the Harrison Act required anyone who sold or distributed narcotics—including importers, manufacturers, wholesalers, and retail druggists, and physicians—to register with the government and pay a small tax. They were required to not only keep detailed records of all transactions, but also to have these ready for inspectors at all times. An infraction could be punished with jail time or a fine. It was hoped that these new sanctions would make the trafficking of narcotics crystal clear to the authorities and confine narcotics selling to the legitimate market.

The vaguely written Harrison Act was the subject of a number of important Supreme Court decisions between 1916 and 1928, one of the most prominent being the 1919 *Webb et al v. United States* case. After a Memphis doctor and druggist were indicted for conspiring to violate the law by prescribing morphine to an addict so he could maintain his addiction, a federal court ruled that they violated the intent of the law and upheld their indictments. Its ruling stated that providing drugs to an addict "not as a 'cure' but to keep the user 'comfortable by maintaining his customary use' was a 'perversion' of the meaning of the act" (quoted in Freidman 1993, 328).

The climax of a generation of concern about drug addiction, the Harrison Act did not stop drug addiction, but drove it underground, making the habit more difficult to maintain. Once the new anti-drug laws went into effect, drug addicts were forced into treatment. The focus would soon be shifted to alcohol in the 1920s.

A number of treaties were signed in the early decades leading up to the passage of the Harrison Act in 1914. Between 1918 and 1925, federal drug arrests rose tenfold, "from under 1,000 to over 10,000" (Reppetto 2004, 188).

As soon as an international regulation system was in place, organized drug trafficking syndicates emerged to supply whichever drug just happened to be in demand. The first drug control efforts were the result of suggestions made at the 1909 Shanghai Opium Conference, which resulted in the International Opium Convention, signed into law in 1912 (Chawla and Pietschmann 2005).

Criminal syndicates stepped into the vacuum created by the Harrison Act and subsequent anti-drug legislation. Just 4 years after the passage of the act, a U.S. Treasury Department agent claimed, "the peddlers appeared to have established a national organization, smuggling in drugs through the Canadian and Mexican borders" (quoted in Lunde 2004, 28).

Other countries soon jumped on the drug prohibition bandwagon. In 1920, Great Britain passed the Dangerous Drugs Act, which targeted access to cocaine, morphine, opium, codeine, hashish, and barbiturates for non-medical purposes. This was followed by the criminalization of cannabis in 1928, almost a decade before the United States passed similar legislation in 1937.

Addiction rates had dropped from a high of 1 per 400 during the "Golden Age" of addiction in 1900 to perhaps 1 out of 6,000 in the 1940s and 1950s, perhaps the lowest rate in U.S. history.[9] However, in the 1960s drug use began to increase due to a number of factors led by the liberalization of the era and the growing counterculture. One thing that did not change from one era to the next was the fact that the typical arrestee was from the poorer classes, whether it was alcohol or crack cocaine. According to Prohibition records, agents concentrated their attention on those "who they could not shake down," usually poor, barely literate, and recent immigrants unable to defend themselves (Behr 1996, 242).

Drugs and the Marginalized

Prohibiting drugs was a harder sell compared to prostitution (Mann Act 1910) and alcohol prohibition (1920). Both had faced a Congress reluctant to pass laws that might infringe on states' rights. The Mann Act was the first enacted, thanks to the publicity of the "white slavery" hysteria. In the early 20th century, there was still considerable debate over the use of opium and the products of coca leaves. Physicians were divided among those who saw medicinal wonders of these drugs, whereas others focused on the negative effects and potential addiction. However, once drug

Opiate Addiction Estimates for Various Groups in the United States (1910)[10]

Group	Addicted (%)
General criminal population	45.48
Chinese	25.0
Prostitutes and their companions	21.6
Prisoners in large jails and state prisons	6.0
Medical profession	2.06
Trained nurses	1.32
Other professional classes	0.684
General adult population	0.18
College/university students	Practically Unknown

prohibition opponents accepted the notion that most users and dealers were from the marginalized classes—Blacks, Asians, southern and eastern Europeans—the tide turned for the prohibition lobby. Drug addiction became objectionable once it became associated with unpopular groups whose morality was already in question, such as Catholic immigrants, machine politicians, urban Blacks, and criminals and lower-class paupers and criminals (Courtwright 1998). One expert posited, "Almost every drug prohibition ever enacted has had some racial or political component" (Gray 1998, 46). In 1875, San Francisco passed the country's first anti-narcotics legislation targeting the Chinese with an opium ordinance. In 1909, supporters of national narcotics legislation used the image of "sex-crazed, drug-crazed blacks" (Gray 1998) to win support in the South (although there was no evidence).

Drug Trafficking in the United States:
The Early Years of the Organized Drug Trade

Drug use and addiction in the United States has a long history, waxing and waning in response to changing population demographics, new legislation, and the availability of new drugs. One mob expert suggested, "The first recorded instance of drug-smuggling in the United States occurred in 1868," when a Chinese merchant in lower Manhattan's Chinatown was arrested for smuggling opium for his opium den (Volkman 1998, 46).

At the turn of the 20th century, opium and morphine and their derivatives were the most frequently purchased drugs, legally available in any drugstore. Opium dens flourished openly in major cities such as San Francisco, New York, Chicago, and New Orleans, where addicts of all races and genders gathered to ingest legal opium. The passage of the Opium Exclusion Act in 1909 opened up new opportunities for syndicated crime in the United States. Subsequent legislation targeted in quick succession non-prescription drugs and the sale of heroin, morphine, cocaine, and other addictive narcotics. Jewish gangsters were the first to grasp the potential of this development, and were soon organizing to smuggle narcotics from the leading supplier of the day—China—then building laboratories to dilute and package the narcotics for retail sales, and forming distribution networks to get the product to the addicts. By 1919, there were an estimated 200,000 addicts in New York City alone. The profits from supplying them were remarkable. In 1923, a kilo (2.2 lbs) of pure heroin cost $3,000 at its Chinese source. Once it was cut and divided up into 15,500 multi-grain capsules, it returned a profit of $300,000 (Volkman 1998).

American organized crime groups had been dealing in narcotics since at least 1909. However, the trade was dominated by Jewish gangsters until the ascendancy of Italian groups in the 1930s. One authority noted that although Jews were disproportionately represented in the cocaine trade, it was not an exclusively Jewish business. However, no matter who was involved in the early cocaine business, it remained decentralized, with few of the attributes typically associated with formal organizations. Historical evidence points to the cocaine trade as an early example of inter-ethnic cooperation (Block 1991).[11]

During the 1920s, Arnold Rothstein moved into the narcotics rackets. The profits were irresistible at a time when a pound of raw opium could be bought for $1,000 and refined to earn 150 times that. He was soon sending agents to Europe and Asia to purchase opium and smuggle it into the United States. One of the leading traffickers of this era was Irving ("Waxey" Gordon) Wexler. He and other traffickers had little to fear from a justice system that until 1956, set a federal maximum sentence of 10 years for narcotics smuggling, although in most cases the perpetrator served 1 or 2 years; suspended sentences were common.

Lepke Buchalter was also deeply involved, reinvesting profits from the garment business into drug-trafficking operations, including a ring that bribed ordinary tourists to carry kilos of heroin and opium in specially marked suitcases waved through by Customs officials bribed by Lepke. However, he would bring his friend Thomas Lucchese into the business—a decision he and his Jewish syndicate members would later regret. Lucchese organized several successful narcotics operations, including smuggling opium and morphine from Mexico to be converted into heroin. By most accounts, he was also careful to respect the Jewish contingent, but other Italian mobsters were less gracious as they got on the narcotics bandwagon. This was especially true by the end of Prohibition in 1933, when organized crime groups were casting about for the next big thing. One ploy that they used to drive out the Jewish competition was to lower prices and take over the distribution networks, so that by the end of the 1940s, New York's crime families were handling most of the heroin coming into the United States (Block 1991). As one observer knowingly put it, "The Mafia rush into narcotics marked the precipitate decline of Jewish organized crime" (Volkman 1998, 48).

Beginning in the 1960s, world drug production and consumption increased, fueled by the rise of international drug trafficking and facilitated by growing globalization and world trade, and improved means of transportation and communication. Further facilitating it were the combined "demand pull" of youth populations from developed nations and the "supply push" "provided by the economic difficulties of a number of producer countries and the discovery of the lucrative illegal drug trade by various warlords, insurgency groups, and organized crime circles" (Chawla and Pietschmann 2005, 162).

Noting the increase of America's drug addicts from 50,000 in the late 1950s to more than 500,000 in the 1970s, in his exhaustive history of the New York crime families, Selwyn Raab opined that none of organized crime's activities "inflicted more lasting distress on American society and damaged its quality of life more than the Mafia's large-scale introduction of heroin" (Raab 2005, 114).

Despite warnings by old-timers such as Frank Costello that engaging in narcotics would void the unwritten "live-and-let-live" agreement between the upper- and underworlds, the syndicates failed to listen. Once Italian American mob involvement in the drug trade became publicized, it became a public-relations nightmare. Compounded by harsh new laws and drug-addled gangsters, what many feared came true, as many became mob informers in the 1970s and 1980s to save themselves, undermining the discipline and secrecy that had protected it for so many years.

SOURCES FOR THE MOST POPULAR ILLEGAL DRUGS
Opium and Its Derivatives

Europeans were probably familiar with the opium poppy 4,000 years ago (fossil remains of poppy seed pods have been uncovered in Neolithic campsites). The Sumerians of the Fertile Crescent referred to it as *hul,* whereas Homer alludes to it in the *Iliad,* and most sources indicated that Arab physicians were familiar with the poppy's therapeutic qualities. The poppy probably came to China from the Middle East sometime in the 7th or 8th centuries, but it was not until the 18th century that opium smoking became epidemic in parts of the Far East and China. Some authorities suggest that opium smoking only became popular with the introduction of tobacco by the Dutch into China in

FIGURE 6.13   Opium Poppy Field in the Middle East
Source: Dorling Kindersley Media Library/Alistair Duncan

the 1600s. It was not long before they were experimenting with mixing opium and tobacco together. Opium can be ingested in a number of fashions—it can be eaten, smoked, or dissolved in alcohol or water for drinking; it can also be used for making heroin, morphine, and other drugs.

Although several countries have legal, government-regulated farms that provide opiates for licit medicines, illegal farms operate in a parallel global marketplace. An annual plant, the opium poppy reaches maturity only once and does not regenerate itself. Each season, a new seed must be planted, and once it grows and flowers, it produces a pod only once. The growth cycle for an opium plant takes roughly 4 months, but it is only the pod or fruit part of the plant that produces opium alkaloids. Farmers typically harvest the opium from the pods while still on the plant, using a special knife to produce a vertical incision. The pod then is left to dry on the stem and the largest and most fruitful pods are cut; finally, its seeds are removed and dried in the sun in preparation for storage until the next year's planting.

In the 16th century, the noted physician Paracelsus prescribed a potion made from opium, alcohol, and spices called *laudanum*[12] to patients. Opium eating was common in Europe in the 1700s, and in 1803 a German pharmacist isolated an opium alkaloid that he called *morphine* (after Morpheus, the Greek god of dreams). Almost 30 years later, scientists isolated *codeine*, another opium alkaloid. By the mid-19th century, morphine and codeine were widely available and popular in the United States and elsewhere. The invention of the hypodermic needle in 1856 along with the expansion of the narcotics trade led to serious abuse of these substances throughout the industrialized world. The end of the American Civil War in 1865 left thousands of wounded veterans with the "soldier's disease," better known as drug addiction.

Opium was popular in England as well in the 19th century, where consumption rose from 1 pound per 1,000 people to 10 pounds per 1,000 people by the end of the century. Considered the aspirin of the era, it was used to treat the full range of medical problems; at 1 penny for 25 drops, it was available for purchase virtually anywhere from the corner store to local market stalls (Carnwath and Smith 2002).

Physicians and others noticed the rapidly mounting abuse problem and began a scientific quest for non-addictive painkillers. In the 1870s, the Bayer Pharmaceutical Company seemed to have found the answer with a new and more potent drug that they named Heroin. By the 1890s, inexpensive needle kits were available for the injection of drugs. In 1897, the Sears Roebuck catalogue famously advertised hypodermic kits for sale that included a syringe, two needles, two vials, and a carrying case for only $1.50 (Inciardi 1992, 5). Further augmenting the nation's population of addicts was the lack of patent medicine regulations prior to the Pure Food and Drug Act in 1906 that required manufacturers to include the ingredients of their drugs.

Opium growing prefers a warm climate with low humidity and needs only a modicum of care after in its early stages. Government-regulated opium is produced on farms in India, Turkey, and Tasmania. However, the illegal and lucrative opium-growing regions are in Southwest Asia known as the Golden Crescent, composed of Afghanistan, Pakistan, Iran, and Southeast Asia's Golden Triangle, covering parts of Myanmar, Laos, Vietnam, and Thailand. Opium growing also takes place in parts of Colombia, Mexico, and Lebanon, and up until the possession of the opium plant became illegal in 1942, also the United States. By most accounts, law enforcement has proved inconsistent in enforcing the law. Poppy seeds are often used in breads and deserts, but cooking them prevents their psychoactive properties in the amount used for cooking. Poppy pods are also used widely in dry flower arrangements. In order to produce a little opium, it takes a substantial number of plants. So, in effect, unless someone grows poppies as a source for opiates, it is unlikely one will be prosecuted.

The Golden Triangle

The *Golden Triangle* is an area in Southeast Asia where the borders of Laos, Myanmar, and Thailand come together, and the region is considered the most important source for the plants due to the convergence of perfect growing conditions. Law enforcement authorities claim this region produces 4,000 tons of opium gum each year. Others have referred to this region as the *Golden Quadrangle* by including segments of Vietnam and China's Yunan Province. Myanmar, the former Burma, produces the majority of the opium, followed by Laos and then Thailand, which is considered the major transit point for opium exports.

Today, Myanmar ranks just behind Afghanistan as the largest producer of opium. It was during the 1960s and 1970s that this region emerged as one the world's largest suppliers of illegal opium. For a number of years, this region dominated the heroin-refining markets of Western Europe. During this period, the Netherlands was used as a principle staging area for the heroin trade, with the smuggling networks controlled by Chinese traffickers. In the late 1970s, rivalries among Chinese drug syndicates together with inroads made by law enforcement and a declining production due to poor crop yields reduced the region's importance to the heroin trade (Inciardi 1992, 64).

The Golden Crescent

The Golden Crescent is considered Central Asia's most important region for the production of illegal opium. This region encompasses the mountainous borderlands of Afghanistan, Iran,[13] and Pakistan, as well as parts of Uzbekistan and Tajikistan. In 2005, the northern province of Balkh, adjacent to Uzbekistan and Tajikistan, was awash in poppies—an area of 27,000 acres, nearly twice the size of Manhattan (Semple 2007). The good news is that by the end of 2007, new strategies had left this province and 12 others virtually poppy-free; the bad news is the fact that a sizable portion

Khun Sa (b. 1934)

Known as the "Opium King" and the "Prince of Death," Khun Sa was born in Myanmar's Shan State. The son of a prince, he was raised in opulence, and by an early age styled himself as "Prince Prosperous." In 1960, he formed his own militia, the *kakweye*, which became nucleus of his Shan United Army (SUA). Within the decade his almost 1,000-man army was fully embroiled in what has been described as a full-scale opium war against competitors in the region. Interviews with the warlord in the late 1970s show him claiming that he was not involved in opium production, but only in the taxing of shipments. Since the transition from Burma's democracy to military dictatorship as Myanmar, Khun Sa has been at war with the country's military leaders. Although he claimed his involvement in the drug trade was to finance his army, which was fighting for the independence of the Shan people, in 1989, a federal grand jury in New York indicted him for smuggling 1,000 tons of heroin, but had little impact. Khun Sa proclaimed himself the leader of an independent Shan State in 1993, but this brought more pressure from neighboring countries. In 1994, Thailand and DEA agents took part in "Operation Tiger Trap," which led to the arrest of some of Khun Sa's important contacts and successfully sealed the border against his drug-trafficking operations. Leading an army that had grown into the tens of thousands, in 1995, Khun Sa decided to step aside, vowing to lay down his weapons and leave the trade. Subsequent negotiations led to his surrender and release without trial. He now lives in Yangon, Myanmar.

of these farmers switched from growing opium poppies in favor of cannabis (the herb that produces marijuana and hashish). By most accounts, Afghan and Western governments focused their attentions on the skyrocketing production of opium while cannabis cultivation rose 40%, from 123,500 acres in 2006 to 173,000 acres in 2007. According to one observer, "Even though hashish is less expensive per weight than opium or heroin, cannabis can potentially earn a farmer more than poppies because it yields twice the quantity of drug per acre and is cheaper, less labor-intensive to grow" (Semple 2007, A23).

Farmers in this region continue to rely on the profits of poppies, despite pressures to shift to more legitimate agricultural products. However, most households have an average of 12 members. If they were to grow legal crops such as wheat, in order to grow enough to feed themselves they would require at least two hectares of land, when most have only about half of that. One observer explained,

> This leaves many trapped in a cycle of debt, exacerbated as each generation subdivides the family land. The legal agricultural economy is all but unsustainable in the absence of other sources of employment, and there are few. Poppy cultivation offered some respite from the trap. (*Economist*, June 21, 2008, 54)

As a result, smugglers not only purchase the opium, but also make loans against future production. Because dried opium lasts up to 2 years, farmers are free to hoard it and sell it when market prices are advantageous.

During the 1990s, the U.S. Department of Justice claimed that Afghanistan was the world's leading producer of opium, with an annual yield of more than 4,000 tons. In 1997, the extremist Muslim Taliban regime banned its cultivation, reducing production by almost 98%. By most accounts, Washington dispersed more than $40 million of humanitarian aid to the country, most probably as a thinly veiled payment for the interdiction efforts. Despite early attempts by the Taliban pre-September 11, 2001, and subsequent Western forces to end Afghanistan's opium trade, 2006 saw an estimated 400,000 acres of opium poppies planted—a 59% jump over the previous year. The following year also set a new record. By most accounts, Afghanistan now supplies more than 92% of the world's opium, the raw ingredient for heroin. It has been estimated that more than half of that country's gross national product comes from the drug trade. It's now believed to funding the re-emergence of the Taliban. This demonstrates if anything how pragmatic religious extremists have become, because the Taliban had ruthlessly instituted a strict policy against the opium trade during the waning years of the regime. Recent evidence shows that there is a growing affiliation between opium smugglers and the Taliban. Much like the FARC in Colombia, the Taliban entered into arrangements with drug smugglers in return for protection, and now tax the harvest in exchange for protecting opium farmers from the government's eradication efforts. This way, the Taliban seeks to win the hearts and minds of the population while reaping the largesse of the drug trade (Anderson 2007, 62).

The Heroin Trade

The trafficking of refined heroin to U.S. ports involved an elaborate organizational web of transportation routes, couriers, and payoffs. In the years preceding World War II and the subsequent Communist Revolution of 1949, American gangsters brought heroin in from Shanghai. However, the outbreak of hostilities made this increasingly difficult, and heroin use soon spread further into China. In 1941, a law was passed calling for the execution of addicts caught in the act. This failed to curb heroin use, but the defeat of the Japanese and the subsequent closing of their pharmaceutical factories in Manchuria and Korea turned off this major source. The Maoist Revolution was most successful at finally eradicating drug use in China. The rise of the Chinese communists led to a ruthless suppression of the drug trade and its concomitant legions of addicts. With opium fields destroyed and the processing factories closed down after the war, it was time to look in another direction in order to resuscitate the narcotics trade. Many of the drug syndicates moved their bases of operation from Shanghai to Hong Kong, and heroin use went up (as opium smoking diminished due to British laws). Hong Kong effectively became the main center for heroin production in the East. Initially, production was controlled by Shanghai, but later was taken over by the Chiu Chau syndicate from Kwangtung. Hong Kong maintained its supremacy until a police campaign in 1974 dismantled organizations, and most chemists and businessmen left for Thailand and Malaysia (Carnwath and Smith 2002, 59).

The Far East heroin market was shattered by World War II and its "revolutionary aftermath," and would not return until the 1950s and 1960s with emergence of Southeast Asia's Golden Triangle. Many authorities suggest that the lack of Asian narcotics in this era "reinvigorated" the Middle Eastern and Mediterranean drug operations (Block 1994).

The biggest problem after the war was finding a new supply of raw opium to manufacture heroin. Few countries grew poppies, and with the United Nation's Opium Protocol of 1953, production was allowed for export in only seven countries—Yugoslavia, Greece, Bulgaria, the USSR, Turkey, Iran, and India. Of these, only Turkey had not tightened control over its huge poppy fields. Lebanese businessmen provided the acumen for mediating its distribution to illegal dealers. Historically, the raw material for most heroin used in the United States came from Turkey, where farmers were licensed to grow opium poppies for sale to legal drug companies. However, the unintended consequence of this arrangement was that many sold their excess poppies to underworld entrepreneurs who manufactured it into heroin and transported it into the United States.

Prior to World War II, the heroin business was in the hands of mostly independent operators based in France operating in conjunction with Corsican gangs located in Marseilles, one of the region's busiest ports. Marseilles had long been an ideal transit point for ships smuggling morphine base from the Far and Near East and had proved adept at organizing the manufacture of heroin. Located in the Western Mediterranean, it was perfectly situated to handle all sorts of illegal trade, particularly the excess opium from Turkey. Illegal heroin labs were operating around the clock in Marseilles by the mid-1930s. The Corsicans in many ways resembled their counterparts in Sicily—clannish islanders sharing an Italian dialect. The difference was that the Corsicans had been involved in the drug trade since the 1930s. Under the supervision of Corsican crime boss Paul Carbone, the French underworld had been at the epicenter of the heroin drug trade for years as well as the source of most heroin entering the United States, eventually earning it the sobriquet of the "French Connection."

With their U.S. connections, the Sicilian Mafia became the Corsicans' best customers. Heroin was transshipped to Sicily, then to the United States, often packed in shipments of traditional Italian import items. Corsicans dominated the Marseilles underworld into the 1950s, but after the war, they soon found their power challenged by the ascendance of the local communist party, which had little in common with the gangsters. As in Italy after the war, the United States became especially alarmed by threat of the communist presence, and soon a secret operation was launched by the nascent CIA to support non-communist aligned Socialists in France. According to one investigator, CIA agents supplied weapons and money to Corsican gangs, who attacked and harassed Communist activists and union officials. In the process, the Corsicans emerged as the leaders of the local underworld. So, in effect, the United States used its clout to "inadvertently create and/or revive the two major groups of international drug traffickers: the American–Sicilian Mafia and the French Corsican underworld" (Jonnes 1999, 171). Between the end of World War II and the 1960s, Hong Kong and Marseilles were the heroin-refining capitals of world; later, it became more dispersed. In the years following the war, the opium–heroin trafficking networks from Southeast Asia and Europe were reestablished as well, and drugs were once more being shipped into American ports (Inciardi 1992, 29).

In February 1947, the largest post-war seizure of narcotics took place in New York when a Corsican seaman was arrested leaving a recently arrived French vessel with 7 pounds of heroin. The following month, a similar case led to the seizure of 28 pounds on another French liner. Over the next year, this process was repeated a number of times—a sign that international drug traffickers were back in business after the war had virtually stopped the trade. U.S. Customs and Bureau of Narcotics investigators blamed "Lucky" Luciano for several cases, but the Corsican connection was even more pronounced because most of those arrested in these aforementioned cases were Corsican nationals.

One drug expert pointed out "that the traditional Sicilian Mafia had not been drug traffickers. It was the separate U.S. policy of deporting its Italian-born American gangsters that introduced international drug trafficking as a new and lucrative criminal activity" (Jonnes 1999, 167). This deportation policy proved convenient from an economic perspective but unfortunately allowed a recurrent supply of American gangsters to bring their underworld specialties to their Italian counterparts (see Chapter 3). None proved more important than "Lucky" Luciano. During an October 12, 1957, meeting of Sicilian and American crime bosses in Palermo, the foundations were agreed on for the organization of the international narcotics trade, especially heroin. This was a growing market, with the United States the biggest consumer. The previously deported "Lucky" Luciano had been organizing the U.S. heroin trade through Havana since 1946, but with Cuba on the brink of revolution in the late 1950s, he needed a new distribution network. Although the Italian-American National Commission formally opposed drug trafficking, the profits were too much of a temptation. Among the most important agreements to come out of the Palermo meeting was the idea for the New York crime families to franchise the entire narcotics business to the Sicilians for an agreed percentage of the profits. This system lasted for the most part until the Pizza Connection was discovered in 1987.

The Pizza Connection

During the 1970s, the Sicilian Mafia entered into an alliance with heroin suppliers in Turkey and established network of refineries in Sicily. They also formed alliances with South American suppliers of cocaine before moving into the lucrative trade in the United States in a big way. The Sicilians came up with the ingenious distribution method known as the *Pizza Connection,* using a nationwide network of pizzerias to market drugs and launder money. Soon they entered a franchise agreement with American organized crime groups and brought thousands of their own people to work at the hundreds of pizzerias. By 1985, the ring was led by Gaetano Badalamenti and Salvatore Catalano. This scheme evaded FBI scrutiny until 1980, and no convictions were made until 1987, following the "Donnie Brasco" FBI undercover operation.

The African Connection: The Globalization of the Heroin Trade in the 21st Century

In the latter part of the 1990s, the New Jersey State Commission of Investigation revealed the Nigerian involvement in the international heroin trade. Their investigation revealed a structure that included a "God Father" who is responsible for six smugglers, or *mules,* transporting money and drugs into the country. The typical operation begins in Nigeria with the mule, preferably a woman or juvenile, who is sent to a "Black Magic House" to receive instructions and swallow the heroin in sealed condoms. During the 1990s, it was estimated that Nigerians received most of their heroin from Southeast Asia, as evidenced by the fact that three out of every five couriers arrested in Thailand in possession of heroin are from Nigeria.

The "African connection" has become increasingly entwined in the international drug trade as Nigeria emerged as a major transshipment point for Southeast Asia heroin heading to Europe and the United States. In June 23, 2002, the *New York Times* indicated that most of the foreign heroin buyers in Bangkok were Nigerians who brokered the drugs to Nigerian gangs and to syndicates abroad. The DEA regarded Nigeria as an "essential" juncture in the heroin trade and "Africa's most significant trans-shipment point" (Naim 2005).

According to one leading commentator on global crime, Nigeria now operates heroin labs that process opium brought in from Afghanistan and Myanmar and has also transited through Pakistan, Uzbekistan, Thailand, or China. Nigerian exporters often stationed in Bangkok procure heroin from a variety of channels through Myanmar or when the Afghan product is more competitive, send couriers to buy it in Pakistan. It is then shipped in quantity to Lagos by ship or air freight. In some cases, the drugs are often brought into the United States in the luggage of European women passing through Frankfurt or Brussels. Nigerians play an important role in the American heroin trade in several cities, especially Chicago. They moved into the heroin business here sometime in the 1980s after the Mexican network was interrupted by police operations (see Chapter 11).[13] They have been able to flourish in Chicago as wholesalers, using the mail, couriers, and other services to supply local dealers, "but at the retail level, the Nigerians vanish" (Naim 2005, 73).

COCAINE[14]

Cocaine is a derivative of the coca plant. Found mostly in Colombia, Bolivia, and Peru, Andean Mountain people traditionally chewed on coca leaves to counter the debilitating effects of high altitudes or in religious ceremonies. Cocaine was first extracted from the leaves in 1855 and was considered one of the era's wonder potions. It attracted so much positive press that personages from Pope Pius X to Sigmund Freud would eventually offer public testimony to its propensity for fighting various ailments as well as "its life-giving properties" (Karch 1998, 46). From its introduction to Europe, probably sometime in the late 1600s, until the invention of the hypodermic syringe in the late 1850s, cocaine was only ingested orally; few had realized it could be snorted for effect (Karch 1998, 46). The original *Coca Cola* contained small amounts of cocaine, and when it hit the market in the 19th century was marketed as "a brain tonic and cure for all nervous afflictions" (Karch 1998, 46). However, by 1904, the members of the medical establishment began to warn that the new drink was another source of addiction for cocaine addicts, and the cocaine was soon removed from the popular soft drink.

Coca plants are harvested up to eight times a year and are most successful when grown at low altitudes. The best-quality drug comes from the more mature leaves. Coca harvesting is labor intensive and time is often at a premium, because the leaves must be dried or processed within 3 days of picking. Once dried, the leaves are taken to a processing laboratory where they are then turned into base. In turn, the base is shipped to another laboratory where chemicals are added to convert it to cocaine. It generally takes 3 metric tons of coca leaves to make from 4 to 7 kilos of cocaine. It is then transported to market in any number of ways.

FIGURE 6.14 Map of Andes Mountain Range
Source: Dorling Kindersley Media Library

FIGURE 6.15 Andean vendor selling coca leaves at Sunday market
Source: Dorling Kindersley Media Library/Jamie Marshall

According to one leading authority, cocaine's "transformation from unregulated medicine to tightly controlled social menace became the foundation for contemporary drug prohibition" (Spillane 2000, 1). Cocaine was legal in most states until after 1900—its growing popularity sparked a movement to regulate its use and distribution, culminating in 1914 Harrison Act and the inauguration of national drug prohibition. Cocaine was in such demand prior to 1914 that many users were forced to buy it from "retailers who specialized in the cocaine trade" (Spillane 2000, 1).

According to a recent history of cocaine,

> The regulated drug market therefore began to develop a number of features more commonly associated with the post-prohibition black market: cocaine selling became increasingly geographically concentrated, usually coexisting with other underground trades in urban areas; the bulk of retail sales shifted from pharmacists to drug peddlers; and the product available to consumers declined in quality and purity. Moreover, the retail price began to separate from the legal price, as the specialized cocaine sellers began to extract a premium for their willingness to cross lines of legitimate trade. (Spillane 2000, 162)

The inflated retail prices of the pre-1914 cocaine market had already demonstrated the profit motive that would drive the modern drug illicit drug trade. Cities such as Chicago had set a minimum amount of cocaine per transaction to discourage consumers from buying it at drug stores; this in turn "accelerated the emergence of dealers" (Spillane 1998, 149) who purchased larger amounts and then resold them in smaller units. Although some sold it to perhaps supplement a meager income, others took it on as a full-time profession; however, none dominated the market. As far as organization, part-time dealers probably carried their stock with them, whereas their more professional counterparts hired employees to sell the drugs in various fixed locations, or were hired to steer customers toward the dealer. At the bottom of the cocaine food-chain were users who resold part of their purchase in order to pay for their own—this was usually accomplished by taking some of it out before reducing the purity of the remainder with some type of addictive (Spillane 2000, 149–153).

Crack Cocaine

This highly addictive drug became popular in the 1980s as an inexpensive alternative to powder cocaine. One recent study of drug prohibition suggested, "Crack cocaine was not so much a creature of pharmacology as a creature of the law—an artifact of Prohibition" (Gray 1998, 109–107). By making cocaine so expensive, the government had unintentionally stimulated dealers to look for better ways to market cocaine. As Mike Gray so succinctly put it, "Dealing in contraband always favors the method that puts the most bang in the cheapest package" (1998, 107). Hitting on the smokable version, where one could get very high on small amount, was a reprise of the 1920s when "white lightening" was sold to alcohol enthusiasts—"adulterated 190-proof synthetic hooch" might blind you, but always got you high (Gray 1998,106–107).

At that time, most of the cocaine entering the United States was being transshipped through the Bahamas. In fact, there was so much cocaine powder pouring through these islands that prices dropped by as much as 80%. In the face of dropping prices, dealers sought new alternatives for marketing the drug and hit on the perfect formula—convert the powder to a smokable form, which became known as *crack*. It was cheap, simple to prepare and use, and returned high profits per dose; by 1981; major cities in the West, Southwest, and the Caribbean were reporting its introduction into the nation's repertoire of illegal drugs. Compared to powder cocaine, which averaged a paltry 55% purity for $100 a gram, at dosage units as low as $2.50 and with 80% purity, crack became the poor man's drug of choice—and most important, it gave an immediate high to the user. Soon Caribbean immigrants, especially Jamaican posse members, were teaching the process of making crack to legions of willing students looking for a lucrative new trade. South Florida became the epicenter for the cocaine trade and a principal staging ground for crack-conversion laboratories. By the 1980s, conversion labs had been busted in an increasing number of states.

Crack and Powder Cocaine Sentencing Disparity

Crack cocaine is the only illegal drug that requires a mandatory sentence for first offense possession. For the majority of illicit drugs, the maximum federal sentence for simple possession is 1 year in prison. By comparison, anyone who is sentenced in federal court for possessing 5 grams of crack, equivalent to 5 Sweet 'N Low® packets, automatically receives a 5-year sentence. Since the late 1980s, critics have targeted the racial and socioeconomic disparity between the sentences for crack users and dealers, who are mostly minorities and poor, with those doled out to powder cocaine offenders–where 500 grams of powder cocaine, equal to more than a one-pound bag of Domino® Sugar, merits the same punishment. As a result, the population in America's prisons are disproportionately made up of African Americans snared on low-level federal drug raps. The juxtaposition is glaring when compared to the fates of those nabbed with more expensive powder cocaine, usually wealthier and more upwardly mobile Whites and Latinos. For example, in 2005, an African-American male was given 30 years in prison for possession of 1 pound of crack, whereas a Latino male received 3 years for possession of 11 pounds of cocaine (Casimir 2007, A7). Much of the current legislation is a result of the "get tough" policies of the drug-plagued 1980s, which led Congress to pass the Anti-Drug Abuse Act in 1986, in turn creating mandatory penalties for federal drug offenses. During this era, lawmakers arbitrarily created more stringent penalties for crack cocaine.

Cocaine increased in popularity in the United States in the 1970s, and in the next decade its use soared to 300 metric tons, a level to which it roughly adhered through the end of the 20th century (Spillane 2000). Although powder cocaine became the drug of choice for middle- and upper-income Americans in 1970s, crack emerged as a cheaper alternative for poorer users, in largely minority urban areas; the drug developed an image as a drug used mostly by violent inner-city youths (Lavoie 2007). It also became "the blue collar drug of choice" for a largely White audience like speed is today (Gray 1998, 107). During the mid-1980s, powdered cocaine sold for half or whole gram packets for $50 to $100, whereas crack was sold as small rocks for as little as $5 and $10.

Criminologists, medical practitioners, and others now agree that the differences between crack and powder cocaine have been largely exaggerated and do not justify the sentencing disparity that has lasted since the 1980s. Most of 1980s laws were based on myths that have since been debunked. When the mandatory sentencing laws were passed, Congress believed there was a direct link between crack use and the commission of violent crimes. Under the impression that crack was instantly addicting, lawmakers feared a generation of "crack babies" would plague nation for years to come. However, it turned out that lawmakers had it mostly wrong (Protass 2007, B7). According to a recent *Journal of the American Medical Association* (JAMA) report to Congress, "crack is pharmacologically indistinguishable from, and produces harm no more severe than powder cocaine, even to the unborn" (Protass 2007, B7). Rather than capturing the travails and misery of babies on crack, the public had for years been treated to the well-documented effects of malnutrition and poverty (tiny trembling infants) (Gray 1998; Protass 2007). Indeed, crack's use never reached the epidemic proportions that so many "experts" predicted, and in the end, its consumption bore no higher correlation to violent crime than did other stimulant drugs. When it came to fighting the organized drug trade, the objectives of targeting high-level dealers largely failed, with the majority of criminal actors doing time coming from the ranks of street dealers, couriers, and lookouts.

Cocaine and Methamphetamine Prices (2007)

In November 2007, the DEA revealed that prices for cocaine and methamphetamine had risen for the fourth quarter in a row, indicating a trend that law enforcement claims suggests that the supply has dropped. A gram of cocaine that went for $93 in October 2007 rose to $137 a year later; likewise, a gram of methamphetamine rose from $133 to $245 in 1 year (*USA Today,* November 8, 2007).

Methamphetamines: America's Most Dangerous Drug?

Unlike the crack epidemic in America's urban centers in the 1980s, which was heavily chronicled by the media and government officials, the methamphetamine ("meth") trade slipped under the radar of law enforcement, mostly because it was confined to rural outposts. Once the province of outlaw motorcycle gangs in the 1960s, since the late 1990s, methamphetamine labs have proliferated in a variety of locations—including among the rural poor and urban gay males. Its monikers reflect the demographics of its users: "Biker's coffee," "chicken feed," "crystal," "ice," "stovetop," and "Tine." Once derided as "poor man's cocaine," methamphetamine has become popular across America. Relatively cheap compared to other drugs, this highly addictive stimulant hooks across the socioeconomic spectrum. Meth comes in both powder and rock form, and produces a powerful rush. It is also very cheap, with several hits costing $25, enough for users to stay awake for days. It started out as mainly a rural problem. Users were called "tweakers": as one DEA agent described the effects of methamphetamine, "the user is mowing his lawn at 3 A.M." (quoted in Will 2001, 135). Compared to the short-lived highs of most other illegal drugs, the longer-lasting high can last up to 12 hours per hit. In 1996, the street value of 1 pound of methamphetamine could provide 90,000 hits. It takes no more than $500 worth of chemicals to make 1 pound of methamphetamine. Fifty to 70 pounds can be produced in a day, using the most spartan labs with recipes downloaded from the Internet. Initially, the meth trade was controlled by OMGs, but intergang feuds and violence opened the trade to new competition from Mexico (see Chapter 11).

Compared to heroin and cocaine, which are products of plants grown throughout parts of Asia and South America, methamphetamine is a "purpose-made" drug, created in laboratories from chemicals found in popular cough and cold remedies. Unlike their fellow traffickers, meth dealers are hostage to government pressure and restrictions on the production of ephedrine and pseudoephedrine, especially because only nine factories create most of the world's supply. Once these sources dry up, the availability of meth often does as well.

In one 2005 survey, more than 12 million Americans have tried methamphetamine, and 1.5 million are regular users. Eighty percent of the meth used in the United States is produced by drug cartels operating superlabs in parts of California capable of producing up to 1 million doses in a 48-hour period (Suo 2004). However, meth-making operations have been uncovered in every state; Missouri leads the list with more than 8,000 meth labs, equipment caches, and toxic dumps seized between 2002 and 2004. Police nationwide now rank it "the No. 1 drug they battle today" (Jefferson 2005, 42). Although these smaller labs outnumber the superlabs, roughly 8,300 to 300, they are only capable of manufacturing less than 300 doses per 48-hour period. In a survey of 500 law enforcement agencies in 45 states by the National Association of Counties, 58% reported meth was their biggest problem, followed by 19% for cocaine, 17% for marijuana, and 3% for heroin. One of the greatest indicators of the drug's popularity has been the decision by most drug retailers to move non-prescription cold pills behind the counter, making it tougher for meth cooks to get the main ingredient for their potions—the active ingredient pseudoephedrine, a chemical derivative of amphetamines. It is extracted from cold pills and cooked with other chemicals (such as iodine and anhydrous ammonia) over high heat in recipes that can be downloaded off Internet.

Methamphetamine was first synthesized by a Japanese chemist in 1919. It was used by most armies during World War II to keep the troops alert; kamikaze pilots reportedly took high doses on their suicide missions. By the 1950s, it was commonly prescribed as a diet aid and to fight depression, leading some modern users to call it the "Jenny Crank diet." Meth was not criminalized until 1970, and soon it turned into a minor West Coast fad controlled by California's Outlaw Motorcycle Gangs. In the 1980s, they controlled about three-quarters of California's meth trade. According to one narcotics official, "they went from a loose-knit bunch of guys to an organized crime family" (Owen 2007, 134). During the days of the biker trade, it was nicknamed *crank,* referring to the popular stash hideaway in the motorcycle crankcases. Legislators attempted to restrict supplies of the core ingredients of meth. In 1980, the drug's main ingredient—phenyl-2-propanone (P2P)—came under federal control. In response, underground chemists (*cooks*) turned to ephedrine, a mild stimulant whose main use was to

"22": The Meth Superlab

According to investigative reporter Steve Suo, the superlabs are distinct not just for their efficiency and sophistication, but for their standardization as well. Most labs feature a 22-liter reaction vessel, originally designed for scientific research and capable of holding the contents of 11 two-liter soda bottles.

> The 22 sits in an aluminum cradle lined with heating coils. . . . Inside the glass ball, a blood-red brew of pseudoephedrine, red phosphorus and hydriodic acid reacts to form meth. The temperature dial is turned up to set the mixture bubbling, then down to cook. Orange hoses stretch like octopus arms from the neck of each 22 to a box filled with cat litter, which absorbs reaction gases. . . . The labs are so standardized that the first time police found high-thread-count Martha Stewart sheets—used to filter solid meth from surrounding liquids—in one lab, identical sheets were discovered the next day in a lab 100 miles away. The smallest detail, down to the way in which hoses are duct-taped together, is replicated from one superlab to the next. (Suo, October 3, 2004)

treat asthma. What they found was completely unexpected—that ephedrine made meth twice as powerful as the older biker version. So the crackdown on P2P not only led to an easier way to make meth, but also made it much stronger. Lawmakers responded once more by targeting ephedrine, and the meth labs simply switched to a related compound called pseudoephedrine.

In the 1980s, a middling Mexican cocaine runner named Amezcua Contreras saw the commercial possibilities of the meth trade and transformed it into a business. By the early 1990s, the Mexican meth trade began taking over superlabs in rural California. These labs could turn out 50 pounds of meth in a weekend. Eight ounces of the substance can get 15 people high (see Chapter 11).

Prior to the mid-1990s and the ubiquity of the Internet, the recipe for making meth was not very widely distributed. If one wanted to process meth it was necessary to learn from experienced chemists or find rare underground publications with the recipes. This all changed with "the great democratizing power of the Internet [that] allowed the recipe to be distributed very nearly without limit" (Langton 2007, 103). Anyone with access to a computer can now find meth recipes through chat rooms, forums, and e-mail. During the 1990s, hundreds if not thousands of "mom-and-pop" entrepreneurs were soon in business. For just "eight dollars worth of cold pills and household cleaners, a few bottles and hoses and the nerve to risk explosions and chemical burns [anyone] could go into the business of making and retailing meth" (Langton 2007, 103).

Meanwhile, the DEA sought tighter control on the precursor chemicals and ended up with a less than stellar compromise. Fighting the powerful pharmaceutical lobby was an uphill battle. In the end, Congress settled on controlling all retail sales of pseudoephedrine products except for those sold in blister packs. The naive reasoning behind this was that officials felt meth dealers would find the process of pushing the pills through their foil wrappers too onerous and time-consuming. However, this would have little effect on California's superlabs. Mexican drug syndicates had a ready market of laborers who preferred pushing the pills through foil to picking strawberries under the harsh sun.

In 1996, Congress passed what became known as the Comprehensive Methamphetamine Control Act (MCA). It forced all U.S. dealers of ephedrine to register with the DEA. Pharmacies were expected to keep products behind the counter and report suspicious transactions. In 2000, the DEA cracked down on the black-market pseudoephedrine sales, but this had little impact on the quality of meth, as French and Canadian pills found their way onto the American market. With no real restrictions on the drug north of the American border, Canadian pharmacies flourished thanks to the cold pills. After bulk sales were restricted, manufacturers began buying hundreds of thousands of boxes of Sudafed and other related drugs; cooks resorted to a practice they referred to as *smurfing,* in which they would go from one store to another, either stealing or purchasing pills. Between 2000 and 2001, imports increased from 37 tons to 154 tons. This reversed after Canada adopted similar restrictions to the United States in 2003. That same year, the World Health Organization (WHO) proclaimed meth "the most widely used illicit drug after marijuana" (Langton

---

Shock Tactics in the War against Meth (2008)

Between 2005 and 2007, Montana officials claimed that the number of teenagers using meth had dropped 45%. Although some might have turned to other drugs, a number of officials have pointed to various advertisement campaigns. The state had one of the country's highest rates of meth use in 2005. Several ad campaigns were developed that resulted in billboards featuring young users "with vacant eyes and waxy skin, pinned to the ground by a faceless man in a dirty shirt" with the caption "15 bucks for sex isn't normal. But on meth it is." Although public complaints forced the state to take it down, other campaigns followed using similar themes. One chilling ad that seemed to be most effective was one targeting 12- to 17-year-olds with "a close-up picture of rotting teeth." These ads, combined with putting cold medicine behind the counter and devoting more money to treatment centers, have been so successful that Montana now ranks 39th for meth use (*Economist,* May 3, 2008, 36).

2007, 113). Also in 2003, the meth trade heated up in Mexico, where the precursors arrived in ever larger doses from Asia. These were then smuggled across the U.S. border into the United States.

In 2004, the DEA outlined its National Synthetic Drugs Action Plan, which detailed how the government planned to fight meth and other so-called "purpose-made drugs like ecstasy" (Langton 2007, 113). However, there was little new here. As usual, the federal government lagged behind the states that had implemented the same restrictions months earlier. Oklahoma was the first to pass legislation limiting the amount of pseudoephedrine that pharmacies could purchase, and forced them to keep the remedies behind the counter. Buyers were required to show identification and sign a register. By the time the federal laws went into effect, 23 states had already made strides towards restricting the sale of meth precursor chemicals (35 states by 2005). One Oklahoma official claimed in 2004 that as a result of its state law, "meth labs have all but disappeared in Oklahoma." Drug arrest reports seemed to support these claims, with a 90% drop in lab seizures since its passage. Today, at least 40 states have restrictions on the sale of pseudoephedrine. Although drug manufacturers continue to fight these restrictions, one promising sign is their attempts at reformulate cold remedies with chemicals that cannot be used to make meth.

Ecstasy (MDMA)

In recent years, so-called party drugs like ecstasy have exploded onto the world drug market. Between 1990 and 2002, global drug seizures almost doubled. Ecstasy, or MDMA, has both hallucinogenic and stimulant qualities and is a popular drug on the youth rave party scene. It is typically ingested in pill form, but can also be snorted and injected, and its effects can last 3 to 5 hours. It gives a high that has been compared to "high energy euphoria" (Chawla and Pietschmann 2005) with mild hallucinogenic effects that makes colors seem brighter, sounds more enjoyable, and the sense of touch more sensitive. Often dealers will heat up a Tootsie Roll®, then unwrap it and put an ecstasy pill inside. They then rewrap the candy and sell the hidden pills.

In February 2000, former Gambino underboss Sammy "The Bull" Gravano was arrested on drug-trafficking charges in Arizona. He had left the Witness Protection Program in 1998 on his own volition and had been relocated to Phoenix. He was arrested for dealing ecstasy and other drugs while mentoring a local white supremacist gang called the "Devil Dogs." He used this gang to help in his trafficking schemes that included steroids, ecstasy, marijuana, and amphetamines.

Ecstasy has been used by almost 8 million people worldwide, with the largest seizures being made in Europe and the United States. The smuggling of this drug is now considered a global phenomenon with a significant impact in Europe, the United States, Oceania, Central America, the Caribbean, South America, East and Southeast Asia, the Near and Middle East, and South Africa. It's mostly produced in Belgium and the Netherlands, but evidence of new production centers elsewhere are increasing (Chawla and Pietschmann 2005).

Most ecstasy seizures occur in road traffic followed by aircraft, reflecting the increasingly international scope of the trade. In March 2002, Europol conducted one of its largest ecstasy investigations using Customs officers from France, Germany, and the Netherlands. Dubbed *Operation Mercure,* it targeted air passengers traveling from Europe to the United States, Canada, and Australia. The main goal of the maneuver was to identify and arrest couriers involved in the smuggling of synthetic drugs such as ecstasy. The subsequent operation netted almost €8 million worth of ecstasy at airports in Amsterdam, Frankfurt/Main, Zurich, Madrid, Brussels, Paris, and Miami (DeVito 2005, 232).

Marijuana

The term *marijuana* is a colloquial Mexican word for the plant known to botanists as *Cannabis sativa.* Testament to its ubiquity is the number of international words used to describe it—*dagga* in Africa, *ma* in China, *hemp* in Europe, and *bhangm ganja* and *charas* in India. Cultivated for at least 5,000 years, the hemp[15] plant is an adaptive and highly successful annual found throughout the temperate and tropical zones of the world. It is also one of the most ancient agricultural products not grown for food (Schlosser 2003). Cannabis is a dioecious plant in that it spawns male and female plants in equal proportion and the flower buds of both produce cannabinoids (containing more than 60 compounds specific to marijuana). Of these, several are psychoactive producing THC, or delta-9 tetrahydrocannabinol. Known by its generic term, *cannabis,* and numerous other terms, its psychoactive use has been recorded dating back to at least the 28th century B.C., when it was prescribed by ancient Chinese physicians as an anesthetic (combined with wine) during surgery.

Americans have been familiar with the multifaceted cannabis plant since at least the Colonial era. Prior to his august career as a general and president, Virginia planter George Washington made several notations in his diary in the 1760s, "Began to pull the seed Hemp—but was not sufficiently

FIGURE 6.16 Leaves and flower from *Cannabis sativa*
Source: Dorling Kindersley Media Library/Neil Fletcher and Matthew Ward

ripe" (quoted in Sloman 1979, 21). Although it is doubtful that the first chief executive and his ilk went as far as using the plant for psychoactive purposes, there is little argument that the plant was used for making paper and sturdy clothing—so much so that its growth as a cash crop was frequently encouraged by colonial legislatures. (Virginia imposed penalties on those who did not in 1762.)

It was not until the first decades of the 20th century that marijuana smoking was defined as a social problem, when reports first alerted Americans that it was coming across the border with Mexican migrants. The moral panic against marijuana in the United States can be traced back to the wave of immigration from revolutionary Mexico in the 1910s. On crossing the border, they were often confronted with prejudice and fear—especially when authorities began to notice that marijuana smoking was a traditional intoxicant south of the border (Schlosser 2003). It wasn't long before an anti-immigrant lobby raised the specter of American schoolchildren smoking pot, turning healthy all-American kids into "sex crazed maniacs" (Schlosser 2003, 19). Among the critics was a notion, "The dominant race and most enlightened countries are alcoholic." By comparison, those who were addicted to hemp "deteriorated mentally and physically" (Schlosser 2003, 19).

Following the end of Prohibition, the nation's moral focus was redirected toward marijuana, and by 1933, 7 states had already banned the "Devil's Weed," with some reformers requesting a national ban. The first local ban on marijuana was passed in the border town of El Paso in 1914, and by 1931 29 states had outlawed it. From its inception in 1930, the Federal Bureau of Narcotics recognized the impossibility of eradicating marijuana, which one observer noted grew "like dandelions" in the United States and attempted to stay out of the fray. However, in 1935, pot was upgraded from a "low priority substance" to a threat "as hellish as heroin" (Gray 1998, 76). FBN director Anslinger was soon appealing for an international ban on the substance, but at a meeting of the League of Nations, every country voted against the ban, recognizing the quixotic nature of such a goal. Anslinger found that the only way to find support at home was through the adoption of a tax law. Anslinger figured that the only solution was to place a prohibitive tax on the selling and buying of the drug, and in 1937 the Marijuana Tax Act went into effect, making the sale and possession of marijuana illegal through federal legislation.

The trafficking of marijuana ranges from decentralized local dealers to international syndicates. The vast majority of it is transported by land (77%). Recent evidence suggests that a number of these syndicates have expanded into the traffic of other drugs. Most sources agree that marijuana is the most widely used illegal drug in the United States. Some estimates place the number of cannabis smokers at perhaps 20 million each year (Schlosser 2003, 14). According to the 2006 National Survey on Drug Use and Health, an estimated 97 million Americans over the age of 12 have tried marijuana. Internationally, it has been estimated that 160 million people ages 15 and above had used cannabis at one time or another (3.4% of the global population). Compared to heroin and cocaine, which are mostly imported, a large percentage of marijuana is grown domestically. It is a rugged plant that is grown in luxurious climates in Hawaii and Northern California as well as broad sections of the nation's heartland from the Appalachian Mountains into Great Plains. In 2001, the value of corn, the country's largest legal cash crop, was about $19 million, whereas the annual marijuana crop has been estimated to bring in between $4 billion and $25 billion annually (Schlosser 2003).

One of the few commodities that have not increased in price since the early 1980s years is an ounce of marijuana, still costing an average of $60 to $80 for an ounce (Schiller 2007). From an economic perspective, considering inflation, marijuana is actually cheaper today than it was in the 1980s. Despite the emergence of powerful designer forms of pot, most of it comes from Mexico.

All indications are that border states such as Texas enable an unlimited supply of marijuana to cross into the United States from Mexico. In early 2007, a drug market analysis by federal, state, and local law enforcement affiliated with the Houston-centered High Intensity Drug Trafficking area reported seizures rising from 85,583 pounds in 2005 to 191,000 pounds the following year in just one 16-county area, enough pot to role more than 171 million joints (Schiller 2007, B3). Currently, marijuana sells for as little as $30 a pound in the far reaches of the Mexican outback;

Grow Houses

Today, it is not uncommon for marijuana dealers to purchase suburban homes to grow pot indoors. Many are completely gutted so that every inch can be used for growing plants. In some instances, growers have run water lines and ducts, installed irrigation systems with timing devices, and brought in water tanks, pumps, generators, and power packs. Lest utility companies become suspicious because of high power usage, growers have even bypassed the electric meters and built their own circuit boxes. Federal agents have raided dozens of "grow houses," where plants are cultivated in houses equipped with tens of thousands of dollars worth of equipment to grow and hide the marijuana. One strategy is to purchase homes in newer neighborhoods where there is more anonymity among neighbors. Although not all houses are connected to organized crime syndicates, there is evidence that many are. One has been connected with a crime syndicate based in San Francisco's Chinatown, whereas another involved 50 grow houses that were part of a network that stretched between Florida and New York. One four-bedroom house in New Hampshire was seized with 10,000 plants inside. More illegal plants are seized in California than any other state, which some authorities suggest is due to the state's "medical marijuana laws that have created a permissive attitude" (Ritter 2007). This, combined with the amount of profits that can be made and relatively light penalties in the state, has made the trade more attractive to organized crime groups. However, critics of the DEA's focus on marijuana (and medical marijuana) suggest its strategies are poorly focused, and that organized crime has been involved in the trafficking on and off for years (Ritter 2007, 3A). What is new is the size and utter boldness of the new suburban operations. Recent court cases have revealed growers paying up to $750,000 for houses in new subdivisions, fully financed without down payments.

smuggled into the Houston area, it sells from $500 to $1000 a pound, depending on the quantities sold (usually more for smaller quantity).

WHY MEXICAN MARIJUANA IS PRICED SO LOW   Mexican marijuana is much cheaper than the American variations. Most evidence suggests that it remains so low because major drug-trafficking cartels generally do not charge smaller dealers fees to do business or to smuggle through their territories. Unlike the cocaine trade, few people are killed over marijuana. As one former dealer put it, "Marijuana is pretty much an open market. Nobody controls it, nobody wants to control it" (Schiller 2007, B3). Others suggest it remains relatively inexpensive because many American drug users do not want to pay for the more-potent pot variations that are grown in the United States. According to one expert, there has been a lack of innovation in Mexico compared to the American growers (Schiller 2007).

Overview

One of the surest ways to provide organized crime groups with a foothold in any country's underground economy is to outlaw a commodity that consumers want. From America's colonial era to the present, there are countless examples of how legal regulations and cultural restrictions helped create a demand and an entrepreneur emerged to take advantage, creating a new criminal industry. Prohibiting various goods and services—in this case, alcohol, gambling, prostitution, and drugs—has always failed to prevent individuals from producing and consuming them anyway. In time, criminal networks flourished as they reaped the profits of rapidly expanding illicit markets. Despite a growing acceptance of certain forms of what

some commentators regard as "vice" in the United States, there has never been a consensus among law enforcement and the American public as to how to regulate or police it.

One of the most pronounced differences between the vice prohibitions was that alcohol and drug prohibition were based on federal laws, whereas prostitution and gambling were not. What transpired in these cases was a host of state laws and local ordinances that made betting and commercialized sex the subject of sanctions in whichever state they occurred in. As a result, every state criminalized these behaviors until Nevada legalized gambling and prostitution (in selected counties) in 1931 (Woodiwiss 2001).

Americans have always exercised a certain ambivalence toward gambling as a vice, especially if one looks at its history in the United States. From a legal perspective, society has taken a cautious approach to gambling, preferring to allow only limited forms and highly regulating them in order to protect against organized crime intrusion. By the mid-1990s, legal gambling revenues in the United States alone approached $40 billion a year, making it among the country's leading entertainment industries. By comparison, amusement parks brought in $7 billion and movie theaters $5.5 billion. Despite the availability of countless forms of legal gambling, by most accounts, illegal gambling continues to flourish in the 21st century. The most popular illegal gambling businesses include the "numbers game" and sports betting, which is thought to be second only to casino games in popularity.

With poker on television virtually non-stop on certain channels, news outlets continue to chronicle the arrest of individuals during gambling raids. In November 2007, one illegal sports-gambling ring was busted while operating out of a high-stakes poker room in an Atlantic City casino. Dubbed "Operation High Roller," the investigation began on a tip in March 2006. Authorities used video surveillance and other methods to determine that illegal gamblers were told with whom to place bets in the Poker Room. Two wire rooms in Philadelphia then took the bets while casino employees associated with the ring essentially ignored exchanges of cash and casino chips in order to evade financial reporting requirements. The members used an ingenious method to launder the money, using casino chips to hide the proceeds from their criminal activity. They took cash and turned it into chips (washing the chips), then placed bets with chips and after a period of time exchanged chips for cash and leaving the premises. Of the 18 who were apprehended, 4 had reputed organized crime connections. According to the New Jersey Attorney General, this ring operated out of the Borgata Hotel Casino & Spa and took in $22 million since the previous March, demonstrating the amount of money that can still be generated in such pastimes in a society that has legitimized such behavior. Operating under the very noses of the casino surveillance system and the state gaming commission for almost 2 years, it was reportedly "so complex that it relied on two wire rooms in Philadelphia and involved perhaps hundreds of bettors"; this was the "first time anyone with alleged organized crime ties was charged with illegal gambling in Atlantic City" (Chen 2007, A18).

Illustrating the dangers of unsanctioned gambling was another incident that same month that resulted in the death of a mathematician and former professor who was killed when gunmen broke into an illegal "floating"

poker game in Manhattan. According to the *New York Times*, "dozens of people, mostly middle-class and well-to-do," were playing poker when a group of men in ski masks barged in with guns. Apparently, it was an open secret that illegal gambling took place regularly in that location, with one person overheard telling investigators, "It's like Atlantic City up there" (Wilson 2007, A15).

One major study in the late 1960s suggested that between the 1940s and 1970s, prostitution as a form of organized crime evolved from an activity requiring a number of third persons "to more of an individual entrepreneurship," making it less organized than in previous eras (Winick and Kinsie 1971, 5). However, recent investigations have revealed that even prostitutes are going high-tech, with one Nassau County, New York, detective remarking, "Technology has worked its way into every profession, including the oldest" (Lambert 2007). His comment was in response to 70 arrests associated with www.Craigslist.org, the website renowned for its employment and for-sale advertisements, but now being used to trade sex for money. The same detective suggested, "Craigslist has become the high-tech 42nd Street, where much solicitation takes place now" (Lambert 2007, A31).

"Officials have revealed that prostitution is flourishing online like never before. On one recent day there were 9000 listings on the Erotic Services category in New York alone" (Lambert 2007, A31). Technology has changed some of prostitution's patterns, with individuals choosing to roam the country, setting up shop for a week or two at a hotel, often near airports, where they use laptops and cell phones to arrange encounters before moving on to another city and repeating the operation.

For decades, local vice officers led the crackdown on prostitution. However, the rise in international sex trafficking rings in the 21st century has some anti-trafficking activists and members of Congress attempting to make it a federal issue, whereas the FBI and other agencies argue that it would divert agents from more important and serious crimes. The biggest dilemma facing law enforcement is distinguishing street-level prostitutes and pimps from international sex trafficking. According to federal agencies, *trafficking* refers to

> holding someone in a workplace through force, fraud or coercion, elements that are required to prove a case under federal law. Trafficking generally takes two forms, forced sex or labor. But some activists argue that all prostitutes, even those not forced to turn tricks, should be defined as trafficking victims and their pimps subject to federal prosecution. (Markon 2007, A25)

Demonstrating that some things never change was the case of New York Police Officer Dennis Kim, who pleaded guilty in 2007 to a federal charge of conspiracy to commit extortion. In 2006, he was arrested along with his partner and several others who operated a house of prostitution. Immigration officials took into custody 16 women charged with prostitution in what one journalist called "one of the city's largest sex-and-bribes protection scandals since more than a dozen officers were implicated a decade ago for protecting a brothel on the West Side of Manhattan" (Hauser 2007, C14). The case against Kim stemmed from his relationship with the owners of several New York City brothels who gave Kim information on competing brothel owners and prostitutes as well as other crimes. In return for closing down competitors, Kim was given gifts and favors. In the ensuing investigation, it was revealed that the brothel owners took in more than $1 million a year, and information provided by brothel owners allowed police officers to make career-advancing arrests (Hauser 2007).

"Scare stories about intoxicating substances have been a staple of American newspapers since the temperance crusades of the nineteenth century" (Owen 2007, 218). Since the late 1980s, numerous op-ed pieces by legal scholars and critics such as conservative political commentator William F. Buckley, Jr., and Nobel Prize–winning economist Milton Friedman have criticized America's "War on Drugs." In 1986, the Bar Association of the City of New York noted that similar to the attempt to prohibit alcohol, "drug prohibition is also a failure that causes more harm than the drug use it is purportedly intended to control" (quoted in Buckley 1994).

Drug trafficking earned organized crime members undreamed-of profits; it also became what some have called "an organizational disaster of the first magnitude" (Volkman 1998). According to one Mafia-watcher, "Of all the forms of racketeering and illicit operations the narcotics trade was virtually impossible to control with the Mafia's traditional central command structure with its rigid divisions of authority; every mobster who sold drugs became in effect his own Mafia family" (Volkman 1998, 307).

A number of mob observers have suggested that the drug trade went a long way toward undermining the discipline of the American crime syndicates and dismantled organizational cohesion. In the end, heavy sentences for those arrested on drug charges proved strong temptations for those who wanted to cut deals with the authorities. From a community perspective, drug-dealing mobsters undercut community tolerance for organized crime fam-

ilies. In the past, many had been willing to overlook illegal gambling parlors, numbers games, and labor rackets—activities that did not threaten the health and safety of the neighborhood's residents. Beginning in the 1970s and 1980s this all changed, as heroin and crack poisoned neighborhoods.

> The United Nations Office of Drug Control estimates that there are about 42 million users of meth and related drugs worldwide, more than any other illegal drug except marijuana and at least double that of those who use cocaine and four times of those who use heroin. (Langton 2007, 20)

It appears that every few years a new "drug epidemic" emerges; typically involving a substance that has been around for some time. The media and public servants are always in the wings to declare the next contemporary plague. Although crystal meth was regarded as the latest drug plague—"missing from media accounts is any sense that drug trends are self-limiting phenomena," such as in the case of cocaine. Evidence suggests that like cocaine addicts, meth addicts do not stay addicts for very long (Langton 2007, 219).

There is a growing chorus of drug-prohibition opponents who counter that "drug prohibition in Bolivia and Afghanistan has done exactly what alcohol prohibition did in America: it has financed organized crime" (Tierney 2006, A23). Advocates argue that the only alternative is to repeal prohibition and let poor poppy farmers from source countries sell opium for legal painkilling medicines, or allow "Andean peasants a legal international market for their crops in products like gum, lozenges, tea, and other drinks" (Tierney 2006, A23). One policy expert even suggested putting "the coca back in Coca-Cola®" (quoted in Tierney 2006, A23). Bolivian President Evo Morales opined that "American imperialists [have been] criminalizing a substance that has been used for centuries in the Andes. If gringos are abusing a product made from coca leaves, that's a problem for America to deal with at home" with more drug-treatment programs (quoted in Tierney 2006, A23). In the end, the United States imports its fair share of health-challenging products—from artery-clogging fast foods to cancer-causing cigarettes and syrupy soft drinks. This country will never be willing to stop these American products; likewise says journalist John Tierney of *The New York Times,* "The Saudis can fight alcoholism by forbidding the sale of Jack Daniels, but we'd think they were crazy if they ordered us to eradicate fields of barley in Tennessee" (2006, A23).

Key Terms

Vice
Progressive Era
Volstead Act
18th Amendment
Demon rum
Blue laws
"Drys" and "wets"
Bootlegging
Moonshiners
Bathtub gin
"Lansky's Law"
Dealcoholized
Rum runners
"Tenderloin"
Jim Colosimo
Raines Law
White slavery
Mann Act
Thomas Dewey
Lucky Luciano
Gaming and gambling
Kefauver Committee
Pari-mutuel machine

Slot machines
Horse racing
Bookmaking
Wire services
Bookies
"Poolroom"
Mont Tennes
Point spread
Policy
Numbers
Stephanie St. Clair
Bumpy Johnson
The leadhouse
Bolita
Cuban Revolution
Las Vegas
Bugsy Siegel
The Flamingo
Frank Rosenthal
Stardust casino skim
The Black Book
Pure Food and Drug Act
Harrison Narcotic Act

Webb v. U.S.
Opiates
Opium Exclusion Act
Morphine
Codeine
"Soldier's disease"
Golden Crescent
Golden Triangle
French Connection
Corsicans
Marseilles
Pizza Connection
African Connection
Cocaine
Crack cocaine
Sentencing disparity
Methamphetamines
Tweakers
Superlabs
Ecstasy
Marijuana
Grow houses

Critical Thinking Questions

1. How did moral reform movements influence various vice prohibition crusades?
2. Why were so many laws directed at vice prohibition during the so-called Progressive Era?
3. Chronicle alcohol use in America prior to 1920. Why was alcohol prohibition passed in 1919 if so many Americans were against it?
4. What was the impact of alcohol prohibition in the United States? Was it successful? How did it effect the different classes of people?
5. Compare and contrast *moonshining* and *bootlegging*.
6. How was the bootlegging business conducted, and what was the role of organized syndicates in the manufacture, distribution, and sale of it?
7. Why was Prohibition considered such a landmark in the evolution of modern organized crime?
8. What has been the historic relationship between organized crime and prostitution? Was it always a major source of income? Was it always illegal?
9. What impact did the hysteria over "white slavery" have on prostitution legislation? Was the Mann Act successful, and did it end white slavery? Was white slavery more imagined than real?
10. What were the roles of nativism, prejudice, and racism in the passage of most vice prohibition movements?
11. Compare and contrast *gaming* and *gambling*. Have they always been illegal? Chronicle the love–hate relationship of Americans with gambling since the mid-19850s.
12. What did the Kefauver Committee reveal about gambling in the United States?
13. What technological advancements made gambling attractive to crime syndicates?
14. Are gambling and prostitution big moneymakers for organized crime groups today?
15. Chronicle the evolution of the policy and numbers rackets in the United States.
16. Discuss organized crime's involvement in the casino business, especially Las Vegas and Cuba.

17. Where are organized crime groups to be most likely involved in gambling enterprises today?
18. Why were narcotics and opiates targeted by the federal government in 1914?
19. Compare the evolution of drug legislation with that of other vices.
20. How did the illegal drug trade change between 1900 and 1960? How did it change after 1960?
21. Which organizations predominated in the various drug-trafficking rings?
22. Why have trends in drug use changed over time?
23. Compare and contrast the crack and meth epidemics.

Endnotes

1. Hearings before the Permanent Subcommittee on Investigations of the Committee on Government Operations, U.S. Senate, 88th Cong., 1st session, Part 2, Oct. 10, 11, 15, and 16, 1963, p. 486.
2. Prior to the 1980s, "the 3-mile limit" referred to the limits of a nation's sovereignty over territorial waters.
3. Recent scholarship traces the term *white slavery* back to its origins in the labor movement of the 1830s, when English and American workers adopted the term to describe the poor pay and conditions under which they worked (Keire 2001, 7).
4. Poolrooms were distinct from billiards parlors, where individuals played pool; in the parlance of the day, a *poolroom* was where someone went to place a bet. The constituency of a poolroom in the early 20th century leaned heavily toward gamblers, hustlers, and assorted unsavory characters. The reputation of poolrooms was tainted by this association well into the 20th century, when legitimate billiard poolrooms fought the stigma of an earlier era as legitimate poolrooms lost their association with the betting parlors.
5. According to Landesco, during this era, many poolrooms had been converted into "full-fledged gambling houses with dice, cards and roulette" (1929, 58).
6. The term *policy* came from the Italian word *polizza,* or lottery ticket.
7. According to Courtwright, similar reasons were given when pot was criminalized and also later described as a narcotic.
8. In 1990, there were an estimated 500,000 opiate addicts in a much larger population.
9. Much of the decline was the result of disrupted smuggling networks during the war that led to scarcity and higher prices in the 1940s. In addition, the Federal Bureau of Narcotics was engaged in a preemptive scheme to purchase most of the Near East opium crop to keep it out of the hands of the Axis powers and to ensure a sufficient supply for Allied medical use (Courtwright, Joseph, and Des Jarlais 1989, 131).
10. This is adapted from estimates in the U.S. Senate *Report on the International Opium Commission and on the Opium Problem as Seen within the United States and Its Possessions* (Washington, D.C.: G.P.O., 1910), 42, 47, reprinted in Courtwright, Joseph, and Des Jarlais 1989, 7).
11. According to former New York Police Commissioner Patrick Murphy, "Decentralization has always been the norm in the distribution end of the narcotics trade." He found little difference between the early 1900 and the 1970s, noting quite presciently,

    > Many sources of raw materials exist. Many organiz-ations, large and small, buy and process the raw materials, import the product into this country, where it is sold to the processors and distributed at retail by a host of outlets, some large and small, chain and owner operated. (Quoted in Block 1991, 45)

12. The term is derived from *laudandum,* Latin for "something worthy of praise."
13. According to one study in 2001, perhaps 2% of Iran's population of 1.4 million is heroin addicts, and more than 500,000 are considered casual users.
14. For detailed coverage of the Mexican and Latin America drug trade, see Chapter 11 on organized crime in Latin America and Mexico.
15. Hemp is often used for making rope. Its name comes from either the Old English *henep* or Old Saxon *hanap.*

CHAPTER 7

Businesses of Organized Crime

Crime syndicates have long used both legal and illegal business activities to earn profits and launder cash. The businesses of organized crime fall roughly into several categories. Chapter 6 discusses the providing of illegal goods and services, mostly those determined by various government-imposed prohibitions, focusing on gambling, drugs, alcohol, and prostitution. In this chapter, we discuss the services of money laundering and usurious money lending, better known as *loansharking,* crimes that often skirt the boundaries between the licit and the illicit, and examine several other categories or syndicate activities—business and labor racketeering and organized theft and fraud schemes. Fraud can involve bankruptcy fraud, a scam better known as the *bust-out,* when criminals buy or intimidate their way into a legitimate business such as a hotel, bar, or restaurant, then place huge orders for merchandise, mortgage the property, or both, before declaring bankruptcy, ultimately leaving creditors to sue front men, who often have no clue to the actual scam they have been indicted on. Organized crime groups have been deeply involved in insurance fraud, weapons smuggling, smuggling of antiquities, diamond smuggling and even organ trafficking. It is beyond the scope of any one chapter to cover every one of these at length. Except for human smuggling and trafficking, the organized crime businesses examined in this chapter are most closely associated with the evolution and persistence of organized crime in the United States.

Organized crime syndicates are always looking for a sure thing; nothing is surer than a monopoly on some commodity, such as trash hauling. During the early days of the wire services, bookmakers gained the upper hand, controlling access to horse-racing results. Although illegal monopolies have been the target of federal prosecutions since the 1890s, organized crime syndicates continued to monopolize various businesses and industries throughout most of the 20th century. Most targets were of the low-tech variety such as garbage collection, newspaper vendors, and the construction trades, where intimidation was often all that was necessary to drive legitimate competition out of the field. In

Staging Motor Vehicle Accidents (2007)

In early 2007, a Houston doctor and two lawyers were among 10 individuals charged in an elaborate ring that staged car accidents to collect motor vehicle insurance money. According to one of the suspects, organization members, referred to by police as a *cell* or *operation,* staged the accidents and then used lawyers and chiropractors to file fraudulent claims. This scheme netted the gang almost $500,000 between 2003 and 2007. One insurance investigator claimed the gangs are using this activity to finance other criminal operations. By most accounts, this cell was only one of nine operations using a similar strategy. The members were arrested after an informant infiltrated the organization and identified two Houston-area gangs as the main players. All 10 were charged with engaging in organized crime activity. Experts indicate this type of fraud can be extremely lucrative. For example, if a crash involved cars with several passengers and drivers, participants average $10,000 per insurance settlement (Villafranca, 2007).

some cases something good can even come out of it, such as when Murray "The Camel" Humphreys suggested to Al Capone in the waning days of Prohibition that the milk market presented a great opportunity, noting its markup was higher than bootleg whiskey and besides had a much larger market. Capone apparently loved the idea. They arranged for the kidnapping of the president of the local Milk Wagon Drivers' Union, demanding a $50,000 ransom. After collecting the money, Capone and Humphreys set up Meadowmoor Diaries and proceeded to undercut the competition by using non-union workers. Soon the prices dropped, and Meadowmoor controlled the milk market in Chicago. One authority opined, "It was a rare example of a gangland takeover that created a social benefit" (Lunde 2004, 142). In addition, this operation introduced the concept of the *sell-by date*.

The beginning of Prohibition in the early 1920s coincided with the intrusion of wealthier and more powerful criminals into labor racketeering who took advantage of the chaos in industrial relations through several rackets. In some businesses they created "trade organizations." Businessmen unwilling to join were threatened until they paid fees guaranteeing protection from union troubles. To facilitate such bargains, syndicates used violence to take over some legitimate unions through an array of intimidation methods not limited to bombings, arson, and murder.

The FBI defines *labor racketeering* as "the domination, manipulation, and control of a labor movement which affects related businesses and industries. The domination may result in the denial of workers' rights and sometimes inflicts economic loss on the worker, industry, insurer and consumer." According to the RICO statutes,[1] *racketeering* consists of

> any behavior or threats involving murder, kidnapping, arson, infiltration of legitimate business (including labor unions), bribery, embezzlement, loansharking (usury), and mail and wire fraud . . . and the criminal act of extortion through the threat of violence. (Racketeer Influenced and Corrupt Organization Act of 1970)

One leading authority chronicled the negative economic consequences of business and labor racketeering, noting how its influence can raise prices, restrict entry, engender fear in customers, and reduce innovation. In addition, this so-called "[indirect] control of one industry can provide opportunities in others," as exemplified by the way garment trucking facilitates jobber loansharking (Reuter 1987, 75). Loansharks have found the garment industry particularly enticing; with sudden changes in fashion, the seasonality of demand for particular garments, the small size of most contractor and jobber firms, employers under these conditions are particularly susceptible to "frequent, acute, short-run liquidity problems [that] conventional sources of finance are unwilling to handle" (Reuter 1987, 72).

The word *racket* "appears to have been applied for the first time in June, 1927, to these unholy alliances between business men, labor leaders, politicians and underworld characters" (Hostetter and Beesley 1929). However, as early as 1925, the Employers' Association of Chicago noticed the trend toward business "rackets," noting,

> Not content with holding the reins of labor monopoly, he [the labor union leaders] has conspired with certain employers and employer groups, and has set up organizations under harmless-sounding names, through which the two are enriching themselves at the expense of a credulous public. . . . These combinations, or super-unions. . . . The unions uses the employer to drive all workmen into its folds, discipline union members, extort money and special privileges, and indulge in practices defying comprehension. . . . The employer uses the union to eliminate competition, fix prices, discipline the employer who shows the least sign of independence, and it generally stabilizes his business. (Hostetter and Beesley 1929, 9–11)

One chronicler of early Jewish organized crime in the United States posited that "Racketeering, 'the art of levying and collecting tribute by violence and intimidation,' was to the 1930s what Prohibition was to the 1920s" (Joselit 1983, 106). Following Prohibition, a number of bootleggers moved to extortion-driven rackets, including many second-generation Jews and Italians who used the skills and contacts acquired over a decade of illegal activity to intimidate business and labor organizations into "working together" with them. What made this marketplace so alluring and facilitated their entry into it was its disorganized structure, which Joselit suggests was "characteristic of the ethnic economy" (1983, 106).

According to Nelli,

> Racketeering did not exist across the entire spectrum of the American business world [in the 1930s], but was concentrated in specific industries and businesses that required modest amounts of capital or skill to enter and contained an oversupply of labor. The tendency of racketeering to appear in small, unstable, and disorganized industries led Walter Lippman to observe in 1931 that it was essentially "a perverse effort to overcome the insecurity of highly competitive capitalism." Thus rather than criminals forcing themselves on their victims, it was often the harried businessman faced with the constant threat of cut-throat competition, who turned to underworld elements and invited their help in dealing with excessive competition. (1970, 243)

Thus, markets that proved most susceptible to labor racketeering were typified by undercapitalized small businesses, more vulnerable to labor strife than more vertically structured enterprises. Especially attractive were industries that were more local than national in nature. Heavy competition and ever-present labor problems made small merchants and industries easy targets for crime syndicates who could promise them higher profits and minimum labor disturbances for a slice of their earnings. Thus, an almost symbiotic relationship developed in which labor unions used criminals for "defensive purposes" as protection against anti-union practices of employers and to help organize and even terrorize workers suspected of disloyalty. Union leaders used gangsters to further their own careers or line their pockets with proceeds from kickbacks and sweetheart contracts with various employers.

Examples of labor racketeering can be found in most major cities. Although it has been well chronicled in Chicago, Kansas City, Detroit, Miami, Philadelphia, St. Louis, and elsewhere, it is beyond the scope of a single chapter to detail these various chronologies. The focus here remains on New York City, which has more labor unions and members, and more organized crime families and associates, than any other major city in the United States. Furthermore, in the words of one of the leading experts on the subject, the labor racketeering problem in New York City "is not qualitatively different than the problems in other U.S. cities with strong union traditions" (Jacobs 2006, 57–58).

During the Depression years, with more than 600,000 Chicago workers unemployed, representing some 40% of its labor force, some small companies dealt with competitive pressures that resulted in a decline in demand for their products (due to the cash crisis) by hiring racketeers. Racketeers such as Gennaro Calabrese filled this position for the local pasta makers by blocking entry of the unaffiliated into the market and by increasing pasta prices at the local markets. Alexander suggests that the macaroni market operated in "sharp contrast to Hollywood portrayals that depict

The Pasta Rackets

During the early 1930s, most of Chicago's Italian American pasta makers were intimidated into paying protection to a mobster named Gennaro Calabrese. Beginning in 1931, Calabrese's "Chicago Macaroni and Noodle Manufacturers Club" began its operations. At this time, the term *macaroni* was used to describe any type or shape of pasta. The *macaroni tax* demanded $0.25 per pound of pasta plus $25 monthly for each macaroni press. The unit tax was paid indirectly by paying for the racketeers product labels. Those who refused to pay were liable to be victims of violence. Manufacturers were also expected to stick to the pasta prices demanded by the racketeer.

The Chicago Macaroni Company was the nation's fourth largest macaroni manufacturer, employing 250 people and operating an estimated twenty-five 500-pound-per-hour pasta presses. Calabrese collected his "sales tax" by selling package labels for $0.25 per pound. Every manufacturer within 50-mile radius of Chicago was expected to use these labels on their pasta. In her research on this racket, Barbara Alexander discovered several cases in which recalcitrant pasta makers were bombed or beaten with baseball bats (1997, 180).

Businesses Targeted in Chicago by Labor Racketeers (1927)[2]			
Window cleaning	Ash and rubbish hauling	Candy jobbers	Milk dealers
		Dental laboratories	Glazers
Machinery moving	Grocery and delicatessen stores	Photographers	Florists
		Bootblacks	Restaurants
Paper stock	Garage owners	Shoe repairers	Fish and poultry
Cleaning and dyeing	Physicians	Butchers	Bakers
Laundries	Drug stores	Window shade men	

gangsters as crude extortionists, whose only refinements tend to be the styles of personal attire and violence. The two-part tariff, the labels, and the price floor, all suggest the operation of some fairly sophisticated" operation (1997, 184).

LABOR RACKETEERING

The earliest attempts to organize modern labor unions in the United States date back to the late 1820s, when Pennsylvania workers tried to negotiate for better wages and conditions from their Philadelphia employers. These attempts were met with hostility by the government and business communities, with some employers sending in armed enforcers to dissolve any attempts at labor unity. As one long-time Mob historian noted, "From the first the labor movement in this country met hostility and violence. A dangerous precedent had been set, one that facilitated the rise of organized crime within the American labor movement" (Bequai 1979, 53). What was perhaps unforeseen was that labor would also enter volatile agreements with networks of goons to fight against the employers, albeit at a steep price for the future of the union movement.

The first labor unions were created just prior to the Civil War (1861–1865). Following the war, as big business and the so-called *Robber Barons* took center stage, labor groups organized to negotiate favorable contracts with their employers. However, a number of labor groups hewed a more extremist stand, following a more Marxist or anarchist disposition. In response, employers confident in their social standing and wealth fought back against the labor groups with virtual armies of hired thugs. Although the rise of labor throughout the Western world was often accompanied by violence, no country had a more violent labor history than the United States in the late 19th century.

Criminal syndicates began infiltrating the labor movement concomitant with the first militant organizing efforts in the 1880s. Employers responded to these efforts by hiring thugs to break up picket lines. The first decades of the 20th century were the heyday for modern unions, with total union membership rising to more than 1 million by 1930. Violence remained part of the equation as criminal gangs were hired to rough up or kill labor leaders sometimes resulting in corrupt bargains between the unions and the mobsters. Syndicates reveled in the new venture, with some crime groups even organizing their own labor unions as fronts to extort employers.

The expansion of organized crime groups into the development of unions was "largely a phenomenon of the 1930s, although entry of criminals into labor-management arena occurred during the 1920s, when trade unions in the garment and fur industries, stymied by both legal and economic obstacles, turned to Lepke and Gurrah of Murder, Inc. for help" (Weinstein 1966, 403). Kelly and others suggest that mobsters typically gravitated toward industries that were small in scale, local, and family based, requiring low skills and mostly simple technologies in the work environment (1999, 131). However, perhaps the biggest factor drawing crime syndicates into the labor rackets was the end of Prohibition, which cut off organized crime's largest revenue source and precipitated the search for new sources of income. None had better prospects than the burgeoning trade unions.

During the 1930s, most of the country's major labor unions were reorganized following a decade of convulsive labor conflict between union leaders and employers who were trying to weaken the movement. Employers eventually found that they could not break the increasingly militant unions and sought arrangements with union officers.

The Second World War era "greatly strengthened the tendency among union officers to surrender their members' interests [to employers]—and also weakened the capacity and will of the rank and file to resist" (Friedman 1982, 15). The major stumbling block for this era's workers was that they had given up the right to strike in order to help the war effort. The companies used this respite to retaliate and break the power of the rank and file by introducing new rules that took away the gains of the 1930s. Employers made union stewards discipline their constituency in support of the company's interests. As a result, a wide gulf developed between the union officers and the workers. In the post-war era, Congress passed the Taft-Hartley Act (under pressure from employers), which reduced the ability of the rank and file to wage struggles on their own (see Chapter 14). This transition was smoothed over in part by the period of relative prosperity that existed from the mid-1940s into the late 1960s (corporate profits high, which in turn meant that even a threat of strike led quickly to wage and other concessions). Because it was the era of the Cold War, it was also easy for employers to discredit union members as communist sympathizers. This way, the union bureaucracy was able to consolidate its power over ranks, and as the economy suffered in the late 1960s, employers expected more from workers, leading to a recrudescence of labor strikes and increasing militancy.

What brought labor racketeering home to the American public was a series of newspaper exposes and the nationally televised McClellan Hearings between 1956 and 1959 that offered sensational revelations about union corruption featuring "union and underworld connections, ghost locals, racketeering practices, sweet-heart contracts, stolen union funds, uncontested local officer elections, failure to hold membership meetings, nepotism and favoritism in assigning desirable work, bombings, and assorted forms of employer and worker harassments" (Bruno 2003, 4).

THE GARMENT TRADE

Throughout most of the 20th century, New York City was the hub of America's garment trade. Criminal gangs entered the equation early, when efforts to organize workers into unions required gangsters to facilitate unionization and in other cases suppress it for the employers. As demonstrated later in the chapter, the garment industry "is not really a single entity," but rather is composed of a number of "distinct components" (Reuter 1987, 70). New York's garment district was one of the first centers of U.S. labor racketeering. By 1890, it employed some 83,000, mostly recently arrived immigrants from Eastern Europe and Italy. Between 1900 and 1930, labor racketeering in New York's garment industry expanded from a sideline business for Lower East Side gangs to a major underworld enterprise.

Born in 1889, Benjamin "Dopey Benny" Fein is regarded as "the first Jewish underworld figure to make labor racketeering a full time and highly profitable business for him and his fellow gang members" (Joselit 1983, 107). His moniker came from drooping eyelids that made him seem lethargic and slow-witted; however, this couldn't be further from the truth. He demonstrated his cunning organizational skills during his 4-year association with the Jewish labor movement in the 1910s while on the payroll of the United Hebrew Trades (UHT). Its position at the epicenter of the Jewish labor movement meant most unions turned to him for assistance. Fein's cooperation and friendship with other ethnic gangs throughout the city presaged the rise of such multi-ethnic criminal organizations as the Chicago Outfit and the Luciano, Lansky, and Siegel confederation in Brooklyn. If a union needed Fein's assistance in protecting strikers from physical attacks by management thugs or to otherwise intimidate non-union workers, he supplied the muscle for $25 to $50 a week for each man and an additional $10 a day after this (Fein deducted $2 from each for himself). Similar to other early New York gangs (such as the Whyos), Fein offered a schedule of prices.

FBI Memorandum, August 19, 1955[3]

During the early 1930s, Buchalter and Shapiro turned to the lucrative rackets that were plaguing the entire New York area. In the years that followed, they built a criminal empire seldom matched in the annals of racketeering. The activities of their Mob became the subject of headline after headline in the metropolitan dailies. With the typical weapons of their ilk, they attacked the poultry, fur, artichoke and clothing industries. Brutality, violence, intimidation and vandalism were their stock in trade as they moved in on flourishing businesses. Lead pipes, stench bombs, bullets and strong-armed bandits were the tools they used.

If the union wanted to have a non-union worker, or *scab,* shot in the leg, it cost $60; breaking an arm, $200; wrecking a non-union shop, between $150 and $500, depending on size; and $500 per murder (Joselit 1983, 109).

Arnold Rothstein is also considered a pioneer in labor racketeering (along with many other crimes) and played an important role in several major strikes in the mid-1920s. Rothstein supplied strikebreakers to the employers then supplied them to the burgeoning unions; he found that profits came from mediating between the two. Murdered in 1928, he never lived to completely infiltrate and organize the garment industry, but left it in the capable hands of Louis "Lepke" Buchalter and Jacob "Gurrah" Shapiro, who in short order gained control of the trucking unions, designer firms, and employer associations affiliated with the garment trade. Of these, the trucking business was a priority—controlling it meant having management and labor at their mercy. The key to the mastery of the garment industry was the control of trucking—transportation of goods held together various aspects of the business—from the contracting, cutting, and finishing of the garments to the distribution. Well versed in the trucking industry, Lepke knew it was an easy business to infiltrate, realizing many Teamsters were either independent or self-employed, thus were more vulnerable to intimidation than workers in factory shops. During the 1920s and 1930s, clothing was not produced in one plant, and unfinished goods constantly needed to be transported between the manufacturer in the garment district and the subcontractors, leaving it especially vulnerable to any trucking problems. As previously noted, fashion depends on timing, so it was essential that deliveries were not interrupted by strikes. In time, the New York crime families set up a trucking cartel called the Master Truckmen of America (MTA), controlled by the Colombo family. The MTA, besides preventing independent truckers from entering the market and charging inflated prices for transport, also specialized in high interest loans to designer firms (Lunde 2004, 41). These costs were passed on to the consumers. Lepke biographer Paul R. Kavieff asserts that he accomplished his preeminence in the garment industry "by participating in the organization of garment-truck owners and self-employed drivers into an employer's trade association, a significant act in the development of business racketeering" (2006, 55).

Both Buchalter and Shapiro earned their nicknames and reputations in Manhattan's mostly Jewish Lower East Side—"Lepke," short for his mother's pet name for him, "Lepkele," and "Gurrah," for his reported inability to coherently say, "Get out of the way" in Yiddish (Stolberg 1995). According to his biographer, Louis "Lepke" Buchalter "was the man chiefly responsible for organized crime's shift from labor slugging to the sophisticated control of the needle-trade unions"[4] during this era (Kavieff 2006, 3). At the height of his power in the mid-1930s, Buchalter allegedly controlled the baking, flour-trucking, dress-making, fur, and garment industries, thanks to the support of a gang of 250 men under the direction of Shapiro (Joselit 1983).

"Lepke" and "Gurrah" entered the union fray as members of the "Little Augie" Orgen gang in the 1920s. Too ambitious to take lower billing in the operation, they engineered Orgen's murder, resorting to encasing his body in concrete and dumping it off a bridge into the East River. By the 1930s, they were at the apogee of the city's industrial rackets. Together with "Lucky" Luciano, who provided much of the financing for a percentage of the profits, they took over the high-risk clothing industry. They also gained a valuable tool for taking over smaller garment makers—loansharking.

John "Johnny Dio" Dioguardi (1915–1979)

Johnny Dio started his long career in the labor rackets as a protégée of "Lepke" and "Gurrah" in the 1930s. Racket-buster Thomas Dewey referred to him as "a young gorilla who began his career at the age of fifteen" (quoted in Sifakis 1987, 110). By his early 20s, he was a well-regarded member of the Lucchese crime family. Dio had a well-earned reputation for violence and by most accounts was responsible for the 1956 acid-blinding attack on labor columnist Victor Riesel. His ability to frighten any potential witnesses led other families, such as Los Angeles' Dragna family, to use him as a consultant. In the case of the Dragnas, Dio came up with a strategy that allowed them to get the edge on competitors who were forced to adhere to strict union guidelines. During the 1950s Senate investigations, Dio was identified along with Jimmy Hoffa as one of the masterminds behind paper locals of the union that eventually took control of the airport trucking business. His name was also featured prominently in Joe Valachi's testimony in front of the McClellan Committee. Valachi recalled, "If I got in trouble, any union organizer came around, all I had to do was call up John Dio or Tommy Dio and all my troubles were straightened out" (quoted in Sifakis 1987, 110). Dio was sent to prison for the last time in 1973 after expanding into stock fraud; he died there in 1979.

Styles change quickly, and the 1920s was no different; as styles changed, companies needed instant cash for new materials to compete. Smaller operations had a hard time obtaining loans to keep up with the changes and were often forced to go to Mob loansharks. Once they fell behind on the exorbitant interest charges, some owners had no choice but to invite "Lepke" and "Gurrah" into their businesses. Prohibition lucre paid for much of the expansion, allowing gangsters to gain a foothold in what would have been difficult industries to penetrate in more prosperous times.

"Lepke" and "Gurrah" were quick to grasp the strategic importance of the "cutter's union and the pivotal role garment trucking played in the process of completing a suit of clothes." The garment industry was organized around something called the *jobber–contractor system,* an arrangement considered "particularly vulnerable to gangster influence" (Kavieff 2006, 51). Contractors make garments or parts of the garments—assigning the work to small transient firms—often not more than "sweatshops" set up in apartments and other settings where work codes were violated and conditions unhealthy (Reuter 1987, 70–71). Jobbers were the firms that designed garments and provided orders for contractors, then sold garments to distributors; they tend to be more substantial firms with revenues in the tens of millions, thus more powerful when it came to negotiating with contractors. It was then up to the truckers to transport fabric to contactors, garments or pieces of garments from contractors to jobbers, and garments from jobbers to distributors. Racketeers were involved in both jobbing and trucking, with as previously mentioned, trucking was the more significant of the two.

To take advantage of the cartel arrangement, members had to abide by certain rules. For example, contractors and jobbers were not allowed to switch trucking firms, trucking prices were set well above the competitive level, and organized crime associates usually owned the firms. Peter Reuter noted how similar this racket was to the customer-allocation agreement in the garbage carting industry, but unlike garbage collection, the racketeers were more directly involved in garment trucking firms (1987).

An Anonymous Critic of the Italian Bread Racket (1934)[5]

The writer is a poor unemployed person and with a large family—nine in all . . . . These grafters will first start with bread, on which the bakers are obliged to apply a ticket, which tickets cost one quarter of a cent per pound. Consider the number of loaves of bread made in one day in Chicago. The bakers must in turn sell at one cent more, being forced to do so by these grafters. Not content with this, a short time ago the producers have started on spaghetti . . . . If some manufacturer does not wish to follow this practice he will meet the same fate of Russo [shot to death after complaining to State's Attorney Office]. (Quoted in Alexander, 1997, 177)

Bioff and Browne and the International Alliance of Theatrical State Employees

Hollywood was home to the nation's fourth largest industry during the Depression era. Especially alluring to organized crime were its numerous trade unions. The Chicago Outfit was the first to move in on these unions. In 1932, while working as a labor specialist for Al Capone and in the midst of trying to organize Chicago's kosher butchers, Willie Bioff became associated with George E. Browne,[6] a business agent for Local 2 of the Stagehands Union, representing movie projectionists, electricians, painters, and other theater workers. Gangsters were nothing new to this union. There were many earlier examples of them running roughshod over locals in New York, Newark, St. Louis, and Chicago. One southern California movie owner had the temerity to complain, "We are being unmercifully persecuted by a notorious method of racketeering by a gang of inhuman scoundrels. Our theaters are being stench bombed, tear gas bombed. Three have been burned. They are broken into at night and motion picture equipment, machines, seats, carpets, draperies are destroyed" (quoted in Fox 1989, 211–212).

In 1934, some of America's leading mobsters[7] arranged for George E. Browne to be elected president of the International Alliance of Theatrical Stage Employees (IATSE), representing the aforementioned movie projectionists, electricians, carpenters, and other theater workers. Browne in turn appointed Willie M. Bioff to a union position, and together they became synonymous with Hollywood extortion rackets in the 1940s and 1950s as they engineered a scheme to extort the Hollywood film studios with the threat of closing down their movie theaters across the country. Bioff had prior experience with the unions as a tough guy bouncing heads for the Chicago political bosses and the Teamsters Union. His connections with the Chicago Outfit landed him in partnership with Browne, joining him in Hollywood in 1935, at a time when "Tinseltown" was rife with hoodlums looking to score through the invariable opportunities of the movie industry (Fox 1989). Benjamin Siegel was already representing movie extras while John Roselli was immersed in strikebreaking for film producers (he called it *labor conciliation*).

During the first year, the Outfit made more than $1.5 million from studio extortions and the 2% union members' surcharges. On top of this, it had selected its own bookmaker for each studio, each taking thousands of bets a month. Subsequently, IATSE members saw their wages decline 15% to 40% over the first 4 years of the scam (Russo 2001).

During the last half of the 1930s, the Bioff and Browne team extracted $1.1 million in bribes to ensure labor peace and prevent work stoppages and strikes related to wage demands. Like other labor rackets, it was the consumer that usually took it on the chin, paying higher prices at the movies to pay for the higher wages demanded by the union honchos. Labor corruption was not new to Hollywood's movie moguls, many of whom were familiar with the workings of the East Coast garment industry and personally knew some of the denizens of the underworld. They were not above using gangsters themselves when the workforce and the unions got out of hand.

In 1941, insurgent union members asked a leading labor attorney in Los Angeles to help break the grip of the Mob on the union. His subsequent investigation revealed a treasure trove of evidence that resulted in a 10-year prison sentence for Bioff. To reduce his sentence, he agreed to testify against his Chicago handlers. A number of gangsters were indicted and served prison terms, and many sources indicate that Outfit boss Frank Nitti committed suicide rather than go to jail over his participation in this racket. Although Bioff changed his name and relocated to Arizona, trying to put his past behind him, he was eventually found out and blown apart in front of his home in Phoenix in 1955 while starting his car.

THE BIG FOUR UNIONS

Organized crime groups have had a long relationship with the American labor movement, particularly its involvement in the affairs of the International Brotherhood of Teamsters (IBT) and the International Longshoremen's Association (ILA). Testament to Mob involvement in labor rackets is the fact that more than one third of those arrested at the 1957 Apalachin conference listed their employment as related to labor or labor management. The McClellan hearings of the late 1950s documented systemic racketeering in both the International Brotherhood of Teamsters and the Hotel Employees and Restaurant Employees International Union (HEREIU). Thirty years later, the President's Council on Organized Crime (PCOC) reported that the Independent Laborers Association (ILA), the Teamsters, HEREIU, and the Laborers International Union of North America (LIUNA) were still dominated by organized crime.

The HEREIU and LIUNA have had a close working relationship with organized crime. LIUNA has had a long relationship with the late Outfit boss Tony Accardo and other Chicago crime figures. In the 1980s, the PCOC documented this long association and chronicled, "The Mob defrauded the union's benefits funds, extracted no-show jobs from LIUNA employers, drew reimbursements for fictitious expenses, and operated construction industry cartels in New York City and Chicago" (Jacobs 2006, 47). In 1994, its officials were the target of a major Department of Justice civil RICO complaint alleging that La Cosa Nostra crime families dominated this 800,000 member union (Jacobs 2006, 222).

Founded in 1891 as the Waiters and Bartenders Union, during its formative years the HEREIU was characterized by internal strife between various factions. During its annual convention in 1896, charges of misappropriation of funds were hurled at various officials. The union soon reorganized but was never to take advantage of the luxury hotel business boom of that era. Although this boom could have provided the HEREIU numerous opportunities for potential bartenders, waiters, maids, cooks, and so forth, its unwillingness to organize unskilled and foreign-born workers held its growth back, and in 1920 it was further weakened when almost one third of its membership lost their jobs after the implementation of Prohibition. There has also been a well-documented relationship between the Chicago Outfit and the HEREIU. Like the other major unions, it has been a frequent target of Mob-affiliated criminals. During the 1930s, for example, "Dutch" Schultz's gang took control of Local 302 (Waiter's Union) and Local 16 (Hotel and Restaurant Employees International Alliance).

In the mid-1950s, members of Congress began to acknowledge widespread corruption in the labor movement, leading to the formation of the Senate Select Committee on Improper Activities in the Labor or Management Field. Chaired by Senator John McClellan and expected to issue a full report after the hearings, it became more commonly known as the Rackets Committee. Robert F. Kennedy was appointed chief counsel. During the 270 days of the McClellan Hearings, more than 1,500 witnesses testified, producing an archive of more than 46,000 pages. Almost one fifth of the witnesses took the Fifth Amendment. Costing more than $2 million, it was the most expensive congressional investigation since the Teapot Dome scandal of the 1920s (Kelly 1999, 53). The hearings revealed systematic racketeering in many unions, including the Bakers, Butchers, Carpenters, Distillery Workers, Hotel and Restaurant Employees, Operating Engineers, Teamsters, and Textile Workers. Of the big four unions, the Teamsters (IBT) and Longshoremen's (ILA) unions are used in this chapter to demonstrate the various relationships between major labor unions and organized crime in the 20th century.

The International Longshoremen's Association (ILA)

New York's harbor is considered one of the world's best natural harbors. It is made up of more than 700 miles of wharves and shoreline and 1,900 piers, including 200 deep-water piers. New York's organized crime families emerged as major powers along the harbor waterfront in 1937 after Anthony "Tough Tony" Anastasio took over control of six harbor locals.[8] There were only 50,000 longshoremen in 1936, but the union's control over the port of New York "gave it leverage beyond its size" (Fox 1989, 191–192).

The Longshoremen's union was first organized in 1892 along the Great Lakes, and by the 1910s it was controlled by New York Locals. Working the waterfront has always been an unpredictable livelihood, but never more than when it was run by organized crime groups. Longshoremen were expected to work at any hour and under any conditions. Workers were selected each day using a

The Waterfront Commission (1953)

Following a series of newspaper exposes and suspected murders of union insurgents, a waterfront commission was convened to do what law enforcement and reformers had been unable to do—challenge organized crime's control of the New York docks. Unlike the Kefauver Hearings that preceded it from 1950 to 1951, Thomas Dewey's 1953 Waterfront Hearings were not televised. Over the course of 7 months, more than 200 waterfront characters called testify before the commission with the overwhelming majority pleading the Fifth Amendment. Soon, a number of reforms were enacted that weakened the grip of the Mob on the waterfront— most important, the elimination of the daily shape-up, and the licensing of pier superintendents, hiring agents, and port watchmen, and the requirement that the Longshoremen register with the commission.

method called the *shape-up.* One crime commission called it "a vicious and antiquated system" that stripped the worker of his dignity (Levy 1989, 509). Here, seniority and skill held little sway over who worked. Little skill was required for loading and unloading ships. So in order to work, the legions of unskilled laborers were expected to kick-back up to 20% of a day's wages to the hiring boss. In some locations, prospective workers wore a toothpick behind their ears to demonstrate they were willing to pay to work. With an oversupply of labor, hiring officials exercised absolute control over who worked. This system facilitated the extortion of money and favors from workers while providing a steady source of employment for friends, gamblers, loansharks, and other denizens of the underworld.

Besides the shape up, there was an abuse unique to the Port of New York known as the *public loading racket,* in which gangs of workers charged usurious fees to move goods between trucks and piers. The shape-up and public loading were two prominent facts of life along the waterfront, and eventually came to the attention of organized crime. According to the collective bargaining agreement between the ILA and the New York Shippers Association (NYSA), only public loaders were allowed to move cargo between a pier and a truck.

The Waterfront Hearings led mobsters to begin looking for greener pastures. As the 1950s moved to a conclusion, air freight and overland trucking "sent the seagoing cargo industry into a tailspin from which it never recovered" (English 2005, 325). Membership of the ILA in New York dropped from its zenith of 40,000 in 1945 to only 18,000 by 1970. As the workers departed for other destinations, the extortionate waterfront rackets of the shape-up, labor racketeering, gambling, loansharking, and the like "were not what they used to be" (Levy 1989). Although more cargo passed through the port in the mid-1980s than in 1953, the percentage had dropped significantly since the 1970s. Another innovation that contributed to the decline was the introduction of containerization. Non-existent in 1953, the practice of packaging a large quantity of goods in one large container became the norm in the 1980s, and as one scholar sagely put it, "The era in which men still used time-honored techniques of loading and unloading, especially brute strength, has given way to an age of high technology and mechanization" (Levy 1989, 515). However, it took little time for the crime families to move into this business, and soon the Gambino and Genovese families controlled the trade organization representing dockside companies that repaired and maintained the containers for the new cargo-handling system (Raab 2005, 571).

Organized crime's persistence along the docks of the Port of New York continued to bring in profits. Much of the evidence was revealed by the Union Racketeering in Ports on the Atlantic and the Gulf Coasts (UNIRAC) investigation. Conducted primarily by the FBI in the late 1970s, it concluded with dozens of arrests, indictments, and convictions of mobsters and union associates. None was more prominent than Anthony Scotto who, in 1963, with the approval of Carlo Gambino, took over Local 1814 and was elected vice president of the ILA, then a 16,000 member union in Brooklyn. Scotto, a college graduate with an air of refinement and a Gambino capo to boot, contrasted sharply with his father-in-law, Anthony "Tough Tony" Anastasio. Scotto was able to mix with high society, and in time cultivated relationships of sorts with Vice President

On the Waterfront (1954)

Based on a screenplay by Budd Schulberg, the movie *On the Waterfront* starred Marlon Brando as dockworker and former boxer ("I coulda been a contenda") Terry Malloy. At the outset, he works as an enforcer for waterfront racketeers, but develops a conscience after a series of incidents and turns against union boss Johnny Friendly, played by Lee J. Cobb. What made the movie so effective was not just its timing, released right after the Waterfront Hearings, but its use of nonprofessional "bit actors" selected from various ILA locals. Its realism and believable dialog was groundbreaking in Hollywood, and garnered several well-deserved Academy Awards. By most accounts, this "torn from the headlines" picture played an important role in turning public opinion and the judicial system against the ILA (English 2005).

Lyndon B. Johnson and New York City Mayor John Lindsay. However, in 1980, he was indicted and convicted on charges of accepting unlawful labor payments and income tax evasion. Despite a parade of witnesses vouching for his integrity and effectiveness as a labor leader, he was convicted of manipulating ILA pension funds and welfare plans, taking payoffs from maritime firms to guarantee labor peace, accepting bribes from businessmen to secure union contracts, awarding union business without competitive bidding to firms owned by relatives, and loansharking among ILA members. He was sentenced to 5 years in prison and a $75,000 fine (PCOC 1986).

THE FULTON FISH MARKET: ON THE WATERFRONT *REDUX*   The venerable Fulton Fish Market, America's oldest and largest wholesale fish market, began operation in 1833, supplying New York City with virtually every type of freshwater and saltwater fish. However, by the 1930s, it was firmly in the hands of organized crime members, none of whom were more prominent than Genovese captain Joseph "Socks" Lanza (1904–1968), who organized a seafood workers' local and reportedly earned his moniker for beating up those who refused to pay for permission to do business in the market (others suggest "Socks" was merely a reference to his earlier baseball playing days). Lanza established his presence in 1923 by taking control of Local 359 of the United Seafood Workers, Smoked Fish and Cannery Union in 1923.

Fifty years later, the Genovese crime family controlled the now $1 billion a year market thanks to its control of the union formed by Lanza (Raab 2005). The crime family ran the enterprise by controlling the quick unloading of perishable seafood for more than 100 trucking companies and 50 wholesalers. The only individuals allowed to unload the fish belonged to the six companies authorized by the crime family to unpack the refrigerated trucks bringing their valuable catches from East Coast ports and fish hatcheries. One long-time observer described the Mob strategy:

> The self-appointed, Mob-approved unloading companies operated without required municipal licenses in the market, on city-owned land. They granted themselves exclusive territorial rights to unload trucks, to set the order in which the vehicles were handled, and to dictate the prices for their services: supplies were not unloaded on a first-come, first-served basis. For prompt delivery to a wholesaler's stall, only a few feet away, the merchant or the trucking company had to bribe the unloaders; otherwise, the seafood was left to spoil on the pavement. (Raab 2005, 565)

The Genovese family also lorded over a similar group of companies called *loaders* who were responsible for moving the sold items from the wholesalers to the customers. They too worked only for Mob-affiliated companies, which were granted permission to supply hundreds of restaurants and retailers. No one in the process was allowed to select a loader or unloader, negotiate prices, or even select a favored parking spot. The legacy of Mob intimidation on the waterfront was enough to cow any merchants or workers from cooperating with the authorities and, "because all vendors and customers were subject to the same conditions, the market functioned on the principle that the jacked-up costs were simply passed along to the consumers" (Raab 2005, 566).

FIGURE 7.1 Two views of Fulton Fish Market
Source: Rough Guides Dorling Kindersley/Nelson Hancock/Dorling Kindersley Media Library/Max Alexander

This system allegedly netted the Genovese family $2 million to $3 million a year in shakedown profits, reflecting the almost 150 million pounds of fish sold each year, bringing in between $800 million to $1 billion in sales, salaries, and services. Much of the profit was funneled to mobsters as partners of the trucking companies or for sheltering wholesalers from union problems through protection rackets. Ancillary activities brought in plenty of lucre as well, such as stealing seafood and providing the 1,000 workers with loansharks and gambling rackets (Raab 2005).

In 1995, Mayor Rudy Giuliani broke with another Mob tradition when he banned unloading companies associated with the Genovese crime family from doing business at the Fulton Fish Market after 60 years. It was hoped that by replacing them with heavily vetted legitimate companies that freight charges would drop, as would the price of fish. The mayor's assistant claimed that a new administration would bring in millions of dollars in revenue by raising rents on wholesalers to fair market value and lower fish prices by 20% by getting rid of the questionable middlemen (Donaldson 1995).

The International Brotherhood of Teamsters

By the end of World War II, some national unions had come under the control of crime syndicates; of these, none became more synonymous with organized crime than the International Brotherhood of Teamsters (IBT) union (Bequai 1979). At one time, the Teamsters Union was one of America's largest and most powerful labor unions representing the nation's trucking industry. Any strike by this union could virtually paralyze the country. During the 1940s, its membership stood at 500,000. In an era when the country's transportation network was making the transition from trains to highways, almost every industry needed trucks and truckers. Teaming and the trucking business was mostly a short-haul business until the passage of a series of federally funded highway acts in the 1950s. It wasn't long before the trucking industry replaced the railroad as the country's main transportation medium. Strikes were capable of destroying smaller industries and could be almost as lethal elsewhere. Any stoppage affecting freight terminals, construction, the poultry industry, taxicabs, and other industries had a deleterious impact on the economy. Perhaps Teamsters nemesis Robert F. Kennedy described the union's ubiquity in American life best in his 1960 book *The Enemy Within:*

> The Teamsters Union is the most powerful institution in this country—aside from the United States Government itself. In many major metropolitan areas the Teamsters control all transportation. It is a Teamster who drives the mother to the hospital at birth. It is the Teamster who drives the hearse at death. And between birth and burial, the Teamsters drive the trucks that clothe and feed us and provide the vital necessities of life. They control the pickup and delivery of milk, frozen meat, fresh fruit, department store merchandise, newspapers, railroad express, air freight, and of cargo to and from the sea docks. Quite literally your life—the life of every person in the United States—is in the hands of Hoffa and his Teamsters. (Kennedy 1960, 161–162)

A small group of Detroit wagon drivers sought some measure of protection against the social costs of industrialization organized Team Drivers International Union in 1898. In 1902, a much larger number of drivers in Chicago rebelled and formed Independent Teamster National Union (Bruno 2003). The following year, in 1903, both unions were brought together, creating the International Brotherhood of Teamsters, Chauffeurs, Warehousemen and Helpers of America (IBT), better known as just the Teamsters Union. *Teamsters* referred to the early members, wagon drivers who commanded a team of horses (Russo 2006, 162). The "locals" were, simply put, unions representing local workers.

IBT members were involved in a number of violent strikes in the early part of the 20th century, including a 100-day against the Montgomery Ward Company in 1905 that left 21 dead and more than $1 million in damages. Nonetheless, the union continued to expand as employer abuse of workers continued, eventually establishing strongholds in Detroit and Chicago. Teamsters developed a reputation for using violence in its "negotiations" whether it was subsuming smaller unions or convincing anti-union companies it was best to come along with them. Its supporters were among the most zealous

What Is a Union Local?

The Teamsters have about 800 locals throughout the United States and Canada, and each union is a group of workers engaged in a similar type activity, usually in the same geographic area. For example, Teamster Local 295 is based at New York's John F. Kennedy Airport and has 2,000 members, including drivers, helpers, and others. Members of each local elect officials that include a president, vice president, secretary/treasurer, recording secretary, and trustees. The president is not always the most important official; typically, that role falls to someone with a less public role, usually a business agent or some other lowly sounding official to deflect surveillance by investigators (Capeci 2002).

workers in America, particularly as the union won for them better working conditions, standardized contracts, shorter working weeks, and the right to overtime pay (Russo 2006, 163).

As the automobile rose in popularity in the 1920s, the IBT expanded to include truck drivers, boosting membership past the 1 million mark before the middle of the 20th century. During the Depression years, unions grew in both size and militancy. None expressed the rage of the forgotten workers more than the Teamsters who earned their stripes in violent clashes with law enforcement and the labor hierarchy. As the union expanded in the 1930s and 1940s it, like the garment workers, steelworkers, and dockworkers before them, came into conflict with the gangsters of organized crime. The relationship was a precarious one, with mobsters sometimes working as strikebreakers and other times as union enforcers, and on occasion performing both tasks at once. It all hinged on who paid the most.

Organized crime's troubled involvement in union issues led the Teamsters to make certain concessions to the Mob, whereby they either earned the Mob's support during strikes or stood by the sidelines during the ensuing violence that accompanied strikes in this era. The official stance was that the union would have no relationship with the syndicates; however, the reality was that several locals were heavily influenced by them. For example, the Outfit-affiliated mobster Joseph John Aiuppa of Local 450 in Chicago or Anthony "Tony Pro" Provenzano in New Jersey's Local 450, who at one time was the highest-paid union official in the world.

THE RISE AND FALL OF JIMMY HOFFA　Born in Brazil, Indiana, the son of a coal driller, James Riddle "Jimmy" Hoffa (1913–1975) grew up without his father, who had died from an "occupational" respiratory infection when Jimmy was only 7. Jimmy quit school before high school and went to work to help support his family at a time when company enforcers, labor toughs, and police shoulder hitters were a constant threat to union leaders. During his well-chronicled life, Hoffa's car was bombed, his office destroyed, and he was even arrested 18 times in one day. However, this was nothing compared to going out "on strike in those days," when the odds were high: "The cops would beat your brains out if you even got caught talking about unions," remembered Hoffa.[9]

The years of Jimmy Hoffa's stewardship of the union were its most troubled. Hoffa rose to prominence with a Detroit local while still in his teens in the 1930s, gravitating to organizing strikes in order to improve working conditions. By the early 1940s, he had presumably made accommodations with the Chicago Outfit and Detroit's east side Mob after asking for the assistance in intimidating an opposing union in the early 1940s. In 1943, he was selected as a trustee in charge of examining the union's financial books; 3 years later, he was elected president of a Detroit local during the reign of corrupt union president Dave Beck.

By most accounts, in 1952, Hoffa promised the Outfit access to the Teamster's pension fund in exchange for supporting his run for office. As a result, he was elected to the Teamster's vice presidency. In effect, Hoffa made a deal with the devil, as the Mob famously took advantage of the pension fund to purchase banks, oil wells, real estate, and casinos in sweetheart deals that usually resulted in bankruptcy and a loss for everyone except the Mob. Some sources even claim that Hoffa and his coterie of followers "were running the union by the mid-1950s," although Beck was still officially president (Liddick 2008, 200). In any case, by the 1950s, Hoffa was clearly in league with many Mob luminaries, including Moe Dalitz (Las Vegas), Sam Giancana (Chicago), Nick Civella (Kansas City), and Tony Provenzano (New Jersey).

During the 1950s, the Teamsters were the target of Congressional hearings into union corruption. Its president, Dave Beck, and his successor, Jimmy Hoffa, were sent to prison for labor-related crimes; their fall from grace began an "unbroken line of discredited union leaders" that lasted from the 1950s until the late 1980s (Bruno 2003, 20). Finally achieving the presidency of the union in 1957, Hoffa became the target of an up-and-coming Robert F. Kennedy, who was then chief counsel for the Senate Rackets Committee. The Senate hearings had firmly placed Hoffa and the Teamsters at the center of its labor investigation into the relationships between the unions and organized crime. Until 1963, he was Hoffa's chief public adversary, zealously focused on linking Hoffa to a pattern of stolen and misappropriated union funds, sweetheart deals with employers who paid off union leaders, the denial of the democratic process during union elections, and intimidation of union critics and members by Mob goons. Although Hoffa went to jail, the Teamsters were forever tarnished by its links to the underworld.

Friends described Hoffa as a relatively simple man when it came to daily living routine, preferring cheap clothing to sartorial fashion statements and eschewing the "flash that his money and position allowed" (Friedman and Schwartz 1989, 195). To the very end, Hoffa maintained his innocence of jury tampering and of defrauding the Central States Pension Fund, but few questioned his guilt. One factor that figured prominently in the government case against Hoffa was the use of wiretap evidence.

When Hoffa went off to prison on March 7, 1967, for jury tampering, he could proudly claim to have increased union membership from 1 million to 2.2 million. Sentenced to 13 years in prison, he was confident he could reclaim his position from his handpicked lackey Frank Fitzsimmons once he returned; after all, Fitzsimmons was selected to fill his throne only while he was away with an understanding that Hoffa was still pulling the strings. Fitzsimmons was considered by insiders a perfect replacement for Hoffa, "a safe choice," as one researcher (Friedman and Schwartz 1989) put it.

In 1971, Hoffa was pardoned by President Richard M. Nixon with the understanding he would not take part in union activities for 10 years. However, he almost immediately announced his comeback for the IBT presidency, although his underworld associates pointedly told him it was not on their agenda. Nonetheless, the ever-confident Hoffa persisted. On July 30, 1975, he disappeared without a trace in Detroit the same day he intended to meet Anthony "Tony Pro" Provenzano for a sit-down meeting. Although Provenzano was always a suspect in Hoffa's death, no conclusive evidence has ever materialized. Over the years, Mob insiders have speculated that Hoffa was kidnapped and murdered to keep him from running against the Mob's man at the helm of the IBT; others suggested his death was linked to Jimmy's wife, who it seemed was apparently openly conducting an affair and Hoffa did nothing about it. This was contrary to Mob tradition, where losing face was unforgivable, particularly when it came to minding your wife and kids. As a result, "Hoffa became a joke to some members of the Mob because he had failed to handle the problem with his wife personally" (Friedman and Schwartz 1989, 192).

HOFFA, PROVENZANO, AND TEAMSTERS LOCAL 560   The son of Sicilian immigrants, Anthony "Tony Pro" Provenzano dropped out of school to become a truck driver while still in his early teens. An amateur prize fighter in his youth, he stepped up to the realm of professional violence as a member of the Genovese crime family. Provenzano joined the union in the late 1940s and served as a business agent from 1948 to 1958, when he became president. As business agent, he directed two Genovese gangsters to attend union meetings and suppress dissent (Jacobs and Santore 2001). Headquartered in Union City, New Jersey, this local was first chartered by the IBT in 1911, and by 1982, it had 10,000 members who worked for any one of 425 different companies. Its daily activities were managed by an Executive Board of seven elected officers—president, vice president, secretary-treasurer, recording secretary, and three trustees. The Board also appointed four trustees to control the Local's Welfare and Pension Funds.

Between the 1950s and 2001, the local was dominated by Provenzano, his two brothers, and assorted others, most of whom were members or associates of the Genovese crime family. By the end of the 1950s, his support of Hoffa's campaign for the IBT leadership led to his elevation to vice president of the union. Meanwhile, he continued to rise through the ranks of his crime family eventually becoming a captain, or *capo*. Over the years, Provenzano earned a reputation for brutality, linked to a number of unsolved murders and disappearances of union foes. His association with Hoffa and leadership of Local 560 enabled him to embezzle millions and enter into sweetheart contracts with trucking companies. In 1963, he boasted a salary of $113,000, reportedly the highest union salary in the world at the time. Later that year he was convicted of extortion and began a 7-year prison stint. Despite being barred from union participation for almost a decade, his two brothers acted as his front at Local 560. In 1978, Provenzano was convicted of ordering the garroting of a rival with piano wire along with other charges and was sentenced to 25 years for the murder and 20 more for labor racketeering. Despite attempts by Provenzano to run Local 560 from prison, in 1984, a federal judge removed the Locals' complete executive board and placed it in trusteeship

The Central States Pension Fund

Jimmy Hoffa was an attractive lure for the Mob. Having created the Central States, Southeast, and Southwest Areas Pension Fund by consolidating dozens of small pension funds in 22 states in 1955, he pulled the strings on millions of dollars in pension funds.[10] In theory, the concept of combining these sources to create a pension fund in which a workers' credits accumulated despite frequent job changes seemed progressive and a vast improvement over traditional industry practices that were characterized by layoffs, frequent job changes, bankruptcies and buyouts (Neff 1990, 215–216).

The Central States Pension Fund board was made up of eight union officials and eight employer representatives. The trustees were charged with deciding how to invest the $2 a month that employers paid into the fund for each Teamster on the payroll. "In reality, the committee was a rubber stamp; Hoffa dictated whom to loan money to" (Neff 1990). Hoffa demanded a "finder's fee" of up to 10% of each loan in return. His handpicked trustees never intervened in his decisions. As for the employer trustees, they had few options either, because any wrong move could result in a strike or business slowdown.

Hoffa and succeeding presidents of the Teamsters used control over the fund to reward business leaders and politicians they thought could help them sometime down the line. The result of this cavalier attitude was the loss of millions of dollars, accomplished with the finesse of Allen Dorfman, the scion of a Chicago insurance company executive and former associate of Al Capone named Paul "Red" Dorfman. With close ties to boss Tony Accardo, "Red" Dorfman had been a major fixture in the Outfit since the 1940s. By most accounts it was the senior Dorfman who introduced Hoffa to the Chicago crime family. In return, Hoffa essentially turned over much of the control to of the Central States Pension Fund to his Mob handlers. He turned over most of the Teamsters insurance business to his son Allen, enriching both Dorfmans substantially. Between 1952 and 1954, they siphoned more than $1.6 million from the pension fund as excessive commission and service fees. Authorities declared the pension fund "the most abused pension fund in America" and as "the Mob's bank" (Neff 1990).

Allen Dorfman famously engineered the funneling of millions of dollars to organized crime real estate investments in southern Florida, southern California, and Las Vegas. Hundreds of millions of dollars of virtually unsecured loans were approved in the 1970s. One of the most glaring examples was a $4 million loan to the Aladdin Hotel secured by only $9 million in IOUs from the casino's gambling tables. Subsequent investigations even found loan applications illegibly written by hand on yellow legal paper (Neff 1990, 216).

Between 1972 and 1976, loans of more than $183 million were approved to Las Vegas casinos.[11] All the fund managers got back, according to one insider, "was a cigar" (Neff 1990, 215). In 1977, one investigation estimated that more than 50 Central States loans were in default and losing almost $15 million a year in interest payments. By the end of the 1970s, it was estimated that it had lost $385 million in loans to organized crime figures that were never paid back. The esteemed *Forbes* magazine proclaimed this the "the scandal of trade union history" (quoted in Neff 1990, 217).

In 1982, Dorfman was arrested following an intensive FBI surveillance operation dubbed PENDORF (Penetration of Dorfman). In January the following year, he was out on bail awaiting sentencing for defrauding the Teamsters pension fund when he was murdered in a Hyatt Hotel parking lot outside Chicago before he could cut a deal with the government.

until the membership was free to nominate and elect its own leaders—which they did in 1986, for the first time in more than 25 years. Provenzano died in prison in 1988.

ENTER ALLEN GLICK: LAS VEGAS FRONT MAN   Seemingly out of nowhere, in 1974, a young law school graduate named Allen Glick purchased the Fremont, Stardust, Hacienda, and Marina casinos with a $62 million loan from the Central States Pension Fund, making him second only to Howard Hughes in Las Vegas casino holdings. Born in 1942, he served auspiciously in Vietnam before getting into the southern California real estate market at the end of the 1960s. Men like Glick were indispensable to organized crime groups that needed front men with spotless records to represent them in legitimate business deals where any impropriety could be a potential deal-stopper. Mobsters were always attracted to cash businesses, and none were bigger than casinos. Because any casino transaction in Las Vegas would be heavily vetted by the Gaming Control Board for Mafia, links the Mob needed someone with a spotless record to buy into the casinos—someone like Allen Glick. Glick was not new to Las Vegas, having purchased real estate on the Strip 2 years earlier with the intention of turning it into a recreational vehicle park. Glick always claimed that he obtained the $62 million loan without any strings attached. However, by most accounts, he obtained the loan only with the endorsement of Milwaukee crime boss Frank "Bal" Balistrieri (under the thumb of the Chicago Outfit). Glick was ordered in no uncertain terms to hire Chicago's Frank "Lefty" Rosenthal to run the operations, who reportedly told Glick, "If you interfere with any of the casino operations or try to undermine anything I do here, you will never leave this [Argent[12]] corporation alive" (Pileggi 1996, 135). Glick reportedly complained to Balistrieri in Milwaukee who told him, "What Mr. Rosenthal told you is accurate" (Neff 1990, 225). Rosenthal's subsequent activities have been well chronicled, especially in Martin Scorsese's movie *Casino* from the eponymous book by Nicholas Pileggi. In any case, over the course of 3 years, the consortium of mobsters from Kansas City, Milwaukee, Cleveland, and Chicago skimmed more than $20 million from the slot machines alone.

In 1978, Glick was forced to sell his share of the Argent Corporation to a more malleable replacement or his children would be killed. He realized a profit in the millions of dollars before heading toward the sunset. In 1982, Glick was caught up in a major FBI investigation and wrangled a deal to testify in return for immunity. His testimony ended in convictions for Teamsters' leader Roy Lee Williams and several high-ranking Mob bosses. Two years later, Glick's testimony corroborated evidence from FBI wiretaps that demonstrated how organized crime leaders engineered the Las Vegas skim, leading to still more convictions in 1986.

Beginning in 1989, the IBT was placed under federal supervision following a federal racketeering lawsuit that named 27 Mafia leaders and 18 of the union's board membership as defendants. The lawsuit claimed that the Mob had controlled four of the union's presidents, including Jimmy Hoffa. Following the government takeover, more than 250 Teamsters officials and members were thrown out of the union.

Garbage Disposal and Waste Hauling

During the early 1980s, one of the worst kept secrets in organized crime was its control of garbage pickups, carting, and dumping in the New York metropolitan area. Most excuses for inaction on the part of law enforcement hinged on the well-founded fears of intimidation and retaliation that kept any potential informers from coming forward. By the late 1990s, New Yorkers had become accustomed to organized crime's control of the garbage-hauling business. Mayor Giuliani charged that a "Mafia cartel" had been "holding New York City's private carting industry hostage" (McGeehan 2007). His charge was supported by a 5-year investigation by the Manhattan District Attorney's Office that revealed that garbage carters had been charging a "Mob tax" adding up to $500 million a year by dividing up the city and thwarting competition (McGeehan 2007).

Until relatively recently, organized crime controlled a number of garbage companies in several major American cities, most prominently in New York. During the second half of the 20th century, racketeers used their influence, mostly through muscle and intimidation, to virtually control

> ## 1988 Deposition of Roy Lee Williams, Concerning Loans for Las Vegas Casinos in the 1970s[13]
>
> **A.** As I said earlier, the pension fund was instituted in '55. We started paying small pensions in '57. I started getting a lot of conversation from Nick [Civella] that he wanted to support particular loans.
>
> **Q.** When was this that you got those requests?
>
> **A.** Sometime later in the later part '58 when the pension started getting a few dollars, and I put up with that and refused to do any of these things that he was asking me to do regarding the pension fund. . . . One night when I'm coming out of a meeting—we were in the old building . . .
>
> **Q.** What city was this in?
>
> **A.** Kansas City.
>
> **Q.** What happened next?
>
> **A.** When I come out to get in my car, there was two men standing, one on each side. They said, "Get in, Mr. Williams, and park your car over in the other lot. Take the keys because we intend to bring you back." They shoved me in a big car, in the middle, between the two of them. About a half block they put a blindfold on me. It seemed like twenty minutes when we stopped. They took me inside of a building. They sat me on a chair. The place was dark. At least it was to me. I couldn't see nothing. And they took the blindfold off.
>
> There was a great big light over my head that showed around about ten feet of my stool that I was sitting on. They told me that I was brought there for a reason. That I was going to have to cooperate closer with Nick Civella. . . . They threatened my family, named my two children. They were both young at the time [daughters six and twelve]. They said if I didn't cooperate, they were going to kill my children, my wife, and you will be the last to go. . . .

the garbage disposal business. Crime syndicates were especially attracted to this business, which featured either small partnerships or family-run businesses. In New York City, many of the small firms were owned by Italian Americans who had passed the business down from generation to generation. In his authoritative 1987 study *Racketeering in Legitimate Industries,* Peter Reuter posited that New York, unlike Los Angeles, which was historically dominated by Armenian and Jewish carters, and Chicago, where many had been of Dutch origin, carters were predominately Italian, which might, according to James B. Jacobs, have "facilitated the Mafia's infiltration of the industry and the creation of the cartel system" (Jacobs 1999, 84, 248; Reuter 1987, 7–8).

Every day, New York City produces 13,000 tons of trash (not including debris generated by construction projects). Garbage collection is a two-stage process using separate industries for both. After garbage is collected (waste hauling) it must be disposed of—typically in an incinerator or a landfill. Residential waste is collected by the city's Department of Sanitation; business or commercial waste hauling is accomplished by the combined might of 300 small firms, consisting of from 1 to 20 trucks. In 1995, this business was a $1.5 billion-a-year industry.

After New York City officials dissolved employer trade-waste associations in 1947, organized crime became involved with this union in a big way—at least, that is, when city officials began receiving

> ## The Garbage and Waste Hauling Rackets: McClellan Committee (1957)
>
> [We] find that garbage collection industry men banded together in associations which eventually . . . invoked monopoly and restraint of trade arrangements with a system of punishments for nonconforming members . . . . In Vincent Squillante,[14] we have presented the picture of a man who traded his association with key underworld characters and his ability to "handle" Local 813, International Brotherhood of Teamsters, to parlay himself into a position where he was the absolute czar of the private sanitation industry in Greater New York. (Adapted from Jacobs 1999, 80)

complaints "that illegal activities were restricting free competition" (Raab 2005) in the industry. During this era, organized crime involvement extended only to the collection of commercial paper products; the rest was left to the city sanitation department. However, in 1957, the city, in order to cut costs, decided to stop collecting garbage from all non-residential enterprises—from the smallest candy store to the largest department store—as a radical step toward cutting the budget of the Sanitation Department. By privatizing commercial waste hauling, the city had unknowingly expanded racketeering opportunities exponentially (Raab 2005). Almost overnight, private carting companies reveled in the existence of more than 50,000 new customers, representing a 70% increase in the customer base, made up of mostly restaurants, stores, office buildings, and light industries (Jacobs 1999, 82–83).

As a result, several large companies that functioned more like cartels were formed by the city's Mafia families and essentially directed the trade over the next 50 years. Furthering their grip on this industry was their domination of Teamsters' Local 813, which allowed the families to dictate the operation of an entire industry. For example, the Lucchese family ran the Long Island cartel until the 1990s after several civil RICO suits were filed against its members. Defendants at the subsequent trials included 64 Lucchese and Gambino members and associates, 44 carting firms, the carters' trade association, and IBT Local 813. In 1994, its waste hauling cartel was placed under federal monitorship. Also significant was the Genovese crime family's association with the Westchester County cartel. In 1997, after a 10-year investigation, more than 60 federal charges were brought against 7 individuals and 14 businesses. Among those who pleaded guilty to concealing their involvement in the rackets with fraudulent transactions and tax statements were Genovese family boss Vincent "the Chin" Gigante and Thomas Milo, who owned the Suburban Carting Corporation, what was then "the country's largest privately held waste-hauling company" (Jacobs 1999, 83). As a result of this case, Westchester County put in place a mechanism for conducting extensive background checks on all carting companies bidding on city contracts.

How did the so-called cartels make money? A number of investigations demonstrated that competition was restricted by carving up the territory and fixing non-competitive prices. Criminals basically policed the cartels, making it well-nigh impossible for outside competition. As a result, for almost a half century, national waste-hauling businesses did not seek business in the New York and Long Island regions; instead, customers were forced to pay exorbitant prices as the cartel used every device to jack up profits. Common strategies included inflating the amount of waste collected to charge higher prices, which then increased collection fees for residents. Auditors in the 1990s estimated that the Genovese and Gambino crime families and their waste-hauling partners took in more than $600,000 in overcharges each year (Raab 2005). Lest there be any doubt about the impact of the New York City–area cartels, in the 1990s, Los Angeles and Boston businesses paid substantially less for every cubic yard of waste hauled away—$9 and $5.30, respectively—compared to $14.70 (Jacobs 1999, 91).

The cartels were so efficient that they enforced their own sanctions on members. For example, if one member took a customer away from another member, he was expected to compensate the member with one of his customers representing an equal or higher value; other times they might pay a penalty. One authority suggests, "the trade association functioned like a court with special power to enforce its decrees" (Jacobs, 1999, 86). One might add that they often served as judge, jury, and executioner, doling out beatings and in some cases murdering insurgent truckers, as in 1982, when "rebel waste hauler" Robert Kubecka aided several investigations, leading to his murder and that of his brother-in-law in 1989. Kubecka had refused to join the Long Island cartel since the end of the 1970s. The New York State Organized Crime Task Force (OCTF) convinced him to assist them in an 18-month investigation that led to the arrest of several leading crime figures, including Lucchese family boss Antonio "Tony Ducks" Corrallo. This and other missteps basically signed Kubecka's death warrant by the Mob.

The waste-hauling cartel enforced what was termed a *property-rights system* that paired every business to one or another of the carting companies. Any attempt to leave the partnership was met with threats or violence. When one merchant decided to haul away his own garbage rather than pay the cartel, garbage was deposited on the doorstep of his business with a warning that bombs would follow if he did not pay the cartel. What made organized crime's control of the waste-hauling industry all encompassing was its control of IBT Local 813, which handled the drivers and collectors who pick up the trash each day.

In 1992, Browning–Ferris Industries (BFI), what was then the nation's second largest waste-removal business, tried to break into New York's waste-hauling industry. However, when the company's local sales manager woke up one morning and found the severed head of a dog on his lawn gripping a message in his mouth of "Welcome to New York," BFI reconsidered its strategy (Raab 2005).

According to New York City officials, by 2007, "the Mob's grip [was] no longer felt" (quoted in McGeehan 2007) in the city's garbage hauling business. It had been more than a decade since the city's Trade Waste Commission declared victory over organized crime and placed lower limits on how much garbage carters could charge. That year, Mayor Rudolph Giuliani lowered the limit from $14.70 to $12.20 per cubic yard, a rate that had not changed 10 years later.[15] According to at least one local politician, the cap was an attempt to control the industry and "freeze out Mob-related

---

Anthony "Tony Ducks" Corallo (1913–2000) and the Long Island Cartel

Well-versed in loansharking and hijackings, Lucchese crime family member Corallo found his true calling in the waste-hauling rackets. He had already earned a reputation for shaking down Garment Center companies by threatening work stoppages and unionization drives. Between 1941 and 1960, he was arrested at least a dozen times for crimes such as murder, robbery, hijacking, and extortion, all to no avail, as each time the charges were dismissed in court. His ability to elude the law and prison and to dissuade witnesses from testifying at trial earned him the moniker "Tony Ducks" (Raab 2005, 237). Commenting on his involvement in the labor rackets, Senator McClellan called him "one of the scariest and worst gangsters we ever dealt with" (quoted in Raab 2005, 237). During his appearance before the U.S. Senate Labor Rackets Committee (McClellan Committee), he invoked his 5th Amendment right more than 80 times in response to his involvement in illegal union activities.

Corallo's prophetic move to the Long Island suburbs following World War II allowed him to exploit the construction companies and developers that accompanied the post-war population and building boom. In the 1950s he focused on gambling and loansharking rackets, and his growing interest in labor rackets led him into collaborations with Jimmy Hoffa and other corrupt union officials who facilitated his extortion in this arena. Hoffa, like other officials, typically had no problem with gangsters looting union funds as long as they could ensure the locals they controlled kept him in power.

During the 1950s, Corallo's greatest source of wealth was his control of Teamsters Local 239 in New York. Among his alleged schemes was the creating of *dummy employees* and collecting their salaries. This was basically a variation of using *ghost employees* or *no shows,* which had long been a staple of the union rackets. In some cases, checks were cut for employees who did not exist, as in the case of Corallo, netting him close to $70,000 a year. In other cases, "workers" were hired and reported for work at construction sites, but did little more than sit around while drawing a full salary. (In the 1930s the Chicago Outfit used a similar scheme during its involvement with IATSE, by requiring every movie theater to hire two projectionists, although it was a one-person job.)

When the building boom stagnated in the 1960s, Corallo shifted his attention to the garbage-carting industry. His luck began to desert him in the 1960s and he served several stints in prison for bribery. Released from prison in 1970, "Tony Ducks," at the age of 57, became the head of the Lucchese crime family. His conduit to controlling the Long Island garbage business was the Private Sanitation Industry, Inc., a "trade association" created by Corallo and his associates. Its stated purpose was to handle collective-bargaining negotiations and promote the growth of the carting business in several area counties (Suffolk and Nassau). However, in reality it was a cartel set up to divide collection routes, rig bids on public trash–removal contracts, suppress competition, and punish insurgents. Each garbage carter paid $5,000 a year for membership, plus whatever secret shakedowns that were imposed. The profits negated these costs because any extra costs and kickbacks were passed along through higher prices to customers. His association with the Gambino-run Teamsters' Local 813, representing most of the industry's workers, further augmented the power of his association. According to Raab, the trade association netted between $200 million and $400 million each year (2005, 239). Corallo's luck ran out for good in the 1980s after investigators placed a listening device inside his chauffeur's Jaguar. Caught on tape discussing Mob business, the tapes came back to haunt him during the RICO-driven Commission Case, and in 1986 he was sent to prison, where he died 14 years later.

companies" (quoted in McGeehan 2007). However, by 2007, the waste-hauling industry began to lobby city hall vociferously to eliminate caps on what haulers could charge hotels, restaurants, office buildings, and other businesses.[16]

Construction

Corruption in the construction industry has plagued New York and other large cities since at least the 1860s, and none demonstrated the excesses of corruption better than the Tweed Ring that dominated Tammany Hall. It has been estimated that it looted the city's treasury of at least $200 million. However, one of the most glaring examples of Boss Tweed's corruption was his involvement in the building of New York's City Hall (see Chapter 5). Organized crime expert Robert Kelly suggests that this type of racketeering is different from its modern incarnations, because "there was no Mafia layer between the contractors and the corrupt politicians" and modern construction workers are employed by their unions, rather than recent immigrants who were part and parcel of the 19th-century political patronage system. In addition, any kickbacks to political figures today do not go directly in their bank accounts, as they did in Tweed's time; today, the money must be laundered to make it untraceable (Kelly 1999, 74–75). A series of *New York Times* articles in 1982 and 1983 chronicled organized crime's grip on the city's billion-dollar construction industry, describing how bids were rigged and how combined union–mobster corruption was costing the city millions of dollars and inflating building costs on major public and private works projects (Raab 2005). Prosecutors at one time even referred to the New York area cement truck driver's union as a "candy store" for the Mob. During John Gotti's heyday, Local 282 of the Teamsters was "contributing" $1.2 million a year to the Gambino family coffers (Greenhouse 2008).

Concrete

Concrete workers are among the least-skilled workers in the construction trade. They were also among the most critical: "any work stoppage or even a slowdown would bring a construction site to a halt as tons of unspread concrete hardened into a useless mass" (Volkman 1998, 145). Lucchese member "Tony Ducks" Corallo was heavily involved in the concrete rackets and deserves recognition for some of his racketeering schemes. He expected contractors to fork over $2,000 a week to prevent strikes and similar labor unrest by the local he controlled. Few declined to cooperate, and soon the concrete business was organized into "the classic Mafia cartel" (Volkman 1998). Corallo decided who did and did not receive contracts as well as price schedules. Subsequently, the price of concrete on Long Island rose to 20% higher than prices elsewhere (the 20% was the so-called Mafia tax).

"Tony Ducks" introduced several concrete scams to further line Mob coffers. For example, the essential ingredient for making concrete is crushed stone, most of which came from Connecticut and then shipped to concrete production plants on Long Island. Corallo's cartel took over the only port handling the stone on Long Island; as a result, they were able to triple the going price for a ton of crushed stone. With no other alternatives available, concrete producers paid the inflated prices. As a result, the higher costs were passed on all the way down the line. Another moneymaker required a construction company to hire a *compressor operator* at each site. This job paid the salary equivalent to highly paid union worker. His job? Switching on the compressor in the morning and turning it off at the end of the day. A similar agreement called for a *gateman* to open and close the fence each day. Corallo, in true fashion, could be persuaded to overlook these provisions if he was instead paid a "labor management fee" (Volkman 1998, 146).

During the early 1980s, one investigation revealed that a cartel of suppliers and contractors with links to OC had made New York's concrete prices the highest in the nation—in fact, they were 70% higher than in other parts of the Northeast (Raab 2005). Real estate owners were forced raise commercial and residential rents to meet the excessive construction costs. State auditors estimated that the building of the Jacob Javits Convention Center would require no more than $18 million in concrete work; Mob control of the industry allowed only two controlled contactors to bid, raising the price between $30 million and $40 million.

Colombo Family Soldier Ralph Scopo[17] and the Concrete Club

Scopo: . . . *The concrete's gotta be twelve million?*

Contractor: Yeah. Why can't I do the concrete?

Scopo: You can't do it. Over two million you can't do it. It's under two million, hey, me, I tell you go ahead and do it.

Contractor: Who do I gotta go see? Tell me who I gotta go see?

Scopo: You gotta see every Family. And they are gonna tell you, "no." So don't even bother.

Contractor: If Tommy goes and talks to them?

Scopo: They'll tell you no. No matter who talks. . . .

(Adapted from New York State Organized Crime Task Force, 1990, 87–88)

LOANSHARKING

Legally referred to as *usury, loansharking,* or *shylocking,*[18] loansharks are also known as *juice men* in Chicago Mob parlance. It has been one of organized crime's mainstays throughout the 20th century and probably still ranks as a multi-billion-dollar-a-year industry. Although the actual origins of racketeer loansharking are still unclear, by most accounts it first became known in New York City in the 1920s (Haller and Alviti 1977). By the end of Prohibition, some bootleggers gravitated to this business as they searched for new rackets to replace the dependable bootlegging business. One study by the Russell Sage Foundation in the 1930s estimated the gross national income from loansharking in New York City at more than $10 million (Nelli 1976). The foundation provided special prosecutor Thomas Dewey with enough leads to begin an investigation of this crime. At this time it was a disorganized racket and victims were more willing to testify against individuals than against the Mob. A string of

---

Legitimate Businesses Infiltrated by Organized Crime (1951)

Advertising	Juke box and coin machine distribution	Coal	Racing and race tracks
Amusement industry	Laundry and dry cleaning	Communications facilities	Radio stations
Appliances	Liquor industry	Construction	Ranching
Automobile industry	Loan and bonding business	Drug stores and drug companies	Real estate
Baking	Manufacturing (gambling equipment, broilers, etc.)	Electrical equipment	Restaurants (taverns, bars, nightclubs)
		Florists	Scrap business
		Food and groceries	Shipping
Ball rooms, bowling alleys, etc.	Nevada gambling houses	Football	Steel
Banking	News services	Garment industry	Surplus sales
Basketball	Newspapers	Gas stations and garages	Tailoring (haberdashery)
Boxing	Oil industry	Hotels	Television
Cigarette distribution	Paper products	Import–export business	Theaters
		Insurance	Transportation

(Adapted from Kefauver Committee Report, 1951)

successful prosecutions led Dewey to proclaim victory against the racket in 1935, although he never actually substantiated the connections between the loansharks and prominent racketeers (Stolberg 1995; Reuter 1983, 90). By the 1970s it was still bringing in more than a $1 billion a year (Talese 1971).

Loanshark interest rates, by most accounts, vary from city. In the 1960s, one study by John M. Seidl[19] compared the loanshark business in New York, Detroit, Philadelphia, Cleveland, Chicago, and Boston and found "the structure of the loanshark industry in each of these cities is a function of the local underworld" (Anderson 1979, 69). For example, in New York, he described the underworld as "oligopolistic," wherein the leaders of the five major families "control the allocation of markets and enterprises among competing criminal organizations" (Anderson 1979, 69). In New York, loansharks received loans from the bosses without strings, allowing him to be the arbiter of each loan, with the only requirement being that he repays the original lender whether his borrower pays or not. However, Seidl described the Detroit underworld as more like a cartel "comprising criminal groups of different ethnic backgrounds" (although it is controlled by Italians). According to this cartel arrangement, criminal operations were "controlled directly by the cartel or indirectly through an extortionate taxing system" (Anderson 1979, 69). It is in this way that it allocated loanshark territories and controlled interest rates. Seidl argued that what distinguished this mode of operation is that it tries to restrict the funds lent by loansharks to those funds the cartel supplied. So, compared to New York City funds (in Detroit) were lent "with more strings" (Anderson 1979, 69). Similar distinctions between loanshark operations in other cities demonstrate that the enterprises followed the character of the organizational patterns that dominated each city's underworld (Anderson 1979, 69).

In essence, *loansharking* involves loaning money at extortionate rates of interest, higher than the maximum interest allowed by law. Involvement in this business allows organized crime members to infiltrate legitimate businesses when owners can't keep up with payments, which allows some mobsters to make the transformation to business respectability. Compared to the drug dealer, the loanshark has more in common with legitimate businessmen, with many clients coming from a more respectable milieu. Those at the top of the chain profited the most and did the least work. All they did was loan the capital to street soldiers, charging them 1% each week. For example, $100,000 could earn the bosses $1,000 back each week, and the soldiers could collect whatever profits were above that. One police official labeled this "the ultimate pyramid scheme" (Reuter 1983). Peter Reuter argued that a definition of *loansharking* should "reflect the perspectives of both lenders and borrowers," and identified four essential elements, including

1. True terms of the loan are not legally recorded.
2. Both the borrower and the lender believe that the true transaction is illegal.
3. The borrower understands that the lender might resort to threats or violence in the event payments are not made on time.
4. The interest rate for the loan is near or above the legal limit.

(Reuter 1983, 87–88)

In contemporary times, interest rates are set by law to make sure customers are not exploited by banks and other lenders. Working outside the parameters of legality, the loanshark devises whatever rates he chooses. At its core, it is a rather simple business. All that is required is an ample bank account, a reputation for violence, and a borrower who can't (or does not want to) get money from a bank due to poor or non-existent credit or the nature of the investment. Profits can run more than 20% per week and higher, with some rates even approaching 150% a year (Capeci 2002).

One of the advantages of the availability of loansharks is the fact that a drug trafficker, gambler, or pimp, virtually anyone with financial problems, can get a loan without any explanation required (Nelli 1976). Loansharking often goes hand in hand with gambling. Cash-starved gamblers with poor credit ratings have few alternatives than the ever-present shylocks. One authority on New York City's Mob families describes loansharking as "the symbiotic partner of gambling operations" (Raab 2005, 313). Gamblers, and particularly compulsive gamblers, have proven an ideal client

Salary Lending

Modern loansharking can be traced back to the practice of *salary lending* in the late 19th century, when individuals could borrow against future salaries at excessive rates of interest. The main difference between the two variations was that salary lenders were not linked with organized crime syndicates. Despite a welter of usury penalties, the salary lender operated in a middle ground where the law was often unclear, making small loans to mostly respectable people at higher than legal interest rates. Borrowers tended to fit the profile of married men with steady jobs and legitimate reasons for needing loans. Loans were typically small and repayment due in a matter of months or weeks—the lower the loan, the higher interest rate. In the event a borrower got too far behind on their loan, they could expect the dreaded "bawler out" to appear at his place of work, where in a loud voice she denounced him for his refusal to repay a loan. In a time when borrowing money was seen as a sign of moral weakness, the mere threat of such tactics usually resulted in a satisfactory resolution for the lender. The salary lender's days were numbered in the first decades of the 20th century as a variety of small loan systems were created in the legitimate banking industry for this clientele, and by 1933, 27 states had passed favorable small loan acts (Haller and Alviti 1977).

base over the years. Compulsive gamblers have few alternatives when they need quick money to pay their bookies. Henry Hill, the subject of Nicholas Pileggi's book *Wiseguy,* remembered,

> The guys used to get paid twice a month—the first and the fifteenth. They were always broke just before payday. I could get ten bucks for every five I lent if payday came after the weekend. Otherwise I got back nine for five. I started up a card game and some dice games and then I lent the losers money and I'd wait at the end of the line and get paid. It was beautiful. I didn't have to chase after anybody. (1990 42)

Hill never had to chase anyone down because one of the unwritten laws of the Mob is that one paid his debts, on time. Having built up a reputation for unabashed violence throughout the 20th century, Cosa Nostra moneylenders could count on a profit; because most borrowers would probably would like to borrow again—drug dealers, gamblers, and others—and wanted to keep on the good side of the loansharks. Besides, a crippled or dead borrower would never pay back a lender.

As loansharks expanded their client pool to include white-collar workers and businessmen who could not get legal loans their schemes became more complex. In one case, members of the Colombo family created a bogus loan company called Resource Capital Group that was subsidized by several Teamsters locals. Using intimidation and typical Mob wiles, they borrowed $1.2 million from the Teamsters. Using this to subsidize their plot, the Colombos reaped a fortune. According to Mob expert Selwyn Raab, one borrower had to pay $14,000 in interest on a loan of less than $700,000; another paid $50,000 for a $400,000 loan over the course of 3 months. FBI investigators later dubbed this enterprise as "a super Shylock operation" (2005, 313–314).

Types of Loans: The Knockdown and the Vig

There are a variety of methods for paying off loans, but there are two that predominate. One type of loan is called the *six-for-five,* or *knockdown,* which requires the client to pay $6 for every $5 borrowed by the end of the week. The protocol for paying it back developed out of a variation considered the brainchild of Thomas "Three Finger Brown" Lucchese in the 1930s. It requires a specified schedule of repayment of the principal and interest, "similar to a legitimate loan but at an astronomical cost" (Raab 2005, 313). For example, a $1,000 loan can be paid pack in 14 weekly installments of $100, equal in the end to $1,400. If the total repayment of the loan, including principal plus interest, is not paid on time, the borrower is sill liable for the interest, which is compounded the next week. As one expert described it, "a loan of $100 requires repayment of $120 seven days later. If this is not possible, the borrower must pay the vig, $20, and this does not count the principal or the next week's

Loanshark Murder Ring: Rio de Janeiro (2007)

Demonstrating that loansharking is not just an American phenomenon, in April 2007, police in Rio de Janeiro reported breaking up a gang that they suspect of killing hundreds of individuals. Eighteen suspects, including police officers, hired gunmen, and businessmen, were charged with committing contract killings for between $500 and $2,500 per contract. According to investigators, the gang had committed almost 200 killings a year between 2002 and 2007, "most linked to loansharking" (BBC, April 13, 2007).

interest." After 1 week, the debt increases to $120; after 2 weeks, to $144; after 3 weeks, to $172.80; and so forth (Abadinsky 2007, 261; Russo 2001, 117). Loansharks are quite willing to allow the victim to pay back the interest (or *vig*) each week while keeping the loan in play for another week. If the loan was not repaid rapidly, interest often accrued to more than the size of the original loan.

Unlike the knockdown, the *vigorish,* or *vig* loan (also called *juice*), has no time limitations for paying it back. However, when a payment is made late, the interest is compounded, and weekly interest payments are raised without a reduction in the principal. On a vig loan, the borrower might owe $20 in interest for the first week on a $100 loan. If the first payment is missed, the interest more than quadruples from $20 in the first week to $107 4 weeks later. In other words, missed payments can result in the interest alone surpassing the entire original loan in a matter of weeks (Raab 2005).

Most loansharks charge customers from 2 to 5 points a week in interest on the unpaid balance of the loan. Therefore, if a customer borrowed $2,000 on a Friday at 5 points a week, the following Friday he would be expected to pay a $100 vig to keep the money in play another week; otherwise he could pay it all off for a $2,100. If he kept it for 6 months, just paying the $100 vig each week, before paying off the loan he would pay $2,600 interest on a $2,000 loan over a 26-week period. Smaller loans are usually 6-payment deals. For $100, the customer makes payments of six $20 payments to meet a $100 loan. Average rates have been known to be as high as 150% a year (Capeci 2002).

Collection Methods of Loansharks

The mention of loansharking usually conjures up images of leg-breaking wiseguys pummeling their clients for being late with payments, breaking arms and legs, and even threatening death. In reality, although there is always a hint of violence in the air whenever one deals with crime figures, academic studies have revealed that many in the business "have shown a great reluctance to make use of violence or to have recourse to explicit threats" (Reuter 1983, 98). In some cases, the actors might not even have access to Mob muscle even if they wanted to use it; in other cases, they might expect the borrower to supply some type of collateral. As Reuter has suggested it seems that it depends on the individual loanshark's personality; some may prefer to use violence, whereas others do not, and when violence is used it typically occurs late in the collection process. Reuter described a process that begins with harassment, with threats becoming increasingly explicit and usually at night when the borrower was at home. After at least a month of this, the pressure is ratcheted up (1983).

In the event it appears that the borrower has no means to pay, other alternatives are worked out. An arrangement can be reached during a *sit-down* with the creditors. Several of these were revealed in a 1965 Report by the New York State Commission of Investigation. One story involved a hairdresser operating a beauty parlor in an upscale part of New York. Unable to meet the demands of the lenders, she began "fingering" clients of hers who wore plenty of gems. She would pass on names, addresses, husband's working hours, maid's day off, and other particulars to the mobsters who could then plan a trouble-free burglary. Another case involved a well-known sportscaster who was in debt to several loansharks. They consolidated the debt and had the individual use his contacts among the affluent and the sporting crowd, essentially working as a "steerer" for a crooked dice game set up by the sharks. A percentage of the winnings then went to paying down his debt. In the case of a small family trucking firm that had been drained financially by an unforeseen medical emergency, the debtors were intimidated into transporting and storing stolen property (Block 1991, 58–60).

San Gennaro Festival

In New York City, for almost 70 years, Little Italy's Feast of San Gennaro was conducted without the presence of a special auditor to ensure that the city received its 20% share of vendor's fees and those other proceeds went to charities rather than to local Mob figures. Hosted by the Society of San Gennaro, the festival has been a city tradition since 1916, when Italian immigrants organized the event to honor Saint Gennaro, the patron saint of Naples. In 1995, this all changed when it was monitored for the first time. The previous year, one observer referred to it in a *Village Voice* piece as "Porkstock '94: Eleven Days of Meat, Merriment, and the Mob" (Bastone 1994). The festival is considered the New York's biggest, yearly drawing almost 3 million visitors. One of the changes in 1995 was that the money traditionally pinned to the statue of Saint Gennaro would be promised to the church. Two weeks before its scheduled opening, a federal grand jury charged the Genovese crime family with controlling vendor admissions to the fair and claiming a percentage of the rental fees. Indictments further specified that this family and other Mafia groups were secret partners in dozens of street fairs and festivals where they get kickbacks on rents from merchants. The indictments were spurred by a joint NYPD and FBI investigation in January 1994 that led to court-authorized bugs and wiretaps in a hangout used by a Genovese crime family member who reportedly controlled the feast on behalf of the Genovese family (Toy 1994, 19). Until being sent off to prison for racketeering in 1993, the main figure behind the feast was a crime family captain who operated out of his own social club, the Andrea Doria. At the time of the 1994 festival, it was still graced by a large sign that could be seen from the street stating, "This Place Is Bugged."

New York City's Community Assistance Unit (CAU) regulates hundreds of festivals each year and requires the event's organizers to submit financial statements chronicling the income generated by vendor's fees. The city is supposed to get 20% to cover city expenses for police, sanitation, and other services. In 1993, festival officials claimed to have rented spaces to 113 vendors along an 11-block section of Little Italy. The director predicted that in 1994 this would grow to 190 vendors and gross fees would total $270,000. That same year, it only donated $10,000 to charity, while its director and another official were each paid $30,000 to direct the feast. They also paid $25,000 for unknown consultants and almost $24,000 to rent an office that is empty and shuttered year round. Because most of the commerce generated by the feast is done in cash, it is impossible to derive any real profit figures from the 11-day bacchanal. In 1994, a *Village Voice* investigation tallied some 368 vendors offering freak shows, games of chance, T-shirts, and selling food. The smallest booths rented for $2,000. By most accounts, the feast brings in hundreds of thousands of dollars more than it reported (Bastone 1994).

FIGURE 7.2   San Gennaro Festival, Little Italy, New York City
Source: Pearson Education/PH College/Eugene Gordon

Infiltrating Legitimate Business: Scamming/The Bust-Out Scheme

Racketeers look to the legitimate sector for a variety of reasons, from reducing risks to achieving a certain degree of respectability. In many cases, a legitimate business is a natural accompaniment to illegal activities. Cash businesses such as bars and nightclubs often function as the conduit to other illegal services, including money laundering or just serving as a meeting place for mobsters and associates. Take, for example, Tony Soprano's fictional Bada Bing Strip Club and John Gotti's Bergin Hunt and Fish Club.[20]

Some syndicates have used the process called *bleeding* in which criminals bleed out a legitimate business of profits causing it to collapse altogether. However, in *bust-out* schemes, criminals open a new business or buy into an existing one. Initially, business is conducted legitimately, with bills paid on time, accruing decent credit ratings. Meanwhile, a pattern develops in which the orders for equipment or supplies become larger and larger. In the end, the mobsters basically liquidate inventories and equipment, forcing the company into bankruptcy, defrauding creditors in the process (Kelly 1999; Pileggi 1990). Henry Hill, the subject of the bestselling book *Wiseguy,* explained the theory behind the bust-out using a restaurant as an example,

> pretty soon Paulie is on the guy's payroll for a couple of hundred a week. . . . Now the guy's got Paulie for a partner. . . . Paulie can put people on the payroll for early parole; he can throw liquor and food buying to friends of his. Plus the insurance. Who handles the insurance? That's always big with the politicians, and the politicians who are close to Paulie get the broker's fees. Plus the maintenance. Who cleans the joint? I mean a wiseguy can make a buck off every part of the business.
>
> And if he wants to bust it out, he can make even more money. Bank loans, for instance. A place has been in business say 20, 30 years. It has a bank account. There's usually a loan officer who can come over and give you a loan for some improvements. Of course, if you can, you take the money and forget about the improvements, because you're expecting to bust the place out anyway.
>
> Also if there is a line of credit, as the new partner you can call up suppliers and have them send stuff over. You can call up other new distributors and get them to send over truckloads of stuff, since the place has a good credit rating. Wholesalers are looking for business. They don't want to turn you down. The salesmen want to make the sale. So you begin to order. You order cases of whiskey and wine. You order furniture. You order soap, towels, glasses, lamps, and food, and more food. Steaks. Two hundred filets. Crates of fresh lobster, crab, and shrimp. There is so much stuff coming in the door it's like Christmas.
>
> And no sooner are the deliveries made in one door, you move the stuff out another. You sell the stuff to other places at a discount, but since you have no intention paying for it in the first place, anything you sell it for is profits. Some guys use the stuff to start new places. You just milk the place dry. You bust it out. And, in the end, you can even burn the joint down for a piece of the insurance if it doesn't make enough. (Pileggi 1990, 60–61)

Human Trafficking and Smuggling: Two Sides of the Same Coin?

The smuggling and trafficking of human beings generates huge profits for organized crime groups. Prices are typically determined by the migrant's wealth and nationality, as well as the associated risks of the journey, the degree of professionalism of the service providers, and the attractiveness of the country of destination. The distinctions between smuggling and trafficking cases are sometimes difficult to ascertain for law enforcement. The difference between *coercion* and *consent* are not always so clear cut. Cases of human trafficking have been known to begin as simple smuggling operations. At some point in the saga unexpectedly a victim might be expected to work forced labor or prostitution to pay for an unforeseen debt.

In 2005, at the 3rd Summit of Heads of State and Government—the Council of Europe Convention on Action against Trafficking in Human Beings defined *trafficking in human beings* as

> the recruitment, transportation, transfer, harboring or receipt of persons, by means of the threat or use of force or other forms of coercion, of abduction, of fraud, of deception, of the abuse of power or of a position of vulnerability or of the giving or receiving of payments or benefits to achieve

Average Costs for Human Smuggling (2005)

North Africa to Spain: €4,000 (€2,000 more for false identity papers)

Hungary/Russia to Western Europe: €8,000–10,000

Slovakia to Italy: $3,000–4,000

Serbia and Montenegro to Western Europe: $1,000

Croatia to Western Europe: €500

China to Italy: $13,000

South Asia to Spain: €6,000 (or double that with false identity papers)

(Adapted from Council of Europe, 2005, 39)

the consent of a person having control over another person, for the purpose of exploitation. Exploitation shall include, at a minimum, the exploitation of the prostitution of others or other forms of sexual exploitation, force labor or services, slavery or practices similar to slavery, servitude or the removal of organs. (Quoted in Council of Europe 2005, 32)

Immigrant smuggling is hazardous for the migrants, whether crossing the Mexican border into Texas, traveling from China to California by ship, or being smuggled into Europe. Hundreds—if not thousands—die each year. Between 1995 and 2005, at least 5,000 people died on the journey between North Africa and southern Europe while crossing the Mediterranean Sea.

A large portion of human trafficking in Southeastern Europe is the province of organized criminal syndicates. This flies in the face of regions such as Southeast Asia, where trafficking "is often informal and managed through personal connections" (Surtees 2008, 47).

Modern organized human trafficking dates back to the early 20th century. In Europe, it began to attract more attention internationally following the breakup of the former communist regimes in the early 1990s. Although *human smuggling* and *trafficking* are often mentioned as synonyms and treated as equivalents, they have a different history and differ substantially from each other. In contrast to the concept of *human smuggling,* with its focus on illegal border crossings, *trafficking in humans* is more about the violation of the rights of the individual through exploitation. Human smuggling, while requiring some element of coercion and subsequent exploitation, often "involves cross-border movement." Both can result in the mistreatment of the migrant, and "a process that starts for the victim as smuggling may end up as trafficking" (Surtees 2008, 43).

Services Required by Successful Trafficking Operations

• Arranging transportation and proper documents
• Providing transport or counterfeit documents
• Acting as a guide to people crossing borders
• Serving as a chaperone on the journey
• Providing information at various stages of the border, such as, "How do you cross the border?"
• Arranging logistics such as bribing guards and officials
• Supervising victims at the destination
• Acting as security or a bodyguard to intimidate victims and to ensure they do not report the crime or run away
• Providing accommodation and food
(Quoted in Surtees 2008, 47)[21]

What Is Human Smuggling?

According to the United Nations Protocol against the Smuggling of Migrants by Land, Sea and Air, *human smuggling* refers to "the procurement, in order to obtain, directly or indirectly, a financial or other material benefit, of the illegal entry of a person into a State Party of which the person is not a national or permanent resident" (quoted in Surtees 2008, 42–43). Of the estimated 130 million international migrants, between 20 million and 30 million are considered "irregular" migrants, and at any time some 4 million are on the move. These figures are probably low. Western Europe is among the more attractive destinations for illegal immigrants, offering a relatively high standard of living and job opportunities, particularly in the 21st century, where fertility levels are below replacement level and there is an aging population. Organized criminal groups are increasingly involved in the smuggling of persons, as previously demonstrated with the snakeheads in China (Asian Organized Crime) and the coyotes of Mexico (Mexico and Latin America).

What perhaps has contributed most to the development of organized smuggling networks has been the tightening of border controls and points of entry in the European Union that has forced illegal migrants to rely on smuggling organizations. Because of immigration control and with few legal alternatives to entry, the unanticipated consequences have pushed refugees into the hands of smugglers. Because most illegal immigrants have put their faith in the traffickers and smugglers they are usually receptive to the coaching that will allow them to elude being caught. Anti-trafficking efforts have changed patterns of movement, especially speedboat routes on the Adriatic. As a result, most immigration takes place overland, taking advantage of the open borders offered by Schengen in Europe and NAFTA on the Mexican-American border, for example.

One of the newest trends in Southern and Eastern Europe is to obtain legal documents and to move the migrants through legal border crossings thereby deceiving them with the documents affording the travel a patina of legitimacy. As one leading expert put it, "Victims unaware of the exploitation that awaits them, often readily accept coaching from traffickers on how to answer questions by border officials and law enforcement officers as crossings and while en route" (Karrstrand 2007, 53). Usually migrants are instructed to respond that the purpose of their travel was tourism; by doing so, their movements from one country to another is considered legal, thereby "[camouflaging] the trafficking process as legal travel [and averting the suspicion of] the victims who, until their arrival at the destination, may not recognize they are being trafficked" (Karrstrand 2007, 53).

One method of keeping the upper hand in respect to their victims is the practice of holding their documents and controlling their use throughout the journey. In the event that one escaped, they would be without the documentation that would allow them to cross borders to return home. Kosovar and Albanian traffickers often traffic victims without documents or with fake papers, thus amplifying their vulnerability in whichever country they are in; victims are more reluctant to approach legal authorities without these papers for fear of arrest or deportation. These fears are intensified by terrible stories of the treatment they could expect from the authorities (Karrstrand 2007).

Human Smuggling: Houston (2008)

In late April 2008, Houston bar manager Oscar Mondragon was sentenced to 15 years in prison for his role in a human trafficking ring that forced illegal immigrants to pay off smuggling debts by working as prostitutes. The bar manager was part of a smuggling ring that brought women and girls from Central America into the United States under the pretext of offering waitress jobs. Investigators claimed that over a 4-year period beginning in 2001, up to 120 women were forced to have sex with patrons of the bar and businesses owned by ring members in Houston. Authorities charged that the conspirators used fear and violence to control the women. The defendants pleaded guilty to sexual assault, increasing their victims' debts, and threatening to harm relatives abroad if they did not pay exorbitant smuggling fees (George 2008, B2).

How Sex Traffickers Recruit: Southeastern Europe—A Case Study

The trafficking of migrants for the purpose of sexual exploitation continues at an alarming rate and is considered a major force driving human trafficking. Primarily women and children are exploited in this fashion through a variety of subterfuge. One investigation of human trafficking in Southeastern Europe revealed that most victims were recruited by someone from their same nationality, although there is a high incidence of multinational cooperation. A country such as Moldova, for example, might be home to a transnational organized crime group made up of Moldovan nationals as well as members from Romania, Russia, Syria, Lebanon, and Egypt (Surtees 2008).

Human traffickers use a variety of methods to recruit potential migrants. Southeastern Europe has become a particular hotspot for sex trafficking gangs. Although there have been some reports of victims being kidnapped, evidence is more anecdotal and it remains uncommon. More likely are schemes that take advantage of an individual's frustration with low salaries and few employment options (Karrstrand 2007, 50), making it easy to convince many of them to seek higher-paying jobs abroad. Other issues might push individuals into immigration, such as family members beset by crises, needing emergency funds to pay for an illness, debts, or other emergencies that require quick money. In some cases, women respond to job advertisements for babysitters, models, cosmeticians, dancers, or waitresses or are recruited by friends or relatives. Transportation and documents are usually provided by organized crime networks. On arrival at their destination, women and girls are often stripped of their identity papers and told they still owe a large debt to the traffickers and that they need to work it off through prostitution. It is not uncommon for violence to be used to coerce them into the sex trade, and reports indicate that women are kept in isolation, beaten, and even raped to "break them." Victims are often resold or traded between criminal groups and countries in order to ensure there is always "fresh meat on the market" (Council of Europe 2005, 33).

One ruse in 2004 and 2005 targeted traditional Romanian dancers who were promised traditional dancing jobs once they reached their destination in Greece. However, once there, some of them applied for positions through a legitimate employment agency and with a legal contract; ultimately, one was beaten and forced into the sex trade, and not even paid (Karrstrand 2007). In other cases, traffickers have targeted women by offering them job as prostitutes. It is still unclear whether recruitment was directed at those already in the sex trades. Promises of marriage have also served well for recruiters; according to one recent study, almost half of Albania's victims in 2004 were recruited with marriage or engagement prospects. In some cases, traffickers have even married women and then forced them into prostitution. There are cases in which Albanian husbands were followed to another country by their "brides," who were then forced into sex trade (Surtees 2005). Still others recruit specific targets with personalized overtures. One was recruited with the promise of a drug rehab program, another with promises of being assisted by a fertility clinic, and still others easily prey on those looking for adventure abroad (Karrstrand 2007).

Deep Throat, the Mob, and the Pornography Business

Until the 1940s, sexually explicit materials were available only in marginal areas of urban centers. In the following decades the protection of the First Amendment was expanded to offer protection to these materials as well as certain literary works once considered obscene. During the years of the Warren Court (1950s and 1960s) it became much harder to prosecute this crime (Winick 1994). Organized crime figures have been involved in the pornography industry for decades, but the expansion that took place in the 1960s and 1970s led to an increasing interest in this lurid business, although none had very long careers in it. By the 1970s, one of the biggest players was a Bonanno *capo* named Michael "Mickey Z" Zaffarano, who had offices on both coasts and operated the Pussycat Cinema chain of adult movie theaters. Targeted by a number of law enforcement agencies, it was the FBI who got to him first on Valentine's Day 1979. Before they could finish cuffing him, he had a heart attack and died.

In the 1980s, Robert "DiB" DiBernardo, a captain in the Gambino crime family, was considered a major porno dealer. His first flirtation with the pornography business was as an enforcer for

Star Distributors in New York City in the 1970s. Star Distributors produced and distributed pornographic materials to adult bookstores and movie theaters throughout the country. By the late 1970s, DiBernardo owned Star News, New York's largest distributor of adult materials, as well as sex shops in Times Square. John Gotti ordered his murder in 1986 (even though DiB participated in Gotti's plot to kill boss Paul Castellano). According to the testimony of Gotti's former underboss Salvatore "Sammy the Bull" Gravano, DiBernardo was lured to Gotti's office, where he was shot twice in the back of the head (Capeci, 2002). He was one of Gotti's first victims as boss.

One investigative journalist most recently asserted, "the sex industry had always attracted people with criminal backgrounds of some sort," for after all, entrepreneurs "concerned about their reputations didn't tend to open adult bookstores with peep booths" (Schlosser 2003, 13). Organized crime figures were drawn to the adult entertainment business after noticing the mounting profitability of adult-related businesses in the liberalized environment of the 1960s and early 1970s. Typical "adult" industry businesses at the time included peep shows in booths at sex shops, feature films shown in movie theaters, books and magazines, mail-order materials, and sex tabloids. Adult bookstores were a milieu onto themselves, where consumers could find a cornucopia of sex-related services. One investigator discovered that employees at such enterprises could often be depended on to supply customers with contacts to mobsters, local drug dealers, prostitutes, bookies, and fences for stolen goods (Potter 1986). In retrospect, these activities seem rather quaint in an unregulated world of Internet pornography, cable television networks, and around-the-clock pay-per-view adult movies.

There were a number of lucrative opportunities for organized crime to pursue from a "strong arm's" distance. One venture was to collect "street taxes" from adult business owners. Because banks were unlikely to fund loans for such prurient businesses, prospective merchants had few options besides local loansharks. However, by most accounts, the sex industry, despite extortion risks, was rather tame compared to the violence associated with gambling and drug running. In his foray into examining the sex industry, Eric Schlosser revealed that criminal organizations found the illegal copying and distribution of popular hardcore films a most lucrative racket, noting it was almost straight profit because no royalties were in order and producers were unlikely to sue for copyright violations due to the questionable legality of the products in question. Interestingly, a number of local hoods pirated copies of *Deep Throat,* unaware that the film was the property of the Colombo family representatives, the Perainos. However, this worked in favor of the legitimate distributors because checkers showed up anyway and collected half the proceeds. In effect "the widespread piracy [of the film] not only facilitated its nationwide distribution, but also spared the Perainos the cost of making new prints" (Schlosser 2003, 138).

Beginning in the 1980s, law enforcement and journalists maintained that the Mafia controlled 90% of the porn industry, citing incredible returns and inflating profits to ludicrous heights. It was true that organized crime had been involved in the business in one way or another since the pre-videotape days of the small, coin-operated machines that were ubiquitous in such places as Manhattan's Times Square. Brothers Joseph and Anthony Peraino[22] processed and distributed these up and down the East Coast. Mob *capo* John "Sonny" Franzese controlled the distribution of 8-millimeter porno shorts in New York City. They and others made money, probably lots of money, but nowhere close to the hundreds of millions of dollars reported in the following reports. One of the biggest popular myths about organized crime is that it at one time or another controlled America's porn industry—just not so (Capeci 2002).

Deep Throat: The Mob and the Movie

The 61-minute hardcore pornographic film *Deep Throat* was released in 1972, establishing a market for "porno chic" as celebrities and couples stood in lines at movie theaters. Reportedly costing only $22,000 to make, according to various sources, it went on to make somewhere between $100 million and $600 million, probably one of the most profitable movies ever made. However, the FBI and the *Los Angeles Times* suggest that profits were closer to the lower figure, citing the fact that the film was banned in most cities and was probably shown in only one theater in a handful of large cities. It must also be taken into account that movie ticket prices hovered between $2.05 in most cities and $5 in New York City.[23]

According to a 1982 *Los Angeles Times* investigation of Mob involvement in the pornography business, *Deep Throat* was "the most successful porno movie ever, estimated to have earned anywhere from $30 million to $100 million since its first release in 1972" (Farley and Knoedelseder 1982). By 1984, with the rise of the home video industry, it was selling 300,000 copies a year at $60 each (Farley and Knoedelseder, Jr. 1982, 3). Prominent movie critic Roger Ebert recently stated, without substantiation, in his review of the documentary *Inside Deep Throat,* that when the film was made and released in the 1970s, most of the nation's porn theaters were owned by crime syndicates, and they probably "inflated box office receipts as a way of laundering income from drugs and prostitution" (Ebert 2005).

The film's producer was Louis "Butchie" Peraino, listed in the credits as Lou Perry. The seed money for the film came from his father, Anthony Peraino, and his uncle, Joe "The Whale" Peraino, both reputed members of the Colombo crime family. All three Perainos became millionaires in the process of distributing the movie. Once the film's successes seemed assured, director Gerard Damiano, who had the rights to one-third of the profits, was forced out with a paltry $25,000 payoff by the Perainos.

The Perainos entered the pornography business at the ground level in the late 1960s. According to some Mob experts, the business turned into "organized crime's most profitable new business venture since it got into narcotics in the 1950s" (Farley and Knoedelseder 1982, 6). One account of the Mafia infiltration of the porn business suggests, "Until 1973, the Mob was involved in pornography only in an ad hoc, local way" (Hubner 1993). The Perainos, according to John Hubner, "were just two more guys in New York City who were financing pornographic films." He argues that rather than an incredible moneymaker like drugs, gambling, and union pension funds, the Mob considered pornography "small potatoes because the films were shown in only a few theaters so the 'handle' was small" (Hubner 1993, 207). Mobsters perceived porno to be more work than it was worth, citing the unreliable milieu of actors and the constant demand by viewers for new faces. However, in 1973, the Mob started to take serious look at porn because of all the new theaters opening up. That same year, the U.S. Supreme Court, under Chief Warren Burger, a stern opponent of adult theaters, dirty book stores, and massage parlors, issued the *Miller v. California* decision, driving a number of pornographers out of business. Before *Miller,* local courts could find a film obscene on "community standards," but lawyers could appeal to a higher court where a national standard, however vaguely defined it might be, was used to determine what was obscene; after *Miller,* the community had the right to determine and write its own laws, and as a result it made it almost impossible to distribute X-rated films across state lines. One of the unanticipated effects of this ruling was that it also gave mobsters the opportunity to get in the business; by distributing such films clandestinely under the table, they not only took the heat off producers, but could copy the films and distribute them themselves (Hubner 1993, 209).

By the early 1980s, the pornography industry was raking in an estimated $5 million or $6 million a year, with half of it, according to law enforcement, going into Mob coffers, ranking it just behind gambling and narcotics as a profit maker. With the profits from *Deep Throat,* the Perainos went on to build a financial empire in the mid-1970s. Profits were invested in a number of legitimate businesses, including garment companies in New York and Miami, investment companies, a chain of porno theaters in Los Angeles, and several music and record publishing companies on the West and East coasts. Among their prize investments was Bryanston Distributors, which was considered "the most highly touted independent movie company in the motion-picture industry" (Farley and Knoedelseder 1982) for 3 years in the mid-1970s, financing, producing or distributing more than 20 non-pornographic films, including the original *Texas Chainsaw Massacre*[24] and Bruce Lee's last film, *Return of the Dragon.*

Despite his reputation in the movie community, which had the *Christian Science Monitor* heaping accolades on Louis Peraino as a "new kind of movie tycoon" whose goal was making "family-oriented" films, and *Hollywood Reporter* referring to him as "one of the successful new breed of independent distributors" (Farley and Knoedelseder 1982), law enforcement had a decidedly different opinion. In 1976, a California Department of Justice confidential intelligence report

Deep Throat *and Creative Accounting Methods*

Initially, Bryanston Distributors distributed the movie to theaters much like it would any other film. The movie was sent by mail or parcel service to various theaters, where owners were expected to maintain box office records and then pay the Perainos' company its share of receipts by check. However, the conservative bent of the Supreme Court by 1973, a year after the release of the movie, stimulated the creation of a new system of distribution in order to evade the increasingly punitive obscenity laws. With the passage of *Miller v. California*, communities were now empowered to create their own obscenity standards, thereby making the legal transportation of hard-core films across state lines a risky proposition, and in 1973 the Perainos introduced a system to bypass the mail and other traditional shipping methods. Journalist Eric Schlosser adroitly pointed out, "The system invited loose accounting and employee theft, [but] had the virtue of eliminating any paper trail, and tens of millions of dollars were collected this way" (2003, 137). The Perainos turned to loyal employees referred to as *checkers* who hand-delivered each print to the movie theater owner. In order to keep track of profits, spies or checkers (*stand-over guys*) counted patrons with clickers to verify ticket sale numbers. At the end of the day, the checker picked up the Perainos cut in cash—typically 50%. Most adult theaters were open 24-hours a day, which required three 8-hour shifts of guys to count the people who walked in (McNeil 2005). Other employees in this elaborate scheme were the *sweepers*, who traveled from theater to theater in cities across the country, collecting the money from the checkers and packing it into suitcases and then personally delivering the suitcases to the Perainos.

identified Peraino's Bryanston Distributors on a list of "key corporations controlled by the Mob" (Farley and Knoedelseder 1982). That same year, a series of federal obscenity cases targeted the movie. The Perainos and several other Mob associates were sentenced to short prison sentences.

By the 1980s, the Perainos' movie business was in shambles, in part due to convictions in 1976 related to transporting obscene materials across the state lines in the *Deep Throat* case. Louis and Joseph Peraino were convicted in Miami on federal obscenity charges and were sentenced to prison terms of 6 and 3 years, respectively. With family legal troubles mounting, Joseph took over much of the Peraino family's business activities. On January 4, 1982, a shotgun ambush left Joseph Peraino in serious condition and his son Joe, Jr., dead on the streets of Manhattan. A number of news sources tied the shootings to a "Mob porn war" (Farley and Knoedelseder 1982). One police investigator told a journalist, "For whatever reason—whether they wanted to take it over [the porno business] or he was making too much money and somebody else wanted it or he wasn't operating it properly—they just wanted him out of it" (Farley and Knoedelseder 1982, 4).

The result is that the Mob found a number of lucrative opportunities in the porn industry, but rather than dominating it, organized crime syndicates and members were just some of the players in the rackets. According to Mob expert Jerry Capeci, some were partners of pornographers, some owned buildings that housed adult stores, and others muscled in on film labs and distribution of videotapes, but the Mafia had no monopoly on the world of porn (2002, 176).

MONEY LAUNDERING

Most accounts trace the beginnings of money laundering to the Prohibition era of the 1920s, when American bootleggers found it necessary to disguise their vast profits from the tax services. Meyer Lansky's biographer and others credit him as a pioneer in money laundering—"the prophet of the voguish new gospel of money laundering," tracing his involvement back to his years as a "one-man think tank" for "Lucky" Luciano in the early 1930s (Lacey 1992, 4–5). Utilizing a series of shell companies and offshore bank accounts, Meyer Lansky made it more sophisticated in the 1930s, allowing him to transfer profits from his slot machines in New Orleans to a Swiss bank account. Lansky established his first Swiss bank account in 1934, to be followed by accounts in the Caribbean and other places. Lansky engineered one scheme called the *loan-back* that exploited the traditionally liberal policies of the Swiss banking system in the 1960s. Couriers carried cash from the United States to

Switzerland to avoid the tax services. The money was then deposited in a Swiss bank account, which was identified only by a distinct number (a practice now frowned on). Lansky then "borrowed" back his own money. Once safely in his coffers, there was little risk of the authorities finding it was taxable.

The euphemism *money laundering* originated sometime in the late 1920s or early 1930s by U.S. Treasury agents investigating Al Capone. During this era, when few homes had running water let alone a washing machine, most people took their clothes to the neighborhood laundry, and Capone's syndicate was supposed to be heavy into this business, controlling hundreds of laundries scattered about Chicago. This business allowed the Capone organization to conceal its illicit income from bootlegging and other sources by declaring it as legitimate income from the laundry business. In 1928 alone, the Capone syndicate made $10 million; by 1931, it was making $50 million (Lunde 2004, 40). Although there were no statutes against money laundering until 1986, Capone was brought to ground for evading federal income tax, demonstrating a close connection between "tax evasion and money laundering" (Mathers 2004, 21–22).

Money laundering is used by organized crime groups to conceal the existence of illegal income (as well as its source and use). Often this is accomplished under the guise of legitimate business. According to the International Monetary Fund, between 2% and 5% of the world's GDP ($500 billion) consists of money being fraudulently laundered (Nackman and Cooperman 2006, 43). As Chapter 15, concerning Hi-Tech Organized Crime, illustrates, much of the fraud can now be accomplished through electronic banking systems, which allows almost instantaneous transfer of funds without one ever leaving an office or entering a bank.

The first meaningful legislation enacted to deal with money laundering came about in 1970 with the passage of the Bank Secrecy Act (BSA), which mandated a series of reporting and recordkeeping requirements designed to track money laundering activities. In theory, it was based on the proposition that unusual transactions of currency at domestic financial institutions and unusual shipments of currency into or out of the United States might be related to criminal activity (Powis 1992, ix). Among its most important requirements was for banks and other financial institutions to report currency transactions over $10,000 by or on behalf of the same person on the same business day. The report must be made to the IRS on IRS Form 4789, better known as a Currency Transaction Report (CTR). Similarly a Customs report must be filed by persons who transport or ship currency or monetary instruments over $10,000 into or out of the country on a Customs Form 4790. Over the years, the laws and penalties related to them have been amended. In 1990, financial institutions were required to obtain identification and maintain records of all purchases between $3,000 and $10,000, including those made with cashier's checks, bank checks and drafts, traveler's checks, and money orders (Powis 1992, xii).

One long-time ruse used to get around these requirements is through structuring, in which large sums of money are broken down into amounts under $10,000 for purposes of conducting transactions at banks and other financial institutions. During the 1980s it became a major tool for drug traffickers. More popular is *smurfing,* which sometimes involves organizations of between 5 and 15 couriers that launder money through a series of structured transactions. Large quantities of cash is given to small groups within the smurfing organization; the groups then travel to various cities where individual members go to a number of banks and buy cashier's checks and money orders for less than $10,000. Continuous purchases done until currency dispenses. Cashier's checks are then shipped back to Miami and deposited into bank accounts. At this point, it is not necessary to file CTRs, as these are required only for cash transactions. The cash is often wired to accounts in countries with strict bank secrecy laws. However, while smurfing is an expensive, time-consuming, and labor-intensive strategy, it is still in use (Powis 1992, 92).

Some authorities argue that money laundering remained a low priority for law enforcement until the avalanche of cash that accompanied the growth of the cocaine trade in the 1970s and 1980s. The United States was the first nation to pass legislation against money laundering, which did not become a federal criminal offense per se in the United States until the passage of the Money Laundering Control Act of 1986. Before then, prosecutors brought cases under a variety of taxation statutes relating to the defrauding of the government, and under the Bank Secrecy Act, which required the reporting of foreign bank accounts and other transactions (Plombeck 1988, 71). In 1986, it was made a separate federal offense punishable by fine of $500,000 or twice the value of property involved, and prison sentence of up to 20 years.

The Process of Money Laundering

The basic process of money laundering involves three stages. *Placement* is the initial step. It is at this point that illicit money is transferred or broken into less conspicuous sums to evade currency transaction reporting. There are various methods for accomplishing this. For example, it can be split into smaller transactions and deposited by employees known as *smurfs,* hence *smurfing.* Once a syndicate eventually produces legitimate paperwork accounting for the cash, the money is withdrawn and collected. During the heyday of organized crime involvement in Las Vegas that lasted from the 1940s to the 1980s, the casinos were ideal instruments for laundering torrents of cash. The most popular method was to have a gang runner purchase a large amount of gambling chips. After gambling away a small portion, the individual then cashed in the rest of the gambling tokens, counting it as winnings. Gang members have been known to buy high-value goods—antiques, luxury cars—for cash and then resell them, the buyer paying by bank transfer into a legitimate account.

The next stage is called *layering,* which involves moving the money through various channels to conceal its real origins and owners, each channel forming another layer to cover the transaction. At this juncture, *shell companies,* registered companies with offices in place such as the Dutch Antilles, Liberia, or Nauru, are often involved. Typically, they serve only as a name for a bank account. Layering often relies on international financial institutions such as offshore banking havens or other jurisdictions that have bank secrecy laws. Essentially, the larger the number of small daily transfers, particularly using falsified sender information, hinders tracing to the source. These offshore companies can then freely invest in real estate and other investments until the criminals decide to convert them to cash somewhere up the line.

The final stage is called *integration,* whereby the original illicit funds have been sufficiently layered and can be returned to the mainstream flow. At this point, the funds can be used in legitimate business enterprises without the attendant suspicion usually accompanying business transaction with large amounts of cash.

OFFSHORE BANKING AND SHELL CORPORATIONS   Any bank located outside the United States is considered *offshore.* Other countries have different laws and regulations in regard to company formation, with many offering extensive provisions for secrecy in this endeavor. These may include rules of nondisclosure of company officers, shareholders, or owners. Among the jurisdictions most favored due their lax requirements are the Isle of Man, Panama, Gibraltar, Bermuda, the Bahamas, the Netherlands Antilles, Hong Kong, Luxembourg, and Switzerland (Madinger 2006, 170).

By most accounts, "shell corporations are the mainstay of money laundering schemes everywhere" (Madinger 2006, 170–171). As one leading authority describes them, shell corporations have "no assets and no liabilities, just a charter to operate. It is easy to set up, can be interlocked all over the place with other shells, and, if established someplace with secrecy laws, can make it almost impossible to identify the owners or directors" (Madinger, 2006, 170–171). Shell banks are not a recent phenomenon. In the 1960s, the Internal Revenue Service discovered a pattern in which shell banking institutions were popping up in the Bahamas, some established by individuals closely connected to "gambling interests, international underworld couriers, James Hoffa and the Teamsters Union" (Messick 1969). The IRS suspected correctly in the late 1960s that much of the money going into the shell banks were proceeds from casino skims in the United States; more important, they were out of American jurisdiction. Underworld figures used this money to finance gambling operations in the Caribbean.

When one appeared at the door of one of these "banks," they found an empty office with the name on the door, or "space retained in the office of the Bahamian lawyer who obtained the charter for the bank" (Messick 1969, 85). Shell banks like these are created expressly for the purpose of concealing the names of depositors through means of secret numbered accounts. Money is alleged to be transported

FATF Blacklist of Countries Considered Below International Standards in Enforcing Money Laundering Legislation (2000)[25]

Bahamas	Nauru	Lebanon	St. Kitts and Nevis
Cayman Islands	Nive	Liechtenstein	St. Vincent and the
Cooks Islands	Panama		Grenadines
Dominica	Philippines	Marshall Islands	
Israel	Russia		

from the U.S. couriers using private planes, boats, and other means. The funds are then redeposited by the shell bank into the more substantial English or Canadian banks located in the Bahamas. Once the funds are secreted into these accounts using the name of the depository shell bank, the funds can be retained in Nassau or forwarded with commission to Switzerland for redeposit in that country.

As recently as 2001, New York's Federal Reserve Bank estimated that more than $800 billion was sitting in Grand Cayman banks. However, in the past few years much has changed here. One leading authority asserts that "today it's harder to launder money in Cayman than it is in the United States," explaining that once the Financial Action Task Force (FATF) dubbed them the leading non-cooperative country in the world as far as enforcing money-laundering laws, the government responded quickly with new money-laundering legislation (Mathers 2004, 159). Established by the G-7 group of industrialized countries in 1989, the FATF is a task force organized under the banner of the Organization for Economic Co-operation and Development (OECD) to fight the scourge of money laundering. In 2000, it declared 29 offshore jurisdictions to be deficient, and labeled the 15 worst "non-cooperative countries and territories" (see box) (Naim 2005, 152).

Banking Fraud: The BCCI Scandal

No case illustrates the collusive nature of major banking fraud better than that of the Bank of Credit and Commerce International, better known as BCCI, or more sardonically, "Bank of Crooks and Criminals International."[26] Founded in 1972 by Pakistani banker Agha Hasan Abedi, it conducted all of its real business in London, although it was incorporated in Luxembourg[27] and financed by a British Sheik from Abu Dhabi. Its incredible ascension in the 1980s was in large part due to its use by the CIA in funding rebels fighting the Russians in Afghanistan between 1979 and 1989. In addition, Abedi, the Pakistani banker, was closely linked to the leader of the Pakistan military at that time, General Mohammed Zia ul-Haq. BCCI reportedly was used by them to launder billions of dollars a year generated by hundreds of heroin laboratories in Pakistan's North West Frontier Province (NWFP), where Afghani opium poppies were processed before being unleashed on the world heroin market. What further complicated the nature of the funds being handled by BCCI was that it was used as the main bank for the flow of British and American weapons to the Afghan "freedom fighters."

During the 10 years of the Afghan War, BCCI's assets grew from an initial financing of $2.5 million to $4 billion in 1980. When it was shut down in 1991, most of its reported $23 billion was missing and unaccounted for. At its zenith, BCCI ran more than 400 branches in 78 countries and had assets of $25 billion. Its headquarters was divided between Luxembourg and the Cayman Islands, both known for their bank secrecy statutes. In 1988, its Tampa, Florida, branch was implicated in laundering drug money, and in 1990, the bank pleaded guilty and paid a fine. Around this time, an internal audit revealed hundreds of millions of dollars were unaccounted for from BCCI coffers. A subsequent investigation dubbed "Sandstorm" and conducted by the Bank of England reported BCCI was involved in "widespread fraud and manipulation" (Kelly Maghan, and Serio 2006). By 1991, the scandal was growing as American and British investigations documented a pattern of money laundering, tax evasion, arms trafficking, terrorism financing, human trafficking, and the illegal purchase of real state and other banks.

Since the mid-1980s, a number of links between BCCI and organized criminal enterprises have been documented. The U.S. government laundered more than $10 billion of Medellin drug money by accepting cash and placing it in certificates of deposit (CDs) in its European, Central American, and South American branches. Bank officials created accounts accessible as loans to the traffickers at other branches that permitted them to withdraw the funds, and then the banks used the CDs to repay the loans. Terrorist for hire Abu Nidal kept $60 million in the London branch of BCCI (Kelly, Maghan, and Serio, 2006).

Ultimately, BCCI was declared worthless after at least $13 billion was found missing and it was shut down in 1991. Perhaps 1 million investors suffered losses. One former Senate investigator, Jack Blum, testified to a congressional committee in 1991,

> This bank was a product of the Afghan War and people very close to the mujahedin have said that many Pakistani military officials who were deeply involved in assisting and supporting the Afghan movement were stealing our foreign assistance money and using BCCI to hide the money they stole; and to market American weapons that were to be delivered that they stole; and to market and manage funds that came from the selling of heroin that was apparently engineered by one of the mujahedin groups. (Engdahl and Steinberg 1995)

Perhaps what was most troubling to many observers was the cast of characters caught up in this monumental web of scandal, ranging from terrorist leader Abu Nidal to former U.S. Defense Secretary and long-time friend to presidents Clark Clifford. Clifford was especially tarnished by his association with the bank, which he claimed he was introduced to by a business partner and long-time friend of President Jimmy Carter, Bert Lance. One BCCI director, James Reynolds Bath, had been a business partner of future President George W. Bush and went on to make millions in complex business arrangements with the family of Osama bin Laden. Despite lawsuits and prosecutions on both sides of the Atlantic, a firm of independent auditors reported in 2002 that BCCI had continued its illegal operations even after its official revelations, using copies of its confiscated records to keep the illicit cash flowing.

Overview

Chapter 6 examines syndicated criminal activities revolving around legally prohibited commerce—drugs, alcohol, prostitution, and gambling. This chapter demonstrates the involvement of organized crime in the traffic of legal goods and the accompanying businesses. "One of the reasons we fail to understand organized crime is because we put crime into a category that is separate from normal business. Much crime does not fit into a separate category. It is primarily a business activity" (Chambliss, 1978, 53, quoted in Wright, 2006, 50). Mob observer Jerry Capeci opined that members and associates of organized crime groups "have long used just about every method they could dream up to turn an illegal buck" (2002, 169). Indeed, the businesses of organized crime are endless and impossible to cover completely in one book, let alone in one chapter. However, this chapter examines a number of proven moneymakers, including money laundering and loansharking, the pornography business, banking fraud, human smuggling and trafficking, and labor racketeering in a variety of industries.

An examination of the business of organized crime reveals the centrality of the so-called protection rackets to most of the more traditional criminal enterprises, both illicit and licit. Italian sociologist Diego Gambetta and others have demonstrated that many individuals from every walk of life "find it in their individual interest to buy Mafia protection. While some may be victims of extortion, many others are willing customers" (Gambetta 1998). Nowhere was this truer than with the burgeoning labor unions, where racketeers either forcefully insinuated their way into the unions or were asked in by the employers or union leaders. Alan Block perhaps hit the nail on the head when he observed, "Modern capitalism created lucrative new enterprises for criminals" (1991, 15). The rise of organized labor and the subsequent reaction of American businesses generated a conflict that provided fertile ground for the seeds of racketeering and organized crime. Crime syndicates provided virtual "mercenary armies" of tough guys willing to use violence to organize workers or thwart strikebreakers. Although a variety of labor unions have been linked to organized crime, four have historically had the closest and most documented relationships with criminal organizations—the IBT, ILA, LIUNA, and HEREIU. The question then comes up as to why some unions and industries are more susceptible to organized crime infiltration than others. The answer lies in the propensity of certain industries for management and labor to bring in racketeers to defend their interests in the struggle over unionization and corporate competition. In some cases, as in New York City's longshoremen and, nationally, various Locals of the Teamsters, gangsters ended up controlling aspects of the union or the industry and in some cases both, after gaining power in key union positions or after forming employer associations.

Businesses and industries most susceptible to labor and business racketeering are usually in smaller or disorganized industries, low-tech ones that require workers with only a modicum of skill and where there is usually an oversupply of labor, such as in garbage hauling and construction (Kelly 1999, 227–228).

Globalization has opened and expanded markets that have reshaped the businesses of organized crime. As Moises Naim most recently noted, "Networks with capabilities to move illicit goods across borders have diversified into new geographies and added new products to their existing ones" (2005, 157–158). Organized crime groups in India and South America, for example have been linked to human organ trade, whereas others have found profits in smuggling endangered species, forged airplane parts, fake pharmaceuticals, and various counterfeit consumer products. Cars stolen in New York have been traced as far away as China. Any attempts at determining the annual volume of the global shadow economy is mere conjecture, because by its very nature, global organized crime is unregulated and unsupervised, leaving few measures to go by.

Every generation produces new opportunities for criminal activity. Typically, at least in American history, the first to grasp these opportunities were the newest immigrants. From Irish, Italian, and Jewish immigrants to today's Central Americans and Eastern Europeans, there are plenty of examples demonstrating how newcomers have been the first to detect and exploit these opportunities even before the established players. According to Naim, "It is the new entrants who often take advantage of untapped market niches that appear thanks to a new source of supply, a new set of customers, or new technologies" (2005, 158). Indeed, new illicit global networks have emerged in the last few decades dealing in such obscure or niche products as human organs, endangered species, hazardous wastes, and stolen art all operated with the same methods used in better-known rackets such as stolen cars, illegal logging, smuggled cigarettes, but without as much official scrutiny or media coverage.

There are signs that organized crime has been shifting much of its attention from drugs and arms trafficking toward human trafficking and smuggling, pursuits that in which the profits remain high but the risk of punishment much lower from weapons, drugs, and other activities. Most crime watchers agree that what is most attractive about the human trade is the fact that there is an unquenchable thirst for immigration around the world, leading to a continuous flow of profits. Although this crime is probably as old as history, world events since the mid-1980s have fueled its growth. Many observers cite globalization for influencing the movement of people from poorer countries to wealthier climes. Poverty, despair, war, and civil crisis all play a central role, as do the economic dislocations that have followed the collapse of communism.

Globally, human smuggling and trafficking remains one of organized crime's major sources of income, and the impact is felt by nearly every country in the world. Those in the trade have exploited wars, civil strife, natural disasters (such as the 2004 Indian Ocean tsunami), and the weakening of law enforcement in various parts of the world. Much of the traffic follows a pattern of rural to urban migration. There are still societies that favor sons over daughters, and where daughters are viewed as economic burdens. It should not be surprising that the majority of those trafficked are women under the age of 25. Sex tourism still flourishes in parts of Asia, and the demand for trafficked women and children for the sex workers, cheap sweatshop labor, and domestic workers remains high. There have even been cases reported in which daughters were sold to traffickers or brothels to avoid paying the dowry it would require to marry them off (Miko 2007, 37).

In 1994, the United Nations identified 18 activities regarded as being endemic in transnational organized crime, most of which are listed in the following box,

Primary Activities of Organized Crime	
Arms dealing	Smuggling women and children for sex
Counterfeiting	Smuggling stolen vehicles
Drug trafficking	Smuggling human organs
Extortion and protection rackets	Smuggling protected flora and fauna
Fraud and corporate crime	Smuggling art and cultural artifacts
Illegal vice	Terrorism
Labor racketeering	Theft, robbery, hijacking, kidnapping
Loansharking	White-collar and corporate crime
Marine piracy	Smuggling illegal immigrants
(Wright 2006)	

No one is impacted by organized crime's infiltration into legitimate businesses more than the consumer, both of illicit and licit commodities, who pay the costs for doing business with mobsters. Not only does it increase living costs for the legitimate consumer, but it also hits criminals and criminal organizations in the pocketbook as well. For example, the U.S. government strategy of following money trail has driven up traffickers' costs of doing business, now paying 6% to 25% to get money "collected, washed, and into his pocket. The downside is that the added expenses are reflected in the street price, and there is a direct correlation between increased street prices and increased street crime" (Robinson 1998, 388–389).

In April 2008, U.S. Attorney General Michael B. Mukasey warned of the rising threat from international organized crime, proclaiming, "a new breed of mobsters around the world is infiltrating strategic industries [and were] capable of creating havoc in our economic infrastructure" (Schmitt 2008). He announced that one of his first law enforcement initiatives since his appointment to attorney general the previous fall was his intention to resuscitate the Organized Crime Council (which last met in the 1990s), first established during the Johnson administration of the 1960s. Mukasey noted that organized criminals "are more involved in our everyday lives than many appreciate, [touching] all sectors of our economy" (Schmitt 2008). Anyone who studies organized crime understands this is long overdue. His stated intentions to go after money launderers, extortionists in the construction industry, human smugglers, and other actors is best understood as the latest phase in an ongoing conflict between organized crime and the justice sector dating back to the 1920s and 1930s (Schmitt 2008).

Key Terms

Rackets
Labor racketeering
Garment trade
Dopey Benny Fein
Lepke Buchalter
Jacob "Gurrah" Shapiro
Johnny Dio
Bioff and Brown
IATSE
The Big Four unions
IBT
ILA
HEREIU
LIUNA
Longshoremen
"Shape up"
Tough Tony Anastasio
Waterfront Commission
Fulton Fish Market
On the Waterfront
Robert F. Kennedy

The Enemy Within
James Hoffa
Teamsters
Tony Provenzano
Teamsters Local 560
Central States Pension Fund
Red Dorfman
Allen Dorfman
Allen Glick
Argent Corporation
Frank "Lefty" Rosenthal
Roy Williams
Waste and garbage hauling business
Rudy Giuliani
The Long Island Cartel
Tony "Ducks" Corallo
Teamsters Local 813
Concrete and cement scams
Loansharking
"Shylocking"
Salary lending

Knockdown
Vig/Vigorish
"Sit-down"
San Gennaro Festival
Bust-out scheme
Human trafficking
Human smuggling
NAFTA
Deep Throat
Peraino Family
Money laundering
Bank Secrecy Act
Currency Transaction Report
Smurfing
Layering
"Shell" companies
Offshore banking
Integration
The BCCI Scandal

Critical Thinking Questions

1. What is the difference between *racketeering* and *organized crime*?
2. What is *labor racketeering,* and what types of unions are most susceptible to organized crime infiltration?
3. Discuss the evolution of the garment trades and the accompanying rackets. What was Louis "Lepke" Buchalter's involvement?
4. How did the Mob infiltrate the motion picture unions? What were the results?
5. What are the Big Four unions?
6. Who controlled New York's waterfront? Discuss the docks and the ILA prior to the 1953 Waterfront Commission.

7. What did the Fulton Fish Market have in common with waterfront rackets? Which crime families were involved?

8. Why and when did the Teamsters come to power? Why did they have such influence? What was the Central States Pension Fund, and how did organized crime syndicates exploit it?

9. What role did Jimmy Hoffa play in the nexus of the union movement and organized crime? Did Hoffa deserve the accolades of the union rank and file?

10. Why is the garbage disposal and waste hauling business so prone to racketeering? What characteristics does it share with other mobbed-up industries?

11. What has been the impact of organized crime on New York City's construction trade unions? Who wins and who loses?

12. Why is loansharking such a lucrative business? How did it become a mainstay for organized crime groups? How does a loanshark racket operate, and does it have any structure?

13. What kinds of payback schemes are available to borrowers? What are the myths and realities of loansharking?

14. What is the *bust-out* scheme?

15. What is the difference between *human trafficking* and *smuggling*? Give examples of each.

16. Why did organized crime get involved in the pornography business? Was it lucrative, and does it remain an important source of revenue?

17. What is *money laundering*? Has it always been illegal? How is it accomplished? Is it easier today than times past?

Endnotes

1. See Chapter 14 for more on RICO statutes.

2. Adapted from John Landesco, *Organized Crime in Chicago* (1929, 149–150).

3. FIOA, Louis "Lepke" Buchalter file, 62-99379-9, Memorandum, Aug. 19, 1955, p. 1, in author's collection.

4. The needle-trades union was synonymous with the garment manufacturing industry in its early years.

5. The Italian bread racket was also run by the aforementioned Gennaro Calabrese.

6. One Mob historian described Browne as "a pickled oaf supposedly capable of drinking a hundred bottles of beer every day" (Fox 1989, 212).

7. These included Frank Nitti, "Lepke" Buchalter, "Lucky" Luciano, "Longy" Zwillman, and others.

8. His brother Albert Anastasia (yes, they spelled their last names differently), headed Murder, Inc., and led the crime family that eventually became the Gambinos.

9. There are a number of excellent sources on Hoffa, including but not limited to Brill, *Teamsters,* 1978; Franco, *Hoffa's Man*, 1987; Hoffa, *Hoffa,* 1975; Moldea, *Hoffa Wars* 1978; and Sloane, *Hoffa,* 1991.

10. Other pension funds were operated more professionally by companies such as Prudential. Contrary to Hoffa's protocol, the insurance giant brooked no interference from labor leaders when it came to controlling investments.

11. These included the Aladdin, Caesar's Palace, Circus Circus, the Desert Inn, the Fremont, the Lodestar, the Stardust, and others.

12. *Argent* was the acronym for Allen R. Glick Enterprises, as well as French for money, although it is doubtful any involved spoke French (besides Glick).

13. Adapted from Jacobs, Panarella, and Worthington, 1994, pp. 189–190. The testimony revolved around the loan requested by Allen Glick to purchase casinos for "his" Argent Corporation. Civella was the boss of the Kansas City family and the agent through whom Williams, later the president of the IBT, was dominated by the Mob.

14. Vincent "Jimmy" Squillante was a close associate of Mob boss Albert Anastasia and rose to prominence as he muscled into the commercial carting industry as a "labor relations expert" in 1953.

15. Rates were only $4.90 per cubic yard in 1974; but Mob infiltration in the business led to a stratospheric increase to almost $15 per cubic yard by the late 1980s.

16. As opposed to business haulers, residential garbage is collected by New York City's Sanitation Department.

17. Colombo construction-business specialist Ralph Scopo was sentenced to 100 years in prison for labor racketeering during the historic Commission case and died in prison.

18. The term *shylocking* is actually a "bastardization" of William Shakespeare's Jewish money-lending antagonist Shylock, in *The Merchant of Venice* (Russo, 2001, 117).

19. See *Upon the Hip—A Study of the Criminal Loanshark Industry,* Ann Arbor, MI: University Microfilms, 1968, p. 239.

20. Selwyn Raab points out that this sardonically named hangout was apparently "a nostalgic misspelling of Bergen Street in East New York, the [Gambino] gang's roots" (2005, 354).

21. This information is adapted from International Labour Organization—International Programme on the Elimination of Child Labour. (2005). *Child Trafficking—The People Involved: A Synthesis of Findings from Albania, Moldova, Romania and Ukraine,* Geneva, ILO-IPEC.

22. Their father Giuseppe was a member of the Profaci family and was killed in 1931.

23. At a $2.05 ticket price, a $600 million box-office return would require every man, woman, and child in the United States to have seen it 1.5 times. In addition, there was no mass video market until the late 1970s.

24. In less than 10 years, *Chainsaw* boasted box office earnings of close to $50 million.

25. Only months after the release of this list, the Bahamas, Cayman Islands, Cook Islands, Israel, Liechtenstein, the Marshall Islands, and Panama took major steps toward complying with the new standards (Naim 2005, 153).

26. Dubbed so by former CIA head Robert Gates in a story in *Time* magazine.

27. This small country between France and Germany is known for its bank secrecy laws and casual regulations.

CHAPTER 8

Homegrown Organized Crime: Outlaw Motorcycle Gangs, Prison Gangs, and Urban Street Gangs

The term *gang* conjures up a number of sinister specters in the 21st century—Outlaw Motorcycle Gangs (OMGs), urban street gangs, and prison gangs to name just the most prominent today. In 1997, the Chief of the FBI's Violent Crime and Major Offenders Section lamented that among the basic obstacles in addressing gang activity "is the absence of a universal definition for gangs, and the difficulty in documenting the nature and extent of gang related activity" (Wiley 1997, 1). The FBI defined a *Violent Street Gang/Drug Enterprise* as a criminal enterprise having an organizational structure, acting as a continuing criminal conspiracy, which employs violence and any other criminal activity to sustain the enterprise (FBI 1997).

During the first three months of 1983, Congress held hearings on organized crime in Washington, D.C.[1] Most of the focus of the hearings related to organized drug trafficking. However, what made these hearings a landmark was the fact that the focus had shifted from traditional organized crime groups such as La Cosa Nostra to the growing prominence of outlaw motorcycle gangs, urban street gangs, and prison gangs. Attorney General William French Smith noted that since the early 1970s, close to 800 outlaw motorcycle gangs had developed in the United States and in foreign countries (1983, 11). Of these, he cited the Hells[2] Angels, the Outlaws, the Pagans, and the Bandidos as the most influential.

French went on to note the emergence of prison gangs as another form of non-traditional organized crime. He traced their origins to the California prison system in the 1960s and 1970s, but noted that although they were "predominately a West Coast phenomenon," there is evidence they are spreading (1983, 11). French argued that the prison gangs like the OMGs, have a "Big Four" as well—La Nuestra Familia, the Mexican Mafia, the Aryan Brotherhood, and the Black Guerrilla Family. Although race still plays a key role in prison gang dynamics, it is overshadowed by organized crime activities in the larger gangs, as they pursue an agenda based on drug running, protection rackets, prostitution, witness intimidation, money laundering, and other criminal acts.

By most accounts, the Aryan Brotherhood was the first of the major race-based prison gangs. Gangs have proliferated only since the 1960s with many new White, Black, Hispanic, and mixed gangs on the scene. One of the best explanations for the expansion of prison gangs was that until the 1960s, most prisons were segregated. However, with the desegregation of the 1960s, mixed prison populations gave birth to ethnic and racially based gangs for protection and criminal racketeering (Anti-Defamation League 2002).[3]

The years 1946 to 1967 are considered to be the formative years of the OMGs, as larger clubs absorbed smaller ones and formal organization structures were put in place allowing the clubs to morph into OMGs. The 1960s were considered most significant due to the prominence and proliferation of the drug culture. It was during this era that the gangs first started using drugs before gravitating to trafficking in them. In the process, the major OMGs have become increasingly sophisticated and have diversified their operations. Although OMGs usually have fewer member than most large street gangs, they are better organized, with numerous chapters with bylaws (constitutions) established by a national or international hierarchy. What is most troubling from a law enforcement perspective is that the leading OMGs have developed international connections that provide them with access to wholesale quantities of illegal drugs. For example, in February 2004, three members of the Dutch Hells Angels were killed following the theft of $11 million in cocaine. A subsequent investigation revealed their international ties to Colombian drug dealers. In this case, the drugs were shipped from the Revolutionary Armed Forces of Colombia (FARC) to Amsterdam via a new Hells Angels chapter on the Caribbean island of Curacao (Marsden and Sher 2006).

In 2006, the National Drug Intelligence Center (NDIC) released its report *Organized Gangs and Drug Trafficking,* and reported that

> street gangs, prison gangs, and outlaw motorcycle gangs (OMGs) have long been and continue to be the predominant organized retail drug distributors; their level of organization is the key factor that renders gangs a significant threat that gangs pose to the nation, their influence with respect to drug smuggling, transportation, and wholesale distribution has increased sharply. (NDIC 2006, 1)

Its strategic findings indicated several important trends, among the most significant concerning organize crime was that street gangs and prison gangs have, to varying degrees, established relationships with Mexican drug-trafficking organizations (DTOs), which enabled these gangs to evolve from primarily retail-level distributors of drugs to significant smugglers, transporters, and wholesale distributors.

According to the NDIC, the estimated number of gang members in the United States has decreased over the past few years[4]; however, the proliferation of gangs and their involvement in drug activity continue to increase throughout the country, particularly in rural and suburban areas. Despite the diminished numbers, by virtue of increasing involvement in drug smuggling, transportation, and wholesale distribution has only augmented the significance of homegrown gangs in the organized crime continuum.

A number of issues have contributed to the evolving street gang phenomenon. Although in the minority, a number of national-level street gangs have evolved from turf oriented gangs to sophisticated, profit-driven, organized crime enterprises that engage in poly-drug trafficking activities as well the aforementioned aspects of the trade, include smuggling, transportation, and wholesale distribution. Some of the more prominent exemplars of these gangs are found in Chicago and Los Angeles. The NDIC recently estimated that some national-level street gangs are highly organized, with as many as 100,000 members and associates. The most highly organized include Latin Kings, Gangster Disciples, and Vice Lords, all featuring centralized leadership cores that direct various enterprises in addition to the drug trade. Although it has been exaggerated by the media, high-profile gangs have proliferated in areas throughout country not previously affected by gang activity, either by means of "emulation, migration, or a combination of both" (NDIC, January 2006).

OUTLAW MOTORCYCLE GANGS

Returning to America from World War II, servicemen were confronted with a changing home front. Many returned with different cultural values than the ones they went off to war with. In the aftermath of the war, "groups of young men, many newly-returned soldiers formed motorcycle clubs and rejected normal civilian lifestyles." As the 1940s moved to conclusion the behavior of these gangs "became not so boisterous as surly, less rebellious than openly criminal" (PCOC 1986, 58). In the aftermath of a highly publicized motorcycle riot in Hollister, California, in 1947, the phrase *outlaw motorcycle* was reportedly used for the first time, referring to the actions of a gang that evolved into the notorious Hells Angels. The July 21, 1947, issue of *Life* magazine featured the story of the "Fourth of July debauch" at Hollister, California. The short piece was emblazoned with the headline, "Cyclists' Holiday: He and Friends Terrorize a Town." Most research on the subject indicates not much actually happened there that day, and when the day was done the bikers paid their fines, accepted their jail terms, and left town. In any case this incident entered biker lore as the "birth of the American biker," if not in reality, at least in the American consciousness. Barely seven years later, Hollywood capitalized on the Hollister incident in the Marlon Brando–vehicle, *The Wild One*,[5] further embellishing the mythology of a growing biker culture. More than a half-century since the "epochal event," the town of Hollister continues to embrace the incident that put it on the map.

Concerned for the image of the nascent motorcycle culture in the 1950s, the American Motorcycle Association issued a proclamation that only 1% of motorcycle owners are criminally inclined desperadoes. Since then, Hells Angels and others have adopted the slogan as a badge of honor by wearing "1%" patches on their vests.

The years between 1947 and 1967 have been called "the formative years" for motorcycle gangs, an era in which "they spawned imitators; major clubs absorbed smaller ones—or pushed them aside; roaming members of chapters called 'Nomads' carried the seeds of new chapters and formulated gang alliances. Formal organizational structures were put in place; leaders developed" (PCOC 1983, 380). In the Vietnam War era, returning vets, much more disenchanted than those from previous wars, returned home by the thousands, but this time they brought with them well-honed weapons and explosives skills. During the 1960s and 1970s the OMGs, especially Hells Angels, began an unprecedented expansion, much of it fueled by the expanding drug business. It was the 1970s that saw OMGs make the transition from mostly participants in the drug subculture as users to major drug traffickers.

What makes OMGs so unique in the world of organized crime is the public display of their colors and other links to their criminality. However, they share with more established organized crime groups most of the traditional characteristics, including maintaining legitimate businesses as fronts for money laundering, a structured hierarchy, drugs and weapons trafficking, sophistication, secret rules and restricted membership, as well as others. Other OMG activities include supplying strippers and prostitutes to night and dance clubs, extortion, organized theft, fraud, and contract killings (Nicaso and Lamothe 2005).

Biker Counterintelligence

At one time OMGs were expert at vetting new members. For many years, gangs such as Hells Angels, prided themselves on their impenetrability—due to a long recruitment process lasting from so-called *hangaround* to prospect to full patch member, coupled with extensive background checks designed to weed out cops and informers. It has long been an accepted part of the club's protocol to conduct full background checks on potential members—including their criminal history and credit cards, conducted through the Internet using special software. In other cases, wives, girlfriends, and associates have found jobs with government agencies, giving them access to this information (Marsden and Sher 2006, 197). More recently, the gangs are showing chinks in their armor as undercover officers have infiltrated each gang. Bikers typically employ private investigators to check out prospects or potential business partners. New members in the Mongols, for instance, are required to submit six years of W-2 tax forms and phone numbers of family members. They even check high school yearbook photos and information. OMGs have been observed by law enforcement conducting surveillance on police officers and prosecutors (Davis 1982).

FIGURE 8.1 Motorcycle gang member displaying colors
Source: Pearson Education/PH College/Charles Gatewood

Structure of OMGs

Chapters are considered the foundation on which most OMGs are structured. Chapters control defined geographic areas where activities are conducted. Each chapter is led by a president and has varying degrees of independence from other chapters. Members are usually Caucasian males—racist and misogynist elements. Prospective members are subject to intense screening to root out informers or undercover agents. Loyalty to the club is demanded; most gangs have bylaws or a constitution that governs behavior both inside and outside the group. Mutual support among all members under all circumstances is expected, especially in the facilitation of criminal activities.

Butch Testifies Before 1983 Organized Crime Hearings[6]

Senator Grassley: What is the role of the intelligence officer in Hells Angels and what type of intelligence information do the Hells Angels maintain?

BUTCH: The intelligence officer was established back in 1974–1973—and it was an office to gather all information they could on the Outlaws, Pagans, any club in the United States, any police officer, any newsmen, anybody that the Hells Angels had a grudge against, and they gathered it up from all the different people they know. The Hells Angels know a lot of people. They call them spies. They bring them information on this or that, and they collect all their addresses and everything. . . . They keep a record of a person, of families, the whole smear [*sic*], addresses, types of cars, what girls they used to go with or whatever, bike clubs. (1983, 411–412)

OMG Hierarchy/Canada

President: Leader of the gang with full authority over the members. The Bandidos refer to him as *El Presidente*.

Vice President: Assumes president's duties in his absence.

Secretary/Treasurer: Handles the money and keeps the books.

Sergeant-at-Arms: Enforces discipline and maintains armory. Referred to as *Sargento de Armas* in the Bandidos.

Road Captain: Rides at the front of the pack and deals with police during events.

Full-Patch Member: Full members of the gang who wear full colors, pay dues, and have voting rights. Must be approved by unanimous vote of full members. The Bandidos also have honorary members who have retired from gang life but are permitted to wear the colors still.

Prospect: Prospective members are sometimes called *strikers* or *probates*. Must perform onerous tasks to prove their value, Can wear some gang badges but not full colors.

Hangaround: Act as associates and guards for gang members. Wear only the city patch for the gang.

Friend: An official status between associate and hangaround in the Hells Angels.

Associate: Someone who has been useful to the gang. May attend parties and events, but can't wear colors.

(Criminal Intelligence Service Canada, 2004)

Women and Bikers

Bikers typically regard women as property. In one case, a member of the Hells Angels nailed his girlfriend to a tree after she refused to turn a $10 trick. Her "brazen" excuse was that the john never showed up (Lavigne 1987). Biker women fall into three categories. *Mamas* or *Sheep* belong to all of the members of the club and are subject to the gang's sexual whims when they are not performing routine tasks in the clubhouse. Some clubs allow them to wear the gang's colors with the inscription "Property of [club]" embroidered on the back. An *Old Lady* is considered a step up the food chain of respect in the notoriously misogynist OMGs. These are wives or steady girlfriends of club members and are off limits to other members. Old Ladies are prohibited from attending club meetings, but in some clubs are permitted to wear the club colors with "Property of [particular biker]" sewn on the back. Finally there is the *Broad,* women viewed as the most disposable, picked up for just an evening's pleasure and humiliation, often in the form of a rape. OMGs use women as couriers for the purchase of weapons, particularly in bars near military bases, where they can convince servicemen to do them favors for sex. Other women are put to work as prostitutes or strippers and are expected to hand all money over to the club.

BIKER FUNERALS   Nothing gets bikers out like a funeral. These are considered major social events as gang members convene from around the country. Like Mafia funerals, law enforcement agents monitor these closely, which are considered a major source for intelligence gathering. Each gang has its traditions. The Outlaws, for example, allow only other Outlaws to toss dirt on the grave. Guns are often fired (in the air) at graveside.

Hells Angels (Motto: "Three can keep a secret if two are dead".)

During its more than 50-year history the Hells Angels made the transition from a club dedicated to partying and bikes to what is now a multinational, multimillion-dollar business. In that time, it has set the standard for OMGs throughout the world. The Hells Angels originated in 1947 as the

---

Legitimate Business of the Hells Angels: Testimony before Congress (1983)

Mr. Short: How much money would you estimate is made by the Hells Angels organization, and is this money used to infiltrate and buy into legitimate business?

Mr. Bertolani: From the several investigations that I have been involved in, it would be safe to say that the Hells Angels motorcycle club's drug operation has produced revenues in the millions and probably the billions. Although it would be almost impossible to determine the exact amount of moneys made through illegal activities engaged in by members . . . we have learned from our investigation that the primary source of income for the Hells Angels is the manufacture and distribution of methamphetamines. . . . A prime example of [legitimate businesses] is the activities of the previously cited [member]. He started off as a motorcycle rider in 1973. He opened a body shop, investing $200,000 in that. He later invested money in a motorcycle shop, sold both of those, and began Siesta Catering in 1976 as a small catering company. . . . After a pattern of intimidation through bombings and fire bombings, he operated the business until about 1980, at which time he sold it for about $6 million. (1983, 368)

POBOBS, or Pissed Off Bastards of Bloomington, under the aegis of Otto Freidli. On March 17, 1948, the Hells Angels opened its first chapter (under the Angels moniker) in San Bernardino, California, better known to biker aficionados as *Berdoo* (also shortened so it would fit on the bottom rocker of their colors). A number of the gang's early members were war veterans who readily named their club *Hells Angels,*[7] a name they were partial to during World War II (the term dates back to the planes of World War I). The 303rd Bombardier Squadron in England christened several planes *Hells Angels.* After the war, some former Angels "exchanged their wings for wheels and formed motorcycle gangs" (Lavigne 1987, 27).

In the mid-1960s, the Angels modified their colors. Members called the crude death's head patch the bumblebee patch. Berdoo originally signified the first chapter formed around 1948. California Angels replaced the bottom rockers bearing chapter names with a generic one bearing only the state name to prevent easy identification by police (Lavigne 1987). During the 1960s the club was considered foundering financially, with most of its members working flunky jobs if they worked at all.

For an anti-establishment organization, the Angels have remained fervently patriotic, in no small part due to its military veteran founders. It is somewhat ironic that a group that served in the war and boasted of its patriotism and 100% Americanism would later adopt swastikas as a prominent symbol—but that would come later.

Hells Angels, Canada

In 2006, the Criminal Intelligence Service Canada (CISC) described the Hells Angels as "the foremost organized crime group in the country, topping traditional Mafia and ethnic gangs" (CBC 2006, 2). The Angels have a much more prominent presence in Canada than in the United States. Canada alone has 32 active chapters with 500 full members. The largest and most prominent chapter of the Hells Angels was established in Montreal, and by 1977 had merged with the local Popeyes OMG. Some experts claim that the Hells Angels and other OMGs took advantage of the vacuum in organized crime leadership left by the 1970s Royal Commission on Organized Crime with its crackdown on Mafia activities, thereby reducing their potential competitors.

In the mid-1980s, the Rock Machine emerged out of Quebec to become the Angels' fiercest rival. During the 1990s, war over the drug trade between the two gangs left 150 dead. As a result of the murders of two prison guards and the death of an 11-year-old bystander in a car bomb attack, the Canadian criminal justice system came down hard on all OMGs. The passage of Bill C-95 led to stiffer penalties for convicted offenders who had tangible links to organized criminal groups. In 2004, the CISC claimed

FIGURE 8.2   Motorcycle parked outside Hells Angels Building in New York City
Source: Pearson Education/PH College/Eugene Gordon

the law was making inroads on gang activity, citing the much lower profiles of the Canadian Outlaws and Bandidos, and the Hells Angels organization in decline through much of Canada (CBC 2006).

Interestingly, in March 2005, the Hells Angels opened its newest official store in Prince Edward Island, joining a chain of stores called Route 81, the 8-1 standing for the letter positions in the alphabet of H-A. The new outlet joined ones already operating in Monkton, Halifax, and Toronto.

Overview of Biker Crime in Canada

- There were 500 members across Hells Angels chapters, of which two chapters in Quebec were listed as "inactive."
- In British Columbia, Quebec, and Ontario, the Angels "remain sophisticated and well established."
- Outlaws and Bandidos have kept a low profile since crackdowns in 2002; the Outlaws had seven chapters in Ontario, but only three of them had any degree of stability; the Bandidos had one full chapter in Alberta—sparking fears the move indicates a potential move against the Hells Angels.
- Although the Angels' influence is growing in British Columbia—their most stable location—and in Ontario—through ties to Italian organized crime groups—it appears to be waning in Alberta, Manitoba, Quebec, and Atlantic Canada.

Criminal Intelligence Service of Canada, 2004 (Nicaso and Lamothe 2005, 227).

Becoming an Angel: Prospect/Striker to Membership

To become a member of Hells Angels, a prospect or striker must undergo a grueling process, beginning at the lowly level as a *hangaround.* At this level, he gets to meet and interact with the gang members. A member of good standing must then nominate him for prospective membership. Once this occurs, then begins a seeming inexorable process of "gofer" and "grunt" jobs, serving every whim of club members to their satisfaction. They are on virtual call 24/7, a process that can range from 6 months to 5 years, with the average time about 18 months. A prospect is prohibited from wearing the Angels colors and bottom rocker, and is typically identifiable by an armband or sleeveless vest with rocker. Once his status is put to a vote, he must garner 100% of the vote. He is allowed three chances to win unanimity, and if he fails after the third attempt, he is unceremoniously kicked out. Once a prospect makes the transition to member, he is usually required to commit a crime to prove his worth. Some chapters have reportedly required a prospect to commit murder to earn his colors, much the same way a wiseguy might garner entrance into a traditional crime family.

In June 2005, the Canadian Hells Angels were officially declared a criminal organization following the verdict in the Lindsay–Bonner case, in which two Hells Angels were accused of conducting an extortion racket while both wore the Angels colors. The judge ruled that

> I am satisfied beyond a reasonable doubt that during the time period specified in count two of the indictment, the HAMC as it existed in Canada was a criminal organization. I am satisfied beyond a reasonable doubt that both Mr. Lindsay and Mr. Bonner committed the offense of extortion in association with that criminal organization. (*R. v. Lindsay,* 2005)

Traditional Rules

Due to its white supremacist leanings, the club does not accept Black members, although there are several Jewish members. A member must be 21 and is expected to own a Harley Davidson (this is no longer true). Women are prohibited from membership. Other prohibitions include those against needle injection of drugs and *mudchecking,* Angel parlance for fighting. When a member moves into another chapter's territory, he is expected to shift his membership to it.

STRUCTURE   Most chapters maintain size limits as a way of controlling its members. Organizationally, the club is hierarchically structured in an attempt to protect and insulate club leaders. Some experts compare the OMG structure with that of traditional organized crime, with which it was aligned in 1970s and 1980s. This includes enforcing a code of silence. The Hells Angels differ from the other groups of the Big Four in that they do not have a national president or national officers to plot the gang's future.

Several observers have remarked on the operational similarities between traditional organized crime and the Commission and the Angels. For example, the club is divided into two factions, with Omaha, Nebraska, the dividing line. Each faction has an annually elected president, vice president,

Hells Angels and Traditional Organized Crime: Hierarchical Comparisons

Chapter President	**Family Boss**
Secretary (most logical member)	*Consigliere*
Vice President	Underboss
Sergeant at Arms	*Caporegima*
Members	Soldiers

recording secretary, and treasurer. The president of the West Coast faction is responsible for chapters on the American and Canadian west coasts, Alaska, Australia, and New Zealand. The East Coast president presides over all other chapters, including those in Europe and South America.

Officers meet every three months in different chapter areas, not unlike the old Commission. When club leaders meet, they discuss family business, such as how to financially assist another chapter, whether a new chapter should be admitted, how many patches need to be ordered, and the like. The discussion of drug deals and crimes are prohibited from the discussion. Both organizations reputedly control the vicinities where they commit their crimes, both are known to corrupt police and public officials, and both use associates and fronts to manipulate and influence people.

Both Hells Angels factions have their own treasuries to which each chapter is expected to contribute. This money is used for legal expenses or to defray travel costs on fact-finding trips to other countries, as well as to purchase confidential police reports.

HELLS ANGELS STRUCTURE AND DUTIES   The prototypical structure of each club begins at the top with the chapter president, who is elected—or, in some cases, self-appointed if he carries enough clout in the overall organizations. He has final say on club business and can overrule any vote by club members. On club runs, he rides in front of the pack next to the center line and beside road captain. Members follow in two columns behind them and do not pass/stray unless they have mechanical problems.

The chapter vice-president is typically selected by the president and is considered heir apparent. He often acts in the capacity of the leader when the president is absent. During a run, he takes his place in the double column behind the president and road captain. The secretary–treasurer's duties include keeping club minutes at meetings, collecting dues and fines, paying club bills, and arranging bond for members who have been arrested. He is also expected to have the list of addresses and phone numbers of members and to keep accurate records on club business.

The sergeant-at-arms is usually the club's most formidable member when it comes to violence and acts as the president's bodyguard, chapter enforcer, and club executioner. It is up to him to keep everyone in line during meetings and outings. During the run, he rides next to curb behind full-color members and ahead of the prospects, associates, and honorary members. Finally, the road captain is considered the club logistician and secretary chief on runs. He plans out routes and strategies for avoiding roadblocks, and responsible for food, refueling, maintenance, and carries club money for bail. In addition, he lets police know of their plans beforehand. He rides next to the president beside the curb.

By 1980, the Angels had expanded to 45 chapters. In less than 20 years it more than doubled the number of chapters to 108, having just established its latest chapter in Manaus in the Brazilian Amazon (*The Economist,* March 28, 1998). Journalists William Marsden and Julian Sher suggest that the Hells Angels are America's major crime export, tracing their membership in 2006 to 25

The U.S. v. Ralph Barger Jr., et al. (1979)

It was not until the late 1970s that law enforcement recognized Hells Angels as an organized crime group. In June 1979, the U.S. government brought RICO charges against 32 members of the gang (including Mr. Barger). In what became known as *The U.S. v. Ralph Barger Jr., et al,* the government outlined a comprehensive case alleging drugs and weapons dealing and contract murder. The "cornerstone of this illegal drug enterprise," according to the government attorneys, "was the large scale manufacture and mass distribution of methamphetamines, also known as speed and crank" (quoted in Lavigne 1987, 46). However, after 11 months, a mistrial was called when the jury failed to reach verdicts on a multi-million dollar case that featured more than 100 prosecution witnesses. Barger soon garnered a reputation that would only be exceeded by John Gotti in his halcyon days as the "Teflon Don." The government continued to go after Barger and the Angles, and in 1981, the jury once again failed to reach a verdict and a second mistrial was declared.

Ralph Hubert "Sonny" Barger (b. 1938)

If anyone has seen Hells Angels leader Sonny Barger in recent years it was probably at a Barnes & Noble bookstore signing his best-selling autobiography, *Hells Angel: The Life and Times of Sonny Barger and the Hells Angels Motorcycle Club*. Barger was born to working-class parents in Modesto, California. It's fair to say his career took him in a different direction. Barger dropped out of school in the tenth grade and enlisted in the army in 1955. He finished basic training, but during advanced infantry training it was discovered he was under age and he was discharged (honorably). He joined the Oakland chapter of Hells Angels in 1957, memorializing the date of his induction with a tattoo on his right shoulder. The following year he was elected as club president after founder Otto Friedli was sent to prison. One of Barger's first moves was moving the mother chapter from Berdoo to Oakland. Sonny worked as a machine operator from 1960 until he was fired for taking too much time off in 1965. According to Barger, between 1965 and 1973, his only income came from advising on the set of several atrocious motorcycle films. He was even featured alongside Jack Nicholson in the 1967 *Hells Angels on Wheels*. That same year, Hunter S. Thompson elevated the Angels to cult status with the publication of *Hells Angels: The Strange and Terrible Saga of the Outlaw Motorcycle Gangs*. During the 1960s, the ever-patriotic Barger wrote President Johnson, offering to form a "crack group of gorillas [*sic*]" to fight behind enemy lines (Lavigne 1987). When this favor was refused, the Angels went after local antiwar protestors at the Berkeley campus instead. Barger has had an unparalleled career as OMG member and biker entrepreneur. Despite his prominence in the club and despite the decades of media attention, Barger was never club president—because the Angels don't have one! When the gang became a beacon for the media in the 1960s, he incorporated the club and sold 500 shares in 1966 for "the promotion and advancement of motorcycle driving, motorcycle clubs, motorcycle highway safety and all phases of motorcycles and motorcycle driving" (Lavigne 1987, 38). On January 4, 1972, the Angels went a step further and patented their flying death's head emblem. In 1973, Barger was sentenced to 10 years in prison for the sale and possession of heroin and marijuana, but was paroled just 4 years later.

In 1983, Barger stepped down to fight his toughest adversary after he was diagnosed with cancer of the larynx. He had it removed and was soon back on the road with the Angels. That same year, he was identified by an agent from the ATF as one of the leaders of the gang who described him thus,

> Except for the fact that he is a Hells Angel and has frequent visitors on motorcycles wearing colors, he would appear outwardly to be an average American. He tries to maintain a low profile and not draw a lot of attention to himself unnecessarily. Barger most recently worked in a health studio in Oakland, and his wife Sharon works in another health studio. Barger's conviction record includes a 1963 conviction for narcotics, a 1966 conviction for assault with a deadly weapon, a 1973 conviction for narcotics, a 1973 conviction for false imprisonment and possession of firearms and he was also tried in a RICO in 1979. It was a hung jury and the charges were dismissed. (OC in America, 98th Cong., 1st session, 1983, 337–338)

countries, including the UK, Australia, and Holland (2006). In 2006, the FBI estimated that the gang earns $1 billion a year just from the sales of narcotics. The Canadian government estimated that it had 1,800 members in 22 countries (CBC 2006, 2).

For the modern Hells Angels, drug trafficking continues to be the main source of income. Members are known to be opportunistic and flexible—and involved in activities that include arson, assault, corruption, gambling, forgery, pornography, international white slavery, loansharking, car and cycle theft—all of which have helped transform them from motorcycle gang to international drug traffickers. During their years of collaborating with New York mobsters, they have also learned that conspicuousness can be a weakness in the drug trade.

The Bandidos (Motto: "We are the people our parents warned us against".)

The Bandidos originated in Houston, Texas, in 1966. Legend has it that ex-Marine Donald Eugene Chambers, who started the gang, borrowed the club moniker from the corn chip commercial featuring the Frito Bandito mascot (Marsden and Sher 2006).[8] More recently, the origin of the term has been tied to Chambers' affection for "Mexican bandits who refused to live by anyone's rules but their own" (Hollandsworth 2007, 134). Since the late 1960s, the gang has grown to 28 chapters in the United States. Its headquarters is in Corpus Christi, Texas.

The Bandidos came to national attention in the late 1970s, when they were incorrectly linked to several high-profile killings in Texas, leading to features on the gang on ABC's *20/20* and in *Newsweek*, which labeled them "the single greatest organized crime problem" in Texas (quoted in Hollandsworth 2007, 226). By the late 1990s, the gang was expanding its operations into Canada, Australia, and Europe

As of 2006, the Bandidos, sometimes referred to as *Bandido Nation*, is the fastest growing OMG in the United States, with 30 chapters and 500 members. The Bandidos are structured around a mother chapter, with a hierarchy of a president, four regional vice presidents, and regional and local chapter officers. Each chapter typically has a president, vice president, secretary–treasurer, sergeant-at-arms, and road captain. In some cases a club may fall below seven members; if so, it usually doesn't have a full complement of officers. The gang's security is handled by what is called a *nomad chapter*, which is responsible for counterintelligence and internal discipline. Members of this elite unit are typically charter members of longstanding. Counterintelligence often takes the form of keeping track of police activities and enemy OMGs.

The Bandidos are heavily involved in a range of organized crime activities including drug and weapons trafficking, contract killing, fencing, extortion, robbery, arson, and welfare and bank fraud. Its most lucrative activities involve the manufacturing and selling of methamphetamines. The club has members who are pilots and easily smuggle the drugs across the border and state lines.

In 1978, the Bandidos allied themselves with the Outlaws motorcycle gang in an attempt to corner drug markets. Both gangs play an important role in the distribution process, with the Outlaws obtaining cocaine from Colombian and Cuban suppliers and then middling it to the Bandidos. Both gangs consider each other brother clubs, and for solidarity also wear the other's tattoos.

The Bandidos group or OMG made its mark most recently due to the Shedden Massacre in Ontario, Canada. On April 8, 2006, four cars containing the bodies of eight gunshot victims were discovered in a rural field outside the village of Shedden. Six of the victims were identified as full Bandido members, including the acting president of the Canadian chapter. In this case, it was an inside job involving other Bandido members.

The Pagans (Motto: "Live and Die".)

The Pagans were established in Prince George's County, Maryland, in 1959. The Pagans are considered more nomadic than other clubs, and differs from the other major gangs in that it does not have a geographically fixed mother chapter. The Mother Club alternates its locations between Suffolk and Nassau Counties in Long Island, New York. A mother club composed of 13 to 18 former chapter presidents who wear black number the 13 to indicate their status leads the organization. The Pagans are the only major OMG without an international chapter (Lavigne 1987, 168; DeVito 2004). Current estimates place membership in the range from 900 to 1,000 members in 44 chapters, mostly on the East Coast.[9]

The Pagan hierarchy includes a president and a vice president who function more as figureheads than as decision makers, although they are known to set the prices for major drug-trafficking activities. According to Lavigne, the gang paid homage to its president recently by paying a salary of $200,000. Besides drug running, the Pagans have made prostitution rackets lucrative activities; however, harking back to the white slave traffic of the early 20th century, apparently not all prostitutes are willing accessories. Although some are girlfriends or female associates, law enforcement has reason to believe some are runaways or are being blackmailed into the life. Pagans are involved in a cornucopia of other criminal enterprises including operating chop shops, fraud, and weapons trafficking. Each local chapter is expected to contribute 10% of its profits to the Mother Club.

One of the difficulties of ascertaining membership is that a number of individuals prefer to remain associates and not full members. The relationship between the two statuses is mutually beneficial and is considered symbiotic. Activities illustrating this dimension include chop shops, tattoo parlors, and firearms and narcotics trafficking (New Jersey, 1989). RICO convictions took some of the luster from the Pagans' reputation when 28 members and associates were convicted or pleaded guilty to racketeering charges.

Positioned conveniently near the inner sanctum of traditional organized crime families, the Pagans are reportedly closer to the New York mob than others of the Big Four. Before the decline of the Scarfo mob in Philadelphia, both organizations cooperated with one another. More recently, they are suspected of operating as drug middlemen, enforcers, bodyguards, and killers for the Genovese and Gambino crime families. Other cooperative efforts include extortion and car-theft racketeering. The Pagans also have taken advantage of their geographic position to distribute and manufacture most of the methamphetamines and PCP in the northeast (DeVito 2004). They boast an elaborate set-up, employing their own chemists and laboratories. In the late 1990s, police sources indicated that the gang was also transporting PCP to the east from Los Angeles using female couriers, private cars, and even the postal system.

The gang has a well-earned reputation for violence and has been hired to intimidate labor unionists. It also has a special hit-team of 13 members called the "Black T-Shirt Gang." The killers' signature includes two bullets to the back of the head and then stomping of the victim. In 1998, Pagans made national news after several were arrested for selling drugs in Pennsylvania's Amish country.

The Outlaws (Motto: "God Forgives, Outlaws Don't".)

The Outlaws were inaugurated in 1959, and by 1983 were regarded as the largest OMG in the United States ((1983, 336). By 1977, the gang had gone international by absorbing a club in Canada. Founded in Chicago, Illinois, the Outlaws also go by the title "The American Outlaw Association." The Outlaws claim 34 chapters with about 900 members in North America, as well as chapters as far away as Australia. Unlike the other large OMGs, the Outlaws are more regional than national, mostly operating east of the Mississippi River, although the westernmost chapter is in Oklahoma City, the headquarters for the southern region. Detroit is headquarters for the northern region, and has been the gang's Mother Chapter since 1984.

The Outlaws refer to their sinister colors as "Charlie," a white skull with crossed pistons on a black background—a fitting homage to the Jolly Roger emblem from the golden age of piracy. According to gang lore, the emblem was borrowed from the jacket worn by Brando in *The Wild One* (it is only visible during a quick fight scene)

The Outlaws are involved in the typical panoply of criminal activities including contract killing, drug dealing, car theft, extortion, weapons running, prostitution, and mail fraud; however, drug dealing is the main source of income. Most prominent is Valium, or "Canadian Blue," manufactured in Ontario and shipped to Chicago for distribution down the chain. The more southern chapters sell cocaine transshipped by Cubans and Colombians. Favoring the vertical integration approach, the Outlaws manufacture and sell methamphetamines in the Florida area.

Each member is required to sell drugs and own at least one handgun, and members are encouraged to work in pairs to avoid mistakes and prevent a situation where several enemies hoping to make a reputation threaten one biker.

Lest there any doubt that OMGs are not considered major organized crime groups, in 1998, a top-ranking member of the Outlaws was placed on the FBI's Top Ten Most Wanted List (and arrested the following year). Harry Joseph Bowman[10] was charged with violating RICO statutes, racketeering, distribution of drugs, and other crimes. By the end of the 1990s, the Outlaws had chapters in more than 30 American cities and close to 20 chapters in at least 4 other countries. Recent estimates place the number chapters at 43 in the United States and 13 internationally (Lunde 2004).

The Outlaws consider Hells Angels to be their biggest rival, and if there was any doubt, in August 2006, around the time of the Sturgis, South Dakota, Motorcycle Rally,[11] both gangs traded gunfire in Custer State Park, leaving four Outlaws wounded. Two Canadian members of Hells Angels were arrested for the assault.

The Great Nordic OMG War: An International Perspective

The Hells Angels and the Bandidos have been engaged in a 10-year war in northern Europe that some experts call the "Great Nordic War." In 1978, the Angels awarded full-patch status to a chapter in Amsterdam. Its leader was Willem van Boxtel, who had started his own biker club in 1973 at the age of 17 and now had his sights set on becoming the Sonny Barger of Europe. Over the next several years he opened new chapters throughout Holland, and by the mid-1990s, controlled the country's biker scene. Under the aegis of van Boxtel, by 2002, there were Hells Angels chapters operating throughout northern Europe, including Denmark, Sweden, Norway, Finland, and even Eastern Europe and Russia (Marsden and Sher 2006). The expansion led to Europe's bloodiest biker war. Headquartered in Amsterdam, the gang took advantage of the country's *laissez faire* attitude toward drugs and built a drug empire. According to chroniclers of the history of OMGs, Hells Angels in effect became "gatekeepers" for the continent's drug trade, comparing it to the "Colombia of synthetic drugs" (Marsden and Sher 2006, 239). Soon after attaining chapter status, van Boxtel aimed at linking up with the hundreds of Scandinavian biker gangs, and in 1979, he gave prospect status to the rather innocuous sounding Galloping Goose gang. By 1980, the Geese were wearing Angels' wings as the first Scandinavian chapter.

In 1989, the Bandidos, who had already made their presence felt in Australia, made their first incursion into Europe, patching a club in Marseilles, France. One of their most lucrative operations was selling used Harley-Davidsons, a rare commodity in Europe, where they could be sold for twice their value. The Bandidos embarked on a strategy to expand their turf. In an attempt to discourage this, several Angels came to Marseilles and killed the Bandido vice president. However, it did not end there, as both gangs began recruiting new members from a neverending supply of recruits eager to wear the colors of American OMGs. In 1993, the Bandidos moved into Denmark, where they patched a gang called the Undertakers[12] and set up two chapters near Copenhagen. Not wanting to go to war and draw the heat of law enforcement, the Hells Angels went along with this as long as the Bandidos agreed to not patch anymore chapters in Scandinavia. Nevertheless, in January 1994, the Bandidos violated the treaty and patched another club in the region, and the war was on. The following month, the first death in the conflict was recorded after Hells Angels entered a Bandido party shooting, beginning a shootout that left one dead and three wounded. The war was about to escalate with the introduction of heavy weapons. Sweden and Denmark are dotted with small armories situated for the benefit of civilian militias. Most law-abiding citizens of these rather placid countries knew these armories were left unguarded—so did the Bandidos, who raided one of the weapons depots, getting away with 16 shoulder-fired light anti-tank weapons; hundreds of hand grenades; and crates of small arms, rifles, and ammunition (Marsden and Sher 2006). This operation would be repeated until law enforcement stepped in. Meanwhile, the Angels were busy arming themselves with Eastern European–rocket launchers and surplus machine guns purchased from former Soviet states. Despite attempts at diplomacy by the American chapters, the European chapters were on a collision course. Between 1994 and 1997, the gangs were involved in more than 400 violent incidents, ranging from bombings to beatings, leaving 11 dead and 100 wounded. At its conclusion, the police proclaimed "the Great Nordic Biker War" ended and estimated the number of dead was probably much higher, with so many missing bodies unaccounted for. OMG experts have yet to explain why "Denmark has the highest concentration of outlaw bikers in Europe and perhaps the world" (Marsden and Sher 2006, 252). In any case, both OMGs doubled in size between 1998 and 2005. The Bandidos had grown from 1 European chapter in 1989 to 70 in 2005. During the same time period, the Angels enjoyed a similar expansion.

PRISON GANGS

There has been a long debate as to whether prison gangs should be considered a form of organized crime.[13] Desegregation and the political awakening among inmates in the 1960s and 1970s made these watershed years for the development of prison gangs. With politicization came polarization between various racial and ethnic groups, diminishing the more traditional and stable prison culture.

As a result, prison gangs based on race flourished. During these years, California's prisons were at the epicenter of the Black Power movement.

Prior to the 1960s, U.S. courts allowed prisons to operate unimpeded by the courts. Much of the blame for the development of prison gangs has been focused on the 1964 U.S. Supreme Court decision *Cooper v. Pate*, which established the precedent that allowed prison inmates to sue state officials in federal court. This and other rulings laid the groundwork for the avalanche of litigation that transformed prison conditions in the 1970s.

Adding to the demographic changes in prisons was the "War on Crime" that contributed to the growing racial disparity among prison population beginning in the 1960s. In 1960, almost 40% of prison inmates were classified as "non-White"; by 1975, this figure grew to almost 50%. Nationwide, Black incarceration rose from 46.3 per 100,000 in 1973 to 65.1 per 100,000 in 1979, a rate more than nine times higher than for whites (Roth 2005, 288–289).

Gangs quickly spread into the new liberal prison environments that prevailed after *Cooper v. Pate*. Prior to the ruling, only Washington and California reported the presence of gangs; by 1984, more than 60% of state and federal prisons reported gang activity. The growth was spurred in part by the free world crack trade. Subsequent tougher sentencing laws in the 1970s and 1980s ensured that unprecedented number of street gang members ended up behind bars and in the process transferred street gangs from the outside to the inside. This transformation however was not entirely new, as James B. Jacobs noted in his seminal study of Stateville Penitentiary. The prison was dominated by ethnic gangs, particularly Italians affiliated with the Chicago Taylor Street mob. However, under the administration of Warden Joseph Ragen, there were no laws mandating the coddling of prisoners and authorities had a free hand in breaking up and controlling gangs. There were few restraints if the authorities wanted to separate inmates, censor mail, monitor visits, or lock up prisoners in solitary confinement (Jacobs 1978, 48).

As early as November 5, 1973, the FBI reported one sagacious source that warned,

> California penal institutions are violently experiencing the powers of criminally oriented groups now operating both within and outside the correctional system. Individuals have grouped themselves into organizations that reflect their ethnic background and language and are directed at prisoner self-protection and control of illegal activities within prison walls and on the streets. These formal tight-knit organizations are composed of convicts and ex-convicts and are known to involve narcotics, extortion, contract killing, robbery, forgery and receiving.[14]

This account is a virtual description of prison activity in the 21st century, more than 30 years later.

By the 1990s, a number of prison gangs had transformed themselves into extremely organized gangs, causing alarm to law enforcement on both sides of the prison walls. They are distinct from past gangs in their demands of absolute obedience to the parent group. As the following sets of rules indicate, these gangs now obtain this obedience by compelling members to make a "death oath" of allegiance to the group, better known as "Blood In, Blood Out." Once a member, you are considered a member for life. The new breed of prison gang also contrasts sharply with earlier incarnations through the adoption of a structure based along paramilitary lines, with the rank of soldier, lieutenant, captain, treasurer, secretary, vice chairman, and chairman. During the 1990s, state prison gangs became increasingly organized to facilitate their various rackets that revolved around narcotics, sex, food, clothing, loansharking, gambling, extortion, and protection.

At the turn of the 21st century, Illinois had "the most gang-dominated prison system in the country" (Hallinan 2001, 95). Although slightly more than half of the state's inmates were considered gang members, when it came to the state's four maximum security institutions—Menard, Joliet, Stateville, and Pontiac—this estimate almost doubled to 90%. The most dominant gangs in the prison system were also well represented on the streets, including the Gangster Disciples, El Rukns, the Vice Lords, and the Latin Kings. Of these, the Gangster Disciples were clearly the most powerful and feared. This is probably demonstrated through the lens of one of its leaders—Ernest "Smokey" Wilson. Except for the lack of freedom, there was little to distinguish his life behind bars for murder from the world outside. It was obvious he wasn't lacking for creature comforts. In 1992, he served as a poster child for what was wrong with the prison system and culture by critics of the correctional system. During a 30-day period, it was revealed that the following items were confiscated from his cell:

- 1 cellular telephone (with charger)
- 1 Nintendo Game Boy
- 1 Motorola pen pager
- $230 in cash
- 15.7 grams of cocaine
- 13 bottles of cologne
- 1 electric digital scale
- 1 six-inch hunting knife
- 1 portable tabletop washing machine
- 1 Casio two-inch color television
- 1 electric iron[15]

Similar to the way major criminal organizations in the free world use associates from smaller gangs, prison gangs often collaborate in crime together. For example, the Aryan Brotherhood (AB), which is small in number and has witnessed few prosecutions until 2006, has used affiliates from gangs such as the Dirty White Boys and the Mexican Mafia (Grann 2004). Other AB associate gangs include the more regionally based Aryan Circle (Texas), the Nazi Low Riders (California), and the Peckerwoods.

Illinois Prison Gangs

By the mid-1970s, Chicago's Blackstone Rangers was the most powerful prison gang in Joliet Prison. In the 1980s, gang members exercised power that had been improbable earlier—spitting on guards, openly defying them, and attacking staff. In 1985, a gang member killed the assistant warden of the Pontiac Correctional Institute. Two years later another one was killed at the very same prison. It was later reported that a new warden acquiesced to the gangs to the extent of quietly cooperating and tolerating the display of gang insignia (Hallinan 2001). Some observers traced the rise of its prominence to Chicago Mayor Richard Daley's campaign against the gang beginning in the late 1960s. Hundreds of members were convicted of serious crimes as a result and ended up in the three maximum security prisons closest to Chicago—Joliet, Stateville, and Pontiac. The two gang leaders—Jeff Fort and "Bull" Hairston—were transferred to Joliet. It was estimated that by the early 1970s that 50% to 80% of the inmates in the aforementioned three prisons had either been formerly members of Blackstone Rangers or recruited inside. Using their organizational skills developed on the political battlegrounds of Chicago, the Blackstone Rangers took advantage of the liberalization policy implemented by the less punitive regime that began with the retirement of Warden Joseph Ragen, who ruled Stateville with an iron grip between 1936 and 1961. Throughout the 1980s, the new administration surmised that because the prison was full of gang members it might be a good idea to give them some say in the operation of the prisons, a decision that would come back to haunt them. Some experts suggest that it was in this manner that gangs gained control of Stateville–Joliet under the well-meaning liberal regime that "tolerated and legitimated their power," and resulted in the creation of a prison population that "would not recognize attempts by future wardens to abrogate this agreement" (Useem and Kimball 1989, 67). In 1985, the U.S. Department of Justice reported that Illinois had "the most gang dominated prisons in the nation." Subsequently, Blackstone Rangers adopted the guise of Islam and changed its name to El Rukns in hopes those members' demands for special privileges as a religious group would be met. The pragmatic former-Rangers demanded the right to wear special emblems, possess El Rukns [gang] literature, and to hold meetings—all under the guise of religious freedom. An unconvinced federal judge eventually ruled against the change of status (Useem and Kimball 1989, 76).

Today, a number of prison officials and police organizations refer to prison gangs as a *Security Threat Group (STG)*. More recently, the Gangs and Security Threat Group Awareness organization asserted that there are six prison gangs nationally recognized "for their participation in organized crime and violence" (Florida Department of Corrections). These include Neta, Aryan Brotherhood, Black Guerrilla Family, Mexican Mafia, La Nuestra Familia, and Texas Syndicate. Besides these groups there is an ever-expanding population of apolitical street gangs, including the vaunted Bloods and Crips.

Although White, Black, and Hispanic gang members adorn their language with racist rhetoric to ensure racial solidarity, a close examination of the larger prison gangs suggests "it is often the desire for power, profit and control that really drives the gangs to action" (ADL, 2006, 10). Prison gangs, for the most part, slipped below the radar of law enforcement for years by using racially charged language to obscure the true nature of their enterprises, including extortion, drug trafficking, and assaults. The best evidence of the profit motive trumping the racist one is the fact that so many white supremacist gangs have formed alliances with Black or Hispanic prison gangs to increase profits. The following gang portraits demonstrate a number of instances where these unexpected alignments take place.

Drug Trafficking in Prison

Gang members are always on the prowl searching for the most vulnerable inmates. Members of the Aryan Brotherhood (AB), for example, search out drug addicts and indebted prisoners and coerce them into becoming "mules" to help bring in drugs. In many prisons it has become easier to get drugs inside than on the outside. In 1995 alone, more than 1,200 Leavenworth prisoners tested positive for heroin use (Grann 2004, 166). The demand for illegal narcotics in prison is so high that the costs are reflected in the exaggerated prices. A gram of heroin, which sells for $65 on the street, can bring as much as $1,000 inside. One AB member told journalist David Grann that the gang was bringing in anywhere from $500,000 to $1,000,000 a year in just one prison (2004, 166).

Prison Gangs in Supermax Prisons

In the 1990s a number of top leaders from the major prison gangs were relocated to *supermax* prisons, where each was held in a single cell with little chance for human contact. Despite the intense scrutiny and security, leaders have been able to communicate with gang members through elaborate coded messages. Some dropped notes to nearby cells, others tapped Morse code on prison bars, still others coerced orderlies to pass messages. Another technique was using a rhyming coded language called *carnie,* which they whispered to each other through wall vents. For example, *bottle stoppers* referred to "coppers" (Grann 2004). Other gang members had women on the outside who were used to pass on messages to gang members on the outside after visits or receiving letters. Some codes were incredibly complex, with one based on a bilateral cipher invented by 17th-century philosopher Sir Francis Bacon.

CELL PHONES BEHIND BARS   There is nothing more valuable in prison these days than a cell phone. Inmates trade them, and some sell for as much as $350. Smuggled phones allow inmates to operate criminal enterprises from behind bars as well as to track the movements of correctional personnel. As they continue to shrink in size, it becomes much easier to hide them. Most are smuggled in by inmates on work-release programs, visiting family members, corrections officers, and contractors working in the prisons. In July 2008, following the successful introduction of cell-phone sniffing dogs in neighboring Maryland and Virginia, The Washington, D.C., Department of Corrections announced plans to train its drug-sniffing dogs to do the same (Morse 2008).

More recently, prison officials have become increasingly concerned over inmates using cell phones. In Texas several incidents brought attention to this problem as far back as 2004. In one case, a letter was intercepted during a routine mail check. In the letter, the convict asked his mother to put more minutes on his cell phone. That same year authorities conducting an undercover investigation using electronic surveillance discovered a member of the Texas Syndicate making and receiving calls. Authorities have expressed concern that inmates were using cell phones to conduct organized crime activities including drug trafficking, extortion, and escape planning. One explanation for the cell phone problem in Texas is the fact that Texas inmates do not have regular access to phones for calling family members and attorneys (only one call every 30 days). Philadelphia authorities became aware of the problem back in 2002 when a sweep of the city's three jails turned up 61 illegal phones. One senior Philadelphia law enforcement official asserted that the main concern was that they were used "for drug deals and arranging crimes" (Butterfield 2004). Family members and guards have been implicated in most of these cases. Attempts at introducing technology to jam the phones have resulted in mixed results due to the fact that it could also jam the radios and communication equipment used by correctional officers. American prison gangs are no match to Latin American gangs when it comes to cell phone use. In 2002, Brazilian inmates used cell phones to organized simultaneous riots in 29 prisons that left 15 dead and thousands held hostage (Butterfield 2004).

Prison Gangs and Religion

A number of prison gangs have taken advantage of the Bill of Rights protection that allows one the freedom to practice religion. This has provided a convenient smokescreen for groups to meet with limited surveillance under the rubric of "religious freedom." Throughout the history of prisons, it has been common for prisoners to find religion behind bars. The earliest groups to take advantage of this were those claiming to be Muslims (although they did not follow Islam). Street gangs such as the Gangster Disciples and the Vice Lords adopted this ruse to plan criminal activity. In recent years prisoners have adopted extremist faiths such as Black Hebrew Israelism or the white supremacist theology of Christian Identity. Once a group of individuals has a particular religion recognized by authorities, they are given access to privileges that often differ from state to state (depending on lawsuits filed). Some western-state prisons allow access to Native American sweat lodges (regardless of ethnicity and race). Some officials grant inmates the opportunity to meet together in chapel. Now groups have claimed adherence to such faiths as Odinism, Wicca, and Asatru, which is considered the main rival to the Christian Identity theology (Pitcavage 2002).

Prison Gangs and Street Gangs

Since the mid 1990s, a number of surveys have attempted to flesh out the presence and activities of American prison gangs. In 1995, the average number of gang members in a prison was 20.5%, with only 7.4% reporting zero gang density (Knox, 1999, 4).[16] A 1999 survey of adult correctional institutions asked, "What are the names of the top three largest [street] gangs that are represented among inmates in your facility?" The gangs most frequently cited in their rank order were as follows:

Crips (various factions)	15.4%
Black Gangster Disciples	13.9%
Bloods/Piru factions	1.7%
Vice Lord factions	7.1%
Aryan Brotherhood	6.8%
Latin King factions	4.5%

(Knox 1999)

WHY THE PRISON GANG IN THE 21ST CENTURY?

At the high-water mark of the post Capone era in the late 1930s America was imprisoning 137 of its citizens for every 100,000 of the population. At the end of the 20th century, this figure had more than tripled to 476 per 100,000 of the population. Broken down further, the federal government predicted in 2000 that 1 of 11 men would spend a stint in prison during their life; however, when it came to African American men, this figure rose to 1 in every 4 men. So, on the cusp of the 21st century, it was fair to say most inmates came from urban areas and were either Hispanic or Black. As Joseph T. Hallinan so persuasively observed in his 2001 book *Going Up the River*, most of the prison-building boom has taken place in America's hinterlands, in communities mostly White, "where guards likely never encountered anyone like them," a phenomenon that was surely be considered a prescription for racial conflict in the prison system (2001, xiii).

NORTEÑOS AND *SUREÑOS*: THE GANGS OF CALIFORNIA

Originally the name *Sureno*, or "southerner," was brandished exclusively by gangbangers in East Los Angeles, before being adopted thousands of Hispanic gang members in the United States and into Central America. However, in the mid-1980s, California Hispanics locked up in the state's correctional system diverged into two opposing factions—southerners and northerners—and entered into a bloody internecine conflict that continues to this day. Southern gang members were from southern California and were usually of Mexican background, whereas northerners were from northern California. The dividing line between the two alliances at one time was considered Bakersfield; however, over time, the movement of *Sureños* into the north has forced the demarcation line to Fresno. Non-aligned prisoners were pressured to join either faction. Gang experts suggest that the *Sureños* are better acclimated to the "prison-gang environment" because most of them had been actively involved in the gangster lifestyle in the barrios of East Los Angeles (Valentine 2000, 100, 111).

Norteños, or "northerners," however, were considered "less sophisticated in gang ways and had values more closely related to agriculture and family" (Valentine 2000, 111). Many had in fact worked as farm laborers and related occupations at one time or another. *Sureños* mocked them as *farmeros*, or farmers. It became common for Hispanics inside and out of prison to adhere to an allegiance to one faction or the other. For this reason, the *Sureños* became the dominant clique, with most newcomers to California adopting *Sureños* tattoos. Some of Los Angeles' most powerful Hispanic gangs—the 18th Street Gang, Sur-13, and White Fence—claim they are allies of the *Sureños*. However, this relationship never precludes gangs within each alliance from warring with each other.

Sureños number in the tens of thousands, but this attests more to the ease of gaining membership than any great criminal acumen. Like other large gangs, its "made members" who have killed or completed an important task, number only in the hundreds. What was once just a California phenomenon has spread to other cities.

HISPANIC PRISON GANGS

The Texas Syndicate (ESE TE)

Francisco Gonzales established the Texas Syndicate (*Sindicato Tejano*) in Folsom Prison in the mid-1970s. The gang started out predominately Mexican American and was created, according to one member, as a protective response against other gangs preying on Texas native inmates in the California correctional system, particularly the Aryan Brotherhood, the Mexican Mafia, and La Nuestra Familia. In recent years, the gang has expanded its criteria to accept other Latinos. In the early 1990s the group was considered among the most feared prison gangs. More recently, a Texas Department of Corrections report noted: "Mexican-American inmates originating from Texas have always been the most feared due to their fierce loyalty to one another" (quoted in Chapa 2006). This

Texas Syndicate Rules

1. Be a Texan.
2. Once a *carnal,* always a *carnal.*
3. Never let a *carnal* down.
4. Right or wrong, a *carnal* is always right.
5. *Carnales* come first. The Texas Syndicate come first.
6. All *Carnales* will respect each other.
7. All *Carnales* will wear the Texas Syndicate tattoo.
8. Do not reveal our thing.
9. A member must respect all other members and their families at all times.
10. A member must never lie to another member.
11. Every member must share all things with other members; there is no exception.
12. Every prospect to become a member must be voted on by every member on every unit.
13. If a member is designated to carry out a hit, then he will have two weeks to do so or else he will be hit himself.
14. When a member is released from prison, he must stay in contact with at least one member of the unit where he went free from.
15. The member who sponsors a prospective member will be forever responsible for the prospective member's actions, should he become a member.
16. The member will carry himself with respect at all times and abide by all the rules.
17. Every prospect will be investigated throughout the system, the Federals and *Califas.*
18. A vote will be taken only once on anything and it will be final; the majority takes the vote.
19. When called to a meeting that pertains to something very important, every *Carnal* must attend, except if he has a good excuse.
20. After the *Carnal* is accepted and has the symbol put on, he will be told and explained about the rules; we will make sure he understands them well.
21. A *Carnal* will not bring heat to the ESE TE just because he has our backing.
22. A *Carnal* will not write another unit, Federal, or *Califas* putting another *Carnal* down.
23. There will be no Marano's turnkeys in ESE TE.
24. The opinion of a *Carnal* will be respected.
25. A *Muleta* or a problem of a *Carnal* is every *Carnales* problem; everything comes in with a *Carnal;* since he is accepted and there is not such a thing as a personal matter about *Carnales;* a *Carnales'* problem is our problem.
26. Only rules 9, 10, 11, 12, and 13 will be shown to prospective members.
27. No one outside the ESE TE shall have the ESE TE *copia.*
28. There will be no more white dudes coming into the ESE TE except the ones already in.

These rules were confiscated by California correctional staff from a known gang member sometime in the 1980s.

loyalty is typically expressed by immediate and absolute retaliation. By most accounts, once freed, Texas Syndicate (TS) members returned to Texas and continued related illegal activities on the outside. The gang is considered well organized and known to abide by a set of rules. Compared to the Mexican Mafia and Nuestra Familia, this group is much smaller, but has not kept them from earning a reputation for violence. A TS member is called a *carnal,* a group of members *Carnales,* a TS recruit is *Cardinal,* and the institution leader is the *Chairman.* TS identifiers include the TS tattoo.

La Nuestra Familia

Robert "Babo" Sosa has been credited with forming *La Nuestra Familia (NF),* or "Our Family," in California's state prison system in 1968.[17] The creation of the NF was a direct result of internecine conflict between northern and southern California Hispanics in the prison system, with the southerners, or *Sureños,* holding the upper hand in the bloodshed. The *Norteños* in response adopted a paramilitary structure and a constitution for their new gang. The structure of NF is made up of a general at the top of the command, followed in descending order by captains, lieutenants, squad leaders, squad members or soldiers, and recruits.

According to its constitution and its 14 rules, only northern Hispanic recruits were welcome. Members refer to each other as *Carnales,* Cs, or *familianos*. Like most other prison gangs they incorporate a "Blood In, Blood Out," policy—once one becomes a *Carnal*, he is expected to belong to the NF for life and be ready to go to war at any moment. First, however, members must go through a "prison education program," in which they learn how to make and conceal weapons, defensive tactics and knowledge of lethal striking techniques, escaping from handcuffs, nonverbal communication, and code writing (Valentine 2000).

The NF's paramilitary leanings included requirements that a member present well-groomed appearance, make his bed each morning, wear shoes while awake, and not fall asleep before lockdown for personal protection. *Carnales* can be identified by the color red. All members were expected to attack their main enemy, the *Mexican Mafia (MM)*, on sight. NF members risked death for showing cowardice, not fulfilling a mission, or leaving the gang.

Over time, most southern California prisoners entering the correctional system became affiliated with the MM, whereas northern California Hispanics gravitated to the NF. Northern California street gang members are identifiable by the number 14, for the 14th letter in the alphabet, N, representing *Norteños* or northerners. Gang members signified their affiliation with the symbols VIV, X\$, 14, and 4 dots.

By the mid-1970s there were only an estimated 600 members and associates in the NF. Like the MM and others, the gang adopted a policy of restricting membership based on quality rather than numbers. During the 1970s, the NF were well entrenched in the usual prison rackets of protection, extortion, prostitution, drugs, and weapons trafficking. Following another outbreak of bloodshed between the NF and the MM, the California Department of Corrections was forced to separate the gangs in different prisons. This led to a boon in recruiting by both gangs.

In 1976, the NF branched out to the hard streets of Fresno, where they organized a "regiment" led by recently released *carnals*. Once outside, veteran gang members entered into an alliance with local Chicano street gang members, many affiliated with the Fresno-14. Unrestricted by the prison regime, NF members trained the earnest gang members how to extort business owners and using the NF rep to sell street protection. The NF also began taxing street dealers. By controlling drug trafficking in the area, the gang's wealth rose to unprecedented levels. By coopting prison staff to traffic drugs inside the prisons, NF members received a return of four to five times that on the streets. However, by bringing their organized crime activities to the streets, it was only a matter of time before they attracted the attention of the authorities, and in 1982, 25 NF gang members were indicted for a litany of acts including extortion, robbery, drug trafficking, murders, and witness intimidation. The NF became the first prison gang federally indicted for violating the RICO act.

What facilitated the government's case was the testimony of defectors, and in the end, only a handful of gang leaders escaped indictment. The RICO indictments and the testimony of informers were a hard lesson, but one the NF would learn from. A strategy was conceived to better insulate leading NF members. By most accounts, a "diversionary" NF was created in hopes that the feds would take to their scent, allowing the actual power structure to operate in peace. The decoy NF, however, was trusted with vetting the ever-ready recruitment pool. This "Northern Structure" was expected to evaluate any potential recruit closely before allowing him to join.

In the meantime, the gang was also restructured under the direction of Robert "Black Bob" Vasquez. The new scheme featured a Regimental Security Department (RSD) as its new security arm. Henceforth, there was also a tendency to refer to the NF as *The Organization* or *The O*. Relatives and friends of the O were expected to find jobs where they could gain access to public records—the telephone company, utility companies, the court system and law enforcement, and corrections. In so doing, they could tap into any number of databases and establish a "foolproof" system for vetting new members or gaining information that could be used to blackmail adversaries (Valentine 2000).

The NF also introduced a new cell system to obscure the identity of ranking members. Category I includes new members or returning members. Here prospects were given their basic training and education, which included reading Sun Tzu's *The Art of War*. Personnel at this level are given the opportunity for advancement, but also barred from knowledge of the higher categories. Promotion to Category II leads to advanced training in the criminal arts and appointment of squad leaders, but recruits at this level are still privy to knowledge of only the bottom two categories. The leading cohort is in Category III, which includes RSD staff, lieutenants, and commanders. At this level, *Familianos* make decisions to be passed down the food chain. The next highest level is La Mesa, dominated by no more than 10 captains. According to gang expert Bill Valentine, at the turn of the 21st century, all of the captains were housed at the Pelican Bay Maximum Security Prison. The highest rung of the O is the General or Nuestro General, who is typically selected by the outgoing General. He has the power to sign treaties, start wars, and promote or demote officers.

Neta

In Puerto Rico's Rio Pedras Prison, Carlos "La Sombra" Torres-Irriarte founded the predominantly Puerto Rican American and Hispanic gang known as *Neta* in 1970. The gang adopted its name from the popular celebration of a baby's birth, when Puerto Ricans traditionally chant "Neta! Neta!" However, others suggest that it is an acronym for "Never Tolerate Abuse." According to prison authorities, it was created to suppress violence between inmates in that prison (DeVito 2005). By most accounts, the gang has adopted the façade of a "cultural organization" and has a tradition of affiliation with street gangs. The gang is considered patriotic to the home country and has been associated with members of the Los Macheteros terrorist group, whose goal is Puerto Rican independence.

A prison-based gang on the East Coast, Neta's reach has expanded from New England to Florida. Each member is expected to find 20 potential members, and on the 30th of each month the group come together to recognize the dead. Gang member affiliation is reflected by the colors red, white, and blue, although black sometimes fills in for blue. Members often display the Puerto Rican flag and carry membership cards. Colors can be demonstrated in a member's clothing or beads. Probationary members can wear only white beads until they are officially members. The Netas are notoriously restrictive in their membership and earned a reputation behind bars for its clandestine activity that allowed the gang to operate under the radar for a number of years.

The Neta preoccupation with keeping a low profile is in stark contrast to other Hispanic groups that are constantly the focus of official attention. Neta's main criminal activities include (but are not limited to) drug dealing, extortion, and contract killings for street gangs (Florida Department of Corrections, 2007). Since the mid-1970s, Neta has established a foothold in a number of America's largest cities and in most prison systems in the United States and Puerto Rico.

Mexican Mafia

By the early 1970s the FBI was investigating the Mexican Mafia for organized crime activity. A report by one Special Agent indicated, "The Mexican Mafia is suspected of being involved in specialized type of crime such as that involving violence as in loan sharking, narcotics, etc."[18]

The Mexican Mafia was established in California's Duel Vocational Center in the 1950s. The purported founders, Rodolfo Cadena and Joe Morgan, conceived the gang as protection against larger White prison gangs, such as the Blue Bird Gang. By the 1960s, the Mexican Mafia was the dominant gang in the California prison system. However, in the late 1960s, the emergence of La Nuestra Familia, the Black Guerrilla Family, and the Aryan Brotherhood cut into its control and established competition. The increasing incarceration of young Hispanic street gang members from southern California, who refer to themselves as *Sureños*, or southerners, revived the strength of the gang. Mexican Mafia members have been identified in prisons across the United States. There has been some confusion among authorities and researchers as to the relationship between the *Sureños* and the Mexican Mafia. Prison experts today consider these two separate phenomena. In order to become a true member of the MM, a prospect must kill or seriously injure a target identified by group leaders. Most estimates indicate perhaps 600 members nationwide (inside and out). However, there are not a lot of requirements for becoming a *Sureños* outside of being of Hispanic heritage. Many are born in gang neighborhoods and are "born into the gang," stepping into a tradition followed by relatives. Others have relocated from south of the border and simply join the gang. Its street gang members are often identified with the symbols XIII, X3, 13, and 3 dots—all inferring the 13th letter of the alphabet—M, for Mexican Mafia. Other identifiers include the color blue and words *Sureno, Sur,* and *Southerner.*

More prominent members of the Mexican Mafia display the symbol of a black hand or *La Eme,* standing for the letter M in Spanish. Members of the Mexican Mafia have partnered up with Italian syndicates and the Aryan Brotherhood. The Mexican Mafia has adopted the code of "Blood In, Blood Out," and is considered the most active gang, incidents wise, in the Federal Bureau of Prisons. Its main prison rivals are the Black Guerrilla Family, Black street gangs, and its main enemy La Nuestra Familia. As previously mentioned, it often casts its lot with the Aryan Brotherhood for business and security purposes. Interestingly, it reputedly provides protection to imprisoned La Cosa Nostra members. Membership is restricted to Mexican Americans and other Hispanics. Women and relatives play an important role as couriers for drug and financial activities. Main criminal activities include drug trafficking, extortion, pressure rackets, and maintaining internal discipline. The Mexican Mafia has won a hard-earned reputation for violence and horrific contract killings.

WHITE PRISON GANGS

Aryan Brotherhood

The Aryan Brotherhood originated in San Quentin Prison in the mid-1960s. Its membership is restricted to Whites and was initially formed to protect them from minority inmates. It is considered one of the nation's most violent prison gangs, and has emerged as a presence outside prisons as well. It has had a long alliance with the Mexican Mafia against their enemies in La Nuestra Familia and the Black Guerrilla Family. In recent years, diverse authorities from law enforcement to the Anti-Defamation League (ADL) have asserted that it has evolved into a criminal syndicate responsible for violent attacks, drug trafficking, and other illegal enterprises and now resembles an organized crime group more than a hate group.

The ABs originated as the Diamond Tooth gang, so-called for the practice of imbedding diamond-shape pieces of glass into their teeth. Its next incarnation was as the Bluebird gang; all members were required to have a bluebird tattoo on their necks. In 1968 the AB was formed out of the hardcore Bluebird members, together with bikers and neo-Nazis. It was then that they gravitated to White supremacist ideology and adopted a paramilitary structure. AB members are recognizable by an identifying tattoo of a three-leaf clover, or shamrock, along with the number 666 across the leaves and underscored by the letters AB.[19]

Unlike most other prison gangs that continually recruit to increase the size of the organization, the ABs limit their membership to only the most powerful and violent inmates, who are expected to kill on command. Being more cloistered than other gangs allowed the ABs to slip under the radar, effectively operating with impunity for years (Grann 2004). Like many other prison gangs, the ABs have a "Blood In, Blood Out" rule. According to this decree, one is expected to shed blood to join and can only quit the gang by dying.

Numbering only about 100, the original ABs managed to stake its claim to be the deadliest prison gang by declaring "open season" to kill all Black inmates regardless of their affiliations. By the early 1970s, California's prison system was beset by an unparalleled spate of murders and violent gang assaults Along with establishing its dominance, it also took over most of the prison rackets, including protection, extortion, drugs and weapons trafficking, and contract killings.

Aryan Brotherhood Rules

1. After reading these rules and you decide you would like to be in the Brotherhood and you are voted in and accepted, there is only one way out, which is death.
2. Once you enter into the AB, do not try to backslide in any way! You are not being given a free ride thru this prison. If you enter with these thoughts in your mind and we find out, it will be your death!
3. After you are sworn into the AB, you will be advised of the social structure of the AB and will be expected to recognize it and abide by its decisions and orders.
4. The AB is exactly what it says, "A Brotherhood." When you see a brother involved in any sort of hassle, you go to his side. You may not be on the best of terms with the man, but he is your brother and will be treated as such. So back him! He is going to do the same for you when you need him!
5. A brother can sometimes be wrong, but in front of a non-brother, he's right! Afterwards when you are alone, his being wrong can be dealt with. But never in front of a non-brother!
6. You will not bullshit or play games with a brother in front of non-brothers. Always show respect to a brother and let everyone around you know that the respect is there!
7. We take care of our own! We don't have time for the games that non-brothers are involved in! You will protect your brother, his property, and the interest of the AB as if it were your own! Your brothers will be doing the same for you.
8. If you are told to do something there is a reason for you being told to do it, so do it!
9. You are in the AB for life! If you hit the streets and come back, you're still in it! You must be willing to do for a brother what you want him to be willing to do for you. No matter where you are!
10. After a certain length of time, it will be necessary to make a donation to a bank account in case any brother is placed on then adjustment center (maximum security detention). A brother is taken care of to the fullest of the AB's capacity! The donations will be reasonable.
11. The purpose of the Aryan Brotherhood is to bring back the respect that is long overdue in coming to this prison and to the White Race! At all costs! We will strive to maintain that respect!

The AB allows the creation of unaffiliated splinter groups, which use the name of their state with the AB moniker, as in "Aryan Brotherhood of Texas." However, ABs in federal and California prisons do not regard them as true members and have even gone so far as to threaten violence if "copycat members" do not cut or burn off AB tattoos.

Prison authorities had once dismissed the ABs as a "fringe white supremacist gang," but now admit that the gang of convicted felons "had gradually taken control of large parts of the nation's maximum security prisons, ruling over thousands of inmates and transforming themselves into a powerful criminal organization" (Grann 2004, 158). Over time, the "Brand" has established drug-trafficking, prostitution, and extortion rackets in prisons throughout the nation. Perhaps one member put it best, explaining that the gang was "no longer about destroying the minorities of the world, white supremacy and all that shit. It's a criminal organization, first and foremost" (Grann 2004, 165).

Other White Prison Gangs (1999)

Aryan Nation	Brothers of the White Struggle (BOWS)
Aryan Warriors	Northridge's (Illinois Prison System)
Aryan Society	Simon City Royals (Midwest)
White Aryan Resistance	Texas Mafia
Ku Klux Klan	White Gangster Disciples
Neo-Nazis	White Supremacists
Various Biker gangs	Young and Wasted
Peckerwoods	Church of the New Song (CONS) (Iowa)

New Kids in the Block": The Nazi Low Riders[20]

The Nazi Low Riders (NLR) were established in the California Youth Authority in the 1970s and 1980s. Its evolution was facilitated by its message of White supremacy, and under the mentorship of the Aryan Brotherhood, NLR members were soon acting as middlemen for the ABs, by taking care of criminal activities while various AB leaders were in administrative segregation. According to the American Defamation League (ADL), this allowed the NLR to become the most powerful gang in the Youth Authority and spread into prisons all along the west coast. The NLR has come a long way, and is now considered the most powerful White prison gang next to the ABs. Like the ABs, the NLR has also allied itself with southern Hispanic gangs against the Black Guerrilla Family and La Nuestra Family in order to control the drug trade. The NLR diverges from other White gangs by accepting members with Hispanic surnames or with Hispanic wives. As one former member put it, "You must have at least half White blood but no Black blood." As prison authorities began to move against the NLR, the gang took a page out of the AB playbook and began recruiting other gangs, in this case the Dirty White Boys and the Skinhead Dogs. At the turn of the 21st century, the NLR had also become a force to be reckoned with on the streets of some West Coast cities, and have been tied to crimes such as drug trafficking and production, robbery, contract killings, weapons trafficking, and witness intimidation.

By the late 1990s law enforcement noticed that the ABs had expanded their racketeering activities outside the prison walls. The AB recruited paroled members and affiliates to operate drugs and weapons trafficking, and to commit contract killings. Although the ABs are racist this has not prevented members from using Black associates to buy and sell drugs to Black prisoners, once again proving that the gang's ideology often comes in second to promoting criminal activity.

Since the mid-1990s, prison authorities have been able disrupt many of the AB's criminal activities. In response, the gang began recruiting young White males imprisoned in juvenile institutions to act as middlemen. In so doing they created a new gang that became known as the Nazi Low Riders. Their association with the ABs allowed them to extend their power in prison and on the outside, basically conducting the criminal activities that the ABs could not accomplish in isolation.

In 2006, four alleged leaders of the ABs went on trial on racketeering charges. The federal prosecutor told jurors that the gang ordered members to start a war against a Black gang that left two of them dead within 12 hours. Prosecutors described how two federal inmates received a letter in 1997 with a message written in invisible ink. When the note was heated the inmates read the message: "War with D.C. from T.D." The initials referred to the D.C. Blacks prison gang and the first two initials of AB leader Tyler Davis "The Hulk" Bingham, currently in prison for robbery and drug trafficking (Flaccus, March 15, 2006, HC, A7).

How Do Gang Members Make Money When Currency Is Prohibited in Prison?

Because cash is not allowed in prison, most inmates pay off their debts to gangs by exchanging contraband or commissary items in lieu of money. Typical items include cigarettes, candy, stamps, and books. Leavenworth Prison has gained a reputation for high-stakes gambling, in which a number of drug kingpins were reportedly given credit for 1 month, betting thousands of dollars at a time. Gamblers were expected to pay gangs such as the Aryan Brotherhood through friends or relatives, who sent untraceable money orders to a designated affiliate outside the prison. One's position as a kingpin did not give him a free pass if he was late on a payment. Prison records have reported a number of severe beatings administered to indebted inmates.

Confederate Knights of America

One of the nation's most heinous racial murders of the late-20th century took place near Jasper, Texas. On June 7, 1998, James Byrd, Jr., was walking alone along a country road when a truck carrying three White males picked him up. He was never seen alive after that. His death has been well chronicled and the perpetrators have been sentenced. However, what has also emerged is the fact that two of the men, King and Brewer, had joined a small White supremacist prison gang during their last stint in prison.

According to the indictment, it was alleged that that gang members were involved in 32 murders and attempted murders since the mid-1970s, with most of them directed by the men on trial. More than a dozen other defendants faced the death penalty at trials coming up, and 19 others had already accepted plea bargains. The attorney for one of the suspected ringleaders noted, "The reality is, federal penitentiaries are violent and dangerous places and all of these guys—white guys— are a small minority and they're just trying to survive" (Flaccus 2006).

Recent estimates by law enforcement place AB membership at 15,000 nationwide. Mark Potok, director of the Southern Poverty Law Center's Intelligence Project, explained, "We keep track of them because they have a racial ideology, but mostly they are a criminal organization" (Korosec 2006, B5).

AFRICAN AMERICAN PRISON GANGS

The 1960s was a benchmark for the development of America's prison gangs, particularly African American ones. The growing politicization of inmates, Black Power and Black Pride, as well as the influence of the Black Muslim movement all played crucial roles in the racial dynamics of the prison in that era. The emergence of the Black Muslim consciousness in the 1960s in the nation's prison system coincided with a newfound appreciation for organization, discipline, and politics among Black inmates, as it became a formidable force. (At this time, prisons were segregated.) Prison administrators were alarmed at the burgeoning solidarity and addressed it by separating Muslim inmates from each other. Threatened by the growing stature of the Black Muslims, in 1962 the American Correctional Association resolved that the group was a "race hatred group" and was therefore "unworthy of the recognition granted to bona fide religious groups" (Hallinan 2001, 25).

Although there were only "fifty-eight documented Muslims" in the prison at the time, no prison exemplified the conflict between administrators and Black Muslims than the Stateville Correctional Center southwest of Chicago, future home of some of the nation's most powerful Black street gangs. Inmates were controlled under the punitive regime of legendary warden Joseph E. Ragen. Harking back to an earlier century, inmates were not allowed to speak to each other in the dining hall or while marching in formation, under the looming threat of corporal punishment. The rules applied to all prisoners at this time. Ragen viewed the Muslims as a looming threat and had them actively investigated. Ragen's "Muslim file" kept a record of "secret conversations" and other accounts gathered through surveillance.

One inmate would test the litigious atmosphere of the 1960s and the growing civil rights movement. In 1962, prisoner Thomas Cooper, a 22-year-old man serving a life sentence for murder and a recent convert to Islam, changed his name to Thomas X. Cooper. Housed in solitary confinement for almost 10 years for assaulting a guard, Cooper sued the warden of Stateville, who was now Frank Pate, Ragen having been promoted to director of public safety. In 1964, Cooper's suit appeared before the U.S. Supreme Court, and against all odds the following year the Court issued the historic ruling *Cooper v. Pate,* a landmark decision with an impact on all of the nation's prisoners. The case unleashed an avalanche of prisoner lawsuits protesting the often-barbaric conditions of prison and led to unprecedented "liberalization" of the nation's correctional facilities.

Black Guerrilla Family

The Black Guerrilla Family (BGF) originated as a radical prison gang in San Quentin Prison in 1966. Founded by the former Black Panther George L. Jackson as the Black Family, many of its early members had formerly belonged to other revolutionary groups in the 1960s. Its foremost goal was to "establish the prison gang as one of the most effective and deadly revolutionary forces in society" (Valentine 2000, 16).

Its initial structure was designed along paramilitary lines, with one leader, who functioned as the supreme commander, a central committee, and a rigid chain of command. Membership was restricted only to Blacks, and members were expected to make a lifetime commitment with a death oath.

The BGF is usually found in adult prisons, although authorities have cited instances of it operating in juvenile facilities, and is centered in California, but also operates in Arizona, Georgia, Indiana, Minnesota, Nevada, New Jersey, Texas, Washington, and Wisconsin (National Gang Crime Research Center 2006).

Its written constitution runs to 16 pages of single-space type and clearly indicates its intent to engage in armed conflict. The Constitution reveals that the Aryan Brotherhood and the Mexican Mafia are its archenemies, describing them as "tools" of the prison administration. The BGF are considered the most politically astute of the major prison gangs, but lacking in originality.

Shortly before his death on August 2, 1971, Jackson adopted the name "Black Dragon," and renamed the BGF the Black Vanguard. Jackson was shot dead in a bloody escape attempt gone awry along with two inmates and three correctional officers. Following Jackson's death, a power struggle erupted within his gang, which had returned to the name BGF. One faction wanted to pursue a more political agenda, whereas the other geared itself toward organized crime activity by controlling various lucrative prison rackets. Eager for financial gain, the BGF began shaking down prisoners selling protection. The group soon moved into selling drugs and weapons, extortion, gambling, prostitution, and contract killings (Valentine 2000).

The BGF eventually joined with the Nuestra Familia in an attempt to take financial control of prison rackets. In turn, the two groups agreed to declare war on the Mexican Mafia and the Aryan Brotherhood. By most accounts they established a "hit-on-sight" policy.

Like the other major prison gangs, BGF began to exert its influence outside prison walls. As inmates left the prison they became involved in kidnappings, bank and armored car robberies, and the murders of police officers. Meanwhile, many of the BGF members on the inside were placed in solitary confinement for assaulting guards. In the 1980s, the war between the BGF and its enemies was not going well and a number of its members formed its own group called "Bay Love" for its affiliation with the San Francisco Bay area. Bay Love would later become the Kumi African Nation, or 415 (telephone area code for the Bay area).

In recent years the BGF is also known as *Jama*, or "family" in Swahili. Many of its members have learned to communicate in the East African language Swahili. Although it is still centered in

Oath of the 415[21]

I, as an active 415 soldier, will come from the bleeding heart of this constitution and flow as a true soldier across the land. I hereby fly the right African solution never before like no other black man, to achieve the goals of African opportunity never before like no African other and embrace "415" African to support the cause of my brothers. And through the years to come I'll honor and do my best by this banner until the job is done. I'll never stop for rest, to be a winner is the faithful test, to be a loser is for the African dead. This is why I fight for the real conquest with the faith of my 415 comrades. If ever I should fail my obligated deeds under this banner that I fly, may this oath prevail and punish me for the reasons I did not try. Forever and ever to the 415.

Oath of the Black Guerrilla Family[22]

If I should ever break my stride,
And falter at my comrade's side,
This oath will kill me.

If ever my world should prove untrue,
Should I betray this chosen few,
This oath will kill me.

Should I be slow to take a stand,
Should I show fear to any man,
This oath will kill me.

Should I grow lax in discipline,
In time of strife refuse my hand.
This oath will kill me.

the Bay area, the gang is active in a number of other states and in the Federal Bureau of prisons. The BGF has become increasingly radicalized and members consider themselves political prisoners or prisoners of war. The group has earned a reputation for its propensity for attacking officers. The BGF reportedly shares its intelligence with other politically oriented groups such as the New Black Panther Party and the Nation of Islam and is still allied with the Nuestra Familia. Prison intelligence has discovered plans by the group to unite all 415 members and members of the Consolidated Crip Organization under the BGF. This scheme is designed to protect prisoners against the expanding Hispanic gangs in the California Prison System.

Brazilian Prison Gangs: An International Perspective

Housing more than 360,000 inmates, Brazil has the fourth largest prison population in the world. With one of the highest urban crime rates in Latin America, it has taken a punitive approach to justice to control crime, leading to prisons overcrowded with violent young men. Compared to South American prison gangs, America's gangs seem rather quaint. Brazil's gangs are so prevalent that many of the country's penologists contend that criminals actually run Brazil's prison system. The Sao Paulo–based First Command of the Capital (PCC)[23] is considered one of the most prominent, and is considered by experts to have evolved into a formidable criminal organization, displaying a high degree of coordination, integration and management of its members (BBC News 2006, 1).

The PCC originated in the Sao Paulo prison by survivors of a 1990s prison massacre of 111 inmates. Although its origins had more in common with a prisoners' union, it eventually took control of a number of prisons. The origins of the PCC contrast with the race- and ethnic-based American prison gangs. PCC has worked to unite all prisoners in improving prison conditions, often through rioting and violent conflict. Today, the gang participates in weapons and drug trafficking, kidnappings, robberies, and prison riots. The introduction of the cell phone has allowed the gang to spread outside the prison as well. Gang leaders have no problem coercing the notoriously corrupt and understaffed prison guards to help them obtain cell phones. Once they have them inside, criminal activities can be directed from the jail cell.

PCC members are expected to pay monthly dues—an equivalent of $23 per month for inmates and $230 a month for those on the outside. When members are unable to pay, they are required to take part in risky attacks on police officers. In 2001 alone, the PCC was involved in 24 riots; in 2005, they killed five of their fellow inmates and tossed the decapitated heads from the rooftop.

There is no consensus at to the number of PCC members, but Brazilian police and media observers estimate that at least 6,000 members pay monthly dues and are considered the nucleus of the prison hierarchy (Hanson 2006). Recently, two members of the Sao Paulo Department of Investigation of Organization reported that the PCC controls at least 140,000 members in Sao Paulo State.[24] The same officials also added that many prisoners acquiesce to gang membership just to keep alive (Hanson 2006). By most accounts, prisoners are terrorized into joining the gang. However, the PCC, like some organized crime groups, "also buys loyalty by helping prisoners get lawyers, medicine, and by handing out the best jobs and cells inside the prison" (Downie 2006, 2).

Like many American prison gangs, the PCC adheres to an ideology, in this case prisoner solidarity, and in 1993 outlined a 16-point Manifesto under the motto, "Liberty, Justice, and Peace." The Manifesto lists discipline guidelines, specifically prohibiting mugging, rape, extortion, or the use of PCC power to resolve personal issues. Some experts have indicated that its "fundamental reason to exist is to improve the rights of prisoners" (quoted in Hanson 2006, 3). This does not preclude criminal activities, with the PCC involved in drug trafficking and other criminal activities in order to raise money to support family members and even put former prisoners through law school.

The PCC hierarchy includes members who pay monthly dues. Members function either as soldiers, *towers*—gang leaders in specific institutions—or as *pilots*—individuals who are responsible for communications. The leader of the PCC since 2002 is a 39-year-old intellectual well versed in Machiavelli's *The Prince* and Sun Tzu's *Art of War*. Marcos Willans Herbas Camacho, known by his sobriquets "Marcola," or "Playboy," is serving a 44-year sentence for bank robbery and has already spent half his life in jail.

What concerns authorities most are the gang's political ambitions and its links to other Latin American criminal groups. Prison officials indicate there is a high-level relationship between the PCC and the Red Command, considered Rio de Janeiro's most prominent drug traffickers. According to journalist Stephanie Hanson, experts are under the impression that the leader of the Red Command supplies Marcola with cocaine, and together the groups control the drug trade in Sao Paulo and Rio de Janeiro. An interesting development has been the merging of criminal political activities, a phenomenon common in other Latin American countries. For example, shortly after the turn of the 21st century, the PCC entered into a relationship with Colombia's FARC, which offered its " kidnapping expertise" to the PCC and also entered into a drugs for weapons exchange with them (Hanson 2006, 5).[25]

URBAN STREET GANGS: THE MODERN ERA

Recent scholarship has attempted to explain the recrudescence of gang activity in New York City in the 1940s and 1950s (Schneider 1999). Among the factors cited were the transformation of the labor market and new demographic patterns that saw European immigration decline due to wartime restriction laws and an increase in African Americans and Puerto Ricans seeking better opportunities. As the nation's first post-industrial city, New York City enjoyed a unique transformation that unlike Detroit, Chicago, and other cities, did not just depend on a handful of heavy industries. In New York City, a growing working class found thousands of service-based jobs—for example, printing, construction, and on the docks.

Increasing gang activity often parallels population movements, no matter whether the migrants are foreign-born or indigenous. Following in the footsteps of Irish and Italian street gangs that proliferated in East Coast cities during the 19th century, African American, Latin American, and other ethnic and racial gangs have settled into similar patterns, albeit in a much more complex world.

In 1998, a trio of criminologists examined whether certain street gangs should be recognized as organized crime groups (Decker, Bynum, and Weisel, 1998). The criminologists ascertained that although several gangs in the study were disorganized and did not reflect this trend,[26] the Gangster Disciples of Chicago clearly "exhibited many characteristics of emerging organized crime groups" (Decker, Bynum, and Weisel 1998, 423). To support their claim, the experts cited such characteristics as the gang's structure, activities, and relationships, including those with prison gangs and other street gangs. Interviews with a number of Gangster Disciples revealed that the gang owned legitimate businesses, providing opportunities for money laundering. As recently as January 2006, the government suggested that the Latin Kings, Gangster Disciples, and Vice Lords are the nation's "most highly organized" street gangs due to their "central leadership cores" (NDIC, 2006, 2).

One of the best definitions has been accepted by the Chicago Crime Commission, most recently in 2006. Home to some of the nation's most powerful and numerous street gangs, the Chicago Police Department's gang intelligence is among the best and most sophisticated among the nation's major police forces. Chicago law enforcement defines *street gangs* as

> an organized group that participates in criminal, threatening or intimidating activity within the community. This anti-social group, usually three or more individuals, evolves from within the community and has recognized leadership as well as a code of conduct. The group remains united during peaceful times as well as during conflict. (2006, 8)

What Are the Characteristics of a Street Gang?

The Chicago Crime Commission identified six characteristics of a street gang, as follows:

- A gang name and recognizable symbols
- A definable hierarchy
- A geographic territory
- A code of conduct
- An organized, continuous course of criminal activity (2006, 8)

But Are They Organized Crime?

The Crips and Bloods are not monolithic gangs but closer to what Robert J. Kelly calls "federations made up of dozens of independent gangs that each claims a territory much like the La Cosa Nostra crime families" (2000, 90). Indeed, for most of their history, urban street gangs have had little in common with "Mafia-type" groups, but crack cocaine did for urban street gangsters what alcohol prohibition did for several urban gangs of the 1920s and 1930s. The crack cocaine trade has given impetus to the transformation of various Blood and Crip sets from neighborhood-oriented cultural gangs to criminal organizations. However, there are still major differences. These particular African American street gangs are rarely involved in "labor racketeering, the infiltration of legitimate businesses, wide-scale political and law enforcement corruption, large scale loansharking, and transnational money laundering"; however, as Schatzberg and Kelly note, neither are Colombians, Mexicans, Russians, Cubans, and Chinese, who are widely considered stalwart examples of organized crime (1997, 185). The following examples from the Chicago's People and Folk Nations offer closer analogues to traditional organized crime syndicates.

Criminal Activities of Major Chicago Street Gangs (2006)

Gang	Activities
Gangster Disciples	Drug trafficking, extortion (taxing independent dealers), mortgage fraud, auto theft, knapping, money laundering, murder, arson, assault, armed robbery
Black Disciples	Drug trafficking, illegal weapons trade, gambling, extortion of independent drug dealers
Latin Kings	Drug trafficking, identity theft, auto theft, robbery, extortion
Vice Lords	Drug trafficking, extortion, auto theft, robbery, murder, mortgage fraud, credit card fraud, money laundering

People Nation Sets

El Rukns	Bishops
Latin Kings	Gaylords
Vicelords	Latin Counts
Spanish Lords	Kents

CHICAGO-INFLUENCED GANG ALLIANCES: PEOPLE AND FOLK NATIONS

As a hotbed of organized crime throughout its sordid history, the emergence of powerful Black street gangs in Chicago in the 1980s and 1990s should not be unexpected. Throughout the 20th century, Irish, Polish, Italian, and Jewish immigrants answered the city's demand for unskilled workers and some joined criminal gangs, particularly as Prohibition approached. Changes in the drug trade likewise stimulated the gangs of the late 20th century, although most of the former immigrant gang members had left the gang life. By the 1980s, many of the leaders and members of Chicago's biggest gangs were ensconced in federal and state penal institutions. With such a cornucopia of gangs behind bars, it was difficult to distinguish enemies from allies. In the 1980s, it was hoped that this was resolved when imprisoned gang members began separating into two alliances. The gangs previously affiliated with the Black P. Stone Nation joined with the People Nation. Those who had been predisposed to the Black Gangster Disciple Nation (BGDSN) aligned with the Folk Nation. In the end, both Nations should be viewed as alliances under which gangs are aligned and not as gangs in and of themselves. The Florida Department of Corrections offers the analogy of the National and American baseball leagues. The teams in each league form the alliance, which is the league; the Baltimore Orioles and New York Yankees are aligned with the American League.

Both alliances share a number of traits, including an "All for One, One for All" philosophy that effectively renders the one-on-one fight obsolete. In addition, both Nations use a similar "Code of Conduct" lexicon that includes phrases such as

- "Folk before Family"
- "I will not let my brother fall to a knee."
- "All is All" and "All is Well" (People)
- "All is One" (Folk)

Both alliances view disrespect from gang rivals through a similar prism. The following acts often require a reprisal:

- Breaking a rival's symbol.
- Showing a rival's hand signal upside down or crossing out rivals' hand sign with another finger.

Folk Nation Sets

Black Gangster Disciples	Latin Disciples
Black Disciples	Maniac Latin Disciples
Gangster Disciples	Simon City Royals
La Raza	Spanish Gangsters
Cobras	Two Sixers
Eagles	

- Drinking from a plastic cup belonging to a rival gang member.
- Striking through a rival's graffiti or spraying it upside down.

Black P. Stone Nation

Chicago's Black P. Stone Rangers was founded in 1959, creating the groundwork for what would become one of modern Chicago's largest criminal syndicates. At its zenith, the gang boasted between 6,000 and 8,000 members (Valentine 1995; Useem and Kimball 1989). However, what is often not mentioned is that the majority of members do little more than wear a Ranger patch and identify themselves as members. In actuality, only about 200 are included in the gang structure in that they participate in day-to-day affairs and know each other.

Early on, Black P. Stone Nation entered into a long-lasting enmity with the Black Gangster Disciples. Under leader Jeff Fort in 1968, the Rangers created an alliance of 21 gangs on the Southside of Chicago united under the mantle of what became Black P. Stone Nation. Hierarchically, the leaders formed a 21-man commission known as the "Main 21" and served as generals in the governing body of the organization. Initially, the group operated under police radar, billing itself as a socially conscious, self-help organization with the goal of uplifting themselves and the community.[27] Under this subterfuge, the organization applied for and received $1.4 million in federal anti-poverty funds to create programs for underprivileged children and former gang members. Instead, this provided early seed money for its nascent criminal activities. In 1968, an investigation led by Senator John L. McClellan discovered that the program was a sham, and that money was being diverted to bankroll extortion and drug trafficking. When a federal grand jury uncovered the ruse in 1972, Fort was convicted of defrauding the government and sent to federal prison. By most accounts, while in prison Fort converted to Islam, and on his return to Chicago renamed the gang El Rukns.[28] The group purchased a theater and four apartment buildings in Chicago that became the group's headquarters, called the "Grand Major temple" as the gang became increasingly radicalized.

Although the gang was now veiled in a Muslim cloak, it did not escape law enforcement that it had become the most prominent organized crime group in the African American community. By the 1980s, it controlled much of the drug trade on the South Side. In 1983, now using the moniker "Prince Imam Malik," Fort ran afoul of the law once more and was convicted and sentenced to a 13-year prison stint for cocaine trafficking; however, he still ran the organization from his cell. In late 1985, El Rukns made a sophisticated attempt to enter legitimate business through a dummy corporation called Security and Maintenance Services (SMS). In this process, the gang hoped to accredit members as security personnel with permission to carry concealed guns as security guards; however, the ATF got wind of the plan and set up a sting operation. The following year, a task force closed down SMS and arrested 18 members for various weapons violations. In 1987, Fort and El Rukns faced their most serious charges when they were indicted for entering an agreement with the Libyan government to perform terrorist acts in the United States for $2.5 million. Fort was sentenced to 80 years in prison. (see *Terror and Organized Crime*, Chapter 13).

Jeff Fort (b. 1947)

Fort was born in Aberdeen, Mississippi, and arrived on Blackstone Avenue in Chicago with his mother in 1955. Growing up in the city's Woodlawn neighborhood, Fort left school in the fourth grade a barely literate kid showing little of the imagination that would take him into the top echelons of Chicago crime. He entered the gang life as leader of Woodlawn's notorious Back P. Stone Rangers (Schatzberg and Kelly 1997).

As the 1980s drew to a conclusion, it was clear that the El Rukns were on the decline. The city had torn down its headquarters and most of the organization's leaders were in prison. They have been eclipsed in recent years by the more powerful Black Gangster Disciples.

Black Gangster Disciples

At the turn of the new millennium, the Black Gangster Disciples (BGDs) had ascended to the top of Chicago's Black underworld, a trek that began when the Black Gangster Disciple Nation (BGDN) was established on Chicago's south side in the early 1960s. Today, the BGDs belong to the Folk Nation group of gangs that formed in response to the emergence of the Black P. Stone Nation conglomeration of gangs who controlled the Englewood section of Chicago. Its co-founders were David "King David" Barksdale, leader of the Gonzanto Disciples, and Larry Hoover, who headed the Supreme Disciples. Both groups joined together to form the BGDN, with Hoover acting as the organization's number two and Barksdale its leader. In 1972, Barksdale was shot down, leaving the organization in the hands of Larry Hoover. However, following the death of Barksdale, Jerome Freeman, who was loyal to his former chief and a former member of the Gonzanto Disciples, established a parallel line of leadership, and the group split in two. Freeman's gang took the name Black Disciples (BD), whereas Hoover's group adopted the name Black Gangster Disciples (BGD). The BGD adopted the Jewish Star of David with upturned pitchforks as its identifying symbol. Under the guiding hand of Hoover, the BGD morphed into one of America's largest criminal organizations, with branches in most Midwestern cities. However, the BDs have stayed rather localized in the Chicago area.

During the mid-1990s, a federal task force targeted the criminal activities of the BGDs and in the process uncovered a drug-running empire. A successful prosecution led to long prison sentences for a number of its leaders. In the 1990s, the gang boasted as many as 30,000 members[29] and became involved in politics in an effort influence the political process, launching several members toward political careers where they could better look after gang activities. The gang had found as did those in New York City in the previous century that, "Because the number of patronage jobs available to elected officials, especially in cities such as Chicago, efforts to penetrate the political process bring considerable benefits" (Decker, Bynum, and Weisel).

The increasingly "politicized" gang, under the guise of the "21st Century Vote" and "Growth and Development," devoted much of its efforts in the late 1990s to passing out leaflets in support of selected candidates, registering voters, and soliciting contributions. The consensus was that the political campaigning was an attempt to assemble support to free Gangster Disciple leader Larry Hoover, who was jailed on federal drug charges in 1997. Although the organization has strived to create a mask of respectability, by most accounts it is a smokescreen to cover involvement in large-scale drug dealing, contract killings, and more sophisticated white-collar crime.

Larry Hoover

Larry Hoover directed a multimillion-dollar-a-year organized crime empire from behind prison bars for almost 30 years. He was shuffled from prison to prison in Illinois, where he was serving a life sentence for killing a competing drug dealer in the 1970s. On the streets of Chicago he attained a mythic status as a "Black Al Capone," but was more often referred to as "King Larry" or "the Chairman." In the late 1990s, the sun began to set on King Larry's empire after the DEA working together with other federal, state, and local law enforcement agencies virtually dismantled the organization sending 40 high-ranking GD to prison. In the aftermath, he attempted to run his syndicate from the Vienna Correctional Center. Correctional administrators ended that by moving him to another prison.

Black Gangster Disciples Bylaws

1. All members shall abide by the code of secrecy and silence.
2. Every member should believe in respect and no disrespect to every member and non-standing members.
3. No member shall take property from any other member or non-standing member.
4. No member shall take any addictive drug.
5. No member shall break and enter any building which may cause institutionalization.
6. All confrontations with any other members or non-standing members will be reported through the proper chain of command whether major or minor.
7. No member will argue with any officers or guards.
8. No member shall gamble unless all merchandise is up front.
9. All members must pay dues.
10. All members are requested to have personal hygiene.
11. All members are required to exercise daily.
12. All members are required to aid and assist when asked to.
13. All members must participate in all meetings and gatherings.
14. No member shall participate in homosexuality.
15. All members are required to be on the money.
16. All members are required to uphold all laws set forth. (Valentine and Schober 2000, 82)

In its heyday at the end of the 1990s, the BGDs contrasted sharply with other African American gangs that were more loosely structured, such as the Crips and Bloods. Hoover sat at the top of the chain of command as "chairman," and under him sat two "boards of directors." One board controlled street activities and the other the prison rackets. Under the directors sat an estimated fifteen "governors," who were expected to supervise "regional operations in hundreds of franchised territories." "Regional bosses" at the next level were divided into "regents" and "coordinators" who were responsible for selling drugs and weapons, supervising security forces and tax collection, and forwarding messages to the top echelons from the street level. "Enforcers" imposed discipline and fines at the next level. At the same level, "shorties" concocted drug deals and strategically armed posts on the gang's turf (Valentine and Schober 2000, 81). This sophisticated structure is credited in part with earning the gang's drug operations in excess of $100 million a year at its zenith.

At the turn of the 21st century, Larry Hoover was still in control of the gang behind prison bars. Voter registration drives led by the Gangster Disciples have registered thousands of young African Americans. By getting out the vote, similar to their Irish and Italian forerunners, the gang created voting blocs to support local ward-level politicians. During the Clinton administration, the BGDs earned a patina of acceptance when Clinton met with Jesse Jackson and Hoover's right-hand man, Wallace "Gator" Bradley, for a photo-op in the Oval Office. Bradley, a character in his own right, insisted that BGD no longer stood for Black Gangster Disciple Nation, but was an acronym for the civic organization now known as "Better Growth and Development." In recent years, the gang has relaxed its Black-only restrictions and has initiated White and Hispanic youths into the gang. The gang continues to participate in numerous criminal activities, including money laundering; drug and weapons trafficking are among their more prominent enterprises.

Recent reports indicate that the Gangster Disciples are still one of Chicago's most structured and largest street gangs, with at least 7,300 local members, with other estimates as high as 30,000. The conviction of most of the leadership has cast the gang's hierarchical structure into a bit of disarray. In any case, the Chicago Police Department identified at least 36 factions in the city in their last report (Chicago Crime Commission 2006, 12). Its main rivals include the Latin Kings and the Vice Lords. However, law enforcement concedes that although each group aligns itself with either

Gang Communication: Survey of Chicago Area Police Departments (81 responses)

Method Used by Gang	Number of Departments Reporting Communication Method
Cell Phones	70
Text Messaging	49
Faxes	5
E-mail	23
Chat rooms	20
Websites	21
Radio Stations	3
Party Lines	13
Other	
Graffiti	2
Walkie-Talkies	8
Instant Messages	1

(Chicago Crime Commission 2006, 99)

the People or Folks, these alliances mean little, and both gangs are not above cooperating with each other when enough money is on the table.

ALMIGHTY LATIN KING NATION

The Almighty Latin Kings, formerly the Latin Kings, originated in Chicago sometime in the 1940s. The gang is considered by most experts to be the oldest and largest Chicago Hispanic street gang. By most accounts, it emerged with the original goal of protecting Hispanics from African American gangs. Its creation was based on racial and ethnic solidarity. Originally, members had to have Latin roots, although most members were Puerto Rican. New waves of immigrants and changing demographics opened membership to Latvians, Italians, Portuguese, Spanish, Caribbean, and South American newcomers. However, for most of its modern history, the Latin Kings have been overwhelmingly Hispanic, although it does have White and African American members. The Latin Kings are involved in a wide range of criminal activity, not limited to drug and weapons trafficking, murder, robbery, extortion, and witness intimidation. They have a well-deserved reputation for ruthlessness and violence.

In recent years, the gang is more formally known as "The Almighty Latin Kings and Queens Nation," and boasts chapters from New York, Florida, and Illinois to New Mexico and California. Its presence can be found in most cities harboring large Hispanic-speaking enclaves.

Gangster Disciples in the Mississippi Delta (2007)

In recent years, Chicago's Gangster Disciples and Vice Lords have been fighting over several streets in the small Mississippi Delta town of Tutwiler. Observers claim that the gangs have been a problem in this poor rural area since the 1980s, linked to familial connections that go back to the Great Black Migration north in the 1940s and 1950s. In 2007, law enforcement were trying to shut down a trade that saw weapons going north and drugs south. Officials expressed surprise when 13 young people were arrested on gun-trafficking charges in 2007. One sociologist surmised that the gangs have evolved outside their typical urban breeding grounds because this region offers young men few legitimate opportunities and is beset by rural poverty (Joyner 2007, 3A).

The Largest Gangs Represented among Inmates in American Correctional Institutions, 1999[30]

In rank order:
Crips (various factions)
Black Gangster Disciples
Bloods/Piru factions
Vice Lord factions
Aryan Brotherhood
Latin King factions

The Latin Kings contrast sharply with other street gangs due to their structure and organization as well as having a written constitution, the 30-page *King Manifesto,* which contains the bylaws of the Almighty Latin King Nation. The Kings have an established hierarchy and chain of command. Leaders have grandiose titles such as "King Blood," "First Supreme Crown," and "King Tone." Its identifying colors are gold and black, representing life and death. In addition, the Kings are one of the rare gangs that allow female members. The gang's motto is "Once a King, always a King."

The Latin King structure has two recognized leaders, each responsible for the north and south sides of Chicago. There are more than 20 factions in Chicago alone. As a People Nation gang, it is often at war with the Imperial Gangsters, the Black Gangster Disciples, and the Maniac Latin Disciples.

The Latin Kings reached an apogee of sorts in the 1980s when gang membership surpassed 2,000. However, its size became its Achilles' heel, resulting in fratricidal bloodletting before the end of the decade. The gang extended its power into prisons in the 1980s with the incarceration of a number of members. Authorities estimate there are more than 15,000 Latin Kings doing time (Valentine 2000). Some gang experts suggest that despite its growing reputation for violence, the Kings "have matured into sophisticated criminal enterprises" (DeVito 2004).

THE CRIPS AND BLOODS

Los Angeles has a rich history of street gang activity, with the earliest progenitors of Hispanic heritage dating back at least as far back as 1900. African American gangs made their appearance sometime in the 1920s. Early gangs of the 1920s and 1930s included the Goodlows, the Kelleys, the Magnificents, the Driver Brothers, the Boozies, and the Blodgettes. By the 1930s, most of these gangs fell apart as members aged out. There were several juvenile gangs prior to the 1950s, but none was involved in organized crime activity. The 1950s and 1960s saw a number of inconsequential gangs, with many young Blacks finding more inspiration in the Black Panthers and Black consciousness-raising organizations rather than street crime.

The Crips and Blood gangs were the most prominent African-American street gangs of the late 20th century, in part because of the attention focused on them by the media. Both gangs emerged from the mean streets of South-Central Los Angeles in the early 1970s. By March 1988, officials estimated that 58.3% of all murders committed in Los Angeles were gang related. Most of the violence was related to controlling the crack cocaine trade. During the 1970s, Bloods and Crips moved into new neighborhoods, expanding their turf and recruiting new members. A number of sub-groups broke away to form their own sets, averaging between 30 and 100 members each. For example, the Five Deuce Hoover Crips were a Crips set, and the Bounty Hunters a Bloods set. One argument that has been used to differentiate street gangs from traditional organized crime is the fact that the gangs themselves do not have a common leader or council to direct the activities of the sets.

Originally, each one generally remained distinct and neighborhood based. However, by the 1990s efforts were being made to unify some of the Crips sets.

Originally, each of the sets got along with each other, viewing the other gang as a common enemy. However, disputes soon arose between various Crips sets, often leading to bloodshed. One of the bloodiest conflicts raged between the Eight Tray Gangsters and the Rollin' Sixties, both Crips sets. During the late 1970s and beyond, hundreds of members and associates were killed and, as gang expert Bill Valentine makes clear, "By the late 1990s more Crip casualties had been inflicted by other Crips than Bloods" (2000, 76).

The introduction of crack cocaine in the 1980s was a watershed of sorts for gangs across the country, with most gang activity directed toward controlling the crack trade. As a result, virtual armies were created replete with the most high-tech weapons to control the lucrative business. Crack cocaine stimulated the creation of some organization within the various territories, because the trafficking system needed a multi-layer of operatives—street-level dealers, soldiers, runners, collectors, enforcers, and counterintelligence—the specialization that marks other syndicates.

During the late 1980s, Bloods and Crips began to expand consciously outside Los Angeles to exploit the market differentials of the drug markets. The Los Angeles Sheriff's Office reported the existence of 25 major Black gangs involved in drug distribution outside of Los Angeles (1990). At that time, an ounce of cocaine was going for $300 in L.A. County and between $800 and $1500 elsewhere. A handful of older Crips and Bloods became virtual godfathers. These *OGs,* or Original Gangsters, reached an apogee where they were actually dealing directly with Colombian cartels. In recent years, LAPD officials reported that they had received inquiries from police departments about the Crips and Bloods from 48 different states.

More recently, both types of gangs have been aligning themselves with the Folk and People Nation based in Chicago, with the Bloods trying to hook up with the People Nation and the Crips with the Gangster Disciples (Valentine 2000). In recent years, a number of Bloods and Crips have dispensed with the showing of colors, preferring to identify by their sets. The Lime Hood Pirus, for one now use Green and Red, whereas the Watts Vario Grape set prefers purple. Gang identifiers have expanded to include particular hair picks, certain brands of shoes, and hair ties. For example, Bloods or Blood Killers prefer the British Knights (BK) brand; likewise, Crip Killers (CKs) prefer CK for Calvin Klein (Valentine 2000).

Crack Cocaine

Best known for the quote, "Read My Lips," President-Elect George H.W. Bush would probably prefer to be remembered for a speech in Los Angeles on May 17, 1988, in which he said, "Gang members and narcotics are a marriage made in hell, and gentlemen, this is one marriage we've got to break up." According to one 1990 report, two drug syndicates in South-Central Los Angeles fought for the control of the local market, resulting in 25 murders in an 8-month period. The syndicates operated a combined 130 "rock" houses, employing hundreds of young gang members as couriers, hit men, and street salesmen. Older former members who had "aged out" of the street scene and were currently operating legitimate business as fronts ran the syndicates. According to records seized from one of the syndicates, it was grossing almost $160,000 each day. In the late 1980s, urban street gangs had become major cogs in the distribution of cocaine, distributing crack cocaine directly from Colombian and Mexican importers. A joint investigation of the Rayful Edmond III cocaine distribution network revealed the prominence of Los Angeles street gangs. This organization attempted to bring hundreds of pounds of cocaine into the Washington, D.C., area. The supply came directly from a Colombian source, which used a member of the West Coast Crips as an intermediary. Much of the evidence for this relationship was drawn from wiretaps. Ultimately, law enforcement seized $600,000 in drug proceeds.

Origin of the Crips Moniker

There are a number of explanations for how the Crips got their name. The most repeated stories suggest that gang leader Raymond Washington adopted it from the Vincent Price film *Tales from the Crypt,* leading to the suggestion that if you messed with this gang you too would end up in a crypt (Valentine 2000). Another suggested the term was borrowed from Superman's fictional nemesis, kryptonite. One popular theory has it that "Crip" evolved from the word "Crib," which, in the 1970s, was a faction of the Slausons, the most powerful Black gang in South Central. Another has it that one of the founders (Raymond Washington) walked with a limp and a cane. When the gang, including the physically challenged member, attacked some Asian visitors, they described the assailants to the police, focusing on the limping member, repeating over and over "a crip, a crip with a stick." If this is to be believed, a reporter then picked up on it and adopted "Crip" to connote the gang. Another closely associated explanation suggests that the name came from the gang practice of using canes to beat their victims until they were crippled. More recently, new members presume the name reflects its political roots, hence the acronym CRIP, or Common Revolution in Progress (Valentine 1995).

The Crips

Of several individuals associated with the founding of the Crips, Raymond "Truck" Washington is the most prominent. Early Crips criminal activity leaned toward robberies, extortions, car thefts, and assaults on non-Crips. Over a rather short time, the Crips earned premier status in the constellation of Los Angeles gangs. As a result, a number of other gangs began to adopt the Crips designation as part of their gang names. For example the Five Deuce (52)[31] Hoovers became the Five Deuce (52) Hoover Crips; the Main Street gang became the Main Street Crips, and so forth. Even though it was clear where a gang's allegiance was, it retained autonomy.

Crips are identified by the color blue, which can be displayed through bandannas, articles of clothing, and hats. According to the LAPD, the color blue was inspired by the color associated with Los Angeles' Washington High School.

The Crips began expanding their reach into other states sometime in the late 1980s. By 1991, the Justice Department reported Crips and Bloods in 32 states and 113 cities. In 2000, these gangs reportedly controlled 30% of the crack trade. The Crips remain the Los Angeles' largest Black street gang, with some 30,000 members (Kelly 2000).

The Bloods

The Bloods gangs developed in order to protect themselves from the dominant Crips gangs. Sylvester Scott and Vincent Owens organized the first Bloods club, calling it the Compton Pirus (West Piru Street in Compton). As the gang established an identity of its own and earned street credibility, other gangs aligned themselves as Bloods gangs, including the Brims, the Bounty Hunters, the Swans, and the Family. Most accounts suggest that the Brims and Pirus typically addressed each other as "Bloods." Both gangs evidently formed an alliance, creating the original Bloods gang.

The Bloods are aligned with the People Nation sets and, unlike the Crips, there has been very little infighting between the various Bloods sets. Today, the Bloods are estimated to be about a third of the size of the Crips, with some 9,000 Latino and Black members. Bloods are typically identified by the color red, often represented by a bandanna or rag, and the word Piru, for the original Bloods gang.

Originally, the gang restricted membership to Blacks only, but in recent years they have accepted other ethnic groups including Hispanics, Whites, Greeks, and Chinese members. Typical criminal activities include drug dealing, car theft, extortion, and murder.

Bloods Organizational Structure

- **First Superior (the leader):** Directs functions and activities of the set and acts as disciplinary officer.
- **Second Superior:** Similar to the relationship between a president and vice president, he assists and advises the First Superior and fills in for him when he is absent.
- **Minister of Defense:** Provides strategies and information to the First Superior concerning the operations of the set.
- **Minister of Information:** Provides information concerning the set and its rivals.
- **Head of Security:** Provides weapons and discipline to all members of set.
- **Commanding Officer:** Relays orders from Superior.
- **Captain:** Relays orders to lieutenants.
- **Head Lieutenant:** Assists and advises the captain and performs his duties when he is unavailable.
- **Lieutenant:** Ensures that the principal soldiers carry out captain's orders.
- **Principal Soldier:** Follows orders from lieutenant at all times and is expected to be at constant war with rival gangs.

(DeVito, 2005)

Mara Salvatrucha (MS-13): America's Most Dangerous Gang?

Initially, MS-13 membership was restricted to Salvadorans, but by the turn of the 21st century, the gang's ranks counted members from Ecuador, Guatemala, Honduras, and Mexico, as well as several African Americans. Most profiles indicate average age ranges widely from 11 to 40 years of age. Members can be identified by a variety of tattoos. Most use the number 13 and typically identify themselves as *Sureños* or southerners, signifying that they are aligned with southern California gangs against their northern rivals. Because there are a number of southern California gangs (and prison gangs) that use the "13" symbol, it is important to recognize an additional "M" or "MS" tattoo.

MS-13 is sophisticated and violent and has been involved in the shootings of peace officers throughout the United States. Members have put their military skills to use by booby-trapping stash houses with explosives. Former gang members have testified that the gang is well structured with multiple leaders. Most members fear deportation to El Salvador, where death squad vigilantes tired of the national crime problem such as the Black Shadow and the Lightening Command await them.

Mara Salvatrucha,[32] or as it is better known, MS-13, was organized in Los Angeles in the late 1980s. It was named for La Mara, a street in San Salvador, as well as for the so-called Salvatrucha guerrillas who fought in El Salvador's violent civil war during the early 1980s. More than 100,000 people died during the conflict, with more than 1 million fleeing to the United States. Many initially settled in southern California and Washington, D.C. (Alvarez 2000). Some of the immigrants had served in the paramilitary Farabundo Marti National Liberation Front (FMNL) during the civil war and were skilled in the military art of bomb making and firearms. Refugees from La Mara and the FMNL banded together to protect themselves from Los Angeles' myriad street gangs, creating Mara Salvatrucha. It wasn't long before the gang evolved into something worse, as it began preying on fellow immigrants in Salvadoran neighborhoods. Gang members are identifiable by the blue and white colors of the El Salvador national flag. Many also wear tattoos on their bodies and faces. However, it is the ones who are not marked that are considered the most dangerous. MS-13 is no longer only a southern California phenomenon. Police reports indicate the gang has spread throughout the country into Alaska, Oregon, Utah, Texas, Nevada, Oklahoma, Michigan, New York, Maryland, Virginia, Georgia, Florida, and Washington, D.C. In addition, the gang has exported its criminal propensities back to Central America. In 2004, there were an estimated 36,000 MS-13 members in just Honduras (Domash 2006).

As early as the 1990s, the Mexican Mafia was using MS-13 members as tax collectors and drug connections. MS-13 first appeared on law enforcement radar in the 1990s, when several members were deported to El Salvador. Back in their home country, members regrouped and many returned to the United States. In early 2005, the National Drug Intelligence Center (of the Justice Department) estimated that there were 8,000 to 10,000 members in America and at least 50,000 internationally (Harman 2005). By the end of 2004, the FBI created a task force to keep track of MS-13 criminal enterprises.

MS-13 has taken advantage of its contacts in El Salvador, where a hand grenade can be purchased for $1 or $2 and sold for more $200 in the United States, a relationship that has provided MS-13 with military hardware and created a thriving weapons trafficking network. Curiously, street intelligence revealed that handguns are less readily available in El Salvador and are considered a valuable commodity. According to one investigator, the demand for them is so high "that MS members will often take handguns as payments for drug transactions," and the guns are sent either back to El Salvador or to the streets of urban America (Valdez 2000, 1).

Mara Salvatrucha is involved in a litany of criminal enterprises, including automobile thefts, which are often traded to South American drug cartels for drugs. One estimate suggests that in 2000, 80% of the cars driven in El Salvador had been stolen in the United States. Besides car theft and weapons and drug trafficking, MS-13 has been connected to home invasion robberies, extortion, rapes, witness intimidation, and carjackings. Drug trafficking products include cocaine, marijuana, heroin, and methamphetamines. Southern California gang investigator Al Valdez asserted, "MS gang members tend to have a higher level of criminal involvement than other gang members" (2000, 1). Members have expanded into other rackets, even going as far as to tax prostitutes.

MS-13 has made the transition from merely another gang culture to organized criminal organization in a rather short time because it is "extremely flexible in its activity, [willing to] do any crime at any time" (Domas 2006, 2). The gang contrasts sharply with other street gangs; according to senior FBI Agent Robert Hart, as MS-13 gangs unite, the results can be catastrophic for law enforcement. Hart said,

> The cliques, instead of operating independently of each other, are beginning to come together. The difference is by doing that, obviously you have a much tighter organization, much stronger structures and, instead of having various cliques doing whatever they want, whenever they want, there is one individual who is the leader and able to control the payment of dues and the criminal acts they engage in. The result is very, very similar to what you would see in what we refer to as traditional organized crime families. (Domas 2006, 2)

What has also made MS-13 so difficult to keep track of is their mobility and ability to adapt to law enforcement strategies. According to one reporter, "when it feels the heat in the U.S., it moves to another state. When it feels heat in El Salvador and Honduras it sets up operations in Mexico" (Domas 2004, 4). One Washington, D.C., right-wing think tank, the Maldon Institute, asserted that the gang "appears to be in control of much of the Mexican border and, in addition to its smuggling and contraband rackets, the gang collects money from illegal immigrants that it helps [move] across the border (quoted in Domash 2004, 4). When it comes to detection, once gang members realize they are under surveillance, they adapt by changing colors and even numbers, substituting 67 and 76 for 13.

Case Study: Gang Members and the Military

Since the mid-1980s, investigators and gang experts have become aware of a growing number of street gang members in the American military. More recently, the *Chicago Sun-Times* reported, "The Gangster Disciples, Latin Kings, and Vice Lords were born decades ago in Chicago's most violent neighborhoods. Now, their gang graffiti is showing up 6,400 miles away in one of the world's most dangerous neighborhoods—Iraq." According to the newspaper, one Department of Defense investigator identified 320 admitted gang members who have served in Iraq since April 2002. Although most of those identified as either Latino or Black, a number of soldiers have been linked to racist groups such as the Aryan Nations. In May 2006, a Wisconsin National Guard sergeant serving in Iraq provided the *Chicago Sun-Times* with photos he took of gang graffiti on buildings and equipment throughout Iraq. According to his reports,

> Armored vehicles, concrete barricades, and bathroom walls all have served as canvasses for their spray-painted gang art. At Camp Cedar, about 185 miles southeast of Baghdad, a guard shack was recently defaced with "GDN" for Gangster Disciple Nation, along with the gang's six-pointed star and the word "Chitown" (Main 2006).

Attempts by soldiers to report the increased activity have been stonewalled by superior officers and have been told "not to ruffle their feathers because they were doing a good job." According to one soldier with gang interdiction experience in the correctional system, gang members make little effort to hide tattoos and gang identifiers, citing the Vice Lords and Simon City Royals of Chicago as examples.

Gang members have also had an impact on military communities in the United States. One report indicated that a dozen soldiers, identified as Gangster Disciples, at bases in Texas and Colorado were sentenced to prison since the mid-1990s after federal investigations into criminal activities (Main 2006). One investigation at Fort Carson in Colorado in 1996 revealed that a retired Army sergeant and Gangster Disciples leader had relocated from Chicago to Colorado Springs, where he maintained contact with gang members serving as non-commissioned officers. ATF agents targeted the sergeant and 25 other Gangster Disciples engaged in a weapons and drug trafficking. The gang associates bought cocaine and marijuana in El Paso, Texas, using an Army contact at Fort Bliss and resold it in Gary, Indiana, where one of the members, an active-duty sergeant, lived. The same individual used his military ID to purchase weapons in Colorado and shipped them back to Gary. Some were later connected to crimes committed in Chicago. The sergeant was arrested and sentenced to 15 years in military prison (Main 2006).

In 2006, the FBI revealed it was concerned about gang activity at Fort Bliss and Fort Carson. One agent in El Paso told the *Sun Times,* "law enforcement agencies there are preparing for a rise in soldiers affiliated with the Gangster Disciples and other 'Folk Nation' gangs" (Main 2006) when they are relocated to Bliss from Fort Hood. In 1999, one soldier was even identified as the "governor" of a 40-member group of Gangster Disciples, including a number of soldiers.

There are a number of experts who suggest that there has been an overreaction to the purported menace suggesting that many of the soldiers who left the gang symbols "had no gang affiliation and little knowledge of how gangs operate." By most accounts, according to a spokesman for the Army's Criminal Investigation Command, "In nearly every one of the cases that we look into, it is a young man or woman who thought the symbol looked cool," adding that, "We have found some people even get gang tattoos not knowing what they really are" (*Chicago Tribune,* 2006). Most Army investigators have admitted that there are gang members in the military, but insist that it is not a problem.

More than a decade ago the national media warned that L.A. street gang members from the Bloods and Crips were infiltrating the military (*Weekly Journal,* 1995; *Newsweek,* 1995). One *Newsweek* investigation claimed that members of the Crips, the Bloods, and Chicago's Folk gangsters were active in all four branches of the armed forces and on more than 50 military bases in the United States. Photos and reports all point to a growing gang threat in the military. During the first Gulf Wars, soldiers were photographed flashing gang signs and on some aircraft carriers some gang members reportedly staked out territory while at sea. Despite such incidents, most gang-related crime has been strictly small time in the 1990s.

Is this simply hysteria or is it a self-fulfilling prophecy? One 1994 Justice Department report warned that some gang members had gained expertise with grenades, machine guns, rocket launchers and military experts that they have used to train gang members on American streets (*Newsweek,* 1995). Since 2006, gang members in Seattle have been caught wearing flak jackets probably stolen from Fort Lewis and on another occasion a soldier linked to a White racist gang was apprehended attempting to ship an assault rifle back to the United States from Iraq. Although these are not master criminals, at least one expert has recorded soldiers involved in drug dealing, gunrunning, and other criminal activity off base (*Chicago Sun-Times,* 2006). Just a month into 2007, an FBI investigator revealed to *Stars and Stripes:* "gang members have been documented on or near U.S. military bases in Germany, Italy, Japan, South Korea, and Iraq" (Robson, 2007). Although there are no official statistics identifying the number of gang members in the military, experts have estimated that one to two percent are gang members, compared just 0.02% of the U.S. population (Robson, 2007).

Overview

The continual demographic changes wrought by global-ization and changing immigration patterns together with the ever-changing demands of illegal market economies have an impact on street gangs and prison gangs that are especially based on race and ethnicity. The increasing flow of undocumented migrants across porous borders, deportations, and improved transportation and commu-nication networks have helped gangs like MS-13 be-come international crime networks (Johnson and Muhlhausen 2005). As a result, the gang scene and its culture are in an almost constant state of fluctuation. Current trends are highly influenced by punitive drug laws that lock up virtual entire gangs in the same prison, where they put whatever organizational skills they have to work much as they would on the streets.

One of the more unforeseen consequences has been the increasing dominance of prison gangs over street gangs. They have been able to flout their new power by exacting street taxes from retail drug distribution net-works and managing the flow of drugs through major Mexican drug-trafficking organizations. According to a 2006 report by the National Drug Intelligence Center, the prison gangs now play the role of broker between the drug syndicates and the street gangs. This symbiosis has been especially rewarding for the Mexican drug-trafficking organizations because by using the gangs to move the drugs, it offers them an extra level of insulation from law enforcement.

A number of studies indicate that some modern gangs have distanced themselves from stereotypical de-pictions. Many of the newly emerging gangs might adopt the names of older gangs, but the similarities often end there. These developments are making the identifi-cation of gang members more difficult in some regions. Recent research suggests that there is a hybrid quality to a number of modern gangs, producing in effect a

> hybrid gang culture . . . characterized by mixed racial and ethnic participation in multiple gangs by a single individual, vague rules and codes of

conduct for gang members, use of symbols and colors from multiple—even rival—gangs, collab-oration by rival gangs in criminal activities, and the merger of smaller gangs into larger ones. (Starbuck et al, 2001)

Many are eschewing the traditional colors and iden-tifiers and keeping a lower profile; the same goes with some OMG members. One official lamented, "They're getting so much smarter. They don't stand out like they used to." Hybrid gangs differ from earlier prototypes in that "they lack the hierarchy and structure of the coun-try's larger, more dangerous gangs" (Wagner 2006).

Outlaw motorcycle gangs have been part of American popular culture since the late 1940s. For more than a half century, they symbolized a renegade culture eschewing the rules of civility. Since the mid-1980s, they have emerged as major drug-trafficking syndicates with all of the trappings of La Cosa Nostra. Some ac-counts suggest that one major OMG chapter modeled it-self after Mario Puzo's potboiler, *The Godfather*. Today, OMGs are clearly major players in international organ-ized crime, with some groups having branches in dozens of countries—part of the trend toward transnational or-ganized crime made possible by new technologies and the growing demand for illegal contraband. Hells Angels is the still the dominant OMG internationally. Recent es-timates place membership at 2,500 members in 23 states and 25 countries on 5 continents (Marsden and Sher 2006, 5).

The biker of the 1960s might not recognize his modern counterpart as they strip off their sinister colors and don the sartorial trappings of a businessman. The other symbol, the motorcycle, has also become a nostal-gic reminder as the modern OMG member waits for the valet to bring him his Lexus. The notion today is that bikes are too obvious for conducting criminal business. Angels' expert Yves Lavigne claims that by the late 1980s, the runs and motorcycles had become *de passé* as well (Lavigne 1987).

Key Terms

Outlaw Motorcycle gangs	Pagans	Aryan Brotherhood
Prison gangs	Bandidos	Texas Syndicate
Hells Angels	La Nuestra Familia	Black Guerrilla
Outlaws	Mexican Mafia	Family Mamas

Sheep	Blackstone Rangers	Latin Kings
Old Lady	Jeff Fort	People Nation
Broad	Bloods	Folk Nation
POBOBS	Crips	Larry Hoover
Colors	Sets	"Growth and Development"
Rocker	Carnal	21st Century Vote
Ralph "Sonny" Barger	"Blood In, Blood Out"	*Norteños*
Great Nordic Biker War	Neta	*Sureños*
Cooper v. Pate	Nazi Low Riders	MS-13
Gangster Disciples	First Command of the Capital (PCC)	Mara Salvatrucha
El Rukns	Vice Lords	

Critical Thinking Questions

1. What are outlaw motorcycle gangs (OMGs)? When did they first appear? Are all motorcycle gangs/groups criminal?

2. What are the major OMGs? Describe their similarities and differences, especially their structure. Why is the Hells Angles the best known of these?

3. Compare the hierarchy of Hells Angels with that of a traditional Italian American crime family.

4. What was the impact of the U.S. Supreme Court decision *Cooper v. Pate* on the establishment of prison gangs?

5. Why did California's prison system spawn most of today's major prison gangs? Why is Illinois's prison system so saturated with gang members?

6. What are the major Hispanic prison gangs? What is distinct about the Mexican Mafia?

7. Describe the evolution of White prison gangs. What distinguishes the Aryan Brotherhood from other prison gangs? Why are they so feared both in and out of prison?

8. What does "Blood In, Blood Out" mean? Which gangs subscribe to this rule?

9. Compare and contrast the Mexican Mafia with the Aryan Brotherhood.

10. Describe the impact of the Black Power movement and *Cooper v. Pate* on the growth of Black prison gangs.

11. Why do urban street gangs persist into the 21st century? Why has it become an international phenomenon? Which countries are most likely to have them?

12. Are street gangs and prison gangs really a form of organized crime? Explain.

13. Describe the influence of Jeff Fort and Larry Hoover on their respective gangs, even though they are in prison.

14. What determines which Hispanic street gang one belongs to in California? Which are considered the most and least sophisticated?

15. Compare and contrast the structure of the Crips and Bloods.

16. What is MS-13?

Endnotes

1. *Organized Crime in America*, Hearings Before the Committee on the Judiciary, United States Senate, 98th Cong., First Session on Organized Crime in America, Part 1. (Hereafter cited as Hearings on Organized Crime, 1983.)

2. Hells Angels dispensed with the apostrophe in "Hell's" a number of years ago.

3. Since then, several states have experimented with "resegregating certain cell blocks as a security measure meant to weaken race-based gangs" (Anti-Defamation League 2002).

4. According to the National Youth Gang Center, estimated gang membership in the United States decreased 6%, from 780,233 in 1998 to 731,500 in 2002.

5. The film was evidently quite popular among bikers. The president of the Hells Angels San Francisco chapter was so enamored he drove down to Hollywood in 1954 and bought the T-shirt worn by Lee Marvin in the film.

6. In 1983, Butch was a 43-year-old member and 14-year veteran of the Cleveland, Ohio, chapter of the Hells Angels. He was also a founding member of the Bandidos in Texas in 1966. He was a high-ranking member of the Angels in the 1970s. At the time of his testimony, he was a federally protected witness.

7. Although it is unsubstantiated, some experts indicate the Hells Angels moniker may have been inspired by the prewar-film by the same name. In 1927, Howard Hughes bought 87 planes for his film project, *Hell's Angels,* starring silent-film star Jean Harlow. The filming of the air combat scenes is considered groundbreaking. The film was a huge success. During World War II, U.S. general Claire Chennault organized the Flying Tigers to help the Chinese fight the Japanese. He divided the group into three squads, including one named the Hell's Angels.

8. According to the online and notoriously unreliable encyclopedia Wikipedia, the story about the Frito Bandito inspiring the club's name is not true, because Fritos did not adopt the image until 1968, two years later.

9. In 1989, the state of New Jersey released the findings of its investigation into OMGs and estimated the membership at between 300 and 400 in New Jersey, Pennsylvania, Delaware, New York, Maryland, West Virginia, Kentucky, Ohio, Virginia, North Carolina and South Carolina.

10. See *United States v. Bowman,* 302 F.3d 1228, 1232 (11th Cir., 2002).

11. The Outlaws' Web site had previously announced that its members would attend the rally, but would not make any display of power, and even claimed to have notified federal law enforcement of their itinerary, including plans to sightsee and enjoy the rally.

12. Marsden and Sher call it the Undertakers (2006, 243), whereas Nicaso and Lamothe refer to it as the Morticians (2004, 228).

13. For example, except for several paragraphs on the Aryan Brotherhood, prison gangs are still not covered in the 8th edition of Howard Abadinsky's *Organized Crime,* 2006.

14. FOIA, Mexican Mafia, December 7, 1973, p. 18.

15. Hallinan, 2001, p. 96; originally featured in November 10, 1996, *Chicago Tribune,* p. 1.

16. These figures reflect about one-third of all adult correctional facilities in the United States. At the same time, gang activity was growing in female correctional institutions, with facilities reporting gang membership from 0 to 50% of populations, with a national mean of 3.1%.

17. Three different sources on prison gangs list three different originating prisons. DeVito cites Folsom State Prison in 1968 (2005, 220); Valentine, in San Quentin in 1968 (2000, 32); and Florida State Prison Gang and Security Threat Group Awareness Web site, asserts Soledad Prison in 1968.

18. FOIA, Mexican Mafia, Dec. 7, 1973, p. 19.

19. The Shamrock originated with an early founder who was obviously proud to be Irish. The tattoo was allowed only after performing a successful first mission.

20. Anti-Defamation League (ADL), *Dangerous Convictions,* 2002.

21. This oath was confiscated during a cell search. New recruits are expected to memorize it within 3 days of their acceptance.

22. The oath rhymes in the form of a poem, just like that of their enemy, the Aryan Brotherhood.

23. Translated from the Portuguese *Primeiro Comando da Capital.*

24. Nationwide, there are 360,000 inmates.

25. Experts estimate the PCC is responsible for three quarters of the kidnappings in Sao Paulo.

26. The authors claimed that the Latin Kings exemplified the cultural gang, where Hispanic culture was more pervasive than any criminal organizational features.

27. In 1969, Fort was invited to President Nixon's inauguration. He did not attend, but sent several representatives.

28. There are a variety of accounts on Fort's conversion. Most suggest that he converted in prison, then returned to the gang and renamed it El Rukns. Other accounts assert Fort was paroled in 1976 and relocated to Milwaukee, Wisconsin, where he joined the Moorish Temple of America and adopted the name Chief Prince Malik, and then returned to Chicago two years later and changed the name of the Black P. Stone Nation to the El Rukns. The name El Rukns was borrowed from the name of the cornerstone of the Kaaba, an Islamic shrine in Mecca, Saudi Arabia.

29. Some sources estimate membership reached 100,000 nationwide by 2000.

30. This information comes from George W. Knox, "A National Assessment of Gangs and Security Threat

Groups in Adult Correctional Institutions; Results of the 1999 Adult Corrections Survey."

31. Street names are typically pronounced as separate words rather than complete numbers, such as Five Deuce instead of 5-2 or 52. See Schatzberg and Kelly 1997.

32. Mara Salvatrucha's etymology is geographically based. The term *mara* refers to a gang in Caliche, and originated in the name of a fiery type of ant called a *marabunta*. *Mara* also refers to the violent gangs of Maraville in East Los Angeles dating back to the 1920s. *Salvatrucha* is a combination of *Salvadoran* and *trucha*, which is Caliche for "being alert" (for police activity or criminal opportunities). Gang expert Bill Valentine offers that the gang's name can be roughly translated as "Beware of the Salvadorans" (2000, 110).

CHAPTER 9

Asian Organized Crime

Asian organized crime groups have been operating in the United States since the end of the 19th century. Long thought to be a recent phenomenon in America, a new generation of scholars has used historical research methods to reveal the roots of Chinese organized crime in America, that predate most of the traditional Italian- and Jewish-American syndicates. In one valuable recent study, Jeffrey Scott McIllvaine unearths evidence demonstrating that Chinese-Americans were engaged in a number of "classic organized criminal enterprises" between 1870 and 1910, including gambling, prostitution, extortion, corruption, and drug trafficking (2004).

Recent scholarship has demonstrated that Chinese-American organized crime began in Chinese communities on the West Coast in the mid-1800s. The first significant Chinese immigration to the United States began in the 1840s, where they found employment as "coolies" or "bitter labor" working in mines and building the Transcontinental Railroad.[1] As job prospects diminished and facing racial hostility and the unionization of white workers, many Chinese immigrants began heading to the East Coast as the century moved to conclusion.

More recently, the end of the Vietnam War era saw an influx of immigrants from Vietnam, Laos, Cambodia, and other parts of Southeast Asia. Although most have assimilated into American society a number went on to form various Indochinese gangs, particularly on the West Coast. What distinguishes most Asian organized crime groups is their predilection for almost exclusively targeting Asian victims.

However, other Asian organized crime groups are even more deeply rooted in their region's historical traditions and patriotic folklore. Chinese Triads can trace their origins back to at least the 17th century, when as resistance fighters they fought the Ching Dynasty.[2] The Japanese Yakuza's roots go back even farther. The term *Yakuza* itself dates back to the beginning of the 1600s. Modern-day Yakuza have been especially inspired by the exploits of the masterless samurai warriors, or *ronin*, who roamed late medieval Japan.

According to the FBI, members of the most dominant Asian criminal groups impacting the United States have links "either directly or culturally" to China, Korea, Japan, Thailand, the Philippines, Cambodia, Laos, and Vietnam. Regarded as adaptable and extremely mobile, they stand out for their multilingual abilities, highly sophisticated operations, and extensive financial resources. Like most groups, they continue to prosper with the continuing globalization of the world economies, facilitated by new communications technologies, generous immigration policies, and international travel opportunities.

CHINESE ORGANIZED CRIME

What Is a Triad Society?

Triad expert Yiu Kong Chu defines *Triad secret societies* as "loose cartels consisting of a number of independent gangs that adopt a similar organizational structure and ritual to bind their members

318

Chinese Concept of *Guanxi*

The Chinese have a deep and abiding reverence for the past. Nothing expresses this more than the ancient Confucian philosophy of reverence for ancestors and name associations. Little business takes place without *guanxi*, which is equivalent to the American concept of networking. This concept is ingrained in Chinese culture. If one does not have *guanxi* in China, it's difficult to get things accomplished—buying certain items, buying airplane tickets, or getting children into a desired university. The Chinese Diaspora that began in the 19th century established communities throughout the world. However, wherever they went, they never lost touch with their roots and traditions and were always welcoming to others who shared their heritage. This allowed Chinese immigrants to create new relationships, establish mutual aid societies, set up schools, and forge partnerships that evolved in some cases into some of the world's largest multinational companies. For law enforcement, deciphering *guanxi* relationships can lead investigators to discover whether a person is hiding a fugitive or providing a car for a smuggling operation, has family obligations that go back generations, or whether there is an ancestral link to the same village or school friendships. The favor must be granted, or the entire extended family could lose face.

together" (2005, 5). Asian gang experts insist that it would be a mistake to assume that all Triad Societies are Chinese criminal organizations, or that all Chinese organized crime members belong to a Triad. Today there is no single Triad movement—only a number of groups often collectively referred to in English as Triads. One authority states, "Most Triads are in fact loosely organized, and shoot-outs and assassinations between rival factions of several gangs using the same name is not uncommon" (Lintner 2005, 90).

The term *Triad* is a purely English designation derived from the sacred emblem of the Society, which consists of a triangle, each side representing the three basic powers of Heaven, Earth, and Ma (Morgan 1960). In Hong Kong, prior to its return to China in 1997, Chinese referred to it as the *Sam Hop Wui* (Three United Association), *Tin Tei Wui* (Heaven and Earth Association), *Hung Mun* (Hung Sect), or *Hak Sh'e Wui*[3] (Black Society Association).

Until the 1960s, most authorities on organized crime traced the first Triad society back to the late Ming/early Ching dynasties, when Shaolin monks formed patriotic resistance in protest against the Manchu rulers who overthrew the Ming in 1644 and formed the Ching dynasty (Morgan 1960). This interpretation has been refuted by Chinese and Western scholars in subsequent decades. In the mid-1960s, evidence in Taiwanese and Chinese repositories revealed that the first such society was probably the Tiandihui—founded at the Goddess of Mercy Temple in Fujian province in 1761. Better known as the "Heaven and Earth Society," it existed more as a mutual aid organization in an unpredictable frontier region rather than a bona fide political organization. Although the majority of "modern" Triads "trace their origins to the Heaven and Earth Society, it was not until 1821 that the name Triad was coined; referring to the magic number 3, which in Chinese numerology denoted the balance between Heaven, Earth and Man" (Murray 1994; Gaylord and Fu 1999).

The British, the Triads, and the Chinese Opium Trade

During the 19th century, China made a concerted attempt to stop the opium trade with India—then a British colony—that had created legions of addicts. Except as a remedy for pain and dysentery, there were few reports of opium addiction in China prior to 1800. In the early 19th century, British merchants were eager to purchase tea, silk, rice, and other commodities from China to feed the growing demand for these products at home. Unfortunately, they had little if any products that the Chinese were interested in buying. In 1773, the British East India Company gained control of India's Bengal opium fields, reportedly the best in the world. During the next century the British inundated China with opium, creating a serious addiction problem among Chinese users who had no familiarity with the drug. In 1839, the Emperor's high commissioner confiscated and destroyed a large trove of opium setting off what would become known as the Opium War. China's defeat by the British in 1842 forced China to accept the free trade of opium within its borders. In order to counter a mounting trade deficit, China allowed the cultivation of its own opium plants beginning in 1880. Although it did away with trade deficits, it also increased the growth of Chinese opium addiction exponentially. It has been estimated that by 1900, at least one-third of the Chinese became users and perhaps 10% were addicted.

Following the 1909 Shanghai Opium Commission and the 1911–1912 International Opium Conference held at The Hague, China began to suppress the domestic cultivation that led to a dramatic shift in the consumption to imported morphine and heroin from Europe and to the centralization of the Shanghai Triads over the illegal opiate trade (McCoy 1992).

Although the British ceased importing opium in 1917, there were still perhaps 150 million Chinese left craving the drug. It was then that Triads and the "Opium King" Tu of the Green Gang moved in to satisfy the demand. So, by the early 20th century, the opium trade had been passed from the British to the Chinese underworld. By the 1920s, Shanghai's drug syndicates were importing 10 tons of heroin from Japan and Europe per year; by the early 1930s, Japanese labs in north China were producing large quantities of heroin. Most accounts suggest that Mao was outraged by the Triad drug trade, which was a chief impetus for driving out the Triads in the 1950s.[4]

Nationalist Period—Overthrow of Manchu, 1911

Hong Kong was considered a private stronghold of Triads and secret societies long before it was ceded to the British in 1842. In earlier days, Triads and outlaw bands took advantage of its prominence as a place of refuge from the Manchu government. Despite a British prohibition against membership, Triads flourished here. First controlling the labor market and then extorting wages from workers. Drugs, gambling, prostitution, and other rackets followed.

Hong Kong's first "homegrown" Triad, the Chung Wo Tung ("Lodge of Loyalty and Righteousness") was founded by Nationalist leader Dr. Sun Yat-sen in the early 20th century. In the late 19th century, the nationalist-Chinese Kuomintang capitalized on the "historical traditions" of the Heaven and Earth Society when its leader, Dr. Sun Yat-sen, began his struggle against Manchu emperors as he attempted to turn China into a republic. By assuming the name "Heaven and Earth Society," Yat-sen more readily found support for his cause and in the process garnered the support of Chinese communities outside of China and from the Ming stronghold of southern China—the home of a majority of Chinese immigrants. Yat-sen played his patriotic credentials to further the political goals of the Nationalists and to make use of Triad muscle (Lintner 2005, 88). Sun Yat-sen traveled the world visiting Chinese communities in search of support for the overthrow of the Manchus and to establish a modern republic, using various Triad organizations overseas to collect funds and disseminate propaganda (Ma 1990).

Following the overthrow of the Manchu government in 1911, the Kuomintang government became more closely affiliated with the Triads. The support of Triads was rewarded with the *de facto* recognition of the society in China. This tacit recognition led to an exponential increase in membership that became so pronounced that a number of officials joined, whereas others were motivated to join for security and profits. It was not much of a leap for Triad activity to make a transition from graft to more blatant criminal activities, so that after the Republican Revolution, the increasingly fragmented Triads became more akin to criminal organizations than patriotic ones.

Chiang Kai-shek

Sun Yat-sen was succeeded by Chiang Kai-shek, a longstanding member of the Green Gang and Triad member, with a resume that included art theft, extortion, and armed robbery (Dubro and Kaplan 1986). In 1926, he was elevated to the leadership of the Kuomintang (Nationalist Party). During the first half of the 20th century, Chiang Kai-Shek's Nationalist government solidified its power by using secret societies such as the Green Gang (see box p. 321,

Shanghai's Green Gang

In contrast with most Triads that have been historically linked to Hong Kong and Taiwan, Shanghai, in mainland China, is home to one of the oldest and most powerful Triads known as the Great Circle Triad. The tremendous growth of this city since the late 1970s has facilitated the rise of the Great Circle Triad and other criminal organizations. From the beginning of the 19th century until the victory of Maoist forces in 1949, the booming international port of Shanghai had a well-deserved reputation as the most decadent city in Asia. For much of this era, an omnipotent criminal underworld controlled the port city in league with the city's wealthiest residents and military satraps. In the 1930s, Edgar Snow reported that in Shanghai, "racketeering flourishes with a velvety smoothness that makes Chicago gangsters seem like noisy play-boys" (Dong 2000, 113).

The most powerful syndicate was known as the Green Gang, which was originally a Triad group. What had once been an organization predominantly composed of peasants and unskilled laborers had morphed into a criminal organization by the end of the 19th century that specialized in drug trafficking, extortion rackets, and bribery. This transition paralleled Shanghai's industrialization in the 1890s, when a growing underclass ensured a legion of willing recruits.

The Green Gang expected new members to take secret oaths and promise unwavering loyalty. Like modern gang members, Green Gang members recognized each other through a sequence of signals that also broadcast the member's position within the gang. Such signals might include a certain way one took a cigarette out of its wrapper or the way one used his eating utensils. Any violation of the gang's rules resulted in severe penalties, ranging from kneecappings and broken bones to severing an ear or execution (Dong 2000).

The Green Gang is notable on several counts, according to Lintner, who asserts that it was "in many ways China's first 'modern' secret society" and should be considered the first Triad to get involved in "the production and distribution of 'modern' drugs such as morphine and heroin" (Lintner 2002, 54).

"Shanghai's Green Gang"), led by the notorious Tu "Big Eared Tu" Yueshang (see box p. 322, "Tu Yueh-sheng"), to manipulate trade unions and the communists in Shanghai (Gaylord and Fu 1999, 119).

In the 1940s, Nationalist government secret police and Kuomintang officers helped create new Triads to fight the rising tide of communism more effectively. Of these, the best known is the 14K Society founded in 1947 by Kuo Gen Kot Sio Wong. The gang's moniker is derived from its original headquarters location at No. 14 Po Wah Road in Guangzhou. By 2005, the 14K was the largest Triad society in Hong Kong, although the Sun Yee On was considered the most powerful (Chu 2005, 5). Today, many experts suggest that the 14K is the world's largest Triad.

Between 1914 and 1939, nearly 300 Triad societies were established in Hong Kong. By the middle of 2005, nearly 50 still existed, 14 of whom were constantly on the police radar, including the Sun Yee On, 14K Hau Group, 14K Tak Group, 14N Ngai Group, Wo Shing Wo, Wo Hop To, Wo On Lok (Shui Fong), and Luen Ying Sh'e.

During the Chinese Civil War, the Nationalists under Chiang Kai-shek ordered the creation of a consortium of all Triad groups that were used to fight against Mao's communist forces using guerrilla warfare.

Communist Victory (1949)

Mao Tse Tung's communist forces emerged victorious from the Chinese Civil War. The victory would have important ramifications for Chinese secret societies and crime syndicates. It is generally accepted that the Communist Revolution ended the country's long plague of drug addiction—but not the Triads. Wherever Chiang fled, Triad members followed—to Hong Kong, Taiwan, and elsewhere. The 14K Society fled to Hong Kong, where many members made new homes in Rennie's Mill, a squalid village on Junk Bay, just east of the old Kai Tai airport.

> ### Tu Yueh-sheng ("Big Eared Tu") c. 1888–1951
>
> Born in one the worst slums of Shanghai, Tu was drawn to the criminal life as a teenager, when he earned a reputation as a contract killer and drug runner. Shanghai was then an international city divided up by three countries. Tu took over a number of gangs and became the second in command of the preeminent Green Gang by the 1910s. His wealth was counted in the tens of millions of dollars as he held sway over most activities on the Yangtze River, Shanghai, and the opium-growing regions. However, it would be his opposition to the increasingly powerful communists that would lead to his downfall. Despite using his gang to rough up or kill literally thousands of students and communist supporters, the ultimate victory by the Maoist forces in 1949 forced him to flee to Hong Kong in 1949, where he died in 1951 (Lunde 2004).

Although it was not much consolation, here the flags of the Nationalist government (now Republic of China in Taiwan) that had fled to Taiwan still fluttered over the run-down slums. Mao consolidated his victory in 1949 by executing or imprisoning many Triad members. Tens of thousands of members fled overseas to Hong Kong and elsewhere. Relocating Green Gang members, once so powerful in Shanghai, were soon replaced in Hong Kong by local syndicates, and the gang faded into memory.

Modern Triads

Modern Triads have been able to operate almost unimpeded by forging alliances with high-ranking members of the army and Communist Party hierarchy, allowing them to continue to operate lucrative gambling and prostitution rackets, minibus services, protection rackets, and even keep a hand in a motion picture industry that "idealizes secret societies and mythical origins" (Lintner 2005, 89).

Triad members have been used by the government to silence critics and exiles, such as Henry Liu. In 1984, an agreement was reportedly made in which security forces delegated killers from the United Bamboo Gang to silence the dissident journalist in exchange for "unofficial" protection for various criminal activities. So, by the 1980s members and non-Triad affiliates filled the role as middlemen, performing sinister tasks for the higher echelons of the social order. The other side of the equation is that although "they are outside the law, [they are] not outside society" (Lintner 2005, 90), and play an important role in suppressing the more unpredictable segment of disorganized criminals who would steal purses and engage in petty crime—both bad for business. Some experts concede that the Chinatowns of New York City and San Francisco are probably the safest parts of town due to similar circumstances in which merchants pay protection to local gangsters to keep order (Lintner 2005, 90).

Hong Kong Reverts to China (1997)

Despite its return to China in 1997, Hong Kong is still center of Triad activity in Asia. At the time of its return, police officials estimated there were as many as 50 Triad societies in Hong Kong, with the 14K and the Wo Sing Wo, the most prominent.

The consensus among law enforcement officials and academics was that following the return of Hong Kong to Mainland China in 1997, there would be a mass migration of Triads to Western nations. Recent scholarship reveals an unexpected phenomenon that finds Hong Kong Triad members entering the Chinese markets (Chu 2005). Most authorities expected an estimated 90,000 Chinese gangsters to flee after the island reverted to Chinese rule in 1997; however, in an unexpected turn of events, "the reverse turned out to be true" (Lintner 2005, 85). Instead of a migration to Canada, Australia, and the United States, Hong Kong Triads entered agreements with the new powers in the former British colony. Paralleling this development Triad groups made inroads on the mainland as

Jackie Chan and the Hong Kong Triads

By the 1990s, Jackie Chan had inherited the mantle once held by Bruce Lee and was the most popular martial arts film star in the world—a profitable commodity in the karate-crazed Far East. Motion pictures mean big profits in Asia. According to one estimate, a successful Chinese film typically turns a 300% profit. When video and foreign sales are included, it can net close to 1,500% profit (Booth 1999, 248). At the start of the 1990s, the Hong Kong film industry was ranked third behind Hollywood and India's Bollywood (Bombay). It was at this point that Triads moved in for a piece of the action. One of their ploys was to coerce leading stars to be in their pictures with threats of violence once friendly entreaties failed. One story recounts how an actress left a film and a Triad member burned her pay in front of her. Others have been raped and kidnapped. Jackie Chan was "told" he should participate in a film backed by the Wah Ching Triad, which is considered an American-Chinese organized crime group. Chan, who had other obligations, desisted. In the midst of filming Burt Reynolds' *Cannonball II* opus, the film's main office in San Francisco was raked with gunfire. The Triad next tried to extort $4 million from Chan "for damages and loss of face" to the gang's leader. When Chan returned to Hong Kong, a member of the 14K Triad attempted to collect the "debt." It is unknown whether this debt was ever paid (Dubro 1992; Booth 1999).

well, taking advantage of the nation's move from old socialist traditions to "cutthroat capitalism." Few could have imagined that Triads would be exploiting legal and illegal markets on mainland China and taking advantage of the economic reforms implemented over the past decades.

Recent trends in Triad activity in Hong Kong include an increasing investment in legitimate businesses such as bars, nightclubs, dance halls, restaurants, and the movie industry. There has also been a move to link up with legitimate entrepreneurs in an attempt to monopolize emerging markets, including interior decoration, sale of new residential property, and intimidation of motion picture stars in an attempt to make inroads in the film business. The film industry has proved a lucrative target for Hong Kong gangsters. Rackets have included protection schemes that impose insurance against exposing film and protecting film props, and stars are forced to pay for security. Foreign productions are also targeted, with demands for rent to film on location and the intimidation of film crews.

Triad Structure

Triad ranks and their corresponding numbers have a deep cultural significance that is still obscure. What is known is that all ranks begin with the number 4, based on an ancient Chinese conception that the world was surrounded by four seas.[5] The leader of a Triad is the Hill Chief (*Shan Chu*), signified by the number 489. He is expected to make final decisions in all phases of Triad society. Occasionally he is assisted by a deputy. Next in command is the Incense Master (*Heung Chu*), represented by number 438. He functions as a high priest and is most concerned with the organization and performance of ceremonial rituals related to initiation and promotion of members. The 415, or White Paper Fan, is drawn from the more intelligent and better educated members of the Triad, and he operates strictly as an advisor and financial administrator. The Red Pole, or the 426, plays the role of enforcer and muscle. He is expected to dole out physical punishments and to take the lead during gang wars. The Straw Sandal fills the role of mediator and messenger. As the 432, he lets members know when there are meetings and facilitates communication between various societies and other branches. The bottom rung is the 49, or ordinary member (the only number not divisible by 3) who functions as a soldier.

Triads are decentralized "in that no one central body is able to unite all Triad societies, or to give universal commands." Over the years, Triad organizational structures have become more flexible and decentralized to the point that the traditional rank system has been largely reduced to several levels—Red Poles and 49s, with a coterie of Blue Lanterns—triad recruits waiting to be initiated—on the fringe. Others suggest that the there are four basic ranks: Red Pole (fighter official), White Paper Fan (Advisor official), Grass Sandal (messenger–official), and 49 (ordinary member). In any case, Red Poles and 49s conduct street-crime activities, whereas larger criminal enterprises are

Other Chinese Organized Crime Groups

- *Sun Yee On:* The Sun Yee On Triad was established by the Chinese minority group, the Chiu Chau, in Hong Kong. Today its members come from a variety of different Chinese ethnic groups. Members have been detected in the United States, Canada, the UK, and Australia. With more than 56,000 members worldwide, it is considered the largest Chinese Triad (Curtis, Elan, Hudson, and Kollars 2003).
- *Wo Shing Wo:* The Wo Shing Wo Triad broke away from the Wo Hop To Triad in 1930. Its membership represents a cross section of Chinese society and includes a small number of local Indian and Pakistani members. Members operate in the UK, the United States, and Canada. By most accounts, they tend to participate in more violent crime than other Triads, and recently some journalists reported it has become the most influential Triad society in Hong Kong (Chu 2005, 11).
- *Four Seas Gang:* The Four Seas Gang Triad is second only to the United Bamboo in Taiwan. It operates in the United States, particularly in southern California. Although it reportedly disbanded in 1997 during an amnesty program, it still operates outside the country and has an estimated membership of 5,000 (Curtis et al. 2003).

directed by mid-rank officials and backed by muscle provided by the 49s and Red Poles. However, one expert cautions that the modern 49s are not your father's thugs of old, but are more likely to be more skilled "with a computer than with a meat cleaver" (Booth 1999, 221).

TRIAD INITIATION AND MEMBERSHIP Typically, like most of today's secret societies and organized crime subcultures, Triad initiation ceremonies have been simplified. In former times, a secret ritual was held to bind initiates into tightly knit brotherhoods to avoid betrayal by fellow members. Most new members today join based on an oral agreement with their Big Brother. Today it is no longer possible for many Triad societies to enforce strict discipline over their members and the transfer of membership between Triads is more readily accomplished than in times past. This breakdown in *esprit de corps* has had other unintended consequences. For example, by most accounts, Triad Big Brothers no longer feel obligated to look after their followers when they encounter problems. However, Triads are still a male-dominated secret society, although there is evidence that a very select number of females may have joined through the formal initiation society. Triads may also allow other races who live in Hong Kong to join their societies as well (Chu 2005).

Big Circle Boys

The Big Circle Boys is one of the newest incarnations of Chinese organized crime. Also known as the Big Circle Gang and Dai Heun Jai, experts consider it a "Mainland-based Triad." What distinguishes this gang from others is its composition of mostly former Red Army guards who had served time in Chinese prison camps. These camps are identified on government maps with big red circles, hence the moniker. There is still some disagreement as to whether members escaped or were banished from China, but in any case, they wound up in Hong Kong. Big Circle Boys are known for their brutality and familiarity with weaponry. They favor criminal activities such as heroin trafficking and jewelry store heists. The Big Circle Gang is not technically a Triad, but most of its members belong to various Triads. One former member named Johnny Kon claimed that he molded Big Circle members into a highly organized gang known as the Flaming Eagles, which specialized in jewelry store robberies and international heroin trafficking. In recent years, members have expanded their activities into Canada, the United States, and South America, where they have diversified into credit card fraud, counterfeiting, and the continuing trafficking in drugs and humans. Recent estimates place membership around 5,000, making it one of the most successful exemplars of the Chinese organized crime tradition (Huston 2001).

Threats of Chinese Criminal Enterprises

- *National and International Network System:* By utilizing their long cultivated international network of criminal contacts, the Chinese criminal enterprises are able to organize and carry out sophisticated transnational criminal activities such as heroin trafficking, human smuggling, counterfeiting, and piracy of intellectual property.
- *The Fluid Nature of the Enterprises:* Many of these groups are loosely organized crime groups consisting of independent criminal cells operated by influential individuals. Several unknown enterprises can emerge and join forces to conduct specific business ventures. On completion of a venture, they dissolve. Sometimes they regroup in different configurations or locations for other profit-making ventures.
- *Sophistication:* Chinese criminal organizations engage in activities that require a high degree of sophistication and knowledge of business, finance, and technology strategies. They are also quite adept at recognizing investigative techniques and in some cases have been observed conducting surveillance against their victims and using counter-surveillance techniques against law enforcement.
- *Mobility:* They take advantage of open borders and are not restricted by geographic boundaries or bureaucratic rules. They see the world as a huge money-making market where boundaries do not exist.
- *Flexibility and Patience:* They change their methods of operation or criminal activities based on each situation or project. They are also patient when it comes to protecting an established venture. Human smugglers have been known to keep aliens at one location for months waiting for the right opportunity for transporting them to the next destination.
- *Multilingual Ability:* Most know at least two languages, which allows them to organize international criminal activities. It also has become an obstacle to American law enforcement due to a lack of interpreters.
- *Financial Strength:* A Chinese project is usually a joint venture that pools the money of several groups together. By forming collaborative alliances with corrupted government and law enforcement authorities with their financial resources, they are able to pursue their goals. Armed with large sums of capital and shielded by legitimate front companies, they have continued to prosper in illegitimate business with little risk.

Adapted from the Asian Criminal Enterprise Program Overview, FBI, U.S. Department of State.

TONGS: AN AMERICAN PHENOMENON

Most sources agree that the word *Tong* means "hall" or "gathering place." One source even traces the term back to *tang*, which means "party" (Valentine 2000). More recently, Lintner explained that *Tong* is derived from the last syllable in Guomindang—*dang* in *pinyin*, which means "hall" or "lodge" (2002, 357). In any case, Tongs are considered the American incarnation of the Chinese Triad. Following in the footsteps of other criminal societies, in time various Tongs became involved in a litany of criminal enterprises, including prostitution, usury, drug dealing, and extortion.

Chinese immigrants began to appear in the United States in the mid-1800s and found jobs building railroads and mining gold in the West. Employers scurried to hire them as cheap labor and for their work ethic. Many sent money home to their families in China. Triad members could be found among their ranks serving as both "exploiters" and "protectors." Chinese immigrants clustered in Chinatowns due to racism, discrimination, and immigration policies. It was here that the Triads gained their first foothold in the United States due to the enormous power they wielded in the Chinese communities. In the United States, these early Triad immigrants formed or became known as *Tongs,* which literally meant "lodges" or "meeting places," and initially to the untrained eye appeared to be nothing more than meeting halls set up in various Chinatowns. Early Tongs served as self-help organizations for Chinese immigrants, although as far back as the 1850s law enforcement considered them criminal enterprises due to involvement in criminal activities such as illegal gambling, prostitution, extortion, and other crimes. In any case, Tong leaders acted as power brokers and mediated disputes in their communities.

There were more than 70,000 Chinese in America by the 1870s, with most located on the Pacific Coast—8 Tongs in San Francisco and 24 others scattered down the coast. By the late 1800s, Chinese immigrants began making their way east, mostly to New York City. In the years following the Civil War, many of them settled in the Five Points neighborhood. In 1880, a small Chinatown of 748 residents had developed in the neighborhood of Chatham Square. Historian Tyler Anbinder has recently noted that of all of the ethnic groups that called the infamous Five Points home during the 19th century, only the Chinese stayed; today, New York City's Chinatown rests on the ghost and bones of the fabled New York City intersection (Anbinder 2001, 396). By 1910, the community was home to 10,000 Chinese residents.

New York City and San Francisco have the richest Tong traditions dating back to the 19th century. The Hop Sing and Suey Sing Tongs in San Francisco, like the Hip Sing and On Leong (see box below, "On Leong Tong") in New York, are credited with establishing their respective Chinatowns. In time, powerful Tongs gained control of the Chinese language press and the quasi-public bodies that governed these two Chinatowns—New York's Chinese Consolidated Benevolent Association (CCBA) and the Six Companies in San Francisco (Kleinknecht 1996).

Each Tong had an identifying name and a membership exclusively composed of Chinese immigrants. Some Tongs were based on the region of China that the immigrants came from, whereas others revolved around a particular job or trade, creating laundry Tongs, railway Tongs, medical/herbal Tongs, and many others. Not all Tongs were operated in a fixed community; for example, the mineworkers Tong had membership throughout America. Over time, Tongs expanded their activities from offering opium and prostitutes to making usurious loans to Chinese immigrants, a practice that was legal in China. Others paid protection to local police officers to protect opium dens and other illicit businesses.

What is often overlooked is the positive influence of the Tongs. From a historical perspective, they served their Chinatowns well by offering loans to merchants, mediated business disputes, and found employment for newcomers, not unlike the services doled out by Tammany to new Irish immigrants. Tongs toed the line between the underworld and the upperworld as they observed their civic and legitimate responsibilities on the surface while running rackets out of view.

Tong Structure

Large Chinese communities gave rise to more than 30 different Tongs. The most common form of hierarchy included in descending order a president, vice president, treasurer, auditor, several elders, and public relations administrator (Chin, Kelly, and Fagan 1994). Tong members were usually self-employed. Tens of thousands of legally employed members paid regular dues. However, members were excluded in the decision-making process, which was the purview of

---

On Leong Tong

New York City's On Leong Tong emerged as the country's most prominent Tong in the 19th century. Tom Lee, born Wong Ah Ling in Canton, organized Chinatown's first Tong (Anbinder 2001). In 1880, Lee and several Chinese merchants went to Albany to legitimize the creation of the Tong, and it wasn't long before Lee, who would later receive a commission as a deputy sheriff, was hitting up local gambling dens for payoffs, threatening to use his police connections or violent street thugs to close their establishments if weekly payments went unmet. Lee's Tong soon diversified into controlling opium dens, gambling parlors, and prostitution. A number of accounts have made comparisons between the On Leong Tong and later Italian-American organized crime syndicates. In the 1890s, a second Tong was established, the Hip Sing. Nevertheless, the On Leong Tong remained unchallenged in New York's Chinatown until the 20th-century Tong wars with the Hip Sing.

only Tong officers and employees. Elections for these positions were held annually or biannually. In any case the vast majority of Tong members were law abiding and gainfully employed workers and merchants.

Outside the Chinese communities there were few opportunities to corrupt city officials—and nowhere approaching the corruption of America's emerging urban centers. Due to the uniqueness of Chinese culture, there were few opportunities outside Chinatown, and what opportunities existed had already been spoken for by Blacks, Hispanics, and Whites. Early on, Tongs sought to control local gangs to impose their authority in the communities.

Tong Wars

New York City's first Tong war broke out in 1899 over the control of the various gambling rackets. By that time, there were more than 200 gambling halls in New York City's Chinatown. According to the rampant corruption of the day, each gambling establishment paid $17.50 per week in protection money to the police to keep operating. Tongs collected 7% of all winnings under $25 from the gambling dens (and 14% over that amount). The On Leong (Peaceful Dragon) Tong, directed by Tom Lee, controlled most of the Chinatown's gambling halls. Lee, who arrived in New York sometime in the 1870s, controlled most of Chinatown's opium dens and gambling rackets. Under his direction, the On Leong Tong developed into a diversified criminal organization, moving away from its roots as a benevolent society. Its main rival was the Hip Sing Tong, which got by with whatever was left over. At this time, only six Chinese residents were qualified to vote despite the omnipresence of the immigrant-friendly Democratic machine. However, Tom Lee controlled the Chinese vote and had friends at Tammany Hall; in return, he was appointed deputy sheriff of New York County.

At the turn of the 20th century, under the leadership of Mock Duck, the Hip Sing Tong challenged the On Leong Tong for control of the gambling rackets. Mock Duck, decked out in protective chain mail and armed with a hatchet and a brace of pistols, was a formidable presence. When he demanded 50% of the gambling establishments the war was on. Using the legitimate power, structure he convinced his connections at City Hall to shut down Lee's gambling halls and brothels; then he reopened them under his name. The bloodshed that ensued was prodigious, and both parties signed a treaty that gave each their own territories. However, in less than a week, the truce faltered and the conflict only ended with government intervention followed by the arrest and conviction of Mock Duck. However, it would not be the last Tong war on either coast.

Recent scholarship suggests that the best-known conflicts between Tongs, or "Tong wars," were more often "the manifestation of conflicts between highly organized Chinese criminal syndicates (McIllwaine 2004, 8). During the 19th and 20th centuries Tong battles of varying degrees of violence erupted in San Francisco, New York, Boston, Chicago, Philadelphia, and Detroit. The two most powerful San Francisco Tongs in the 1800s were the Sum Yops and the Sue Yops. The former was heavily involved in gambling, drugs, and "white slavery." Fung Jing Toy, who made his early reputation as a "highbinder" or "hatchet man," ran the latter.[6] Both Tongs engaged in open warfare at the end of the 19th century. The San Francisco Tong wars only ended when Chinese government officials informed the more powerful Sue Yop that their relatives in China would be executed if they harmed another Sum Yop.

The Modern Tong

Following the passage of the Immigration and Naturalization Act in 1965, a new wave of Chinese immigrants landed on American shores. Among them were the future progenitors of the modern Chinese street-gang phenomenon. As America's cities became more diversified in the second half of the 20th century, Asian communities flourished throughout urban America in cities as varied as Boston, Chicago, Los Angeles, New York City, and San Francisco. What had once been an East/West Coast phenomenon had expanded into Chicago and Houston and other cities closer to the

FIGURE 9.1 Manhattan Chinatown Scene of Gang Warfare
Source: Dorling Kindersley Media Library/Max Alexander

nation's midsection. In 1966, the Wah Ching street gang emerged and soon dominated vice rackets in the Chinatowns of Los Angeles, San Francisco, and New York. Observers compared their extortion methods to those of older mafia syndicates in the heyday of America's Little Italies. In 1989, the Wah Ching was severely tested by the arrival of the Wo Hop To Triad from Hong Kong to San Francisco. Subsequently, both groups made concessions, consolidated their strength, and have emerged as a force to be reckoned with.

Chinese Street Gangs

Tongs would have a difficult task controlling various rackets if not for the assistance of Chinese street gangs. By most accounts, these gangs, particularly in New York City, are hierarchically organized. In New York City, Tongs recruit from a ready supply of street criminals. The individual

---

Chinese Ambassador Reports on Tong Wars (c. 1930s)

Narcotics and gambling are the causes of the tong wars. The tongs are generating unlimited amounts of income from operating opium and gambling dens. The tongs are so rich that a tong would spend tens of thousands of dollars for a building, and a tong's annual expenditures could be more than a million dollars. The tongs are well organized, their leaders very dignified. Each has about twenty or thirty branches, with ten to twenty thousand members. The tongs recruit a bunch of thugs (hatchetmen) to run opium and gambling dens and to revenge and kill when the situations call for action. If a thug kills a person, the tongs will reward him with several thousand dollars. A hatchetman's subsidy is higher than a senior government official's. A group of hatchetmen is similar to a regular army, and the tongs resemble the warlords.[7]

The Golden Dragon Massacre (1977)

San Francisco's Chinatown has been plagued sporadically by gang warfare over the past 150 years. Rarely, however did it merit front-page news in this cosmopolitan city by the bay. This all changed when turf warfare over illegal fireworks sales resulted in a shootout in the Golden Dragon Restaurant which left 5 dead and 11 wounded. This carnage was the product of an ongoing dispute between the J Boys and the Hop Sing Boys and Wah Ching Tongs.

who is tasked by Tong bosses with coordinating and organizing the street gangs is referred to as the *Dai Dai Lo*, or "Big, Big Brother." He serves as a buffer between the Tong bosses and the street criminals, essentially insulating them from direct involvement in criminal activity. He in turn supervises the street-level commander, the *Dai Lo*, or "Big Brother." In descending order, this individual could also be a *Yee Lo*, or "Second Brother," or *Saam Lo*, or "Third Brother." Under the control of the street-level boss are young men, variously referred to as *Mai Jai* ("Horse Boys") or *Leng Jui* ("Little Kids"). These youths belonged to various gangs with names such as Ghost Shadows, the Flying Dragons (see following box, "The Flying Dragons"), and the White Tigers, each with its own codes of behavior and oaths of loyalty. Most of these gangs were ephemeral in nature—each disappearing or subsumed by another name once the gang "had outlived its usefulness, its activities been exposed, or its members arrested or killed" (Lintner 2002, 359).

The Chinese street gangs allowed Tongs to continue criminal activities unimpeded by police and unchallenged by business owners. Tongs could shakedown restaurants, nightclubs, and gambling halls under the guise of juvenile street gangs; but more than likely, the gangs are collecting debts and protection from Tong-supported prostitution and gambling rackets (Chin, Kelly, and Fagan 1994).

To ensure security, great steps are taken to prevent *Mai Jais* from learning the identities of *Dai Los* and their superiors. Street-level *Dai Los*—the *Yee Los* and *Saam Los* are the highest level that actual street members might be familiar with. The only opportunity that *Mai Lais* have to observe higher levels in the Tongs is during induction initiation ceremonies.

The genesis of Chinese street gangs in the 1960s is tied to the power of the Tongs and the need for muscle in the Chinatown rackets. As long as these gangs performed well for their employers, Tong members looked the other way and even supplied lawyers as gangs branched off and committed violent robberies and other crimes. In a number of cases, gang members have been inducted into the Tongs. According to one investigative journalist, a former gang member testified before a congressional subcommittee that he had been inducted into the Ghost Shadows gang and the On Leong Tong at the same time (Kleinknecht 1996, 95).

One of the earliest identifiable Chinese gangs was the "Bugs" formed in Chicago in the late 1950s. In 1964, young Chinese immigrants established San Francisco's "first foreign born Chinese gang" (Chin, Kelly, and Fagan, 1994). The Wah Ching, or "Youth of China," was apparently organized to protect American-born Chinese. With the passage of new immigration laws the following years, the

Major Tongs and Their Headquarters in the United States (2004)

On Leong	New York City
Hip Sing	San Francisco
Ying On	Los Angeles
Hop Sing	Pacific Coast/East Coast offices
Suey Sing	Pacific Coast/East Coast offices

The Flying Dragons

By the 1990s, the Flying Dragons were considered New York City's most violent Chinese gang. It began its affiliation with the Hip Sing Tong under godfather Benny "Uncle 7" Ong in the 1970s. He used the gang to guard Hip Sing gambling dens and for collecting protection money.

Wah Ching became the largest Chinese gang in California within less than two decades. In the 1960s and 1970s, Chinese street gangs made the transition from self-help clubs to predatory marauders who preyed on their own communities, shaking down merchants, stealing food, and robbing illegal Tong gambling dens. Tongs had no other choice than to channel their energies in their direction, hiring gangsters as street soldiers to protect their own rackets. By the 1980s, powerful Asian gangs had established themselves in a number of cities, with New York City claiming more than any other city. Chinese street gangs flourished in the wake of the lifting of immigration restrictions in the 1980s. The Fuk Ching[8] gang was considered one of the most prominent exemplars of this type of Asian organized crime. Members were readily distinguishable by their black clothing and brightly streaked hairstyles as they loitered in black BMWs on various street corners in Chinatown. To protect themselves from police shakedowns they usually had their girlfriends carry weapons and contraband for them. Experts concede that it is now the power base of Chinese organized crime in the United States.

Tong Rackets and Chinese Gangs

In the United States, Tongs and Chinese gangs have combined forces in a number of lucrative, but illicit activities. Besides an ongoing involvement in illegal gambling parlors, promoting prostitution, and human smuggling, they are also identified with drug smuggling, especially the importation of heroin, and various protection rackets. Tongs have had a hand in gambling probably longer than any other activity. Gambling parlors offer games running from low stakes betting to higher stakes clubs, where street-gang members are typically present for security. The Tongs generally own the houses where the gambling takes place—receiving a 5% commission in return.

Extortion has been long regarded one of the most prevalent forms of crime and has received much attention by scholars such as Ko Lin Chin. Chin enumerated four types of gang intimidation, including protection, extortion, forced sales at exorbitant prices, and refusing to pay for food and services. In the case of protection, it corresponds to a gang member demanding a fixed payment from a businessman to forego disruption of his business. This can be accomplished with either one large payment or a series of regular payments. Paying protection has been so widespread that it has contributed to a drop in disorganized crime, making Chinatowns seem more orderly than other similar immigrant communities. Merchants are sometimes given "offers they can't refuse," in which gang members force them to purchase plants, cakes, and firecrackers during holidays, at substantially marked-up prices (Chin 1992).

Snakeheads and Human Smuggling

The term *snakehead,* or *shetou,* is a Chinese term used to denote entrepreneurs who specialize in human smuggling—the moving of undocumented workers from one country to another. One snakehead described the origin of the term as a result of watching "smuggled immigrants slither through the wire fences strung along borders" and as they emerged morphed into a shape that "looks like a snake" (Keefe 2006). Chinese Snakeheads smuggle prospective immigrants illegally across borders for a fee, often amounting to tens of thousands of dollars. In this network, Snakeheads are divided into the "little Snakeheads" who function as local recruiters for the "big Snakeheads."

When it comes to human smuggling, China has a distinct tradition from other countries. Unlike forced migration or human trafficking, human smuggling is considered a voluntary but

Crimes Committed in the United States by Asian Gangsters

- Victimization of Vietnamese immigrants through extortion and home invasions
- Theft of and counterfeiting of credit cards, identification cards, and payroll checks
- Counterfeiting videotapes, CDs, and DVDs
- Cloning cellular phones
- Auto theft and chop shops; carjackings to order
- Killers for hire, especially among Viet-Ching gangsters
- Computer chip thefts
- Wholesale marijuana cultivation and distribution by Hmong and Laotians
- Kidnapping for ransom
- Cigarette smuggling from the United States to Canada
- Auto insurance fraud
- Smash and grab robberies at gun and jewelry stores
- Fencing stolen goods
- Drive-by shootings, weapons violations, drug trafficking, street crime

(Adapted from Valentine 2000, 127.)

often illegal activity (see Chapter 7). A significant number of those smuggled abroad come from a tiny patch of China about the size of Delaware. The Fujian province is located conveniently on the country's southern coast. It has been estimated that of the 55 million Chinese who relocated overseas, 85% originate from here. In the United States, the number is even higher at 90%, with most of them coming from the provincial capital of Fuzhou. A successful operation led to a guarantee of more follow-up business. As each immigrant paid off his debts to the Snakeheads, a process that could take years, the immigrant then began saving to bring over other family members. In the end, this process might relocate an entire village or clan overseas. In any case, family members continue to send money back to their villages "for the construction of multi-story houses [that served as] monuments to the filial loyalty of 'overseas Chinese'" (Keefe 2006). According to one journalist, "In status-conscious small towns, this inspired other villagers to emigrate" (Keefe 2006).

Although Chinese immigrants have traveled to the United States since the mid-19th century, the modern Snakeheads emerged only in the 1960s and 1970s, when citizens fled the mainland to the British colony of Hong Kong for a number of reasons including *push factors,* such as political repression, Chinese policies of sterilization and forced abortion, as well as the *pull factors* of America's capitalist system (Keefe 2006). This onslaught of migration that began in the 1960s saw the population of New York's Chinatown increase tenfold by the 1980s, from 20,000 to 200,000. During this era, the new denizens were sometimes derided as "$18,000 men," reflecting the going rate of the 1980s.

However, it was the period between 1988 and 1993 that saw "the largest influx of illegal Chinese in the country's history" (Keefe 2006) into America. According to a study by the United Nations, in the mid-1990s this added up to a $3.5 billion windfall for the Snakeheads. The continued prosperity of the Snakeheads can be traced to changes in U.S. immigration policy in the 1980s that made residency requirements much easier and green cards available to undocumented aliens. On top of this, the Tiananmen Square massacre of 1989 led President George H.W. Bush to issue an executive order granting amnesty to Chinese students in the United States while giving "enhanced consideration" to asylum application from Chinese nationals who disagreed with China's family-planning strategies. By most accounts, this basically meant that any Chinese adult could meet the standards for refugee status.

By the late 1990s, China was enjoying relative economic prosperity, which some experts suggest has only increased the divide between the rich and the poor. In any case, between 1997 and

Sister Ping

Reportedly born to a Snakehead father in 1949, Cheng Chui Peng emerged from the small farming village of Shengmei to international prominence as a Snakehead in her own right. Ping was charged with partnering in the purchase of *The Golden Venture*, whose 17,000 mile voyage from Thailand came to an abrupt halt off the coast from the Rockaway peninsula in Queens, resulting in the deaths of 10 passengers. Despite little formal education or knowledge of the English language, the 1981 immigrant became a prominent businesswoman in Manhattan's Chinatown. In 2005, Sister Ping became the 23rd person convicted in this operation, and in March 2006 was sentenced to 35 years in prison. FBI sources estimate that she made almost $40 million over a 20-year period. She was part of a huge network that included affiliates in China, Hong Kong, Thailand, Belize, Kenya, South Africa, Guatemala, Mexico, and Canada, and is credited with setting up the route from China to Chinatown in the 1980s that brought thousands of illegal workers into the United States (Keefe 2006).

1999 there was a notable increase in the number of illegal immigrants apprehended while trying to enter the United States. On top of this, the costs of passage have skyrocketed to perhaps $70,000 per person, which necessitated new smuggling networks. One of the more interesting incarnations was a syndicate made up of Fujianese and Mohawk Indians who reportedly smuggled thousands of refugees through the "sovereign reservation" that lies between the United States and Canada. Some reports suggest this network made $175 million in a 2-year period (Keefe 2006).

Chinese Triads have dominated human smuggling operations from China, including the 14K, United Bamboo, and Sun Yee On Triads. More recent players include "ethnic Taiwanese entrepreneurs," who are distinguished from the Triads in that they are more involved in legitimate enterprises, and effectively run these smuggling activities like a business, absent the Triad penchant for secret initiation and involvement in traditional organized crime activities (Mabrey 2003, 7). Most recently, Chinese street gangs have taken over many of the smuggling enterprises, particularly the Fuk Ching gang, which played a role in the *Golden Venture* debacle in 1993. This incident left an indelible imprint on the American public's consciousness that had previously been innocent to the hidden costs of human smuggling. On the morning of June 6, 1993, a ship named the *Golden Venture* carrying human cargo ran aground on a sandbar some 150 yards from a New York beach, not far from midtown Manhattan and Wall Street (Smith 1997). With little adieu, crew members unlocked the sealed cargo hold and encouraged the 300 passengers to jump into the 53° waters and swim to shore. Of the 200 who initially complied, at least 8 drowned. The rest stayed on board and waited for U.S. Coast Guard rescue. The smuggling of Chinese immigrants to America has a long history, but this case had a resonance thanks to the power of a mass media focused on the incident.

It soon emerged that the trip to America was much worse than the denouement. Many of the passengers began their journey on the other side of a mountain range that took them from Burma to Thailand, and thence on a 3-month journey by sea to the United States. Although they would subsequently ask for political asylum, almost one third were deported back to China, and initially only 30 were given political asylum.[9]

By most accounts, Snakeheads have made fortunes bringing illegal immigrants to Japan by sea. The Snakehead gang led by Yong Zhang smuggled an average of 20 illegal immigrants into the UK a month at £15,000 each, and was estimated to have made in the neighborhood of $20 million over a 3-year period (Lunde 2004). Since 1978, there has been a large increase of Chinese living in Japan. In 1998, alone officials estimated that some 70,000 of Japan's 230,000 Chinese immigrants were living there illegally, including students with expired visas and immigrants illegally smuggled into the country (Lintner 2003). Once there, these immigrants become fair game for extortion, robbery, theft, and other crimes by Chinese gangsters in the immigrant communities. Authorities believe that as the Japanese Yakuza's power has diminished somewhat in recent years, that Chinese gangsters are "changing the criminal landscape of China" (Lintner 2003, 180).

Sample Smuggling Routes Used by the Fukienese to the United States (1995)[10]

"Northwest Passage"

- Fuzhou to Hong Kong to Vancouver to San Francisco
- Fuzhou to Hong Kong to Vancouver to Toronto and New York
- Fuzhou to Hong Kong to Vancouver to Toronto to Niagara Falls to New York
- Fuzhou to Shanghai to Vancouver to Toronto to Champlain to New York

"Bangkok Connections"

- Fuzhou via land transport to Hong Kong, by air to Bangkok, by air to Canada
- Fuzhou to Yunnan, smuggled over the border to Burma, smuggled over border to Thailand and taken to Chiang Mai flown to Bangkok, and flown to the United States
- Fuzhou to Bangkok to Colombo to Zurich to New York
- Fuzhou to Hong Kong to Bangkok to Seoul to Vancouver to Toronto to New York
- Fuzhou to Hong Kong to Bangkok to Copenhagen to Newark
- Fuzhou to Hong Kong to Bangkok to Moscow to Havana to Managua to Tucson
- Fuzhou to Hong Kong to Bangkok to Kuala Lumpur to Singapore to Dubai to Frankfurt to Washington, D.C.

"Straits Ways"

- Fuzhou to Hong Kong to Kuala Lumpur to Frankfurt to Amsterdam to Belize to New Orleans

"European Gateways: Germany"

- Fuzhou to Hong Kong to Frankfurt to Amsterdam to Mexico City to San Diego
- Fuzhou to Hong Kong to Frankfurt to Amsterdam to Guatemala to San Salvador to Mexico City to San Diego
- Fuzhou to Hong Kong to Frankfurt to Antigua, Virgin Islands to New York

By Ship

- Fukien by chartered ship to Mombassa, new ship to South Africa and on to New York

(Adapted from Huston 1995, 184–185).

JAPANESE ORGANIZED CRIME

The origins of the modern Yakuza are still a subject of much debate. More often than not, experts trace the roots of Japanese organized crime back to the early Tokugawa period beginning in the1600s, an era highlighted by the existence of a class of Samurai warriors. The Samurai of this era certainly run against type, preferring to wear outlandish costumes and hairstyles, speaking an elaborate patois and brandishing long swords. Some observers regarded them as *kabuki-mono*, or "crazy ones"; others referred to them as *hatamoto-yakko*, or "servants of the Shogun." Legends developed around them as bandit heroes akin to the Robin Hood tales of Norman England. By some estimates, nearly 500,000 unemployed Samurai wandered through Japan during the years of peace that characterized the Tokugawa era (1600–1867). Unfettered by officials or masters, a number of them turned to banditry and plundering towns throughout the shogunate, earning the name of *ronin,* or "wave man," indicating a masterless Samurai. With little in the way of leadership, some *ronin* reportedly plagued communities as violent thieves; modern Yakuza prefer to remember these ancestors as servants of the town who protected the poor and the defenseless as veritable medieval Robin Hoods.

Modern scholarship, however, suggests that these Samurai were not really the forebears of the Yakuza tradition. The Yakuza seemed to have emerged sometime in the late 1700s. Today's Yakuza is a product of two unique traditions, embracing both gamblers, or *bakuto*, and traveling peddlers or stall keepers, or *tekiya*.[11] Both groups were often suppressed during the Tokugawa period, although officialdom more often regarded these individuals from a more pragmatic

FIGURE 9.2 Samurai
Source: Dorling Kindersley Media Library

perspective by viewing them "as useful agents of social control and sources of intelligence" (Hill 2005, 97). In any case, both terms are still used to describe Yakuza members. In the years following World War II, a third group was added to the mix—*gurentai*, or gangsters. The three types emerged from similar backgrounds—typically from the poor dispossessed classes, delinquents, and misfits. For most of their existence, the *bakuto* stuck to the highways and small towns and the *tekiya* mostly to the markets and fairs of Japan; by adhering to a particular territory, it eliminated conflict between these two groups.

Yakuza

The etymology of the generic term *Yakuza* itself refers to a losing hand of cards in a game called *oicho-kabu*—eight, nine, and three—or *ya ku sa*, hence its affiliation with the gambling tradition. In this variation of the game of Blackjack, numbers adding up to 20 is a losing hand of cards. Over time the term *Yakuza* was used to describe a worthless person, a loser, or a misfit, an image that some members used to embellish their image as underdogs and societal rejects (much as today's Outlaw bikers relish their reputation as "Born to Lose" outsiders). "Gambling bosses frequently also operated as labor brokers to the central government's ambitious construction projects while local *tekiya* bosses were responsible for the organization of stall-holders at festivals within their territories" (Hill 2005, 97).

With the decline of the Tokugawa regime, a wealthy business class with money to burn emerged; it was during this era of political and military turmoil in the late 1800s that gambling syndicates emerged capable of summoning up veritable small armies of fighting men to prop up the "new or old" central governments (Tokugawa or Meiji). In one celebrated incident, a syndicate with 500 armed gamblers took part in capturing a city for the new Meiji regime (Hill 2005, 98).

The restoration of the Meiji regime also reintroduced a strong central government, which then turned against the gambling groups as in an earlier era, leading to a decline in their numbers.

Korean Yakuza

Koreans face discrimination in most parts of Japanese society, despite the fact that Japanese-born people of Korean ancestry represent a significant segment of the national population. During the first half of the 20th century, thousands of Koreans were sent to Japan as forced labor. Large numbers were never repatriated, and because of few professional opportunities, many found refuge in the Yakuza. In any case, in such a homogeneous society, they are still viewed as resident aliens and often find barriers to finding employment in legitimate occupations. However, the Yakuza welcomes them as fellow outsiders into the criminal brotherhood. Koreans became an important cog in the Yakuza underworld, facilitating the spread of this underworld into South Korea, where Yakuza members have infiltrated the docks and construction industry, the illegal disposal of toxic waste, the drug trade, and weapons and drug smuggling. The most prominent Korean Yakuza was Hisayuki Machii. Born in Japanese-occupied Korea in 1923, he worked his way up from petty street crime to take over many black market rackets in post-war Japan. A diplomat at heart, he forged a number alliances with Yakuza bosses. Perhaps his crowning achievement, in 1948, he created the *Tosei-kai,* or "Voice of the East Gang," and gained control of the lucrative Tokyo Ginza district, often compared to New York City's Times Square. His power allowed him to come to favorable arrangements with the Yamaguchi-Gumi, who were interested in getting a piece of the Tokyo market. His formidability also paved the way for him to broker deals between the Yakuza and the Korean government that allowed Japanese criminals to set up rackets in anti-Japanese Korea. Ever acquisitive, Machii ran a syndicate engaged in an extensive range of rackets involving tourism, entertainment, bars, restaurants, prostitution, real estate, and even oil importing. One of his biggest coups was the acquisition of the largest ferry service between South Korea and Japan (and shortest route), thanks to his political connections. Machii retired in the 1980s.

However, as before, history conspired to reintroduce the gambling syndicates in the first decades of the 20th century. It was during this period between 1900 and 1920 that Japan experienced modern industrialization and race riots as the Bolshevik Revolution cleaved Russia to its west. In response to these threats of destabilization, the government turned once more to the Yakuza gangs, by forming them into a "Pan-Japanese" syndicate for the purpose of using them as strikebreakers and to break up left-wing protests. However, this arrangement was short-lived, in part due to internal bickering and failure to meet the government's expectations (Hill 2005, 98). Nevertheless, Yakuza groups continued to fill a role in far right movements throughout the 1930s until an authoritarian government renewed its suppression of the Yakuza.

Post–World War II

In the years following Japan's defeat in World War II, the nation's formal economy was in virtual ruins. Together with a weak police force and the availability of a large number of unemployed and hopeless former soldiers, most brutalized by the war, a black market emerged run by neighborhood strongmen and demobilized constituents. These conditions proved rife for the development of organized mafia-style gangs in many eras and countries (Gambetta 1993; Varese 2001; Whiting 1999). The new gangs were characterized as *gurentai,* meaning racketeers or hoodlums (Hill 2005). Not formally Yakuza gangs, *gurentai* groups either "absorbed Yakuza gangs or adopted many of their cultural symbols and norms," which included their distinctive full-body tattoos and finger amputation as a demonstration of contrition (Hill 2005). With few available business opportunities, a number of gambling organizations adopted what were formerly regarded as *gurentai* business activities.

In the aftermath of the war, Yakuza members earned a degree of acceptance and respect in Japanese society. Most members carried a business card and rented office space, which was typically emblazoned with the renter's name and title, often in the same buildings as legitimate stockbrokers and lawyers.

Yoshio Kodama (1911–1984)

At the height of his career in the 1970s, Yoshio Kodama was considered "the most powerful man in Japan." However, his fall from grace was assured in 1976, when he was implicated in the Lockheed scandal. Kodama had earned millions of dollars representing the Lockheed aircraft corporation in Japan and establishing links between the Yakuza and politicians. He was paid a reported $2.1 million dollars to discredit an All Nippon president who was forced to resign, thereby allowing Lockheed an opportunity to grab a foothold in the market (from McDonnell-Douglas and Boeing). Before he could be imprisoned, Kodama was felled by a stroke in 1976 and died 8 years later. Kodama had a lifelong predilection for subterfuge, exercising it during World War II directing a spy and espionage network in Asia. In the course of directing this operation, he was able to provide Japan with radium, copper, nickel, and other sources needed for Japan's war machine while lining his own pockets at the same time. He also became embroiled in heroin trafficking, which he was able to do using the legitimate façade provided by the Japanese government. At the end of the war, he was worth an estimated $175 million and had been accorded the honorary rank of rear admiral.

Classified as a war criminal by the Allies he was sentenced to 2 years in prison. Released as part of a general amnesty in 1948, his diplomatic skills were used by the U.S. government as an intermediary between the allied forces intelligence corps (G-2) and the Yakuza. During the late 1940s and the 1950s, Kodama was able to marshal Yakuza thugs for political bosses and the Allies when needed. His power extended from Japan into much of Asia, and was sufficient to mediate a truce between several powerful Yakuza clans, including the Yamaguchi-Gumi and the Tosie Kai. As a result, he earned the reputation as the criminal world's "visionary godfather" and continued to make peace between other warring factions. In his early career Kodama had participated in ultra-nationalistic activities and became a rabid anti-communist, a feature of most Yakuza groups. By most accounts, his peacemaking among the gangster groups was due in part to a perception that warring Yakuza groups represented a threat to the country's anti-communist unity.

Japan's economy recovered in the 1950s and crime syndicates focused on new financial opportunities represented by the increasing number of new bars, clubs, restaurants, and sexually oriented businesses. Other Yakuza groups targeted as labor brokers providing laborers to docking and construction industries. These emerging opportunities led to conflict between various gangs between 1950 and 1963, which police referred to as the "gang-war period" (Hill 2005, 98).

Despite the passage of new legislation to rein in the gang carnage, the Yakuza flourished due to a confluence of factors including alliances between gangsters and politicians at all levels of government, inadequate policing, and fear of extreme left-wing activity among students and labor groups. The government once more used the vehemently anti-communist Yakuza as a tool to suppress radical activities. By most accounts, Yakuza membership peaked at 180,000 in 1963 before declining to 120,000 by the end of the 1960s (Hill 2005). Larger syndicates profited from the disbanding of a number of gangs in the 1960s, growing more powerful and sophisticated. As Yakuza scholar Peter Hill put it, new police countermeasures and new gambling laws facilitated the growth and diversification of certain groups "at the expense of the small, locally based traditional gambling groups" (Hill 2005). During the 1970s the Yakuza expanded its operations in response to the police crackdown on gambling, moving into the lucrative amphetamine trade.

By most accounts, all Yakuza own handguns but rarely carry them unless there is a gang war raging, preferring to leave them in another location or at a non-member's apartment. In recent years, a bodyguard bearing a weapon is forced to keep some distance from his boss due to new legislation that prosecutes the boss as well as the guard if firearms statutes are violated.

JAPANESE ORGANIZED CRIME IN THE MODERN ERA   Yakuza activities since the late 1970s run the gamut from illegal to legal rackets, including corporate extortion, gambling, loansharking, prostitution and sex tours, gun and drug trafficking, slavery, sports, money laundering, stock manipulation, and pornography. Although Yakuza groups operate across the country, they are most powerful in major cities such as Tokyo, Kyoto, and Kobe, which is home to the nation's largest, the Yamaguchi-Gumi

Sokaiya Activities

In the 1970s and 1980s, the Yakuza became more involved in corporate extortion or *sokaiya* (shareholders' meeting men) activities. They have reaped millions of dollars in the process. Typically these individuals purchase a small number of shares in a company so that they can attend shareholders' meetings. Prior to attending, the *sokaiyo* collect damaging information about the company and its officers—perhaps information about secret mistresses, tax evasion, pollution, or unsafe factory conditions. A representative then threatens to divulge this information at the meeting unless they are "compensated." In cases where the corporate managers refuse to pay, the *sokaiyo* disrupt the meeting, shouting down speakers and yelling out scandalous information. In a society where individuals fear embarrassment more than physical violence, it does not usually come to this, with executives paying the extortion demands. Other extortion scams include posing as business magazine publishers who target certain companies with promise to report favorably on the company if they purchase ads and subscriptions. Most executives pay, due to past incidents where ersatz magazine salesmen followed through on their threats and published embarrassing articles critical of the company. Corporate extortion schemes have included forcing corporate managers to purchase block of theater tickets at usurious rates and organizing golf tournaments and beauty pageants to shakedown corporate sponsors. Other *sokaiya* are paid to protect companies from competing groups.[12] Those companies not depending on *sokaiyo* protection typically employed Yakuza members in that capacity. The process by which this protection operates is similar to the definition of *mafia* described by Gambetta (1993). In 1982, new legal reforms aimed at the *sokaiya* diminished their numbers from an estimated 6,738 to 1,682 in just 1 year (Hill 2005).

(see box on next page). The Yakuza has lost much of its prestige and respect as a Japanese institution. In 1992, the government passed the Act for Prevention of Unlawful Activities by Boryokudan Members.[13] Aimed at organized crime groups, this legislation attempted to ban any organization made up of a certain percentage of members with criminal records, or those harboring members with violent or criminal propensities. In response, the Yakuza adopted a strategy of masquerading as businessmen and legitimate entrepreneurs, even going as far as publishing a book entitled *How to Evade the Law*, which reportedly became required reading for members of the Yamaguchi-Gumi. Testament to its popularity is the fact that more than 75 gangs associated with the Yamaguchi-Gumi are registered as either religious or business organizations.

During the 1990s, Yakuza family members and supporters went on the offensive to protest new legislation clearly aimed at them. Most supporters drew parallels between the modern gangsters and medieval Samurai warriors—a tired argument that could not surmount the public dissatisfaction with Yakuza thugs, particularly after members stabbed revered movie director Itami Juzo, who had the temerity to make the film *Minbo no Onna* (A Woman Yakuza Fighter), highly critical of the Yakuza.

Nevertheless, the Yakuza have not been without defenders in the legitimate community, with dozens of lawyers and religious ministers protesting what they believed were unconstitutional laws infringing on basic human rights. In recent years, Japanese citizens have joined the crusade against the Yakuza. In the 1980s, most Japanese parents prohibited their children from playing and interacting with the children of Yakuza. More recently, citizens in some cities have begun videotaping the

October: Gang Roundup Month

One law enforcement tradition that persisted well into the 1980s was the annual roundup of gangsters in October, which was designated "Intensive Roundup Month" by the Japanese police. By the mid-1980s, this effort to attract the attention of the press and the public had lost its luster, with few actually paying attention (Jameson 1985).

Yamaguchi-Gumi

Japan's largest organized crime group grew out of the syndicates that organized labor on Kobe's docks in the early 1900s.[14] Members of the Yamaguchi-Gumi are identifiable by a diamond-shaped badge that in gangland circles amounted to a sign of prestige in the underworld (Jameson 1985). The badge typically bears the Japanese characters *yama* (mountain) and *guchi* (mouth). For years, one could walk down to the Yamaguchi-Gumi headquarters, just three doors down from the Kobe District Court, and read the names of its leaders on boards posted on the walls (the names of jailed members were posted in red). As Japan's version of "Lucky" Luciano, Kazuo Taoka (1913–1981) is credited with laying the foundation for this syndicate, running it with an iron fist for almost 35 years. Orphaned in his youth, Taoka was forced to work on Kobe's docks by a local gang lord. During this period, he earned the moniker of *Kuma,* or "the bear," for his predilection for clawing out his opponents' eyes with his fingers. By the early 1980s, the Yamaguchi-Gumi controlled an estimated 2,500 business bringing in close to $500 million per year. The gang was able to flourish due in part to its political connections and willingness to innovate and diversify. Under Taoka's leadership, legitimate businesses were forced to accept the presence of Yakuza members. He also encouraged the transition to the drug trade. The organization received perhaps its best publicity following the 1995 Kobe earthquake by providing relief to the city residents before the government. In the 1990s, the Yamaguchi-Gumi expanded into the Tokyo area despite a longstanding agreement with the Inagawa-Kai not to open offices in the city. In response, members opened legitimate business fronts and operated without official gang headquarters, making it impossible for officials to gauge the actual number of Yakuza in Tokyo. Estimates range from 750 to 4,000 members. During this era, hundreds of members became involved in loansharking, real estate, and construction rackets. By 2002, the number of members in Tokyo had more than doubled.

movements of Yakuza at their buildings and headquarters—anyone who went in or out of these so-called "Black buildings," particularly those dressed in flashy clothes, with short hair and tattooed arms. In the city of Hamamatsu, some 130 miles from Tokyo, gangsters retaliated against citizens by breaking windows and stabbing citizen watchdogs.

According to Japanese police figures for 2002, there were 84,400 Boryokudan members, half of whom were considered full members and the others were associates. There were nearly 100,000 more members in the heyday of the Yakuza in 1963, but it has seen a rise in membership since its lowest membership of just more than 79,000 in 1995 (Hill 2005, 106). After the anti-crime legislation of 1992, it became increasingly difficult to keep track of the Yakuza, because members take precautions to obscure their status from authorities.

More recently, Yakuza groups have been using right-wing gangs as fronts for their activities. These groups, known as *uyoku dantai*, preach an anti-American, anti-communist, and ultranationalist message. Members of the 900 or so right-wing gangs are estimated to number up to 10,000. Police estimate that more than half of them are fronts for organized crime groups. The ascendance of Japan's far right has been accompanied by several high-profile incidents, but none has been more prominent than the 2007 murder of the left-leaning mayor of Nagasaki by a prominent Yakuza member in broad daylight.[15] The murder of Mayor Itcho Ito has been described as a "threat to democracy," although law enforcement views it more a sign of desperation on the part of the Yakuza rather than a demonstration of power. In 2007, the Yamaguchi-Gumi was still

Largest Yakuza Groups (2004)

Yamaguchi-Gumi [group]	17,500 members	750 clans
Inagawa-Kai	7,000 members	300 clans
Sumiyoshi Rengo [alliance] Kai	7,000 members	170 clans
Kyokuto Kai	1,700 members	

Slaying Spotlights Yakuza Violence in the Corporate World

Well into the 1990s, Japanese corporations and banks were targeted by Yakuza violence. One notable 1994 case illustrated what happens when anyone attempts to stand up to the gangsters. In this case, a board member and manager of Sumitomo Bank's Nagoya Branch was found dead with a gunshot wound to his head. This was only the most recent report of violence against corporate members of one of Japan's biggest industrial groups. Law enforcement authorities recorded almost two dozen attacks on Sumitomo group offices and executives' homes in less than 2 years. According to speculation, the bank was a big lender during the "so-called bubble economic expansion" of that period and "cash-strapped borrowers could be the source of violence" (Forman 1994, A10). However, journalists opined that this was the third murder of a Japanese corporate executive in the previous 2 years, and suggested that as the country's economic downturn continued corporate extortionists (*sokaiyo*) were "becoming increasingly desperate." This, together with the public campaign on corruption, have made it difficult with the *sokaiyo,* and as one business commentator suggested, the bank "may have tried to cut itself off from the underworld, but it may have turned against them" (Forman 1994). Others have been quick to point out that some companies had begun to stand up to the gangsters, citing the case of a Fuji Photo Film executive hacked to death by sword-wielding gangster the previous year (Forman 1994).

considered Japan's largest criminal syndicate. In April of that year, the organization garnered more unwanted publicity when Tetsuya Shiroo, a senior member of the syndicate, gunned down Nagasaki's mayor in a brazen attack at a city train station. However, by most accounts the attack was the result of a personal score between the two. Shiroo later told police that he killed the mayor because the city refused to compensate him after his car was damaged at a public works construction site (Tabuchi 2007). However, officials described Shiroo's demands as "more of a gangster shakedown," suggesting that the mobster initially demanded 600,000 yen to repair the car, but soon increased the demand more than threefold to 2 million yen ("Nagasaki Mayor Itoh dies," 2007). This syndicate is best known for its involvement in construction rackets related to government construction projects. With the Japanese government investing less in construction and the new get-tough measures on corruption, there is less money for the criminal gangs. In an act of contrition after the mayor's slaying, the leader of the syndicate approached the police with promises to disband the organization.

Yakuza Structure

Compared to the hierarchy of the traditional mafia, the Yakuza's is fairly complex. Yakuza are organized into paternalistic "families" based on the *oyabun-kobun*, or parent–child relationship. The *oyabun,* or father figure, is also the supreme boss, who gives advice, helps, and protects gang members in a paternalistic relationship in which his minions are his *kobun*, or children. Every new member is expected to accept this relationship, including unquestionable obedience to his *oyabun.* Until the mid-1980s, it was common for 5,000 youths to join the gangs each year, roughly the same number that left, or "washed their feet," each year (Jameson 1985).

Immediately under the *oyabun* is a senior advisor (*saiko komon*), and then a headquarters chief (*so-honbucho*), and then a number-two man—the *wakagashira*, a regional boss responsible for supervising a number of gangs. He is assisted by the *fuku-honbucho*, who also governs several gangs. Other members of the hierarchy in descending order include a lesser regional boss, or *shateigashira,* and his assistant, or *shateigashira-hosa.* In the prototypical Yakuza family, there are dozens of younger brothers, or *shatei,* and junior leaders, called *wakashu.*

Prior to the mid-1960s most Yakuza groups were regarded as autonomous, governing small territories. However, many of these groups have since been subsumed by larger groups. Police have begun to distinguish them from the smaller groups calling them *Koiki* ("wide area"). From this perspective, another way of looking at the structure is as a pyramid, with a multi-strata power structure headed by a "godfather" and his henchmen. At the next level in descending order are the bosses, followed by lieutenants. Of the three most powerful *Koiki*, the Yamaguchi-Gumi is the largest, with a membership estimated at 23,000 in 1992. Not bad for a gang that began in Kobe with 15 members in 1915. The other two *Koiki* are the Inagawa-kai and the Sumiyoshi-Kai (Yokoyama 1999).

MEMBERSHIP   Traditionally, any prospective member is required to take part in an initiation ritual where the initiate drinks *sake*, a rice wine, which some have made parallels with the Italian Mafia tradition of pricking one's finger and smearing a picture of a saint with blood. The initiate and the *oyabun* meet face-to-face as *azukarinin*, or guarantors, prepare the drinks, which is carefully mixed with salt and fish scales and poured into cups. This is all done in front of a Shinto altar. The boss's glass is completely filled, whereas the initiate is given much less, symbolizing their relative positions. Each takes a sip from his cup and then swaps cups and takes another sip. This process cements the *kobun's* membership in the family, and from that day on his wife and children would become secondary to his Yakuza family.

In recent years standards have been lowered in order to fill the ranks, and as a consequence the Yakuza lost some of its traditional luster and power. Where in times past the Yakuza could depend on a ready supply of prime recruits, today's members are more likely to be drawn from the *bosozoku*, or street tribes, ordinary street hoodlums recognized for their devotion to motorcycles. In the modern era, the Japanese National Police Agency make less of a distinction between the Yakuza and other criminal organizations, referring to them all generically as *Boryokudan*, the violent ones. Yakuza members are not pleased, considering it an insult to their proud traditions.

Promotion is another matter, according to Yakuza scholar Peter Hill, who asserted it is not based on rationale or merit, but on "whether the boss likes you or not" (Hill 2003, 288, n.4).

Unlike most organized crime groups that prefer to conduct their myriad activities in the shadows, the modern Yakuza had clearly marked social clubs and headquarters embellished with signs and logos.

YAKUZA CUSTOMS   Finger amputation, or *yubitsume*,[16] is probably the best-known Yakuza custom. Its use can be traced back to the medieval era when it was used to weaken one's grip on a sword, "limiting self-defense ability." More recently Yakuza expert Peter Hill noted the adverse impact on an amputee's golf swing (Hill 2003, 76).[17] In this traditional ritual, a gang member who has offended or failed in some way is expected to cut off a finger joint, usually the little finger, and present it to his chief, or *oyabun,* to ask for forgiveness. With his hand damaged and unable to hold his weapon appropriately, the Samurai symbolically becomes more dependent on his boss for protection. Until the 1990s, this was a common and well-reported custom. According to one 1971 estimate, 45% of *gurentai* were missing a finger joint, and 30% of *tekiya* had performed the apology more than once. Stigmatized at home and abroad, digitless Yakuza now frequently undergo operations to replace the digit, in some cases with the little toe. In recent years, *yubitsume* has become less common among newer members, who opt for paying a fine instead. In 1994, Japanese police reported that the average of finger amputees amongst *boryokudan* had decreased to 33%. There are several explanations for this. Perhaps one of the best reasons is to avoid the identification aspects. Others suggest it could be the "weakening of the Yakuza ethos" (Hill 2003, 75).

Bosozoku

In Japan, teenage bike gangs, or *bosozoku*, have been blamed for a significant rise in violent crime during the 1990s. In the past, the Yakuza could count on the *boryokudan* and Koreans for new members, but in recent years the Yakuza has also recruited the motorbike-affiliated teens. Those that are not Yakuza members are expected to pay protection money to continue criminal activities.

Yubitsume: Finger Amputation (1984)

Yakuza Witness (YW): The actual procedure is to take a—what they in Japanese Yakuza call a little silver knife in a table and you pull it towards you and bend over and your body weight will snap your finger off.

Interrogator (I): What do you do with the severed part of the finger?

YW: The finger that is severed is put in a small bottle with alcohol and your name is written on it and it is sent to whoever you're repenting to as a sign that [you are sorry].

(President's Commission on Organized Crime: Asian Organized Crime, Oct. 1984, 228).

With the government suppression of the Yakuza and the increasing stigmatization of its members, some doctors have carved out an interesting niche repairing missing fingertips. More than a decade ago a doctor created this medical specialty. This service has become increasingly popular as hundreds of Yakuza attempt to rejoin law-abiding society, only to be turned down once the missing digits were observed. The operation cost more than $10,000 in the 1990s, and once more also required the patient giving up a toe for transplantation. It was estimated that in the mid-1990s some 90,000 Yakuza were missing at least a portion of one finger (Fingers Inc. 1995).

Tattooing is not a required activity, but as one Yakuza informant suggested, it demonstrates that an individual "has endured a tremendous amount of pain." The typical tattoo can take up to 100 hours. Most are performed in the traditional manner, which includes the use of bamboo tools, a painful process indeed. According to a Yakuza who testified in front of the 1984 President's Commission on Organized Crime, during the tattooing process, "Japanese needles are imbedded roughly one-quarter of an inch under the skin, it is indelible and therefore it also shows that the man has committed to becoming a Yakuza for life" (1984, 226–227).

Unlike many American organized crime groups, one can leave the organization without fear of recrimination. The same aforementioned informant described the resignation process as beginning when either the member tells the organization he is resigning or the syndicate tells the member. After the proclamation, a letter (called the "red letter") is sent to all Yakuza clans reporting the change in status. From then on, contact between the individual and the organization was prohibited.

The Yakuza in the United States

The Yakuza first arrived on American soil in the early 1900s, when a major Japanese drug distribution network began selling opium-based products and amphetamines to California criminal syndicates, primarily in the Los Angeles area. In recent years, Yakuza members have predominated in Hawaii, where they have established relationships with local crime syndicates. There and elsewhere they are involved in all aspects of the entertainment business, as well as shaking down and exploiting Japanese tourists. Yakuza members began appearing in Hawaii sometime in the 1960s, taking menial service-related jobs in restaurants, bars, and related business. By the 1970s, Yakuza members had become affiliated with Hawaii's underworld and partnered in a range of activities, including weapons and drug trafficking and pornography—typically smuggled from the United States into

Pavement Hijacking

One of the more common methods used in contract killings is to throw an unaware victim into oncoming traffic. According to one source, the Yakuza used the so-called "pavement hijacking" method to kill 1,367 individuals in the city of Okayama in 1 year (Japanese Yakuza 2003).

The Yakuza in America

Former President George H.W. Bush's older brother, Prescott Bush, Jr., was caught unawares when he was implicated in a Yakuza real estate transaction in which he received $250,000 finder's fee and another $250,000 per year for 3 years for helping a Tokyo-based real estate firm purchase the Houston-based software firm Quantum Access and Asset Management International Financing and Settlement, out of New York City. He was reportedly innocent of any knowledge that the real estate company, West Tsusho, was part of a company run by the Inagawa-kai Yakuza (Sterling 1994).

Japan. In Hawaii, the Yakuza have been active in prostitution and extortion rackets. Nevada, New York, and California have reported Yakuza activities as well.

Hawaii has been the predominant American destination of Yakuza members, in no small part because they easily blend in with the droves of Asian tourists and immigrants. The Yakuza have invested billions of dollars in real estate and drugs and weapons smuggling. In Hawaii, they partner with local criminals by directing tourists to gambling parlors, brothels, and sex shows for a percentage of the action.

One Los Angeles detective reported in 1984 that Yakuza engaged in cases of homicide, prostitution, prison escapes, gun smuggling, and money laundering in southern California (1984, 240). In one 1980 murder, a heavily tattooed body was discovered some 60 miles from Los Angeles, and although still unidentified in the mid-1980s, city detectives suspected he was a Yakuza.

In 1991, former director of the FBI William Sessions testified to a U.S. Senate committee investigating Asian organized crime that "the *Boryokudan* have built one of the world's largest criminal organizations" (quoted in Myers 1995). He cited a National Japanese Police report that estimated that Japanese syndicates grossed close to $10 billion in revenue in 1988 alone; one third was from the distribution of crystal methamphetamine, which sold on the street as "ice." *Boryokudan* reportedly were responsible for 90% of this drug in Hawaii.

Criminal Activities

The Yakuza are engaged in a wide spectrum of illicit activities. Today the drug trade and extortion are the leading moneymakers, followed by gambling and racketeering.[18] Extortion schemes range widely. One of the more diabolical is to force someone in debt to the syndicate to sign a life insurance policy with the Yakuza as recipient. The debtor is often murdered, typically while out of the country, and the gangsters collect. However, the typical scheme is extorting money from prospective business operators—mom-and-pop enterprises or young couples who opened a new sushi restaurant are often targeted and might include these payoffs as part of their monthly budget. Yakuza members have been known to use harassment, arson, and extortion to help landlords get rid of unwanted renters.

By most accounts, the Yakuza were slow to seek opportunities outside of Asia, mostly due to cultural factors. However, this all changed in the 1960s as a new generation came to the fore. Many spoke English and were well schooled in the popular culture of Western society. As the world became more internationalized, the Yakuza expanded sex tours aimed at Japanese men that took them throughout Asia.

WEAPONS TRAFFICKING Japan has some of the stiffest gun control laws in the world.[19] Currently, the Yakuza operate a lucrative gun trade between Japan and the United States, with bullets going for up to $15 each. More recently, cheap Chinese weapons brought $3,000 each, with U.S. machine guns going for more than triple that. Since the 1970s, the Yakuza have invested billions of dollars in real estate in North America.

During the Senate Hearings on Asian Organized Crime in 1984, it was revealed that at least one U.S. Army veteran had been convicted of running guns to Japan. During his trial, he explained to authorities that he had begun taking small loans from a Korean while in the Air Force. One thing led to another, and the veteran was in debt and agreed to recover a shipment of amphetamines lost in Japan. When he was unsuccessful, Yakuza members beat him and put a gun in his mouth. He later found the package and made another similar trip as well from Korea to Japan. When the ex-serviceman returned to the United States, he began fielding threatening calls from Yakuza and proceeded to have his number unlisted. Within 3 days they had the new unlisted number. This time, the Yakuza coerced him into smuggling 250 weapons to Japan on military and commercial aircraft. At that time, each gun could bring up to $1,500. According to the vet, over a 2-year period the Yakuza made a net profit of $250,000 on this racket alone. In later testimony the ex-serviceman explained, "The American Mafia is kind of like, it is kind of funny to say but it is like a kid's game, they [Yakuza] are very strict in their codes, they are very strict in what they do" (1984, 235).

TOURISM AND ENTERTAINMENT   There have been a number or reports where Japanese tourists in the United States were lured into Yakuza-run gambling games. When the gambler needs money, traditional organized crime loansharks are often at their willing disposal. Some victims have fled to Japan, presuming that the long arm of American syndicates will not follow. In such cases Yakuza members are expected to collect for them and return it to the American syndicate (President's Commission 1984, 230).

Yakuza members have been involved in the so-called White slavery racket, in which advertisements are placed in American showbusiness magazines looking for singers and dancers interested in performing in Japan. Once they arrive, they are typically beaten and threatened with worse if they did not work for them as prostitutes.

SEX-RELATED ENTERPRISES   During World War II, Yakuza were active in trafficking women for the pleasure of Japanese troops in the occupied territories of China and Manchuria. Following the war, they opened brothels for U.S. soldiers during the occupation of Japan. Since the mid-1950s, sex-oriented businesses have been popular enterprises for Yakuza. Whether it be smuggling pornography into Japan from abroad or running prostitution rings and forcing young Asian women into working as "comfort workers."

Japanese sex customers have a preference for young women. Yakuza have bought unwanted female children in China (during the heyday of one-child policy) for as little as $5,000 and then forced them to work in Yakuza-owned nightclubs, bars, and restaurants, in what observers call the *mizu shobai*, or "water business." Prospective prostitutes are lured from impoverished villages in the Philippines and elsewhere with promises of good jobs, but when they arrive in Japan, they are forced to take jobs as strippers and sex workers. For years, the Yakuza have been offering sex tours, a popular entertainment in East Asia. They have extended these activities to offering sex hotels in Bangkok, Manila, Seoul, and Taipei, where adventurous tourists can have fantasies fulfilled by prostitutes. More recently, various campaigns have diminished the sex-tour industry, but the demand for sex-related businesses persisted, so the Yakuza began trafficking in young women for the Japanese sex industry at home.

DRUG TRAFFICKING   One mob expert suggested that as early as the 1930s, "Japan held a position similar to that of Colombia today," as a drug producer and distributor aiming much of their product at the United States (Lunde 2004, 102). The Japanese made the transition from moving heroin in the 1930s to trafficking in opiates and amphetamines during World War II and the subsequent American occupation. Today, the amphetamine trade is the dominant drug business in Japan, with "speed" and "ice" the most popular. However, to obscure their participation in the drug trade, Yakuza members have established drug production factories in other countries.

MINBO   Since the 1980s there has been an increase in *minbo*, or "the violent intervention in civil affairs." A number of Yakuza have been able to ride their reputation for brutality to earn financial

The Yakuza and the Kobe Earthquake (1995)

The Japanese government had much explaining to do after a 1995 earthquake leveled one of the country's biggest cities. What was most embarrassing was trying to explain why the Yakuza was running a huge operation to provide food and supplies to quake victims. Most observers lauded the Yakuza for handing out water, food, and diapers with an efficiency that trumped government efforts during the first week. Yakuza publicists claimed to be handing out 8,000 meals a day from a parking lot adjacent to its headquarters, including powdered milk, eggs, water, and bread. Members used motor scooters, boats, and a helicopter to transport goods throughout the ravaged city.

rewards in myriad civil disputes (Hill 2005, 100). A typical strategy might include a Yakuza getting in a traffic accident "accidentally on purpose," wherein a Yakuza purposely crashes his car into another driver and claims damages. By most accounts, the Japanese criminal justice system runs at a glacial pace and litigants often negotiate out-of-court settlements. With a Yakuza as an adversary, most settlements are adjudicated in favor of the reputed gangsters, or, as Yakuza expert Peter Hill put it, "when a driver is handed a name-card bearing a Yakuza crest and the suggestion made that he pay compensation for the damage caused by his reckless driving, there is no doubt what is going on, but no direct threat has been made" (Hill 2005, 100). Once the victims discerns a missing finger or elaborate tattooing, there is little doubt that these markers come with a reputation for violence—in other words, the threat remains implicit and is almost impossible to adjudicate under criminal law. Other examples include a Yakuza charging a laundry with having ruined his expensive clothes. *Minbo* comes in other incarnations as well, cases where they actually offer a service in return for payment. These take the form of debt collection and financial and corporate racketeering (Hill 2005).

One of the most rewarding forms of *minbo* beginning in the 1980s has been *jiage*, or "land sharking." Traditionally, Japanese law has looked unfavorably on a free market in real estate, which makes it almost impossible to evict tenants in order for a landlord to profit from an impending real estate deal. Unable to force out tenants themselves, landlords have hired Yakuza to "encourage" residents to vacate, or for small landowners to sell their properties. If successful, a Yakuza can expect a return of a 3% commission. According to Peter Hill, these ventures netted the Yakuza a significant fortune during the real estate bubble that characterized the 1980s.

VIETNAMESE AND OTHER SOUTHEAST ASIAN GANGS AND ORGANIZED CRIME GROUPS

Vietnamese Organized Crime and Street Gangs

Following the Vietnam War, thousands of Asian refugees, mostly from Vietnam, emigrated to the United States. Among the émigrés were many with prior ties to the former South Vietnamese government and the United States military. Others included corrupt government officials, former military officers, and black market profiteers who had gotten rich from the decade long conflict. The first wave of these immigrants came to the United States in 1975, with successive movements targeting destinations in Canada, Australia, England, France, and Germany. The majority of the first wave settled in California, which offered a year-round temperate climate and generous government benefits. Subsequently, hundreds of thousands of "boat people" fled the socialist Vietnamese state for the States and elsewhere. More recently, scholars have noted that this wave of emigration to the United States "had the unintended consequences of transferring ancient conflicts with the Chinese to the United States" (Woodiwiss 2001, 366). Violence between the two groups was also an ongoing problem in other cities, including Boston and Toronto. One of the best examples of this conflict was the Chinese Ghost Shadows opening fire on Vietnamese mourners at the funeral of Vinh Vu (discussed later).

Like their earlier counterparts, they were welcomed in America and provided similar dispensations, although the communist government characterized them as mostly hard-core criminals and spies. By most accounts, the first wave of immigrants was part of the merchant and business classes. Although they faced an uphill battle assimilating and winning acceptance, many made impressive strides toward early success, starting restaurants and other businesses as their children made equally impressive adjustments, earning reputations for academic success only years after gaining fluency in the English language.

It should not be unexpected that the corrupt cogs of the corrupt South Vietnamese regime would turn to their old tricks in the new environment. A number of former South Vietnamese Army (SVA) personnel reportedly organized anti-communist brigades for a war against the communists that would never take place. This became a front operation to extort money from businessmen who faced being branded unpatriotic if they did not dole over "contributions." It was not much of a transition for these groups to become "extortion" gangs. Attempts by Vietnamese critics in their communities to end this practice were met with violence. Between 1980 and 1995, at least nine crusading journalists were murdered.

The criminal element among the new immigrants found sanctuary among already established Asian criminals who had preceded them from China and Vietnam. Established Chinese syndicates used the newcomers as collectors and enforcers. Vietnamese organized crime has not evolved beyond its roots as a scattering of violent street gangs, often engaged in murder, extortion, and drug trafficking (Lintner 2003). Much of their activities are affiliated with the more organized and influential Chinese syndicates (similar to Australia). Many of the immigrants were themselves ethnic Chinese from Vietnam, better known as Viet Ching. Their ability to communicate with both segments of the Asian community made the Viet Ching valuable commodities in Asian communities. In New York, leading Chinese gangs including the Wah Ching, Flying Dragons, and Ghost Shadows employed them as enforcers.

During the 1984 PCOC Hearings on Organized Crime of Asian Origin, the source quoted in the next box, a lieutenant with the Garden Grove Police Department, was asked whether there "are any Vietnamese-American police officers in the State of California?" He soon followed up with, "I don't know of any officers in California that can speak Vietnamese fluently" (PCOC 1984, 326).

Among the best-known Vietnamese gangs in California are the Natoma Boyz, the Santa Ana Boyz, the Chosen Brothers, and Nip Family. They have female counterparts such as the Natoma Girlz, Chosen Sisters, Innocent Bitch Killers, South Side Scissors, and Midnight Flowers. Vietnamese gangs are perhaps most unique for not adhering to specific boundaries, preferring to move from neighborhood to neighborhood in various "Little Saigons," where they can prey on fellow immigrants and are less likely to be identified than in the dominant Caucasian and African-American communities. Their lack of strong ties to any community and almost constant mobility made them a unique phenomenon in organized crime in the 1980s and 1990s. Although Vietnamese gangs are not known for their

---

Vietnamese Gangs According to the Garden Grove, California, Police

On October 11, 1981, at approximately 1:30 in the morning, three male Vietnamese entered a local restaurant and opened fire with shotguns. The result here was one dead and five wounded. This case has not been solved [as of 1984]. The investigation centered on Vietnamese gang warfare, fighting over territorial jurisdictions. The case catapulted Vietnamese organized crime into the newspapers again and fueled the fear of the Vietnamese criminal element. During this time, the crimes being reported confidentially were murder, torture, arson, extortion, gambling, prostitution, auto theft, welfare fraud, and narcotics. Often these schemes were reported to involve political fronts alleging to involve efforts to finance freedom for the homeland. . . . We also noted at this time that a "gangster" was generally adult male Vietnamese, mid-twenties to fifty years old. They generally had a war record, generally claim alliance to a military source such as the Frogmen.

PCOC, *Organized Crime of Asian Origin*, October 1984, pp. 319–320.

organizational qualities, some gangs made the transition to well-disciplined robbery and extortion gangs that traveled to various Asian communities throughout the United States. However, for the most part, they were less formally structured than most other Asian organized crime groups.

Vietnamese gangs achieved a certain prominence for their penchant toward home-invasion robberies. A rare type of crime before the Vietnamese exodus to the States, its popularization led other Asian gangs to follow suit. A typical home-invasion robbery entails identifying prominent Asian businessmen and then making a forced entry into his home, ransacking it for jewels and valuables. It was often unlikely that these crimes would be reported, because many immigrant families keep valuables at home to avoid paying taxes. Gang members make sure to make the heists as terrifying and threatening as possible to ensure the victims did not report the crime, lest they risk a replay by gang members.

In the 1980s, Vietnamese gangs were involved in more sophisticated enterprises, including but not limited to stealing computer chips and cars, Medicaid and credit-card fraud, loansharking, and bookmaking. Toward the end of the 1980s, authorities noted that the average Vietnamese gang member had become much younger, ranging in age from 12 to 25.

BORN TO KILL (BTK)   In the mid-1980s, a group of Vietnamese teens left the orbit of the Chinese underworld and formed the Born to Kill (BTK) gang,[20] a name adopted from the slogan worn on the helmets of many American soldiers during the Vietnam War. BTK members identified themselves with five dots, representing *tien* (money), *tinh* (sex), *thuoc* (drugs), *toi* (crime), and *tu* (jail) and were also recognizable by the emblem of three lighted candles on a coffin. Most of these youths were already considered outsiders having not made the requisite assimilation as the majority of their fellow immigrants did and turned to a variety of criminal activities. BTK members were identifiable by their trademark black clothing and ponytails. Despite their predilection for violence and criminal behavior, the BTK were never able to make the jump to an organized underworld cartel.

David Thai

Of Viet-Ching heritage, Thai is considered the organizer of the Born to Kill gang. Most accounts have him running away from a foster home in Indiana in the 1970s and making his way to New York City. He spent several nights sleeping in the Port Authority Terminal before finding employment as a dishwasher at a Long Island nursing home. Subsequently, he spent a stint at NYU, worked several menial jobs, and experienced a failed marriage. Sometime in the 1980s during this succession of events, New York's Chinatown gang, the Flying Dragons, apparently recruited him. By the late 1980s, Thai left the gang and set about recruiting Vietnamese gang members for what would become the Canal Boys, so-named for its turf that extended down Canal Street to the west of central Chinatown. More widely known as the BTK, it was here on Canal Street the gang began extorting protection payments from the numerous merchants and vendors. Observers concluded it was just a matter of time before Thai was retaliated against for leaving the Flying Dragons without the consent of Hip Sing leader, the venerable Benny "Uncle Seven" Ong.[21] However, by most accounts, local Tongs decided to wait and watch, unwilling to start a bloody conflict between the Chinese and Vietnamese gang members. Thai gained a reputation as a modern-day Fagin as he supported a legion of famished youngsters more than willing to learn the modus operandi of street extortion and robbery from the cagey Thai (Kleinknecht 1996, 192). Gang members were given free room and board at safe houses from Manhattan and Brooklyn to the Bronx and Jersey City. Like gangs elsewhere, these formerly homeless young men found a sense of family in these new conditions. One of Thai's most accomplished killers was 30-year old La Ngoc Tran, who federal agents labeled the "Poet of Death," due to his habit of expounding on his latest murder with a poem or two. Thai did not shrink from the public eye—tooling around town in fancy cars, he ran a counterfeit Rolex factory out of his home. Although Thai dreamed of creating a nationwide syndicate and even working with the traditional mob, an informer sidetracked his ambitions. Thai and "the Poet" were sentenced to life in prison in October 1992 after being found guilty following a 20-count RICO indictment.[22]

When Thai's second in command, Vinh Vu, was killed leaving a Canal Street massage parlor in the early hours of July 25, 1990, it signaled a ratcheting up of the violence. During his funeral and burial 3 days later, rival gang members opened fire on the mourners, killing five. Reports indicated that two or three men posed as mourners and as they approached the throngs of BTK supporters, they tossed aside memorial flowers, pulled out a shotgun and 9-millimeter handgun, and shot at the more than 100 onlookers, with some escaping by jumping into open graves. Subsequently, the BTK became increasingly violent, going as far as killing witnesses during robberies in Chinatown.

Prior to the demise of Thai and most of his leadership in 1992, many BTK members had already relocated to other parts of the country, where they continued the tradition of home-invasion robberies, extortion rackets, and computer chip robberies.

NGUYEN CAO KY AND THE DARK SIDE   One of the most controversial revelations from the 1984 PCOC hearings was the testimony of a witness obscured by a screen to protect his identity, who claimed that he was a member of a Vietnamese anti-communist organization with chapters across the country known as the Dark Side. According to the witness, its reputed leader was none other than the former South Vietnamese prime minister and military leader Nguyen Cao Ky. Other members of the hierarchy included former high-ranking officers from the South Vietnamese Army (SVA). Although the organization's stated purpose was to fight communism, it had also made the transition to criminal activities, engaging in robbery and extortion to fund rebels in Vietnam. The witness invoked the names of four gangs, which he said were sponsored by the Dark Side—the Black Eagles from San Francisco, the Fishermen in Houston, the Eagle Seven in Chicago, and the Frogmen out of Orange County (PCOC 1984, 328–344).

To those who followed syndicated columnist Jack Anderson, this revelation was less startling. Almost 2 years earlier (1982), Anderson published a column claiming Ky was indeed a crime boss who had fled Vietnam with up to $8 million in gold, diamonds, and currency (Kleinknecht 1996). By most accounts, Ky was no newcomer to the "dark side," having played an important role in the smuggling of raw opium from the Golden Triangle to Saigon while prime minister in the 1960s (McCoy 1972; Kleinknecht 1996). Despite all of these charges, there was a lack of consensus among the law enforcement community as to whether he was a "Vietnamese godfather," for if he was, "he's the poorest godfather in America"—in reference to Ky's current occupation at that time, which was running a liquor store in Garden Grove and actually tending the counter himself (quoted in Kleinknecht 1996, 182).

Organized Crime and Gangs in Taiwan

The origins of organized crime groups in Taiwan can be traced back at least as far as the 17th century, when dispossessed farmers and others left the Fujian coast and crossed the sea to Taiwan, which was at that time inhabited by non-Chinese "Austronesian aboriginals" (Lintner 2003, 45). Due to the island's strategic location near the coast of China and along the water-route to Japan, the Portuguese, who describe the land as "Beautiful Island" or "Ihla Formosa," had established trading outlets here in the 16th century.

According to one authority, organized gangs and criminal groups became "an obvious fact of life" in Taiwan soon after 1945, after China recovered the island from Japan. Ko-Lin Chin asserts that the first gangs were formed by newcomers from mainland China in an attempt to protect themselves from the indigenous Taiwanese. Native Taiwanese gangs were referred to as *jiaotou*,[23] and were more likely than the newcomers to be involved in the extortion of local merchants and illegal gambling (2003, 5–6). Conflict between the two types of gangs led to a government crackdown, which became known as "sweeping away black societies." Subsequently, the heads of the Bamboo United and the Four Seas, the two largest mainlander gangs, were imprisoned. Nonetheless, both the mainland and *jiaotou* gangs continued to flourish and penetrate the legitimate business community.

The murder of the Chinese-American writer Henry Liu in California in 1984 by three Bamboo United leaders led to an unprecedented gang crackdown across the country called "Operation Cleansweep."[24]

Until 1985, Taiwan was ruled by an authoritarian establishment. However, that year, President Chiang Ching-kuo (son of Chiang Kai-shek) announced the end of martial law (which had begun in 1949 after the government moved from the mainland to Taiwan) and that none of his lineage would enter the political ring, essentially taking the family out of the country's political process. As a result of these momentous reforms, most of the social control mechanisms, including curfews, censorship, and prohibitions on public demonstrations, were lifted (Chin 2003).

According to one local police chief the onset of the reforms also opened up the country to organized crime, suggesting, "Before the abolishment of martial law, the crime problem in Taiwan was a minor one. At that time, our main concern was the existence of gambling dens and commercial sex establishments," which he maintained were not much of a problem. However, the end of martial law in 1986 led to reduced coastal patrols and opened up the island's coasts to drugs and weapons smuggling that "completely changed the crime scene here" (quoted in Chin 2003, 6).

CAN THESE GANGS BE REGARDED AS ORGANIZED CRIME GROUPS? One way to discern whether a gang or group is a form of organized crime is to consult the country's organized crime laws, which typically are used against such criminality. In 1996, Taiwan introduced the Organized Crime Prevention Law. Taiwanese criminal organizations officially fall into three types. The organized type is the largest and best organized and for the most part originated from the mainland Chinese who moved to the island with Chiang Kai-shek in 1949. These gangs include the most powerful syndicates including the Bamboo United; the Four Seas; and the Celestial Alliance, which is considered the only Taiwanese organized gang. Unlike traditional American syndicates, these groups typically do not control certain territories, but are active across the island and internationally. On the other hand, the second group—the *jiaotou* type, is territorial and members are mostly Taiwanese. These groups are smaller, with between 20 and 50 members as opposed to the hundreds and thousands of the "organized-type" groups. The third type is the "loosely knit" group, with even fewer members, ranging from a handful to more than 20. They are also composed mostly of Taiwanese, but do not control a particular territory (Chin 2003, 9–11). Into the early 2000s, few organized gangs of any standing were indicted as organized crime groups. According to one government source, the government takes a pragmatic approach, suggesting, "Organized gangs are organized crime groups; most *jiaotou* groups and loosely knit groups are not well organized, so we need to examine them case by case to determine whether they are organized crime groups or not" (Chin 2003). The following are brief descriptions of Taiwan's three largest organized crime groups.

THE UNITED BAMBOO GANG In 1956, the United Bamboo Triad originated in the suburbs of Taipei as the Bamboo Woods League. It took its moniker from local Bamboo Forest Road neighborhood, where 17 teenagers, predominately scions of Chiang Kai-shek's military officers, banded together to rectify the humiliation they felt from the Nationalist defeat and retreat from mainland China. It reached its apogee in the early 1980s, when it counted up to 40,000 members scattered between Taiwan and the rest of Asia as well as the United States, Canada, Australia, and Europe (Lintner 2003).

According to the gang's rules established in 1957, members were expected to focus on their conflict with the Four Seas Gang, staying united, and contributing weekly to their local treasury. Today, Bamboo United is a well-ordered syndicate with a headquarters and various local branches in Taiwan. According to a 1985 investigation, headquarters is home to the gang boss, or "Ultimate Gang Leader," and his two immediate subordinates: the "Ultimate Enforcer," who enforces gang protocol, and the "Ultimate Superintendent," responsible for overseeing gang activities and members (National Central Police University 2005). In 25 years, the number of gang branches has increased from 8 to more than 60 branches.

A typical branch or Tong hierarchy consists of a Branch Leader, Deputy Branch Leader, and members, referred to as *brothers*. However, there are variations between branches, with some now featuring sub-branches or "guardian units" or "combat units." Some also feature other officers, including Right-arm and Left-arm Enforcers, Internal Regulator, and Communications and War Officers. Bamboo United branches are located in urban environments. It is not unusual

United Bamboo Members' Code of Ethics

1. Harmony with the people is first priority. We have to establish good social and personal connections so as not to create enemies.
2. We have to seek special favors and help from uncommitted gang members by emphasizing our relationships with outside people. Let them publicize us.
3. Gambling is our main financial source. We have to be careful how we handle it.
4. Do not take it upon yourself to start things and make decisions you are not authorized to make. You are to discuss and plan all matters with the group and "Elder Brother."
5. Everyone has their assigned responsibility. Do not create confusion.
6. We do not divulge our plans and affairs to outsiders, for example to our wives, girlfriends, etc. This is for our own safety.
7. We have to be united with all our brothers and obey our Elder Brother's orders.
8. All money earned outside the group must be turned over to the group. You must not keep any of it for yourself. Let the Elder Brother decide.
9. When targeting wealthy prospects, do not act hastily. Furthermore, do not harass or threaten them. Act to prevent suspicion and fear upon their part.
10. If anything unexpected happens, do not abandon your brothers. If arrested, shoulder all responsibility and blame. Do not involve your brothers.

Los Angeles Sheriff's Department (DeVito 2005, 322–323).

for branches to engage in fratricidal skirmishes over debt collection and other rackets. Recent evidence suggests there are no real requirements for membership, nor are there formal registration or initiation ceremonies. A National Police Survey revealed that most members simply became members by fraternizing with current members over a period of time (National Central Police University 2005, 14).

The United Bamboo is involved in a number of traditional organized crime activities, including extortion, loansharking, protection schemes, and prostitution and gambling rackets. As goes the Taiwanese economy, so goes the gang. During the 1980s and into the 1990s, the economy was booming, increasing opportunities for the nation's gangs. In this post-industrial era, new rackets emerged in the entertainment, video, communications, and film industries. Other stand-bys prospered as well, many in the legitimate world involving construction, futures trading, and even the funeral business. According to the best source on the United Bamboo, "the level of professionalism within the gang is not as high as the public has imagined, [and] does not even employ a lawyer, an accountant, or a professional" (National Central Police University 2005, 15–16).

FOUR SEAS GANG The Four Seas Gang ranks behind the United Bamboo Gang as one of Taiwan's leading gangs. Membership is estimated at more than 2,000, compared to the United Bamboo's 10,000. This gang has prospered in recent years expanding to more than 40 different Tongs. Each gang is structured with a leadership hierarchy of chairman, deputy chairman, and standing committee members. These leaders rule over the Four Seas Tongs. Each Tong is ruled by a Tong master, a deputy Tong master, "big brothers," and "brothers." However, it is the chairman who has the ultimate say, relaying rulings and decisions to the various Tongs.

Similar to its other Taiwanese counterparts, it is no great feat to become a member, although some Tongs have used probationary periods to vet new recruits. Initiation ceremonies seem to be more onerous than others, often involving a ceremony that includes taking oaths, pricking fingers, drinking wine mixed with blood, adapting to new rules, and meeting old members. The Four Seas gang also enforces a list of gang prohibitions against drug use, rape and kidnapping, eating free meals, cheating and fraud, robbery and theft, compromising national interests, and a host of others (National Central Police University 2005, 22).

Cambodian Gangs

Thousands of Cambodians (ethnic Khmers) fled Cambodia after the emergence of the Khmer Rouge in 1975. Many joined the other Southeast Asians displaced by the Vietnam War in the United States. According to gang expert Bill Valentine, Cambodian gang members differ from Vietnamese gangs by emulating American street gangs. They prefer to claim their own territory and have adopted the graffiti and oversized clothes familiar to inner city Black and Hispanic gang members. One of the best known of these is the Korat Boyz, or K-Bs, in Long Beach, California. Conflict with other gangs is typically predicated on ethnic affiliation; for example, the K-Bs engaged in warfare with the Mexican-American East Side Longos beginning in 1989 (Valentine 2000).

CELESTIAL (HEAVENLY) ALLIANCE Following a roundup of gang members in 1984, many were locked up in prison rehabilitation programs. Many found a common goal in protecting themselves from United Bamboo members and in 1986 established the "Heavenly Alliance." By 2004, it had more than 30 branches. These branches are structured in familiar fashion. Using the Sun Branch as an exemplar, its leadership in descending order is made up of a Branch Leader, Deputy Branch Leaders, Advisers, Special Combat Teams, Unit Chiefs, and members. By most accounts, the Heavenly Alliance mimics most of the recruiting tactics of the leading gangs, including recruiting high school students and other low achievers. However, it is unknown how long these particular members stay in the gang.

The Heavenly Alliance does not utilize any complicated initiation ceremony but does require new members take a pledge consisting of four rules:

- Help "heaven" in dispersing justice, that is support the weak and help the poor
- Be honest and candid with other members, that is to be united
- Follow the example of heaven and earth, that is to assist the world with empathy and justice, and
- Fly as high as possible, that is to travel around the world and do "just" things (National Central Police University 2005, 18–19)

The Heavenly Alliance participates in myriad criminal activities, from operating sex and gambling rackets to debt collection, bid rigging, waste land disposal, and extortion schemes. However, it is most prominent in its virtual dominance of the country's lottery business, which is considered its most lucrative enterprise.

Korean Gangs and Organized Crime

The official use of the term *organized crime* in South Korea typically refers to "an organized violent band or group," in which gang members exhibit "a minimum level of organization and employ violence as a tool" (Lee 2006, 63). Like most countries with a contemporary organized crime problem, its roots can be traced back hundreds of years. Historians traced the first use of the terms *hoodlum* and *violent bands* to the Ko-ryo Dynasty, which lasted from 918 to 1392. However, these were mostly opportunistic bandits who preyed on local citizens when the moment was right. As a number of Korean cities emerged as urban centers in the 1800s, these centers became home to a number of small street gangs, or *keondal,* what one observer has compared to a Korean version of America's Bowery Boys (Lee 2006). Many of the members had been drawn to these cities for jobs but found few opportunities, poor housing, and little in the way of public assistance. Gangs of young men found employment in the demimonde of the Korean underworld.

The 1950s are considered "the first golden era of organized crime in South Korea, as two dominant gangs battled for control of Seoul" (Lee 2006; Jung 1997). By the 1960s, the *keondal* numbered in the thousands and some had joined larger gangs with a hierarchy and chain of command.

They were especially active in the entertainment industry. Politicians also used them for security and to attack opponents. After a police crackdown, the *keondal* went underground in the South Korean prison system and in the 1970s reemerged as crime "families." They formed alliances with other Asian crime families as well as with Korean immigrant groups around the world.

Bloody conflict for the streets of Seoul in 1975 between two factions armed with fish knives and iron bars resulted in the ascendance of the Ho-Nam Faction, which over the next few years splintered into three subgroups—the Seo-bang Faction, the Yang-eun Faction, and the OB Faction (Lee 2006, 65). What distinguished the warfare between Korean gangs from other Asian underworlds was the absence of modern weapons in these bloody clashes, with members preferring to use medieval weapons and martial arts. There are a number of authorities who have suggested that rather than a certain noblesse oblige for the past, these tactics were rather the result of strict Korean laws against gun possession. As the 1970s moved to conclusion, Korean organized crime groups became increasingly more violent and hierarchically structured.

Despite subsequent crackdowns and roundups, the *keondal* are considered a considerable force today, with an estimated 12,000 members in some 400 families (Nicaso and Lamothe 2005). The bread and butter for these gangs include drug and weapons trafficking, loansharking, and extortion. The most popular drug activities involve pharmaceuticals and methamphetamine. Among the most prominent syndicates are the *Tongsongno-pa* and the *Shinsangsapa,* which recently engaged in the methamphetamine trade with Yakuza members, especially smuggling these drugs into North Korea (Nicaso and Lamothe 2005).

Organized crime in Korea became prominent once more in the 1980s due to the opportunities offered by Korea's hosting the 1986 Asian Games and the 1988 Seoul Olympics. Following the assassination of the South Korean President Jun-Hee Park in 1979, the government proclaimed martial law and a curfew—a serious blow to organized crime activities. In 1982, the curfew was lifted and Korea entered an era of relative prosperity that left the citizens with more leisure time and money for entertainment. Besides the entertainment business, Korean mobsters found new profits in the construction industry and real estate speculation, heralding what one criminologist labeled "a second golden era" of South Korean organized crime (Lee 2006, 66).

Today's Korean syndicates have a global presence from Africa to the United States and are active in the importation of methamphetamine, ice, counterfeit goods, as well as murder contracts and credit card fraud. A number of these acts are committed with the complicity of Korean gangsters in the United States. Sex-trade gangs have brought women from Korea to North America and in some cases American military men have been paid (between $3,000 and $5,000) to marry a prospective prostitute to facilitate her delivery to America. Some of the more prominent gangs include the Korean Killers, the Korean Fuk Ching, the Green Dragons, and the Korean Power.

According to the 2000 census, there are more than 1 million Koreans living in the United States, making them one of the nation's largest immigrant populations. The first immigrants arrived in Hawaii in 1903. Korean immigrants began to emigrate in the thousands until the Korean government stopped the flow in 1905 when word filtered back of the poor treatment they received in Hawaii. The large-scale immigration of Koreans only commenced following the passage of the 1965 Immigration Act that eliminated reference of national origin as a criterion for immigration. By most accounts, the majority of the Korean immigration occurred since the mid-1970s.

One early study of Korean criminal gangs focused on "shoeshine gangs" that were organized into territories used for criminal and business purposes. As the name suggests, these gangs pursued legitimate shoe-shining businesses as well as various rackets in Korea (Kang and Kang 1978). Most gang members were from the impoverished and disenfranchised classes and the gang created a bond and offered opportunities that were otherwise limited due to the social and economic conditions that existed. By most accounts, these gangs were highly organized, hierarchical, with a strong leadership. Positions ranged in descending order from the *wang cho,* or leader, to the generals, *daejang,* and then the older brothers, or *hyung him,* and then the oaji, or fathers (Covey 2003). The gangs operated similar to a crime syndicate and offered young men opportunities to move up in rank. Most important to these gangs was the control of territory or turf, which they would defend with violence in order to keep control of their rackets.

More recent research suggests that Korean crime groups can be classified in three tiers, each distinguished by age. The top tier is composed of adults ranging from 25 to 60 who basically control the gang's activities. Some accounts identify these actors as former Korean Intelligence Agency members (Choo 2007; Leet, Rush, and Smith 2000). This group is reportedly violent and aggressive and favors the extortion of Korean businessmen. The other two groups in descending order include a young adult group ranging from 13 to 17 years of age, and finally a juvenile clique, with members as young as 13.

Korean gangs diverge from their Asian counterparts particularly when it comes to structure. Most Asian gangs act separately from adult gangsters, especially Vietnamese, Taiwanese, and Korean immigrant gangs that have been established in American communities. According to Choo, "Compared to Tong affiliated gangs, [these other Asian gangs] seem to be less organized, smaller in size, younger in age, less cohesive and with fewer ties to neighborhood traditions" (2007, 21).

Into the 1990s, the Korean Power Gang (KPG) was considered one of the more prominent Korean organized crime groups in the States. One scholar compared the structure of this gang to that of the Chinese Tongs, but with the caveat that it is probably not under the control of the Korean Merchant Association (Choo 2007). In its formative years, the KPG served as protection for Korean-owned nightspots before moving into gambling and extortion rackets. One observer reported that the KPG extorted some $20,000 per month from Korean businesses in Manhattan's and Flushing's Koreatowns. However, by 2007, this activity had stopped after a heavy crackdown on Asian gangs by the New York Police Department. The success of this crackdown has emboldened Korean businessmen who are now more apt to call 911 at the first hint of extortion (Choo 2007, 75).

Due to close contact with Chinese communities, the Chinese subculture has exerted a larger influence on Korean gangs. Indeed, it is quite common for Korean-Americans to join Chinese gangs. Reasons for this include the higher name recognition of the gangs and more opportunities provided by more financially secure gangs (Choo 2007). One of the results of the aforementioned police crackdown was that gang members are more difficult to identify now, with most eschewing identifiers such as tattoos, hand signs, and certain clothing styles. Today's Korean gang members are likely to be involved in non-traditional crimes including credit card and check fraud, as well as escort services. More traditional crimes such as extortion and protection rackets have fallen by the wayside in favor of more brutal crimes including home invasion and taxicab robberies.

Overview

Asian organized crime groups represent a distinct form of ethnic and cultural criminality. It is not enough to evaluate its various dimensions with the same perspectives used to explain Italian, African and Hispanic crime groups. Similar to any discussion of the aforementioned, this chapter demonstrates the importance of understanding the historical and cultural traditions that fostered the development of these unique groups. Although Chinese organized crime syndicates share a number of proclivities, it would be hasty to assume that the Triads are international organizations. Although many gangs around the world have adopted monikers used by high-profile Triads such as the 14K, the Wo On Lok, and Big Circle Boys, it does not necessarily mean they are part of a worldwide network. Similar to the way American street gangs move about the country and use the name of urban gangs such as the Bloods and Crips to evoke fear, Chinese syndicates have discovered that the very mention of these gangs can earn instant respect from local thugs while sending fear through local disorganized crime and local police (Lintner 2005).

One leading scholar argues that

> Unlike other ethnic gangs—which operate in deteriorated, poor neighborhoods—Chinese gangs flourish in rapidly developing and economically robust communities that are tied closely to Chinese societies in Southeast Asia. It is this link to communities outside the United States that makes many Asian gangs distinct from other ethnic-American counterparts, which are "hampered by both the lack of lucrative criminal opportunities in their own neighborhoods and the absence of contacts outside those neighborhoods. (Chin 1990, 140–145)

Law enforcement and others have recognized several trends among Asian organized crime groups. Asian gangs are now much more likely to cooperate across ethnic and racial heritage lines. Some gangs and criminal groups have begun to structure their groups more hierarchically in order to remain more competitive as their operations become increasingly globalized. Another trend finds these groups increasingly engaging in white-collar crimes as they consolidate their illegal and legal business ventures. Nonetheless, traditional crimes such as extortion, murder, kidnapping, gambling, prostitution, loansharking, human smuggling, drug trafficking, auto theft, and money laundering continue as their main stock in trade.

Key Terms

Triads	Tong Wars	*Oyabun*
"Heaven and Earth Society"	Hatchet men	*Bosozoku*
Sun Yat-sen	Highbinder	*Boryokudan*
Chiang Kai-shek	Mock Duck	*Yubitsume*
Four Seas	*Dai lo*	Born to Kill
"Big Eared Tu"	Snakeheads	David Thai
Green Gang	Yakuza	Ko-lin Chin
Big Circle Boys	*Bakuto*	*Jiaotou*
Tongs	*Tekiya*	United Bamboo gang
On Leong Tong	*Sokaiya*	Shoeshine gangs
Hip Sing	Yamaguchi-Gumi	

Critical Thinking Questions

1. What are Triads, and how do they differ from Chinese street gangs?
2. What does the Chinese concept of *Guanxi* have to do the study of Chinese organized crime?
3. What was the impact of opium on Chinese society and organized crime?
4. What was the impact of the Chinese Revolution on organized crime?
5. What distinguishes the Big Circle Boys from traditional Chinese crime groups?
6. What differentiates Asian gangs in the United States from other ethnic and racial gangs?
7. What are Snakeheads, and how do they operate?
8. What are the characteristics of the Yakuza groups, and why are they distinct from other Asian groups?
9. What role does the Yakuza play in Japanese society?
10. Contrast Vietnamese street gangs with other Asian street gangs.

Endnotes

1. In his 1962 book *Hatchet Men*, Richard Dillon traced the word *coolie* back to the Bengali or Tamil word *kuli*, which was synonymous with "burden bearer."
2. In 1644, the Ming Dynasty lost control of China to the invading Manchu Dynasty. The Manchus swept in from Manchuria to the North, signaling the beginning of 268 years of rule by the outsiders.
3. The *Hak Sh'e Wui* is considered the most recent of these. By the 1960s, it reflected a public consensus that the Society had a rather sinister connotation

rather than earlier incarnations that were regarded closer to a mystic brotherhood of man (Morgan 1960).

4. Interestingly, Mao had no problem with the drug trade as long as it was directed at the West. He hoped this would quicken the decline of the West.

5. Some of this is connected to the ancient Chinese science of numerology.

6. Sometime around 1880, a San Francisco police officer coined the term *highbinder* for Chinese gangsters. Subsequently, another incident led to the adoption of the term *hatchet men* after one of the so-called highbinders brandished a hatchet in a violent encounter. See Dillon, 1962 p. 52.

7. Quoted in McIllwain, *Organizing Crime in Chinatown*, 2004, p. 194. Originally translated by Ko-lin Chin in *Chinese Sub-culture and Criminality*, 1990, p. 63.

8. *Fuk Ching* is an abbreviation of Fukien Chingnian, or "young Fujianese."

9. In 1997, President Bill Clinton responded to the public outcry by relenting and releasing the remaining refugees to federal supervision pending adjudication.

10. According to the best estimates, the average trip from China to the United States takes 89 days and has an average of 2.6 transit points, often involving air, land, and sea travel (Chin 2001).

11. One recent historian suggests that the *tekiya* was "medieval Japan's version of snake oil salesmen" (Hill 2005).

12. According to Hill, during the 1980s only about one third of the *sokaiyo* were actually Yakuza members.

13. These countermeasures are referred to as the *Botaiho*.

14. Parallels can be drawn with the rise of "Lucky" Luciano in New York City in the same era.

15. This was not the first assassination attempt on a Nagasaki mayor. In 1990, Itoh's predecessor, Hitoshi Motoshima, was shot in front of city hall by a right-winger who was upset that Motoshima had made derogatory remarks about Emperor Hirohito and his responsibility for World War II. However, Motoshima survived the shooting.

16. In the Yakuza community, this process is called *enkozume*.

17. By removing the smallest finger, it weakens the hand holding the traditional Samurai long sword, the *katana*, which is gripped properly requires the pinkie as the strongest finger in the grip.

18. According to police arrests from 2001.

19. Japan's gun control tradition can be traced back to at least the 17th century, when Japan rejected Western influence and closed itself to the outside world. Since then, gun ownership has remained within the purview of the government authorities. Some experts suggest that this policy is designed to concentrate the power of the state and limit violence.

20. According to Kleinknecht 1996, BTK members have also used the moniker, "Canal Boys."

21. Ong's moniker, "Uncle Seven," refers to his being the seventh son of his family. Ong was born in Harbin, China, in 1907, and came to America while still in his teens. He served several prison stints, including a 17-year sentence for murder and shorter terms for bribery. When he became the leader of New York's Hop Sing Tong in 1974, he was considered the "godfather" of Chinese organized crime. However, at the time of his death at the age of 87 in 1994, he was more figurehead than actual leader.

22. For more on Thai, see T.J. English (1995). *Born to Kill: America's Most Notorious Vietnamese Gang, and the Changing Face of Organized Crime*, New York: William Morrow.

23. In 1998, the National Police of Taiwan counted a total of 1,274 gangs, *jiaotou*, and other criminal groups.

24. Liu had written an incendiary biography of President Chiang Ching-kuo. As a result, the head of the country's Intelligence Bureau of the Ministry of National Defense ordered the three gangsters to commit the assassination.

CHAPTER 10

Organized Crime in Russia and Europe

Europe contains probably more sovereign countries than any other continent but yet is smaller than all the others except for Australia. Bordered by a handful of great bodies of water—the Atlantic Ocean, the Mediterranean Sea, the Black Sea, and the Caspian Sea—the more than 40 countries of Europe are home to perhaps one-seventh of the world's people and is surpassed only by Asia in population density. The sheer number of cultures, traditions, and languages has unique implications for organized crime. When one considers the totality of threats to national security and law enforcement, it becomes overwhelming, particularly when one takes into account the potential for conflict with so many borders, ethnic groups, and immigration and trade issues (Albanese, Das, and Verma, 2003). What often gets lost in the consideration of the organized crime problem in Europe are the historical ramifications from a continent that has been rent by wars and conflicts over the centuries but for many groups remain a source for conflict into the 21st century. One need look no farther than the bloodletting in the Balkans and former Yugoslavia in the first half of the 1990s as well as the region's long reputation as a tinderbox for internecine conflict that predates World War I.

One criminologist describes the European organized crime world as "murky, fragmented, and often contradictory because of factual differences, scattered and often incompatible differences, and culturally induced differences in perceptions and conceptualizations," suggesting, "The concept of 'organized crime' is an American invention that has been superimposed on a heterogeneous European crime landscape" (2005, 403). Fijnaut and Paoli agreed noting that "the term organized crime was rarely used in Europe before the early 1980s (2004, 21). However, does this mean organized crime did not exist here prior to this era? Definitely not! An historical examination of most European countries reveals a number of continuities with modern organized crime dating back more than a century."[1]

It is beyond the scope of this chapter (or any chapter) to cover every country in Europe. Italy is covered in Chapter 3, and Ireland, Spain, and Turkey are heavily chronicled in relationship to the convergence of terrorism and organized crime in their countries in Chapter 14 concerning terrorism. This chapter focuses on regions and countries at the center of Europe's organized crime problems in the 21st century not discussed elsewhere in the book, primarily in Russia and the countries of the former Soviet Union, the Baltic Region, the Balkans, Turkey, and a number of Western European countries, such as Britain and the Netherlands.

When it comes to the former Soviet Union republics, there is still a significant disparity between the living standards across the entire spectrum of its former states. Some countries such as Tajikistan in Central Asia have social indicators comparable to the poorest countries in Africa, whereas the nations of the Baltic region have developed at a relatively high rate. One leading authority suggests that crime in many of these countries has been marked by "new forms of criminality not previously known or not known on [such a] large scale" (Fijnaut and Paoli 2004), citing the rise of human trafficking for sexual and labor exploitation, as well as a tremendous surge in human smuggling, part of a larger tapestry that demonstrates the zeal with which residents wish to migrate outside the former USSR and Eastern Europe by any means necessary, even illegally.

When one considers Central and Eastern Europe, much of its rampant criminality is associated with its transition to a new economic system, the liberalization of foreign trade and investment, and the concomitant privatization process. The majority of organized criminality in these regions is related to economic crime, the drug and weapons trade, and illegal immigration. Chief among the economic crimes are the embezzlement of state property, violation of tax laws, bankruptcy of companies, crimes against intellectual property, and business fraud, most of which committed with the collusion of high-ranking officials and members of the private sector (Csonka 2003).

CENTRAL ASIA

Strategically located between the narcotics producing region of the Golden Crescent (Afghanistan and Pakistan) and major drug markets in Russia and Europe, the Caucasus Republics of Central Asia have become an important corridor for the narcotics trade. Uzbekistan and Turkmenistan are transit points for heroin precursor chemicals headed for Afghanistan, whereas Uzbekistan opiates are transported through Estonia bound for Finland. Operating on the periphery of Europe, Central Asian organized crime revolves around the lucrative drug trade. One explanation for this "was that unlike the Caucasus, Central Asian states were kept in one-crop economies during the Soviet era." As a result, their organized crime activities have not diversified their illegal economies to the extent they have elsewhere (Soderblom 2005, 5). A convergence occurred in which members of Central Asian organized crime groups prosecuted during the Soviet era were released soon after the fall of the USSR, when the region was most vulnerable to organized crime and feasted on the opportunities presented by the new markets.

WESTERN EUROPE

Organized criminal activity in Europe can be traced as far back as the Pre-Industrial Era with some even claiming as far back as the Roman Empire. Woodiwiss (2001, 16) argues, "Criminal enterprise was itself deeply embedded in the machinery of Roman law and government" during the early first century, citing examples of its leaders and officials using their administrative positions to "cheat, intimidate, and steal from the general population," and goes on to assert that in most cases, continuous criminal enterprise was characterized in this era by "networks of accomplices with powerful connections" that used force and threat of force to carry out an agenda of extortion, intimidation, bribe taking, fraud and illegal enterprise (Woodiwiss, 2001, 18).

The majority of European countries can find some type of organized criminal activity in their histories. What has changed in the modern era is the addition of non-indigenous crime groups ranging from the Middle East and Asia to Africa and South America. Most groups—whether from Colombia, Nigeria, Russia, or Turkey—maintain strong links to their countries of origin. These groups were just as likely to fall into conflict with each other as they were to cooperate.

According to a 2005 report by the Council of Europe, representing 46 member countries, the most common forms of organized crime in Europe today are fraud and other forms of economic crime, drug production and trafficking, and the smuggling and trafficking of individuals (2005, 28). Although the drug trade has been synonymous with organized crime for many years, the smuggling and trafficking of humans is a recent development, as is fraud and other economic crimes.

SMUGGLING TRADITIONS

Smuggling activities have a long history throughout the world. A number of activities have been geared to sell commodities without paying excise taxes. As early as the 13th century, some Dutch cities were requiring taxes on certain luxury goods, like salt and sugar. As a result, a shadow economy developed in which smugglers supplied these goods without paying taxes and thus added to their profits. The trafficking of cigarettes has become a big moneymaker for syndicates throughout the world. A number of organized groups emerged to take advantage of the increasingly high excise taxes in Europe. Governments used the tactic of increasing taxes to make the smoking habit cost-prohibitive; however, this has only created a parallel market for cheaper cigarettes that are shipped without paying duties, a form of bootlegging not unlike the response to other vice prohibitions throughout history.

Western Europe features a variety of well-established participants in the illegal drugs and weapons trade—some more than a century old, such as the Italian crime groups; others more than a half century old, including the Basque ETA and the IRA. These groups are among the welter of groups that responded to modern international police pressure and new criminal opportunities by extending and revising their lines of cooperation with other groups, even in some cases transcending the traditional animosity that once divided such antagonists as the Albanian and Italian groups (Curtis and Karacan 2003).

Cigarette trafficking is a cross-border affair, with production facilities typically located in the Far East and Eastern Europe and the markets in high excise countries such as Britain and Ireland. The Netherlands and Belgium are two of the main transit countries in the cigarette pipeline to Western Europe (Van Dijck 2007). Most of the cigarettes are transported by trucks. Sometimes they are professional truckers supplementing their incomes with some smuggling, whereas at other times they are more permanent members of the smuggling group. This form of crime proved popular among a cross-section of the population. Offenders range from retirees and heads of families to professional criminals engaged in drug trafficking, music piracy, and money laundering. Operations ranged from a more bureaucratic style employing a convoy of trucks and a number of warehouses to someone working out of the trunk of his car. One recent investigation in the Netherlands concluded that many of those involved "coexist without much awareness," and that in common with other "non-violent markets there is plenty of room for both professionally operating trafficking groups and small-time smugglers" (Van Dijck 2007, 14).

European Drug Trade

Europe's drug problem became more pronounced in the years between World War I and World War II (1918–1939). This was an era in which steps were taken to restrict the manufacture of addictive drugs such as opium, morphine, heroin, and cocaine. There is little doubt that when steps were taken to "more narrowly define legitimate drug consumers and to discipline legitimate drug firms, pharmaceutical traders and dealers" (Block 1994) that organized criminal syndicates formed to take advantage of the prohibition much the way American syndicates responded to alcohol prohibition. Although European crime groups played an important role in the international drug trade, they were never without competition from mostly Asian syndicates. In any case, "European criminals played crucial roles in the years of the greatest structural change in the production and trafficking of narcotics" (Block 1994, 94).

During this era between the wars, Germany, France, and Switzerland and, to a lesser degree, Great Britain, Italy, and the Netherlands were the most prominent European producers of refined drugs. According to Block, at least 20 German, Swiss, and French factories produced either one or combinations of morphine, heroin, cocaine, dicodide, dilaudid, and oxycodone (1994, 97–99).

By 1931, a series of international provisions had stopped the production of most of these drugs in Europe, and Turkey, Yugoslavia, and Greece stood alone as suppliers of opium to the European market. One explanation for the recalcitrance of Turkey in this matter was that for the prior century it had seen its territory diminished to a fraction of its size before World War I and the dismantlement of the Ottoman Empire, and as the country's economy dwindled along with its borders, "the relative significance of opium production [naturally] increased" (Block 1994).

From an early era, European drug syndicates drew on the expertise of those with connections to the broader international community. Similar to what is taking place in much of Europe post-1991, in the 1920s and 1930s these syndicates were "notable for their adaptability, the semi-independence of many members, the ephemeral nature of gangs, and for the unique blending of nationalities and ethnic minorities" (Block, 1994, 108).

It has become increasingly clear that the same people who traffic in narcotics are "very often the same people who will use the infrastructure to move human beings as illegal migrants, traffic in weapons, and smuggle other high value items" (Curtis and Karacan 2002). In the words of one organized crime expert, "It's like being a good trucker. You don't want to travel the return leg with an empty truck. If you use this sort of analogy, you have drugs coming out one way and that produces money and that buys the weapons and the weapons go back in" (quoted in Curtis and Karacan 2002, 2–3).

Human Smuggling and Trafficking

The fall of the Berlin Wall in 1989 opened the borders between Eastern and Western Europe, leading to an increase in various forms of illegal smuggling, including the trafficking in people. The wars in Yugoslavia only added to the human trafficking problem. It was not uncommon in the early 1990s for women to be trafficked in that region for sexual purposes, which included being used to provide sexual services to peacekeeping and civilian personnel as well as the combatants themselves. Like the earlier crisis in the former Soviet Union, the break-up of Yugoslavia was followed by a leap in unemployment, rising inflation, and an economic downturn. One recent investigator said, "Unregulated transition from a state-controlled to a market economy often resulted in massive unemployment (particularly of women), a breakdown in social assistance and widespread poverty" (Surtees 2008, 40).

The free movement of people has increased migration between states and has also created opportunities for organized crime groups to establish links with communities based outside their home territories. An examination of the human trafficking problem today reveals that the countries of Southeast Europe, including Moldova, Albania, Romania, and Bulgaria, are the preeminent source countries for those being trafficked into or through Bosnia-Herzegovina, Croatia, Macedonia, Serbia, Montenegro, and Kosovo. More recently, the corridor of immigration has expanded to include the rest of the European Union, the Middle East, Russia, and Turkey. One recent study notes:

> The demand for prostitution and other sexual services has increased in western Europe, while at the same time the former socialist countries of eastern Europe, with their current economic and social problems, form a source area from which trafficking to western Europe can be organized far more easily and more economically than from the old sources areas" of Southeast Asia, West Africa, and Latin America. (Lehti and Aromaa 2007, 124)

The structure of trafficking operations in Southeastern Europe varies. Some are low-level organizations mainly composed of individuals acting alone, whereas others are local criminal groups (mid-level) and even well-organized criminal networks (high level). The high-level organizations "tend to use well-developed methods of planning and control. They typically set prices and finance the costs of transfer but avoid becoming directly involved in transporting victims or crossing borders" (Surtees 2008, 47). They establish trade relations with other high-level groups (in the same country or in other countries) and cooperate in the exchange of victims or set up contracts with medium-level groups for the supply of various services such as transportation (Surtees 2008).

Weapons Trafficking

Thanks to an increased demand due to the expansion of ethnic and regional conflict since the late 1980s, the illegal trade in weapons has become a huge international business mostly controlled by organized crime groups. However, their success would be impossible without the collusion of individuals and institutions outside the criminal organizations such as national defense ministries, national security agencies, banks, legitimate arms dealers, and a number of other groups each vying for power within particular countries (Curtis and Karacan, 2002, 2). Much of the illegal trade is the result of the collapse of the rule of law in former communist states in Europe, especially in Yugoslavia, Albania, and the former Soviet Union. This, combined with open borders, the collapse of currencies, and the growth of terrorist financing schemes, played a role in the expansion of the weapons trade. Following the fall of the Berlin Wall, arms brokers became much more entrepreneurial; no longer guided by ideological leanings, they became in turn freelance businessmen interested only in making a profit. The massive Soviet arsenal fell into the hands of former Soviet Republics, but none profited more than Ukraine, which became the center of the global weapons trade. Economic woes easily convinced these new states to sell off anything to get hard currency. It has been estimated that between 1992 and 1998, more than $30 billion worth of weapons disappeared from former Soviet arsenals, including helicopters, AK-47 assault rifles, grenades, mortars, machine guns, and ammunition. A measure of how lucrative the arms business is can be discerned in the sale of an AK-47 rifle, which can be purchased for $20 and sold for $300 (including ammunition). Payment was typically made in untraceable cash or diamonds. In an attempt to restrict the sale of weapons, documentation, called the *End User Certificate (EUC),* is required that purportedly guarantees the destination of the weapons. A certificate must accompany every shipment, but most reports indicate these can be easily bought from corrupt countries for a percentage of the eventual profit. Arms trafficking organizations have flourished in no small part due to the labyrinthine bank arrangements they have concocted to protect themselves, making it one of the more highly profitable businesses of organized crime (Lunde 2004). More successful smugglers ship their weapons under the guise of legitimate business, sometimes marking crates of ammo as "perishable fruit." According

Viktor Bout (b. 1967): "Lord of War" and Weapons Trafficker Extraordinaire

No weapons dealer was more prominent than a Tajikistan-born Russian named Victor Bout. With monikers such as the "Merchant of Death"[2] and the "Embargo Buster," one observer described Bout as "the McDonalds of arms trafficking—he was the brand name" (Lunde 2004). Bout is thought to be the inspiration for the weapons dealer played by Nicholas Cage in the 2005 movie *Lord of War.* Born in Soviet Tajikistan to Russian parents, he entered the military as young man and rose through the ranks before earning a degree in economics from Moscow's Soviet Military Institute of Foreign Languages. Reportedly fluent in six languages, a number of sources suggest he was probably affiliated with the KGB at one time or another and that he was on assignment in Angola in 1991 when the Soviet Union collapsed. The following year he made his first arms deal. Between 1992 and 1995, he was estimated to have earned more than $50 million by supplying Afghani fighters from the Northern Alliance with Russian military weapons. However, most of his early dealings were in sub-Saharan African nations beset by civil wars, coups, and rebellions such as Sierra Leone, Congo, Liberia, and the Ivory Coast. In 1993, he started the TransAvia Export cargo company, which sold weapons to Belgian peacekeepers in Somalia. Several years later, he founded the Trans Aviation Network Group in Ostend, Belgium, which supplied weapons in the Iran-Contra operations. Bout next supplied the Taliban and continued in the weapons trade, but in 1997 finally appeared on police radar in his current home country of Belgium, and he moved his operations to the United Arab Emirates. A crossroads of East–West trade and an important financial center, Bout found this a much more suitable headquarters from which to conduct business. However, after the September 11, 2001, terrorist attacks and revelations that Bout had been supplying the Taliban with weapons, arrest warrants were issued for him by Interpol and Belgian authorities and his bank accounts were later frozen by the United Nations (DeVito 2005; Kelly, Maghan, and Serion, 2005). Bout was finally arrested March 6, 2008, in Bangkok during a U.S.-led sting operation while trying to procure weapons for Colombia's FARC guerrillas. Although the United Nations linked him over the years to weapons deals to help fuel wars in Afghanistan and throughout Africa, he has never stood trial for these allegations. Bout continually denied the charges, and in 2002 even went on Moscow radio to insist he was innocent and comparing the accusations against him to a Hollywood movie script. American officials claim he owned that largest private fleet of former-Soviet cargo aircraft in the world, and that over the years he used his company to operate an international arms bazaar (Johnston and Mydans 2008, A6).

to several experts on the enterprise, weapons shopping lists are trafficked clandestinely through networks of individuals who fill the orders for cash on delivery. Bribes are usually given to officials and military officers to look the other way (Kelly, Maghan, and Serio, 2005, 113).

Structure of Organized Crime Groups and Networks in Europe

By most accounts, ethnicity is no longer a central criterion for identifying organized crime groups, which have become increasingly multi-ethnic. A variety of organized crime structures have been identified. One 2002 study by the United Nations found 5 types of structures in the 16 countries in its study. In years past, a pyramidal/hierarchical model was most dominant. These groups are typically "ethnically homogeneous, formally and hierarchically structured, multi-functional bureaucratic criminal organizations" (Shaw 2002). This typology is best exemplified by the Cosa Nostra family-type organizations in Sicily and groups in the former Soviet Union that demonstrate a clear division of tasks, such as the Russian "thief in law." Another example is the British "firm-type organizations with permanent members, distinct roles and clear chains of command." Today, organized crime groups in Europe are more likely to be "more loosely structured [cooperating] in varying compositions for particular criminal enterprises" (Council of Europe 2005, 50–51).

Today, Europe is probably the most profitable market globally for the drug trade and remains the most important organized crime activity of the region's crime networks (Council of Europe 2005). Most of the heroin consumed in Europe is based on Afghanistan opium, most of which is funneled through the Balkan route, but as the Russian Federation and other Eastern European countries develop larger consumer markets, the Silk Road from Afghanistan through Central Asia has become more important. Ethnic Albanian criminal syndicates are linked with a large portion of Europe's heroin trade. Spain and the Netherlands are considered the leading entry points for cocaine (Council of Europe 2005, 29–30).

What Is the European Union?

The European Union (EU) is a treaty-based framework that defines and manages economic and political cooperation among its member states. The internationalization of organized crime has been

---

Organized Crime Groups in the European Union (2005)

- Indigenous organized crime (OC) groups still pose the main threat to EU.
- Italian Mafia–type OC groups are particularly dangerous for their ability in infiltrating the public and economic sectors.
- Lithuanian groups forge alliances with international OC and rapidly expanding all over the EU; they are extremely skilled in money counterfeiting.
- Dutch OC groups are specialized in drug production and trafficking.
- German OC groups are involved in types of crimes that require a vast network of international connections.
- Russian and other former Soviet Union OC groups are involved in all types of crime; highly sophisticated in the area of financial crime, fraud, and money laundering.
- Turkish OC is mainly involved in heroin production and trafficking to the EU.
- Chinese OC groups are well established in the EU, and are involved in illegal migration, trafficking of human beings (THB), and non-cash payment fraud.
- Moroccan groups are major provider of cannabis to EU drug market, and are also involved in THB and illegal migration.
- Colombian OC groups control cocaine production and global trafficking.
- Outlaw motorcycle gangs are present in force in Nordic countries, Germany, and Belgium, but are now expanding activities into new Members states.

(Adapted from European Council report by Europol 2005, 49–50.)

influenced by the strengthening of the EU, with recent steps toward lowering of internal border controls between states. The creation of a single European Market began in 1993, with its goal of furthering the region's economic integration by allowing the free movement of goods, services, people, and capital between member states. This process was intended to create a single space of mobility for EU citizens to live, travel, and work in Europe. The unintended consequence of this policy and similar schemes such as the 1985 Schengen Agreement was to facilitate smuggling operations of criminal groups intent on expanding their operations in terms of markets and territory. Today, 27 countries—Austria, Belgium, Bulgaria, Cyprus, the Czech Republic, Denmark, Estonia, Finland, France, Germany, Greece, Hungary, Ireland, Italy, Latvia, Lithuania, Luxembourg, Malta, the Netherlands, Poland, Portugal. Romania, Slovakia, Slovenia, Spain, Sweden, and the United Kingdom—have full membership status in the EU.

RUSSIAN ORGANIZED CRIME

Although some authorities date the roots of Russian organized crime back at least as far as the 19th century, when by most accounts it flourished outside the legitimate framework (Rawlinson 1998), others identified Russian criminal organizations as far back as the 15th century. However, these should not be confused with the modern phenomenon of organized crime. The 17th century saw the introduction of the so-called thieves' traditions, or thieves' law and thieves' slang. During this era, Moscow became the epicenter for Russia's burgeoning criminal gangs. Most observers trace the foundations of Russia's criminal underground to Tsarist Russia, when thieves' and beggars' guilds controlled petty crime (Varese, 2001; Applebaum, 2003). During the reign of Peter the Great (1682–1725), a vast network of Russian prison camps was created. It was here that hardened criminals banded together, spreading in time throughout the Gulag Archipelago. Members were bound together by a rigid code of conduct that prohibited them from working a legitimate job, paying taxes, fighting in the army, and from cooperating with authorities. According to several studies in the 1990s, researchers suggested that that the first Russian criminal organizations were inspired by *artels*—"an old Russian social institution, a cooperative set up to organize joint labor activity" (Gilinsky and Kostjukovsky 2004, 185). *Artels* became a well-entrenched form of organization in Russia, particularly during the Soviet era and the rise of communal culture. By the mid-19th century, *artels* of thieves came into prominence, especially horse thieves. The main difference between these criminal *artels* and the traditional legal ones (besides their illegitimacy) was the clandestine nature of their activities. However, it was not until the 1930s that the rudiments of modern organized crime groups and the evolution of the modern thieves in law were discernable.

As recently as the 1980s, it was a Soviet tradition to downplay the existence of organized crime and little was done to combat it. More recently, experts have traced the foundations of Russian organized crime back to the 70 years of the Soviet system itself. Between 1920 and the early 1990s the Soviet labor camps gave birth to an extensive criminal fraternity. During their incarceration a number of prisoners became bound up in their own system of rules and behavior that they viewed as a "thieves' world." Out of this emerged an elite band of criminals, or *vory-v-zakone,* who lived according to a "thieves' law." By most accounts, modern-day Russian organized crime grew out of this movement as well as the government organization and its high level officials. Individual *apparatchiks* developed mutually beneficial relationships with these criminals. By the 1960s, modern Russian organized crime groups had emerged, thanks in part to the state apparatus that "encouraged, facilitated and protected it" (Wright 2006, 148).

In the years leading up the communist revolution, free members of the *vor* brotherhood inspired Lenin's gangs to rob banks to fund the revolution. By the time Stalin came to power, he was laying plans to annihilate them. During World War II, he found just the right opportunity by recruiting them to fight for the homeland. Despite the prohibition against serving the country in any capacity, many fought; Stalin paid them back by tossing them back into the prison camps at the war's conclusion. Behind barbed wire, those who fought were considered traitors by the hardcore *vor* who refused to serve, resulting in bloody gang conflict. The *"Vor Wars,"* or "Bitches' War," lasted from 1945 until the death of Stalin in 1953 (Friedman 2000). Some accounts suggest that by 1953, only the hardcore survived and by then had virtually taken control of the prison system. Due to the conditions of the early years of the Soviet regime,[3] hundreds of thousands of orphaned street children resorted to thievery and petty crime to survive and provided a ready supply of hoodlums to fill the ranks of developing crime syndicates.

During the years of the Brezhnev regime in the 1970s and early 1980s, an era referred to as the *zastoi,* or "time of stagnation," it became clear to an increasingly dissatisfied public that the country was being run by a corrupt "kleptocracy" of Communist bureaucrats. It was during the latter part of this era that it became fashionable to brand the corruption as "Mafiya." Rather than referring to a monolithic hierarchy, the term referred to the daily inequities of life in the Soviet Union exemplified by the power structure and the inequities of the Russian communist system—whether a retail sales manager, a clerk, physician, or automobile mechanic—any of these occupations could be branded "mafiya" simply for the fact that they all controlled certain services or commodities. Whether placing high-quality merchandise or food under the counter to sell or exchange through the underground economy, or simply taking the goods out the back door, scarce supplies and services were controlled by individuals even at the middle echelon of the economy. One journalist summed it up in 1989, when he reported, "We apply 'mafiya' to practically anything—shops, creative unions, hospitals, diplomats, prostitutes, butchers, chess players, cities, regions and republics."[4] In any case, the Soviet system had indeed institutionalized a culture of thievery and an underground economy that became the foundations for a black market that could supply prospective consumers with almost anything from medicine to food.

Prior to the advent of the recent market economy, state property had little cachet among the common people and Russians typically took part front and center in a shadow economy that included off-the-books factories, nascent food-co-ops, and even construction companies. Those without access to this market were stuck with the inferior goods that marked consumer culture in the Soviet empire. In the mid-1980s, *Krokodil,* a satirical Soviet magazine, published a piece that characterized this dilemma, demonstrating how store management and other employees could be regarded as mafiya, "Dear customer, in the leather goods department in our store, a shipment of 500 imported women's purses has been received. Employees of the store have bought four hundred and fifty of them. Forty-nine are under the counter and been ordered in advance for friends. One purse is in the display window. We invite you to visit the leather department to buy this purse."[5]

Beginning in the late 1980s and continuing through the 1990s, the release of price controls that marked the Soviet economy led to more open markets exemplified by thousands of merchants who opened up shop in Moscow and elsewhere. Many were from the distant regions of Armenia, Georgia, Chechnya, and Dagestan. Others came from Central Asia and beyond. In any case, these fledgling entrepreneurs, migrants, and refugees were often drawn into the orbit of developing crime syndicates that tightly controlled most of the nation's markets. Perspicacious crime bosses used the newcomers to move narcotics, imitation liquor, and other underground commodities. Meanwhile, the merchants were free to engage in their own rackets, with a percentage turned over to local crime lords. It was during this era that the term *mafiya* was applied in a more familiar environment, as ethnic Russian citizens fed up by high prices, rising crime, and filthy streets of the market areas hung the pejorative label on these individuals.

In the final two decades of the 20th century, emerging crime syndicates and gangs operating out of the former Soviet Union were branded mafiya by a newly minted "free press." The use of such nomenclature, however, obscured the fact that not all gangs were equal in structure, power, and influence, leading to the misconceptions that there is one monolithic Russian mafiya. A number of syndicates took advantage of this confusion and postured as syndicate bad guys, despite evidence to the contrary.

Besides the criminal underworld, *mafiya* could be applied to the Communist Party as well as the State. Industrial and agricultural managers were considered part of the country's most powerful mafia networks, as were directors of large state ministries and factories—any enterprise that controlled the exploitation of the nation's tremendous natural resources as well as the production and distribution of goods. Few doubted that bribery and corruption were required to move up the economic ladder or to attain wealth.

In recent years, it has become *de rigueur* to blame the rapid growth of organized crime on Russia's eagerness to develop a free market economy before creating a civil society in which such a market could safely operate (Lintner 2003; Handelman 1994).

Despite his good intentions, Gorbachev played into the hands of Russian organized crime (ROC) with such poorly thought-out strategies as an anti-alcohol campaign that opened up opportunities for Russian gangsters along the lines of those offered by American Prohibition in the 1920s and 1930s. In the words of one authority, "Attempts to encourage economic reform through cooperatives had in practice provided new opportunities for racketeering, money laundering and loan sharking" (Lintner 2003, 206).

Following the collapse of the Soviet Union, hundreds (if not thousands) of new criminal groups emerged in Russia to take advantage of the latest opportunities presented by the democratization process. The new gangster class included poorly paid former KGB agents and military defectors, government specialists, and former prison inmates, who merged to form criminal organizations that have been collectively described as the Russian Mafiya or the Vodka Dons. In 1991, Yeltsin banned the Communist Party, and out of the rubble of the former Soviet Union emerged 15 new republics.[6] This development facilitated the expansion of Russian organized crime syndicates, who took advantage of the confused state of affairs and the shortage of goods as they created a black market that would eventually spread westward into Eastern Europe, Western Europe, and the United States.

Like Cuba under Fidel Castro, Boris Yeltsin began cleaning out his prisons under the guise of humanitarian reform, but instead of allowing Jews to emigrate, a number of the country's leading criminals were allowed to bring their criminal acumen overseas. A number of Russian émigrés landed in Israel and the United States. Russian gangsters flourished from Boston, New York City, and Miami to Los Angeles, Sacramento, and San Francisco.

In 1993, the findings of "the first comprehensive sociological study of crime and its effects on Russian society" were published. In response to its dire predictions, then–Vice President Alexander Rutskoi proclaimed, "The present sweep of crime already poses a threat to the existence of the state, its institutions, and more so, to the people itself (Rawlinson 1998, 95).

The collapse of the Soviet system opened the floodgates for the international expansion of ROC. As early as 1994, the FBI had identified gangs operating in New York City, Chicago, and a handful of other major American cities. The Russian Ministry of Interior estimated that as many as 110 Russian crime groups were operating in 44 countries in the 1990s. By 2000, journalist Robert I. Friedman claimed 30 Russian crime syndicates were operating in at least 17 American cities. Perhaps New York state tax agent Roger Berger said it best when he noted that ROC members "didn't come here to enjoy the American dream, they came here to steal it" (Friedman 2000, xix).

Although several powerful criminal organizations have emerged, there is no evidence of a single gang or group of gangs who control the post-Soviet underworld. In the decade leading up to 2005, literally thousands of small criminal gangs composed of professional criminals, petty crooks, politicians, businessmen, and bureaucrats emerged to prey on the Russian economy.

Among the few organizations with a recognizable hierarchy is Moscow largest group, the *Solntsevo*. Named after the suburb where it was created, in the mid-1990s it had almost 9,000 members, although others put the number at no more than half this figure (Dunn 1997). Operationally, it is "an umbrella organization of different crews active in different countries" (Varese 2001). According to Varese, the *Solntsevo* has a supreme council, composed of 12 individuals who are considered significant leaders of various factions. It meets on a regular basis and is open to only "made *vory*" (2001, 170–171). Nonetheless, although there is a wide variation in size estimates for this group, it runs against the typical Russian organized crime group profile that most current authorities describe as rather small in numbers (Serio 2008, 216–218).

> ### *Kryshas:* The Protection Business, Russian Style
>
> Any discussion or organized crime in Russia must acknowledge the persistence of the *krysha*, or "roof," which operationally speaking is an organization or individual that can provide the protection and patronage that is necessary to carry on business or government activities (think New York City's Boss Tweed). The *krysha* system dates back to organized crime practices in the former Soviet Union, when the "state itself started to sell private protection" (Varese 2001). As Federico Varese described it, by the late 1980s the Interior Ministry issued an order that allowed local Soviet policemen to enter into contracts with various industrial enterprises, collective farms, and ministries to provide security services for commercial establishments (Varese 2001, 59). Lamenting the pervasiveness of the *krysha* in Russia, one Moscow crime boss reportedly complained, "It's gotten impossible to work; one place the cops are providing roofs; somewhere else it's the KGB, and yet another place it's Korzhakov's boys[7] or the Alfa group. Who can make sense of it anymore?" (CSIS 1997, 30). As the Communist Party collapsed in 1991, *kryshas* filled an organizational void, leading in effect to one variant of corrupt patronage replacing another. However, membership in a *krysha* came with a price—a percentage of profits or some future and yet unidentified service or favor that was owed by the member corporation or individual to the *krysha*. In return for payment, individuals and corporations receive service in return—guaranteed personal security, protection from attacks and shakedowns from another *krysha*, handling of payoffs and deals, intimidation of real or potential enemies and competitors, and advancement of the interests of the recipient for the established price.
>
> A *krysha* is mistakenly is thought of as only criminal, a mafiya group that uses force or the threat of force, but it is just as likely to be governmental. A slang word for "protection," *krysha* today refers "to protection against ordinary criminals and 'unprofessional' racketeers, unruly business partners, and competitors" (Varese 2001, 59). In 1996, U.S. hearings on Russian organized crime noted that in order to operate a business successfully in Moscow, "you must pay the right government officials under the table." If one wants to operate a successful business, one must buy *krysha*, or protection. According to this report, "The more important you are, the higher the 'roof' must be. In Moscow, organized crime provides the roof" (quoted in Finckenauer and Waring 1998, 134; Varese 2001, 59). By the late 1990s, *kryshas* flourished throughout the former Soviet Union.

What Is Russian Organized Crime?

Investigative journalist Stephen Handelman is credited with popularizing the alternate spelling of mafia—as in *mafiya*—his attempt to distinguish this post-Soviet incarnation of organized crime from the traditionally accepted Western experience. The term Russian *mafiya* is brandished by officials and experts; however, the term obscures the fact that ROC is composed of diverse ethnicities and cultures, including Ukrainians, Lithuanians, Georgians, Armenians, Chechens, and Dagestanis. In the early 1990s, a high-ranking official with Russia's Organized Crime Control Department asserted, "there is no classical 'mafia' in Russia. The 'mafia' is a very centralized organization with a rigid hierarchy. Here in Russia, thank God, we do not have a single center that would coordinate all these groups. We will not allow this to happen."[8] According to some Russian mob experts, "the world had adopted the word 'Russian Mafia' for convenience's sake."[9]

Others use the term *mafiya* as an all-inclusive term for mobsters from the Soviet Union. However, its use dates back to the 1970s, when the expression was used to refer to corrupt Communist Party officials, but since the collapse of the Soviet Union has broadened its meaning to including prominent businessmen and oligarchs who have acquired huge fortunes inside Russia (Handelman 1995).

More recently, Federico Varese countered supporters of the so-called Russian mafiya model with the conclusion, "The Russian Mafia is not a single crime group," explaining, "a mafia group stretched across a vast country would find it difficult to operate" (2001, 187). Vadim Volkov, however, rejects the term *mafiya*, preferring to refer to these new groups as "violent entrepreneurs," suggesting that using the label *mafiya* is "a convenient mechanism for putting a disproportionate amount of responsibility for the rise in criminal groups on the legacy of communism instead of

Red Mafiya

In 1995, Russian criminologist Alexander Gurov coined the term *Red Mafiya*, in reference to Russian organized crime in Germany and an ongoing car theft racket that witnessed the theft of between 18,000 and 20,000 expensive cars each year in the early 1990s (Siegel 2003, 59).

blaming the ill-conceived reform policies of Gorbachev and Yeltsin" (2002, 18). In any case, there is a growing consensus that the term *mafiya* now refers more to a method than a group, and its true meaning can be found in the countless cases of torture, extortion, and murder by a wide range of actors in Russia, including politicians, businessmen, and gangsters (Serio 2006).

As recently as 2001, experts were still unable to come up with a universally accepted definition of ROC (Finckenauer and Voronin 2001). In 1998, a Russian Organized Crime Task Force (ROCTF) found that Russia's definition of *organized crime* was substantially different from that of the American FBI. According to the FBI, *organized crime* is

> any group having some manner of a formalized structure and whose primary objective is to obtain money through illegal activities. Such groups maintain their position through the use of actual or threatened violence, corrupt public officials, graft, or extortion, and generally have a significant impact on the people in their locales, region, or the country as a whole. (FBI, Organized Crime Glossary 2009)

The Russian Ministry of the Interior (MVD), however, defined *organized crime* as "an organized community of criminals ranging in size from 50 to 1,000 persons, which is engaged in systematic criminal business and protects itself from the law with the help of corruption" (ROCTF 1997, 23–24).[10] The ROCTF adopted a definition combining parts of the Russian MVD and American FBI definitions. Most definitions of ROC share a number of characteristics with its counterparts in other parts of the world, including the following (Finckenauer and Voronin 2001, 6):

- Use and threat of violence
- Hierarchical structure
- Limited or exclusive membership
- Specialization in types of crime and a division of labor
- Military-style discipline, with strict rules and regulations

By the late 1990s, ROC was substantial but hardly quantifiable. The Russian MVD estimated that the number of organized gangs had increased from 785 in 1990 to more than 8,000 in 1996. Gang membership was estimated at more than 120,000, with more than 3 million people associated in various capacities (Dunn 1997). At the approach of the new millennium, some analysts suggested that ROC controlled up to 40% of the Russian gross national product (GNP), making it indistinct from the country's economy. The most recent scholarship on ROC examines the "numbers game" that has stimulated the discussion of the phenomenon since the early 1990s, when the MVD reported "criminal gangs controlled 40,000 businesses including 1,500 in the state sector, over 500 joint ventures, and more than 1,800 banks." ROC authority Joe Serio (2008) rightly points out that the widespread acceptance of these figures seemed to indicate that "the profound distrust of statistics from the Soviet Union seemed to vanish" as these figures took on a life of their own in the post-Soviet era and are still used by many sources today with unquestioning acceptance. Between 1990 and 1995, the MVD and other official spokesmen reported the number of organized crime groups rising from 2,000 to 5,000, and again to 8,000 by 1996. What was never made clear was what groups fell under the rubric of organized crime groups, whether these numbers included gangs, mafiya clans, criminal societies or associations, bandit groups, or whatever. By the end of the 1990s,

Among the many unique signs of a Russian gangland killing is the chopping off of a victim's fingers and placing them in a glass of beer to hinder identification (Handelman, 1195, 262).

estimates placed the number of groups as high as 10,000; since then, these numbers have continued to fluctuate wildly.

There are various views on whether the term *Russian Mafiya* is an appropriate appellation. Rawlinson, for example, suggests that ROC "operates as a syndicate, that is, a hierarchical organization based entirely on business relations as opposed to the 'family' of nepotistic structures of the Sicilian mafia" (1998 113). In other parts of the former Soviet Union, particularly in the Central Asian republics, there are organized crime groups that follow the traditional structures associated with the mafia phenomenon. More common were the binds of ethnicity or geographic origin.

What has become increasingly clear is that the very nature of ROC makes any estimates unreliable. More realistically, it is the very structure of (Russian) crime groups and their interaction with each other that makes it difficult to distinguish one from the other and further complicates the numbers game. Serio offers the example of the Izmailovo group in Moscow. It had been previously linked to the Solntsevo group, which consisted of the Golianov and Perov groups and engaged in the sharing of membership. One could easily discern figures ranging from one to four groups. By any reasonable standards, this situation defies quantification and it would seem reasonable to conclude that the "Russian mafiya" "was really a hodgepodge of criminal groups that were highly flexible and mobile," with small core memberships and frequent cooperation with each other when it seemed profitable (Serio 2008).

Several years ago a leading expert asked, "What has become of the Russian mafiya?" (Serio 2006). Indeed, over the past several years the Russian mafiya seems to have vanished from the headlines. There are several explanations. One is that it has ceased to exist (or never actually existed). In reality, ROC never demonstrated a "central apparatus" or a commission of bosses. Rather, it had always been a number of small, loose knit groups that were adaptable, flexible, if not amorphous. Others have pointed to the fallout from the "Great Mob War" of 1992–1996, when many mobsters either disappeared or were killed. These individuals more probably fanned out across the globe as the media focused its attention on terrorism and Iraq. Out of this turmoil, "new rules of the game emerged" as gangsters made the transition to legitimizing their ill-gotten profits as they became "part of the social, political, and economic fabric of society." As a result, the gangster made the transformation to businessman—pillar of the community—to philanthropist supporting social causes (Serio 2006). As one recent observer put it, "A very large part of the Russian economy has criminal origins and a number of former godfathers are now locomotives of the Russian economy" (Lapenkova 2007).

Prison Camp Origins of the *Vory-v-Zakone*

During the Soviet era an estimated 18 million individuals served time in the massive prison system. Sometime in the late 1920s a criminal fraternity known as the *vory-v-zakone,* or "thieves with a code of honor," developed in the Soviet prison system. By most accounts, the *vory-v-zakone* were well established by the early 1930s (Varese 2001, 146). What made them distinct from other groups of prisoners was their involvement in a secret criminal fraternity, with its own rules, rituals, and code of behavior. These thieves, or *vory,* refused to work in the labor camps. This fraternity flourished for almost 30 years before camp authorities embarked in a war against them between 1948 and 1953.

In Soviet Russia's vast gulag system, a hierarchy existed among the criminal elements in which professional "big-time" criminals were considered dominant. Referred to as *urki,* or *blatnoi* if they were of the elite criminal class, they were regarded as *vory-v-zakone,* or "thieves-in-law," who lived according to a distinct set of rules and customs "which preceded the Gulag, and which outlasted it" (Applebaum 2003, 282). They clearly considered themselves a class apart and had little to do with petty criminal types. There was little love lost between these milieus, as the ordinary criminals hated them as well.

The Thieves' Code

A thief is bound by the code to

- Forsake his relatives—mother, father, brothers, sisters, etc.
- Not have a family of his own—no wife, no children; this does not however, preclude him from having a lover.
- Never, under any circumstances work, no matter how much difficulty this brings—live only on means gleaned from thievery.
- Help other thieves—both by moral and material support, utilizing the commune of thieves.
- Keep secret information about the whereabouts of accomplices (e.g., dens, districts, hideouts, safe houses).
- In unavoidable situations (if a thief is under investigation) take the blame for someone else's crime; this buys the other person time of freedom.
- Demand convocation of enquiry for the purpose of resolving disputes in the event of a conflict between oneself and other thieves, or between thieves.
- If necessary, participate in such enquiries.
- Carry out the punishment of the offending thief as decided by the convocation.
- Not resist carrying out the decision of punishing the offending thief who is found guilty, with punishment determined by the convocation.
- Have good command of the thieves' jargon.
- Not gamble without being able to cover losses.
- Teach the trade to young beginners.
- Have, if possible, informants from the rank and file of thieves.
- Not lose your reasoning ability when using alcohol.
- Have nothing to do with the authorities, not participate in public activities, nor join any community organizations.
- Not take weapons from the hands of authorities; not serve in the military.
- Make good on promises given to other thieves.

Translated from *Dictionary: Prison, Camp, Blatnoi, Jargon* (Speech and Graphic Portraits of Soviet Prison, compiled by Dantsik Sergeyevich Baldaev, Vladimir Kuz'mich Belko, and Igor Mikhailovich Isupov.)

By the late 1920s, Soviet prison camps had expanded to such an extent that the legions of professional criminals had created their own society, adhering to a strict behavioral code that prohibited them from having anything to do with the Soviet state. If one was to be taken seriously as a thief-in-law, one was expected to refuse to work, refuse to own a passport, and refuse to collaborate with officials in any way unless it involved exploitation. More recently, historian Anne Applebaum, in her magisterial *Gulag: A History,* asserts that the prototypical "indoctrination and re-education programs of the early 1930s were in fact directed at thieves-in-law rather than political prisoners" (2003, 282). However, by the end of the 1930s, Soviet authorities gave up on this goal, recognizing the impossibility of reforming professional criminals. Instead, officials came up with the idea of using thieves-in-law to control and intimidate other prisoners, such as counter-revolutionaries, in much the way prison tenders were used in the American prison system. Applebaum suggests that this arrangement existed from 1937 until the conclusion of World War II.

By the 1950s, the "thieves' world" lured younger prisoners attracted by its place in the prison hierarchy and the accommodations it offered. Prison and police officials claim that by this era, new members of the criminal society were swearing an oath to live by the code of the thieves' rules and at every step defy camp discipline. Once accepted, the thief was given a nickname, if he did not already have one, and the prison grapevine let it be known that the new convert would be accorded respect throughout the system.

Russian Prison Tattoos

- Barbed wire across one's forehead: a prison lifer
- Cat's head: a good luck emblem
- Double lightning bolts: Signify Nazi runes, indicating one is not an informer
- Skull on finger: denotes a murderer
- Stars on each shoulder: the number of points correspond to years served in jail
- Illustrations of playing cards or card suits: Professional gambler
- Tree branch tattoo: An independent criminal who works outside a gang

A number of observers throughout the Soviet era commented on a particular type of labor camp inmate who was identifiable by a particular sartorial style and accompanying behaviors. One inmate remembered those who wore "home-made aluminum crosses round their necks and waist-coats" (Applebaum 2003). They were typically bearded and wore their shirts outside their trousers, with one or more waistcoats above. These particular inmates were recognizable by tattoos covering their bodies and spoke a common jargon. Members of the thieves' world were recognizable for their slang, clothing, and bizarre fashion sense. These fashions changed over time, but always had the power to intimidate other inmates. According to one source, "In the twenties, the thieves wore trade-school caps; still earlier, the military officer's cap was in fashion. In the forties, during the winter, they wore peakless leather caps, folded down the tops of their felt boots, and wore a cross around the neck" (quoted in Applebaum 2003, 287).

However, what most distinguished the thieves from other prisoners was their distinctive use of tattoos that identified where each prisoner stood in the thieves' world. One expert suggests the use of tattoos increased after the Communist Party took over the country. It was one of the rare ways prisoners could "express their political beliefs, demonstrate their positions in the complex prison hierarchy, and most importantly, proclaim their personalities, talents, and plans" (Serio 2008, 162). Tattoos proclaimed one's homosexuality, drug addiction, or criminal past. Although the majority of tattoos were chosen by the inmates, sex offenders and other marginalized offenders were forcibly tattooed with the image of a knife running across their shoulder blades and through their necks. In some cases, prison inmates were tattooed head to toe while a *vory* might have negligible tattooing, outside of the identical eight-point stars tattooed on each side of the torso just below the collarbone, or one the knees—the mark of the *vory-v-zakone*.

Russian organized crime expert Joe Serio asserts that the collapse of the Soviet Union also led to the end of several *vory* trademarks, not the least being a new disdain for all aspects of the prison experience. Where in the past it was considered a badge of honor or rite of passage, the modern *vory* considers it a duty to avoid prison at all costs. Other traditions, such as tattooing, are crumbling as well. Indeed, in times past they were expected to abstain from owning an apartment or house and other material objects; the new *vory,* however, can often be seen cruising major cities in luxury vehicles and even having suits tailor made and shipped from Paris (Serio 2008).

Odessa

The mostly Jewish port city of Odessa was once considered Russia's smuggler's capital and "played in the development in the thieves' culture" (Applebaum 2003, 286). As late as the 1970s, the city's first secretary of the party committee was sentenced to death for black marketeering (Friedman 2000). One leading authority insists it still has a reputation as a *mafiya* paradise (Serio 2007).

Brighton Beach: Odessa by the Sea

The working-class community of Brighton Beach in Brooklyn emerged as the country's largest Russian neighborhood in the 1980s, boasting as many as 100,000 Eastern European immigrants. The community became known as "Little Odessa" or "Odessa by the Sea," due to its affinity for Russian culture, language, and a distrust of government authorities. As in most immigrant communities, an overwhelming percentage of them were law-abiding citizens, but they were well aware of the criminal element that lived among them. Despite killings among the gangsters, most residents adhered to the adage, "The bad kill the bad; the good stay together." Like similar ethnic enclaves, Brighton Beach was a tightly knit community bound together by shared language and culture and distrustful of government representatives. There were already 40,000 Russian Jews residing here in the 1970s; by the 1980s, it had become the center of Russian mob activity in America. Among the monikers used to describe these early Brighton Beach gangsters was the "Potato Bag Gang," referring to a ruse used on new immigrants. Fresh off the boat immigrants were given the "opportunity" to trade their rubles for cash. Once the transaction was completed, the newcomer was typically left holding a bag filled with potatoes (Kelly 2000).

In contrast to 1989, when Russian authorities estimated there were 512 *vory-v-zakone* (about half in prison), by 2005, these numbers had declined by more than half, to about 200. According to Serio and others, the drop can be explained in part by killings during the 1992–1994 Great Mob War as well as natural causes; but what was probably more reasonable was that many had fled overseas either to escape law enforcement or to establish new operations.

FUEL EXCISE SCHEME/GASOLINE BOOTLEGGING   ROC groups have been involved in numerous sophisticated criminal enterprises. Turkish and Greek immigrants pioneered gasoline-bootlegging rackets in the 1960s. At that time, the operation consisted of collecting taxes at the pumps and pocketing the profits rather than turning them over to the government. By the time IRS agents caught on, the perpetrators were gone. However, by most accounts, "Fuel tax-evasion cases are the largest and best-known cases of crime involving Soviet émigrés" in the United States (Finckenauer and Waring 1998, 149). Some of these fuel-fraud schemes earned billions of dollars in the process and had a tremendous impact on both consumers and the business community, not only in the United States, but abroad as well. There are three basic types of fuel tax evasion. The more simple ones involve fuel substitution and the sale of adulterated fuel. There are a number of different fuel oils, the difference being that only fuel used for motor vehicles is hit with the special taxes that are supposed to be used for highway construction and repairs. Taxes are placed on the fuel at all three levels of government, creating significant returns. However, the collection of the taxes is complicated on a number of levels. Those directed at the consumer might include placing additives in diesel fuel to increase the amount of fuel or rigging fuel pumps. For example, diesel oil used in cars is taxed; however, it is virtually the same substance used for heating homes, which is not taxed as high. This creates opportunities for substituting one for the other to avoid taxes. When drivers pump gas into their cars, there is no way to know what exactly is going in the tank. A number of investigations revealed that it is not uncommon for polluted petroleum to be sold at the pump. These "diesel cocktails" are often a combination of truck diesel oil and used crankcase oil, or other mixtures that violate government standards. At different times members of the Gambino, Lucchese, and Genovese crime families collected waste oil from service stations and tank cleaning companies, mixed it with clean oil, and sold it as fuel (Kelly 1999, 180).

The most lucrative schemes involve defrauding federal and state governments of taxes excised over motor fuel. In some cases this might include falsifying tax forms, but the most popular is the "daisy chain" scam. By most accounts, Russian organized crime appeared on America's law enforcement radar during an investigation of a fuel excise scheme. Selwyn Raab suggested it was the Russians who first discovered the flaw in the tax process. They noticed that only the last company that sold gas to the retailer collected the taxes (included in total cost at each pump transaction).

Russian Mobsters and the Colombo Family: Unwanted Partners

Sometime at the beginning of the 1980s, Colombo crime family *capo* and future informant Michael Franzese was asked by several Russian mobsters to help collect a large debt stemming from one of their gas tax frauds. Franzese was amazed when he saw how much money this racket produced and began to move in on the Russians, a move they could not refuse; in return, he would guarantee the collection of all debts. Making use of his connections with state officials, Franzese was able to facilitate the daisy chain scam by obtaining the licenses needed by the counterfeit gas dealers. Soon he was collecting three quarters of the profit. In his later testimony, Franzese reported receiving $9 million a week in cash in paper bags from his Russian confederates, and at its zenith he was collecting $15 million a month (Raab 2005).

In the mid-1980s this was almost 30 cents a gallon in New York. Fuel must pass through a number of steps as it makes its way from refinery to the station pump, and each step in the process is an invitation for fraud. Russian gangsters soon created daisy chain companies in which they transferred gas back and forth between each other in a number of paper transactions. Although it looked on paper like a number of legitimate companies were involved, the gas never changed hands. When taxes came due, the transfer records listed a company as making the final sale to retail stations and collecting the requisite taxes. When the authorities came looking for overdue taxes, they found that the company headquarters was a dummy or "burn" company, little more than an address and a mailbox, empty store front, or a vacant lot (Raab 2005).

Until the Russians got involved, the scam had pretty much worked unimpeded. However, the Russian penchant for casino gambling and expensive cars soon brought them to the attention of the IRS, who put two and two together and figured out they were losing millions of tax dollars. A leading chronicler of the New York mob claimed, "Russian immigrants invented the gasoline bootlegging racket" (Raab 2005). The convergence of increasing Russian immigration and New York State's decision to shift the burden of collecting and forwarding gas taxes from the gas station owner to the wholesaler who delivered the fuel unwittingly led to the daisy chain scam. In the years leading up to 1982, New York State's myriad gas stations were responsible for collecting state and federal taxes—as high as 28 cents per gallon—and then turning it over to the proper officials.

Semion Mogilevich: The Most Dangerous Gangster in the World?

Born in Kiev, Ukraine, in 1946, Semion Mogilevich came to the attention of Russian police in the 1970s. The "Brainy Don" has an economics degree and is thought to be worth more than $100 million. Most of his early criminal escapades were strictly small-time, but this did not prevent him from serving a 3-year prison stint for selling currencies on the black market. Mogilevich made his first big score in the 1980s by purchasing the possessions of Russian Jews emigrating to Israel, promising to send them their profits after selling the goods. They never saw their money. By the 1990s, he was considered one of the world's most feared crime bosses, and was accused of involvement in weapons and drug trafficking as well as numerous murders. Wanted by the FBI, Interpol, and UK police, he was finally arrested by Russian police on January 23, 2008, outside a Moscow shopping center. At the time of his arrest, he was going by "Sergei Schnaider," one of at least six pseudonyms he used. His arrest was in connection with an investigation into an alleged $2 million tax evasion scheme run in connection with Arbat Prestige, a successful chain of cosmetic stores. The owner of the stores was arrested along with the 61-year-old Mogilevich. Others suggest that the real motive behind the arrest was his involvement in the clandestine multi-billion-dollar natural gas trade between Russia and Ukraine, in which he appeared to play an important part. Authorities have also linked him to the trafficking in nuclear materials, drugs, prostitutes, precious gems, and stolen art, as well as running hit squads in the United States and Europe (Horton 2008; Faulconbridge 2008).

Due to widespread fraud, legislation was passed in 1982 that placed the responsibility for tax collection on the state's some 400 gasoline distributors. These distributors were supposed to assess the fuel before it was moved to the stations. Unknowingly, authorities had set up an even larger score by allowing Russian gangsters to set up fake distributorships. At the scam's apogee, Russian mobsters were selling $150 million in fuel each month and pocketing more than $30 million in unpaid taxes (Robinson 2000).

Far Eastern Russia/Eurasian Organized Crime

One international gang specialist suggests, "Russia is as much a European as an Asian country that spans several time zones" (Covey 2003, 135). Some authorities use the term *Eurasia* to describe a region composed of five Central Asian countries, including Kazakhstan, Kyrgyzstan, Turkmenistan, Tajikistan, and Uzbekistan, as well the former Soviet republics of the South Caucuses (Armenia, Azerbaijan, and Georgia). The FBI currently uses the term *Eurasian* to refer to organized crime groups in the former Soviet Union or Central Europe. Eastern Russia is contiguous with several

Vyacheslav Ivankov

No one exemplified the gangster tradition of this region more than Vyacheslav Ivankov, who some sources arguably once considered the most prominent crime boss in Russia's Far East. Born in Vladivostok in 1938, he was given the moniker of "Yaponchik," or "Little Japanese," by police for his faintly Asian appearance. At least one source suggests that he was named after a legendary Russian-Jewish criminal from Odessa also named "Yaponchik" (Nicaso and Lamothe 2005, 162).[11] Ivankov enjoyed a long criminal career in the former Soviet Union before arriving in the United States in 1993. He came to prominence as the leader of the *Solontsevskaya* gang in Moscow in 1980, heading a crew that specialized in masquerading as police officers and robbing the homes of wealthy Muscovites.[12] Arrested and convicted for these activities, Yaponchik was sentenced to 14 years in a Siberian prison, but was able to bribe his way out in 1991 and subsequently landed in the welcoming confines of New York City.

Ivankov was among the crime lords clamoring for a more energetic participation in the Eurasian drug trade, even advocating conflict with the Chechen and other Caucasian groups who controlled much of the narcotics trade in the early 1990s. He was not without important political connections that continued from the Soviet era into the 1990s, counting at least one high official of the Russian Supreme Court and a former Soviet deputy internal affairs minister as his patrons. Although American authorities were reportedly warned of his prospective immigration plans, he was able to arrive unimpeded, claiming to be involved in the motion picture industry.

Following his release from prison he hoped to use his reputation to shore up a base of criminal support in Brighton Beach and create a formidable syndicate. Although some accounts suggest he was sent to the United States "with instructions from his peers to explore business opportunities" (Handelman 1995, 29), most authorities doubt it. More recently, experts suggested it was more likely Ivankov was trying to keep one step ahead of Chechen mobsters, Turks, and investigators who had different plans for the erstwhile *vory* (Nicaso and Lamothe 2005). Although Ivankov's gang was considered the most powerful Russian syndicate in New York City, the conditions in the United States were not as conducive to crime as the ones he left behind in Russia. His success in the United States was short-lived, and in 1995 he was among a group of gangsters convicted with wiretap information chronicling an attempted extortion of a Manhattan investment firm owned by several Russian-born businessmen. As for the legacy of Ivankov—although most agree he was a formidable criminal, the reality is that he was never a monolithic crime boss in the model of the traditional mafia don; his gang was more like a dozen or so loosely affiliated gangsters who engaged in organized crime activities. Yaponchik has not fared well in prison, and by some accounts became addicted to heroin (Lintner 2003). According to an interview Ivankov gave in prison, the hyperbolic gangster suggested that the FBI created the myth of the Russian mafiya and the Ivankov personality cult, noting that the FBI is "only tilting at windmills." When it comes to organized crime in Russia, he compared the country to "one uninterrupted criminal swamp" (DeVito 2005, 170).

Asian countries and its crime syndicates are often coterminous with their crime syndicates. More recently, investigative journalist and Asian mob expert Bertil Lintner noted, "The presence of the Yakuza, the Triads and the North Koreans shows that the Russian Far East has, at long last, become incorporated in a larger East Asian fraternity," and that although the former Russian "godfathers" took a more racist view and shied away from working with Chinese and Japanese gangsters, "a younger generation of more business-oriented gang leaders sees all sorts of advantages in cooperating" with the more established Triads and Yakuza in Eastern Russia (Lintner 2003, 215).

Recent estimates indicate that there are anywhere between 150,000 and 2 million ethnic Chinese living in Russia, mostly in the Far Eastern cities of Vladivostok, Khabarovsk, and Blagoveschensk. In some Far Eastern towns there are more Chinese residents than Europeans. Regardless, due to a constant threat of deportation and a lack of opportunities because of racism, many of these immigrants often have little choice but to work for Triad-affiliated ethnic Chinese gangsters.

Eastern Siberia is another region of recent Asian–Russian organized crime convergence. Located in the center of post-Soviet Russia, this region has proven a valuable transit route for smuggling syndicates. In eastern Siberia, a number of transport routes converge, including those from the Far East, North and South Eastern Asia, as well as from the central parts of Russia and Middle Asia (Repetskaya 1999, 123). Rich in natural resources, this region has long attracted Russian syndicates. Among the criminal opportunities presented by such resources has been the theft and trafficking of strategic fuel and energy resources, illicit trafficking in gold, poaching, and transporting cattle from frontier regions. In 1996, for example, a train bearing 5,000 tons of petroleum disappeared without a trace after leaving Vladivostok.

Abundant in correctional facilities and penal camps, it has been estimated that perhaps one third of discharged prisoners relocate here, contributing to what one observer has called the "criminalization of the territory" (Repetskaya 1999, 123). As elsewhere, organized crime varies throughout Siberia, with the Irkusk Region the center for organized crime activity. In 1996, Eastern Siberian authorities reported the existence of 99 organized crime groups with almost 400 members. What has become most alarming has been their affiliation with Chinese and Mongolian crime groups. Ethnic crime groups have proliferated as well from Georgia, Azerbaijan, and elsewhere.

Chechen and Cossack Syndicates

Since the 1980s, Russian syndicates have had to contend with increasingly more powerful Chechen and Cossack gangs. The Russian *vory* tradition "never influenced ethnically based criminality," according to one Chechen gangster, who claimed, "We have nothing of this sort. We do not accept laws of the *vory*, we recognize only our national traditions" (Varese 2001, 178). Chechen gangs first began appearing in Moscow in 1987, shortly before the breakup of the Soviet Union. In the 1990s, three Chechen groups, the *Tsentral'naya*, *Ostankinskaya*, and *Avtomobil'naya*, splintered out of a larger organization. These gangs controlled various territories in Moscow, specially the northeast quadrant of the city, relying mostly on extorting protection money from small business owners and vendors (Dunn 1997). In the 1990s the Russian army, short on troops in the Caucasus and border enclaves, began recruiting from local Cossack groups, going as far as passing legislation in 1997 that allowed them special rights to carry weapons and to "operate as suppliers of private protection" (Varese 2001, 179). They used these powers to maintain law and order in the Rostov region and have even incorporated the public whipping of malefactors. Among the cities vying for Cossack services was Moscow, which used them to patrol railroad stations and markets. The Cossacks have taken their powers a step further and became involved in operating protection rackets and other criminal endeavors. There have been instances of local criminals joining the Chechen syndicates. As far back as 2001, organized crime expert Federico Varese warned of the looming potential of Cossack groups forming "an umbrella uniting different brands of criminals, supplying these individuals with common and recognizable 'trademarks,' such as a patriotic mission, ideology, uniforms, and rituals alternative to those of the *vory*" (2001, 180). As of 2007, this scenario has yet to be fulfilled.

Another nexus between Russian and Asian organized crime has involved the weapons trade. Host to a number of military units, the 1990s found organized criminal bands, including some composed of former soldiers, looting arsenals and selling explosives, ammunition, and automatic weapons to the Mongolians and Chinese. The drug trade also abounds here, as traffickers transport raw poppy and poppy straw from Middle Asia and marijuana from Burytania (Repetskaya 1999).

ORGANIZED CRIME IN THE BALTIC REGION: ESTONIA, LATVIA, AND LITHUANIA   Organized crime in the Baltic region, in the words of one authority, "was shaped by its Soviet past, the rapid social and economic restructuring in the early 1990s, its geographical location making it a transit region for both legal and illegal goods and the process of reintegration with the western community" (Karrstrand 2007, 6). In the late 1990s, a pattern emerged that saw organized crime syndicates moving into a number of semi-legitimate ventures in business and finance while maintaining a strong interest in lucrative trafficking schemes (Curtis 2003, 53). During the late Soviet era, the "Baltic corridor" was an important route for smugglers. However, in the decade after the breakup of the Soviet Union, the Baltic countries joined the ranks of the few former Soviet republics that have made the most progress toward eliminating conditions that promote organized crime.

Situated between Russia and Western Europe, the three Baltic states of Estonia, Latvia, and Lithuania experienced a strong resurgence of organized crime in the wake of the end of the USSR, but were somehow less affected by this type of crime than other former Soviet countries. There is a variety of explanations for this. Some observers point to the existence of alternative elites at the time of transition, and the country's previous experience of democracy and state-hood. Others point to the existence of an independent media, which is "an important factor in providing accountability and restraining organized crime" (Karrstrand 2007, 9); still others suggest it was the absence of violent conflicts such as those that raged in the Balkans, the Caucasus, and Central Asia (Karrstrand 2007, 9). However, one should not rule out that the concomitant forces of globalization and reintegration into the Western community created new opportunities for Baltic organized crime as well; particularly narcotics traffickers who used the region as a transit country smuggling in directions, both east and west, taking advantage of neighboring Nordic countries' drug consumers as well as for local consumption. By most accounts, the organized crime that now exists in the Baltic countries, although less than elsewhere, it is more professional than it was in the Soviet era. Contemporary groups are more likely to be associated with other domestic and international groups and are markedly more sophisticated, organized, and capitalized. The process of globalization has led to an increase in transnational crime in the following areas:

- Production and distribution of counterfeit money
- Thefts
- Smuggling and illegal production of cigarettes and narcotics
- Legal and illegal migration and trafficking in human beings
- Narcobusiness
- Prostitution
- Economic and financial crimes (Karrstrand 2007, 27)

Recent investigations by Lithuanian operational intelligence suggests that Lithuania alone is home to least 13 organized criminal associations, about 30 organized criminal groups, and several dozen small organized criminal gangs, totaling more than 1,500 members and an equal number of outside affiliates. One of the best examples of organized crime syndicates "Baltic style" is Lithuania's *Smaugliai* group, an "independent, well-organized criminal groups composed of five persons. It was characterized by strict hierarchy and distribution of roles and territories" (Karrstrand 2007, 37). The groups used violence as a preventive measure and for discipline in its drug transactions. Besides narcotics trafficking, it was engaged in murder, document fraud, illegal disposal of weapons, and extortion of property. Another group is based in Vilnius and has about 25 members. Officials regarded it "as a criminal alliance, arranged to maintain long-term relationships." Much of its attention was focused on securing weapons for its robbery operations. From 1991 to 1997, it was identified in a variety of organized assaults and murders, as well as the theft of weapons, explosives, and personal documents (Karrstrand 2007, 37–38).

WESTERN EUROPE

With its close proximity to the Balkans and the former Warsaw Pact states, Western Europe offers a range of conditions that have facilitated the continuation of the drug, weapons, and human trade as well as other smuggling operations as many of the trafficking routes from the Soviet period and the subsequent lawless 1990s remain intact. What is perhaps most favorable toward the continuation of this trend is the availability of "a very highly developed and integrated transportation and communications infrastructure and many concentrated urban centers combining large lower-class and immigrant populations with sophisticated commercial operations" (Curtis and Karacan 2002, 3). The ongoing globalization since the late 1990s enabled groups to take advantage of variation among nations in standards and effectiveness of law enforcement (Williams 2001, 58). At the same time, security and police agencies continue to evolve into more effective barriers against international crime-trafficking networks.

Great Britain

Organized bands of criminals have been present in Britain for much of its recorded history, although the degree to which they were organized is the subject of much conjecture. For example, by the mid-18th century, the existence of gangs of robbers had become so threatening that early police reformer Henry Fielding was moved to introduce his *Enquiry into the Causes of the Late Increase of Robbers.* However, the real turning point in the transformation of British organized crime occurred in the years surrounding World War I and World War II. By the time war broke out in 1939, racecourse-based extortion, illegal drinking clubs, and prostitution were long-established alternative institutions (Thomas 2003). Various groups of territorially based criminals had for centuries regarded the center of London as prize, but with the onset of World War II, "established groups of criminals, often with reputations acquired via violent exploits as racetrack enforcers, thieves, and extortionists," found wartime leisure demands a lucrative opportunity (Hobbs 2004, 414). The shortages in a wide range of essential and non-essential products—from building materials to food and clothing—as well as a thriving black market further stimulated the growth of criminal enterprises.

Until World War II, there were few opportunities for powerful and sophisticated organized crime networks in Great Britain. The demands of the wartime economy, however, created a tremendous black market that allowed criminal gangs to expand their present markets and develop new ones. Between 1918 and 1939, the five Sabini bothers controlled anything in the London area resembling an organized crime network with international ties. The half-Italian and half-Scots brothers controlled some racing tracks by protecting bookmakers before expanding into nightclubs and gambling rackets with a well-organized robbery here and there. One chronicler of the era described the Sabini gang as "a full-service syndicate," engaged in burglary and armed robbery, protection rackets, extortion, gambling, prostitution, fixing horse races, and running nightclubs (Newton 2007). During the war, their Italian roots came back to haunt them and they were interned under wartime regulations (regulation 18B) after Italy joined the Germans in the war.

Throughout the war, shortages and rationing provided the impetus for organized crime groups who led a thriving underground economy for extra food, clothes, cigarettes, forged identity papers for army deserters, and gasoline coupons. They also engineered raids on government offices for ration books. By end of the war in 1945, a handful of powerful criminal associations had been established. Originally formed as "territorial imperatives," they expanded their operations as they became more responsive to market demands of the new era.

Prior to the 1960s, British criminal organizations were traditionally not known for their international connections (Morton 1998). In fact, by most accounts there is little evidence of a monolithic or widespread organized crime fraternity except at local levels, where an influential group of criminals who had established themselves during the war remained highly influential throughout the post-war decades (Pearson 1973, 84–99). The Kray twins were among those who emerged during the post-war era and were well established by the 1960s; however, their "legendary empire failed to extend much beyond their own community" (Hobbs 2004, 416). Nevertheless, the media and particularly the popular press was complicit in concocting the imagery of the post-war based gangster as a predominant form of British organized crime, firmly ensconced in a defined working-class neighborhood, and extorting elements of big-city vice. What is more clear is that the British incarnation of organized crime in the post-war era was dominated by transactions between networks of small but flexible firms rather than any type of hierarchically based syndicate (Hobbs 2004).

Modern organized crime in Britain is no longer "a family affair," if it really was to begin with. Like most incarnations of organized crime in the contemporary era, criminal enterprise was typically the result of a group of important criminals who operated without reference to a dominant criminal group or "crime family." Of the continuing family groups, none exemplified the family concept better than the Adams family. Beginning in the 1980s, the Clerkenwell crime syndicate, better known as "The A Team," became the most powerful criminal group in Britain (McKay 2006). Led by the three Adams brothers—Terry, Patrick, and Thomas—it operated a variety of criminal networks including drugs, extortion, securities fraud, and armed robbery. It distinguished itself for hiring Afro-Caribbean enforcers who are blamed for more than 25 murders (see Chapter 12 on Afrolineal organized crime). During the 1980s, the Adams family started trafficking in cocaine and marijuana, adding ecstasy in the 1990s. They established links with Colombian cocaine syndicates

The Kray Brothers and the Firm[13]

Reggie (d. 2000) and Ronnie Kray (d. 1995) were identical twins born on October 24, 1933. They were England's most prominent gang bosses of the 1960s. Their father deserted from the British Army during World War II and remained in hiding for more than a decade. Meanwhile, the brothers drifted into a life of juvenile crime and also became adept amateur boxers. Chips off the old block, when they were drafted in 1951, both repeatedly deserted, eventually earning dishonorable discharges. Ronnie showed early signs of mental illness, and his reputation for erratic and brutal acts of violence led clinical prison psychiatrists to brand him clinically insane. They soon sorted out their troubled lives and purchased a pool hall, and established a lucrative protection racket in their Bethnal Green neighborhood (East London). By the 1960s, they had branched out into armed robbery, hijackings, arson for profit, and investments in nightclubs and other real estate. In time, their gang became known as "the Firm." According to their biographer, "the twins appeared intent on following the pattern of the big organizing criminals in the United States, [especially] the way American crime syndicates brought in their gunmen from another city" (Pearson 1973, 110). Much of their profits came from protection rackets foisted on nightclubs and restaurants in London's West End, but they also began expanding their operations beyond London into Birmingham and Leicester. It was estimated that by the mid-1960s, they were taking in protection money from between one half and one third of all of London's illegal gambling clubs. In its early stages, the Kray brothers ran the Firm like a company, using board meetings to collect profits from club managers under their aegis. However, it was around this time that the Krays came under official scrutiny as they mixed with celebrities and other denizens of the English underworld. In a climate of homophobia, Ronnie Kray's sexuality became an issue when he was linked to a British politician in 1964. In 1966, Ronnie shot to death a member of the opposition Richardson gang after he called Ronnie a "fat poof" in front of several witnesses in the Blind Beggar pub in East London. In 1968, after a series of murders and other assorted crimes, the brothers were arrested, and they were sentenced to 30 years in prison the following year (Newton 2007; Lunde 2004). As to whether the Kray gangs should be considered organized crime, one British crime expert suggests, "they were such only in terms of a loosely-coupled oligarchy, characterized by charismatic leadership and pre-bureaucratic in form, [but] it is still valid to apply the term 'organized' to such structures" (Wright 2006, 173).

and Jamaican Yardie groups, laundering their proceeds with a stable of corrupt financiers, account-ants, lawyers, and others while investing heavily in real estate and other legitimate business. A number of sources suggest that the gang regularly bribes members of the London Metropolitan police. Terry Adams was considered its leader, with former associates describing him "a Machi-avellian ruler who exercises control through both cunning and violent force" (Amoruso 2007). Others have compared him to John Gotti, late of New York City's Gambino crime family. Like Gotti, Adams eventually was sentenced to prison. After his arrest and subsequent trial for money laundering, tax evasion, and dealing in stolen goods, he was sentenced to 7 years in prison in March 2007 (Amoruso 2007).

Participation in the international drug trade has been a major factor in distinguishing today's British gangs from those of the pre-1960s era. With the emergence of global drug markets and inter-national economic crimes, it has become clear that the activities of modern British organized crime groups differ from times past. One authority posited that these groups were likely to "maintain their local character," but in stark contrast to earlier eras, were more apt to pursue opportunities in other parts of the world such as the rest of Europe and the United States (Wright 2006, 174–175).

Despite these marked changes, the "criminal family firms" that characterized the earlier gangs persisted into the 21st century. According to the leading expert on this phenomenon, this structure continues because it offers "some measure of dependability and consistency in a socio-economic realm marked by fragmentation and uncertainty." What one sees today is the "permutation of old es-tablished brands, first generation felons, legitimate businesses in the process of criminal mutation, and a multitude of venture capitalists, their peers and subordinates in confederations at various stages of formation and disintegration" (Hobbs 2001, 556–557; quoted in Wright 2006, 175).

One of the best examples of this transition to more transnational criminal activity has been the activities of Liverpool's Curtis "Cocky" Warren (b. 1963), who in 2000 was listed as Britain's wealthiest criminal. Warren's success lay in his ability to merge his sweeping neighborhood crimi-nal connections with his links to major global players in Colombia, Turkey, Morocco, and else-where in Europe. At the apogee of his drug-trafficking career, Warren was worth an estimated £185 million, and was Britain's main supplier of cocaine, heroin, and ecstasy. After several close brushes with the law, Warren moved his operations to Holland. Despite unremitting surveillance and wiretap-ping by the authorities, police were unable to break his code, which never used names of colleagues, just monikers such as "Macker and Tacker," "the Egg on Legs," "Twit and Twat," "the Werewolf and the Vampire," "Badger," "Boo," and others (Amoruso 2007).

Warren's network was made up of *joeys* or *gophers* that were responsible for handling tasks such as bribing police and other officials wherever necessary. In some schemes, he concocted "a cellular structure of companies, connections and associates" to provide him with multi-layered pro-tection that allowed him to complete major drug transactions. One of the best examples of this struc-ture was a 1995 cannabis operation that brought the drug to Britain from Morocco through Spain. In this operation the structure included "a front company, an overseas fixer, a regular driver and several odd-job men to complete the operation" (Wright 2006; Barnes, Elias, and Walsh 2000).

In 1996, Dutch SWAT units raided Warren's home and those of several accomplices. The raid uncovered 1,500 kilos of heroin, 50 kilos of ecstasy, and $600,000 in cash. Together with a cache of weapons, police estimate that that the seizure was worth £125 million. The following year, Warren was sentenced to 12 years in a Dutch prison.[14] His stay behind bars has been marred by several serious infractions. Despite being charged with running an international drug smuggling enterprise from his prison cell, he was released from prison 7 years early in 2007 and sent on his way back to Liverpool. However, if it was thought this kindness would change his ways, it did not. In July 2007, he was charged with conspiracy to import £300,000 worth of drugs into the British Isle of Jersey near France (Amoruso 2007).

The years since the late 1990s has seen a groundswell of ethnically based criminal syndicates in Great Britain. Among them are the Yardie gangs that originated among the Jamaican expatriate com-munity in the late 1980s. Although a number of Jamaican criminals remain affiliated with these gangs,

Long-Firm Fraud

Long-firm fraud (LF) dates back to the 1920s, when British criminal groups obtained goods on increasing credit until the company went bankrupt. The gang sold most of the goods that were fraudulently obtained through the London street markets. During the 1960s, some long-firm frauds were bringing profits of more than £100,000. The Kray brothers were among those who made a killing on this scheme. According to the brothers' biographer, this was a simple scam. First, a "front man," whose job was to set up and manage a fraudulent but fully operable wholesale company and register it under a fictitious name was selected. The next step required renting a warehouse or an office and printing company letterhead. Then letters were written to prospective suppliers of wholesale goods. Once these were all tended to, it was time to go into action. The front man visited local banks and got to know the manager, explaining that he was an entrepreneur about to open a new business and would soon be depositing a substantial amount of money as his firm's capital. Over the ensuing weeks, the money was redrawn and redeposited, suggesting to the bank that the business was indeed successful. Assured of the support of the bank manager, the front man placed orders with manufacturers and started trading. In its initial stages, it was incumbent for the long-firm players to act legitimately, paying suppliers on time, placing ads in trade journals, and selling goods to shops and customers. Soon the fraud took a more ominous turn, when the Krays ordered the front man to place maximum orders with all the suppliers. The warehouse eventually filled up, and the goods were sold to cash customers at greatly reduced prices—bargains on everything from washing machines and other modern appliances to crates of wine. After the warehouse was cleaned out, the actors disappeared, but only after withdrawing the rest of their money from the bank. Meanwhile, bills from suppliers piled up outside the now empty offices (Pearson 1973, 106–107).

most members belong to the next generation of British-born Afrolineal criminals (see Chapter 12 concerning Afrolineal organized crime for more). In addition to the Caribbean gangs, there has been an increase in organized crime activity among immigrants from China and much of the former British Empire. Since the fall of communism (1991) and the expansion of the European Union (1994), criminals from Eastern and Central Europe have become much more prominent (Wright 2006).

The Netherlands

Most of the features of the traditional organized crime paradigm are missing in the Netherlands. Recent investigations concluded: "No criminal groups at either a national or local level had gained control of legitimate sectors of the economy by taking over crucial businesses or trade unions." In addition, there is little evidence of protection rackets and political corruption (Kleemans 2004, 307). What emerged instead is what one criminologist refers to as *transit crime,* suggesting that criminal groups in the Netherlands are indeed organized, but are mostly involved in international trade and smuggling activities. Transit crime is regarded as a distinct form of organization that focuses on trade and crossing borders. In this way, a group involved in transit crime can be viewed as a profitable and successful organization without needing to control specific territories or economic sectors (Kleemans 2004, 325).

Taking advantage of the country's strategic position as a "logistical node" in Europe, the availability of the port of Rotterdam and the Amsterdam Schiphol Airport created "an excellent opportunity structure for organized crime" (Kleemans 2004, 307). Most of the activities associated with organized crime here are related to smuggling drugs, illegal immigrants, weapons, stolen vehicles, cigarettes, and women for the sex trade. There is also a parallel structure requiring expertise in money laundering and evading taxes. The drug trade has been facilitated by the emigration of people from a number of countries in the 1960s and 1970s who later became leading producers or transit dealers of major drugs for the European market in the 1980s and 1990s. Of these, heroin comes from Turkey, whereas Suriname, the Netherlands Antilles, and Aruba are an important link for Colombian cocaine headed for Europe from South America, and Morocco is a leading producer of hashish.

Klaas "De Dominee" Bruinsma (1953–1991): The First Dutch Godfather

According to the foremost authorities on Dutch organized crime, Klaas Bruinsma "was the one person in the history of Dutch organized crime who aspired to be the equivalent of a stereotype American crime boss" (Fijnaut, Bowenkerk, Bruinsma, and van de Bunt, 1998, 75). The scion of a wealthy Dutch businessman, Bruinsma entered the drug trade full-time selling hashish in 1974. After a stint in jail for dealing, he changed his name on release to Frans van Arkel and made up for lost time in the drug business. He formed the "Organization" with several other confederates. By the 1980s, Bruinsma had expanded his customer base beyond Holland and was also going into legitimate business in a big way in order to launder his profits. Despite frequent spells in prison for increasingly more violent crimes, he managed to hold sway over the Organization; by the late 1980s, he commanded more than 200 men and became the most important drug supplier in Europe (Amoruso 2007). He became increasingly erratic and paranoid after losing several huge seizures to the authorities. He soon had designs on the entire Amsterdam underworld. One of his schemes was to force every coffee shop to buy his slot machines. One policeman said if one refused, Bruinsma "sent over some Yugoslavians with Uzis." He also directed his attention to the red-light district. However, his increasingly violent behavior soon caused his Organization to unravel. Not only were his competitors and former associates gunning for him, but the Dutch equivalent of the IRS and other investigators had him firmly in their sights as well. In 1991, at the age of 37, Bruinsma was gunned down by an ex-cop hitman working for a Yugoslavian syndicate.

The ongoing integration of a number of ethnic minorities is mirrored by the increasingly diverse nature of Dutch criminal syndicates. In the Netherlands, the traditional bureaucratic model is more the exception than the rule. Rather than a criminal network composed of hierarchical positions and specialized units, "the term *criminal network* is better suited to characterize the structure of cooperation, in that offenders cooperate on certain projects, but the structure of cooperation is fluid (and flexible) and changing over time" (Kleemans 2004, 309).

Prostitution is endemic in the Netherlands. It has never been illegal in the Netherlands as long as it has been voluntary, and clients are not regarded as breaking the law unless it involves minors. The Netherlands has 12 "red-light" districts, where women take part in "window prostitution." Other prostitutes work the streets in "toleration zones," or *tipplezones,* which were created in the 1980s and 1990s in an attempt to reduce the problem elsewhere and to increase the safety of the prostitutes. Other forms of prostitution include escort services; "independent entrepreneurs" who run brothels, sex clubs, sex-farms, massage parlors, and similar establishments; and those who work out of their homes using the Internet and cell phones. At the end of the 1990s, there were an estimated 25,000 prostitutes working in the Netherlands, with almost 70% coming from foreign countries. Geopolitics played an important role in determining which country they came from. In the 1970s, they came mostly from Thailand and the Philippines. The end of the Soviet Union brought in many from Central and Eastern Europe. By the end of the 1990s, the majority were from the Dominican Republic, Colombia, the Czech Republic, Romania, and Poland (Zaitch and Staring 2007). More recently, new trends have been established. One 21st-century investigation asserts, "More than 90% of the suspects in the criminal women trafficking cases had residence in the Netherlands, but the majority of the apprehended traffickers were born in Central and Eastern Europe, especially Bulgaria and Albania" (Zaitch and Staring 2007, 18).

When it comes to the criminal side of the sex trade, prostitutes and others trafficked in the sex trade are often recruited using coercion and deception, or have been recruited under false pretenses for other unrelated jobs. Others had to pay exorbitant prices for transportation and housing, and rarely saw much of the money they earned. Numerous cases verify that many are forced through blackmail and violence to work as prostitutes once arriving in the Netherlands (Fijnaut, Bowenkerk, Bruinsma, and van de Bunt. 1998).

After the European borders were opened, female sexual labor came from Eastern and Central Europe due to a number of important push factors. Many were fleeing rampant unemployment, changes in family structure, and the situation for prostitutes and ethnic minorities in their countries of origin. Many enter the country illegally with forged documents or with travel visas. The trafficking of women for prostitution does not always require organized crime networks (Fijnaut et al. 1998). During the 1990s one national study on organized crime in the Netherlands revealed four different types of organization. In some cases no criminal group was involved, but is just a sex club owner in the Netherlands making contact with Eastern European criminals. In other cases, middlemen have been identified who put sex club owners in touch with individuals recruiting women for the sex trade in St. Petersburg, Russia. According to this 1990s study, organized groups of individuals were identified from the former Yugoslavia, who, with the help of affiliates in central Europe, brought sex workers into the Netherlands. This study concluded that the variations of sex trafficking in the Netherlands ranged from "relatively unorganized small-scale transactions to much larger commercial activities by fixed groups that do undoubtedly have many of the features of organized crime" (Fijnaut et al. 1998, 106).

When it comes to the drug trade, a variety of groups or structures have been identified. In some cases, single-line groups transport a drug like hashish on one circuit from Morocco, Lebanon, or Pakistan directly to the Netherlands. A boss manages the daily routine, with groups membership ranging as high as 40, but in some cases half that. The personnel include couriers, mechanics, debt collectors, and so forth. In some case a number of these circuits are operated simultaneously by multi-line groups, in which the structure is more complex, making use of sub-groups to further insulate the operation leaders. In such cases one group might act solely as the go-between for producers and buyers and is responsible for arranging shipment from one continent to another without passing through the Netherlands. Another group might be in charge of multiple lines, where the hashish is transported either by lorry or in specially prepared containers by ship for Dutch market and elsewhere in Western Europe. This structure is very flexible and involves between 100 and 150 individuals. In between these two structures are mixed groups made up of a few hardcore members who take part in a cornucopia of activities and are adept at constantly creating new lines for an assortment of drugs (Fijnaut et al. 1998, 75–76).

Germany

Germany's tradition of organized crime can be traced back at least as far as the late 19th century, when the government officially registered convict associations known as *Ringvereine,* which "served as an underworld-government and maintained close ties to police officials, judges and politicians" (von Lampe, 2002, 1). By most accounts, examples of organized crime in Germany contradict the notion of sophisticated criminal organizations such as mafia-type syndicates associated with Italy and Albania.

Paoli's research into the illegal drug trade in parts of Europe found that the vast majority of drug deals were carried out by "relatively small and often ephemeral enterprises" (2003, 20). In her investigation, these drug rings were structurally similar to *crews,* which she describes as "loose associations of people which form, split, and come together again as each opportunity arises. In crews, positions and tasks are usually interchangeable and exclusivity is not required. Indeed many crew members have overlapping roles in other criminal enterprises" (Paoli 2003, 22). This view is confirmed in an interview with a Frankfurt policeman:

> The structures, the stable hierarchic structures or family structures that are frequent in Italy do not exist in Germany. . . . As far as organized crime in Germany is concerned, specialists talk about a network structure and this is a correct representation that we can prove in our investigations. If some people want to commit a crime, they look for people specialized in the required tasks; the latter are asked and eventually recruited. Afterwards, the booty is divided and each of them goes their own way. Very, very rarely you can find steady gangs, which for a long time commit a series of crimes. (Quoted in Paoli, 2003, 22)

The overwhelming consensus is that loose networks of actors predominate in the German underworld, with authorities having little luck in identifying any vertical trafficking structures in German trafficking operations, whether it is drugs, stolen cars, immigrants, or the exploitation of women. During the first few years of the new millennium, German police discovered that the majority of crimes committed in Germany were by foreign nationals. One leading expert suggests that this goes against the "commonly held belief about ethnic homogeneity among organized criminals," because most of these cases involved multi-national crime syndicates. In this case, they were connected to Germany's three largest immigrant communities—Turks, those from former Yugoslavian states, and Italians (von Lampe 2002, 16).

GERMAN ORGANIZED CRIME TYPOLOGIES   Soon after the transition to the new millennium, one German criminologist identified four types of criminal networks in Germany. At the most basic level is foreign-based criminal networks, which lack any social support structure within the country in which they operate. Von Lampe chronicles the existence of burglary gangs that operate from home bases in Poland and Romania, describing their activities as a type of "crime tourism," in that they come to the country for the specific purpose of committing crimes that include the robbing of ATMs and the burglarizing of businesses and private homes. Once they are finished, they return to their country of origin (2002, 19). It has been well established that this type of crime is not uncommon in Europe since the fall of the USSR. Investigations revealed that the German transnational burglary gangs demonstrate a complex hierarchical organizational structure replete with "a military-like hierarchy and a clearly defined division of labor between sub-units." Von Lampe suggests that this structure indicates that the gangs were created and trained in their home nations, where they had little to fear from law enforcement (2002, 20).

Next are "subculturally based networks"—criminal networks rooted in distinct cultures and are "more or less set apart from mainstream society and its institutions." This type is exemplified by groups found in ethnic minority neighborhoods as well as in distinct subcultures such as red-light districts. Von Lampe finds this typology among Germany's large Turkish and Kurdish communities, where newcomers created "parallel universes in which a system of ethnic businesses and cultural; institutions allow [them] to a considerable extent to live in seclusion from the German host culture." These conditions, where barely one in five speaks German, facilitated the growth of criminal networks (von Lampe 2002, 20).

The third typology includes "criminal networks rooted in mainstream society," which are made up of individuals who on the surface conform to the legitimate social order and are not restricted from taking advantage of the opportunities presented by "the legitimate social infrastructure." These groups are most similar to white-collar criminals as they prey on a system through investment or insurance fraud. What also makes these networks distinct is that "they consist of circles of decreasing awareness of illegality" (von Lampe 2002), where outside the core of criminal actors most others are unaware of criminal ramifications of their actions.

Hungary

In 2001, it was estimated that more than 160 criminal groups were active in Hungary. Observers point to the country's well-developed transportation and communications infrastructure and its fast-growing commercial ties with the West, and its geographic location in the center of Europe. A number of criminal ventures have been tied to Russian groups and have led to "considerable instability and violence in Hungary's underworld, while diminishing the ethnic homogeneity of individual criminal operations" (Curtis, 2003, 43). Hungary, like Bulgaria and Romania, is an important stop in the primary narcotics route from Southwest Asia to Western Europe. At the end of the 20th century, Interpol reported, "Hungary had the third-largest amount of transited narcotics in the world," with as many as 64 groups involved in the trafficking.

Finally, there are criminal networks that are well-established in the "power elite." What makes this typology most distinct is the direct access these powerful individuals have

> to socially relevant decision-making processes in politics, business and the media." Most examples of this typology can be found in myriad political scandals at every level of government, usually involving public contracts and permits, illegal party financing and the personal enrichment of politicians, lobbyists and other officials. (von Lampe, 2002, 19–20)

NORWAY AND SCANDINAVIA   Rarely considered a hotbed of organized crime activity, Norway and Scandinavia are distinct from the rest of Europe in that "Illegal distilling and smuggling of alcohol, not drug trafficking, has been Norway's principal organized problem for years." Finland and Sweden have also grappled with the problem of illegal alcohol markets in different eras. Finland and Sweden went through a period of prohibition or rationing between 1919 and 1933, allowing the creation of black markets. Structurally, the illegal alcohol trade has been viewed as "flexible, informal, autonomous and short lived." Today, the drug trade is viewed as a developing business in this region. Scandinavia is also distinct for lacking

> traditions of criminal extortion or "protection." Most observers suggest that the efficiency of the regions law enforcement and judiciary has prevented the emergence of these rackets, although there is some evidence of it today among recent immigrant groups that do not trust the authorities. But compared to other regions of Europe Scandinavia has been less threatened by organized crime. (Johansen 2004, 203–204)

ORGANIZED CRIME IN THE BALKANS

Unlike the hierarchically structured traditional Cosa Nostra, there is no single Balkan mafia. According to the FBI, Balkan crime groups have brought their clan-like structure to the United States, where they have become increasingly involved in gambling, money laundering, drug trafficking, human smuggling, extortion, violent witness intimidation, robbery, and murder.

The end of the Yugoslavian war and its subsequent humanitarian crisis in 1999 had the unanticipated consequence of stimulating the growth of more sophisticated crime than had existed previously. These new types included organized crime, economic crime, prostitution, and arms and drug trafficking. The countries of the Balkans experienced a rise in organized crime activity during the 1990s and into the next decade. The Balkans region encompasses Albania, Bosnia-Herzegovina, Croatia, Kosovo, the former Yugoslavian Republic of Macedonia, Serbia and Montenegro, Bulgaria, Greece, and Romania. Some observers refer to this region as "the soft underbelly of the European narcotics market." Organized crime in this region can be traced back to traditional clan structures that characterized most of these rural nations, where people banded together into clans with large familial ties for protection and mutual assistance. Beginning in the 15th century, clans operated under the *kanun,* or "code," which values loyalty, and *besa,* or "secrecy." Any cooperation with the authorities would be considered a violation of *besa,* which in turn could lead to a blood vendetta or *gjakmarria*. It is not uncommon for these blood feuds to last for generations (Nicaso and Lamothe 2005). Each clan established itself in different territories and controlled most activities in that territory. In the course of protecting their own interests, clans often fell into violent feuds. Modern-day organized crime in this region is built in part on the structure of the earlier clans and ethnic solidarity (FBI, Balkan Organized Crime, 2008).

Balkan organized crime groups have been linked to a variety of types of narcotics trafficking, human trafficking, and other actions. The two primary ethnic groups involved in organized crime in this region are Turkish and Albanian crime syndicates. There is plenty of evidence suggesting that these two groups are allied in various smuggling schemes. One explanation is that a large number of Turks in the western part of the country have Albanian ancestors, thus sharing a cultural, religious, and ethnic background.

The Balkan Route

Until the outbreak of the Yugoslavian conflicts, most of the European drug market was supplied with narcotics being brought in through the Balkan route, which began in Pakistan, Iran, Pakistan, and Turkey, where the narcotics were processed. The road then led through Greece, Bulgaria, former Yugoslavia republics (Serbia, Croatia, and Slovenia), Romania, Hungary, the Czech Republic, and Slovakia, until reaching final destinations in Austria, Italy, Switzerland, and the rest of Western Europe. The outbreak of hostilities in the region led Albanian syndicates to blaze new paths to Europe in order to avoid the warfare. A southern route began in Turkey and then through Bulgaria, former Yugoslavian republics, Kosovo and Albania to Italy and other countries. The northern route went from Turkey through Bulgaria, Romania, and Hungary to the Czech Republic, Slovakia, and Western Europe. Once the war ended, the old Balkan route was re-established; however, the new conduit for drug smuggling stayed, and the entire network was expanded by Kosovan Albanians and Turkish groups (BIA 2003).

Yugoslavia remained a semi-totalitarian country from the end of World War II until the death of its leader Marshal Tito in 1980. The next two decades saw the country dismantled by civil war, culminating in the hostilities of the early 1990s that saw Yugoslavia disintegrate into various countries (Serbia, Croatia, Bosnia-Herzegovina, and Kosovo). Many Yugoslavian gangsters who had fled the country during the Tito regime moved back to take advantage of wartime rackets. Following the signing of the Dayton Accords that ended the war between Serbia and Bosnia in 1995, the traffic in illegal arms increased exponentially, as former soldiers became middlemen for the various arms trafficking networks. Using weapons-smuggling routes that were well established by 1995, traffickers took possession of weapons caches, and former enemies entered into cooperative ventures.

Recent investigations indicate that the war in former Yugoslavia, together with sanctions and embargo regimes imposed on the warring republics, led to a proliferation of organized crime related to smuggling, trafficking, and illegal trade in southeastern Europe. During the subsequent war, the various republics laid some of the groundwork for what was to come in the process setting up and arming their newly created armies. Most had only one alternative to arming themselves—through the illegal weapons trade. According to one report, "The party-leaders and high-ranking figures in the Yugoslav Army and secret service "largely tolerated these activities and in their turn contributed to the development of a stable smuggling system." The system that developed was built both "vertically (from political leaders to smuggling system) and horizontally (it included the whole chain of smuggling channels, passing across the new state borders and connecting through common interests the political elites in all post-Yugoslav republic)" (Center for the Study of Democracy, 2003, 9).

In the more vertically structured networks, the elites in the republics were actively involved in development and organization of smuggling channels, demonstrating at least a "temporary symbiosis between the authorities and organized crime" (Center for the Study of Democracy 2003, 4) as transitional states were created. However, a free hand was given to organized crime groups in the war-ridden Balkans, ultimately impacting other countries on the peninsula, particularly during the United Nations–imposed trade and weapons embargos. In the end, it fostered the development of a regional network of smuggling channels, with gangs in Bulgaria, Romania, and Albania playing crucial roles in process.

Balkan Crime Syndicate Structures

In the 21st century, Balkan organized crime groups have transformed themselves from a hierarchical model toward more loosely organized networks. By 2007, most European investigators acknowledged that Serbian and ethnic Albanian clans controlled the heroin coming north out of Afghanistan, weapons smuggled through the Balkans, and prostitutes trafficked from Africa to

Copenhagen (Fleischman 2006). Trafficking groups are considered very flexible, able to adjust their "operations according to the risks to their business, all in an effort to maximize economic gain" (Council of Europe 2005). In various parts of the Balkans, as law enforcement adapts their anti-smuggling strategies, it seems that trafficking networks are responding by using "a managerial model, which involves large investments and mobilizes legal channels and tools, such as legal documents and regular transportation." Above all, what this demonstrates is the increasing professionalism of organized crime in the region as they reinvest profits in legitimate business as well as other forms of trafficking. As these groups become more enmeshed in legitimate business through the purchase of real estate, tourist agencies, nightclubs, and other businesses, it complicates the investigative process as well as "provides logistical support for criminal activities, facilitates money laundering and allows for legitimate contacts with public authorities" (Council of Europe 2005, 55). What's more, traditional organized crime groups rarely monopolize all segments of a trafficking business, with "non-criminal agencies active at various stages such as initial recruitment through job agencies and later transportation" (Karrstrand, 2007, 48).

Like others emerging from communist dictatorships in the mid-1990s, Bulgaria experienced organized crime activity and endemic corruption. Similarly, declining economic conditions combined with a class of former communist officials and weak domestic law enforcement and civil institutions gave rise to a variety of drugs, weapons, and money-laundering networks. Although lax policing allowed the formation of criminal gangs throughout the region, wars and sanctions in parts of Yugoslavia provided new opportunities for smuggling fuel, cigarettes, alcohol, and stolen cars from Bulgaria into Yugoslavia. Meanwhile, money-laundering laws were almost non-existent.

Few countries in the Balkan region have thwarted the expansion of Albanian groups. Their impact is felt from Greece and Bulgaria to Bosnia-Herzegovina. Bulgaria is one of the transitional states that emerged from the collapse of communism in 1989. Subsequently, local Bulgarian crime networks evolved into an essential link supporting powerful Turkish and Albanian networks trafficking drugs from Asia and Afghanistan to the EU along the Balkan transit route (Curtis 2003).[15] Bulgarian syndicates are known to cooperate with gangs from EU countries as far as Brazil. Next to the drug trade and the trafficking in women, Bulgarians are also involved in large-scale activities such as currency counterfeiting and CD piracy.

Greece has proved especially vulnerable to non-indigenous organized crime groups, mainly because of its proximity to both Western Europe and the eastern end of the Mediterranean, corruption at high levels of government, and the existence of a number of domestic organized crime syndicates (Karacan 2003, 134). Its long coastline and numerous islands are especially inviting, and its location along the old Balkan route permits illegal goods to flow into Europe from the Middle East. Balkan groups have made themselves known in Greece. Albanians have been linked to organized burglaries and the drug trade there; Turkish groups with illegal immigrant trafficking from Pakistan and the Middle East, and Romanians with illegal prostitution, and Bulgarians with forgeries and scams.

Greece has served as a transit stage and destination for the trafficking of women from both the former Yugoslavia and former Soviet Union. It is also considered an important transit stop in the international arms trade. Greek authorities have linked the weapons trade to Albanian, Italian, and Russian organized crime groups. In 2001, one Greek journalist wrote, "Guns and narcotics are shipped to Greece from nations of the former USSR and then shipped to European nations through Italy" (quoted in Karacan 2003, 135). More recently, Greek police have reported a heavy infiltration of Balkan groups in Athens, specializing in the drug trade and organized burglaries. More and more Balkan syndicates are laundering money in legitimate businesses there, such as bars and nightclubs, strip shows, and real estate. Police sources have admitted these gangs are the primary organized crime threat in the country. Much of their attention has focused on the weapons trade, most of which comes from Albania. The drug trade has become an increasing problem as the price of heroin dropped. In 2001, Greece had the lowest heroin prices in Europe (Michaletos 2008).

Bosnia-Herzegovina has also become a haven for organized crime. With endemic corruption ranging from the abuse of police power and suspicious privatization deals to involvement in the

The Patriot League

In 1991, at the start of the Yugoslavian conflict, Bosnian Muslims created a paramilitary organization called the Patriot League. One scholar has suggested that this group "used patriotism as a cover for their criminal activities during the war." Subsequently, this group made the transition from criminals to Islamic extremists and continued to participate in the drug trade and other smuggling activities to fund their terrorist activities in the region. The association of the terrorists with the criminal syndicates has demonstrated the existence of a "mujahedin connection" for the trafficking of heroin into the EU (Trifunovic 2006).

smuggling of high tariff goods, copyright piracy, gunrunning, and human trafficking, this state has been the site of substantial organized crime activity. Its involvement in the drug trade is among most serious problems in the EU. Seventy percent of heroin comes by way of three Balkan routes. Bosnia-Herzegovina is an important stop on one of these routes; more recently, it has become a storage zone for illegal narcotics and now offers an emerging consumer market. Local syndicates are connected with Albanian, Kosovar, Serbian, Turkish, and Bulgarian organized crime groups.

Albania and Kosovo

Since the mid-1980s, there has been a recrudescence of medieval practices that have hamstrung Albania's ability to conform to European security models. Harking back to the earlier communist era, the rules of the "Kanun scripture" have reemerged as important societal institutions. Laid down by Roman Catholic priests in the 15th century, Kanun rules depicted obligations of every male, which included orders to participate in vendettas and revenge actions. It apparently resurfaced in Northern Albania, where "Kanun is steadily becoming the code of conduct for members of organized crime groups that are paralyzing state security and creating a framework similar to that of Sicily in another era" (Michaletos and Markos 2007).

Albania has become home to well-developed crime networks since the collapse of communism. It has further profited from the instability and war in the Balkans since 1992 to "become the fastest growing ethnic presence in Europe" (Curtis, 2003, 33). Albania is plagued by corruption in the police force, the tax service, and the judiciary system, which is run by poorly paid civil servants susceptible to bribes and pressure from criminal gangs. One recent investigation revealed the tremendous amount of money funneled into the country noting that according to economic reports, since 2003, legal investments average some €200 million, compared to more than €1 billion on the illicit market. Transparency International claims that 80% of Albania's economy is a parallel economy; that for every €100 of documented capital, another €80 are never accounted for, most of it from organized crime activities (Michaletos and Markos 2007).

Today, Albania is considered the epicenter for Balkan money-laundering and drug-trafficking activities. During the Communist era, 15 families, or *fils,* controlled organized crime smuggling activities in Albania, mostly through corruption and bribery. The fall of the country's government and military led to chaos everywhere except within these 15 crime families. The end of the Cold War unleashed an exodus of emigrants that by 2000 had seen immigrant communities sprout up and flourish throughout Europe and the United States. Besides the more than 500,000 ethnic Albanians in America, an estimated 400,000 have settled in Germany and 30,000 in the U.K.

Albanians are the majority in both their own country and in neighboring Kosovo, a territory once claimed by both Albania and Serbia, and one of the six republics that emerged from the breakup of Yugoslavia. What has become most alarming are reports by various European intelligence agencies asserting there is "close interaction between the leading members of the Kosovo-Albanian society and the domestic and international underworld" now centered in Pristina, Kosovo (Michaletos 2008).

Albania, like most countries, has always had a criminal element, but unlike today, they were formerly confined within their own borders by a repressive government that made it difficult for natives to leave and foreigners to enter. Following its Italian occupation during World War II, Albania resurfaced under the tyrannical rule of Enver Hoxha. Besides giving a cold shoulder to most communist influences, by the 1960s he had declared war on all religious institutions as well leading to Albania being turned into "the world's first atheist country" (Thomas 2005, 341). Throughout the Hoxha years, journalists and Americans were prohibited from entering its borders; and there were no private cars, no inflation, no priests or mullahs, not even private taxation. Well into the 1980s, Albania remained one of the least economically developed and most isolated countries in Europe, a situation that continued even after the death of Hoxha in 1985. By the summer of 1999, the conflict in Kosovo led some observers to view the Balkans as the "Colombia of Europe," as officers and supporters of the Kosovo Liberation Army (KLA) became a major force in international organized crime (Roth 2000, 7).

Although Albanian criminal groups did not arrive on the European organized crime scene until the early 1990s, they made up for lost time by pursuing an especially aggressive and risky campaign to consolidate their heroin- and arms-trafficking networks. With no tangible border between Kosovo and Albania during the conflict (or, for that matter, between Kosovo and Macedonia), the besieged enclave became a magnet for some of the world's most notorious drug barons. Turkish, Russian, and Italian gangsters found it a veritable paradise. Drug trafficking saw its first major escalation in the region in 1993, when Yugoslavia lost its membership in Interpol after the imposition of international sanctions. Problems worsened after the ensuing conflict left the region without viable law enforcement or custom controls. During the 1990s, Kosovo became the heroin gateway to the West. At the same time, it was estimated that perhaps two-thirds of the cars and motorbikes in Albania were stolen property (unlike stolen cars, motorbikes are typically not driven, but disassembled and carried into Albania in sacks). What is most remarkable is that Albania, as one of Europe's poorest countries, with almost 80% of the population living below the poverty line, had one of the highest per capita ownership rates of Mercedes automobiles.

Albanians came to prominence as couriers for established Italian smuggling groups, offering their familiarity with routes that avoided border patrols during the Yugoslavian conflicts of 1992–1995. They quickly made the transformation to running their own drug- and human-smuggling networks, and even going as far as acquiring their own heroin processing and distribution systems. Diversification into other activities such as stolen cars and illegal cigarettes soon led to agreements with Italian organizations, especially in Calabria, Apulia, and Naples. From Italy, the Albanians expanded their heroin- and arms-smuggling as well as their money laundering into the rest of Europe. However, expansion and ethnic integration weakened the structure and solidarity of these traditional ethnic criminal organizations, as well as led them into conflict with other groups in Eastern Europe (Curtis 2003, 35–36).

According to the members of the U.S. Army's Task Force Hawk installation at Tirana airport, crime ranked as a higher threat to troops in Albania in the 1990s than even the opposition forces. During the 1990s, armed gangs hijacked vehicles at gunpoint, committed armed robberies, and smuggled cigarettes without paying taxes.

Albanian gangs proved particularly adept at war profiteering, playing an important role in the clandestine arms trade, shipping weapons from Italian and Spanish ports to Adriatic harbors for transshipment to Bosnia and Serbia (Roth 2000, 8). Albanians control much of the drug trade in Europe, as well as the trafficking of women and children from the Balkans to Western Europe. Both of these activities are complementary to each other, and frequently groups switch from one activity to another (Michaletos, February 3, 2007).

It is almost impossible to establish the total number of criminal groups and their membership; neither is there sufficient intelligence to gauge the size and structure of Albanian crime syndicates. A number of recent cases have revealed close connections with Italian, Greek, and Bulgarian criminals in the drug trade. Since the early 1990s, Albanian criminals have been collaborating with Italy's Apulian mafia and pseudo-mafia groups such as the Sacra Corona Unita. The Apulian beaches are especially attractive to Albanian smugglers because they are only 41 nautical miles across the Adriatic Sea from Otranto to Albania (Hysi 2004, 545).

Albanian groups are distinct for their general preference for acting on their own—only buying and selling illegal goods from foreign criminals. They are also known to be particularly cruel and violent—both against competitors as well as trafficked customers in human-smuggling rings. Albanians are extensively involved in smuggling illegal migrants, trafficking in women and children for the purposes of exploitation, trafficking in stolen cars, drug trafficking, and a variety of economic crimes. All of these activities flourish thanks to the country's favorable location, which established it as a major transit point in 1990s for undocumented migrants bound for the EU. Once foreign nationals, mostly Turks and Kurds, arrive in Albania, they are passed on to criminal entrepreneurs often working in tandem with Apulian smugglers in Italy. Operationally, they often use family members, relatives living on the Adriatic coasts who have no other livelihood to guide and provide shelter. Much of this activity is now directed toward the drug trade.

In the mid-1990s, Albanians established their role as couriers for Italian smuggling groups. Their acumen was especially helpful during the 1992–1995 conflict, when routes were needed to avoid the war zones. At this time, Albanians acquired own heroin processing and distribution systems and diversified their smuggling operations to include migrants, stolen cars, cigarettes, and so on (Curtis 2003). These cooperative arrangements with Italian groups were especially noteworthy. In the aftermath, they reached an agreement to share operations in Calabria, Apulia, and Naples as Albanians continued to migrate west, especially into northern Italy, where there is no dominant organized crime group, to take advantage of lucrative opportunities in the more economically developed Milan and Florence. Albanian groups have spread from Italy into other areas of EU, and now dominate heroin trade in Switzerland, as well as money laundering and arms smuggling. However, their expansion has not been without its problems. It has demonstrated how "expansion and ethnic integration tend to weaken the structure and solidarity of the traditional ethnic Albanian groups; and expansion into markets in Hungary had brought resistance from various Russian groups as well" (Curtis 2003, 36; Galeotti 2001).

One type of organized criminal activity that distinguished Albanian gangs is their burglary networks. Police sources have identified a hierarchy of specialized actors such as *climbers,* who climb on detached houses or apartment blocks early in the morning and steal money, jewels, electronic devices, and other valuable commodities. However, what sets these burglars apart is their predilection for breaking into houses without making sure tenants are absent (like Roman burglary networks). As a result, it is not uncommon for simple burglaries to turn into robbery and even murder. Sources indicate that the "public is afraid to sleep with windows open" (Antonopoulos 2003, 7).

The population of Kosovo is almost 90% Albanian, as is the neighboring region of northwest Macedonia. For many years, this region was characterized by extreme economic disorder, substantial displacement of Albanian populations by war, and nationalist aspirations to promote the recruitment of young people for the illicit activities of organized crime groups. This all came to a head with

Daut Kadriovski (b. 1955)

Born in Macedonia, Daut Kadriovski entered the criminal world as a heroin smuggler during the 1970s, operating a network that ran from Turkey to Yugoslavia. His involvement in several legitimate businesses gave him the cover he needed to launder his proceeds in Germany, Hungary, Italy, and the United States. Subscribing to the family structures of Albanian organized crime, he tried as much as possible to work with only blood kin other countries. When he was arrested in Albania in September 2001, he was regarded as the boss of one of Albania's "15 Families." Other nations filed charges against him as well. Because Italy claimed him first, he was extradited there in 2002. He was tried, convicted, and sentenced to 12 years in prison (Newton 2007).

Kosovo's independence in February 2008. In 2000, one European media outlet described Kosovo as a "gangster's paradise," comparing its crime rate to that of Los Angeles. One report argues that the expansion of Albanian organized crime in Kosovo is directly related to KLA terrorist activities, whose leaders have used their authority to gain control over various illegal rackets (BIA 2003, 10). In 2003, these activities included trafficking in drugs, weapons, cigarettes, and human beings, as well as participation in the human organs trade and the transportation of stolen vehicles; they are also involved in blackmail, violence, and illegal taxing. Intelligence sources suggest that Albanian criminals play an increasingly vital role in organized crime activities in many European countries, most notably in the drug trade, although they are also heavily into corruption, money laundering, and economic criminal acts. Like Albania, most criminal activities are the domain of the family clans who are closely connected to crime groups in other European countries, especially Turkey, Albania, and Bulgaria, due to their proximity to their smuggling routes. The Kosovan clans control specific territories, but as in other countries, there always those trying to acquire more power and thus engage in bitter rivalries with other clans that often take the form of blood feuds, or vendettas. Activities include trafficking in drugs, arms, and human beings, as well as dealing in stolen vehicles, cigarettes, and fuel and excise goods.

Turkey

Turkey's strategic location between Asia and Europe, along with its proximity to the opium-producing areas of Afghanistan and Pakistan, assured the country a central role in the world narcotics trade. Today, this takes place mostly in heroin trafficking. Turkish organized crime is rooted in criminal traditions that date back to the 13th century, when cultural traits emerged that encouraged "courage, fearless manliness and a code of honor" (Yesilgoz and Bovenkerk 2004). Modern international organized crime involving Turks and Kurds is of fairly recent vintage, dating back no further than the 1960s, as immigrant colonies were established in various European countries such as France, Cyprus, Germany, the United Kingdom, Belgium, the Netherlands, and Spain (Yesilgoz and Bovenkerk 2004, 203). Descriptions of the earlier incarnations of "honorable men" resonate strongly in descriptions from Sicily and other agricultural countries still weighted down by cultural baggage from a feudal past. For example, consider the *kabadayi,* or "urban knights" of the Ottoman Empire, who sold their protection, settled disputes, and protected the disenfranchised from oppressive governments, sounding in many respects close to the description of the Sicilian enforcers or *gabelloti* of a much later era.

Turkey was an opium producer for generations. However, in the early 1970s, international pressure encouraged Turkey to restrict the growing of opium only for pharmaceutical purposes. Turkish crime syndicates operate mostly as coordinators, financiers, and facilitators in the drug trade. Their experience in areas such as transportation, company formation, and facilitation management allowed the country to become an important transit country for illegal immigration to the EU.

Turkish crime organizations are known to participate in a wide range of legal businesses that come in handy for laundering proceeds from the heroin trade, including restaurants, bars, fast-food franchises, real estate agencies, travel agencies, and vehicle repair shops.

No Turkish group is more prominent in organized crime circles both at home and abroad than the Kurdish Workers Party (PKK). Better known for its terrorism than criminal activities, since its inception in 1978 the organization has made the transition from terrorist organization to a hybrid combination of crime group/terrorist paramilitary organization (Roth and Sever 2007). The drug trade has proved a particularly attractive business for the PKK, with heroin its most profitable commodity. Captured Turkish drug cartel members have revealed much about the PKK's participation in the illegal drug trade. Records of the National Central Bureau of Interpol (Interpol Ankara) reveal that between 1984 and 1993, Interpol Ankara investigated a total of 503 persons connected with the PKK for drug trafficking. Of these, 188 were cleared, whereas 298 were arrested and charged. A breakdown of the 12 countries where the arrests took place suggests the widespread involvement of the PKK in transnational organized crime.[16]

The current organizational structure of the PKK and the existence of immigrant Kurdish communities in European countries provided an environment and strategic transit point for transnational organized crime activities, especially for drug trafficking. The most popular drug routes from Asia traditionally passed through this region for generations (Sahin 2001). According to one 1998 Turkish National Police Report, Hakki Kitay, a leader of one of Turkey's biggest drug-trafficking cartels, frequently delivered profits to Selim Curkkaya, who was responsible for handling PKK financial affairs in the late 1990s.[17] Kitay even claimed to have sat in at meetings discussing the transportation of heroin from Turkey to Europe. Further suggesting his ties with the PKK, he also revealed that his brother was a member of the PKK, and had been killed in a shoot-out with Turkish security forces. He added that his own son joined the PKK after being trained in a PKK camp in Bekaa (Lebanon) in the 1990s (Turkish National Police 1998).

It is estimated that 80% of the drugs produced in the Golden Crescent, which is composed of the region of Afghanistan, Pakistan, and Iran, are trafficked to the European market through Turkey. Most sources assert that the PKK plays an important role in the transportation process via the Balkan route (Alkan 2004). Experts suggest that the PKK benefited generously from the proximity of Turkey to narcotics sources in South and Central Asia. Furthermore, the PKK often collaborates with other major criminal groups from the Istanbul, Turkey, vicinity (Curtis and Karacan 2002).

A number of investigations and reports linked the PKK to involvement in the illegal drug trade. According to the 1996, 1998, and 1999 annual reports of *The International Narcotics Control Strategy,* prepared by the U.S. State Department, the PKK used heroin production and trafficking to support its terrorist activities. These reports indicate that the PKK not only is directly involved in transporting and marketing narcotics in Europe, but also extracts "revolutionary taxes" from narcotics traffickers and refiners in order to finance terrorist actions (U.S. Department of State 1999).

In April 2004, Yvon Dandurand and Vivienne Chin prepared a report entitled *Links between Terrorism and Other Forms of Crime,* in which it states that investigations have shown that the PKK is deeply involved in illicit drug trafficking, production, and street dealings as well as in extorting commissions from drug traffickers (Dandurand and Chin, 2004).

The PKK's involvement in illegal immigrant activities is well documented. It provides them with not only a source of revenue, but also utilizes it as a method of recruitment. The organization uses its drug trade routes to smuggle illegal immigrants from South Asia to Europe. Investigators Curtis and Karacan have noted the "nexus" between terrorists and organized crime in Western Europe, and have found that the PKK's complicated human smuggling network generates a significant amount of money, as it transports refugees from northern Iraq to Italy via Turkey. The three most popular routes include Istanbul–Milan, Istanbul–Bosnia–Milan, and Turkey–Tunisia–Malta–Italy (Alkan 2004; Curtis and Karacan 2002).

Interpol estimates PKK profits from illegal immigration and people smuggling as ranging from €2,000 to €3,000 for each individual (Interpol Ankara). Following the new millennium, the Italian police became increasingly involved in suppressing these activities. In January 2002, Italian officials accused the PKK of involvement in these activities. In one case, the Security Directorate of Trieste (northern Italy) reported one illegal smuggling operation with PKK connections transported 9,000 Kurdish people from Anatolia to Europe via land and sea in 2001 (Hurriyet Daily Newspaper 2002). According to the special branch of Italy's Guardia Finanza, the PKK people smuggling operations often begin in northern Iraq, passing through Turkey and Greece, to the ultimate destination in Western Europe, particularly Italy and Germany via Albania (Andalou News Agency 2000).

More recently, in 2005, the Romanian daily newspaper *Adevarul,* reported that the Romanian police destroyed a PKK-affiliated human smuggling ring that had been transporting people through Turkey, Romania, Hungary, Austria, Britain, and France. Police found faked passports and bank documents during a search of the operation's headquarters. Each individual was reportedly expected to pay €6,000 to €7,000 per person for transportation to Berlin, Vienna, Paris, or London. According to the Romanian police, the money generated from smuggling was being transferred to PKK camps in Northern Iraq. As previously noted, the PKK is involved in forging passports and documents. People are then smuggled using these documents (visas, passports, traveling documents).

The trafficking in illegal cigarettes has been another moneymaking operation for the PKK. The PKK, as well as other terrorist organizations, including Hezbollah, the Real IRA (RIRA), Al Qaeda, and Hamas have been linked to the smuggling of contraband cigarettes with forged tax stamps. Evading tax on wholesale cigarettes and then selling them for retail prices results in significant profits; according to one account, cigarette smugglers can earn up to $60USD per carton in this fashion (Billingslea 2004). In 2000, Turkish law enforcement agencies participated in a raid on a house in eastern Turkey suspected of being used for PKK operations. Expecting to find firearms, ammunition, and explosives, they were surprised when they found a gravure printing press for creating counterfeit tax stamps and other fraudulent documents.

In a 2002 lawsuit, *European Union (EU) v. RJR Nabisco,* it was alleged that between 1990 and 2002, RJR Nabisco participated in an agreement with Audeh Trading and Consultancy Service and IBCS to smuggle cigarettes into Iraq through the towns of Dohuk and Zakho. Although this case was later dropped, the proceedings revealed that PKK units in northern Iraq were collecting tax on all cigarettes trafficked into Baghdad and the rest of Iraq. The EU also alleged that Saddam Hussein's late son Uday controlled distribution of this illicit business and grossed enormous profits (Kochan 2005).

Overview

Most members of the EU admit the existence of domestic criminal organizations operating within their borders since the mid-1980s. Nevertheless, the foreign origin of many of these groups remained a distinct characteristic of organized crime in this region. Explanations for this phenomenon are related to the various historical, cultural, and geographic factors that influence the distribution of crime syndicates of foreign origin throughout the EU. For example, Spain and Portugal have historic and cultural links with South American countries of Colombia and Argentina. The Netherlands has links to its former colony of Suriname, also in South America. In both cases, these can be considered causal factors for the trafficking of cocaine from South America to Western Europe through the Netherlands. In other cases, the proximity of countries to Eastern Europe, such as in the case of Germany, Austria, and Greece, goes a long way to explaining the origins some of these domestic groups with international origins. In the mid-1990s, 11 of the then 15 EU states referred to Russian organized crime and 9 to former Yugoslavian nationals. The organizational structures of these groups varied as well, with domestic groups more likely to be based on family relationships or ad hoc relationships with local criminals, whereas others were more hierarchical (van der Heijden 1996).

Several factors contributed to the growth of modern organized crime in Europe. One of the key developments has been the collapse of socialism throughout Europe, along with the dismantling of the Soviet Union, which led to the removal of the geopolitical East–West division that had been in place since the end of World War II, resulting in independence for a number of states that are now teeming with transnational crime networks. A second important development was the closer integration of Europe through the evolution of the European Union (EU). Out of these changes and others came new opportunities for criminal organizations based both in and out of Europe.

More and more contemporary developments are shaped by the increasing influence of "non-indigenous" criminal networks. Organized crime in Europe features an immense "variance in terms of numerical and ethnic composition, organizational structure, operational methodology, and the scope and scale of operation" (von Lampe 2005). Although evidence clearly suggests there are a number of intricate criminal organizations operating in Europe, by most accounts, European organized crime groups are more often characterized by

webs of personal relations that are flexibly used by criminals for the commission of crimes. Cooperation typically occurs either on a contractual basis, in the form of supplier-consumer or ephemeral employer–employee relations, or on a partnership basis in pairs or small groups with little overall horizontal or vertical integration. (von Lampe, 2005, 406–407)

Since the mid-1980s, perceptions of Russian organized crime activity in the former Soviet Union have undergone a sea change; from the mid-1980s when Soviet police debunked the existence of ROC as exaggerated, to 1995, when the "'Russian mafiya' was considered one of the dominant powers within not just Russia, but the global underworld, and it had become a staple of the post–Cold War thriller" (Galeotti 2005, 54–55). During the mid-1990s, most Russian officials accepted the notion that the so-called mafiya controlled up to 40% of the nation's economy. At the same time, the expansion of ROC garnered headlines throughout the world. However, much had changed by the beginning of the new millennium. With the economy growing at an estimated rate of 6% per year, foreign investment increased substantially, and by some accounts gangland carnage decreased dramatically (Serio 2006).

More recently, some scholars conclude that the Russian underworld is "maturing, as larger, more professional networks" subsume the hundreds of smaller organizations and gangs that emerged in post-Soviet Russia (Galeotti 2005, 55). On top of this, President Putin differed vastly from his predecessors Yeltsin and Gorbachev, and was less likely to accept the freewheeling conditions that marked the early 1990s. Despite these developments, Russian organized crime remains unique for "precisely how disorganized it is." Today, ROC is just as likely to include Chechen syndicates as seemingly legitimate "business empires built on the back of money laundering and rigged privatization auctions" (Galeotti 2005, 55).

Many of the new countries and republics to emerge from the Balkan wars and the breakup of the Soviet Union have proved hospitable for the growth of organized crime activities. In most cases, this is the result the lack of strong government institutions such as the police and the judiciary as well as the vacuum in authority that typically occurred in the periods between the arrival of multinational forces and the establishment of a new legal system and control of the borders.

Overall, organized crime has continued to flourish in great swaths of the former Soviet Union and the former Yugoslavia. The best explanations for this has been globalization and the increasing sophistication of the networks, combined with their ability "to take advantage of weak customs systems, poorly guarded borders, corrupt officials, poverty stricken national economies, and well-established shadow economies" (Curtis 2003, 88).

Following a familiar pattern that holds true in much of the developing world today, organized crime thrives wherever the state apparatus is weak, corrupt, disorganized, and non-transparent. This is especially true during the transitional period from the disintegration of former totalitarian states to free market economies, where the lack of state interference (in sharp contrast to former times) results in a vacuum in authority that is often filled by organized crime structures.

In addition, one must consider geopolitical and domestic conditions that provide such a tantalizing range of opportunities. This can be demonstrated by the extreme poverty in some parts of Europe that has only increased the supply of women for transnational traffickers; the collapse of a major superpower that left large poorly guarded arsenals of weapons in countries needing money and luring arms dealers. Finally, one cannot overemphasize the fact that widespread corruption, smuggling routes, and shadow economies were well-established in the former Soviet system, and that many of the nations that have proved most hospitable to organized crime were products of this tradition.

Key Terms

Viktor Bout
"Lord of War"
European Union
Thieves' law
Vory-v-zakone
Vor
Gulags
Soviets
Tsarist
"Bitches' War"

Solntsevo
Kryshas
Red Mafia
Russian Mafiya
Thieves' Code
Brighton Beach
Little Odessa
"Daisy chain" scam
Semion Mogilevich
Eurasian

Vyacheslav Ivankov
Chechens
Baltic states
Adams family
"A-Team"
The Firm
Kray Brothers
Long-firm frauds
Klaas Bruinsma
Tipplezones

Critical Thinking Questions

1. What was the impact of the dissolution of the Soviet Union on organized crime in Europe?
2. What are the most common forms of organized crime in Europe?
3. Discuss the evolution of smuggling activities.
4. What are the structural differences between the various European crime syndicates?
5. Is there a "Russian Mafiya"? If so, what is it? If not, why is the term so popular, and what does it actually refer to?
6. What relationship did the former Soviet Union have to subsequent creation and certain acceptance of Russian crime syndicates?
7. What are the origins of the *vory-v-zakone*? What is a *vory*?
8. Why is organized crime more rampant in the Balkan region than in the rest of Western Europe?
9. Is the PKK closer to a terrorist group or an organized crime group? Discuss the differences and similarities to both.
10. What is the *Krysha* system?
11. Is organized crime common throughout the former Soviet Union? What conditions promote or block the development of organized crime activity here?

Endnotes

1. See, for example, in Fijnaut and Paoli 2004; Florike Egmond, "Multiple Underworlds in the Dutch Republic of the 17th and 18th Centuries," pp. 77–109; "Banditry in Corsica: The 18th to 20th Centuries," pp. 151–180; Yakov Gilinskiy and Yakov Kostjukovsky, "From Thievish *Artel* to Criminal Conceptions: The History of Organized Crime in Russia," pp. 181–202; and Yucel Yesilgoz and Frank Bovenkerk, "Urban Knights and Rebels in the Ottoman Empire," pp. 203–224.
2. His best-known sobriquet came from a United Nations report delivered in 2003 by the British Foreign Office Minister Peter Hein, in which he declared Bout "the leading merchant of death" between Eastern Europe and Africa (Newton 2007, 175).
3. Many had lost parents to the revolution and civil war that followed; others through the system of collectivization that led to massive starvation and dislocation.
4. Yuri Shchekochikhin, "Mafia," *Soviet Life,* March 1989, p. 5; quoted in Joe Serio, unpublished manuscript, "The Russian Mafia," 2006, p. 13.
5. Quoted in Serio, 2008.
6. These included Armenia, Azerbaijan, Belarus, Estonia, Georgia, Kazakhstan, Kyrgyzstan, Latvia, Lithuania, Moldova, Russia, Tajikistan, Turkmenistan, Ukraine, and Uzbekistan.
7. Referring to General Aleksandr Korzhakov, who formerly led the Presidential Security Service and at one point directed one of Russia's biggest *kryshas*.
8. Unpublished transcript, "Press Briefing by the Interior Ministry Regarding the Activities of the Russian Mafia Abroad," April 1995, p. 9; Joe Serio, *Investigating the Russian Mafia,* Durham: Carolina Academic Press, 2007.
9. Interview with Joe Serio, August 18, 2006.
10. Joe Serio suggests that KGB documents and MVD officials put the membership of the Solntsevo at closer to 450–700.
11. Ivankov has also been awarded sobriquets such as "The Red Godfather," the "Father of Extortion," and even "The Assyrian Son-in-Law," referring to his reported marriage to an Assyrian woman.
12. Named for a Moscow suburb and with a reported 9,000 members, it is considered one of the most powerful gangster cliques in Russia.
13. For a fascinating, if not disturbing photographic chronicle of the modern Firm, see Jocelyn Bain Hogg's 2003 book, *The Firm.*
14. Holland has very lax drug laws.
15. Bulgaria is along the route between the Black Sea and the Republic of Yugoslavia.
16. This breakdown includes 154 in Germany, 82 in Turkey, 17 in the Netherlands, 12 in the Czech Republic, 8 in France, 7 in Italy, 5 in England, 3 in Belgium, 3 in Spain, 3 in Switzerland, 2 in Denmark, and 2 in Portugal. The remaining 17 of the 503 were discovered to have connections to other terrorist groups.
17. Selim Curukkaya, known as "Tilki" within the PKK, was sentenced to death by the organization and fled to Germany, where he testified that he profited greatly through the drug business.

CHAPTER 11

Organized Crime in Mexico and Latin America

As recently as late 2007, the Washington Office on Latin America (WOLA) declared, "Throughout Latin America, organized criminal networks exercise a significant degree of influence over the state" (Washington Office on Latin America, October 2007, 2). The geographic region comprising Central and South America and the Caribbean has nurtured drugs, weapons, and human smuggling organizations for decades. What has become most alarming in the 21st century has been the emergence of Central America as an important link in the region's drug trade. Most observers have noted that many of these same countries are only recently emerging from more than a decade of civil conflict and are on the cusp of falling back into similar conditions as the countries' capacities to maintain and enforce the rule of law have eroded.

Since the end of the Cold War at the start of the 1990s, there has been a noticeable increase in the overlapping of politically inspired violence and organized crime activity in Latin America. According to one leading scholar, "The establishment of the military dictatorships beginning in the 1960s was certainly the most important stimulus to the onset and development of organized crime in Latin America, for it generated the institutional conditions criminals needed to operate freely" (Gaio 2008, 132). As the dictatorial regimes suppressed civil dissent and liberties among the segments of society they feared most—the middle classes, professoriate, civil libertarians, and intelligentsia—rising crime among other classes received scant interest. Following on the heels of the state terrorism, guerrilla warfare, and counter-insurgent activity that so characterized the era 1960–1980, and was the cause of the region's organized violence, a number of countries made great strides toward democracies. However, citizens of these countries were often disappointed if they expected a return to the rule of law. Government control actually diminished during the 1990s as huge territories became "out of bounds to police—areas where drug lords impose their political control, collecting taxes, setting curfews, carrying out recruitment and making seizures" (Manrique 2006). Crime rates have increased between 400% and 600% in the 10 countries of Latin America that provide the most reliable comparative figures. Organized violence and crime by a host of players—irregular militias, narco mafias, urban gangs, and paramilitary forces—continues to bedevil large swaths of the region's social and political institutions. Of the various organized crime activities, none has the capacity for generating corruption, violence, and political instability like the drug trade (Manrique 2006).

Organized crime, particularly at the transnational level, has persisted through parts of Latin America since the early 1960s. The Andean region in particular has been home to the cocaine trade, enveloping nations including Colombia, Bolivia, and Peru. One leading expert suggests, "Illegal drugs have become a permanent feature" of these three societies (Thoumi 2003, 1). Like earlier generations that grew up recognizing that their countries were internationally known for traditional commodities such as coffee, tin, fishmeal, sugar, and copper, for the younger generation (those under 35), "illicit drugs have taken the role of those earlier export commodities [and they] do not have a memory of their countries without illicit drugs" (Thoumi 2003, 1). These countries have also

The Cartel Debate

There is still a lack of consensus among economists, criminologists, policymakers, and others who study organized crime as to whether Latin America's drug organizations functioned as true cartels in the economic sense. Among those who have subscribed to the "cartel" explanation is America's Drug Enforcement Administration, which defines *cartels* as "independent trafficking organizations that have pooled their resources." These groups are able to control prices, eliminate competition, and avoid prosecution through the use of violence and corruption, and use criminal and legitimate businesses to launder drug profits. In 1995, organized crime expert Louise Shelley agreed, stating,

> Colombian organized crime is quite different from the other organized crime groups because it operates as a cartel—its business is the monopolization of the illicit international narcotics trade. A cartel takes advantage of a monopoly position in the market to artificially control prices. (Shelley 1995, 479)

During the 1970s, several independent drug-smuggling outfits in Colombia did indeed band together into what some have labeled *cartels* for want of a better title. The leaders of the Cali and Medellín cartels offered the drug world a vision and a business strategy. Shipments were organized so that if one was confiscated, others would surely get through. Therefore, if one trafficking unit was busted, only those participants were apprehended. Typically, they had only limited information, because the units (like cells) were isolated from each other and the primary leaders (Nicaso and Lamothe 2005). Several experts say that the term *cartel* "suggests a close, corporate bond between its participants, who may engage in concerted efforts to limit the size of the market" (Fuentes and Kelly 1999, 348). If this definition is applied to the Colombian permutations of the cartel, in Cali and Medellín groups, the opposite prevails. Thus, on examining the Colombian cartels, the term applies to a "geographically confined, loose federation or coalition of major drug trafficking organizations that have formed alliances for the self-serving purpose of reducing the risky nature of the business which they participate in" (Fuentes and Kelly 1999, 348). For example, when necessary, the members can come together to suppress the threat of kidnapping by profit-seeking insurgent groups; in other cases they can share trafficking routes or pool resources in major drug shipments to reduce the risks for individual groups (Fuentes and Kelly 1999, 348). In any case, there is little doubt that the strategies of the pioneers in the drug trade allowed the expansion of the cocaine business to unimagined levels. The 1990s saw the Andean cocaine industry go through rapid transformation. The Medellín and Cali organizations that had developed in Colombia during the 1970s and controlled a large share of the cocaine business in the following decade were decapitated in the 1990s. However, by focusing on these two organizations as major cartels leaves the impression that there were few others involved. In reality, there were dozens if not hundreds of smaller cocaine trafficking organizations at work contemporaneously alongside the Medellín and Cali syndicates.

The Medellín and Cali Drug Trafficking Organizations Were Not True Cartels

Today, there is probably more concordance than ever over the notion that the cocaine business between the 1970s and the present was never the province of a handful of drug cartels in Colombia and then Mexico. One critic of the cartel myth (Kenney 2007) asserts that the reality behind a cocaine trade run by a "handful of massive, vertically integrated cartels that restricted production and set international prices" is a misconception and a "longstanding illusion." He argues:

> The cartel myth achieved remarkable staying power in American popular culture, in part because the vivid imagery it conveyed was plausible—and useful—to politicians eager to pass drug-control legislation, law enforcers hoping for greater drug war resources, investigative journalists searching for profitable news copy, and citizens fearful of the harmful effects of drug abuse and addiction. (Kenney, 2007, 25)

In the end, despite the destruction of the so-called Cali and Medellín cartels, cocaine is as cheap and plentiful as ever. If these organizations did indeed control the industry as a traditional cartel, this should have at least been a major disruption of the product into the United States and elsewhere. In reality, the Colombian trade was never dominated by monolithic cartels but was the result of hundreds of small, independent enterprises that became increasingly diffuse and decentralized after the fall of Escobar and the Rodriguez Brothers. Subsequent interviews with imprisoned cocaine kingpins lend credence to the cartel

(continued)

myth. Most have debunked the notion of a cartel dominating the cocaine trade, setting production limits, and fixing prices internationally. As one imprisoned Medellín associate explained it, "The cartels never existed until they were created by the media and the U.S. government" (Kenney 2007, 25).

Drug Networks as Non-Traditional Cartels

One of the leading authorities on the Andean cocaine trade refers to these organizations as *export syndicates*, noting they "are not cartels in the traditional economic sense because they do not control raw material production and most distribution systems in their main markets," therefore these organizations "could not prevent a large increase in coca cultivation and a long-term decline in coca prices" (Thoumi 2003, 94). As export syndicates, these trafficking networks are organized to share risks and guarantee a lucrative return on the product for each partner. So in effect, they are risk-minimizing structures created in lieu of the ability to plan production quotas or ensure that orders are carried out as planned through several layers of production and distribution. Thoumi argues that the definition of *cartel* is not applicable here because the main actors in the production of cocaine— those who gather coca leaves and manufacture coca paste, transport it, refine it, and distribute to the key markets "tend to be fluid [as] the structure of the industry adapts itself to changes in the business environment brought about by the activities of law enforcement agencies and other factors" (Thoumi 2003, 95). Although there is little doubt that cocaine traffickers would love to control the market forces, it is really beyond their control to conspire to negate any major attempts to create a suppliers' market agreement or cartel.

become staging areas for the movement of illegal immigrants and various illicit commodities into the United States from China and the Middle East (Liddick 2008).

One common misconception is that the destruction of the Cali and Medellín cartels led to the fragmentation of the cocaine business. However, this began much earlier, as the more prescient traffickers recognized that the larger the organization was, the more vulnerable it was to attack. So, one of the dominant and least-mentioned trends was that drug gangs formed smaller and more controllable organizations, and (like many terrorist groups) began compartmentalizing their responsibilities. Separated into cells, workers knew little about the workings of other cells, better insulating the leaders of the syndicates from the law. For example, one group takes care of smuggling the contraband from Colombia to Mexico. Others control jungle laboratories, whereas other gangs handle the transportation of coca base from the fields to the labs. The most recent additions to this equation are the links with Colombia's Marxist guerrillas, who are often tasked with guarding the fields and labs in exchange for a generous tax from the drug trade. However, right-wing paramilitary groups are suspected of also controlling coca fields, labs, and smuggling networks. One recent estimate by the DEA and the Colombian National Police estimates that Colombia is now home to more than 300 active drug-trafficking groups.

Peru and Bolivia increased their participation in the refining and trafficking of cocaine as Colombia became the premier coca producer. Due in part to the fact that the American cocaine market stagnated in the late 1980s, cocaine merchants diversified their markets and products and began looking for new markets in Europe, the former Soviet Union, and South America. At the same time, Colombia became the leading importer of heroin into the United States (Thoumi 2003).

The 1990s represented a sea change for drug trafficking in Mexico and Latin America as new and smaller drug-trafficking networks emerged. Coca production declined in Peru and Bolivia at this time. The end of the Cali and Medellín cartels[1] created less of a demand for coca paste in Peru because the smaller syndicates preferred to purchase paste in Colombia. However, more important was the fact that the coca production decline in Peru was mainly the result of the abandonment of coca fields in response to the sharp price decline as well as the expansion of coca plantings in Colombia. Mexico stepped in to play a leading role in some of the Colombian smuggling pipelines into the United States. Soon, Colombian guerrillas and paramilitaries replaced the traditional cartel networks as the main players in the drug trade, and Andean drug syndicates linked up with European crime groups (Thoumi 2003).

Despite recent attempts by the Calderón administration, Mexico remains mired in corruption as it continues its prominence as a major producer of heroin, methamphetamine, and marijuana. As a result, Mexican drug traffickers now control much of the U.S. methamphetamine market, while perhaps half of the cocaine enters the United States across the Mexican border. Crime syndicates use the porous border also for smuggling weapons, tobacco, stolen cars, alcohol, and counterfeit goods.

Mexico was among the countries of the region that was not beset by dictatorships; but institutional corruption continues to plague efforts of the criminal justice system to rein in organized crime activity. Corruption stimulated the growth of organized crime syndicates much in the way that has in other corrupt democracies. Mexico was dominated by one political party for decades. The Institutional Republican Party (PRI) ran the country with little competition into the 1990s; so, in Mexico, organized crime groups flourished thanks to the stimuli of the nation's political officials.

A lack of cooperation between Mexico and the United States has hampered the War on Drugs for years. Mexico has a long tradition of distrusting the United States government dating back to the Mexican-American War between 1846 and 1848, when Mexico lost half its territory to the northern invaders. Partially as a result, the Mexican military has traditionally refused most American aid; the animosity was so deep rooted that Mexico has not participated in joint military exercises or allowed bases on its territory. However, this began to change during the administration of Vicente Fox (2000–2006). Of course, it did not hurt that his grandfather was American and that Fox had studied in the United States when he was younger. As a result of his rapprochement, the United States almost tripled its aid to its southern neighbor, from $15.7 million in 2000 to nearly $46 million in 2006. On top of this, Fox outdid his predecessors by extraditing more alleged drug traffickers than ever before. During his administration relations began to improve, and for the first time Mexico started to allow U.S. military personnel to offer counterterrorism training. Subsequently, the new president, Felipe Calderón, increased cooperation substantially and recently handed over several organized crime figures. In fact, it was Calderón who first suggested a mutual drug-control strategy with the United States at a March 2007 summit meeting in Mexico with President George W. Bush (Hawley 2007, 10A).

The Caribbean is a major transshipment route for passage of illegal contraband ranging from weapons and drugs to illegal migrants. It also became home to major offshore banking centers used for tax evasion and money laundering. During the 1970s, Cubans landed in Florida in increasing numbers. As conditions in many Central American countries deteriorated, they were joined by refugees and immigrants from Mexico, Nicaragua, Guatemala, and El Salvador.

Central America is a major channel for drug traffickers and illegal immigrants heading to the United States. Central America is the main base for the smuggling of people into the United States, and U.S. officials estimate that alien smuggling networks bring in more than $1 billion annually. More than 100,000 migrants cross the Central American corridor, along with perhaps one-third of the cocaine shipments into the United States.

Rules for Drug Dealers to Live By

- Live quiet life with family
- No outward display of wealth or power
- Blend into neighborhoods
- Open small businesses
- Drive modest cars
- Keep homes up
- Rent or purchase houses were electric meters are on the outside
- Have garages with direct access to the house (for going in and out)
- Do not conduct business when kids are around (might talk to friends in school)
- Perform a reconnaissance of city to determine which lawyers, accountants, and banks to use
- Determine which police and judicial officers are corrupt

(Nicaso and Lamothe, 2005)

MEXICO

Mexico: Home of the World's Most Powerful Drug Cartels

Historically, Mexico has long been a haven for outlaws and criminals and a staging ground for border smugglers. Links to Mexican drug-smuggling operations can be discerned as early as the first decades of the 20th century. The passage of the Harrison Narcotics Tax Act in 1914 further stimulated the smuggling of opium from Mexico, where it was still legal, and where poppies had been cultivated since the late 19th century (Owen 2007). Similar to other eras, "Prohibition on one side of the U.S.–Mexico border and legal commerce on the other created the conditions for drug trafficking" (quoted in Owen 2007, 147).

Throughout its history, Mexico has been burdened by economic inequality that today places most the country's wealth in the hands of perhaps three dozen families, whereas a fifth of the population lives on less than $1 a day (Gray 1998, 134). During almost 70 years of one-party rule, the PRI regularly stole elections, a "significant factor in promoting criminal activity" at all levels of society (Hudson 2003, 163). Mexican organized crime flourished thanks to a culture of corruption that characterized the nation's military and politicians for decades. One expert on narcotics noted in 2005 that Mexican drug gangs make between $10 billion and $30 billion annually from the cocaine trade alone. The bottom line is that there is just too much money to be made. In the case of President Vicente Fox, his 6-year term was due to expire after the 2006 election. Traditionally, corruption in Mexico increases during the president's last year in office. As a consequence, it is common for police and army officers to do anything they can to supplement their looming retirement, because most realize they will be out of a job after a new administration takes over (Pinkerton and Grillo 2005).

Geographically, Mexico ranges from an easily accessible Rio Grande River to remote and inhospitable desert along the southwest border of the United States. The problem is further complicated by the presence of teeming urban centers that straddle both sides of the border, such as San Diego–Tijuana and El Paso–Juárez. Inadequate policing, dense legitimate commerce and traffic, and multiple jurisdictions further confound any attempts to stifle organized crime in this region and contribute to its reputation as America's "soft underbelly." Mexican criminal groups take advantage of its more than 3,300 kilometer border and the legitimate commercial travel between Mexico and the United States to bring in illegal immigrants, heroin, cocaine, marijuana, and counterfeit goods.

Latin American drug lords have long resorted to torture and gruesome killings, but had nothing on the Mexican groups when it came to violence and intimidation.[2] The Juárez cartel was known for cutting off the fingers of snitches and stuffing them down their throats. Others were bestowed with a "Colombian necktie," where the victim has his throat cut and his tongue is pulled through the opening in his throat. To be sure, these were brutal and sent a message, but were never epidemic in numbers as in Colombia (Watson 2007, A19). In 2007, Mexican drug gangs adopted a new strategy of terrorism in an attempt to stop newly elected President Calderón's nationwide crackdown on drug trafficking. No incident captured the brutality more than the execution and beheading of two police officers and the placing of their heads on spikes in clear view of the public with a sign warning, "So that you learn to respect," written in bold black letters. Previously, drug gangs killed only each other; however, the 21st century unveiled a criminal underworld without limits. A number of indicators suggest that the terror campaign might be working, with police resigning in record numbers and newspapers censoring their coverage of organized crime.

The North American Free Trade Agreement

The North American Free Trade Agreement (NAFTA) fulfilled its promise of opening trade routes—but no business has taken advantage of it more than the drugs, weapons, and human-trafficking networks. Using their years of success smuggling various types of contraband across the border, the advent of NAFTA made these talents, "already exceptional, the keys to an unprecedented bonanza" (Naim 2005, 75). When the United States, Mexico, and Canada signed the agreement that was hoped would make commercial and tourist movement faster, few expected that in 2007 drug gangs would be warring over turf from Mexico into southern Texas. One official recently referred to the agreement as the "North American Free Trafficking Agreement" (quoted in Callahan 2005).

Mexican organized crime groups had one economic advantage that no other country in Latin America could claim—control of the territorial approaches to the border, which was "the single most lucrative bottleneck in the drug supply chain, the point where the value is added" (Naim 2005, 75). Mexican drug-smuggling routes became increasingly lucrative after NAFTA as they quickly took advantage of the new opportunities presented by globalization that allowed them adapt to the changing economics of the smuggling business and squeeze "the maximum value from their territorial advantage" (Naim 2005, 75). The larger the traffic of legitimate trade, the more opportunity to ship bulk loads of drugs in the millions of vehicles that cross the border each year. According to one 2005 estimate, 5 million trucks and 92 million personal vehicles crossed the border between Mexico and the United States. Perhaps 90% of the cocaine is brought into the country in this manner. Prior to NAFTA, cocaine was typically transported across the Caribbean in overloaded Cessnas, a risky and expensive proposition to say the least. By comparison, today the cocaine is unloaded from ships in Mexico and often "shotgunned" across the border by traffickers in very small increments, lessening the risk for all involved (Dermota 2007, 24).

With the control of the strategic border-crossings at Tijuana, Mexicali, Juárez and Laredo, the Mexican organizations have been able to negotiate with other international smuggling organizations from an unprecedented position of strength, leading to various partnerships with established Colombian groups as well new players brought into the picture through globalization such as the Russians, the Ukrainians, and the Chinese. Whereas Colombia remained focused on a single product—cocaine— Mexico's focus on controlling the border allowed it to participate either directly or indirectly in a variety of criminal enterprises from heroin, marijuana, and cocaine to human trafficking and money laundering (Naim 2005, 75).

Paralleling the growing demand for cocaine, marijuana, and heroin in the United States during the 1960s and 1970s was the emergence of a number of entrepreneurs ready to supply these drugs. One study characterized this era as "a pioneering time when the drug trade in Mexico was neither controlled by cartels nor carefully regulated by either the army or the main federal police force" (O'Day and Venecia 1999, 424).

Beginning sometime in the post–World War II years of the 1940s, the Herrera Family was considered Mexico's preeminent crime family. By the 1990s it was led by Jaime Herrera, a former police officer; at its zenith, his heroin smuggling operation employed almost 5,000 members— 2,000 related by blood or marriage. One expert suggests that it resembled "a cartel-type drug trafficking organization long before the Colombians came on the scene" (Kelly 2000, 216). According to most sources, major Mexican drug networks are fairly centrally organized. Some have even gone as far as suggesting that many of the Mexican groups resembled Colombian cartels in "their most unsubtle aspects: the vendettas, corruption, and extreme violence" (Naim 2005, 75).

In 1969, the Mexican drug trade was targeted by President Richard Nixon with a plan dubbed "Operation Intercept." During a 3-week period border guards stopped and searched some 5 million travelers. Despite its good intentions, not one seizure was made. The United States next took a different tact, offering Mexico a $1 million reward if it would destroy the country's drug plantations. This effort failed as well, and by the mid-1980s Mexican drug cultivators had spread out of the mountains to Veracruz, Baja California, and Sonora. By the next decade, Baja emerged as the main route for smuggling drugs into the United States from Mexico and Colombia. No case exemplified these conditions more than the 2003 discovery of two tunnels running under the border between Tijuana and Otay Mesa in California. One of these tunnels was more than 500 feet long, replete with electricity and air conditioning (Morton 1998).

In the 1970s, most of America's marijuana supply was smuggled in from Mexico. Mexico became the world's leading exporter of heroin in the early 1970s after the Turkish government banned the growing of opium in 1973. However, this began to change after a joint military style operation by the United States and Mexico engaged in an eradication program in 1975 that targeted Mexico's marijuana and poppy fields. The spraying of these fields with the toxic herbicide Paraquat disrupted if not ended this particular trade once reports of pot smokers being sickened became publicized. By the end of the 1970s, what was once the major source of marijuana in the United States had fallen to only 11%, and by 1981, it plummeted further to 4% (Owen 2007).

Mexican Organized Crime in the 21st Century

In 2006, street battles between rival Mexican cartels (Gulf and Sinaloa) left more than 2,000 dead.[3] However, 2007 was even bloodier, with 1,000 drug-related slayings reported for January through April. Journalists have been forced to tone down any criticism of the cartels or face the prospect of death. As a result, some journalists spy for the cartels and give crime bosses advanced warnings of pending stories or threaten other reporters. In cities such as Nuevo Laredo,[4] cartel henchmen attacked the newsroom of the city's largest newspaper. In response, the paper cut back substantially on its coverage of drug-related crime. Despite a barrage of publicity abroad by the foreign press, local reports give a false impression of diminished violence. As one local pundit put it, Nuevo Laredo is under the thumb of the Gulf Cartel, and "wants the city to appear calm so they won't send more federal police here" (Castillo 2006). Police have been so reluctant to get involved they often do not issue news releases or comment on specific drug-related crimes. Since 2000, more than two dozen reporters and editors have been killed in Mexico, and by 2007 it had become second only to Iraq in the slayings of journalists. Formerly a tourist oasis, even Acapulco has been among the hardest hit, with 300 gangland killings in 2006 alone (Lloyd 2007, A1).

Mexican peace officers have been killed by the hundreds since the mid-1990s. It is widely held that these killings continue because "Mexican police do a poor job of protecting their own" (McKinley 2006). Of the dozens killed in 2006, for example, only a handful of arrests were made; most remain unsolved due to the reluctance of witnesses to testify. Police officers admit they often fail to follow certain leads in order to protect themselves and their families. This led critics to suggest that the Mexican police have become "cowed by assassinations." In 2006, besides the dozens of local police victims, cartel killers also assassinated 8 police chiefs and 16 state and federal police commanders across Mexico, together with 2 judges and 2 federal prosecutors, all handling drug cases. Most were ambushed either in their cars or outside their homes (McKinley 2006).

Mexican officials suggest that the elevated killings are a sign that they have made progress in dismantling the major cartels. Some experts point to the arrest of several kingpins and their top lieutenants as the spark that has ignited a struggle among lower ranking mobsters for control of drug trade routes. With the old order in disarray, those who are left are either killing each other or plotting new alliances to fill the power vacuum (McKinley 2006, A1). In addition, local Mexican markets come into play as the country experiences a rising tide of drug addiction. In any case, there is little doubt that the power vacuum within the criminal organizations following the imprisonment of a number of drug kingpins contributed to the growing chaos and deterioration of public safety in certain areas of Mexico (Pinkerton and Grillo 2005).

Mexican drug organizations continue to flourish on both sides of the border by spending an estimated $3 billion in bribes each year for protection from local, state, federal officials. As a result, the cartels are now more transnational than ever, often involved in elaborate alliances with other national groups, such as Colombian and Dominican syndicates. The FBI and other law enforcement agencies note that besides the drug trade, Mexican organized crime groups are involved in money laundering, armed robbery, kidnapping for ransom, extortion, and illegal weapons trafficking. Mexican drug traffickers even elevated their targets in an attempt to influence political campaigns by kidnapping and threatening candidates to steer election results.

President Calderón's campaign against the Mexican drug cartels together with the weak American economy led a number of traffickers to look toward Europe, where the Euro is strong, law enforcement less aggressive, and the markets more open (Schiller July 4, 2008, A1). However, by the middle of July 2008, most observers labeled Calderón's crackdown on organized crime a total failure. Since the campaign began in December 2006, almost 5,000 people have been slain in gangland-related violence, with almost 2,000 in the first 6 months of 2008 alone. Among the victims were at least 500 policemen. Some officials suggest that many of them were killed more for their relationships with the cartels rather than in crime fighting (Althaus, July 12, 2008). Targeted killings of police chiefs and officers have led many to abandon their posts altogether, with many seeking asylum north of the Mexican border. The whole police force of Puerto Palomas, just over the border with Columbus, New Mexico, quit after a barrage of death threats in March 2008 (Althaus, May, 15, 2008, A1).

However, there were rare successes to report in the campaign by Mexican police against regional crime organizations in 2008. In late July, Mexican marines seized a cocaine-filled mini-submarine 120 miles off the Pacific Coast. The Colombian vessel was described as a 30-foot long semi-submersible vessel. Almost 6 tons of cocaine was seized, valued at between $50 million and $100 million (Althaus July 19, 2008, A21). Homemade subs are just the latest in a string of transportation schemes. They first appeared in the late-1990s, but were rather primitive. Although they don't fully submerge, the new incarnations are considerable more advanced. In 2006, U.S. officials detected three such subs, but now are sighting an average of 10 each month. Made of fiberglass and manned by four crew members, they typically unload the cargo onto fast speedboats for the final stages onto shore. Some sources suggest that the Colombians adopted these vessels in an attempt "to win back from their Mexican rivals-cum-partners a bigger slice of the profits from drugs" (*Economist*, May 3, 2008, 48). This Colombian innovation is just the most recent attempt to take back control of the retail-distribution business that had been taken over by Mexicans in the 1990s as shipment routes were forced from the Caribbean to land routes on the Mexican-American border.

As 2008 dawned, to most observers it seemed that Mexico had gone to war, as thousands of troops laden with the accoutrements of war streamed toward the border with the United States. During the first 2 weeks of the year, bloody skirmishes between federal troops and drug cartel soldiers have been almost daily occurrences in towns such as Rio Bravo and Tijuana. However, as one reporter noted, "What is

The Kidnapping Racket

One of America's leading security companies, Kroll Associates, has estimated that half of the world's kidnappings take place in Latin America. In 2003, there were more than 4,000 kidnappings in Colombia (the world leader at that time), followed by Mexico with 3,000 and Argentina with 2,000. More recently, kidnappings have declined in Colombia and increased in Mexico. By most accounts, the majority of victims come from prosperous neighborhoods featuring residents of Spanish, Lebanese, and Jewish origin. Now even members of the upper-middle class are being targeted as well for ransoms averaging around $100,000. The darker side of these figures is that many families in Mexico refuse to report these crimes because they fear a corrupt security apparatus that has itself been linked to kidnappings. What has become even more troubling is that the torture and mutilation of victims has become more commonplace. One explanation suggests that "this is due to a kind of class war in which kidnappers of the lowest social classes take out social vengeance on their victims" (Manrique 2006, 2). Hostages are typically tortured in order to force relatives to meet the demands for ransom. In some cases, a finger has been cut off as "proof of life" and sent to the family. In other cases, a victim might be forced to listen on the phone as his wife is raped (Billeaud 2008). Over the past several years, kidnapping "has moved across the border into the United States," as fellow drug and human smugglers kidnap each other (and family members) for six-figure ransoms. These are seen as prime victims because their occupation guarantees they can raise large cash ransoms quickly. In many cases, the kidnapping is not even reported, because it typically involves the kidnapping of a drug trafficker and the ransom being paid by his family. One veteran police sergeant noted, "We have never had a victim that we have investigated that has been as clean as the new driven snow" (Billeaud 2008, A7). Phoenix, Arizona, is currently the hot spot in the United States, reporting 340 of these type kidnappings in 2007, but law enforcement asserts they are vastly underreported.

happening is less a war than a sustained federal intervention in states where for decades corrupt munici-pal police officers and drug gangs have worked together in relative peace" (McKinley 2008, A1).

It was hoped that this unprecedented offensive would break up the cozy relationship between local police and officials and the drug cartels. However, what was once thought to be a straightfor-ward operation met surprisingly staunch resistance by drug gang members not willing to give them-selves up as federal forces hunt down cartel leaders and Zeta gunmen and their ilk. More than 6,000 troops were sent into the Tamulpais state, to the south of east Texas. Home to crews of Zeta assas-sins, they are considered such a threatening presence that Mexico has a hard time finding state offi-cials to fill important positions in the state. Federal police commanders are especially vulnerable and must keep on the move to stay alive.

Zetas

Formerly part of the Mexican Army's elite, a number of Zetas joined the drug cartels as hitmen in the late 1990s. It is easy to see why because they went from making a monthly army salary of $700 to $15,000. Oth-ers have asserted that in the past, most desertions were the result of mistreatment in the army, or that they were perhaps reluctant to fill the role of policeman. The former theory has been supported by the fact that of the almost 5,000 soldiers assigned to the federal police force by former President Vicente Fox (2000–2006), "all but ten deserted." Since this crossover to the "dark side" began, more than 120,000 Mexican soldiers[5] have reportedly deserted, creating an additional pool of military-trained killers for the country's brutal drug gangs. It is unknown how many of the recent army deserters have joined, but as one security analyst put it, "Even if just 5 percent of those join the cartels, that's an army of hitmen" (Lloyd June 18, 2007). These ex-commandoes have trained hundreds of gunmen to act as transporters, collectors, and killers. One new phe-nomenon is the emergence of *zetillas,* teenage enforcers for the Gulf cartel, trained by Zetas (Carroll 2007). In recent years, Zeta leader Heriberto Lazcano won a well-earned reputation for ruthlessness. Lazcano was a Mexican army recruit from Veracruz who in the 1990s was selected as a member of the elite Special Forces group fighting drug traffickers on the eastern border. Sometime toward the end of the 1990s he along with more than 30 others began working for Osiel Cárdenas' Gulf Cartel as enforcers. Once Cárdenas was extra-dited to the United States in 2007, the shackles came off and the group became more independent.

In 2004, the so-called "El Verdugo (the Executioner)" murdered a prominent Tijuana publisher in front of his two children. The following year, Zetas raided a federal prison in Matamoras. Here they blindfolded and handcuffed six prison employees and then shot them in the head. Under Lazcano, Zetas have even used rocket-fired grenades to attack police stations with military precision. Rumor has it that Lazcano has fed captives to his pet lions and tigers that he maintains on private ranches (Padgett 2005). Since 2006, the Zetas have become so influential that their former handlers are losing their grip on them, leading one expert to express the opinion that they "have clearly become the biggest, most serious threat to the nation's security. Now they want to control the nation's drug routes and along the way topple the traditional cartel leaders" (Corchado 2007). Besides extending their territory into Acapulco, Monterrey, and Veracruz, they are now operating in conjunction with former Guatemalan death squad members known as *Kaibiles.* As a result, the Zetas have become a more than 2,000-man paramilitary organization with influence throughout Mexico and are even operating in several American cities, such as Dallas.

In 2007, a new organization emerged in response to the Zetas. Called *La Gente Nueva,* or "New People," this group of former Mexican police officers is reportedly bankrolled by the Sinaloa cartel in opposition to the rival Gulf cartel and backer of the Zetas. By most accounts, this new group is motivated by revenge for the hundreds of police killed by the Zetas. It has also earned a reputation for bloodthirsty efficiency and torture. Some observers have compared them to Colombian vigilante group *Los Pepes,* formed in the 1990s to help track down Pablo Escobar. Subsequently, it morphed into the paramilitary group the United Self-Defense Forces of Colombia, or AUC, which like the Mexican groups continues to plague its homeland. If one doubted the resolve of *La Gente Nueva,* they need look no further than a 2007 message to Veracruz officials, who they accused of complicity with the Zetas. This message was left along with a decapitated head; it said "[The offi-cials] who work for the disgusting Zetas are going to end up just like this guy" (Corchado 2007).

Juárez Cartel

It has been suggested that the modern Juárez cartel has been "transformed into a new 'Golden Triangle Alliance,'" led by drug kingpins from the American border states of Chihuahua, Durango, and Sinaloa (Newton 2007, 117). Based in the border town of Ciudad Juárez, the Juárez cartel rose to prominence under the leadership of Amado Carrillo Fuentes (1956–1997), who earned the nickname "Lord of the Skies" for his strategy of using more than 20 retrofitted Boeing 727 airliners to transport cocaine (as well as heroin and marijuana) for Colombian cocaine kingpins. During the 1990s, the Juárez organization was Mexico's most powerful drug-trafficking organization. It is estimated that during his 4 years at the top, he earned $25 billion, leading American drug officials to brand him "Mexico's most powerful drug trafficker" in his heyday. Like his counterparts, Fuentes used his extensive ties to military and government officials to build his operations in the 1990s and had "protected" use of an assortment of municipal and rural airports and landing strips. One major investigation in 1997 revealed that a number of military officers were on Carrillo's payroll, along with other allegations of pervasive military corruption (Downie 1997).

Carrillo took over the operation after the death of its founder Rafael Aguilar Guajardo in 1993 and led it to its apogee of power. Formerly a member of the Guadalajara drug cartel, he was sent to Colombia as their representative to Pablo Escobar, who taught him the nuances of cocaine trafficking. Not content as a mere underling, he later left the Guadalajara group and resurfaced as leader of the Juárez cartel after the death of Aguilar.

The Juárez cartel used regional bases in Guadalajara, Hermosillo, and Torreón for storage shortly before goods were to be shipped to locations along the American border. Carrillo was used to gallivanting around the world in luxury. However, a concerted effort by American and Mexican authorities forced him to try and change his appearance. He purportedly died during plastic surgery at a hospital in Mexico City on July 3, 1997. His death has been shrouded in controversy, with some claiming he died from a malfunctioning respirator or from anesthesia; others suggest he was killed by his bodyguards; still others suggests he is still alive and a corpse was substituted for him for subsequent forensic tests and photographs. Whatever is the case, his three brothers took over and were quickly replaced by a string of other traffickers, none of whom reached the heights of the Carrillo era.

Testimony to the cartel's reach into the highest levels of government was the case of Mario Villanueva, former governor of the Yucatan Peninsula state, home to major tourist destinations. He was convicted of receiving $30 million from the Juárez Cartel for offering political and police protection during his administration between 1993 and 1999. Following a 6-year sentence, he was released in 2007 and almost immediately rearrested by Mexican authorities as preparations were made to extradite him to the United States for trial. According to federal charges awaiting him in the United States, he is accused of being part of a conspiracy to smuggle 200 tons of cocaine through southern Texas while he was governor Yucatan's Quintana Roo state. Villanueva and his son were originally apprehended thanks to a cooperative investigation between the two countries. U.S. officials were tipped off when word surfaced that they had been possibly laundering money through New York brokerage and investment firms.

Sonora Cartel

Based in Sonora, Mexico, bordering Arizona, the Sonora cartel is most identified with Miguel Caro-Quintero's family. Although it is involved in marijuana, amphetamine, and cocaine traffic, it has specialized more in the cultivation, production, and distribution of marijuana. Centered in Caborca and Hermosillo, Mexico, it is from here that a number of outposts are controlled on both sides of the border, maintaining active smuggling routes in Arizona, California, Nevada, and Texas.

This organization's key to success (aside from bribes and corruption) is its ability to synchronize air operations using small single-engine airplanes used to transport marijuana and cocaine from deep inside Mexico to Sonora on the border with Arizona. The drugs are reportedly stored in northern Sonora

Enrique "Kiki" Camarena Salazar (1948–1985)

Perhaps the best known casualty in the "War on Drugs," the DEA agent was kidnapped and tortured to death in Guadalajara by "cocaine cowboys" of the Sonora cartel. Camarena was born in Mexicali, Mexico, and brought up in California. After joining the DEA, he was posted to Guadalajara, where he developed a program to monitor marijuana crops on the outskirts of the city. Subsequently, "Operation Miracle" led to a 1984 raid that retrieved 20 tons of marijuana. The following year, he testified to a congressional investigation that drug trafficking–related corruption in Mexico reached into the highest levels of government. Just before his revelations were printed, he was abducted outside a bar in Guadalajara. Almost 3 months later, his terribly mutilated body was found near the compound of a prominent Mexican legislator named Manuel Bravo Cervantes. When law enforcement tried to query Cervantes, a gunfight broke out when shots were fired from inside his estate. Cervantes, his wife, and two children were killed in the subsequent gun battle. Giving in to American pressure, Mexican officials arrested a former policeman named Raúl Lopez Alvarez, who confessed to his role in the Caro-Quintero–engineered slaying. Attempts to extradite him and several others to Los Angeles were held up by a vacillating Mexican government. The FBI approved a plan to kidnap the suspects using private bounty hunters. Alvarez was convicted and sentenced to three life terms. However, Caro-Quintero was tried in Mexico (the torture took place in his home) and sentenced to 40 years in prison (Phillips and Axelrod 2000, 39; Newton 2007).

until it they can be transported along the international border by means of packhorses and backpackers. Tons of drugs were smuggled in this fashion each month during the late 1980s and into the 1990s.

The Sonora cartel became notorious following the kidnapping and torturing of DEA agent Enrique "Kiki" Camarena Salazar in 1985. Soon afterward, authorities in Costa Rica arrested Caro-Quintero for drug trafficking. Although indicted on numerous charges in several American states, Mexico had jurisdiction in the case and found him guilty, resulting in the country's maximum sentence of 40 years. Despite a number of key convictions of cartel leaders, several siblings continue to run the organization.

Sinaloa Cartel

In January 2008, the government scored a victory with the capture of Alfredo Beltrán Leyva, one of five brothers who are considered high-ranking leaders in the Culiacan-based cartel. Authorities now believe the Sinaloa cartel is "the country's most important drug trafficking organization" (Althaus 2008, A12). Based in the Sinaloa state capital of Culiacan, the cartel is now under the ostensible control of Joaquin "El Chapo" Guzman Loera. Sinaloa has long been a key location for growing opium poppies, the raw material for heroin. The Sinaloa cartel has long dominated this locale. Guzman escaped from prison in 2001 and went to war over the strategic border town of Nuevo Laredo with the Gulf cartel. Both organizations are fighting for control of this key smuggling route. Gulf cartel members have long argued that the federal government favors its enemies from Sinaloa. However, whether this is true is a matter of opinion, because the Gulf cartel has the upper hand with a nearly 2–1 advantage in gunmen. Nuevo Laredo is an important position for the drug trade, mainly because the city offers extensive trade facilities, processing more legitimate cargo than any other crossing point along the 2,000 mile border between Mexico and the United States. In 2004, almost $90 billion worth of legitimate goods from 60 nations passed through Laredo into the United States (compared to almost $43 billion that crossed in El Paso and $22 billion in San Diego). Drugs are then transported up route 35 to Dallas, Texas, and from there it is distributed to the East Coast. The war over Nuevo Laredo drew international attention in 2003 and 2004 as murders spiraled out of control. The gang war even reached into the country's prison system, as cartel members took their outside conflicts inside with them (Pinkerton and Grillo, 2005).

Tijuana Cartel

Based in Tijuana, this cartel has been considered one of Mexico's most brutal drug-smuggling organizations for more than decade. It has long been under the control of the extended Arrellano Félix family. Miguel Angel Felix Gallardo, however, is considered the founder of the Tijuana cartel. During his prime, the drug trade was considered small that it could be controlled by one man, in this case Felix Gallardo (Wallace-Wells 2008). Imprisoned in 1989 for his involvement in the death of DEA agent Enrique "Kiki" Camarena, his organization was divided among his subordinates and family members. Subsequently, American interdiction efforts forced Colombian groups to abandon the Caribbean corridor for the presumed safety of the Southwest border of the United States. Unable to control the evolving drug trade from prison, Gallardo reportedly met with his lieutenants and divided Mexican border crossings between them. One recent investigation asserted that he gave Tijuana to his nephews, whereas other lieutenants were given Sinaloa–Arizona and Laredo–Nuevo Laredo; El Paso–Juárez was given to Amado Carrillo Fuentes (Wallace-Wells 2008).

Beginning in the 1990s, the Tijuana cartel dominated the flow of cocaine, marijuana, and heroin into California and the West Coast. In 2006, Mexico extradited Francisco Rafael Arellano Felix, the first time Mexico extradited a major drug lord to the United States to face trial on drug charges. He had already served a 10-year sentence in Mexico. He was the oldest of the seven brothers and four sisters in a family that has been accused of running one of Mexico's most notorious drug-smuggling organizations during the 1990s. Most of the brothers have either been killed or arrested, but despite its losses it continues to transport tons of cocaine and marijuana across the border from Tijuana.

At one time, the Tijuana cartel was considered Mexico's most ruthless and feared drug organization. It gained a reputation for grisly ways of eliminating rivals and witnesses, methods that included dismembering bodies and dissolving the bodies in acid. However, since the killing of Ramon Arellano-Félix during a shootout with police in 2002 and the arrest of the cartel's "patriarch," Benjamín, several weeks later, its influence has diminished. In September 2007 (5 years after his arrest in 2002), Benjamín Arellano Félix was sentenced to 22 years in prison. DEA agents had been trying to get their hands on him for at least 15 years. He has been linked to dozens of murders and was recently indicted by a jury in San Diego on 28 counts of drug smuggling and money laundering. The U.S. government has been particularly interested in the drug boss, accusing him of working closely with the Revolutionary Armed Forces of Colombia (FARC) while attempting to turn Mexico into the premier drug corridor into the United States.

The Gulf Cartel

Based in Matamoras, Mexico, the Gulf cartel was created in the early 1980s. By most accounts, it was modeled after the Cali cartel, compartmentalized into small cells to protect its clandestine transactions. The brainchild of Juan García Abrego, it now operates in 17 Mexican states under the leadership of his brother. The award-winning film *Traffic* was reportedly based on his rise and fall from power. His organization dealt mostly in cocaine and marijuana, and probably flourished thanks in large measure to handsome payoffs to high-ranking members of the Mexican government. According to a 1996 episode of the PBS television show *Frontline,* he had ties to the brother of former Mexican President Raúl Salinas de Gortari.

Abrego was known for a number of idiosyncrasies such as ordering murders on the 17th of each month and was known by a number of monikers, including "Dollface," "the Doll," "the Lord," "the Director," and "the Boss." Indicted in the United States several times in the early 1990s, by 1995 he was on the FBI's Top Ten Most Wanted List. He was arrested the following year and extradited to America, where he is now serving 11 life sentences for his role in the drug trade. During Abrego's halcyon years, he guaranteed Colombian cartels that their cocaine would reach destinations for 50% of each load, assuming all risks and amassing a bankroll approaching $10 billion. However, there is evidence his organization was in decline at the time of his arrest, as measured by the Cali cartel's decision to cut off his cocaine supply due to his notoriety and the unreliability of new government officials who were supposed to protect the trade.

In the beginning of 2007, the former federal policeman Osiel Cárdenas Guillen, 39, the suspected head of the Gulf Cartel in the Tamulpais state, was extradited from Mexico to stand trial in the United States for narcotics trafficking and threatening to kill U.S. agents. Known to some as the "Friend Killer" and to others as "Crazy Man," U.S. officials claimed Cárdenas directed a trafficking network that each month brought between 4 and 6 tons of cocaine across the southern Texas border. Initially, his operations were centered in Matamoras on the border. Following his arrest, he continued directing the syndicate from a federal prison near Mexico City. He joined the Gulf Cartel in the early 1990s when it was under the aegis of Juan García Abrego. He was first arrested in 1992 for smuggling more than 5 pounds of cocaine across the border into the United States, but charges were later dropped. Following the arrest and extradition of Abrego in 1996, Cárdenas took control through a campaign of murder. However, perhaps one of his greatest accomplishments was luring dozens of members of the Zetas from the army to his syndicate. They adopted the name *Zetas* in homage to their original leader, who was killed in 2002 and used the radio call-name *Zeta*. This well-known gang of hitmen was critical to establishing the Gulf Cartel as one Mexico's most powerful organized crime groups (Lloyd and George 2007, A8). As killers and bodyguards, the Zetas were considered the elite. Rumor had it that some had even been trained by the U.S. army. The Zetas were originally tasked with protecting drug shipments and killing competitors.

When Cárdenas was arrested in 2003, he was placed in a federal prison along with the already incarcerated kingpin Benjamín Arellano Félix. Usually, these two would be at each other's throats. However, they put aside their differences and joined forces in order to run their businesses from prison (thanks to banned cell phones). Following in the footsteps of other drug kingpins, such as Colombia's Pablo Escobar, Cárdenas earned a reputation as a Robin Hood even while in prison, bestowing games, bicycles, and toys on thousands of children who had been displaced by a flood in April 2004. He followed up his Children's Day Party the next month with a Mother's Day celebration for border town women, giving away kitchen appliances and furniture (Scharber 2007, A8).

Osiel Cárdenas Guillen

Born in Matamoras, Mexico, in 1968, Cárdenas left school after junior high school before entering a series of occupations—city police officer, mechanic, federal informant—before his ascendance in the world of Mexican drug trafficking. Cárdenas had his first brush with organized crime while still in his teens, when he regularly took care of a car for a hitman known as "the Nice One," for his penchant of letting victims know their imminent deaths were not personal, "just business." Also known as "Fantasma," or "Ghost," and "El Patron" ("The Boss"), Cárdenas was convicted by the Mexican government for organized crime activities before his extradition to the United States, where authorities have charged him with leading the Gulf cartel and threatening to kill several federal agents and a sheriff's deputy. His extradition to the United States was viewed as a message to other cartel kingpins, letting them know, "If they can get the man nicknamed the 'Ghost,' they can get anyone." His extradition in January 2007 ended the reign of one of Mexico's most violent drug kingpins. He is considered the most prominent drug trafficker to be extradited from Mexico. American drug agents tracked Cárdenas for a decade when he was still on his way up as a go-to man in a corrupt branch of the federal police. He put his profits into the drug trade. What separated Cárdenas from his counterparts was his unwillingness to build alliances with other cartels and his reluctance to keep a low profile (Schiller Feb. 18, 2007).

Guadalajara Cartel

Founded by the four Amezcua-Contreras brothers, the Guadalajara drug organization specializes in the illegal methamphetamine traffic. According to the DEA, at its zenith, the Amezcua organization was probably the largest producer of methamphetamine in the world. During the 1990s it was able to buy huge quantities of the precursor drug ephedrine from India and Thailand. The product was then distilled in laboratories on either side of the border. In the late 1990s, three of the brothers were arrested along with almost 100 others for drug trafficking. Raids led to the seizure of more than 130 pounds of methamphetamine, 1,100 kilos of cocaine, several drug labs, and several million dollars in cash. What was most troubling was that one of the labs operated less than 200 yards from a busy school and daycare center, and another near a California equestrian center. Despite the arrests of the brothers, the network continues to flourish.

It has been estimated that 80% of the methamphetamine in the United States is produced by Mexican drug gangs working in rural Central and Southern California, a region that one Fresno prosecutor dubbed "Colombia for meth" (Suo 2004).[6] In the mid-1990s, the Mexican cartels introduced the industrial-scale production of methamphetamine in what police have called *superlabs*.[7] Thanks to professional lab equipment and hundreds of pounds of precursor chemicals, these labs are capable of producing from 100,000 to 1 million doses in 48 hours, as compared to the typical mom-and-pop user lab that might be able to produce 280 doses in a batch. Although superlabs represent only 4% of the meth labs, they account for all but 20% of the meth produced nationally (Suo 2004).

The methamphetamine business was particularly attractive to Mexican organizations. For years they had moved Colombian cocaine for a percentage of the profits; with methamphetamine, there was no sharing. So, in effect they made the transition from middlemen to vertically controlling every aspect of the business, from production and distribution to sales. Unlike the marijuana, heroin, and cocaine trades that depended on a large agricultural labor force and the capriciousness of the growing seasons, synthetic drugs such as methamphetamine could be produced inside a lab leading to a cost–price ratio of 10–1. As former director of the DEA Thomas Constantine put it in 1997, "Unlike the cocaine business, where traffickers from Mexico are just one link in a chain, methamphetamine is one rung they can control from beginning to end. And because they are in complete control, they can keep 100 percent of the profits" (quoted in Owen 2007, 149).

The Amezcua-Contreras Organization: The Mexican Methamphetamine Business

Not everyone in the illegal drug business lamented the drop in the cocaine and crack trade that took place in the late 1980s. Among those who saw it as a no-lose opportunity were the Amezcua Brothers—Luis, José de Jesús, and Adán Amezcua-Contreras, who would revolutionize the methamphetamine trade eventually producing methamphetamine in superlabs on a larger and more structured scale than ever seen before. In the 1990s, the Mexican press heralded their global drug-trafficking network by dubbing the brothers *reyes de la metanfetamina* ("the kings of methamphetamine"). Both began their trafficking careers rather ignominiously, smuggling immigrants across the border, before they made the transition to middlemen in the cocaine trade. They had learned their lessons well as traffickers for Colombian organizations, and by 1992 had established international contacts for chemical precursors.

The Amezcua-Contreras brothers were only one of a handful of Mexican organizations that moved into the methamphetamine business in the 1990s. Both the Tijuana and Juárez cartels had made overtures to the methamphetamine trade, but the Amezcuas became the most important because they were the first to grasp the commercial potential of the trade and adapted quickly to the vicissitudes of the marketplace, such as making the switch from ephedrine powder to pseudoephedrine pills. In 1995, when the DEA moved to get Congress to control ephedrine, which disrupted the production of methamphetamine, the Amezcuas responded to the watered-down legislation by switching to pills; when these sources dried up, they then found new ones in

Canada. However, what most distinguished this group was its ability to get along with its competitors. One need look no further than their arrangements and alliances with the Tijuana and Juárez cartels. For years, much of their profits went toward bribing Mexican police, customs officials, judges, prosecutors, and politicians to look the other way so their drugs could get through. They had an epiphany that would change the methamphetamine trade—"the secret to making the big money . . . was making the drugs, not retailing" (Langton 2007). It was no secret that the Mexican climate was inhospitable to coca plants, and that better marijuana was now being grown in California, a market already saturated; besides, it took tons of pot to equal the profits of a pound of pure cocaine. However, with methamphetamine increasingly popular in the United States and with its main ingredient ephedrine now closely monitored, there was a huge market for illicit methamphetamine. It was relatively easy, considering Mexico's lax internal and border security systems, to import ephedrine to Mexico. In the early 1990s, they were purchasing huge quantities of the chemical legitimately from source factories in Germany, India, the Czech Republic, and Switzerland. In 1993, Jesús personally traveled throughout Asia searching for factories that manufactured ephedrine. In India, he discovered sources where he could buy it for an eighth of what it cost in Mexico (Owen 2007). It was shipped first into Mexico and then through Tijuana and Mexicali into Central and Northern California. In the beginning, they resold the ephedrine to established cooks, but eventually tired of sharing the profits. They soon began to import ephedrine as well as the cooks and chemists, who had perfected the manufacture of methamphetamine before sending it north. It was not long before they opened huge methamphetamine factories in California. They selected California because the penalty for importing ephedrine into United States was a misdemeanor, whereas importing methamphetamine was a felony. They knew well that this region was home to thousands of migrant laborers, with miles of rural real estate. Soon, superlabs were seemingly all over California. The product entered the polydrug Mexican distribution networks already trafficking marijuana, heroin, and cocaine coast to coast, and cartels were no longer wrapped up in one drug, as they became trafficking organizations capable of smuggling anything for profit.

The success and longevity of the Amezcua-Contreras organizations was in no small part attributable to an insulated structure in which they heavily recruited relatives, extended family members, and long-time friends. In addition, the second tier of operatives recruited individuals to engage in the dangerous cooking of the meth, as well as the risky activity of smuggling either chemicals or meth into the United States (DEA 1998).

In the 1990s, federal legislation and law enforcement stopped the supply of chemicals needed to make methamphetamine.[8] As a result, the drug became harder to get, and many of the crimes previously associated with the drug as well as hospital admissions plummeted. However, in less than a year, drug cartels found new ways to get the ingredients and the methamphetamine epidemic was worse than ever. For law enforcement, this was a battle that should have been easy to win. Methamphetamine is different from cocaine and heroin—drugs that are distilled from plants in South America

Roller Coastering

The passage of the Comprehensive Methamphetamine Control Act in 1996 extended its restrictions to the transmission of ephedrine and similar chemicals by mail or courier to non-pharmaceutical individuals; this covered the sale of powdered pseudoephedrine, but not the sale of cold tablets. Sales of cold remedies accelerated. However, most of the purchases at the retail level were done in small amounts to avoid suspicion. Mexican nationals were often schooled in a technique called *roller-coastering*. One expert described the technique: "Individuals who pretended not to know each other arrived at a drugstore at about the same time and all bought the same thing—cold remedies containing pseudoephedrine—then hopped into a van, moved on to another drugstore and repeated the process" (Langton 2007, 102).

and Asia; the methamphetamine business is something else, in that it depended on the chemicals ephedrine or pseudoephedrine, the main ingredients of cough and cold remedies. With less than a dozen factories manufacturing most of the world's supply, if they could be shut down or better regulated, it would shut down the superlabs that make methamphetamine (Suo 2004).

The reality is that in the mid-1980s, methamphetamine trafficking was mostly the purview of California biker gangs, particularly Hells Angels. Within a decade, Mexican drug gangs would control most of the trade. By most accounts it is now America's biggest drug problem, thanks in no small part to lobbyists for the pharmaceutical companies. Some DEA agents had tried to convince Congress to pass legislation to regulate the drug's precursor chemicals—ephedrine and pseudoephedrine, legal drugs used for cold medicines and produced in fewer than a dozen factories worldwide. Despite attempts to convince the Reagan administration, the lobbyists for the drug industry had the final say in the legislation that was finally passed. The bill proposed to Congress required companies to keep records on the import and sale of the chemicals. However, the pharmaceutical industry needed pseudoephedrine and ephedrine to make their profitable cold remedies, a $3 billion industry. In a compromise, Congress ended up passing a watered-down bill that monitored the sale of these chemicals, but created an exemption for the selling of the chemicals in tablet form—a loophole that ensured a steady stream of profits to the drug companies. This new law sparked two major changes in the illegal methamphetamine market. First, dealers began to look overseas for their supply of ephedrine. The Mexican cartels were quick to recognize this emerging market and were able to duck American restrictions on the chemicals by importing it from legitimate companies in China, India, and Europe, and then smuggling it across the Mexico–United States border to the outlaw motorcycle gangs that had traditionally distributed methamphetamine. Second, the chemical companies began moving huge amounts of the drugs to the West Coast in the form of cold and cough medicine (pills). As one recent investigative reporter put it, "The Reagan administration had unwittingly helped accelerate a new epidemic" (quoted in Wallace-Wells 2007, 103).

Coyotes: Human Smuggling Mexican-Style

One Arizona Department of Public Safety detective compares human smuggling rings to organized crime syndicates, noting, "It's an illegal enterprise, a scheme. . . . It's not your poor immigrant being smuggled by another poor immigrant. It's an organization with significant structure and assets" (quoted in Wagner 2006). Human smuggling ranks just behind drugs and weapons smuggling as the world's most lucrative illegal trades. The *coyote* is the Mexican permutation of the Chinese Snakehead. Smugglers have participated in the illegal smuggling of immigrants, often desperate migrants and refugees from Central America and Mexico, into the southwestern United States for generations. In Arizona alone, this black market business was estimated to bring in between $1 billion and $2 billion annually (Wagner 2006). In 2005, Arizona authorities estimated that 1 million illegal immigrants passed through the state, with a daily rate approaching at least 3,000 to 4,000. In 2006, Phoenix-area investigators placed the number of coyotes in their region at more than 1,000. In earlier years, it was relatively easy for someone to cross the border into Arizona and Texas undetected, with the help of others for several hundred dollars; but during the late 1990s, conditions changed, as officials began to take notice and clamped down on illegal migration. This in turn drove prices up and attracted professional criminals to the business. Various operations became streamlined and professionalized— veritable crime syndicates adopting modern surveillance and communications systems.

Prospective immigrants are referred to as *goats, furniture,* and *pollo,* or "chicken." Costs have soared to between $1,200 and $2,500 to be guided across the border. These new organizations scared off or killed most of the small-time "mom-and-pop" smugglers.

Today's smuggler is much better armed than earlier incarnations, more likely to be armed with assault weapons than traditional pistols and knives. Such firepower is necessary both to intimidate recalcitrant clients and to protect their valuable cargo from bandits or *bajadores,* who would seek to kidnap the immigrants and hold them for ransom, with fees ranging up to $1,600 per *pollo* (Wagner 2006).

TABLE 11.1 Drug-Trafficking Organizations or Criminal Groups Operating in the United States

Region	Cocaine	Methamphetamine	Heroin	Marijuana	MDMA
Great Lakes	Mexican Colombian African American	Mexican Asian	Mexican Colombian Nigerian African American	Mexican Asian Middle Eastern African American Caucasian	African American Asian Caucasian
Florida/ Caribbean	Colombian Mexican Dominican Caribbean-based Venezuelan Haitian Puerto Rican Jamaican Bahamian Cuban Honduran Panamanian Nicaraguan Salvadoran Guatemalan Caucasian African American European Street Gangs	Caucasian Mexican	Colombian Dominican Caucasian Venezuelan Cuban Honduran Panamanian Nicaraguan Salvadoran Guatemalan Puerto Rican Street Gangs African American	Mexican Jamaican Colombian African American Caucasian Cuban Haitian Honduran Panamanian Nicaraguan Salvadoran Street Gangs	Israeli Caucasian Colombian Dominican African American Cuban Street Gangs
Mid-Atlantic	African American Caucasian Colombian Dominican Mexican Puerto Rican	Caucasian Hispanic Mexican	African American Asian Caucasian Colombian Dominican Mexican Puerto Rican West African	African American Asian Caucasian Cuban Colombian Dominican Mexican Puerto Rican	Asian Caucasian Dominican Israeli
New England	African American Caucasian Colombian Dominican Haitian Honduran Panamanian Nicaraguan Salvadoran Guatemalan Jamaican Mexican	Cambodian Chinese Laotian Vietnamese Caucasian Mexican Outlaw Motorcycle Gangs Puerto Rican	Cambodian Chinese Laotian Vietnamese Caucasian Colombian Dominican Haitian Honduran Panamanian Nicaraguan Salvadoran Guatemalan Mexican	African American Cambodian Chinese Laotian Vietnamese Caucasian Colombian Dominican Haitian Honduran Panamanian Nicaraguan Salvadoran	Cambodian Chinese Laotian Vietnamese Caucasian Outlaw Motorcycle Gangs

Region	Cocaine	Methamphetamine	Heroin	Marijuana	MDMA
New England	Outlaw Motorcycle Gangs Puerto Rican		Outlaw Motorcycle Gangs Puerto Rican	Guatemalan Jamaican Mexican Puerto Rican	
New York/ New Jersey	African American Caucasian Colombian Dominican Jamaican Mexican Puerto Rican Street Gangs	Caucasian Filipino Mexican	African American Asian Caucasian Colombian Dominican Mexican Pakistani Puerto Rican West African Nigerian Street Gangs	African American Asian Caucasian Colombian Dominican Jamaican Mexican Street Gangs	Caucasian Colombian Dominican Jamaican Mexican Street Gangs Vietnamese
Pacific	Mexican Caucasian Outlaw Motorcycle Gangs Vietnamese Samoan Tongan African American Street Gangs	Mexican Caucasian Outlaw Motorcycle Gangs African American Street Gangs	Mexican Caucasian Outlaw Motorcycle Gangs African American Street Gangs	Caucasian Mexican Vietnamese Indonesian Malaysian African American Street Gangs	Vietnamese Caucasian Outlaw Motorcycle Gangs Indonesian Malaysian African American Mexican
Southeast	Mexican African American	Mexican Caucasian African American Hispanic Asian Outlaw Motorcycle Gangs	African American Mexican Caucasian Street Gangs	Mexican African American Caucasian Asian	Vietnamese Mexican
Southwest	Mexican Colombian African American	Mexican Asian	Mexican Colombian	Mexican Jamaican Asian Caucasian	Asian
West Central	Caucasian Hispanic Mexican Street Gangs	Caucasian Hispanic Mexican Native American Outlaw Motorcycle Gangs Street Gangs	Asian Caucasian Hispanic Mexican Street Gangs	African American Caucasian Hispanic Mexican Vietnamese Outlaw Motorcycle Gangs Street Gangs	Asian Caucasian Vietnamese Street Gangs

National Drug Intelligence Center, *National Drug Threat Assessment,* 2007.

Today most of the smugglers are Mexican nationals, lacking legal residency credentials in the United States. What has become clear to investigators is that each smuggling ring has member responsible for specific duties. Some are recruiters, guides, drivers, drophouse managers, cooks, and guards; others are document specialists and money collectors. Insulating the leaders at the top is the propensity of these rings to operate in family networks, with the boss typically ensconced south of the border. Once undocumented immigrants arrive on America soil, they are usually taken to *drophouses* while the coyotes collect the cash, arrange for transportation, and fend off other smugglers who would steal migrant clients for ransom. If someone cannot come up with the money, women may be assaulted, children separated from parents, and immigrants even killed (Wagner 2006).

The typical coyote organization takes part in the entire operation, providing individuals on both sides of the border who make sure that the immigrants reach a specific destination. It remains a deadly business, not just between various smuggling groups, but between the immigrants and their supposed benefactors as well, who often retract their original agreements once in the United States and have it doubled. The only option is to pay. The payment system relies on fees being paid to the coyotes through the relatives and friends of the *pollos*. The Attorney General's Office claimed that 95% of coyote transactions are conducted in wire-transfer businesses, with more than half using fictitious Social Security cards. In 2001, the Arizona State Attorney's Office began requiring transaction data from money senders and receivers like Western Union and MoneyGram. In 2005, wire transfers to Arizona from several specific states totaled more than $50 million, compared to the amount of money sent from Arizona to these states. For example, Delaware customers sent 60 times more transfers than they received from Arizona; South Carolina, 38 times more; and New Jersey, 31 times more than was received (Wagner 2006).

Phoenix police blamed the 45% rise in homicides in 2003 and 41% increase in home invasions on *bajadores* and coyotes (Wagner 2006). In response, the police force launched Operation ICE Storm late that year, doubling agents in the Valley who were teamed with local police. In 18 months, they arrested 374 people and captured more than 8,000 immigrants and $7.4 million in cash; as a result, murders dropped 30%.

However, the more zealous law enforcement becomes, the more the profit; corrupt officials can demand more money and landlords raise their normal rents to smugglers. Virtually every human smuggling ring is supported by contacts in the legitimate community who are prepared to accept false identification while keeping records off the books. Coyotes are familiar with which businesses launder cash, who are the auto dealers and travel agents who will help with transportation for financial incentives, Department of Motor Vehicle workers willing to supply fake documents, and border inspectors who look the other way for the right price.

Today, the border is so heavily patrolled and potentially lethal that most immigrants feel they have little choice but to hire professional coyotes. One of most important aspects of this business is the use of extortion and bribery on both sides of the border, "prerequisites for setting up and maintaining human trafficking rings" (Nunez 2007). On top of the costs associated with corrupting local officials is the more onerous payments required by drug syndicates if the coyotes expect to operate in their regions. Dubbed *quotas,* these payments range from $5,000 to $15,000 a month.

In recent years, the *coyotaje* business has gone under a facelift, as increasingly more women have risen to the top of the smuggling operations. Testament to the new era is the fact that in 2006, more than 3,400 women were arrested for smuggling undocumented workers along southwestern American border. Some of the women coyotes have begun to branch out into drugs and weapons trafficking as well (Nunez 2007). Mexican coyotes have found it safer to smuggle immigrants through border crossings rather than more hazardous mountain or desert crossings. According to one female coyote who specializes in smuggling women and children in this manner, "It costs more, but it's safer. That's why they come to us. We don't mess around with walking for three lousy days in the desert" (Nunez 2007).

After weighing the risks and benefits of this lifestyle, prospective smugglers often select human smuggling over drugs and weapons, because penalties in the United States are for the most part lighter, ranging from a 1-year prison stint or probation to the steepest punishment, which can be a maximum of 10 years and up to a $250,000 (or both). As a result, potential immigrants are expected to cough up between $2,000 and $5,000 for the assistance of a professional coyote. Although interviews with female coyotes reveal a number of explanations for their growing participation in human smuggling—poverty, luxurious lifestyles, excitement, to support drug habits[9]—others suggest its "a lust for power [that drives] women to enter the U.S.–Mexico trafficking business" (quoted in Nunez 2007).

COLOMBIA

The World's Top Producer of Cocaine

Colombia had the "longest democratic history in Latin America" well into the 1990s (Fukumi 2003, 93). The same freedom that allowed the economy to flourish in the free market also set the stage for the evolution of that country's drug-trafficking organizations in the 1970s and 1980s. Despite its democratic tradition, the country has also been wracked by six interparty wars during the 1800s and two in the 20th century. Today, Colombia is considered the most violent nation in the Western Hemisphere. A combination of high unemployment and social factors such as the massive displacement of the rural population has resulted in a country where more than 50% of the people live below the poverty line (Hudson 2003). These conditions furnish a ready recruitment pool for organized crime groups.

As the home of the coca plant, Colombia is the source for most of the world's cocaine industry and the main exporter of the drug into the United States. Along with cocaine, Colombian traffickers also market heroin and counterfeit American dollars. Over several decades, Colombia's cocaine cartels terrorized the country, killing politicians, policemen, and journalists at will, even blowing up a passenger airline in flight, killing more than 100 passengers and crew.

Since the mid-1960s, guerrillas, paramilitary groups, and drug cartels have been in bloody conflict with each other, the government, or sometimes both at one time or another. Much of the warfare has been fueled by organized crime groups through "a variety of mutually beneficial support activities carried on with the other groups" (Hudson 2003, 155). This symbiosis led to an environment of interdependency between drug-trafficking syndicates and the guerrilla and paramilitary groups.

According to one 1983 CIA intelligence report, Colombian guerrillas and paramilitaries initially eschewed the narcotics trade, "except to condemn the corrupting influence of drugs on Colombian society" (Bowden 2001). However, over the following years they became increasingly active in the drug trade, typically by extorting protection money from the cartels for the purchase of weapons. It was during this formative era of the cocaine trade that Pablo Escobar and other traffickers began collaborating with the Colombian army against FARC, the ELN, and M-19. Like the organized crime groups, they were becoming the pragmatic guerrillas, and soon found that it would be more profitable to work with the drug cartels instead of against them. FARC and others made the transition from the protection rackets to making arrangements to guard the coca fields and processing labs. This often led the guerrillas in some regions to establish quotas, taxes, wages, and rules of their own for the workers, producers, and owners of the coca fields (Bowden 2001, 43).

Despite the decapitation of the vaunted Medillín and Cali organizations in the 1990s, drugs still roll out of Colombia thanks to left-wing FARC guerrillas and their right-wing opposition, the AUC "self-defense forces," and hundreds of other drug gangs. Paramilitaries and guerrillas control vast territories of coca crops, provide clandestine labs, and make the majority of their money from the drug trade. The remnants of the former cartels can be discerned today in a number of smaller organizations that have stepped in to fill the demands of the cocaine trade and gone on to establish relationships with international organized crime groups in order to distribute narcotics, purchase weaponry, and launder vast sums of money.

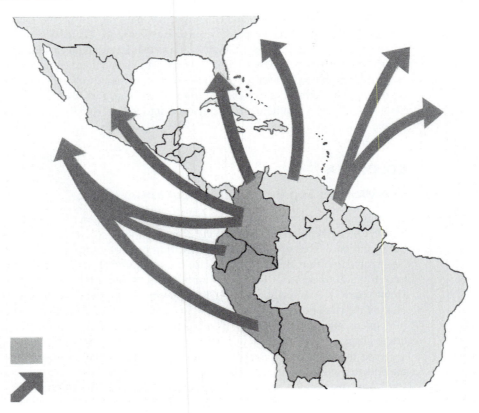

FIGURE 11.1   Map of South American Drug Routes
Source: Dorling Kindersley Media Library

Colombia, the sole South American country with coastlines on both the Caribbean and the Pacific Ocean, is perched at the northern tip of South America, a strategic corridor into Panama and the Caribbean—long part of the smuggling chain used to traffic drugs and contraband. Furthermore, the country's borders with its five neighboring nations are marked by sparsely populated jungle territory.

In recent years, Colombian traffickers have tried smuggling cocaine undersea, as they search for new ways to avoid authorities, particularly as anti-drug agents make record seizures on conventional vessels. Authorities claim to have apprehended at least eight submarines or semi-submersibles (craft that are mostly hidden underwater) since the mid-1990s. In 2000, Colombian officials uncovered a warehouse in the mountains outside Bogotá. Inside was a submarine under construction that when finished would have been 78 feet long, capable of traveling at depths of 300 feet (deep enough to avoid sonar), able to travel some 3,000 nautical miles at sea for almost 2 weeks. Most recently a submarine-like vessel was seized off the Pacific Coast of El Salvador loaded with 5.5 tons of cocaine valued at more than $350 million. What makes underwater smuggling so threatening is the fact that because submarines and semi-submersibles move more slowly, without leaving much of a wake, it makes them almost impossible to locate by radar and eyesight. By contrast, the traditional method uses boats to transport drugs to and from drop-off points on various coasts before heading back to "mother ships" farther out at sea, all easily traceable by sight and radar. As drug traffickers become savvier in their search for alternative transportation by sea, they have even experimented with attaching large containers to vessels with cables. These are typically filled with cocaine and towed like fishing lures undersea to the ship's destination. To avoid law enforcement, traffickers can cut the line when agents move in (Otis 2007).

What Is the Medellín Cartel?

Questioned in an interview with the television show *Frontline*, former Medellín member Juan David Ochoa was asked, "What does that mean—the 'Medellín cartel'?" he responded, "That's a name given by the authorities or the press, because in itself, there was no group or association that was 'the cartel of Medellín.' . . . I never heard any of us say 'the cartel of Medellín' or 'the cartel of Cali.'"

In September 2007, as the United States remained tightly focused on the "War on Terror," Colombia's Vice President Francisco Santos warned that its attention should be refocused on the spreading influence of the Latin American drug cartels. Santos had firsthand experience with the sway of the cartels, having been kidnapped in 1990 by cocaine drug lord Pablo Escobar. By most accounts, as 2007 came to an end, drug cartels were looking to Peru, Bolivia, and other countries to expand coca crops.

Plan Colombia

In the late 1990s, the United States and Colombia launched "Plan Colombia," a joint effort to diminish the output of coca. Although it has been effective in its campaign against the various paramilitary and guerrilla warlords, coca production increased by 16% in 2007, the highest rise since 2001. Most of the cultivation increase in the Andes comes from Colombia. As one journalist put it, "Attacking the drug supply is a job for Sisyphus" (*Economist* June 21, 2008, 50).

The Medellín Organization, aka "Cartel"

***PLANO* OR *PLATO*, "SILVER OR LEAD," "CASH OR DEATH"**   Centered in Medellín, Colombia, this organization was formed by the Ochoa family, Pablo Escobar, Carlos Lehder-Rivas, and José Gonzalo Rodríguez Gacha. According to several authorities the consolidation of this group in the mid-1980s was Latin America's "first relevant experience of politicizing organized crime" (Rubio and Ortiz 2005, 430; Gugliotta and Leen 1989). Each figure added a different dimension to the alliance. For example, Gacha, known as "The Mexican" for his love of everything Mexican, hired Israeli counterterrorism specialists to train the cartel's paramilitary personnel and hitmen, and perhaps even to make bombs. He was responsible for killing informers and competitors and hiring local farmers to grow coca plants. He could be depended on to arrange for FARC protection of the narcotics operations and laboratories. By most accounts, he headed the organization's West Coast distribution, purchased airstrips, and was the boss of the Bogotá operations. In 1989, Gacha was killed by Colombian police during a raid on his ranch in Tolu. The Ochoas, however, were skilled distributors, who in the late 1980s set up thousands of Colombians in cells that were crucial to distributing cocaine to key markets in the United States and Europe. Medellín trafficker Carlos Lehder, above all, was considered one of the pioneers of the cocaine trade. He purchased the small island of Norman's Cay in the Bahamas as a "sort of bridge for the trafficking of drugs" (*Frontline,* "Drug Wars," 5). Lehder was captured in 1987 and extradited to the United States, where he was convicted and sentenced to 135 years in prison. However, 5 years later he agreed to incriminate Panamanian president Manuel Noriega, and his sentence was reduced to 55 years. Following Lehder's arrest, Pablo Escobar took the reins.

More recently, the Medellín organization, or *La Compañia* ("the company"), as some called it, has been compared to a "loose federation of underground corporations"; others compare it to a cartel. Although this is still a matter of debate, it had many but not all of the characteristics of a cartel. It was well-structured and highly organized, with specialized units responsible for obtaining raw materials for the production of cocaine, and groups responsible for security and transportation.

The George H.W. Bush administration became obsessed with Escobar, who they blamed for "industrializing the cocaine trade" in the 1980s. During the 1970s, the cocaine business was the purview of individual operators who flew small planes loaded with the drug, or used "mules" to smuggle small batches through customs. This changed in 1981, when a Marxist guerrilla organization made the fatal mistake of kidnapping the sister of a major drug lord. Kidnapping for ransom to finance revolutions and the like has a long tradition in Latin America that continues to this day. As one observer put it, "These narcotraffickers were not your ordinary capitalists" (Gray 1998, 120). Rather than pay a ransom, more than 200 organizations banded together to create a new organization that they called *Muerto a Secuestradores*, or "Death to Kidnappers." Each gang agreed to put 10 men at its disposal. In the next 3 months, the 2,000 man hit-team waged war on the Marxists, killing anyone they suspected of collaborating with them, including young children, women, union organizers, and guerrilla sympathizers tied to the university. If they couldn't get to the kidnappers, then a relative or friends would do nicely instead. Soon, announcements were handed out and air-dropped throughout the region proclaiming the new strategy. In February 1982, the hostage was safely returned without any money being exchanged.

The defeat of an entrenched guerrilla army by a consortium of drug traffickers emboldened Escobar, and convinced him—at least for the time being—it would be worth transcending some of the old rivalries with other drug traffickers. In 1982, Escobar joined the Ochoa Family of Medellín and Gonzalo Rodríguez Gacha of Bogotá and inaugurated the Medellín & Compañía syndicate. In the beginning, Gacha was responsible for the raw material in Peru, whereas the Ochoas were responsible for transportation, distribution, and money laundering. Escobar was tasked with reorganizing the manufacturing process. One example of his ingenuity was revealed by the army raid on the laboratory of Tranquillandia, where they uncovered an incredible complex of buildings deep in the jungle offering air-conditioned offices for management, dormitories, recreational facilities, a pilot's lounge, 6 landing strips with hangars, maintenance facilities, and 14 laboratories capable of processing 20 tons of cocaine a month. The raid revealed something much more distressing—the ability of Escobar to infiltrate the highest levels of government. Although only a handful of top officials knew of the raid in advance, by the time it went down, there was not a soul at the base (Gray 1998).

In 1989, Escobar set his sights on an incorruptible candidate for president, Carlos Galán. Most polls indicated he would win the election. Despite extensive security, Galán was gunned down in front of 10,000 supporters during a rally in Bogotá. This assassination finally galvanized the government to go full bore after the drug traffickers. Escobar and his lieutenants were out of the country on vacation when the Colombian army was ordered to go after all of their assets. In the process, they confiscated ranches, private islands, vintage cars, and racehorses along with the rest of the ostentation paid for in cocaine and bullets. Escobar "picked up the gauntlet" and issued a press release, stating, "Now the fight is with blood," and it was signed by "The Extraditables."[10] For the next several weeks, the country was rocked with bombings and bank robberies on a daily basis, with traffickers even hunting down the wives and children of politicians and police not already in their pockets. In February 1989, the mayor of Medellín was killed after an anti-drug rally. The government had its successes as well in 1989, cornering and killing Gacha in a gun battle near the coastal town of Tula, along with his teenage son and more than a dozen bodyguards. In addition, when Panama's Manuel Noriega was captured 5 days later, this finally got the attention of drug kingpins—they too could be extradited to America. The leaders of the Medellín organization soon reached out to make a deal with Colombia's new president, César Gaviria. His offer—turn themselves in and they will be tried in Colombia, not the United States, in effect terminating the current extradition treaty.

Escobar waited to make a better deal for 6 months. Gaviria agreed to all of his demands in 1991, including his request to be "imprisoned" in a specially constructed prison according

Interview with Juan David Ochoa, Principal Member of the Medellín Cartel[11]

Interviewer: Can you describe the details that make the business work? You had distributors on one end, and you had producers. . . .

Ochoa: The business worked in the following way. The supply people would bring it initially from Peru and Bolivia, and they would process it in labs here in Colombia. From there, you would buy the cocaine and you would contract it with someone to send it to the United States. Maybe it was through air or perhaps some maritime way, and there someone would receive it. The agent would be in charge of sending it to other clients, from California, from New York, from different states. The person in the United States would be in charge of receiving the money and sending it back to Colombia. That's the way it would work.

Interviewer: What part of the business did you own outright, and what part did you have to contract with other for?

Ochoa: I had several ways of doing this. One way was to buy the cocaine and to send it the way I explained, and my partner would sell it there. The other way would be to have your own lab where you could process it. You'd have your own way of transporting it, a plane or a boat or something like that. You send it at your own cost. Another way, you'd end up having to subcontract with other people to do the different stages, like processing, transport, and the transfer of sales to the person that you had contracted in the United States.

Adapted from *Frontline*, "Drug Wars," p. 2.

to his specifications, which the media wasted no time in dubbing "Club Medellín." This agreement soon backfired on both parties when it was revealed that Escobar continued to control his smuggling organizations (as well as conduct executions) from the safe confines of his fortress. Gaviria had no choice but to act; Escobar was apparently tipped off, and vanished into the jungle.

Interview with Carlos Toro[12]: Getting the Drugs to Market in the United States

Toro

We had to find alternative ways of doing it, which is a small private aircraft that will bring 1,000 kilos at a time. And when you leave out of Colombia on, let's say, a King Air or 640, you can only go so far when you have 1,000 keys of cocaine, a pilot, a copilot, and maybe another man with weapons trying to save the load. That plane would be able to fly as far as somewhere in the Caribbean, air drop the load to a waiting boat, and go and refuel somewhere. . . . Once we get it to the island on the Bahamas (Norman's Key), we're home pretty much . . . the flight to the American coast is not very long. . . . The drugs would land at an airstrip either at Atlanta, in Georgia, or in Florida. From there we would transport the drugs. There were many ways of doing it, and there were many plans that we executed at different times, depending on how we were prepared, and what we expected and anticipated—from RVs, to just private automobiles in several shipments. . . . The drugs went to a stash house. We had a house where the drugs were welcome. We would take the load, and the load comes with a shipping manifesto, just like any other shipping company. We had a bill of lading. And we had the name of the parties that were the recipients of that cocaine—that would be the distributors. And that all came coded. No specific names. But we knew who they were, because we knew the codes. . . . Then we'll call someone and say, "The shipment is here." He'll tell us where to bring it. . . . so we'll do the same thing we did with exchanging the money. We'll bring a vehicle with 100 kilos, and exchange automobiles. And this man will take his load to California or New York. . . .

Adapted from *Frontline*, "Drug Wars," pp. 7–8.

Pablo Emilio Escobar-Gaviria (1949–1993)

Formerly a bit player in the cocaine trade, by the end of the 1980s, Colombia became the premier global source of cocaine. An admirer of Al Capone,[13] Escobar eventually personified the drug trade, achieving an almost cult-like status at home and abroad. Capone, who had set up soup kitchens for the unemployed in Depression-era Chicago, had nothing on his Colombian incarnation. Escobar built more public housing in Medellín than the government; put up hundreds of two-bedroom cement-block houses, new schools, sewers, streetlights, clinics, sports plazas, and planted 50,000 trees in the barrios. He saved the best for himself—at the height of his power; he had 16 houses in Medellín and a country house capable of sleeping 100, as well as his own 7,000-acre spread that boasted the country's finest zoo, replete with camels, lions, giraffes, bison, llamas, and a kangaroo that could play soccer (Gray 1998, 119).

This former stealer of grave tombstones[14] and automobiles became a master of subterfuge. His ingenious escapades included concealing a landing strip under mobile houses on wheels; residents pushed them aside for a plane to land and unload, and then moved the mobile homes back into place on departure. Escobar cultivated his own personal "Murder, Inc.," and pioneered new methods of killing, such as putting assassins on the back of motorcycles, "well-suited to snarled Bogotá traffic" (Naim 2005, 74).

Escobar's emergence was also important to the developing "War on Drugs" during the Bush Administration of the late 1980s by putting a human face on the formerly anonymous enemy, and led to his demise in 1993. After the downfall of the Medellín and Cali organizations, the balance of power in the cocaine trade shifted. At the local level, paramilitary movements took over, whereas the part of business with the highest added value—moving product into the United States—shifted into Mexico.

During the 1980s and early 1990s, Escobar was one of the world's preeminent drug traffickers. The former car thief and small-time hood emerged as one of the most powerful crime figures of the late 20th century. In 1989, *Forbes* magazine even reported he was the world's seventh richest man (his partners were not far behind). Escobar's rise to the head of the Medellín cartel was matched by his god-like status among the poor and marginalized, a significant part of Colombia's population. In 1983, they elected him to congress, representing his home state of Antiquia. However, the following year he began his slide to fugitive status when the United States demanded his extradition for trial on drug-trafficking charges. The Colombian government had begun extraditing lower-level dealers, but Escobar was another story, being capable of declaring war on his own government. In the end, Escobar's decision to wage an all-out war against the Colombian state led to his death and the end of the Medellín cartel. Some estimates suggest that Escobar's war against Colombia left 1,000 judges and officials dead. Escobar engineered the murders of several presidential candidates who favored his extradition, and he was probably behind the takeover of Bogotá's Palace of Justice in 1986 that left 11 Supreme Court justices[15] dead, along with 79 others. He upped the ante exponentially in 1989, when he masterminded the bombing of an Avianca passenger plane, killing all 110 passengers, as well as the killing of presidential candidate Galán later that year. It was around this time that the United States became involved, sending financial support to the Colombian government to cover the costs of the manhunt for Escobar, who had become "public enemy number one in the world" (Bowden 2001).

In 1991, Escobar surrendered after an agreement was reached in which he would be jailed in a facility of his own making, replete with nightclub, satellite television, gourmet food, and women, all the while running the drug network and moving tons of cocaine into the United States and ordering the deaths of anyone who got in his way. However, when word reached Escobar in 1992 that he was to be repatriated to a military prison, Escobar walked away from his "jail," leading to a massive manhunt by both Colombian and American agents. Soon the agencies of legal law enforcement were joined by a vigilante group that became known as LOS PEPES, an acronym for "People Persecuted by Pablo Escobar." This group ratcheted up the pressure on Escobar. So as Escobar waged his war of terror on the Colombian government in an attempt to get a favorable deal, LOS PEPES

Sicarios

Sicarios refers to the hired killers employed by the drug cartels to carry out assassinations and guerrilla-style warfare. They are typically young men, who despite their youth are well trained and professional. At the height of its drug trade, Medellín was home to 6,000 *sicarios* between the ages of 12 and 20 who worked for 500 different smuggling groups. One report indicates the Medellín cartel paid for more than 600 killings between 1989 and 1991 at an average of $13 per victim (Fukumi 2003).

vowed that every time an innocent person was victimized, they would strike back at Escobar's family and friends. For many observers, LOS PEPES seemed too perfect. Many suspected that the competing Cali cartel had the most to gain in the hunt for Pablo Escobar. Even his biographer, Mark Bowden, suggested that LOS PEPES was most probably composed of members of competing drug gangs and financial backers of the Cali cartel, and that they were helped along by information shared by the Colombian National Police, who had lost hundreds of members to Escobar gunmen in the early 1990s. With a large reward on his head and a concerted hunt by U.S. and Colombian agents, he was able to stay in one place for only a few hours. Ever the family man, he called his family on December 1, 1993, allowing authorities to trace the call to his position. He was finally located and killed in a shootout the following day (Bowden 2001).

THE CALI ORGANIZATION, AKA "CARTEL"

The Cali organization was founded in the 1970s by brothers Gilberto and Miguel Angel Rodriquez-Orejuela, José Santa Cruz Londono (1942–1996), and several others. Also known as "the Chess Player," Gilberto, the older brother, postured as a legitimate businessman. The brothers were businessmen first and foremost. Gilberto is a former banker who had once run a chain of drugstores and bought influence at an unprecedented rate. His extraordinary business acumen together with his younger brother's handling of daily operations and business affairs allowed the Cali cartel to become the preeminent of the Colombian cocaine cartels after the death of Escobar. Miguel, often referred to as "the Master," micromanaged each aspect of the drug trade. As the "Transportation Specialist," he oversaw production, transportation, wholesale distribution, and money laundering.

Initially a small criminal syndicate located 200 miles south of Medellín, the early Cali organization was focused on kidnapping and counterfeiting, but gradually expanded into smuggling cocaine base from Peru and Bolivia to Colombia to be converted into cocaine. In its heyday, the Cali cartel was the most powerful criminal syndicate in Colombia. For almost 15 years it flourished with relative impunity, controlling most of Cali's business leaders and politicians. It has been estimated that at one time it was responsible for 80% of the world's cocaine supply, with estimated earnings approaching $7 billion. It was distinct from the Medellín cartel in a number of ways; first, it was never as violent as its counterpart, and second, it was run different structurally. Whereas the competing Medellín cartel resorted to violence and brutality, in its daily activities, the Cali cartel earned a well-deserved reputation for towing a more civil line by relying more on bribery and cunning. By most accounts, its relationship with government officials went all the way to the top.

At its zenith, the Cali organization controlled some of the region's airports, taxi systems, and phone companies and ran a global enterprise through a sophisticated network with the help of faxes, pagers, computers, and the requisite violence. Run similar to a commercial franchise chain, the cartel was created around a cell-like structure, with each cell consisting of 6 to 10 trusted subordinates. In addition, this structure served to better insulate the drug lords from the workers.

For the number three man in the Cali cartel, Santacruz-Londono kept a remarkably low profile, all the while earning the respect of his underlings. He was among a number of drug kingpins who underwent plastic surgery on several occasions, earning the moniker *Mil Rostros* or "Many Faces." This was due in no small part to his reputation for violence and his ability to create enemies. He was closely involved in intelligence gathering. Over a 20-year period, he accumulated billions of dollars. Arrested in 1995, he escaped 6 months later. He was killed in a shootout with the Colombian National Police on March 5, 1996.

The DEA estimated that in the mid-1990s the brothers were worth more than $200 billion after a decade of drug trafficking, and that they were clearing almost $8 billion a year. However, once the Medellín cartel was dismantled, the American government together with the Colombians targeted the brothers. Gilberto was arrested in 1995, and his brother and the remaining principals the following year. The Cali cartel was dismantled in the mid-1990s and other, smaller groups have taken over as the market became more fragmented.

Revolutionary Armed Forces of Colombia (FARC)

Narcoterrorism (see Chapter 13 for more on terrorism), a term coined by Peru's President Belaude Terry in 1983 to describe attacks on anti-narcotics investigators, was first documented in Latin America. There is a lack of consensus over its actual meaning today. What is probably more accepted is that it refers to terrorism that is linked to the production of illegal drugs, either through the use of drug profits to fund political violence or the use of violence and terror to protect and preserve illegal drug production (Kushner 2003, 251). Today, the Revolutionary Armed Forces of Colombia (FARC) exemplifies its adoption as a tactic. In the 1970s, coca became the major cash crop for many Colombian peasants at the same time the FARC was entering the picture. These guerrillas were intent on fomenting a Marxist revolution and driving government forces from their territory. Once in control of remote areas, they were able to become the de facto government authority in the region, and also entered the drug-trafficking business. It began by exacting a "tax"—extortion payments—from all landowners in the area, whether they were coca or coffee growers. Once they realized that revenues were much higher from coca, traffickers made the transition from taxing to offering protection to coca markets, labs, and airstrips from government attack. As Kushner puts it, "For the narcoguerrilla, the illegal nature of both the drug trade and the rebellion were complementary; untrammeled by national or international law, guerrillas can openly offer traffickers their services" (2003, 252).

FARC continues to be a strong and troubling presence in Latin America. No longer solely an "Andean insurgency," it now threatens the regional security from Argentina to Mexico. At the end of 2006, Colombian officials reluctantly admitted that FARC had established a presence in Peru's northern borderland regions. Both countries share a 1,010-mile border. One regional leader accuses FARC of implementing a de facto draft, noting, "The young people dedicated to the trafficking of drugs and the illegal extraction of wood are drafted . . . they tattoo them on the shoulder in such a way that they can never leave the guerrillas" (Logan and Morse 2006, 4). What was once a regional problem has begun to spill over into neighboring countries as well. Besides supplying Mexican drug syndicates with cocaine, FARC has made great strides in creating an integral transshipment point in Venezuela. In addition, Peru and Ecuador have become welcoming places of retreat, recruitment, and coca cultivation (Logan and Morse 2006).

FARC has solidified its association with Mexican syndicates over the past few years after the Colombian government tightened its border controls and the traditional Pacific port of Buenaventura was lost to paramilitary trafficking organizations. One expert suggested, "the transition that led to FARC's downstream integration in Mexico came about as conditions for trafficking directly out of Colombia worsened" (Logan and Morse 2006, 14).

Venezuela

Its remote and porous 2,200 kilometer border with Colombia has facilitated the growth of Colombia's cocaine and heroin traffickers. Tons of drugs are smuggled across the border through

Black Market Peso Exchange (BMPE)

Recently, a peso broker in Colombia arranged for other colleagues to collect cash in New York and then turn it over to another who would use it to purchase truck parts from a junk yard in Lindenhurst, New York (which he owned). The parts were then shipped to Venezuela and Colombia and resold for pesos (Neumeister 2006). This is the gist of the Black Market Peso Exchange (BMPE).

In the early days of the cocaine trade, cash was flown back to Colombia in the very same planes that transported cocaine. On its return, it was easily converted into pesos at friendly banking institutions or simply held until needed. In the 1980s, U.S. cocaine distributors were likely to transport huge amounts of cash into U.S. banks. Others flew cash to offshore banking havens in the Bahamas, Aruba, the Caymans, and the British Virgin Islands, where it was deposited. Although this method is still used, enforcement at airports and seaports have made it increasingly risky. One IRS agent in South Florida reported in the early 1980s, "We had twelve individuals in Miami who were depositing $250 million or more annually into non-interest bearing checking accounts" (Zill and Bergman 2008). The U.S. government did not pass its first money-laundering laws and suspicious transaction reporting requirements until the early 1970s; however, by most accounts these were ignored by banks until much later. By the 1980s, IRS agents had begun to catch on to the money side of the drug business and began clamping down on banks that did not initially comply. As a result, drug dealers found ways around the legitimate banking protocol.

Colombian drug lords rarely venture from their safe havens in Colombia, preferring the security of places like Medellín and Cali. Nevertheless, they require pesos for their extravagancies and day-to-day costs. More important, they need to pay off corrupt politicians and support the costs of producing and smuggling cocaine. Huge amounts of cash are collected on the streets of America, dollars that must be converted into pesos. Due to Colombia's restrictive currency controls and tax laws, a thriving black market used to exchange currency has existed for Colombian businessmen for many years. Colombian drug lords have infiltrated the BMPE to launder their drug money.

The Black Market Peso Exchange (BMPE) is a trade-based money-laundering scheme that has become "the largest money laundering system in the Western Hemisphere" (Office of Public Affairs, May 15, 2000). By all accounts, it is considered one of the most successful laundering methods ever devised (Zill and Bergman 2008). As far back as 2000, it was estimated that this system was used to launder more than $5 billion annually. This scheme is used predominantly by Colombian drug networks and Colombian importers to avoid paying Colombian tariffs and taxes on smuggled commodities. Assisting these two groups are peso brokers who help complete the sometimes multimillion-dollar transactions beyond the reach of Colombia's legitimate financial system.

1. The process begins with the shipment of drugs into the United States.
2. The drugs are then sold, resulting in large volumes of U.S. currency.
3. In order to get the money back into Colombia, the cartel sells the U.S. currency to the Colombian BMPE broker's agent in the United States.
4. On delivery of dollars to a U.S.-based agent of the peso broker, the peso broker in Colombia deposits an agreed-on equivalent in Colombian pesos into the cartel's account in Colombia.
5. The Colombian broker and his agent now assume the risk for introducing drug dollars into the U.S. banking system, usually through covert transactions.
6. The Colombian BMPE broker now has a pool of laundered funds in U.S. dollars to sell Colombian importers, who use the dollars to purchase goods, either from the United States or other markets; these are then smuggled into Colombia and sold on the black market.
7. Finally, these goods are smuggled into Colombia and sold on the black market.

(Office of Public Affairs, May 15, 2000)

Venezuela every year using a variety of routes that include the Pan-American Highway, the Orinoco River, the Guajira Peninsula, and hundreds of remote airstrips. According to counter-drug officials in 2007, a third of Colombia's cocaine passes through Venezuela each year, twice the amount as from the 1990s (Forero 2007). Organized crime groups have found it safer and more profitable to buy their heroin and cocaine from the Colombians than to produce it themselves. As a result, Venezuelan syndicates have begun setting up their own operations to transport and then distribute the drugs in foreign markets. Bearing testament to this new strategy has been the arrest of Venezuelan traffickers in Holland, Spain, Ghana, and other countries (U.S. Department of State 2006). Although Venezuela has not been involved in the cultivation of coca leaves, located on South America's northern fringe, along with Ecuador and Central America, Venezuela has long been a transit point for neighboring Colombia's cocaine trade. Among the new trends has been an increasing alliance between the drug kingpins and Venezuelan military officers who are using their country as a transit point for smuggling cocaine into the United States and Europe. What has made matters worse is the poor relations between the United States and Venezuela during the Hugo Chávez era.

Venezuela continues to be an influential stop for drugs leaving Colombia. What increased its influence beginning in 2005 is the rampant corruption in the highest levels of policing and a weak judiciary. More recently, intelligence sources revealed a number FARC training camps inside Venezuela. In 2004, DEA agents accused National Guard members of corruption and involvement in the drug trade. Dubbed the "Sun Cartel," it is named after the Venezuelan National Guard insignia of the rank of general, the sun. Separated from Colombia by a porous 1,367 border, some smugglers refer to it as "the gateway to heaven" due to the absence of border security. Further augmenting the increasing criminal activity is America's poor relationship with the Hugo Chávez government. Previously, Venezuela was considered a minor stop on cocaine routes; it is now recognized as the

---

The Triborder Region (TBA)

This border frontier between Argentina, Brazil, and Paraguay has received recent attention due to the activities of Islamic terrorist organizations in a region with Latin America's largest concentration of Muslims (see Chapter 13, Terrorism). However, it has long been a haven for organized crime groups and an active corridor for the smuggling of weapons, drugs, and now counterfeit goods. In 2000, it was estimated that some $12 billion was being laundered each year. Porous borders have made it relatively easy to transport stolen cars from Brazil and Argentina into Paraguay via the TBA.

Besides the indigenous groups, there is an increasing presence of foreign crime organizations from Chile, Colombia, Corsica, Ghana, Italy, Ivory Coast, Japan, Korea, Lebanon, Libya, and Taiwan—a melting pot of sorts for syndicated crime. Many of them have been tied to corrupt Paraguayan business leaders, politicians, and military officers (Hudson 2003, 173). Thanks to widespread corruption in the criminal justice system, open or poorly guarded borders, human rights abuses, and weak money-laundering laws, it has proved an attractive haven for criminal enterprises.

Most of the criminal activity is centered in three closely connected population centers at Puerto Iguazu, Argentina; Foz de Iguaçu, Brazil; and Ciudad del Este, Paraguay. Testament to the region's diversity was a 2001 census in Foz de Iguaçu, which determined there were 65 different nationalities living there. This trend began almost a decade earlier. In 1994, for example, Ciudad del Este recorded 7,000 Lebanese, 4,000 Koreans, and 6,500 Chinese residents. In the 1990s, groups from mainland China became more prominent, including the Fuk Ching, Big Circle Boys, Flying Dragons, and Tai Chen. Chinese syndicates apparently focus most of their attention on the large legitimate Chinese business community, who they charge for protection, force to purchase certain imports from them, or tax containers imported by the merchants from China. A 2002 investigation revealed that five Chinese mafias operating in São Paulo, Brazil, earned $1.6 billion from extortion and protection rackets from Chinese businessmen. One expert described these cities as "ideal for the operation of terrorist or criminal groups" (Hudson 2003, 175). Beginning in the 1970s, at attempt was made to profit from the tourist industry at Iguazu Falls by establishing a free-trade zone in the boomtown of Ciudad del Este. It soon earned a reputation as a lawless center "dominated by the illegal acts of mafias and Islamic terrorist groups" (Hudson 2003, 174).

primary country used by the FARC and other groups to export South American cocaine (Logan and Morse 2006, 13).

Argentina

Although it is not considered a major drug-producing nation, Argentina serves as a valuable transit country for the trafficking of cocaine from Bolivia, Peru, and Colombia. Most of the product is destined for European destinations. Argentina is also considered a valuable stop on the route for Colombian heroin being sent to the United States, especially New York. The country has also earned a reputation as a source for precursor chemicals, thanks to the availability of advanced chemical production facilities. Cocaine-related seizures by Argentine authorities have risen each year since 2004 (U.S. Department of State 2006). More recently, international drug-trafficking organizations have become more active in the trafficking of children, human smuggling, the car theft business, insider trading, fraud, and tax evasion as organized crime becomes an increasing concern for law enforcement (Hudson 2003).

Bolivia

Bolivian farmers have grown coca leaf for traditional use for centuries. By law, the government allows 12,000 hectares of legal coca cultivation to supply the legitimate market. Beginning in the mid-1990s, Bolivia was a principal supplier of cocaine to the world market. However, in the late 1990s, the administration of President Banzer (1997–2001) oversaw the reduction of cocaine production by nearly three fourths (from 255 to 70 metric tons). Since 2001, Bolivian coca cultivation increased each year. Although the government vigorously pursued various eradication programs and is committed to counternarcotics policies, it has been hamstrung due to the recurring political challenges to democratic governance. From 2000 to 2006, Bolivia had five different presidents (U.S. Department of State 2006).

Brazil

Today, Brazil is a major transfer country for illegal drugs destined for Europe and, to a lesser degree, the United States. Although it is not considered an important drug-producing country, it remains a channel for cocaine base and related products to be transported to Europe, the Middle East, and Brazilian cities, as well as heroin being moved to the United States and Europe. In recent years, drug traffickers have avoided flying over Brazilian territory due to its shootdown law, which allows the Brazilian Air Force to use lethal force in the interdiction of suspected aircraft. Meanwhile, cocaine and marijuana are smuggled into Brazil via Paraguay and Bolivia by organized crime syndicates located in Sáo Paulo and Rio de Janeiro. Brazilian syndicates traffic the contraband throughout the country. It is believed that proceeds from this enterprise finance the purchase of weapons for the gangs that rule slums, or *favelas*, of the major urban centers (U.S. Department of State 2006). According to Hudson, more than half of the business software and CDs sold in the country are counterfeit, perhaps 40% of the cigarettes consumed are purchased on the black market, and one fifth of the drugs on sale in pharmacies were manufactured illegally (2003, 190).

What started out as a prison soccer team in 1993 has morphed into one of Latin America's largest criminal organizations. The First Capital Command (PCC) is considered Brazil's leading organized crime group. With an army of 140,000 men at its disposal, it expanded its activities and has now even set its sights on the political system. Accounts have surfaced of members taking competitive exams for civil service positions that they hope can lead to running as candidates in future elections (Manrique 2006). Founded inside Sáo Paulo's sprawling Taubate Penitentiary, it spread throughout the country's scandalously brutal and corrupt correctional system. Like other prison gangs around the world, this gang was created for self-defense, but soon gravitated to economic profit. It is probably "the largest gang in the Western Hemisphere" (Insideprison.com, 2006). The gang moved beyond prison walls and into São Paulo's seething slums, running both with brutal efficiency. They are also capable of funding smaller crime groups to commit robberies for a hefty profit. Like other prison gangs around the world, it adopted its own 16-point constitution that declares war on the "penal establishment." It has now set its sights much higher, eyeing a place in the political system. Following in the footsteps of a number of other crime groups, the PCC has begun to portray itself as a political party rather than a gang, with members referring to each other as "brothers." One prison lawyer has even suggested that it "doesn't just want to challenge the government's power. It wants to take that power" (quoted in Insideprison.com 2006).

Recent evidence points to the fact that the PCC developed a number of alliances with other gangs to keep out competition and created a crime monopoly. *Reuter's News* (quoted in Insideprison.com, "First Command," 2008) noted that the PCC uses discipline, technology, and business alliances to monopolize its control over organized crime in Brazil. The gang flourishes on both sides of the walls, thanks to the assistance of corrupt correctional officers who provide members with weapons and cell phones—strategic tools for any major prison gang. Each gang member "contributes" a $22–$27 (USD) monthly fee, which gives them access to legal help and food for the inmates and their families. However, once they are freed, they pay 10 times that amount, up to about $230. These fees not only are used to purchase weapons and drugs, but also to finance the bail for other members. Anyone wishing to join the PCC must be formally introduced to the organization by current members.

More recently, Brazil has become world's second leading destination (United States is number one) for cocaine. As a result, cocaine that formerly would have been transshipped from the country is now staying there to feed the increased demand for the popular drug. The PCC used this opportunity to grow even stronger through its control of much of the drug trade (Dermota 2007, 25).

Much of the country's crime activity takes place in the capital city of São Paulo. With more than 20 million inhabitants, it is among the world's largest cities. Crime has become so widespread that business executives are afraid to travel by car. As a consequence, the city is home to more heliports than New York City. São Paulo is also the world's largest purchaser of armored cars for civilian use.

In 1993, the city of Rio de Janeiro recognized the existence of a national organized crime syndicate, describing it as

- Complex and hierarchical
- Economically motivated
- Extending across the national territory
- Following an entrepreneurial type program
- Manages large volume of resources
- Maintains close relationships with national political powers
- Utilizes corruption and violent methods to maintain hegemonic power
- Acts with the objective of absorbing the constitutional state into the criminal state (Frossard, 2007, 182)

Like the Sicilian mafia, this organization is run by a *cupola*, made up of the most intimidating individuals who also wield the most power. It also has an armed wing of enforcers who carry out the orders of the cupola and enforce an unwritten code of honor. Since the mid-1960s, the leaders have become better known as the "bankers of the animal game," a reference to their participation in the illegal lottery known as *jogo dos bichos*. In 1993, this game was the only one that fell under the legal definition for *organized crime*.[16]

What Is *Jogo dos bichos?*

Jogo dos bichos is an illegal lottery that originated in 1886 with the opening of Rio de Janeiro's first zoo. In order to attract plenty of visitors, it was decided that admission tickets would be numbered, with each one corresponding to a particular animal. When the day was done, a ticket was drawn, and whoever held the winning numbered ticket won a prize. From this came the idea to create the "Animal Game," or *jogo dos bichos*. It was not long before booking agents were selling tickets outside the zoo, inaugurating the illegal lottery. By the 20th century, the game had become popular throughout Brazil thanks to an organization of booking agents, dealers, and players. Despite periods of repression, the game has continued into the 21st century. Many of the game's characteristics are almost unchanged from the original version. Players continue to exchange whatever money they decide to bet for an opportunity to play several versions of the game. The lottery uses a list of 25 animals, with each one corresponding to either a number or set of numbers. What has changed is the way the numbers are selected. In the 1890s, it was considered a side bet to the legal lottery. By the 20th century, it was disassociated with the legal lottery, and instead bakers or *banquieros* operate a secret drawing of the winner each day.

During the game's early years, each individual involved in the illegal lottery was known as a *bichiero*, responsible for taking numbers and paying winners. However, the success of the early gambling groups led to increased competition and accompanying bloodshed. By 1941, the violence had become so pronounced that the government issued a new penal violation that ruled the game was a crime and punishable with a fine and a prison sentence of up to 4 months. By the end of the 1940s, the *bichiero* had devolved into more of a paid worker in the organization. The more powerful members became "the Bankers." They did not take bets on the games, but were responsible for managing the prize money of the game's organizers.

Like the illegal policy and numbers rackets in certain parts of the United States, this game has taken its place as "one of Brazil's most ubiquitous cultural practices" (Chazkel 2005). In the minds of many Brazilians today, the *jogo do bichos* organization is just as likely to be associated with the drug trade as it is with the lottery (although this has yet to be proved empirically). Players today have more alternatives than ever if they want to play—from the street corner to the telephone and the Internet—but it is still a misdemeanor crime

(Chazkel 2008, 88–93; Frossard 2007).

Chile

Chile remains an important transport stop for cocaine and heroin originating in the Andean region and destined for the United States and Europe. In recent years, the country has been plagued by its own drug consumption problem. Chile is also considered a source for the essential chemicals needed for coca processing.

Ecuador

Due to its poor border controls and a coastline that extends from Colombia and Peru, Ecuador has become a strategic transit point for the trafficking of illegal drugs and chemicals. What is more, the country's weak institutions, endemic corruption, and a poorly regulated banking system have left the country open to organized crime activity. Recent seizures of partially harvested opium poppies indicate that planters are testing the feasibility of this drug crop's cultivation in Ecuador. Colombia's Revolutionary Armed Forces (FARC) has extended its dominance over the drug trade south into northern Ecuador. According to the U.S. State Department, this region has become an important stop for the trafficking of cocaine, chemicals, and supplies to the FARC and other Colombian crime organizations. The recent trend has been to use "Ecuadorian-flagged vessels" to ship tons of drugs at a time (U.S. State Department 2006).

Paraguay

Paraguay is regarded as an important country for the shipment of drugs from Latin America. One of the country's biggest victories was the capture and extradition to the United States of Ivan Carlos Mendes Mesquita, the head of a major drug-trafficking syndicate with links to Colombia's FARC. Other traffickers have been extradited to Brazil as well. Much of the cocaine being shipped from Colombia, Bolivia, and Peru to Argentina, Brazil, Europe, Africa, and the Middle East passes through Paraguay. Law enforcement sources place Brazilian nationals at the head of regional groups that purchase cocaine from FARC in return for currency and arms. One of the biggest weapons wielded by Paraguayan police agencies is the national Anti-Drug Secretariat's (SENAD) Major Violator Unit (MVU). Its campaign to identify the "Most Wanted" drug traffickers elicited numbers of leads. In 2005, together with the Brazilian National Police, SENAD captured Luis Alberto Da Cunha, a fugitive on Brazil's Ten Most Wanted List. Despite several pyrrhic victories, the country is still plagued with government and police corruption (U.S. State Department 2006).

Peru

Despite surpassing its coca eradication goals, the cultivation of coca continues to increase in Peru. Coca farmers, or *cocaleros*, seem to have become more violent and better organized and have become affiliated with the Shining Path, or *Sendero Luminoso,* which reemerged in 2006 after a long absence. Analysts assert that the remnants of this terrorist organization now work as a protection force for organized crime groups, watching over Peruvian coca crops in the Huallaga Valley and elsewhere. Most

---

Political Bosses, Latin American Style: The *Coronelismo* and the *Cacique*

America does not have a monopoly on powerful political bosses with outsize power and influence; Latin America has had more than its fair share of this archetype. Most recently, the death in Brazil of Antonio Carlos Magalhaes, "a senator who dominated the political life" of the northeastern state of Bahia for almost 50 years, demonstrated the passing of the "old-fashioned political bosses" known as colonels or *coronelismo*. The term originated from the custom of 19th-century landowners/politicians of purchasing the control of the local national-guard unit. In the poorer regions, they were likely to control access to education and jobs, much like their American counterparts in an earlier era. In a similar vein, most explanations for the diminution of the political bosses in Brazil was the fact that Brazilians were better educated and informed than in times past, and voters are less dependent on the local bosses because of new social programs instituted at the federal level to help the previously disenfranchised classes (*Economist*, July 27, 2007, 50).

The Mexican incarnation of the American political boss lives on in the person of the *cacique*, described by one journalist as "local kingpins and kingmakers who have helped hold society here [Mexico] since before the Spanish conquest" (Althaus 2006, A29). Less an urban phenomenon that a rural one, these influential men ruled their lands and fiefdoms "with willpower and wile," and when necessary, with violence as well. *Caciques* come from a variety of backgrounds—union bosses, ranchers, drug dealers, and sometimes governors. As one *cacique* put it, "Some call me a *cacique*. Well, if building schoolrooms and streets and bridges, if bringing progress to the people, is a *cacique,* then I am one." One Mexican economist explained their persistence into the 21st century this way: "Democracy does not appear miraculously. This is the passage from a primitive country to a modern one." Most caciques have never held public office or stood election but have the power to make sure streets are paved, schools are built, funerals paid for, doctor bills are paid, and supporting candidates for office (Althaus 2006). Although President Vicente Fox vowed to make the *caciques* "relics," 6 years into his term, they continue to flourish in rural Mexico, as does a bribery culture that has been around for centuries. Here, a bribe is typically referred to a *la mordida*, or "the bite," which many observers suggest "is often the most efficient—or the only—way of getting things done in Mexico" (Pinkerton 2006, A29).

La Mordida ("the Bite"): Bribes for Favors[17]

Cost of Bribe	Favor Received
$1,000–$2,000	Dismiss a driving while impaired case
$40–$100	To buy a counterfeit car insurance certificate
$500	Obtain Texas license without passing test
$10,000	Award a county jail contract
$300	Allow undocumented immigrant to cross international bridge without papers
$500	To fix a traffic ticket
Up to $3,965	Obtain a building permit

(Pinkerton, 2006, A1)

coca-related products are transported out of Peru to Mexico, Bolivia, Brazil, Colombia, Ecuador, and Chile using air, river, land, and ocean routes. Regional sources suggest that 70% of all illegal drugs from Peru are hidden along with legitimate cargo in maritime shipping routes. Like elsewhere in Latin America, Mexican drug traffickers have emerged as important cogs in the shipments of larger loads of drugs to Mexico and the Caribbean (U.S. State Department 2006).

Bribery of Politicians, Justice Officials, and Media Owners and Executives[18]

Politicians

Members of Congress	Bribe (Monthly)
Frente Popular Agricola del Peru (FREPAP)	$20,000
Partido Aprista (APRA)	$50,000
Peru Posible (PP)	$10,000
Avancemos (A)	$15,000

Members of the Executive Branch	
Prime Minister	$10,000
Minister of Justice	$ 5,000

Justice Officials

Position	Bribe (Total)
Director, Judicial Reform Office	$55,000
Justice on the National Elections Board	$50,000
President of the Supreme Court	$35,000
Superior Justice	$25,000
Judge	$10,000

Media Owners and Executives

Media Outlet	Bribe Estimates
America Television (Channel 4)	$9 million in a signed contract
Frecuencia Latina (Channel 2)	$3 million in a signed contract
Panamericana Television (Channel 5)	$9 million
Expreso	$1 million
La Chuchi (popular press)	$8,000 weekly

CENTRAL AMERICA

In 2004, the presidents of Honduras and El Salvador proclaimed its tens of thousands of criminal gang members "as big a threat to national security as terrorism is to the United States" (Thompson 2004). Like Mexico, Central America's economic growth and democratic development is threatened by rising organized crime activity. Home to more than 30 million people, with almost 60% under 25 years old, Central America is composed of the countries of El Salvador, Guatemala, Honduras, and Nicaragua. Likewise, almost half of Mexico's 9.6 million people are under 25. Both regions are plagued by unemployment. Most of this region's *maras*,[19] or youth gangs, "have transcended the borders of Central America, Mexico, and the United States and evolved into a transnational concern" (USAID 2006, 5). Unlike a previous era when gangs adhered to territorial borders, a new age of globalization and technological advances has allowed these gangs to spread beyond the confines of their communities of origin. Today, gangs such as Mara Salvatrucha and the 18th Street Gang (formerly Barrio 18), both having originated in the Los Angeles barrios, flourish throughout Central America unfettered by national identities. There is little consensus among analysts on whether the *maras* features vertical command and control structures, or whether they are simply independent groups that operate as franchises of larger gangs such as MS-13 (Manrique 2006). In any case, today each country in this region has a variation of the gang problem. However, each country shares a number of factors that stimulated the growth of this problem, including "a lack of educational and economic opportunities, marginalized urban areas, intra-familial violence and family disintegration, easy access to drugs and firearms, overwhelmed and ineffective justice systems, and the 'revolving door' along the U.S.–Mexico border" (USAID 2006, 5–6).

Gangs such as MS-13 and the 18th Street Gang engage in transnational organized crime involving kidnapping, extortion, trafficking of people and contraband, and even assassinations. Recent research blames some of the problem on the American policy of deporting gang members without sharing information about them with the government officials in the nation receiving them. It is well known that many gang members fear being deported, knowing that they face an uncertain future once identified at home. In El Salvador, for example, there is a rogue unit of police and military personnel known as the "Black Shadow," or *Sombra Negra,* which functions as a vigilante group targeting criminals and gang members (USAID 2006, 6, 20).

A number of transnational gangs originated in Los Angeles, created by immigrants who left conflict-ridden Central America in the 1980s. Many young men eventually were exposed to gang life and when they were deported back to their countries of origin they brought with them knowledge of American gang culture. Today, these international links have served only to spread gang culture. It is estimated that the four Central American countries are home to 60,000 gang members.

Estimated Number of Gang Members in Mexico and Central America (Predominantly MS-13 and 18th Street Gang)

Country	Gang Membership
El Salvador	10,500
Honduras	36,000
Nicaragua	2,200
Guatemala	14,000
Southern Mexico border	3,000
Northern Mexico border	17,000

Adapted from USAID. Central America and Mexico Gang Assessment, April 2006, p. 17.

Guatemala

In 2002, Amnesty International described Guatemala as a "Corporate Mafia State [constructed] on an alliance of traditional sectors of the oligarchy, new entrepreneurs, police and military officers, and common criminals" (Washington Office on Latin America, October 2007, 8). Located between two oceans and Central and North America, Guatemala stands out as a transit corridor for hundreds of tons of cocaine that each year pass from Colombia to Mexico and then into the United States. It was hoped that after more than 200,000 deaths and 36 years of a civil war that began in 1960, Guatemala could look forward to an era of civility and prosperity. However, this would not take place; there would be no peace dividend. Guatemala's homicide rate was nearly seven times that of the United States' between 2001 and 2004, with that pattern continuing into 2005. Following the civil war era the region is awash in guns. In 2006, this small country of 14 million reported almost 6,000 murders, giving it one of Latin America's highest homicide rates. One official called the country "a good place in which to commit murder" (Washington Office on Latin America, October 2007, 7), referring to a solution rate of only 2%. Many are killed during political feuds, but most are related to powerful drug-trafficking organizations that are trying to make inroads on the nation's political system. This battle for Guatemala's institutions is most pronounced near the Mexican border, where there is evidence that cartels support various local candidates. Some observers compare the constituencies of local politicians to something akin to feudal kingdoms with very little control from the federal government.

The ascendance of Guatemala's drug cartels parallels changes in the drug transportation routes that have made the tiny country a critical transit point for Colombian cocaine. It has risen in importance as it has become increasingly difficult to bring drugs into Mexico and Florida. According to law enforcement, traffickers have found sanctuary and protection in the Guatemala's lawless jungles and unprotected coastlines (Schwartz 2007, A21).

Although the gang problem is considered less severe than in neighboring countries, there is much concern due to the fact that almost half of the population is under 20 years old. The majority of gang members are under 24 years of age and declining. Similar to its neighboring countries, Guatemala's gangs, thanks to deportation of gang members from the United States, porous borders, and new technologies such as the Internet and cell phones have become increasingly transnationalized.

Guatemala's new crime organizations have used their political connections and relationships with military and police officials to intimidate competitors as they pursue profits from state corruption, car theft, drug trafficking, money laundering, and other activities. Today, Guatemala has perhaps the worst extradition record in the region. Since the time of the Clinton administration, Guatemala has failed to extradite anyone on drug charges.[20] This is especially troubling, because a

Manuel de Jesús Castillo Medrano: Mayor or Crime Boss?

Manuel de Jesús Castillo Medrano was elected mayor of the small town of Jutiapa, strategically located for criminal activities near the border with El Salvador and the Pacific Coast. According to one 2007 report, the mayor's involvement in organized crime activities ranges from car theft and human smuggling to drug trafficking and extortion. In 2000, he was linked to the delivery of a shipment of Colombian cocaine. He was present along with his brother and others armed with AR-15 assault rifles when it was unloaded. It was then that he appeared on the radar of various counter-drug officials (the DEA and its Guatemalan counterpart). In 2007, the nation's national police tied him to the murders of three El Salvadoran politicians (which were followed by the murders of the assassins hours after being imprisoned). More than 300 calls were made between Castillo and the killers in the days preceding the killings. Although he is currently being investigated, he has not shirked the spotlight, traveling everywhere with an entourage of more than a dozen bodyguards (Logan October 2007).

Kaibiles

Following the end of the Central American conflicts in the 1980s, numerous mercenaries, death squads, and militants were looking for new opportunities, including the *Kaibiles*—the Guatemalan equivalent of Mexico's Zetas. Like their counterparts, but in smaller numbers, the *Kaibiles* are special forces deserters who become hired guns for Mexico's Gulf cartel (along with Zetas). What is most troubling has been the presence of *Kaibiles* in Mexico, "an additional foreign element" in the Mexican drug wars, along with MS-13 from El Salvador and Calle 18 gangsters from Guatemala (Offnews.info 2006). They have a hard-earned reputation for cruelty, and have established a reputation for their unconventional tactics, such as biting the heads off live chickens during training exercises. They were investigated for civil rights abuses committed during the country's civil war. During the 1980s, they were among the most feared special forces in Latin America. In 2006, the Guatemalan army began reorganizing, and in an attempt to further the reconciliation process, dropped the name *Kaibil* from its special forces unit. Recent interviews have revealed that *Kaibiles* trained a number of Mexican special operations soldiers between 1994 and 1999, and it is suspected that some of these later became Zetas.

U.S. report suggested that "between two thirds and three fourths of all cocaine being trafficked to the United States from Colombia and other Andean nations" passes through this small republic south of Mexico (Smyth 2007).

El Salvador

El Salvador experienced one of Latin America's bloodiest armed conflicts during the civil war that raged between 1980 and 1992 and claimed more than 75,000 lives. The country was beset with a wave of crime after the war, partially attributable to the large number of demobilized veterans of the war who had to find some way to survive with few job opportunities and an embarrassment of military hardware. It became common to solve most disputes with violence. In most of the country, there was a paucity of social services as well as public security, an environment than emboldened gangs to "take on roles normally reserved for the state," including "taxing businesses and bus drivers" (USAID 2006, 1).

The connections between former paramilitary groups and organized crime activity have been recognized for more than a decade, with numerous reports focusing on the organizational structure and access to military hardware that have allowed former death squad members to enter organized crime activities including drugs and weapons trafficking and kidnapping. According to one 1994 investigation, the death squads underwent "a process of 'mutation and atomization'" that saw them transform "into more decentralized organized criminal structures both at the regional and national levels" (WOLA 2007, 4).

The El Salvador gang problem is considered severe and international in scope. MS-13 and the 18th Street Gang are rooted here and demonstrate transnational characteristics. This activity has escalated faster than any other country in the region, partially the result of deportations from the United States. El Salvadoran gangs have flourished, and indeed, some have evolved into organized crime networks, thanks to their role in the international drug trade. The country is now considered a prominent transshipment point for Colombian drugs marketed in the United States.

El Salvadoran officials claim that state infiltration of the gangs has revealed their argot and codes. Furthermore, it seems that the constant media attention given to the gang problem has acted more as a recruiting tool. Although MS-13 and the 18th Street Gang have previously worked in association with drug cartels, more recently it appears they are attempting to work directly with the Colombians to establish drug routes through Mexico and Central America. One of the most

Characteristics of El Salvadoran Gangs

- Use minors to commit crimes
- Jailed gang members expanding networks while in prison
- Extortion fees demanded from bus drivers and business owners
- Stronger links with organized crime
- Competition for drug trafficking replacing competition for territories
- Fluid communication between gangs in El Salvador and the United States
- Communication using Web sites and coded language between street and prison
- Displacing coyotes and narcotraffickers

Adapted from *USAID. Central America and Mexico Gang Assessment*, 2006, p. 47.

extensive gang assessments of the region suggests that the gang problem has grown faster here, and that some are becoming more sophisticated, but the majority of the gangs do not have a high level of sophistication. One of the main structures of the gangs is the decentralized *clicka*, a smaller unit that controls a small territory. By contrast, the 18th Street Gang has been identified with a structure that includes national leaders called *ranfla*, leaders with no tattoos, strong discipline, and they are required to commit murders and traffic in contraband, or *runners*, and *clickas* gang members referred to as *missionaries* (USAID 2006, 47).

Honduras

Although Honduras escaped its own civil war during the 1980s, it did not escape unscathed, because it played host to anti-Sandinista Nicaraguan Resistance fighters, better known as the Contras. During the 1980s, Honduras was regarded as a repressive state with rampant abuses of human rights. It is one of the region's poorest nations and one of the most violent countries in Latin America. Much of the crime and violence has been attributed to juvenile gangs, organized crime, drug trafficking, and endemic social violence. A 2006 USAID gang assessment report judged the country's gang problem as severe and "among the worst in Central America." MS-13 and the 18th Street Gang have been well-entrenched here since the early 1990s, a period that paralleled high legal and illegal immigration to the United States, followed by deportations back home, a recurring cycle familiar elsewhere, in which Honduran gang members copied the Los Angeles gang culture brought home by deportees. Gangs have been transformed in response to a series of anti-gang laws passed in 2001. Among the most noticeable changes are that they have become less territorial and changed their regalia. Others have fled for America and El Salvador; still others have found work as hired guns and drug distributors.

Contrary to media exaggerations, some officials believe the gangs have not matured beyond the bottom of the food chain and have no ties to the Colombian drug trade. By focusing on youth gangs, it obscures the activities of much more prevalent organized crime groups and white-collar crime. More likely, gang members work for neighborhood drug wholesalers, without any direct association with international traffickers (USAID 2006, 93). Others suggest that the country's gang has become a social and security problem as they become increasingly intertwined with the drugs and weapons trade. In 2006, Honduras was placed on the U.S. State Department's "primary concern locations"[21] for money laundering (Martinez, Guatemala, 2007).

More recently, the U.S. Department of State has tagged Honduras as a preferred transit point in Central America for shipments of cocaine heading to the States. In addition, it regards the country in the high range of countries as an origin for human trafficking to the United States and as a transit point for victims trafficked to Mexico and the United States.

Nicaragua

Nicaragua is considered the poorest country in Central America (second poorest in Latin America), with 70% of its population living in extreme poverty. Together with a young population and the amount of weapons left over from conflicts in the 1980s, it comes as a surprise that Nicaragua has experienced less violence than its neighbors. In the early part of the 21st century, gangs became involved in narcotrafficking that existed for decades along Caribbean coast. Its proximity to the Colombian island of San Andre has made it a natural transit point for the cocaine trade (USAID 2006, 125).

Although the gang problem is severe, it is fortunately localized and has been decreasing for years. Nicaragua is distinct from its neighbors to the north in that it has one of the lowest homicide rates in Central America. However, its fragile economy has lured more youths to gang activity. "While most youth gangs have not made links to organized crime, some are hired by political parties to cause disturbances at rival political and social events" (USAID 2006, 125). One explanation for why gangs have not gained such a grip in the country is that as Nicaragua transitions to a democratic system, lingering socialist structures such as the neighborhood watch and the crime prevention role of the police has made it less hospitable to gang culture.

THE CARRIBEAN REGION

Ranging from the southern tip of Florida to northwest Venezuela, some 25 countries make up the Caribbean region, including hundreds of small islands. The region's proximity to the United States has made it a significant staging area for organized crime between Latin and North America, particularly in respect to the drug trade, money laundering, and human smuggling. In 2004, the U.S. State Department identified the Bahamas, Jamaica, and the Dominican Republic as major transshipment points for the entry of narcotics into the United States from South America and elsewhere. The most popular route for cocaine traffickers runs through Jamaica[22] and Haiti, thence through Puerto Rico, the Bahamas, and the Dominican Republic. Jamaica was once the main source of marijuana from the region, but in recent years Colombians have moved into the trade in a big way. Caribbean routes also have facilitated the trafficking of synthetic drugs into the United States (and Europe).

This region is considered a tax haven for money launderers. Financial institutions in the Caribbean typically require little if any tax burden and provide strict secrecy laws to protect against scrutiny from outside investigators. In addition, the Caribbean offers a large banking and financial hub, offering low incorporation fees, the free movement of currency in and out of the country, and has few laws that criminalize money laundering and other financial crimes. It should not be surprising that drug traffickers favor this region for laundering their profits. Offshore banking has been especially identified in Aruba, the Bahamas, Curacao, and most British independencies (Wilson 2008).

Illegal arms and human trafficking flourish in this region, with many weapons traffickers affiliated with the drug trade as well. Haiti is considered a prominent center for the arms trade. Human trafficking ranks just behind drugs and weapons trafficking as a source of income for crime syndicates.

The Dominican Republic

The Dominican Republic is one of the most impoverished countries in the world. Dominican drug traffickers started out in the retail cocaine trade in American neighborhoods with high density of Dominican immigrants, particularly New York City's Washington Heights, in the 1970s. The Dominican Republic shares the island of Hispaniola with the equally poor country of Haiti. In 2000, Haiti was second only to the Dominican Republic when it came to poverty in the Western Hemisphere, with average income close to $1,000 per capita. Like many of the countries in this region, it is vulnerable to corruption at every level of society and government, providing numerous opportunities to organized crime groups.

Cuba and American Organized Crime

Prior to the Cuban Revolution in 1959, "Cuba was virtually a Mafia fiefdom" (Galeotti 2006, 45). For almost 30 years, it was one of American organized crime's biggest gambling producers. This Caribbean island had been attracting land speculators, mobsters, tourists, and outside entrepreneurs since at least the early 1920s. Following the military coup referred to as the "Revolt of the Sergeants" led by Fulgencia Batista y Zaldivar (1901–1973) in 1933 that would in turn install him as dictator, mob moneyman Meyer Lansky joined the first international visitors to Havana to offer his congratulations and "pay his respects." It was around this time that he landed control of the gambling concession at Havana's Hotel Nacional, the first in a string of such establishments. Several leading organized crime scholars cite this as the Mafia's "first major international venture" (Lyman and Potter 2004, 473).

Beginning in 1933, organized crime emerged as a powerful force on the island. According to recent investigations, during the 1930s criminal enterprises in Havana operated under "mafiosi with Sicilian, Corsican, Jewish, or U.S. origins" (Cirules 2004, 17). The following decade saw Cuban nationals being brought into this arrangement that cemented ties with the country's political elite. According to a recent prize-winning investigative work, "from the 1930s until the end of 1958, no significant political event or big business deal occurred in Cuba without [Meyer Lansky's] involvement" (Cirules 2004, 18).

During the 1930s and 1940s, American Mafia groups found Cuba "its safest stop on the drug route" that brought heroin and cocaine into the United States. Once in Cuba, it was almost guaranteed they would reach the United States, thanks to the compliance and connivance of Cuban politicians and military leaders, who placed military airports and private runways at the disposal of drug traffickers (Cirules 2004). By the 1940s, transnational syndicates were evaluating the role Cuba would play in the growing narcotics business. During the Kefauver Hearings in the 1950s, the commission revealed that by 1942, arrangements had been in place to expand the drug corridor in order "to bring heroin from Marseilles via Cuba to Kansas City for distribution in the Midwest" (Cirules 2004, 64).

In truth, Batista persevered thanks to covert U.S. aid for a number of years, and even before he became dictator, he was helping rumrunners smuggle outlawed liquor from Cuba to the United States. It was during this period that he made the acquaintance of Meyer Lansky, "Lucky" Luciano, Santos Trafficante, Sr., and other luminaries of the underworld. During the 1930s, his American supporters decided that Batista needed to eschew the trappings of a military dictatorship in favor of democracy. Between 1934 and 1940, five presidents were elected and deposed "democratically" as Batista pulled the real strings of power. In 1940, Batista ran for president himself and won, but with the adoption of a new constitution that prohibited a second term in 1944, he left Cuba for Miami, where some sources suggest he consorted with Lansky in the illegal casino rackets.

By the 1950s, the American government seemed wary of an increasingly liberal-leaning Cuba and looked the other way as Batista used Florida to launch a *coup d'etat* in 1952, reimposing himself on the tropical island. His return in 1952 significantly increased the organized crime presence in Havana, and soon the city's nightlife offered tourists wholesale prostitution and drugs to go along with the numerous casinos. However, not everyone basked in the nightlife. Despite the fact that in the 1950s Cuba had the fastest growing economy in Latin America, wealth still remained the province of a wealthy few. It was *de rigueur* for journalists to make light of the fact that this impoverished island boasted "more telephones, televisions, and new Cadillacs per capita than any U.S. city."

In 1958, it became clear to more perspicacious gangsters that Batista's administration was on the brink of collapse and began selling off their Havana operations. The more repressive the Batista regime became, the more popular Che Guevara, Castro, and other anti-government interests became among the majority peasant class. Soon even the United States refused to prop up the dictator.

After Fidel Castro took over in 1959, Batista, Lansky, and most others connected to the dictatorship and mob rackets left the island. Lansky's brother Jake was among the few to stay behind, but only to try and arrive at some type of understanding with Castro that would allow the return of casino gambling. Jake was thrown into jail and in subsequent years his brother along with other crime figures supposedly joined the CIA in several plots to kill the dictator (dubbed "Operation Mongoose"). A $1 million bounty was supposedly placed on "The Beard" by Lansky. However, as the first decade of the 21st century moves to its conclusion, Castro has outlived and outlasted all who plotted against him. Despite the machinations of seminal

(continued)

mob figures Santo Trafficante, Jr., Carlos Marcello, Sam Giancana, John Roselli, and Meyer Lansky, Castro's presence looms the largest over modern-day Cuba.

One of the unforeseen phenomena of American–Cuban relations has been the evolution of Cuban organized crime syndicates in the United States, particularly since the 1980 Marielito boatlift. Long accused of running a police state, in October 1980, Castro opened the port of Mariel to anyone that wanted to leave for the United States. Over the next 200 days more than 125,000 Cuban immigrants left for American shores. What was unexpected was that Castro had actually used the boatlift to deport inmates from overcrowded prisons and psychiatric facilities along with political dissidents. Although many were locked up for years in processing centers on the Gulf Coast and elsewhere, a number managed to elude the net and formed the nucleus of a nascent "Cuban mafia." Although the amount of actual crime and criminals associated with this event has been exaggerated, with only about 1 in 10 immigrants associated with criminal activity or mental illness, recent scholarship insists that the "arrival of a small core of hardened criminals with nothing to lose but much to gain did galvanize Cuban organize crime in the United States" (Galeotti 2006, 53).

The emergence of Cuban organized crime activity on American shores dates back to the 1959 exodus of gangsters from Cuba. The "Corporation" originated around 1964, but its roots can be discerned earlier in the decade following the Bay of Pigs debacle in 1961. By the late 1990s, the Corporation was among the largest Hispanic crime syndicates in the United States. In the 1980s, it controlled the numbers racket from New York to Florida. According to the 1985 President's Commission on Organized Crime (PCOC), its New York profits alone approached $45 million per year. The syndicate favored the numbers game *bolita*, a mainstay of Hispanic communities. By 1986, José Miguel Battle (1929–1997), the reputed head of the Corporation, was one of Dade County, Florida's richest men, with a net worth approaching $180 million. Over the years, Battle insulated himself from law enforcement by organizing his group like a "crime family" and relying on "corrupters" who bribed politicians and other officials to look the other way. During the 1990s, the Corporation became increasingly diversified as it expanded into territories once controlled by Italian-American crime families. Known as "the Godfather" or "El Padrino," Battle ironically started out as a police officer in Havana in the 1950s, where he made acquaintances with Meyer Lansky and Santos Trafficante Sr., connections he would later use to open gambling operations in Florida. Battle has been connected to a number of murders, and in 1997, at the age of 68, he was sentenced to prison for violating his parole. He died from kidney disease soon after.

By the 1980s, perhaps 500,000 Dominicans had ended up in Washington Heights, Queens, and Brooklyn, New York; Paterson, New Jersey; and Lawrence, Massachusetts, looking for better opportunities and fleeing the grinding poverty of their home country. Over the next decades they moved into other cities in the Northeast corridor. This tidal wave of immigration happened to coincide with the boon years of the Colombian drug trade. Drug couriers working for the Colombian couriers smuggled wholesale cocaine north to the markets dominated by Dominicans. There, crack dealers from New England to the Chesapeake found a dependable source for their regional markets. During the mid-1980s, the Cali cartel provided wholesale shipments of cocaine, relying on Dominicans to facilitate distribution. As the Dominicans prospered, some made the transition from street dealing to wholesale distribution, functioning as middlemen for the Colombians and other ethnic syndicates. Dominican drug syndicates are distinguished by their policy of moving operatives in and out of the United States after a 2-year hiatus (Liddick 2008).

Trinidad and Tobago

Trinidad and Tobago has become a key transit site for the illegal drug trade, especially cocaine and less so with heroin. With an advanced petrochemical sector requiring the import and export of precursor chemicals, it is feared these might be diverted to groups needing them for the manufacturing of cocaine hydrochloride. Criminal organizations from Syria, China, and Russia are known to operate here, but Venezuela appears to be its linchpin in the drug trade. The so-called

Manuel Noriega and Panama: A Case Study

Born in Panama City in 1938, Manuel Antonio Noriega Moreno was the first head of state to be convicted of felony charges by the United States. Scion of a poor family, he entered the military in his 20s and rapidly moved up in the ranks. His participation in suppressing a 1969 coup against then-President General Omar Torrijos proved a turning point when he was selected to head Torrijos' intelligence services. He exploited this position to rise in the nation's military and political hierarchy. Torrijos died in a mysterious plane crash in 1981, and 2 years later Noriega was in control of Panama, a position he would use over the next few years to become wealthy through the international drug trade and other criminal activities.

As America's drug problem worsened in the 1980s, President George H.W. Bush was forced to act, freezing Panamanian assets in U.S. banks and cutting all military and economic assistance to Panama. In 1985, one well-known government critic was kidnapped, tortured, and beheaded after publicly accusing Noriega of complicity in the drug trade. In 1988, a U.S. Senate report revealed Noriega's association with Colombian drug cartels. Noriega's doom was probably sealed much earlier, but when he publicly declared that a state of war existed between Panama and the United States in 1989, tensions were ratcheted up significantly. After an American soldier was killed by Panamanian Defense Force troops American forces invaded Panama in "Operation Just Cause," with the main goal of arresting Noriega in order to bring him back to the States to stand trial for racketeering and drug trafficking. He was captured on January 3, 1990, but not before thousands of Panamanian citizens were killed in the process. Noriega was taken to Miami, and over the next 2 years investigators made their case against him.

During an 8-month trial that some observers depicted as the "drug trial of the century," more than 100 prosecution witnesses testified, including Colombia cocaine kingpin Carlos Lehder-Riva. In April 1992, a jury found Noriega guilty on 8 of the 10 counts against him and was sentenced to 40 years (reduced to 30 years on appeal in 1999) in federal prison for his role in money laundering and protecting Colombian cocaine traffickers who had been using Panama as a transshipment point for bringing drugs into the United States.

Venezuelan *Tucupita* cartel is thought to be the main link between Trinidadian and Colombian drug cartels (Martinez 2007, 1). In 2007, Trinidad and Tobago was among the 10 countries with the highest kidnapping rates in the world—between 2001 and 2004, kidnappings increased from only 10 to 150.

Jamaica

For a more in-depth discussion of Jamaica and its links to organized crime, see Chapter 12 on Afro-lineal Organized Crime.

Overview

A number of observers have expressed fears that "the borders of crime in Latin America are dissolving" (Franco, USAID 2005), citing the region's slow economic growth rates and levels of income inequality. Others fear the porous borders now threaten regional democracy, stability, and security, resulting in what some of called the "transnationalization" of the problem. Nations throughout this region are at the same time dealing with the debilitating threats from organized crime networks, narcotrafficking, youth gangs, high levels of corruption, and ineffective legal systems. It is no wonder that the "divide between youth gang violence and organized narco-crime is becoming increasingly blurred" (USInfo.State.Gov. 2005, 4).

In 2003, the DEA reported that with the assistance of Cuban crime syndicates, Latin American and Caribbean criminal organizations have coordinated in the transportation of Colombian cocaine and marijuana into the United States through Florida (Galeotti 2006). Although Cuban networks have conveyed these drugs into cities and regions with "significant Cuban crime presence" (Galeotti 2006), their participation in the drug trade pales in comparison to Dominican and Mexican drug syndicates. The drug networks continue to flourish as they sink more and more money into their own research and development projects. Despite some victories and billions of dollars in drug eradication efforts on the part of the United States, Colombian coca growers have been able to make up for their diminished acreage by using the most modern agronomy techniques to boost productivity and create new strains of coca that are resistant to most herbicides. As a result, the new incarnations are leafier than and twice as tall as the traditional variety, producing a much higher quality and stronger cocaine (Naim 2005).

One sign of the diminished strength of the so-called Colombian cartels was the results of a 2006 trial of Gilberto and Miguel Rodriguez Orejuela. Already convicted on drug charges in their native country in 1995, they were indicted in Miami in 2003, charged with running their Cali empire from inside prison. Now in their 60s, the two brothers who had headed the Cali cartel pled guilty in a Miami court in September 2006 to drug trafficking and money laundering, which American officials proclaimed was a "major milestone in the government's war on drugs" (Anderson 2006). Both agreed to hand over billions of dollars in assets as they prepared for 30 years in an American prison. Their cartel was once responsible for 80% of the cocaine smuggled into the United States and became the leading cartel after the death of Pablo Escobar in 1993.

The threat and reality of extradition to the United States has become one of the greatest tools for law enforcement in organized crime hotbeds such as Colombia and Mexico. Mexico has only recently permitted extradition, and it has paid some dividends already. However, as a caveat, criminals are required to complete their Mexican sentences before being transferred to the United States (Althaus 2007).

One of the unexpected consequences of the Mexican government campaigns against the major trafficking groups has been the emergence of "microcartels." The capture of stalwart leaders such as Felix in 2002 and Cárdenas in 2003 has led to a "recomposition" of the larger organizations. Some experts refer to this process, in which the big cartels break up into smaller groups, as *atomization*. As a result, the gangs that once

employed thousands of people in the 1980s and 1990s have given way to ferocious syndicates such as the Zetas; all arrayed to battle each other (and the remnants of various cartels) over the lucrative drug trade. What made the Zetas so treacherous was their military discipline, modern weapons, and wiretap ability, together making them more dangerous than traditional drug gangs. Although the government claims to have killed or arrested half of the original Zetas, the group's ability to recruit and train *Zetitas*, or "Little Zetas," has enabled them to hold on to its former authority. By 2006, the violence between these gangs, all vying for control of the drug trade, was spilling into formerly placid cities such as Nuevo Laredo, which reported 60 gang-style killings in 2004, and continued to increase each year since. Like many organized crime groups around the world, the once sacrosanct rules against victimizing women and children no longer apply today (Padgett 2005).

According to a 2007 National Drug Threat Assessment report, Mexican drug-trafficking organizations "are the most influential and pervasive threats with respect to drug transportation and wholesale distribution in nearly every region of the country and continue to increase their involvement in the production, transportation, and distribution of most illicit drugs" (NDIC 2006).

Organized trafficking networks continue to use well-established overland transportation routes to transport cocaine, pot, methamphetamines, and heroin to drug markets throughout the United States. More important, their strategic location on the American border has allowed them to respond quickly to changes in the U.S. drug market. For example, when locally produced methamphetamines decreased substantially in the United States, "the supply of the drug was virtually uninterrupted as they almost immediately stepped up the production of Mexican methamphetamine" (NDIC 2006). In similar fashion, Mexican drug-trafficking organizations have begun producing pot with higher THC levels than in the past to respond to growing market demands for higher potency pot. In recent years, Mexican drug gangs have moved into other drugs, particularly methamphetamine. Officials suggest that this drug will be even better for the gangs because they would not have to pay the Colombians anything and would have complete control. Mexican groups continue to demonstrate great ingenuity—including building tunnels under the border—and have become more difficult to track as they resort to cheap disposable cell phones.

Although new President Felipe Calderón deployed more than 24,000 troops and Federal police into the strongholds of the Mexican cartels, the bloodshed related to the drug trade has continued undiminished. Between January and June of 2007, it claimed more than 1,200 lives (Althaus 2007). Calderón made extradition the centerpiece of his anti-organized crime campaign. Once in the United States, some of the extradited kingpins have provided valuable intelligence during the course of plea bargains that have facilitated the destruction of some of the gangs.

In Mexico, there have been a few glimmers of hope in the war against the drug traffickers. Early in 2007, the four main kingpins of the Gulf cartel were arrested and extradited to the United States, "the first time in the history of Mexico that they have extradited to the United States what amounts to a clean sweep geographically of the cartel leadership"; among this group was the successor to Juan García Abrego, Osiel Cárdenas-Guillen, who officials claim was responsible for the transporting 4 to 6 tons of cocaine into the United States each month (Lozano 2007). After taking office in December 2006, President Felipe Calderón adopted strategies that saw some success in Colombia in the 1990s. Although others before him took on the cartels unsuccessfully, Calderón opted to use the military to take back regions where drug dealers control local officials and continues to extradite top cartel members to the United States while eradicating marijuana and opium poppies. Even observers inside Mexico note that he is the first leader to attempt such a concerted effort with so many resources (McKinley 2007).

In late 2007, it was announced that Mexico and the United States had agreed to terms on a proposed $1 billion, 2-year package to help fight Mexican drug traffickers. As drug violence runs unchecked from the Texas border deep into Mexico, Calderón has made the crime crackdown the centerpiece of his administration, but has failed to stem the almost unremitting violence. Despite sending in thousands of troops, underworld feuds left more than 2,500 dead in 2007. Dominated by the Gulf cartel and its army of Zeta hitmen, much of the current violence has taken place in the state of Tamulpais, which borders South Texas from Laredo to the Gulf of Mexico (Althaus 2008).

Sandra Avila Beltrán: The Diva Drug Lord

A resident of Guadalajara and Hermosillo, throughout the 1990s Sandra Avila Beltrán operated under police radar for a number of years. However, in 2001, police discovered nine tons of cocaine on a ship docked on the Pacific Coast at Manzanillo. A subsequent investigation tied the shipment to 46-year-old Beltrán and her 39-year-old lover, Juan Diego Espinoza Ramírez, known to law enforcement as "the Tiger." Arrested in October 2007, Sandra Avila Beltrán, dubbed the "Queen of the Pacific," was suspected of spending more than 10 years using her whiles and beauty to insinuate herself into Mexico's male-dominated drug trade and uniting Colombia's Norte del Valle cartel with and Mexico's Sinaloa organization (Rodriguez 2007, A15). More recently, Beltrán became the subject of a recent folk ballad, or *narcocorrido*, about drug trafficking, referring to her as "a top lady who is a key part of the business."[23] What is most interesting about this *telenovela*-in-the-making is her unprecedented role as a female leader of an organization (officials claim she was head of public relations for the Sinaloa cartel). Because her uncle is Miguel Angel Felix Gallardo, a former leading Mexican drug lord, now serving 40 years for smuggling and the murder of DEA agent Enrique Camarena, some observers have suggested that the drug trade was in her blood (another uncle, Juan José Quintero Payan, was extradited to the United States on drug charges in 2006).

Key Terms

Cartels	NAFTA	Juárez cartel
Medellín cartel	Herrera Family	Sonora cartel
Cali cartel	Zetas	"Kiki" Camarena

Salazar	AUC	Maras
Sinaloa cartel	"Silver or lead"	MS-13
Tijuana cartel	*La Compañía*	Kaibiles
Gulf cartel	LOS PEPES	18th Street Gang
Juan García Abrego	Sicarios	Cuban organized crime
Guadalajara cartel	Black Market Peso Exchange	Marielitos
Amezcua-Contreras organization	Triborder Region	Manuel Noriega
"Roller-coastering"	First Capital Command	Felipe Calderón
Coyotes	Favelas	
FARC	*Jogo dos bichos*	

Critical Thinking Questions

1. Are the Medellín and Cali drug organizations cartels? Why is there still a debate over whether they are actually cartels?
2. When did the fragmentation of the Colombian cocaine business begin? What impact has the involvement of various paramilitary groups had on the cocaine trafficking business in Latin America?
3. Why has Mexico been plagued with corruption for so long, despite never having suffered a dictatorship?
4. What has changed in Latin America that has allowed Mexican cartels to become such prominent players in various smuggling operations? Discuss the tradition of smuggling on the Mexico–United States border.
5. How has the North American Free Trade Agreement (NAFTA) facilitated the ascendance of the Mexican drug cartels?
6. Who are the Zetas, and what are their roles in the Mexican drug trade?
7. Compare and contrast the various Mexican cartels. Select at least three organizations. Which have become more diversified and proved to be the most pragmatic?
8. What characteristics do coyote organizations share with other organized crime groups? How are they different?
9. What has happened to the Cali and Medellín cartels since the mid-1980s? Contrast their modern incarnations with the days of their zenith. What led to their demise?
10. What makes Colombia such a strategic location for the drug trade and other organized crime activities?
11. What is the Black Market Peso Exchange? How does it operate, and why is it necessary?
12. What is narcoterrorism, and what does it have to do with organized crime?
13. How did a soccer team in Brazil evolve into one of Latin America's largest criminal organizations?
14. What was Cuba's importance to American crime syndicates, and why did it come to an end?

Endnotes

1. The best definitions of a *cartel* refer to a group of independent organizations that collude to control production, pricing, and the marketing of goods by its members. The term *cartel* is often misapplied to Mexican organized crime groups. However, the term is used in this book when referring to organizations that are called *cartels* by most Mexican and international media (e.g., Gulf cartel, Tijuana cartel).
2. The best example is how the Mexican gangs virtually stole the methamphetamine trade from Hells Angels in the 1990s. One report indicated that DEA agents rubbed this in the face of the bikers, letting them know how embarrassing it

was that they had allowed non-Americans to come in and take over their trafficking operation (Owen 2007).

3. These tolls are considerably higher than the 1,304 recorded in 2004 and 1,080 in 2001.

4. The Nuevo Laredo border crossing is a veritable "smuggler's paradise," with more than 20,000 cargo trucks and cars passing through it each day in transit for the Interstate 35 route through the United States. It is impossible to keep most contraband from getting through border checkpoints.

5. According to investigative journalist Idalia Gomez, prior to the mid-1990s, an average of 50,000 deserted during each 6-year presidential administration. During the 1994–2000 term of former President Ernesto Zedillo, that figure rose to 114,000.

6. *Oregonian* writer Steve Suo's 2004 Pulitzer-Prize nominated series, "Unnecessary Epidemic," is a must for anyone seeking to understand the 1990s methamphetamine problems. In it, Suo argues that greedy drug companies put profits above public safety by using lobbyists to defeat the DEA's strategy to regulate methamphetamine precursor chemicals.

7. The DEA defines a *superlab* as "a clandestine laboratory operation which is capable of producing 10 pounds or more of methamphetamine in a single production cycle" (Suo 2004).

8. The *Oregonian* newspaper discovered that federal authorities cut off the flow of methamphetamine precursor chemicals to the drug cartels in 1995–1996 and 1998–1999. The investigative journalists found that in each case, it corresponded with a drop in crime and addiction, as well as an increase in price (Suo 2004).

9. One Mexican organization called Integral Family Development, out of Nogales, has reported that almost 90% of the women arrested on the border have been drug addicts (Nunez 2007).

10. Former Medellín leader Juan David Ochoa claims the "extraditables" included all those who had indictments hanging over their heads in the United States, but asserts that it was Escobar alone who waged the terrorist campaign that was connected to the threat of extradition, and that only certain members of the Medellín group agreed to these acts. In sum, according to Ochoa, "the extraditables terrorist group was Pablo Escobar" (interview with David Ochoa, *Frontline* 2008).

11. Along with his brothers Jorge and Fabio, Juan David was a key member of the Medellín cartel. In 1991,

he turned himself in to authorities. He currently resides in Medellín.

12. Carlos Toro was recruited by his childhood friend Carlos Lehder in the early 1980s. He served in a number of capacities, including public relations, managing political bribes, and money laundering. He was interviewed for *Frontline*'s Drug Wars documentary.

13. When his so-called prison at La Catedral was raided, Escobar had already fled, leaving behind pictures of him attired as a 1920s gangster, replete with Tommy gun.

14. The "myth" of Escobar as tombstone thief has been disputed by his biographer (Bowden 2001, 18–19).

15. These same eleven judges had coincidentally all voted in favor of the extradition treaty with the United States.

16. More recently, Denise Frossard (2007 183) argued that although there are drug-trafficking groups in Brazil, "they have been erroneously defined as criminal associations; in reality these groups are only the 'managers' for a 'stock company' with as-yet-unidentified 'stockholders' and major 'investors.'"

17. These examples are drawn from actual cases recorded in the Rio Grande Valley.

18. This table was adapted from Washington Office on Latin America, Special Report, *The Captive State,* October 2007, p. 21. These are examples of selected bribes paid by Vladimiro Montesinos of the Peruvian Congress. Original source is John McMillan and Pablo Zoido, "How to Subvert Democracy: Montesinos in Peru," *Stanford Institute for Economic Policy Research*, July 1, 2004. Montesinos was a captain in the Peruvian army who was cashiered out in the 1970s for various criminal activities. He reappeared as an expensive defense attorney associated with the cases of drug traffickers and powerful politicians and military officers facing fraud charges. He met future Peruvian President Fujimori in 1990, and was soon selected as the head of Peru's National Intelligence Service. It has been well chronicled how Montesinos used bribery, blackmail, and intimidation to create an elaborate criminal network involving money laundering, weapons smuggling, and drug trafficking. One expert described the country under Fujimori and Montesinos as a "mafia state" (quoted in Washington Office on Latin America, November 2007, 17).

19. Youth gangs, referred to as *maras* in Central America, and adopted their name from the *marabunta*, which

is a gluttonous horde of ants that destroys everything in their way.

20. Some critics suggest that the United States stopped trying to extradite Guatemalan drug suspects in 1994, after the country's chief justice was assassinated. His death apparently stemmed from an attempt to extradite a Guatemalan Army lieutenant colonel accused of smuggling 500 kilograms of cocaine into Florida. Nine days after the murder of the judge, the surviving justice denied the extradition.

21. This refers to countries where "financial institutions engage in transactions involving significant amounts of proceeds from all serious crime" (Martinez, Guatemala, 2007).

22. See Chapter 10 for more on Jamaica in the context of Afrolineal organized crime.

23. Following her arrest, a video clip of her telling police that she was only a businesswoman and housewife surfaced on YouTube, and in its first week was seen 40,000 times.

CHAPTER 12

Afrolineal Organized Crime

In this chapter, the term *Afrolineal* refers to organized criminal activity rooted in countries that are predominately African or of African descent, originating from outside the United States. For organizational purposes African American street gangs that evolved on the streets of urban America are covered in Chapter 8, with its emphasis on homegrown organized crime. This chapter focuses on crime groups emanating from the continent of Africa and the countries of the Caribbean. Many of these countries have been beset by a cornucopia of factors often stimulating the development of organized crime, including political instability, economic chaos, high illiteracy, poor communication, and the breakdown of the rule of law. Since the 1980s, much of Africa has been plagued by violent conflicts—warfare between the MPLA and UNITA in Angola, the northern Nilotics and southern Bantu tribes in Uganda, northern Arabs and southern Africans in Sudan, Moslems and Christians in northern Nigeria, the RENAMO and FRELIMO in Mozambique, and so forth.

As with many Third World countries (and former communist countries) making the transition to democracy and undergoing tremendous social change, such as urbanization and democratization, new conditions not only tend to result in more crime but new types of crimes (for these regions). The process of societal and economic development is often concomitant with increased desire for wealth. It also makes new products available for organized stealing, such as cars and bicycles, electronic equipment, and other commodities now in demand by the new prosperous classes, as well as a large pool of indigent with few outlets for economic mobility but the same desire for luxury goods. Parasitic crimes also accompany this transition, including prostitution and drug trafficking as new markets become available. New crimes of development favored by organized syndicates include currency counterfeiting and the forging of bank checks. Most accounts indicate a correlation between increased economic activity and drug-related crime, such as addiction and trafficking. The illicit smuggling of contraband across borders is a typical byproduct of modernization and economic development. Faster communication facilitated by the automobile and telephones, and now the Internet, enabled certain new forms of organized crime to flourish.

Although it has been fashionable to blame organized crime activity on a lack of economic opportunities and the existence of poverty and corruption, in certain regions of the world the persistence of military coups and civil wars has often obscured the linkage between politics and crime. West Africa, for example, has been plagued by these phenomena since the 1980s. It is no coincidence that a parallel growth in syndicate activities is discernable. In this environment of civil disorder, few legitimate companies are willing to invest in the troubled economy. Without their economic input, there are few alternatives to create jobs and concomitant economic growth. It is just such a setting that often encourages individuals to seek wealth by any means and as quickly as possible, rather than investing in a meaningful long-term effort.

Charles Taylor: Crime Lord or Politician?

Charles Taylor, the warlord-turned-president of Liberia, on the West Coast of Africa, was arrested by Nigerian security officials on March 29, 2006, and is considered the first African head of state to be indicted for war crimes. Educated in the United States, Taylor led an army in the Liberian civil war, in which he rose to prominence for his strategy of using child soldiers, or "small boy units." During his years in power, his government "became a functioning criminal enterprise," exploiting Liberia's natural bounty for himself and his acolytes (Farah 2004, 15). Taylor first registered on the tyrant radar screen in 1991, when he sponsored the bloody civil war in Sierra Leone, where young soldiers under the age of 15, fueled by amphetamines and homemade gin, ravaged the country. As warlord, Taylor controlled Liberia's diamond-rich regions in western Lofa county and eastern Sierra Leone, as well as timber concessions, iron ore deposits, and rubber plantations. American sources estimated in 1996 that between 1990 and 1994, Taylor brokered close to $75 million a year in financial transactions stemming from his iron-fisted control of these sources. On assuming the presidency of Liberia in 1997, his income grew exponentially to more than $100 million per year until he was unseated in 2003. Under his tenure, Taylor oversaw the despoliation and rape of the country's natural resources while pillaging the national treasury. During this era, he spent heavily on weapons and creating a mercenary army to look after his interests. International officials traced his banking accounts to institutions throughout West Africa, Europe, Panama, and the Caribbean islands. Authorities believed he used at least 30 front companies to hide his assets, with large shipments of cash being transferred by couriers. During his years as warlord and president, Taylor helped destroy two of West Africa's most prosperous countries—Liberia and Sierra Leone—while establishing links with various organized crime syndicates and terrorist organizations. For example, in 2000, organized crime groups from China, Israel, Russia, South Africa, and Ukraine operated simultaneously in Liberia with the full blessing of Taylor.

In regions such as West Africa, where there is full-scale war in many countries, including Sierra Leone and Liberia, it has been necessary for military forces to resort to organized criminal activities to fund hostilities. Separated by a porous border, Sierra Leone and Liberia are both considered failed states, where "chaos is the norm and war is a way of life. Insofar as there is a government, it operates in a way similar to an organized crime syndicate" as it becomes a welcoming beacon to "non-state actors" such as drug syndicates, criminal organizations, and terrorist organizations (Farah 2004, 20).This goes for lower-intensity conflicts as well. According to one United Nations study, it has been suggested that this process can result in professional criminals taking control of the state itself, citing the case of Charles Taylor, who ruled Liberia between 1997 and 2003 (United Nations 2005).

The Caribbean has proved to be particularly vulnerable to organized crime due to its geographic proximity between South and North America. Further contributing to its presence is the region's porous borders, as well as an ease in travel that has been exemplified by traditional patterns of migration between interdependent Caribbean states that have unintentionally facilitated greater mobility and aided in the expansion of both legal enterprise and transnational organized criminal activities.

Factors Aiding the Spread of Organized Crime in the Caribbean

- The presence of political, economic, and social inequalities that create large-scale migration flows that encourage organized crime syndicates to follow and exploit these situations.
- The ability of international syndicates to buy influence in domestic political systems.
- The increasing availability of more sophisticated weaponry and technologies.
- The difficulties of fragile and economically strapped governments to manage and safeguard their modern nation states. (Ramdin, 2007)

AFRICAN ORGANIZED CRIME

African countries share with other poor nations a number of characteristics that make them hospitable to organized criminal activity. Among the most important factors are the persistence of high levels of income inequality—and Africa is made up of many of the most unequal societies on the planet. Rapid urbanization has been a factor worldwide as well since the beginning of the 20th century, and Africa is urbanizing at almost twice the global rate. With almost 44% of Sub-Saharan Africans under the age of 15, African countries feature a high share of unemployed young men, fertile recruiting for criminal gangs. Add to this formula the fact that its poorly resourced criminal justice systems featuring low conviction rates and a paucity of police, it should be no surprise that there has been an increase in organized crime activity on the continent since the mid-1990s.

One explanation for the rise in African organized crime that has gained increasing currency is that many criminal enterprises beginning in the 1980s took advantage of the globalization of the world's economies and the incredible advances of communication technologies. Together with easier international travel and expanded world trade, crime syndicates found it easier to branch out of local and regional crime to target international victims and develop criminal networks with more prosperous nations.

In 2000, the U.S. government released an *International Crime Threat Assessment* that characterized the conditions that made Africa ripe for transnational crime, stating:

> Porous borders, ample routes for smuggling drugs, weapons, explosives, and other contraband, and corruptible police and security forces makes Sub-Saharan Africa and inviting operational environment for international criminals, drug traffickers and terrorists. Major Sub-Saharan cities with extensive commercial, financial, and sea and air transportation links to Europe, the Middle East, and Asia are hubs for international criminal activity," citing cities that included Nairobi and Mombassa, Kenya; Addis Ababa, Ethiopia; Abidjan, Ivory Coast; Johannesburg, South Africa; and Lagos, Nigeria. (Berry and Curtis 2003, 2)

One of the most convincing explanations for the soaring rates in organized crime begins with a discussion of failed nation-states and widespread poverty, which is then magnified by the persistence of deeply rooted corruption and tribal and ethnic rivalries.

In Africa, a high premium is placed on one's tribal or ethnic background. Quite often, criminal gangs and organized crime groups are bound together by these built-in loyalties. In the same way, conflict arises between these gangs that often can be traced to events that occurred during or even before colonialism and the members' living memories. In November 2006, more than 10 people were killed and 600 homes burned to ashes in a bout of gang violence between Kenyan gangs in Nairobi. By most accounts, the bloodshed was sparked by a bootlegging dispute that was exacerbated by ethnic rivalry (Gettleman 2006). The two adversaries were the Mungiki from the Kikuyu tribe, one of the nation's largest, and the Taliban, from the Luo, also an important tribe. According to one resident, this conflict was less over criminal rackets and more about tribal rivalries, issues that are lost on foreign interpreters of this bloodshed.

The "epicenter" of the dispute was Mathare, a slum housing almost 500,000 people on the edge of downtown Nairobi and an affluent area home to a number of foreign ambassadors. Over the years, this area became well-known "as a pocket of anarchy" in a city considered orderly by African urban standards. This locale was dominated by street gangs of young boys often dreadlocked and bearing machetes who extorted a street tax from local residents at various checkpoints. Throwing up his hands in disgust, one resident lamented, "You pay security, you pay electricity, you pay for toilets and what do you get?" (Gettleman 2006).

One of the gangs is called the Mungiki, which is considered "a secretive, quasi-religious sect" (Gettleman 2006) with a predilection for cutting out their enemies' navels, and who follow a leader they believe came from outer space. Their opponents in the dispute are a group of vigilantes known as the Taliban, although they are all Christians and have nothing to do with Islamic extremism.

What Makes African Societies Vulnerable to Organized Crime?

- Presence of established smuggling networks
- Lack of opportunities for economic activity
- Availability of battle hardened and unemployed combatants with military training
- Legacy of "strong men" and warlords controlling various geographic locales
- Ongoing civil wars and state sponsored violence that generates disrespect for rule of law

(Shaw and Wannenburg 2005, 370–372)

In any case, the dispute was set off when the Mungiki attempted to compel a higher street tax on the brewers of outlawed homemade liquor known as *chang'aa* and revered for potency higher than vodka. The brewers were reluctant to cave in and gathered up Taliban members to defend them. In the resulting skirmishes, houses were burned down and victims were killed with machetes or shot. It took the intervention of Kenyan police and soldiers and a dusk-to-dawn curfew to stem the violence—for now (Gettleman 2006).

What has become clear in the new millennium is that transnational crime syndicates have taken advantage of the "artificial, colonial-era borders that divide ethnic groups in virtually all African countries" (Berry and Curtis 2003, 3). According to one survey, "no fewer than 177 ethnic 'culture areas' in Africa are divided by national boundaries," citing examples of the Nigerian–Cameroon boundary, which divides 14 tribes, and those of Burkina-Faso, which run through the boundaries of 21 tribes. However, this might not seem of utmost geopolitical significance, but "kinship, ethnic, and economic links are far stronger than the national identity" (Reader 1998, 575–576). The process of transnational crime is facilitated by the migration of populations back and forth across said borders and in the process becoming part of the transportation process that transfers illicit and stolen materials. With globalization, most countries have new immigrant communities residing within their borders. Organized crime groups have taken advantage of these by utilizing new legal commerce networks to shield deep-rooted trafficking networks that control the trafficking of illegal goods between various African host countries and their home countries abroad. Such relationships have been well chronicled among Chinese, Indian, Nigerian, and Russian communities in southern Africa, and likewise among Indian and Middle Eastern groups in East and West Africa (Berry and Curtis 2003).

West Africa

The countries most plagued by organized crime in West Africa are Côte d'Ivoire, Ghana, Nigeria, Senegal, and Sierra Leone. Criminal syndicates partake in a host of activities including drug and weapons trafficking, advanced fee and Internet fraud, human trafficking, diamond smuggling, forgery, cigarette smuggling, armed robbery, the smuggling of oil, and the illegal manufacture of firearms (United Nations 2005). West Africa encompasses a large chunk of Africa made up of a number of cultures speaking a range of languages. However, these countries share some common traits. Most important, except for Liberia,[1] all the countries had been colonized by European countries in the late 19th century.

After the West African countries received independence in the 1950s and 1960s, each nation attempted to develop strong national institutions that it was hoped would stimulate a diversified economy. Nigeria and Côte D'Ivoire (the Ivory Coast) emerged as the most successful in this regard. However, other countries did not share in the progress and were notably shackled by political instability, many facing military coups or becoming one-party states. Organized crime in the region became more prominent in the 1970s, "contemporaneous with the oil price rises of that decade, the

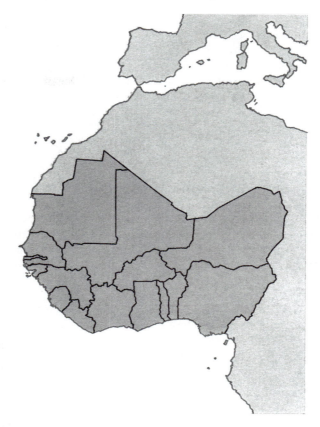

FIGURE 12.1 Map of West Africa
Source: Dorling Kindersley Media Library

Latin American Drug Smugglers Ferrying Cocaine through West Africa (2008)

Throughout at least 2008, West Africa has become a major transit point for cocaine from South America heading for Europe. Early in 2008, the French Navy intercepted a Liberian-registered ship off the coast of West Africa laden with 2.4 tons of pure cocaine. Investigators believed it was bound for Nigeria, but had developed mechanical problems for completing its Atlantic journey (Mbachu 2008). In July 2008, a passenger plane loaded with 1,540 pounds of cocaine was found abandoned at Sierra Leone's main airport. The plane was registered in South America. Authorities, still searching for its pilots, believed that with cocaine prices escalating in Europe higher than the United States, drug smugglers are now bringing cocaine into West Africa, where it is divided up among hundreds of traffickers who transport it north to Europe (*Houston Chronicle*, July 14, 2008).

Recent evidence suggests that cocaine is often stored in West Africa until it is time to ship to Europe and in some cases North America. Once the cocaine arrives by either air or ship from its source in South America, it is trafficked to Europe by either of two routes. One route follows a traditional hashish smuggling route by speedboat north of Morocco to Europe. Others prefer to use couriers who ingest the contraband or hide it in their luggage before boarding commercial flights for Europe. One the most glaring examples of this method involved the arrest of 32 drug couriers who landed on the same plane from Morocco to Amsterdam in 2006. According to European law enforcement, West Africans make up 90% of all Africans arrested for drug trafficking (Mbachu 2008).

de-linking of the dollar from gold, high inflation, and the rapid spread of debt in the developing world" (United Nations 2005, 4).[2]

From a historical perspective, European crime syndicates operating in this region can be considered precursors to modern African organized crime, as they experimented with setting up intercontinental crime bases back in the colonial era. For example, the Ivory Coast was utilized by Corsican gangs engaging in cigarette smuggling and enlisting women for prostitution in France years before independence in 1960 (United Nations 2005). By the 1970s, most West African countries were beginning to recognize new crime trends. Some could be blamed on the wars raging in Liberia and Sierra Leone, or the subsequent civil war in Nigeria, all facilitating an increasing weapons and drug trade. One expert even suggested that wherever there is full-scale war, "it becomes difficult to distinguish between organized crime and political violence" (United Nations 2005, 8). Others have suggested, "Armed conflict has encouraged certain forms of organized crime to flourish under guise of political struggle" (United Nations 2005, 3).

Most evidence points to the fact that there are few examples of hierarchical groups with long-standing associations (except maybe for oil bunkering). In 2004, one researcher explained the operational structure of West African syndicates, reporting at a United Nations conference in Dakar:

> The organizational structure may be similar to [that] employed by legitimate small scale enterprises found [among] ethno-cultural groups disproportionately arrested for drug trafficking. First the enterprises usually involve masters [entrepreneurs] and apprentices [those training to become traders or suppliers in particular goods and services]. Second, there is cooperation among the enterprises/entrepreneurs, such that if goods are not available in a given shop it is collected and supplied from another entrepreneur. Third, many of the entrepreneurs have relations or acquaintances abroad that facilitate payment for the imported goods, usually for a commission. (United Nations 2005, 16)

In any case, the consensus seems to indicate that West African criminals are rarely part of any well-structured syndicates but "tend to be highly flexible and individualistic in their methods."

By March 2007, West African gangs based in Ireland had become major players in the international drug trade. According to a high-ranking customs official, these gangs were "highly

Human Smuggling: Senegal

West African syndicates have become major players in African human smuggling in recent years, with most immigrants heading for European Union (EU) countries. The prospective immigrants sell everything they own for the opportunity to start new lives. The smugglers, however, have different motivations—to make as much money as possible off the misery of their "clients." In one recent case, a vessel broke down carrying some 400 migrants to Europe, but made it no farther than Mauritania. By the time the ship's engines had ground to a halt, the smugglers were on their way after clearing of hundreds of thousands of Euros in cash. Reports indicate that the mostly Asian migrants from Guinea had paid between €6,000 and €10,000 for their trip to Europe. Typically, even once the migrants safely arrive at their destination, smugglers often extort additional funds from their charges even after the original payment has been made. In the aforementioned case, the smugglers allegedly made close to €300,000. Smuggling rings work best in failed states with poor economies and rampant corruption, with protection often supplied at the highest levels of government. Networks of human smugglers have emerged uniting transnational organized crime groups with small-scale smuggling rings. In one year alone, Spanish intelligence officers reported destroying 15 African gangs, with links to Mauritania, Gambia, Senegal, Morocco, and as far as Asia. Crime syndicates are often drawn to human smuggling because it carries less punitive punishments than drugs and weapons trafficking (Gangs profit, 2007).

The Adaptability of West African Gangs

Virtually every law enforcement source characterizes the West African syndicates as *adaptable*, referring to their ability to change their strategies and methods in order to continue criminal operations. In Ireland, police created a profile of a typical drug smuggler (or *mule*), noting that it was usually someone with low socioeconomic standing. It wasn't long before the syndicates caught on to this and adapted by hiring Caucasians from Eastern Europe and White South Africans of low status instead (Burke 2007).

sophisticated, clever and adaptable" (Burke 2007). In the process, West African syndicates based in Ireland were "challenging the traditional dominance of expatriate Irish criminals in the supply of illegal drugs" (Burke 2007).

One cannot explain West African organized crime without reference to the historical and contemporary legacy of corruption. One Ghanaian investigator remarked: "Even those who work for the Narcotics Control Board . . . are scared to confront the levels of corruption in the criminal justice system" (quoted in United Nations 2005, 7). According to the 2003 Corruption Perceptions Index, Ghana was ranked at 50, Senegal 66, Ivory Coast at 71 (the same ranking as India and the Russian Federation), and Nigeria stood at 101— "the second most corrupt country in the world" (United Nations 2005, 7).

HUMAN TRAFFICKING Human trafficking in West Africa occurs in a number of guises. For example, some immigrants have been forced into virtual "agricultural slavery," working on the cocoa plantations, whereas others have been imported from India to work on Sierra Leone plantations thanks to the connivance of Indian and Lebanese businessmen. In addition, there is a strong tradition in the region in which young dependents are placed with the most extended part of the family or kinship group as an unpaid ward or apprentice, but in the end for someone's financial profit.

The region has also earned prominence as a transit point for human traffic attempting to bypass international controls on immigration. In one recent case, six Chinese nationals were caught along with a Nigerian national who was smuggling them into the United Kingdom in 2003. Following interrogation, the trafficker admitted working in a partnership with a Chinese entrepreneur in Nigeria. Sierra Leone, with its almost constant environment of chaos, has proved especially attractive for international traffickers who are able to transport labor migrants disguised as refugees (United Nations 2005).

Other types of human trafficking are related to the sex trade in the form of prostitution and sex slavery. Sierra Leone and Nigeria have featured most prominently in this crime. In Nigeria, young women from the Edo State are smuggled into Europe and the Middle East, as prospects for legitimate employment at home greatly diminished in the 1990s. The directors of this trade are usually former Nigerian prostitutes who made enough in the trade so that they could rise to madams. In this role, she is responsible for organizing the recruitment of prostitutes in West Africa under false pretenses. This might include promising rural girls jobs in the hotel business in Europe and other opportunities. The madam is expected to obtain false travel documents and to bribe immigration officials, and to hire *trolleys,* who serve as guides. One of the final steps before leaving the country is to pay a fetish priest to administer

> a quasi-traditional oath of secrecy to potential prostitutes and finally a lawyer is paid to draft a contract between the madam and her prostitute. Typically what bind the relationship are claims by the madam that she has invested tens of thousands of dollars in travel expenses that are expected to be reimbursed through participation in sex trade activities. (United Nations 2005, 27)

> ### Cigarette Smuggling: The Wansa Group in Sierra Leone
>
> Cigarette smuggling in West Africa typically predominates between states where at least one is marked by a higher excise tax than its neighbors, thus offering a lucrative opportunity to organized smugglers. One of the leading exemplars is the Wansa group, headquartered in Sierra Leone. It is led by an entrepreneur referred to as the *Guinea Wansa*. As leader of the operation, he has solidified a relationship with border officials that allows him to bring in cigarettes to Guinea legally from abroad. Then, under nightfall and to avoid customs controls, the cigarettes are loaded onto boats (locally known as *pampas*) and transported to Sierra Leone, which has a high excise tax on the commodity. Once in country, the product is dispersed to four distributors. Once they reach these strategic locations, the product is smuggled back and forth, hidden along with legitimate commerce. Membership in this syndicate is regarded as restricted, with ties based on kinship and ethnic relationships.
>
> Some anthropologists and social scientists have questioned whether this and other smuggling operation can be truly regarded as organized crime. According to African experts, this trade is dominated by Fula merchants who are highly engaged in commerce, and except for evading excise taxes when possible, are devout Muslims and law abiding in almost every respect. Traders eschew violence and the least attractive characteristics of the milieu, and prefer bribing their way out. These Fula traders who operate on the border between Guinea and Sierra Leone usually began as legitimate traders, and as their profits increase, are considered to have branched into cigarettes to diversify their portfolios (in Western patois) and take advantage of excise inequalities between the two states (United Nations 2005, 28–29).

DIAMOND SMUGGLING

There are no fingerprints on diamonds.

Almost three-quarters of the world's rough diamonds are mined in Africa. A number of international syndicates have become involved in the smuggling of diamonds, including Russian, Chinese, Italian, and African organizations. In war-ravaged Africa, host to a number of bloody civil wars, insurgents, criminals, and even government officials have been embroiled in the smuggling of diamonds and other precious gems. Diamonds, like gold, have a high value on international markets and are an internationally accepted medium of exchange, trailing only hard currency in the world of black market dealings, and are virtually untraceable.[3]

Diamond smuggling has plagued parts of Africa since they were first mined in the 19th century. In the 1880s, a Select Committee in South Africa was appointed to investigate the illegal diamond trade, resulting in the passage of the Diamond Trade Act in 1882, which offered punitive measures and doubled the police force in order to suppress the impulses of anyone toward illicit profiteering. More recently, in 2003, African governments accepted the Kimberly (South Africa) Process Certification Scheme that was geared toward preventing the trade in diamonds to fund conflicts, hence the references to *conflict* or *blood diamonds*. However, recent research suggests that although it makes it more difficult to smuggle diamonds from rebel-held regions to the international markets, the trade in the illicit gems continues due in no small part to weak diamond controls in some diamond-producing countries. Experts estimate that the illicit trade in diamonds in Sierra Leone represents close to 20% of the total trade. As a result, the illicit diamond trade continues to fund terrorist groups and facilitate the laundering of money (Kimberly Process 2006).

The diamond mines of Angola, Sierra Leone, and the Congo are especially productive. Some syndicates trade weapons for diamonds. The smuggling of diamonds is a rather simple process in which bags of uncut stones are transported by air from their place of origin and then split into smaller packages and shipped to one of the major diamond markets, including Tel Aviv, Bombay, and Antwerp. One source has Osama bin Laden's al-Qaeda network converting $20 million into untraceable gemstones prior to the September 11, 2001, attacks.

FIGURE 12.2   Replica of largest diamond ever found (located in Kimberly Mine Museum)
Source: Dorling Kindersley Media Library/Roger de la Harpe

In West Africa, Sierra Leone[4] has become central to the illegal diamond market. Although the country produces only 4% of the world's diamonds, unlike other diamond-rich parts of Africa, in West Africa, "high-quality alluvial diamonds can be mined with no more equipment than a spade and a sieve," and deficiencies in government regulation result in smuggling on a massive scale (United Nations 2005, 27).

By most accounts the main profits from diamond smuggling comes after the extraction of the diamonds—when the stones are exported to international wholesale and cutting centers. Of these the most prominent site is Belgium. Most of the West African diamond trade is dominated by outsiders, many coming from Middle Eastern countries such as Israel, Syria, and Lebanon.

Why Is a Diamond Valuable?

In his magisterial history of diamonds, Matthew Hart argues that diamonds are "sublimely useless," stating that it is "Tradition [that] supports a diamond's value," citing the De Beers Company advertising campaign that created the image of their inherent value (2001, 139). Although billions of dollars' worth of diamonds are harvested, a substantial number are kept in storage to keep the prices high artificially. The De Beers Company, founded in 1880 by British merchant Cecil Rhodes, continues to dominate the diamond trade and is able to discourage competition by flooding the market and causing prices to drop at the hint of new market competition (Farah 2004, 21). In any case, the most profitable aspect of the diamond trade begins after the stones are extracted, during the export process that takes them to wholesale and cutting centers outside the continent, especially in Belgium. Once the diamonds leave West Africa, the gems fall into the hands of foreign traders, most notably the Lebanese and the Syrians, who have been well represented in West Africa for decades, and to a lesser extent Israeli traders (United Nations 2005).

The diamond trade intersects with organized crime activity in several ways. The smuggling of untraceable diamonds is a great source for laundering money. Omnipresent rebel groups often resort to the trade to finance their war plans and weapons. There is evidence to suggest that Sierra Leone's diamonds were a significant source of financing in the Lebanese civil war. The illegal diamond trade is not new. As far back as the 1950s, Ian Fleming, creator of the James Bond novels, wrote in his book *The Diamond Smugglers* that the smuggling of diamonds from Sierra Leone was "the greatest smuggling operation in the world" (United Nations 2005, 28; Fleming 1957, 126).

More recently, other crime syndicates have entered the diamond business at various levels. One of the most prominent newcomers has been the Sicilian Mafia, which used front companies to purchase a diamond cutting and polishing license and gained a foothold in Namibia's diamond-cutting industry. According to a recent investigation, the licenses were obtained with the help of a former National Central Intelligence Services operator, who denied any knowledge of organized crime involvement. What has become most troubling to the authorities is that any legitimate involvement in the diamond industry offers the Mafia incredible money-laundering opportunities. Because the Sicilian syndicates were attempting to launder dirty money, it could offer 30% above market prices for rough diamonds. Once these are cut, they would be almost untraceable among the millions of carats of cut diamonds traded internationally (Grobler 2007).

Nigeria

Almost one-fifth of Africa's Sub-Saharan population live in Nigeria, the continent's most urbanized country. On top of this, Nigeria has 75 mutually "un-understandable" tribal languages, with few Westerners who can translate them. By most accounts, Nigeria can be better compared to an amalgamation of tribal states more than a natural country, citing the artificial natural borders forced on the region by British authorities at independence in 1960 (Robinson 2000). In less than a decade, the teeming nation descended into post-colonial disorder brought about by military coups and ethnic-based warfare.

It has been estimated that Nigerian gangs have been active in 80 different countries. In 1996, a survey of international business executives ranked Nigeria's government as the most corrupt in the world (Liddick, Jr. 2004). This would not be surprising to most Africa scholars because Nigerians have long been recognized as the best traders in Africa, harkening back to the slave-trading era with the Arabs. Congressional Hearings on Intelligence and Security refer to Nigerian criminal enterprises as "adaptable, polycrime organizations," noting, "They launder money in Hong Kong, buy cocaine in the Andes, run prostitution and gambling rings in Spain and Italy, and corrupt legitimate business in Great Britain with their financial crimes" (Winer 1996). Although the FBI has identified criminal syndicates operating out of other African countries such as Liberia and Ghana, no African country is more prominent when it comes to organized crime than Nigeria. Some experts traced elements of organized crime activity to pre-1975 schemes to falsify imports in order to transfer funds outside the country, a violation of international currency regulations. This was a rather sophisticated enterprise for the era that required either overcharging or importing substandard goods for delivery to government departments in return for kickbacks to government officials. This could be regarded as precursors to the frauds that characterize Nigerian organize crime in the modern era (United Nations 2005, 5).

Corruption and financial malfeasance has deep roots in Nigeria, dating back to the colonial era, when Nigerians saw government institutions as White man's business—"an alien system that could be plundered when necessary." One Nigerian scholar explained,

> There was thus nothing seriously wrong with stealing state funds, especially if they were used to benefit not only the individual but also members of the community. Those who had the opportunity to be in the government were expected to use the power and resources at their disposal to advance private and communal interests. (Meredith 2006, 174)

Following independence, the same philosophy prevailed as "every facet of Nigerian society was eventually permeated by corruption," leading one official to surmise, "You bribe to get your child into school; you pay to secure your job and also continue to pay in some cases to retain it; you pay ten per cent of any contract obtained; you dash the tax officer to avoid paying taxes; you pay a hospital doctor or nurse to get proper attention; you pay the policeman to evade arrest" and so forth (Meredith 2006, 175).

The 1980s provided the greatest stimuli for the development of Nigerian crime syndicates, which Nigerian expert Etannibi E.O. Alemika attributed to the corruption of the civilian government from 1979 to 1983 and the inauguration of a new economic adjustment program in 1986 that led to more intense poverty, unemployment, and emigration. Moreover, the rapid and poorly planned restructuring of the financial sector, including the introduction of poorly regulated financial instruments, increased opportunities for money laundering and fraud. The same era witnessed the first reported cases of heroin smuggling as well (United Nations 2005, 5; Jones 1993).

In recent years, the U.S. State Department suggested that Nigerian criminal gangs work as subcontractors for Russian, Chinese, and Colombian criminal organizations (Liddick Jr. 2004). FBI investigators revealed partnerships between various Nigerians and Russian organized crime syndicates, further contributing to the Nigerian reputation as "the most relaxed of all organized crime groups when it comes to forming strategic alliances with other criminals" (Robinson 2000, 282). Nigerian criminal gangs have established themselves as major players in the distribution of cocaine, heroin, and marijuana. For more than three decades, Nigerians have been both a source country and transshipment point for narcotics into the United States, especially heroin. Since the mid-1980s, more than 1,000 Nigerian nationals have been convicted of trafficking heroin into the United States, and in 1994, Interpol stated, "Nigerians are the third largest ethnic smuggling groups in the world" (Liddick 2004, 35). Before the end of that decade, the International Narcotics Control Strategy Report went one step further, painting Nigeria as the "hub of African narcotics traffic" (quoted in Richards 1998, 285).

In 1998, African organized crime expert Phil Williams testified before a Congressional committee on "Combating International Crime in Africa."[5] Much of his testimony was focused on Nigerian organized crime groups, which he asserted were notable for their ubiquity, pointing out, "Nigerian criminal groups are more pervasive around the globe than those of any nation" (Williams 1998, 15). Nigerian crime groups are regarded as adaptable, innovative, and flexible, and "adapt easily to the host country."

NIGERIAN SYNDICATE STRUCTURE   Nigerian crime syndicates appear in a number of incarnations, with most maintaining a modicum of organization that can include a leader at the top with lieutenants acting under his orders, with almost all having some affiliation with government officials or agencies. However, unlike traditional organized crime groups that often subscribe to a more monolithic structure, Nigerian gangs more closely resemble "cell-like syndicates, often breaking apart and reforming in other criminal initiatives with interchangeable members" (Nicaso and Lamothe 2005, 239). Among the more immutable characteristics of Nigerian syndicates is their predilection for linkage across tribal lines or family ties.

One recent United Nations report states that West African syndicates in general rarely follow "the hierarchical, corporation-like model," preferring a type of organization that is project based (United Nations, 2005, 15). According to this report, criminal enterprises are more likely to operate in a manner similar to legitimate traders and merchants. The process is centered on an individual entrepreneur who uses success in one endeavor to inveigle others, often relatives and dependents, to join his business as it becomes a money machine. This type of operation tends to develop strong ties based on family, lineage, and ethnic group. Perhaps investigator Etannibi E.O. Alemika explained it best, noting, "The organizational structure may be similar to [that] employed by legitimate small scale enterprises found [among] ethno-cultural groups disproportionately arrested for drug trafficking" (2005, 16). The investigator went on to describe the structure of the enterprise, explaining,

> The enterprises usually involve masters (entrepreneurs) and apprentices (those training to become traders or suppliers in particular goods and services). Second, there is cooperation among the enterprises/entrepreneurs, such that if goods are not available in a given shop it is collected and supplied from another entrepreneur. Third, many of the entrepreneurs have relations or acquaintances abroad that facilitate payment for the imported goods, usually for a commission. (United Nations 2005, 16)

One Nigerian investigator suggests that most of the crime gangs have a core nucleus of no more than three to five individuals, corresponding to the notion of a master and a few apprentices (United Nations 2005, 16).

According to the entrepreneurial model previously mentioned the corresponding application of this model to the drug trade would look something like the following. Drug traffickers hire others to accomplish certain tasks on a one-time or sporadic basis (rather than on a permanent basis)—possibly as drivers or couriers/mules. Because this ad hoc connection does not adhere to a particular pattern, there is little risk of detection. It is common for police interrogation of drug couriers to reveal very little. The mule is typically carrying drugs across a border for several thousand dollars on a one-time basis and knows next to nothing about the larger picture. Rather than hiring individuals based on long-term relationships, traffickers are more likely to hire a courier using an assumed identity to give instructions to carry the drugs to a destination, or to wait for further instructions. No other information is provided (United Nations 2005).

Transnational crime expert Phil Williams delineates a well-organized structure among the Nigerian gangs and identified three types of structures. The first he considers an "old-fashioned pyramid of hierarchy," in which crime czars in Lagos and elsewhere can be connected with criminal operations around the world. They usually coordinate or support these activities and earn a substantial profit. Nigeria has weak money-laundering laws, and crime bosses are often part of the elite and ruling class, so there is little to prevent illicit profits from reaching their coffers once the crimes are committed.

The second structure is more flexible and composed of a smaller more tightly knit group typically linked by tribal or family affiliations. However, each of these groups operates "within a larger network that resembles trade associations rather than traditional mafia hierarchies." This larger network is capable of offering both support and potential contacts (Williams 1998, 15–16).

A third type of organization resembles a self-contained cell, with each component assigned to certain tasks. Compared to the previous structures, this group has more autonomy and flexibility, which allows creating and taking advantage of criminal opportunities.

WEST AFRICAN KINSHIP NETWORKS AND ORGANIZED CRIME What is often misunderstood by Western observers is that crime groups that recruit through kinship associations based on the village or region of origin allows the crime network to function outside the parameters of Western relationships. These networks are almost impenetrable to outsiders who are unfamiliar with the cultural codes of the region. According to a recent study by the United Nations, examples of these codes include "the practice of administering oaths sworn by reference to religious oracles, and the use of local languages or dialects that make infiltration by outsiders extremely difficult," and making it virtually impossible for non-West African police to infiltrate these groups (2005, 17).

Over time, the persistence of recruiting through personal associations resulted in the connection of certain illegal trades with specific places and tribes. This is exemplified by the association of Nigerian prostitution rings being connected to the Edo State and Benin City, "because those individuals who pioneered the trade have kept it in the hands of networks of kin and associates" (United Nations, 2005, 17) to the exclusion of outsiders. The result of all this is that an impression is forged that certain types of commerce are dominated by particular ethnic groups. For example, Nigerian police assert that most drug-trafficking syndicates are dominated by Igbo-speaking people from southeast Nigeria and Yoruba from the southwest, along with southern minority groups.

ADVANCE FEE, OR 419 FRAUD Since the mid-1990s, Nigerian criminals have become identified with advance fee, or "419" frauds, which has earned its own moniker—"the Nigerian scam." In fact, it has become so widespread that it has become part of the criminal justice lexicon, as in he is a "419er," or someone was "419ed" (Nigeria—419 Coalition 2007). One observer suggested that this scam "represents the perversion of talent and initiative in a society where normal paths of opportunity are closed to all but the well connected" (Packer 2006, 72). According to one account, 419 scams began as a lark among students who lost jobs during Nigeria's 1980s oil bust. Others argue that this is too simplistic, and that it is difficult to substantiate the origins of this scheme, outside of the fact that it began in Nigeria (Chaudhuri, March 10, 2007). More likely, advance-fee frauds began in the late 1980s, when they "developed from the prior existence of corrupt dealings in foreign exchange and the transfer of stolen funds through foreign businesses and entrepreneurs" (United Nations 2005, 6).

Initially, fraudsters used the mails to send thousands of handwritten letters to physicians, lawyers, and other professionals. Although the writers seemed barely literate, they persisted in asking for details of the recipient's bank accounts and accompanying materials to be sent back to the Nigerian capital of Lagos.[6] Typically, prospective victims were told that a large sum of illegally earned money needed to be transferred into a Western bank account. In return for his participation, the recipient would earn a substantial commission. With the inauguration of the Internet, the numbers of schemes have only increased. Today, it has become one the world's most insidious financial frauds.

The "419" refers to a particular Nigerian criminal statute—Nigerian Decree 419, which made the fraud illegal in 1980 (Robinson 2000). Almost anyone with a computer or a fax can be a victim. Typically, the scam is inaugurated through an e-mail or fax purporting to be from some deposed African leader or other luminary who wants to share a fortune with you if only you hand over a bank address/fax/telex number, your bank account number, and private phone number. Characteristically, the message goes on to say that in return for this information and (in some cases) a few sheets of company letterhead, the victim could expect to reap up to 30% of the money. However, to show good faith, first the mark was expected to send an advance payment to guarantee the fictitious money transfer. In the vast majority of cases, once the victim sends the money, the Nigerian partner breaks off contact. Most individuals lose money when the fraud artist asks for cash to pay bribes or last-minute fees and taxes to complete the transfers. Individuals in more than 60 countries have been victimized by this scam, including small and large corporations, religious organizations, and individuals. According to the U.S. Secret Service and the State Department, this scam nets hundreds of millions of dollars each year. The Secret Service created a task force in cooperation with the Nigerian police to target these individuals.

In some cases, victims have been killed while attempting to recover their losses. In June 1995, an American was enticed to Nigeria in an advance-fee fraud and was killed in Lagos. In another case, an American financial consultant flew to Lagos to supervise what he thought was a legal and lucrative business opportunity that came his way through a Nigerian contact. However, following his arrival, the consultant was asked for more and more cash; when he saw the ruse for what it was, he refused to pay another cent. He disappeared and was found "necklaced" not far from his hotel, with a car tire placed around his neck, covered with gas, and set on fire. According to British journalist Tony Thompson, at least 17 individuals have been killed since the mid-1990s after venturing to Nigeria to salvage what they lost to the fraudsters (Sommer 2001; Thompson 2005, 145).

Nigerian fraudsters conduct extensive research before selecting targets. It is typical for unknowing observers to paint victims of the 419 scams either as greedy or naïve. However, what has become increasingly clear is that many fall victim due to humanitarian concerns, which the fraudsters have picked up on and have exploited. It is not uncommon for the scammers to refer to God

Typical Categories of Business Proposals Employed in 419 Scams

- Assistance escaping the country with accumulated wealth
- Transfer of funds from "over-invoiced" or "overestimated" contracts relating to resources, medical equipment, Turn Around Maintenance (TAM), or infrastructure
- Efforts to defraud government on "forgotten" or "former regime" accounts
- Contract fraud
- Conversion of hard currency or money laundering
- Sale of crude oil or other commodities at below-market prices
- Transfer of accounts of now defunct companies
- Require money for chemicals to "clean" large amounts of marked currency
- Purchase of real estate: *The Nigerian National Petroleum Company has discovered oil, and as government employees we want to acquire the land, but we need a front man to purchase it for us.*
- Deposed leaders and their families (widows and sons) and associates (aides, lawyers)
- Over-invoiced contracts and government employees: *The Nigerian government overpaid on some contract, and we need a front man to get it out of the country before they discover the error.*
- Forgotten accounts, wills, and inheritances, or death-bed claims of wealth
- Trade deals
- Assistance getting stolen assets out of country: *My father left me $40 million in his will, but I have to bribe government officials to get it out.*
- Gifts or bequests to charitable or religious organizations: *Your charity has been named as a beneficiary in the will of a wealthy Nigerian. You just need to send the necessary "proofs of identity."*
- Scholarships
- Lottery winnings
- Relative in World Trade Center left a fortune
- Bogus job offers with rebate of wage overpayment using third-party checks

Nigerian E-mail Scams, p. 8.

while targeting religious victims. Others exploited humanitarian impulses. In an increasingly depersonalized world, fraudsters have expanded their repertoire with offers of romance.

During the 1996 Atlanta Summer Olympics, Nigerian syndicates had individuals come to the United States and create an infrastructure that included setting up addresses to facilitate the transfer of money and letters stateside. It was not until later that police investigators pieced together the reasons behind the disappearance of most of the telephone directories, business directories, and Yellow Pages from the region's hotels. Law enforcement eventually deduced that a number of competing athletes and fans had been paid a bounty to take them back home in their luggage. As a result,

Common Senders of Advance-Fee Fraud Contact Letters[7]

- Senior civil servant in one of the Nigerian Ministries, such as the Ministry of Aviation, Finance, Petroleum Resources, etc.
- Nigerian royalty or political insider, such as "the son of the President of Nigeria."
- The spouse, relative, aide, or confidante of a deposed leader.
- A Nigerian businessman or lawyer with an impressive title, such as "Chief," "Barrister," or "Dr."
- An auditor or accountant with strong ties to Nigerian officials.
- A religious figure, such as a Deacon, Brother, Pastor.

Human Costs of the Nigerian Scam (2006)

On March 22, 2006, a popular church parson by the name of Matthew Winkler was found shot to death in his church in a rural Tennessee town. The following day, his wife Mary was arrested more than 300 miles away in Alabama as she fled with her three daughters. Although various explanations were offered by the defense, the prosecution was convinced that the wife was the perpetrator, suggesting that bank managers were closing in on a check-kiting scheme that she wanted to hide from her husband. According to the prosecutor, the wife had been caught up in the swindle known as the "Nigerian scam," which promises riches to victims who send money to cover the processing expenses. Mary Winkler was tried and convicted for the murder (Krajicek 2008; Haines 2006).

almost like clockwork, the Atlanta area was deluged by 419 letters 3 months after the Olympics (Robinson 2000).

According to an investigator for a Nigerian Secret Service Task Force, 419 fraud was so popular in Nigeria in the new millennium that "On any given day, you may have a hundred people, ranging from amateur crooks to organized criminals, all using the same Internet café to send out 419 e-mails" (Thompson 2005, 151).

Prior to the advent and ubiquity of the Internet, most 419 letters were posted out of Lagos, where they are mailed to postal hubs throughout the Western world. However, postal authorities soon caught on and were able to filter many of the letters out of the mail systems. American inspectors were annually taking 3.2 million of the 419 letters out of the system by the end of the 1990s. Although the U.S. Postal Service was legally required to deliver all legally posted letters, they found a loophole revealed by British counterparts that allowed them to take the letters out of the mails prior to delivery. It was the British National Criminal Intelligence Service (NCIS) that recognized that the letters were posted with counterfeit stamps. The 419 fraudsters have been quick to adapt to other devices or to target other less-developed mail systems in regions such as Hong Kong, where at one time inspectors estimated that 95% of the mail from Nigeria consisted of 419 letters. In 2000, one investigator estimated that about 1% of those who received letters responded, with an average loss reaching $200,000.

The Nigerian Repackaging Scam

This scam attempts to bypass restrictions of overseas shipping companies such as FedEx, DHL, and UPS, which all limit shipments to West Africa due to the widespread fraud problems. Those involved in the fraud usually solicit gullible Americans to serve as intermediaries instead. According to the Nigerian—419 Coalition, victims receive the goods, often unaware of its origins, and then send them on to Europe, where other scammers receive the goods and ship them on to Nigeria. In return, victims, who are often drawn in by initial promises of international romance, are promised reimbursement for shipping expenses, but this is never the case. Ever careful in selecting their targets, scammers find a ready supply of potential victims who answer spam and work-at-home advertisements. In one well-publicized case, an Oregon man met a woman on the Internet and their online relationship led to plans for a committed relationship and the woman moving to Oregon. However, first she asked him to help transship some packages to the UK. Once the lovestruck mark agreed, she sent him the goods with instructions on how to repackage them for the next step of the shipping to Europe. Fortunately, an online businessman in Texas recognized the scam and alerted authorities, who intervened and nixed the deal before it (and the relationship) was consummated. According to a Eugene, Oregon, investigator, participants in this scam "offer you a job repackaging and mailing things for, say, $6,000 per month. After you mail a whole bunch of things, they send you a check and, of course, it's bogus" (Nolan 2007).

By 2006, the United States had become the most lucrative 419 market, with losses estimated at almost $800 million a year, considered a 10% increase over the previous year (Chaudhuri, March 9, 2007).[8] Most of the scams originate in Nigeria, the Netherlands, the UK, or South Africa. More recently, India has become the third fastest growing market for the fraud, as perpetrators reach into Asian markets. In 2006, Indian victims lost $32 million, almost 10 times the amount from the previous year.

Illegal Export of Oil: Oil Bunkering

The illegal export of oil, more commonly known as *bunkering,* has become a major problem in Nigeria,[10] which for many years was the region's only producer of oil. The term *bunkering* refers to filling a ship with oil, which has become progressively more illegal. According to one 2004 estimate by Nigerian government sources, every day as much as 300,000 gallons of oil are exported illegally, amounting to more than $1 billion a year.[11] Due to the sophistication required for such schemes,

---

Sample 419 Letter[9]

The Presedency
Office of the Chief Auditor to the President
International Credit Settlement Dept.
Federal Minsitry of Finance

Attention,

This is to officially inform you that we have verified on your contract inheritance file and found out that why you have not received your payment is because you have not fullfilled the obligations giving to you in respect to your contract/inheritance payment.

Secondly we have been infromed that you are still dealing with the none officials in the bank so such illegal act like this have to stop if you wishes to receive your payment since we have decided to bring a solution to your problem, right now e have arranged your payment through our swift card payment ecnetr asia pacific, that is the latest instruction by the president chief, Olusegun Obasanjo (GCFR) Federal Republic of Nigeria.

This card center will sned you an ATM card which you will use to withdraw your money in any ATM machine in any part of the world, but the maximum is four thousand dollars per day, so if you like to receive your fund this way plase let us know by forwarding the following informations;

1. Your full name
2. Phone and fax number
3. Address were you want them to send the ATM card (p.o. box not accepted)
4. Your name and current occupation,

The ATM card payment center has been mandated to issue out $80,000 usd for your information you have to stop any further communication with any other persosn(s) of office(s). This is to avoid any hitches in finalizing your payment.

E-mail back as soon as you receive this important message for more direction on this regards on how to contact the swift card consult payment center for immediate issuing of your ATM

Card note: that because of imposters, we hereby issued you our code of conduct,
Which is (001) so you have to indicate this code on all future correspondence.

Chief Auditor to the President.
Barrister John Scott.

Sample 419 Letter

Dear Friend

I'm happy to inform you about my success in getting those funds transferred under the cooperation of a new partner from Paraguay. Presently I'm in Paraguay for investment projects with my own share of the total sum meanwhile, I didn't forget your past efforts and attempts to assist me in transferring those funds despite that it failed us some how.

Now contact my secretary, his name is _____ on _____ ask him to send you the total $800.000.00 which I kept for your compensation for all the past efforts and attempts to assist me in this matter. I appreciated your efforts at that time very much. So feel free and get in touched with my secretary and instruct him where to send the amount to you.

Please do let me know immediately you receive it so that we can share the joy after all the sufferness at that time. In the moment, I am very busy here because of the investment projects which me and the new partner are having at hand, finally, remember that I had forwarded instruction to the secretary on your behalf to receive the money, so feel free to get in touch with _____ he will send the amount to you without any delay.

With best regards,
Barrister Nweze Agu

---

some government critics cite the complicity of government officials at high levels of the Nigerian government.

Oil bunkering in West Africa is typically associated with the warfare between competing gangs in the Niger Delta Region attempting to control the territory. The control of the "bunkering turf" is a necessity for the illegal oil transactions to take place. According to one 2004 paper delivered at the meeting of the United Nations Office on Drugs and Crime in Vienna, the population that reside in the Delta region of Nigeria have seen little of benefit from the oil trade and, not surprisingly, "collaborate in the illegal export of oil" (United Nations 2005, 8, 31).

Most of the gangs involved in bunkering operate internationally, involving nationals from Morocco, Venezuela, Lebanon, France, and Russia, many of whom with connections to larger networks of organized criminality. Oil bunkering is often coterminous with the illegal exchange of cash, drugs, and weapons for oil. In one notable case in April 2004, a Nigerian navy vessel stopped a ship containing 8,000 metric tons of crude oil and lacking the appropriate papers. The crew of eight was arrested (United Nations 2005).

According to one recent anti-corruption commission, almost $380 billion worth of oil was stolen or wasted between Nigerian independence in 1960 and 1999. Another way of looking at it is that this is equivalent of 5 years national output, or "if American leaders had walked off with, say, $50 trillion" (Guest 2007, A21).

Foreign Exchange Fraud

Syndicates take part in colossal illegal foreign exchange transaction schemes, which has allowed wealthy Nigerians to move large amounts of cash outside the country to foreign bank accounts, usually with the help international companies. The United Nations asserts that this became a major enterprise in the mid-1970s practiced by Lebanese, Asian, and European companies, which included the Johnson Matthey Bank (United Nations 2005, 13).

The Black-Money Scam

The "black-money scam" is one of the more popular scams being run by Nigerian gangs in various European cities, particularly Amsterdam (Thompson 2004). Although this fraud is not exclusive to Nigeria, experts have traced the "Black Currency Scam" to a centuries-old traditional West African con called the "Red Mercury" scam (Marked Currency/Black Money 2007). The scam involves convincing an unsuspecting mark that a specific chemical concoction can "clean" money that banks have reportedly painted black in preparation for disposal or in some cases had been painted or stamped for security purposes. The alleged money is shown to the victim, who explains how the bills can be cleaned with a special compound. The chemical is variously referred to as SSD Solution, Vectrol Paste, Lactima Base 98%, microtectine, and Tebi-Matonic. A victim is approached and convinced to buy "black money" and then the chemical so the money can be cleaned. According to the usual "agreement," once this purchase is done, the money will be split between the two parties. The victim is then shown a few real, blackened $100 (USD) notes and the special chemical is actually only an ordinary cleaning fluid that reacts with the black mixture of Vaseline and iodine. Several of these notes are "randomly" selected from the stash of money and are washed to reveal real banknotes, whereas the rest of the paper is just worthless black paper cut to the form of actual cash. The victim is asked to provide between $50 and $100,000 to purchase bulk supplies to clean the rest of the money, which the offenders offer to deliver from an additional location.

Since the mid-1990s, this scam has been reported in the United States—mostly on the East Coast. According to one 2001 indictment, two West Africans were indicted in San Antonio, Texas, on one count of possessing altered U.S. currency and one count of possessing fictitious obligations in order to commit fraud in a fraudulent black money scheme. These two individuals allegedly approached a victim and showed him three $20 (USD) bills coated with a black substance. They then showed the victim how the black substance could be removed using a liquid solution that would leave the currency looking new. Next, they showed the mark what they said was $2.5 million in currency and said they needed money to acquire more solution in order to clean the money. The bundled currency ultimately proved to be black paper cut to the size of U.S. currency. West Africans have introduced this fraud to the far corners of the world, including Malaysia, Boston, Great Britain, Italy, Hong Kong, and Thailand.[12]

Nigerian Internet Fraud: The Kakudu Group

The Nigerian-led Internet fraud syndicate known as the Kakudu group operates out of Sierra Leone, but has affiliations with a number of West African countries, including Guinea, Gambia, Nigeria, and the Ivory Coast. However, it finds most of its victims beyond the African continent. The Kakudu group was directed by the Nigerian Raphael Ajukwara, who went by the alias James Kakudu. Residing in Sierra Leone, he worked in the automobile business. He owned a computer and possessed sufficient technical knowledge thanks in part to brief college education. Kakudu's accomplices included three other Nigerians and a Ghanaian, as well as the leader's local girlfriend. All were said to be well-educated, which allowed them to perpetrate a series of 419 frauds and earn a substantial profit, which they went on to invest in legitimate commodities from Nigeria that they would sell in Freetown. The fraud worked as follows: Members targeted prospective marks through the Internet, using the lure of non-existent gold and diamonds. However, the demise of the racket began when they targeted a European businessman in the Caribbean who reported the scam to the Sierra Leone police. Although Kakudu was responsible for the computer side of things, the others masqueraded as prominent individuals, one even going as far as to offer himself as the son of a former finance minister of Ghana. The gang was well aware of the paucity of local legislation of computer crimes as well as the lack of skill in handling this activity by the police. As a result, they made a fatal blunder by not seeking political protection, police, or judges. The subsequent investigation linked the group to associates in Ghana, Gambia, Ivory Coast, and Nigeria (adapted from United Nations 2005, 14)

SOUTHERN AFRICA

The region of Southern Africa is composed of the countries Botswana, Lesotho, Mozambique, Namibia, South Africa, and Swaziland. Countries in this region are characterized by long national borders and coastlines, offering ample opportunities for transnational criminal syndicates. Of these countries, South Africa is the most economically viable and is the focus of this regional study. The other nations are poor and remain underdeveloped, with little capital to invest in educational, health, and policing programs.

By most accounts, indigenous criminal syndicates had developed throughout South Africa by the 1980s, taking advantage of the *Apartheid* government fixation on political dissent to establish various criminal enterprises. Despite the presence of strict border controls, evidence beyond the anecdotal suggests the expansion of transnational crime links between local syndicates and gangs in bordering states.

South Africa

South Africa has a long history of organized criminal gangs dating back to the 19th century. Today, it is considered "one of the most crime-ridden societies in the world" (Kynoch 2005, 1). What has exacerbated this trend is the persistence of unemployment, often between 30% and 50%. Recent estimates suggest that there are more than 300 organized crime syndicates working in South Africa, with 10% specializing in "cash-in-transit-heists." The Institute for Security Studies (ISS) warns that these syndicates are a threat to national security. Between April 2005 and March 2006, these heists increased by almost 75% (People's Daily Online 2006).

At the turn of the millennium, by some reports, South Africa ranked just behind Russia and Colombia in the frequency of organized crime (Kynoch 2005, 163). Most criminal syndicates operate in the major urban centers of Johannesburg, Durban, and Cape Town. The discovery of diamonds and gold only stimulated the establishment of more organized syndicates. Sometime late in the 19th century, an Australian immigrant named Scotty Smith emerged as one of the region's first major highwaymen and gang leaders, conducting large-scale stock thefts in the Northern Cape and Orange Free State. South African authorities credit the Smith Gang with participating in "one of the first transnational criminal operations in South Africa" (Gastrow 1998), when the gang smuggled a large herd of horses across the South African border to German Cavalry troops in German South West Africa. In the first decades of the 20th century, the Foster Gang achieved prominence after a violent series of bank and post office robberies. However, their run was preempted when the gang all committed suicide in a Johannesburg mine dump in 1914.

JOHANNESBURG   Following World War II, South Africa experienced rapid industrial development and urbanization, setting the stage for the development of a legion of street gangs. In Johannesburg and Pretoria, these gangs were known as *tsotsis*, which in some cases grew into organized crime syndicates over time. In the vicinity of Durban's harbor, the smuggling of contraband and *dagga* (marijuana) contributed to an increasing sophistication of gang members, as did a similar process in Cape Town. During the 1940s, some former members of the "coloured" Cape Corps returned home to find few opportunities, and turned to illicit activities and established gangs such as the Goofies and the Red Cats.

The Msomi Gang, which originated in Alexandra, was one of South Africa's most formidable syndicates in the 1950s, participating in murders, protection and extortion rackets, and robberies. One contemporary South African journalist compared the gang to its American counterparts, writing, "The Msomi gang introduced a new era in our crime. Here were the first signs of organized gang activities, based on lessons from the American gang world" (Gastrow 1998). Wealthy gang leaders included Shadrack Matthews, who before he met his fate on the gallows made a fortune in extortion rackets. Matthews, who was given the moniker "Prime Minister," ran his gang with a combination

The Marashea Gangs

The Marashea, which translated means "Russians," is a South African mutual-aid-cum-criminal society for migrant workers from Lesotho that originated in the 1940s. According to Gary Kynoch, the foremost authority on the gang, its members, called Lerashea, adopted the moniker for the organization during the World War II era after serving in the British military, where they developed an ample respect for the "formidable" Russian soldiers.[13] One distinguishing feature of the Marashea gangs is that they are composed of mostly adult members, although "no age cohort dominated." The consensus among authorities on the Marashea is that "it began as a fighting association of Basotho migrants who banded together on the Rand in the 1940s and 1950s for protection from urban criminals and ethnic rivals, to obtain control over migrant Basotho women, and to celebrate their identity as Basotho" (Kynoch, 2005, 10).[14]

Prospective members were expected to participate in elaborate admission rituals where they agreed to meet the expectations of the gang. By most accounts, the only requirement to joining was the facility to speak Sesotho. Once joining, the new member was expected to contribute money to the gang for the rest of his life, as well as to serve in battle if called on by the gang's elected leaders. Although the Marashea provided financial aid from the organization's coffers for members' medical, legal, and burial debts, the gang feasted on other township residents through robbery and protection rackets, when they were involved in internecine conflict with other ethnically organized gangs.

of cunning and terror. He earned a reputation for brutality in various gang wars, particularly a running conflict with the 250-member Spoilers.

During the 1950s, Johannesburg gave birth to the Sheriff Khan Organization, led by its namesake Sheriff Khan, who by most accounts became the most powerful gangster in the region, running an extensive gambling empire.[15] Recent scholarship asserts that the Msomi and Sheriff Khan organizations flourished because of their close contacts with police.

DURBAN As South Africa's largest port city, Durban offered crime syndicates a multitude of opportunities and was particularly attractive to drug smugglers. The evolution of organized crime in Durban followed a sequence familiar to most other cities, beginning with a handful traditional street gangs that ruled recognized territories. The drug *dagga* played "an important role in the development of organized crime structures" in the vicinity of Durban (Organized Crime in South Africa 1998). In the 1960s, an international demand for South African *dagga,* which went by the brand name of "Durban Poison," led to the establishment of lucrative drug syndicates that soon became involved in the trafficking of other drugs as the requisite coordination and contacts were made. An illicit trade with Europe and Australia brought LSD and other drugs into South Africa through the port of Durban.

Tsotsis

South African youth gang members are often referred to as *tsotsis* or *bo-tsotsis*. According to Glaser, *tsotsis* were heavily influenced by the American gangster prototype and rejected the middle-class values of work, family, and education in favor of accumulating wealth (2000). This phenomenon can be traced back to the street-corner gangs that emerged in the 1940s and 1950s following the cascade of Black immigration to the cities during the war years. Some of the more prominent gangs were the Black Swines, Pirates, and the Hazels. Typically bereft of legal income and family support, many banded together in neighborhoods with high unemployment and seemingly in a perpetual state of social disarray. However, these wannabe gangsters had not made the transition to true organized criminality. Nevertheless, for many, their years of petty crime prepared them for a career in big-time crime as they evolved into professional criminals.

The most prominent Durban drug syndicate was led by an individual named "Brasco." Its success hinged in part on the small inner circle of members that formed the core of the organization. According to South African law enforcement, at least 17 syndicates depended on Brasco for the distribution of drugs, which were often smuggled into Durban onboard yachts and passenger liners. However, Durban's internal drug trade paled in significance compared to Johannesburg and Cape Town, with the port city performing as transit point. Other syndicates focused on other less lucrative enterprises including robbery and burglary of businesses. Of these, the Young Americans were prominent.

CAPE TOWN   The expansion of organized gangs in the Cape Town region was stimulated by the relocation of a large segment of the "coloured" community from various neighborhoods of the city to the townships of the Cape Flats in the 1960s and 1970s. The removal of families, as well as neighborhood gang members, and the destruction of their communities found the forced emigrants in a new environment, where some of the former gangs disintegrated and some members joined other gangs, whereas others kept their nucleus and established their dominance in the new area.

In the 1970s, a number of different types of gangs could be distinguished on the Cape Flats. Criminologist Don Pinnock identified four distinct types of gangs, of which the most prevalent were established to defend its members and turf from other gangs. Pinnock calls these *defense gangs*. These types engaged in organized activities including payroll robbery, housebreaking, and the theft of weapons and automobiles.

Another category of gangs Pinnock refers to as *reform gangs,* which are similar to the defense gangs but were established in reformatories instead of the streets. Members typically ranged from 12 to 20 years old, but are considered more advanced due to the shared "brotherhood" created by prison detention. The boss was usually an older if not more accomplished criminal. These types of gangs became part of the "supergang" demimonde, exemplified by the Cape Town Scorpions and the Born Free Kids. Robbery and burglaries were their preferred activities.

Pinnock's third group is what he refers to as the *mafias.* These are more sophisticated, organizationally speaking. Many of the mafias were the outgrowth of the dislocation and concomitant breakdown of social relationships stemming from the Cape Town dislocations. Blocked from opportunity and upward mobility, families "transformed themselves into the mafias of the Cape Flats" (Pinnock 1984, 1997). Exemplars of these include the Mongrels and Cisco Yakis, which can be traced back to their former family networks (Organized Crime in South Africa 1998). The mafias were distinguished from the reform and defense gangs by their ability to take on more-complicated and larger-scaled criminal operations. They also operated beyond the confines of their turf to create rackets larger in scope and territory. In addition, their access to more capital allowed them to get into the more lucrative drug rackets.

Thug Life

In April 2007, a 47-year-old South African reflected on his life as a gangster. He reported that he started his career by joining the Junior Young Ones (JYO) gang while still in his early teens. Convicted of multiple murders in 1974, he was sentenced to 20 years in prison, where he fell in with the 28s, considered one of South Africa's most formidable prison gangs. Reminiscing about his gangster life, he noted,

> Most of the guys are dead now: either shot or stabbed by rival gangsters, or hung on the gallows. I was crazy back then and didn't even think that killing people was wrong. I was stabbed once when I was 14 years old and decided that enough was enough; it was never going to happen again. If people wanted to kill me, I killed them first, and the alcohol used to tell me I was right. But when I left prison in 2000 I was tired of the life and wanted to change—I have kids and I don't want them to end up in jail, or worse. (IRIN In-Depth, 2007, 2)

Boere Mafia

The Boere Mafia, or "Farmer's Mafia," attained a certain prominence in the 1980s as tightly organized and ethnically based organized crime groups emerged in South Africa. Members employed a diverse number of criminal activities. In time, police infiltration led to its diminished importance. One interesting phenomenon associated with this organization was the Boere Mafia's recruitment of former security forces members (Shaw 1998).

Pinnock's fourth category is harder to pigeonhole. He defines them as *merchant syndicates,* which are considered "the most professional and profitable organizations on the Cape Flats" (Pinnock 1984). These syndicates were essentially groups of businessmen who banded together to monopolize an illegal commodity—in this case, Mandrax, or methaqualone, was the preferred commodity. Formerly the province of Asian gangs, in the 1970s African syndicates became more involved in the trade. In the beginning, it was the Asians that set up the supply routes from Pakistan and India, but the drug was typically handled by other middlemen who redistributed it to street dealers. However, the *dagga* market was almost solely an African operation, with various gangs obtaining the product from rural farmers in the Transkei. Profits could be as high as 3,000% "on the farm price of *dagga*" (Organized Crime in South Africa 1998). Merchant syndicates often used these "mafia" gangs as distributors who sold the product to defense or reform gangs to sell on the streets.

SOUTH AFRICA POST-APARTHEID   It is generally understood that organized criminal activity spreads more rapidly in times of political transition and violence. The most prominent example of this is the growth of organized crime in Russia following the collapse of the Soviet Union. South Africa endured a similar crisis not long after the policy of *Apartheid* was replaced by a constitutional democracy in 1994. During the preceding years, the authoritarian nature of the police state stemmed the expansion into the country by international syndicates, although homegrown groups flourished. During the 1980s, while the security apparatus was busy chasing down political opposition indigenous organized crime groups expanded within the nation's borders and in the face of stringent border controls, organized crime increased significantly, spreading into neighboring countries. By most accounts, *Apartheid* "created the opportunity for both indigenous and international organized criminal groups to exploit the new low-risk environment that South Africa provided criminals" (Gastrow 1999, 3). As the country made the transition from police state to democracy, it was necessary to reorganize the police institutions, which took time—time those criminals took advantage of. As South Africa became more tourist-friendly, its open borders and new trading partners offered new links for criminal syndicates.

ZIMBABWE   Located in southern Africa and surrounded by South Africa, Zambia, Mozambique, and Botswana, Zimbabwe, although rich in natural resources and the like, has been hit particularly hard by organized criminal activity. As a result of the plundering of the rich landscape, much of the country has been denuded by deforestation and soil erosion, and much of its once flourishing herds of wildlife have been seriously depleted by organized poachers. For example, the country once boasted of the largest concentration of the black rhinoceros in the world, but by the 1990s, the animal was on the brink of extinction. The local elephant population has also been substantially reduced due to the incidence of ivory smuggling. The transnational smugglers have been assisted by the ties between various ethnic communities on both sides of the border that facilitate the transportation of illicit goods between countries by creating an informal market system used to move animal parts from one country to another. According to one source, some of these gangs are so dangerous and well organized that even police hesitate to become involved (New African 1991).

The Firm

Prior to 1994 and the end of *Apartheid,* a number of Western Cape gangs fought turf battles over a nascent and expanding drug trade. Over time, gang leaders recognized that this internecine feuding was detrimental to their activities, but persisted in such behavior nonetheless. However, with the relaxation of border controls that accompanied the new political environment, a number of West Cape syndicates decided to pre-empt the entrée of foreign crime syndicates by forming a cartel that would reduce local conflict and make possible the purchase and distribution of larger drug shipments according to a prearranged protocol. Cartel members agreed not only to order drugs in larger shipments but also to adopt a price structure that all could agree on. The cartel became known as the Firm, and by the following year, it had changed the nature of organized crime in the Western Cape (Shaw and Wannenburg 2005). Increasing profits led to more sophisticated activities, such as money laundering, and the Firm began investing in real estate along the coast and in the interior. One of the more aggressive syndicates that made up the cartel was the gang known as the "Hard Livings," which began establishing branches of their gang in a number of other towns and communities and entered into affiliations with Chinese triads and Sicilian mobsters. This transition from money collectors to organized syndicates exemplifies the "typical path of progression of a common criminal gang moving up the ladder of sophistication on its way to becoming a well-organized criminal group" (Gastrow 1999, 8–9). The Hard Livings reportedly formed as early as 1971 under the leadership of the Staggie twins, Rashaad and Rashied. Rashied was better known as "Mad Dog" for his affinity for violence. With the explosion of gang violence following the end of *Apartheid,* vigilante groups formed to counter them in the Cape Flats. One of the better known was the People Against Gangsterism and Drugs, or PAGAD. In the late 1990s, this primarily Muslim group took matters into their own hands and shot down and killed Rashaad, and later seriously wounded his brother (Robinson 2000, 288).

Other major activities include drug trafficking, motor vehicle theft, passport fraud, money laundering, and armed robbery. By most accounts, one of the most popular forms of organized criminal activity involves foreign nationals who enter the country using false documents and then entice locals to marry them to validate their residency. One recent investigation revealed the five most popular foci of corruption, which include customs and excise, the passport office, the vehicle and licensing department, the police service, and local officials. Furthermore, the investigation demonstrated that "a Zimbabwean passport was the easiest document to get, as staff in the passport office can be bribed to issue unofficial passports" (ZimObserver 2006). Under the current Mugabe regime, the nation's corruption laws have been unevenly applied, with the poor typically getting the short end of justice.

Since the 1980s, the drug trade has emerged as a national problem. Prior to this time, marijuana, locally known as *mbanje,* was grown for medicinal purposes or for personal consumption. In the 1980s, drug networks emerged to traffic in psychotropic substances such as mandrax or methaqualone. In 1981, 100,000 tablets of the substance were seized in a bust at the Harare International Airport. During the following decade, an increase in drug consumption and trafficking plagued Zimbabwe, made only worse by the availability of new and harder drugs such as cocaine, heroin, and, of course, mandrax. However, by most accounts, Zimbabwe is mainly used as a transshipment point for hard drugs destined for South Africa. The country's main problem is the large-scale trafficking in Indian hemp, known as *dagga.* It reaches Zimbabwe by every mode of transportation. By the mid-1990s, new technologies allowed syndicates to compress the substance into bricks and cubes, much easier for transportation and smuggling (Chihuri 2003).

Legitimate businesses are used either as a cover or as a means to operate underground rackets. In Zimbabwe, for example, it is not uncommon for an individual to own a fuel business with a legitimate license and import the fuel. However, at the same time this liquid fuel was quite rare on the open market, because most of it is sold on the illegal parallel market. More recently, reports have filtered out that burglary syndicates and armed robbery gangs were emerging and terrorizing residents

(All Africa 2006). Other gangs terrorize motorists and businessmen and with the help of prostitutes corrupt police officers and other officials.

MOZAMBIQUE   In the 1980s, indigenous crime networks emerged in most South African countries, many linked together in cross-border networks that trafficked in stolen cars, drugs, and weapons. By the 1990s, a number of international syndicates banded together to take advantage of opportunities afforded by the weakened states of the region. Of these, South Africa and Mozambique were considered the most vulnerable, in no small part due to the vagaries of political transitions accompanying the end of *Apartheid* and the like. Most gangs were drawn to the opportunities of South Africa, which possessed the region's richest natural resources and most developed infrastructure. Mozambique's proximity to South Africa, its ports, and its almost 1,550-mile-long coastline made it attractive as a transit country whose banking system could be manipulated for syndicates looking to launder their illicit profits.

Like many other poor countries that offer accessible ports and airports, the very existence of unrelenting poverty, low salaries, and an environment of corruption, the result has been a culture of bribery and corruption of police, border officials, and government leaders. In addition, Mozambique offers routes and ports that are not effectively monitored for smuggling networks. Besides the drug trade, the country has also experienced a flourishing trade in stolen cars and weapons. One clue to the amount of money laundering that takes place in Mozambique is the fact that the country has many "more banks and foreign exchange bureaus than can be justified by the size of the legal economy and the need to exchange sizable foreign aid funds" (Berry and Curtis 2003, 21).

By the early 1990s, Mozambique finally witnessed the conclusion of a protracted period of civil war and was experiencing an increased demand for material goods and immigrants. Along with the accompanying immigration and rise in trade came the region's syndicates that used the country as a transit point for narcotics. Located northeast of South Africa, it became an important entry point for drugs coming from South Asia on their way to Europe, and for cocaine shipments from South America heading to both Europe and East Asia. In addition, methaqualone came from South Asia or was locally manufactured before moving on to South Africa. Hashish was also smuggled in from Southeast Asia, at an estimated 200 tons per year during the last part of the 1990s. Investigators reported one seizure in 2001 of more than 6 tons. The national law enforcement authorities have had few victories in suppressing organized crime, and of course, it is of little solace when one of the larger traffickers has previous ties to national police agencies. In 2003, it became clear how drug-trafficking syndicates were operating unimpeded when the president's son was implicated in illegal import and currency transactions as well as murder during a high-profile trial (Berry and Curtis 2003).

EAST AFRICA

In recent years, terrorism activity in East Africa has captured the attention of law enforcement officials worldwide. However, religious and political terrorists are just the newest players on the international crime scene. This region has a long tradition of illegal smuggling thanks to the long coastline afforded by proximity to the Indian Ocean. East African countries function as pivotal transit points for various contraband smugglers. Significant amounts of drugs and other smuggled goods flow through the ports of Mombassa, Kenya, and Dar es Salaam, Tanzania. These are complemented by the airports in Nairobi and Addis Ababa.

As far back as the 1990s, East Africa was ensnared in the Southwest Asian heroin trade. East Africa became an important transit point for Southwest Asian hashish and heroin as other African regions clamped down on drug trafficking in the 1990s. Among its greatest lures is its access to international transportation, commercial connections, and persistence of ineffective law enforcement. To make matters worse, East African countries have been more preoccupied with regional conflicts and domestic crises as well as concomitant high crime rates. It is no coincidence that terrorists targeted the U.S. Embassies in Kenya and Tanzania in 1998; more likely was the attraction of poor border controls and immigration protocol that allowed the terrorists to move materials and personnel into the area unimpeded.

Furthermore, this region has long suffered from weak state institutions, corrupt politicians and police, porous borders, high rates of poverty, and ethnic groups who have deep relations with their brethren in neighboring countries. Many of the countries in this region have endured domestic and transnational conflicts for years, which in the process as weakened law enforcement and border controls. Although Kenya, Tanzania, and Uganda have been relatively stable, other countries have not been so lucky. Intertribal warfare between Tutsis and Hutus in Rwanda and Burundi, conflict in the Sudan, and insurgent movements in the Congo are just a few of the small conflicts that have created opportunities for traffickers in weapons, drugs, and people in recent decades.

Trade routes have linked East African ports with South Asia for centuries. Smugglers and terrorists alike have taken advantage of the long coastline, regular airline service to Europe and North America, close proximity to the Middle East and South Asia, and the increasingly radicalized Muslim communities to pursue their criminal activities (Berry and Curtis 2003, 9).

One of the more troubling forms of organized crime has been the emergent weapons trafficking, particularly in Kenya, Somalia, Sudan, and Uganda. Some experts suggest that the trading of livestock for guns has become an accepted part of life in East Africa, citing a 2002 report that asserted that these weapons "filter beyond armies and police forces to criminal organizations, private security forces, vigilante squads, and individual citizens" (Berry and Curtis 2003, 13). Another study named a Russian arms dealer headquartered in the United Arab Emirates as a major source for these weapons.

East Africa plays a crucial role in various drug-trafficking networks. Located along popular trade routes from the east to the west, Kenya, Tanzania, and Ethiopia remain popular stops for drug traffickers eager to take advantage of the various water ports and airports, as well as land-transshipment locations.[16] Ports such as Mombasa, Kenya have proved a key entry spot for the transfer of drugs from Asia to Europe and from India to South Africa. Among the most popular drugs are cocaine, heroin, mandrax, and marijuana. By most accounts, mandrax is shipped from India by land routes through Kenya, Tanzania, and Zambia. During the 1990s, hashish from Pakistan and Afghanistan entered Kenya by way of ocean routes from Pakistan to Sri Lanka and then on to the port at Mombasa. The drug trade in East Africa has many parallels with organized syndicates elsewhere, as drug networks find newer ways to launder money and corrupt local officials. One 2002 report indicates that Ethiopia "was ranked first among African nations in volume of heroin trafficking" (Berry and Curtis 2003, 15). Addis Ababa's Bole Airport is considered a major transit point, as flights arrive frequently from most parts of Asia and thence to other African and European destinations (Opala 2002).

NORTH AFRICA

If we exclude terrorist activity from the equation, the two North African countries with the strongest ties to organized crime are Egypt and Morocco. One explanation is that these two nations "at North Africa's corners [are] closest to the Middle East and Europe respectively" (Berry and Curtis 2003, 4). As recently as 2002, Morocco was cited as "the world's largest exporter of cannabis, [with an estimated] 75 percent of [its] total output of 2,000 tons" being shipped to Europe and representing three fourths of the product entering the region (Berry and Curtis 2003, 6). A number of international narcotics experts suggest that Morocco's trade in hashish resin and oil is the country's "largest single source of foreign currency" (Berry and Curtis 2003, 7).

Morocco and Nigeria are considered home to the continent's best organized drug-trafficking networks. Cannabis products are transported from Morocco through Spain before dispersal to the rest of Europe. The most popular Mediterranean ports involved in the trafficking are Oued Lalou, Martil, and Bou Ahmed. Products are also delivered by motor vehicles to Spain by means of ferries.

Morocco is also considered an important transit point and a destination for the transnational trafficking of women into the sex trade, and is also a departure point for illegal migrants seeking entry to Europe. It has been estimated that some 200,000 women work as prostitutes in the country, many of them working for criminal syndicates. As recently as 2002, Morocco did not even have a law prohibiting trafficking in humans. Most of the cross-border crime networks have been able to prosper with the collusion of police, border guards, and well-connected nationals. Only 8 miles from Spain, the proximity has proved both a curse and blessing to those looking for opportunities by legitimate or illicit means. The international community has been notoriously timid in its dealings with the Moroccan government, mitigated by the country's standing as "a primary bulwark against Islamic fundamentalism in the Muslim world" (Berry and Curtis 2003, 7–8).

CENTRAL AFRICA

Since the mid-1990s, criminal syndicates have extended their reach into Central Africa, a region surrounded by Angola, Namibia, Botswana, Zimbabwe, Mozambique, Malawi, Tanzania, and Congo. Crime in this region has not only increased in virulence, but in sophistication as well, and has become a national and international problem. Organized criminal activity runs the gamut from auto theft, commercial poaching, bank fraud, and money laundering to weapons and drug trafficking. Transnational criminal syndicates operate freely between this region and South Africa.

Zambia personifies the problems of Central Africa and is surrounded by the aforementioned countries (Ndhlovu 2003). Most organized crime in this landlocked country includes vehicle theft, drug and weapons smuggling, commercial poaching, bank fraud, and money laundering. Motor vehicle theft plagues most African countries and continues to flourish due to the exigencies of social conflict, porous borders, and weak law enforcement. Most stolen vehicles are either stolen or carjacked. They are then transported across the borders to Zimbabwe, Namibia, Botswana, Malawi, Mozambique, South Africa, and Congo (or vice versa) and traded for other commodities, cash, and drugs (Ndhlovu 2003, 408).

The movement of stolen cars and car parts is facilitated by alterations to identifications numbers, forged documents, and the cooperation of corrupt officials bribed by the syndicates. Many of the syndicates operating out of Zambia are led by Zambians in collusion with foreign nationals from other African countries. One prominent case involved a resident known as Winsome Yedo Kasoka, who was accused of leading a gang transporting stolen vehicles in and out of the country. In the so-called Yedo Case, proceedings revealed a preference for the latest Japanese vehicles, which are much in demand in Zimbabwe. According to court documents, Yedo bought a mansion while leading a gang of six fellow Zambians and a handful of Zimbabweans. Their modus operandi included using AK-47 weapons to steal vehicles and then driving them east through Mozambique to Harare, Zimbabwe, where Yedo awaited the carjacked vehicles and brokered deals with waiting clients. The profits were then taken home and divvied among the gang members.

Investigators revealed a tapestry of corruption that included police, customs officers, and city council members. Yedo gangsters began their operations by obtaining signed original blue books from the Lusaka City Council's revenue office with the connivance of its employees. Legitimized by these documents, the cars were smuggled with ease through customs. Ultimately, the entire gang was rounded up and tried for a litany of offenses (Ndhlovu 2003).

Zambia is also considered both a market and a transit point for illegal drugs ranging from cannabis, hashish products, and *khat* to opium, mandrax, cocaine, and morphine. Some are manufactured in clandestine labs, whereas others are transported from Southeast Asia and other parts of Africa. Proximity to South Africa has only augmented the growing problem and led to an unprecedented crime increase. Syndicates are international in scope, with local dealers and distributors representing a microcosm of the world cultures—Asians, West Africans, Greeks, Lebanese, and so forth.

Zambia: The Mabenga and Kunzley Syndicate

A handful of entrepreneurs from Zambia and Switzerland formed a partnership to harvest emeralds in a corner of Zambia. It has been estimated that the country loses more than $200 million per year through the illegal emeralds trade that flourishes alongside other illicit trade, including weapons trafficking and stolen cars (Ndhlovu 2003). The erstwhile emerald smugglers needed seed money to finance their entry into the field. This was facilitated first by a lucrative trade in smuggled weapons. The only Swiss member left Zambia for South Africa, where he contacted his Zambian partners and told them that he had finagled an export order and would provide the documentation that would facilitate the weapons transaction in the Congo. He then was supplied with a tourist's import permit from the Zambians that allowed him to stay in the country legally. In due course, the partners were able to provide him with all of the necessary paperwork that allowed him to "legally" purchase the weapons for the impending transaction. By most accounts, throughout the exchange the customers were under the impression that the deal was legal—for, after all, the Swiss dealer presented what seemed to be the appropriate firearms licenses (by way of forged documents). The subsequent police investigation led to the arrest of syndicate members and the recovery of 17 firearms. In any case, authorities discovered the conspirators were using the Mukumbe Mining Limited as a front for laundering their profits. In 1995 and 1996, police recovered more than 125 weapons obtained with forged firearms certificates (Ndhlovu 2003, 412–414).

THE CARIBBEAN

Some Afrolineal Caribbean syndicates are often referred to as *West Indian organized crime,* with many members originating in the Bahamas, the British or U.S. Virgin Islands, Trinidad, the Greater Antilles, the Lesser Antilles, Belize, Barbados, Grenada, and the Cayman Islands. New Jersey law enforcement noticed that Bahamians and Virgin Islanders often gravitate to the Jamaican Posses (http://www.mafianj.com, 2007). Jamaica is considered one of the most impoverished countries in the Western Hemisphere, with almost half the population considered illiterate. A rising crime rate over the past decades has been blamed on a population explosion coupled with few opportunities. In response, many of the island's youths have migrated to the United States illegally and legally, where some became embroiled in organized criminal activities. Between 1996 and 2001, the United States deported more than 4,000 criminals to Jamaica. Once they returned to the island, many reportedly joined up with others deported from regions of the former British Empire—primarily Canada and Great Britain—and have joined homegrown street gangs, exacerbating the island's crime problem (Covey 2003; Erlich 2001).

In recent years, human trafficking has become a concern in the Caribbean, with reports of this activity surfacing in Barbados, the Bahamas, Guyana, Jamaica, St. Lucia, the Netherlands Antilles, and Suriname. Other countries in the region are drawn in as they become involved as source, transit, or destination countries. According to government sources, the Caribbean has functioned more as a source country for human cargo, but more recently has become an important destination for women trafficked from Europe and North America (Ramdin 2006).

Located between a major illegal drug supply source (South America) and a major market for the product (the United States), it is not surprising that Caribbean syndicates have become involved in the lucrative drug trade. This region is also an important transit point for the shipment of drugs to Europe, which is reportedly the destination for almost half the drug supply. The Caribbean narcotics trade has become increasingly entangled with other forms of organized crime, including weapons and human trafficking. The illegal transit of weapons contributed to an escalation in the region's violence. Academic studies of homicide in Latin America and the Caribbean indicate a murder rate double the world's average, with more than 150,000 reported annually (Ramdin 2006). One 2005 report estimated that 90% of the cocaine emanating from South America is transported by sea, with the majority of it traveling through a transit zone of 6 million square miles that includes the Caribbean Sea. According to the Organization of American States, seven Eastern Caribbean nations form the eastern perimeter of the transit zone.[17]

West Indian Organized Crime: The Padmore Group

The Padmore Group was a Trinidadian organized crime syndicate led by Wade Padmore and located in East Orange, New Jersey. According to the New Jersey State Police, at its apogee in the late 1980s there were 300 active members chiefly involved in cocaine trafficking. At one time, the gang supplied cocaine to various Jamaican drug dealers in northern New Jersey. The group was extensively involved in smuggling cocaine from Trinidad to the United States, and reportedly had invested in a substantial amount of real estate. Padmore's legitimate interests included three bars, three grocery stores, a flower shop, five ice cream stores, a property management firm, and other businesses located mostly in Northern New Jersey and Brooklyn, New York. Wade Padmore was murdered by Guyanian hit men at the request an African American–based gang in Essex County (New Jersey Commission of Investigation 1989).

Jamaican Organized Crime

Jamaica is the third largest island in the Caribbean. At one time it was the world's leading source for bauxite, the main source for aluminum, but a decline in the demand for bauxite in the 1960s had a catastrophic effect on the island's economy, leading to waves of migration from the hinterlands into the cities, especially the already overcrowded capital city of Kingston. It was here in an environment of unrelenting poverty and epidemic marijuana use (especially among those that embraced Rastafarianism) that gangs were created based on neighborhood boundaries and political affiliations.

During the 1960s and 1970s, urban armed gangs were recruited by politicians to get out the vote and enforce party loyalty. Initially, these gangs were based in Kingston and then Spanish Town. It was not much of a stretch for these gangs to morph into criminal syndicates and play important roles in the international drug trade. However, the transition from gang to "posse" was a gradual process.

By the early 1980s, posses had emerged in the United States and Yardies in Great Britain. Great Britain was especially attractive due to the similarities in cultural, sporting, and religious values, all of which had driven the legitimate immigration of earlier years. However, as the criminal syndicates became increasingly successful, the United States became the more popular destination. In recent years, American law enforcement became increasingly aware of the Jamaican gangsters and has made it more difficult for them to enter the United States. Great Britain became the next best choice, where they could more readily obtain new identities and fraudulent passports and enter the United States.

In the 1980s, government budgets were so diminished that less money was available for ruling political parties to fund the armed gangs. It was at this point that many turned to the drug trade and organized criminal activities. The exodus of Jamaican gang members to the United States and Britain in the early 1980s followed the defeat of Michael Manley's[18] People's National Party (PNP), which they had backed in the earlier national elections. However, when the victorious Labor Party took over, local gangsters were targeted by the government and blamed for the 500 murders that accompanied the election. Since the mid-1980s, violence has not relented as the country continues to have one of the highest homicide rates in the world.

Laurie Gunst spent almost a decade (beginning in 1984) in what she referred to as "A Journey through the Jamaican Posse Underworld." She spent more than a decade of ethnographic research on posses in Jamaica and the United States. Perhaps this Harvard-educated writer described put it best, noting,

> Their Jamaican beginnings were in some ways only a prologue to what they became here [in the United States], an apprenticeship in the ways of badness. But, they had been taught essential lessons in Jamaica—by the politicians who used them, by the police who gunned them down when their brief period of usefulness was over, and by a poverty from which death is often the only release. (Gunst 1995, xxii–xxiii)

Posses

The earliest posse members have been in the United States since the early 1970s but appeared on police radar screens only in the mid-1980s. The consensus is that Jamaican gang members were so enthralled by the American Western genre popular in the 1950s and 1960s that they adopted the name *posse* for their gangs. One estimate suggested the presence of 10,000 posse members in 40 different gangs in the United States in the 1990s (Valentine 1995, 107), virtually all located in urban centers. Posses took their names from their communities back in Jamaica. For example, the Jungle Posse and the Jungle Lites Posse originated in a township called the Jungle, a neighborhood known for violent criminals who are referred to locally as *Junglelites.* One expert suggests that the best way to understand the structure of a posse is to compare it with a football team, wherein the name of the team reflects a certain location but membership can come from a variety of locales. The only requirement for joining the posse is to be from Jamaica. Once in the United States, Jungle Posse recruits, for example, can come from all over America, but must originally be from Jamaica (Valentine 1995).

The U.S. Bureau of Alcohol, Tobacco, and Firearms (ATF) has been chronicling the activities of the posses since they first arrived in the United States in the 1980s, and by the mid-1990s, the ATF estimated the gangs were responsible for some 4,500 killings during that period.

Beginning in 1989, a number of non-Jamaican gangs adopted the *posse* moniker, whereas the real posses began calling their groups *massives.* Some even adopted the term *crews* to refer to lower-echelon drug distributors operating under the second-tier leaders (e.g., New York's Tower Hill Crew).

The first posses to operate in the United States were the Untouchables, from Tecks Lane in the Kingston neighborhood of Racetown, and the Dunkirk Boys, who originated Kingston's Franklin Town. The two most prominent posses in the United States and in Jamaica were the Shower and Spangler posses, considered the best organized posses operating stateside. The key to comprehending the emergence of posses in Jamaica is to understand the country's governmental politics leading

---

Active Jamaican Posses in the United States (1995)

Black Bush Posse	Paneland Posse
Banton Posse	Public Enemy Number One
B & E Posse	Reema Posse
Bilbour Posse	Renkers Posse
Bushmouth Posse	Riverton City Posse
Cuban Posse	Rude Boys
Dog Posse	Samocan Posse
Dreadnox	Shower Posse
Dunkirk Posse	Southie Posse
Exodus Posse	Spangler Posse
Flethees Land Posse	Spanish Town Posse
Forties Posse	Stiker Posse
Jungle Posse	Super Posse
Jungle Lites Posse	Superstar Posse
Lockie Daley Organization	Tel Aviv Posse
Markham Massive	Tivoli Gardens Posse
Marvally Posse	Tower Hill Crew
Montego Bay Posse	Trinidadian Posse
Nanyville Posse	Waterhouse Posse
Okra Slime Posse	

Valentine 1995, 108.

up to the bloody 1980 elections. In the 1960s, Tivoli Gardens was conceived as Jamaica's first housing project, a first step toward delivering jobs and housing to the impoverished Kingston neighborhood of Trench Town—a forlorn ghetto. Leading the campaign for this project was Edward Seaga, one of the coming leaders of the ruling conservative Jamaica Labor Party (JLP). Ultimately, the construction project rewarded his supporters with jobs. This is an important moment; like the patronage-obsessed politics of mid-19th-century New York City, the Tivoli Gardens project established Jamaican political parties as a dispenser of jobs and housing, and political access. Although gangs seemed to have been around forever, they did not become politicized until the housing projects were built. As a result, Tivoli Gardens became an important power base for the JLP and the residence of the Shower Posse.

In 1972, the JLP lost the national election to the socialist People's National Party (PNP), resulting in the inauguration of Michael Manley as Prime Minister. Manley pursued a socialist agenda that included many reforms; meanwhile, the Tivoli Gardens project was left uncompleted. To reward his followers, Manley instead took a page out of the JLP playbook and began the construction of Arnett Gardens to reward his supporters with jobs and housing. Not only did this locale, known as *the Concrete Jungle* or just plain *the Jungle,* become a Manley stronghold, but also the sanctuary of the Spangler Posse. As he pursued a platform of socialist reform, Manley created alliances with various Third World and Communist countries, while at the same time solidifying his support in Kingston neighborhoods such as Tel Aviv in central Kingston, habitat of the Tel Aviv Posse.

By 1976, with posse violence out of control in Kingston, Manley was forced to declare a state of emergency, leading to the arrest and detention of the area's most prominent top-ranking gunmen (Pincomb and Judiscak 1998). However, this strategy did little to ease the violence. One of the most famous victims was reggae sensation Bob Marley, who was shot and wounded shortly before a Kingston concert. The Jamaican economy continued to founder, and in 1980, Seaga's JLP, thanks to financial support from supporters in Miami, won the elections. Seaga used his position to try to tame the posse violence. Like his predecessor, he targeted the top-ranking gunmen, and even engaged them as enforcers for his administration. Subsequently, Seaga began encouraging posse members to move to the United States, where a lucrative marijuana and cocaine trade awaited them.

The first inkling of Jamaican gangsters in America began as early as the mid-1970s, when a group was identified selling marijuana in Kansas City. By the end of the decade they were fighting indigenous American gangs over the drug trade in South Florida. By the mid-1980s, posses had become well established in the United States, and began migrating from their bases in Brooklyn and Miami and started appearing in the smaller cities throughout the country, where they were credited with spreading the crack epidemic. In 1985, Kansas City felt the impact of this migration as an estimated 450 members arrived and set up crack houses. Between 1985 and 1987, the city's homicides increased from 91 to 131 (Kleinknecht 1996). In 1988, the U.S. Department of Justice blamed the posses for 1,400 drug-related murders from 1985 to 1988 nationwide.

According to leading posse experts, members "subscribe to what are seen as status symbols in Jamaica," often leading to a preference for brand name items, including Volvo, Mercedes-Benz, Nissan Maximas, and BMWs when it came to cars, or Heineken beer. When it came to weapons, top-of-the-line 9-millimeters handguns were the guns of choice. Posses are very weapons-centric, and are known to have smuggled thousands of automatic weapons into southern Florida. The Shower and Spangler posses remain the two largest groups in the United States; however, successful prosecutions have diminished their power, and other posses have filled the vacuum once held by the two.

Few organized crime groups have such a well-earned reputation for violence as the Jamaican posses. Members reportedly torture others to obtain information with gunshots to the ankles, knees, and hips before unceremoniously killing them. Others have been scalded to death. Home invasions have resulted in the killing of every living thing in a house, including pregnant women, children, and pets. In February 1988, Washington, D.C., police responded to an emergency only to find four children under 3 years old crying near the bodies of four murdered Jamaican women. Police officers

Caribbean Organized Crime and Crack Cocaine

Colombian cartels began shipping cocaine through the Bahamas to the United States toward the end of the 1970s. Unfortunately, a byproduct of the transshipment route was that cocaine was soon diverted into the local population. It was during this era that cocaine became in demand among local residents. To make it affordable and quickly digestible, it was cooked into freebase or mixed with baking soda and water to make crack. In her groundbreaking study of Jamaican posses, Laurie Gunst (1995, 137) asserted that although "the Caribbean origins of crack are still under debate," most evidence suggests that the Bahamas was one of the first locales hit by the addictive substance, probably around 1980. However, it should be emphasized that American users had already been experimenting with smokable cocaine—witness comedian Richard Pryor setting himself on fire while smoking it in 1980. The Jamaican–Bahamian connection is an important one, because Jamaicans have always traveled between the two islands, as no visa was required for Jamaicans. Experts suggest that they may have stumbled onto the new chemical process in Bahamas and then introduced it back home in Kingston. The next step was shepherding the drug into urban America in the 1980s, and thence into more rural communities.

were not immune either. There are a handful of accounts of bounties up to $25,000 for the killing of law enforcement agents. Posses have been known to use a variety of counter-surveillance schemes to identify police investigators and learn personal information including telephone numbers and addresses (Valentine 1995).

THE SHOWER POSSE   The Shower posse is a gun-loving group that rose out of the Tivoli Gardens section of Kingston and earned its moniker for its reputation for "showering" its opponents with gunfire. Its members found solidarity supporting the Jamaican Labor Party (JLP). In 1984, it moved its base of operation to southern Florida. Led by Vivian Blake and Lester "Jim Brown" Coke (so called out of respect for the American football hall-of-famer), the Shower became major players in cocaine and marijuana trafficking between Miami and New York. By the time he arrived in Florida, Coke had a hard-won reputation as a killer in his home country, especially after he led 20 Shower members in an attack on a Kingston neighborhood that left 12 dead. Soon after arriving in the United States he was robbed in what he thought was a drug-rip off. Suspecting the people in the house from which he bought some cocaine, he went back to it and killed all six people with gunshots to the head. It took the authorities until 1987 to link him to the killings.

THE SPANGLER POSSE   Once known as the Bibo due to their love of jewelry, the Spangler posse originated in Kingston's Matthews Lane community. Its early members found common ground in their support of Jamaica's Peoples National Party (PNP). The late Glenford "Early Bird" Phelps, gunned down in 1990, led the posse's transition to New York City in the 1980s. Its main criminal activities involve drug trafficking, particularly marijuana, cocaine, and crack cocaine.

The posses' arrival coincided with the growing cocaine trade in the 1980s, and they quickly filled a niche for Latin American cartels that required street-level dealers to move the cheap new

Jointing

One way that Jamaican drug trafficking rings have been able to ensure loyalty from subordinates is the threat of violence to them and their families. A survey of New Jersey police organizations in the late 1980s even documented cases of what is referred to as *jointing*. Gang members who cooperated with the authorities have been dismembered at the joints and shipped back in pieces to the family back in Jamaica.

Demise of the Gulleymen Posse (1990)

By the late 1980s, the McGregor Gulleymen posse held the turf around Sterling Place and Schenectady in New York's Crown Heights. Members traced their origins to the similarly named neighborhood, McGregor Gulley, in Kingston, where it was aligned with the PNP. The posse became a "natural enemy" of the PLP-supporting Renkers posse, and both engaged in an open war for drug turf. In December 1990, the Gulleymen posse was decimated when 42 of its core members were indicted by a federal grand jury in Brooklyn: there were 35 indictments for conspiracy, 16 indictments for money laundering, and 3 indictments for fraudulent passport charges. FBI spokesman James M. Fox estimated that the Gulleymen had carried out close to a dozen murders (Gunst 1995). Among the indicted was a U.S. State Department employee who assisted the gang in obtaining fake passports. According to authorities, at its apogee, the gang was bringing in more than $100 million, thanks to the trafficking of heroin, cocaine, crack, and marijuana in New York, Washington, and Dallas during a 5-year period (NJSCI 1990, 21).

---

product called *crack*. Gambino family crime boss John Gotti testified in a 1986 trial that posse leader "Delroy Edwards deserves a special place in history as one of the first drug dealers to introduce crack to the streets of New York" (Gunst 1995, 160). The vertical structure of posse drug trafficking that allows them to control the product from its manufacture to its distribution results in a high profit margin. According to one gang specialist, a posse managing 50 crack houses can expect a profit reaching $9 million per month (Valentine 1995).

Jamaican gangs penetrate urban communities in a number of ways. According to one strategy, a member may select a particular African American woman and offer sumptuous gifts, money, and drugs. Once she falls for the bait, she is then expected to allow her home to be used as a base for drug operations. Another tactic involves paying certain individuals "rent" to use their apartments for criminal activities. Also popular is the creation of "gatehouses"—fortress-like bases typically set up in abandoned buildings. These serve a dual role as protection from both police and competitors. Meanwhile, the operation can employ dozens of people in positions that include lookouts, carpenters, and drug packagers, retailers, and wholesalers (Kelly 2000).

By most accounts, a number of Jamaican posses are vertically structured, which allows the flexibility to control costs and sell drugs at lower prices than competitors. Some posses have a multilayered structure, whereas others are less structured or primarily based on family and kinship ties. More recently, it has been suggested that "Each of the posses is an alliance of autonomous core groups spread across the country which utilize continuing criminal conspiracies to attain the goals of accumulation of wealth and individual power through illegal, quasi-legal, or legal means" (Pincomb and Judiscak 1998, 396).

JAMAICAN WEAPONS TRAFFICKING   The Jamaican reverence for high-powered weapons has been well chronicled. Some sources suggest the roots of their gang activity in the United States coincided with earning money to buy weapons to control their home neighborhoods. The posses have used their tolerance for violence and guns as an effective recruiting tool for their various drug operations. Weapons are acquired in a number of mostly illegal ways. Outright purchases usually include having a member or affiliate set up a residence and acquiring required documentation in states where residence requirements are less than 90 days.[19] Subsequently, residency allows the member to purchase plenty of weapons that can then be transported to other states, where they can be sold on the streets for a substantial profit.

Posses have acquired weapons by raiding gun dealerships, in home invasion robberies, hijacking vehicles carrying guns, breaking into military armories, and by stealing weapons shipments sent through the mail/shipping systems. In any case, the destination of these weapons once they are in the hands of Jamaican gang members is typically the market with the greatest potential for profit. In

Other Notable Posses

Renkers Posse

In her 1995 book *Born Fi' Dead*, Laurie Gunst chronicled the rise and fall of the Renkers posse, so named for the smell of urine on a wall. The gang originated in Kingston's Southside ghetto and supported the Jamaica Labour Party. Gunst interviewed its incarcerated leader, Delroy "Uzi" Edwards, at Rikers Island, where he explained the posse's moniker—*Renkers* meant "stinky"—"It's like the smell when you piss against a wall" (Gunst 1995, 5). Edwards left Jamaica for Brooklyn after the 1980 election and organized the Renkers Posse around the crack trade, a business lucrative enough to offer profits of $50,000 to $100,000 a day (Valentine 1995). In 1989, Edwards was tried for a host of felonies. His conviction on RICO charges is considered "the first successful prosecution of a Jamaican posse leader under the RICO statute" (Gunst 1995, 7). He was sentenced to 501 years without parole and fined more than $1 million.

Tel Aviv Posse

The Tel Aviv posse originated in the Tellerville neighborhood of Kingston, where it rose to prominence as the Skulls. This gang has affiliations with the Jungle posse, and both posses, like the Spanglers, support the Peoples National Party. This has led authorities to surmise that the three probably interact in various drug distribution schemes.

Waterhouse Posse

The Waterhouse posse took its name from the neighborhood in Kingston, Jamaica, where most of the members called home. In early 1980s they appeared in several northern New Jersey cities, where they trafficked in marijuana. By the early 1990s, members were major distributors of cocaine and crack through a network of street dealers.

many cases, this results in the weapons ending up in Jamaica, which, due to strict gun laws, offers a much higher return on each purchase. Weapons are smuggled onto the island along with food and other goods inside commercial containers, using small planes, or shipping inside cars destined for Jamaica from the United States (Grennan and Britz 2006).

FRAUDULENT ENTERPRISES   Jamaican gangsters have responded to virtually every attempt to suppress their activities with great cunning and success, particularly when it comes to hiding money. Due to currency transaction regulations, especially the requirement to fill out IRS 8300 forms whenever U.S. currency is used in a purchase of more than $10,000. To get around this, posse members have been known to purchase automobiles legally in the United States and then send them to Jamaica to be sold on the open market. The member stateside is then reimbursed once the car is sold. Posses have been known to send cash back to Jamaica using overnight express mail or by *smurfing,* sending several cash shipments under $10,000 to avoid the Currency Transaction Reports. This can be accomplished using several wire transfer companies.

Operation Rum Punch (1987)

By 1987, posse members had been linked to more than 600 drug-related murders, earning the reputation as one of America's most violent organized crime syndicates. In October 1987, the ATF led a raid named "Operation Rum Punch" on Jamaican posses. It resulted in the arrest of 124 members in 11 major metropolitan areas from Philadelphia to Los Angeles. Many of them belonged to prominent Kingston posses such as the Spanglers, the Shower, and the Tel Aviv posses.

POSSES: STREET GANGS OR ORGANIZED CRIME?   As newer generations of Jamaicans fill the posse ranks, former political linkages have become less important than criminal racketeering. In the mid-1990s, New Jersey State Police investigators revealed that Spangler and Shower posse members were cooperating in drug activities in order to increase profits (NJSCI 1990, 21). There is still a considerable amount of debate over whether the posses are more street gang, or more organized crime; nevertheless, few quibble with the fact that they are more sophisticated than a typical street gang. Some scholars argue that posses are locally organized syndicates with affiliations that allow them to expand their drug-trafficking networks. However, unlike organized crime, posses typically operate autonomously and are less cooperative with each other than organized crime families. Posse competition over the drug trade has, if anything, detracted from any attempts at organized networking. In any case, posses never came close to monopolizing any criminal enterprises, and although they clearly used violence and fear, there is little evidence that they had any great success corrupting American officials or infiltrating existing organizations, such as businesses or unions. On top of this, except for reinvesting in some restaurants, nightclubs, record stores, boutiques, and garages in local Jamaican communities, there is little evidence that posses have entered into legitimate businesses in any great way (Gay and Marquart 1993; Grennan and Britz 2006).

Since the mid-1990s, Jamaican authorities have assisted the United States by cracking down on posse drug syndicates. By most accounts, this has resulted in a drop in murder in recent years, although it is probably more the result of community initiatives to moderate gang violence. Various strategies have also included the utilization of troops to maintain anti-gang checkpoints. Jamaica is still far from gang-free, and as recently as 2002 the Jamaican government had to supply Queen Elizabeth with an armed security detachment to ensure her protection in a visit to urban slums.

Camden Police Detective Testifying about Jamaican Posses (1990)

Q. Is the Jamaican criminal activity in Camden organized?

A. Yes. The term . . . posse . . . picked up by our local drug . . . sets, . . . [originally came] from the Jamaican posses.

Q. In what types of criminal activity are the Jamaican posses involved?

A. They deal basically in the sale of marijuana and cocaine, and they've also been involved in numerous weapons violations.

Q. Have you been able to identify the Jamaican gangs that operate in Camden?

A. [I]ntelligence information has identified elements of the two major posses (the Spangler and Shower posses), but at this time the term *posse,* as an individual group, is fading away and what you are seeing now is the search for the money. Everything is developed on the profits.

Q. Do these Jamaican drug dealers interact with any of the African-American sets or other operations in Camden?

A. Yes, several of the Jamaican drug dealers do interact with the sets in Camden by selling marijuana. In addition to their own sources of supply for cocaine in New York City, the Jamaican dealers in Camden have obtained cocaine from members of the Junior Black Mafia operating out of Philadelphia, and they also maintain their own marijuana supplies.

Q. How do Jamaican drug dealers launder their drug profits?

A. Within the last two to three years the Jamaicans involved in drug distribution have tripled their legitimate business operations. They own and operate several bars, clothing stores and small food stores in the Camden area.

Q. Do these Jamaican groups . . . cooperate with these other non-Jamaican groups in Camden? Do they divide up the territory, or is this not as organized as that?

A. They are extremely organized. They are nationally connected. As a matter of fact, I would even go as far as to say internationally connected as far as the United States. Their network is as far reaching from Camden as Texas, Florida, Baltimore, New York, Kansas City (NJSCI 1990, 22).

Rastafarian Beliefs

- Ras Tafari is the living God.
- Ethiopia is the Black man's home.
- Repatriation is the way of redemption for Black men.
- The ways of the White men are evil.
- Eating pork is forbidden.
- The herb marijuana, or *ganja,* is a gift of God, who enjoined us to smoke it.
- Beards and long hair are enjoined on men; it is a sin to shave or cut the hair.
- Alcohol and gambling are prohibited.

(Valentine 1995, 106–107)

RASTAFARIANS   Rastafarianism, inspired by the ascendance of Ethiopia's ruler Haile Selassie, originated in the late 1930s, when Ethiopia was the only African country unshackled by European colonialism. Born Lij Tafari Makonnen, Selassie was appointed governor of Ethiopia's Sidamo Province while still in his teens. It was here that he became Ras ("Duke") Tafari. Those who followed Rastafarianism saw Selassie as the living incarnation of the Black man's true God—Negus. During the 1920s, as Tafri, he became immersed in foreign affairs and saw the country admitted into the League of Nations in 1928. He garnered his highest praise in 1935 when he fought back against the technologically superior Italian army invasion engineered by Mussolini. Selassie was always cognizant of the plight of Black Africans outside of Africa, and over the years encouraged them to return to their roots on the African continent. As his following increased, so did his ego, to the effect that he declared himself a living god. Selassie's message had a particular resonance on the island of Jamaica where almost 90% of the population was of African origin.

The Jamaican Rastafarians rebelled against most of the island's social conventions, including Christianity and "air-straightened Afro-Saxon primness" (Gunst 1995, 76). Recognizable for their dreadlocks, police reveled in arresting them and cutting their hair off. Jamaican posse members have had a long feud with the Rastafarians and brought the conflict with them from Jamaica to the United States. Toward the end of the 1990s, police intelligence revealed that the Rastafarians favored the production and sale of marijuana in Jamaica, but opposed the production of cocaine and its derivatives by posses. This feud was further provoked with the movement of both groups to America, where the Rastafarians originally controlled much of the drug market in New York City.

YARDIES   Jamaican immigration to England began in the 1950s as the country encouraged immigration to fill jobs during the post-war economic boom. The lure of a better life was seductive. However, on their arrival, recent immigrants typically found only unskilled jobs waiting for them. Earning low wages, immigrants were clustered in poor inner-city communities, a pattern repeated in industrialized countries around the world. Police relations were always strained, but with the arrival of a new wave of immigrants in the 1970s, relations deteriorated even further. Unlike the earlier immigrants, this generation was not interested in taking the traditional paths to social mobility, but was more interested in criminal activities. Over time, these individuals became known as "Yardies," which distinguished them from the hard-working and law-abiding Jamaicans. According to one recent study, more than a third of the UK's ethnic gang members (the majority of gang members there are White) were "mainly black African and Caribbean" (Bennett and Holloway 2004, 319).

The bonds forged by colonialism between Great Britain and Jamaica have inextricably linked the histories of both countries since the beginning of the 19th century. Among the results of this relationship, according to England's National Criminal Intelligence Service (NCIS), is the recent development of Afro-Caribbean organized crime. The most prominent of these groups are the

Yardies, a term that can be traced back to its slang origins in the ghettos of Kingston, Jamaica. In Jamaican street argot, a *yard* or *backyard* refers to back home in Jamaica. Another scholar suggested that the term referred to government yards of two-story concrete homes with shared cooking facilities (Covey 2003; Womersley 2002). When Jamaicans first immigrated, especially to England, they referred to themselves as *Yardies,* reflecting their Jamaican roots.

According to Scotland Yard, Yardies are typically between the ages of 18 and 35, and often eschew legitimate employment, although a number of them claim to be involved in the recording industry as musicians, singers, disc jockeys, and record producers. Many Yardies enter the country illegally, usually using false papers. British law enforcement has been hampered in its identification of members due to the Yardie predilection for using only street names and forged credentials (Ramm 2007).

Yardie drug gangs first registered on British radar screens in 1987, when they were linked to the crack cocaine in Black housing estates and the media publicized the first Yardie-linked homicide. By the 1990s, the NCIS recognized that these groups can no longer be regarded as "disorganized," when the Yardies began moving their base of operations to expand the crack cocaine trade into provincial markets to avoid increasingly more sophisticated police operations (Tendler 2000, 4).

In 1998, a network of drug traffickers directly linked to the Yardie gangs in the English Midlands appeared on the Scottish radar screen in Fraserburgh, which some authorities referred to as "the new heroin capital of Scotland" (Urquhart 1998). British authorities estimated the cocaine and crack cocaine market in this region to be worth £10 million a week. John Davidson reported some of the anti-Yardie operations by the British police in his 1997 book *Gangsta,* which focused on the strategies of Operation Dalehouse, which combined intense surveillance with computer analysis.[20]

Despite the rising violence associated with the Yardie phenomenon, police sources were still cautious about putting the blame on organized crime or drug wars. Indeed, there is little consensus concerning the sophistication of Yardie operations and whether they actually represent a monolithic form of organized crime (Roth 2000). About the only thing that Scotland Yard and the law enforcement establishment can agree on is that Afro-Caribbean gangsters made the transition in the 1990s from urban drug markets to smaller communities. Some journalists have suggested that the "Yardie gangs are being blamed for what is really an outbreak of anarchy among young urban black men" (Phillips 2000).

Over the years, England's Afro-Caribbean communities became established in relatively poor inner-city locales, which in many areas were in a state of gentrification. As upwardly mobile White professionals moved into these same communities and partook in the rich Afro-Caribbean cultural nightlife, young Black men became increasingly trapped with few opportunities in the same neighborhoods. Bedeviled by high unemployment rates, the little support provided by traditional community structures had diminished as well.

Overview

African and Caribbean countries have been plagued by a number of problems that are regarded as precursors and stimuli for the development of organized criminal groups. In these settings beset by ineffective law enforcement, a weak judicial process, armed ethnic militias, and masses of unemployed young people, criminal syndicates have a built-in recruiting ground for new members. With the last barrier to extensive organized crime removed with the end of South African *Apartheid* in the early 1990s and its accompanying restrictions lifted, virtually the entire continent of Africa is open for illegal syndicates. Africa is currently in the grips of tremendous socioeconomic and political changes made more glaring by the omnipresence of drought, famine, civil war, and corruption. Beset by a high population growth rate of between 3% and 4% a year, the continent's population doubled between 1985 and 2000 to more than 360 million people, almost two-thirds of whom are younger than 25. In 2000, it was estimated that there were close to 32 million street children—fodder for Africa's rapidly growing urban street gangs and ready recruits for various military groups (Urban Management Programme 2000).

More recently, journalist Tom Masland examined the bloody chaos in Sierra Leone, where he chronicled the participation of "child soldiers" in numerous atrocities against the local civilian populations and exhibited behavior one would correlate with the development of criminal and street gang behavior (2002). Together with

"an implied lack of sense of community, absence of legitimate economic opportunities, poor schooling, and the glaring multi-level governmental corruption, it is no wonder that organized criminal syndicate activity seems a welcome alternative to the rampant poverty that exemplifies the continent" (Covey 2003, 176).

By most accounts, the power and fear evoked by the 1980s and 1990s Jamaican gangs has diminished with the changing drug markets, new waves of criminal entrepreneurs, political changes, and a successful campaign by various law enforcement agencies.

Key Terms

Charles Taylor	Oil bunkering	The Padmore group
Warlords	Black-money scam	Posses
Agricultural slavery	Kakudu Group	Yardies
Wansa group	Marashea gangs	Rastafarians
Blood diamonds	*Tsotsis*	Kingston
Kimberly Process	*Dagga*	People's National Party
West African gangs	Msomi gang	Labor Party
Nigerians	Defense gangs	Massives
Sierra Leone	Reform gangs	Shower posse
Liberia	"The mafias"	Spangler posse
Kinship networks	Merchant syndicates	Jointing
Advance Fee Fraud	*Apartheid*	Renkers posse
419 Fraud	The Firm	
Nigerian repackaging scheme	West Indian gangs	

Critical Thinking Questions

1. What is *Afrolineal organized crime*?
2. What conditions in Africa has made it so welcoming to organized crime syndicates?
3. Is Charles Taylor more similar to a crime boss or to a politician? What is the differentiation?
4. Discuss the impact of ethnic and tribal rivalries on the African version of organized crime.
5. Why is West Africa the epicenter of organized crime on the continent? Discuss the various groups.
6. What types of organized crime structures exist in Africa? Why are they rarely well structured?
7. Discuss the role of diamond smuggling networks in Africa. Where are they located? Who runs them? Is it only an African network?
8. Why is Nigeria so central to the story of organized crime in Africa? Discuss their syndicate structure.
9. What is the *advance fee* fraud? What other criminal enterprises are popular in Nigeria?
10. What makes Southern Africa susceptible to transnational organized crime? Chronicle the history of criminal gangs in South Africa. Why is the country considered one of most crime-plagued regions in the world?
11. What was the impact of the end of *Apartheid* on South African organized crime?
12. What does East Africa's proximity to the Indian Ocean have on its peculiar organized crime problems? What impact has the rise of terrorism had?
13. What types of organized crime flourish in Central Africa?
14. Why is the Caribbean region included in this chapter? What has been its role in the drug trade?

15. What type of organized crime groups emerged from Jamaica? What were their characteristics? What was their relationship to the various political parties?

16. Compare and contrast illegal weapons trafficking in Africa and the Caribbean region. What differences are there?

Endnotes

1. Liberia was settled by immigrants by American immigrants who received international status for their own republic in 1847.
2. Some of the new seeds for organized crime were sown even earlier in Nigeria.
3. For more on the nexus between the diamond trade and terrorist funding, see Chapter 11 on Organized Crime and Terrorism.
4. This region's diamonds have figured prominently in literary works, most prominently in Graham Greene's *The Heart of the Matter* and Ian Fleming's non-fiction work, *Diamond Smugglers* (Farah 2004, 22).
5. "Combating International Crime in Africa," Hearing Before the Subcommittee on Africa of the Committee on Africa of the Committee on International Relations, House of Representatives, 105th Cong., Second Session, July 15, 1998. Further references are identified as Williams 1998.
6. Lagos is currently the world's third largest city, with a population nearing 15 million (http://www.punchng.com/Articl.aspx?theartic=Art2008123133011821).
7. There is a listing of more than 2000 variations of names used in Nigerian Advance Fee Fraud letters and e-mails on the Nigerian E-mail Scam Web site, http://www.crimes-of-persuasion.com.
8. According to the Dutch-based company Ultrascan Global Investigations, the United Kingdom comes in second at $530 million.
9. Received by author May 2007, and copied verbatim with errors.
10. Nigeria is not the sole oil producer of the country, nor is it the only one plagued by oil bunkering. For example, in 2000, Angola is estimated to have lost $1 billion in accounted for revenue.
11. Insiders suggest this is an understatement.
12. There are dozens of examples of this fraud on the Marked Currency Web site, http://www.crimes-of-persuasion.com/Nigerian/marked_currency.htm.
13. For a short time, another group called itself the *Majapane,* or "Japanese," in deference to that country's fighting men.
14. Most Basotho men came from Lesotho. They were distinct from other migrant groups that settled in South Africa due to their predilection to settle in urban centers.
15. This organization was actually the product of an alliance between former members of the "Durban" and "Y" gangs. Both had previously been at war with each other before hitching their guns to Sheriff Khan's organization.
16. For example, heroin is transported from Afghanistan through Pakistan to Tanzania before being smuggled to Europe and North America by a host of air routes, often by Nigerian couriers.
17. These include Antigua and Barbuda, Barbados, Dominica, Grenada, St. Kitts and Nevis, St. Lucia, and St. Vincent and the Grenadines.
18. In his 1982 book *Struggle in the Periphery*, Manley dedicated it to the 750 young men killed during the 1980 election.
19. Most weapons purchases take place in the southern states of Florida, Georgia, Texas, and Virginia, with most ending up on the streets of New York City.
20. See John Davison, *Gangsta: The Sinister Spread of Yardie Gun Culture*, London, 1997.

CHAPTER 13

Terrorism and Organized Crime: An Evolving Relationship

A recent United Nations High Level Panel on Threats, Challenges, and Change released a report that suggested (among other conclusions) that security threats including organized crime and terrorism "were more interrelated today than ever before" (quoted in HUMSEC 2006). In a 2003 report, the United Nations Secretary General suggested, "It is necessary to set up measures against transnational terrorism and organized crime" (quoted in HUMSEC 2006). These links became the focus of criminologists and police officials in the 1980s when the term *narcoterrorism* was created to distinguish the use of terrorism in Colombia and Peru by large drug syndicates trying to protect their investments. This represented a turning point in the examination of these two phenomena.

Previous investigations viewed most criminal groups and syndicates as pragmatic rather than ideological. In the late 1990s, terrorism scholar Bruce Hoffman suggested what distinguished the two was that

> the criminal is not concerned with influencing or affecting public opinion; he simply wants to abscond with his money or accomplish his mercenary task in the quickest and easiest way possible so that he may reap his reward and enjoy the fruits of his labors. By contrast, the fundamental aim of the terrorist's violence is ultimately to change "the system"—about which the ordinary criminal, of course, couldn't care less. (Hoffman 1998, 42)

In recent years, the ideological motivations of terrorist groups have eroded to the point of blurring any distinction from organized criminal organizations, or as two recent researchers observed, "the lines of separation are no longer unequivocal" (Shelley and Picarelli 2005, 52). Perhaps DEA administrator Steven W. Casteel put it best when he suggested, "Whether a group is committing terrorist acts, trafficking drugs or laundering money, the one constant to remember is that they are all forms of organized crime" (quoted in Mathis 2004, 105).

Researchers across the spectrum have increasingly turned their attention to the process by which criminal syndicates and international terrorists adopt each other's organizational and operational characteristics. Scholars have long recognized that terrorists have engaged in transnational organized crime activities. However, the question that comes up is, when does a criminal enterprise become a terrorist group (or vice versa)? Terrorist groups have used physical violence in hijackings, kidnappings, and murders, and have participated in weapons- and drug-trafficking networks, immigrant smuggling, and money laundering. More recently, groups have established "illegal multinational criminal organizations" (White 2005, 66). However, there are still a number of critics who refuse to classify terrorism as criminal activity (Wilkinson 1974; Cooper 1978; Laqueur 1999). In 2004, Raphael Perl of the Library of Congress' Congressional Research Center added his voice to the debate, arguing, "It is

477

> ### Differences between Terrorist and Organized Crime Groups
>
> • Terrorist groups are usually ideologically motivated, whereas organized crime groups are profit oriented
> • Terrorist groups often wish to compete with governments for legitimacy, whereas organized crime groups do not
> • Terrorist groups usually seek media attention, whereas organized crime groups do not
> • Terrorist victimization is usually less discriminate than violence used by organized crime groups (Schmid 2005, 5)

important to recognize that we are dealing with two distinct and separate phenomena, linked mainly for convenience" (quoted in Mathis 2004, 105). However, others insist that the "merger of transnational crime, terrorism and corruption is profound," and that the notion that these "ideas can be discussed separately is problematic" (Shelley 2004). Government officials have been even more forthcoming in linking the two, with one State Department official warning, "Transnational crime is converging with the terrorist world" (quoted in Kaplan 2005, 1), whereas a spokesman for the United Nations Office of Drugs and Crime suggested, "The world is seeing the birth of a new hybrid of organized crime—terrorist organizations" (Kaplan, Fang, and Sangwan 2005, 1).

Shelley and Picarelli (2005) devised a multi-stage process that explains the evolution of the "terror–crime relationship." The earliest stage begins when the two begin to actively buy and sell services from each other, borrowing methods from each other in a process that the authors call *activity appropriation*. In the next stage, both groups begin to work more closely in a symbiotic relationship once they mutually recognize their shared methodologies and motivations. In some regions of the world, such as the Tri-Border area of Paraguay, Brazil, and Argentina and Chechnya, there is so much of both activities that it is impossible to distinguish one behavior from the other, because many individuals partake in both activities.

However, what seems most likely is that although terrorism and organized crime are indeed separate phenomena, both use overlapping networks and often cooperate in various enterprises. One recent survey by the Pentagon has gone as far as to suggest, "The phenomenon of the synergy of terrorism and organized crime is growing because similar conditions give rise to both and because terrorists and organized criminal use similar approaches to promote their operations" (Milton 2006). Indeed, both groups use many of the same strategies to promote their operations; both rely on an underworld of black markets and laundered money; both rely on shifting networks and secret cells to accomplish objectives; and both need weapons, false documents, and safe hiding places.

WHAT IS TERRORISM?

Like organized crime, there is a lack of consensus as to the definition of *terrorism*. As one authority recently suggested, the issue is in the problematic definition: We can agree that terrorism is a problem, but we cannot agree on what terrorism is (Cooper 2002). In the mid-1970s, a scholar predicted this dilemma when he suggested that all efforts to define terrorism would not end with a consensus, and that the term would retain its uncertainty in the minds of people (Laqueur 1977). Leading authority Jonathan White (2002) argues that a terrorist is any organization that engages in any terrorist activities, including the funding of the organization.

National definitions vary according to basic criteria. For the United States, a *terrorist organization* must demonstrate three basic characteristics:

• Individuals are gathered for the same purpose.
• These individuals belong to an anti-government or a sub-national revolutionary or autonomous non-state movement.
• They have to use violence in order to achieve their aims (Advisory Panel of Congress 1999).

Similarities between Terrorist and Organized Crime Groups

- Both operate secretly and usually from an underground network.
- Both use "muscle and ruthlessness" on primarily civilian victims.
- Both use intimidation.
- Both use similar tactics, such as kidnapping, assassination, and extortion.
- In both cases, the control of the group over the individual is strong.
- Both use front operations, such as legitimate businesses or charities (Schmid 2005, 5–6).

Turkey, however, passed an Anti-Terror Law in 1991 that stated that a terrorist organization is considered operational when at least two people gather with the same goals. The term *organization* includes formations, associations, armed associations, gangs, or armed gangs, as described in the Turkish Penal Code and in the provisions of special laws.

In any case, most definitions mention acts of a violent nature, conspiracy, providing transportation, safe houses, false identifications, weapons, or training to individuals who commit terrorist acts (U.S. State Department 1999). Terrorism has been regarded as distinct from organized crime for decades due to the emphasis on terrorism's political and ideological motivations, which have previously rendered it distinct from definitions of organized crime. The U.S. Department of Justice has obscured the differences between the two by offering the FBI's definition: "The unlawful use of force or violence against persons or property to intimidate or coerce a government, the civilian population, or any segment thereof, in furtherance of political or social objectives" (FBI, U.S. Department of Justice 1998).

There is still a lack of consensus among law enforcement agencies as to how close the cooperative links are between organized crime and terrorist groups. What is abundantly clear is that terrorists support their activities through whatever avenues that are convenient and profitable, and can include legal employment, accepting voluntary donations, social assistance, or criminal activity, or through any combination of the aforementioned. Most of these activities do not endanger the operational security of terrorist organization. Some terrorists resort to low-profile criminal activity, including petty thefts or social assistance frauds, whereas others prefer a more organized network of criminality, one that is preferably confined only to close associates.

One's level of devotion to political and religious extremist groups often determines what type of organized crime organization and activities are preferred. Those who are more "professional terrorists" might be more inclined to place operational security over profit margin, or might be less or more likely to resort to activities considered morally repugnant, such as trafficking in sex and drugs. Others make the judgment based on the level of scrutiny that some activities might bring from law enforcement, or whether it will impede their terrorist activities. Those who consider themselves professional terrorists or are more devoted to a particular cause might lean toward minimizing their links to organized crime groups for ethical reasons that could alienate their supporters.

A number of authorities agree that a cooperative link ties many terrorists with organized crime groups, but it is more likely to occur in cases where guerrilla or insurgent groups exert control over drug-producing regions. However, in most other cases the ties seem to be more tenuous and become so blurred that it is difficult to distinguish the terrorist group from its criminal activities and vice versa. For example, in the 1980s the Provisional IRA and Loyalist paramilitary groups in North Ireland resorted to criminal fundraising efforts that were formerly the province of organized crime groups, leading one observer to remark, "It wasn't a case of terrorists being linked to organized crime groups; they were themselves organized crime groups in direct competition with what British authorities sometimes described as 'ordinary decent criminals'" (Strang 2004, 3).

The goals of transnational criminal groups and terrorist groups often dovetail when it comes to raising money. For example, it is easier to traffic in drugs through zones of civil conflict, and separatists and other extremists have discovered that drug trafficking is an important source for purchasing weapons, organizing terrorist attacks, and maintaining armed terrorist squads.

Another contribution to the convergence between the two is the huge gap in development levels between countries. Typically, patterns of migration move from poor to rich states. As a result, the have-nots of other countries join the ranks of the have-nots of another, often joining the socially deprived who support international terrorists (Kudryavtsev 2005, 88).

Prior to the end of the Cold War, the labels *terrorist* and *criminal* had been generally clear cut, but in the post-Soviet era, the distinction has become less clear (Clutterbuck 2004). In the mid-1990s, a State Department employee eloquently lamented that in his travels he "had seen in Colombia that hybrid organizations, with parents of both terrorist and organized crime pedigrees, are a stark reality" (Schweitzer 1998, 288–289). The same links can be made between modern organized crime syndicates and terrorists in most other regions of the world. Globalization and the collapse of the Soviet Union are among the factors that have increased links between terrorist and transnational criminal organizations. With the decline in state sponsorship of terrorism, a number of terrorist groups have turned to a variety of criminal enterprises that were formerly the province only of organized crime syndicates to finance their myriad activities (Hamm and Van de Voorde 2005).

Scholars first began to make the connections between the two phenomena in the 1970s and 1980s, an era when leftist terrorist groups in Latin America began forging relationships with drug cartels (Makarenko 2003). These relationships were characterized under a new rubric—*narcoterrorism* (Ehrenfeld 1990). By the early 1990s, Western law enforcement agencies reported an "increasing reliance on criminal activity by terrorist networks around the world" (Mili 2006, 1). However, as early as 1993, French authorities uncovered evidence that illegal drug sales in Muslim slum areas were under the direction of Afghanistan War veterans with ties to Algerian terrorist groups (Kaplan 2005).

According to one study, organized drug trafficking financed at least 30 terrorist campaigns around the world at the start of the new millennium (Calvani 2001; Landau 2003). A wide range of terrorist groups have resorted to organized crime to finance their activities, including the radical Islamic groups Hezbollah and Hamas, both of which have been cited for participation in complex schemes involving money laundering, arms and drug smuggling, and intellectual property rights piracy (Landau 2003; Gribben 2003; Pollard 2002). For Islamic terrorist groups, the adoption of criminal enterprises has been troubling to most devout Muslims. However, contemporary terrorists have weathered this critique by using the writings of the 13th-century scholar Ibn Taymiyya as "religious justification for their acts, criminal or otherwise." In 1998, Osama bin Laden announced that jihadists should kill Americans and "plunder their money wherever and whenever they find it" (Mili 2006, 3).[1]

More recently, definitive links have demonstrated how Islamic extremist groups use organized criminal activities to fund operations. The terrorists who planned the 2004 Spanish train bombings, for example, funded the bombings with hashish and ecstasy sales. Evidence points to their contacts with major drug dealers with a network that runs from Morocco through Spain, Belgium, and the Netherlands. However, although the costs of this bombing ranged to about $50,000, police raids uncovered almost $2 million in drugs and cash linked to the jihadists (Kaplan, Fang, and Sangwan, 2005).

Relationships between Organized Crime and Terrorist Actors/Groups

In 1997, Colombian President Ernesto Samper announced, "The terrorist group FARC has financed its activities with $600 million from the Colombian drug dealers" (quoted in Schweitzer 1998, 165). It is incredibly expensive to run a terrorist campaign, particularly one that is well organized and equipped, widespread and active, and ultimately successful. As recently as July 2007, a U.S. military spokesman accused Iran of attempting to establish a "Hezbollah-like network of cells in Iraq" (Hennessy-Fiske and Susman 2007). The amount of money required for this operation exemplifies

Most Prominent Examples of Organized Crime Associations with Terrorists	
Organized Crime Group	**Terrorist Group**
Albanian mafia	Kosovo Liberation Army
Colombian cartels	Revolutionary Armed Forces of Colombia (FARC)
Dawood syndicate	Al Qaeda, Tamil Tigers
Central Asian syndicates	Islamic Movement of Uzbekistan

the financial resources needed by terrorist groups. In this case, it was estimated that it cost between $750,000 and $3 million a month for a unit of Iran's Revolutionary Guards to operate and train prospective terrorists in three camps near Tehran. Although Iran's government is able to meet these expenses, most terrorist groups do not have the luxury of state sponsorship and are forced to gather funds by any means possible. This may include charities and donations, but is more likely through criminal enterprises. Indeed, today, more groups rely on crime strategies over state sponsorship as they diversify their resource base (Scherpenberg 2001, 4).

Although terrorist and organized crime groups have similar requirements for moving people, money, and materials across international borders, historically there has been only minimal cooperation between the two. However, both share a reliance on the drug trade to generate funding, and there is often cooperation between the two in acquiring forged identification and travel documents.

As one expert noted recently, "The illegal nature of terrorist groups makes the collecting of funds uncertain, leading them to engage in sporadic alliances with groups that may not share their dissident views" (Garces 2005, 86). Nevertheless, there is still a debate among academics and law enforcement authorities as to whether there is anything resembling "a systematic organized crime–terrorism nexus" (Williams 2001, 97; Schmid 2005, 2). By most accounts, the strongest links between the two has been between drug traffickers and terrorist/guerrilla groups. One scholar found a link between armed conflict and illicit drug trafficking in 30 out of 100 countries (Schmid 2005, 2).

Although each group borrows strategies from the other or they occasionally cooperate with each other, the most common reciprocity is for terrorist groups to use organized crime activities to fund their operations. However, as expert Phil Williams suggests, each group might borrow tactics and strategies from the other when practical, but this "does not necessarily mean that there is a convergence" between the two. In the mid-1990s, Williams declared, "In many areas of the world, the distinctions between organized crime which is essentially profit driven—and terrorism—which is about the pursuit of political change through use of violence—remain clear and distinct" (quoted in Garces 2005, 87), citing parts of Africa, Central Asia, the Balkans and the countries of Afghanistan, Burma, and Colombia. However, what has muddied the issue has been the "complex mixture of insurgency, factionalism, warlordism, terrorism, crime and corruption" (quoted in Garces 2005, 87) that has accompanied the process of globalization.

IMPACT OF GLOBALIZATION ON ORGANIZED CRIME/TERRORISM NEXUS

One 2003 investigation examined countries in Africa, the former Soviet Union and Eastern Europe, South Asia, Western Europe and Italy, and the Western Hemisphere, and in each region, researchers found example of the confluence of organized crime and terrorism. What has become most clear is that since the mid-1990s, both types of organizations have "globalized and diversified their operations" (Berry, Curtis, Hudson, Karacan, Kollars, and Miro 2003). In many cases, this has required basing operations in countries offering the maximum opportunities for survival and expansion of their criminal operations, demonstrating the "fragility of a globalized world" (Chanda 2007).

Domestic Elements Making a Nation Hospitable to Transnational Organized Crime and Terrorism

- Official corruption
- Incomplete or weak legislation
- Poor enforcement of existing laws
- Non-transparent financial institutions
- Unfavorable economic conditions
- Lack of respect for the rule of law in society
- Poorly guarded national borders
- Geographic location
- Proximity to traditional smuggling routes

(Adapted from Berry and Curtis, 2003)

Globalization has been both a boon and a pox on international economies. Chief among its negative consequences has been the decreasing capacity of many national governments to prevent and confront transnational crime and terrorism. In his recent book, *Bound Together: How Traders, Preachers, Adventurers, and Warriors Shaped Globalization,* Nayan Chanda asserts that *globalization* is basically a new word used to describe an old process. Although the term was introduced in the late 1970s, it has gained increased currency since the turn of the 21st century. To study human history is to examine the process by which people become more and more enmeshed in a web of interconnectedness. More than a century ago, explorer David Livingstone noted that, "The extension and use of the railroad, steamships, and telegraphs break down nationalities and brings peoples geographically remote into close connection commercially and politically" (quoted in Chanda 2007). However, "the closer the connections between the parts, the more vulnerable the system becomes to any major wobbles" (Chanda 2007), such as the attacks on September 11, 2001. Both terrorists and syndicates flourished as this process became more advanced. As one observer so eloquently noted, "Threats today from superbugs like SARS, Islamic terrorism, can go global faster than any threats in the past" (Chanda 2007).

Albanian Organized Crime and the Terrorist Connection

In 2005, one leading expert on the links between organized crime and terrorism noted, "The most illustrative nexus between a criminal and terrorist group—one in which a mutual relationship has proven integral to the operation of both entities—is the relationship between the Albanian mafia and the Kosovo Liberation Army (KLA) during the Kosovo conflict" (Makarenko 2005, 132). In 1996, the terrorist group known as the Kosovo Liberation Army (KLA, or the Albanian-derived acronym UCK) emerged out of the chaos that was once Yugoslavia and instigated a war between Kosovo and Serbia, with the goal of winning Kosovo's independence from Serbia. More than 90% of Kosovo's population is of Albanian ethnicity, reflecting the collective identity shared with neighboring Albanians. One Interpol officially suggested, "It is this element, based on the affiliation to a certain group which links organized Albanian crime to pan-Albanian ideals, politics, military activities, and terrorism" (Mutschke 2000, 3).

The following year witnessed the collapse of the Albanian government. The process of democratization that began in 1990 resulted in a progressively out of control environment, as many Albanians who had formerly disrespected the rule of law as practiced by the communist regime were increasingly drawn into the orbit of developing criminal syndicates. At roughly the same time, Albanian drug syndicates were consolidating their control over the Balkan heroin-smuggling routes. Toward the end of the 1990s, the relationship between the two groups had become well established, and a major concern for international law enforcement. By most accounts, it was at this point that the contacts between the KLA and the Albanian syndicates morphed into "a well-oiled arrangement," in which millions of dollars in drug profits from the Pristina cartel were turned over to the KLA, where the lucre was used to purchase armaments, "often in 'drugs-for-arms' arrangements" (Makarenko 2005, 132).[2]

The fall of the Albanian government followed some four decades of communist rule. Subsequent events resulted in conditions of anarchy and chaos as a welter of warlords from Albania's mountain region together with corrupt police, military, and government officials along with black marketeers, drug traffickers, and assorted gangsters ran roughshod over the country. Taking advantage of the concomitant unrest in neighboring Croatia and Serbia and the Yugoslavian war, Albanians took advantage of their geographic position to establish alternate Balkan routes for heroin traffickers looking to bypass the civil conflict raging next door. By most accounts, more than 50% of European heroin came by this route, and from then on it has been smuggled through Albania, over the Adriatic into Italy, and from there to Northern and Western Europe.

Conditions in 1997 plummeted to the extent that the breakdown in civil authority in Albania gave crime syndicates virtual free rein to loot military arsenals of thousands of automatic weapons. The marketplace in the region was clamoring for such weapons. In a short time, some criminal syndicates used the guise of paramilitary units to acquire a patina of legitimacy. When war broke out in Kosovo as the 1990s came to conclusion, the ersatz paramilitaries-cum-drug-traffickers took advantage of the unrest by creating smuggling operations to support the KLA (Nicaso and Lamothe 2005).

The KLA's stated objectives included the secession of Albania from Serbia and ultimately the creation of a "Greater Albania" that would include Kosovo, Albania, and the ethnic minority of neighboring Macedonia. The KLA had deep support in the Albanian communities and used its financial support to buy weapons that were then smuggled across the Albania–Kosovo border. Reprisals and a crackdown by Serbian forces only increased support for the KLA.

As the 1990s moved toward conclusion, the KLA–Albanian relationship continued. Between 1996 and 1999, it is estimated that at least half the funds reaching Kosovo came from the drug trade. It is thought that legitimate fundraising for the cause was used to launder drug money. In 1998, the United States State Department went so far as to declare the KLA a terrorist organization after reporting that it financed its campaigns with heroin profits and from loans from Islamic countries and extremists such as bin Laden (Mutschke 2000, 8).

A number of links between terrorists and the drug gangs in this region surfaced in the late 1990s. By 1998, the KLA was regarded by Interpol as a major player in the trade of drugs for weapons, charging that the KLA helped "transport 2 billion USD worth of drugs annually into Western Europe" (Mutschke 2000), using a complex network of banks and companies to transfer the funds.

By the summer of 1999, the conflict in neighboring Kosovo led some critics to declare the region the "Colombia of Europe," as officers and supporters of the KLA became a major force in international organized crime. During the late 1990s, the rule of law had ceased throughout much of Albania, leading one observer to deride the nation's legislature as "the Kalashnikov Parliament," referring to rampant weapons trade between Albanian gangs and the KLA. The United Nations announced that it had found 200,000 Kalashnikov automatic weapons stolen from Albanian armories in the KLA arsenal, leading one observer to lament, "It's easier to buy a modern machine gun in the Balkans today than a Toblerone chocolate bar" (quoted in Roth 2000, 8).

What is most probable but seldom mentioned is that organized crime groups hoped their participation in the campaign would provide them with a safe haven in the Kosovo region. More recently, Pristina has emerged as an important transit point in the Balkan trade route and as a shelter for the heads of Balkan crime syndicates. Further contributing to this criminogenic environment has been high unemployment and persistent industrial decay that have led the population to be more tolerant of illegal activities. Indeed, the local heroin trade has even revitalized some local economies.

SOUTH ASIAN ORGANIZED CRIME AND TERRORIST NETWORKS

Organized crime in South Asia runs the gamut, from drug and weapons trafficking to extortion, money laundering, and kidnapping. In recent years, the links between organized crime and terrorist groups have been well documented, particularly in the region's urban centers in India and Pakistan. Since the mid-1990s, these localities have witnessed an alarming increase in terrorist attacks coordinated with the help of various crime syndicates. The 1993 Mumbai (formerly Bombay) attacks best illustrates this partnership. The most prominent organized crime group in South Asia is known as the *Dawood Gang* or *D Company,* under the aegis of the region's most wanted gangster, Dawood Ibrahim. He commands a crime network of more than 4,000 members, half of whom are located in Mumbai (Lal 2005, 296).

Dawood Ibrahim: South Asia's Al Capone

In 2003 the U.S. Treasury Department designated Dawood Ibrahim, formerly India's most prominent gangster, a "global terrorist" for allowing al Qaeda to use his smuggling routes, supporting jihadists in Pakistan, and participating in the March 12, 1993, terrorist attack in Mumbai that killed 257 and injured more than 700. It is now believed that the 1993 serial bombings were masterminded by Dawood and his brother Anis in retaliation for the deaths of hundreds of Muslims during riots blamed on the right-wing Hindu Shiv Sena party. Ibrahim is now thought to be hiding in Pakistan, where he has developed links with al Qaeda and another banned extremist group. Although links between terrorist and organized crime groups seems like a recent development, in reality, Dawood had been financing Islamic militant groups working against India since the early 1990s (Zaidi 2002; Profile 2006).

What was least expected by investigators was that the ensuing investigation would lead to the crime boss regarded as South Asia's Al Capone (Kaplan, Fang, and Sangwan 2005). By most accounts, Ibrahim directs a criminal empire that includes a small army of contract killers, smugglers, and extortionists that reaches across 14 countries. However, one unintended result of Ibrahim's forays into terrorism has been the splintering of his group, as a number defected in condemnation of the mass killings and formed the rival Hindu gang under the leadership of the criminal Chhota Rajan (Lal 2005).

Little known in the West, Dawood Ibrahim now runs criminal gangs from Bangkok to Dubai from the relative safety of his Pakistan hideout, sheltered by India's foremost adversary. His hardly sinister sounding "D Company" syndicate is involved in strong-arm protection, drug trafficking, extortion, murder-for-hire, and now supplying jihadists with weapons and financial support. He is considered India's most wanted man. A 2005 *U.S. News and World Report* investigation has revealed

---

Black Friday: The Mumbai Bombings, March 12, 1993

Several prominent South Asian crime syndicates have been identified with the attacks that killed 257 people on March 12, 1993, in Mumbai, India. Most notable were Dawood Ibrahim and Tiger Memon. The planning and carrying out of this murderous attack is a graphic lesson in how terrorists and organized criminals cooperate. Both gang bosses recruited members to be trained for the attacks in Pakistan. To ensure security, they were transferred first to Dubai and thence to Pakistan under false documentation received in Dubai. Once at the training camps, the recruits were skilled in the use of various automatic weapons, hand grenades, rocket launchers, and a potent explosive additive known as RDX (Zaidi 2002). With the assistance of corrupt customs officials, the weapons were landed in the ports near the target center. The subsequent attacks, concluded political scientist Rollie Lal, would not have been possible without the collusion of "Pakistani officials and the corruption of various Indian agencies" (2005, 297).

Names Added to List of Drug Kingpins According to U.S. Kingpin Act (2000)

- Dawood Ibrahim (India)
- Fahd Jamil Georges (Brazil)
- Ali Naway (Iran)
- Dawood Ibrahim Organization (India/Pakistan/UAE)
- Amezcua Contreras Organization (Mexico)

what many already suspected—"terrorists worldwide are transforming their operating cells into criminal gangs" (Kaplan, Fang, and Sangwan 2005).

Born in 1955, Dawood is one of eight sons of a struggling policeman. He rose from petty crime to gang boss by eliminating rivals at the head of his own gang on the means streets of Bombay and is now one of the world's most wanted terrorists. His D Company gang's nucleus came from the minority Muslim population of Bombay. He built Bombay's most formidable syndicate by smuggling black market gold and other commodities into India's closed economy, and bullied his way into the country's Bollywood film industry (Kaplan et al, 2005).

Ibrahim left India for Dubai to avoid prosecution and to run his empire from the welcoming environment of the United Arab Emirates. He flourished considerably in Pakistan, where he has maintained a number of legitimate and illicit businesses, leading to his emergence as the "don of Karachi," where his organization made huge investments in real estate and plays an important role in the country's parallel credit system business, the *hundi*. Some have even credited him with having rescued Pakistan's Central Bank by providing loans that saw it through a financial crisis at one point. Gold- and drug-smuggling schemes as well as cricket-match fixing are among his more lucrative endeavors (Raman 2003, 8).

In the 1980s and 1990s, Ibrahim was the acknowledged kingpin of the Mumbai underworld, directing a multi-billion-dollar vice empire involving prostitution, drugs, and gambling. His connection to the Bollywood film industry ensured that no star would refuse his request to appear in one of his films. According to Pakistani journalist Ghulam Hasnain, Ibrahim "lives like a king" in Pakistan in a palatial home spread over 6,000 square yards. The 5′4″ kingpin prefers designer clothes and expensive cars and wears a 500,000-rupee Patek Phillipe watch (Profile 2006).

Ibrahim's syndicate has been linked to large-scale shipments of narcotics to the UK and Western Europe, and shares smuggling routes from South Asia, the Middle East, and Africa with the al Qaeda network. Conversely, bin Laden has also used routes established by Ibrahim's syndicate over the years (Raman 2003). Dawood Ibrahim is one of the rare players on the international scene who is regarded as both a crime kingpin and a terrorist leader.

Aftab Ansari: Kidnapper and Financial Supporter of Terrorists

Aftab Ansari, a Dubai-based criminal, has been linked to terrorist financing in South Asia. Indian authorities reportedly intercepted an e-mail indicating that he sent $100,000 to terrorist financier Sayed Omar Sheikh through Dubai in August 2001. Insiders are confident that some of this money was sent to 9/11 hijacker Mohammed Atta in exchange for a promise that Sheikh would offer weapons training to Ansari's kidnapping network (Lal 2005). Sheikh and Ansari met while in prison together in the 1990s. Following Ansari's release, he went to Pakistan. The former prisoners reconnected soon after and came to an arrangement by which Ansari sent recruits for terrorist training in Army of Mohammed training camps in Pakistan, and Sheikh responded by allowing Ansari to use his terrorist network in his various criminal enterprises. The $100,000 sent to Sheikh was part of the $830,000 ransom paid to Ansari for the release of a kidnapped shoe manufacturer (Lal 2005).

Funding Sources for Selected Terrorist Groups

- **Revolutionary Armed Forces of Colombia (FARC):** Narcotics, kidnapping, and extortion
- **National Liberation Army (ELN):** Colombian Marxist guerrillas funded by kidnappings, extortion, and drug trafficking
- **United Self-Defense Forces (AUC):** Colombian right-wing paramilitary force involved in drug trafficking and gasoline smuggling
- **Abu Sayyaf (Philippines):** Kidnapping, extortion, drugs, and cigarette smuggling
- **Jemaah Islamiyah (Southeast Asia):** Armed robbery and credit card fraud
- **IRA (Northern Ireland):** Bank robbery, fraud, extortion, counterfeiting, cargo theft, and cigarette and gasoline smuggling
- **Kurdistan Workers Party (PKK):** Turkish group tied to heroin trafficking, kidnapping, and extortion
- **Hezbollah:** Lebanese-backed militia trafficking in heroin and hashish; also engages in cigarette smuggling, counterfeiting, extortion, and fraud
- **Chechen Rebels:** Smuggling and trafficking in drugs, weapons, and counterfeit currency
- **Islamic Movement of Uzbekistan (IMU):** Drug-related activities
- **Moroccan Islamic Combatant Group (GICM):** Drugs, financial fraud, counterfeiting
- **Salafist Group for Call and Combat (GSPC):** Kidnapping, armed robbery, extortion, drugs, human smuggling, and fraud in Algeria and Europe
- **Iraqi Insurgents:** Extortion, kidnapping for ransom, theft, and smuggling of oil
- **Al Qaeda:** In Pakistan and Afghanistan; engage in kidnapping, antiquities smuggling, robbery, and financial fraud
- **Taliban:** Drug trafficking
- **D Company (Southeast Asia):** Indian mafia; engages in narcotics trade, extortion, arms smuggling, contract murder and kidnapping

Adapted from "The Rackets of Terror," *U.S. News and World Report,* December 5, 2005, Vol. 139, Issue 21.

Ansari and Sheikh later joined forces in the attack on the American Center in Calcutta in 2002. That same year, Ansari was arrested and confirmed his ties to terrorist funding and Sheikh.

Hawala and the Financing of Terrorist and Criminal Networks

It is one thing to earn illicit money, but it is another just as hazardous challenge to send it through whatever channels are available to its ultimate destination—whether banking institutions, individuals, or other criminal and terrorist networks. Underground banking arrangements have operated beside legitimate banking systems for centuries. *Hawala* originated in early medieval commerce in the Near and Middle East in an era that was marked by substantial long-distance trade by sea and by camel caravans. *Hawala* played an important security role when robbers and pirates were always on the prowl for merchant commodities in transit. The utilization of this method meant traders could count on a system of monetary transfer based solely on trust and grounded in Islamic propriety. This allowed traders and travelers alike to conduct business in foreign countries without having to physically carry the necessary currency (Mabrey 2003).

Underground banking networks have been variously referred to as *alternative remittance systems, informal funds transfer systems,* and *informal value transfer systems.* Different types of underground banking systems have evolved in various parts of the world, including *hawala* and *hundi* in South Asia and *fei-ch'ien* in China. However, these informal networks operate from Hong Kong to South America and from the Himalayas to North America (McCusker 2005).

The exchange of money through the seemingly informal *hawala* underground banking network is common throughout much of South Asia and the Middle East. Attempting to track funding through *hawala,* although not impossible, has been compared to trying to catch smoke or "electronic blips as they fly through the atmosphere" (Madinger 2006, 391). Because these transfers of money leave no paper trail, any estimate of the money exchanged is meaningless.

Hawala is particularly useful for the transmitting of illegal funds from criminal activities and terrorist organizations because, like other underground systems, it "is a rational choice for the transfer of money because it has the same structure and operational characteristics as the formal banking sector without any of its attendant bureaucracy or external regulatory scrutiny" (McCusker 2005, 4).

Hawala transactions are similar to money wire transfers facilitated through banks and companies such as Western Union. For example, when al Qaeda wants to move large amounts of money from one place to another to pay for members' living expenses or for upcoming operations, it has usually gone through a trusted member of the local Muslim community, such as in Pakistan to assist in the transaction. The *hawala* businessman provides a chit receipt for the funds and telephones or faxes instructions to a contact in another country to provide money to the intended recipient, minus his fee. *Hawala* networks operate through traditional ties of religion, ideology, or family connections to the terrorist or organized crime networks.

However, since 9/11, this ancient and traditional trading system has come under close scrutiny due to its association with terrorist groups. Al Qaeda is among the more prominent groups to have used this system to move funds garnered from illicit activities such as credit card fraud, which brings in more than $1 million a month (Mabrey 2003, 26). According to one authority, the money trail begins with Algerians in Europe who handle the money through *hawala* operators in Pakistan, then transfer the profits to Islamic extremist cells linked to al Qaeda (Gunaratna 2002).

The *hawala* system remained virtually unchanged until the emergence of modern banking systems. There are basically only two groups that depend on this system today—expatriate workers who need to send money home to family members, and those involved in money laundering. In times past, *hawala* was the domain of tight-knit extended families that could trust and confide in each other; however, in recent years this has undergone a transition, with family units being replaced by more commercial figures who use various businesses as a façade for their activities, including travel agents, laundries, small grocery stores, and money exchanges. In 2002, Dubai boasted more than 100 exchange operations. Today, human smugglers, terrorists, and illegal organ smugglers are more likely to use this system than any legitimate business. In the end, this system is still simple, quick, safe, and effective, with no necessity to save documents that can be shredded easily (Mabrey 2003).

UNITED STATES

Bombs, Black Handers, and Beer Wars: Syndicates and Terror Tactics

American criminal syndicates have adopted what today would be regarded as terrorist activities since they first began to appear sometime in the late nineteenth century. Although Black Hand operatives were more local extortionists than monolithic syndicates, they introduced the power of the bomb to induce terror and to gain profit. Bombings soon accompanied tense political campaigns and labor racketeering activities.

In the early 1900s, dynamite was a favorite for those with extortion on their minds. Dynamite replaced blasting power as the explosive of choice at construction sites, and was thus available for anyone enterprising enough. It was not a great feat for a laborer to pocket an unexploded stick or two for his own motivations, leading one Black Hand historian to suggest, "There was always a profitable market for them among the blackmailing gangs" (Pitkin 1977, 33).

The crime families that emerged in the 1920s and 1930s adopted some of the terroristic inducements once only the purview of the Black Handers. During the infamous mob "Beer Wars" in Chicago, both sides used bombs (called *pineapples*) to move into the other's rackets. In the so-called

1928 Pineapple Primary, both sides in the Chicago Republican primary used bombs so readily that the primary earned its fabled sobriquet. Al Capone supplied a good percentage of the terrorists as he attempted to head off the defeat of mobbed-up Mayor Big Bill Thompson and State's Attorney Robert E. Crowe. One Chicago reporter captured the violence with the couplet: "The rockets' red glare, the bombs bursting in air, Gave proof through the night that Chicago's still there" (Sifakis 1999, 291).

In the 1970s, bombs made an unwelcome return to underworld conflicts. By then they were referred to as *Apache Indian jobs,* referring to the desolation often left in the wake of frontier Apache attacks on lonesome homesteads (Sifakis 1999). As gangs moved onto new turf, they sometimes resorted to bombings in order to gain acquiescence from recalcitrant businesses.

Domestic Terrorism and Organized Crime

WHITE SUPREMACIST GROUPS/RIGHT-WING GROUPS   In 1982, the First International Congress of Aryan Nations converged on Hayden Lake, a White-supremacist Woodstock of sorts. One of the major lures of the convention was the publication of the book *The Turner Diaries*[3] by a former Oregon State University physics professor by the name of William Pierce. The book, published under the pseudonym "Andrew McDonald," provided a virtual blueprint for using organized crime activities to fund a right-wing revolution. The heroes of the saga belonged to an underground group called the Order, from which a real group would later draw inspiration and adopt the name.

THE ORDER/SILENT BROTHERHOOD   During the 1980s, White supremacist extremists launched a terrorist and criminal campaign in support of the creation of a "White Bastion" in the Pacific Northwest. None was more prominent or more criminally inclined than the Silent Brotherhood, or Order. At first, the group used legitimate work to fund the group, even winning a contract to clear trails for the U.S. Forest Service. However, the labor took more time than expected and when snow fell, members looked for other means of support—ones with a quicker and more lucrative return. In 1983, the Order "embarked upon one of the most profitable crime sprees in America history" (Hamm and Van de Voorde 2005, 27; Flynn and Gerhardt 1990).

The Silent Brotherhood distinguished itself from other racist groups that were typically better at talking than planning, and rarely participated in a successful scheme to raise money through illegal channels. Robert J. Mathews (see the box entitled "Members of the Order Sentenced for Organized Crime Activity") had a ready supply of angry young White men who saw few prospects in the economy of the Reagan era. Some had been members of other White supremacist groups; others associated on the periphery of membership. By the time the Order went into action, it had almost 50 members, although fewer than 10 were considered to be part of the "inner circle" or "action group." Following the script provided by the *Turner Diaries* members began compiling a list of high-profile Jewish targets and went on a crime spree to fill its coffers to carry on the White revolution. Although Mathews had borrowed a cell-like structure to guard against informants, it would ultimately be an informant that brought down the organization.

During its almost 1-year heyday, the Order demonstrated a sophisticated criminal organization unmatched by its right-wing counterparts. Members were trained to live underground, acquire false identity papers and code names, and learned to move from hideout to hideout without leaving a paper trail. According to one FBI agent, "The Order was the most organized group of terrorist-type people ever to have operated in the United States" (quoted in Hamm and Van de Voorde 2005, 29).

Although the crimes of the Order have been often chronicled, it took almost 20 years for someone to scrutinize the group's criminal agenda. In 2005, two scholars offered a detailed analysis of the crime spree that actually demonstrates more sophistication than previously realized. Taking some pages from the organized crime playbook, the Order robbed drug dealers and pimps, and then an adult book store—all supposedly targeted for their association with the "moral decay" sweeping

Members of the Order Sentenced for Organized Crime Activity

Andrew Virgil Barnhill: Sentenced to 40 years for racketeering, conspiracy, armored car robbery, and transporting stolen money

Randy Duey: Sentenced to 100 years for racketeering, conspiracy, robbery, and other charges

Richard Kemp: Sentenced to 60 years for racketeering, conspiracy, and armored car robbery

David Lane: Sentenced to 40 years for racketeering and conspiracy, as well as 150 years for murder

Ardie McBrearty: Sentenced to 40 years for racketeering and conspiracy

America in the 1980s. The group finally hit the big-time with armored car heists and counterfeiting, which Hamm and Van de Voorde describe as "unique for their time" (2005, 30). Further demonstrating a criminal acumen far above other political extremist groups of the era, the Order adopted tactics such as counter-surveillance on police scanners, adopting disguises, and trying to elude the forensic tools of the era (such as fingerprinting).

In the mid-1980s, almost two dozen members of the Order were arrested and charged with 67 separate counts of racketeering, including conspiracy to commit robbery, counterfeiting, and murder. The trial cost more than $1 million and featured more than 1,500 items of evidence and the testimony of almost 300 witnesses. Defendants faced a range of charges that included robberies, arson, bombings, counterfeiting, murder, conspiracy to commit robbery affecting interstate commerce, and transporting stolen property across state lines. When totaled, these crimes amounted to 176 acts that established the requisite "racketeering activity" specified in the Racketeer Influenced and Corrupt Organization Act (RICO). Thirteen defendants pleaded guilty before they went on trial; 10 were sentenced to long prison stints. This case proved significant by setting a legal precedent. Formerly, the statute had only been used against organized crime kingpins. The Order case was the first time RICO was used in a political case (Flynn and Gerhardt 1990).

Robert Jay Mathews (1953–1984): Crime Kingpin or Terrorist?

Robert Mathews was no newcomer to racist extremism, having joining the John Birch Society before even entering high school. By his late teens he had formed the Sons of Liberty paramilitary group, but he soon disbanded this group and moved from Arizona to a neo-Nazi enclave in Metaline Falls, Washington, where he joined the National Alliance and immersed himself in extremist right-wing literature. He found his greatest inspiration in William Pierce's *Turner Diaries*, which featured the violent overthrow of the U.S. government and a subsequent race war to establish an Aryan nation. In the early 1980s, he had become a well-known visitor to the Aryan Nations compound in Hayden Lake, Idaho. Both Mathews and the Aryan Nations hoped to create a White country in the Pacific Northwest. It was here that Mathews went about creating the *Bruder Schweigen*, better known as the Silent Brotherhood or the Order. Interestingly, Mathews' vision was inspired not only by the *Turner Diaries,* but also by the violent crimes committed by far-left radicals who counted among their ranks Blacks and Jews.[4]

In 1983, the Order put its theories into action and began a campaign of bombings, robberies, and a counterfeiting operation. In little more than a year, the gang had a war chest of almost $4 million and had assassinated prominent Jewish radio talk show host Alan Berg in Denver, Colorado. During what seemed like a series of successful armored car heists, Mathews dropped one of his weapons and it was traced back to a fellow member of the Order. This put the FBI on their trail. The final nail in the Order's coffin was inserted when one of the members became an FBI informant after he was caught passing counterfeit money in Philadelphia. In December 1984, Mathews was tracked down and killed during a siege at his Puget Island hideout.

Hate Groups and Organized Crime Activity

Group	Founder	Activities	Time Period
Minutemen	Robert DePugh	Bank robbery, murder	1960s
The Order	Robert Mathews	Armored car and bank robberies, counterfeiting, weapons trafficking	1980s
Posse Comitatus	Henry L. Beach	Counterfeiting, weapons trafficking	1970s

According to a journalist investigating the Aryan Brotherhood (AB) since the mid-1990s, one long-term member of the gang told authorities that he had been approached at the supermax prison in Colorado and asked by gang members for technical help making bombs. The informant told authorities that the ABs were planning a series of terrorist attacks against federal buildings throughout the United States. He reportedly told his handlers, "It's become irrational. They're talking about car bombs, truck bombs, and mail bombs" (Grann 2004, 170).

NARCOTERRORISM: THE MELDING OF DRUG TRAFFICKING AND TERRORISM

The term *narcoterrorism,* first recognized in Latin America, was coined by Peru President Belaunde Terry in 1983 to describe violent attacks on anti-narcotics police by Shining Path (*Sendero Luminoso*) insurgents in Peru (Lupsha and Cho 1999). A number of Latin American countries, most notably Colombia, borrowed the term for their own devices, mostly in reference to the links

Urban Street Gangs in an Age of Terrorism

The El Rukns–Libya Connection: *USA v. Trammell Davis et al.,* 86-CR-572

On March 11, 1986, four of the top lieutenants of the Chicago-based El Rukns— Jeff Fort, Reico Cranshaw, Trammell Davis, and Melvin Mayes—flew from Chicago to Casablanca and, despite travel prohibitions at the time, then to Tripoli, Libya. The Libyan government picked up all expenses. They had evidently promoted the El Rukns as an organization that had the ability to carry out acts of terrorism against American imperialism. A deal was made for Gadhafi to pay the gang $2.5 million for their services. According to the testimony of a former high-ranking member of El Rukns, Jeff Fort had been offered $2.5 million by Libya to plant bombs on American airplanes. In order to finalize the arrangement, Gadhafi telephoned the Chicago headquarters of El Rukns and the call was then transferred to the federal prison holding Fort. In addition, members of the El Rukns purchased an anti-tank missile from undercover FBI agents. The FBI moved in and made arrests after the missile was transferred to the gang armory, located in an apartment building.

In September 1986, a 50-count indictment was handed down naming 6 members of El Rukns as defendants who were indicted for conspiring to transport explosives and commit violent acts in the United States on behalf of or at the direction of representatives of the government of Libya. The defendants were also charged with receiving and possessing firearms and weapons, including hand grenades, fully automatic weapons, and anti-tank weapons. Sentences ranged from 80 years in prison and a $225,000 fine for Fort and 63 years and $241,000 fine for Reico Cranshaw to a suspended sentence for Trammell Davis and the dropping of charges against Melvin Mayes. These convictions, however, are considered the first time in American history where citizens had been found guilty for planning terrorist acts on behalf of a foreign government for money (MIPT Terrorism Knowledge Base 2006).

FIGURE 13.1   Typical garb/weaponry of Colombian paramilitaries
Source: Dorling Kindersley Media Library/Jamie Marshall

between drug traffickers and guerrillas. There is a lack of consensus as to what actually constitutes narcoterrorism, with critics suggesting that the word connotes "too broad a range of activities to be definitive for a particular form of terrorism" (Kushner 2003, 251). On one side are scholars who argue that it refers to all insurgent actors involved in the drug trade; on the other side are those who argue this definition only clouds the issues linking terrorism and drug trafficking. In one of the most detailed definitions of the narcoterrorism phenomenon, Lupsha and Cho suggest that *narcoterrorism* refers to

> acts of violence and terror against persons and property—frequent agents of the State or media influentials—in order to further the political, economic, and social agendas of drug traffickers by intimidating or coercing governments, their agents, individuals, groups or elite populations to influence and change their behaviors and policies. (1999, 424–425)

Most authorities agree that *narcoterrorism* refers to a type of terrorism linked to the production of illicit drugs. This terrorism can be achieved in two ways: either by using drug profits to support political violence or by using it to protect continuing illegal drug production. It must also be remembered that the drug trade was not just the business of the leftist guerrillas, as right-wing forces depended on it to fund their operations through taxing and extorting dealers and providing protection for the traffickers as well.

Narcoguerilla: Criminal or Terrorist?

One controversy that continues to receive attention is whether some criminal groups are primarily criminal syndicates that masquerade as political movements. During the 1980s, Peru found itself in a virtual war with the supposedly "communist inspired" Shining Path and Tupac-Amaru (MRTA) revolutionary movements. Police and military forces were also waging a parallel campaign against the same region's drug traffickers. The initial story rested on the presumption that these two revolutionary movements were legitimate, and that their involvement in the drug trade was due to their reliance on drug lords who helped finance their operations. Out of this relationship came the notion promulgated by a 1985 U.S. government report of the "'narcoguerilla' as an 'alliance between drug smugglers and arms dealers in support of terrorists and guerrillas' and as an instrument of Soviet influence in Latin America" (Clawson and Lee 1996). However, more recent scholarship suggests that the Shining Path and MRTA movements were conceived not as political movements, but as "original, full-fledged creations of the local drug lords, who set the movements up as 'armed insurrection' organization to help them fight against" the drug eradication campaign of the president of Peru (Nakamura 1999, 100).

Colombian Cartels and Narcoterrorism

Following the fall of Chilean leader Salvador Allende in 1972, a military regime took over and suppressed the country's drug trade. The Colombian drug trade took off soon after, when Chilean-based associates of the drug trade, including chemists and entrepreneurs, relocated to more open countries such as Colombia and Bolivia. By the turn of the 21st century, government officials estimated that Colombian cartels were responsible for 80% of the cocaine and 70% of the heroin in the United States. Some estimates suggest that FARC nets as much as $600 million a year through related protection rackets involving poppy growers and are slowly eliminating some of the cartel middlemen and organizing its own distribution system (Hill 2000, 5–6).

Beginning in the early 1980s, members of the Medellin cartel embarked on a campaign to obtain power and respectability through legitimate channels. However, under the direction of Pablo Escobar, the cartel became synonymous with violence. The cartel never hesitated to use violence against the public who opposed it or attempted to enforce laws as their duties required. Many observers trace Escobar's campaign of terror to the fallout from the 1984 murder of justice minister Rodrigo Lara Bonilla, who had the temerity to run against Escobar for a congressional seat. Up to that time, President Belisario Betancur had been averse to extradition, but subsequent to the assassination, he began to extradite traffickers to the United States. By most accounts, it was then that the cocaine kingpins turned to acts labeled *narcoterrorism* that included public bombings and the murders of judges, policemen, journalists, presidential candidates, and virtually anyone who seemed affiliated against the drug cartel (Thoumi 2003). However, what is just as likely was the 1984 Tranquilandia raids that saw the immolation of more than 12 tons of cocaine and millions of dollars worth of investments. Just 2 months later, the campaign of narcoterrorism was ignited (Cho and Lupsha 1999).

Throughout the 1980s and into the early 1990s, huge bombs were detonated at public places and monuments to government security such as police stations. Following a string of assassinations of political candidates, judges, and acting politicians, the new administration of President Virgilio Barco declared "an all-out war against the 'narco-terrorists'" (Thoumi 2003, 206).

Unlike previous crackdowns, this strategy seemed to damage the seemingly indestructible Medellin cartel, seizing property, arresting hundreds, and extraditing its leaders. However, the cartel

Silver or Lead (*Plata o Plomo*)

During the 1980s, gangsters working for the Medellin cartel offered Colombian judges who were trying drug cases the choice of *plata o plomo*—silver or lead. In other words they would receive money if they allowed the defendant to walk free, or would receive a bullet for a conviction. By most accounts, judges opted for the former option. The brutality of the Medellin cartel contrasted sharply with the Cali cartel's philosophy, which, according to one of its kingpins, was, "We don't kill ministers or judges; we buy them."

responded with a declaration of "total and absolute war" against the forces aligned against it, and in the late 1980s continued its campaign of terror. Among its most egregious attacks was the wanton 1989 bombing of an Avianca passenger jet, killing 111 people and the leveling of the 12-story headquarters of the National Security Forces in Bogotá, which left more than 70 dead and hundreds wounded.

South America's Tri-Border region: Argentina, Brazil, and Paraguay

The *Tri-Border region,* also known as the *Triple Frontier* or *La Triple Frontera,* has proved to be a sanctuary for criminals, terrorists, and all manner of miscreants. An open border established by the Common Market of the South (MERCOSUR), with members Argentina, Brazil, Paraguay, and Uruguay, has been a boon to the region's economy while allowing free movement of member citizens. At the same time, a lack of adequate border patrols, government corruption, and rampant smuggling operations has placed the region's security at risk (Sverdlick 2005).

Three cities meet at this juncture—Puerto Iguazu, Argentina; Foz de Iguaçu, Brazil; and Ciudad del Este, Paraguay. Contraband typically enters Ciudad del Este from two directions, depending on original source of lading. Commodities from the Far East come through Foz de Iguaçu after arriving from the Brazilian harbors of Santos and Paranagua. When coming from Miami, the ports of entry are Santos, Montevideo, Uruguay; and Buenos Aires, Argentina (Sverdlick 2005). Brazilian authorities suggest there are perhaps more than 100 illegal airstrips on the Paraguay frontier, estimated to bring in more than $1 billion worth of contraband a year.

Of the three cities cited, Foz de Iguaçu is considered the main center for money laundering followed by Ciudad del Este. It was estimated that in 2000–2001 close to $12 billion of drug money was laundered, while other sources estimate twice that amount. The money laundering that accompanied the illegal drug traffic is a major nexus in which organized criminals, terrorists, and corrupt politicos come together to disguise dirty money, and Paraguay remains the main center for this activity (Sverdlick 2005).

Also key to the terrorist–organized crime nexus are other illegal activities such as other forms of contraband smuggling and various counterfeiting schemes involving electronic equipment; information technology; pirated music, clothing, beverages, toys, textiles, and perfumes; and tobacco, cars, and people. The motor vehicle theft problem is emblematic of the porous border controls and ineffective law enforcement, which allows stolen vehicles to be easily trafficked unimpeded between countries in the region. By most accounts, luxury automobiles can be bought in Ciudad del Este 15 hours after being stolen. Buyers are plentiful, especially with $50,000 Mercedes-Benzes going for a fifth of their value (Sverdlick 2005, 88).

The Triple Frontier and Islamic Extremists

Recently, a U.S. diplomat suggested, "There is no question about it; funding for Islamic terrorist groups is being provided in the Tri-Border Region" (ISVG 2003, 32). According to Sanderson (2004), the 1992 and 1994 truck bombings of the Israeli Embassy and the Jewish Cultural Affairs Center in Buenos Aires are some of the examples of terrorist attacks with ties to state sponsorship and organized crime. The Tri-Border Region between Argentina, Brazil, and Paraguay has earned a reputation as a no-man's land open to drug trafficking, money laundering, and other enterprises. The center for much of this activity is Ciudad del Este, where the three borders meet. There, members of Hezbollah, Hamas, and al Gamaat al Islamiyah have taken full advantage of the region's lawlessness and the existence of a rich local Muslim community. A full investigation by Argentine intelligence revealed that the trucks and explosives used in the 1992 and 1994 attacks were purchased in the Tri-Border zone and conveyed to Buenos Aires with the help of regional criminal syndicates.

Today, more than 15,000 people of Middle Eastern descent reside in this region. Brazil has the largest Muslim population in South America. Recent research studied "Islamicization in Latin

Ciudad del Este, Paraguay

In Ciudad del Este, Paraguay, the three borders of Argentina, Paraguay, and Brazil come together—three disparate countries representing the best and worst of South America. This city of more than 250,000 has become a haven for all manner of businessmen seeking to avoid the region's high taxes and take advantage of the porous borders that make it "a smuggler's paradise." Created by former Paraguayan dictator Alfredo Stroessner in 1957 as Puerto Flor de Lis, its name went through several changes in homage to the strongman before being tagged with its more familiar Ciudad del Este (Sverdlick 2005). It has been estimated that more than 40,000 people travel unimpeded across the border every day, all contributing to a shadow economy that has flourished for years. According to one regional report, "The daily average currency movement [is at least $12 million, making it] the third largest commercial city in the world, only surpassed by Hong Kong and Miami" (quoted in Sverdlick 2005, 85–86). Some organized crime experts suggest that the region has become a meeting place for the Yakuza and Latin American crime groups who exchange drugs through Ciudad del Este that then wind up in the ports of Brazil, Argentina, and Uruguay (Shelley and Picarelli 2005, 61). Not surprisingly, it has also drawn representatives of terrorist groups, including al Qaeda, Hezbollah, Islamic Jihad, al Gamaat al Islamiyah, and FARC.

America," citing successful campaigns of Islamic proselytism in the regions of poor indigenous tribes and populations by Shia and Sunni religious leaders and activists (Herzliyya 2006).

Law enforcement officials suspect that terrorist sleeper cells may be present in the Tri-Border Region. According to a 2003 report by the Institute for the Study of Violent Groups, Islamic extremists from Hezbollah, Hamas, and al Gamaat al Islamiyah are using this permeable region as a base for funding terrorist operations. These activities are possibly facilitated through contact with Iranian embassies in Brazil and Argentina.

Both terrorist and criminal groups have taken advantage of the spotty border security that allows thousands of individuals to move at will without requisite documents. This cooperation became particularly revealing in 1998, when the leader of the Egyptian group al Gamaat al Islamiyah was arrested in connection to exchanges with Colombian rebels involving weapons and drugs. The following year witnessed the arrest of an Egyptian terrorist in Uruguay after he was seized with a Malaysian passport acquired in Paraguay. Sa'id Hasan Ali Muhammed Mukhlis was charged with a $2 million fraud scam in the Tri-Border Region. South American officials suspect he was raising money for various Egyptian extremist groups. More recently, a Lebanese citizen was arrested in Beirut in 2003 carrying a Paraguayan passport and 20 kilos of cocaine. According to intelligence, he was also part owner of the region's largest shopping malls and was a close associate of a suspected Hezbollah financier who was living in the Tri-Border Region (ISVG 2003, 32).

If anything is evident, it is that terrorists have found it "logical and cost effective to use the skills, contacts, communications and smuggling routes of established criminal networks rather than trying to gain the requisite experience and knowledge themselves" (Shelley and Picarelli 2005, 63). Smuggling routes are apparently shared by both groups, with terrorists moving weapons and drugs along the same routes pioneered by car traffickers, a major business in the region. One recent report suggested that almost half the cars purchased annually in the region are obtained illegally (Berry, Curtis, Hudson, and Kollars 2002, 16). Some researchers have categorically connected Hong Kong crime syndicates with Hezbollah cells operating in the Tri-Border Region. Shelley and Picarelli (2005, 63) assert that the Asian syndicates involved in "large scale trafficking of counterfeit products such as music albums and software" have colluded with Hezbollah representatives in the region. By most accounts contraband goods are smuggled into the area from Hong Kong and then sold by terrorist associates who use the profits to fund their terrorist activities. Most accounts place profits in the millions of dollars, with much of it making its way into coffers in Canada, Lebanon, and other countries.

Revolutionary Armed Forces (FARC): A Hybrid Group?

The Revolutionary Armed Forces of Colombia (FARC) was founded in 1966 by Manuel "Sureshot" Marulanda. Its membership has been estimated to range between 10,000 and 18,000. Since the mid-1960s, it has proved itself to be one of the most durable and powerful rebel forces in the world. Over the years it has begun to take on an increasingly "hybrid" appearance, toeing the line somewhere between terrorist and organized crime group. Its coffers are consistently replenished by a variety of organized crime activities not limited to kidnapping for ransom, extortion (revolutionary taxes), and robbery. However, drug manufacturing and trafficking is by far the greatest money-maker for FARC, bringing in an estimated $300 million a year. By taking part in the most important stages of the drug manufacturing and distribution process, FARC ensures itself a significant profit. In addition, FARC taxes cultivators of coca plants and controls manufacturing laboratories. By some accounts, the group makes a profit through a "Tax for Peace" on any Colombian citizen with assets exceeding $1 million.

During the administration of former President Andres Pastrana, FARC consolidated and expanded its activities thanks to a number of concessions made by the government, which included establishing a demilitarized zone and a crackdown on the opposition paramilitary groups. According to the Institute for the Study of Violent Groups, FARC also received assistance from members of the IRA, noting that in 2001 several Irish nationals were arrested in Colombia for helping train FARC members (ISVG March 2003).

EUROPE

Northern Ireland

SICILY WITHOUT THE SUN   Both Protestant and Catholic paramilitary groups have long participated in organized crime activities to support their operations. However, their participation in organized crime has become significantly more pronounced since the Catholic and Protestant leaders in Northern Ireland signed a permanent ceasefire in 1998. In fact, it has become so pervasive that some observers have referred to the region as "Sicily without the sun" (Alvarez 2005).

Although many may disagree that the IRA and its political wing Sinn Fein together represented a terrorist organization, their actions speak for themselves, because the IRA and its various incarnations have used car bombings and attacks on civilian targets. So, what explains this evolution from political extremists to extreme criminality? Among the most often cited explanations is that the ongoing peace process stripped the IRA and its counterparts of its political mission, with the result being an army without a war. For centuries, professional soldiers have been occupationally stranded by wars. For some, organized crime has been a logical choice, particularly when legitimate employment is scarce.

According to a 2004 report by the Independent Monitoring Commission, tasked with tracking paramilitary activity in Ireland,

> Seldom in the developed world has this high proportion of the most serious criminals been associated with groups originating in terrorism with an organizational structure and discipline, and the experience of planning, learning and conducting sophisticated clandestine operations, methods of handling money, and with traditions of extreme violence. (Alvarez 2005)

Such expertise explains why groups such as the IRA so easily launder money and smuggle goods while at the same time using terror to control informants and frustrate prosecution.

In 2003, it was estimated that nearly 100 criminal gangs were operating in Ulster, and at least two thirds of these were linked to the Provisional IRA, the Ulster Defence Association, or other paramilitary groups (Ulster Terror Gangs 2003, 16). The IRA has used criminal activities to fund its operations since the 1970s. Smuggling operations and counterfeit rings have been estimated to have netted the IRA as much as $20 million a year (Sennott 2005). According to police investigators and

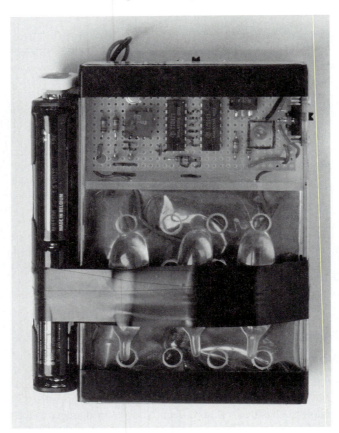

FIGURE 13.2 IRA bomb
Source: Dorling Kindersley Media Library/Geoff Dann

analysts, since its ceasefire, the IRA has easily made the transition from a sophisticated and discipli-nary paramilitary organization into "an organized crime syndicate." Crime specialists encouraged the Police Service of Northern Ireland (PSNI) to "confront the IRA less as a terrorist organization and more as a Mafia family" (Sennott 2005). According to one consultant to the PSNI, "the struc-ture of the IRA—its discipline, its hierarchy, and its members' skills—lends itself to the classic structure of organized crime" (Sennott 2005, 2).

Testimony to this transition has been the recent conviction of three IRA members for training narcoterrorists in Colombia. In August 2001, Colombian officers arrested the three explosives ex-perts in Bogotá. British intelligence estimates that FARC paid IRA contacts nearly $2 million into offshore accounts for weapons and urban warfare training. Intelligence analysts suspect that this has been going on since at least 1998. According to 2002 testimony by the Chief of the Colombian Joint

Organized Crime Activities of the IRA

- Kidnapping for ransom
- Extortion
- Armed robbery
- Money laundering

Who Did It? The December 20, 2004, Bank Robbery

Although no one has been convicted of this bank robbery, investigators believe that it had the earmarkings of the IRA, although IRA and Sinn Fein leaders claim it could be just as likely have been "disgruntled" police officers. With its sophistication, lack of fingerprints, the use of hostages, and the "strongarming" of a bank employee who lived in an IRA-friendly neighborhood, it seemed a clear-cut case, albeit an unsolved one. The robbery began on December 19, with several men dressed as police officers arriving at the home of a senior North Bank executive with the news that a relative had died in an accident. Once the door was opened they pounced and took the wife away as a hostage, leaving her husband tied up. They repeated this ruse at the home of another employee, and both employees were then told to cooperate in the robbery the following day or their relatives would die. The following day, both employees arrived at work and let the staff go home early—an early Christmas gift. Around 6 P.M., the men used their secure passes and keys to enter the inner vault of the bank, filled to the rim with cash from the city's ATM machines. In a test run, they carried out $2.2 million (USD) in a bag, then brought out the remainder of the $50 million (USD) in a number of receptacles and handed them to an individual whose face was concealed by a scarf and hat. The loot was taken to a white Ford truck and the thieves got away. The hostages survived, but none of the money was recovered (Alvarez 2005).

Chiefs of Staff, seven IRA members trained Colombian, Cuban, Iranian, and possibly Basque militants how to use weapons for terroristic purposes. It is also suspected that together with FARC, the IRA was also supplying guns to Nicaraguan insurgents in 2000 (Curtis and Karacan 2002, 6).

The IRA, like many successful terrorist groups and crime syndicates, is made up of a large number of well-armed and trained men and has a propensity for organization and discipline. These attributes come in handy when building a criminal domain. The IRA is suspected of demonstrating its criminal acumen in 2004, when an "unidentified" gang robbed the Northern Bank in Ulster of £22 million in Bank notes, one of the largest robberies in the country's history.[5] Authorities suspect the IRA was involved with this robbery because it has long been involved in funding its operations through bank robberies. In addition, there are few groups that could have pulled of the heist with such aplomb.

IRA extortion rackets run the gamut from shaking down illegal entrepreneurs such as drug dealers to pushing protection on legitimate businessmen. By most accounts, members have

The Shankill Butchers

Demonstrating that the IRA was not the be all and end all when it came to terroristic violence, throughout the 1970s Protestant paramilitaries unleashed a wave of terror against the Catholic community in Northern Ireland unequaled by any group in this long-running conflict. The Ulster Volunteer Force (UVF) was established in the years leading up to World War I for the purpose of defending Ulster against Home Rule (by the Catholics). However, the war intervened and its members distinguished themselves in battle. Yet within the 36th Ulster Division was a nucleus of a junior wing that emerged as the Young Citizen Volunteers. After the war, it adopted a structure similar to that of the IRA. Into the 1920s most of the organization's direction went toward the communal and sectarian violence in Belfast neighborhoods. The so-called Shankill Butchers who operated out of a number of pubs in the Shankill Road area of Belfast began killing Catholics in July 1972, and were not arrested until 1977. Their moniker was derived from their abduction and subsequent torture and murder of Catholic victims with butcher knives and axes. Following a lengthy trial, the 11 Loyalists that made up this gang were sentenced to life for 112 offenses that included 19 murders. Although its most prominent member and leader was Lenny Murphy, the gang continued to operate despite his imprisonment in 1976 (Dillon 1989).

successfully placed taxes on local drug dealers, who had few alternatives to paying. It is in this way that the IRA can profit from the drug trade without being directly involved in dispensing the poison on the streets. A number of security companies do business in Belfast, many owned by IRA affiliates. It's no problem convincing businesses that it would be a good idea if they hired IRA personnel.

Northern Ireland paramilitary groups have turned to some of the more traditional organized crime activities including the sex trade. Organized prostitution rings have flourished by luring hundreds of women from Eastern Europe on the pretense of good job opportunities, only to be forced into the sex trade. Where once IRA leaders and their counterparts used their crimes to purchase weapons, today it is more likely they will spend the money on self-fulfillment—buying status symbols such as lavish houses and expensive cars. This in turn has created tensions within the communities that once protected them as well as within the organizations themselves.

Police have been hard-put to stamp out this recent phenomenon. Witness protection has proved difficult in such a small and insular country, and it is less likely that local residents will come forth with information against former paramilitaries living off their reputations for violence. As a result, extortion remains the "cornerstone of financing," with police estimating that two-thirds of its victims fail to take action (Ulster Terror Gangs 2003, 16).

Other Northern Irish Paramilitary Organizations Using Organized Crime Activities

Irish National Liberation Army

Established in 1975 as the paramilitary wing of the Irish Republican Socialist Party (IRSP), the Irish National Liberation Army (INLA) is composed of between 30 and 50 disaffected members of the Official IRA and the Provisional IRA who disagreed with the ceasefire of 1975. Paramilitary in structure, it is known to have extensive contacts in the Irish underworld. In Northern Ireland alone, there are at least 100 crime groups with ties to terrorist groups (ISVG 2006). Limited in legitimate funding sources, the INLA relies heavily on organized crime activities, including large-scale armed robberies, smuggling, money laundering, extortion, drug trafficking, and intellectual property crime. Compared to other paramilitary terrorist groups, the INLA has been more inclined to using and selling drugs. One if its more interesting schemes is a variation on kidnapping called *tiger kidnapping,* in which a hostage is abducted in order to coerce another person to commit a crime (ISVG 2006, 62–63).

Continuity Irish Republican Army

Established in the 1990s following a fracture with the mainstream republican organization, the Continuity Irish Republican Army (CIRA) made itself known in 1996 when it came out in opposition against the Provisional Irish Republican Army (PIRA) ceasefire. Some observers suggest this split was more subterfuge than anything else, and that it was done to provide PIRA members a cover if they were accused of breaking the ceasefire (ISVG 2006, 47). Recent evidence asserts that the small group of some 30 members has been able to flourish thanks to organized crime activities. Others suggest that the group has used its structure to make the transition of criminal syndicate participating in armed robberies, hijackings, alcohol and cigarette smuggling, drug dealing, and extortion.

Loyalist Volunteer Force

More than 300 members support the Loyalist Volunteer Force (LVF), a Protestant extremist group with links to other Ulster groups. Northern Ireland authorities claim the group earns an estimated $4 million (USD) annually from drug trafficking, extortion, and armed robbery. In 2003, it was linked with one of the country's largest drug busts. It also operates legitimate business as fronts, mostly relating to the entertainment industry, including pubs, clubs, and taxi companies.

> ## 22 October Group of the Corsican National Liberty Front (FLNC-22)
>
> The Corsican National Liberty Front (FLNC-22), an extremist group, was founded in 2002 to combat French policies on the island of Corsica. Although it is relatively small with less than 50 members, it makes up for it with an arsenal of weapons and its participation in the European weapons smuggling trade. It has funded its operations with a number of criminal enterprises, including drugs and weapon trafficking, extortion, and misappropriation of government funds. In 2003, FLNC-22 achieved fleeting prominence after Club Med revealed that it had been victimized by an extortion scheme, in which they paid protection to avoid being targeted by violent attacks from the organization.

The ETA (*Euskadi ta Askatasuna*/Basque Fatherland and Liberty)

Since 1959, the ETA (*Euskadi ta Askatasuna*/Basque Fatherland and Liberty), a group of separatists, has been trying to win independence from Spain. Over more than 40 years this group waged a campaign of violence that left more than 800 dead through bombings and targeted assassinations. Authorities have linked this group to drug trafficking since at least 1984, and have even found evidence that Basque groups have fought among themselves for the control of the Spanish narcotics market. Next to the IRA, they have been the longest lasting terrorist group in Europe, and similarly use the heroin and cocaine trade to pay for the illegal weapons needed in their terrorist operations.

In recent years Italian officials have revealed an association between the ETA and the Naples-based Camorra crime organization. According to a 2001 agreement, the Camorra offered to supply heavy weapons (missile launchers and missiles) in exchange for large shipments of cocaine and hashish. The Neapolitans were supposed to receive the weapons via Pakistan and Uzbekistan using military contacts in the Czech Republic a month or so after receiving the drugs. The narcotics were apparently delivered weekly to Genoa in special drums rigged to the bottom of the ship. Although much of the investigation has not yet been revealed, sources suggest that if this exchange took place between the ETA and Italian organized crime groups, "it would provide the Basque terror organization with arms from the diverse trafficking sources in Eastern Europe and the former Soviet Union" (Curtis and Karacan 2002, 10).

The Kurdish Workers Party (PKK): A Case Study

The Kurdish Workers Party (PKK) was inaugurated in 1978. Built on Marxist–Leninist principles during the radical foment of the 1960s, by the mid-1980s the organization had begun a guerrilla campaign against the Turkish government with the avowed goal of establishing a Kurdish state. Although there is a tendency for pundits to conclude that the transition from terrorist group to organized crime occurred after the disintegration of the Soviet Union, there are a number of observers who have linked the PKK to international drug trafficking prior to this event. In the mid-1990s, one German magazine reported that the PKK had been involved in the drug trade in Europe throughout the previous decade, and were using the proceeds to fund "its bloody guerrilla fight" (Focus 1994).

The PKK has taken advantage of Turkey's central location at the crossroads of Asia, the Middle East, and Europe, bordering eight countries, including Iran, Iraq, Georgia, Armenia, Syria, Greece, Bulgaria, and Azerbaijan. Turkey also offers access to 5,000 miles of coastline. One expert estimated the PKK's annual income derived from criminal activities at $86 million at its peak in the 1990s (Radu 2001). The PKK has resorted to a cornucopia of organized crimes, including drug trafficking, arms smuggling, robbery, extortion, human smuggling, and money laundering, leading one Turkish security officer to observe, "The cooperation between the PKK and Kurdish criminal clans has been similar to the cooperation among Sicilian mafia families." Furthermore, The PKK should be considered as "multilevel business organization that is involved in all phases of the narcotics trade from production to retail distribution" (Curtis and Karacan 2002; Roth and Sever 2007).

Organized Crime Activities of the PKK

- Extortion
- Drug trafficking
- Human smuggling
- Weapons smuggling
- Money laundering
- False passports and documents
- Murder and threat of violence
- Corruption
- Illegal cigarette smuggling
- Blood smuggling

As noted by Abadinsky (2007), extortion is the main activity of organized crime gangs. Extortion, in both Turkey and Europe, is one of the most commonly reported organized crime activities engaged in by the PKK. This terrorist group found a ready source of income by means of intimidating and forcing people of Kurdish origins in eastern and southeastern Turkey to pay extortion fees. Those who have dared resist or complain to the authorities have been kidnapped and murdered, and in some cases their businesses and properties have been burned and vandalized (Alkan 2004).

Although drugs, humans, and weapons smuggling along with extortion and money laundering are considered the "bread-and-butter" of the PKK's organized crime activities, they are also involved in a number of non-traditional smuggling schemes. However, it is doubtful that any is more bizarre than a longstanding blood smuggling operation chronicled by Turkey's weekly news magazine *Aksiyon* in April 2005. In this operation, the so-called Kurdish Red Crescent (*Heyva Sor a Kurdistan*) founded by the PKK has been involved in collecting blood in southeastern Turkey under the auspices of charity. It is collected only from citizens of Kurdish origin. The blood is often smuggled abroad, where it is sold for a profit. This report also discussed similar activities in the Turkish cities of Diyarbakir, Mardin, Batman, and Sanliurfa. Apparently, disputes have arisen among the PKK affiliates on how to share the profits from the scam (Kochan 2005; Curtis and Karacan 2002, 21).

Since the mid-1980s, the PKK has taken advantage of the existence of immigrant Kurdish communities in European countries. These communities have provided the PKK an environment and strategic transit point for its various transnational criminal enterprises, especially illegal immigration, human smuggling, and drug trafficking.

Shared Organizational and Operational Characteristics of Organized Crime and Terrorist Groups

- Involved in illegal activities and often need access to similar resources
- Use and threat of violence
- Commit kidnappings, assassinations, and extortion
- Act in secrecy
- Challenge the state and laws (unless state funded)
- Have back-up leaders and foot soldiers
- Are exceedingly adaptable and open to innovations (Sanderson 2004)
- Threaten global security
- Quitting either group can have deadly consequences for members

Interpol and Turkish authorities have revealed the widespread involvement of the PKK in organized crime activities. It is estimated that 80% of the drugs produced in the Golden Crescent (Afghanistan, Pakistan, and Iran) are trafficked to the European market through Turkey. As far back as 1993, the British National Service of Criminal Intelligence (NCIS) estimated that the PKK's income from drug smuggling in Europe was equivalent to 56 million Marks (Roth and Sever 2007). Official sources assert that the PKK plays an important role in the transportation process via the Balkan route, allowing the organization to profit from its proximity to narcotics sources in South and Central Asia. It has also been established that the PKK collaborates with other major criminal groups form the region of Istanbul (Curtis and Karacan 2002).

By 1995, the terrorist group was recognized by the U.S. Drug Enforcement Agency (DEA) as well established in the production and distribution of a variety of opiate products, and to be deeply involved money laundering. PKK involvement in both organized crime and terrorism has been well documented since the mid-1990s. According to its imprisoned leader, Abdullah Ocalan, and other high-ranking members, the organization relies heavily on organized crime to fund its activities. Of these, the most profitable has been the drug trade, which is used to purchase weapons.

THE PKK AND HUMAN SMUGGLING The PKK has used the trade in humans as not only a source of income but as an avenue of recruitment as well. The group uses its drug trade routes to smuggle illegal immigrants from South Asia to Europe. Its complicated human-smuggling network generates a significant amount of money as it transports refugees from Northern Iraq to Italy via Turkey (Alkan 2004; Curtis and Karacan 2002). Interpol estimated that the PKK earns €2,000 to €3,000 for each individual. According to Italian officials, one smuggling operation alone involved bringing in 9,000 Kurdish people from Anatolia to Europe via land and sea in 2001 (Roth and Sever 2007).

Human trafficking is an incredibly organized activity. The PKK is involved in forging passports and documents for those being smuggled. Along the route, they are registered in a variety of PKK front organizations that promise them food, lodging, and employment—every immigrant's ultimate goal. During this process, it is common for members to extort from each refugee a "membership fee" (Alkan 2004). There have been a number of cases in Germany where the PKK has forced Kurdish children between 10 and 14 to sell drugs for them, in an attempt to evade the limits of penal responsibility.

THE PKK AND EXTORTION The PKK has been successful extorting money from drug dealers. In both Turkey and Europe, extortion is one of the PKK's most commonly reported organized criminal activities. It collects funds by intimidating people of Kurdish origin living in certain regions of Turkey. Those who resist have been kidnapped and killed. Like other terrorist groups that have turned to organized crime, the PKK has found that its well-structured network is suited to both types of crime. Members extort citizens of Kurdish origin, usually of Turkish origin, outside Turkey as well. However, the group prefers the terms *revolutionary tax* and *voluntary contribution* to crime-laden expressions like *extortion*. In 1993 alone, the PKK extorted £2.5 million from Kurdish immigrants and businessmen in Great Britain. This money was reportedly used to fund a 1996 terror campaign in Turkey. One source indicated the PKK ran an intricate protection racket in Green Lanes in Northern London where many restaurants must pay "insurance fees" or face retaliation (Kochan 2005, 92; Roth and Sever 2007).

THE PKK AND MONEY LAUNDERING In 1996, Scotland Yard and the Belgian Police launched Operation Sputnik. Raids were conducted in London and Brussels as well as in Germany and Luxembourg. The operation was predicated on the alleged money laundering activities of the Med TV Broadcasting Company, which was suspected as acting as a front for the PKK. This satellite television station was inaugurated in May 1995 through London's Independent Television Commission. Although it claimed to be a private company and downplayed links to PKK, it regularly

The Sicilian Mafia as Terrorists: A Case Study

In 1982, a law was passed that allowed Italian authorities to confiscate Mafia wealth. Soon after, Mafia boss Toto Riina was overheard saying, "We must make war in order to be able to mould the peace" (Dickie 2004, 409). By most accounts, the Sicilian Mafia reached a decision at a meeting in 1991 to wage war against the Italian state by striking at the nation's cultural heritage—museums and churches. It was the first time in its history that it had taken this tact, in an attempt to cause economic damage by ruining the tourist industry.

On May 27, 1993, a car bomb exploded outside Florence's famed Uffizi gallery, killing five people and wounding dozens. By 1995, only 3 of the 15 damaged rooms had been reopened to the public. By then, Italy had spent some $10 million to repair structural damage. By one estimate, it would take another year and $7 million more to restore the 16th-century palace that is home to the world's greatest collection of Renaissance art. The bombing of the Uffizi was followed up that summer by bombings at two churches in Rome and a modern art gallery. Vandalism against Italy's cultural legacy "was wedded overnight to terrorism" (Bohlen 1995). This was just another series in a chain of bombings, kidnappings, and murders that have shaken Italy to the core since the mid-1970s.

Unlike terrorist groups, which typically claim responsibility for their actions, the Mafia does not. However, links to the bombing of the Uffizi were drawn from the bomb itself. It was described as a sophisticated 500-pound device installed in a stolen Fiat, and was similar to bombs used in attacks in Sicily. On top of this, was the information provided by a rapidly growing list of informers, or *pentiti*.

showed programs spouting PKK propaganda. Subsequent to the operation, police seized 350 million Belgium francs ($11 million US) from a Med TV account that they were able to link to drug, weapons, and human smuggling activities as well as to Belgian nationals and companies who paid extortion payments or revolutionary taxes to the PKK. Belgian police discovered that the PKK conducted its activities through 15 different companies that laundered illicit profits. Operation Sputnik also uncovered a revenue stream that was used by Med TV and the conveniently named "Kurdish Parliament in Exile."

In 2002, Belgian and French investigators targeted more PKK money-laundering activities. In the process, a Paris-based company was charged with money laundering, faking documents, and corruption. The case was cracked after several PKK members confessed under interrogation that money had been transferred to the PKK under the auspices of a company called the Kurdish Foundation Trust. The Anatolia News Agency reported that this company was located on the British-controlled Jersey Islands, known as an offshore haven for international money laundering (Kochan 2005; Roth and Sever 2007).

COUNTERFEITING, TERRORISM, AND ORGANIZED CRIME GROUPS

Counterfeiting plays an important part in the organized crime networks that support terrorist groups. One Interpol official suggested that "terrorist groups who resemble organized crime groups" are drawn to counterfeiting because it is possible to "invest at the beginning of the counterfeiting cycle and extract an illicit profit at each stage of the counterfeiting process from production to sale, thus maximizing returns" (Interpol 2003, 7). According to one 2000 study from the Global Anti-Counterfeiting Group in Paris, at least 11% of the world's clothing is fake. Counterfeiting surfaced in a number of normally legitimate activities, including DVDs, CDs, clothing, cigarettes, alcohol, and even cosmetics. Although most of these items alone seem harmless, once one understands that the various counterfeit rackets are operated under the auspices of criminal organizations that also engage in drug trafficking, child prostitution, human trafficking, and terrorism, the activities seem less benign. According to the secretary general of Interpol, the profits from the sale of counterfeit goods have funded operations by groups connected with Hezbollah, Northern Ireland paramilitary

Why Intellectual Property Crime Receives Low Priority from Law Enforcement

- Lack of generalized expertise in investigating counterfeit and pirated goods
- Wide range of products vulnerable to counterfeiting and piracy
- Widespread demand for pirated products due to a perception that buying these goods is not really criminal
- Large market of individuals seeking to engage in low-risk criminal activity
- It is a relatively easy criminal activity
- Low costs and high profit margins

organizations, and Colombia's FARC. Terrorism experts have gone as far as to suggest that "Profits from counterfeiting are one of the three main sources of income supporting international terrorism" (Thomas 2007, B7).

Intellectual Property Crime and Terrorist Financing

Due to a number of factors, intellectual property crime has become an increasingly important resource for terrorist funding. Some estimates suggest that the profits from counterfeiting are close to those made in drug trafficking, placing the estimate at €10 for every €1 invested. Others are of the opinion that counterfeiting can be even more lucrative, using the example of 1 kilo of CDs valued at €3,000 versus 1 kilo of cannabis resin valued at only one third that. Another comparison notes that a computer game costs €20 to produce and sells for €45, whereas cannabis costs €1.52 a gram and sells for €12. What is just as persuasive is the fact that the level of risk involved is much lower for counterfeiting. Using France as an example, the prison term for counterfeiting is closer to 2 years with a €150,000 fine, compared to a 10-year jail sentence and a €7,500,000 penalty for selling drugs. The Secretary General of Interpol put it best, noting, "It follows that the profit/risk ratio is attractive not only to criminals but to networked terrorist groups, [who] do not have the capacity to generate funds through sophisticated criminal activity" (Noble,, 2003, 7).

Experts categorize intellectual property crime and its relationship to terrorist financing in two ways. *Direct involvement* refers to a specific terrorist group implicated in the production, distribution, or sale of counterfeit goods, which subsequently relays a large proportion of the funds to the terrorist group to find its operations. According to Interpol, terrorist organizations subscribing to this methodology "include groups who resemble or behave more like organized criminal groups" (Noble 2003). Northern Ireland paramilitary groups are exemplars. However, other groups are characterized by *indirect involvement,* in which case supporters or militants involved in intellectual property crime pass on some of the funds to terrorist groups using the façade of a third party. Hezbollah and the Salafist Group for Call and Combat exemplify this strategy (Noble, 2003, 4).

Northern Ireland

In June 2003, a published report on organized crime in Northern Ireland reported, "Pubs, clubs, and taxi firms who operate in districts influenced by paramilitary groups are known to facilitate a lucrative trade in counterfeit goods" (quoted in Thompson, 2003).Various paramilitary groups have take part in counterfeit cigarette trafficking, but it is unknown how much goes to terrorist groups and how much is kept as criminal profit (Noble, 2003).

Interpol estimates that the counterfeit products' market in Northern Ireland costs the economy millions each year. Northern Ireland's police authorities reported in 2003 that they seize more

Popular Counterfeit Goods in Northern Ireland

- Clothes
- Computer games
- CDs, DVDs, and videos
- Cigarettes
- Currency
- Vodka

(Observer, UK, 2003)

counterfeit goods than all other UK police forces combined, but believe this represents only 5% of the total market (Thompson 2003).

Counterfeit goods are often sold by door-to-door salesmen. In one case, a man was stopped at Belfast International Airport in June 2003 after debarking a flight from Singapore with $500,000 (US) worth of counterfeit DVDs. Counterfeit currency that originated in this region has been found throughout the world, including copies of sterling, Euros, and dollars. Experts report the British sterling's counterfeited watermarks and foil strips are virtually undetectable.

There is a dark side to the counterfeit trade, because a number of goods are produced using harmful ingredients. For example, customs officials revealed cigarettes made in the Far East containing not just tobacco, but harmful fillers as well. Bogus vodka has also been produced using watered-down industrial alcohol.

The illegal trade in smuggled fuel has proved a profitable enterprise for the former terrorist groups turned criminal gangs. According to customs officials, almost two thirds of Northern Ireland's gas stations have sold illicit fuels. In some cases, counterfeiting skills have come in handy, such as the case where one gang made an exact replica of a fuel tanker, replete with company logo, license plate, and livery of an existing vehicle. The vehicle was discovered only after suspicious Customs agents tailed it along a highway and phoned the driver on his mobile, only to discover the real vehicle was 100 miles away (Thompson, 2003).

KOSOVO   A number of reports indicate a long-standing affiliation between criminal syndicates and local ethnic-Albanian extremist groups, with relationships built on family and social ties. In Kosovo, the sale of counterfeit goods has been relatively open, taking advantage of weak law enforcement and the low priority given this crime. A substantial amount of the country's consumer goods—ranging from CDs and DVDs to shoes, clothing, cigarettes, and computer software—have been labeled counterfeit by investigators. Funds generated by this trade benefit both terrorist and crime groups (Interpol 2003).

CHECHNYA   In 2000, Russian police, along with officials from private industry, shut down a counterfeit CD plant that had been financing Chechen separatists. The Chechen organized crime group that ran the factory was estimated to have earned between $500,000 (US) and $700,000 (US) per month, further demonstrating the alliance between terrorists and crime syndicates. During the police raid, a number of weapons and explosives were seized as well (Interpol 2003).

NORTH AFRICAN EXTREMISTS IN EUROPE   Interpol investigators suggest that radical extremist networks operating in Europe have added intellectual property crime to their wide range of criminal activities used in support of funding terrorist operations. Sources indicate that the funds are donated in the guise of charitable giving through mosques, Imams, and non-profit organizations supportive of radical fundamentalist causes. Because these funds make their way to groups as cash, there is rarely a paper trail to follow. The typical pattern is for those directly involved in the criminal side of the activities to keep a portion of the money given to the radicals, similar to the methods used by other syndicates (Interpol 2003).

HEZBOLLAH　Interpol linked Hezbollah to several cases of intellectual property crime and terrorist funding in South America. These cases involved ethnic-Lebanese who sent funds to Hezbollah from South America. Their operations involved the distribution and sale of counterfeit goods, but not the manufacturing and fabrication of the commodities, which was handled by organized crime. In one case, the counterfeit goods were produced in Europe and sent to free-trade zones in South America by Lebanese supporters of Hezbollah. These goods were then transshipped into another country to avoid import duties. The goods were then sold through a network of terrorist sympathizers, mostly of Middle East origin. In one case, an individual sold counterfeit CDs and video game discs to fund a Hezbollah-affiliated terrorist organization. Investigators recovered discs with images and short films showing terrorist attacks and interviews with suicide bombers, all part of a propaganda campaign to generate support for the groups (Interpol 2003).

FAKE COSMETICS　It has been estimated that counterfeit cosmetics and toiletries reap more than $200 million (US) annually, and officials cite this as a potential operation to be exploited by terrorists. Most of the fake cosmetics are produced in the Middle East and China.

Drug-Dealing Jihadists

JEMAAH ISLAMIYAH　Al Qaeda's affiliate in Southeast Asia, Jemaah Islamiyah, engages in bank robbery and credit card fraud. It partially financed the 2002 Bali bombing through jewelry store robberies that netted more than 5 pounds of gold. In the past, many terrorist groups would have eschewed these tactics, afraid of tainting their image. However, crimes against non-believers have become increasingly acceptable. According to Jemaah Islamiyah's spiritual leader, "You can take their blood; then why not take their property?" (Kaplan, Fang, and Sangwan 2005).

THE MADRID TRAIN BOMBINGS AND ORGANIZED CRIME　The terrorists behind the Madrid train bombings, representing the Moroccan Islamic Combatant Group (GICM), were major drug dealers with a network that stretched from Morocco through Spain to Belgium and the Netherlands. Its leader was Jamal "El Chino" Ahmidan, the brother of one of Morocco's biggest hashish dealers. Ahmidan's cell purchased the bomb materials by trading hashish and cash with a former miner. When police raided one member's home, they seized 125,800 ecstasy tablets—one of the largest busts in the history of Spain. Authorities eventually recovered almost $2 million in drugs and cash from the group. However, the Madrid bombings, which killed almost 200 people, cost only a fraction of this—almost $50,000.

New Associations: Mara Salvatrucha (MS-13) and al Qaeda

In 2004, Honduran Security Minister Oscar Alvarez made news when he announced that al Qaeda might be trying to recruit Central American gang members to help terrorists infiltrate America. In February 2005, Salvadoran President Tony Saca added that he could "not rule out a link between terrorists and Central American gang members" (Harman 2005, 4A). However, an FBI Task Force convened to investigate MS-13 responded that it could find no connections between the two—but this did not end the debate. In January 2005, Rep. Solomon Ortiz of Texas acknowledged, "We know from El Salvadoran law enforcement that al Qaeda is meeting with violent gang leaders in El Salvador." FBI Task Force Director Robert Clifford haughtily responded, "To have something as sophisticated as al Qaeda overtly align and identify itself with a group of misfits is improbable." However, Clifford did admit that MS-13 still should be considered a threat to national security because it has been spreading rapidly through the country in recent years (Harman 2005, 4A).

AFRICA: A REGIONAL EXAMINATION OF THE TERRORIST–ORGANIZED CRIME NEXUS

The existence of weak state institutions, widespread poverty, weak border controls, and transnational ethnic networks as facilitated a parallel growth in terrorist activities on the African continent (see Chapter 12, AfroLineal Organized Crime). According to an *International Crime Threat Assessment* report,

> Porous borders, ample routes for smuggling drugs, weapons, explosives, and other contraband, and corruptible police and security forces make Sub-Saharan Africa and inviting operational environment for international criminals, drug traffickers, and terrorists. Major Sub-Saharan cities with extensive commercial, financial, and sea and air transportation links to Europe, the Middle East, and Asia are hubs for international criminal activity. . . . These include Nairobi and Mombasa in Kenya, Addis Ababa in Ethiopia, Abidjan in Cote d' Ivoire, Johannesburg in South Africa, and Lagos in Nigeria. (U.S. Government 2000, 34)[6]

In terms of terrorism, North African countries have been most hospitable to the growth of the organized crime–terrorism nexus. Algeria's flirtation with terrorism began in the mid-1950s with the country's war for independence against France. The 1990s saw a recrudescence of the terrorist phenomenon as extremist Islamic groups tried to overthrow the secular government. The most prominent in terms of criminal trafficking activities has been the Salafist Group for Call and Combat (GSPC), which has links with weapons traffickers within and outside Algeria. Neighboring Morocco has been linked to the exportation of marijuana into Europe, shipping an estimated 70% of the cannabis into the continent. Morocco is hospitable to the cultivation of highly drought-resistant crops, such as cannabis, and is also a source of hashish resin and oil. Recent research suggests that drug traffickers "entered symbiotic relationships with Islamic groups in and around the port of Tangier" (Berry and Curtis 2003, 6–7). Although both groups have different motivations, they share a common disdain and distrust of the secular government, which has come down hard on both groups.

With its long coastline and unrelenting poverty, East Africa has long been a favorite for smugglers and criminal syndicates. Its geographic proximity to the Middle East has long been a boon to Southeast Asian traffickers and Muslim extremists. According to one British expert, as some of these countries, such as Kenya, continue to experience economic problems, the region will be "susceptible to Islamic radicalization" (Harman 2002, 8). Kenya is home to a small but "restive Muslim population," whose members have maintained commercial and family ties to their countries of origin, which facilitated the hashish and heroin trade alongside a lucrative legitimate trade. The Muslim communities of a number of East African countries have been under scrutiny by their governments, and in the process shifted their allegiances to co-religionists and become popular recruiting grounds for extremist groups.

An illegal weapons trade flourished on the east coast of Africa for generations. In more pastoral regions, livestock in Kenya, Sudan, Uganda, and Somalia are traded for small arms,[7] which in many cases have spread throughout the conflict-plagued region of the Horn of Africa. According to Berry and Curtis, the availability of illegal weapons in this area "filters beyond armies and police forces to criminal organizations, private security forces, vigilante squads, and individual citizens" (quoted in Berry and Curtis 2003, 13), as well as burgeoning terrorist movements. The easy availability of illegal firearms has also been linked to the activities of Sudanese groups such as the Lord's Resistance Army, the Allied Democratic Forces of Uganda, and the Sudan People's Liberation Army. Most reports indicate perhaps a quarter of small arms come from the UK, with another 30% coming from other European Union countries. Sudanese weapons traffickers are able to freely move between their country and other east African countries, particularly in Uganda. Investigators tracked the black market in weapons from Uganda, Ethiopia, Somalia, and Sudan into Kenya, where an estimated 11,000 guns are sold annually. According to researchers, a prominent Russian arms dealer headquartered in the United Arab Emirates was linked to the sale of weapons in this region. In any case, the persistence of porous borders and corruption allowed substantial numbers of weapons throughout this conflict- and crime-plagued region, with many of the weapons ending up in the hands of terrorists. American intelligence has even accused the Somalia's al-Ittihad al-Islamayah (Islamic Unity) group with having provided sanctuary to al Qaeda operatives in the days leading up to the twin embassy bombings in August 1998 (Berry and Curtis 2003, 14).

In recent years, Muslim communities in South Africa have crossed the line into organized crime and terrorist activities. One of the most notorious groups is People Against Gangsterism and Drugs (PAGAD). Although it originated as an organization to fight the drug trade and street gangs, it has now morphed into "a full-fledged terrorist organization" with links to Iran, Libya, and Sudan. Further exacerbating the rise of organized criminals and terrorists has been the atmosphere of confusion and transition that followed the end of the *Apartheid* era (Berry and Curtis 2003, 25–26).

Heavily chronicled in Chapter 12, West Africa is at the center of some of the most prominent organized crime and terrorism activity in Africa. Virtually every predisposing condition is found here—poor border security, corruption, poverty, and the presence of myriad armed groups. An illegal weapons trade between Eastern Europe and the former Soviet Union and Liberia ensures the existence of well-armed criminal groups. What most attracts these various elements to the region is the region's substantial supply of rich natural resources, ranging from diamonds and precious stones to oil and timber—all there for the taking and the right price. As a result, the region has been a consistent presence on criminal radar screens as unscrupulous entrepreneurs from Europe and criminal and terrorist syndicates continue to flourish here.

Al Qaeda has been tied to the illegal diamond trade for a number of years. Since the 1990s, there have been a number of reports indicating a European-based trade in weapons for diamonds with various rebel groups. Some dealers have been suspected of providing terrorist groups with firearms. Researchers believe that in 2002, an Algerian arms dealer with links to the extremist Islamic group Call to Combat received funding from al Qaeda and was able to "take advantage of the sparse population and limited law enforcement capability" of several nations in the interior of West Africa" (Berry and Curtis 2003, 30).

Al Qaeda and Terrorist Financing

By late summer 2008, al Qaeda in Iraq was increasingly "embracing extortion and kidnapping to finance its operations, as cash carried by its dwindling foreign fighter network is drying up" (Hess, 2008). Terrorist organizations need funding. Funding comes from a variety of sectors, both legitimate and illicit. The more complex and larger groups need more funding than small cells. The four primary means of funding terrorist groups consists of government sponsorship (Afghanistan/Taliban), income from legitimate businesses, donations, and contributions (Madinger 2006). Al Qaeda also benefited from Afghanistan's flourishing opium and heroin trade. By most accounts, as government, Taliban, and Saudi funding dried up, the organization was forced to seek more criminal enterprises. When bin Laden joined up with the Taliban in Afghanistan in 1996, he brought with him the keys to various fundraising operations that by the end of the decade stretched "from the tropical diamond fields of West Africa to the gold markets of the United Arab Emirates, from the money merchants of Pakistan to the suburbs of Washington, D.C." (Farah 2004, 1).

One journalist recently chronicled the pragmatic tendencies of the al Qaeda financing operations, noting how "terrorists understood how to take advantage of the rapid deregulation that came with globalization, where international financial transfers are instantaneous and hard to trace" (Farah 2004, 2). However, it took a hard-learned education to achieve its current success. Initially, al Qaeda and the Taliban kept its funds in the formal banking sector. In the wake of the U.S. embassy bombings in East Africa, the Clinton administration was able to locate and freeze almost $250 million that the groups kept in Western banks. This was a turning point for bin Laden and his counterparts, because they recognized the vulnerability of adhering to traditional banking systems. They soon discovered, if not pioneered, the transfer of cash into almost untraceable commodities that could be trafficked from failed states into the world market. By the turn of the millennium, al Qaeda leaders oversaw the transition from a cash-based trade to one that depended on diamonds, gold, emeralds, and sapphires—goods that were "easy to transport, smuggle, and convert" (Farah 2004, 2–3).

Four Main Sources of Terrorist Financing

- Criminal activity
- Charitable contributions/donations
- Legitimate or semi-legitimate business
- Government or state sponsorship

(Madinger 2006)

Terrorist Financing and Money Laundering

In his magisterial 2006 tome *Money Laundering,* John Madinger offers the rhetorical question, "What does terrorist financing have to do with money laundering?" By most accounts, terrorist financing and money laundering share a number of characteristics, and this boded well for law enforcement in an earlier time, when they could borrow from traditional crime-fighting techniques. Today, globalization has made investigation of funding much more complex.

Since the terrorist attacks of September 11, 2001, al Qaeda representatives have found themselves engaged in a race against time as they attempted to convert their cash into goods that could not be attached by American retaliation. This shift in tactics baffled most investigators, who had been under the impression that bin Laden was bankrolling the terror network with his own funds. This turned out not to be the case at all, leading one high-ranking member of the National Security Council in the late 1990s to admit that American intelligence knew "almost nothing" about terrorist financing prior to 9/11. In time, al Qaeda had found a foolproof method for hiding its assets outside financial institutions.

Al Qaeda involvement in the West African diamond trade could not succeed without the participation of high-ranking politicians who protected the operation. Of these, one of the most prominent was Liberia's Charles Taylor, who authorities have verified had been providing a safe haven for al Qaeda and Hezbollah members for a number of years (Farah 2004).

THE ILLICIT TANZANITE TRADE Tanzanite is a rare gem that can be found only in a small parcel of land in northeastern Tanzania. This gem, like diamonds and emeralds, can be sold for cash, avoiding the paper trail left by traditional banking transactions. According to one Tanzanian investigator, bin Laden has been linked to the "smuggling of rough tanzanite through Kenya to bazaars in the Middle East." The official asserted, "Beyond any doubt, I am 100 percent sure these Muslim gem traders are connected to Osama bin Laden" (Farah 2004, 65–66). Even local miners recognized the bin Laden connection to the illegal tanzanite trade, with one veteran miner noting the popularity of al Qaeda among the diggers and even going as far as to suggest that Muslim extremists had established "a mafia to dominate the trade" (Farah 2004, 66).

DIAMONDS ARE A TERRORIST'S BEST FRIEND: THE ILLEGAL DIAMOND AND WEAPONS NEXUS Al Qaeda's involvement in the West Africa's illegal diamond trade followed in the footsteps of other savvy Middle Eastern groups such as Hezbollah, who had been financing their crusades with diamonds thanks to the assistance of an underworld of Russian weapons traffickers, British mercenaries, retired Israeli military officers, and Western merchants all eager to play their parts in the diamond trade (Farah 2004).

In 2002, Belgian investigators arrested an al Qaeda contact on charges of diamond smuggling and illegal weapons trafficking following an examination of the suspect's computer and other records that revealed tens of millions of dollars linked to the al Qaeda purchase of diamonds. However, what was probably most disturbing was evidence that suggested that this lucre was part of a plot to purchase high-tech weapons in Central America from Nicaraguan army contacts, with the assistance of

Israel: A Case Study

In Israel, a *terrorist act* is defined as "the indiscriminate use of lethal violence against persons for the attainment of political objectives" (Landau 2003, 145). During the recent Intifada, there have been a number of examples in which Palestinians used organized crime to fund activities. Drug trafficking was the most prominent example, but other activities included illegal weapons trafficking, human smuggling, and motor vehicle theft.

The illegal arms trade demonstrates the links between terrorism and organized crime. According to one Israeli scholar, Palestinian terrorist groups purchased M-16 rifles, ammunition, and other weapons from Palestinian gangsters during the Intifada. In 2002, in one well-publicized case, an Israeli military officer was indicted for planning to steal a number of rifles and ammunition from a kibbutz. In another case, various soldiers have been charged with selling stolen army ammunition to Palestinians (Landau 2003).

Palestinian and Jewish gangsters have taken advantage of the separation between the Palestinian Authority (PA) and Israel. Beginning in the 1990s and continuing into the new millennium, the massive theft of autos stymied Israeli investigators, because the PA is beyond the reach of the Israeli criminal justice system. Stolen cars are typically taken from across the border to "chop shops," where cars are stripped and the parts sold on the black market. Some accounts suggest that the better vehicles end up in the hands of high-ranking PA officials. Others, bearing their original Israeli license plates, are used to transport suicide bombers to their targets inside Israel (Landau 2003).

The drug trade has clearly proved the most lucrative criminal activity. There is evidence that groups such as the Popular Front for the Liberation of Palestine (PFLP) have been involved with traffickers in Lebanon. Drug routes into Israel from Egypt and Jordan have also been utilized for smuggling weapons, explosives, and illegal immigrants (Pollard, 2002).

---

an Israeli weapons dealer located in Central America. Investigative journalist Douglas Farah noted this "proposed deal shows how global the black market" for weapons has become (2004, 79).

HEZBOLLAH'S CIGARETTE SMUGGLING SCHEMES Two native Lebanese brothers,[8] Mohammed and Chawki Hammoud, were convicted of smuggling cigarettes, racketeering, and money laundering in North Carolina in 2002. When arrested in 2000, Mohamed Hammoud, described as the leader of a terrorist cell, became the first person to be tried under a 1996 U.S. law that prohibits support for terrorist groups. The brothers were accused of smuggling $7.9 million worth of cigarettes out of North Carolina, where taxes are low, and then reselling them in Michigan for a huge mark-up, and in the process violating the tax laws. The scheme involved purchasing truckloads of cigarettes from North Carolina, where the tax is $0.05 per pack—the nation's lowest tax. The cigarettes were then delivered to Michigan, which had one of the highest taxes, at almost $0.75 per pack (Farah 2004). In this way, the brothers cleared up to $10 per carton, with each van representing a profit of $13,000. Prosecutors were able to prove at the trial that some of the profits ended up in the hands of Hezbollah leaders (Roig-Franzia 2002).

ORGANIZED CRIME, TERRORISTS, AND WEAPONS OF MASS DESTRUCTION: AN UNHOLY TRINITY?

In 2006, two organized crime experts published an opinion piece subtitled, "How organized crime is a nuclear smuggler's new best friend" (Shelley and Orttung 2006). The investigators conducted research in Russia, Georgia, Turkey, and the United States, and revealed a number of factors leading to a "widening access to nuclear materials" among criminal groups. This was underscored by the 2005 report by Georgia's Chief of Nuclear Radiation, "that on several occasion his agency had confiscated small quantities of smuggled, Russian-origin highly enriched uranium on Georgian territory," and in another case apprehended smugglers trying to leave Georgia with nuclear materials through its Turkish border (Shelley and Orttung 2006, 22). Other revelations from these two researchers included,

- News reports that suggest it is possible to gain entrance into closed cities, where some nuclear facilities are located, for as little as a $5 bribe.
- With the influx of drugs through Central Asia and Russia from Afghanistan, officials have noticed an increase in drug abuse among nuclear workers in one closed city. What makes this most challenging is the potential for narcotics kingpins associated with organized crime to take advantage of vulnerable addicts.
- Russian construction companies have hired large numbers of undocumented illegal immigrants, many of whom have been targeted by Islamic recruiters. There was a report that the construction foreman at one Russian project to protect a nuclear materials site was murdered for refusing to cooperate with organized crime.

More recently, a U.S. ambassador declared that "smuggling and loose border control associated with Georgia's separatist conflicts" pose a threat "not just to Georgia, but to all the international community" (Sheets and Broad 2007, A19). His comments were made in response to recently revealed intelligence detailing how illicit smuggling continues unimpeded in this former Soviet republic, as tiny separatist regions "have broken away to become lawless criminal havens" (Sheets and Broad 2007, A19).

Among certain analysts, North Korea has become a major threat in the shadowy underworld of nuclear smuggling. The United States is just one of 11 countries now tracking North Korea's criminal capabilities. Among the most sinister threats is the chance that North Korea will sell or trade some of its nuclear prowess to the highest bidder—no matter criminal or terrorist. It already sells missiles to Middle East countries and its technology is credited with providing the date used by Pakistan to improve its missile capabilities. According to American intelligence, it is already suspecting North Korea of considering trading weaponry for Afghanistan opium. By some accounts, the country is using pharmaceutical factories to process opium into heroin; these same factories are also suspected of manufacturing synthetic drugs. One American observer has gone as far as to brand the country as "the mafia masquerading as a government" (Nicaso and Lamothe 2005, 119).

Are the concerns of nuclear weapons being smuggled on the black market legitimate, or just a case of police officials "crying wolf"? There is little doubt that the small arms market is a worldwide concern. However, the illegal market for state-of-the-art weaponry increases each day as syndicates, nation states, and warlords vie for the latest tanks, radar systems, missiles, and what one researcher calls "the makings of the deadliest weapons of mass destruction" (Naim 2003, 31). According to the International Atomic Energy Agency, there have been more than a dozen substantiated cases (as well as hundreds of unsubstantiated cases) of smuggled "nuclear-weapons-usable material" since the mid-1990s. No one knows how much stolen material for weapons of mass destruction (chemical, biological, and radiological) materials and technology is available on the black market. However, there is little doubt there is a growing demand for the products in the congruent world of organized crime and terrorism. A recent report by investigative journalist Moises Naim reveals, "More than one fifth of the 120,000 workers in Russia's former 'nuclear cities'—where more than half of all employees earn less than $50 a month—say they would be willing to work in the military complex of another country" for the right price (Naim 2003, 31).

What Would Happen if a Criminal or Terrorist Group Acquired Nuclear Materials?

One of America's leading authorities on terrorism is of the opinion "with complete confidence that it would be nearly impossible for a terrorist organization that did not have the support of a government to produce the fissionable uranium or plutonium for a fission bomb from raw materials"

(Kushner 2003, 263). Plutonium is regarded as one of the deadliest poisons ever known. Even without a nuclear bomb, its effects can be catastrophic. Inhaling as minute an amount as 0.0001 gram can lead to lung cancer or leukemia.

Experts in the field agree that the technologies required to extract plutonium from irradiated nuclear fuel from a reactor is "too complex, dangerous, and expensive for a small group to master" (Langiewiesche, December 2006). That being said, there is a real threat that other less-destructive devices could be created that could still exact a tragic loss of life and economic calamity to a modern city unmatched by any weapon since Hiroshima or Nagasaki. Nuclear experts warn that a nuclear explosion and its blast effects would cause destruction on an enormous scale, and that the detonation of even a small nuclear weapon in a crowded city center could kill tens of thousands of people and injure many more. Lest one wonder why one has not been unleashed by criminal forces, the simple explanation is that it is incredibly difficult to make even a small nuclear weapon. One need only consider the massive undertaking that it took in the 1940s to build the first nuclear weapon. The most perplexing part of its manufacture involves acquiring the requisite amount of fissionable material.[9]

If a terrorist/criminal group could obtain the required materials and have access to scientists, engineers, and other required actors they "could probably make a nuclear device with an explosive yield approaching the weapons used against Japan" (Kushner 2003, 263). However, the probability is that it would be too large a device to drop from an airplane or launch with a missile; in that case, it would be necessary to transport it by some unwieldy conveyance such as a truck, railroad car, or container on a ship.

Despite these aforementioned challenges, it is not out of the realm of possibility that terrorists, with the help of criminal syndicates, can acquire materials to create a nuclear explosion, albeit not on the scale of Hiroshima or Nagasaki.

Scenario 1   The potential for stealing uranium and plutonium from countries with nuclear weapons is real. Tests in the United States carried out by highly trained strike teams were successful in half their attempts to penetrate security barriers at facilities harboring these materials and were able to confiscate dangerous quantities of nuclear materials (Kushner 2003).

Scenario 2   Russia remains one of the best targets for those seeking nuclear materials. It has been well chronicled how poor security conditions are, and combined with the low morale and low salaries of scientists, it presents a strong incentive for anyone willing to make a buck. There have been numerous reports of thefts of fissionable materials from Russia that although are not substantiated, still infer a major threat.

Scenario 3   Terrorists might acquire operational nuclear weapons through force, bribery, or theft (Kushner 2003, 263). Although countries place the highest priority on protecting their stock of weapons, there have been few if any tests revealed to the public that demonstrate whether security could be breached to steal a weapon (as in Scenario 1).

German Police Seize Weapons-Grade Plutonium

In 1994, German police reported the arrest of a plutonium black-marketeer, the fourth such seizure that summer. The year before, Germany reported 123 "known cases of illegal nuclear-materials trading in Germany" (Walsh and Boudreaux 1994, 24A). The 1994 arrest took place at Munich airport, where 10.5 to 12.25 ounces of the material were confiscated, making it up to that point the largest seizure of illicit weapons-grade plutonium. Police accounts confirmed that the substance was brought into Germany aboard a Lufthansa jet from Moscow. The dealers were supposed to receive $250 million for 8.8 pounds (4 kilos). Nuclear experts asserted that to fashion a nuclear device, it would take a group of "unsophisticated" assemblers 13.2 to 17.6 pounds (6–8 kilos) of the weapons-grade plutonium.[10]

Scenario 4   During the halcyon days of the Cold War, the two major superpowers had vast stockpiles of smaller nuclear weapons, or *suitcase bombs,* that could be carried by one or two individuals. Although they were well guarded, at one time there have been a number of enquiries that suggest this is less true in the former Soviet Union. During the 1990s, a Russian military officer even testified in front of the U.S. House of Representatives and admitted that dozens of these weapons were missing from the Russian arsenal. Although this was subsequently downplayed by Russian officials, it still leaves analysts and other observers somewhat skeptical.

Scenario 5   The final scenario involves what is called an *improvised radiological weapon,* usually referred to as a dirty bomb. Unlike its more destructive counterparts, this weapon is designed to spread hazardous nuclear material over a vast area. Although most analysts suggest that the effects would be rather small, it would create enough havoc and population dispersal to put a dent in a local economy and even make some areas unlivable for long periods of time. Such a device would consist of an explosive charge attached to some receptacle containing radioactive materials, which can be acquired both legitimately and illegally. What makes this scenario so likely is that it would require much technical sophistication. This type of weapons is more difficult to control, so its impact would depend on weather conditions and the quality and quantity of materials used.

The Reality

Despite the prognostications and doomsday scenarios posited by everyone from academics and law enforcement officials to novelists and screenwriters, "the existence of suitcase bombs has never been proved, and there has never been a single verified case, anywhere, of the theft of any sort of nuclear weapon" (Langwiesche 2006, 83). Of course it's possible, but the odds seemed stacked against it. Recent investigations by journalists and other researchers have uncovered a number of explanations why it is so challenging. Of these, the most convincing has been the examination conducted by William Langwiesche which revealed the following:

- Nuclear weapons need regular maintenance and any still on the black market are probably "duds."
- Because of this and other time limitations, "the very lack of a terrorist strike thus far tends to indicate that nothing useful was ever stolen."
- Nuclear weapons in Russia and other countries are protected by advanced locks "that would defeat almost any attempt to trigger them."
- Plutonium is difficult to handle, requires shielding, and extremely dangerous if breathed in, swallowed, or absorbed through body wounds.
- Uranium would be "the perfect fuel for a garage-made bomb (although it is the heaviest element on Earth, almost twice as heavy as lead, and 2 pounds of it amounts to about three tablespoonfuls).
- So the answer to the question, "Why have terrorists and criminals not succeeded in getting their hands on a nuclear weapon sixteen years after the fall of the Soviet Union?" is rather simple according to Langwiesche: Either they are "ignorant, incompetent, and distracted," or nuclear weapons and materials are better protected that was previously assumed (2006, 80–98).

Overview

There are few dissenters when it comes to the realization that most active terrorist groups use criminal activities to fund some of their activities. Experts have recounted attributes shared by terrorist and organized crime groups, as well as a tendency for them to borrow from each other. Terrorist groups are most pragmatic when it comes to obtaining funding. One scholar pointed out the increasingly difficult task of distinguishing one group from the other because organized crimes involving theft, fraud, drug smuggling, money laundering, and other financial offenses have become commonplace among "interconnected and self-perpetuating terrorist networks" (Cronin, 2004, 291). By most accounts, the nexus between the two forms of crime are most pronounced in regions with porous borders and unstable governments—regions that provide a perfect environment for the convergence of terrorist groups with criminal activities. This is especially true in post-conflict regions and failed states—areas where criminal and terrorist groups readily exploit any vacuum in authority.

What troubles law enforcement agencies is the potential threat posed by the convergence of both types of actors as well as concerns that today's terrorist group will someday morph into tomorrow's criminal syndicate, albeit with the weapons and power to threaten the rule of law in some regions. In fact, what has become increasingly more obvious is that since September 11, 2001, most organized crime groups have been able operate well under the radar, as many Western government devote their resources and attention to counter-terrorism.

The studies of various cases documenting the cooperation between both groups suggest that in some cases, organized crime members might be willing to "adopt or be converted to the ideological leanings of terrorists" through joint activities and contact in prison. However, they are just as likely to cooperate with each other without sharing the same political or religious leanings (Lal 2005, 299). In any case, money is one commodity that transcends the barriers of religious and political doctrine.

According to a 2006 report by the National Drug Intelligence Center,

> It is possible that some U.S.-based OMGs, street gangs, and prison gangs may associate with foreign terrorists for the purpose of conducting drug trafficking and various criminal activities. Moreover the potential for such relationships exists primarily among U.S. prison gangs, whose members seem to be particularly susceptible to terrorist and other extremist recruitment. (NDIC 2006, 3)

Internationally, the convergence of organized crime and terrorist activities has led a number of countries to consider terrorism to be a crime, and expand legislation to strengthen the efforts to confront it. The nature of the threat from both phenomena is constantly changing. What has most aided the congruence of the two has been their transformation or transition from traditional hierarchical structures to more complicated "network forms of organization" (Clutterbuck 2004, 157).

Regardless where one stands on the issue of convergence, the simple fact remains that terrorist organizations need money to operate, and that the more financing, the better chances for success. Costs include weapons, which in most cases must be purchased on the black market and then smuggled into the country. Security requires expenditures for maintaining safe-houses and protecting weapons stashes. Communications costs are often prohibitive, with groups such as al Qaeda utilizing satellite technology, computers, and cellular phones. However, the highest costs involve paying personnel, which in many cases includes supporting the families of jailed or deceased members (Madinger 2006).

Key Terms

Hezbollah	The Order/Silent Brotherhood	"Sicily without the sun"
Globalization	*The Turner Diaries*	IRA
Organized crime/terrorism nexus	Robert Mathews	Ulster terror gangs
Albanian mafia	El-Rukns/Libya connection	Shankill Butchers
Kosovo Liberation Army	Narcoterrorism	ETA
Yugoslavian Conflict	Narcoguerilla	PKK
Mumbai attack	Shining Path	Intellectual property crime
Dawood Gang	Cartels	Madrid train bombings
Dawood Ibrahim	Pablo Escobar	MS-13 and al Qaeda
Black Friday	*Plato o plomo*	Diamond smuggling
"D Company"	Tri-Border Region	Cigarette smuggling
Aftab Ansari	Ciudad del Este	WMDs
Hawala system	FARC	Nuclear scenarios

Critical Thinking Questions

1. What is terrorism? What is the difference between *organized crime* and *terrorism*? What is the definitional discussion on the subject?

2. Why are terrorism and organized crime more interrelated than ever in the 21st century?

3. What has the interrelationship between terrorism and organized crime done to the understanding that organized crime is not ideologically motivated? How should the definitions of *organized crime* be readjusted to bring them up to date?

4. What are the major differences between organized crime and terrorist groups? What are their similarities? Is there much overlapping?

5. Does the religious and extremist nature of a terrorist group determine what crimes is will or will not commit?

6. What impact did the end of the Cold War have on the convergence of terrorist and organized crime activities?

7. What are the most popular organized crime activities of terrorist groups?

8. Where was the convergence of terrorism and organized crime first observed? Does it persist today?

9. What elements make a nation hospitable to organized crime and terrorism?

10. What conditions stimulated the link between Albanian gangs and KLA terrorists?

11. Why is *hawala* an important ingredient for transferring money between countries? How does the system work?

12. What is *narcoterrorism*? Are its actors more terrorist or criminal?

13. Discuss the persistence of organized crime and terrorist groups in South America's Tri-Border Region. What illegal activities predominate?

14. What has been the role of organized criminal activity in the struggle between Catholics and Protestants in Northern Ireland? How have organized crime activities evolved as the peace movement gathered strength? Why do they still commit crimes?

15. What are the goals and activities of the PKK? Are they more a terrorist group or an organized crime group? What shared organizational and operational characteristics do they display?

16. Discuss intellectual property crime and its prevalence among terrorist and organized crime groups. Why does this type of crime receive such low priority from law enforcement?

17. Why is the terrorist–organized crime nexus so strong in Africa? What are the most prevalent activities?

18. What are the chances of a terrorist group getting a weapon of mass destruction through organized crime contacts?

Endnotes

1. According to this 13th-century Islamic jurist, it is acceptable to seize enemy property during *jihad*.

2. Interpol reported that Albanian drug lords in other parts of Europe had been contributing to the "national cause" since the 1980s, but beginning in 1993, these funds were to a great extent invested in weapons for the KLA.

3. Since its original 1978 publication, *The Turner Diaries* has sold hundreds of thousands of copies. The publisher of the book has attempted to mollify its critics after winning a suit on the grounds of the First Amendment by adding a foreword condemning the book's hateful views and donating $1 from each sale to a gun control organization.

4. See, for example, the activities of the Black Liberation Army and the May 19 Communist Organization.

5. The bank responded with alacrity by recalling all notes of the denominations stolen in the robbery and issuing new ones that are substantially different in color and design, making the stolen lucre of little value.

6. This interagency law enforcement working group in the U.S. government has been widely cited, especially by Berry, Curtis, Hudson, Karacan, Kollars, and Miro, 2003.

7. *Small arms* includes weapons that can be carried by one person or perhaps in small vehicle.

8. Both Mohammed and Chawki Hammoud entered the United States illegally and misrepresented their status by paying American women to marry them to gain permanent resident status. They then helped other nationals into the country using the same ruse.

9. One must obtain a type of uranium known as U^{235}, so-named because it contains 235 protons and

neutrons. What is most difficult is separating the lighter variety (U^{235}) from the heavier variety (U^{238}). Once the separation succeeds, the prospective bombers can make the bomb from it directly or can use it to build a nuclear reactor that uses neutrons to irradiate U^{238} and make plutonium^{239} (Pu^{239}). In 1945, the bomb dropped on Hiroshima was made of U^{235}, and several days later one with Pu^{239} was dropped on Nagasaki.

10. However, in the more advanced nuclear arsenals, 8.8 to 11 pounds (4–5 kilos) is sufficient to build a more advanced device.

CHAPTER 14

Investigating and Responding to Organized Crime

America's justice system has produced an array of organized crime control strategies since the turn of the 20th century, with varying degrees of success. More recently, one legal scholar referred to these strategies as "the prosecutor's toolbox" (Nardini 2006, 528). New police investigative methods, including electronic surveillance, undercover operations, and a Witness Security Program, have further widened the investigative net. However, new laws such as RICO and immunity statutes and a series of crime commissions at different levels of government together with mob informants have been the most effective of all.

In recent years other countries have begun to borrow some of the pages from America's organized crime fighting playbook. For example, in late 2002, the British Home Office published an extensive examination of the U.S. Racketeer Influenced and Corrupt Organizations Act (RICO), considering its applicability to the growing organized activity in England and Wales (Levi and Smith 2002).

Law enforcement and the rest of the criminal justice system became interested in organized crime in fits and starts beginning in the late 19th century. One of earliest efforts came out of investigations by the New York City Police Department's Italian Branch at the turn of the 20th century, when an Italian Squad of almost 30 officers was created under the direction of Italian-born Joseph Petrosino. The Treasury Department saw some successes thanks to the IRS during Prohibition investigations into Al Capone, and during the 1930s, a special racket group led by prosecuting attorney Thomas E. Dewey secured convictions of prominent gangsters such as "Lucky" Luciano and Lepke Buchalter. However, for the most part, the investigation and prosecution of organized crime during the 20th century was rarely conducted "on a continuous, institutionalized basis" (Task Force Report 1967, 456) and was haphazard at best.

Traditional organized crime did not go away after Prohibition, and by the 1960s it was considered one of the country's leading crime problems, in part because of a hysterical media campaign following several high-profile Congressional hearings. Congressional attention had turned to organized crime beginning with the Kefauver Committee hearings in 1951 and the McClellan Committee hearings in 1963 (see Chapter 1). A number of other hearings continued to debate the various pieces of organized-crime legislation, and although the Department of Justice chimed in during the early 1960s after Robert Kennedy became attorney general in 1961, his reign was short lived.

Despite the Kefauver, McClellan, and other congressional committees, FBI Director J. Edgar Hoover refused to devote significant resources well into the 1960s. His recalcitrance in this matter has never been fully explained; whether it was his desire to go after more important enemies during the Cold War, or was afraid his august force might be tainted by corruption, or if he had been compromised by Cosa Nostra somehow, no one knows for sure. A proliferation of achievements fighting organized crime had to wait until his death in 1972, removing an intractable barrier; beginning in the late 1970s and gathering steam through the 1980s, a serious of investigations decimated whole organized crime families, most significantly in the Commission case, *United States v. Salerno.*

As a result of federal law enforcement's late start, it was forced to play catch-up as its organized crime control program evolved at a glacial pace until the 1980s. There were, however, pyrrhic victories along the way; Attorney General Robert Kennedy (1961–1964) resuscitated the Organized Crime and Racketeering Section (OCRS) of the Department of Justice and the Task Force on Organized Crime of the President's Commission on Crime and Administration of Justice (1967) produced an in-depth but probably exaggerated report on the power and organization of organized crime, leading to the establishment of organized crime strike forces. The 1968 Omnibus Crime Control and Safe Streets Act provided a standard and a protocol for legal electronic surveillance that by the 1980s allowed the FBI to develop some of the most effective cases against organized crime families.

However, it was the Organized Crime Control Act in 1970 that galvanized the fight against organized crime. Although narrowly focused, it nonetheless gave the law enforcement establishment two of its greatest weapons—RICO and the Witness Security Program (more commonly known as Witness Protection Program). Prior to the passage of the Act, Congress enacted several statutes authorizing more punitive punishment for traditional organized crime activities such as illegal gambling rings, loansharking, interstate transportation of stolen goods, and extortion. However, what was missing was legislation that specifically punished the very act of committing organized crime.

Traditionally, the most effective approach to organized crime control had been long prison sentences. However, it had little impact on the operations of the more powerful syndicates that were well prepared to replace one boss with another. It would require a new remedy, "one that aimed at syndicates and systemic criminality," which, according to one leading authority on the subject, was RICO (Jacobs, Fiel, and Radick 1999, 223–224). RICO, with its goal of targeting "a pattern of racketeering activity," and not used until the 1980s, made it possible to bring to a single trial whole criminal groups and families, all those who participated in the affairs of the same enterprise (crime family or union local) through a pattern of criminal activity and laid the foundation for a series of organized crime mega-trials in the 1980s.

Until the 1980s, the results of federal, state, and local organized crime initiatives had been rather lackluster. Few (if any) local police departments and prosecutors were equipped to mount the types of sustained investigations and prosecutions necessary to reel in powerful crime syndicate figures, and when they did, it was typically an individual figure. As a result, crime syndicates continued to function with a new set of leaders, demonstrating the power of organizations with a self-perpetuating leadership. By the end of the 1980s, "the inconceivable had become commonplace," as leading La Cosa Nostra figures, such as Gambino underboss Sammy "the Bull" Gravano, became cooperating witnesses in exchange for leniency and admission into Witness Protection Program.

One of the first organized crime investigations and prosecutions with international implications was the 1985–1987 *U.S. v. Badalamenti case,* better known as the Pizza Connection case, in which a cooperative effort of American, Italian, Swiss, Brazilian, and Spanish law enforcement agencies closed down a massive international drug trafficking and money-laundering conspiracy involving American and Sicilian Mafia members.

Academics, police, policy experts, and politicians have never reached a consensus on a definition of organized crime and continue to debate its issues into the 21st century. Many argue that targeting a handful of Italian-American organized crime groups is a rather narrow-minded approach to the problem; however, this has been the foundation for most organized crime fighting efforts over the past century. One of the biggest problems with organized crime control efforts well into the 1990s was that they were too narrowly focused on the usual "bogeymen" of traditional organized crime. This parochial view continues, as Michael Woodiwiss submits, dumbing-down the American discourse on the subject (2001, 227–311). Commenting on the successful RICO prosecutions of the 1980s, one of the biggest critics of the "Mafia myth" concluded,

> No neat and tidy hierarchy of capos, consiglieres, and soldiers can explain the tidal wave of crime and violence associated with gangsterism and other forms of systematic illegal activity. Had Mafioso controlled organized crime in the United States, then Blakey's [G. Robert Blakey, architect of RICO] conceit may have been justified. However, since they [bosses of the five families] only participated in a much larger and more complex criminal environment encompassing both legal and illegal markets, there is no reason to believe that locking up scores of aging patriarchs or Gotti-type upstarts has made even a marginal impact on the extent of organized crime activity in America. (Woodiwiss 2001, 291)

This chapter examines the evolution of organized crime control strategies in the United States at various levels of government, the barriers faced by those targeting organized crime, and the future of international cooperation in these efforts.

CONSPIRACY LEGISLATION: FROM RACKETS TO RICO

Prior to the implementation of RICO, it was often difficult to meet the requirements of burden of proof—the proving of the beyond a reasonable doubt standard. "Not even the most sophisticated civil prosecutions by federal authorities were able to deal effectively with organized crime" (Strasser 1988). The traditional approach to crime fighting was limited in that it was powerless to stop a criminal enterprise from flourishing, replacing various criminal participants from a ready pool of replacements in urban America. Its self-perpetuating nature and continuity facilitated the expansion of organized crime activities. It was difficult to prove the existence of racketeering operations because historically, criminal law was narrowly drawn and narrowly interpreted, designed to reach only specific kinds of criminal conduct. Courts and juries were rarely allowed to hear or review proof of a criminal enterprise involved in a variety of illicit activities; therefore, criminals had the capacity to evade prosecution. If convicted, they could rely on the financial clout or reserves of the organization to avoid severe sanctions by "lawyering up." By most accounts, defendants usually faced little threat of confinement and relatively small fines when convicted of these offenses (Fox 1989; Chambliss 1988). Not until Congress enacted RICO in 1970 was there legislation that facilitated large-scale prosecutions and the destruction of criminal organizations (Urbina and Kreitzer 2004).

Anti-Racketeering Act of 1934

A precursor of the Hobbs Act in both language and intent, the Anti-Racketeering Act of 1934 followed on the heels of hearings conducted by a sub-committee of the Committee on Commerce entitled "investigation of the Matter of So-Called Rackets with a View to their Suppression" from 1933 to 1934. Among those testifying before the committee was a labor representative who noted, "The definition [of racketeering] apparently as accepted by the committee, is that a racketeer is one of a group who conspires to do something which is in the interests of man" (quoted in Grindler 1975, 308). Another testified that racketeering was "synonymous with organized crime" (quoted in Grindler, 1975, 308). Others were more specific in their appraisal of labor racketeering, defining it as the "extortion of money from persons engaged in legitimate business, or otherwise by the use of force" (Grindler 1975, 308). Ultimately, "the hearings failed to clarify the meaning or scope of the offense and contributed to the amorphous quality of racketeering" (Grindler 1975, 308), with all parties agreeing the definition was too broad. What perhaps confused the issue more than anything was the frequent use of the word *rackets,* which some interpreted as synonymous with organized crime, whereas others more specifically defined it as related to the extortion of money (using force or threats) from individuals engaged in legitimate business. The term *rackets* was widely and carelessly used prior to the 1960s, much like the term *mafia* is today. There were beer rackets, poultry rackets, milk rackets, food rackets, and so forth. As a result, it became "difficult to derive a notion of what conduct the Anti-Racketeering Statute was meant to reach" (Grindler 1975, 308). More important, the Assistant Attorney General in 1934 insisted that the local nature of racketeering activities should restrict federal involvement in its control, noting that enforcing racketeering laws "is not and should not constitute a federal problem (Grindler 1975, 309). Substantial limitations of the Act eventually induced Congress to pass the Hobbs Act.

The Hobbs Act (1946)

The Hobbs Act is considered the first piece of federal legislation designed to fight organized crime specifically by discouraging two activities—labor extortion and obstruction of the movement of individuals across state lines for the purpose of marketing their goods, leading one scholar to refer to Hobbs as "Teamster-targeted" legislation (Bruno, 2003, 21), because it seemed to be aimed at the commercial trucking industry.

Two elements must be proved for a Hobbs Act conviction; that there was either a robbery[1] or extortion,[2] and that there was an effect on interstate commerce by such extortion or robbery. Hobbs makes interference with interstate commerce for criminal purposes a federal crime punishable by 3 years in prison or a $10,000 fine, or both. Today, it is one of many statutes used to expand the scope of federal criminal jurisdiction. The Hobbs Act has expanded extensively since the 1940s, and between 1946 and 1970, this legislation was the most frequently used anti-racketeering legislation. However, with the passage of the Organized Crime Control Act in 1970 that introduced RICO, it has lost much of its luster.

Response to racketeering activities in the labor movement prohibits criminal conspiracies that impeded interstate commerce through use of extortion or robbery. The act also forbids the coercion of broadcasting companies to hire employees whose services are not needed. Hobbs initially emphasized interstate commerce. Its sponsor stated in 1945, "I want to make it perfectly clear that the sole and simple purpose of this bill is to do the best we can to protect interstate commerce and free the highways and streets of this country of robbers" (quoted in Grindler 1975, 310).

Hobbs paved the way for future organized crime statutes that started out more specific, but over the years saw their interpretations broadened by prosecutors, eventually winning the support of the courts. In similar fashion, critics continue to rail against this open-ended legislation, arguing that it affords prosecutors the ability to broadly interpret the law, often leading to "haphazard application of the criminal statute" (Grindler 1975, 322). The following story of RICO elucidates the conundrums of organized crime legislation.

CONSPIRACY LAWS: FROM POULTERERS' CASE TO RICO

Conspiracy laws have played an increasingly important weapon in the war against organized crime. They also provide the government with significant advantages in every stage of the criminal process. In many cases they can prevent a major violator from escaping punishment through guile and insularity. During a conspiracy prosecution, individuals can be incriminated although seemingly playing only fringe roles in the criminal operation, not directly involved in the crime. As a result, conspiracy cases have been targeted by civil libertarians because of the risks of innocent defendants being convicted due to less stringent procedural requirements.

The development of modern conspiracy laws is the outgrowth of the 1611 Poulterers' Case, in which defendants conspired to accuse a man falsely of robbery. The man was so obviously innocent that the grand jury refused to return an indictment.

> As a defense to a subsequent damage suit, the poultry merchants claimed no conspiracy existed because the crime never took place and the accused was not indicted nor stood trial. But the court demurred, stating that simply conspiring together as they did constituted the basis of the crime rather than the actual lodging of an indictment followed by a formal acquittal. Over the next century

the crime of conspiracy expanded as part of the common law to include agreements to commit any criminal or otherwise unlawful activity. Courts usually applied the rationale established by the Poulterers' Case, ruling that the gist of the crime of conspiracy was the agreement among the plotters and that no additional overt acts were required. Today, it is the conspiring together, the agreement to commit a crime, which furnishes the basis for most conspiracy liability, and the crime is complete when the agreement is entered into, the overt act being a less significant element of proof. The key to the successful prosecution is proving the nature of agreement and the involvement of the participants. (Campane 1981, 26)

Wheel and Chain Conspiracies

One of the main advantages of conspiracy laws is the ability of the prosecution to use the statements of a conspirator against others in the conspiracy. The three most common types of conspiracies are the wheel, chain, and enterprise conspiracies (see RICO later in the chapter for more on enterprise conspiracies). The *wheel conspiracy* involves an individual or group of people known as the *hub*. The hub is involved in illegal activities with various others, like the spokes in the wheel. The spokes are generally not involved in illegal activity except for their involvement with the hub. The prosecution of a wheel conspiracy hinges on whether the prosecution decides there is one large conspiracy revolving around the hub, or a number of smaller conspiracies between the different spokes and the hub. It is up to the prosecution to prove each spoke was cognizant of the existence and cooperation of the other spokes in the conspiracy. Failure to prove this point typically results in the court regarding the other spokes as individual members of multiple conspiracies. Crimes most likely to fall under a wheel investigation are bribery, theft, and fraud. A more modern interpretation requires each member to know some of the other members, but not all of them. According to one leading authority, the wheel conspiracy is

> often utilized by terrorist and drug smuggling organizations when the leadership finds it necessary to reveal the identities of some of the other members for operational purposes. Ultimately, each member is criminally liable for the actions of all members of the group. (Lee 2005, 31)

Chain conspiracies can be best visualized as a large group of individuals, known as *links*, dealing with a single subject matter rather than a single hub. Each link represents a series of agreements between sellers, middlemen, wholesalers, retailers, and ultimately purchasers. Although each member of the conspiracy is directly linked to only one or two others, and members do not all of the other members, theoretically all members can be charged with the criminal acts committed in furtherance of the conspiracy. These types of conspiracies are usually found in the illegal drug trade and counterfeiting operations, where the object of the conspiracy is to place the contraband goods into the hands of a paying consumer. Ultimately, no one in the chain profits unless each link fulfills its obligations in the process of supplying the consumer. For the government to prove a single conspiracy, it must show the links knew about the other links in the chain.

Organized Crime Control Act: Enterprise Conspiracies and RICO

The Organized Crime Control Act (OCCA) of 1970 was an outgrowth of the recommendations made by President Johnson's Commission on Law Enforcement and the Administration of Justice, which ran from 1965 to February 1967. The Commission's report highlighted more than 20 recommendations for federal action against organized crime. The OCCA contained a number of new tools for attacking large-scale criminal organizations. Among its most important provisions was RICO, which introduced new racketeering laws that enabled prosecutors to link numerous members of criminal syndicates in a single overarching charging document (conspiracy). In addition, it can establish that their combined association to commit multiple crimes constitutes a pattern of racketeering activity worthy of its stiff sentencing guidelines. A federal RICO violation carries a maximum

**Organized Crime Control Measures Recommended
by the President's 1967 Task Force**

- Investigative grand juries in jurisdictions with major organized crime activity
- General witness immunity statute broad enough to assure compulsion to testify
- New wiretap and bugging legislation
- Harsher sentences for involvement in a "continuing illegal business"
- Regular procedures to protect witnesses from reprisals for testifying against organized crime groups

penalty of 20 years, which increases to potential life in prison if the underlying acts themselves include offenses such as murder or large-scale drug trafficking, which on their own carry life sentences (100-year sentences for crime bosses became *de rigueur* in the 1980s).

According to a 1977 report by the Government Accounting Office (GAO) entitled "War on Organized Crime Faltering—Federal Strike Forces Not Getting the Job Done," the GAO found the OCCA to be a disappointing failure, stating, "In essence, there is no coordinated Federal effort to fight organized crime" (quoted in Block 1980, 56). It went on to suggest that the nation's federal law enforcement agencies (e.g., DEA, FBI, IRS) "all conduct their own private and basically uncoordinated campaigns" (Block 1980, 56). Although some of this is true, it should be noted that the backing of the U.S. Supreme Court and the Executive office (under President Ronald Reagan) in the 1980s forced critics to reexamine their previous notions.

Racketeer Influenced and Corrupt Organizations Act

Despite the passage of a litany of organized crime legislation during the 20th century, the overwhelming majority were ineffective. However, in 1970 Congress passed the Racketeer Influenced and Corrupt Organizations (RICO) Act, as Title 9 of the Organized Crime Control Act of 1970, revolutionizing the war on organized crime (although it would take nearly a decade to learn how to implement RICO). Most scholars consider it to be "the most sweeping criminal statute ever passed by Congress" (Atkinson 1978, 1). The brainchild of G. Robert Blakey, its main purpose was to allow a single prosecution of a multi-defendant criminal group for its myriad criminal activities, specifically targeting organized crime enterprises. Born and raised in Burlington, North Carolina, Blakey came of age in the Jim Crow South of the 1930s and 1940s. After graduating from Notre Dame University with honors, he won a scholarship to its law school, graduating second in his class in 1960. He accepted a position as a Special Attorney with the Justice Department in Washington, where he found himself assigned to the Organized Crime and Racketeering Section. Although Blakey has never specifically confirmed or denied it, it has been speculated that the name and acronym RICO was in homage to the movie *Little Caesar,* featuring a gangster modeled after Al Capone named "Rico" (played by Edward G. Robinson). In any case, as the architect of RICO, Blakey once inferred in an early interview that although its primary intent was to target organized crime, Congress never intended it to merely apply to the Mob, noting, "We don't want one set of rules for people whose collars are blue or whose names end in vowels, and another set for those whose collars are white and have Ivy League diplomas" (quoted in Sanders and Painton 1989).

Initially, RICO did not create any new substantive offenses, but instead consolidated 35 existing offenses (8 state offenses and 27 federal offenses) under the rubric of *racketeering activity*. All of the crimes punishable under RICO already existed under extant federal and state laws (Urbina and Kreitzer 2004, 296). However, this statute is distinct for taking an array of state and federal crimes and mandating that if an individual commits two of these offenses, the person is guilty of racketeering activity and subject to severe penalties. As a result, individuals can face penalties under RICO that are more punitive than for the actual crimes that constitute the definition of *racketeering*

Attorney General William French Smith on RICO (1983)[3]

The Chairman (CH): In 1970, the Congress enacted the Organized Crime Control Act. Included in that act is a section more commonly known as RICO. This is certainly an important tool in prosecuting organized crime figures in groups. Does the Department of Justice fully utilize the civil forfeiture provision of the statute, and is the Civil Division of the Department involved in this process?

Attorney General William French Smith (AG): Well, the civil forfeiture provision is primarily a private action. In other words, it is not primarily utilized by the Government, although, under that act, we do what we can to monitor cases, and we would have the authority, of course, to intervene in civil forfeiture proceedings. At the present time, or up to the present time, we have not yet done so. We are primarily concerned, of course, with criminal forfeiture, rather than civil forfeiture. . . .

CH: Recently, the Department of Justice conducted a training seminar in Washington dealing with the civil forfeiture provisions of the RICO statute. Does the Department have any plans to continuing training additional attorneys in the area of civil forfeiture so that this very important tool in the war on organized crime can be more effectively utilized?

AG: Yes, although that program, of course, involved forfeiture of all kinds, criminal as well as civil.

activity. There are three criminal penalties for RICO violations, all of which can be applied simultaneously, including a fine of not more than $25,000, imprisonment for not more than 20 years (per racketeering count), and forfeiture of any interest acquired or maintained in violation of the statute. A number of states have enacted their own "little RICO" laws that like the federal counterpart, specifically target the activities of organized crime with strict penalties.

Although RICO became law in 1970, it was not used for almost a decade. Some observers blame this on the very nature of law enforcement itself: "Trapped inside an old way of thinking—trying to tie mob bosses to specific crimes instead of going after the organization itself—law enforcement was unable to see how it needed to reconceive the war against the mafia" (Lawson and Oldham 2006, 45).

Scholars, politicians, lawyers, and law enforcement have debated RICO's benefits and negative consequences almost since its inception. Although some suggest it met its stated objectives, others argued it failed to meet its goals (Urbina and Kreitzer 2004). Its original intent was to allow the government to allege and prove the entire history of a criminal organization beyond the normal statute of limitations. Designed to meet the challenge of criminals who at times move beyond the illegitimate world to infiltrate, invest, and acquire legitimate businesses, the architects of RICO wanted to destroy the economic foundations of organized crime in a manner that more traditional penalties had failed to do by authorizing draconian penalties. RICO in effect released the shackles

Racketeering Activities According to RICO

Hobbs Act violations	Mail fraud
Bribery	Wire fraud
Sports bribery	Obstruction of state or federal justice
Counterfeiting	Contraband cigarettes
Embezzlement from union funds	White slavery
Loansharking	Bankruptcy fraud
Drug violations	Acts of terrorism
Money-laundering	Obscenity (added in 1984)

from federal prosecutors, allowing them to attack entire Mafia families through the introduction of two new concepts: *criminal enterprise* and *pattern of racketeering.* After mob boss Joe Bonanno published his tell-all book on his life of crime, Rudolph Giuliani, former U.S. attorney for the Southern District of New York, famously observed, "If he can write a book about the commission, I can prosecute them." He would do just that, taking down the heads of New York's vaunted Five Families in a series of trials in the 1980s.

Criminal Enterprise

A central element of a RICO violation is the existence of an enterprise with which the defendant has some connection. An *enterprise* is any "association in fact" and is composed of two or more people whose purpose was to engage in a "pattern of racketeering." An enterprise can be a legitimate or an illegitimate group, such as Cosa Nostra.[4] In 1981, the Supreme Court ruled in *U.S. v. Turkette* that an illegal organization could indeed be tried as an enterprise, which the statute broadly defines as "any individual, partnership, corporation, association, or other legal entity, and any union or group of individuals associated in fact although not a legal entity" (*United States v. Turkette* 1981; McNabb Associates 2008). The concept has changed the way organized crime investigations were conceived and executed. It enabled prosecutors to make case once they could prove an "association in fact." Prosecutors have a tremendous edge in a RICO trial against organized crime because they are free to introduce extensive evidence about criminal activities using charts and tables illustrating the structure of a crime family. By most accounts, jurors are quite impressed by this method. However, by law, this information "must contain some structure distinct from the pattern of racketeering activity that is identified in the charge, its groups must have a common or shared purpose, and there must be at least some continuity of structure or personnel" (*United States v. Turkette* 1981; McNabb Associates 2008).

Pattern of Racketeering

In order to obtain a conviction under RICO, the government must show the defendant engaged in a pattern of racketeering activity, which was defined as "at least two acts of racketeering activity, one of which occurred after the effective date of this chapter and the last of which occurred within ten years (excluding any period of imprisonment) after the commission of a prior act of racketeering activity" (RICO, 18 U.S.C. 1961 (5), 1970).

Over the years since the inception of RICO, Congress has deemed increasingly more criminal behaviors to be related to organized crime, and the number of predicate crimes has grown from 35 to more than 60, with more on the table. Title 18 lists the individual criminal acts that lead to a charge of violating RICO, otherwise known as *predicate acts* (18 USC Sec. 1961, Jan. 3, 2007). A *racketeering act* or *RICO predicate* is defined as almost any serious federal felony and most state felonies. Predicate acts are related if they "have the same or similar purposes, results, participants, victims, or methods of commission, or otherwise are interrelated by distinguishing characteristics and are not isolated events" (quoted in Tarlow 1998).

H.J. Inc. v. Northwestern Bell Telephone Co. (1989): *Continuity Plus Relationship Test*

In 1989, the U.S. Supreme Court instructed federal courts to follow the "continuity plus relationship test" in order to determine whether the facts of a specific case give rise to an established pattern of racketeering. In the 1989 case of *H.J. Inc. v. Northwestern Bell Telephone Co.,* the court ruled that in order to prove a pattern of racketeering activity for RICO purposes, the government must establish both the relationship and the continuity of predicate acts.

A *pattern of racketeering* is defined as any two violations of state or federal laws from a list of crimes, including murder, mail fraud, and gambling. One of the crimes must have been committed within the preceding 5 years, but the second crime could have been committed within the preceding 10 years. For example, a mobster who was found guilty of operating an illegal gambling operation in 2006, sharing the proceeds with his bosses, and who also was involved in an extortion scheme headed by the same bosses in 1997, could be found guilty of racketeering. As a result, mob bosses, who had been previously so well insulated from prosecution, could now be convicted of racketeering while running a crime family, even though although not directly involved in individual criminal acts.

Over the past several decades criminal organizations have continued to expand activities into the legitimate world, where it is often hard to detect and prosecute them. RICO was intended to counter the trend of organized crime's infiltration of the legitimate business world. Subsequently, its criminal and civil provisions have been used in a wide array of fraud cases. When applied in financial crimes, the statute outlaws, in general, the investment of ill-gotten gains in another business enterprise, or the acquisition of an interest in an enterprise through certain specified illegal activities, including illegal interstate gambling, drug trafficking, money-laundering, prostitution, and other crimes. Its powerful criminal penalties require stiff fines and jail terms as well as forfeiture of all illegal assets. Civil penalties include triple damages, attorney's fees, dissolution of the offending enterprise, and other remedial measures. Prison sentencing is so punitive under RICO it has tempted a number of mobsters, including such high ranking ones as Sammy "the Bull" Gravano and Philadelphia's Philip Leonetti, to cooperate with authorities in return for lighter sentences or entry into the Witness Protection Program. Leonetti served almost ten years for 30 murders and assorted other crimes.

Constitutional Objections to RICO

One of the most heavily debated features of RICO is its inherent complexity, which to a great extent was the result of efforts to avoid the constitutional problems that voided most attempted anti-racketeer legislation in the 1930s. From a constitutional vantage point, the justice system found the offending 1930s provisions unconstitutional because they punished the mere "status" of being a gangster, rather than any specific criminal conduct. RICO was created with the clear intention of avoiding this obstacle by basing its definition of *racketeering* and enhanced penalties on "patterns" of conduct defined in the statute. Most of the constitutional objections to RICO pertain to its broadly worded definition, the vagueness of its forfeiture provisions, its application to activities outside the purview of organized crime, and its standards of double jeopardy and multiplicity.[5]

In 1989, the Justice Department revised its RICO guidelines so that homes and businesses would not be confiscated in all cases and innocent third parties ruined by zealous investigators. However, critics were still concerned that it could be applied to political situations. One of the unintended consequences of RICO has been its application in cases unrelated to traditional organized crime. In April 1998, a jury verdict in the Federal District Court for the Northern District of Illinois ruled in favor of several abortion clinics, awarding the plaintiff $86,000, based on RICO claims of

The Elements of a RICO Offense

- Two or more predicate acts of racketeering activity
- Pattern (controversial)
- Enterprise (controversial)
- Effect on interstate commerce
- Prohibited acts
- Scope of outsider liability

extortion, conspiracy, and threats of violence. Following the ruling of *National Organization for Women v. Scheidler,* several unsuccessful post-trial motions by anti-abortion forces claiming RICO was used to deny them free speech and equating their protest with racketeering were struck down.

Although RICO was clearly intended to deal primarily with organized crime, as part of the Organized Crime Control Act, nowhere in RICO (or the Organized Crime Control Act) is there a definition of organized crime. Although it proscribes specific conduct, it does not proscribe the status of being involved in organized crime. According to one early court interpretation (in 1976), "if conviction under RICO depended on membership in organized crime, the statute would probably be unenforceable or unconstitutional," because its violation would hinge on "a matter of status and would probably be a denial of equal protection" (Atkinson 1978, 10).

CIVIL RICO

Some of the federal government's most important crime control initiatives were brought as civil RICO suits. Some sought restraining orders and injunctions and in other cases trusteeships in order to free labor unions and legitimate companies from the grip of organized crime (Jacobs 1999). One advantage the government has in seeking civil as opposed to criminal remedies is that it is faced with a lesser burden of proof. In a civil case, the government must make a case based only on the preponderance of the evidence as opposed to proving beyond a reasonable doubt. Other advantages include the fact there is no requirement of jury unanimity, and the government can appeal a verdict in favor of the defendant.

Civil RICO also allows for "extensive pretrial discovery [depositions and documents], which can provide a wealth of information from corrupted companies and unions" (Jacobs, Fiel, and Radick 1999, 224). RICO's most controversial feature has been its civil provisions, which can be used by the government or private individuals against any private party injured by a defendant's business or property. Critics have long complained that private-party suits have been used to reach wealthy defendants, such as accounting firms who cannot be categorized as racketeers, or to coerce unwanted settlements from innocent defendants who fear the possibility of paying *treble damage judgments,* referring to payment of three times the amount of damages to the entity damaged by the defendant. However, its supporters argue otherwise, contending that a plaintiff cannot recover unless he or she proves fraud or certain identified criminal acts.

Trusteeships and Consent Decrees

James B. Jacobs asserted, "the most important innovation brought about by the extensive use of civil RICO has been the court appointment of monitors or trustees to carry out the terms of the court orders or negotiated settlements" (1999, 224). He underscores this with the observation that the courts were inspired to use this innovation against organized crime by "the techniques and strategies of organizational reform, developed in the school desegregation and unconstitutional prison conditions cases," noting,

> Like the special masters appointed to oversee school desegregation or the remediation of deplorable prison conditions, the court appointed trustees carried out the judge's mandate to transform an organization, for example, purging a union local of corruption and racketeering and restoring union democracy to the rank and file. (Jacobs, Fiel, and Radick 1999, 224)

Several strategies for preventing organized crime infiltration of labor unions were recommended by the 1986 President's Commission on Organized Crime (PCOC). When there is evidence that a business or labor union has been infiltrated or controlled by organized crime members, under civil RICO statutes the government can seek a court-appointed trusteeship. Once a consent decree has been reached after mediation between the government and the defendants and a resolution to fix the problem is agreed to by both sides, the government can remove the leadership of a union and a trustee is selected to run the operation on behalf of the court. The best exemplar of this was its use against the International

Brotherhood of Teamsters. In 1988, a suit was filed in New York federal court charging the union had been dominated by criminal syndicates since the 1950s; the PCOC hearings alleged this as well.

Most trusteeships have been appointed in labor-racketeering cases. RICO trustees have been imbued with significant powers, including powers to subpoena books and records and compel testimony under oath. Trustees are typically appointed for an indefinite term, but if there was a trial, the trustees' powers are shaped by a judge; in the event of a negotiated settlement, the powers are dictated by other parties. In any case, the mandate is usually the goal of removing organized crime from mobbed-up labor organizations. Trustees are often drawn from a pool of former prosecutors and law enforcement personnel, many of whom, in places like New York City, came to the job well versed in the requirements of organized crime investigation. The use of trusteeships has not been without its critics, some of whom have raised a host of legal and philosophical issues, particularly in cases where trustees have voided elections or expelled union members for consorting with organized crime figures. In other cases, trusteeships have been less than successful, sometimes getting bogged down in the minutiae of union administration, at other times failing to receive adequate court support or to find appropriate techniques (Jacobs, Fiel, and Radick, 1999, 227).

THE WITNESS SECURITY PROGRAM

The stirrings of the Witness Security Program (WITSEC) can be traced back to the testimony of Joseph Valachi before the McClellan Committee in 1964. Facing the death penalty for a number of convictions, he made a deal with federal agents that would allow him to be taken out of the country for protection in return for testifying against the Mafia. However, in the years preceding WITSEC, all he ended up getting was solitary confinement for protection and $15 a month prison pay. Valachi tried to kill himself several times once the government failed to follow through with their promises. In subsequent years, protected witnesses have been kept safe in "remote, highly secured sections of federal prisons or in remote county jails, safe houses and hotel rooms" (Moushey 1996, 4).

Over time the protocol changed, and in the 1980s the Justice Department built the first of what would be five special prison units in Otisville, New York. Once witnesses left this prison, they were given new names, Social Security numbers, and transportation to their new homes. They typically received monthly stipends of $2,000 for a year and a half or until the government decided that they had achieved some type of stability in their lives. Although many were able to find anonymity and solace in their new lives others could not move away from their lives of crime. Several audits in the 1980s concluded that protected witnesses had been involved in a range of crimes including murders. Henry Hill and Sammy Gravano are among the most celebrated gangsters to have entered (and left) the WITSEC program.

Created by the Organized Crime Act of 1970, WITSEC, together with the RICO statutes, have been two of the most important steps taken against organized crime. It is administered by the U.S. Marshals Service with the assistance of the Bureau of Prisons in the Department of Justice. Its mission is to protect government witnesses and their families when there is reason to believe that because of their testimony or their lives are in danger. The majority of the prosecutions that require that witnesses be protected involve organized crime.

WITSEC provides witnesses and their families with a number of services, including temporary protection, relocation, establishing a new identity, providing documentation to support the new identity, and limited financial and employment assistance. By 1981, almost 3,500 witnesses and 8,000 dependents were in the program. However, it was beset by internal problems almost from the very beginning. During a Senate Hearing in 1981, witnesses reported how inexperienced and untrained members of the U.S. Marshals Service caused serious breaches in security, how witnesses were often given inaccurate descriptions of how they would be treated, that documentation for the witness and his family was often incomplete or slow in arriving, the difficulties in finding adequate employment for witnesses, and the lack of procedures for registering complaints for "perceived mistreatment."

Aladena "Jimmy the Weasel" Fratianno (1913–1993) and WITSEC: A Case Study

Prior to Gambino underboss Sammy "the Bull" Gravano, Fratianno, a member of the Los Angeles crime family, was the highest-ranking mob figure to turn informant. Fratianno earned his moniker "Weasel" in his youth, when his ability to outrun pursuing police conjured up images of a speedy weasel, but lived up to his moniker for other reasons during his long career in organized crime. He won respect as a killer for hire that had no compunction about murdering close friends. The media referred to him as the "Mafia's executioner on the West Coast," even though no murder case had ever been made against him. Fratianno became a made member of the Los Angeles family in 1947, and then transferred back to Chicago but returned to Los Angeles in 1975. When Jimmy returned to Los Angeles in 1975, he apparently posed as the acting boss while the real boss Dominic Brooklier was in prison (Capeci 2002).[6] He used his position to line his pockets and set up deals, all the while feeding the FBI information about mob activities in Chicago, Los Angeles, and elsewhere. In 1977, Brooklier learned of his scheme, and a contract was placed on Fratianno. He ran to the FBI for protection and shortly after, he agreed to enter the witness protection program.

According to his plea agreement, he had to serve 19 months in prison and earned a reputation with his handlers in the U.S. Marshals Service WITSEC operations branch as "a royal pain in the ass" (Earley and Shur 2002, 170). Once paroled in 1979, Fratianno was given the alias "Jimmy Marino" and relocated to Boise, Idaho. This didn't work to his liking and he began a rather peripatetic existence in WITSEC. Nevertheless, during a 5-year period, his testimony in a series of high-profile Mafia trials led to the conviction of six crime bosses in the early 1980s and dozens of minor gangsters. He soon became a nationally recognized celebrity, interviewed on television's *60 Minutes* and other news shows. He also collaborated on his bestselling memoir, *The Last Mafioso,* with Ovid Demaris in 1981.

Jimmy was in high demand in the early 1980s after the Supreme Court gave prosecutors more power under RICO as it became an important tool against organized crime. His handler in the program said, "He was an expert at manipulating the system [and] made more money milking WITSEC than he ever did committing crimes" (Earley and Shur 2002, 170), citing the special favors he received, including paying his telephone bills for years, monthly subsistence checks to his mother-in-law, breast implants for his wife, and for himself, a facelift and capped teeth (Earley and Shur 2002, 170).

Fratianno's demands from the program were so onerous that they tried to convince him to leave the program after his first 5 years. Finally a deal was hammered out in which he would receive a yearly salary for two more years ($33,477 tax-free), plus a payout of $411,300 to pay for his numerous personal expenses such as insurance, gasoline, and real estate taxes. However, the diplomacy between the erstwhile killer and WITSEC continued for several more years as he began to show early signs of dementia. Thrown out of the program after 10 years in 1989, longer than anyone else up to that time, he had finally worn out his welcome. The Department of Justice later reported that during his decade as a witness, he received almost $1 million in support (Earley and Shur 2002).

U.S. Marshals and the Witness Protection Program: The Department of Justice

U.S. Marshals are appointed by the president to 4-year terms in each judicial district, with the advice and consent of the Senate. They in turn appoint their own deputies. Today, U.S. Marshals are responsible for moving prisoners; apprehending fugitives; executing court orders; providing security to the court and its personnel; and most important, for supervising WITSEC. Its $20 million annual budget and elaborate programs to provide participants with new identities, Social Security numbers, and homes in distant locales makes it "the gold standard of witness protection programs" (Kocieniewski 2007, 24). Since the inception of WITSEC in 1970, the U.S. Marshals have relocated almost 8,000 witnesses along with 10,000 family members. During its history, not one participant has been harmed (Kocieniewski 2007).

RICO in Action: The Commission Case, *U.S. v. Salerno* (1986)

In *U.S. v. Salerno*, the heads of four of the five New York crime families (and other key figures) were prosecuted together for constituting and operating a *Commission*, similar to a national board of directors for organized crime. The indictment charged the bosses and some of their leading subordinates with operating this Commission. The case hinged on placing the defendants within "the history of Cosa Nostra" (Jacobs, Panarella, and Worthington 1994, 79). Although for years law enforcement insisted that this board of directors did in fact exist, they could not prove it until the former boss of the Bonanno crime family, Joseph Bonanno, had the temerity to chronicle his life story in *A Man of Honor* in 1983. In it, he gives a virtual blow-by-blow account of the evolution of the Commission from its inception in 1931. He insisted that the last time it met was in Apalachin, New York, in 1957, but since then it was made up of only the five New York bosses.

The genesis of *U.S. v. Salerno* began in 1980, when FBI agents from its New York City office initiated Operation GENUS with the intention of constructing RICO cases against each of the five families. More than 200 agents ultimately took part (along with a bevy of assistant U.S. attorneys). This massive operation coordinated members from federal, state, and local agencies—from FBI agents to New York Police Department detectives—and "utilized electronic surveillance on a scale previously unknown" (Jacobs, Panarella, and Worthington 1994, 80). Almost 4,000 hours of conversation from 171 court-authorized wiretaps and bugs revealed the inner workings of high-ranking crime figures. The surveillance of the Bonanno family was especially productive, especially after Joseph Pistone, as "Donny Brasco," reported the disorder in the family that led the commission to take it over. For 5 years, the investigators compiled information that gave an unprecedented picture of the structure, hierarchy, and activities of the crime families.

In February 1985, indictments named "more Cosa Nostra leaders than had ever before been indicted at one time" (Jacobs, Panarella, and Worthington 1994, 81). The defendants included Paul Castellano (head of the Gambino family), Anthony Salerno (head of the Genovese family), Anthony Corallo (head of the Lucchese family), and Carmine Persico (head of the Colombo family), as well as their underbosses and other ranking members. Because the Bonanno family was not represented on the commission at that time due to internal conflict, its boss was the only one left off the indictment.

The government's case was built on the notion that Cosa Nostra's commission constituted a criminal enterprise, meaning each of the defendants was either a member or functionary of the commission. Each of the defendants was tied to the commission of two or more acts of racketeering in support of the organization. The prosecution described their predicate racketeering acts in three categories: management of multi-family bid rigging and extortion in New York's concrete industry, conspiracy to organize loansharking territories, and the murders of Bonanno boss Carmine Galante and two associates as part of a commission strategy to resolve the ongoing leadership dispute within the family (Jacobs 2002, 81).

What would become a 9-week trial began on September 8, 1986. The linchpin to the government's case was proving the existence of the organization. Although the defendants and their lawyers vigorously denied the history of Cosa Nostra as outlined in the government case, the vivid testimony of witnesses and informants such as Joe Pistone and former family members bolstered the case further, as they testified about the traditional rules and structure and the existence of the continuing enterprise known as Cosa Nostra. The aforementioned predicate offenses were clearly laid out and substantiated through direct testimony and dozens of taped conversations.

The defense's case rested on trying to discredit the witnesses and argued that the wiretap evidence might have shown the existence of an organization, but not in the participation of any criminal activities. Despite attempts to discredit the informers and witnesses who made up part of the case, the existence of so many government photographs showing defendants together with intercepted references to commission meetings as well as recordings of concrete extortion schemes and murder plots were too powerful for the defense to overcome, and on November 19, 1986, the jury found the defendants guilty of all 17 racketeering acts and 20 related charges involving extortion, labor payoffs, and loansharking. In the word of Rudolph Giuliani, "The verdict reached today has resulted in dismantling the ruling council of La Cosa Nostra" (quoted in Jacobs, Panarella, and Worthington. 1994, 86). All the defendants except for one (who was sentenced to 40 years) were sentenced to 100 years in prison. Fines ranged from $50,000 to $250,000 for each individual.

PROSECUTING ORGANIZED CRIME

Beginning in the 1980s, the U.S. government finally made inroads against American organized crime groups using a panoply of powerful legal tools. Together with personnel and structural changes in the Department of Justice and the FBI, and initiatives supported by presidents and attorneys general, some of the most important advances in organized crime control were instituted. Besides the obvious impact of RICO and WITSEC, prosecutors have been aided by prosecutorial tools and innovations as well as court decisions that have greatly expanded the use of witness immunity and forfeiture sentencing in organized crime trials.

Grand Juries

According to the U.S. Constitution, American citizens have the right not to be charged with a felony (a criminal offense punishable by more than 1 year in prison) unless the charges have been approved by a grand jury. The 5th Amendment requires a grand jury indictment for federal criminal charges, and the federal grand jury is the investigative apparatus used to initiate criminal cases in federal court. There are two types of grand juries in the federal system. Both types are equal in authority, with their only major differences being the reasons they are convened and the time period in which they sit (Taylor 1983).

Regular grand juries sit for 18 months, although a special grand jury called for a specific purpose or investigation may sit for twice as long a period. In terms of organized crime cases, the investigative grand jury has proved the more effective of the two due to its expansive powers. These are called into existence to investigate if organized crime is occurring in the community in which it sits. According to the Organized Crime Control Act of 1970 a special grand jury must be convened at least every 18 months in federal judicial districts of more than one million people. Once empanelled, it can investigate organized drug trafficking, government corruption, and a host of other organized criminal activities. Once a special grand jury establishes that organized criminal activity has been taking place within its borders, it can charge the individuals responsible for the activity or it can issue a report chronicling the criminal operations. Once it issues a report, the special grand jury must submit the report to the court that supervises the grand jury. It is then up to the court to decide whether the report can be made public.

About half the states now have grand juries investigating organized crime, especially drug trafficking. For the most part, their activities are similar, except the state-level grand jury might investigate organized crime activity but is not limited to a particular jurisdiction.

A typical grand jury is composed of 23 ordinary citizens who meet secretly behind closed doors to determine whether there is probable cause to return an indictment. Grand jurors are selected from the same pool of potential jurors as any other jury panels and in the same manner. Unlike potential jurors in regular trials, they are not screened for biases or other factors. The grand jury has extraordinary investigative powers that have been evolving since the 1950s. Its wide, sweeping, almost unrestricted power is the cause of much criticism.

After the grand jury is selected and sworn in, the proceedings are secret. During the hearings, only the jurors, the prosecutor, the court reporter, and the witness are present. There are no lawyers present to represent the witness allowed in the grand jury room. However, in most grand juries, with certain limitations, it is acceptable for the witness to leave the room to consult with an attorney outside the room before answering a question, but an abuse of this right can be met with a contempt citation (Taylor 1983, 121). The grand jury does not even have to give a reason why it has subpoenaed a witness or physical evidence, nor does it have to advise the witness of the nature of the investigation, who is being investigated or, generally, the relevancy posed to him.

Because the proceedings of the grand jury are secret, witnesses are typically instructed by court officers not to reveal anything that went on during their time in court. However, because federal rules expressly prohibit the imposition of secrecy on a witness, it is up to the discretion of the witness once he leaves the court whether to follow the instructions.

The Grand Jury and Double Jeopardy

Double jeopardy does not apply to a grand jury—it applies only to jury trials. Grand juries do not convict or acquit individuals, but simply meet with the prosecutor in a secret proceeding and decide on the evidence presented whether there is enough evidence for an indictment (and subsequent jury trial). In effect, the grand jury is more like an investigation than a formal accusation. The protection against double jeopardy is enshrined in the 5th Amendment, which states that no person shall be "twice put in jeopardy of life and limb" for the same offense. Until June 1996, the courts often favored a judicial interpretation of the double jeopardy ruling in forfeiture cases—that it was double jeopardy to punish a defendant criminally and take the defendant's property away for the same crime. However, in *U.S. v. Ursery,* the U.S. Supreme Court resolved many of the questions over double jeopardy in favor of law enforcement, essentially ruling that forfeiture was a "device for denying someone the fruits of their criminal behavior" rather than a punishment (Vecchi and Sigler 2001; Abadinsky 2007, 349).

A special investigative grand jury is not a court of law, but should be considered an extension of a state's prosecuting agency. Thus a grand jury can investigate cases independently and in secret (like a prosecutor does), can interrogate witnesses, and, like a prosecutor, can file indictments for public offenses. The main difference between a prosecutor-driven investigation and a grand jury–driven prosecution is the subpoena power of the latter. The grand jury is empowered to subpoena a witness and compel him to testify under oath. Refusal to comply can be punished with incarceration for civil or criminal contempt. Nonetheless, it is easy to see why prosecutors are more than happy to opt for the more unwieldy and expensive, but often more successful, grand jury protocol over traditional prosecutorial tools.

If a prosecutor wants a grand jury to charge someone, the prosecutor must reserve time with the grand jury and then present evidence to them, trying to persuade the grand jurors that individuals have committed certain crimes. Evidence can include testimony from witnesses, documents, video and tape recordings, and results of scientific tests such as DNA and photographs. The grand jurors then must decide whether there is probable cause to charge a defendant with the crimes charged by the prosecutor. They then vote on the proposed charges of *indictment* (meaning "returning a true bill") that was drafted by prosecutor and given to grand jurors.

The Refusal to Testify: Civil and Criminal Contempt

If a witness refuses to appear before the grand jury, the witness can be held in contempt of the court that issued the subpoena to testify. Technically speaking, *contempt* refers to the power of a governmental body to compel enforcement of its decrees and orders. In 1831, Congress passed a statute defining the exact scope of the criminal contempt power for American federal courts, a statute that remains in effect today. According to this statute, "a federal court may punish by fine or imprisonment only misbehavior in or near the court's presence, misbehavior of a court officer in an official transaction, or disobedience of a lawful court write, rule, or order" (Livingston 2002, 157).

Contempt issues typically come into play in organized crime cases when the authority of a court is used to either punish or coerce individuals who violate its commands or offend the dignity of the judicial process. There have been a number of court cases in which individuals have been granted immunity to testify, but then refuse to do so. Because *contempt* also refers to situations when an individual shows disrespectful or disobedient behavior toward the court, a civil or criminal contempt charge can be proffered when the witness refuses to cooperate.

When it comes to criminal contempt, most state and federal courts are expected to follow the appropriate criminal procedures before imposing a criminal contempt sanction. What this means is that the defendant should be accorded full Constitutional protections against self-incrimination, right to counsel, presumption of innocence, proof of the violation beyond a reasonable doubt, and the right to a jury trial for serious sanctions. However, this has not always been true. Throughout much of the 20th century, many trial courts did not give defendants full criminal procedural protections before sanctioning them with criminal contempt fines and imprisonment. Between 1911 and 1968, a handful of Supreme Court cases gradually expanded procedural protections in such cases.

During the 1990s the Supreme Court was faced with concerns over the possible judicial abuse of the contempt power, particularly in regards to the power of a trial court to label its contempt sanction as civil in order to avoid affording the defendant full criminal procedural protections. Unlike the criminal contempt proceeding, a jury trial is not used in a civil contempt proceeding. After a grand jury decides that a witness has indeed committed contempt, and despite a grant of immunity refuses to testify as previously agreed on, the civil sanction can result in a period of confinement during the life of the grand jury (typically 18 months).

Immunity and the 5th Amendment

Any witness called before federal or state grand jury is protected by the 5th Amendment and has the right to refuse to answer any question that he feels might incriminate him. Likewise, the prosecutor has the burden of establishing an answer is not damaging, "an almost impossible burden in most cases" (Taylor 1983, 116).

Historically, American citizens have had the right to refuse to testify if called to do so by the prosecution as a witness concerning criminal activities. Protected by the 5th Amendment to the U.S. Constitution from incriminating himself: ". . . nor shall (any person) be compelled in any criminal case to be a witness against himself". Courts have typically upheld this right, despite the fact that the testimony of that witness would be lost to the prosecution. In 1857, this began to change when the first federal immunity statute was passed granting complete *transactional immunity*. The new law was designed to protect a witness testifying before Congress or one of its committees from prosecution. This *blanket immunity* was respected even if the witness testified about a crime such as a murder or robbery he had committed.

Over the next several years this immunity system was widely abused, leading to a new statute in 1862 in which a witness was protected from having his testimony used against him only in a future criminal prosecution. In effect, he could still be prosecuted for the crime for which he testified. According to the new statute, then, the prosecution could not use the defendant's testimony before the congressional apparatus, but would be open for future prosecution using "derivative evidence" gleaned from that testimony, otherwise known as *use immunity* (Taylor 1983, 3–4). The original statute in 1857 established transactional immunity, meaning the witness will never be charged for any offense as a result of his testimony. The amended law laid the groundwork for what is now known as *use immunity,* in which no testimony obtained from the witness while he is immunized may be used against him in a later prosecution. However, with use immunity, law enforcement officials were free to grant immunity to a suspect, force him to divulge incriminating information, and then use it to obtain other evidence and then prosecute the defendant using the derivative evidence.

Several U.S. Supreme Court cases took up the constitutionality of use immunity leading Congress to pass the Immunity Act of 1893 (27 Stat. 443), which "reintroduced transactional immunity in the federal system." Under this act, "no witness compelled to testify could be 'prosecuted or subjected to any penalty or forfeiture for or on account of any transaction, matter or thing, concerning which he may testify, or produce evidence, documentary, or otherwise'" (Taylor 1983, 5). During the next century, Congress authorized compelled testimony before federal administrative bodies by passing dozens of similar immunity schemes such as those found in the Securities Exchange Act (1934) and the Narcotic Control Act (1956). At the same time, a number of states were passing their own immunity statutes.[7]

The various types of immunity at different levels of government created much confusion. For example, "If an individual was granted immunity in one jurisdiction would it be binding in other jurisdictions?" (Taylor 1983). In 1964, the Supreme Court held in *Murphy v. Waterfront Commission* that it was indeed binding, but only as far as use immunity. In 1970, the Organized Crime Control Act consolidated into one comprehensive transactional immunity law all the various federal immunity statutes. Beginning with this landmark act, "federal authorities were authorized to force a witness to appear and give testimony, and then go ahead and prosecute the witness for crimes concerning which he incriminated himself, so long as no direct or indirect use was made of the testimony" (Taylor 1983, 8). One of the biggest critiques of immunity statutes was the possibility that a witness might take an *immunity bath*—that is, admit to every crime he ever committed, thus leaving the prosecution without much hope of a future prosecution.

In the late 1960s, the Nixon administration set its sights on creating tougher immunity laws in order to attack the leadership of organized crime. Nixon protégé John Dean helped draft the 1970 OCCA, and in it he made immunity uniformly applicable in the investigation of any federal crime by giving congressional committees for the first time the formal power to grant immunity. More controversially, the act "dropped from federal law the traditional 'transactional' immunity, which provided complete protection from prosecution" (The Immunity Game, *Time* 1973) in favor of use immunity, which meant only that a witness could not be prosecuted on the basis of his own specific testimony or evidence developed as a result of it (The Immunity Game, *Time* 1973).

Since the passage of the OCCA of 1970 (all federal jurisdictions must abide by its provisions), there has been a trend toward decreasing constitutional protection, reflecting the more punitive nature of the "law-and-order" era. As a result, a grant of immunity is now more likely to be found valid. In 1963, the Department of Justice obtained transactional immunity for 12 witnesses; 10 years later, it had increased to more than 3,000, after the passage of federal use immunity provisions. Use immunity offers less protection than transactional immunity because there is nothing to preclude the state from prosecuting the witness after he has given the incriminating testimony. The protection extends only to the "use" of the witness' testimony, and does not protect him from being prosecuted for the offense concerning which he testified. Therefore, the state attorney could elicit incriminating evidence about a crime from a defendant and then investigate it further. The defendant could then be prosecuted with the new evidence, but not the original testimony. It is indeed a powerful prosecutorial tool.

Forfeiture

The concept of assets forfeiture[8] dates back to biblical and English common law traditions. Although the concept itself is centuries old, it first appeared in the guise of civil forfeiture in the concept known as the *deodand,* from the Latin *Deo Dandum,* "to be given to God." Over time, it evolved into the English common law practice of forfeiting the value of one's material property to the English Crown. Today, *assets forfeiture* refers to something surrendered as a penalty for unlawful activity and without compensating the owner in return (Vecchi and Sigler 2001). In recent years there has been a growing trend for countries to introduce civil forfeiture in response to the nature of organized crime activity (e.g., Australia, the UK, Ireland, Israel, Italy, South Africa).

Before the 1970s, the only federal law that included criminal forfeiture provisions in the United States was the Civil War–era Confiscation Act of 1862, which targeted the estates of Confederate soldiers with the full support of the Supreme Court. Forfeiture was revived as an important weapon in the war against the drug trade in the 1970s with the Comprehensive Drug Abuse Prevention and Control Act of 1970, which contained criminal forfeiture provisions in Title 1 (RICO) and Title II (the Controlled Substances Act) of the act.

By most accounts, the Controlled Substances Act (CSA) contained the basic anti-drug forfeiture provisions for the forfeiture of controlled substances and collateral materials such as manufacturing equipment; precursor chemicals; and transportation equipment, such as motor vehicles, boats, and airplanes. In 1978, the CSA was amended with the Psychotropic Substances Act (PSA), which required forfeiture of all monetary instruments intended to be furnished in exchange for controlled substances. It also allowed for the forfeiture of all profits linked to the illegal activity.

Since the mid-1980s, forfeiture has been a major weapon in the federal government's "War on Drugs." In 1984, the Comprehensive Crime Control Act amended the CSA once more by adding provisions that allow the seizure of all real property that was used or was intended to be used in furtherance of drug trafficking. Two years later, the 1986 Anti-Drug Abuse Act extended civil forfeiture to include proceeds from money-laundering activities. Forfeiture provisions were added throughout the 1990s; as a result, there are more than 130 drug- and money-laundering–related federal statutes that contain either civil or criminal forfeiture provisions (or both). Between 1986 and 1996, the mean total of net assets going into the Department of Justice Assets Forfeiture Fund (AFF) was $420.44 million (Vecchi and Sigler 2001).

Several issues have arisen during challenges to civil and criminal forfeiture statutes. A number of critics pondered whether criminal punishment of an offender in the guise of imprisonment or fines together with the confiscation of property constitutes either a violation of the 5th Amendment's double jeopardy clause or the 8th Amendment's ban against excessive fines. In the vast majority of cases, the Supreme Court has ruled against such challenges, making forfeiture an important tool in the campaign against drug trafficking.

There is little doubt that forfeiture is a potent deterrent and a valuable revenue resource for law enforcement. However, what has become increasingly clear since the 1980s are the potential risks associated with it, because it offers far fewer procedural safeguards than the criminal law. Civil liberties groups have filed suits targeting civil forfeiture laws that allowed motorists to lose their cars when arrested for drunk driving, carrying drugs, or picking up prostitutes.

Most forfeiture activity occurs under federal law, and most of it is connected to drug trafficking. The Department of Justice established the National Assets Seizure and Forfeiture Fund in 1985 and realized $27 million from drug-related forfeitures that year; by 1992, forfeitures were at $875 million. The law mandates that the profits from confiscated cash and property on its resale be spent on the War on Drugs, funding state and local law enforcement activities. Many states followed with their own civil forfeiture programs based in part on federal statutes. Cities and other municipal governments have used such laws on their own to deal with local concerns ranging from unsafe housing to prostitution and drunk driving.

Civil versus Criminal Forfeiture

Civil Forfeiture

Almost all contemporary forfeiture statutes are civil rather than criminal in nature. Criminal forfeiture operates as punishment for a crime, and therefore requires a conviction, after which the state takes the assets in question from the criminal. However, civil forfeiture lowers the threshold of proof necessary for the forfeiture of such property. Civil forfeiture rests on the provocative assumption (legal fiction) that the property itself, not the owner, has violated the law. Thus this proceeding is directed against the *res,* or the thing involved in some illegal transaction specified by statute.

Unlike criminal forfeiture, *in rem* forfeiture does not require a conviction or even an official criminal charge against the owner. This is the source of contention over its abuse and constitutionality.

Criminal Forfeiture

In Personam, or criminal forfeiture, is a punitive action taken by the government against an offender as part of the sentence following conviction. Criminal forfeitures are predicated on the guilt of the offender and require the government to prove charges beyond a reasonable doubt. By comparison, civil forfeitures require only that the government establish probable cause that money, instruments (property used in the commission of a crime), or real property was related to illegal drug transactions.

Although the criminal conviction requires the government to prove guilt "beyond a reasonable doubt," civil forfeiture is subject to a lower burden—"preponderance of the evidence." The burden shifts to the defendant once the government demonstrates that the defendant acquired the property around the time of the crime and no other likely source existed. The owner has the right to contest seizure after it has occurred, but must prove money or property was earned through legal activities—that is "prove on a preponderance of the evidence"—that it is unrelated to crime.

A Forfeiture Allegation (2007)

An indictment was returned by a federal grand jury in New Haven, Connecticut, in June 2007 charging 29 individuals and several entities with various violations of federal law. The indictment alleged these individuals were involved in racketeering in the waste hauling industry in Connecticut and eastern New York. Charges included mail and wire fraud and extortion. Also contained in the indictment was a forfeiture allegation based on the racketeering charges:

if the assets' owners are convicted, the assets would be forfeited to the United States. The listed assets include 25 trash carting and related businesses; two parcels of real property, 24 personal bank accounts in the name of GALANTE and his family members; six race cars; and $418,153 cash that was seized in July 2005 from GALANTE'S home and business offices during the execution of multiple search warrants by federal agents. The indictment also seeks a money judgment of at least 100 million dollars. Since June 2006, in connection with the forfeiture allegations, the United States Marshals Service has been monitoring the operations of the indicted businesses to assure both that the businesses continue to serve their customers, and that they conduct all operations in compliance with the law. (FBI June 14, 2007)

Forfeiture and the USA PATRIOT act (2001)

The passage of the USA PATRIOT act of 2001 enjoyed widespread support at its inception, but by the end of the decade much of its luster was gone as various constituencies targeted controversial provisions. Its passage removed many of the barriers that formerly prevented law enforcement and intelligence operations from collaborating, and created several new money-laundering crimes and increased penalties for some existing money-laundering violations. The PATRIOT act

- prohibits the laundering of any proceeds from foreign crimes of violence or political corruption.
- prohibits the laundering of proceeds of cybercrime and offenses relating to the support of terrorist organizations.
- prohibits bulk cash smuggling, and lays out procedures for the forfeiture of smuggled bulk cash shipments.
- revises the language that had previously required the government to show that the defendant knew a business was operating illegally. This was changed to include anyone who "knowingly conducts, controls, manages, supervises, directs, or owns all or part of an unlicensed money transmitting business" (Madinger 2006, 57–58).

Most large drug-trafficking networks must contend with smuggling bulk cash shipments. Although it was already illegal to fail to report to Customs the movement of large amounts of cash or monetary instruments in and out of the United States, the 1998 court decision *United States v. Bajakajian* prevented the government from forfeiting large amounts of cash unless the government could demonstrate the funds were the result illegal activities. In order to remedy what law enforcement considered a serious loophole in the forfeiture legislation, a change was made in the PATRIOT act that made the smuggling or shipment of large amounts of currency a separate criminal violation, a felony punishable by 5 years in prison. What's more, the new law made it a crime to transport or attempt to transport or transfer more than $10,000 in currency or monetary instruments into or out of the United States if the funds were both "concealed on the person, in a container, or in a conveyance" and the funds were "transported with the intent to avoid the CMIR reporting requirement"[9] (Madinger 2006, 58). Clearly, the intent was to prevent money launderers from moving their profits offshore, where they were easier to conceal, layer, and integrate.

The PATRIOT act dramatically expanded forfeiture laws, which, although directed toward terrorist organizations, were just as applicable to organized crime groups. According to the new legislation, the government could seize all property in the United States that is identified as being connected with a number of foreign crimes and provide for the domestic enforcement of foreign crimes, and more. In addition, in response to the 1998 *Bajakajian* decision, an individual caught smuggling large amounts of currency out of the country without reporting the transfer to Customs can be charged with a crime, and the entire cash shipment can be seized and forfeited.

The USA PATRIOT Act[10]: RICO Redux?

As demonstrated previously Chapter 13 on Organized Crime and Terrorism, new laws that have been directed toward the challenges of terrorism have also found applicability in regards to organized crime. In both cases they have been found to be controversial. Criticisms of the PATRIOT act have resonated strongly among the critics of RICO, many of whom have branded it unconstitutional.

The PATRIOT act, which was overwhelmingly approved in Congress and signed into law in 2001, armed law enforcement with new tools to detect and prevent terrorism. Many of these tools have already been used for decades to suppress organized crime and narcotics trafficking. When then-Senator Joe Biden found out how difficult it was for the FBI to obtain wiretaps against terrorist groups, he exclaimed, "The FBI could get a wiretap to investigate the mafia, but they could not get one to investigate terrorists. To put it bluntly, that was crazy! What's good for the mob should be good for terrorists" (*Cong. Rec.*, October 25, 2001).

Almost as soon as it went into effect, critics were comparing it to RICO, with some even suggesting, "It may go down in the record books [with RICO] as two of the most notorious laws in U.S. history" (Shelton and Hall 2002). Others have branded it a "knee-jerk reaction to a seemingly insurmountable problem" (Shelton and Hall 2002). One observer said that modifying existing laws to expand the powers of the federal government in areas such as surveillance and information gathering made the United States "a nation of potential suspects" (Shelton and Hall 2002).

The PATRIOT act established several new laws that dovetailed with the campaign against organized crime, such as new anti-money-laundering laws and granting extensive powers to the U.S. attorney general. These rules have been highly controversial, particularly when it comes to detaining foreign citizens and others without citizenship, as well as for simplifying procedures for using wiretaps and other surveillance measures.

Other criticisms target the following:

- Detention of terrorist suspects indefinitely without having to file formal charges
- Roving warrants (Section 206) that allow law enforcement to potentially gain access to the electronic data of innocent citizens
- "Sneak and Peak" warrants (Section 2130) that allow law enforcement to secretly search a private residence and if showing good cause could indefinitely delay notifying the property owner of the warrant

More recently, one scholar at Georgetown University argued that the law "runs roughshod over constitutional freedoms, discriminates against foreign nationals, and eliminates checks and balances on executive power" (Cole 2004)). Others suggest critics are overreacting to its "Orwellian name" (Cole 2004)). Supporters emphasize that it has not created any great revolution in government powers and merely contains "a series of evolutionary changes in law enforcement that improve upon, and expand, existing powers already exercised by the government" (Yoo 2004).[11] One Justice Department spokesman asserted, "Delayed-notification search warrants are a long-existing crime-fighting tool upheld by courts nationwide for decades in organized crime, drug cases and child pornography" (Stambaugh 2007). Indeed, proponents of the PATRIOT act have pointed to the fact that the same surveillance and search tools used against drug dealers and the Mafia were now simply being adjusted and modernized to fight a new threat. Often cited is the fact that before the act the government had to seek an individual warrant for each communication device used by a suspected terrorist; and each time the target traveled to a new judicial district, a new warrant was required. In the past, law enforcement used delayed notification—for example, in drug and organized crime cases so as not to alert the surveillance targets. The implementation of the PATRIOT act allowed for continuing surveillance of the terrorist even if he switched communications devices and methods; meanwhile, the warrants now allowed for nationwide surveillance. So far, federal courts have upheld these "roving" wiretaps as consistent with the 4th Amendment (Yoo 2008).

ELECTRONIC SURVEILLANCE

The term *wiretapping* refers to the traditional methods for intercepting telephone conversations. Much has changed in the telecommunications business, with a fax or data communication just as useful a target. In earlier eras, *eavesdropping*—overhearing a conversation without the knowledge of the participants—and letter opening—opening, reading, and copying of written messages without the knowledge of the parties involved—served a similar function. The modern telecommunications revolution "unified and systematized these practices" (Diffie and Landau 1998, 151).

Wiretapping was first used in the 19th century, when individuals obtained information by intercepting telegraph messages, such as the California stockbroker who violated a state statute in 1864 and was prosecuted for illegally obtaining market information in this way. New York City police began tapping telephones as early as the 1890s (despite an 1892 state statute that considered it a felony).

In the Prohibition era, it was common for authorities to use wiretaps to gather evidence on prominent bootlegging gangs. Among those benefiting from the largesse of illegal liquor was Seattle's leading bootlegger and former police lieutenant Roy Olmstead. Federal agents brought a case against him based on wiretap evidence. In 1928, the case went to the U.S. Supreme Court and in *Olmstead v. United States* five of the nine justices supported the agents, finding that warrantless wiretaps were legal, and Olmstead went to prison. *Olmstead* would stand until 1967 when *Berger v. New York* held that a New York eavesdropping statute did indeed violate Berger's 4th and 14th Amendment rights.

In 1934, Congress formally banned wiretapping with the Federal Communications Act (FCA), prohibiting the interception and divulgence of material gathered from wiretaps. However, it did not explicitly state that the ban applied to the "interception and divulgence" of communications "transmitted by wire" to federal agents. Federal agents therefore continued to use wiretaps during criminal investigations for several years. However, in the aftermath of several rulings in 1937 and 1939, the Supreme Court stated in *Nardone v. U.S.* that the wiretapping ban applied to federal agents as well, and that indictments that hinged on illegally gathered wiretap evidence should be dismissed.[12]

During wartime, FBI Director Hoover persuaded President Franklin D. Roosevelt that the omnipresent threat of spies, subversives, and saboteurs required the use of electronic surveillance against foreign agents, but with the caveat that the information would not leave the government. As a result, the *Nardone* decision was reinterpreted to mean, "It was not unlawful to intercept communications as long as the contents were kept within the U.S. government" (Diffie and Landau 1998, 179). The FBI was granted the authority as long it kept records of its wiretapping activities. After the death of FDR in 1945, President Harry S Truman was convinced to expand the national security limits of wiretapping to include domestic security and situations that imperiled human life. This was significant, because it laid the groundwork that would later allow the use of this surveillance against organized crime.

Wiretapping and Organized Crime

Electronic surveillance has figured prominently in almost every organized crime prosecution since the late 1970s, with some prosecutions based almost exclusively on intercepted conversations.[13] Since the mid-1950s, police have relied heavily on wiretaps as a method for penetrating the inner sanctums of the usually clandestine underworld and its code of silence. By its very nature, most organized crime activities involve supplying illegal goods and services to myriad citizen customers. As a result, "the consensual nature of these crimes means that 'law enforcement lacks its staunchest ally, the victim'" (Diffie and Landau 1998, 167), and investigation tools such as bugging and wiretapping stepped to the forefront of organized crime investigations.

In the late 1950s, the FBI wiretapped the headquarters of the Chicago Outfit and passed on the intelligence to its Washington headquarters. Subsequent bugging operations targeted mob figures in San Francisco, Pittsburgh, Las Vegas, and New England. This campaign ground to a halt in 1965,

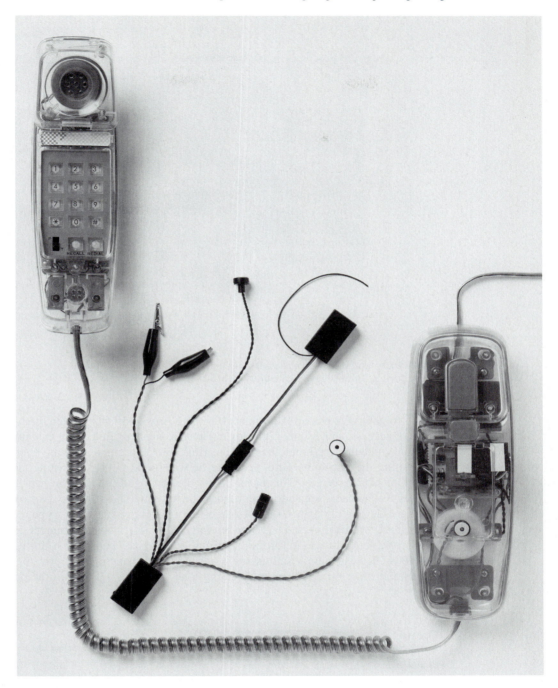

FIGURE 14.1   Wiretapped telephone
Source: Dorling Kindersley Meida Library/Geoff Dann

when President Lyndon Johnson prohibited wiretapping without approval from the attorney general and placed a 180-day limit on eavesdropping.

Upon taking the reins of the justice system as attorney general in 1961, Robert Kennedy made it one of his first points of business to launch a major campaign against organized crime. However, with weak federal anti-racketeering laws granting him limited authority in this arena, his

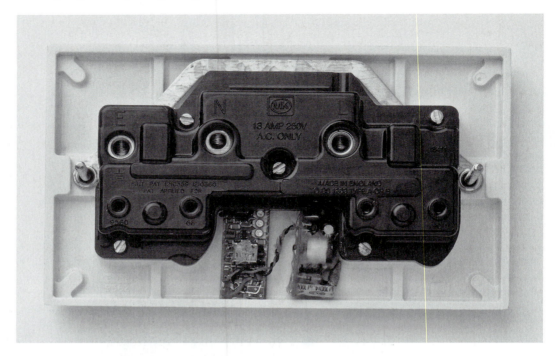

FIGURE 14.2 Bug disguised as a wall socket
Source: Dorling Kindersley Meida Library/Geoff Dann

crusade to convict a welter of prominent crime bosses and labor leader Jimmy Hoffa held slim chance of success, and despite his heady objectives, Kennedy failed. For example, Hoffa was convicted of jury tampering rather than racketeering, and Chicago boss Joseph Aiuppa was sentenced for violating the Migratory Bird Act, after he was found guilty of owning more than the legal limit of mourning doves (Theoharis 2000). Following Kennedy, the next attorney general, Nicholas Katzenbach, created a special organized crime task force to coordinate his anticrime campaign. He quickly approved FBI requests for wiretaps; but for it to be a successful crime-fighting tool, wiretapping had to be made available to other law enforcement groups.

Urban America was embroiled in racial conflict and civil unrest throughout the mid- to late 1960s. A clearly anti-establishment and law enforcement ethos prevailed among campus radicals and other militant groups, creating a new political climate in the process, and in the

---

Charles Katz v. the United States (1967)

In 1967, Charles Katz made a $300 bet from a phone booth in Los Angeles (violating the Hobbs Act), innocent to the fact that the FBI had previously placed an electronic bug in the booth while investigating interstate gambling. However, the conversation was recorded without a search warrant. Katz's conviction was overturned by the Supreme Court in *Charles Katz v. U.S.*, ruling the investigation violated his 4th Amendment protections. Many thought the Supreme Court was "heading down a one-way path to greater privacy protection" (Diffie and Landau, 1998, 151). However, this was far from true. During the 1980s, electronic surveillance resulted in the most successful prosecutions of organized crime figures of the 20th century. What *Katz* did was change "the doctrine underlying US wiretap law" (Diffie and Landau, 1998, 167), ruling wiretaps were illegal without a search warrant but permissible as long as the limitations and protections of the 4th Amendment were respected.

late 1960s Southern Democrats and conservative Republicans pushed for a law-and-order regime. This new dynamic led to the enactment of the Omnibus Crime Control and Safe Streets Act (OCCSS) of 1968, and the Racketeer Influenced and Corrupt Organization Act (RICO) in 1970; both revolutionized law enforcement by centering responsibility at the federal level (Theoharis 2000, 36).

In 1967, the Presidential Task Force on Organized Crime recommended the legalization of electronic surveillance as part of major federal legislation against organized crime. This was met by ardent opposition from Attorney General Ramsey Clark, who prohibited the use of wiretaps by all federal law enforcement officers and made it clear to Congress that he thought it was too expensive and ineffective, arguing, "I think it may well be that with the commitment of the same manpower to other techniques, even more convictions could be secured [against organized crime]" (quoted in Diffie and Landau, 1998, 192) A number of other high-ranking officials at various levels of government seemed to agree, including Detroit Police Commissioner Ray Girardin and the attorneys general of California, Delaware, Missouri, and New Mexico. Although the debate was heated, the tenor of the times won the day, as national security concerns in the turbulent 1960s trumped the opposition. For the first time in its history, Congress legalized wiretapping as a law enforcement tool in criminal cases. Under Title III of the Omnibus Crime Control and Safe Streets Act of 1968, electronic surveillance by law enforcement would be allowed under strict conditions, and in less than 20 years turned out to be a critical component of the government's attack on Cosa Nostra. The use of wiretaps and bugs during criminal inquiries was limited to court-approved warrants, although broad permissive language affirmed the president's constitutional right to authorize wiretaps during "national security" investigations (see the discussion of the PATRIOT act).

Title III

First, it should be remembered that private eavesdropping is prohibited and can be used by federal officials and prosecutors only in states that allow it (Abadinsky 2007). To apply for a Title III, a law enforcement officer must first prove that all other intelligence gathering methods have been exhausted, and electronic means are the last resort before obtaining a warrant to initiate a wiretap. It could be used only against certain crimes where there is probable cause to believe the subject is committing or has committed a crime, such as bribery, kidnapping, robbery, murder, extortion, fraud, drug dealing, or conspiracy to commit any of these offenses. There must also be probable cause that information concerning one or more of these offenses will be obtained by the bug or wiretap. Finally, the phone, fax, computer, or place being placed under surveillance must have been used in criminal activity and likely to be again. The application for the court order is prepared by a government attorney, and must then be approved by a member of the Department of Justice at or above the level of Deputy Assistant Attorney General.

Once the court order for the wiretap is approved, it is brought to a service provider such as a utility company for execution. The provider is expected to assist in placing the wiretap and compensated for the work. In most cases, these are approved for 30 days or less; an extension necessitates a new court order. State and local law enforcement in most states have similar recourse to wiretaps, albeit with more restrictive requirements. More important, in the aftermath of the Hoover FBI predisposition for keeping secret files, Congress mandates that electronic surveillance records be opened up to members of the public.

INVESTIGATING ORGANIZED CRIME

The first members of law enforcement to specialize in organized crime investigation were Italian-born members of the New York Police Department. By the turn of the 20th century, New York City was home to more than 500,000 Italians (out of a total population of 3 million). Most of the police on the force were Irish (with some Jewish officers as well). In 1883, the Italian-born Joseph "Joe" Petrosino (1860–1909) joined the New York Police Department. After several years as a beat cop, he was promoted to detective and devoted the rest of his life to investigating Italian-related syndicate activities. After Petrosino went to his superiors telling them there were more Italians in New York than in Rome, and few policemen could speak the language, Police Commissioner William McAdoo directed the creation of an Italian Squad, consisting of four Italian-speaking detectives. Most of their activities were directed against Black Hand extortion gangs, and by 1896, the Italian Squad numbered more than a dozen. Petrosino eventually traced some of the activities to Sicily, and with the approval of top brass, he traveled to Palermo to investigate. What was supposed to be a clandestine mission turned into a debacle after newspapers leaked word of the trip while he was onboard a ship headed to Sicily. Less than a month after his arrival, he was assassinated in a Palermo park. Petrosino was the first New York City detective killed outside the United States. His murder led to the dismissal of police chiefs in New York and Palermo. By most accounts, his funeral in Manhattan drew more than 200,000 people (Petacco 1974).

In the century since Petrosino's death, police at every level—federal, state, and local—have been confronted by organized crime activities. Law enforcement uses two basic strategies in response to criminal activity. *Reactive policing* basically depends on waiting for a crime to happen and then reacting, whereas *proactive policing* involves police actually going out and seeking out criminals, such as during undercover operations, prior to the crime occurring. Of the two, proactive policing has the best chance of leading to police corruption, as undercover officers pretending to be criminals are difficult for their handlers to control. The findings of the 1972 Knapp Commission reinforced this view, noting, "At the time of the Commission's investigation, plainclothesmen bore primary responsibility for enforcing anti-gambling laws, and it was among plainclothesmen that the Commission found the most pervasive and systematic police corruption, particularly in relation to gambling" (Knapp Commission 1972, 73).

Police Corruption

There is nothing more important in an organized crime investigation than preserving its secrecy as long as possible. Once targets find out they are being investigated, they have the potential to intimidate witnesses, destroy incriminating evidence, or interrupt their criminal activity at least temporarily to stifle the probe. Any leaks of information can endanger the lives of undercover agents and cooperating witnesses. One recent case underscores how one corrupt officer can ruin an investigation. In 2002, after a long and drawn out trial, former FBI Special Agent John Connolly was convicted of racketeering, obstructing justice, and making false statements to federal investigators. Evidence was introduced during the trial that proved Connolly had leaked the proceedings of a grand jury to Boston gangster James "Whitey" Bulger. Warned of his impending indictment, Bulger had time to make his getaway and remains on the FBI's Ten Most Wanted List. In another related case, the FBI was using a court-ordered wiretap to track calls from Bulger's brothers' telephones. Massachusetts State Trooper Richard Schneiderhan found out about the surveillance and passed the information on to Bulger associates. In 2003, Schneiderhan was convicted of obstructing justice (Nardini 2006).

Informants

In the early 1950s the Supreme Court approved the use of confidential informants, and it became a major tool in the war on drugs and organized crime. It is unknown how many informants are used by law enforcement agencies. At the national level, the FBI reported it employs 15,000 secret informants and the DEA about 4,000 at any given time. However, state and local agencies do not release this information to the public, although the majority track contacts with informants using internal databases. According to one recent survey, "federal law enforcement agencies seem much more

Two Cops Who Murdered for the Mafia

In 2006, two highly decorated former New York Police Department detectives were convicted of "moonlighting as hitmen for the mob" (McShane 2006, A12). It was one of the most sensational cases of police corruption in New York history. Louis Eppolito and Steven Caracappa were convicted for their roles in eight murders committed between 1986 and 1990, while simultaneously working for the New York Police Department and for Lucchese family crime boss Anthony "Gaspipe" Casso. According to the prosecution, the two were paid $4,000 a month to help the Mafia (more if they killed someone). Prosecutors demonstrated how the two detectives committed at least two murders themselves after pulling over victims at traffic stops. In other cases, they delivered victims to their Mafia executioners. Eppolito and Caracappa were convicted of RICO charges that included racketeering conspiracy, witness tampering, witness retaliation, and obstruction of justice. Caracappa, who had retired in 1992, helped establish the New York Police Department's unit for Mafia murder investigations, although his partner was the son of a Gambino crime member and a much-praised street cop, Eppolito went out of his way to broadcast his family ties to the Gambino family in his book *Mafia Cop*. After he retired in 1990, he had a small part in the movie *Goodfellas*. Since their retirement, the detectives lived in homes on the same block in Las Vegas. Neither took the stand in their own defense. Later that year, in a stunning turn of events, a federal judge threw out key racketeering conspiracy convictions against the "Mafia Cops," convictions that included their participation in eight murders between 1986 and 1991 due to a "conflict with the federal five-year statute of limitations" (DeStefano 2006, 1). According to the judge, the trial overwhelmingly established their guilt, but that legal issues compelled him to acquit them. A new trial was ordered for both men on charges of drug dealing and, in Eppolito's case, money-laundering. The defendants were indicted in 2005, but their most recent killing took place in 1991, and generally, under federal criminal law, crimes alleged in a racketeering conspiracy must have occurred within 5 years of the indictment (Destefano 2006; McGrath 2006; McShane 2006; Lawson and Oldham 2006).

likely to rely on informants than do local agencies" (Fox 2008). This is probably the result of federal sentencing guidelines that recognize cooperating with authorities only as a basis for winning sentencing leniency (Fox 2008).

According to one observer, "Without informants, law enforcement authorities would be unable to penetrate and destroy organized crime syndicates, drug trafficking cartels, bank frauds" (Fox 2008) and other forms of crime. However, critics counter that this practice has become a "dangerous public policy, compromising the integrity of police work, endangering both informants and innocents, and often producing band information" (Fox 2008). Civil libertarians and legal scholars argue that the use of informants often leads to "false convictions, shoddy police work and an erosion of trust in high crime, low income communities" (Fox 2008). Nevertheless, there are just as many proponents who would argue that informants are an "invaluable investigative tool" and that their diminished use would "have the unintended effect of driving the officer–informant relationship further underground" (Morton 1995, 301). Even esteemed legal scholar Alan Dershowitz admits it is a necessary evil, noting, "Informers are very important. They give you leads and tips. They tell you where the guns are buried. That's all fine. It's when the informant's word, his credibility, is used in court—that's the problem" (quoted in Morton 1995, 301).

By most accounts if, anyone considering using informants should remember two things: "They should never be trusted" and "their motive should always be considered" ("Death Under Cover," 2007). Police departments around the country adopted several safeguards to protect the integrity of the narcotics enforcement process. For example, undercover officers in many cases are prohibited from registering contraband by themselves. This is accomplished by a backup team under a supervisor, who directs the vouchering process for confiscated drugs and cash. In other cases, rules mandate that any payment to a confidential informant be witnessed by at least two officers (Fox 2008).

Informants U.K. Style: Supergrasses

English police refer to their informants as *supergrasses*. Although the origin of the term is somewhat obscure, it was probably derived from the rhyming of the American slang for policeman—copper—with grasshopper. Others suggest that it comes from the phrase *in the grass*, which could mean being on the run from the police or prison (Morton 1995). Police forces around the world use informants to make cases. Since the mid-1980s a number have adopted witness protection systems as well. Witnesses in the context of organized crime investigations are placed into three categories by the London Metropolitan Police:

1. Resident Informants are active participants in a series of serious crimes and have agreed to identify and testify against other criminals involved in those and similar offenses.
2. Protected Informants are individuals informing on associates involved in crimes, but whose identity and activity is already exposed.
3. Protected Witnesses are individuals who can provide important evidence about the most serious offenses and a substantial threat exists on their lives. (Morton 1995, 306–307)

FEDERAL LAW ENFORCEMENT AND ORGANIZED CRIME

There was little national interest in the problem of organized crime until 1950 when the U.S. Attorney General convened a national conference on organized crime, leading to the Senate Special Committee under Senator Kefauver (see Chapter 1). In 1954, the Department of Justice followed with the formation of an Organized Crime and Racketeering Section (OCRS) to continue prosecutorial efforts that followed the Kefauver hearings. It is considered the first federal law enforcement unit dedicated solely to investigations of organized crime, but efforts to institutionalize an anti-racketeering intelligence program were hindered by a lack of coordination and interest by some Federal investigative agencies. The stated purpose of the OCRS was to "coordinate enforcement activities against organized crime, initiate and supervise investigations, accumulate and correlate intelligence data, formulate general prosecutorial policies, and to assist federal prosecuting attorneys throughout the country" (quoted in Ryan, 1994, 343). Despite its good intentions, it accomplished little in the 1950s, but between 1967 and 1971, the OCRS established 18 federal strike forces throughout the country in response to the goals of crime control enumerated by the President's Task Force on Organized Crime.

In 1958 (after the 1957 Apalachin Conference), an Attorney General's Special Group on Organized Crime was created within the Department of Justice with regional offices from which intelligence information was gathered and grand jury proceedings conducted concerning the Apalachin attendees. However, its methods were mostly reactive in nature. It was soon after subsumed by the OCR Section.

The Department of Justice did not turn its attention to organized crime until Robert Kennedy's tenure as attorney general in the early 1960s, when he announced that fighting organized crime would be his top priority. As demonstrated in Chapter 4, the revelations of the Apalachin Conference and the heavy influence of the media in 1957 had finally energized federal law enforcement into action. What is perhaps just as important, according to Alan Block, was Kennedy's attitude toward organized crime, which he suggests were the result of his background as a "Cold Warrior [who] framed his actions through a deep-seated belief in subversive conspirators" (1980, 42). Kennedy, like others in his position, was of the opinion that it was fruitless to concentrate on coming up with a substantive definition when all that he thought was required was, "Don't define it, do something about it" (quoted in Block, 1980, 43).

In 1960, FBI began to supply the OCR Section with regular intelligence reports on 400 of the nation's organized crime figures (mostly Italian). However, it was understaffed from the beginning, with only 17 attorneys and minimal intelligence information from other federal agencies, and could not fulfill its functions, which included coordinating all federal law enforcement activities against organized crime, accumulating and correlating all necessary data, initiating and supervising investigations, formulating general prosecutive policies, and assisting federal prosecuting attorneys throughout the country. In 1961, the OCR Section expanded its organized crime program, greatly increasing staff and its convictions. However, it must be said that it was not the result of any one agency, but rather reflected the rare cooperation and information sharing between federal agencies, with most investigative leads emanating as tax cases from the Internal Revenue Service. Between 1961 and 1965, more than 60% of the convictions developed in this manner. A number of others resulted from the efforts of the Federal Bureau of Narcotics (Katzenbach 1965, 1158; McClellan 1963–1964, 652).

In the mid-1960s, the campaign against organized crime at the federal level lost some of its momentum after the Department of Justice and the Treasury Department were accused of using illegal electronic surveillance extensively in several tax cases and in racketeering investigations in Las Vegas. In 1966, President Johnson ordered a review of the "national program" against organized crime (1967).

The *Organized Crime Intelligence: Executive Summary* report, published in 1976 by the Department of Justice, indicated that in 1972, the national strategy against organized crime was made up of four parts, including the Organized Crime Strike Force; international efforts against organized crime; recent legislation, such as the Omnibus Crime Control and Safe Streets Act of 1968 and the Organized Crime Control Act of 1970; and the national Council on Organized Crime. However, by the time it was published in 1976, "only the strike forces and the federal legislation remained in existence" (Block 1980, 44).

Department of Homeland Security: Immigration and Customs Enforcement

Immigration and Customs Enforcement (ICE) is the largest investigative arm of the U.S. Department of Homeland Security. ICE is responsible for identifying criminals and organizations involved in human smuggling and trafficking. ICE developed a number of initiatives in recent years that focus on attacking the infrastructure that supports smuggling organizations as well as the assets that are derived from these illicit activities, including the seizure of currency, property, weapons, and vehicles. One of its most powerful new tools is the issuance of Civil Asset Forfeiture Reform Act (CAFRA) notices to property owners whose properties have been identified to have facilitated smuggling or the harboring of aliens (http://www.ice.gov).

Department of Homeland Security: U.S. Secret Service

The first general law enforcement agency of the federal government, the U.S. Secret Service (USSS) was created in 1865 under the Treasury Department for the purpose of combating counterfeiting. Since that time, it has seen its charge expanded to include a variety of other activities (including the protection of the president, the president's family, and other dignitaries). Today, its stated mission is "maintaining the integrity of the nation's financial infrastructure and payment systems" (http://www.secretservice.gov, 2008). Its mandate has been broadened by several laws passed in 1982 and 1984 that made it responsible for investigating access device fraud, including credit and debit card fraud, and gave it parallel authority with other federal law enforcement agencies in identity crime cases. The USSS is the primary authority for the investigation of computer fraud. Following the passage of the PATRIOT act, in 2002, it was charged with establishing a nationwide network of Electronic Crime Task Force (ECTF). The USSS was transferred to the Department of Homeland Security effective March 1, 2003. Today, the service employs 3,200 special agents, 1,300 uniformed division officers, and more than 2,000 support personnel. This change has increased its role in investigating cybercrime and organized crime. Since 2003, the Secret Service has made almost 30,000 arrests for counterfeiting, cybercrime, and other financial crimes and seized close to $300 million in counterfeit currency (http://www.secretservice.gov, 2008).

> ## Primary Offenses Investigated by the U.S. Secret Service
>
> - Credit card/access device fraud (skimming)
> - Check fraud
> - Bank fraud
> - False identification fraud
> - Passport/visa fraud
> - Identity theft

Major crime-fighting initiatives since the 1990s have been directed at new organized ethnic criminal groups from West Africa, Asia, and Eastern Europe who have been at the forefront of a number of financial criminal schemes, particularly Nigerian advance fee fraud (see Chapter 12 concerning Afrolineal Organized Crime).

Department of Justice: The Federal Bureau of Investigation

Prior to the 1960s, the Federal Bureau of Investigation (FBI) regarded organized crime as a local police problem involving independent gangs of hoodlums and beyond the mandate of the Bureau. The well-chronicled embarrassment of the Apalachin Conference in 1957, in which New York State troopers discovered the meeting of dozens of national mob leaders in upstate New York, forced J. Edgar Hoover to bring the FBI into the organized crime maelstrom. Hoover intensified agency involvement in mob investigations beginning with the Top Hoodlum program, which required each FBI field office to identify the 10 major mob figures in its area and closely monitor their activities. The primary goal of the program was to gather information about organized figures, not necessarily to arrest and prosecute them. Having denied the existence of organized crime for so long during the 1950s, it was time to play catch-up on the intelligence front. Just as it had in its earlier security operations, the FBI resorted to electronic bugs and wiretaps without warrants. Although the evidence was inadmissible in court, the FBI went ahead with it anyway. The Chicago field office was one of the first to use bugs in the Top Hoodlum Program. In 1959, investigators placed a bug in one of the Outfit's meeting places, and over a 5-year period delivered a wealth of information about organized crime in Chicago and elsewhere. Its success led other FBI field offices to adopt this technique as well. In the end, the program produced few results, in no small part because the FBI lacked resources and any real interest in conducting a war on organized crime. When Robert F. Kennedy became attorney general in the early 1960s, this changed, as he successfully lobbied Congress to expand federal efforts in this direction. However, it would take the death of Director Hoover in 1972 to energize the Bureau and free up the required sources in the fight against organized crime.

In 1978, the FBI took part in one of the modern era's most massive attacks against mob-controlled enterprises. The investigation dubbed *UNIRAC* investigated the Longshoremen's Association on East Coast and other labor unions, construction companies, restaurants, and mobbed-up industries resulting in the indictments of 22 labor union indictments in Miami for kickbacks, embezzling, and other schemes. Among those convicted was Longshoremen's Union leader and organized crime figure Anthony M. Scotto. Two years later, the operation code-named *BRILAB* directed by New Orleans Strike Force with the help of the FBI led to political corruption and bribery indictments of New Orleans boss Carlos Marcello and others. In one of its most lengthy organized crime investigations, known as the "Pizza Connection," beginning in 1984, FBI agents documented the international connections of organized crime syndicates in the United States and their use of pizza parlors as a front for laundering heroin money. In 1987, 18 organized crime figures, including a leading Sicilian crime boss, Gaetano Badalamenti, were convicted for their roles in the heroin ring.

Joseph D. Pistone (b. 1939): AKA Donnie Brasco

The grandson of Italian immigrants, Pistone joined the FBI in 1969 and worked in the Jacksonville, Florida, and Alexandria, Virginia, field offices. At the Quantico FBI Academy, he was trained in undercover work. In 1974, he was assigned to the New York City office, where he was selected to infiltrate the Mafia as deep-cover agent Donnie Brasco—an assignment that lasted almost 6 years (1976–1981). It was the most successful infiltration of a mob family by a government agent. Posing as a jewel thief and a con man, he became an associate of the Bonanno crime family. A natural at playing a tough guy, he won the trust of a growing number of Cosa Nostra figures from Milwaukee (the Balistrieri family) to the Chicago Outfit and Florida's Trafficante family. Brasco was eventually put up for membership, but first had to complete a murder contract, something the federal government prohibited. Fearing for his life, the FBI pulled Pistone out in 1981 (as well as the murder target). Over the next several years, Pistone participated in mob trials throughout the country. Despite the 1970 RICO statute, officials did not really figure out how to use it until the Pistone investigations of the Bonanno family. Revelations from his investigation sent more than 100 mobsters to prison. A $500,000 contract was put on his head. He resigned from the FBI in 1986, and 2 years later he published *Donnie Brasco: My Undercover Life in the Mafia.* He decided not to enter WITSEC, preferring to change his family's name and move far from New York City. The 1997 film *Donnie Brasco,* starring Johnny Depp, is said to depart somewhat from the real story only when the FBI agent was portrayed as assuming the morality and sensibility of a mobster, something that Pistone has denied ever took place.

Department of the Treasury: Internal Revenue Service

The Internal Revenue Service (IRS) employs more than 100,000 people. However, when it comes to investigating organized crime activities such as money-laundering, the investigation is handed over to IRS–Criminal Intelligence (CI). Today, it has almost 2,900 agents, a steep decline from its 3,744 in 1996 (due to the budgeting crunch). The IRS has long been one of the unsung heroes in the crusade against organized crime. Its CI unit was established in 1919 and was involved in its first narcotics investigation (of an opium trafficker in Hawaii) at the beginning of the 1920s, resulting in tax evasion charges against the organization's leader. Financial investigations have usually been at the root of many complex investigations—tax evasion, health care fraud, and drug-trafficking cases—all crimes that revolve around money. No investigation was as heralded as its case against Public Enemy Number 1, Al Capone, in the 1930s. The IRS-CI has sole jurisdiction over criminal violations of the Internal Revenue Code (IRC). Asset forfeiture proved to be one of its most effective tools against organized crime, drug trafficking, and money-laundering. It wasn't until the 1960s that investigators started carrying guns, which signaled a shift toward the role of criminal investigators as they made the transition from focusing exclusively on "pure tax crime" to investigating organized crime, hunting drug traffickers, and investigating money-laundering. In times past, the IRS would have handed over many of these cases to the Department of Justice, but by the late 1990s, the IRS was more likely to turn the cases over to CI, as it became more adept at handling "street law enforcement action, [meaning] making arrests, executing search warrants, and participating in raids" (Foster 1998).

Net Worth Method

The IRS developed several methods of proving a taxpayer had received income even though it had no direct evidence of this income. These "indirect methods" of establishing income are used to prove criminals had received income illegally and present this information at trial. It is considered very convincing to a jury when prosecutors can show how an alleged drug kingpin purchased a mansion and a Ferrari without being employed. Several methods have been used to prove income came from criminal sources. The net worth method is the best known method. According to one expert, "every criminal case against a major organized crime figure routinely involves a net worth investigation of his income, assets and expenditures" (Kelly 1999, 204–205). The concept of net worth hinges on a rather simple formula—the difference between a person's assets and liabilities; in other words, the investigator seeks to ascertain significant differences between legal income and actual expenditures. You basically take what a person owns, subtract what the person owes, and you have the figure of what that person is worth. A net worth case begins with the identification of the subject's assets, liabilities, and living expenses. One can usually find a paper trail that provides the financial information needed—loan applications, real estate records, court records, financial statements, credit card information, employment records, and so forth.

U.S. v. Alphonse Capone

The career of Al Capone is well-chronicled in Chapter 5. However, it is instructive to observe how the IRS created its case against him, especially when no other law enforcement entity had been able to do so. In the course of the Capone case, investigators searched over more than 2 million separate records, hunting for documents that could be used to convict him. The intention was to prove that Capone had income between 1924 and 1929 but paid no taxes on it. The problem for lead investigator Frank Wilson was proving this to a jury.

As Summer 1930 loomed on the horizon, investigators had already pored through half the records, including many seized from the Capone organization. Although they had identified plenty of his expenditures, they had yet to find any proof of income. Surveillance teams and informants did little better at linking Capone to illegal income.

Throughout the late 1920s, a number of ledgers and records documenting the businesses of the Capone organization had been seized in police raids. These records provided damaging evidence concerning Capone's consortium of brothels, gambling joints, and liquor manufacturing plants. It wasn't until Wilson began looking through some of these documents in 1930 that he came across a ledger in a disused file cabinet. In that ledger, Wilson found notations describing a gambling operation that posted net profits of more than $500,000 in an 18-month period. More important, were references of payments to "Al."

Wilson was well aware of Capone's caution when it came to bookkeeping. He knew Capone never signed anything, had no bank accounts, nor a single parcel of property titled in his name. He was also known to use aliases in his various transactions to conceal his involvement. All of his financial acquisitions were made by his trusted inner circle and family members. His Miami mansion and home in Chicago were titled in his wife's name. Investigators faced two barriers. Capone had managed to bribe, threaten, or permanently silence most of the witnesses who could have been used in the net worth case that Wilson was constructing. Second, they had literally "too much evidence" to examine; still, a witness was needed. That man turned out to be one of Capone's bookkeepers, who had been hiding out in Miami. Finally after a 3-year investigation, the case against Capone was ready for trial.

Capone thought that he had the requisite amount of insurance after bribing the entire list of prospective jurors. The trial took place during 4 days in October 1931. Capone must have been apoplectic when he found out that the judge switched the jury pool at the last minute. A procession of witnesses testified to Capone's lavish spending. The government ultimately proved that between 1924 and 1929, Capone netted more than $1 million, which should have paid about $215,000 in income tax. On October 17, 1931, the untainted jury returned with a guilty verdict after 8 hours. Capone's ride at the top of the Chicago underworld lasted 6 years. Just 1 week after his conviction, he was sentenced to 11 years in a federal penitentiary, effectively ending the career of one of America's most legendary organized crime figures. He would never have to answer for the dozens if not hundreds of murders that went unsolved during his years as crime boss. If there is a lesson here, it is, "Pay your taxes." More than 70 years later, the IRS continues use similar investigative techniques, a combination of financial sleuthing, informants, and other traditional investigative techniques (Spiering 1976; Madinger 2006; Russo 2001).

Frank J. Wilson (1887–1970)

Frank Wilson joined the Treasury Department's Intelligence Unit soon after its inception in 1920, and over the next three decades he became one of its most formidable investigators. In 1930, he was selected by the head of the Intelligence Unit, Elmer Irey, to build a tax evasion case against Al Capone. During the next year, he uncovered a paper trail that exposed the sources of Capone's illicit fortune; more important, Capone had never paid taxes on these profits. In October 1931, Capone was indicted on income tax evasion of more than $215,000, leading to his conviction and imprisonment shortly after. Sentenced to 11 years, Capone was released in 1940 suffering from the effects of syphilis. In 1932, Wilson made headlines once again during his investigation of serial numbers on ransom money related to the Lindbergh kidnapping case. In 1936, he was selected to lead the Secret Service, the Treasury Department's leading police agency. He retired in 1947 (Spiering 1976).

Department of Justice: U.S. Drug Enforcement Administration

The origins of the U.S. Drug Enforcement Administration (DEA) can be traced back to the early 20th century, when the federal government began to institute gradual restrictions on dangerous drugs such as heroin and cocaine. In 1915, just a year after the passage of the Harrison Narcotics Act, drug law enforcement was placed in the hands of the Bureau of Internal Revenue. During the 1920s, the association of the Narcotics Division with the Prohibition Bureau led to public disenchantment with the bureau, in part because of the unpopularity of Prohibition as well as the ineptitude of its enforcement. At the inauguration of Prohibition in 1920, the Narcotics Division of the Prohibition Unit of the Revenue Bureau consisted of 170 agents and 17 offices. In 1922, the drug agents saw their power expanded with the passage of the Narcotic Drugs Import and Export Act. Following a scandal in which drug agents were arrested for taking payoffs from drug dealers, Congress established the Bureau of Narcotics in 1930, removing drug enforcement from the Prohibition Bureau and creating a separate agency in the Treasury Department—the forerunner of today's Drug Enforcement Administration, the Federal Bureau of Narcotics (FBN). Initially, its powers were limited; in fact, in the 1930s, few states had any drug control laws. However, with the emergence of the new federal bureau, the states followed with their own legislation. The next year, every state had introduced laws to restrict the sale of cocaine (and most to restrict opiates). However, drug enforcement was hampered by the lack of uniformity in state statutes and weakness of law enforcement strategies.

Harry Anslinger (1892–1975) was the first commissioner of the bureau (he retired in 1962). Anslinger was the architect of what became a get-tough policy against drug abusers and led the crusade against marijuana that culminated in the Marijuana Tax Act in 1937. During World War II, he made unsubstantiated claims that the Japanese were using an "opium offensive" as part of a strategy to enslave conquered nations through drug trafficking. Alarmed at this prospect, the U.S. government granted him access to the Coast Guard, the U.S. Customs Service, and the Internal Revenue Service in the crusade against the narcotics trade (Roth 2005).

Although there were some similarities with the much larger and powerful FBI, they were mostly superficial. Particularly distinctive were the agents themselves. Although FBI agents were typically cast of WASP stock with "middle American" backgrounds, by contrast, FBN agents were just as likely to be drawn from urban ethnic communities, boasting Black and Asian agents long before the FBI. Tactics distinguished the two as well, with the FBI more likely to chase after traditional criminals with traditional tactics; FBN agents, or *narcs,* were often assigned undercover investigations, something Hoover particularly disdained, fearing the corruptive influence of consorting with criminals. It should not be surprising that the FBN was chasing after organized crime syndicates years before they registered on Hoover's radar screen following Apalachin in 1957 (Reppetto 2004; Valentine 2004).

Buy-and-Busts and the Mafia Book

Recent evidence asserts that the FBN never had more than five informers in the Mafia as they tried to make heroin cases against mob bosses in the 1940s and 1950s. One of the barriers to creating informers was the fact that most of them were acquired "through the plodding process of 'two buys and a bust'; two buys being required by law to transcend entrapment and prove intent" (Valentine, 2004, 82), an arduous process if there ever was one. Although FBN attempts to find addicts who might help snare discontented Mafioso failed to reveal any great international drug conspiracies, it did result in the most comprehensive record of biographic data on Mafia members ever recorded. Eventually, the "two-buys-and-a-bust" strategy paid off. Enough information was collected from these busts that an astonishing amount of data on drug traffickers in the United States and abroad was compiled in several volumes. A two-volume leather-bound blacklist was divided into a dark brown *National List* containing the names and records of all domestic violators; their foreign counterparts were listed in the burgundy *International List*. The books were published by the Treasury Department and handed out to FBN operatives. However, it was a separate Mafia Book that specifically covered known Mafia members and associates that was the crown jewel of the FBN archive. Together, the books offered encyclopedic insight into the aliases, associates, and methods of operation of almost 800 drug traffickers. According to the leading expert on the FBN, this rogues' gallery was the first organizational chart of the underworld. It showed relationships that revealed corporate veils, and offshore businesses and bank accounts. Moreover, by enabling federal agents to check the passenger lists of ocean liners and merchant vessels for known smugglers, it sometimes allowed them to anticipate deliveries and make significant seizures. Best of all, the book impressed politicians. By 1950, the FBN had made good use of its blacklists, stable of informers and contacts in law enforcement around the world, allowing them "to put more bodies in prison than any other federal agency" (Valentine 2004, 82). In 2007, Harper and Collins published a facsimile copy of the original Mafia Book with an introduction by the son of Chicago Outfit boss Sam Giancana.

Although the recreational use of marijuana was made illegal, it did not become much of an issue until the 1960s and the explosion of the counterculture, leading to a vociferous anti-drug lobby. In 1973, the DEA was created, resulting in the merger of several agencies. As a branch of the Department of Justice, the DEA was given the single mission of enforcing (the unenforceable) federal drug statutes and investigating major drug traffickers. Today, the DEA has 19 field offices located in cities across the United States, as well as offices in close to 50 countries. Its staff has grown from 1,470 at its inception to more than 5,000 today. Its expanded responsibilities have led the DEA into investigations involving money-laundering, drug trafficking, terrorism, as well as collaboration with other law enforcement agencies in a variety of capacities (see Chapter 6 concerning Prohibition).

Interagency Cooperation

State, local, and federal law enforcement have historically been embroiled in turf battles and other rivalries that have severely curtailed their success in the war against organized crime (and other targets). At the center of each controversy is typically the question as to who or which office will investigate, arrest, and prosecute. As one authority on task forces noted, "The potential for conflict is born of the very nature of criminal activity; much of it transcends jurisdictional boundaries" (Kelly 1994, 348).

ORGANIZED CRIME STRIKE TASK FORCES (1967) Since the 1960s, a number of joint task forces have targeted organized crime with varying levels of success. The task force concept is intended to unify anti-crime operations across the entire United States, combining the efforts of any mixture of federal, state, and local law enforcement agencies. Over the years, there have been bank robbery task forces that focused on major theft, joint terrorism task forces that focused on violent fugitives, and Safe Street Task forces that focused on violent street gangs.

In 1970, the former Attorney General under Lyndon Johnson, Ramsey Clark, was of the opinion that the Organized Crime Strike Task Forces had exceeded their expectations and that more federal indictments were returned against organized crime figures in a few months than in preceding decades. Each strike force obtained more indictments in its target city than all federal indictments in the nation against organized crime in as recent a year as 1960 (Clark 1972, 63).

The first federal Organized Crime Strike Task Force was inaugurated in Buffalo, New York, in 1967, targeting the Magaddino crime family. This task force was composed of agents from 11 different federal agencies including the FBI; DEA; IRS; Customs; U.S. Marshals; U.S. Postal Services; the Secret Service; Labor Department; the Bureau of Alcohol, Tobacco, and Firearms (BATF); the Security and Exchange Commission (SEC); and the Immigration and Naturalization Service (INS). This model was put to use in 18 cities over the next 4 years. By 1976, strike forces were operating in Boston, Brooklyn, Buffalo, Chicago, Cleveland, Detroit, Kansas City, Los Angeles, Miami, Newark, Philadelphia, San Francisco, and Washington, D.C.

Targeting the hierarchy of the Buffalo crime family (known as "the Arm"), the strike force concept was initially viewed as a successful strategy. By going after the mob leaders, it was hoped this would incapacitate the criminal operations of organized crime groups across the nation. Early on, investigations were inaugurated by one of the participating agencies in the local task force. This would be followed with an indictment and prosecution. However, by 1983, almost 80% of the case initiations resulted not from local members, but by federal investigators from the BATF, DEA, FBI, and the IRS. By most accounts the task force structure was successful due to its ability "to place prosecutorial resources across jurisdictional boundaries" eliminating some of the turf battles that had blocked previous law enforcement efforts (Ryan, 1994; Jacobs, Panarella, and Worthington, 1998).

A number of criticism were leveled at the task forces in the late 1970s and early 1980s, including their inability to define organized crime, for chasing after low priority targets, and for lacking the authority to control the investigative agencies which they depended on (Jacobs, Panarella, and Worthington, 1994, 14). By the end of the 1980s, Attorney General Edwin Meese had developed a plan to get rid of the strike forces "because their investigations were autonomous and competed with the activities of local U.S. attorneys in the 94 federal judicial districts across the country" and by 1990 the strike forces had disappeared, subsumed into the offices of U.S. attorneys (Ryan, 1994).

The New York State Organized Crime Task Force

The operations of New York's Organized Crime Task Force (OCTF) demonstrated how a small agency was sometimes better suited than a large bureaucracy to develop innovative crime-fighting strategies. Created in 1970, it had some limited successes early on but by the end of the 1970s was essentially on life support. It was reorganized in 1981 with headquarters in White Plains and field offices in Buffalo and Albany. According to one leading authority, "Unlike the U.S. Attorney's Offices and the New York City District Attorney's Offices, after its restructuring the OCTF became a hybrid investigative and prosecutorial agency" (Jacobs 1999, 6). OCTF had state-wide jurisdiction and can carry out investigations. In addition with the consent of the local district attorney can bring state-court prosecutions anywhere in New York. For most of its history the OCTF operated unfettered by federal, state, and local law enforcement agencies. However, this is not to say that it was able to win victories without cooperation from various federal and local investigative and prosecutorial offices. According to James B. Jacobs OCTF, "made an enormous contribution by reconceptualizing organized crime investigation along the lines suggested by Blakey [creator of RICO]" (1996, 133). Over the next 15 years the OCTF reached its apogee, employing some 140 attorneys, investigators, analysts, and accountants as well as other staff (Raab 2005). However, after the September 11, 2001, attacks, organized crime took a backseat to terrorism, and the staff was gradually reduced by almost two thirds. In quick succession, the agency was stripped of its autonomy and "folded into the state attorney general's office" without a separate budget and often reduced to working investigations unrelated to organized crime (Raab 2005, 698).

Somerset County, New Jersey, Organized Crime and Narcotics Task Force

Formed with the goal of upholding New Jersey's narcotic, gambling, and racketeering laws, this task force employs a variety of investigative techniques including undercover and surface interventions, physical and electronic surveillance, search warrant executions and a number of information gather strategies. Its members are full-time detectives from the Somerset County Prosecutor's Office as well as police officers assigned by city police departments and the sheriff's office on a rotating basis. It also employs two assistant prosecutors as full-time legal advisors. The task force works closely with other state and federal law enforcement agencies and its efforts have paid off with the arrest of a number of suspects involved in mid-to-high-level drug distribution networks. In 2002 and 2003, Operations "Greenhouse," "Villagers," "Spring Clean-Up II," and "Trap Door" were among the most prominent cases.

ORGANIZED CRIME DRUG ENFORCEMENT TASK FORCE The Organized Crime Drug Enforcement Task Force (OCDETF) Program was created in 1982 as a federal drug enforcement program under the aegis of the Attorney General and the Department of Justice. Its primary tasks are disrupting major drug trafficking networks and solving related crimes including money-laundering, tax and weapon violations, and violent crimes. Today, almost 2,500 agents work for the force. Structurally it combines the resources and skills of other federal agencies including the FBI, ICE, BATF, the U.S. Marshals Service, the IRS, and the U.S. Coast Guard. OCDETF is considered the Attorney general's "centerpiece" in his drug supply reduction strategy. The program's stated purpose is to focus its resources "on coordinated, nationwide investigations, targeting the entire infrastructure of major drug trafficking" operations (DEA Programs, Organized Crime Drug Enforcement Task Force, 2008). It also assisted in the development of the Attorney General's Consolidated Priority Organization Target (CPOT) list, a unified agency target list of international "command and control" drug traffickers and money launderers. Since its inception, its operations as of 2006 have led to more than 44,000 drug-related convictions and the seizure of more than $3 billion in cash and property assets. Each of the nation's 93 judicial districts is placed into one of 9 OCDETF regions based on geographic location. A core city is designated within each region (see box below).

International Organizations

In an era of global organized crime groups and terrorists, international law enforcement cooperation is of manifest importance. Europe has developed a variety of cooperative schemes over the years, with Interpol and Europol being the most prominent. Transnational criminal matters have stimu-

OCDETF Regions

Task Force Region	Core City
New England	Boston
New York/New Jersey	New York City
Mid-Atlantic	Baltimore
Great Lakes	Chicago
Southeast	Atlanta
West Central	St. Louis
Florida/Caribbean	Miami
Southwest	Houston
Pacific	San Francisco

lated cooperation between international police agencies for over a century. However, it was only in the years following World War I that a true organization apparatus was created to further police cooperation between foreign countries with the creation of Interpol.

INTERPOL Founded in Vienna in 1923, the International Criminal Police Organization, or Interpol, was disbanded in 1938 and then resuscitated after World War II in 1946. In 1956, *Interpol* was adopted as its formal name and has since become synonymous with international police cooperation and investigation. With more than 185 members, today it is second only to the United Nations as an international organization. It helps introduce, coordinate, and cooperate in helping law enforcement officials from different police forces and countries work together to solve transnational crimes. However, because it is an international organization, its charter prohibits employees to engage in any investigation or coordination of a political, military, religious, or racial character. More recently, its focus is directed toward terrorism, organized crime, drug trafficking, human smuggling and trafficking, money-laundering, corruption, and financial and hi-tech crime. Located in Lyons, France, the organization operates simultaneously in English, French, Spanish, and Arabic; it receives, and stores, analyzes, and disseminates criminal intelligence 24 hours a day, 7 days a week, making it the single largest international criminal database in the world.

EUROPOL Based on the Interpol model, the European Police Office, better known as Europol,[14] was established in the Maastricht Treaty on European Union in 1992, mainly as a response to problems of European transnational crime. Situated in The Hague, The Netherlands, it initially focused on the illegal drug trade, but in 1994, its mandate was enlarged to prevent trafficking in nuclear and radioactive substances, money-laundering, immigrant smuggling and trafficking, and motor vehicle theft. In July 1996, European member states ratified Europol. Europol's main objective was to improve police cooperation between member states to combat terrorism and serious forms of international crime. Each member state is expected to establish its own national unit tasked with facilitating the exchange of information and aiding investigations among member states. They are also responsible for maintaining a computerized system of collected information and to obtain, collate, and analyze information and intelligence. Like Interpol, its agents have no powers of arrest, although members have been allowed to participate in operations.

BARRIERS TO INTERNATIONAL POLICE COOPERATION In the current post-industrial era, with new conceptions of policing, and with national boundaries often less marked and clear, there is need more than ever for police organizations to cooperate. First steps have already been taken to form bilateral and multilateral agreements, such as Europe's Schengen Agreement. Organized

The Budapest Project (2000)

Innovative approaches to cooperative law enforcement have had mixed results. However, one recent program has resulted in a number of successes. In April 2000, the FBI–Hungarian National Police Organized Crime Task Force was created in Budapest, Hungary. Its declared focus was to investigate and dismantle organized crime groups that had begun to headquarter in Central Europe after the fall of communism. Budapest proved particularly attractive to eastern European crime syndicates due to its sophisticated banking system and high standards of living. One of the task force's first major successes saw Ukrainian-born crime kingpin Semion Mogilevich flee from Budapest back to Moscow, one step ahead of Philadelphia organized crime strike force indictments charging him and three others with money-laundering, securities fraud, and RICO conspiracy. In the initial stages of the Budapest Project, four FBI agents worked together with seven elite officers from the Hungarian National Police. It is now considered the most elite investigative unit in Hungary (FBI, October 31, 2003).

criminal activities that transcend national borders create numerous problems and challenges for law enforcement. Among the most recurrent challenges are the following:

- *Language differences* can be a barrier to effective communication and can discourage or interfere with conducting a timely interrogation or translation of documents.
- *Respect customs and national sovereignty* with proper sensitivity toward differences in religion, ethnicity, ideology, cultural uniqueness, customs and culture, and national and political history.
- *Governmental and police corruption*
- *Regional conflict and civil war* causes refugee crises that can present excellent cover for the movement of crime syndicates and diverts law enforcement sources from performing in its traditional capacities.
- *Police organizational culture* varies in rank and decision making, varying procedures, and types of centralization; police officials must know who their counterparts are in unfamiliar countries.
- *Inter-organizational coordination* is often hampered by competing objectives, a lack of agreements on institutional objectives, and poor coordination between the public and private sectors.
- *Variation among legal traditions* (e.g., civil, common, Islamic, and socialist law)
- *Technological disparities* between developed and developing countries often interferes with proper interaction between police services.
- *Variation of time zones* may not allow timely response from all countries.
- *Fiscal limitations and financial barriers*
- *Traditional privacy regulations*
- *Porous border controls*
- *Geographic barriers such as long coastlines and mountain ranges*
- *Different political systems*
- *Variations in information sharing*
- *Political instability and ungoverned territory*
- *Sharing intelligence* has long been the Achilles' heel of international policing (Roth and Sever 2007).

INTERNATIONAL FORFEITURE COOPERATION   The increasingly international character of organized crime syndicates has obviated against a number domestic organized crime measures designed to control this type of crime at home. Because most major organized crime groups operate across national borders, it has been necessary to expand efforts and legislation to take the profit out of these illegal enterprises. Toward the end of the 1990s, the Department of Justice placed the development of international forfeiture cooperation among its highest priorities (Viano 1999, 196). Mirroring the importance of sharing forfeited wealth among domestic law enforcement agencies is the attempt to accomplish on an international basis. Several bilateral and multi-lateral agreements providing mutual forfeiture on an international basis were ratified in the 1990s. For example, the United States was involved in mutual assistance treaties with 22 jurisdictions ranging from the Caribbean and Mexico to Morocco, Philippines, Italy, Spain, Switzerland, Thailand, and Uruguay. It is hoped that with time these agreements will lead to the standardization of international forfeiture cooperation. Among the more promising developments was Article V of the Vienna Convention (The United Nations Convention Against Illicit Traffic in Narcotic Drugs and Psychotropic Substance), which listed the obligations of the parties seeking forfeiture of funds and instrumentalities from drug traffickers and money launderers; each signatory was expected to enact laws with domestic and international application (Viano 1999, 197).

THE LAW ENFORCEMENT STRATEGY TO COMBAT INTERNATIONAL ORGANIZED CRIME (2008)   In response to a 2007 International Organized Crime (IOC) Threat Assessment, a new federal strategy was announced, called the Law Enforcement Strategy to Combat International

Organized Crime. The strategy entailed a comprehensive detailed plan that enables the Department of Justice and nine federal law enforcement agencies to gather their collective resources to most effectively fight international organized crime. The IOC Threat Assessment identified and defined eight strategic threats. International organized criminals

- have penetrated the energy market and other strategic sectors of the U.S. and world economy. As U.S. energy needs continue to grow, so too should the power of those who control energy resources.
- provide logistical and other support to terrorists, foreign intelligence services, and foreign governments, all with interests adverse to those of U.S. national security.
- traffic in people and contraband goods, bringing people and products through U.S. borders to the detriment of border security.
- exploit the U.S. and international financial system to move illegal profits and funds, including billions in illicit funds through the U.S. financial system annually. To continue this practice, they seek to corrupt financial service providers worldwide.
- use cyberspace to target U.S. victims and infrastructure, jeopardizing the security of personal information, the stability of business and government infrastructures and the security and solvency of financial investment markets.
- are manipulating securities exchanges and engaging in sophisticated fraud schemes that rob U.S. investors, consumers, and government agencies of billions of dollars.
- have successfully corrupted public officials around the world, including countries of vital strategic importance to the United States and continue to seek ways to influence—legally or illegally—U.S. officials.
- use violence and the threat of violence as a basis of power. (Adapted from Kouri, 2008).

Overview

The RICO statute and related legislation has been so effective against American organized crime groups that authorities in Canada, Italy, and other countries have followed it with similar laws intended to fight organized crime. With most of America's traditional crime families destabilized and decapitated, RICO attention has turned to the newer incarnations of organized crime in America, a trend that has been in the making since the mid-1970s. For example, in 2004, ICE, under the Department of Homeland Security, charged two Chinese organized crime groups with multiple offenses. According to indictments, 51 defendants were charged with wide-ranging criminal activity, including RICO offenses, attempted murder, conspiracy to commit murder, extortion, conspiracy to commit extortion, alien smuggling, conspiracy to commit alien smuggling, conspiracy to take hostages, extortionate debt collection, conspiracy to use extortionate means to collect extensions of credit, money-laundering, trafficking in counterfeit goods, and the operation of large-scale illegal gambling businesses. Furthermore, the indictments sought a total of $11 million in forfeiture from the 16 defendants charged with RICO offenses. The indictments were the result of coordinated investigations during a 2-year period by ICE, the FBI, and the New York Police Department (http://usinfo.org/, 2004).

In late April 2008, U.S. Attorney General Michael B. Mukasey turned his attention from the "War on Terrorism" to the almost forgotten "War on Organized Crime." This was the first time the Organized Crime Council[15] ever convened to focus on the threat of international organized crime (Kouri 2008). The Organized Crime Council existed in various forms since 1970, and has usually been involved in establishing priorities and formulating a national unified strategy to combat organized crime. Except for the PATRIOT act and other legislation focused on terrorism (sometimes as a form of organized crime), most discussion of organized crime had dropped off the front pages of American newspapers. The late Attorney General Robert Kennedy would have probably been pleased to hear Mukasey rail against the rising threat from international organized crime, asserting, "a new breed of mobsters around the world was infiltrating strategic industries, providing logistical support to terrorists and becoming capable of 'creating havoc in our economic infrastructure'" (Schmitt 2008).

Key Terms

Prosecutor's toolbox
"Mafia myth"
Anti-racketeering Act of 1934
Hobbs Act
Rackets
Conspiracy laws
Wheel conspiracy
Chain conspiracy
Enterprise conspiracy
Organized Crime Control Act
RICO
G. Robert Blakey
Pattern of racketeering
Civil RICO
Trusteeships
Consent decrees
Witness Security Program
U.S. v. Salerno

U.S. Marshals Service
Joseph Bonanno
Grand juries
Double jeopardy
Civil contempt
Criminal contempt
Use and transactional immunity
Forfeiture
USA PATRIOT act
Wiretapping
Olmstead v. U.S.
Katz v. U.S.
Title III
Informants
Supergrasses
Department of Homeland Security
ICE
U.S. Secret Service

Department of Justice
FBI
Donnie Brasco
Department of Treasury
IRS
Net worth method
U.S. v. Alphonse Capone
Frank Wilson
DEA
FBN
Harry Anslinger
Buy and busts
OC Strike Task Forces
Interpol
Europol
OC Drug Enforcement Task Force

Critical Thinking Questions

1. When did law enforcement first target organized crime?
2. How successful were federal, state, and local organized crime initiatives prior to the 1980s?
3. What is a *conspiracy,* and what does it have to do with organized crime activity?
4. What was the purpose of the Hobbs Act? What is the legacy of this act from a modern perspective?
5. What are the differences among *wheel, chain,* and *enterprise* conspiracies?
6. What is the Organized Crime Control Act? What has been its impact on organized crime?
7. What is RICO? Why has it been so successful? What are the controversies surrounding this statute?
8. What is a *pattern of racketeering,* and what does it have to do with organized crime?
9. What is the difference between civil RICO and criminal RICO suits?
10. What is the Witness Security Program? Discuss its evolution and use.
11. What was the importance of the Commission Case, *U.S. v. Salerno*?

12. What do grand juries do? What happens if one refuses to appear before the grand jury?
13. What role do immunity, contempt, and forfeiture play in organized crime cases? What is the difference between civil and criminal forfeiture and contempt statutes?
14. What role does the USA PATRIOT act play in the war against organized crime? Contrast and compare RICO with the PATRIOT act.
15. Discuss the evolution of electronic surveillance in America as well as the laws surrounding its use. Has wiretapping been an important tool against organized crime?
16. What federal agencies are most involved in fighting organized crime? What is the role played by their major organizations, such as the FBI and DEA?
17. Discuss the various organized crime task force programs.
18. What are the major barriers to police cooperation in the battle against international organized crime syndicates?

Endnotes

1. *Robbery,* as defined by Hobbs, meant

   the unlawful taking or obtaining of personal property from the person or in the presence of another, against his will, by means of actual or threatened force, or violence, or fear of injury, immediate or future, to his person or property, or property in his custody or possession, or the person or property of a relative or member of his family or of anyone in his company at the time of the taking or obtaining. [18 U.S.C. 1951 (1948)]

2. According to Hobbs, the term *extortion* means "the obtaining of property from another, with his consent, induced by wrongful use of actual or threatened force, violence or fear" [18 U.S.C. 1951 (1948)].

3. See testimony in *Organized Crime in America* hearings, 98th Cong., 1st Sess., 1983, pp. 19–20.

4. *United States v. Turkette* (1981) established that it could apply to illegal groups.

5. *Multiplicity* refers to the charging of a single offense in several counts; as opposed to *duplicity,* which refers to "the joining of a single count of two or more distinct and separate offenses" (Atkinson 1978, 69, n. 60).

6. There is actually some debate about his relationship with Brooklier. Some sources suggest that he had actually named Fratianno acting boss while he was in jail, and that when he found out he had used this opportunity to make profitable deals for associates outside Los Angeles, Brooklier placed a contract on him (Earley and Shur 2002, 153–155).

7. It must be remembered that the 5th Amendment had not yet been applied to the states by the Supreme Court, and that decisions involving immunity referred only to federal immunity statutes. Each state was therefore free to adopt its own version of *compelled testimony.*

8. Some jurisdictions use the term *confiscation.*

9. This refers to U.S. Customs form 4790, "Report of International Transportation of Currency or Other Monetary Instruments" in an aggregate amount exceeding $10,000 at any one time into or out of the United States.

10. USA PATRIOT act is the acronym for "Uniting and Strengthening America by Providing Appropriate Tools Required to Intercept and Obstruct Terrorism Act.

11. Many observers trace these practices back to the Foreign Intelligence Surveillance Act established by Congress under President Jimmy Carter in 1978.

12. President Franklin Roosevelt privately concluded that this limitation did not apply to national defense investigations, and in 1940 secretly authorized the FBI to wiretap individuals suspected of subversive activities against the United States.

13. See, for example, *United States v. Gotti* and the Pizza Connection case.

14. TREVI was the acknowledged forerunner to Europol, but unlike its current incarnation, the former was without a headquarters, budget, secretariat, and permanent staff, but simply revolved around a system of confidential meetings in which top European police officers shared experiences and information, in the process enhancing cooperation between various European police forces. Ultimately, the creation of Europol led to the dissolution of TREVI.

15. It consists of the Deputy Attorney General, the Assistant Attorney General for the Criminal Division, and the leaders of nine participating federal agencies.

CHAPTER 15

Organized Crime in a High-Tech World

Virtually every new technology has "created a new crime alongside it" (McCusker 2006, 260). Since the advent of the optical telegraph in 1794 and its electrical ancestor some 50 years later, criminals have managed to keep abreast of the latest innovations in technology. In many cases they grasped these advantages before the law enforcement community, which has been playing catch-up ever since. In 1888, one Chicago policeman remarked, "It is a well-known fact that no other section of the population avail them more readily and speedily of the latest triumphs of science than the criminal class" (quoted in Standage 1999, 105).

In the 1830s, stock market information was already being transmitted by optical telegraphs in France. Soon after, several French bankers bribed telegraph operators "to introduce deliberate but recognizable errors into the transmission of stock market information" (Standage, 1999, 106–107) that would signal whether the stock market in Paris had gone up or down that day. According to Standage, "By observing the arms of the telegraph from a safe distance as they made what appeared to everyone else to be nothing more than occasional mistakes, the bankers could gain advance information about the state of the market without the risk of being seen to be associating with their accomplices" (1999, 106–107). It operated for 2 years before the scheme unraveled in 1836.

Communication and the transfer of information could travel only as fast as a horse, ship, or train could take it prior to the advent of the telegraph. Its arrival removed most distance barriers and offered criminally minded schemers an "information imbalance," allowing them to exploit "situations where financial advantage can be gained in one place from exclusive ownership of privileged information that is widely known in another place" (Standage, 1999, 106–107). Nothing exemplifies this better than modern horse racing, where the result of the race is known at the racetrack as soon as it declared. Before the invention of telegraph, information could take hours, even days, to reach bookmakers in other parts of the country. Anyone with results before it reached bookies could place a guaranteed bet on winning horse. Almost from the beginning, rules were passed prohibiting this type of information from being relayed by telegraph, but "criminals tended to be one step ahead of rule makers" (Standage 1999, 106–107).

In the 1960s the invention of the *blue box* became a money maker for the high-tech criminals of the era. This tone-generating device signaled telephone company equipment that a call had ended, when in reality, the call had actually continued and the user was not billed for the added time. Over the years other refinements to this telephone fraud gave rise to a *black box* that emitted an electronic signal that a call did not go through, although it had; and then a *red box* that simulated the sound of coins being loaded into a pay phone. These devices are regarded as the precursors to devices used by modern hackers, or *phreakers* who have employed schemes to defraud telephone companies around the world out of millions of dollars (Newton 2004).

Cyberspace has become a busier and more dangerous place since the early 1980s. During that time, the information and communication technologies (ICT) have become central to the lives of people around the world. Between 1999 and 2005, Internet users tripled from 300 million to almost 900 million. By the end of 2005, there were almost 200 million cellular subscribers in the United States alone (Grabosky 2007). Concomitant with societies becoming increasingly dependent on the Internet are the potential threats from *cybercriminals* who commit crimes with the anonymity of the Internet. In 2004, the main source countries of computer-driven attacks began with the United States, followed in descending order China, Canada, Australia, Germany, the United Kingdom, and France.

Organized crime has shown a remarkable ability over the years to adapt and utilize new opportunities and technologies. It is well chronicled that organized crime groups follow the money. Since the early 1980s, they have found big profits in computer passwords, identities, intellectual property, and cash from compromised credit cards and bank accounts. As one expert put it, "The Russian mafia and U.S. mobsters have done the math and moved in" (Fox 2005, 6). Organized crime's interest in exploiting digital technology has been stimulated by the waning of opportunity in a number of traditional venues due to either decriminalization or policy changes that created a more hostile climate, pushing and pulling organized crime into new spheres of activity (Grabosky 2007).

Considering the depersonalization of contacts, ease of access, and rapidity of electronic transactions, new technologies have proved to be an attractive tool for money laundering. Virtual casinos, smart cards, online banking, and the possibility to conduct various stock transactions online offer a plethora of avenues for money laundering. New innovations in technology have benefited both sides of the organized crime divide. "Almost every new technology has brought great benefits attached with some risks. To each 'technology' there is an anti-technology, making it a double-edged weapon" (Mishra 2003, 1). Although mobsters come up with shrewd new techniques for milking various components of local, national, and world economies, law enforcement is just behind them developing sophisticated new technologies to suppress and investigate organized high-tech crime schemes. One expert on cybercrime used the example of advances in security by the car industry and law enforcement agencies that allowed them to put a damper on car theft. Car thieves with traditional skill sets who were initially ahead of the security curve found they were outmatched by newly developed car immobilizers and other new devices that made it difficult to steal cars. In response, the car thieves found they could beat this technology by stealing identities and either renting or buying cars with this fraudulent information, thereby committing the crime with less effort and risk (Warren and Streeter 2005).

There is still major debate as to whether cybercrime and the cyberspace continuum should be considered organized crime at all. One leading voice is of the opinion that "high tech crime is an oxymoron; a classic contradiction in terms. . . . It's not about technology, it's about people" (quoted in McCusker 2006, 264–265). Furthermore, "the very nature of cyberspace is inconsistent with hierarchy. Cyberspace is a network, or, more properly, a network of networks. Networks are lateral, diffuse, fluid, and evolving. Hierarchies are vertical, concentrated, and tend to be rigid and fluid" (quoted in McCusker 2006, 264–265). Others argue, "The Internet with its anonymity and lack of physical geography does not lend itself to bossy leaders or compounds in the woods. Locally autonomous groups can also better refine their message to fit the markets, which further fuels fragmentation" (Johnson, 2005).

New York City's Five Families Go High-Tech: "Sleeping with the Phishes"

According to the deputy assistant director David Thomas of the FBI Cyberdivision, the American Mafia made $360 million in 7 years through e-crime by using search engines to hack into secure files and pull out credit card details, or by producing their own algorithms to generate "legitimate" credit cards. Traditional organized crime groups have never been far behind innovations in technology by both law enforcement and the business community. From the telegraph and the wire services to the automobile and the Thompson submachine gun to the modern Internet and e-commerce, criminal groups have continued to flourish, thanks to the latest advances in technology. New York's organized crime families had a head start in the digital world by running several online sports betting sites. It has come to light that in 1998, one family set up a business offering services to companies to prepare them for the year 2000 (Y2K) problem. The consultancy firm had its own Web site and toll-free number, and by most accounts had a great solution for the Y2K bug. Once the company's programmers got into a client's financial software, they adjusted it so that the company's funds were redirected to other offshore mob accounts (Lilley 2006, 112). That same year, just 5 years after John Gotti was sent away to prison for life, his son and mob heir John Jr. and 39 others were charged in Federal District Court for crimes that included telephone calling-card fraud (Weiser 1998).[1]

At the turn of the 21st century, New York's vaunted crime families were also making the transition to the high-tech world through a number of diverse schemes ranging from telephone bill and phone card fraud to counterfeit CDs and credit card copying. The son and heir of Gambino underboss Frank Locasio, Salvatore Locasio and nine underlings were charged with stealing more than $200 million in 5 years from unknowing customers. According to the scheme, the gangsters lured thousands of victims to sample adult entertainment, including sex-chat lines, dating services, and psychic readings. The theft operation was based on a tactic that had been around for years known as *cramming,* described by one expert as "a trap in which callers were clipped for up to $40 a month on their phone bills after being deceived by 'free trial' advertisements" (Raab 2005, 696). According to the following investigation, the gangsters set up a labyrinth of shell companies that billed callers indirectly through local telephone utilities. Callers were under the impression they were responding to sample services from psychic phone lines, telephone dating services, and adult chat lines (Rashbaum 2004). The head of the FBI's Gambino Squad described this case as among the largest perpetrated by the Mafia, adding, "The profit from the fraud alone makes the Gambinos look like a Fortune 500 company" (quoted in Raab 2005, 697). According to law enforcement officials, this case demonstrated how traditional organized crime has moved beyond enduring mob moneymaking schemes of the 20th century to the far more sophisticated Internet era (Rashbaum 2004).

What facilitated this huge scam were the new methods of paying telephone service providers. Today, many telephone-related services are paid through the local phone company's monthly bills, with the companies passing on the payments to the service providers. The Gambino members figured that they could use one company to consolidate billings for service providers, which would allow them to bill through local phone companies and collect their fees, "fees with innocent-sounding titles like 'voice mail services' hidden deep within the phone bills, unnoticed by all but the most dogged consumers" (Rashbaum 2004).

The Gambino family has also found the phone card industry to be a huge moneymaker, making millions of dollars by setting up companies to sell prepaid phone cards. Members sold the cards through various retail distributors, usually in neighborhoods with a large number of immigrants who need them to call their countries of origin. Each card reportedly was sold for $20, but most became worthless after only $2 or $3 worth of calls were made; in reality, the cards had never been programmed for the promised amount. No one was ever prosecuted for the crime, with many illegal immigrants afraid to report the ruse to authorities (Raab 2005).

The Genovese family reaped a fortune from counterfeiting compact discs ($2.5 million a year for several years) until it was busted. In another operation, Genovese soldiers were able to obtain copies of credit cards with the help of store clerks and cashiers. Employees were paid $50 for every stolen number. The duplicated cards were then sold for $1,000 each to individuals who quickly maxed out the cards before the victim became aware. Another crew managed to take over a company that handled medical, dental, and vision care programs for a number of employers and unions.

The scheme involved strong-arming administrators into approving excessive fees for questionable medical services, which went into mob coffers (Raab 2005).

Russian Organized Cybercrime

Russia's shadow economy in the Soviet era contributed to a tradition in which licit and illicit entrepreneurs evaded official restrictions (such as paying taxes) through any number of schemes. In fact, modern cybercrime can be traced back to this cultural phenomenon or "way of life," and by the digital era networks to commit such crimes were well established (Ward 2005). Organized crime adopted the skill sets provided by new technologies and in many cases morphed into more loosely organized and fluid groups.

One of the unanticipated consequences of Western restrictions on technology transfers to the Soviet Union in the 1970s and 1980s was that it gave rise to a generation of computer specialists adept at taking apart, assembling, and hacking American computer systems in order to see how they worked so they could be made functional on Soviet systems. The KGB played an important role in actively recruiting hackers and unemployed scientists who together provided "a great recipe for a skilled, criminally minded digital underground" (Ward 2005).

Further contributing to this rapidly developing expertise was the weak economies of the former Soviet Union with few opportunities for computer experts. This was aggravated in 1998, with the collapse of the ruble and the loss of many jobs in the computer-related sectors of the economy. Subsequent investigations identified a 50-year old unemployed university professor who, along with several others, was arrested for operating an Internet pornography ring; in another case, a 63-year-old former programmer organized a gang of computer hackers to help steal money from Western credit cards (Serio and Gorkin 2003, 193).

A number of authorities recognized "the enormously successful tech savvy gangs" (Ward, 2005) operating out of Russia, Romania, Estonia, Latvia, and Lithuania. When it came to phishing attacks, criminal groups hired technicians for each job and utilized their expertise to create systems online to support phishing attacks. Participants in different nations apparently develop in different ways. For example, Russian phishing gangs are more likely to be "tight communities that prefer communicating within closed circle chat programs" (Ward, 2005), although Romanian gangs are considered "more open and instead use well-known Internet Relay Chat rooms to keep in touch" (Ward 2005).

Goodbye Pizzo (Protection Money): Challenging the Mafia Online

In 2004, a number of Palermo businessmen and merchants joined forces in rebelling against the Sicilian mafia's traditional demands for protection money, or *pizzo*. One recent investigation of this practice discovered that street vendors pay between €50 and €100[2] each month, whereas local bread stores pay €150–€250; clothing stores about €250; a jewelry store, €1,000; and so forth. The success of their movement has sapped the crime organization of one of its most dependable sources of income. The business community found safety in numbers and in the anonymity of the Web with the site *Addiopizzo,* or "Goodbye Pizzo." The rebels have found support inside the politically influential industrialists' lobby, *Confindustria*, which threatened to expel any of its members caught paying protection money. Although only 230 businesses out of thousands of stores, factories, and offices signed on initially, it has inspired a similar movement in Catania, Sicily's second largest city. Extortionists found this work lucrative for decades, with many earning monthly salaries of almost $3,000, way above the island's standard of living. However, the more they pushed, with arsons, beatings, and threats, the more a number of victims resisted. In one high-profile case, the owner of one of Palermo's most prominent restaurants, one that specialized in the local delicacy, sandwiches stuffed with calf's spleen and lung, paid almost $2 million purchasing supplies from friends of a gangster who had moved into his business. He went to the police and identified to the racketeers who had been extorting him, resulting in long prison sentences for each of them. He is now under police protection (D'Emilio 2008).

From Traditional Crime to Cybercrime

There is a remarkable continuity between many of the crimes committed online and their counterparts in the pre-computer era. Although the tools are different, the intent, goals, and motivations remain the same. In former times it was common for merchants in various immigrant communities and ethnic enclaves to pay protection money to organized gangs under threat of harm or business disruption. Today, organized criminals are just as likely to threaten the disruption of e-business if a ransom is not paid. Bank robbers still rob banks and security vans, a dangerous avocation. Others have found it safer to simply hack into a bank's computer system and transferring money using electronic payment systems.

Criminals adapted quickly to the telephone as a tool for calling potential victims pretending to be from the security branch of a bank, often asking victims for passwords and credit card numbers. This has since been replaced by *phishing,* much more anonymous e-mails that are designed to direct the victim to a Web site run by the criminal that looks exactly like the legitimate bank. The customer is then asked to reveal similar information then is then used by the criminals.

At one time, criminals were not above checking through garbage cans to find credit card statements and utility bills that could then be used for subterfuge. This has been replaced in many cases with online credit card theft, in which cybercriminals steal thousands of credit card numbers at one time by hacking into company databases. One old standby of traditional organized crime was the *boiler-room share scam,* in which criminals pretended to be brokers, selling shares by telephone at an artificially inflated price, or shares of companies that did not even exist. More prominent today are *pump-and-dump scams,* in which criminals purchase shares in companies and use online share sites to issue false statements to "pump up" the price before unloading them for a profit.

The burglar has been a mainstay in the world of crime since there was something to steal. Methods included knocking on a front door to see if anyone was home, or adopting the façade of a legitimate businessman while a confederate sneaks in the back door and steals valuables. The high-tech version works similar online. As one security group puts it, "the back door on a PC is opened up through illegal hacker behavior, enabling viruses to spread easily and infect a machine" (McAfee 2005, 8).

Operation Firewall

In late 2004, the U.S. Secret Service announced that it had cracked a "global organized cybercrime ring," arresting 28 individuals, including citizens of 8 U.S. states and 6 foreign countries. The suspects were charged with identity theft, computer fraud, credit card fraud, and conspiracy. Those involved in the case alleged that the organization had as a group sold at least 1.7 million stolen credit card numbers, resulting in losses to financial institutions totaling more than $4 million. *Operation Firewall* began in 2003 as a national operation, but soon expanded into a transnational investigation of global credit card fraud and online identity theft. The underground groups involved have been identified as ShadowCrew, CarderPlanet, and DarkProfits. They operated Web sites that sold counterfeit credit cards and false identification information and documents. Assisting the U.S. Secret Service were police officials from Bulgaria, Belarus, Poland, Sweden, the Netherlands, and Ukraine, as well as Europol, the Royal Canadian Mounted Police, and the UK's National Hi-Tech Crimes Unit (Verton 2004).

The cybergang known as ShadowCrew was considered one of the modern exemplars of organized cybercrime by the U.S. Secret Service and other agencies, and were charged with identity theft, robbery, extortion, and other crimes; they are suspected of stealing and reselling millions of dollars' worth of stolen credit card numbers and personal identification documents (Zambo 2007).

OPERATION BUCCANEER   Founded in Moscow in 1993 by two hackers known as *deviator* and *CyberAngel,* DrinkOrDie (DoD) rose to prominence in the underworld of digital piracy by releasing a cracked copy of Windows 95 over the Internet several weeks before Microsoft's official release. Never considered a "for-profit" organization, it competed with other pirate groups for prestige. Nevertheless, software companies lost $50 million (retail) to the mostly teenage consumer market. A 4-month undercover operation against the DoD piracy group resulted in simultaneous raids in 7 countries in 2001 against high-level Warez[3] leadership and members. DoD is thought to have 40 members worldwide. Its strategies include decoding antipiracy measures in software and the release of the code on the Internet before or at the same time of the product is released. In 2007, after fighting extradition for 3 years, its leader, Australian Raymond Griffiths,[4] better known in pirating circles as *Bandito,* pleaded guilty in U.S. federal court to one count each of criminal copyright infringement and conspiracy to commit criminal copyright infringement.

RECRUITING INFORMATION TECHNOLOGY EXPERTS   The recruiting of information technology (IT) experts has become increasingly sophisticated in recent years. Today, members of international crime groups are likely to monitor online chat rooms and newsgroups deciding who would be likely recruits. Besides offering high financial incentives, there have been instances where individuals have been intimidated into cooperating. Organized crime has also been successful in recruiting from certain Web sites popular among those in the IT industry, who use them to post their resumes. Here gangsters can sift through the curricula vitae before contacting those that fit their required skill sets. Lured by lucrative job offers, it is doubtful that many recognize what they have gotten into at first. In the words of one veteran cyber investigator, "If organized crime is looking for a particular skill set and the Internet is a wonderful resource, we should anticipate that it's going to make use of it at the source" (Warren and Streeter 2005, 36).

After the recruits have been reeled in by paychecks beyond their wildest dreams, they typically enter a variegated enterprise where they might be expected to manage Web sites, develop phishing scams, or operating denial of service attacks. There is evidence to suggest that certain syndicates are not beyond paying the way through university for aspiring talent, although others operate a type of "Research and Development Department." One source explained, "This unexpected criminal enthusiasm for higher education is confirmed by one hacker who had links with a London-based syndicate in the 1990s," in which the daughter of one member was put through school with the intent of setting her up in banking, where he could utilize her access to the banking network (Warren and Streeter 2005, 37–38).

Computer-Assisted Crimes

Theft of telephone services	Video and software piracy
Copyright	Vandalism (through virus attacks)
Spying and industrial espionage	Terrorism
Fraudulent transfer of electronic funds	Hacking
Denial of Service (DoS)	Cross-border crime
Extortion and blackmail	Cloning mobile phones and phone cards
Credit card and accounting fraud	Stalking and harassment
Money laundering	Investment fraud
Telemarketing fraud	Sale of stolen goods
Identity theft	Gambling
Tax evasion	Conspiracy

(Warren and Streeter 2005)

One of the most fertile recruiting grounds has been Eastern Europe and the former Soviet states. Leading authorities explain that gangs emanating from these regions have been more "technologically inclined than some others," noting "Russian organized crime is the first post-modern form of organized crime to explode in the modern era" (quoted in Warren and Streeter, 2005, 38). With few prospects in the commercial sector, a vast pool of well-educated individuals exists that is more likely to be technologically adept than traditional crime group members. Russia's leading gangs such as *Solntsevo* usually hire IT specialists only when their services are required, rather than bringing hackers into the organization's inner core.

British cyber-intelligence sources have revealed that a number of organized crime groups are organized around a cell-type structure in which the technical staff is just one group supervising technology-related issues, although other cells are devoted to other specific tasks such as security or recruiting; at the same time, each cell is unaware of the workings of the others, or unaware of the broader structure of the overall syndicate operations.

One leading cybercrime researcher notes a new trend emerging among Russian cybercriminals that he calls *virtual organized crime groups,* whereby the groups are set up by and wholly consisting of IT experts, unlike the other cases where existing gangs have simply diversified into high-tech crime. According to Mark Galeotti,

> With these technology groups we are now at a cusp point. Until now, the computer people still had their own jobs during the day. Now they are at a point where there is enough activity for them to drop those jobs. Ironically, however, there are areas of business for these virtual gangs where they need to turn to the experts in existing gangs—for example, in the longstanding problem of how to launder stolen money. (Galeotti 2005, 41)

Criminal Organizations in Cyberspace

Grabosky identifies a variety of distinct forms of criminal organization in cyberspace. Most recognizable are the so-called traditional criminal groups that have adopted digital technology in pursuing criminal activities. This is best exemplified by the Japanese Yakuza's use of Internet fraud and Colombian cocaine traffickers using encryption, which enables the user to transmit information hidden inside digital photos and files (2007, 11).

Other high-profile groups are organizations that only came into existence with the digital revolution. What makes these groups distinct from the previous ones is the fact that their crimes take place exclusively online. More prominent exemplars include the DrinkOrDie piracy conspiracy, the Wonderland child pornography ring, and the ShadowCrew identity theft organization.

Other organizations were created with legal intentions, but over time adopted corrupt criminal practices after the company "principals [chose] to lead them down a corrupt path" (Grabosky, 2007, 11). Examples date as far back as the 1980s, when "a large pharmacy chain utilized a computer-generated double-billing scheme to overcharge governments for health insurance reimbursements" (Grabsosky, 2007, 11). In other cases, legitimate businesses, particularly in the finance sector, have been infiltrated by criminal actors. In some instances an organized crime group insinuates members into the organization or corrupts what was once a legitimate member of the company. Once corrupted, these individuals are capable of sharing access to IT systems, account details, and furthering check counterfeiting and fraudulent funds transfers (Grabosky 2007; Carwile and Hollis 2004).

At the highest levels, sovereign states are capable of operating as a criminal organization in cyberspace; for example, North Korea used digital technology in the alleged production and laundering of counterfeit currency.[5]

Over the years there have been a number of examples of organized crime groups creating what on the surface seemed legitimate organizations as fronts for their criminal activities. Passas and others assert that the Bank of Credit and Commerce International (BCCI) exemplifies this scheme. Grabosky suggest a scenario in which "a criminal entrepreneur might, for example, become an Internet service provider, in order to allow criminal communications to avoid hindrance or scrutiny that might otherwise be directed against them" (2007, 12).

A vast array of organizations last for only a short time before breaking up. Examples of this behavior can be found in the techniques of swarming for the purpose of creating mass disturbance, organized stalking, and mail bombing.

One of the world's leading computer anti-virus companies identified a virtual food chain of cybercriminal structures. At the bottom of the hierarchy are groups that are not necessarily economically motivated and are considered less technologically astute. The *Script Kiddy,* for example, is typically under the age of 20 and usually does not know how the program they execute works; in most cases, they are using a macro file or other lists of commands written by someone else to exploit computer vulnerabilities. *Cyberpunks* basically are more youthful individual with computer skills to break into computer systems and networks and financial gain is not their primary motivation.

Hackers and *crackers* are a different story, however. *Hackers* are quite often skilled programmers "with a libertarian bent to their politics" (McAfee, 2005, 10) individuals who enjoy learning programming languages and acquiring more skills. The term *hacker* has developed a mostly negative connotation, referring to anyone who gets unauthorized access to a computer or network. In order to make some type of distinction, hackers refer to the aforementioned as *crackers*. Hackers argue that they usually work alone and are motivated by social goals more than economic gain; they are more interested in their standing in the hacker community.[6]

During the life of the Internet, there has been a documented change in the "division of labor in the organization of cybercrime" (Wall 2007, 155). Together with the fact that hackers from one country can easily commit crimes against companies, governments, and individuals without leaving their keyboards, "asymmetric" relationships have developed in which a single offender can victimize a number of victims simultaneously. Although it is probably still valid to assume that most cybercriminals act alone or outside a conventional group structure, reports from the Council of Europe in 2004 and 2005 "indicate organized forms of cybercrime [have become] more frequent" (2005, 43).

Increasingly immersed in the traditional markets of organized crime such as protection and extortion rackets, some of these gangs "are often highly skilled and organized and thus possibly part of organized crime structures" (Council of Europe, 2005, 43). One structure used to facilitate the stealing, buying, and selling of millions of credit card numbers and identifications includes a hierarchical arrangement, with *Administrators/Managers* making decisions and enforcing protocol. Under them are *Moderators,* responsible for operating discussion groups; *Reviewers,* who judge the quality of the stolen merchandise; *Vendors,* who then sell the stolen merchandise and related services to paying customers; and finally, *Members,* who provide the merchandise as well as share information with others in the group. Favored *modi operandi* include encrypted communication, the use of proxy servers, money laundering, and, at times, intimidation (Council of Europe 2005, 43–44).

CYBERGANGS   The groups most germane to organized crime are the *cybergangs,* defined by one antivirus giant as

> Groups of career criminals and hackers who have acquired the computer skills necessary to move their activities into cyberspace. Very often the groups are based in countries with weak cybercrime laws, but they can also be loose, fluid networks of criminals located in a number of different countries who agree to cooperate for a particular operation. (McAfee 2005, 10)

What distinguishes them from the traditional hackers is that their curiosity about computers has been replaced with committing financially motivated crimes using computers. Thanks to the ubiquity of the Internet, groups of these individuals have formed cybergangs while sharing their criminal knowledge and skills with like-minded individuals, suggesting, "cybergangs are the new form of the Mafia in the twenty-first century" (Zambo 2007).

Some observers note how highly organized these groups are becoming, with some going as far as to compare them to the traditional Mafia. A number of revelations came out of Operation Firewall, which divulged the structure common to cybergangs (see the box entitled "ShadowCrew: Case Study of a Web Mob"). Zambo continues to assert that because cybergangs pursue monetary gain, they are no different from the Mafia. In a similar vein, he suggests that the RICO statutes should be applied to groups such as ShadowCrew, because they display similar structures to traditional organized crime (2007, 574).

At a 2006 Defcon hacker conference in Las Vegas, a cyber-investigator said, "cybercriminals have been taking a page from organized crime, adopting the same organizational structures as these older crime groups." Using the group CarderPlanet as an exemplar, the speaker asserted that this group "organized themselves into the same structure as the Italian Mafia" (McMillan 2006). At this time, CarderPlanet, which has since been closed down, was only a part of a larger organization of online criminals referred to as the *International Carder's Alliance,* whose calling card was the use of established Web sites and Internet Relay Chat channels to coordinate online attacks. The investigator noted, "This is really the heart of organized cybercrime" (McCusker 2006, 259). His foundation for such a claim was the very fact that traditional organized crime was becoming increasingly affiliated with online crime. These claims have been challenged in some quarters by those who argue that any attempt to compare cybercriminals (such as CarderPlanet) with traditional organized crime groups does nothing but muddy the "definitional waters" of organized crime (McCusker 2006, 259).

CYBERGANGS AND THE MAFIA: COMPARATIVE STRUCTURES?   One 2007 study claimed, "Cybergangs are structured very similarly to the Mafia, the only real difference being that cybergangs operate entirely online" (Zambo 2007, 558). Basing much of his research on the definitions from the 1986 President's Commission on Organized Crime (PCOC), Zambo argues that both groups in effect restrict their membership to those with specific characteristics: the Mafia through race, ethnicity, and criminal acumen, and cybergangs through technical skills. What ties the cybergangs into this definition is the fact that only "prolific or experienced computer hackers" (Zambo 2007, 558) are recruited. Members of both incarnations of organized crime are rewarded both monetarily and with the pride in belonging to such a restricted group.

Individually, the *Boss* of a Mafia family is equivalent to the cybergang members known as *Administrators,* in that both remain outside the daily routines and still earn a percentage of the illegal activities committed by other members. In descending order, the Mafia *Underboss* has no analog in the cybergang, but develop easily over time (Zambo 2007, 559). Mafia *Captains* are comparable to cybergang *Moderators;* both supervise criminal activities and are "trusted to realize their earning potential in the organization" (Zambo 2007, 559). Unlike the Mafia *Soldiers* at its lowest level, who commit street crimes but usually are "unproven as financial contributors," there is no direct analog in the cybergang's membership. The largest numbers of Mafia family affiliates are called *Associates.* Not limited to restrictions of ethnicity and other requirements, they can only participate at the behest of a family member who puts his own neck out by vouching for the associate. This sponsor is comparable to the role played by the *Vendor* in the cybergangs. Other similarities include continuity through leadership changes and the use of intimidation to achieve goals.

Among the traits that most distinguish real-world mobsters from their counterparts in cyberspace is their tangible ability to use physical force against others. Cybercriminals and their other high-tech counterparts will continue to adapt to the changing opportunities of organized criminality. Organized crime groups—both terrestrial and digital—have demonstrated a capacity for some time now to break the mold of traditional structures by coming together for short periods of time to achieve certain goals and then disbanding and going their separate ways. Legal scholar Susan W. Brenner even suggested, "The individual cybercriminal's ability to operate independently is in some ways analogous to the small-scale criminal activities Mafia soldiers operate to generate personal profits" (Brenner 2002, 44), although in the long run, the cybercriminal is "more autonomous than a member tied to the protocol and traditions of a larger criminal organization" (Brenner 2002, 44). Brenner goes on to forecast the evolution of new types of "disorganized" criminal organizations, what she calls "Mafias of the moment," as opposed to the more traditional "geographically [and] genetically fixed Mafia entities" (2002, 44).

More recent studies by the Web security company Finjan suggest that

> Cybercrime companies that work much like real-world companies are starting to appear and are steadily growing. . . . Forget individual hackers or groups of hackers with common goals. Hierarchical cybercrime organizations where each cybercriminal has his or her own role and reward system" is what should be worrying companies. The security company even claims that "the employee structure that these cybercrime companies employ as being similar to the Mafia. (Protalinski 2008)

CYBERBANGERS   Internet Web sites have been used by pedophile gangs, software piracy gangs, organized crime groups, and urban street gangs to organize physical or online gatherings. Details are often hidden by encryption, which makes the information available only to members aware of the messages or those who have access to the group's servers. This venue provides them with a rather anonymous ability to circulate information about their activities as well as to publicize their symbols and accomplishments.

One of the more recent trends in street gang crime has been the adoption of the Internet for what police now refer to as *cyberbanging,* where gang members openly boast about gang affiliations, cutting class, doing drugs, and fighting with rivals. Police officials in the Washington, D.C. area are particularly alarmed by the numerous postings from purported Mara Salvatrucha (M-13) members. Although police acknowledge that it is difficult to tell the phony gang members from the real ones, anything dealing with MS-13 should be taken seriously. As one investigator put it, "If you portray yourself as being MS-13 and you're not, when they find out about it, they kill you just as if you're a rival gang member" (Klein 2006, A11).

According to a recent investigation of gang-related Web sites, the *Washington Post* discovered that most of these Web pages feature teens who prefer to design their sites with "flash in-your-face images of gang flags, hand signs, marijuana, women, stacks of cash and 'original gangster' scrolls certifying them as legitimate" (Klein 2006, A11). There is nothing illegal about these sites, but they have proven a boon to gang investigators, offering revealing insights into local gangs and previously unknown gang members. One investigator claimed to have identified 1,300 gang members and associates in Maryland's Prince Georges County alone.

ILLEGAL "WAREZ" ORGANIZATIONS AND INTERNET PIRACY   Beginning in the early 1990, groups of likeminded individuals working in underground networks organized themselves into competitive gangs that obtained software illegally and posted it on the Internet for other members of the group. The software was stripped of its various forms of copy protection, more commonly known as being *cracked* or *ripped* before being posted on the Web. A network of groups and individuals evolved into the *Warez scene* or *community,* eventually numbering in the thousands.

Operation Buccaneer by the Department of justice's Computer Crime and Intellectual Property Section (CCIPS) revealed the structure of some of these Warez groups. The top of the chain was helmed by several "release" groups that were the first to acquire, crack, and distribute recent software, games, movies, and music to the Warez community. Often releases hit the Internet before they are commercially available. The CCIPS claims that

> The top-level release groups are highly structured organizations with defined roles and leadership hierarchy. These organizations generally have a Leader, who oversees and directs all aspects of the group; three Council members or Senior Staff, who direct and mange the day-to-day operations of the group; 10 to 15 Staff, who frequently are the most active and skilled contributors to

the group's day to day release work; and finally, the general membership, whose functions and involvement in the group vary. Members generally only interact via the Internet and know each other only by their screen nicknames. (CCIPS n.d., 2)

Once new releases are posted on the Web on large file transfer sites (FTPs), pirated versions of copyrighted products can be found on thousands of Web sites. They begin to bring in the real money when they appear on pay-for-access Web sites from China to the United States, where users pay monthly or per-purchase fees to download unauthorized copies.

The CCIPS reports that Warez releases are a dependable source of income for counterfeit hard goods criminal organizations. By most accounts, almost every PC or console game is cracked and available on Warez sites before or within 24 hours of its release, or *0-Day Releases*. These are typically downloaded by hard good syndicates in China and Russia, for example, and then mass produced at an optical disc manufacturing plant. The goods are ready for foreign markets sometimes weeks before the official release date. This activity is capable of financially ruining the market for legitimate products.

In order to maximize impact and profits, it is essential for the Warez group to quickly prepare and package new pirated software for release and distribution as fast as possible. This is usually accomplished in four stages and as quick as a few hours. The first step begins with a member, or *supplier*, posting an original digital copy of new computer software to the group's Internet drop site—usually a computer where the software is posted for retrieval for members of the group. Next, once on the drop site, another member known as the *cracker* retrieves it and removes or circumvents all embedded copyright protection, which can range from serial numbers, tags, and duplication controls to digital protections and security locks. Third, the software is tested to make sure it is fully operational, and then *packed*, or broken into file packets that are more readily distributed to other group members. After the software has been cracked, tested, and packed, it is returned to the drop site, where individuals are waiting for new contraband in preparation for distributing the pirated goods across the Internet. After the packers (or "*pre-ers*"[8]) pick it up, it is distributed to Warez locations throughout the world (CCIPS n.d.).

WEB MOBS The digital revolution has given birth to new organized crime groups dubbed *Web mobs* by high-tech observers. Law enforcement officials describe a *Web mob* as "a highly organized group of criminals" (Gage, 2005) that unlike traditional organized crime groups operates only in the digital realm. The most prominent during the first years of the 21st century have been CarderPlanet, StealthDivision, DarkProfits and the ShadowCrew. Their chief enterprise involves buying and selling credit card information, social security numbers, and identification documents of millions of individuals. Most sell for only $10 each. These groups are also capable of creating sites and services to facilitate the creation of similar skilled and motivated organizations.

In 2005, the FBI and U.S. Secret Service busted the U.S.-based ShadowCrew, operating from a home in suburban New Jersey. Investigations reveal that carder groups are structured similar to traditional organized crime groups. In order to join the group, one must provide a certain number of newly stolen credit card numbers. Once they join, the member pledges to provide a certain number of stolen card numbers each week. The ShadowCrew apparently used threats of violence if the goods were not delivered or if faulty numbers were provided (although there is no evidence that they went through with the threats). Carders hire virus writers to infect computers around the globe in order to harvest credit card information from PCs or other computers on a network. ShadowCrew was busted after it was infiltrated by a federal agent (Vamosi 2005).

A number of other cybergangs besides the ShadowCrew have emerged since the early part of this century. The "Muzzfuzz" was involved in some credit card and identification theft schemes as before it was busted in 2004. The group known as StealthDivision was shut down the same year and counted among its members ShadowCrew members who evaded the police dragnet that caught its leaders. They were able to operate for a longer period due to their ability to make it seem like they were operating

ShadowCrew: Case Study of a Web Mob[9]

Between 2003 and 2005, ShadowCrew grew to an organization of 4,000 members. The U.S. Secret Service reported that their worldwide marketplace offered for sale 1.5 million credit card numbers, 18 million e-mail accounts, and untold numbers of identification documents ranging from drivers' licenses to passports, all available to the highest bidder. By most accounts, whoever purchased credit card numbers did not plan on paying for their purchases. In 2004, the U.S. Secret Service put their Web site out of service (http://www.shadowcrew.com). Although the organization caused more than $4 million in losses, if they had not been stopped the losses would have approached the hundreds of millions of dollars.

Law enforcement authorities assert that the typical profile of a Web mob member is a 20-something, technically savvy and circumspect individual who works behind the façade of a *nic,* or nickname, such as "BlackOps" or "Kingpin." Eschewing traditional methods of communication, members recognize each other only by their Web aliases, their only venue of communication. In this way, they are fluid and flexible, and capable of setting up an electronic marketplace to sell their contraband with several keystrokes, and just as quickly can disband it. Researchers compare the Web mobs to the American Mafia, noting that members

> don't have to break into a bank to rob it. Instead they provide a framework and services for criminals to trade in their chosen stock-stolen credit cards ad identity documents. And their efforts, including the "commerce" sites where they trade stolen "merchandise," will only accelerate what is already a thriving trade in numbers that are regarded on the Web as currency. (McCormick and Gage 2005, 2)

The demise of the ShadowCrew began with the assistance of an informant positioned in the upper hierarchy. His access to one of the group's servers allowed the U.S. Secret Service to set up an undercover operation that led them to several of the key players. Soon after, the informant engaged 30 members in simultaneous online chats. Firmly fixated by their digital partners, they were unprepared when a joint force of federal agents barged into their homes armed and wearing bulletproof vests. In one location agents found several loaded assault rifles. According to the criminal complaint behind the investigation, these groups were quite distinct from traditional hackers, having more in common with an "international criminal organization" (McCormick and Gage 2005).

Reporters for the online-journal *Baseline* cobbled together the structure of the ShadowCrew organization after examining court documents and interviewing various agents and experts. Upper management consisted of anywhere from two to six members. This level controlled the organization, deciding which businesses to engage in and how to sell the stolen merchandise, as well as who could join the operation and what type of access each member should be given to the Web site and its forums. Daily operations were usually in the hands of a dozen members, or *Moderators,* who directed information and discussion forums. Forums offered advice for successfully stealing and forging credit cards and creating false documents such as driver's licenses, training certificates, and college diplomas. Only members who had a record of achievement in this arena were allowed to moderate questions from members.

At the next level were *Reviewers,* tasked with judging the quality of the illegal goods, especially credit card numbers and passports. In order to find out if a card worked, Reviewers were responsible for testing the cards to test if they were valid. *Vendors* were members who sold the illegal products, including credit card numbers and insurance health cards. They also provided money-laundering services and access to retailers' credit card validation systems. The lowest level consisted of thousands of *General Members,* whose affiliation was based on using the ShadowCrew Web site to improve and share skills related to aforementioned criminal activities. Although anyone in effect could register to join, more sensitive information was protected by passwords. If a Member wanted to deliver a sales pitch to the group, the individual needed a well-respected member of the group to vouch for him first. Members had opportunities for promotion based on a record of providing quality goods (valid credit cards and passable IDs), or by introducing members to innovative fraud strategies. However, those who habitually came up with poor-quality goods or were deemed disloyal were subject to punishment by designated enforcers.

The investigation of ShadowCrew and other Web mobs offers tangible evidence that these groups are indeed "highly structured and very well organized" (McCormick and Gage 2005, 5). What was most striking was the way the cyber organization conducted business. For example, in one case, a Member hacked

(continued)

into the mobile provider T-Mobile's computer systems and stole 400 accounts. When the Vendor received the stolen information, the merchandise had to be examined by a Reviewer. In the case of goods in the electronic format, the Vendor merely sold a file to an inspector. However, if it was plastic or paper, the goods were supposed to be moved along through a string of "drop boxes" located in retail stores such as Kinko's or UPS. The boxes were rented out to aliases and the locations were often changed to avoid detection.

When the Reviewer gets the products in his hands, it becomes his job to vet the product. This could be accomplished by the *dump check*, which involves hacking into merchant's cash register system. The cards are tested using small denomination bills to ascertain whether the cards were declined. If it turned out the charges were accepted, the dump was considered good. According to McCormick and Gage, it was then up to the Reviewer to write a report detailing the descriptions of the stolen goods. They describe this process as similar to listing the qualities of a used book on Amazon. For a driver's license, for example, the description might include the quality of photos, the hologram, the printing of names and numbers, color scheme, and even card thickness. Finally, the product is ready for sale. Goods are usually shipped in limited numbers, but in some case it is done in bulk. On one occasion in 2004, a ShadowCrew member sent 110,000 credit card numbers at one time. Cards were sold according to limits, with those with, for example, a $10,000 limit going for as little as $1 to $10. Until the ShadowCrew's Web site was shut down in 2004, the goods would be listed with prices online. In another case vendors used an approach much like eBay through an auction forum. Sales might include "three counterfeit Arizona driver's licenses," and the starting and ending times for the auction. Although the Web mobs proved to be highly skilled and organized, others suggest these groups are mid-tier players "whose bark is worse than its bite" (quoted in McCormick and Gage, 2005, 9). By comparison, Russian mobsters, said one security analyst, "managed to roam around for up to five years inside the computer systems of Citibank during the 1990s" (McCormick and Gage 2005, 9).

from another country. By using computers and servers in Malaysia, investigators took a while to catch on. Before its demise, StealthDivision had more than 300 members. A group called "Boatfactory" was blamed for $2.5 million in credit card losses, and DarkProfits reportedly created several worms that were used as tools for future extortion and denial of service attacks. If anything has been learned from the successful investigations against these groups, it is the fact that "members who evaded police capture do not stop their criminal activities, but form new cybergangs" (Zambo 2007, 561).

Cybercrime: From Hackers to Crackers

Cybercrime is a crime related to technology, computers, and the Internet. According to a 2006 FBI estimate, cybercrime robs legitimate businesses of $67.2 billion each year. *Consumer Reports* noted that during one recent 2-year period, American consumers lost more than $8 billion to viruses, spyware, and online fraud schemes (*USA Today* October 12, 2006, 1B).

Despite the wealth of research on cybercrime, there are still dissenters who dislike the term and reserve particular disdain for its association with the term *organized*. Detractors argue, "Cybercrime is nothing more than ordinary traditional crime enhanced in terms of its distribution and impact by the facilitation of technology" (McCusker 2006, 260). Whether one calls it *high-tech* or *cybercrime,* most computer crime falls into two general categories. Some use computers as a tool, such as when reproducing copyrighted materials or stalking someone. In other cases the computer is the target, wherein someone tries to steal passwords and social security numbers or interfere with computer network service. One leading expert asserts that cybercrime actually falls into three categories:

1. Conventional crimes committed with computers, such as digital child pornography, piracy, or intellectual property theft, and forgery
2. Attacks on computer networks
3. Conventional criminal cases such as drug trafficking, in which evidence exists in digital form (Grabosky 2005, 146)

Prominent Forms of Organized Cybercrime

- **Cracking:** Gaining unauthorized access to computer systems to commit a crime. This can happen in a variety of ways, including digging into the code to make a copy-protected program run without a password or a valid license string, flooding Internet sites and denying service to legitimate users, erasing information, corrupting information, and deliberately defacing Web sites.
- **Piracy:** Copying protected software illegally.
- **Phreaking:** Using a computer or other device to manipulate phones system for free calls.
- **Cyberpornography:** Producing or distributing pornography using a computer.

The birth of computer criminality began with the hackers who gravitated toward *phone phreaking* in the 1960s and 1970s. However, unlike modern groups, hackers were less concerned with the profit motive and more interested with the intricacies of computer networks, seeing hacking as an intellectually stimulating hobby. From the beginning, there was a divide between those who used their knowledge to rip-off phone companies, albeit on a small scale, and those who did not. The advent of phone phreaking also led to the criminalization of hacking. It was not long before mobsters heard that money could be made by manipulating telephone networks, launching the age of digital organized crime. One observer referred to this confluence of criminals and hackers as *cross-fertilization,* where "You had criminals, organized crime, gangsters in fact, who were able to communicate with fellow gangsters without paying money" (Warren and Streeter 2005, 22). More important, however, was the fact that besides setting up free phone call services, they also had a new service they could sell to others.

As more cybercriminals went to jail for short spells, their contacts with the criminal underworld brought them and their technical skills to the attention of more crime syndicates. Gangsters might not be well educated, but they knew a good thing when they saw it, as well as the implicit opportunities of technology for future crime ventures. As more businesses dabbled in e-commerce, so did the targets for criminal groups. According to infamous hacker Kevin Mitnick, who for a brief time was on the FBI's Most Wanted List and now consults for security companies, it was inevitable that "When the Internet went commercial and there was money involved—business transaction from B2B (business to business) and B2C (business to consumer)—it was going to attract criminal elements" (quoted in Warren and Streeter 2005, 33).

globalHell (gH)

The organization globalHell (gH), a hackers' syndicate, according to federal prosecutors in 1999, was "a real gang, just like the Crips and Bloods" (Meeks 1999; Newton 2004, 128). For the most part, government investigators overreacted to this group that was little more than a loose coalition of 15 to 20 members between 13 and 29 years of age. The members represented Belgium, Canada, Southeast Asia, and the United States and rose to prominence in 1999, when it unleashed cyber attacks that shut down the White House and FBI Web sites for 24 hours. The somewhat hyperbolic response by law enforcement personnel belied the fact that there was little to link the members to criminal activities for profit. The FBI described one leading member as "a known street gang member in the Houston area" (Meeks 1999; Newton 2004, 128). In 2000, one gH member known as "Coolio" was linked to some denial of service attacks on some of the Internet's largest commercial business sites, including Yahoo!, eBay, and Amazon.com. In 2001, Coolio pleaded guilty to several misdemeanor accounts and was sentenced to up to 1 year in jail and a $15,000 payment of restitution. In recent years, most of the members have backed away from defacing Web sites, thanks in part to improved security and training in the realm of digital policing (Meeks 1999; Newton 2004, 128).

Pirates with Attitude

By the end of the 20th century, federal prosecutors described Pirates with Attitude (PWA) as "one of the oldest and most sophisticated networks of software pirates anywhere in the world." Formed in the early 1990s, the organization was motivated by economic profit from the very beginning. Members ranged the world from the United States and Canada to Sweden and Belgium. Members communicated through the private Internet Relay Chat (IRC) channels "#pwa" and "#tude." The group used a number of file transfer protocol (FTP) sites on the Internet that were set up to facilitate the movement of pirated software stored in bulk on numerous sites. PWA members operate one site called "Sentinel," considered to be among the first FTP sites on the Internet. Between 1995 and 2000, Sentinel was operated out of Canada's University of Sherbrooke specifically as a Warez site, a Web site trafficking in stolen software and available only to authorized users who were first vetted by a PWA leader in Massachusetts. Once an individual was approved, they had access to downloading programs as long as they uploaded software from other sources. In a subsequent investigation, authorities found that at least 100 individuals had been approved through the Massachusetts member. From 1998 to 2000, more than 5,000 copyrighted software programs were illegally stored and traded through the Sentinel site in violation of U.S. and international copyright laws. Visitors reportedly downloaded operating systems; utilities; applications, including word processing and data analysis programs; and games and MP3 music files, such as programs published by Adobe, IBM, Lotus, Microsoft, Norton, Novell, and Oracle.

The organization featured a structure based on specialization. *Suppliers,* for instance, funneled software programs to the group from major companies, although *Crackers* eliminated copy protection embedded in the software. *Packagers* tested the programs and readied them for sale, although *Couriers* transferred the software to the organization's FTP sites. Among the suppliers was a Microsoft employee known as "Warlock," who not only stole the software but also used his access to the company's internal network to allow others to penetrate Microsoft's network with his identification and password codes. By 1998, PWA had enlisted several Intel Corporation employees to provide computer hardware necessary for maintaining the Sentinel FTP storage capacity after it turned out that the Sentinel site's hardware was limited in terms of its memory capacity. The employees shipped the hardware to Canada, at Intel's expense and without the company's permission, in order to evade Canadian customs. One of the members configured Intel's servers to produce software that was readily accessible in exchange for free access to Sentinel. In January 2000, a combined FBI and Canadian task force busted the organization, charging 17 defendants with conspiracy to infringe on copyrights on more than 5,000 computer software programs worth more than $1 million. Federal prosecutors proclaimed the arrests as "the most significant investigation of copyright infringement involving the use of the Internet conducted to date by the FBI" (Newton 2004, 247–248).

Cybercrime Forums

A *Cybercrime forum* is just another name for a clearinghouse for the trade in digital criminal strategies, methods, and techniques. At its zenith in 2004, almost 4,000 members of ShadowCrew shared what became the "established standard for cybercrime forums" (Acohido and Swartz 2006, 2B). Offering well-designed and interactive Web pages "run much like a well-organized co-op" (Acohido and Swartz 2006, 2B), members posted and exchanged information, sent private messages on certain topics, and essentially found a forum where hackers could "congregate, collaborate and build their reputations," albeit in a virtual realm (Acohido and Swartz 2006, 2B).

Credit Card Cloning

In the majority of credit card thefts, the crime is quickly reported and it can be blocked in less than an hour. Criminal groups in the early 2000s discovered it was more lucrative to *clone* an existing card, copying it rather than stealing it, because this gives them a larger window of opportunity to use it. As one source put it, "With a cloned card you can pretty much relax. It hasn't been stolen so no

Typical Costs of Goods and Services in Forums

$1,000–$5,000: Trojan program that can transfer funds between online accounts

$500: Credit card number with PIN

$80–$300: Change of billing data, including account number, billing address, SSN, home address, and date of birth

$150: Driver's license

$150: Birth certificate

$100: Social security card

$7–$25: Credit card number with security code and expiration date

$7: PayPal account log-on and password

4%–8% of the deal price: Fee to have an escrow agent close a complex transaction

(Adapted from *USA TODAY*, October 12, 2006, 2B).

one is looking out for it" (Thompson 2004, 174). By 2000, card cloning had become a huge industry, costing hundreds of millions of dollars each year. An army of waiters, gas station attendants, and hotel staff were willing to use hand-held scanners to skim details from cards given them by customers for gangsters who would pay them an average of $100 for each card. In Europe, many card-cloning gangs have been linked to Russian and Eastern European crime syndicates.

By most accounts, this crime is on the decline as credit card companies develop automated computer systems that can detect unusual spending patterns. Cloned cards often trigger alarm bells

John Draper: From "First Alleged Criminal Hacker" to High-Tech Millionaire

Generally accorded the distinction as the inventor of the Blue Box, Draper was one of the pioneers of phreaking, or ripping-off phone companies on long distance charges. He was among the first hackers to become involved in phone-line manipulation and among the first to be sent to prison for wire fraud in the cyberage (Newton 2004). Most sources allude to him as "the first alleged criminal cracker to come to the attention of the popular North American media" (Schell and Martin 2004, 7).

Working under the alias "Cap'n Crunch," Draper rose to cult status and high-tech prominence when he used a Cap'n Crunch cereal box whistle to emit a 2,600-Hz tone that allowed him to reproduce the exact tone used by American Telephone and Telegraph (AT&T) and other long-distance providers to indicate the line was available.

Draper's exploits were chronicled in journalist Ron Rosenbaum's 1971 *Esquire* article, "Secrets of the Little Box."[8] According to Draper, he learned from blind friends that by covering the holes and blowing on the free whistle, it produced the 2,600-Hz frequency that allowed him to make free phone calls. The way it apparently worked was that when any phone that emitted this tone, the switch controlling the call was tricked into thinking a call had ended and all billing ended there as well, allowing Draper and his pals to call each other long distance without paying.

Draper was eventually arrested and sent to jail. While in jail, he refused to cooperate with Mafia members who wanted to use his skills and was badly beaten. However, although he refused to cooperate with organized figures while in prison, he later reported, "I went out of my way to teach every criminal I came in contact with on how do this" (Warren and Streeter 2005, 22). On his release from prison, he hooked up with his old friend Steve Wozniak, the developer of the Apple Two computer. Wozniak convinced him to trade his phreaking skills for computer programming. In 1981, Draper's career came full circle when he wrote the Easy Writer word-processing program that was sold along with IBM personal computers, leading him on the path to multimillionaire status.

Computer Chips: "The Dope of the 1990s?"

Organized crime's interest in new technologies appeared on California law enforcement radar screens in the early 1990s during a string of computer chip robberies that netted Asian gangsters more than $1 million. Referring to the highly sought 486-series computer chips in 1994, one police sergeant in California's Silicon Valley said, "Computer chips are the dope of the 90's. They're easier to steal than dope. Worth more money than dope. And for the people who steal them, here's the best part: Once stolen, they're almost untraceable" (Webster 1994, 54). Between 1992 and 1994, it was estimated that the costs of computers continued to rise "solely due to organized chip thievery." During this period computer chips were considered the "most valuable commodity on the international black market" (Webster 1994, 54).

The computer industry was undergoing an $80 billion annual boom in the silicon chip technology in the early 1990s, as they became integral parts of cars, computers, toys, medical equipment, and even greeting cards. The 486-series chip was considered the best performing chip, capable of sorting 150 million electronic instructions per second. During the mid-1990s, it was estimated that in Silicon Valley alone, businesses were losing $1 million a week. Easily transported and completely legal to possess, computer chips seemed at face value to be the ideal trafficking commodity, especially when compared to the risks of drug trafficking. As of 1994, only 2% had serial numbers. The following year, Intel, the world's largest manufacturer of computer chips, took steps to thwart this problem by placing serial numbers on its more expensive microprocessors and began placing tracking devices on higher-priced products. In 1995, Intel announced that it would work "with the semi-conductor industry on a standard bar code identification system for computer chips, making them as identifiable as a human fingerprint and a lot less attractive to buyers on the black market" (Riley 1995).

With Intel's newest Pentium chips costing £600, they were more valuable than heroin (Riley 1995). Violent organized robberies began in 1991 throughout the computer industry from Japan to Oregon. Gangs forced their way into factories in "takeover" style robberies, stealing chips and intimidating witnesses. In 1992 and 1993, more than $40 million worth of chips were stolen, and in one robbery, $1 million worth of 486 chips were put into a gym bag in less than 12 minutes. Subsequent investigations revealed that most of these robberies were facilitated with inside help from temporary workers or security guards.

Once the chips were stolen, they changed hands more than a dozen times in less than 3 days. Ultimately, many arrived in Asia, where they are used to make "knock-off" computers that are sold back to the United States. According to one middleman, he makes several trips from southern California to Asia each year, making stop-offs in Singapore, Tokyo, Bangkok, and other cities. For less than 5% of the value of the chips, he takes the goods to various transit sites, where they are divided up and distributed to destinations in Asia. He admitted that his largest shipment was $2.7 million worth of 486-series chips (Webster 1994).

Since the 1990s chip manufacturers have substantially curtailed organized chip theft rings by introducing unique identifiers such as Processor Serial Numbers (PSNs) and a new generation of chips that can transmit unique identification numbering when online (which has been opposed by privacy activists). More recently new chip protection has gone "beyond serial numbers." In 2008 a new technique was introduced that replaced bar codes and outdated serial numbers with something called a Radio Frequency Identification (RFID) tag. Chips are burned with a unique serial number, "an almost invisible computer chip that goes beyond serial numbers" by linking chips to sound and pictures" (Hart, 2008).

as a result. In addition, the old-style magnetic-stripe cards that were perfect for cloning are set to be replaced by more secure "chip and pin" cards. When this was inaugurated in France in the late 1990s, it cut fraud by 80% (Thompson 2004).

Phone Card Piracy

Major telephone carriers such as Sprint, MCI, and AT&T estimate their annual losses related to phone card piracy at more than $100 million. One of the earliest and most damaging international networks was discovered in 1994. Following extensive investigation, it was revealed that members

Cybernarcotics?

Some computer experts envision the development of cybernarcotics that rather than being ingested orally or taken as an injection, come in the form of digital stimulants. One would ingest these by hooking up to a special machine that stimulates the brain's pleasure centers directly. FBI authorities suggest that these products could be more addictive than heroin and cocaine. One source suggests the digital stimulants might be transmitted across the Internet or by using radio waves and would be available whenever someone wants to turn on (Thompson 2004).

of the ring, which also included telephone company operators using screen names such as Killer, Phone Stud, and Major Theft, stole more than 140,000 phone card numbers over the prior 2 years. The numbers were then sold through online bulletin boards for about $1 each. It was estimated than $1,000 in illegal long distance calls were placed on each number. The leader of the gang was an Illinois resident who eventually plea bargained for a lesser sentence after being faced with 5 years in jail and a $250,000 fine (Newton 2004).

Phishing and Variants

The explosion of hacker Web sites that sell phishing kits contributed to the growth of phishing and other related Internet criminal schemes. According to one spokesperson for the Anti-Phishing Working Group, "There's a whole underground economy of trading credit card information back and forth and the tools for doing credit card fraud." What has made this increasingly difficult to investigate domestically is the fact that many attacks originate in foreign countries in Asia, Russia, and Eastern Europe.

Phishing involves sending fraudulent e-mails that appear to come from a legitimate organization such as a bank, credit card company, online merchant, or Internet service provider. These e-mails ask the recipient to share personal information such as birth dates, social security numbers, or personal identification number (PIN) codes. Once criminals get this information, victims are hit with identity theft, monetary losses, and credit card fraud. Originally, it was delivered through crude typo-ridden e-mails by relative amateurs; however, it has since developed into a wide range of sophisticated methods engineered by professionals capable of tricking experienced computer users. E-mails might include eye-catching logos and the exact language used on Web sites of respected financial institutions or electronic commerce retailers. These e-mails make Web sites look like the real thing. They may also contain personal or account information gleaned from other sources. Phishing has become so rewarding that organized crime groups around the world now use it as a new method of theft, extortion, and blackmail. Variations of phishing include *vishing*, in which computer users are talked into calling a phone number to give up personal information directly to waiting criminals; *spear phishing* refers to when criminals obtain access to a corporate network or social networking site, and obtain e-mail addresses of individuals familiar to the potential victims and create messages that purport to come from direct bosses and close friends. In the case of *pharming*, criminals are able to manipulate legitimate Web sites or use tools that redirect traffic to fraudulent sites that collect victims' information or take over their machines (Koch 2007).

Phishing groups move quickly, in many cases taking less than a week from creating fake sites and sending the e-mails to the collecting information and the actual thefts. Some sites are up for as little as 2 or 3 days, with most activity coming within a day of the first messages sent. What has proved so attractive to phishing groups is the ratio of risk to reward. One need not be especially technically sophisticated, and the rewards are huge compared to the low risk of

Phishing Activity (2005)

	January 2005	October 2004
Active phishing sites	2,560	1,186
Brands hijacked	64	46
Percentage of attacks on financial services	80	74

(Anti-Phishing Working Group; Fisher, 2005)

being caught. Organized crime groups in Brazil and Eastern Europe have purportedly assembled "crews of crackers, fences and code writers who handle everything from creating and sending fraudulent e-mails to converting ill-gotten goods into hard currency" (Fisher 2005, 20). Both the FBI and the U.S. Secret Service are involved in suppressing this activity and other types of electronic fraud.

In May 2004, the UK's National High-Tech Crimes Unit arrested 12 Russian-speaking people who had been recruited by Russian organized crime groups to take part in a phishing scam. They were from Russia, the Baltic republics, and Ukraine. They set up bank accounts in which money stolen from these schemes was deposited. The money was later transferred back to syndicate members in Russia or used to buy goods. The suspects had been recruited in Internet chat rooms and through local Russian-language publications in Great Britain.

Brazilian police launched a massive coordinated investigation targeting that country's growing phishing underworld. Subsequent police raids in four Brazilian states led to the arrest of more than 50 suspects. Police called the group "a sophisticated, organized criminal ring" (Fisher 2005, 20) reputed to have stolen more than $30 million. The scheme used by the Brazilians involved sending thousands of messages to customers whose addresses had been taken from a list stolen by a bank employee. The customers were sent email s notifying them that they needed to update their online banking information and included an attachment that was in reality a Trojan. When the user opened up the attachment, the Trojan modified the PC's host file to point the machine to a malicious Web site instead of the legitimate banking site (Fisher 2005, 20).

One recent investigation identified the structure and actors of a phishing network, comparing their methodologies to "those of organized crime deployed for the purpose of money laundering. Among the actors are *Mounting agents,* who provide technology to begin the attacks. These agents design the software that attracts potential victims to fraudulent Web sites, and in the process infects their computer systems with malicious software. *Hosting attack agents* are expected to collect credentials. They compromise Web servers and design phishing sites and other attacks that are designed to get users to reveal their credentials. *Intermediaries* impersonate fooled customers and transfer assets to financial agents or foreign accounts such as offshore accounts. *Financial agents* are responsible for transferring funds to these bank accounts. Finally, there are *Confidants* who are expected to withdraw the transferred funds (Birk, Gajek, Grobert, and Sadeghi. 2007).

Cyberspace

Cyberspace refers to all types of computer-mediated communications, even traditional telephone systems, which are currently digitized and "fall within the ambit of cyberspace" (Mishra, 2003, 2). The following are all components of cyberspace:

- Digital computers
- Voice, fax, telex, video, and other forms of communication systems

- Digitally operated transportation systems such as cars, trains, airplanes, elevators, etc.; these can be remotely monitored or controlled over a network
- Digital control systems, such as are applied in chemical processes, health care of energy provision
- Digitally operated appliances such as watches, microwave ovens, digital cameras, and video recorders; Bluetooth technology allows some of these systems to be connected to the Internet and act "intelligent"
- Robots that run automated systems independently
- High-tech weapons systems, missiles, global positioning systems (GPS), space vehicles and satellites, etc.
- Communication technologies that include switching systems, broadcasting, various audio-visual devices, local area networks, cellular/WLL phones, modems, satellite systems, laser/microwave/HF/VHF/UHF radio systems, and optical fiber and other cable systems (Mishra 2003)

Computer Viruses, Botnets, and Zombie Computers

Generally speaking, a *computer virus* is an executable code that attaches itself (infecting) to some other code within a host computer in a bid to replicate itself. *Malware* or *malicious viruses* are specifically created to alter or erase data, crash the host system, and other related motivations. Organized crime gangs have used their access to mostly home-based PCs with broadband connections to launch a variety of criminal schemes involving extortion, threat of denial of service, and phishing techniques. However, this would not be possible without the use of "zombie PCs" to spread viruses and spam through fraudulent e-mails. When a target receives an e-mail from one of these units, it looks like it is coming from a legitimate source, because it is. Especially alluring to phishers and others is the general lack of awareness among many Internet users, and they are becoming experts at getting account information and passwords in response to e-mails coming from legitimate financial retailers and institutions. This information is then sold on the black market. Unbeknownst to thousands of users, their infected computers are being controlled by remote spammers. By one estimate, during the first half of 2004, 30,000 PCs a day were being turned into zombies (Krim 2004). In 2005, the going price for temporary use of an army of 20,000 zombie PCs cost between $2,000 and $3,000 (Spring 2005).

A number of law enforcement organizations around the world have identified organized crime groups with *botnet* (a collection of software robots, or bots, that run autonomously and automatically) gangs. For example Russian, Turkish, and Moroccan gangs have been linked with hiring *botmasters* (hackers who control large numbers of zombie PCs) "much as one might enlist a hit-man" (Rigby 2005, page). One of the most important tools used by criminal cybergangs is the creation of zombie computers, which essentially run programs that give control to another user over the Internet. In this way, a cybercriminal can take direct control over these computers. This is accomplished by deliberately infecting the targeted computers with a virus that allows the perpetrator control various functions of the computer without the actual owner being aware. Once this is accomplished, they then can use them to launch denial of service attacks and hide fraudulent activities behind these zombie PCs. More recently, this scheme has become increasingly prominent, but what has become even more alarming has been the creation of armies of "zombie PCs directly under their control which can then lead to large scale attacks on targeted businesses when they are commanded to perform a malicious function" (Zambo 2007, 551). This tactic is used in extortion schemes in which cybergangs or criminals threaten to take down a company's Web site if a ransom is not paid.

Some cybercriminals use malicious programs called *Trojan horses* to create botnets. Although botnets first appeared in the late 1990s, by most accounts, "the first organized attempt

Leading Computer Viruses

Virus	Year	Damage
LoveBug	2000	$8.75 billion
MyDoom	2004	$5.75 billion
Netsky	2004	$3.75 billion
Sasser	2004	$3.6 billion
SoBig	2003	$2.75 billion
Zotob	2005	$850 million
Mytob	2005	$500 million

(Bryan-Low 2006, A1)

to create large-scale Botnets" (Koch 2007) took place in 2003. It all supposedly began with the SoBig e-mail worm, and by 2007 estimates of PCs under the control of hackers approached at least 1 million. They range in size from a few hundred compromised machines to 50,000 infected computers (Koch 2007). One Dutch case involved a botnet using 1.5 million computers (Iiett 2005). Other estimates suggest extortion gangs control hundreds of thousands of computers, using personal computers of individuals with high-speed DSL lines or cable modems. They gained control of the PCs with the help of a series of worms[10] and viruses[11] that are most adept at spreading to machines without necessary protections. Once infected, these computers listen for instructions from a new program or order them to check with master machines. Together, these legions of computer *bots,* short for *robots,* are utilized for spreading spam and stealing financial information as well as launching denial-of-service attacks (Menn 2004, 2). In 2008, the FBI Cyberdivision warned potential victims to be on the lookout for spam e-mails spreading the Storm Worm malicious software, a form of what is known as *malware.* Once the recipient clicks to download what is advertised as an electronic greeting card, the malware is downloaded to the Internet-connected device and causes it to become infected and part of the Storm Worm botnet, "a network of compromised machines under the control of a single user" (FBI, Storm Worm Virus, 2008).

Pump-and-Dump Schemes

Organized crime has become especially interested in the new life digital technology has given to traditional *pump-and-dump schemes,* which begin with criminals purchasing stocks of companies whose shares sell for pennies and are typically sold over the counter rather than on legitimate exchanges. Next, they hire spammers to send mass e-mails inviting investors to take advantage of these undervalued companies. Because the prices and trading volumes of penny stocks are so low to begin with, it does not take much trading activity to pump up the stock price. Then the criminals sell their stocks, causing the stock price to cash. In one 2006 example, hackers were able to break into accounts at two large U.S. brokerages to execute fraudulent trades. On December 15, 2006, shares of Apparel Manufacturing Associates were trading at 6 cents a share. A 3-day spam campaign pumped the price up to 19 cents, and trading volume on December 18 rose to 484,500 shares. The stock price peaked at 45 cents on December 20. Two days later, the price dropped to 30 cents, and trading volume decreased to 36,450 shares. In March 2007, the SEC suspended trading on the stock and 34 others for 10 business days, citing "suspected manipulation" (Koch 2007).

Child Pornography

Schlegel and Cohen examined modern technology's impact on the crime of pedophilia, noting that pedophiles invariably include collecting and disseminating child pornography or through physical contact with them. They assert that these crimes have evolved over time "in response to important advances in image technology," beginning with the first Polaroid Land Camera in 1947, allowing individuals for the first time to instantly produce photographs (2007, 25). Previously, if one wanted a pornographic image of a child, they had to navigate the intricacies of traditional negative-to-film printing or have an associate in the film-developing business. However, it was difficult for an individual, let alone an organization, to trade the photos once in hand, and as a result, most of the commercially available photos were found in poor-quality magazines imported into the United States. Law enforcement was often successful at suppressing this crime until the introduction of Beta- and VHS-format video cameras in the late 1970s and 1980s. Unlike the still images of times past, the alarming trafficking in amateur child pornography and the new technology "allowed contact offenders to memorialize their behaviors as never before" (Schlegel and Cohen 2007, 25–26).

Today, the Internet and digital technology not only make it easy to produce child pornography on a worldwide scale, but also proved a boon to maintaining anonymity and a means for offenders to communicate with each other and their victims through myriad chat rooms, Webcams, social networking sites, and forums. Pornography has proved to be one of the Web's biggest businesses. During a survey taken in 2001, more than 17.5 million Americans visited Internet pornography sites, a 40% increase over the previous year. These figures, like subsequent surveys, reflect visits only to legal porn sites, where images of only certified adults are posted. The only area of pornography that has been tethered by legal restrictions is related to child pornography. No federal child pornography prohibitions were instituted until the adoption of the Sexual Exploitation of Children Act in 1977, which banned the production, interstate shipment, and advertisement of related products. Seven years later, the Child Protection Act of 1984 determined that a *child* is defined as anyone under the age of 18. Over the next several years other restrictions followed, including the Child Sexual Abuse and Pornography Act in 1986 and the Child Protection and Obscenity Act of 1988 that prohibited the use of computers for the transmission or advertisement of child pornography. In 1990, the interstate or foreign shipment of three or more child porn images by any means, including computers became a federal crime. The rise of the Internet and the digital revolution led to the Telecommunications Act of 1996, which banned the use of any communications medium to solicit acts of sex from minors. One of the most controversial pieces of legislation and a continuing target of civil libertarians was the Child Pornography Prevention Act of 1996, which expanded the definition of *child pornography* to include "any simulated depiction of children having sex—even if the models are themselves legal adults or the images include only nonexistent virtual children" (Newton 2004, 59–60).

Despite the litany of child pornography laws, child or "kiddy" pornography remains a lucrative business. The growth of child pornography has become an important moneymaker for organized criminals, with criminal networks sharing child pornography online and operating fee-based sites. It is considered to be one of the fastest growing markets, with a volume ranging from $3 billion to $20 billion globally. In 2004, 55% of the material originated from the United States and 23% from Russia.

Among related innovations in the production and distribution of child pornography has been computer software that can digitally alter images of child pornography to enhance or change the image, for example, "sexualizing content by removing clothing. Similarly, in contrast to software that digitally ages missing children, images of child porno can be created by de-aging images of adult porno" (Criminal Intelligence Service Canada, 2007, 3). "Criminals have been known to use steganography to conceal information, like child porn, and distribute it in a secure fashion" (Criminal Intelligence Service of Canada 2007, 3).

Spam

The first e-mail was sent in 1978 over the Defense Department's network, the ARPAnet, considered the precursor to the Internet. The birth of the Internet was accompanied by a new generation of *spam*[12]—mass mailings sent over a variety of channels. Originally only advertisements, today they are a popular tool of computer criminals that use e-mail; newsgroups; instant messaging; and the comment fields in blogs, cell phones, and other devices to send messages to a huge group of recipients and potential victims. The trend has been for spam to become more malicious as criminals adopt it as a carrier for an array of scams, ranging from identity theft to fraud and software designed to take control of a victim's computer. The advent of instant messaging has also given rise to a related spam called *spim* (Koch 2007).

Over the past several years, spam has continued to evolve from its origins as essentially as an advertising nuisance to something more illegal and malicious. When the online security firm Clearswift first confronted it in the early 1990s, it was dominated by a witches' brew of pornography, financial, healthcare, and direct product spam. Soon gambling and scam-related spam flourished as well. Today, spammers are aiming even higher with financial and pharmaceutical spam, which grew from 21.8% in 2004 to 69.6% in 2005. Paralleling this has been a large drop in pornographic spam, with Web users more typically being targeted by cheap Viagra offers and low interest loans. Observers suggest this trend indicates the growing sophistication of spammers and the movement of more criminals toward the digital world. More troubling is the movement of organized crime groups shifting their operations online. Spam has proved to be the tactic of choice "to direct e-mail users onto disreputable sites" (Gamba 2005, 1), while at the same time evading the prying eyes of law enforcement. This led one digital authority to assert. "Spam is now a hotbed for a variety of financial scams, such as phishing and pump and dump stock tipping, and serves as a black market for illegal goods such as fake pharmaceuticals and counterfeit software" (Gamba 2005, 1).

Internet Extortion

Internet extortion, also referred to as *digital extortion* and *cyberextortion,* involves making certain demands of an individual or groups of individuals under the threat of harm. Although the demands are typically financial in nature, there are cases that have involved non-financial considerations such as sexual favors. The vast majority of cases have targeted wealthy organizations and individuals (Deflem and Hudak, 2008, 289).

Besides the extortion threats, cybercriminals added a new twist by e-mailing individuals with threats to kill them if they did not pay a large amount of money. In late 2006, the FBI reported e-mails were surfacing in London claiming to be from the FBI, warning the target that the recipient's information was found on a subject linked to several contract killings in the United States and the UK, and identified the recipient as the next victim. He was then requested to contact the FBI in London. This ruse depends on a social engineering technique that uses the FBI's name to intimidate and convince the recipient the e-mail threat is legitimate. In response, the FBI claims it never sends out e-mails soliciting information from citizens (FBI, January 4, 2008).

CYBER BLACKMAIL Cyber blackmail is increasing. Criminals focus on specific computer users and send them e-mails that threaten to delete essential files or install pornographic images on their work computers unless they pay a ransom. This scam emerged around 2003 and has been used to indiscriminately attack anyone on the corporate ladder who has a PC connected to the Internet. According to one authority, it begins with an e-mail telling a victim that someone has the power to take over his work computer and usually demands a small fee (usually less than $60), or perpetrator will attack the victim's PC with some type of file-erasing program or download image of child pornography on his machine. However, like the 419 scams (chronicled in Chapter 12 concerning Afrolineal Organized Crime), the scam only works if some of the recipients actually follow through and pay up.

TARGETING ONLINE GAMBLING   In 2006, more than two dozen individuals were busted in a $3 billion gambling operations that used the Internet, offshore computer services, and "good old-fashioned mob muscle" (Moore and Shiftel 2006). The FBI seized more than $7 million in cash and closed down the popular sports betting site called Playwithal.com. The New York Police Department claimed, "It is the largest illegal gambling operation this department has ever encountered" (Moore and Shiftel 2006). This operation was significant because it was the first bust made after a law went into effect in October 2006 that made it more difficult for bettors to use their American-based credit cards and banks to fund their Internet gambling accounts. Playwithal.com set up a system that relied extensively on cold cash. Bettors would be given a secret code to use the secret Internet site by a network of 2,000 traditional bookies, thereby allowing users to bet on all types of sports. At the end of each week, bookies either paid off or collected from customers. Members of this syndicate were able to sock away millions of dollars using shell corporations and bank accounts ranging from Central America and the Caribbean to Switzerland and Hong Kong (Moore and Shiftel 2006).

Online gambling sites were among the early businesses hit by digital extortion rackets. As far back as 2003, messages were sent to sports and gambling Web sites threatening to shut down their site unless they met certain financial demands. The consensus is that there is some type of organized crime affiliation with some of these schemes. An executive for one security services group noted, "Organized crime has always been about money, and there is definitely money at the end of a hostile or fraudulent Internet attack" (Germain 2004). Although some operations are relatively expensive, others require large amounts of capital. Super Bowl Sunday has proved to be fraught with extortion schemes because it is the heaviest betting day of the year. These "distributed denial-of-service" (DDoS) attacks threaten recipients with shutting down betting sites or parlors unless protection money is paid. The trade-off between wiring a $40,000 payoff to the millions at stake often convinces the victims to pay, preferring to seek hardware solutions in time for the next year's game.

The NFL Super Bowl is the most lucrative sports-wagering event, bringing in more than $2 billion each year and an important event for both legal and illegal gambling. However, the advent of online betting has given rise to a number of schemes that are capable of unleashing denial-of-service attacks on online sports betting, which gleans millions of dollars from Internet gamblers. Those in the business suggest that these groups can be more of a threat than traditional organized criminals "because they hide behind a computer screen from anywhere on the planet" (quoted in Walker 2005, 3). Many compare this new type of extortion to a high-tech protection racket. Cyber-extortionists have been successful at disabling a number of well-respected sites, including bluegrasssports.com, betcasade.com, pinnnaclesports.com, Caribsports.com, vipsorts.com, and betgameday.com. In 2004, after making a bundle during football season, extortionists then went after horse bookmakers and European sites during the soccer championship in Portugal. One e-mail threat demanded $15,000 for 6 months of protection: "If you wait to make a deal with us when the attacks start, it will cost you $25,000 for six months protection, lost revenues and your site will stay down until the $25,000 is received" (quoted in Walker 2005, 3).

One of the main lures of the online gambling industry is that it is unregulated, making operations vulnerable to shakedowns. Unlike state lotteries and government-regulated casinos, it is illegal to place bets for monetary gain over a wire transfer in the United States.[13] Organized crime is well aware of this Achilles' heel. Because most casinos and online sports sites are located outside U.S. jurisdictions, these gambling operations have little recourse when it comes to meeting extortion demands. However, this has not stopped them from attacking legal gambling firms based in England and Australia. Once every major betting firm had been hit at least once, one of the businesses went to Scotland Yard's High-Tech Crime Unit in 2004 and agreed to participate in a sting operation. Soon, British authorities picked up the money trail and in tandem with the Russian Interior Ministry, arrested several members of the ring. Although it consisted of less than a handful of members who communicated exclusively online, the group realized profits in the hundreds of thousands of dollars through their extortion schemes. On top of these profits, the gang caused $90 million in damages to several major banks, bookmakers, and other targets (Menn 2004).

DENIAL OF SERVICE EXTORTION   What was once a business identified with brass knuckles and bludgeons has for a new generation of extortionists morphed into a business in which the leg breakers do not even have to leave the sanctuary of their computer rooms. One of the latest lucrative cybercrimes involves the protection/extortion rackets, in which gangs of computer hackers threaten to stop traffic to Web-based sites if the operators refuse to meet their demands. Digital extortionists now have the power to launch coordinated attacks on thousands of computers that can knock businesses off the Web for weeks at a time. By most accounts, businesses often pay the protection demands, which total in the millions of dollars. Initially, the cybergangs trained their sights on gambling and pornographic Web sites, but are increasingly targeting traditional e-commerce businesses.

HIGH-TECH FRAUD   Traditionally, Italian mafia bosses used a combination of the carrot and stick approach—offering bribes or threatening violence—when it came to election time. In 2003, mobsters tried adopting 21st-century technology to make an impact on the outcome of regional elections by using video phones. Although the idea never quite got off the ground in time for this election, it demonstrated the transformation through technology of a number of Mafia activities. The plan in this case was to use a new third-generation video phones (3G). Voters would be instructed by local Mafiosi to take the 3G phones to the voting booth and send back images confirming they voted as instructed. Known for its obsession with mobile phones, the Italians were among the first consumers to have access to video phones capable of handling huge quantities of data, such as video clips, TV news broadcasts, share-price information, and city maps (BBC 2003).

ELECTRONIC MONEY LAUNDERING   In the global economy of the 21st century, billions of dollars in money transfers are conducted every day through electronic impulses. This is widely utilized by banks shipping money to each other, stock exchanges, brokerages, commodities dealers, credit card companies, money remitters, governments, and wealthy individuals. Today, the three major electronic funds transfer (EFT) systems are CHIPS, SWIFT, and Fedwire, which combined handle almost $2 trillion in transfers each day (Madinger 2006, 225).

The spread of electronic banking and e-payment systems has been a godsend to money-launderers. Digital technology has done for money laundering that it has accomplished in the legitimate economy with online retail selling. Most observers assert that organized crime groups are at the forefront of adopting and developing technologies to facilitate money laundering. As one authority put it, "From pay as you go mobile phones for anonymous communication to transacting business through the Internet, all the tools and techniques that are available to global business are similarly available to global criminals" (Lilley 2006, 108–109). Digital technology allows money to move around the world at the speed of light. Utilizing such a route, criminals have the advantage of jurisdiction shopping for countries and regions where transaction regulations are less than rigorous. Once this is done, the money trail soon grows cold for investigators (Grabosky 2007).

Electronic money laundering offers a number of ways for criminals to move illicit cash. Sometimes they use legitimate online services such as auctions, where a buyer and seller can team up in order to transfer "phantom" items at a previously agreed-on price, thus criminal proceeds are transformed into cash due to the sale of a legitimate commodity. Others use online gambling services to create an account with service providers using illicit income, and then eventually cashing out the account and collecting the funds as winnings. Another popular ruse is to widely advertise online with come-ons such as, "Earn money while working at home." Once an unwitting recruit responds, he is often ensnared in schemes to transfer money electronically to offshore accounts, using the technique of *smurfing,* in which they only transfer amounts less than the required transaction reporting amount (usually under $5,000). These "mules" receive a small fee for their help (Grabosky 2007).

Some organized crime groups have even set up their own telecommunications companies to commit fraud and money laundering. Others have accepted the fact that some groups were probably putting their own people into mobile companies. One leading security services officer in the UK recently pointed out,

> If a criminal gang in eastern Europe makes 200,000 pounds from drugs sold to the UK and needs to move the "dirty money" back to eastern Europe, it can make calls using prepaid mobiles from the UK to personal numbers (which enable users to receive calls anywhere) it runs in eastern Europe. It will then receive a share of the revenues these numbers have generated for the UK mobile operator which it used for its prepaid calls. It could end up with a "clean" cheque from a UK mobile operator for 150,000 pounds. (Quoted in Shillingford 2004, 6)

ELECTRONIC BANKING FRAUD   In 1995, Russian hacker Vladimir Levin was arrested for the world's first reported attack on the bank's network (Warren and Streeter 2005). Using a PC in St. Petersburg, he and members of his hacking group were able to get access to Citibank's U.S. network. After appropriating the names and passwords of customers, they moved more than $3 million into personal accounts they set up in other parts of the world. There is some evidence that Levin was operating at the behest of organized crime. In any case, he was arrested and most of the money was returned to the bank. According to one knowledgeable source, Levin returned home from a night on the town in St. Petersburg to find several Russian mobsters waiting for him. Then they made their pitch offering him either "a small amount of money or an attitude correction course" (Warren and Streeter 2005, 34).

In 2004, London's Financial Services Authority warned there was evidence that criminals were trying to place staff inside banks with the intention commit identity theft (Devi 2005). In March 2005, British police uncovered a "high-technology crime ring" attempting to steal $421 million from the London offices of the Japanese banking group Sumitomo. The investigation began the previous October, when it was discovered that a gang had gained access to the bank's computer systems and was attempting to transfer cash electronically to 10 other bank accounts around the world. Fortunately, the scheme was uncovered before transactions could take place. In the aftermath of that investigation, authorities warned London financial institutions to be on the lookout for criminals using devices called *keyloggers* to record each keystroke on the computer, thereby stealing passwords to the computer systems. Keylogging programs allow criminals to copy the keystrokes of computer users and send the information, including passwords, back to criminals who can assume a user's identity.

The investigation expanded to Israel, where the gang had tried to transfer some of the money. Police arrested the individual whose business account was slated to receive some of the loot. According to Israeli police, the man was charged with money laundering and deception in trying to transfer $27 million. One banking official and fraud consultant said, "The rise of the keyloggers poses a real threat to companies and this may be the first time we have evidence of organized criminals using the equipment to attack a bank" (Larsen 2005, page).

Keyloggers were especially prominent in other cases in 2005, particularly in the case of the Zotob virus, which antivirus companies began noticing. This particular virus infected computers by taking advantage of a weakness in some versions of Microsoft Corporation's Windows operating system. Not only did it slow down and repeatedly reboot infected computers, but more threateningly, it also opened the door for other malicious software to be installed, including keylogging programs that record what a PC user types into a computer. Cybercriminals were able to exploit this to steal credit card numbers and information that could be sold to organized crime groups. One source suggests that Zotob affected more than 100,000 companies, including those of several major media companies (Bryan-Low 2006).

In February 2006, Brazilian police arrested 55 people for illegally loading keylogging software onto hundreds of computers, getting away with almost $4.7 million from 200 different accounts at 6 banks before they were apprehended (Nackan and Cooperman 2006). According to one

2006 estimate, more than 80 million individuals had their accounts compromised in just the United States in 2005. One of the more massive intrusions involved a group stealing 145,000 records from a U.S. data broker called CheckPoint while masquerading as a legitimate customer.

USING COMMUNICATIONS ADVANCEMENTS TO EVADE SURVEILLANCE   Until 1984, the majority of American local and long-distance telecommunications services were carried by AT&T. As long as one company dominated the industry, there was "a uniform system of equipment and analog technology" that allowed law enforcement to conduct surveillance operations easily on private telephone lines. The dismantlement of AT&T in 1984 severely compromised the ability of law enforcement to monitor what used to be a fairly uncomplicated protocol. In its place emerged thousands of different providers and a revolution in the telecommunications industry, as it made the transition from analog to digital technology. This transformation further complicated electronic surveillance.

Drug-trafficking organizations, particularly in Latin America, have been forced to contend with the scrutiny incumbent in America's "War on Drugs." A number of organizations have been crippled in recent years, but others have adopted new telecommunications advances to stay one step ahead of law enforcement. From the 1980s to the early 1990s, Colombian syndicates utilized pagers and created password systems to communicate times and locations for transactions. Supplementing these were payphones that offered a "virtually untraceable medium when live voice communication was required" (Nolin 2006, 3). During the 1990s, cartel leaders added pre-paid phone cards and faxes to their communications arsenal, always adapting to the newest advancements in technology, including cell phones, which they purchased in quantity and periodically threw away after using them for short spells.

Mexican and South American drug organizations invested their vast resources in technological advancements that would help facilitate the drug-smuggling operations using clandestine communications. Since the mid-1980s, these organizations have made frequent use of payphones in foreign countries because they were usually free from law enforcement surveillance. Other devices were adopted as well, including two-way pagers, push-to-talk or walkie-talkie communications, pre-paid phone cards, and cellular phones, all of which were reliable alternatives for criminals who needed to communicate within an organization and needed to evade the prying ears of law enforcement. Drug kingpins also use satellite phones, which they have found can make calls anywhere in the world in conjunction with almost untraceable pre-paid phone cards. A number of advancements in cell-phone technology have also been used to conceal incriminating conversations such as call waiting, call forwarding, conference calling, three-way calling, and call transfer. Christopher Nolin chronicled how these basic techniques have been used to evade surveillance, noting, "criminals use call forwarding to redirect calls outside of the same line loop, rendering the information virtually untraceable. By manipulating conference call holding features, agents may evade surveillance while coordinating criminal activities from remote locations or even prison" (2006, 5). Other methods avoid direct conversation by first using an agreed-on ring signal to convey messages to each other. After this, they have incoming calls directed to their cell-phone's voice mailbox and later retrieve the messages from an outside payphone. More recently, instant messaging services have become popular due to their speed and freedom from surveillance (Nolin 2006, 5).

COUNTERFEITING TECHNOLOGIES

By the end of the 20th century, advances in technology had revolutionized and expanded illegal counterfeit organizations. For example, currency counterfeiting used to be a specialized industry. The advent of computers, laser printers, and scanners expanded the capability to make passable bank notes. One estimate in 2004 suggested that perhaps 7% of the entire world's trade involved counterfeit goods (Lunde 2004, 48). The list of counterfeit goods is encyclopedic; let it suffice to say that if a profit can be made from a commodity, it will be counterfeited.

Music Piracy in a High-Tech World

The introduction of optical discs, including such devices as the CD and the DVD, has radically changed the landscape of music piracy. Like other businesses in the intellectual property sector, the music industry is targeted by international organized crime groups who reap profits from illegally selling pirated music to fund other crimes. According to the International Federation of the Phonographic Industry (IFPI), which represents the worldwide recording industry there is plenty of evidence linking "music piracy and other crimes, such as people trafficking, money laundering, violence, drug smuggling and terrorism" (IFPI 2004, 2). In 2004, it was estimated that the annual sales of pirated music was close to 2 billion units, worth between $4 billion and $5 billion. This means that roughly two units of each five recordings are illegal. No region of the world has been exempt from music piracy operations, and they have become increasingly more sophisticated since the mid-1990s.

As far back 1999, Southeast Asia authorities identified several sophisticated organizations working between Macao and Hong Kong. One of their methods was to store bootleg discs in sealed oil drums in underwater locations in preparation for picking up by smugglers, a method also favored by drug-trafficking organizations. The size of one operation was illustrated by the interception of a fishing boat from mainland China entering the harbor at Hong Kong from Macao. Inspectors found the ship was towing a submerged object. Hong Kong Police had it floated to the surface, revealing a 14-meter concrete bridge support that had been customized to transport pirated optical discs. In this instance, it concealed several hundred thousand discs valued at more than HK$5 million (IFPI 2004, 12).

In 2002, Ukrainian Tax Police and IFPI investigators collaborated in a raid on a pirate network operating in Odessa, where one location housed three clandestine workshops equipped with compact disc recorders (CDRs) duplicating pirated discs 24 hours a day. The investigation was noteworthy for demonstrating that music piracy had moved away from pressed-disc piracy in parts of Eastern Europe to the CDR method. This transition was chalked up to increased law enforcement pressure on this type of crime. The following year, a raid in Spain led to the arrest of 40 persons involved in the mass duplication of CDRs. A number of the suspects were illegal immigrants from China who had purposely been brought to Madrid by members of a Chinese crime group. The investigation revealed that that the Chinese gang relied on illegal immigrants to duplicate the discs as well as several computer shops and restaurants to launder the money earned from the illegal activity (IFPI 2004, 8).

The Camorra and Music Piracy

One of the unanticipated results of the Yugoslavian conflicts between 1991 and 1999 was that the increasing naval presence in the Adriatic interrupted the traffic of contraband cigarettes from the Balkans to Italy, and activity that was managed by Italian organized crime groups. In cities such as Naples, cigarette smuggling had been an important source of income for the Camorra for a number of years. The collapse of the illicit cigarette trade resulted in a downturn in employment and income for organized crime groups. This coincided with technological development in CD counterfeiting with the introduction of faster and cheaper CD burners. The convergence of these two trends saw the Naples underworld move from trafficking in cigarettes to the counterfeiting of music CDs. By the turn of the 21st century, Naples was Italy's epicenter for music piracy, putting out 70% of the country's counterfeit CDs. Camorra families had already become acquainted with this business in the 1990s by copying music cassettes, but with the shift to CDs, the production system became highly sophisticated and its supply chain well structured.

In 2002, Operation Jessica revealed the existence of large-scale organized crime involvement in the counterfeiting market and the leading role played by the Frattasio family. The investigation demonstrated the importance of the family in an operation that produced and imported counterfeit music cassettes and CDs, as well as extensive involvement in the importation of the raw materials required (recordable CDs, blank music and video cassettes) from Eastern Europe.

The Frattasio Family and Structure of Music Counterfeiting Operation

Operation Jessica established the operational structure that ran the enterprise. It featured a pyramidal hierarchy with the Frattasio family at the top. Under them were local crime bosses or others selected by the family to control particular territories in Naples and the Campania region. The local bosses operated with autonomy, but were ultimately answerable to the family. The Frattasio family delegated control over production and sale in a single district to a specific boss. Once the local boss received this backing, his gang was responsible for managing the district-level production of the counterfeit music and could allow others to produce CDs and cassettes for themselves, as well sell the products directly to consumers. All the while, this level paid a street tax to the primary actors. A range of actors depended on the local boss for the music products, especially non-indigenous groups who were involved in the immigrant street vendors' network.

The local bosses managed a number of smaller affiliate groups and families. These "cells" had usually requested permission to counterfeit CDs and cassettes in their own homes. Operation Jessica demonstrated that the most important cells were those responsible for obtaining the master copy of the track to be illegally reproduced. Other cells were involved in obtaining copying hardware or in charge of distributing the master to local production centers and controlling the production process. Still other cells controlled warehouses and the movement of the CDs outside the region, whereas the distribution of the final product and the sale process was in the hands of the cell most directly involved with street vendors and non-indigenous immigrant groups. Italian investigators noted a striking similarity between the logistical infrastructure used by this organization and those used by the earlier tobacco-smuggling operations.

As the Frattasio family counterfeiting empire expanded, it had to create the necessary financial structure to pay for the raw materials and launder profits. Operation Jessica revealed the existence of a number of dummy companies and corporate structures that were used to purchase the equipment and raw materials legally for the music duplication. By using a legitimate front, it was possible to purchase directly from legal wholesalers without drawing suspicion from agencies tasked with monitoring purchases of unusual quantities or raw materials by unregistered groups or individuals. As the operation expanded, it developed links outside the region into northern Italy and east to Ukraine.

Operation Jessica concluded with the arrest of four Frattasio brothers who were convicted and sentenced to $4^1/2$; years for criminal conspiracy and violating Italian copyright laws; 17 other members of the Frattasio family were sentenced to a combined 39 years in prison. Since then, a number of other Neapolitan Camorra gang bosses have been arrested in connection to similar schemes. The denouement of the investigation also revealed international links between the Frattasio organization and Ukrainian criminal groups (*Jane's Intelligence Review,* 2007).

Counterfeiting of Currency and Documents

Advancements in computer technology have virtually revolutionized the counterfeiting of currency and documents. Color scanners and printers, state-of-the-art word-processing and graphics software suites, and computer-driven color photocopiers not only expanded counterfeiting networks, but have also made their products much more difficult to identify. At one time, the $100 bill was the most frequently counterfeited currency in the world. As a result, global markets were awash in counterfeit $100 bills. In response, the U.S. Treasury Department redesigned it and added a watermark and other security devices. However, in less than a month, counterfeit $100 bills were being reproduced and used successfully in Eastern Europe, thanks to high-resolution color scanning that can reproduce the watermarks and colors of fibers in the paper (Taylor, Caeti, Loper, Fritsch, and Liederbach. 2006).

Counterfeit Medicine

One of the more alarming examples of high-tech fraud is the sale of counterfeit drugs, which often either contain the wrong ingredients or are missing the active ingredients. Southeast Asia has been a center for this activity, with much attention focused on a counterfeit anti-malaria drug. When composed of the proper ingredients, artesunate, which is produced primarily in southern China by Guilin Pharma, is considered one of the most highly effective treatments for malaria. However, one researcher studying counterfeit drugs in the region documented at least seven distinct variations of fake artesunate. There are no figures on the number of deaths resulting from fake pharmaceuticals. Other studies in 1999–2000 found that 38% of a random 104 samples were fakes and contained none of the active ingredient. The more impoverished regions of the world remain an easy target for criminal groups selling fake pharmaceuticals. Until recently, Chinese drug counterfeiting operations have faced only small fines, which gangs write off as just a cost of doing business. By most accounts, a number of narcotics-trafficking organizations whose members face the death penalty have switched to this activity due to its less severe sentencing (Aldhous 2005).

The sale of counterfeit medicines is the province of both individuals and organized groups. In 2005, indictments were issued by the United States against an organization led by two Indian nationals who repackaged controlled substances that had been physically smuggled into the United States and sold on online pharmacy Web sites. This scheme distributed millions of dosage units around the world. According to the indictment, authorities were seeking the forfeiture of 41 bank accounts in the United States, India, Singapore, the Channel Islands, the Isle of Man, Nevis, Antigua, and Ireland (Grabosky 2007, 8).

Software Piracy

The distribution of counterfeit Microsoft software has been the target of recent FBI activity. What is most troubling about the latest arrests was that it was the first serious effort to copy Microsoft's new edge-to-edge hologram security feature illegally on the software CDs. Four of those arrested belonged to an Asian organized crime group that has been active in California's San Gabriel Valley for some time. According to FBI spokesperson Cheryl Mimura, the software was smuggled into the United States from Asia, and the four arrested had been involved in the pickup and distribution of the software. A subsequent search turned up counterfeit copies of software estimated to be worth more than $10 million. A former DEA veteran now leading Microsoft's Worldwide Piracy Investigations notes that 6.6 million units of counterfeit software with a retail value of $2 billion has been seized worldwide in a 2-year period. Microsoft has pinpointed Asia as the epicenter for these activities, noting that although legal discs are manufactured in replication plants in Asia, there is substantial "leakage." According to the former DEA agent, the counterfeiting of DVDs and CDs has strong appeal for organized crime groups, and some groups have made the transition from the drug trade to this form of counterfeiting, noting, "Profits are high, and the risk is very low. It's unlike

Operation Cyber Chase

In April 2005, U.S. and international law enforcement agencies took part in Operation Cyber Chase. They targeted an Internet pharmacy based in India that had reportedly been selling controlled drugs to thousands of people online to the tune of $20 million. The only requirement for purchasing the drugs was a credit card and an address. The foreign distributor sold drugs on 200 Web sites and shipped the drugs in bulk to sites in Philadelphia and other parts of the United States, where the drugs were repackaged and shipped to customers. The subsequent raids seized $7 million from banks and 7 million doses of drugs. More than 20 individuals were arrested in the United States, India, and Canada. The investigation revealed that most buyers paid higher-than-market prices, indicating most were "abusing the drugs" (McAfee 2005, 9).

alien smuggling or drugs, where it's hard to get a legitimate cover. But an office in Silicon Valley has an air of respectability" (Gates 2001, page).

Policing the Internet and Fighting Cybercrime

Law enforcement has been playing catch-up since phishing became a serious problem in 2003. The burgeoning Internet has created special task forces staffed with investigators trained to detect electronic crimes, but these groups are poorly staffed, in many cases forced to hire help from the private sector. One leading authority admitted, "The feds have a prosecution-driven culture, so a crime has to be committed for them to get involved. And there are more economic crimes of a sizable nature than there are resources" (quoted in Fisher 2005, 24).

In 2005, the research firm Computer Economics claimed that computer-based crimes resulted in $14.2 billion in damages worldwide, including lost business and repairs. Since the turn of the millennium, the FBI has expanded its campaign against cybercriminals outside American jurisdiction. Following in the footsteps of previous crusades against transnational organized crime and terrorism, the transition reflects the global threat posed by computer crimes, including the unleashing of viruses, worms, and other rogue programs that allow criminals to disrupt or steal information from personal computers. During the early 2000s, the FBI created Cyber Action Teams (CATS) composed of roughly 25 individuals including agents, computer forensic experts, and specialists in computer code. By 2005, the FBI had assigned 150 agents to 56 offices around the world to handle computer intrusions, terrorism, and other crimes.

By most accounts, these responses and others have been rather unsuccessful in stemming the expansion of organized cybercrime. The FBI claims that its third highest priority (just behind terrorism and espionage) is protecting the United States "against cyber-based attacks and high technology crime" (Krebs, 2007). According to the FBI's 2009 budget request, it was seeking $258.5 million in funding for cybercrime, enough to fund 659 field agents and only a 1.5% increase over the previous year. What is most worrisome to those in the cyber community is that this is only 659 agents out of a total of 11,868 agents nationwide—meaning only 5.5% of agents would be used for fighting its third highest priority.

U.S. LAW ENFORCEMENT AGENCIES AND ORGANIZED CRIME ON THE INTERNET   At the highest levels of the American criminal justice system the Department of Justice (FBI) and the Department of Homeland Security's U.S. Secret Service investigate the criminal use of electronic and digital technologies. The U.S. Department of Justice Computer Crimes and Intellectual Property Crime Section (CCIPS) works with other government agencies, the private sector, academic institutions, and foreign counterparts to prevent, investigate, and prosecute computer crimes. The FBI is tasked with investigating cyberattacks by foreign enemies (and terrorists), and endeavors to prevent criminals and malicious actors from utilizing the Internet for fraud or theft. Its cyber division coordinates and supervises FBI investigations of federal violations involving the Internet or computer networks for espionage, terrorism, or criminal operations. The FBI has also created InfraGuard, a program of partnerships between the FBI field offices and private companies to support these investigations. By 2005, the program had enrolled 14,800 private-sector members in 84 local chapters across the country. In addition, the FBI supports a number of Regional Forensic Computer Labs (RCFL) that provides technical assistance to local law enforcement involved in examining digital evidence.

The Financial Crimes Division's Electronic Crimes Branch of the U.S. Secret Service houses equipment and specialists for electronic investigations and offers services to special agents posted in more than 125 domestic and foreign offices. These investigations often include unauthorized computer access, cellular and land-line telephone fraud, the manufacture of fraudulent identifications, counterfeit currency, and other crimes (McAfee 2005, 18).

In its budget justification for 2008, the Justice Department consolidated the headquarters and field resources of the FBI's Cyber Program into a "single entity" that allows the Cyber Program "to coordinate, supervise, and facilitate the FBI's investigation of those federal violations in which the Internet, computer systems, or networks are exploited as the principal instruments or targets of terrorist organizations, foreign government-intelligence sponsored intelligence operations, or criminal activity" (quoted in Krebs, 2007). What worries some critics of the FBI digital investigation process is the organization's historic focus on violations of the Innocent Images National Initiative, which, although listed last in priorities, claims the attention of almost one third of the agency's cyberagents. There is little argument that this program targeting child pornography is a worthy priority. However, compared to other cybercrimes, in 2006, this program accounted for a "major share of the FBI crime convictions and pretrial diversions" (Krebs 2007). According to the FBI, that year there were 1,018 convictions and plea agreements related to child pornography, compared to only 118 convictions or pleas for computer intrusions that same year. Among those chiding the government to increase the number of agents and analysts supporting overall cyber-investigative efforts is a former White House cyber-security adviser for the Bush administration, who lamented, "When we have as many problems going on as we have today, with China and Russia and organized crime and white-collar criminals involved in computer crimes, we don't have nearly enough agent workforce to take on the problem" (Krebs, 2007). Others suggest that the FBI "should focus mainly on the larger cyber criminal operations" (Krebs 2007).

CHALLENGES TO POLICING INTERNATIONAL CYBERCRIME One of the biggest handicaps faced by police forces around the world when responding to organized cybercrime is the fact that many of these acts take place internationally. For example, in one case a bank reported a robbery in Sweden after customers were infected with a Trojan, leaving the bank with a loss of €1 million. An investigation suggested that the Trojan was created by someone in Russia, although he never personally used it. However, he did offer a Web page with advice on how to use it for a fee. Individuals paid the fee and used it to attack the Swedish bank. This type of scenario requires investigations in three different countries (Weinberg 2007). If this had been a case involving the FBI, agents would not be allowed to travel overseas unless they were asked by a particular country, and once they do, they have no special powers to make arrests, but are available for technical and investigative help. In the cyber era, foreign police departments have noted improved interaction and reciprocity with the FBI. For example, in late 2006, the FBI reported the breaking up of a credit card theft ring involving the United States, Poland, and Romania. During the investigation, the FBI temporarily stationed agents with their Polish and Romanian counterparts to help with surveillance and information sharing. This contrasts with past practices of stationing FBI agents at U.S. consulates and embassies in other countries. Currently, the FBI posts a full-time agent with Australia's high-tech crime center.

These relationships can also result in distrust and conflict between the police forces. In one case in 2002, the Russian police accused an FBI agent with computer hacking after the agent downloaded evidence from a seized computer in Russia without prior official approval. However, by most accounts, these turf battles are anomalies (Bryan-Low 2006).

PROSECUTING CYBERGANGS In 1984, the first Computer Fraud and Abuse Act (CFAA) was signed into law. From the beginning it was criticized as "vague and too narrow in scope" (Zambo, 2007, 562). Congress revised the Act in 1986 by differentiating between *computer trespass*, which was not regarded as criminal, and computer crimes that were more malicious. It was also amended by specifying computer fraud, trafficking network passwords, and hacking as felonies. Minor amendments followed over the next few years, and in 1994, two felonies were added. By 1996, the Act was expanded to include a larger number of crimes and changing the loss requirement from $1,000 to $5,000. The passage of the USA PATRIOT Act in 2001 expanded the Act to include provisions related to threatening national security and stricter punishments.

Today, the CFAA criminalizes seven computer crimes:

1. Espionage
2. Unauthorized access of a government agency's computer and obtaining information used by financial companies and credit agencies

3. Unauthorized access to any non-public computer used by a department or agency of the federal government
4. Computer fraud
5. Intentionally transmitting commands or programs to cause damage, including the use of a virus, worm, or other program
6. Password trafficking
7. Extortion (Zambo 2007, 564–565)

Among the more glaring weaknesses of the CFAA has been the lack of distinction made between cybercrime and non-cybercrime.

SATELLITE TRACKING TECHNOLOGY   By 2005, advances in satellite tracking system technology had come to the attention of the international trucking industry. For decades, thieves commonly stole freight trailers full of goods and the victim lost both the truck and the goods. A number of companies are fitting their vehicles with a satellite tracking system, pioneered by General Electric (GE) equipment services division. In one case, a truck was stolen in Sweden and within 2 days was located 1,000 miles in Russia. The tracking device helped guide Russian police to a freight yard where it was parked, resulting in the recovery of the truck and the apprehension of the thieves. Telematics now helps companies make their supply chains more efficient by removing the uncertainty where goods are and when they will arrive. This fast-growing market has attracted the interest of IBM, Qualcomm, and other technology groups. Wal-Mart has equipped most of its 46,000 U.S. trucks with GE's service called VeriWise (Ward 2005).

In another instance, a crime syndicate operating out of Mozambique was stealing petroleum tankers from South Africa and driving them across the border to Lesotho, hoping to evade the tracking companies. After letting them sit for several days, they were driven through Swaziland to Mozambique. Most groups have gotten wise to this strategy and avoid trucks fitted with tracking devices when possible. One company, DigiCore, fits trucks with a panic button that a driver can use to alert the control room a hijacking has taken place or might be imminent. The alarm also goes off if someone tries to disable the tracker. Authorities lament it is just a matter of time before crime syndicates are able to infiltrate the call center of one of these companies, allowing them access to the list of vehicles, locations, vehicle make, and where the tracker unit is located (Ryan 2005).

Taking steps to thwart or at least combat increasing piracy on the high seas, beginning in 2004, the United Nations Maritime Organization required all passenger vessels and cargo ships of more than 300 tons to transmit an Automatic Identification System (AIS) signal. This tracking technology has already been adopted by various coast guards. Ships equipped with this device sent out regular radio broadcasts that informed authorities and other ships of their coordinates, identifying information, origins and destination, as well descriptions of their cargo. It was hoped that eventually this technology would become ubiquitous, allowing ships to identify each other; however, it has also given pirates a new tool for identifying cargoes as well. One British security expert noted, "There is no technology that will entirely prevent piracy" (Knight and Crystall, 2005). Proof of this is the low-tech strategy used in hijacking many ships by simply bribing the crew or placing a "sleeper" operative on the inside (Knight and Crystall 2005).

As police become more involved in counterterrorism activities, their focus has often been directed at the tens of thousands of ships plying millions of square kilometers of ocean at any given time. Shipping has become of special interest to both pirates and terrorist groups, hoping to take advantage of "the most unregulated of spaces—the sea" (Knight and Crystall 2005, 3). Ocean-going vessels can be used to ship weapons and terrorists, or can launch an attack on a port using tankers filled with hazardous chemicals and capable of causing massive economic disruption. The U.S. government's Defense Advanced Research Projects Agency (DARPA) suggests that the best solution to these threats is the utilization of satellite surveillance along with a host of "sophisticated intelligence algorithms that to spot rogue operations" (Knight and Crystall 2005, 3). The manager of one prototype surveillance system explained how applying algorithms based on pattern recognition operate, noting, "Commercial maritime ships follow motion-based patterns. If you think of a single voyage as consisting of a sequence of events, you can identify movement and other activity patterns that correlate with these events" (quoted in Knight and Crystall 2005, 4). This pattern analysis proved successful in other surveillance operations. For example, banks have used it to identify credit card fraud by identifying uncharacteristic changes in a customer's card use behavior.

RETAILERS USING TECHNOLOGIES TO COMBAT ORGANIZED SHOPLIFTING   Losses from organized retail theft have tripled to $30 billion each year, three times the amount of the 1990s. Organized groups of thieves often target large department stores and urban places heavily populated by malls and retailers with easy access to highways for a quick getaway. Members are responsible for specific tasks, such as distracting a sales clerk as another steals clothes. In other cases, they are capable of reproducing facsimiles of receipts to return stolen goods for cash, and still others remove inexpensive items from its box and fill it with higher-priced goods, then seal it up and pay for the cheaper item. Retailers are now taking advantage of the latest technologies to gain an edge on this costly criminal enterprise. Some are working together to establish a joint database of crimes so companies can prove the scope of theft of a particular group, resulting in a more punitive prosecution. Others are spending huge sums on security systems that range from software that tracks patterns of theft regionally to high-tech fixtures that prevent multiple packages from being removed at once. Other retailers, such as Wal-Mart Stores, Target Corp., and Lowe's, have gone even farther, setting up their own organized crime divisions (Access Control and Security Systems 2005).

Overview

New technologies have played a major role in the trend toward globalization, whether it is more efficient ships, new loading and unloading tools, roll on–roll off cargo containers vessels, improved logistics, advances in refrigeration or new packaging materials, or satellite navigation and tracking. One authority on illicit world trade said, "Traffickers have added creative applications of their own" (Naim 2005, 21), citing higher-quality latex condoms, which reduce the risks of lethal breakages once filled with drugs and inside a smuggler's digestive tract. Furthermore, "Aggressive and inventive adoption of new technologies has helped traffickers to lower risk, increase productivity, and streamline their business" (Naim 2005, 21).

The drug trade is one arena that has taken advantage of the opportunities presented by the spread of new technologies. In order to communicate, drug traffickers can choose instant messaging, Web mail accounts, and chat rooms to arrange drug sales, often from the anonymity of a public cybercafé. Alternatively, they can simply use a disposable cell phone that can be tossed in the garbage after a short time of use. If a drug trafficker wants to know whether a shipment has arrived or has been held up, they can track the shipment online; in doing so, they can take evasive action if it seems a shipment has been compromised, often one step ahead of law enforcement.

New technologies have also had an impact on drug markets by allowing new competitors to get into the action. For example, at one time the most sought after marijuana came from Mexico and Colombia. This has since been surpassed by British Columbia bud, grown thanks to advanced hydroponics and cloning techniques in special nurseries capable of providing year-round optimal growing conditions. The effort is worth it, with the better-quality marijuana selling for $3,500 a pound in California. Once it is ready to be distributed, kayakers load up to 100 pounds of marijuana at a time and coordinate deliveries by means of BlackBerry two-way devices (Naim 2005, 70).

Several organized crime researchers recently commented on the relationship between technology and criminality, noting, "In many respects, modern technology in the 21st century is no different from modern technology of the Middle Ages, and so forth: the invention and modification of tools continues to be applied to relieving victims of their money and/or property, and to moving property and money quickly" (Schlegel and Cohen 2007, 23).

What distinguish today's criminal adoption of technology is the increasing challenges faced by law enforcement following what is often an obscure or almost untraceable money trail, thanks to the skills of cybercriminals. The global nature of computer crimes and the blurring of electronic borders have led the FBI and other law enforcement agencies to reach out beyond the United States to improving cooperation with other agencies in pursuit of cybercriminals (following strategies from the "War on Terrorism"). The FBI currently ranks cybercrime as its third priority behind terrorism and espionage.

Authorities have been tracking organized online crime for a number of years now. However, what is most alarming is the skyrocketing number of malicious software or malware attacks. McAfee, the security software security company, estimated that the number of phishing Web sites had increased 784% over the previous year during the first quarter of 2007. The FBI estimated the total cost of cybercrime in 2006 at $67 billion. One widely heralded research paper in April 2007 conducted by a Google security team found more than 450,000 Web pages that included malicious code during a "digital hunt" (Blitstein 2007).

There are a number of challenges to fighting international computer crime, beginning with the fact that it often thrives in countries with weak computer crime laws and lax law enforcement. Law enforcement is severely limited in its response against international cybercrime, in part because hackers can hide their tracks by commandeering computers far away and routing their activities through machines around the world. In addition, many cybercrimes, particularly those affecting prominent financial institutions, go unreported, with corporations often unwilling to admit to their trusting customers, stockholders, and business partners that their networks were compromised from outside sources.

Technology continues to be a double-edged sword for organized crime groups and law enforcement, as each takes advantage of technical advances to thwart or counter the other. Most of the larger and more sophisticated gangs currently employ computer technicians and

engineers, and probably subscribe to trade journals to keep up with recent advances in forensic and technological science. There is enough anecdotal evidence to suggest that some criminals have their residences and cars swept regularly for recording devices.

According to Russian security experts Eugene and Natalya Kaspersky, although it has become fashionable to blame Russian organized crime groups with many organized computer exploits, "Traditional criminals are not in touch with computer criminals, probably because they still don't understand how to manage it. With the traditional mafia, it's drugs, it's prostitution, it's illegal weapons trading" (quoted in Weinberg 2007). In the end, these experts branded that the notion of the Russian mafiya being behind global computer crime is "a myth" (Weinberg 2007). When queried as to the where most computer criminal activity was coming from, the Russian security experts responded that the Chinese were the biggest threat, citing their development of multi-vector backdoor Trojans, and Trojans that steal data from online games. After the Russians, Spanish-speaking countries and Brazil were rated second, with most of the activity directed at stealing from personal banking accounts. Surprisingly, they placed Turkey at third, just ahead of Russia (Weinberg 2007).

Most authorities are convinced that cybercrime Information and Communications Technology (ICT) is not only changing the shape of organized crime, but the way individuals organize themselves to commit certain crimes as well. According to one Council of Europe report, "Cybercrime does not require control over a geographical territory, requires less personal contacts and thus relationships based on trust and enforcement between criminals" and less formal organization. "The classical hierarchical structures of organized crime groups may even be unsuitable for organized crime on the Internet. ICT may favor those organizations which are based on flat-structured networking" (2005, 43).

Key Terms

Blue box
Black box
Red box
Telegraph
ICT cybercrime
Pizzo
Operation Firewall
Operation Buccaneer
ShadowCrew

Warez
Cyberspace
IT
Crackers
Hackers
Cybergangs
Vendors
Moderators
Reviewers

"Disorganized criminal
organizations"
"Mafias of the moment"
Cyberbangers
Cracked
Ripped
Web mobs
CarderPlanet
Carders

Phreaking

Phishing

Cyberpornography

Hackers' syndicate

Cybercrime forums

Credit card cloning

Vishing

Spear phishing

Pharming

Viruses

Botnets

Zombies

"Pump-and-dump" schemes

Spam

Child pornography

Cyber blackmail

Cyber extortion

Denial of Service (DOS)

Keyloggers

Music piracy

Counterfeit medicine

Software piracy

Computer Fraud and Abuse Act

Critical Thinking Questions

1. What is *cyberspace,* and why has it become a more dangerous place in recent years? Should cyberspace and cybercrime continuum even be considered organized crime? Explain.
2. How have organized crime groups adapted to new technologies to commit crimes over the past several decades? How have New York's five crime families gone high-tech?
3. Chronicle the role of the telephone and the telegraph in the development of high-tech organized crime.
4. Why has high-tech crime become so prominent in the former Soviet Union? How have these gangs expanded their reach?
5. What is a *cybergang*? Does it have an identifiable structure? Compare and contrast cybergangs to the traditional Mafia structures.
6. How do organized crime groups recruit IT experts? Where do they usually find them?
7. What types of criminal organizations and structures has Peter Grabosky identified in cyberspace?
8. Discuss *Web mobs* and why law enforcement considers them groups of organized criminals; focus especially on ShadowCrew.
9. How and why did *hackers* give way to *crackers*? What role do they play in the organized crime continuum?
10. What are the differences in *phishing, vishing,* and *pharming*?
11. How do organized crime groups use computer viruses, botnets, and zombie computers?
12. What are the most prominent forms of organized crime activity on the Internet? Who is responsible, and how do they profit from the crime?
13. Discuss Internet extortion and blackmail. How does this affect the online gaming industry?
14. What new counterfeiting technologies have been used by organized crime groups? Discuss the use of technology in music piracy, document counterfeiting, and software piracy.
15. How successful has law enforcement been at policing the Internet? What kinds of cybercrime fighting tactics have worked? What strategies have been established to deal with cybercrime?

Endnotes

1. Prosecutors alleged that Gotti and his associates, including former Cy Young award-winning pitcher Denny McClain, were involved in a scheme to sell worthless telephone calling cards to customers and sought to defraud the phone companies that sold long-distance services. They used a McClain-owned telecommunications company to market the inoperable cards.
2. In 2008, €1 was worth $1.50.
3. *Warez groups* specialize in the illegal distribution of copyrighted software programs, computer games, and movies on the Internet.
4. At 44 years old, he was much older than typical profile that is usually in their 20s.
5. The U.S. government reportedly intercepted telecommunications indicating this activity, but it was done without a warrant (Grabosky 2007; Sims 2006).

6. In Hacker jargon it is popular to use a "z" instead of an "s" to demonstrate the plural, as in *Warez* (software), *hackz* (hacking techniques), and *crackz* (software that can remove license restrictions from software).

7. Those who are responsible for dividing the programs into small files and distributing them to various release sites (Lee 2002).

8. McCormick and Gage, "Web Mobs," 2005, is among the best examinations of the structure of digital organized crime groups.

9. Ron Rosenbaum, "Secrets of the Little Box," *Esquire*, October, 1971, pp. 116–125.

10. *Worms* "are wholly contained viruses that travel through networks, automatically duplicate themselves and mail themselves to other computers whose addresses are in the host computer. They propagate by sending copies of themselves to other computers via e-mail or Internet Relay Chat" (McAfee 2005, 18).

11. A *virus* is a program of piece of code that spreads from computer to computer without the users consent. They usually cause an unexpected and negative event when run by a computer.

12. The term *spam* was inspired by Monty Python's "Spam Song" routine in which Spam, the canned pork product, dominated a café menu and was sung repeatedly; hence, modern spam's identification with "something that keeps repeating . . . to great annoyance."

13. Online gambling is legal in Great Britain.

REFERENCES

BOOKS

Abadinsky, Howard. (2007). *Organized Crime*. Belmont, CA: Thomson Wadsworth.

Ackerman, Kenneth D. (2005). *Boss Tweed: The Rise and Fall of the Corrupt Pol Who Conceived the Soul of Modern New York*. New York: Carroll and Graf.

Albanese, Jay S., Dilip, K. Das, and Arvind Verma (Eds.) (2003). *Organized Crime: World Perspectives*. Upper Saddle Hill. NJ: Prentice Hall.

Albini, Joseph. (1971). *The American Mafia: Genesis of a Legend*. New York: Meredith Corporation.

Alexander, Michael. (2001). *Jazz Age Jews*, Princeton: Princeton University Press.

Allen, Oliver E. (1993). *The Tiger: The Rise and Fall of Tammany Hall*, Reading, MA: Addison Wesley.

American-Italian Historical Association. (1970). *An Inquiry into Organized Crime*, Proceedings of the Third Annual Conference, October 24, 1970, Columbia University.

Anbinder, Tyler. (2001). *Five Points*. New York: Free Press.

Anderson, Annelise G. (1979). *The Business of Organized Crime: A Cosa Nostra Family*, Stanford: Stanford University Press.

Anderson, Jack, and Fred Blumenthal. (1956). *The Kefauver Story*. New York: Dial Press.

Andrews, Kenneth R. (1979). "The English in the Caribbean, 1560–1620," in *The Westward Enterprise: English Activities in Ireland, the Atlantic and America, 1480–1650*, Kenneth Andrews, N.P. Canny, and P.E.H. Hair (Eds.). Detroit: Wayne State University Press.

Angiolillo, Paul F. (1970). *A Criminal as Hero: Angelo Duca*, Lawrence, KS: The Regents Press of Kansas.

Anslinger, Harry J. and William F. Tompkins. (1953). *The Traffic in Narcotics*. New York: Funk and Wagnall's.

Anti-Defamation League. (2002). *Dangerous Convictions: An Introduction to Extremist Activities in Prisons*. New York: Anti-Defamation League.

Applebaum, Anne. (2003). *Gulag: A History*. New York: Doubleday.

Arlacchi, Pino. (1986). *Mafia Business: The Mafia Ethic and the Spirit of Capitalism*, London: Verso.

———. (1993). *Men of Dishonor: Inside the Sicilian Mafia*. New York: William Morrow and Company.

Asbury, Herbert. ([1927] 1970). *The Gangs of New York*. New York: Capricorn Books.

———. (1938). *The French Quarter*, Garden City, NJ: Garden City Publishing.

———. ([1940] 1986). *Gem of the Prairie: An Informal History of the Chicago Underworld*, Dekalb, IL: Northern Illinois University Press.

Ashton, John. ([1898] 1969). *The History of Gambling in England*, Montclair, NJ: Patterson Smith.

Barnes, M. R., Elias, and P. Walsh. (2000). *Cocky: The Rise and Fall of Curtis Warren, Britain's Biggest Drug Baron*, London: Milo.

Becker, Howard. (1963). *Outsiders: Studies in the Sociology of Deviance*. New York: The Free Press of Glencoe.

Behr, Edward. (1996). *Prohibition: Thirteen Years that Changed America*. New York: Arcade Publishing.

Bequai, August. (1979). *Organized Crime: The Fifth Estate*, Lexington, MA: Lexington Books.

Bergreen, Laurence. (1994). *Capone: the Man and the Era*. New York: Simon and Schuster.

Bernstein, Lee. (2002). *The Greatest Menace: Organized Crime in Cold War America*, Amherst: University of Massachusetts Press.

Berry, LaVerle, Glenn E. Curtis, Rex A. Hudson, Tara Karacan. Nina Kollars, and Ramon Miro. (October 2003). *Nations Hospitable to Organized Crime and Terrorism*, Federal Research Division, Washington: DC: Library of Congress; pp. 1–252.

Berry, LaVerle, Glenn E. Curtis, Rex A. Hudson, and Nina A. Kollars, *A Global Overview of Narcotics-Funded Terrorist and Other Extremist Groups*, Federal Research Division, Washington, DC: Library of Congress, May 2002, pp. 1–142.

Binder, John J. (2003). *The Chicago Outfit*, Charleston SC: Arcadia Publishing.

Block, Alan. (1980). *East Side/West Side: Organizing Crime in New York, 1930–1950*, Cardiff: University College Cardiff Press.

Block, Alan, and Constance A. Weaver. (2004). *All Is Clouded By Desire: Global Banking, Money Laundering, and International Organized Crime*, Westport, CT: Praeger.

Blumenthal, Ralph. ([1988] 1989). *Last Days of the Sicilians: The FBI's War Against the Mafia*. New York: Simon and Schuster.

Bonanno, Bill. (1999). *Bound by Honor: A Mafioso's Story*. New York: St. Martin's Press.

Bonanno, Joseph. (1983). *A Man of Honor: The Autobiography of Joe Bonanno*. New York: Simon and Schuster.

Bonsanto, Vincent S. (1991). *Street Gang Paraphernalia Searches*.

———. (1991). *Street Gang Investigative Guide*.

Booth, Martin. (2003). *Cannabis: A History*. New York: St. Martin's Press.

———. (1999). *The Dragon Syndicates: The Global Phenomenon of the Triads*. New York: Carroll and Graf.

———. (1996). *Opium: A History*. New York: St. Martin's Press.

———. (1990). *The Triads: The Growing Global Threat from the Chinese Criminal Societies*. New York: St. Martin's Press.

Botting, Douglas. (1978). *The Pirates*, Alexandria, VA: Time-Life Books.

Bowden, Mark. (2001). *Killing Pablo: The Hunt for the World's Greatest Outlaw*. New York: Atlantic Monthly Press.

Brandt, Charles. (2004). *"I Heard You Paint Houses": Frank "The Irishman" Sheeran and the Inside Story of the Mafia, the Teamsters, and the Last Ride of Jimmy Hoffa*, Hanover, NH: Steerforth Press.

Bresler, Fenton. (1981). *The Chinese Mafia: The Most Frightening New Organization in International Crime*. New York: Stein and Day.

———. (1993). *Interpol*, Toronto: Penguin Books.

Brotherton, David C., and Luis Barrios. (2004). *The Almighty Latin King and Queen Nation: Street Politics and the Transformation of a New York City Gang*. New York: Columbia University Press.

Bruno, Robert. (2003). *Reforming the Chicago Teamsters: The Story of Local 705*, DeKalb, IL: Northern Illinois University Press.

Bryce, James. (1908). *The American Commonwealth*, Vol. II. New York: MacMillan Co.

Buell, J.W. (1883). *Metropolitan Life Unveiled: Mysteries and Miseries of America's Greatest Cities*, St. Louis: Historical Publishing Company.

Burnstein, Scott M. (2006). *Motor City Mafia: A Century of Organized Crime in Detroit*, Charleston, SC: Arcadia Publishing.

Callow, Alexander B. (1966). *The Tweed Ring*. New York: Oxford University Press.

———. (Ed.) (1967). *The City Boss in America: An Interpretive Reader*. New York: Oxford University Press.

Campbell, Rodney. (1977). *The Luciano Project: The Secret Wartime Collaboration of the Mafia and the U.S. Navy*. New York: McGraw Hill.

Capeci, Jerry. (2002). *The Complete Idiot's Guide to the Mafia*, Indianapolis: Alpha.

Carnwath, Tom, and Ian Smith. (2002). *Heroin Century*, London: Routledge.

Cashman, Sean Dennis. (1981). *Prohibition: The Lie of the Land*. New York: Free Press.

Chalfant, Frank E. (1997). *Galveston: Island of Chance*, Houston: Treasures of Nostalgia.

Chambliss, William J. (1988). *On the Take: From Petty Crooks to Presidents*, Bloomington, IN: Indiana University Press.

Chanda, Nayan. (2007). *Bound Together: How Traders, Preachers, Adventurers, and Warriors Shaped Globalization*. New Haven: Yale University Press.

Chandler, David Leon. (1975). *Brothers in Blood: The Rise of the Criminal Brotherhoods*. New York: E.P. Dutton.

Chepesiuk, Ron. (2007). *Gangsters of Harlem: The Gritty Underworld of New York's Most Famous Neighborhood*, Fort Lee, NJ: Barricade Books.

———. (2007). *Black Gangsters of Chicago*, Fort Lee, NJ: Barricade Books.

Chicago Crime Commission. (2006). *The Gang Book: A Detailed Overview of Street Gangs in the Chicago Metropolitan Area*, Chicago: Chicago Crime Commission.

Chin, Ko-Lin. (2003). *Heijin: Organized Crime, Business, and Politics in Taiwan*, Armonk. New York: M.E. Sharpe.

———. (1996). *Chinatown Gangs: Extortion, Enterprise, and Ethnicity*. New York: Oxford University Press.

———. (1990). *Chinese Sub-culture and Criminality: Non-traditional Crime Groups in America*, Westport, CT: Greenwood Press.

Choo, Kyung-Seok. (2007). *Gangs and Immigrant Youth*. New York: LFB Scholarly Publishing.

Cirules, Enrique. (2004). *The Mafia in Havana: A Caribbean Mob Story*, Melbourne, Australia: Ocean Press.

Clark, Ramsey. (1972). *Crime in America: Observations on Its Nature, Causes, Prevention and Control*. New York: Pocket Books.

Clarke, Donald Henderson. (1929). *In the Reign of Rothstein*. New York: Vanguard Press.

Clinard, Marshall B. (1964). *Anomie and Deviant Behavior*. New York: Free Press.

Cloward, Richard A. and Lloyd B. Ohlin. (1960). *Delinquency and Opportunity: A Theory of Delinquent Gangs*. New York: Free Press.

Cohen, Albert K. (1955). *Delinquent Boys: The Culture of the Gang*, Glencoe, IL: Free Press.

Cohen, Mickey. (1975). *In My Own Words* (as told to John Peer Nugent). Englewood Cliffs, NJ: Prentice-Hall.

Cohen, Rich. (1998). *Tough Jews: Fathers, Sons, and Gangster Dreams*. New York: Simon Schuster.

Cook, Fred J. (1964). *The FBI Nobody Knows*. New York: Macmillan.

Cordingly, David. (1995). *Under the Black Flag: The Romance and Reality of Life among the Pirates*. New York: Random House.

Courtwright, David, Herman Joseph, and Don Des Jarlais. (1989). *Addicts Who Survived: An Oral History of Narcotic*

Use in America, 1923–1965, Knoxville: University of Tennessee Press.

Covey, Herbert C. (2003). *Street Gangs throughout the World*, Springfield, IL: Charles C. Thomas Publisher, Ltd.

Cox, Donald. (1992). *Mafia Wipeout: How the Feds Put Away an Entire Mob Family*. New York: SPI Books.

Cressey, Donald. (1969). *Theft of a Nation: The Structure and Operations of Organized Crime in America*. New York: Harper and Row.

Cronin, Audrey Kurth, and James M. Ludes. (2004). *Attacking Terrorism: Elements of a Grand Strategy,* Washington, DC: Georgetown University Press, 2004.

Dash, Mike. (2007). *Satan's Circus: Murder, Vice, Police Corruption, and New York's Trial of the Century*. New York: Crown.

Davison, John. (1997). *Gangsta: The Sinister Spread of Yardie Gun Culture*, London.

Decker, Scott H., and Barrik Van Winkle. (1996). *Life in the Gang: Family, Friends, and Violence*. New York: Cambridge University Press.

Deitche, Scott, M. (2004). *Cigar City Mafia: A Complete History of the Tampa Underworld*, Fort Lee, NJ: Barricade.

———. (2007). *The Silent Don: The Criminal Underworld of Santo Trafficante Jr.* Fort Lee, NJ: Barricade.

DeNeal, Gary. (1998). *A Knight of Another Sort: Prohibition Days and Charlie Birger*. Carbondale IL: Southern Illinois University Press.

DeStefano, George. (2006). *An Offer We Can't Refuse: The Mafia in the Mind of America*. New York: Faber and Faber.

Diagnostic and Statistical Manual of Mental Disorders, 4th ed. (1994). Washington, DC: American Psychiatric Association.

Dickie, John. (2004). *Cosa Nostra: A History of the Sicilian Mafia*, London: Hodder and Stoughton.

Diffie, Whitfield, and Susan Landau. (1998). *Privacy on the Line: The Politics of Wiretapping and Encryption*. Cambridge, MA: The MIT Press.

Dillon, Martin. (1989). *The Shankill Butchers: The Real Story of Cold-Blooded Mass Murder*. New York: Routledge.

Dillon, Richard H. (1962). *Hatchet Men: the Story of the Tong Wars in San Francisco's Chinatown*. New York: Coward-McCann.

Dong, Stella. (2000). *Shanghai, 1842–1949: The Rise and Fall of a Decadent City*. New York: Morrow.

Dorsett, Lyle. (1968). *The Pendergast Machine*. New York: Oxford University Press.

Drzazga, John. (1963). *Wheels of Fortune*. Springfield, IL: Charles C. Thomas.

Dubro, James. (1992). *Dragons of Crime: Inside the Asian Underworld*. Markham, Ontario: Octopus Publishing Company.

Duffy, Maureen P. and Scott Edward Gillig (Eds.) (2004). *Teen Gangs: A Global View*. Westport, CT: Greenwood Press.

Dunkley, Michael. (1930). *X Marks the Spot: Chicago Gang Wars in Pictures*. Chicago: Spot Publishing Co.

Earle, Peter. (2003). *The Pirate Wars*. New York: St. Martin's.

Earley, Pete, and Gerald Shur. (2002). *WITSEC: Inside the Federal Witness Protection Program*. New York: Bantam.

Edmonds, Andy. (1993). *Bugsy's Baby: The Secret Life of Mob Queen Virginia Hill*. New York: Birch Lane Books.

Ehrmann, Herbert B. (1933). *The Untried Case: The Sacco–Vanzetti Case and the Morelli Gang*. New York: Vanguard Press.

Einstein, Stanley, and Menachem Amir (Eds.) (1999). *Organized Crime: Uncertainties and Dilemmas*. Chicago: Office of International Criminal Justice.

Eisenberg, Dennis, Uri Dan, and Eli Landau. (1979). *Meyer Lansky: Mogul of the Mob*. New York: Paddington Press.

Ellis, Edward Robb. (1966). *The Epic of New York City*. New York: Kondasha International.

English, T.J. (2005). *Paddy Whacked: The Untold Story of the Irish American Gangster*. New York: Regan Books.

———. (1995). *Born to Kill: America's Most Notorious Vietnamese Gang, and the Changing Face of Organized Crime*. New York: William Morrow.

———. (1991). *The Westies: The Irish Mob*. New York: St. Martin's Paperbacks.

Fabian, Ann. (1990). *Card Sharps, Dream Books, and Bucket Shops*, Ithaca, New York: Cornell University Press.

Farah, Douglas. (2004). *Blood from Stones: The Secret Financial Network of Terror*. New York: Broadway Books.

Farrell, Joseph. (1995). *Leonardo Sciascia*, Edinburgh: Edinburgh University Press.

Farrell, Ronald A., and Carole Case. (1995). *The Black Book and the Mob: The Untold Story of the Control of Nevada's Casinos*. Madison: University of Wisconsin Press.

Fentress, James. (2000). *Rebels and Mafiosi: Death in a Sicilian Landscape*, Ithaca, New York: Cornell University Press.

Ferrell, Robert H. (1996). *Harry S Truman: A Life*. Columbia: University of Missouri Press.

Fiaschetti, Michael. (1930). *You Gotta Be Rough: The Adventures of Detective Fiaschetti of the Italian Squad*. New York: Double Day and Doran.

Fijnaut, Cyrille, Frank Bowenkerk, Gerben Bruinsma, and Henk van de Bunt (Eds.) (1998). *Organized Crime in the Netherlands*. The Hague: Kluwer Law International.

Fijnaut, Cyrille, and Letizia Paoli (Eds.) (2004). *Organized Crime in Europe: Concepts. Patterns and Control Policies in the European Union and Beyond*. Netherlands: Springer.

Finckenauer, James O. and Y.A. Voronin. (2001). *The Threat of Russian Organized Crime*. Washington, DC: US Department of Justice.

Finckenauer, James O. and Elin J. Waring. (1998). *Russian Mafia in America: Immigration, Culture, and Crime*, Boston: Northeastern University Press.

Findlay, John M. (1986). *People of Chance: Gambling in American Society from Jamestown to Las Vegas.* New York: Oxford University Press.

Fleming, Ian. (1960). *The Diamond Smugglers*, London: Pan.

Flynn, Kevin, and Gary Gerhardt. (1995). *The Silent Brotherhood: The Chilling Inside Story of America's Violent, Anti-Government Militia Movement.* New York: Signet Books.

Fox, Stephen. (1989). *Blood and Power: Organized Crime in Twentieth-Century America.* New York: Morrow.

Fried, Albert. (1980). *The Rise and Fall of the Jewish Gangster in America.* New York: Holt.

Friedman, Allen, and Schwarz, Ted. (1989). *Power and Greed: Inside the Teamsters Empire of Corruption.* New York: Franklin Watts.

Friedman, Lawrence. (1993). *Crime and Punishment in American History.* New York: Basic Books.

Friedman, Robert I. (2000). *Red Mafiya: How the Russian Mob Has Invaded America.* New York: Little, Brown, and Company.

Friedman, Samuel R. (1982). *Teamster Rank and File: Power, Bureaucracy, and Rebellion at Work and in a Union.* New York: Columbia University Press.

Furfey, Paul Hanley. (1926). *The Gang Age: A Study of the Pre-Adolescent Boy and His Recreational Needs.* New York: Macmillan Co.

Galeotti, Mark. (Ed.) (2005). *Global Crime Today: The Changing Face of Organized Crime*, Routledge.

———. (Ed.) (2002). *Russian and Post-Soviet Organized Crime,* Aldershot UK: Ashgate Publishing.

Gambetta, Diego. (1998). *The Sicilian Mafia: The Business of Private Protection.* Cambridge: Harvard University Press.

Gambino, Richard. (1977). *Vendetta.* New York: Doubleday.

Gardiner, John. (1970). *The Politics of Corruption: Organized Crime in an American City.* New York: Russell Sage Foundation.

Gatewood, Jim. (2004). *Captain Will Fritz and the Dallas Mafia,* Garland, TX: Mullaney Corporation.

———. (2002). *Benny Binion: The Legend of Benny Binion, Dallas Gambler and Mob Boss.* Garland, TX: Mullaney Corporation.

———. (2006). *A Pickpocket's Tale: The Underworld of Nineteenth Century New York.* New York: Norton.

Gilfoyle, Timothy J. (1992). *City of Eros: New York, Prostitution, and the Commercialization of Sex, 1820–1920.* New York: W.W. Norton.

Glaser, C. (2000). *Bo-Tsotsi: The Youth Gangs of Soweto, 1935–1976,* Portsmouth, NH: Henneman.

Goddard, H.H. (1914). *Feeblemindedness: Its Causes and Consequences.* New York: Macmillan.

Goldfarb, Ronald. (1995). *Perfect Villains, Imperfect Heroes: Robert F. Kennedy's War Against Organized Crime.* New York: Random House.

Gori, Umberto, and Ivo Paparela (Eds.). (2006). *Invisible Threats: Financial and Information Technology.* IOS Press.

Goring, Charles. (1913). *The English Convict.* London: His Majesty's Stationary Office.

Gottfredson, Michael R., and Travis Hirschi. (1990). *A General Theory of Crime,* Stanford: Stanford University Press.

Gottschalk, Jack A., Brian P. Flanagan, Lawrence J. Kahn, and Dennis M. Larochelle. (2000). *Jolly Roger with An Uzi: The Rise and Threat of Modern Piracy.* Annapolis MI: Naval Institute Press.

Grabosky, Peter. (2007). *Electronic Crime.* Upper Saddle River. NJ: Pearson.

Gray, Mike. (1998). *Drug Crazy: How We Got into This Mess and How We Can Get Out.* New York: Random House.

Griffin, Dennis N. (2006). *The Battle for Las Vegas: The Law vs. the Mob.* Las Vegas: Huntington Press.

Griffin, Sean Patrick. (2003). *Philadelphia's "Black Mafia": A Social and Political History.* Dordrecht. Netherlands: Kluwer Academic Publishers.

Gunaratna, Rohan. (2002). *Inside Al-Qaeda: Global Network of Terror.* New York: Columbia University Press.

Gunst, Laurie. (1995). *Born Fi' Dead: A Journey Through the Jamaican Posse Underworld.* New York: Henry Holt.

Hagedorn, John M. (1988). *People and Folks: Gangs, Crime and the Underclass in a Rustbelt City,* Chicago: Lakeview Press.

Halberstam, David. (1993). *The Fifties.* New York: Villard Books.

Hallinan, Joseph T. (2001). *Going Up the River: Travels in a Prison Nation.* New York: Random House.

Hamm, Mark S. (1994). *American Skinheads: The Criminology and Control of Hate Crime,* Westport, CT: Praeger.

Handelman, Stephen. (1995). *Comrade Criminal: Russia's New Mafiya.* New Haven: Yale University Press.

Hart, Matthew. (2001). *Diamond: A Journey to the Heart of an Obsession.* New York: Walker and Company.

Haskins, James. (1974). *Street Gangs: Yesterday and Today.* New York: Hastings House.

Haysom, Nicholas. (1981). *Towards an Understanding of Prison Gangs,* University of Cape Town, Institute of Criminology, Social Justice Research Project, http://web.uct.ac.za/depts/sjrp/publicat/prisgang.htm.

Hazlehurst, Kayleen, and Cameron Hazlehurst (Eds.). (1998). *Gangs and Youth Subcultures: International Explorations.* New Brunswick, NJ: Transaction Publishers.

Helmer, William J. (1969). *The Gun That Made the Twenties Roar.* New York: Macmillan.

Helmer, William J., and Arthur J. Bilek. (2004). *The St. Valentine's Day Massacre: The Untold Story of the Gangland Bloodbath That Brought Down Al Capone.* Nashville: Cumberland House.

Herbert, D., and H. Tritt. (1984). *Corporations of Corruption: A Systematic Study of Organized Crime,* Springfield, IL: Charles C. Thomas.

Herrnstein, Richard J., and Charles Murray. (1994). *The Bell Curve: Intelligence and Class Structure in American Life.* New York: Free Press.

Hershkowitz, Leo. (1977). *Tweed's New York: Another Look.* New York: Anchor Press.

Hess, Henner. (1973). *Mafia and Mafiosi: The Structure of Power,* Lexington, MA: Lexington Books.

Hill, Peter B.E. (2003). *The Japanese Mafia: Yakuza, Law, and the State.* New York: Oxford University Press.

Hirschi, Travis. (1969). *Causes of Delinquency,* Berkeley: University of California Press.

Hobsbawm, E.J. (1959). *Primitive Rebels: Studies in Archaic Forms of Social Movements in the 19th and 20th Centuries.* New York: Norton.

Hoffer, Peter Charles. (2000). *The Brave New World: A History of Early America,* Boston: Houghton Miflin.

Hogg, Jocelyn Bain. (2003). *The Firm,* London: Trolley Limited.

Hooten, Earnest A. (1939). *Crime and Man,* Cambridge: Harvard University Press.

Hornung, Rick. (1998). *Al Capone.* New York: Park Lane Press.

Hostetter, Gordon L., and Thomas Quinn Beesley. (1929). *It's a Racket!* Chicago: Les Quin Books, Inc.

Hubner, John. (1993). *Bottom Feeders: From Free Love to Hard Core—The Rise and Fall of Counterculture Heroes Jim and Artie Mitchell.* New York: Doubleday.

Hunt, Thomas, and Martha Macheca Sheldon. (2007). *Deep Water: Joseph P. Mancheca and the Birth of the American Mafia.* New York: iUniverse, Inc.

Huston, Peter. (1995). *Tongs, Gangs, and Triads: Chinese Groups in North America,* Boulder: Paladin Press.

Ianni, Francis A.J. (1974). *Black Mafia: Ethnic Succession in Organized Crime.* New York: Simon and Schuster.

———. (1972). *A Family Business: Kinship and Social Control in Organized Crime.* New York: Russell Sage Foundation.

Inciardi, James A. (1992). *The War on Drugs II,* Mountain View, CA: Mayfield.

Jackson, Joy J. (1969). *New Orleans in the Gilded Age: Politics and Urban Progress—1880–1896,* Baton Rouge:

Jacobs, James B. (2006). *Mobsters, Unions, and Feds: The Mafia and the American Labor Movement.* New York: New York University Press.

Jacobs, James B., C. Fiel, and R. Radick. (1999). *Gotham Unbound: How New York City Was Liberated from the Grip of Organized Crime.* New York: New York University Press.

Jacobs, James B., C. Panarella, and J. Worthington. (1994). *Busting the Mob: United States v. Cosa Nostra.* New York: New York University Press.

Jankowski, Martin Sanchez. (1991). *Island in the Street: Gangs and American Urban Society,* Berkeley: University of California Press.

Jeffers, H. Paul. (1994). *Commissioner Roosevelt: The Story of Theodore Roosevelt and the New York City Police, 1895–1897.* New York: John Wiley and Sons.

Jewkes, Yvonne (Ed.). (2007). *Crime Online,* Portland, OR: Willan Publishing.

Johnson, Curt, and R. Craig Sautter. (1998). *The Wicked City: Chicago from Kenna to Capone.* New York: Da Capo Press.

Johnson, David R. (1995). *Illegal Tender: Counterfeiting and the Secret Service in Nineteenth Century America,* Washington: Smithsonian Institution Press.

Jonnes, Jill. (1999). *Hep-Cats. Narcs, and Pipe Dreams: A History of America's Romance with Illegal Drugs,* Baltimore: Johns Hopkins University.

Joselit, Jenna Weissman. (1983). *Our Gang: Jewish Crime and the New York Jewish Community, 1900–1940,* Bloomington: Indiana University Press.

Karch, Steven B. (1998). *A Brief History of Cocaine,* Boca Raton, FL: CRC.

Karlin, J. Alexander, "New Orleans Lynchings of 1891 and the American Press," *Louisiana Historical Quarterly,* 24 (January 1941): 202–203.

Karraker, Cyrus H. (1953). *Piracy Was a Business,* Rindge, NH: Richard R. Smith.

Katcher, Leo. (1959). *The Big Bankroll: The Life and Times of Arnold Rothstein.* New York: Harper and Brothers.

Kavieff, Paul R. (2006). *The Life and Times of Lepke Buchalter: America's Most Ruthless Labor Racketeer,* Fort Lee, NJ: Barricade Books.

———. (2000). *The Purple Gang: Organized Crime in Detroit, 1910–1945,* Fort Lee, NJ: Barricade.

Keefe, Rose. (2003). *Guns and Roses: The Untold Story of Dean O'Banion, Chicago's Big Shot Before Al Capone.* Nashville: Cumberland House.

Keen, David. (1998). *The Economic Functions of Violence in Civil Wars,* London: Oxford University Press.

Kellner, Esther. (1971). *Moonshine: Its History and Folklore,* Indianapolis: Bobbs-Merrill.

Kelly, Robert J. (2000). *Encyclopedia of Organized Crime in the United States,* Westport, CT: Greenwood Press.

———. (1999). *The Upper World and the Underworld: Case Studies of Racketeering and Business Infiltrations in the United States.* New York: Kluwer Academic.

Kelly, Robert J., Chin Ko-Lin, and Rufus Schatzberg (Eds.). (1994). *Handbook of Organized Crime in the United States,* Westport, CT: Greenwood Press.

Kelly, Robert J., Jess Maghan, and Joseph Serio. (2005). *Illicit Trafficking,* Santa Barbara: ABC-CLIO.

Kemp, John R. (1981). *New Orleans: An Illustrated History,* Woodland Hills, CA: Windsor Publications, Inc.

———. (1977). *Martin Behrman of New Orleans: Memoirs of a City Boss,* Baton Rouge: Louisiana State University Press.

Kenney, Michael. (2007). *From Pablo to Osama: Trafficking and Terrorist Networks, Government Bureaucracies, and Competitive Adaptation,* University Park: The Pennsylvania State University Press.

Kessler, Ronald. (1996). *The Sins of the Father: Joseph P. Kennedy and the Dynasty He Founded.* New York: Warner Books.

King, Rufus. (1969). *Gambling and Organized Crime,* Washington, DC: Public Affairs Press.

Klein, Malcolm W. (1971). *Street Gangs and Street Workers,* Englewood Cliffs, NJ: Prentice Hall.

Kleinknecht, William. (1996). *The New Ethnic Mobs: The Changing Face of Organized Crime in America.* New York: Free Press.

Kneeland, George J. (1913). *Commercialized Prostitution in New York City.* New York: Century.

Knox, George W. (1994). *National Gangs Resource Handbook: An Encyclopedic Reference,* Bristol, IN: Wyndham Hall Press.

Kobler, John. (1974). *Ardent Spirits: The Rise and Fall of Prohibition,* London: Michael Joseph.

———. (1971). *Capone: The Life and World of Al Capone.* New York: Putnam and Sons.

Kushner, Harvey W. (2003). *Encyclopedia of Terrorism,* Thousand Oaks, CA: Sage.

Kynoch, Gary. (2005). *We Are Fighting the World: A History of the Marashea Gangs in South Africa, 1947–1999,* Athens: Ohio University Press.

Lacey, Robert. (1992). *Little Man: Meyer Lansky and the Gangster Life.* New York: Little, Brown and Company.

Landesco, John. (1978 [1929]). *Organized Crime in Chicago: Part III of the Illinois Crime Survey,* introduction by Mark Haller. Chicago: University of Chicago Press.

Langewiesche, William. (2004). *The Outlaw Sea: A World of Freedom, Chaos, and Crime.* New York: North Point Press.

Langton, Jerry. (2007). *Iced: Crystal Meth, The Biography of North America's Deadliest New Plague,* Toronto: Key Porter Books.

Laqueur, Walter. (1999). *The New Terrorism: Fanaticism and the Arms of Mass Destruction.* New York: Oxford University Press.

Lavigne, Yves. (1987). *Hell's Angels: "Three Can Keep a Secret If Two Are Dead,"* New York: Lyle Stuart.

Lawson, Guy, and William Oldham. (2006). *The Brotherhoods: The True Story of Two Cops Who Murdered for the Mafia.* New York: Scribner.

Lee, Gregory D. (2005). *Conspiracy Investigations: Terrorism, Drugs and Gangs,* Upper Saddle River, NJ: Pearson Prentice Hall.

Leet, D.A., G.E. Rush, and A.M. Smith. (2000). *Gangs, Graffiti and Violence,* Incline Village, NV: Copperhouse Publishing Company.

Lemert, Edwin. (1951). *Social Pathology: A Systematic Approach to the Theory of Soiciopathic Behavior.* New York: McGraw-Hill.

Lender, Mark Edward, and James Kirby Martin. (1987). *Drinking in America: A History.* New York: Free Press.

Lerner, Michael A. (2007). *Dry Manhattan: Prohibition in New York City,* Cambridge: Harvard University Press.

Lewis, Alfred Henry. (1904). *The Boss.* New York: A.L. Burt Company.

Lewis, Brad. (2007). *Hollywood's Celebrity Gangster: The Incredible Life and Times of Mickey Cohen.* New York: Enigma Books.

Lewis, Lloyd, and Henry Justin Smith. (1929). *Chicago: The History of Its Reputation, 1833—Centennial Edition—1933.* New York: Blue Ribbon Books.

Liddick, Don. (1999). *The Mob's Daily Number: Organized Crime and the Numbers Gambling Industry,* Lanham, MD: University Press of America.

Liddick, Donald, Jr. (2004). *The Global Underworld: Transnational Crime and the United States,* Westport, CT: Praeger.

Lilley, Peter. (2006 [2001]). *Dirty Dealing: The Untold Truth about Global Money Laundering, International Crime and Terrorism,* London: Kogan Page.

Lindberg, Richard. (1985). *Chicago Ragtime: Another Look at Chicago, 1880–1920.* South Bend, IN: Icarus Press.

Lintner, Bertil. (2003). *Blood Brothers: The Criminal Underworld of Asia.* New York: Palgrave Macmillan.

Longrigg, Clare. (1997). *Mafia Women,* London: Chatto.

Lunde, Paul. (2004). *Organized Crime: An Inside Guide to the World's Most Successful Industry.* New York: DK Publishing.

Maas, Peter. (1997). *Underboss: Sammy the Bull Gravano's Story of Life in the Mafia.* New York: Harper Collins.

———. (1986). *The Valachi Papers.* New York: Pocket Books.

Macdonald, Andrew. (1980). *The Turner Diaries,* 2nd ed. New York: Barricade Books.

Macintyre, Ben. (1997). *The Napoleon of Crime: The Life and Times of Adam Worth.* New York: Farrar, Straus & Giroux.

MacKenzie, Norman (Ed.). (1967). *Secret Societies.* New York: Holt, Rinehart, and Winston.

Maharashtra Control of Organised Crime Act. (1999). Maharashtra Act No 30-OF 1999. http://www.satp.org/satporgtp/countries/india/document/actandordinances/maharashta1999.htm.

Mannheim, Herrman (Ed.). (1972). *Pioneers in Criminology,* Montclair NJ: Patterson Smith.

Marsden, William, and Julian Sher. (2006). *Angels of Death: Inside the Bikers' Global Crime Empire,* London: Houghton and Stodder.

Mathers, Chris. (2004). *Crime School: Money Laundering—True Crime Meets the World of Business and Finance,* Buffalo: Firefly Books.

Mays, G. Larry. (1998). *Gangs and Gang Behavior,* Chicago: Nelson Hall.

McCorkle, Richard C., and Terance D. Miethe. (2001). *Panic: The Social Construction of the Street Gang Problem,* Upper Saddle River, NJ: Prentice Hall.

McCoy, Alfred W. (1972). *The Politics of Heroin in Southeast Asia.* New York: Harper and Row.

McDonald, John. (1880). *Secrets of the Great Whiskey Ring and Eighteen Months in the Penitentiary,* St. Louis: W.S. Bryan.

McFeely, William S. (1981). *Grant: A Biography.* New York: Norton.

McIllwain, Jeffrey Scott. (2004). *Organizing Crime in Chinatown: Race and Racketeering in New York City, 1890–1910,* Jefferson, NC: McFarland and Company.

McKay, Reg. (2006[2004]). *The Last Godfather: The Life and Crimes of Arthur Thompson,* Edinburgh: Black and White Publishing.

McNeill, William H. (1980). *The Human Condition: An Ecological and Historical View,* Princeton: Princeton University Press.

Meredith, Martin. (2006). *The State of Africa: A History of Fifty Years of Independence,* London: Free Press.

Merriner, James L. (2004). *Grafters and Goo Goos: Corruption and Reform in Chicago: 1833–2003,* Carbondale: Southern Illinois University Press.

Messick, Hank. (1972). *John Edgar Hoover: An Inquiry into the Life and Times of John Edgar Hoover and His Relationship to the Continuing Partnership of Crime, Business and Politics. N*ew York: David McKay.

———. (1968). *Syndicate in the Sun.* New York: Macmillan.

———. (1967). *The Silent Syndicate.* New York: Macmillan.

Mezzrow, Milton (Mezz). (1946). *Really the Blues.* New York: Random House.

Miller, Nathan. (1998). *Star Spangled Men: America's Ten Worst Presidents.* New York: Scribner's.

Miller, Wilbur R. (1991). *Revenuers and Moonshiners: Enforcing Federal Liqiour Law in the Mountain South, 1865–1900,* Chapel Hill: University of North Carolina Press.

Miller, Zane L. (2000). *Boss Cox's Cincinnati: Urban Politics in the Progressive Era,* Columbus: Ohio State University Press.

Mitgang, Herbert. (2000). *Once Upon a Time: Jimmy Walker, Franklin Roosevelt, and the Last Great Battle of the Jazz Age.* New York: Free Press.

Moore, Joan W. (1991). *Going Down to the Barrio: Homeboys and Homegirls in Change,* Philadelphia: Temple University Press.

———. (1978). *Homeboys: Gangs, Drugs, and Prison in the Barrios of Los Angeles,* Philadelphia: Temple University Press.

Moore, William Howard. (1974). *The Kefauver Committee and the Politics of Crime, 1950–1952,* Columbia: University of Missouri Press.

Morgan, H. Wayne. (1974). *Yesterday's Addicts: American Society and Drug Abuse, 1865–1920.* Norman: University of Oklahoma Press.

Morgan, John. (1985). *Prince of Crime.* New York: Stein and Day.

Morgan, W.P. (1960). *Triad Societies in Hong Kong,* Hong Kong: Government Press.

Morris, Ronald L. (1980). *Wait Until Dark: Jazz and the Underworld, 1880–1940,* Bowling Green: Bowling Green Popular Press.

Morton, James. (1998). *Gangland International: The Mafia and Other Mobs,* London: Little, Brown and Co.

———. (1995). *Supergrasses and Informers: An Informal History of Undercover Police Work,* London: Little, Brown and Co.

Mueller, G.O.W., and Freda Adler. (1985). *Outlaws of the Ocean: The Complete Book of Contemporary Crime on the High Seas.* New York: Hearst Marine Books.

Murray, Dian H. (1994). *The Origins of the Tiandihui: The Chinese Triads in Legend and History,* Stanford: Stanford University Press.

Mushanga, Tibamanyamwene (Ed.). (1992). *Criminology in Africa,* Publication No. 47, Rome: United Nations Interregional Crime and Justice Research Institute.

Naim, Moises. (2006). *Illicit: How Smugglers, Traffickers, and Copycats Are Hijacking the Global Economy.* New York; Anchor Books.

Neff, James. (1990). *Mobbed Up.* New York: Dell.

Nelli, Humbert S. (1976). *The Business of Crime: Italians and Syndicate Crime in the United States.* New York: Oxford University Press.

Newark, Tim. (2007). *Mafia Allies: The True Story of America's Secret Alliance with the Mob in World War II,* St. Paul, MN: Zenith Press.

Newton, Michael. (2007). *The Encyclopedia of Gangsters: A Worldwide Guide to Organized Crime.* New York: Thunder's Mouth Press.

———. (2004). *The Encyclopedia of High-Tech Crime and Crime-Fighting.* New York: Facts on File.

Nicaso, Antonio, and Lee Lamothe. (2005). *Angels, Mobsters & Narco-Terrorists: The Rising Menace of Global Criminal Empires,* Mississauga, Ontario: John Wiley & Sons Canada, Ltd.

Nown, Graham. (1987). *The English Godfather: Owney Madden,* London: Ward Lock Limited.

O'Connor, Richard. (1986). *Hell's Kitchen: The Riotous Days of New York's West Side.* New York: Old Town Books.

Owen, Collinson. (1931). *King Crime: An English Study of America's Greatest Crime Problem,* London: Ernest Benn Ltd.

Owen, Frank. (2007). *No Speed Limit: The Highs and Lows of Meth*. New York: St. Martin's Press.

Pacyga, Dominic A. (1986). *Chicago, City of Neighborhoods,* Chicago: Loyola University Press.

Paoli, Letizia. (2001). *Illegal Drug Trade in Russia,* Freiburg, Germany: Max Planck Institute.

Partridge, Eric. (1950). *A Dictionary of the Underworld*. New York: MacMillan Company.

Pasley, Fred D. (1931). *Muscling In*. New York: Ives Washburn.

———. (1930). *Al Capone: The Biography of a Self-Made Man*. New York: Garden City Publishing.

Pennell, C.R. (Ed.). (2001). *Bandits at Sea: A Pirate Reader*. New York: New York University Press.

Petacco, Arrigo. (1974). *Joe Petrosino: The True Story of a Tough, Turn-of-the Century New York Cop*. New York: Macmillan.

Peterson, Virgil W. (1983). *The Mob: 200 Years of Organized Crime in New York*. Ottawa, New York: Green Hill Publishers.

Pietrusza, David. (2003). *Rothstein: The Life, Times, and Murder of the Criminal Genius Who Fixed the 1919 World Series*. New York: Carroll Graf Publishers.

Pileggi. Nicholas. (1996). *Casino*. New York: Pocket Books.

———. (1985). *Wiseguy: Life in a Mafia Family*. New York: Simon Schuster.

Pitkin, Thomas M., and Francesco Cordasco. (1977). *The Black Hand: A Chapter in Ethnic Crime*. Totowa, NJ: Rowan and Littlefield.

Pollard, N.A. (2002). *Terrorism and Organized Crime: Implications of Convergence,* Terrorism Research Center, Internet edition.

Porrello, Rick. (1998). *To Kill the Irishman: The War That Crippled the Mafia,* Cleveland: Next Hat Press.

———. (1995). *The Rise and Fall of the Cleveland Mafia,* Barricade Books.

Porteous, Samuel. (1998). *Organized Crime Impact Study,* Public Works and Government Services of Canada.

Potter, Gary W. (1986). *The Porn Merchants,* Dubuque, IA: Kendall-Hunt.

Powers, Richard Gid. (1987). *Secrecy and Power: The Life of J. Edgar Hoover*. New York: Free Press.

Powis, Robert E. (1992). *The Money Launderers,* Chicago: Probus Publishing Company.

Raab, Selwyn. (2005). *Five Families*. New York: St. Martin's Press.

Rafter, Nicole Hahn. (1997). *Creating Born Criminals,* Chicago: University of Illinois Press.

Reader, John. (1998). *Africa: A Biography of the Continent*. New York: Knopf.

Rediker, Marcus. (2004). *Villains of All Nations: Atlantic Pirates in the Golden Age,* Boston: Beacon Press.

———. (1987). *Between the Devil and Deep Blue Sea,* Cambridge: Cambridge University Press.

Reid, Ed, and Ovid Demaris. (1974). *The Green Felt Jungle*. New York: Pocket Books.

Reppetto, Thomas. (2006). *Bringing Down the Mob: The War Against the American Mafia*. New York: Henry Holt.

———. (2004). *American Mafia: A History of Its Rise to Power*. New York: Henry Holt.

———. (1978). *The Blue Parade*. New York: Free Press

Reuter, Peter. (1987). *Racketeering in Legitimate Industries: A Study of the Economics of Intimidation,* Santa Monica: The Rand Corporation.

Reuter, Peter. (1983). *Disorganized Crime: The Economics of the visible Hand,* Cambridge, MA: MIT Press.

Reynolds, George M. (1936). Machine Politics in New Orleans, 1897–1926. *New York: Columbia University Press.*

Richards, James R. (1998). *Transnational Criminal Organizations, Cybercrime, and Money Laundering,* Boca Raton, FL: CRC Press.

Ridgeway, James. (1991). *Blood in the Face: The Ku Klux Klan, Aryan Nations. Nazi Skinheads, and the Rise of a New White Culture*. New York: Thunder's Mouth Press.

Riis, Jacob A. (1957). *How the Other Half Lives*. New York: Hill and Wang.

———. (1900). *A Ten Year's War,* Boston: Houghton Mifflin Co.

Riordan, William. (1994). *Honest Graft: The World of George Washington Plunkitt,* St. James. New York: Brandywine.

Ritchie, Robert C. (1986). *Captain Kidd and the War Against the Pirates,* Cambridge: Harvard University Press.

Robb, Peter. (1996). *Midnight in Sicily*. New York: Vintage.

Robinson, Charles Alexander, Jr., and Charles Alexander Robinson. (1980). *Athens in the Age of Pericles*. Norman: University of Oklahoma Press.

Robinson, Jeffrey. (2000). *The Merger: The Conglomeration of International Organized Crime*. New York: Overlook Press.

Rockaway, Robert A. (1993). *But—He Was Good to His Mother: The Lives and Crimes of Jewish Gangsters,* 6th ed. New York: Gefen Publishing.

Roemer, William F. (1994). *The Enforcer: Spilotro—The Chicago Mob's Man Over Las Vegas*. New York: Ivy Books.

Rorabaugh, William J. (1979). *The Alcoholic Republic: An American Tradition*. New York: Oxford University Press.

Rose, Al. (1982). *Storyville, New Orleans,* 3rd ed. University of Alabama Press.

Rosecrance, John D. (1988). *Gambling Without Guilt: The Legitimation of an American Pasttime,* Pacific Grove, CA: Brooks/Cole Publishing.

Roth, Mitchel P. (2005). *Crime and Punishment in American History,* Belmont, CA: Thomson.

Rothstein, Carolyn. (1934). *Now I'll Tell*. New York: Vanguard Press.

Ruggiero, Vincenzo. (1996). *Organized Crime in Europe: Offers That Can't Be Refused,* Aldershot UK: Dartmouth Publishing Company.

Ruggiero, Vincenzo, Nigel South, and Ian Taylor (Eds.). (1998). *The New European Criminology: Crime and Social Order in Europe,* London: Routledge.

Russo, Gus. (2006). *Supermob: How Sidney Korshak and His Criminal Associates Became America's Hidden Power Brokers.* New York: Bloomsbury.

———. (2001). *The Outfit: The Role of Chicago's Underworld in the Shaping of Modern America.* New York: Bloomsbury.

Salerno, Joseph, and Stephen J. Rivele. (1990). *The Plumber: The True Story of How One Good Man Helped Destroy the Entire Philadelphia Mafia.* New York: Knightsbridge Publishing.

Salerno, Ralph, and John S. Tompkins. (1969). *The Crime Confederation.* New York: Popular Library.

Sanchez, Gonzalo, and Donny Meertens (translated by Alan Hynds). (2001). *Bandits, Peasants, and Politics: The Case of "La Violencia" in Colombia,* Austin: University of Texas Press.

Sante, Luc. (1991). *Low Life: Lures and Snares of Old New York.* New York: Vintage Books.

Schatzberg, Rufus. (1993). *Black Organized Crime in Harlem, 1920–1950.* New York: Garland Publishing.

Schatzberg, Rufus, and Robert J. Kelly. (1997). *African American Organized Crime: A Social History.* New Brunswick, NJ: Rutgers University Press.

Scheim, David E. (1983). *Contract on America: The Mafia Murders of John and Robert Kennedy.* Silver Spring, MD: Argyle Press.

Schell, Bernadette H., and Martin Clemens. (2004). *Cybercrime: A Reference Handbook,* Santa Barbara: ABC Clio.

Schlosser, Eric. (2003). *Reefer Madness: Sex, Drugs, and Cheap Labor in the American Black Market.* New York: Houghton Mifflin.

Schneider, Eric C. (1999). *Vampires, Dragons, and Egyptian Kings: Youth Gangs in Postwar New York.* Princeton: Princeton University Press.

Schoenberg, Robert J. (1992). *Mr. Capone.* New York: William Morrow and Company.

Schwartz, David G. (2006). *Roll the Bones: The History of Gambling.* New York: Gotham Books.

Schweitzer, Glenn E., and Carole C. Dorsch. (1998). *Super-Terrorism: Assassins, Mobsters, and Weapons of Mass Destruction.* New York: Plenum.

Scott, Kenneth. (1957). *Counterfeiting in Colonial America.* New York: Oxford University Press.

Serio, Joseph D. (2008). *Investigating the Russian Mafia,* Durham NC: Carolina Academic Press.

Servadio, Gaia. (1976). *Mafioso,* London: Secker and Warburg.

Shanty, Frank G. (Ed.). (2008). *Organized Crime: From Trafficking to Terrorism,* Santa Barbara, CA: ABC Clio.

Shaw, Clifford R., and Henry D. McKay. (1931). *National Commission on Law Observance and Enforcement, Report on the Causes of Crime,* Vol. II. No. 13, June 26, Washington, DC: United States Government Printing Office.

Shelden, R.G., S.K. Tracy, and W.B. Brown. (1997). *Youth Gangs in American Society,* Belmont, CA: Wadsworth.

Short, James F., Jr., and Lorine A. Hughes (Eds.). (2006). *Studying Youth Gangs,* Lanham, MD: Rowman and Littlefield.

Short, James F., Jr., and Fred L. Stodtbeck. (1974). *Group Process and Gang Delinquency,* Chicago: University of Chicago Press.

Sifakis, Carl. (1992). *Encyclopedia of American Crime.* New York: Smithmark.

———. (1987). *Mafia Encyclopedia.* New York: Facts on File.

Sleeper, Gary W. (2006). *I'll Do My Own Damn Killin': Benny Binion, Herbert Noble, and the Texas Gambling War,* Fort Lee, NJ: Barricade Books.

Smith, Alison J. (1954). *Syndicate City: The Chicago Crime Cartel,* Henry Regnery Co.

Smith, Paul J. (Ed.). (1997). *Human Smuggling: Chinese Migrant Trafficking and the Challenge to America's Immigration Tradition,* Washington, DC: Center for Strategic and International Studies.

Smith, Tom. (2007). *The Crescent City Lynchings: The Murder of Chief Hennessy, the New Orleans "Mafia" Trials, and the Parish Prison Mob,* Guilford, CT: Lyons Press.

Sondern, Frederic, Jr. (1972 [1959]). *Brotherhood of Evil.* New York: Manor Books.

Spergel, Irving. (1995). *The Youth Gang Problem.* New York: Oxford University Press.

Spillane, Joseph F. (2000). *Cocaine: From Medical Marvel to Modern Menace in the United States, 1884–1920,* Baltimore: Johns Hopkins University Press.

Standage, Tom. (1999 [1998]). *The Victorian Internet: The Remarkable Story of the Telegraph and the Nineteenth Century's On-line Pioneers.* New York: Berkley Books.

Stanford, Sally. (1966). *The Lady of the House: The Autobiography of Sally Stanford.* New York: Putnam.

Steffens, Lincoln, (1968 [1904]). *The Shame of the Cities.* New York: Hill and Wang.

———. (1931). *Autobiography.* New York: Harcourt Brace.

Steinberg, Alfred. (1972). *The Bosses.* New York: Macmillan Company.

Steinberg, Jonny. (2004). *Nongoloza's Children: Western Cape Prison Gangs During and After Apartheid,* Centre for the Study of Violence and Reconciliation, http://www.csvr.org.za/papers/papjonny.htm.

Sterling, Claire. (1994). *Thieves' World: The Threat of the New Global Network of Organized Crime.* New York: Simon and Schuster.

Stevens, Steve, and Craig Lockwood. (2006). *King of the Sunset Strip: Hangin' with Mickey Cohen and the Hollywood Mob.* Nashville: Cumberland House.

Stille, Alexander. (1995). *Excellent Cadavers: The Mafia and the Death of the First Italian Republic.* New York: Random House.

Stolberg, Mary M. (1995). *Fighting Organized Crime: Politics, Justice, and the Legacy of Thomas E. Dewey,* Boston: Northeastern University Press.

Summers, Anthony. (1993). *Official and Confidential: The Secret Life of J. Edgar Hoover.* New York: Putnam.

———. (1981). *Conspiracy.* New York: McGraw-Hill.

Sutherland, Edwin H. (1947). *Criminology,* 4th ed. Philadelphia: Lippincott.

Taylor, Lawrence. (1983). *Witness Immunity,* Springfield, IL: Charles C. Thomas.

Taylor, Robert W., Tory J. Caeti, D. Kall Loper, Eric J. Fritsch, and John Liederbach. (2006). *Digital Crime and Digital Terrorism,* Upper Saddle River, NJ: Pearson.

Thachuk, Kimberly L. (Ed.). (2007). *Transnational Threats: Smuggling and Trafficking in Arms, Drugs, and Human Life,* Westport, CT: Praeger,

Thompson, Buddy. (1983). *Madam Belle Brezing,* Lexington, KY: Buggy Whip Press.

Thompson, Tony. (2005). *Gangs: A Journey Into the Heart of the British Underworld,* London: Hodder and Stoughton.

Thoumi, Francisco E. (2003). *Illegal Drugs, Economy, and Society in the Andes,* Washington, DC: Woodrow Wilson Press.

Tosches. Nick. (2005). *King of the Jews.* New York: Harper Collins.

Thrasher, Frederic M. (1927). *The Gang: A Study of 1,313 Gangs in Chicago,* Chicago: University of Chicago Press.

Thrower, Rayner. (1980). *The Pirate Picture,* London: Phillimore.

Train, Arthur. (1912). *Courts, Criminals, and the Camorra.* New York: Scribner's.

Turkish National Police Department, Department of Anti-Smuggling and Organized Crime. (1998). *Drug Report—1998* (Ankara, Turkey: Turkish National Police).

Turley, Hans. (1999). *Rum Sodomy and the Lash: Piracy, Sexuality and Masculine Identity.* New York: New York University Press.

Turner, William. (1970). *Hoover's FBI: The Men and the Myth,* Los Angeles: Sherbourne Press.

Urban Management Programme. (2000). *Street Children and Gangs in African Cities.* Nairobi: Kenya: Urban Management Programme, United Nations, Centre for Human Settlements.

USAID Bureau for Latin American and Caribbean Affairs Office of Regional Sustainable Development, *Central America and Mexico Gang Assessment,* April 2006: 159 pp.

Useem, Bert, and Peter Kimball. (1989). *States of Siege: U.S. Prison Riots, 1971–1986.* New York: Oxford University Press.

Valentine, Bill. (2000). *Gangs and Their Tattoos: Identifying Gangbangers on the Street and In Prison,* Boulder: Paladin.

———. (1995). *Gang Intelligence Manual: Identifying and Understanding Modern-Day Violent Gangs in the United States,* Boulder: Paladin Press.

Valentine, Douglas. (2004). *The Strength of the Wolf: The Secret History of America's War on Drugs,* London: Verso.

Van Duyne, Petrus C., Klaus von Lampe, Maarten van Dijck, and James L. Newell (Eds.). (2005). *The Organised Crime Economy: Managing Crime Markets in Europe.* Netherlands: Wolf Legal Publishers.

Van Duyne, Petrus, Klaus von Lampe, and James L. Newell (Eds.). (2003). *Criminal Finances and Organising Crime in Europe,* Netherlands: Wolf Legal Publishers.

Varese, Federico. (2001). *The Russian Mafia: Private Protection in a New Market Economy,* Oxford: Oxford University Press.

Viano, Emilio C. (Ed.) (1999). *Global Organized Crime and International Security,* Aldershot, UK: Ashgate.

Volkman, Ernest. (1998). *Gangbusters: The Destruction of America's Last Great Mafia Dynasty,* Boston: Faber and Faber.

Volkov, Vadim. (2002). *Violent Entrepreneurs: The Use of Force in the Making of Russian Capitalism,* Ithaca, NY: Cornell University Press.

Vyhnanek, Louis. (1998). *Unorganized Crime: New Orleans in the 1920s,* Lafayette, LA: Center for Louisiana Studies.

Wall, David S. (2007). *Cybercrime: The Transformation of Crime in the Digital Age,* Cambridge, UK: Polity.

———. (Ed.). (2001). *Crime and the Internet,* London: Routledge.

Walters, Ronald G. (1978). *American Reformers, 1815–1860.* New York: Hill and Wang.

Warren, Peter, and Streeter, Michael. (2005). *Cyber Alert: How the World Is Under Attack from a New Form of Crime,* London: Vision.

Wendt, Lloyd, and Herman Kogan. (1971). *Bosses in Lusty Chicago: The Story of Bathhouse John and Hinky Dink,* 2nd ed. Bloomington: Indiana University Press.

Whyte, William F. (1955). *Street Corner Society.* Chicago: University of Chicago Press.

Wilkinson, Paul. (1974). *Political Terrorism.* New York: Wiley.

Will, George F. (2001). *Woven Figure: Conservatism and America's Fabric, 1994–1997.* New York: Scribner's.

Williams, Neville. (1961). *Contraband Cargoes: Seven Centuries of Smuggling,* Shoe String Press, Inc.

Williams, Phil, and Ernesto U. Savona (Eds.). (1996). *Transnational Organized Crime.* London: Taylor and Francis.

Williams, Phil, and Dimitri Vlassis (Eds.). (2001). *Combating Transnational Crime: Concepts, Activities and Responses,* London: Frank Cass.

Willoughby, Malcolm F. (1964). *Rum War at Sea,* Washington, DC: Government Printing Office.

Winick, Charles, and Paul M. Kinsie (1971). *The Lively Commerce: Prostitution in the United States.* Chicago: Quadrangel Books.

Winston, Alexander. (1969). *No Man Knows My Grave: Privateers and Pirate, 1665–1715.* New York: Houghton Mifflin.

Wolfgang, Marvin E. (1960 [1958]). *Patterns in Criminal Homicide.* Oxford: Oxford University Publishing.

Woodard, Colin. (2007). *The Republic of Pirates: Being the True and Surprising Story of the Caribbean Pirates and the Man Who Brought Them Down.* New York: Harcourt.

Woodiwiss, Michael. (2001). *Organized Crime and American Power,* Toronto: University of Toronto Press.

Wright, Alan. (2006). *Organised Crime,* Devon, UK: Willan Publishing.

Yablonsky, Lewis. (1997). *Gangsters: Fifty Years of Madness, Drugs, and Death on the Streets of America.* New York: New York University Press.

———. (1962). *The Violent Gang.* New York: McMillan and Co.

Zaidi, S. Hussain. (2003). *Black Friday: The True Story of the Bombay Bomb Blasts.* New Delhi: Penguin Books.

Zink, Harold. (1930). *City Bosses in the United States.* Durham: Duke University Press.

Zion, Sidney. (1994). *Loyalty and Betrayal: The Story of the American Mob,* San Francisco: Collins Publishers.

ARTICLES

AAPA Statement on Biological Aspects of Races. (1996). *American Journal of Physical Anthropology,* 101: 569–570.

Acohido, Byron (Aug. 24, 2007). Cyberthieves stole 1.3 million names. *USA TODAY,* p. 1B.

Acohido, Byron, and Jon Swartz. (Oct. 12, 2006). Cybercrime flourishes in online hacker forums. *USA TODAY,* pp. 1B–2B.

Albanese, Jay S. (Summer 2005). Fraud: The Characteristic Crime of the Twenty-First Century. *Trends in Organized Crime,* 8(4), 6–14.

———. (March 1988). Government Perceptions of Organized Crime: The Presidential Commission, 1967 and 1987. *Federal Probation,* pp. 58–63.

Aldhous, Peter. (2005, March 10). Murder, by Medicine. *Nature,* 434, 132–136.

Alexander, Barbara. (April 1997). The Rational Racketeer: Pasta Protection in Depression Era Chicago. *Journal of Law and Economics,* 40(1), 174–202.

Alkan, N. (2004). Teror Orgutlerinin Finans Kaynaklari [Financial Sources of Terrorist Organization]. *Polis Dergisi* [Police Review], 40, 28–35.

AllAfrica, Inc. (Aug. 10, 2006). Zimbabwe: Organized Crime on the Rise. *The Herald,* retrieved January 31, 2007.

Aloisi, Silvia. (Aug. 15, 2007). Brazen killings show power of Italian 'Ndrangheta. *Reuters,* retrieved September 30, 2007.

Althaus, Dudley. (Jan. 27, 2008). Mexico says crackdown is pressuring cartels. *Houston Chronicle,* A25.

———. (Jan. 22, 2008). Alleged leader of powerful Mexican drug cartel nabbed. *Houston Chronicle,* A12.

———. (Jan. 10, 2008). Calderon: "Close ranks" against crime. *Houston Chronicle,* A16.

———. (June 22, 2007). Ex-governor in Mexico faces U.S. charges. *Houston Chronicle,* A20.

———. (June 11, 2006). Bosses still call shots on local level. *Houston Chronicle,* A29.

Alvarez, Lizette. (Jan. 19, 2005). Police Fear IRA Is Turning Expertise to Organized Crime. *The New York Times,* A3.

Amoruso, David. (2007). Curtis Cocky Warren. August 16, http://gangstersinc.tripod.com/CurtisWarren.html, retrieved November 28, 2007.

———. (2007). Terence Terry Adams. April 5, http://gangstersince.tripod.com/TerryAdams.html, retrieved November 28, 2007.

Andalou News Agency. (2005). Italian Police Report: PKK obtains money from people illegally and use this money in human smuggling. http://zeus.hri.org/news/turkey/andalou/2000/00-08-03.andalou.html, retrieved April 27, 2005.

Anderson, Jon Lee. (July 9, 16, 2007). The Taliban's Opium War. *The New Yorker,* pp. 60–71.

Anderson, John L. (2001). Piracy and World History: An Economic Perspective on Maritime Predation. In *Bandits at Sea: A Pirate Reader,* C.R. Pennell, (Ed.). New York: New York University Press, pp. 82–106.

Antonopoulos, Georgios A. (Nov./Dec. 2003). Albanian Organised Crime: A View from Greece. *Crime and Justice International.* pp. 5–9.

Arlacchi, Pino. (1998). Some Observations on Illegal Markets. In *The New European Criminology,* Ruggiero et al. (Eds.). London: Routledge, pp. 203–215.

Atkinson, Jeff. (1978). Racketeer Influenced and Corrupt Organizations, 18 U.S.C. 1961–68: Broadest of the Federal Criminal Statutes. *The Journal of Criminal Law and Criminology,* 69 (1): 1–18.

BBC News. (April 13, 2007). Brazil Breaks up "killing" firm. http://www.news.bbc.co.uk/i/hi/world/Americas, 6552727, April 13, 2007, retrieved December 10, 2008.

———. (May 15, 2006). Brazil's mighty prison gangs. http://bbc.co.uk/2/hi/americas/4770097, retrieved January 10, 2007.

———. (May 16, 2003). Mafia turns to 3G video phones. http://newsvote.bbc.uk/mpapps/pagetools/print/news.bbc.co.uk/2/hi/technology/303355, retrieved March 13, 2008.

Baldaev, Dantsik, Belko Sergeyivich, Vladimir Kuz'mich, and Igor Mikhailovich Isupov. (n.d.). Dictionary: Prison, Camp, Blatnoi, Jargon [Speech and Graphic Portraits of Soviet Prison], http://www.fas.org/irp/world/para/docs/rusorg3.htm, retrieved December 10, 2008.

Barra, Allen. (March 1999). Gangster. http://www.americanheritage.com/articles/magazine/ah1999/3/1999_3_55, retrieved December 10, 2008.

Barry, Dan. (Oct. 18, 1998). At Fish Market, Tradition Is Giving Way to Tension. *The New York Times.*

Bastone, William. (Sept. 1994). Porkstock '94: Eleven Days of Meat, Merriment, and the Mob. *Village Voice,* p. 18.

Bell, Daniel. (1992). Crime as an American Way of Life. In *The Antioch Review,* 13, pp. 131–154.

Bennett, Trevor, and Katy Holloway. (2004). Gang Membership, Drugs and Crime in the UK. *British Journal of Criminology,* 44: 305–323.

Berman, Jay S. (1981). The Taming of the Tiger: The Lexow Committee Investigation of Tammany Hall and the Police Department of the City of New York. *Police Studies,* Winter: 55–65.

Berry, LaVerle, and Glenn E. Curtis. (Oct. 2003). Africa. In *Nations Hospitable to Organized Crime and Terrorism,* Federal Research Division, Library of Congress, pp. 2–31.

Billeaud, Jacques. (Jan. 12, 2008). With abductions, criminals target their own. *Houston Chronicle,* A7.

BIA (Security Information Agency). (Sept. 2003). Albanian Terrorism and Organized Crime in Kosovo and Metohija. Belgrade, http://www.kosovo.net/albterrorism.htmn, retrieved February 21, 2008.

Billingslea, W. (2004). Illicit Cigarette Trafficking and the Funding of Terrorism [Electronic version], *The Police Chief,* 71(2).

Birk, Dominik, Sebastian Gajek, Felix Grobert, and Ahmad-Reza Sadeghi. (2007). Phishing Phishers—Observing and Tracing Organized Cybercrime. Second International Conference on Internet Monitoring and Protection (ICIMP).

Blitstein, Ryan. (Nov. 23, 2007). Pearl Harbor of cybercrime has already happened. *Charleston Gazette.* http://www.wfdnvr9.webfeat.org/KtxeJ1735/url=http://infoweb.newsbank.com/iw-serach/we, retrieved March 27, 2008.

Block, Alan. (1994). European Drug Trafficking: Between the World Wars. In Alan Block (Ed.), *Space, Time and Organized Crime.* New Brunswick: Transaction, pp. 93–125.

———. (1994). Organized Crime: History and Historiography. In Kelly, Chin, and Schatzberg (Eds.), *Handbook of Organized Crime in the United States,* Westport: Greenwood Press 1994, pp. 40–74.

———. (1991). Organizing the Cocaine Trade in Progressive-Era New York. In *Perspectives on Organizing Crime: Essays in Opposition,* Alan Block (Ed.). Boston: Kluwer, pp. 33–49.

———. (Winter 1980). The Organized Crime Control Act, 1970: Historical Issues and Public Policy. *The Public Historian,* 2(2): 39–59.

Boyle, Robert H. (Sept. 3, 1962). The Bookies Close Shop. *Sports Illustrated,* 17(10): 18–20.

Brenner, Susan W. (Fall 2002). Organized Cybercrime? How Cyberspace May Affect the Structure of Criminal Relationships. *North Carolina Journal of Law and Technology,* 4(11): 1–50.

Bryan, Anthony T. (Oct. 2000). Transnational Organized Crime: The Caribbean Context. Working Paper No. 1, http://www.miami.edu/nsc, retrieved April 17, 2007.

Bryan-Low, Cassell. (Nov. 21, 2006). To Catch Crooks in Cyberspace, FBI Goes Global. *The Wall Street Journal,* pp. A1, A11.

Buckley, William F. (Sept. 27, 1994). Reefer Madness at the Bar on the Right. http://www.drugsense.org/tfyl/buck_bar.htm, retrieved December 10, 2008.

Burke, John. (March 18, 2007). African Gangs Play Big Role in Drugs Trade. *THE POST.IE,* http://archives.tcm.ie/businesspost/2007/03/18/story/21974.asp, retrieved April 16, 2007.

Butterfield, Fox. (June 21, 2004). Inmates Keep Tie to Outside with Smuggled Cellphones. *New York Times,* p. A15.

California Department of Justice. (Dec. 1995). Fuel Theft Alert. *Intelligence Operations Bulletin,* 71: 15–18.

Callahan, Nora, (2007). Certifiably Stupid. http://www.november.org/razorwire/rzold/05/0504.html, retrieved January 3, 2009.

Camilleri, Andrea. (April 21, 2006). When a Godfather Becomes Expendable. *New York Times,* p. A23.

Carroll, Susan. (April 15, 2007). Cartel Hiring Teens in Texas as Hitmen. *Houston Chronicle,* pp. A1, A10.

Carwile, K.P., and V. Hollis. (2004). The Mob: From 42nd Street to Wall Street. *Journal of Financial Crime,* 11(4): 325–341.

Casimir, Leslie. (Sept. 27, 2007). Sentencing Disparity for Cocaine under Attack. *Houston Chronicle,* p. A7.

Castillo, Mariano. (Sept. 29, 2006). Nuevo Laredo Media Go Silent on Violence. *Houston Chronicle.*

CBC News Online. (April 10, 2006). Biker Gangs in Canada. http://www.cbc.ca/news/background/bikergangs, retrieved January 10, 2007.

Center for the Study of Democracy. (2003). Corruption, Contraband, and Organized Crime in Southeast Europe. Sofia: Center for the Study of Democracy, 2003.

Chapa, Sergio. (May 19, 2006). Police: Man Killed During Gang Initiation. http://www.free[rublic.com/focus/f-news/1635182, retrieved December 10, 2008.

Chaudhuri, Pramit Pal. (March 10, 2007). Indian BPOs Feeding 419 Scamsters. *Hindustan Times,* http://home.rica.net/alphae/419coal/news2007.htm, retrieved April 16, 2007.

———. (March 9, 2007). U.S. to Find Means to Stop Spread of 419 Fraud. *Hindustan Times,* March 9, 2007, http://home.rica.net/alphae/419coal/news2007.htm, retrieved April 16, 2007.

———. (March 7, 2007). India an Emerging Market for Nigerian Fraudsters. *Hindustan Times,* http://home.rica.net/alphae/419coal/news2007.htm, retrieved April 16, 2007.

Chawla, Sandeep, and Thomas Pietschmann. (2005). Drug Trafficking as a Transnational Crime. In *Handbook of Transnational Crime and Justice,* Philip Reichel (Ed.), Thousand Oaks, CA: Sage, pp. 160–180.

Chazkel, Amy. (2008). The Jogo do Bicho: Brazil's Illicit Lottery. In *Organized Crime: From Trafficking to Terrorism,* Frank G. Shanty (Ed.), Santa Barbara: ABC-CLIO, pp. 88–93.

Chen, David W. (Nov. 15, 2007). 23 Charged in Illicit Ring at Casino, Official Says. *New York Times,* p. C18.

Chicago Tribune. (May3, 2006). FBI Probes Military Gangs. [Electronic edition], retrieved April 16, 2008.

Chihuri, Augustine. (2003). Organized Crime: A Perspective from Zimbabwe. In *Organized Crime: World Perspectives,* Jay Albanese et al. (Eds.), Upper Saddle River NJ: Prentice Hall, pp. 427–437.

Chin, Ko-Lin. (2001). Chinese Gangs and Extortion. In *The Modern Gang Reader,* Jody Miller et al. (Eds.), Los Angeles: Roxbury Publishing Company, pp. 134–143.

———. (2001). The Social Organization of Chinese Human Smuggling. In *Global Human Smuggling: Comparative Perspectives,* David Kyle and Rey Koslowski (Eds.), Baltimore: Johns Hopkins University Press.

Chin, Ko-Lin, Robert J. Kelly, and Jeffrey Fagan. (1994). Chinese Organized Crime in America. In *Handbook of Organized Crime in the United States*, Robert J. Kelly, Ko-Lin Chin, and Rufus Schatzberg (Eds.), Westport, CT: Greenwood Press, pp. 213–244.

Chu, Yiu Kong. (Spring 2005). Hong Kong Triads after 1997. *Trends in Organized Crime,* 8(3): 5–12.

Clark, Mark. (2005). Organised Crime: Redefined for Social Policy. *International Journal of Police Science and Management,* 7(2): 98–109.

Clutterbuck, Lindsay. (2004). Law Enforcement. In Audrey Kurth Cronin and James M. Ludes (Eds.), *Attacking Terrorism.* Washington, DC: Georgetown University Press, pp. 140–161.

Cole, David. (n.d.). The Patriot Act Violates Our Civil Liberties. http://encarta.msn.com/sidebar_701713501/is_the_patriot_act_unconstitutional_.html, retrieved 5/15/2008.

Coll, Steve. (Dec. 25, 1987). Jimmy the Weasel: Ex-L.A. Crime Boss Angry over Being Dropped from Federal Payroll. *Los Angeles Times,* Part II, pp. 1, 4.

Cooper, H.H.A. (1978). Terrorism: The Problem of the Problem Definition. *Chitty's Law Journal,* 26: 105–108.

Corchado, Alfredo. (June 11, 2007). Cartel's Enforcers Outpower Their Boss. *Dallas Morning News,* http://www.dallasnews.com/sharedcontent/dws/news/world/stories/o61107dnintzetas.3a36, retrieved January 19, 2008.

Council of Europe. (Dec. 2005). Organized Crime Situation Report 2005: Focus on the Threat of Economic Crime, Strasbourg, France: Department of Crime Problems.

Criminal Intelligence Service of Canada (July 19, 2007). The Organized Crime Marketplace in Canada. http://www.cisc.gc.ca/annual_reports/annual_report2005/technology_an_crime_2005, retrieved February 28, 2008.

Csonka, Peter. (2003). Organized Crime: A Perspective from the Council of Europe. In Albanese et al. (Eds.), *Organized Crime: World Perspectives,* Upper Saddle River NJ: Prentice Hall, pp. 212–235.

Center for Strategic and International Studies (CSIS). (1997). Russian Organized Crime: Global Organized Crime Project. http://www.csis.org, retrieved December 10, 2008.

Curtis, Jack H. (1953). Gabriel Tarde. In *Social Theorists,* Clement S. Mihanovic (Ed.): Milwaukee, pp. 142–157.

Curtis, Glenn E. (Oct. 2002). Involvement of Russian Organized Crime Syndicates, Criminal Elements in the Russian Military, and Regional Terrorist Groups in Narcotics Trafficking in Central Asia, the Caucasus, and Chechnya. Federal Research Division, Washington, DC, pp. 1–36.

Curtis, Glenn E., and Tara Karacan. (Dec. 2002). The Nexus among Terrorists. Narcotics Traffickers, Weapons Proliferators, and Organized Crime Networks in Western Europe. Federal Research Division, Washington, DC: Library of Congress, pp. 1–30.

Curtis, Glenn E., Seth L. Elan, Rexford A. Hudson, and Nina A. Kollars. (April 2003). Transnational Activities of Chinese Criminal Organizations. Federal Research Division, Washington, DC: Library of Congress, pp. 1–68.

Dandurand, Y., and V. Chin. (2004). *Links Between Terrorism and Other Forms of Crime,* Report submitted to Foreign Affairs Canada and the United Nations Office on Drugs and Crime, 2004, http://www.dfait-maeci.gc.ca/internationalcrime/menu-en.asp, retrieved February 19, 2005.

Davis, Robert S., and Gary W. Potter. (1991). Bootlegging and Rural Criminal Entrepreneurship, *Journal of Crime and Justice,* 14(1): 145–159.

Davis, Roger H. (Oct.–Nov. 1982). Outlaw Motorcyclists: A Problem for Police. *FBI Law Enforcement Bulletin,* 1–9.

Davy, Monica. (April 26, 2005). In Mob Sweep, Feds Hope to Send Up the Clown. *New York Times,* pp. A1, A13.

Drug Enforcement Administration (DEA). (June 2, 1998). Press Release, DEA Confirms Arrest by Mexican Authorities of Amezcua-Contreras Bothers, http://www.fas.org/irp/agency/doa/dea/product/pr980602, retrieved January 26, 2008.

WhosARat.com. (Feb. 28, 2007). Death Under Cover: The Danger of Rats. *Arkansas Times,* Little Rock AR, http://www.websitetoolbox.com/tool/post/whosarat/vpost?id = 1734610, retrieved May 23, 2008.

Decker, Scott H., Tim Bynum, and Deborah Weisel. (Sept. 1998). A Tale of Two Cities: Gangs as Organized Crime Groups. *Justice Quarterly,* 15(3): 395–425.

DeCeur, Marissa. (Nov. 30, 2007). More States Debate End to Blue Laws. *USA Today.* p. 3A.

Deflem, Mattieu, and Brian Hudak. (2008). Internet Extortion and Information Security. In *Organized Crime: From Trafficking to Terrorism*, Frank G. Shanty (Ed.), Santa Barbara: ABC CLIO, pp. 289–292.

D'Emilio, Frances. (2008). Challenging the Mafia . . . Online. ABC News, http://abcnews.go.com/print?id=4127845, retrieved March 13, 2008.

Dermota, Ken. (July–Aug. 2007). Snow Fall. *The Atlantic*, 24–25.

Destefano, Anthony M. (July 1, 2006). USNY: New York City Judge Throws Out Cops Conspiracy. http://www.mapinc .org/drugnews/vo6/n873/a07.html, retrieved May 23, 2008.

Devi, Sharmila. (March 18, 2005). Police Continue Hunt for High-Tech Gang Sumitomo Bank. *Financial Times London*, http://www.FTnewspaper.com, retrieved October 3, 2006.

Dishman, Chris. (2001). Terrorism Crime and Transformation. *Studies in Conflict and Terrorism*, 24.

Domash, Shelly Feuer. (2005). America's Most Dangerous Gang. *Police Magazine*, http://www.policemag.com/Articles/ 2005/02/America-s-Most-Dangerous-Gang.aspx, retrieved December 10, 2008.

Donaldson, Greg. (Oct. 24, 1995). The Last Waterfront. *Village Voice*, pp. 41–45.

Downie, Andrew. (July 29, 1997). Mexico Says 34 in Military Accused of Drug Crimes. *Houston Chronicle*, p. 8A.

Downie, Andrew. (May 16, 2006). Brazil Gang Takes on State. *The Christian Science Monitor*, May 16, 2006, online edition, retrieved January 15, 2007.

Dreyfus, Pablo G. (Nov. 1999). When All the Evils Come Together: Cocaine, Corruption, and Shining Path in Peru's Upper Huallaga Valley, 1980–1995. *Journal of Contemporary Criminal Justice*, 15(4): 370–396.

Driscoll, Joseph. (Nov. 1933). Men of Action. *New Outlook*, 103.

Driver, Edwin, D. (1972). Charles Buckman Goring. In *Pioneers in Criminology*, Montclaire NJ: Patterson Smith, pp. 429–442.

Drori, I., and D.J. Gayle. (1990). Youth Employment Strategies in Jamaican Sugar Belt Area. *Human Organization*, 49(4): 364–372.

Duffy, Maureen. (2004). Introduction: A Global Overview of the Issues of and Responses to Teen Gangs. In *Teen Gangs: A Global View*, Maureen P. Duffy and Scott Edward Gillig (Eds.), New York: Greenwood Press, pp. 1–12.

Dunn, Guy. (1997). Major Mafia Gangs in Russia. In *Russian Organized Crime: The New Threat?* Phil Williams (Ed.), London: Frank Cass, pp. 63–87.

Duradand, Yvon, and Vivienne Chin. (April 2004). Links between Terrorism and Other Forms of Crime. Report submitted to Foreign Affairs Canada and the United Nations Office on Drugs and Crime, pp. 1–37.

Earlier Manifestations of Organized Crime Groups. (n.d.). http:// www.iss.co.za/Monograph/No28/CriminalGroups.html, retrieved December 10, 2008.

Ebert, Roger. (Feb. 11, 2005). Inside Deep Throat. Movie review, http://rogerebert.suntimes.com, retrieved December 10, 2008.

Economist. (July 28, 2007). Extinct or Just Adapting? pp. 50–51.

El-AbouAdy, Mohsen Mohamed. (2002). The Crime of International Bribery. Al-Ahram Center for Political and Strategic Studies (ACPSS), Strategic Papers 115, Year 12.

Emsden, Christopher. (March 15, 2001). Arrest Is Seen as Tightening Noose around Mafia Boss. *Italy Daily*, p. 1.

Engdahl, Bill, and Jerry Steinberg. (Oct. 13, 1995). The Real Story of the BCCI. *Executive Intelligence Review*.

Erlich, R. (April 9, 2001). Jamaican Gangs Give Peace a Chance. *The Christian Science Monitor*, p. 8.

Farah, Douglas. (n.d.). The Use of Gold, Diamonds and Other Commodities in Terrorist Finances. http://www.douglasfarah .com/articles/use-of-gold.shtml, retrieved May 26, 2007.

Farley, Ellen, and William K. Knoedelseder, Jr. (June 13, 1982). Family Business, Episode One: The Porn Brokers. *Los Angeles Times Calendar*, pp. 3–13.

Faulconbridge, Guy. (n.d.). Semion Mogilevich Facing Tax Evasion Charges. http://www.businessspectator.com.au/bs .nsf/Article/Semion-Mogilevich-facing-tax-evasion, retrieved March 3, 2008.

Fingers, Inc.: Japan's Surgical Handiwork. (Sept. 1995). *Details*, p. 63.

Fisher, Dennis. (March 27, 2005). Phishing, Inc. *EWEEK*, pp. 20–24, http:// www.eweek.com.

Flaccus, Gillian. (March 15, 2006). White Supremacists Could Get Death in Prison Gang War Trial. *Houston Chronicle*, A7.

Florida Department of Corrections. (n.d.). Major Prison Gangs, http://www.dc.state.fl.us/pub/gangs/prison.html, retrieved January 10, 2007.

Focus. (Oct. 24, 1994). PKK Members Were Involved in Drug Trafficking.

Fong, Robert S., and Ronald E. Fogel. (Winter 1995). A Comparative Analysis of Prison Gang Members, Security Threat Group Inmates, and General Population in the Texas Department of Corrections. *The Journal of Gang Research*, 2(2): 1–12.

Forero, Juan. (Oct. 28, 2007). U.S: Colombia Cocaine Trail Goes through Venezuela. *Houston Chronicle*, p. A17.

Forman, Craig. (Sept. 15, 1994). Sumitomo Bank Director's Death Is Investigated. *The Wall Street Journal*, p. A10.

Foster, Sarah. (Dec. 21, 1998). Armed and Dangerous. *WorldNetDaily*, http://www.worldnetdaily.com/index.php? fa, retrieved May 22, 2008.

Fox, Aubrey. (Feb. 20, 2008). Delving the Murky World of Police Informants. *Gotham Gazette*, http://www.gothamgazette.com, retrieved May 23, 2008.

Fox, Steve. (Sept. 26, 2005). High-Tech Mobsters. *InfoWorld*, p. 6.

Franco, Adolfo. (April 20, 2005). Crime Hinders Development, Democracy in Latin America. http://usinfo.state.gov/dhr/ARCHIVE/2005/Apr/21-965427.html, retrieved November 19, 2007.

Frontline. (n.d.). Interview with Carlos Toro. *Drug Wars*, pp. 1–11, http://www.pbs.org/wgbh/pages/frontline/shows/drugs/interviews/toro, retrieved January 17, 2008.

Frontline. (n.d.). Interview with Juan David Ochoa. *Drug Wars*, pp. 1–24, http://www.pbs.org/wgbh/pages/frontline/shows/drugs/interviews/och, retrieved January 17, 2008.

Frossard, Denise. (2007). Women in Organized Crime in Brazil. In *Women and the Mafia: Female Roles in Organized Crime Structures,* Giovanni Fiandaca (Ed.). New York: Springer, pp. 181–204.

Fuentes, Joseph R., and Robert J. Kelly. (November 1999). Drug Supply and Demand: The Dynamics of the American Drug Market and Some Aspects of Colombian and Mexican Drug Trafficking. *Journal of Contemporary Criminal Justice,* 15(4): 328–351.

Fukumi, Sayaka. (2003). Drug-Trafficking and the State: The Case of Colombia. In *Organized Crime and the Challenge to Democracy,* Felia Allum and Renate Siebert (Eds.), pp. 93–111.

Gage, Deborah. (March 7, 2005). Shadowcrew: Web Mobs. Baseline, http://www.baselinemag.com/c/a/Security/Shadowcross-Web-Mobs/, retrieved January 12, 2009.

Gaio, Andre Moyses. (2008). The Relationship between Politics and Organized Crime in Latin America. In *Organized Crime: From Trafficking to Terrorism,* Frank Shanty (Ed.). Santa Barbara: ABC-CLIO, 132–136.

Galeotti, Mark. (Spring 2006). Forward to the Past: Organized Crime and Cuba's History, Present and Future. *Trends in Organized Crime,* 9(3): 45–60.

Gamba, Remi. (2005). Organized Crime Taking Over Spam—Survey. Digital Media Europe, http://www.dmeurope.com/default.asp?ArticleID=2364cachecommand=bypass&Print, retrieved November 28, 2007.

Gans, Herbert J. (1997). Best-Sellers by Sociologists: An Exploratory Study. *Contemporary Sociology,* 26: 131–135.

Garces, Laura. (Winter 2005). Colombia: The Link between Drugs and Terror. *Journal of Drug Issues*, 83–105.

Gastrow, Peter. (2001). Triad Societies and Chinese Organized Crime in South Africa. Organized Crime and Corruption Program, Institute for Security Studies. Occasional Paper No. 48, http://www.iss.co.za/Pubs/Papers/48/48.html, retrieved April 16, 2007.

———. (1999). Main Trends in the Development of South Africa's Organized Crime. *African Security Review,* 8(6). http://www.iss.co.za/pubs/ASR/8No6?MainTrends.html, retrieved April 25, 2007.

———. (August 1998). Organized Crime in South Africa. ISS Monograph Series, No. 28, Institute for Security Studies, South Africa.

Gates, Dominic. (Aug. 13, 2001). FBI Busts Four Alleged Software Pirates. *Industry Standard*, http://www.pcworld.com/printable/article/id,57883/printable.html, retrieved March 10, 2008.

Gay, B.W., and James W. Marquart. (1993). "Jamaican Posses: A New Form of Organized Crime," *Journal of Crime and Justice,* 16(2): 139–170.

Gaylord, Mark S., and Hualing Fu. (1999). Economic Reform and "Black Society": The Re-Emergence of Organized Crime in Post-Mao China. In *Organized Crime: Uncertainties and Dilemmas*, S. Einstein and M. Amir (Eds.). Chicago: Office of International Criminal Justice, pp. 119–134.

George, Cindy. (April 29, 2008). Bar Manager Gets 15 Years for Role in Smuggling Ring. *Houston Chronicle*, p. B2.

Germain, Jack M. (March 23, 2004). Global Extortion: Online Gambling and Organized Hacking. http://www.technesworld.com/story/33171.html, retrieved February 28, 2008.

Gettleman, Jeffrey. (Nov. 10, 2006). Chased by Gang Violence, Residents Flee Kenyan Slum. *New York Times International,* p. A4.

Gilinsky, Yakov, and Yakov Kostjukovsky. (2004). From Thievish *Artel* to Criminal Corporation: The History of Organized Crime in Russia. In *Organized Crime in Europe,* C. Fijnaut and L. Paoli (Eds.). Netherlands: Springer, pp. 181–202.

Gilinsky, Yakov. (2006). Crime in Contemporary Russia. *European Journal of Criminology,* 3(3): 259–292.

———. (1999). Organized Crime in Russia: Domestic and International Problems. In *Global Organized Crime and International Security,* Emilio Viano (Ed.), Aldershot, UK: Ashgate, pp. 117–122.

———. (1998). The Market and Crime in Russia. *The New European Criminology,* Vincenzo Ruggierio et al. (Eds.), London: Routledge, pp. 230–241.

Glaberson, William. (April 26, 1998). Goodfellas Meets the Government in the Talk Captured on 7,000 Gotti Tapes. *New York Times,* http://nytimes.com, retrieved January 10, 2007.

Goldberg, Jeffrey. (Feb. 8, 1998). Jimmy Hoffa's Revenge. *The New York Times Magazine,* pp. 38–45, 62, 67–68, 76–77.

Gomez-Cespedes. (Nov. 1999). The Federal Law Enforcement Agencies: An Obstacle in the Fight Against Organized Crime in Mexico. *Journal of Contemporary Criminal Justice,* 15(4): 352–369.

Gordon, Robert. (1976). Prevalence: The Rare Datum in Delinquency Measurement and Its Implications for the Theory of Delinquency. In *Juvenile Justice System*, Malcolm W. Klein (Ed.), Beverly Hills: Sage Publications, pp. 201–284.

Grabosky, Peter. (Oct. 30, 2007). The Internet, Technology, and Organized Crime. *Asian Journal of Criminology: An*

Interdisciplinary Journal on Crime, Law and Deviance in Asia, http://www.springerlink.com/content/d361354j58h05u35/fulltext.html, retrieved February 28, 2008.

———. (2005). The Global Dimension of Cybercrime. In *Global Crime Today: The Changing face of Organized Crime,* Mark Galeotti (Ed.). London: Routledge, pp. 146–157.

Grann, David. (February 16 & 23, 2004). The Brand: How the Aryan Brotherhood Became the Most Murderous Prison Gang in America. *The New Yorker,* pp. 157–171.

Gribben, M.C. (Ed.) (2003). *Terror and Organized Crime,* http://www.organizedcrimeabout.com.

Grindler, G.S. (Sept. 1975). Prosecution under the Hobbs Act and the Expansion of Federal Criminal Jurisdiction. *The Journal of Criminal Law and Criminology,* 66 (3): 306–324.

Grobler, John. (March 23, 2007). Mafia Linked to Namibian Diamonds. *The Namibian,* http://dusteye.wordpress.com/2007/03/23/mafia-linked-to-namibian-diamonds, retrieved May 26, 2007.

Guest, Robert. (May 1, 2007). Oil and Democracy Don't Mix Well. *Wall Street Journal,* p. A21.

Hagedorn, John M. (2006). The Global Impact of Gangs. In *Studying Youth Gangs,* James F. Short, Jr. and Lorine A. Hughes (Eds.). New York: Altamira Press, pp. 181–192.

Haller, Mark H. (Summer 1991). Policy Gambling, Entertainment, and the Emergence of Black Politics: Chicago from 1900 to 1940. *Journal of Social History,* 24 (4): 719–739.

———. (1990). Illegal Enterprise: A Theoretical and Historical Interpretation. *Criminology,* 28 (2): 207–235.

Haller, Mark H., and John V. Alviti. (April 1977). Loansharking in American Cities: Historical Analysis of a Marginal Enterprise. *The American Journal of Legal History,* 21 (2): 125–156.

Hamm, Mark S., and Cecile Van de Voorde. (Winter 2005). Crimes Committed by Terrorist Groups: Theory, Research, and Prevention. *Trends in Organized Crime,* 9 (2): 18–51.

Hamill, Pete. (March 11, 2007). Raging Thirst. *New York Times Book Review,* p. 9.

Handelman, Stephen. (March–April 1994). The Russian "Mafiya," *Foreign Affairs,* 83–95.

Hanson, Stephanie. (n.d.). Brazil's Powerful Prison Gang. http://www.cfr.org/publication/11542.

Harman, Danna. (Feb. 24, 2005). U.S. Steps up battle against Salvadoran gang MS-13. *USA Today,* p. 4A.

———. (Dec. 6, 2002). Why Radicals Find Fertile Ground in Moderate Kenya. *Christian Science Monitor,* p. 8.

Hart, Richard. (Jan. 28, 2008). New Chip Goes Beyond Serial Numbers. http://abclocal.go.com/kgo/story?section+news/drive_to_discover&id=5918380, retrieved January 13, 2009.

Hasnain, Ghulam. (Sept. 2001). Portrait of a Don. *Newsline,* http://www.newsline.com.pk/NewsSept2001/coverstory2.htm, retrieved April 10, 2007.

Hauser, Christine. (Dec. 28, 2007). Officer Pleads Guilty in Scheme That Thwarted a New York Brothel's Competitors. *The New York Times,* C14.

Hawley, Chris. (Oct. 9, 2007). Mexico's Drug-Control Initiative Reflects More Trust in U.S. *USA TODAY,* p. 10A.

Hays, Tom. (Nov. 16, 2006). New York Gambling Ring Busted. http://www.reviewjournal.com/lrrj_home/2006/Nov-6-Thu-2006, retrieved December 10, 2008.

Helfand, Neil S. (July 2003). *Asian Organized Crime and Terrorist Activity in Canada, 1999–2002,* Federal Research Division, Washington, DC: Library of Congress.

Hennessy-Fiske, Molly, and Tine Susman. (July 3, 2007). U.S. Says Iran Backs Hezbollah Militants in Iraq. *Houston Chronicle,* p. A7.

Herzliyya Institute for Counter-Terrorism Research Paper. (Nov. 7, 2006). Expert on Hizballah, Al'Qaida Threaten to Recruit Latin American Terrorists.

Hess, Pamela. (July 29, 2008). U.S: Iraqi Fighters Extort, Kidnap to Raise Funds. Associated Press, http://abcnews.go.com/Politics/wireStory?id=5476566, retrieved January 15, 2009.

Hill, Peter. (2005). The Changing Face of the Yakuza. In *Global Crime Today,* Mark Galeotti (Ed.). London: Routledge, pp. 97–116.

Hirschi, Travis, and Michael J. Hindelang. (1997). Intelligence and Delinquency: A Revisionist Review. *American Sociological Review,* 42: 572–87.

Holmes, Stephanie. (Aug. 16, 2007). A Mafia Family Feud Spills Over. *BBC NEWS,* http://news.bbc.co.uk/2/hi/europe/6949274.stm, retrieved September 30, 2007.

Hopkins, A.D. (n.d.). The Cowboy Who Pushed the Limits. In *The First 100 Persons Who Shaped Southern Nevada,* http://www.1st100.com/part2/binion.html, retrieved September 30, 2006.

Horton, Scott. (Feb. 1, 2008). Mogilevich Arrested and Charged. *Harper's Magazine,* http://www.harpers.org/archive/2008/02/hbc-90002296, retrieved March 3, 2008.

HUMSEC. (n.d.). Theoretical Framework. http://www.etc-graz.at/cms/index.php?id=336, retrieved November 9, 2006.

Hurriyet Daily Newspaper. (Jan. 1, 2002). Italy Accuses the PKK of Human Smuggling.

Hysi, Vasilika. (2004). Organised Crime in Albania: The Ugly Side of Capitalism and Democracy. In *Organized Crime in Europe,* Fijnaut and Paoli (Eds.). Netherlands: Springer, pp. 537–562.

Ianni, Francis A.J. (Oct. 24, 1970). Mafia and the Web of Kinship. In *An Inquiry Into Organized Crime,* Liciano J. Iorizzo (Ed.). Proceedings from the American Italian Historical Association Third Annual Conference, pp. 1–22.

Iiett, Daniel. (Nov. 9, 2005). The Organized Crime Gangs That Covet Your Computer Network. *Financial Times*. FT Report–Digital Business, p. 9.

IRIN In-Depth. (April 16, 2007). South Africa: Gang Culture in Cape Town. http://www.irinnews.org/Report.aspx?ReportId =70038, retrieved April 16, 2007.

Insideprison.com. (2006). First Command of the Capital: Prison Gang Profile. http://www.insideprison.com/prison_gang_ profile, retrieved January 4, 2008.

ISVG. (April 2003). The Tri-Border Region. *Crime and Justice International*, p. 32.

———. (March 2003). Revolutionary Armed Forces. *Crime and Justice International,* p. 29.

Jackson, Joy J. (Summer 1968). Crime and the Consciousness of a City. *Louisiana History.*

Jacobs, James B. and David N. Santore. (March–April 2001). The Liberation of IBT Local 560. *Criminal Law Bulletin*, 125–158.

Jameson, Sam. (May 20, 1985). Japan Gangs Not Really Underworld. *Los Angeles Times,* pp. A1, A10.

Jane's Intelligence Review. (June 1, 2007). Pirate Gold—Music Counterfeiting in Italy. pp. 1–6.

Japanese Yakuza. (January 2003). *Maxim,* p. 93.

Jefferson, David J. (Aug. 8, 2005). America's Most Dangerous Drug. *Newsweek*, pp. 41–48.

Johansen, Per Ole. (2004). Organised Crime, Norwegian Style. In *The Organised Crime Economy,* Van Duyne et al. (Eds.). Netherlands: Wolf Legal Publishers, pp. 189–208.

Johnson, Kirk. (April 6, 2005). New Tactics, Tools and Goals are Emerging for White Power Organizations, *TIME Magazine online.* http://query.nytimes.com/gst/fullpage .html?res=9400E5DF163EF935A35757C0A9639C8B63&s ec=&spon=&pagewanted=all.

Johnson, Stephen, and David B. Muhlhausen. (Fall 2005). North American Transnational Youth Gangs: Breaking the Chain of Violence. *Trends in Organized Crime,* 9(1): 38–54.

Johnston, David, and Seth Mydans. (March 7, 2008). Russian Held and Charged with Trying to Sell Arms. *New York Times,* p. A6.

Jones, Mark. (1993). Nigerian Crime Networks in the United States. *International Journal of Offender Therapy and Comparative Criminology,* 37(1): 59–73.

Jung, Y.S. (1997). Organized Crime in Contemporary Korea: International Implications. *International Journal of Comparative and Applied Criminal Justice,* 21 (1): 91–102.

Kang, G.E., and T.S. Kang. (1978). The Korean Urban Shoeshine Gang: A Minority Community. *Urban Anthropology,* 7: 171–183.

Kaplan, David E. (Sept. 12, 2006). The Mafia: A 21st-Century Cosa Nostra. *USNEWS.com,* LexisNexis(TM) Academic, http://http://www.usnews.com/usnews/news/badguys/ 060912/the_mafia_a_21stcentury_cosa_n.htm, retrieved January 31, 2007.

Kaplan, David E., Bay Fang, and Soni Sangwan. (Dec. 5, 2005). Paying for Terror, *U.S. News and World Report,* 139 (21): http://http://www.usnews.com/usnews/news/articles/ 051205/5terror_10.htm, retrieved January 23, 2007.

Karrstrand, Klas. (May 9–10, 2007). Countering Narcotics and Organized Crime in the Baltic Sea Region. Report from the Silk Road Studies Program Workshop, Tallinn, Estonia, http://www.silkroadstudies.org.

Keefe, Patrick Radden. (April 24, 2006). The Snakehead. *New Yorker*, 82(10). http://http://www.newyorker.com/archive/ 2006/04/24/060424fa_fact6.

Keire, Mara L. (Autumn 2001). The Vice Trust: A Reinterpretation of the White Slavery Scare in the United States, 1907–1917. *Journal of Social History,* 35(1): 4–51.

Kelley, Louise. (August 2001). Corruption and Organized Crime in Mexico in the Post-PRI Transition. *Journal of Contemporary Criminal Justice,* 17(3).

Kendall, John Smith. (April 1939). Who Killa de Chief? In *The Louisiana Historical Quarterly,* 22(2).

Kimberly Process Website. (n.d.). Combating Conflict Diamonds. http://www.globalwitness.org/pages/en/the_ kimberley_process.html, retrieved May 26, 2007.

Klein, Allison. (April 15, 2006). Gangs Use Internet to Deliver Threats. *Houston Chronicle,* p. A11.

Klein, Malcolm, Cheryl Maxson, and Lea Cunningham. (1991). "Crack," Street Gangs and Violence. *Criminology,* 29: 623–650.

Knight, Will, and Ben Crystall. (Dec. 10, 2005). Pirates Ahoy. *New Scientist.*

Knox, George W. (Fall 2001). Gang Profile Update: The Black P. Stone Nation (BPSN). *Journal of Gang Research,* 9 (1): 53–76.

———. (n.d.). Gangs, Guerrilla Warfare, and Social Conflict: The Potential Terrorism Threat from Gangs in America. http://http://www.ngcrc.com/introcha.html, 37 pp. retrieved July 22, 2006.

Koch, Christopher. (June 4, 2007). A Brief History of Malware and Cybercrime. http://www.cio.com/article/print/116250, retrieved March 10, 2008.

Kocieniewski, David. (Oct. 28, 2007). Vital and Vulnerable, Many Witnesses Receive Scant Protection. *New York Times,* p. 24.

Korosec, Thomas. (Sept. 11, 2006). Slayings Spotlight Dallas-Area Aryan Gang. *Houston Chronicle,* pp. A1, B5.

Kouri, Jim. (April 26, 2008). Enforcement Strategy to Combat Growing Threat of Organized Crime. www.canadafreepress. com/index.php/article/2774, retrieved May 1, 2008.

Krebs, Brian. (Sept. 24, 2007). Is Cyber Crime Really the FBI's No. 3 Priority? http://blog.washingtonpost.com/securityfix/ 2007/09/is_cyber_crime_a_distant_3rd_p.html, retrieved March 13, 2008.

Krim, Jonathan. (Nov. 11, 2004). E-Mail Authentication Will Not End Spam, Panelists Say. *The Washington Post,* p. E01.

Kudryavtsev, Vladimir, Viktor Luneyev, and Viktor Petrishchev (translated by Aram Yavrumyan). (2005). Terrorism and Organized Crime under Globalization Conditions. *Social Sciences*, 1: 84–94.

Lacey, Marc. (Feb. 18, 2007). Haiti on Offensive Against Gangs. *Houston Chronicle*, p. A23.

Lal, Rollie. (Spring 2005). South Asian Organized Crime and Terrorist Networks. *Orbis*, pp. 293–304.

Lambert, Bruce. (Sept. 9, 2007). Craigslist Is Becoming Prostitution's New Frontier. *Houston Chronicle*, p. A31.

Landau, Simha H. (2003). The Effects of Terrorism on Crime Patterns in Society: The Case of Israel. *Global Organized Crime*, D. Siegel et al. (eds.). Netherlands: Springer, pp. 137–148.

Landler, Mark, and Ian Fisher. (Aug. 16, 2007). German Police Link 6 Dead Men to an Italian Mob Feud. *New York Times*, http://www.nytimes.com/2007/08/16/world/europe/16italians.html, retrieved September 30, 2007.

Langewiesche, William. (Dec. 2006). How to Get a Nuclear Bomb. *Atlantic Monthly*, pp. 80–98.

Lapenkova, Marina. (Jan. 31, 2007). More Brain, Less Brawn: Russian Mafia Gets Into Big Business. *Agence France Presse*, http://www.mafia-news.com/russian-mafia-gets-into-big-business, retrieved online January 31, 2007.

Larsen, Peter Thal. (March 17, 2005). Gang Targeted Sumitomo in UK. *Financial Times London*, http://www.acpo.police.uk/asp/policies/Data/Fraud%20in%20the%20UK.pdf, retrieved online October 3, 2006.

Lavoie, Denise, (Dec. 25, 2007). Dangers of Crack vs. Coke Are in Dispute Decades Later. *Houston Chronicle*, p. A22.

Lee, Jennifer. (July 11, 2002). Pirates on the Web, Spoils on the Street. *New York Times online edition*, http://query.nytimes.com/gst/fullpage.html?res=9804E1D81530F932A25754C0A9649C8B63.

Lee, Rensselaer W. III, and Francisco Thoumi. (2003). Drugs and Democracy in Colombia. In *Menace to Society: Political–Criminal Collaboration Around the World*, Roy Goodson (Ed.). New Brunswick: Transaction Publishers.

Lee, Seungmug. (Spring 2006). Organized Crime in South Korea. *Trends in Organized Crime*, 9(3): 61–76.

Lehti, Martti, and Kauko Aromaa. (Fall 2007). Trafficking in Humans for Sexual Exploitation in Europe. *International Journal of Comparative and Applied Criminal Justice*, 31(2): 123–145.

Levi, Michael, and Alaster Smith. (2002). A Comparative Analysis of Organized Crime Conspiracy Legislation and Practice and Their Relevance to England and Wales. London: Home Office, pp. i–18.

Levy, Peter B. (July 1989). The Waterfront Commission of the Port of New York: A History and Reappraisal. *Industrial and Labor Relations Review*, 42(4): 508–523.

Liddick, Don. (Spring 1997). Race, Ethnic Succession, and Organized Crime: The Ethnic Composition of the Narcotics Gambling Industry in New York City. *Criminal Organizations*, 10(4): 13–18.

Lieberman, Paul. (Oct. 7, 1991). How the Mafia Targeted Tribe's Gambling Business. *Los Angeles Times*, pp. A1, A22, A23.

Light, Ivan. (Dec. 1977). Numbers Gambling among Blacks: A Financial Institution. *American Sociological Review*, 42(6): 892–904.

Lintner, Bertil. (2005). Chinese Organized Crime. In *Global Crime Today: The Changing Face of Organized Crime*, Mark Galeotti (Ed.). London: Routledge, pp. 84–96.

Lloyd, Marion. (June 18, 2007). New Fear in Mexico: Soldiers Fleeing for Cartels. *Houston Chronicle*, pp. A1, A9.

———. (Feb. 24, 2007). Calderon's Plan for Drug War Has Mixed Outcome. *Houston Chronicle*, pp. A23.

———. (Feb. 7, 2007). Gunmen Kill 7, Fuel Acapulco Drug War. *Houston Chronicle*, pp. A1, A4.

———. (May 10, 2007). Mexico 2nd Only to Iraq in Journalist Slayings. *Houston Chronicle*, pp. A1, A18.

Lloyd, Marion, and Cindy George. (January 23, 2007,). Alleged Mexican Kingpins in Court. *Houston Chronicle*, pp. A1, A8.

Logan, Samuel. (October 19, 2007). Governance in Guatemala Increasingly Threatened by Organized Crime. http://www.pinr.com/report.php?ac=view_printable&report_id=703&language_id=1, retrieved November 19, 2007.

Logan, Samuel, and Ashley Morse. (Dec. 2006). The FARC's International Presence: An Overview. http://www.samuellogan.com, retrieved January 19, 2008.

Lozano, Juan A. (January 23, 2007). 4 Extradited Mexican Drug Lords, 11 Others Appear in U.S. Court, Associated Press Online.

Lozzi-Toscano, Bettina. (2004). Italy. In *Teen Gangs: A Global View*, Maureen P. Duffy and Scott Edward Gillig (Eds.), New York: Greenwood Press, pp. 105–120.

Lunden, Walter A. (May–June 1958). Emile Durkheim. *The Journal of Criminal Law, Criminology and Police Science*, 49: 1.

Lupo, Salvatore. (Spring 1997). The Allies and the Mafia. *Journal of Modern Italian Studies*, 2(1): 21–33.

Lupsha, Peter A. and Cho, Sung-Kwon. (1999). The Future of Narco-Terrorism: Colombia—A Case Study. In *Organized Crime: Uncertainties and Dilemmas*, S. Einstein and M. Amir (Eds.), Chicago: Office of International Criminal Justice, pp. 423–437.

Lupsha, Peter A. (1981). Individual Choice, Material Culture, and Organized Crime. *Criminology*, 19: 3–24.

Mabrey, Daniel. (March 2003). Human Smuggling in China. *Crime and Justice International*, pp. 5–11.

Main, Frank. (May 15, 2006). Troops do Double Duty in Gangs: One Soldier Allegedly Helped Buy. *Chicago Sun–Times*, electronic edition, http://www.suntimes.com.

Makarenko, Tamara. (2005). The Crime–Terror Continuum: Tracing the Interplay between Transnational Organized Crime and Terrorism. *Global Crime Today: The Changing Face of Organized Crime,* Mark Galeotti (Ed.). London: Routledge, pp. 129–145.

———. (2003). "The Ties That Bind": Uncovering the Relationship between Organized Crime and Terrorism. In *Global Organized Crime: Trends and Developments,* de Bunt, Siegel, and Zaitch (Eds.). Netherlands: Kluwer Academic Publishers, pp. 159–173.

Manrique, Luis Esteban G. (2006). A Parallel Power: Organized Crime in Latin America. *Real Instituto Elcano,* Madrid, http://www.realinstitutoelcano.org/analisis/1049.asp, retrieved January 17, 2008.

Markon, Jerry. (Nov. 30, 2007). Lawmakers Want FBI to Get Involved in Prostitution Fight. *Houston Chronicle,* p. A25.

Martinez, Angelica Duran. (May 2007). Guatemala. *FRIDE Comment,* pp. 1–7.

———. (May 2007). Trinidad and Tobago. *FRIDE Comment,* pp. 1–7.

Masland, Tom. (May 13, 2002). We Beat and Killed People. *Newsweek,* pp. 24–29.

May, Allan. (Oct. 2006). Anthony Giordano—St. Louis Hot Head. http://www.americanmafia.com/Allan_May_7-26-99.html, retrieved Oct. 1, 2006.

———. (Oct. 2006). The History of the Kansas City Family. http:/crimemagazine.com/kcfamily, retrieved October 12, 2006.

———. (2005). The St. Louis Family. http://www.crimelibrary.com/gangsters_outlaws/family_epics/louis/1.html, retrieved Oct. 1, 2006.

McAfee. (July 2005). McAfee Virtual Criminology Report, http://www.mcafee.com, retrieved March 13, 2008.

McCafferty, Dennis. (Sept. 1, 2004). Organized Cyber-Crime. Web Host Industry Review, http://www.thewhir.com/features/organized-cybercrime.cfm, retrieved March 13, 2008.

McCormick, John, and Deborah Gage. (March 7, 2005). Web Mobs: They Operate Under Names Such as Carderplanet, Stealthdivision, Darkprofits and the Shadowcrew. Baseline, http://web.lexis-nexis.com.unx1.shsu.edu:2048/universe/-document?_m=c8258faf1a266agd, retrieved October 3, 2006.

McCusker, Rob. (2006). Transnational Organized Crime Cyber Crime: Distinguishing Threat from Reality. *Criminal Law Soc Change,* 46: 257–273

McGeehan, Patrick. (Feb. 12, 2007). New York to Revisit a Cap on Rates for Hauling Trash. *New York Times,* p. A19.

McGrath, Ben. (May 1, 2006). Kiss City: The Unmaking of the Mafia Cops. *The New Yorker,* pp. 54–65.

McGuire, Phillip. (April–May, June–July, 1986). Outlaw Motorcycle Gangs: Organized Crime on Wheels. *National Sheriff Magazine,* pp. 1–14.

McKinley, Jr. James C. (January 22, 2008). Mexico Hits Drug Gangs with Full Fury of War. *New York Times,* pp. A1, A9.

———. (January 27, 2007). Mexico's Latest War on Drug Gangs Is Off to a Rapid Start. *New York Times,* p. A10.

———. (October 26, 2006). With Beheadings and Attacks Drug Gangs Terrorize Mexico. *New York Times,* pp. A1, A10.

McMillan, Robert. (August 6, 2006). FBI: Cybercriminals Taking Cues from Mafia. *PCWORLD,* http://www.pcworld.com/printable/article/id,126664/printable.html, retrieved April 8, 2008.

McNabb Associates. (2008). When the FBI Comes Calling. http://www.federalcrimes.com/rico.htm#top, retrieved January 9, 2009.

McShane, Larry. (April 7, 2006). 2 Ex–NYPD Detectives Convicted of Being Mafia Hitmen. *Houston Chronicle,* p. A12.

McShane, Larry. (Oct. 24, 2004). Junior Gotti's Midlife Mob Crisis. *Houston Chronicle.*

Meeks, Brock. (Sept. 7, 1999). globalHell says it's going legit. Tech News on ZDNet, http://news.zdnet.com/2100-9595_22-501316.html?legacy=zdm, retrieved March 21, 2008.

Menn, Joseph. (October 26, 2004). Digital Mafia Hitting Web Sites in Protection Racket. *Los Angeles Times,* http://www.houstonbeats.com/board/archive/index.php/t-39727.html, retrieved March 13, 2008.

Merton, Robert K. (Oct. 1938). Social Strain and Anomie. *American Sociological Review,* 3: 672–682.

Meyer, Maureen (with contributions from Coletta Youngers and Dave Bewley-Taylor). (Nov. 2007). At a Crossroads: Drug Trafficking, Violence and the Mexican State, Washington Office on Latin America (WOLA). 12 pp.

Michaletos, Ioannis. (Feb. 14, 2008). Greece Battles Balkan Organized Crime. http://www.serbianna.com/columns/michaletos/028.shtml, retrieved February 21, 2008.

———. (Jan. 27, 2008). Kosovo Underworld Rising. http://www.serbianna.com/columns/michaletos/027.shtml, retrieved February 21, 2008.

———. (February 2, 2007). An Outlook of Organized Crime in the Southern Balkans. http://www.serbianna.com/columns/michaltos/009.html, retrieved March 26, 2007.

Michaletos, Ioannis, and Stavros Markos. (March 7, 2007). Albania and EUROPOL Sign Agreement on Organized Crime, http://www.worldpress.org/print_article.cfm?article_id=2827&dont=yes, retrieved February 21, 2008.

Miko, Francis T. (2007). International Human Trafficking. In *Transnational Threats,* Kimberly Thachuk (Ed.).Westport: Praeger, pp. 36–52.

Mili, Hayder. (January 12, 2006). Tangled Webs: Terrorist and Organized Crime Groups. *Terrorism Monitor,* http://www.jamestown.org/terrorism/news/article.php?articleid=2369, retrieved April 16, 2007.

Millard, Candice. (June 3, 2007). Pirates of the Caribbean: The Rise and Fall of Captain Morgan, Blackbeard and Other Swashbuckling Rogues. *New York Times Book Review,* pp. 28–29.

Miller, Walter B. (1980). Gangs, Groups, and Serious Youth Crime. In *Critical Issues in Juvenile Delinquency*, David Shichor and Delos H. Kelly (Eds.). Lexington, MA: Lexington, pp. 115–138.

Miller, Walter B. (1958). Lower Class Culture as a Generating Milieu of Gang Delinquency. *Journal of Social Issues,* 14(3): 5–19.

Miller, Zane L. (March 1958). Boss Cox's Cincinnati: A Study in Urbanization and Politics, 1880–1914. *Journal of American History*, 54: 823–838.

Milton, Pat. (Oct. 3, 2006). U.S. Worrying about Collaboration. *The China Post*, http://www.chinapost.com.tw/editorial/detail.asp?onNews=&GRP=i, retrieved November 9, 2006.

MIPT Terrorism Knowledge Base. (Dec. 10, 2006). Key Leader Profile: Jeff Fort, http://www.tkb.org/KeyLeader.jsp?memID=5393, retrieved January 18, 2007.

Mishra, Stitanshu. (July–Sept. 2003). Exploitation of Information and Communication Technology by Terrorist Organizations. *Strategic Analysis: A Monthly Journal of the IDSA,* 27(3); http://wf2dnvr2.webfeat.org/gxrQI1465/url, retrieved September 30, 2007, 13 pp.

Moore, Joan. (1988). Gangs and the Underclass: A Comparative Perspective. In *People and Folks*, John M. Hagedorn (Ed.). Chicago: Lake View Press, pp. 3–16.

Moore, Robert F., and Scott Shifrel. (No. 16, 2006). You Lose! 3B Ring Bashed. *New York Daily News*, p. 7.

Murphy, Kim. (June 29, 1987). The L.A. Mob: Eking Out a Living Working Streets. *Los Angeles Times*, Part I, pp. 1, 18.

Mutschke, Ralf. (Dec. 13, 2000). Links Between Organized Crime and "Traditional" Terrorist Groups. Testimony to U.S. House Judiciary Committee, Subcommittee on Crime, pp. 1–26, http://www.russianlaw.org/Mutschke.htm, retrieved June 25, 2007.

Myers, III, Willard H. (Sept. 1995). The Emerging Threat of Transnational Organized Crime from the East. *Crime, Law and Social Change,* 24(3): 181–222.

Nackan, Allan, and Jonathan Cooperman. (Nov.–Dec. 2006). New Directions in Fraud Investigation. *The Secured Lender,* pp. 43–46, 68.

Nagasaki Mayor Itoh Dies; Suspect Held Grudge. (April 17, 2007). *The Asahi Shimbun,* http://www.asahi.com/emglish/Herald-asahi/TKY200704180347.html, retrieved April 19, 2007.

Naim, Moises. (Jan.–Feb. 2003). The Five Wars of Globalization. *Foreign Policy.* 134: 28–37.

Nakamura, Rodolfo Mendoza. (1999). The Use of the "Shining Path" Myth in the Context of the All-Out War Against the Narco-Guerilla. In *Global Organized Crime and International Security,* Emilio C. Viano (Ed.). Aldershot: Ashgate, pp. 99–116.

Nardini, William J. (2006). The Prosecutor's Toolbox: Investigating and Prosecuting Organized Crime in the United States. *Journal of International Criminal Justice,* 4: 528–538.

National Central Police University, Taipei, Taiwan. (Spring 2005). Organized Crime in Taiwan. *Trend in Organized Crime,* 8(3): 13–23.

National Drug Intelligence Center. (Jan. 2006). National Drug Threat Assessment 2006: Organized Gangs and Drug Trafficking, http://www.usdoj.gov/ndic/pubs11/18862/gangs.htm, retrieved January 10, 2007.

———. (Oct. 2006). National Drug Threat Assessment 2007: Drug Trafficking Organizations, http://www.usdoj.gov/ndic/pubs21/21137/dtos.htm, retrieved January 10, 2007.

National Gang Crime Research Center (NGCRC). (2000). Bomb and Arson Crimes among Gang Members: A Behavioral Science Profile, http://www.ngcrc.com/bombarson.html, 40 pp. retrieved July 22, 2006.

Naylor, R.T. (1997). Mafias, Myths and Markets: On the Theory and Practice of Enterprise Crime. *Transnational Organized Crime,* 3(3): 6.

Ndhlovu, Francis K. (2003). Organized Crime: A Perspective from Zambia. In *Organized Crime: World Perspectives,* Jay Albanese et al. (Eds.). Upper Saddle River NJ: Prentice Hall, pp. 406–426.

Neumeister, Larry. (Oct. 19, 2006). Authorities Break Up Colombian Money-Laundering Ring. *Houston Chronicle,* p. A10.

Noble, Ronald K. (July 16, 2003). The Links Between Intellectual Property Crime and Terrorist Financing. Text of speech from Interpol director, http://www.interpol.int/Public/ICPO/Speeches/SG20030716.asp.

Nolan, Rebecca. (Feb. 16, 2007). Man Seeking Love Finds Nigerian Scam. *Eugene Oregon Register–Guard,* http://home.rica.net/alphae/419coal/news2007.htm, retrieved April 16, 2007.

Nolin, Christopher A. (Fall 2006). Telecommunications as a Weapon in the War of Modern Organized Crime. *Catholic University of America CommLaw Conspectus,* pp. 1–30.

Nunez, Claudia. (Dec. 27, 2007). Women Are the New Coyotes. *New American Media,* http://arizonasportsfan.com/vb/showthread.php?t=104452, retrieved January 15, 2008.

O'Day, Patrick, and Rex Venecia. (Nov. 1999). Cazuelas: An Ethnographic Study of Drug Trafficking in a Small Mexican Border Town. *Journal of Contemporary Criminal Justice,* 15(4): 421–443.

Offnews.info. (2005). Kaibiles: The New Lethal Force in the Mexican Drug Wars. http://www.offnews.info/imprimir.php?contenidoID=4703, retrieved January 19, 2008.

Old Habits Die Hard. (May 19, 2007). *The Economist,* p. 63.

Opala, Ken. (Aug. 1, 2002). The Case for a More Effective Approach. *Daily Nation,* http://www.mapic.org/ccnews/v02/n1429/a05.html?347, retrieved May 11, 2007.

Otis, John. (Aug. 24, 2007). Run Silent, Run Deep, Run-Down. *Houston Chronicle,* p. A13.

Packer, George. (Nov. 13, 2006). The Megacity: Decoding the Chaos of Lagos. *The New Yorker,* pp. 62–75.

Padgett, Tim, et al. (April 18, 2005). The Killers Next Door. *Time,* 165(16): 140–141.

Paoli, Letizia. (2005). The "Invisible Hand of the Market": The Illegal Drugs Trade in Germany, Italy, and Russia. In *Criminal Finances and Organizing Crime in Europe,* Van Duyne et al. (Eds.). The Netherlands: Wolf Legal Publishers.

Paoli, Letizia. (1999). The Future of Sicilian and Calabrian Organized Crime. In *Organized Crime: Uncertainties and Dilemmas,* Stanley Einstein and Menachem Amir (Eds.). Chicago: University of Illinois, OICJ, pp. 155–186.

Paoli, Letizia. (1998). The Pentiti's Contribution to the Conceptualization of the Mafia Phenomenon. In *The New European Criminology,* Ruggiero et al. (Eds.). London: Routledge, pp. 264–286.

Phillips, Mike. (Aug. 6, 2000). This Time Its Personal. *Sunday Times,* p. 6.

Pincomb, Ronald A., and Daniel L. Judiscak. (1998). The Threat of the Jamaican Posses to the United States in the 1990s. In *Gangs and Gang Behavior,* G. Larry Mays (Ed.). Chicago: Nelson Hall, pp. 396–405.

Pinkerton, James. (April 28, 2007). Mexican Cartels Thought to Be Stockpiling Arms for Turf War. *Houston Chronicle,* p. A26.

———. (Dec. 16, 2006). Bribe Culture Seeps into South Texas. *Houston Chronicle,* pp. A1, A29.

Pinkerton, James, and Ioan Grillo. (May 8, 2005). The Fight for Nuevo Laredo. *Houston Chronicle,* pp. A1, A16.

Pinnock, Don, and Mara Douglas-Hamilton. (1998). Rituals, Rites and Tradition: Rethinking Youth Programs in South Africa. In *Gangs and Youth Subculture,* Cameron Hazlehurst and Kayleen Hazlehurst (Eds.). Piscataway NJ: Transaction Publishers, pp. 307–341.

Pitcavage, Mark (Interview). (Winter 2002). Behind Prison Walls: An Expert Discusses the Role of Race-Based Gangs and Other Extremists in America's Prisons. Southern Poverty Law Center Intelligence Report, http://www.splcenter.org/intel/intelreport/article.jsp?=sid55.

Plombeck, Charles Thelen. (1988). Confidentiality and Disclosure: The Money Laundering Control Act of 1986 and Banking Secrecy. *International Lawyer,* 22.

Pollard, N.A. (2002). *Terrorism and Organized Crime: Implications of Convergence,* Terrorism Research Center, Internet Edition.

Popkin, James. (Aug. 23, 1993). Gambling with the Mob? *U.S. News & World Report.*

Popkin, James, and Katia Hetter. (March 14, 1994). America's Gambling Craze. *U.S. News & World Report,* 42–43, 46, 48–56.

Profile: India's Fugitive Gangster. (Sept. 12, 2006). *BBC News,* http://newsvote.bbc.co.uk/mpapps/pagetools/print/news.bbc.co.uk/2/hi/south_asia/477553, retrieved June 17, 2007.

Prosecution under the Hobbs Act and the Expansion of Federal Criminal Jurisdiction. (Sept. 1975). *The Journal of Criminal Law and Criminology,* 66(3): 306–324.

Protass, Harlan. (Nov. 5, 2007). Finish the Job Equalizing Crack Cocaine Sentencing. *Houston Chronicle,* p. B7.

Raab, Selwyn. (Dec. 20, 2005).Vincent "The Chin" Gigante, "Oddfather," Mob Boss, 77 *New York Times* obituary, http://www.nytimes.com/2005/12/20/obituaries/20gigante.html.

———. (Oct. 17, 1995). Crackdown on Mob Leads to Chaos at Fish Market. *The New York Times.*

———. (Sept. 3, 1995). With Gotti Away, the Genoveses Succeed the Leaderless Gambinos. *New York Times,* pp. 1, 12.

Raman, B. (Oct. 19, 2003). Dawood Ibrahim: The Global Terrorist. *South Asia Analysis Group,* http://www.saag.org/papers9/paper818.html, retrieved June 17, 2007.

Ramm, A.C. (n.d.). The Yardies: England's Emerging Crime Problem, http://www.gangland.net/yardies.htm, retrieved April 16, 2007.

Rapetto, Jr., U. (2006). Transnational Crime: Challenges for Law Enforcement. In *Invisible Threats: Financial and Information Technology Crimes and National Security, Volume 10 NATO Security through Science Series: Human and Societal Dynamics,* Umberto Gori and Ivo Paparela (Eds.). Birmingham AL: IOS Press, pp. 63–68.

Rashbaum, William K. (Feb. 11, 2004). Officials Say Mob Stole $200 Million Using Phone Bills. *New York Times,* p. A1.

———. (Jan. 10, 2003). After Mob Defections, U.S. Indicts Man It Calls Boss. *New York Times,* p. A22.

Rawlinson, Paddy. (1998). Criminal Heirs—Organised Crime and Russia's Youth. In *Gangs and Youth Subculture,* Cameron Hazlehurst and Kayleen Hazlehurst (Eds.). Piscataway NJ: Transaction Publishers, pp. 95–115.

Rawlinson, Patricia. (1998). Russian Organized Crime: Moving Beyond Ideology. *The New European Criminology,* Vincenzo Ruggierio et al. (Eds.). London: Routledge, pp. 242–263.

Rediker, Marcus. (2001). The Seaman as Pirate: Plunder and Social Banditry at Sea. In *Bandits at Sea: A Pirate Reader,* C.R. Pennell (Ed.). New York: New York University Press, pp. 139–168.

Repetskaya, Ann L. (1999). Regionalization and Expansion: The Growth of Organized Crime in East Siberia. In *Global Organized Crime and International Security,* Emilio Viano (Ed.). Aldershot, UK: Ashgate, pp. 123–127.

Retailers Use Technology to Combat Organized Shoplifting. (2005). *Access Control and Security Systems,* Oct. 1: 11.

Rider, Barry A.K. (2001). Cyber-Organised Crime—The Impact of Information Technology on Organised Crime. *Journal of Financial Crime,* 8(4): 332–346.

Rigby, Rhymer. (Dec. 9, 2005). The Whiz-Kids and Wiseguys of Cyber Crime. *Financial Times,* Business Life section, p. 14.

Riis, Jacob A. (July 1899). The Genesis of the Gang. *Atlantic Monthly,* pp. 302–311.

Riley, Christopher. (Jan. 14, 1995). Chip Giants Turn Up the Heat on Hoodlums. *New Scientist Magazine,* http://www .newscientist.com/article/mg14519600-chip-giants-turn-up-heat-on-hoodlums, retrieved January 13, 2009.

Ritter, John. (Feb. 7, 2007). Pot Growing Moves to Suburbs. *USA TODAY,* p. A3.

Robson, Seth. (January 17, 2007). FBI Says U.S. Criminal Gangs Are Using Military to Spread Their Reach. *Stars and Stripes*, European edition, Internet copy.

Rodriguez, Olga R. (Oct. 5, 2007). Arrest of Alleged "Diva" Drug Lord Proves as Scintillating as a *Telenovela. Houston Chronicle,* p. A15.

Roig-Franzia, Manuel. (June 23, 2002). Man Convicted of Using Smuggling to Fund Hezbollah. *The Washington Post.*

Roth, Mitchel. (March 2008). Organized Crime in the Balkans. *Crime and Justice International,* pp. 7–8.

———. (Oct. 2000). The Emerging Yardie Problem. *Crime and Justice International,* pp. 5–6.

Roth, Mitchel, and Murat Sever. (Oct. 2007). The Kurdish Workers Party as Criminal Syndicate. *Studies in Conflict and Terrorism.*

Roth, Mitchel, and Murat Sever. (2007). Barriers to International Police Cooperation in the Age of Terrorism. In *Understanding and Responding to Terrorism,* Huseyin Durmaz et al. (Eds.). Amsterdam: IOS Press, pp. 42–55.

Rubio, Mauricio, and Roman Ortiz. (2005). Organized Crime in Latin America. In *Handbook of Transnational Crime and Justice,* Phil Reichel (Ed.).Thousand Oaks, CA: Sage, pp. 425–437.

Ryan, Patrick J. (1994). A History of Organized Crime Control: Federal Strike Forces. In *Handbook of Organized Crime in the United States,* Robert J. Kelly, Ko-Lin Chin, and Rufus Schatzberg (Eds.). Westport, CT: Greenwood, pp. 333–358.

Sampson, Robert J., and W. Byron Groves (1989). Community Structure and Crime: Testing Social Disorganization Theory. *American Journal of Sociology,* 94: 774–802.

Sanders, Alain L., and Priscilla Painton. (Aug. 21, 1989). Showdown at Gucci, http://www.time.com/time/magazine/article/0,9171,958402-1,00.html, retrieved December 10, 2008.

Sanderson, T.M. (2004). Transnational Terror and Organized Crime: Blurring the Lines. *SAIS Review,* 24(1): 49–61.

Schelling, Thomas C. (Autumn 1971). What Is the Business of Organized Crime? *The American Scholar,* pp. 643–652.

Schiller, Dane, (Dec. 24, 2007). Mexican Marijuana Plentiful and Cheap. *Houston Chronicle,* pp. A1, A3.

———. (Sept. 26, 2007). Colombian Official Warns of Drug Cartels' Growing Reach. *Houston Chronicle,* p. A10.

———. (Feb. 18, 2007). Prosecutors Set to Take on Suspected Gulf Cartel Leader. *Houston Chronicle,* p. A37.

Schlegel, Kip, and Charles Cohen. (2007). The Impact of Technology on Criminality. In *The New Technology of Crime, Law and Social Control,* James M. Byrne and Donald J. Rebovich (Eds.). Monsey, New York: Criminal Justice Press, pp. 23–47.

Schmid, Alex. (Jan. 27, 2005). Links Between Terrorism and Drug Trafficking: A Case of "Narco-Terrorism"? http://english.safe-democracy.org/causes/links-between-terrorism-and-drug-trafficking-a-case-of-narcoterrorism. html, retrieved June 25, 2007.

Schmitt, Richard B. (April 24, 2008). Attorney General Targeting International Organized Crime. *Los Angeles Times,* http://www.latimes.com/news/nationworld/washingtonc/la-na-crime24apr24, retrieved May 1, 2008.

Schneider, Jane, and Peter Schneider. (Aug.–Oct. 2005). Mafia, Antimafia, and the Plural Cultures of Sicily. *Current Anthropology,* 46(4): 501–520.

Schwartz, Jeremy. (Sept. 9, 2007). Guatemala's Run for Democracy. *Houston Chronicle,* p. A21.

Segal, David. (March 1992). Dances with Sharks. *The Washington Monthly,* 24: 26–30.

Semple, Kirk. (Nov. 4, 2007). Cannabis Thrives in an Afghan Province. *The New York Times.* http://www.nytimes.com/2007/11/04/world/asia/04cannabis.html?_r=1, retrieved December 10, 2008.

Sennott, Charles M. (Jan. 17, 2005). Robbery Spurs Look at IRA Criminal Ties. *Boston Globe,* http://www.boston.com.

Serio, Joseph. (Nov.–Dec. 2006). Has the Market Tamed the Mafia? *Crime and Justice International,* p. 47.

———. (Sept. 2002). Post-Soviet Crime Groups in the Computer Realm: A Real Threat? *Crime and Justice International,* pp. 7–8, 27.

Serio, Joseph, and Alexander Gorkin. (July 2003). Changing Lenses: Striving for Sharper Focus on the Nature of the "Russian Mafia" and Its Impact on the Computer Realm. *International Review of Law Computers & Technology,* 17(2): 191–202.

Shaw, Mark. (Sept. 2002). Typologies of Transnational Organized Crime Groups. Centre for International Crime Prevention, United Nations Office of Drugs and Crime, http://www.undoc.org/pdf/crime/training/typologies.pdf, retrieved June 15, 2008.

———. (Jan. 1998). Organized Crime in Post-Apartheid South Africa. Safety and Governance Program, Institute for Security Studies, Occasional Paper No. 28, http://www.iss .co.za/pubs/PAPERS/28/Paper28.html, retrieved April 16, 2007.

Shaw, Mark, and Gail Wannenburg. (2005). Organized Crime in Africa. In *Handbook of Transnational Crime and Justice,* Philip Reichel (Ed.). Thousand Oaks CA: Sage, pp. 367–385.

Sheets, Lawrence Scott, and William J. Broad. (Jan. 26, 2007). Smuggler's Plot in Georgia Boosts Fear over Uranium. *Houston Chronicle*, p. A19.

Sheldon, Henry D. (1898). The Institutional Activity of American Children. *American Journal of Psychology*, pp. 425–428.

Shelley, Louise. (2002). The Nexus of Organized International Criminals and Terrorism. *International Annals of Criminology*, 20 $\frac{1}{2}$: 85–92. Online at: http://pagesperso-orange.fr/societe .internationale.de.criminologie/pdf/Intervention%20Shelley. pdf, retrieved December10, 2008.

Shelley, Louise, and Robert Orttung. (Sept./Oct. 2006). Criminal Acts: How Organized Crime Is a Nuclear Smuggler's New Best Friend. *Bulletin of the Atomic Scientists*, pp. 22–23.

Shelley, Louise I., and John T. Picarelli. (Winter 2005). Methods and Motives: Exploring Links between Transnational Organized Crime and International Terrorism. *Trends in Organized Crime*, 9(2): 52–67.

Shelton, Lee R., and James Hall. (Feb. 4, 2002). Patriot Act Another RICO? http://www.enterstageright.com/archive/ articles/0202/0202patriot.htm, retrieved May 15, 2008.

Shillingford, Joia. (Nov. 14, 2004). Inter-Operator Fraud Warning. *Financial Times Limited*, p. 6.

Siegel, Dina. (2003). The Transnational Russian Mafia. In *Global Organized Crime Trends and Developments*, Dina Siegal et al. (Eds.). Boston: Kluwer, pp. 51–62.

Sims, J.C. (July 7, 2006). What NSA Is Doing . . . and Why It's Illegal. *Hastings Constitutional Law Quarterly*, 33(2 and 3): 101–136.

Singer, Mark. (Aug. 12, 2002). The Gang's All Here. *The New Yorker*, pp. 56–61.

Smith, Denis Mack. (Nov. 30, 1995). The Ruling Class. *New York Times Book Review*, p. 7.

Smith, Jr., Dwight C. (1994). Illicit Enterprise: An Organized Crime Paradigm for the 1990s. In *Handbook of Organized Crime in the United States*, Robert J. Kelly, Chin Ko-Lin, and Rufus Schatzberg (Eds.). Westport, CT: Greenwood Press, pp. 121–150.

———. (Jan. 1976). Mafia: The Prototypical Alien Conspiracy. *The Annals*, 423: 75–88.

Smith, John L. (n.d.).The Double Life of Moe Dalitz. In *The First 100 Persons Who Shaped Southern Nevada*, http:// www.1st100.com/part2/dalitz.html, retrieved September 30, 2006.

Smith, Simon. (May 1996). Piracy in Early British America. *History Today*, pp. 29–36, 55.

Smyth, Frank. (March 9, 2007). Bush's Brush with Latin America's Drug Lords. *The Nation*, http://www.thenation .com/docprint.mhtml?i=20070326&s=smith, retrieved November 19, 2007.

Soderblom, Jason D. (Sept. 19, 2005). Eurasia's Organized and Transnational Organized Crime, http://www.World-ICE.com.

Sommer, Samantha. (March 18, 2001). With E-Mail, African Scams Proliferate. *Austin-Statesman*, p. B14.

Spillane, Joseph. (Autumn, 1998). The Making of an Underground Market: Drug Selling in Chicago, 1900–1940. *Journal of Social History*, 32(1): 27–47.

Spring, Tom. (Aug. 25, 2005). Web of Crime: Who's Catching the Cybercrooks? *PCWORLD*, http://www.pcworld.com/ printable/article/id,122245/printable.html, retrieved April 8, 2008.

Stanley, Alessandra. (Jan. 11, 2007). Where Hit Men Better Mean It When They "Yes Ma'am" the Boss, http:// query.nytimes.com/gst/fullpage.html?res=9905EED6113AF 932A25752C0A9679C8B63, retrieved June 21, 2007.

Stambaugh, J.J. (Aug. 13, 2007). Sneak-and-Peek Warrants Debated. *Knoxville News Sentinel*, http://www.knonnews .com/news/2007/Aug/13/sneak-and-peak-warrants-debated, retrieved May 15, 2008.

Standing, Andre. (Feb. 2003). Organised Crime: The Evolution of a Mainstream Definition, http://www.iss.co.za/Pubs/ monographs/No77/Chap3.html, retrieved October 22, 2006.

Starbuck, David, James C. Howell, and Donna J. Lindquist. (Dec. 2001). Hybrid and Other Modern Gangs. U.S. Department of Justice, Juvenile Justice Bulletin, pp. 1–8.

Starkey, David J. (2001). Pirates and Markets. In *Bandits at Sea: A Pirate Reader*, C.R. Pennell (Ed.). New York: New York University Press, pp. 107–124.

Steffensmeier, Darrell, and Jeffrey T. Ulmer. (2006). Black and White Control of Numbers Gambling: A Cultural Assets—Social Capital View. *American Sociological Review*, 71: 123–156.

Strang, Steven. (2004). Dispelling the Myths about Terrorism. *Royal Canadian Mounted Police Gazette*, http://www .gazette.rcmp.gc.ca/print.php?article_id=64&page_id=51& lang_id=1, retrieved June 24, 2007.

Strasser, F. (1988). State Racketeering Laws Are Giving Prosecutions a New Weapon Against Crime. *Governing*, April: 42–47.

Sung, Hung-en. (2004). State Failure, Economic Failure, and Predatory Organized Crime: A Comparative Analysis. *Journal of Research in Crime and Delinquency*, 41(2): 111–129.

Suo, Steve. (Oct. 3, 2004). Hidden Powerhouses Underlie Meth's Ugly Spread. *Oregonian*, http://www.house.gov/larsen/ meth/press_20041003_oregonian_hiddenpowerhouses .shtml, retrieved January 26, 2008.

Suro, Roberto. (March 18, 1986). Sicily and the Mafia. *The New York Times Magazine*, pp. 47–65.

Surtees, Rebecca. (2008). Traffickers and Trafficking in Southern and Eastern Europe. *European Journal of Criminology*, 5(1): 39–68.

Sverdlick, Ana R. (2005). Terrorists and Organized Crime Entrepreneurs in the "Triple Frontier" among Argentina, Brazil, and Paraguay. *Trends in Organized Crime*, 9(2): 84–93.

Tabuchi, Hiroko. (April 18, 2007). Mayor of Nagasaki Is Killed in Attack. *Houston Chronicle,* p. A10.

Tarlow, Barry. (Dec. 1999). RICO Report, http://www .criminaljustice.org/public.nsf/ChampionArticles/99dec07? OpenDocument, retrieved January 9, 2009.

Tendler, Stewart. (Aug. 3, 2000). Yardie Gangs Move into the Provinces. *The London Times,* p. 4.

The Immunity Game. (June 11, 1973). *TIME.* http://www.time .com/time/magazine/article/0,9171,907427,00.htm, retrieved December 10, 2008.

Theognis. (n.d.). Fragments, Lines 0429-0438, http://www .poemhunter.com/ebooks/pdf/Theognis, retrieved December 15, 2008.

Thomas, Dana. (Sept. 3, 2007). Counterfeits Are Literally Terrorism's Purse Strings. *Houston Chronicle,* p. B7.

Thompson, Ginger. (Sept. 26, 2004). Shuttling between Nations, Latino Gangs Confound the Law. *New York Times,* http://http://www.nytimes.com/2004/09/26/international/ americas/26honduras.html?_r=1&scp=1&sq=Shuttling% 20between%20nations,%20Latino%20gangs%20confou nd%20the%20law&st=cse, retrieved November 19, 2007.

Thompson, Tony. (June 15, 3003). Ulster Terror Gangs Links Up with Mafia, http://www.guardian.co.uk/2003/jun/15/ northernireland, retrieved June 20, 2008.

Tierney, John. (1998). Reading the Coca Leaves. *New York Times*, September 26, 2006, p. A23.

Toy, Calvin. (1998). A Short History of Asian Gangs in San Francisco. In *Gangs and Gang Behavior,* Larry Mays (Ed.). Chicago: Nelson Hall, pp. 228–245.

Toy, Vivian S. (1994). Deal Reached to Monitor Street Fair. *The New York Times,* p. 19.

Trifunovic, Darko. (n.d.). Terrorism and Organized Crime in Southeastern Europe: The case of Bosnia-Herzegovina— Sandzak, Kosovo and Metohija. Belgrade University, Faculty of Security Studies, unpublished paper online, retrieved 2/21/2008.

Ulster Terror Gangs Link Up with Mafia. (2003). *Crime and Justice International,* July/August, p. 16.

Urquhart, Frank. (Nov. 7, 1998). UK: Yardies Linked to UKP10 Trade in Scotland's Heroin Capital. *Scotsman.*

USInfo.gov. (Nov. 12, 2004). U.S. Authorities Target Two Chinese Organized Crime Groups. http://usinfo.gov/utils/ printpage.html, retrieved May 15, 2008.

Valdez, Al. (n.d.). Mara Salvatrucha: A South American Import. http://www.nagia.org/Gang%20Articles/Mara%20Salvatrucha. htm, retrieved January 10, 2007.

Vamosi, Robert. (Sept. 6, 2005). A Virtual Den of Thieves. Security Watch, http://reviews.cnet.com/4520-3513_7-6312067- 1.html, retrieved March 12, 2008.

Van de Velde. (1996). The Growth of Criminal Organizations and Insurgent Groups Abroad Due to International Drug Trafficking. *Low Intensity Conflict and Law Enforcement,* 5 (3).

Van Dijck, Maarten. (2007). Cigarette Trafficking and Traffickers in the Netherlands. *Crime and Justice International,* December: 4–14.

Van Duyne, Petrus. (2003). Organizing Cigarette Smuggling and Policy Making, Ending Up in Smoke. *Crime, Law & Social Change,* 39: 285–317.

Van Duyne, Petrus, and Alan A. Block. (1995). Organized Cross-Atlantic Crime: Racketeering in Fuels. *Crime, Law & Social Change,* 22: 127–147.

Van Scherpenberg, Jens. (2001). *Combating the Terrorist–Criminal Nexus,* American Institute for Contemporary German Studies, Johns Hopkins University, pp. 1–10.

Varese, Federico. (2006). How Mafias Migrate: The Case of the 'Ndrangheta in Northern Italy. *Law & Society Review,* 40(2): 411–444.

Verton, Dan. (Oct. 28, 2004). Secret Service Busts Online Organized Crime Ring, http://www.computerworld.com/ action/article.do?comand, retrieved March 12, 2008.

Viano, Emilio C. (1999). The Criminal Justice System Facing the Challenges of Organized Crime. In *Global Organized Crime and International Security,* Emilio Viano (Ed.). Farnham, Surrey, UK: Ashgate Publishing, pp. 185–206.

Villafranca, Armando. (Feb. 7, 2007). 10 Charged in Auto- Accident Scam. *Houston Chronicle,* http://www .accessmylibrary.com/coms2/summary_0286-30449892_ITM.

Vine, Margaret S. Wilson. (1972). Gabriel Tarde. In *Pioneers in Criminology,* 2nd ed, Hermann Mannheim (Ed.). Montclair: Patterson Smith, pp. 292–304.

Volkov, Vadim. (2000). The Political Economy of Protection Rackets in the Past and Present. *Social Research,* 67(3): 709–744.

Von Lampe, *Definitions of Organized Crime,* http://www .organized-crime.de/OCDEF1.htm/, retrieved October 21, 2008.

Von Lampe, Klaus. (2005). Organizing the Nicotine Racket: Patterns of Criminal Cooperation in the Cigarette Black Market in Germany. In *Criminal Finances and Organising Crime in Europe,* Van Duyne et al. (Eds.). The Netherlands: Wolf Legal Publishers.

Wagner, Denise. (July 23, 2006). Human Trafficking's Profits Spur Horrors, http://www.azcentral.com/arizonarepublic/ news/articles/0723drophouse-main2.html, retrieved January 15, 2008.

Wagner, Matt. (2006). Do We Have a Gang Problem? *News- Leader.com,* http://www.news-leader.com/apps/pbcs.dll? article?Date=20060219&Category=NEWS01, retrieved September 2, 2007.

Walker, Clarence. (2005). Russian Organize Crime Targets NFL Superbowl in Multi-Billion Dollar Gambling Scheme, http://www.americanmafia.com/Feature_Articles_293.html, retrieved March 13, 2008.

Wallace-Wells, Ben. (2007). How America Lost the War on Drugs. *Rolling Stone*, December 13: 91–119.

Walling, Joseph K. (1926). The Profession of Bootlegging. *The Annals, Modern Crime: Its Prevention and Punishment,* Philadelphia: American Academy of Political and Social Science, May: 40–48.

Walsh, Mary Williams, and Richard Boudreaux. (Aug. 17, 1994). German Police Seize Weapons-Grade Plutonium. *Houston Chronicle,* p. A24.

Walters, Stephen. (2007). Contemporary Maritime Piracy. *Crime and Justice International,* February: 10–16.

Ward, Mark. (Sept. 28, 2005). Boom Times for Hi-Tech Fraudsters. BBC News, http://newsvote.bbc.co.uk/mapps/pagetools/print/news.bbc.co.uk/1/hi/technology/428627, retrieved March 13, 2008.

Washington Office on Latin America (WOLA). (2007). *The Captive State: Organized Crime and Human Rights in Latin America.* October, 28 pp.

Watson, Julie. (April 13, 2007). Campaign of Fear Hits Public Stage. *Houston Chronicle,* p. A19.

Webster, Donovan. (Sept. 18, 1994). CHIPS Are a Thief's Best Friend. *New York Times Magazine,* pp. 54–59.

Weekly Journal. (July 27, 1995). LA Street Gangs Infiltrate US Army: The Crips and Bloods Have. http://www.streetgangs.com/topics/1995/072795cpblmil.html, retrieved January 17, 2007.

Weinberg, Neal. (Feb. 1, 2007). Kasperskys on Cybercrime: Don't Blame the Russian Mafia and Why We Need Anti-Anti-Anti-Virus Software. NETWORKWORLD, http://www.networld.com/cgi-bin/mailto/x.cgi?pagetosend =/export/home, retrieved March 13, 2008.

Weinstein, Paul I. (1966). Racketeering and Labor: An Economic Analysis. *Industrial and Labor Relations Review,* 19(3): 402–413.

Weiser, Benjamin. (Jan. 22, 1998). U.S. Charges John Gotti Jr. with Extortion. *The New York Times.*

Wellford, Charles. (1975). Labeling Theory and Criminology: An Assessment. *Social Problems,* 22(3): 332–345.

Williams, Phil. (2001). Organizing Transnational Crime: Networks, Markets and Hierarchies. In *Combating Transnational Crime: Concepts, Activities and Responses,* Phil Williams and Dimitri Vlassis (Eds.). London: Frank Cass, pp. 57–87.

———. (2001). Transnational Criminal Networks. In *Networks and Netwars: The Future of Terror, Crime and Militancy,* John Acquila and David F. Ronfeldt (Eds.). Rand Corporation.

———. (2000). Terrorism and Organized Crime: Convergence. Nexus, or Transformation. In *Hype or Reality? The New Terrorism and Mass Casualty Attacks,* Brad Roberts (Ed.). Alexandria VA: Chemical and Biological Arms Control Institute.

Williams, Phil, and Ernesto U. Savona. (1995). Introduction: Problems and Dangers Posed by Organized Crime in the Various Regions of the World. *Transnational Organized Crime,* 1(3).

Willing, Joseph K. (1926). The Profession of Bootlegging. *Modern Crime: Its Prevention and Punishment: The Annals,* Philadelphia: The American Academy of Political and Social Science, pp. 40–48.

Willing, Richard. (Feb. 9, 2007). Dramatic Mob Trials Still Fill the Seats. *USA Today.*

Wilson, Michael. (Nov. 4, 2007). Mathematician Shot at Illegal Poker Game. *Houston Chronicle,* p. A15.

Winick, Charles. (1994). Organized Crime and Commercial Sex. In *Handbook of Organized Crime in the United States,* Robert J. Kelly et al. (Eds.). Westport, CT: Greenwood Press, pp. 289–310.

Wiseman, Paul. (Jan. 22, 2007). Macau Leads Las Vegas in Gambling. *USA Today,* p. A1.

Wolfgang, Marvin E. (1961). Cesare Lombroso. *Journal of Criminal Law, Criminology, and Police Science,* 52 (4): 232–294.

Xhudo, Gus. (1996). Men of Purpose: The Growth of Albanian Criminal Activity, *Transnational Organized Crime,* 2(1): 1–20.

Yokoyama, Minoru. (1999). Trends of Organized Crime by Boryokudan in Japan. In *Organized Crime: Uncertainties and Dilemmas,* S. Einstein and M. Amir (Eds.). Chicago, OICJ, pp. 13–154.

Yoo, John. (n.d.). The Patriot Act Is Constitutional. In *Is the Patriot Act Unconstitutional?* http://encarta.msn.com/encnet/refpages/RefAuxArt.aspx?refid=701713501, retrieved May 15, 2008.

Zaitch, Damian, and Richard Staring. (2007). Trends and Policies on Women Trafficking in the Netherlands. *Crime and Justice International,* December: 15–22.

Zaluar, Alba. (2001). Violence in Rio de Janeiro: Styles of Leisure, Drug Use, and Trafficking. In *International Social Science Journal,* 169: 369–378.

Zambo, Scott. (2007). Digital La Cosa Nostra: The Computer Fraud and Abuse Act's Failure to Punish and Deter Organized Crime. http://ZAMBO_FINAL_MACRO.Doc, retrieved May 14, 2007.

ZimObserver. (Aug. 14, 2006). Organized Crime in Zimbabwe on the Rise. *ZimObserver News Zimbabwe,* http://www.zimobserver.com/index.php?mod=article&cat=Lifestyle&article=141&page_0, retrieved April 17, 2007.

GOVERNMENT DOCUMENTS AND REPORTS

Computer Crime and Intellectual Property Section (CCCIPS) of the U.S. DOJ. (n.d.). Operation Buccaneer: Illegal warez organizations and Internet Piracy. http://www.cybercrime.gov/ob/0Borg&pr.htm, retrieved February 28, 2008.

Combatting Organized Crime. (1966). A Report of the 1965 Oyster Bay, New York, Conferences on Combatting

Organized Crime, Albany, New York: Office of the Counsel to the Governor.

Corruption and Racketeering in the New York City Construction Industry: The Final Report of the New York State Organized Crime Task Force. (1990). New York: New York University Press.

DEA Programs, Organized Crime Drug Enforcement Task Forces. http://www.justice.gov/dea/programs/ocdetf.htm, retrieved May 15, 2008.

18 USC Sec. 1961 (Title 18, Part 1, Chapter 96, Sec. 1961), retrieved January 3, 2007.

Freedom of Information Act (FOIA). *Aryan Nations.*

Freedom of Information Act (FOIA). *Mexican Mafia.*

FBI, June 14, 2007, Investigation into Connecticut and New York Waste Hauling Industry Results in Superseding Indictment. http://newhaven.fbi.gov/dojpressrel/2007/nh061407a.htm, retrieved May 15, 2008.

FBI, An increase in Internet schemes claiming to be from the FBI. http://www.fbi.gov/cyberinvest/escams.htm, retrieved March 10, 2008.

FBI, Storm Worm Virus. (Feb. 11, 2008). http://www.fbi.gov/cyberinvest/escams.htm, retrieved March 10, 2008.

FBI, Balkan Organized Crime. http://www.fbi.gov/hq/cid/orgcrime/balkan.htm, retrieved December 10, 2008.

FBI, Labor Racketeering. http://www.fbi.gov/nq/cid/orgcrime/lcnindex.htm, retrieved December 10, 2008.

FBI, Organized Crime Glossary. http://www.fbi.gov/hq/cid/orgcrime/glossary.htm, retrieved January 3, 2009.

FBI, U.S. Department of Justice, Terrorism definition, 1998, http://denver.fbi.gov/nfip.htm, retrieved December 10, 2008.

Katzenbach (Atty. Gen.) Nicholas (Testimony of). (1965). *Long Comm. Hearings*, 89th Cong., 1st Sess., pt. 3.

Lexow Committee Hearings (1895). See *Report and Proceedings of the Senate Committee Appointed to Investigate the Police Department of the City of New York.*

[McClellan Committee Report]. Hearings before the Permanent Subcommittee on Investigations of the Committee on Government Operations, U.S. Senate, 88th Cong. 1st and 2nd Sess. Pt. 3, Oct. 10, 11, 15, 16, 1963.

National Commission of Law and Observance. (June 26, 1931). *Report on the Causes of Crime,* II(13). Washington, DC: U.S. Government Printing Office.

National Prohibition Act. (1920). http://www.johnsonsdepot.com/Chicago/volstead.pdf, retrieved December 10, 2008.

New Jersey State Commission of Investigation (SJSCI). (Nov. 29, 1990). Afro-lineal Organized Crime, http://www.state.nj.us/sci/pdf/afro.pdf, retrieved April 25, 2007.

New York State Organized Crime Task Force. (1990). *Corruption and Racketeering in the New York City Construction Industry.* New York: New York University Press.

Organized Crime and Human Rights in Latin America. October 2007, pp. 1–27.

Office of Public Affairs, Treasury Under-Secretary for Enforcement James E. Johnson, Remarks before the Wine Institute, May 15, 2000, http://www.treas.gov/press/releases/ls627.htm, retrieved January 12, 2008.

Organized Crime in America, Hearings Before the Committee on the Judiciary, U.S. Senate, 98th Congress, 1st Session, January 27, February 16, March 2 and 3, 1983. Washington, DC: U.S. Government Printing Office.

President's Commission on Law Enforcement and Administration of Justice. (1972). *The Challenge of Crime in Free Society,* 3rd ed. New York: Avon.

President's Commission on Organized Crime. (October 1984). *Organized Crime of Asian Origin,* record of Hearings III, October 23–25, 1984. New York, Washington, DC: U.S. Government Printing Office.

President's Commission on Law Enforcement and Administration of Justice. (1967). *Task Force Report Organized Crime,* Washington, DC: U.S. Government Printing Office.

President's Commission on Organized Crime. (1986). *The Edge: Organized Crime, Business and Labor Unions,* Washington, DC: U.S. Government Printing Office.

R. v. Lindsay. (2005). http://www.canlii.org/on/cas/onsc/2005/2005onsc14135.html, retrieved January 10, 2007.

Ramdin, Albert R. (2007). Assistant Secretary General of the Organization of American States Address at Conference on Organized Crime: A Threat to the Caribbean. March 20, http://www.oas.org/speeches/speech.asp?sCodigo=07-0028, retrieved April 25, 2007.

Report and Proceedings of the Senate Committee Appointed to Investigate the Police Department of the City of New York, 5 vol. (1895). Albany: James B. Lyon; reprinted by Arno Press, 1971.

RICO. Racketeer Influenced and Corrupt Organizations Act, 1970.

Shaw, Mark. (September 2002). *Typologies of Transnational Organized Crime Groups,* Centre for International Crime Prevention, UNDOC.

State of California. (November 15, 1950). *Final Report of Special Crime Study Commission on Organized Crime,* Sacramento, CA.

———. (January 31, 1950). *Third Progress Report of the Special Crime Study Commission on Organized Crime,* Sacramento, CA.

———. (March 7, 1948). *Second Progress Report of the Special Crime Study Commission on Organized Crime,* Sacramento, CA.

———. (March 1, 1948). *First Interim Reports of the Special Crime Sudy Commission on Organized Crime,* Sacramento, CA.

State of New Jersey, Commission of Investigation, Afro-Lineal Organized Crime. http://www.mafianj.com/afro/westindian.shtml, retrieved April 16, 2007.

United Nations Office on Drugs and Crime, Vienna. (2005). *Transnational Organized Crime in the West African Region.* New York: United Nations.

United Nations Office on Drugs and Crime. Vienna. (September 2002). *Global Programme against Transnational Organized Crime: Results of a pilot survey of forty selected organized criminal groups in sixteen countries,* UNDOC.

United Nations Office on Drugs and Crime. (2000). Convention against Transnational Organized Crime, http://www.uncjin .org/Documents/Conventions/dcatoc/final_documents_2/ convention_eng.pdf, retrieved May 6, 2007.

U.S. Department of State. (2006). *International Narcotics Control Strategy Report,* March: 1–33, http://www.state.gov/ p/inl/rls/nrcrpt/2006/vol1/html/62106.htm, retrieved January 17, 2008.

U.S. Government. (2000). *International Crime Threat Assessment,* Washington, DC: http://clinton4.nara.gov.

United States v. Turkette, 452 US, 576, 586, 589, 1981.

USINFO.STATE.GOV. (April 21, 2005). Crime Hinders Development, Democracy in Latin America, U.S. Says. http://uninfo.state.gov/dhr/Archive/2005/Apr/21-965427 .html, retrieved November 19, 2007.

Winer, Jonathan. (1996). Congressional Hearings on Intelligence and Security. Statement of Deputy Assistant Secretary for International Narcotics and Law Enforcement Affairs before the Subcommittee on Africa of the House International Relations Committee, Washington, DC, September 11, 1996, http://www.fas.org/irp/congress/1996_hr/h960911w.htm, retrieved April 16, 2007.

Witness Security Program. (1981). Report of the Committee on Governmental Affairs United States Senate made by its Permanent Subcommittee on Investigations, 97th Con. 1st Sess. Report No. 97-300, Dec. 14. Washington, DC: U.S. Government Printing Office.

INDEX